WEBSTER'S NEW WORLD™

RHYMING DICTIONARY

Clement Wood's Updated

Edited by Michael S. Allen and Michael Cunningham

MACMILLAN • USA

Macmillan General Reference
A Simon & Schuster Macmillan Company
1633 Broadway
New York, NY 10019-6785

A Webster's New World™ book

MACMILLAN is a registered trademark of Macmillan, Inc.

Manufactured in the United States of America

03 02 01 00 99 — 5 4 3 2 1

ISBN: 0-02-862626-5

This book is a complete update of the original *Clement Wood's Unabridged Rhyming Dictionary* © 1943 World Publishing Company, published by Simon & Schuster.

Wood, Clement, 1888–1950.
    [Unabridged rhyming dictionary]
    Webster's New World rhyming dictionary : Clement Wood's updated / edited by Michael S. Allen and Michael Cunningham.
       p.   cm.
    ISBN 0-02-862626-5 (pbk.)
    1. English language—Rhyme—Dictionaries.   I. Allen, Michael S., 1947– . II. Cunningham, Michael, 1969– . III. Title.
PE1519.W62   1998
428'.1—dc21   98-42859
                                       CIP

Table of Contents

Foreword x

Acknowledgments vii

The Mechanics of Rhyme 1

Part One: The Rhyming Dictionary 13

   Single Rhymes (Masculine Rhymes) 13

   Double Rhymes 166

   Triple Rhymes 684

Part Two: Guidelines for Effective Rhyme 817

   Where Does Poetry and Song Come from? 819

   Guidelines to Using the Language 821

   Some Warnings 827

Rhyme 832

   Some History about Rhyme 832

   The Function of Rhyme 833

   Types of Rhyme 834

   A Mental Rhyming Dictionary 843

Rhythm 845

   Early Accent Verse in English 845

   Metric Verse 849

   Free Verse 857

   Line Length in Verse 859

Stanza Forms 860

   One-Line Stanzas 860

   Stanzas of Two Lines: The Couplet 860

   Stanzas of Three Lines: The Triplet or Tercet 862

Stanzas of Four Lines: The Quatrain 863

Stanzas of Five Lines: The Cinquain 866

Stanzas of Six Lines: The Sestet 866

Stanzas of Seven Lines: The Septet 867

Stanzas of Eight and More Lines 868

The Fixed Forms 871

Rules for Formal Verse 871

Sonnets 872

Syllable-Count Forms 878

Miscellaneous Forms 882

Line-Repetition Forms 886

Chain Verse 889

The Lai Group 890

Text-Embroidering Group 893

The Troilet-Rondeau Family 897

The Ballade Family 901

The Sestina 907

Index 911

Foreword

Foreword to the 1943 edition:

The desire to write poetry and acceptable verse is practically universal. The rules for accurate versification are far simpler than the rules and procedures for playing contract bridge or solving crossword puzzles. They are incredibly easier than mathematics or any science. It is far simpler to be a master in versification than to learn to be a qualified mechanic, lawyer, doctor, pharmacist, trained nurse, stenographer, or cook. The rules for writing verse are as simple as the rules for writing prose. Writing good verse is as easy as writing good prose.

All the rules are contained in the three explanatory sections of this volume: The Vocabulary of Poetry; The Complete Formbook for Poets; and Versification Self-Taught. [Now contained within the Guidelines to Effective Rhyme—eds.] They are stated clearly and amply illustrated. When these three sections are absorbed, the versifier can fairly regard himself as a master.

As for the main portion of this book, let me quote from its summary: "The Unabridged Rhyming Dictionary is the most complete and modern rhyming dictionary ever written."

"It is strictly phonetic, and thus satisfies the first half—the repetition half—of the definition of rhyme."

"For the first time it eliminates the danger of using identity instead of rhyme, by grouping the words in each rhyme sound under the appropriate consonantal opening."

"For the first time it includes all types of mosaic rhymes, based upon rhymes constructed of two or more words."

"It has simplified the rules for accurate rhyming to one simple rule: *Choose and use only one word from each group.* By following that, your rhyming will be flawless."

The volume is thus indispensable to poets, versifiers, writers of song lyrics, advertising verses, and all other forms of verse, to instructors and students of poetics, libraries, librarians, and all interested in perfecting this more concentrated half of our verbal expression. It can make the technique of verse and rhyming as automatic as the technique of walking; and thus, as I have written elsewhere, "the poetic energy will be proportionately released for the more effective creation of poetry."

Clement Wood
Bozenkill,
Delanson, NY

Acknowledgments

From the 1943 edition:

Among those who have contributed immensely to the making of this compendium, and have thereby earned my resultant gratitude, are Etta Josephean Murfey, Marcia Jones, Stephen Schlitzer, Diana Douglas, Alfred Turner, Amy Wheeler Morgan, Aimee Jackson Short, and John Thornton Wood. For earnest and painstaking collaboration throughout each stage of the work, thanks beyond my power of expression are due to Assistant Editor Gloria Goddard.

From the updated edition:

The following authors and publishers have generously given permission to use these poems and song lyrics in their entirety from the following copyrighted works.

Atomic Pantoum, Peter Meinke, first appeared in *Poetry* © 1983 by The Modern Poetry Association and is reprinted by permission of the Editor of *Poetry.* From *Liquid Paper: New and Selected Poems,* by Peter Meinke © 1991. Reprinted by permission of the University of Pittsburgh Press.

Ballade of the Grindstones, Judith Johnson Sherwin. Reprinted by permission of Sheep Meadow Press.

Beer Bottle, Ted Kooser, from *Official Entry Blank* © 1969 University of Nebraska Press. Reprinted by permission of the author.

Chant Royal, Robert Morgan, first apppeared in *Poetry* © 1978 by the Modern Poetry Association and is reprinted by permission of the Editor of *Poetry.* From *At the Edge of Orchard Country* © 1987 by Robert Morgan, Wesleyan University Press. Reprinted by permission of University Press of New England.

Death of a Vermont Farm Woman, Barbara Howes, from *Collected Poems 1945–1990* © 1995 Barbara Howes. Reprinted by permission of University of Arkansas Press.

Eastern Guard Tower and *To Write a Blues Song*, Ethridge Knight, both from *Poems from Prison*. Reprinted by permission of Broadside Press.

Epitaph for Someone or Other, and *The Aged Lover Discourses in the Flat Style,* J.V. Cunningham, from *The Collected Poems and Epigrams of J.V. Cunningham*. Reprinted by permission of Swallow Press.

Politics, William Butler Yeats, from *The Collected Works of W. B. Yeats, Volume 1: The Poems,* revised and edited by Richard J. Finneran © 1940 by Georgie Yeats; © renewed 1968 by Bertha Georgie Yeats, Michael Butler Yeats, and Anne Yeats. Reprinted by permission of Scribner, a Division of Simon & Schuster, and A.P. Watt, Ltd.

Rondel, Philip Dacey, from *How I Escaped from the Labyrinth and Other Poems*. Reprinted by permission of the author.

Rondel, George Moore, from *Anthology of Pure Poetry.* Reprinted by permission of W.W. Norton.

Through the Icy Glaze, Neca Maria Stoller, from *Tanka-Sijo-Haiku Muse*. Reprinted by permission of the author.

To a Steamroller, Marianne Moore, from *Collected Poems of Marianne Moore* © 1935 by Marianne Moore; © renewed 1963 by Marianne Moore and T.S. Eliot. Reprinted by permission of Simon & Schuster.

Triolet, Sandra McPherson, from *The Year of Our Birth* © 1973, 1974, 1975, 1976, 1977, 1978 by Sandra McPherson. Reprinted by permission of The Ecco Press.

We Real Cool, Gwendolyn Brooks, from *Blacks* © 1991. Published by Third World Press. Reprinted by permission of the author.

*The editors at Webster's New World have made reasonable efforts to contact authors of the poems and song lyrics used in this book. Due to the age of the previous edition of this book, our efforts in some cases proved unsuccessful. If you are the author of a poem or song lyric within this book and are not mentioned above, please contact the publisher so that we may update our records and print the appropriate acknowledgements on reprint.

The Mechanics of Rhyme

Rhyme Defined

Rhyme is the repetition of an identical accented vowel sound and all the consonantal and vowel sounds that follow it. What differentiates rhyming words from each other is the difference in the consonantal sounds that immediately precede the accented vowel sound. Rhyme is a matter of sound only; spelling doesn't matter.

The accented vowel sound is usually the last vowel sound receiving a major accent, as in (vowels are in bold):

> a**ce**, f**ace**; sp**oken**, br**oken**; w**ea**rily, dr**ea**rily

Notice how all the consonants and vowels following the accented vowel sound repeat in a full rhyme. If any of the sounds had been different (as in wearily and tearfully), then we would have consonance, not full rhyme.

Rhyme can also be a matter of a minor accent, as in these pairs of rhymes from Shakespeare's "Sonnet cxxv":

> canopy, honour**ing**, etern**ity**, ruin**ing**

Rhyme can start before the last major accent, but these compound rhymes must also include the last major accent; some examples are:

> w**eary song**, ch**eery song**; z**ealous he**; j**ealously**; b**urn it you**'re, f**urniture**; l**ot o' news**, hyp**otenuse**; y**earning to hold you fast**; b**urning to hold you fast**.

Rhyme often affects meter, and vice versa. In classical scansion, the accented vowel which starts the rhyme must also start the last foot of the line. Therefore, in sonnet meter, which requires five feet, the line "While Time's dull candle, slowly guttering," would be correct if it rhymes with wing, since "-ring" of guttering is the last accented syllable:

> While Time's | dull can- | dle, slow- | ly gut- | tering,

However, if guttering were rhymed with muttering, the rhyme would throw off the scansion of the line, making it only four feet long:

> While Time's | dull can- | dle, slow- | ly guttering.

If the poem were to stick to sonnet form, another foot would have to be added.

The Two Elements of Rhyme

Rhyme, therefore, has two elements:

1. The accented vowel found in the two or more words, and all the following sounds; and

2. The different consonants preceding that vowel sound.

This rhyming dictionary differentiates all rhymes according to both of these elements. (Not all guides to writing poetry do that!) Here's how the dictionary works:

1. The rhyming sounds, for one-, two-, or three-syllabled rhymes, are all collected under the phonetic symbol for that sound.

2. In each collection of rhyme-sounds, all of the words are grouped according to the different opening consonant sounds.

A word rhymes only with the various words collected under the phonetic symbol of its vowel-sound (except for those in its own consonant group, which are called identities and not regarded as true rhymes), and not with any word in any other vowel sound. To rhyme accurately, only one rule is necessary:

In any given vowel-sound, choose and use only one word from each consonant group.

Need for Differentiation by Consonantal Openings

The ballade and other strict French forms forbid identities—the repetition of the same opening consonantal sound in a rhyme. Identity instead of rhyme, is simply not as much fun—it is perceived to show a lack of imagination in poetry. In this rhyming dictionary, by selecting only one word from each consonant group within a given vowel sound, the use of identities becomes impossible.

Sometimes identities show up unexpectedly. Look at these examples:

light, polite; through, overthrew; queue, cue

The different spellings make it seem at first that these words are rhymes and not identities. But look at the consonants before the rhymed vowels: Light and lite have the same opening consonant; so do through and threw; and so do queue and cue. Remember that in rhyme, sound is what matters, not spelling; "qu" and "cu" are thee same consonant sound.

The division into syllables with hyphens, as given in most dictionaries, also can be unreliable when it comes to rhyme. Hyphenation is sometimes for a printer's convenience, not for accurate pronunciation. Sometimes the words exonerate, exaggerate, exasperate, etc., are hyphenated so that the last syllable is -ate; so, you might think that they belong in a group of rhymes under "ate." However, in rhyme, each rhyme must begin with a consonant, and for these words in a rhyming dictionary, the last syllable must be rate. The same applies to the last syllable of such words as fortunate, exorbitant, animate, the syllable before the last in exaggeration, and so on.

In this volume, the words are grouped strictly according to pronunciation, not according to ordinary syllabification.

Composite or Mosaic Rhymes

Rhyme may involve more than two or more single words. We have accurate rhyme in following pairs:

> heel, feel
>
> satin, matin
>
> happily, snappily

We also have accurate rhyme in these pairs:

> he'll; she'll
>
> sat in, that inn; wholesale, soul sail
>
> end of it, blend of it; heartbroken, part broken;
>
> finding her, blinding her; Pocono, smoke? O, no.

When using these mosaic or composite rhymes, be sure to have the accents match. At times, this may require the use of italics, to indicate where you wish the accent to fall.

This book for the first time includes types of mosaic rhymes for all rhyme sounds which can be made in this way. In using mosaic rhymes, make sure that the opening consonantal sounds are different (and avoid identities). For example, satin rhymes with that inn, but not with its identity, sat in.

Mosaic rhymes may be used, often effectively, in light verse, by using parts of words instead of complete ones. For example:

Peers shall teem in Christendom.
>   And a duke's exalted station
Be attainable by com-
>   Petitive examination.

>>   Finale to Act I, *Iolanthe*, W. S. Gilbert

Who would not give all else for two p-
Enny worth of beautiful soup?

>>   "Soup of the Evening," from *Alice in*
>>   *Wonderland*, Lewis Carroll

Sun, moon, and thou vain world, adieu,
>   That kings and priests are plotting in;
Here doomed to starve on water gru-
>   El, never shall I see the U-
>   Niversity of Gottingen,
>   Niversity of Gottingen

>>   *Song of Rogero*, George Canning

By '45, Canton and Kalamazoo,
Boise City and Baton Rou-
Ge, Indianapolis, clear to the coast
Will lift the ululated boast. . .
Flee Scylla's pains, and then ad lib dis-
Card your fear, and wed Charybdis.

>>   *The Greenwich Village Blues*, Clement Wood

Mama throw a nickel,
And the man will pick a l-
Ittle tune you love.

>>   "The Man with the Mandolin" (popular song)

Sang out with gusto,
And just o-
Verlorded the place.

>>   *Johnny One Note*, Lorenz Hart

The countless mosaic rhymes involving split words are not included in this volume. The can easily be created, however, following the above examples. Both types of mosaic rhymes are valuable, to increase the limited rhyming facilities of the language.

Finding Consonance in a Rhyming Dictionary

Another way to increase the rhyming facilities in the language is consonance (also called off rhyme and near rhyme): Consonance is the repetition of all the consonant and vowel sounds following an accented vowel sound in a word—the difference is in the accented vowel sound preceding the repeated sound elements.

Consonance is, therefore, close to the reverse of rhyme—instead of looking for different consonants (as in rhyme), consonance depends on different vowels.

There are 18 possible groups of words in consonance with any given word: The 18 other vowel sounds, followed by identical consonants and other sounds. Finding consonance in a rhyming dictionary is a slower process than finding rhymes, of course, but the effort often justifies the results.

For example, to find consonance word for feel, we would look up the following sounds in the rhyming dictionary:

> al, āl, äl; el, ēl; il, īl, ōl, ôl, oil, ool, o͞ol; ul, ūl, əl

For strict consonance, three of these must be eliminated—al, el, ul—because they only appear with an r before them: arl, erl, url. But the rules of consonance can bend, and l word can be matched with rl words. Therefore, going down our list of l sounds, we could get the following list:

> fail, Sal, morale, fell, vile, will, soul, soll, bawl, toil, full, foul, rule, dull, (and our rl words:) snarl, curl (there being no erl word).

Note that several of these words—fail, full, foul—have the same opening consonant as our original word, feel. This is permissible in consonance, since the difference is in the accented vowel sounds, the preceding consonants may be identical.

Similarly, if we needed two-syllable words in consonance with winter, we might select:

> painter, scanter, enchanter, dissenter, saunter, anointer, counter, hunter.

The same process my be applied to three-syllable rhymes.

Additional Rhymes

To avoid a proliferation of lists in this dictionary, possessives, plurals, and other accurate rhymes are often grouped together with a plus followed by a typical example, at the end of each list. For example, after the list under ATZ, we might have:

> Plus Kate's, etc.
>
> Plus AT+s.

These notes indicate that possessives like "Kate's" also may be rhymed with ATZ word sounds, and that words ending with the AT sound and a plural ending (AT+s) will also rhyme with the ATZ sound.

Sometimes there are words that often sound so similar that they can be rhymed. Therefore, at the end of some lists, the additional word or group of words is introduced by a Cf. (the Latin confer, meaning "compare"). For example, after the list under OUR, we might find:

> Cf. OU'ur.

Similarly, after the list under ON'ur, we might find:

> Cf. donor.

Archaic Words

To make this rhyming dictionary complete, it also includes archaic words and word forms: welkin, abhorreth, dost, etc. However, each of these words is marked with an asterisk (*) to warn the reader against using them in any poem other than period verse.

Opening U Sounds

The general rule of rhyming in this dictionary is to use only one word from each group. There is, however, an exception to this rule (as there are exceptions to many rules in poetry!). Some words with the long u sound are pronounced as if they have a y sound before them: use, beauty, view, tune. There are, therefore, examples in the u sections where words grouped together form perfect rhymes, such as:

> tune, spitoon
>
> booty, beauty
>
> doable, reviewable

By careful examination of the long u rhymes, you can often locate perfect rhymes even in the same groups. This is the one and only exception to the general rule for the use of this book, that you should select and use only one word out of each group.

Using the Phonetic Alphabet

The pronunciations given in this dictionary are those widely used by good speakers of American English. It is a fact, however, that good speakers do not always pronounce the same words in the same way. These variations in pronunciation occur in everyday speech, and even on newscasts, and other spoken recordings. One pronunciation is not necessarily correct and the others wrong; the differences are due largely to the fluid nature of language and the existence of regional dialects. Because these various pronunciations are widely used by good speakers, the varying pronunciations must be considered as acceptable.

By using phonetic spelling in this dictionary these differences in pronunciation can be more accurately categorized and utilized in the search for an exact rhyme. A phonetic alphabet "spells" words according to the way they are pronounced rather than the way they have come to be traditionally spelled over time. This is done by using the letters of the alphabet, and some additional symbols, according to very strict rules so that one letter (or symbol) represents only one sound. In a phonetic alphabet, for example, there is no difference in the spelling of *trough* and *off* (except for the initial consonants, of course!) like there is in the regular alphabet. Phonetically, they are spelled trôf and ôf. The following key to phonetic spelling and pronunciation describes the way the sounds in words are "spelled" phonetically. Unlike the regular alphabet, the phonetic alphabet has hard and fast rules and is entirely constant. It will take a little time to become familiar with these rules and how they make words appear, but the effort, for the sake of accuracy is well spent.

Throughout the word lists in this dictionary, the possibility of alternate, regional pronunciations are marked with a plus (+) symbol following the word in question. The following guidelines discuss the variations you are most likely to hear and outlines what alternate phonetic spellings these variations are likely to be found under.

The Key to
Phonetic Spelling
and Pronunciation

a: at, carry, gas

ā: ate, day, tape

ä: ah, car, father

b: bed, able, tab

ch: chin, archer, march

d: dip, idea, wad

e: end, berry, ten

ē: eve, be, me

f: fit, after, if

g: get, angle, tag

h: he, ahead, hotel

i: is, hit, lid

ī: ice, bite, high

j: joy, agile, edge

k: kid, oaken, take

l: lid, elbow, sail

m: met, amid, aim

n: no, end, pan

ng: ring, anger, drink

ō: own, tone, go

ô: horn, all, law

oi: oil, coin, toy

oo: look, pull, good

ōō: tool, crew, moo

ou: out, how, our

p: put, open, tap

r: red, part, far

s: sell, east, toss

sh: she, cushion, wash

t: top, meter, sat

th: thin, nothing, truth

TH: the, father, scythe

u: up, bud, cut

ʉ: urn, fur, cur

v: vat, over, have

w: will, away, wit

y: yet, onion, yard

z: zebra, lazy, haze

zh: azure, leisure

ə: a neutral vowel sound, like **a** in ago, **e** in over, **i** in sanity, **o** in comply, **u** in focus

Explanatory Notes

ä: This symbol represents the usual sound in American English of the letter *a* in words like *ah, car,* and *father.* In words like *car,* however, some speakers use a sound between the sound of the *a* in *ah* and the sound of the *a* in *at.* In British English the usual sound of the letter *a* in words such as *grass* and *path* is the same as the sound of *a* in *ah.* Some American speakers pronounce such words with an a sound that lies between the sound of the *a* in *at* and the sound of the *a* in *ah.* In words like *alms* and *hot,* the usual sound in American English of the letters *a* and *o* is the same as the sound of *a* in *ah.* Many speakers, however, use a sound that approaches or is the same as the sound of the *o* in *horn.* The symbol *ä* is meant to include such wide variations in pronunciation and is marked with a plus (+) symbol.

c: This symbol represents two distinct sounds, *s* or *k* in words like *circle, circus,* and *cat.* However, the letter *c* does not appear as a distinct symbol in a phonetic alphabet. In this dictionary words regularly spelled with a letter *c* are listed phonetically with the symbols *s* or *k* as appropriate.

ch: This symbol represents the sound of the letters *ch* in words like *church, catch,* and *cherry.* In words like *Christian* and *Archimedes,* however, the letters *ch* is pronounced as *k.*

d: This symbol represents the sound of the letter *d* in words like *date, ides,* and *card.* In past tenses and other inflections, *d* after *ch, s, f, k,* and *p* is pronounced *t.*

e: This symbol represents the sound of the letter *e* in words like *end, berry,* and *ten.* In words like *care* and *vary,* the sound of the letter *a* often ranges from the sound of the letter *e* in *ten* to the sound of the letter *a* in *at.* Some speakers pronounce the *a* in such words like the *a* in *tape.* The symbol *e* is meant to include all such variations.

ē: This symbol represents the sound of the letter *e* in words like *eve, be,* and *me.* In words like *lucky* and *pretty,* the usual sound in American English of the letter *y* is the same as the sound of the initial letter *e* in *eve.* In British English the usual sound of the letter *y* in such words is the same as the sound of the letter *i* in *is.* A considerable number of American English speakers also pronounce it this way. The symbol *ē* is meant to include such variations.

i: This symbol represents the sound of the letter *i* in words like *is, hit,* and *lid.* The first syllables of words like *deny* and *review* often have a neutral vowel sound that verges on *i,* as do the final syllables of words like *courage* and *goodness.* In words like *dear* and *mere,* some speakers use a vowel sound that is the same as the sound of the *e* in *me.* The symbol *i* is meant to include these variations.

': The apostrophe is used immediately before the symbol *l* or the symbol *n* to indicate that the *l* sound or the *n* sound is a syllabic consonant. A syllabic consonant is a consonant pronounced in such a way as to form a complete syllable, or the main part of a syllable, entirely or almost entirely by itself, with little or no perceptible sound of a vowel in that syllable. Words in which a syllabic *l* occurs are words like *cattle, ladle,* and *turtle.* Words in which a syllabic *n* occurs are words like *button, hidden,* and *satin.* When, in words like those just specified, the *l* or the *n* is not pronounced as a syllabic consonant, a spelled consonantal sound immediately preceding the spelled *l* or *n* typically begins the syllable. The syllable then continues with a vowel sound and ends with the ordinary nonsyllabic sound of the *l* or *n.* The word satin, for example is pronounced by some as *sa-tin* rather than as *sat'n.* Indication of only a syllabic *l* or *n* in words like *ladle* and *satin* is not meant to exclude the acceptability of an alternate nonsyllabic *l* or *n* in the pronunciation of such words.

The consonant *m* is sometimes pronounced as a syllabic consonant as in *chasm,* but the occurrence of a syllabic *m* in American English is much less common than the occurrence of a syllabic *l* or a syllabic *n.* Indication of only a nonsyllabic *m* in words like *chasm* and *prism* is not meant to exclude the acceptablility of an alternate syllabic *m* in the pronunciation of such words.

In words like *apple* and *cabin,* the consonants *l* and *n* are sometimes pronounced as syllabic consonants, as they also are in certain other kinds of consonant combinations. But unless the consonants *l* and *n* are frequently pronounced as syllabic consonants (as they regularly are when following a stressed syllable ending in a *d* sound or a *t* sound), they are not transcribed as syllabic consonants in this dictionary. Indication of only a nonsyllabic *l* or *n* in words like *apple* and *cabin* and in words involving certain other kinds of consonant combinations is not meant to exclude the acceptability of an alternate syllabic *l* or *n* in the pronunciation of such words.

ng: This symbol represents the single sound of the two spelled letters *ng* in words like *bang, long,* and *ring.* Likewise, this symbol represents the same sound of the single spelled letter *n* in words like *pink, rank,* and *sunk,* as it also does in words like *angry, finger,* and *tangle.*

ô: This symbol represents the vowel sound generally used in words like *horn, all,* and *law.* In words like *auto* and *lawn,* some speakers use a sound identical with or close to the sound of the letter *a* in *ah.* In words like *glory* and *more,* a considerable number of speakers use a sound similar to that of the letter *o* in *go.* The symbol *ô* is meant to include these variations.

q: This symbol is usually paired with the letter *u.* Together they represent both the *k* sound in words like *Albuquerque,* and the *kw* sound in *quirk, quack,* and *cumquat.* Words with the letter *q* and *qu* combination have generally been derived from languages such as French or Spanish. Their spelling has been retained from their parent language. In this dictionary these words are listed phonetically under *k* and *kw* as appropriate.

r: This symbol represents the sound of the letter *r* in *red, part,* and *far.* Most speakers in the U.S. and Canada regularly pronounce the *r* in most words that include an *r* in their spelling. All speakers of all varieties of English pronounce any spelled *r* that occurs as the first letter of a word such as *red,* or that occurs immediately after a pronounced consonant such as *bring.* In words like *part* and *far,* however, the spelled *r* is usually not pronounced by speakers of standard British English, nor by most native speakers of American English typically occurring in much of the southern and extreme eastern parts of the U.S. In this dictionary the symbol *r* is regularly used for each occurrence of an *r* sound in a word, in accordance with the way the word is usually pronounced by most speakers in the U.S. and Canada. It is to be understood that speakers who normally do not pronounce the *r* of words like *part* and *far* will disregard the symbol *r.*

x: This symbol represents the sound of *z* in the initial position in words like *xenia* and *xerxes.* More generally, it represents the sounds *gs* or *ks* in words like *exit, axe,* and *ox.* In this dictionary these words are listed phonetically under *z, gs,* or *ks* as appropriate.

ə: The schwa: This symbol represents an indistinct, neutral vowel sound without any stress, often used at the beginning, middle, or end of words. Some speakers replace the neutral schwa sound with the distinct vowel sound of the spelled vowel. Indication of only a schwa for a vowel is not meant to exclude the acceptability of an alternate distinct vowel in place of the schwa shown.

(Choose only one word out of each group.)

Single Rhymes
(Masculine Rhymes)

(Monosyllables and Words Accented on the Last Syllable)

A

Words including the following accented vowel sounds:

a as in at; also in plaid (plad), bade. In rhyming, the *a* heard in *tolerant* is similar.

ā as in fate; also in laid, gaol, gauge; great, eh, veil, prey.

ä as in far, father; also in heart, sergeant, memoir.

For the vowel sound *a* heard in *fall, paw, talk, swarm, haul,* and *caught,* see under *o.*

For the vowel sound *a* heard in *want* and *wash,* see under *o.*

Ā

Vowel: aye+, BA, Concanavalin A, CETA, couturier, D.A., DEA, DNA, dossier, eh, ERA, habitue, HLA, MA, NEA, NTA, Perrier, PSA, RDA, RNA, roturier, TBA, USA, VGA.

b: bay, bey, Bombay, dapple bay, disobey, flambé, loblolly bay, obey, sorbet, Thunder Bay.

br: brae, bray.

d: alackaday*, Ascensionday, bidet, birthday, Christmasday, coudé, day, D day, dey, doomsday, Easterday, firstday, Friday, haladay, galaday, good-day, heyday, high-day*, holiday, judgment day, Labor Day, lackaday, Ladyday, Lord's-day, marketday, May Day, Memorial Day, midday, Monday, noonday, O'Day, payday, playday, quarterday, Saturday, settlingday, seventhday, Sunday, Thursday, today, trystingday, Tuesday, wedding day, Wednesday, weekday, welladay, workaday, workingday, yesterday.

dr: dray.

f: au fait, auto-da-fé, café, coryphee, fay, fey, Santa Fe.

fl: flay, souffle.

fr: affray, defray, fray.

g: assagai, distingué, gay, nosegay.

gl: agley*.

gr: dapple-gray, émigré, gray, grey, hodden-gray, iron-gray, leaden-gray, silver-gray.

h: Haigh, hay, hey.

hw: whey.

j: DJ, J, jay, popinjay.

k(c): K, Biscay, bouquet, communique, croquet, Kay, Kaye, okay, risque, roquet, saskay, sobriquet, Tokay, tourniquet.

kl: clay, fire clay.

kw(qu): qua+.

l: allay, Beaujolais, belay, Bordelais, cabriolet, Calais, cervelas, cervelat, Chevrolet, crème brûlée, delay, forelay, forlay, inlay, interlay, lai, lay, Leigh, Malay, Mandalay, mislay, outlay, overlay, relay, roundelay, underlay, unlay, uplay, virelai, virelay, waylay.

m: consommée, dismay, entremets, gourmet, Marseilles+, may, résumé, Salomé.

n: beignet, Cabernet, catalogue raisonné, Chardonnay, Cloisonné, dejeuner, dragonné, hogmanay, matinee, nay, ne, née, neigh, raisonné.

ny: garconniere.

p: coupé, dead pay, overpay, pay, prepay, repay, toupée, toupet, underpay.

pl: display, fair play, horseplay, interplay, Passion play, play, stage play, underplay.

pr: bepray, Dupré, pray, prey, unpray.

r: array, bewray*, disarray, Doré, foray, Honoré, hooray, Monterey, Monterrey, ray, soirée, Wray, X ray.

s: assay, essay, foresay, gainsay, hearsay, missay, passé, say, soothsay, undersay, unsay, visé.

sh: bouchée, brochée, crochet, Montrachet, O'Shay, papier-maché, ricochet, sachet, shay.

skr: scray.

sl: bob sleigh, slay, sleigh, sley.

sp: spay, strathspey.

spl: splay.

spr: feather spray, spray.

st: astay, bobstay, forestay, mainstay, outstay, overstay, stay, upstay.

str: astray, stray.

sw: sway.

t: conté, crudités, prêt-à-porter, satay, tay, velouté, verité, video verité.

TH: they.

tr: betray, distrait, entrée, estray, outré, portray, tray, trey.

tw: tway*.

v: convey, corvée, inveigh, purvey, survey.

w: airway, away, aweigh, bridleway, byway, caraway, castaway, causeway, crossway, fairway, footway, galloway, Galway, gangway, getaway, halfway, highway, leeway, midway, Milky Way, outweigh, pathway, railway, runaway, steerageway, stowaway, subway, thereaway, tramway, waterway, way, weigh, wellaway*, wey.

y: Chevalier+, yea.

z: exposé, San Jose, visé.

zh: bichon frisé.

Ä

a: A a, ah+.

b: baa, bah+.

bl: blah.

br: braw, chapeaubras, port de bras.

d: da, lah-di-dah.

f: fa, sol-fa.

h: aha, ha, ha-ha.

j: Jah.

k(c): Kaa.

kl: claw, declaw, eclat.

kw(qu): qua+.

l: la.

m: grandmamma, ma, mama+, mamma+.

p: faux-pas, pa, pah, papa+, pas.
r: hurrah, last hurrah, Ra.
s: sah, yessah.
sh: padishah, pasha, shah.
sp: spa
th: Ptah.
y: ja, Jah, yah.
z: huzza.
zhw: bourgeois.

AB

Vowel: abb, Moab.
b: bab, Babb, baobab.
bl: blab.
d: bedab, dab.
dr: drab.
f: confab, prefab.
fr: frab.
g: baffle gab, gab.
gr: grab.
h: Ahab.
j: jab.
k(c): cab, pedicab, taxicab.
kr: crab.
l: lab, Skylab.
m: mab*, Mab.
n: knab*, McNabb, nab.
r: rab.
sh: shab.
sk(sc): scab.
sl: slab.
st: stab.
t: Cantab, tab.

ĀB

Vowel: Abe.
b: babe, foster-babe.
l: astrolabe, cosmolabe.

ÄB

b: bob, cabob, nabob,
thingamabob, thingumabob.

bl: blob.
d: daub+.
f: fob.
g: gob
h: hob.
j: job, McJob, nose job.
k(c): cob, Cobb, corncob.
kw: quab.
l: lob.
m: mob.
n: hob-and-nob, hobnob, knob, nob.
r: rob.
s: sob.
skw(squ): squab.
sl: slob.
sn: snob.
st: stob.
sw: swab.
thr: athrob, heartthrob, throb.
w: nawab+.

ABZ

Vowel: abs.

ÄBZ

b: ods bobs.
d: Dobbs.
h: Hobbes, Hobbs.
k(c): Cobbs.
sk: scobs.
  Plus ob+s.

ACH

b: batch.
bl: Blatch.
br: brach*.
h: crosshatch, hatch.
k(c): catch.
kl: kaffee klatsch.
kr: cratch.
l: latch, potlatch, unlatch.

m: match, overmatch, percussion match, shooting match, shouting match.

p: crosspatch, dispatch, patch.

r: ratch*.

sk(sc): scatch*.

skr(scr): scratch.

sl: slatch.

sm: smatch*.

sn: snatch.

t: attach, detach, tach*.

th: thatch.

ĀCH

Vowel: aitch, H.

ÄCH

b: botch

bl: blotch.

g: gotch

h: hotch.

kr: crotch.

n: notch, topnotch.

p: hotch-potch.

sk(sc): hopscotch, Scotch.

spl: splotch.

sw: swatch.

w: anchor watch+, deathwatch, dogwatch, harbor watch+, larboard watch+, outwatch, overwatch, starboard watch+, stopwatch, watch+, wristwatch.

ACHT

h: hatched.

t: attached, semidetached.
   Plus ach+ed.

AD

Vowel: add, chiliad, Lusiad, Olympiad, superadd.

b: bad, bade, forbade, unforbade.

br: brad.

ch: Chad, Tchad.

d: bedad, dad, Trinidad.

f: fad.

g: begad*, egad*, gad.

gl: englad, glad.

gr: grad, Leningrad, Petrograd, undergrad.

h: had.

k(c): cad, CAD.

kl: clad, heath-clad, iron-clad, ivy-clad, moss-clad, pine-clad, unclad, winter-clad, yclad*.

l: lad.

m: hebdomad, mad, MAD.

p: footpad, pad, tongue pad.

pl: plaid.

r: rad*.

s: sad, unsad.

sh: shad.

sk(sc): scad.

t: tad.

ĀD

Vowel: Ade, aid, co-aid, lemonade, orangeade, underaid.

b: bade, gambade.

bl: blade, Damascus blade, grass blade.

br: abrade, abraid*, braid, unbraid, upbraid.

d: dade*, McDade.

f: fade.

fl: flayed.

fr: afraid, unafraid.

g: brigade, fire brigade, renegade.

gl: glade.

gr: Belgrade, centigrade, degrade, grade, make the grade, planti-grade, retrograde.

h: hade.

j: bejade*, jade.

k(c): alcaide, ambuscade, arcade, barricade, blockade, brocade, cade, cascade, cavalcade, cockade, decade, estacade, falcade, saccade, stockade.

kw(qu): McQuade.

l: accolade, Adelaide, deep-laid, defilade, delayed, enfilade, escalade, fusillade, grillade, inlaid, interlaid, lade, laid, marmalade, overlaid, pistolade*, scalade*, underlaid, unlade, unlaid.

m: dairy maid, handmaid, made, maid, mermaid, milkmaid, new made, old maid, pomade, ready-made, sea maid, self-made, serving maid, undismayed, unmade, unmaid.

n: bastinade, cannonade, carronade, cassonade, colonade, dragonnade, esplanade, fanfaronade, flanconnade, gabionnade, gasconade, grenade, harlequinade, lemonade, marinade, panade*, pasquinade, promenade+, serenade.

p: croupade, escapade, overpaid, paid, postpaid, prepaid, unpaid, unrepaid.

pl: displayed, plaid, played, overplayed, underplayed, undisplayed, unplayed.

pr: prayed, preyed, unprayed, unpreyed.

r: arrayed, bewrayed*, camerade, charade, corrade*, masquerade, parade, raid, rayed, tirade, unarrayed, unrayed.

s: ambassade*, assayed, camisade*, crusade, essayed, glissade, harquebusade, lancepesade*, palisade, passade, pesade, unassayed, unessayed.

sh: nightshade, overshade, shade.

sl: slade.

sp: spade, spayed.

spl: splayed.

spr: sprayed.

st: overstayed, stade*, staid, storm stayed, unstaid.

str: strayed.

sw: dissuade, overpersuade, persuade, suade*, suede.

t: croustade, rodomontade.

tr: balustrade, free trade, trade.

v: evade, invade, pervade.

w: unweighed, wade, weighed.

Plus a+ed.

Plus they'd, etc.

ÄD

Vowel: od, odd*.

b: baad, bod.

d: Dodd.

f: Eisteddfod.

g: begod*+, demigod+, god+, river god+, sea god+, ungod+.

h: hahad, hod*.

k(c): cod*, Codd*.

kl(cl): clod+.

kw: quad*, quod*.

l: ballade, roulade.

m: chamade*.

n: nod*, promenade+.

p: lycopod*, platypod*, pod*.

pl: plod.

pr: prod.

r: Aaron's rod, charade+, divining rod, emerod, goldenrod, hurrahed+, piston rod, rod.

s: facade, glissade+, lancepesade, sod.

sh: dry-shod, pshad, reshod, rough-shod, shod, slipshod, unshod.

skr(scr): scrod.

t: tod.

tr: estrade, trod, untrod.

v: couvade, Eisteddfod.

w: wad.

y: noyade.

z: huzzahed.

Plus ah+ed or ah'd.

ADZ

Vowel: ads, adze.

sk(sc): scads.

Plus ad+s.

ĀDZ

Vowel: AIDS.

ÄDZ

Vowel: odds.

r: emerods.

Plus od+s.

Plus rod's, etc.

AF

ch: chaff+.

dr: draff.

g: gaff, penny gaff, shandygaff.

gr: actinograph, agraffe, anagraph, autograph, ballistocardiograph, calligraph, cardiograph. chronograph, cinematograph, cryptograph, diagraph, dictograph, eidograph, epigraph, graf, graff*, hagiograph, heliograph, holograph, ideograph, idiograph, lithograph, monograph, paleograph, pantograph, paragraph, phonograph, photograph, polygraph, stenograph+, stereograph+, telegraph, telephotograph.

h: behalf+, better half+, half+, half-and-half+.

k(c): calf+, moon calf+.

l: belly laugh+, laugh+.

r: carafe+, giraffe+, raff, riffraff.

s: Saph.

st: cross-staff+, fly staff+, half-staff+, quarter-staff+, staff+, tipstaff+, whipstaff+.

str: strafe+.

t: cenotaph, distaff, epitaph+.

ĀF

ch: chafe, enchafe.

s: safe, unsafe, vouchsafe.

str: strafe.

w: waif.

ÄF

Vowel: long field off+, mouth off+, off+, pairing off+, sign off+, take off+.

ch: chaff+.

d: doff+.

g: golf+.

gr: graf, stenograph+, stereograph+.

h: behalf, better half, haaf, half+, half-and-half+.

k(c): calf+, moon calf+.

k(w): coif+.

l: belly laugh+, laugh+.

pr: prof.

s: soph.

shr: shroff.

sk(sc): scoff+.

str: strafe+.

t: toff+.

tr: trough+.

AFT

Vowel: aft+.

b: abaft+.

ch: chaffed+.

d: daft.

dr: draft+, draught+, overdraft+.

gr: engraft+, graft+, ingraft+.

h: haft+.

kr(cr): craft+, fellow craft, handicraft, priestcraft, river craft, seacraft, witchcraft.

kw(qu): quaffed+, quant+.

l: laughed+.

r: raft+.

sh: shaft+.

str: strafed+.

t: Taft.

w: waft+.

Plus af+ed.

ÄFT

Vowel: aft+.

b: abaft+.

ch: chaffed+.

dr: draft+, draught+, overdraft+.

gr: engraft+, graft+, ingraft+.

h: haft+.

kr(cr): craft+, priestcraft, seacraft.

kw(qu): quaffed+, quant+.

l: aloft+, hayloft+, laughed+, loft+.

r: raft+.

s: soft+.

sh: shaft+.

str: strafed+.

t: toft+.

w: waft+.

Plus af+ed.

AG

ag: Ag.

b: bag, saddle bag.

br: brag, Bragg.

dr: drag.

f: fag, fish fag.

fl: battle flag, flag, red flag.

fr: frag.

g: gag.

h: hag, night hag.

j: jag.

k(c): cag.

kr: crag.

kw(qu): quag+.

l: lag, gulag+.

m: mag.

n: Brobdingnag, knag, nag.

r: bullyrag, chew the rag, do-rag, rag, Wragg.

s: sag.

sh: shag.

shr: shrag*.

skr(scr): scrag.

sl: slag.

sn: snag.

spr: sprag*.

st: stag.

sw: swag.

t: ragtag, tag.

w: scallawag, wag.

z: zag, zigzag.

ĀG

h: Hague.

pl: plague.

v: vague.

ÄG

b: bog+.

d: bulldog+, dog+, dog-eat-dog, hot dog+, prairie dog+, sun dog+.

f: befog+, defog+, fog+, pettifog+.

fl: flog+.

fr: frog+.

g: agog, demagogue, Gog, mystagogue, pedagogue, synagogue.

gr: grog.

h: groundhog+, hedgehog+, hog+, quahog+.

j: jog.

k(c): cog+.

kl(cl): clog+, reclog+, unclog+.

l: analogue+, apologue+, catalogue+, dialogue+, gulag+, log+, travelog+.
n: eggnog, nog.
pr: Prague, prog.
sl: slog.
sn: snog.
t: tog+.
w: golliwog, poliwog.

AGD

t: betagged.
Plus ag+ed.

ĀGD

pl: unplagued.

ÄGD

f: defogged+.
fr: frogged+.

ÄGZ

t: togs+.

AJ

b: badge.
f: fadge.
h: hadj.
k(c): cadge.
m: Madge.

ĀJ

Vowel: age.
g: disengage, engage, gage, gauge, preengage, ram gauge, reengage, weather gauge.
k(c): cage, discage, encage, uncage.
m: mage.
p: compage*, foot page, page, rampage.
r: enrage, outrage, rage.

s: presage+, sage, unsage.
st: stage, backstage, on-stage.
sw: assuage, swage.
tr: arbitrage.
w: wage.

ÄJ

d: dodge.
h: hodge.
l: dislodge, horologe, lodge, unlodge.
n: espionaje+.
p: hodgepodge.
r: raj.
spl: splodge.
st: stodge.
Cf. aj, badge, etc.

ĀJD

g: disengaged, engaged.

AK

Vowel: ammoniac, bivouac, cardiac, demoniac, dipsomaniac, Dyak, egomaniac, elegiac, hypochondriac, kayak, kleptomaniac, manic, monomaniac, Pontiac, pyromaniac, salammoniac, symposiac, umiak, zodiac.
b: aback, bac, back, bareback, biofeedback, callback, comeback, drawback, fallback, flashback, fullback, greenback, halfback, hardback, hatchback, horseback, huckaback, humpback, hunchback, kickback, laid-back, leatherback, outback, paperback, pickaback, piggyback, razorback, stickleback, throwback, wetback, zweiback.
bl: black, nonblack.
br: brach*, bricabrac, ladybrach*.
ch: chack.
d: dak, kodak, NASDAQ.

fl: flak.

h: hack.

hw: whack.

j: applejack, blackjack, bootjack, crackerjack, hijack, jack, leather jack, lumberjack, Monterey Jack, natterjack, shipjack, skyjack, slapjack, Union Jack, yellowjack.

k(c): ipecac, macaque.

kl: clack, claque.

kr: crack, jimcrack, thundercrack.

kw(qu): quack.

l: alack*, Fond du Lac, good lack*, lac, lack, lakh.

m: Mac, tokamak, yashmak.

n: almanac, knack, knicknack.

p: pack, radiopaque, unpack, wool pack.

pl: plack, plaque.

r: rack, sea wrack, tamarack, wrack.

s: cul-de-sac, gripsack, Hackensack, haversack, ransack, rucksack, sac, sack, sacque, wool sack.

sh: shack.

sl: slack.

sm: smack.

sn: snack.

st: haystack, stack.

t: attack, hackmatack, tack, ticktack.

thr: thrack.

thw: thwack.

tr: off-track, track.

v: Slovak.

w: Wack.

y: yack.

ĀK

Vowel: ache, backache, bellyache, earache, heartache, stomachache, toothache.

b: bake, hardbake.

bl: Blake.

br: antilock brake, barley brake, brake, break, daybreak, disc brake, heartbreak, outbreak, upbreak, waterbreak.

dr: drake, mandrake, sheldrake.

f: fake.

fl: cornflake, flake, snowflake.

h: hake.

j: jake.

k(c): cake, hoe cake, johnnycake, seed cake, shortcake, tea cake, wedding cake.

kr: crake, water crake.

kw(qu): earthquake, quake.

l: lake.

m: make, on the make, unmake.

p: opaque, Pake.

s: forsake, namesake, sake.

sh: shake, sheik.

sl: aslake*, slake.

sn: blacksnake, coral snake, garter snake, milk snake, rattlesnake, ribbon snake, snake, water snake.

sp: forespake*, spake*.

st: stake, steak, sweepstake.

str: strake.

t: betake, mistake, overtake, partake, take, undertake, uptake, wapentake.

w: awake, robinwake, wake.

ÄK

Vowel: Antioch.

b: Bach, bock.

bl: auction block, Bloch, block, chock-a-block, stumbling block.

br: brock.

ch: chock.

d: doc, dock, langue d'oc, Medoc, undock.

fl: flock.

fr: frock, unfrock.

h: hoc*, hock, hollyhock, Mohock.

j: jock.

k(c): acock, Babcock, Bankok, billy cock, half-cock, Hitchcock, peacock, petcock, poppycock, shuttlecock, spatchcock, turkeycock, turncock, weather-cock, woodcock.

kl: clock.

kr: croc, scrock.

l: belock, deadlock, fetlock, firelock, flintlock, forelock, havelock, interlock, loch, lock, lovelock, padlock, percussion lock, relock, unlock.

m: amok, bemock, mock.

n: knock.

p: pock.

pl: plock.

r: acid rock, baroque, bedrock, Little Rock, Painted Rock, Plymouth Rock, punk rock, Ragnarock, roc, rock, weeping rock.

s: soc, sock, tube sock.

sh: shock.

sm: lady's smock, smock.

st: alpenstock, laughingstock, penstock, restock, stock, understock.

t: tick-tock.

w: Sarawak.

AKS

Vowel: ax, battle-ax.

f: fax, Halifax.

fl: flax.

l: Analax, lax, parallax, relax.

m: anticlimax, climax.

n: Astyanax.

p: pax.

s: Sachs, Saxe, Tay-Sachs.

sl: slacks.

t: excise tax, income tax, overtax, pretax, post-tax, sales tax, surtax, syntax, tax, value-added tax.

thr: anthrax.

w: beeswax, earwax, sealing wax, wax.

z: zax.

Plus ak+s.

ĀKS

j: jakes.

l: Great Lakes.

Plus ak+s.

ÄKS

Vowel: ox.

b: ballot box, band box, box, Christmas box, dialog box, hatbox, mailbox, paddle box, pillar box, powder box, signal box.

d: heterodox, orthodox, paradox.

f: fox, Foxx.

fl: phlox.

k(c): Cox.

n: equinox.

p: chickenpox, pox, small pox.

s: sox.

v: vox+.

Plus ok+s.

Plus lock's, etc.

AKT

Vowel: abreact, act, counteract, enact, entracte, overact, react, reenact, retroact, underact.

b: backed, humpbacked, saddle-backed.

br: bract.

d: redact.

f: fact, matter-of-fact.

fr: diffract, infract, refract.

h: hacked.

h(w): whacked.

p: compact, impact, pact.

r: cataract.

s: sacked.

str: abstract.

t: attacked, intact, tact.

tr: attract, contract, detract, distract, extract, protract, retract, subtract, tract, untracked.

z: exact, transact.

Plus ak+ed.

ĀKT

b: baked, half-baked.

Plus ak+d.

ÄKT

k(c): concoct, decoct, recoct.

AL

Vowel: Al.

b: bal, cabal.

d: dal.

g: gal.

h: Hal.

k(c): Cal, low-cal, Pascal.

n: canal

p: pal.

r: corral

sh: shall+.

ĀL

Vowel: ail, ale, gingerale.

b: bail, bale.

br: brail, Braille.

d: Bloomingdale, dale.

dw: dwale.

f: fail, pass-fail.

fl: flail.

fr: frail.

g: Abigail, farthingale, Gael, Gail, gale, martingale, nightingale, regale.

gr: engrail, grail.

h: all hail, exhale, hail, hale, inhale.

hw: whale.

j: engaol, enjail, gaol, jail.

k: kail, kale.

kw(qu): quail.

m: blackmail, camail, mail, male.

n: canaille, hobnail, nail, tenaille.

p: bepale, dead pale, deathpale, empale, impale, interpale*, pail, pale.

r: derail, handrail, monorail, rail.

s: assail, foresail, grisaille, mainsail, outsail, sail, sale, topsail, wholesale.

sh: shale.

sk(sc): enscale, Richter scale, scale, sliding scale.

sn: snail.

sp: spale.

st: stale.

sw: swale.

t: aventail, betail, bobtail, cocktail, curtail, detail, disentail, dovetail, draggletail, entail, fairytale, pigtail, retail, tael, tail, tale, trundletail*.

TH: they'll.

thr: thrale.

tr: entrail*, trail.

v: avail, countervail, inveil, overvail, paravail, prevail, travail, unveil, vail, vale, veil.

w: bewail, wail, wale.

y: Yale.

Plus Mav'll, etc.

ÄL

Vowel: vitriol+.

d: dahl, dal, baby doll+, doll+.

h: alcohol+.

l: loll.

k(c): protocol+.

kr: kraal+.

m: gun moll, moll.

r: fol-de-rol, morale.

s: consol, entresol, girasol+, La Salle, parasol+.
t: atoll, extol+.

ALB

Vowel: alb.
d: De Kalb.

ĀLD

Vowel: ailed.
h: haled, unhaled.
s: assailed, sailed, unassailed.
t: bobtailed, short-tailed, tailed.
w: bewailed, unbewailed, wailed.
    Plus al+ed.

ÄLD

Vowel: auld+.

ALF

Vowel: Alf, Alph.
r: Ralph.

ALK

f: catafalque+.
t: talc.

ALKS

k(c): calx.
    Plus alk+s.

ALP

Vowel: alp.
p: palp.
sk(sc): scalp.

ALPS

Vowel: Alps.
    Plus alp+s.

ALT

sh: shalt*+.

ÄLT

v: gevalt.

ALV

s: salve+.
v: bivalve, priming valve, safety valve, univalve, valve.

ÄLV

s: absolve+, solve+.
v: circumvolve, convolve, devolve+, evolve+, intervolve, involve+, revolve+.
z: dissolve+, resolve+.

ÄLVD

s: unsolved+.
z: undissolved+, unresolved+.
    Plus olv+d.

ĀLZ

s: Marseilles+.
tr: Trails.
w: Wales.
    Plus al+s.

AM

Vowel: am, The Great I Am.
b: Alabam.
bl: blam.
ch: cham.
d: Amsterdam, cofferdam, dam, damn, madame, McAdam, Rotterdam, Scheidam.
dr: drachm, dram.
fl: flimflam, oriflamme.
fr: diaphragm.

g: cryptogam, gam.

gr: anagram, angiogram, ballistocardiogram, cablegram, cryptogram, diagram, epigram, gram, monogram, parallelogram, radiogram, stereogram, telegram.

h: Abraham, Birmingham, Cunningham, ham, Nottingham.

hw: wham, whimwham.

j: jam, jamb, Ramajam.

k(c): cam, camb.

kl: clam.

kr: cram.

l: lam, lamb

m: ma'am, Mam.

p: Pam.

pr: pram.

r: battering ram, dithyramb, ram, RAM.

s: Sam, Uncle Sam.

sh: Petersham, sham.

shr: shram.

skr: scram.

sl: slam.

sp: Spam.

sw: swam.

t: tam.

tr: tram.

y: yam.

z: Nizam.

ĀM

Vowel: aim.

bl: blame.

ch: Chaim.

d: dame.

dr: melodrame.

f: defame, disfame, fame.

fl: aflame, flame, inflame.

fr: frame, mainframe.

g: game.

gr: Graeme.

h: hame.

k(c): became, came, overcame.

kl: acclaim, claim, counterclaim, declaim, disclaim, exclaim, proclaim, reclaim.

l: lame.

m: maim, Mame.

n: filename, misname, name, nickname, surname.

s: same, selfsame.

sh: ashame, shame.

t: entame, tame.

ÄM

b: balm, bomb, embalm, gas bomb.

d: dom.

fr: from+, therefrom+.

gr: pogrom+.

gw̄: Guam.

k(c): becalm, calm, sitcom.

kw(qu): qualm.

l: Islam, salaam.

m: imam, ma'am, malm.

n: phenom.

p: impalm, palm, pompom.

pl: aplomb+.

pr: prom.

r: rhomb, ROM.

s: psalm.

sw: swom.

AMB

Vowel: choriamb.

g: gamb.

r: dithyramb.

ĀMD

bl: blamed, unblamed.

fr: framed, unframed.

kl: claimed, unclaimed, unreclaimed.

n: named, unnamed.
sh: ashamed, shamed, unashamed.
t: tamed, untamed.
    Plus am+ed.

AMP

Vowel: amp.
ch: champ.
d: afterdamp, damp, deathdamp, firedamp, mine damp.
g: gamp, guimpe.
k(c): camp, decamp, encamp.
kl: clamp.
kr: cramp.
l: Davy lamp, lamp, safety lamp, signal lamp.
r: ramp.
s: samp.
sk(sc): scamp.
st: enstamp, stamp.
t: tamp.
tr: tramp.
v: revamp, vamp.

ÄMP

k(c): comp.
p: pomp.
r: romp.
sw: swamp.
tr: trompe.

AMPT

d: damped, undamped.
k(c): camped.
    Also amp+ed.

ÄMPT

k: accompt*.
pr: imprompt*, prompt.
    Plus omp+d.

AMZ

j: jams.

ĀMZ

Vowel: Ames.
j: James.
    Plus am+s.

ÄMZ

Vowel: alms.
    Plus am+s.

AN

b: ban, corban.
br: bran.
ch: chan.
d: Dan, echinidan, foo young dan, Ramadhan, redan, sedan, shandrydan.
f: fan.
fl: flan+.
fr: Fran.
g: began, tzigane.
gr: Gran.
h: Han, Isfahan.
j: Jan.
kl: clan, Klan.
kr: cran.
l: Ameslan, castellan, Catalan, LAN, Milan, ortolan.
m: serving man, signalman+, superman+, talisman, tallyman, unman, wherryman.
n: Nan.
p: frying pan, hardpan, Japan, Matapan, moo goo gai pan, pan, trepan, warming pan.
pl: plan.
r: Alcoran, Aldebaran, also-ran, catamaran, foreran, outran, overran, ran, veteran.
s: Parmesan+, partisan.

sk(sc): CAT scan, scan.

sp: C-SPAN, inspan, outspan, span, spick-and-span.

t: orangutan, tan.

TH: than.

v: caravan, divan, luggage van, pavan, prison van, van.

w: WAN.

z: bartizan+, courtesan+.

ĀN

Vowel: Aisne, ane, Cockaigne, Duane, inane.

b: bane, Bayne, fleabane, henbane, inurbane, urbane.

bl: blain, Blaine, chilblain.

br: betweenbrain, brain, featherbrain, forebrain, hindbrain, lamebrain, membrane, midbrain, scatterbrain.

ch: chain, enchain, interchain, unchain.

d: coordain, Dane, deign, disdain, foreordain, ordain, prordain.

dr: drain.

f: aerophane, aeroplane, allophane, cellophane, diaphane, fain, fane, feign, hydrophane, lithophane, misfeign, profane.

fr: refrain.

g: again*, gain, regain.

gr: engrain, grain, ingrain.

j: jain, Jane, Jayne.

k(c): Cain, Caine, cane, chicane, cocaine, Duquesne, hurricane, sugar cane.

kr: crane, water crane, weather crane.

l: chatelaine, Elaine, delaine, lain, lane, McLain, McLean.

m: amain, chowmein, dalmane, demesne, domain, germane, humane, immane, legerdemain, main, Maine, mane, Mayne, mortmain, remain.

p: campaign, campane, champagne, champaign, counterpane, elecampane, frangipane, pain, Paine, pane, Payne.

pl: aeroplane, aquaplane, Champlain, complain, explain, hydroplane, plain, plane, pursuit plane.

r: acid rain, arraign, Bahrain, bearing rein, bridle rein, deraign, interreign, Lorraine, mediterrane, moraine, pertain, quatrain, rain, reign, rein, subterrane, suzerain, terrain, unrein.

s: insane, sane, Seine.

sh: Duchesne, Shane.

sk(sc): skein.

sl: slain.

sp: Spain.

spr: sprain.

st: abstain, bestain, stain.

str: andromeda strain, constrain, restrain, strain.

sw: boatswain, coxswain, swain.

t: appertain, ascertain, attain, contain, detain, entertain, maintain, obtain, pertain, retain, sextain, soutane, sustain, ta'en*, tain.

th: bower thane, thane, thegn.

tr: battering train, detrain, distrain, entrain, pleasure train, train, uptrain.

tw: atwain*, twain.

v: vain, vane, devein, vein, vervain, weathervane.

w: Charles's Wain, Gawain, wain, wane.

z: Zane.

ÄN

Vowel: encomion, hereon, thereon, whereon.

b: bonbon, corban.

d: dawn+, don, glyptodon, iguanodon, mastodon.

f: Bellerophon, chiffon.

fl: flan+.

g: decagon, heptagon, hexagon, octagon, Oregon+, paragon+, pentagon, polygon, tarragon, undergone+, woe-be-gone+.

j: demijohn, John, Littlejohn, Micklejohn, Saint John.

k(c): con, Helicon+, irenicon+, lexicon+, Rubicon+, silicon+, stereopticon+.

l: Babylon+, Ceylon, echelon, encephalon+, gonfalon+.

m: "mon."

n: anon, diazinon, dies non, Parthenon+, phenomenon+, prolegomenon+, sine qua non+.

p: hereupon, put upon+, thereupon, upon+, whereupon.

r: Oberon+.

sh: outshone+, shone+.

sw: swan+.

t: cretonne.

v: chicken divan, Darvon, von, Yvonne.

w: Saskatchewan+, wan.

y: yon.

z: amazon+, Luzon.

ÄNK

bl: beurre blanc, blanc de blancs, boudin blanc, chenin blanc, fumé blanc, sauvignon blanc.

ANCH

bl: blanch+.

br: branch+.

h: haunch+.

l: avalanche.

m: manche.

r: ranch.

st: stanch+, staunch+.

ÄNCH

bl: blanch+, Blanche, carte blanche.

br: branch+.

fl: flanch.

g: ganch.

h: haunch+.

kr: craunch+.

skr(scr): scranch.

st: stanch+.

ANCHT

st: stanched, unstanched.
    Plus anch+ed.

AND

Vowel: and.

b: aband*, band, contraband, disband, imband, saraband.

bl: bland.

br: brand, firebrand.

d: deodand.

f: fanned.

gl: gland, goat gland, monkey gland.

gr: grand, Rio Grande.

h: bridle hand, first-hand, four-in-hand, hand, master hand, minute hand, overhand, second hand, secondhand, underhand, unhand, upperhand.

k(c): multiplicand, Samarcand.

l: abbeyland, Disneyland, fairyland, farmland, fatherland, Holy Land, land, lotus land, overland.

m: command, countermand, demand, full-manned, ill-manned, manned, remand, reprimand, self-command, unmanned.

p: expand.

r: rand.

s: ampersand, sand.

sk(sc): scanned, unscanned.

st: stand, understand, washstand, withstand.

str: strand.

　Plus an+ed.

　Plus man'd, etc.

ĀND

br: brained, feather-brained, hare-brained, hot-brained, muddy-brained, rattle-brained, scatter-brained, shallow-brained, shatter-brained.

ch: chained, unchained.

d: disdained.

dr: drained, undrained.

f: diaphaned, feigned, profaned, unfeigned, unprofaned.

m: maned.

pl: planed, unplained*, unplaned.

r: reined, unreined.

st: blood-stained, stained, travel-stained, unstained.

str: constrained, restrained, self-restrained, strained, uncon-strained, unrestrained, unstrained.

t: ascertained, sustained, unascertained, unsustained.

tr: trained, untrained.

v: interveined, veined.

　Plus an+ed.

ÄND

b: bond, vagabond.

bl: blond, blonde.

d: donned.

f: fond, overfond, plafond.

fr: frond.

g: unparagoned.

m: demimonde.

p: pond.

r: Gironde+.

sk(sc): abscond.

sp: correspond, despond, respond.

w: wand.

y: beyond, yond*.

　Plus on+d.

　Plus don'd, etc.

ANG

b: bang, gobang, shebang, slap-bang.

ch: Chang.

d: dang.

f: fang.

g: gang.

h: hang, overhang, uphang.

hw: whang.

kl: clang.

l: Lang.

n: Penang.

p: pang, trepang.

r: boomerang, harangue, meringue, rang, serang.

s: sang.

sl: slang.

sp: spang.

spr: sprang.

st: stang.

sw: swang.

t: mustang, orangoutang, sea tang, tang.

tw: twang.

v: vang.

w: Wang.

ÄNG

d: ding dong+.

g: gong+.

k(c): Hong Kong+, King Kong+.

l: long+.

t: tong+.

ANGD

b: banged.
l: langued.
p: unpanged.
   Plus ang+ed.

ANGK

b: bank, embank, mountebank, savings bank.
bl: blank, point-blank.
br: brank.
ch: chank.
d: dank.
dr: drank.
fl: flank, outflank.
fr: franc+, frank.
h: hank.
kl: clank.
kr: crank.
l: lank.
pl: plank.
pr: prank.
r: enrank, outrank, rank.
s: sank.
sh: shank.
shr: shrank.
sl: slank.
sp: spank.
st: outstank, stank.
t: tank, water tank.
th: thank.
tw: twank.
y: yank.

ÄNGK

h: honk+.
k(c): conch+, conk+.

ANGKS

m: Manx.
   Plus angk+s.

ÄNGKS

br: Bronx.
   Plus ongk+s.
   Plus honky-tonk's, etc.

ANGKT

s: sacrosanct.
sh: spindle-shanked.
sp: spanked, unspanked.
   Plus angk+ed.

ANJ

fl: flange.
l: phalange.

ĀNJ

ch: change, counterchange, exchange, interchange, sea change.
gr: grange.
m: mange.
r: arrange, derange, disarrange, enrange, free-range, range, rearrange, target range.
str: strange.
tr: estrange.

ANS

ch: bechance, chance+, main chance, mischance, perchance.
d: barn dance+, country dance+, dance+, death dance+, folk dance+, square dance+.
fr: France+.
gl: glance.
h: enhance.
l: ambulance+, demilance, elance*, fer-delance, lance, petulance+, sibilance+, vigilance+.
m: mance, romance.
n: Nance.
p: expanse.
pr: prance.

sk: askance.

st: circumstance, stance.

t: concomitance, heritance, incogitance, inhabitance, inheritance, precipitance.

tr: entrance, penetrance, trance.

v: advance, irrelevance, relevance, Vance.

Cf. ant+s.

ÄNS

Vowel: insouciance.

ch: chance+.

d: barn dance+, country dance+, dance+, death dance+, folk dance+, square dance+.

fr: France+.

l: fer-de-lance.

n: nonce.

sh: bonne chance.

sk(sc): ensconce, sconce.

sp: response.

Plus ont+s.

Plus font's, etc.

ANT

Vowel: ant+, aunt+.

b: bant, Corybant.

br: brant.

ch: chant, disenchant, enchant.

d: commandant, confidant, confidante.

f: hierophant.

gr: grant.

h: ha'nt.

k(c): cant, can't, decant, descant, Kant, recant.

kw(qu): quant+.

l: nonchalant+.

m: adamant+.

p: pant.

pl: deplant, implant, plant, sensitive plant, supplant, transplant.

s: complaisant+, corposant+.

sh: shan't.

sk(sc): askant, scant.

sl: aslant, slant.

t: extant+, tant*.

v: gallivant, Levant.

ĀNT

Vowel: ain't.

d: daint*.

f: faint, feint.

h: hain't.

kw(qu): acquaint, quaint.

m: mayn't.

p: acrylic paint, bepaint, depaint, paint.

pl: complaint, liver complaint, plaint.

r: Geraint.

s: besaint, saint, unsaint.

str: constraint, distraint, restraint, self-restraint, straint, unconstraint.

t: attaint, taint, teint.

ÄNT

d: daunt+.

f: font.

g: gaunt+.

h: haunt+.

k(c): can't+.

m: romaunt+.

p: Dupont, Helles-pont, pont.

s: bien pensant.

sh: shan't+.

t: ataunt+, debutante+, taunt+.

v: avaunt*+, idiot savant, vaunt+.

w: want+.

ANTH

Vowel: amianth.

k: tragacanth.

r: amaranth.

ANTS

h: Hants.
p: hot pants, pants.
　Plus ant+s.
　Cf. ans.

ANZ

b: banns.
　Plus an+s.
　Plus Dan's, etc.

ĀNZ

k(c)r: cremains.
h: Haines.
r: Raines, Raynes.
　Plus an+s.
　Plus Cain's, etc.

ÄNZ

b: bonze.
br: bronze.
j: Johns, St. John's.
p: pons.
　Plus on+s.
　Plus John's, etc.

ÄNZH

l: melange.

AP

Vowel: app, lagniappe.
ch: chap.
d: dap.
dr: drap.
f: Fap.
fl: flap, flipflap.
fr: frap.
g: agape, gap, gape, stop gap.
h: hap, mayhap, mishap.
j: Jap.

k(c): ASCAP, cap, foolscap, forage cap, handicap, nightcap, percussion cap, wishing cap.
kl: afterclap, clap, thunderclap.
kr: crap.
l: lap, Lapp, overlap, unlap.
m: map.
n: genapp, genappe, knap, nap.
p: pap.
r: enwrap, gangsta rap, rap, unwrap, wrap.
s: sap.
skr(scr): scrap.
sl: slap, SLAPP.
sn: snap.
str: bestrap, shoulder strap, strap.
t: heel tap, tap, water tap.
tr: claptrap, entrap, rattletrap, trap.
w: wapp.
y: lagniappe, yap.
z: zap

ĀP

Vowel: ape.
ch: chape.
dr: drape.
g: agape, gape.
gr: grape.
j: jape.
k(c): cape, escape, fire escape, uncape.
kr: crape, crèpe.
l: Lape.
n: nape.
p: pape.
r: date rape, rape, stranger rape.
sh: bent-out-of-shape, shape, shipshape, transshape, unshape.
sk(sc): landscape, scape, seascape.
skr(scr): scrape.

t: audio tape, cassette tape, red-tape, tape.

tr: trape.

ÄP

Vowel: co-op, photo op.

b: bop

bl: blop.

ch: chop.

dr: bedrop, dewdrop, drop, eavesdrop, snowdrop.

f: fop.

fl: flipflop, flippity-flop, flop.

g: gaup.

gr: grop.

h: hop.

hw: whaup+, whop.

k(c): cop.

kl: klop-klop.

kr: aftercrop, crop, riding crop.

l: galop, lop.

m: mop.

n: knop.

p: ginger pop, lolipop, pop, soda pop.

pl: plop.

pr: prop, underprop.

s: sop, soursop, sweetsop.

sk(sc): scaup.

sh: head shop, shop, workshop.

sl: slop.

st: stop, unstop.

str: strop.

sw: swap.

t: atop, desktop, estop, foretop, mizzentop, overtop, tank top, tiptop, top.

w: wop.

y: yawp+.

APS

aps: apse.

h: perhaps.

kr: craps.

l: collapse, elapse, illapse, interlapse, lapse, relapse.

shn: schnapps+.

Plus ap+s.

Plus Jap's, etc.

ĀPS

Vowel: apes.

m: Mapes.

n: jackanapes.

tr: traipse.

Plus ap+s.

Plus ape's, etc.

ÄPS

k(c): copse.

p: pops.

shn: schnapps+.

Plus op+s.

Plus chop's, etc.

APT

Vowel: apt, inapt.

d: adapt.

k(c) : capped, moss-capped, snow-capped.

r: enrapt, rapt, wrapt.

str: bestrapped.

Plus ap+ed.

ĀPT

Vowel: aped.

Plus ap+d.

ÄPT

Vowel: co-opt, opt.

d: adopt.

k(c): copped, Copt.

kr: outcropped, uncropped.

st: unstopped.

Plus op+d.

Plus crop'd, etc.

AR

Vowel: air+, Ayr+, ayre*+.

d: dare+.

h: hair+, hare+, maidenhair+, mohair+.

m: mare+.

ÄR

Vowel: are, caviar, CPR, jaguar LTR, NPR, R, VCR, VFR, VTR.

b: axlebar, bar, cinnabar, debar, disbar, embar, Excalibar, Malabar, saddlebar, shacklebar, unbar, upbar, Zanzibar.

ch: char.

d: dar, deodar, hospodar, jemadar, subahdar, zamindar.

f: afar, far, Farr.

g: cigar, gar.

j: ajar, jar, nightjar.

k(c): car, jaunting car, Lascar.

lw: Loire.

m: cymar, mar, tintamarre*.

n: canard, gnar, knar.

nw: film noir, pinot noir.

p: par, parr.

sk(sc): scar.

sp: feldspar, spar, unspar.

st: daystar, evening star, falling star, instar, lodestar, morning star, north star, pilot star, sea star, shooting star, star.

str: registrar.

t: avatar, catarrh, guitar, scimitar, steel guitar, tar, tartare.

tr: registrar.

ts: tsar.

v: boulevard+.

w: jaguar.

z: bazaar, czar, hussar.

ÄRB

b: barb.

g: garb.

y: yarb.

ÄRCH

Vowel: arch, inarch, overarch.

l: larch.

m: countermarch, dead march, march, outmarch, overmarch.

p: parch.

st: starch.

ÄRD

Vowel: briard, milliard.

b: bard, bombard, close-barred.

ch: chard.

f: fard*.

g: afterguard, avant-garde, blackguard, bodyguard, disregard, enguard, guard, lifeguard, regard, unguard.

h: hard.

k(c): calling card, card, charge card, debit card, discard, green card, placard, wedding card.

l: foulard, interlard, lard.

m: marred, unmarred.

n: Bernard, canard, nard, spikenard.

p: camelopard, pard.

r: Gerard, Girard.

s: sard.

sh: shard.

sk(sc): scarred, unscarred.

sp: sparred, undersparred.

st: evil-starred, starred.

t: dynamitard, petard, retard, tarred, unitard.

v: boulevard.

y: backyard, chickenyard, front yard, poultry yard, yard.

Plus ar+ed.
Plus star'd.

ÄRF

Vowel: arf-and-arf.
l: larf.
sk: scarf.

ÄRJ

b: barge, embarge*.
ch: charge, discharge, encharge*, overcharge, surcharge, uncharge, undercharge.
f: Farge, La Farge.
l: enlarge, large.
m: marge, seamarge
s: sarge.
sp: sparge.
t: targe.
th: litharge.

ÄRJD

b: barged.
ch: charged, discharged, undischarged.
Plus arj+ed.

ÄRK

Vowel: arc, ark, Asiarch, ecclesiarch, heresiarch, hierarch, matriarch, patriarch.
b: bark, barque, debark, disembark, embark.
d: bedark, dark, endark*.
g: oligarch.
h: hark.
k(c): cark.
kl: Clarke.
l: lark, meadow lark, sea lark, skylark.
m: easymark, floodmark, footmark, marc, mark, marque, remark, watermark.

n: irenarch, knark, narc.
p: dispark, impark, park.
s: sark.
sh: shark.
sn: snark.
sp: spark.
st: stark, Starke.
v: aardvark.

ÄRKS

m: Marx.
Plus ark+s.

ÄRKT

b: barked.
m: marked, unmarked.
Plus ark+ed.

ÄRL

h: harl.
j: jarl.
k(c): carl, Karl.
m: Albermarle, marl.
n: gnarl.
p: imparl, parle*.
sn: snarl.

ÄRLZ

ch: Charles.
Plus arl+s.

ÄRM

Vowel: arm, axle arm, disarm, firearm, forearm, unarm.
b: barm.
ch: becharm, charm, countercharm, decharm, disencharm, love charm, uncharm.
d: gendarme.
f: county farm, farm, poor farm.
h: harm, unharm.

l: alarm, false alarm.
m: marm, schoolmarm.

ÄRMD

Vowel: armed, forearmed.
l: alarmed, unalarmed.
  Plus arm+ed.
  Plus arm'd, etc.

ÄRMZ

Vowel: Armes, assault-at-arms, gentleman-at-arms, king-at-arms, man-at-arms.
  Plus arm+s.
  Plus harm's, etc.

ÄRN

b: barn, imbarn*.
d: darn.
k(c): in carn.
m: Marne.
s: consarn.
t: tarn.
y: yarn.

ÄRNZ

b: Barnes.
  Plus arn+s.
  Plus yarn's, etc.

ÄRP

h: harp.
k(c): carp, epicarp, escarp, monocarp, pericarp.
sh: sharp.
sk(sc): scarp.

ÄRS

f: farce.
p: parse.
s: sarse.
sp: sparse.

ÄRSH

h: harsh.
m: marsh.

ÄRT

Vowel: art.
b: bart, Bart.
ch: chart.
d: dart, indart.
f: fart.
h: flintheart, hart, heart, lionheart, sweetheart, unheart.
k(c): cart, Descartes, quarte, uncart, watercart.
m: mart.
p: apart, counterpart, depart, dispart, impart, part.
s: sart.
sm: outsmart, smart.
st: start, upstart.
t: tart.

ÄRTH

g: Applegarth, garth.
h: hearth.

ÄRTS

h: Harz.
  Plus art+s.
  Plus art's, etc.

ÄRV

k(c): carve.
l: larve.
st: starve.

ÄRZ

l: Lars.
m: Mars.
  Plus ar+s.
  Plus tar's, etc.

AS

Vowel: ass.

b: bass+, rubasse, thorough bass.

br: brass+.

fr: sassafras.

g: gas.

gl: flint glass+, gallo glass+, glass+, hourglass+, isinglass+, looking glass+, minute glass+, object glass+, waterglass, weather glass.

gr: after-grass+, eel grass+, GRAS, grass+, sparrowgrass+.

kl(cl): airman first class, class+, declass+, distribution class, first-class+, lower-class, middle-class+, upper-class, working class+, world-class.

kr: crass, hippocras.

l: alas, bonnilass*, lass, paillasse.

m: Allhallowmas, amass, en masse, mass.

p: Khyber Pass+, overpass+, pass+, surpass+, underpass+.

r: cuirass, morass.

s: garden sass, sass.

str: strass.

t: demitasse+, tarantass, tass+.

v: crevasse, kavass.

y: yas.

ĀS

Vowel: ace.

b: abase, base, bass+, database, debase, freebase, rheobase.

br: brace, embrace, unbrace, underbrace.

ch: chase, enchase, steeplechase.

d: dace.

f: aface, boniface+, deface, efface, face, in-your-face, outface.

gr: begrace, disgrace, grace, scapegrace.

k(c): basket case, case, encase, ukase, uncase.

kr: idiocrase.

l: anelace, belace, enlace, interlace, lace, unlace.

m: grimace+, mace.

p: apace, carapace, footpace, outpace, pace.

pl: birthplace, commonplace, displace, hiding place, misplace, place, plaice, replace, resting place, trysting place.

r: chariot race, erase, foot race, horse race, race, rat race.

sp: breathing space, interspace, outer space, space.

thr: Thrace.

tr: retrace, trace.

v: vase+.

ÄS

Vowel: os.

b: boss+, emboss+.

br: brass+.

d: DOS.

dr: dross+.

f: fosse+.

gl: flint glass+, gallo glass+, glass+, gloss+, hourglass+, isinglass+,looking glass+, minute glass+, object glass+, waterglass+, weather glass+.

gr: after-grass+, eel grass+, grass+, sparrowgrass+.

j: joss+.

kl(cl): class+, declass+, first-class+, middle-class+, working class+.

kr: cross+, fiery cross+, rosy cross+, weeping cross+.

kv: kvass.

l: coloss*, loss+.

m: en masse, Hallowmas+, moss+, seas moss+.

p: Khyber Pass+, overpass+, pass+, surpass+, underpass+.

pr: pross.

t: demitasse+, tass+, toss+.

tr: albatross+.

ASH

Vowel: ash, mountain ash, weeping ash.

b: abash, bash, calabash, squabash.

br: brache*, brash.

d: balderdash, bedash, berdache, dash, interdash, slapdash, splatter-dash.

f: fash.

fl: flash, news flash.

g: gash.

h: hash, rehash.

k(c): cache, cash, cold cash.

kl: clash.

kr: crash.

l: calash, lache, lash, unlash.

m: mash.

n: gnash, Nash.

p: calipash, pash.

pl: plash.

r: rash.

s: sash.

sl: slash.

sm: smash.

spl: splash.

t: moustache, patache, sabretache.

thr: thrash.

tr: trash.

ĀSH

kr(ċr): crèche+.

ÄSH

b: bosch+, bosh, debosh, kibosh.

fr: frosh.

g: gosh+.

j: josh.

kw(qu): musquash+, quash+.

l: galosh.

m: mosh.

skw(squ): squash+.

sl: slosh.

spl: splosh.

sw: swash+.

t: mackintosh, McIntosh, tosh.

w: awash, bellywash, bewash, hogwash, wash+.

ASHT

b: abashed.

d: dashed, undashed.

l: lashed, unlashed.

thr: thrashed, unthrashed.

Plus ash+ed.

Plus lash'd, etc.

ÄSHT

b: caboshed+.

w: "great unwashed," unwashed+.

Plus osh+d.

ASK

Vowel: ask+.

b: bask+, basque.

fl: flask+, hip flask+, powder flask+.

k(c): cask+, casque, watercask+.

m: Bergamask, mask+, masque+.

t: task+.

ÄSK

Vowel: ask+, kiosk.

b: bask+, bosk, imbosk*.

fl: flask+, hip flask+, powder flask+.

k(c): cask+, casque, watercask+.

m: antimask, bemask, Bergamask, immask*, mask+, masque+, mosque, unmask.

p: Pasch.

t: overtask, task+.

ASKT

Vowel: asked+, unasked+.
b: basked+.
m: masked+, unmasked+.

ÄSKT

Vowel: asked+, unasked+.
b: basked+.
m: masked+, unmasked+.
  Plus ask+ed.

ASP

Vowel: asp.
g: gasp.
gr: engrasp+, grasp+.
h: hasp+.
kl: clasp+, enclasp+, unclasp+.
r: rasp+.

ÄSP

gr: engrasp+, grasp+.
h: hasp+.
kl: clasp+, enclasp+, unclasp+.
r: rasp+.
w: wasp+, WASP.

AST

Vowel: ecclesiast+, elegiast+, encomiast+, enthusiast+, orgiast+, scholiast+, symposiast+.
b: bast, bombast.
bl: blast+, counterblast+, stormblast+.
d: dast.
f: emberfast+, fast+, hand-fast, holdfast, steadfast+, unfast+.
fr: metaphrast, paraphrast.
g: aghast, flabbergast, ghast*+.
h: hast*+.
k(c): cast+, caste+, downcast, forecast, high-caste, low-caste, overcast, recast+.

kl: iconoclast, idoloclast, theoclast.
l: last+, outlast.
m: amassed, foremast+, half-mast, jury mast, mainmast+, massed, mast+, mizzen mast+.
p: passed+, past+, repast+, surpassed+, unpassed+, unsurpassed+.
pl: metaplast, protoplast.
s: sassed.
tr: contrast.
v: avast, devast, vast+.
  Plus as+ed.

ĀST

b: abased, baste, lambaste, self-abased.
br: braced, unbraced.
ch: chased, chaste, unchaste.
f: apple-faced, bare-faced, brazen-faced, defaced, double-faced, doughfaced, fair-faced, freckle-faced, furrow-faced, hard-faced, hatchet-faced, horse-faced, Janus-faced, lean-faced, lily-faced, mottle-faced, pale-faced, paper-faced, pickle-faced, pie-faced, pimple-faced, pippin-faced, platter-faced, plump-faced, pudding-faced, pug-faced, sad-faced, shamefaced, sheep-faced, smock-faced, smooth-faced, smug-faced, tallow-faced, triple-faced, two-faced, undefaced, unshamefaced, vinegar-faced, weasel-faced, whey-faced, wizen-faced.
gr: graced, undisgraced, ungraced, well-graced.
h: haste, posthaste.
k(c): cased, uncased.
l: laced, straight-laced, unlaced.
p: impaste, leaden-paced, paste, slow-paced, snail-paced, thorough-paced.

r: erased, raced.

sp: spaced.

t: after-taste, distaste, foretaste, taste.

tr: retraced, traced, untraced.

w: waist, waste.

Plus as+d.

ÄST

b: embossed+.

bl: blast+, counterblast+, stormblast+.

f: emberfast+, fast+, steadfast+, unfast+.

fr: frost+.

g: ghast*+.

h: hast*+.

k(c): accost+, cast+, caste+, cost+, Lacoste+, Pentecost+, recast+.

l: last+, lost+, unlost+.

m: foremast+, mainmast+, mast+, mizzen mast+.

p: passed+, past+, repast+, surpassed+, unpassed+, unsurpassed+.

t: betossed+, sea-tossed+, tempest-tossed+.

v: vast+.

w: wast*+.

Plus as+ed.

AT

Vowel: at, caveat+, hereat, thereat, whereat.

b: acrobat, at-bat, bat, brickbat, fruit bat, vampire bat.

bl: blat.

br: Bradt, brat.

ch: chat, fallow chat.

d: dis and dat.

dr: drat.

f: fat, marrow fat, phat.

fl: a flat, flat.

fr: frat.

g: forgat*, gat.

h: hat, high-hat, hi-hat, top hat, unhat.

k(c): cat, civet cat, hellcat, kitty-cat, Magnificat, MCAT, polecat, pussycat, requiescat, ring-tailed cat, tabby cat, tomcat.

kr: aristocrat, autocrat, bureaucrat, democrat, monocrat, plutocrat, theocrat.

m: automat, diplomat, GMAT, mat, Matt, matte.

n: assignat, gnat, Nat.

p: bepat, pat, pit-a-pat.

pl: plait, plat, Platt, Platte.

pr: dandiprat, Pratt.

r: Ararat, rat, Surat, waterrat.

s: LSAT+, sat.

sk(sc): scat, SCAT.

sl: slat.

sp: spat.

spr: sprat, Spratt.

st: heliostat, hydrostat, rheostat, thermostat.

t: habitat, tat, tit-for-tat.

TH: that.

v: cravat, vat.

ĀT

Vowel: abbreviate, absinthiate, accentuate, actuate, affiliate, alleviate, ampliate, annunciate, appreciate, appropriate+, asphyxiate, associate+, ate, attenuate, aureate, aviate, calumniate, chalybeate, circumstantiate, conciliate, create, delineate, denunciate, depreciate, deviate, differentiate, dissociate, effectuate, eight, emaciate, emoliate, enunciate, evacuate, evaluate, eventuate, excoriate, excruciate, expatiate, expatriate, expiate, extenuate, fluctuate, fructuate, glaciate, graduate, habituate, humiliate, immateriate*, impropriate+, inchoate, increate, individuate, inebriate, infatuate, infuriate, ingratiate, initiate, insatiate, insinuate, intermediate, irradiate, laureate, licentiate, lixiviate, luxuriate, mediate, negotiate, novitiate, obviate, officiate, opiate+, palliate, permeate, perpetuate, procreate, professoriate, propitiate, provinciate, punctuate, radiate, recreate, remediate, repatriate, repudiate, retaliate, roseate, satiate, secretariate, situate, spoiliate, substantiate, superannuate, transubstantiate, uncreate, variate, vicariate, vitiate.

b: abate, approbate, bait, bate, debate, exacerbate, incubate, rebate, reprobate, stylobate.

br: celebrate, invertebrate+, lucubrate, vertebrate+.

d: abnodate*, accommodate, antedate, candidate+, consolidate, date, deodate*, depredate, dilapidate, elucidate, intimidate, inundate, invalidate, liquidate, predate, sedate, validate.

f: caliphate, fate, fete+.

fl: conflate, efflate, inflate, reflate, sufflate.

fr: affreight, freight.

g: abnegate, abrogate, aggregate, arrogate, Billingsgate, castigate, congregate, conjugate, corrugate, delegate+, derogate, extravagate, floodgate, fumigate, gait, gate, instigate, interrogate, investigate, irrigate, levigate, litigate, mitigate, navigate, obligate, profligate, promulgate, propagate, relegate, runagate, Sea Gate, segregate, subjugate, subrogate, supererogate, variegate.

gr: disintegrate, emigrate, grate, great, immigrate, ingrate*, integrate, migrate, regrate.

h: hate, Haight.

k(c): abdicate, abjudicate, ablocate*, advocate+, allocate, altercate, applicate, auspicate, authenticate, cate, certificate+, collocate, communicate, complicate, confiscate, dedicate, deprecate, diagnosticate, dislocate, domesticate, duplicate, educate, equivocate, eradicate, excommunicate, extricate, fabricate, hypothecate, implicate, imprecate, inculcate, indicate, intoxicate, invocate, Kate, locate, lubricate, masticate, placate, pontificate, predicate, prevaricate, prognosticate, quadruplicate, reciprocate, rusticate, silicate, spifflicate, suffocate, supplicate, syndicate+, vacate, vindicate.

kr: consecrate, crate, desecrate, execrate, krait.

kw(qu): antiquate, equate.

l: absquatulate, accumulate, acidulate, adulate, alveolate, ambulate, angulate, annihilate, annulate, apostolate, articulate+, assimilate, assimulate*, belate, bimaculate, binoculate, calculate, campanulate, cancellate, capitulate, cardinalate, circulate, coagulate, collate, confabulate, congratulate, consulate, copulate, correlate, crenellate, delate, depopulate, depucelate*, desolate+, dilate, disconsolate, dissimulate, ejaculate, elate, emasculate, emulate, etiolate, expostulate, flagellate+, foliolate, formulate, funambulate, gesticulate, granulate, gratulate*, immaculate+, immolate, inarticulate+, incastellate*, inoculate, insulate, interpolate, inviolate, isolate, lanceolate, late, legislate, manipulate, matriculate, modulate, mutilate, oscillate, osculate, peculate, peninsulate, perambulate, percolate, populate, postulate+, recapitulate, regulate, relate, reticulate, scintillate, sibilate, simulate, somnambulate, speculate, stellulate, stimulate, stipulate, stridulate, tabulate, titillate, translate, triangulate, ululate, undulate, vacillate, vassalate, ventilate, vermiculate, violate.

m: acclamate*, acclimate, amalgamate, animate+, antepenultimate, approximate+, casemate, checkmate, classmate, consummate+, cremate, decimate, estimate+, first mate, helpmate, inanimate+, intimate+, legitimate+, mate, messmate, playmate, proximate, schoolmate, shipmate, stalemate, sublimate, ultimate+.

n: abacinate, abalienate, abominate, acuminate, affectionate+, agglutinate, alienate, alternate+, assassinate, cachinnate, carbonate+, comminate, compassionate+, concatenate, conditionate, contaminate, co-ordinate+, coronate, criminate, culminate, denominate+, designate+, detonate, devirginate, diaconate, discriminate+, disseminate, dominate, donate, effeminate+, eliminate, emanate, exterminate, extortionate, fascinate, foreordinate, fulminate, gelatinate, germinate, hibernate, illuminate, immarginate, impersonate, importunate, incriminate, indeterminate, indiscriminate, indoctrinate, ingerminate, innate, inseminate, intercessionate*, interminate, intonate, machinate, magnate, marinate, Nate, nominate, originate, ornate, oxygenate, patronate, peregrinate, personate, predestinate, predominate, procrastinate, ratiocinate, recriminate, rejuvenate, ruminate, terminate, vaccinate, vaticinate, vertiginate.

p: anticipate, constipate, dissipate, dunderpate, emancipate,

episcopate, exculpate, extirpate, participate, pate, rattlepate, syncopate.

pl: armor plate, contemplate, copperplate, dial plate, electroplate, nickelplate, plait, plate, silver plate.

pr: prate.

r: accelerate, accurate, adulterate, aerate, agglomerate, ameliorate, annumerate*, aspirate, asseverate, augurate*, berate, birth rate, camphorate, collaborate, commemorate, commiserate, confederate+, conglomerate+, considerate, co-operate, corporate, corroborate, death rate, decolorate, decorate, degenerate, deliberate, derate, desiderate, desperate, deteriorate, directorate, discount rate, doctorate, elaborate, electorate, enumerate, evaporate, exaggerate, exasperate, exhilarate, exonerate, expectorate, federate, first-rate, generate, illiterate, immoderate, inaccurate, inaugurate, incarcerate, incinerate, incommensurate, inconsiderate, incorporate, indurate, inmensurate*, intemperate, intenerate, inveterate, invigorate, irate, iterate, itinerate, lacerate, levirate, liberate, literate, macerate, moderate, narrate, obdurate, obliterate, operate, orate, overrate, pastorate, perforate, perorate, preponderate, prime rate, prorate, protectorate, protuberate, rate, rectorate, recuperate, refrigerate, regenerate, reiterate, remunerate, reverberate, saturate, second-rate, rediscount rate, separate, stearate, suppurate, temperate, third-rate, tolerate, transliterate, triturate, triumvirate, ulcerate, underrate, venerate, verberate, vituperate, vizierate, vociferate, water rate.

s: compensate, improvisate, marquisate, pulsate, sate, tergivesate.

sk(sc): cheapskate, roller skate, skate.

sl: slate.

sp: spate.

st: instate, overstate, reinstate, restate, state, understate, unstate.

str: demonstrate, remonstrate, straight, strait.

t: agitate, amputate, annotate, capacitate, capitate, cogitate, crepitate, debilitate, decapitate, devastate, dictate, digitate, estate, excogitate, exorbitate, facilitate, felicitate, gravitate, habilitate, hesitate, imitate, incapacitate, ingurgitate, irritate, meditate, necessitate, palpitate, potentate, precipitate, premeditate, regurgitate, rehabilitate, resuscitate, rotate, sanitate, Tait, Tate, tête-a-tête, vegetate.

tr: arbitrate, concentrate, frustrate, illustrate, impetrate, magistrate, orchestrate, penetrate, perpetrate, trait, prostrate, recalcitrate.

v: aggravate, captivate, cultivate, derivate, elevate, enervate, estivate, excavate, innovate, motivate, renovate, salivate, titivate.

w: await, dead weight, featherweight, heavyweight, lightweight, middleweight, overweight, paperweight, penny-weight, underweight, wait, weight.

ÄT

Vowel: compatriot+, patriot+.

b: bott.

bl: blot.

br: Bradt.

d: dot.

g: begot, first-begot, forgo, got, Gott, hard-got, ill-got, misbegot, unbegot*, unforgot, ungot.

gl: polyglot.

gr: grot.

h: fiery hot, hot.

hw: somewhat+, what+.

j: jot.

k(c): apricot, cocotte, cot.

kl: clot.

kw(qu): aliquot, comquat, kumquat, kumquate, loquat, quot.

l: alot, cachalot, calotte, Camelot, eschalot, Kalat, Khelat, Lancelot, lot, sans culotte, shallot, Shalotte.

m: bergamot, witenagemot.

n: forget-me-not, Huguenot, knot, loveknot, not, reknot, shoulderknot, unknot.

p: Capot, gallipot, inkpot, pot.

pl: counterplot, grassplot, plot, underplot.

r: dry rot, garrote, rot, tommyrot.

s: besot, sot.

sh: cheap shot, grapeshot, overshot, passing shot, shot, sighting shot, slap shot, undershot.

sk(sc): Scot, Scott.

skw(squ): asquat, squat.

sl: slot.

sn: snot.

sp: beauty spot, plague spot, spot.

st: Stott.

sw: swat, SWAT.

t: Hottentot, tot.

tr: dogtrot, jogtrot, trot.

v: gavotte.

w: wat*, watt, wot*.

y: yacht.

ATH

g: Gath.

h: hath*.

m: aftermath, math, philomath.

p: allopath, homeopath, osteopath, physiopath, psychopath.

sn: snath.

ĀTH

b: bathe.
f: blind faith, faith, good faith, ifaith*, misfaith, unfaith.
l: lathe.
r: rathe*, waterwraith, wraith.
sk(sc): scathe.
sn: snathe.
sp: spathe.
sw: swathe, unswathe.

ÄTH

m: behemoth+.
sl: sloth+.
tr: betroth+, troth+.
w: wrath+.

ATS

gr: congrats.
st: stats.

ĀTS

b: Bates.
f: fates.
k: Cates.
st: States, United States.
y: Yates, Yeats.
     Plus at+s.

ÄTS

pl: plotz.
w: WATS.

ĀTTH

Vowel: eighth.
     Plus hate'th*, etc.

AV

h: have+.
k: calve+.
s: salve+.

sl: Slav+.
sw: suave.

ĀV

br: brave, outbrave.
d: Dave.
dr: drave*.
g: forgave, gave, misgave.
gl: glaive.
gr: engrave, grave, ungrave.
h: behave, have+, misbehave.
k(c): cave, concave, encave.
kl: angusticlave, enclave+.
kr: crave.
l: belave, élève, lave.
n: knave, nave.
p: impave, pave.
pr: deprave.
r: rave.
s: save.
sh: shave.
sl: beslave, enslave, galley slave, Slav+, slave, wage slave.
st: stave.
sw: suave.
thr: thrave.
TH: they've.
tr: architrave, trave.
w: waive, new wave, rayleigh wave, wave.

ÄV

Vowel: zouave.
h: halve+.
k: calve+.
kl: enclave+.
s: salve+.
sl: Slav+.
sw: suave.

AZ

Vowel: as, whereas.
h: has.
j: jazz.
r: razz.
sp: spaz.

ĀZ

Vowel: a's.
b: baize, bays.
bl: ablaze, beacon blaze, Blaise, blaze, emblaze, outblaze, upblaze.
br: braise, braze.
d: adaze, days, daze, nowadays, thenadays.
dr: drays.
f: faze, fease, phase.
fl: flays.
fr: fraise, metaphrase, paraphrase, phrase.
g: gaze, ingaze, outgaze, upgaze.
gl: glaze.
gr: Grays, graze, overgraze.
h: Haas, Hayes, Hays, haze.
j: jays.
k(c): 'caze.
kl: clays.
kr: craze.
l: lays, laze, malaise, Marseillaise.
m: amaze, maize, Mayes, Mays, Maze, wondermaze*.
n: mayonnaise, naze, polonaise.
pr: appraise, bepraise, chryso-prase, dispraise, praise, self-praise, underpraise, unpraise.
r: raise, rase, rays, raze, upraise.
sh: chaise.
v: vase.
   Plus a+s.
   Plus clay's, etc.

ÄZ

m: Lamaze.
r: Shiraz.
v: vase+.
   Plus a+s.
   Plus Shah's, etc.

AZD

j: jazzed.
r: razzed.

ĀZD

d: adazed.
gr: overgrazed.
m: amazed, bemazed, unamazed.
pr: unpraised.
   Plus az+d.

ĀZH

t: cortège+.

ÄZH

fl: camouflage, persiflage.
l: collage.
n: badinage, espionage+, ménage.
r: barrage, entourage, garage, mirage.

AZM

Vowel: demoniasm, enthusiasm, miasm, orgiasm.
f: phasm*.
g: orgasm.
k(c): chasm, sarcasm.
kl: iconoclasm.
n: pleonasm.
pl: bioplasm, cataplasm, ecto-plasm, metaplasm, plasm, protoplasm.
sp: spasm.
t: phantasm.

(Choose only one word out of each group.)

E

Words including the following accented vowel sounds:

e: as in ebb, heifer, leopard, friend, Aetna, feather, asafoetida; also as in care, air, prayer, bear, e'er, heir, where.

ē: as in eve; also in feed, seam, believe, receive, people, key, elite, Caesar, quay, phoebe; also as in mere, drear, weird.

Ē

Vowel: A&E, advowee, arrowy, ASAP, avowee, billowy, DOE, drawee, employee, facetiae, LSAT+, minutiae, pillowy, PSAT, REIT, R.I.P., SAT, shadowy, sinewy, willowy.

b: A.B., B, bawbee, be, bee, bumblebee, CB, GLB, honeybee, Niobe, OTB, PBB, PCB, scarabee.

bl: blea.

br: debris.

ch: litchi, tai chi, vouchee.

d: 4WD, attendee, B.V.D., C.O.D., Chaldee, chickadee, D, D.D., Dee, fiddle-de-dee, grandee, killdee, M.D., on dit, Ph.D, Tweedle-dee, vendee, bastardy, comedy, custody, GED, jeopardy, LCD, Lombardy, malady, melody, monody, Normandy, OD, parody, perfidy, Picardy, psalmody, remedy, rhapsody, STD, subsidy, TBD, threnody, tragedy.

dr: dree, heraldry.

dw: lange d'oui.

f: antistrophe, apostrophe, atrophy, biographee, biography, catastrophe, confit, coryphee, fee, geography, McFee, philosophy, pornography, telegraphy, theosophy, topography.

fl: flea, flee.

fr: fancyfree, enfree, free, heart-free, unfree.

g: G, ghee, McGee, PG.

gl: glee.

gr: agree, degree, disagree, external degree, filigree, pedigree, third degree.

h: bohea, he, tehee.

hw: whee.

j: analogy, apogee, apology, astrology, bargee, biology, burgee, chronology, doxology, effigy, elegy, energy, eulogy, G, gee, geegee, genealogy, geology, lethargy, liturgy, mortgagee, mythology, N.G., obligee, O.G., ogee, perigee, pledgee, pongee, prodigy, refugee, salvagee, strategy, theology, trilogy, zoology.

k(c): anarchy, ASCII, Cherokee, junkie, key, Manichee, marquee, master key, McKey, monarchy, quay, raki, synecdoche.

kr: Cree, decree.

kw(qu): colloquy, olboquy, soliloquy.

l: absorbingly, abusively, accordingly, accurately, acidly, affectedly, affectionately, aimlessly, airily, alee, alluringly, allusively, ambitiously, amusingly, anciently, anomaly, appeallingly, appellee, ardently, assertively, atrociously, auspiciously, awfully, bailee, banefully, becomingly, befittingly, beggarly, belee, besottedly, bespottedly, bewailingly, bitterly, bloodlessly, bloomingly, bloomlessly, blushingly, blushlessly, bodily, bootlessly, bouilli, boundlessly, boyishly, brainlessly, breathlessly, broodingly, brotherly, brutally, bumptiously, carefully, carelessly, changelessly, chirpingly, chokingly, churlishly, civilily, clownishly, complainingly, concludingly, conclusively, condescendingly, conducively, confoundedly, confusedly, confusely, consummately, convivially, countlessly, cousinly, cowardly, cravingly, crouchingly, crownlessly, cruelly, crushingly, cumbrously, Cybele, dastardly, daughterly, decorously, deductively, defencelessly, deliciously, delusively, devotedly, disapprovingly, discernibly, discerningly, disorderly, distastefully, distrustfully, divergently, divertingly, doggedly, dolefully, doubtfully, doubtingly, dreamfully, dreamily, dreamingly, dreamlessly, drippingly, droopingly, dustily, dustlessly, easterly, elusively, endurably, enduringly, engagingly, engrossingly, eternally, Eulalie, exclusively, expansively, extensively, exteriorly, extortionately, extraordinarily, extravagantly, extremely, extricably, extrinsically, exuberantly, exultantly, exultingly, facsimile, fadelessly, fairily, faithfully, faithlessly, familiarly, family, famously, fancifully, fantastically, farcically, fascinatingly, fatalistically, fatally, fatherly, faultily, faultlessly, favorably,

fearfully, feasibly, feelingly, felicitously, ferociously, fervidly, feudally, feverishly, fictitiously, fiercely, fierily, figuratively, filially, filthily, fishily, flagrantly, flashily, fleur-de-lis, flexibly, flightily, flippantly, floridly, flossily, flouringly, flourishingly, flowerily, fluently, flurriedly, flushingly, flutteringly, foolhardily, foolishly, foppishly, forcefully, forebodingly, foreknowingly, forgetfully, forgivingly, formally, formerly, formidably, forsakenly, fortunately, foxily, fragilly, fragmentarily, fragrantly, frantically, fraternally, fraudulently, freakishly, frenziedly, frequently, fretfully, frightfully, frigidly, frivolously, frostily, frothily, frugally, fruitfully, fruitily, fruitlessly, fulsomely, functionally, funnily, furiously, furtively, fussily, futilely, gainfully, Galilee, gallantly, garrulously, gawkily, generally, generically, generously, genially, genteelly, genuinely, giddily, gingerly, girlishly, glacially, gladsomely, glamorously, glassily, gleefully, gloomily, gloriously, glossily, gluttonously, godlily, goldenly, gorgeously, gracefully, graciously, gradually, grandiosely, graphically, gratefully, gravelly, greasily, greedily, grimily, grittily, gropingly, grouchily, groundlessly, grudgingly, gruesomely, grumblingly, grumpily, guilefully, guilelessly, guiltily, guiltlessly, gushingly, gustily, gutturally, habitably, habitually, haggardly, handily, handsomely, haplessly, happily, hardily, harmfully, harmlessly, harmonically, harmoniously, hastily, hatefully, haughtily, hazardously, hazily, healthfully, healthily, heartbrokenly, heartily, heartlessly, heartrendingly, heavenly, heavily, heedlessly, helpfully, helplessly, hereditarily, heretically,

hexagonally, hideously, histori-
cally, homelessly, homily, honestly,
honorably, hopefully, hopelessly,
horizontally, horridly, humanely,
humanly, hungrily, hurriedly,
hurtfully, hyperbole, hypocriti-
cally, hysterically, ideally,
identically, idiotically, ignorantly,
illegibly, illogically, illusively,
imaginably, immeasurably,
immediately, imminently,
immoderately, immodestly,
immorally, immortally, immovably,
impartially, impatiently, impecca-
bly, impenetrably, imperatively,
imperially, impersonally,
impetuously, impiously, impishly,
implicitly, imploringly, impolitely,
importantly, impossibly, impotently, improbably, improperly,
imprudently, impudently,
incessantly, incidentally, inclu-
sively, incoherently, incompe-
tently, increasingly, incredulously,
indecently, independently,
indignantly, indirectly, individu-
ally, indulgently, industrially,
industriously, infamously,
infernally, infinitely, ingeniously,
inherently, inhumanly, injuriously,
innocently, insanely, insensately,
insipidly, instantly, instinctively,
instructively, insultingly, intelli-
gently, intermittently, intrepidly,
intrinsically, inwardly, irksomely,
ironically, Italy, jauntily, jealously,
jokingly, joyfully, joyously, jubilee,
judicially, judiciously, juicily,
knowingly, laboriously, laggardly,
lastingly, laughingly, lavishly, lea,
lee, legally, legendarily, leisurely,
levelly, ley, li, liberally, lifelessly,
light-footedly, limpidly, literally,
loathingly, loathsomely, locally,
logically, lonesomely, loungingly,
lovelessly, loverly, lovingly, loyally,
lucidly, luckily, lucklessly,
ludicrously, luridly, luringly, lustily,
lustrously, luxuriously, lyingly,
lyrically, magically, maidenly,
malevolently, maliciously,

manfully, manifestly, mannerly,
masterfully, masterly, materially,
maternally, matronly, meagerly,
meaningly, meltingly, menially,
mercifully, merrily, mindfully,
misgivingly, mistakenly, mistrustfully, mistrustingly, mockingly,
moderately, modestly, monopoly,
morally, morbidly, mortally,
motherly, mournfully,
mournsomely, munificently,
murderously, musingly, mutually,
mysteriously, mystically, mythically,
nakedly, namelessly, narrowly,
nationally, natively, naturally,
nebulae, necessarily, needily,
needlessly, neighborly, nervelessly,
nervily, neutrally, niggardly,
noiselessly, noisily, noisomely,
normally, northerly, northwardly,
numerally, obediently, objectively,
obligingly, obnoxiously, obsequi-
ously, obstreperously,
obstructively, obstrusively,
obtrusively, obviously, offensively,
officiously, omnivorously,
onerously, openly, opposingly,
oppressively, opulently, orderly,
ordinarily, outlandishly, outra-
geously, outwardly, overly,
overtoppingly, overweeningly,
owlishly, painfully, painlessly,
palidly, papulae, paramountly,
parently, partially, passively,
pathetically, patiently, peacefully,
peculiarly, peerlessly, peevishly,
pellucidly, peremptorily, perfectly,
perilously, pervertedly, petulantly,
piquantly, pitifully, plaintfully*,
plaintlessly*, plastically, playfully,
pleadingly, pleasantly, pleasingly,
plentifully, pliantly, pluckily,
poetically, pointlessly, popularly,
portentously, positively, potently,
powerfully, prayerfully, preco-
ciously, prepossessingly,
pretendingly, previously,
primarily, privately, productively,
properly, propitiously, provokingly
prudently, publicly, puissantly,
pungently, pursuantly, quarterly,

querulously, quiescently, rabidly, radically, rapidly, rationally, readily, ready-wittedly, really, recklessly, recurrently, refulgently, rejoicingly, relentlessly, reluctantly, remorsefully, remorselessly, reservedly, resolutely, responsively, restively, revengefully, righteously, rigidly, rippingly, ripplingly, roaringly, Rosalie, rottenly, rovingly, royalty, ruefully, ruffianly, ruggedly, rustically, satisfactorily, savagely, scandalously, scenically, scholarly, scornfully, scowlingly, secretively, secretly, secularly, seducively, seductively, seemingly, self-accusingly, self-consciously, selfishly, sensitively, separately, seriously, severally, shadily, shakily, shallowly, shamefully, shamelessly, shapelessly, sharp-wittedly, sheepishly, shiftlessly, shockingly, shrewishly, Sicily, signally, silently, similarly, simile, sinfully, singularly, sisterly, skilfully, skilligalee, slanderously, sleepily, sleeplessly, slouchily, slovenly, sluggishly, smilingly, smokily, sneeringly, snobbishly, soakingly, soberly, socially, soldierly, solemnly, solidly, somberly, sordidly, sorrily, sorrowfully, soulfully, soundlessly, southwardly, specially, speciously, speedily, spherically, spirally, spiritually, splendidly, spoonily, sportfully, sportily, sportively, spotlessly, springily, spuriously, squanderingly, squeamishly, startlingly, statically, steadfastly, steadily, stickily, stingily, stirringly, stockily, stolidly, stonily, stormfully, stormily, stormlessly, straightforwardly, strenuously, stridently, strikingly, stringently, stubbornly, studiedly, stuffily, stupendously, stupidly, sturdily, stylishly, suddenly, sulkily, sultrily, sunnily, superficially, superhumanly, superstitiously, sure-footedly, suspiciously, swarthily, swimmingly, swinishly, swollenly,

sylvanly, systematically, systole, tactually, tardily, tastefully, tauntingly, tearfully, tediously, tenderly, testily, thankfully, thanklessly, Thermopylae, thornily, thoroughly, thoughtfully, thoughtlessly, threateningly, thumpingly, thunderously, tidily, timelessly, timidly, tirelessly, tolerantly, tonelessly, topically, torpidly, totally, touchily, tranquilly, treacherously, tremendously, trenchantly, trippingly, triumphantly, troublesomely, troublously, trustfully, trustily, trustingly, truthfully, truthlessly, tunefully, tunelessly, turbidly, typically, ultimately, unbecomingly, unbendingly, unbiddenly, unblushingly, unboundedly, unceasingly, uncertainly, unchangingly, uncloudedly, uncommonly, unconsciously, unequally, unerringly, unevenly, unfailingly, unfaithfully, unfeelingly, unfeignedly, unflaggingly, unguardedly, unknowingly, unlovingly, unluckily, unmaidenly, unmannerly, unmindfully, unmotherly, unnaturally, unneighborly, unresistingly, unswervingly, unweariedly, unwittingly, unwontedly, unyieldingly, urgently, usurpingly, utterly, venially, verbally, verily, vernally, viciously, vigilantly, vigorously, violently, virtually, visually, vividly, vocally, voluntarily, vulgarly, wantonly, warily, warningly, wastefully, watchfully, waywardly, wealthily, wearily, wholesomely, willfully, windily, winsomely, wishfully, wittingly, wontedly, wordily, worthily, worthlessly, woundily*, wrathfully, wrongfully, yearningly, yeomanly, yieldingly, youthfully, zealously, zestfully.

m: academy, agronomy, alchemy, antimony, appendectomy,

astronomy, atomy, autonomy, BCME, bigamy, blasphemy, blossomy, bonhomie, deutero-gamy, Deuteronomy, economy, endogamy, enemy, epitome, infamy, neurotomy, phlebotomy, physiognomy, polygamy, Ptolemy, taxonomy, trichotomy, zootomy.

n: accompany, Agapemone, agony, aknee, Albany, anemone, assignee, balcony, barony, Bimini, botany, bouquet garni, bryony, calumny, Chinee, choucroute garnie, colony, company, consignee, destiny, domine, donee, ebony, epiphany, Eugenie, euphony, Euphrosyne, examinee, felony, Germany, Gethsemane, gluttony, gurney, harmony, hegemony, ignominy, irony, Japanee, jinnee, kidney, knee, ladrone, larceny, litany, macaroni, mahogany, Melpomene, monotony, mutiny, nominee, patrimony, Pawnee, petitionee, progeny, rani, Romany, scrutiny, simony, symphony, tyranny, villainy.

p: agape, allotropy, calipee, Calliope, callipee, canopy, cap-a-pie, EMP, entropy, epopee, FTP, HTTP, hydrotherapy, jalopy, MCP, misanthropy, P, pea, Penelope, philanthropy, rappee, recipe, rupee, SCP, therapy, topee, toupee.

pl: panoply, plea.

pr: dupree.

pw: point d'appui.

r: adultery, anniversary, archery, armory, artery, artillery, augury, bain-marie, bakery, battery, beggary, boiserie, boulangerie, bravery, bribery, burglary, calory, Calvary, cartulary, cautery, cavalry, century, chancery, chickaree, chivalry, complimentary, compulsory, contradictory, corroboree, debauchery, delivery, demonry, devilry, diablerie, diary,

directory, discovery, dissatisfac-tory, dissuasory, drapery, drudgery, dungaree, effrontery, elementary, elusory, enginery, equerry, extempore, factory, faerie, feathery, fernery, fiery, finery, flattery, flowery, flummery, foppery, forestry, forgery, gallery, heathery, hickory, history, hostelry, husbandry, illusory, imagery, infirmary, injury, ivory, jamboree, jewelry, jugglery, knavery, livery, lottery, luxury, machinery, Marie, masonry, mastery, memory, mercury, mimicry, misery, mockery, mummery, mystery, notary, nursery, palmary, parliamentary, passerie*, passementerie, penury, peppery, perfumery, perfunctory, perjury, phylactery, pillory, popery, potpourri, precursory, priory, professory, prudery, pugaree, quackery, quandary, raillery, rapparee, recovery, rectory, referee, refractory, revelry, reverie, ribaldry, rivalry, robbery, rockery, roguery, rookery, rosary, rosemary, rudimentary, salary, sangaree, satisfactory, Saulte St. Marie, savagery, scenery, seigniory, shivery, silvery, slavery, slippery, snuggery, sorcery, stingaree, sugary, summary, Terpsichore, testamentary, theory, thievery, thundery, tracery, transferee, treachery, treasury, trickery, trumpery, unsavory, usury, valedictory, vapory, victory, votary, waggery, watery, wintery, witchery, yeomanry, zephyry.

s: abbacy, ABC, ADC, addressee, AFDC, agency, Anglice, apostasy, argosy, aristocracy, ascendency, BCC, bioequivalency, brilliancy, C, cadency, clemency, cogency, complacency, consistency, conspiracy, constancy, contin-gency, contumacy, conveniency,

corespondency, courtesy, curacy,
decency, democracy, dependency,
diplomacy, discordancy, discourtesy, discrepancy, divorcee,
EBCDIC, EC, ecstasy, EEOC,
efficiency, embassy, equivalency,
expectancy, expediency, fallacy,
fantasy, felo-do-se, fervency,
flagrancy, flippancy, fluency,
foresee, fragrancy, frequency,
fricassee, galaxy, heresy, hypocrisy,
idiocy, idiosyncrasy, illiteracy,
impendency, importunacy,
inadvertency, inclemency,
inconsistency, inconstancy,
indecency, indelicacy, independency, infancy, insufficiency,
insurgency, intestacy, jealousy,
legacy, leniency, lessee, licensee,
lunacy, luxuriancy, malignancy,
Marshalsea, NBC, normalcy,
obeisancy, Odyssey, OTC, oversea,
oversee, papacy, Parsee, PC,
Pharisee, piracy, pliancy, poesy,
poignancy, policy, potency,
prelacy, privacy, proficiency,
promisee, prophecy, pungency,
quiescency, recumbency, regency,
regeneracy, releasee, renascency,
repellency, resplendency,
Sadducee, sea, see, secrecy,
solvency, stagnancy, subsistency,
sufficiency, supremacy, sycee,
sycophancy, tenancy, tendency,
Tennessee, theocracy, TMC,
truancy, unforesee, urgency,
vacancy, vagrancy, valiancy,
verdancy, WC.

sh: banshee, debauchee,
garnishee, she, ski.

sk(sc): ski.

skr(scr): scree.

sn: snee, snickersnee.

spr: bel esprit, esprit, joie d'esprit,
spree.

st: mestee, mustee.

t: ability, absentee, absurdity,
acclivity, acerbity, acidity, acridity,
activity, actuality, adaptability,
adversity, advisability, affability,
affinity, agility, alacrity, allottee,
ambiguity, amenability, amenity,
amicability, amity, amnesty,
animosity, annuity, anonymity,
antiquity, anxiety, applicability,
appointee, aridity, asperity,
assiduity, atrocity, audacity,
austerity, authenticity, authority,
avidity, AZT, barbarity, basmati,
Benedicite, benignity, BLT,
bootee, brevity, brutality, calamity,
capability, capacity, captivity,
casualty, catholicity, causticity,
cavity, celebrity, celerity, certainty,
changeability, chariotee, charity,
chastity, Christianity, civility,
coatee, combustibility, comity,
commodity, community, compatibility, complexity, complicity,
comprehensibility, conformity,
connubiality, consanguinity,
contiguity, contrariety, conventionality, convexity, credulity,
criminality, crotchety, crudity,
cruelty, cupidity, curiosity, debility,
declivity, dedicatee, deformity,
deity, density, depravity, deputy,
devotee, dexterity, dignity, dimity,
dishonesty, disparity, dissimilarity,
diversity, divinity, docility,
domesticity, dubiety, duplicity,
dynasty, EFT, elasticity, electricity,
enmity, enormity, entity, equality,
equanimity, equity, eternity,
extremity, facility, faculty, falsity,
familiarity, fatality, fatuity,
fecundity, felicity, ferocity, fertility,
festivity, fidelity, fidgety, fixity,
formality, fortuity, fragility,
fraternity, frigidity, frivolity,
frugality, futility, futurity, gaiety,
garrulity, generosity, geniality,
gentility, goatee, grantee, gratuity,
gravity, grotty, guarantee, heredity,
hilarity, honesty, hospitality,
hostility, humanity, humility,
identity, imbecility, immaturity,
immensity, immodesty, immorality,
immortality, immunity, imparity,
impassivity, impecuniosity,

impetuosity, impiety, importunity, impropriety, impunity, impurity, inability, incapacity, incomparability, incompatibility, incomprehensibility, incongruity, incredulity, indignity, individuality, inebriety, infallibility, infelicity, inferiority, infertility, infidelity, infinity, infirmity, ingenuity, inhumanity, iniquity, insanity, insincerity, insipidity, insularity, integrity, intensity, interrogatee, intrepidity, jocundity, jollity, joviality, juvenility, laity, laxity, legality, legatee, lenity, levity, liberality, liberty, limpidity, lubricity, lucidity, luminosity, majesty, majority, manatee, modesty, moiety, morality, mortality, mutuality, nativity, nebulosity, neutrality, nonentity, normality, nudity, objectivity, parity, passivity, patentee, permittee, picotee, piety, pontee, presentee, privity, proclivity, prolixity, propensity, propinquity, propriety, purity, Q T, quality, quantity, receptivity, remittee, repartee, sanity, settee, sincerity, suttee, T, tea, tee, temerity, tensity, torpidity, trepidity, trinity, triviality, trustee, utility, warrantee.

th: allopathy, antipathy, apathy, homeopathy, sympathy.

TH: the+, thee.

thr: three.

tr: ancestry, artistry, axletree, barratry, barretry, bigotry, bijoutry, Christmas tree, coquetry, coventry, deviltry, errantry, gallantry, gallows tree, geometry, harvestry, idolatry, industry, infantry, knight-errantry, merchantry, ministry, pageantry, palmistry, peasantry, pedantry, pleasantry, poetry, psychiatry, sophistry, symmetry, tapestry, tenantry, tree, weeping tree, whiffletree, whippletree.

tw: étui.

v: ATV, AV, CV, HIV, HTLV, joie de vie, levee, RV, TV, vis-a-vis.

w: ennui, we, wee.

y: employee, payee, ye.

z: A-to-Z, bourgeoisie, chimpanzee, devisee, fusee, recognizee, scuzzy, Zuyder Zee.

EB

Vowel: ebb.
d: deb.
k(c): keb.
n: neb.
s: Seb.
w: cobweb, web, Webb, World Wide Web.

ĒB

dw: dweeb.
gl: glebe.
gr: grebe.

EBD

Vowel: ebbed.
w: cobwebbed, webbed.

EBZ

Vowel: ebbs.
d: Debs.
pl: plebs.
    Plus eb+s.
    Plus deb's, etc.

ĒBZ

th: Thebes.
    Plus glebe's, etc.
    Plus eb+s.

ECH

Vowel: etch.
f: fetch.
fl: fletch.

k(c): Jack Ketch, ketch.

l: lech, letch.

r: retch.

sk(sc): sketch.

str: outstretch, stretch.

t: tetch.

v: vetch.

w: wetch.

ĒCH

Vowel: each.

b: beach, beech.

bl: bleach.

br: breach, breech, unbreech.

fl: fleech.

k(c): keech.

kw(qu): queach.

l: leach, leech.

p: impeach, peach.

pl: pleach.

pr: preach, unpreach.

r: forereach, overreach, reach, seareach.

s: beseech.

skr(scr): screech.

sl: sleech.

sp: forespeech*, speech.

t: foreteach*, teach.

ECHD

f: far-fetched.

Plus ech+ed.

ĒCHD

bl: unbleached.

p: unimpeached.

Plus ech+ed.

ED

Vowel: coed, Ed, continued*, phys ed, sorrowed*, wearied*, winnowed*.

b: abed, bed, deathbed, embed, surbed, truckle bed, trundle bed.

bl: bled.

br: anadama bread, bread, bred, gingerbread*, highbred, homebred*, inbred, pilot bread, shewbread, thoroughbred, true-bred, underbred, well-bread.

d: dead, bediamonded, diamonded, garlanded, heralded, jeoparded, shepherded.

dr: adread*, dread.

f: fed, full-fed, overfed, underfed, well-fed.

fl: fled.

fr: afraid, Fred, Winifred.

h: ahead, acidhead, arrowhead, behead, billethead, blackhead, blunderhead, bullethead, checklehead, copperhead, deadhead, death's-head, dunderhead, featherhead, figurehead, fountainhead, go-ahead, head, head-to-head, jollerhead, loggerhead, lowlihead*, maidenhead, masterhead, negrohead, overhead, poppy head, thunder-head, timberhead, trundle head, unhead, wooly head.

k(c): ked.

l: lead, led, misled.

m: mead.

n: Ned.

pl: plead, pled.

r: read, red, redd, unread.

s: aforesaid, foresaid*, said, unsaid, witnessed*.

sh: shed, watershed.

shr: shred.

sl: sled.

sp: sped, unsped, well-sped.

spr: bedspread, bespread, outspread, overspread, spread.

st: bedstead, bestead, instead, stead.

t: attributed, ballasted, barren-spirited, base-spirited, bigoted, bold-spirited, bonneted, breakfasted, carpeted, contributed, coveted, crescented, discomfited, discomforted, discredited, disinherited, dispirited, disquieted, distributed, exhibited, faceted, fine-spirited, forfeited, gay-spirited, helmeted, high-spirited, inhabited, inherited, inspirited, light-spirited, limited, low-spirited, mean-spirited, merited, patented, pirated, poor-spirited, profited, prohibited, public-spirited, quieted, ringleted, signeted, soft-spirited, spirited, talented, ted, tenanted, turreted, unballasted, unbonneted, uninhabited, uninhibited, unlimited, unmerited, unprofited, unrespited, untenanted, visited, weak-spirited.

thr: rethread, thread, unthread.

tr: tread.

w: rewed, unwed, wed.

z: zed.

ĒD

Vowel: Ead.

b: bead, Bede.

bl: bleed.

br: brede*, breed, crossbreed, halfbreed, inbreed, interbreed, upbreed.

d: deed, indeed, misdeed.

f: feed, off his feed, overfeed, underfeed, unfeed.

fr: freed.

gl: glede, gleed.

gr: greed, pedigreed, unpedigreed.

h: he'd, heed.

kr: creed, decreed, undecreed.

kw(qu): Queed.

l: invalid, lead, mislead, uplead.

m: Ganymede, mead, Mede, meed, Runnymede.

n: knead, knock-kneed, need.

p: centipede, impede, millipede, stampede, velocipede.

pl: implead, interplead, plead.

r: bourride, bur-reed, jereed, misread, read, Reade, rede*, reed, Reid, reread.

s: accede, aniseed, antecede, concede, exceed, intercede, precede, proceed, recede, retrocede, secede, seed, succeed, supersede.

sh: she'd.

skr(scr): screed.

sp: dispeed*, godspeed, outspeed, speed.

spr: spreed.

st: steed.

sw: Swede.

t: teed.

tr: treed.

tw: tweed.

w: seaweed, we'd, weed'.

y: ye'd.

Plus e+d.

Plus sea'd, etc.

EDST

dr: dread'st*.

f: fed'st.

fl: fled'st*.

l: led'st.*

s: said'st.

spr: bespread'st*, overspread'st*.

thr: thread'st*.

tr: tread'st*.

w: wed'st*.

EDTH

br: breadth, hairbreadth.

Plus bespread'th*, etc.

ĒDZ

Vowel: Eades.
l: Leeds.
   Plus Mede's, etc.

EF

Vowel: f, TAF, TGIF.
d: deaf.
f: enfeoff, feoff.
j: Jeff.
kl: clef.
n: nef.
sh: chef.

ĒF

b: beef.
br: brief.
ch: chief, handkerchief, neckerchief.
f: fief.
gr: grief.
l: bas relief, belief, disbelief, interleaf, leaf, lief, relief, unbelief.
r: reef, shereef, Teneriffe.
sh: sheaf.
st: digestif.
th: thief.

EFT

Vowel: eft.
d: deft.
f: enfeoffed.
h: heft.
kl: cleft.
l: aleft, left.
r: bereft, reft, unbereft.
th: theft.
w: weft, wheft.

EG

Vowel: egg, goose egg, scotch egg.
b: beg, beglerbeg, philibeg.
dr: dreg.
k: keg.
l: leg.
m: Meg.
p: peg, unpeg, Winnipeg.
sk: skeg.
t: teg.
y: yegg.

ĒG

gr: Grieg.
kl: klieg.
l: colleague, enleague, league.
n: renege.
t: fatigue, McTeague.
tr: intrigue.

EGD

l: spindlelegged.
   Plus eg+d.

ĒGD

t: fatigued, overfatigued.
   Plus eg+d.

EGZ

l: sea legs.
m: Meggs.
   Plus eg+s.
   Plus Meg's, etc.

EJ

Vowel: cutting edge, edge, reedge, unedge.
dr: dredge.
fl: fledge.
h: enhedge, hedge.
j: "jedge."
k: kedge.
kl: cledge.
l: allege, ledge, privilege, sacrilege.

pl: impledge, interpledge, pledge.
s: sedge.
sl: sledge.
t: cortège+, tedge.
w: wedge.

ĒJ

l: liege.
s: besiege, siege.

EJD

Vowel: double-edged, two-edged.
h: unhedged.
s: sedged.
   Plus ej+d.

EK

b: beck, Kennebec, Quebec.
ch: check, cheque+, Czech.
d: bedeck, deck, quarterdeck, undeck.
fl: fleck.
gr: à la grecque.
h: by heck, heck.
k(c): keck.
n: breakneck, leatherneck, neck, neck-and-neck, rubberneck.
p: henpeck, peck.
r: bewreck, reck, shipwreck, wreck.
sp: spec, speck.
t: biotech, lab tech, Tech, Teck.
tr: trek.

ĒK

Vowel: eke, caique.
b: beak.
bl: bleak, oblique.
ch: cheek, chic.
d: Deke.
fr: freak.
gl: gleek.

gr: Greek.
k(c): cacique.
kl: cleek, clique.
kr: creak, creek.
l: aleak, leak, leek, relique.
m: comique, demi+, Martinique, meak, meek, Mozambique.
n: clinique, unique.
p: afterpeak, apeak, Chesapeake, peak, pique.
r: areek, reek, wreak.
s: hide-and-seek, seek, Sikh, upseek.
sh: sheik.
shr: shriek.
skw(squ): bubble-and-squeak, squeak.
sl: sleek.
sn: sneak.
sp: bespeak, forespeak, speak, unspeak.
str: streak.
t: antique, critique, teak.
tw: tweak.
w: Holy week, Passion week, weak, week.
z: physique, bezique.

EKS

Vowel: ex, Exe.
b: becks.
d: bedecks.
fl: circumflex, flex, inflex, reflex.
h: hex.
k(c): kex.
l: lex.
m: Mex.
n: annex.
pl: complex, multiplex, perplex.
pr: prex.
r: rex.
s: Middlesex, sex, unsex.
t: Celotex.

v: convex, vex.
Plus deck's, etc.
Cf. ek+s.

ĒKS

br: breeks.
sn: sneaks.
Plus ek+s.
Plus creek's, etc.

EKST

n: next.
pl: perplexed, unperplexed.
s: sexed, sext, unsexed.
t: pretext, text.
v: unvexed.
Plus eks+d.
Plus deck'st*, etc.

EKT

ch: checked, rechecked, unchecked.
d: bedecked, decked, undecked.
f: affect, confect, defect, disaffect, disinfect, effect, infect, perfect, prefect, refect*.
fl: deflect, genuflect, inflect, reflect.
gl: neglect.
j: abject, adject, conject, deject, eject, inject, interject, object, project, reject, subject, traject.
l: analect, collect, dialect, elect, intellect, nonelect, prelect, recollect, select.
n: annect*, connect, disconnect.
p: expect, prospect, suspect.
r: arrect*, correct, direct, erect, incorrect, indirect, misdirect, porrect, resurrect.
s: bisect, dissect, exsect, intersect, sect, trisect.

sp: circumspect, disrespect, inspect, introspect, respect, retrospect, self-respect.
t: architect, detect, protect.
tr: trekked.
Plus ek+d.

ĒKT

ch: cherry-cheeked, rosy-cheeked.
p: peaked.
r: unwreaked.
Plus ek+d.
Plus beak'd, etc.

EKTS

p: pects.

EL

Vowel: A. W. O. L., El, ell, Emmanuel, Immanuel, L, vielle.
b: bel, bell, belle, bonnibel*, Canterbury bell, claribel, deathbell, dinner bell, diving bell, gabelle, harebell, heather bell, Isabel, Jezebel, minute bell, passing bell, rebel, sacring bell, sanctus bell, vesper bell.
d: asphodel, citadel, cordelle, dell, fricandel, HDL, infidel, LDL, rondelle.
dr: quadrelle*.
dw: dwell.
f: Astrophel, befell, fell, NFL, refel*.
h: hell, NHL.
j: jell, gel.
k(c): kell.
kw(qu): quell.
l: parallel.
m: béchamel, caramel, HTML, hydromel, intermell*, pall-mall, pell-mell, philomel.
n: Abarbanel, coronel*, Crannell, crenelle, fontanel, jargonelle,

knell, Lionel, mangonel, Nell, Parnell, personnel, petronel, pimpernel, Purnell, sentinel, villanelle.

p: compel, dispel, expel, impel, lapel, pell, propel, repel.

r: chanterelle, cockerel, doggerel, mackerel, nonpareil, tourelle*, URL.

s: alpha cells, cell, daughter cell, excel, pennoncelle, pucelle, sell, resell, undersell.

sh: cockleshell, inshell, seashell, shell, unshell.

sm: smell.

sn: snell.

sp: love spell, spell, unspell.

sw: ground swell, swell, upswell.

t: bagatelle, boatel, brocatel, Chaumontel, clientele, dentelle, foretell, hotel, immortelle, muscatel, tell.

v: caravel.

w: farewell, ne'er-do-well, well.

y: yell.

z: carrousel, damoiselle*, damoselle*, demoiselle, gazelle, mademoiselle, Moselle, zel, Zell.

Cf. miracle, etc.

ĒL

Vowel: eel.

b: automobile, Beale, deshabille, Mobile.

ch: chiel.

d: deal, deil, interdeal*, misdeal, redeal.

f: feal, feel, forefeel.

h: allheal, heal, heel, he'll.

hw: balance wheel, dial wheel, driving wheel, flywheel, paddle wheel, wheal, wheel.

j: congeal, uncongeal.

k(c): keel, Kiel, vakil.

kr: creel.

l: leal, Lille.

m: barley meal, Camille, camomile, Emile, meal.

n: anneal, chenille, cochineal, kneel, Neal, Neil, Neill, O'Neal, O'Neill.

p: appeal, peal, peel, repeal, thunderpeal.

r: real.

s: conceal, difficile, enseal, imbecile, Lucille, privy seal, seal, seel, unseal, unseel*.

sh: O'Sheel, sheal, she'll.

skw(squ): squeal.

sp: speel, spiel.

st: bastille, Castille, pastille, steal, steel.

sw: sweal.

t: genteel, infantile, shabby genteel, teal.

TH: thee'll*.

tw: tweel.

v: reveal, veal.

w: commonweal, weal, weel, we'll.

z: alguazil, zeal.

Plus sea'll, etc.

ELCH

b: belch.

skw(squ): squelch.

w: welch, Welsh.

ELD

Vowel: eld*.

b: belled.

g: geld.

h: beheld, held, unbeheld, upheld, withheld.

j: jelled.

kw(qu): unquelled.

l: unparalleled.

m: meld.

n: unknelled.

s: seld*.
w: weld.
    Plus el+d.
    Plus yell'd, etc.

ĒLD

f: afield, baseball field, battlefield, center field, Chesterfield, corn field, Dangerfield, Delafield, field, football field, harvest field, left field, right field, soccer field, wheat field.
n: annealed, unaneled*.
p: unrepealed.
sh: enshield, shield.
w: weald, wield.
y: yield.
    Plus el+d.
    Plus squeal'd, etc.

ELF

Vowel: elf.
d: delf.
gw: Guelph.
p: pelf.
s: herself, himself, itself, mineself*, myself, oneself, ourself, self, thyself*, yourself.
sh: mantel shelf, shelf.

ELFT

d: delft.

ELFTH

tw: twelfth.

ELK

Vowel: elk.
hw: whelk.
y: yelk.

ELM

Vowel: elm.
h: dishelm, helm, unhelm, weatherhelm.
hw: overwhelm, whelm*.
r: realm.

ELP

h: help, self-help.
hw: whelp.
k: kelp.
sk(sc): skelp.
sw: swelp.
y: yelp.

ELPS

f: Phelps.
    Plus elp+s.
    Plus help's, etc.

ELS

Vowel: else.
    Cf. elt+s.

ELSH

w: Welsh.
    Cf. elch.

ELT

b: belt, Snowbelt, Sunbelt, unbelt.
d: dealt.
dw: dwelt.
f: felt, heartfelt, unfelt, veldt.
g: gelt.
k(c): Celt, Kelt.
m: melt.
n: knelt.
p: pelt.
s: Celt.
sm: smelt.
sp: misspelt, spelt.

sv: svelte.
sw: swelt*.
v: veldt.
w: welt.

ELTH

h: health.
st: stealth.
w: commonwealth, wealth.
   Plus dwell'th*, etc.

ELV

d: delve.
h: helve.
sh: shelve.
tw: twelve.

ELVZ

Vowel: elves.
s: ourselves, selves, themselves, yourselves.
   Plus elv+s.
   Plus helve's, etc.

ELZ

Vowel: Elles.
n: Dardanelles.
s: Lascelles.
sh: Seychelles.
w: Welles, Wells.
   Plus el+s.
   Plus spell's, etc.

EM

Vowel: a.m., em, 'em, requiem.
c: ALCM.
d: anadem, bediadem, condemn, diadem.
f: femme.
fl: phlegm.

h: ahem, Bethlehem, hem.
j: begem, Brummagem, gem, stratagem.
kl: clem.
kr: crème de la crème.
m: mem.
n: ad hominem.
p: LPM, p.m.
r: theorem.
sh: Shem.
st: stem.
t: ATM, contemn, pro tem.
th: apothegm.
TH: them.

ĒM

b: abeam, beam, embeam*, moonbeam.
br: bream.
d: academe, deem, misdeem, redeem.
dr: daydream, dream.
f: blaspheme, grapheme.
fl: fleam.
gl: gleam, weathergleam.
j: régime.
kr: cream, ice cream.
l: leam.
pr: supreme.
r: ream, reem, riem.
s: beseem, enseam, seam, seem, unbeseem, unseam.
sk(sc): scheme.
skr(scr): primal scream, scream.
st: steam.
str: stream.
t: centime, disesteem, dream team, esteem, self-esteem, team, teem.
th: anatheme, theme.
tr: distream, extreme.

EMD

d: undiademed, uncondemned.
Plus em+d.
Plus gem'd, etc.

ĒMD

d: unredeemed.
dr: undreamed.
Plus em+d.
Plus cream'd, etc.

EMP

h: hemp.
k: Kemp.

EMS

t: temse.

EMT

Vowel: exempt, preempt.
dr: adreamt, dreamt, undreamt.
k(c): kempt, unkempt.
t: attempt, contempt, self-contempt, tempt.

EMZ

t: temse, Thames.
Plus em+s.
Plus hem's, etc.

ĒMZ

s: meseems.
Plus em+s.
Plus dream's, etc.

EN

Vowel: cayenne, Cheyenne, Darien, equestrienne, Parisienne, tragedienne, Valenciennes, varsovienne.

b: ben, ISBN.
d: den.
f: fen.
g: again.
gl: glen.
h: hen, prairie hen, sage hen, turkhen, water hen.
hw: when+.
j: halogen, hydrogen, nitrogen, oxygen.
k(c): ken.
l: Len, Magdalen.
m: aldermen, amen, cyclamen, men, regimen, specimen.
n: CNN.
p: brevipen, ESPN, fountain pen, impen, pen, unpen.
r: wren.
s: ISSN, sen, sensen, SSN.
t: ten.
TH: then.
w: wen.
y: yen.
z: citizen, denizen.

ĒN

Vowel: can, e'en*, goode'en*, Halloween.
b: bean, been, shebeen.
br: Breen.
ch: Capuchin.
d: almandine+, amandine+, codeine+, dean, dene, dudeen, gabardine, Geraldine, gradine, Gunga Din, incarnadine+, sardine.
f: caffeine, Josephine, trephine.
fr: Peek Frean.
g: Beguine, carrageen.
gl: glean, gleen*.
gr: bowling green, chagrin, evergreen, grass green, green, long green, peregrine, putting

green, sea green, shagreen, wintergreen.

h: fellahin.

j: alpigene, Eugene, gazogene, gene, heterogene, indigene, Jean+, porphyrogene, quadragene*, seltzogene.

k(c): keen, lymphokine, nankeen.

kl: clean, come clean, unclean.

kw(qu): fairy queen, harvest queen, May queen, meadow queen, palanquin, quean, queen, unqueen.

l: aniline, baleen, bandoline, colleen, crinoline, lien, Evangeline+, gasoline, Ghibelline+, lean, lene*, Magdalene+, naphthalene, opaline, Pauline+, scalene, tourmaline+, uplean, vasoline.

m: demean, demesne, mean, melamine, mesne, mien, misdemean.

n: mezzanine+, nectarine+, quinine+.

p: atropine, fillipeen, pean, peen, Philippine, spalpeen.

pr: impregn*, preen.

r: Algerine, anserine, aquamarine, careen, chlorine, Irene, margarine, marine, mazarine, moreen, Nazarene, nectarine, oleomargarine, Palmyrene, pistareen, serene, submarine, subterrene, superterrene, tambourine, terrene, tureen, ultramarine, wolverine.

s: damascene, Eocene, epicene, fascine, foreseen, kerosene, Miocene, Nicene, obscene, overseen, Pleistocene, Pliocene, scene, seen, seine, unforeseen, unseen.

sh: machine, praying machine, Shean, sheen, voting machine.

skr(scr): bescreen, on-screen, screen.

spl: spleen.

st: Ernestine, langoustine, stein.

t: Argentine, argentine+, Augustine, barkentine, bottine, brigantine, Byzantine+, canteen, carotene, Constantine, duvetyn, eighteen, fifteen, Florentine+, fourteen, galantine, gelatine, guillotine, infantine+, lateen, libertine+, NC-17, nicotine+, nineteen, PG-13, Philistine+, poteen, preteen, quarantine, retine, routine, St. Augustine, sateen, serpentine, seventeen, sixteen, teen, thirteen, umf'teen, velveteen.

tr: Holstein+, leukotriene, yestreen*.

tw: atween, between, go-between, tween.

v: advene, contravene, convene, intervene, margravine, ravine, subvene, supervene, visne.

w: overween, wean, ween*.

y: yean.

z: benzene, benzine, bombazine, compazine, cuisine, magazine, nouvelle cuisine, Stelazine, 'zine.

ENCH

b: bench.

bl: blench.

dr: bedrench, drench, redrench.

fl: flench.

fr: French.

kl: clench, unclench.

kw(qu): quench.

r: monkey wrench, wrench.

skw(squ): squench.

st: stench.

t: tench.

tr: intrench, retrench, trench.

w: wench.

ENCHD

bl: unblenched.
Plus ench+d.
Plus stench'd, etc.

END

Vowel: anend*, end, gable end, minuend, tag end, up-end, year-end.

b: bend, South Bend, unbend.

bl: blend, hornblende, interblend, pitchblend.

d: dividend.

f: defend, fend, forefend*, offend, weather fend.

fr: befriend, friend, imfriend.

h: apprehend, comprehend, misapprehend, reprehend, subtrahend.

k(c): kenned, unkenned.

l: lend.

m: amend, commend, emend, mend, recommend.

p: append, depend, expend, impend, penned, perpend, prepend*, stipend, unpenned, vilipend.

r: rend, reverend.

s: ascend, condescend, descend, Godsend, send, transcend, upsend.

sp: misspend, spend, suspend.

t: attend, contend, distend, extend, intend, obtend, Ostend, portend, pretend, repetend, subtend, superintend, tend.

tr: trend.

v: vend.

w: wend.

z: Zend.
Plus en+d.
Plus hen'd, etc.

ĒND

f: arch-fiend, fiend.

p: piend.

t: tiend.
Plus en+d.
Plus scene'd, etc.

ENDZ

Vowel: loose ends.

b: bends.

m: amends.
Plus end+s.
Plus end's, etc.

ENGK

sh: Schenck.

ENGKS

j: Jenkes, Jenks.

sh: Schenck's.

ENGTH

l: full-length, length.

str: strength.

ENJ

h: Stonehenge.

v: avenge, Montezuma's revenge, revenge.

ENJD

v: avenged, revenged, unavenged.
Plus stonehenge'd, etc.

ENS

Vowel: affluence, confluence, convenience, disobedience, expedience, experience, incipience, incongruence, inconvenience, inexpedience, inexperience, influence, insipience, mellifluence, nescience, obedience, omniscience, precipience, prescience, prurience, resilience, salience, sapience, subservience.

d: accidence, coincidence, condense, confidence, dense, diffidence, dissidence, evidence, impudence, incidence, coincidence, nonresidence, providence, residence, self-confidence, subsidence.

f: defense, fence, offense, self-defense.

h: hence.

hw: whence.

j: diligence, exigence, indigence, intelligence, negligence.

kw(qu): blandiloquence, breviloquence, consequence, eloquence, grandiloquence, inconsequence, magniloquence.

l: benevolence, corpulence, equivalence, excellence, flatulence, flocculence, fraudulence, imprevalence, indolence, insolence, malevolence, opulence, pestilence, prevalence, quantivalence, redolence, somnolence, succulence, truculence, turbulence, violence, virulence.

m: commence, immense, vehemence.

n: abstinence, continence, eminence, immanence, imminence, impertinence, incontinence, permanence, pertinence, preeminence, prominence, supereminence.

p: dispense, expense, pence, prepense, propense*, recompense, suspense.

r: circumference, conference, deference, difference, indifference, inference, irreverence, preference, reference, reverence.

s: beneficence, common sense, concupiscence, frankincense, incense, innocence, magnificence, munificence, reticence, sense.

sp: spence.

t: competence, impenitence, impotence, incompetence, intense, omnipotence, penitence, plenipotence, pretence, subtense, tense.

TH: thence.

Plus Lent's, etc.

Cf. ents.

ENST

Vowel: experienced, inexperienced, influenced.

d: condensed, evidenced.

f: fenced.

g: against, 'gainst.

m: commenced.

n: anenst, forenenst.

p: dispensed.

r: reverenced.

s: incensed, sensed.

Plus ens+d.

Plus fenc'd, etc.

ENT

Vowel: accipient, affluent, ambient, aperient, circumambient, circumfluent, confluent, congruent, constituent, convenient, diffluent, disobedient, emollient, esurient, expedient, gradient, incipient, incongruent, inconvenient, inexpedient, influent, ingredient, insentient, insipient, lenient, mellifluent, obedient, orient, percipient, prescient, prurient, recipient, refluent, resilient, salient, sapient, sentient, subservient.

b: bent, unbent.

bl: blent.

br: brent.

d: accident, coincident, confident, dent, diffident, dissident, evident, improvident, impudent, incident, incoincident, incompetent, indent, occident, precedent, president, provident, resident.

f: fent.

g: Ghent.

gw: Gwent.

j: diligent, exigent, gent, indigent, intelligent, negligent.

k(c): accent, Kent, unkent*.

kw(qu): acquent, consequent, eloquent, frequent, grandiloquent, inconsequent, magniloquent, subsequent.

l: benevolent, corpulent, equivalent, esculent, excellent, flocculent, fraudulent, gracilent*, indolent, insolent, leant, lent, luculent, malevolent, opulent, pestilent, prevalent, redolent, relent, somnolent, succulent, truculent, turbulent, vinolent, violent, virulent.

m: abandonment, abolishment, accompaniment, accomplishment, accouterment, acknowledgment, admeasurement, admonishment, advertisement, affamishment*, affranchisement, aggrandisement, aliment, apportionment, arbitrament, argument, armament, astonishment, augment, babblement, banishment, battlement, bedevilment, bedizenment, betterment, bewilderment, blandishment, blazonment, blemishment, botherment, brabblement, cement, chastisement, cherishment, comment, complement, compliment, condiment, dazzlement, decipherment, decrement, dement, demolishment, detriment, development, devilment, diminishment, dimplement, disablement, disarmament, discouragement, disfigurement, disfranchisement, disparagement, dispiritment, distinguishment, divertisement, document, element, embarrassment, embattlement, embellishment, embezzlement, embitterment, emblazonment, embodiment, emolument, empanelment, enablement, encompassment, encouragement, endangerment, endeavorment, enfeeblement, enfranchisement, enlightenment, ennoblement, enravishment, entanglement, envelopment, environment, envisagement, establishment, excrement, experiment, extinguishment, famishment, ferment, filament, firmament, foment, foremeant, fosterment, franchisement, garnishment, government, habiliment, harassment, hereditament, impediment, imperilment, implement, impoverishment, imprisonment, increment, instrument, integument, inveiglement, lament, languishment, lavishment, ligament, lineament, liniment, management, measurement, medicament, merriment, monument, muniment, nourishment, nutriment, ornament, parliament, pediment, pesterment*, prattlement, predicament, premonishment, presentiment, punishment, ravishment, regiment, relinquishment, replenishment, rudiment, sacrament, sediment, sentiment, settlement, supplement, temperament, tenement, testament, torment, tournament, tremblement, unmeant, vanishment, vanquishment, vehement, wanderment*, well-meant, wilderment*, wonderment, worriment.

n: abstinent, anent, continent, eminent, fornent, immanent, imminent, impertinent, incontinent, permanent, pertinent, preeminent, prominent, supereminent, there-anent.

p: pent, repent.

r: belligerent, deferent, different, indifferent, irreverent, rent, reverent.

s: absent, ascent, assent, beneficent, cent, consent, descent, dissent, innocent, magnificent, maleficent, missent, munificent, reticent, scent, sent, unsent.

sp: forespent*, misspent, overspent, spent, unspent, well-spent.

spr: besprent*, sprent.

st: stent.

t: attent*, competent, content, detent, discontent, extent, ignipotent, ill-content, impenitent, impotent, intent, malcontent, miscontent, omnipotent, ostent, penitent, plenipotent, portent, tent, untent, well-content.

tr: Trent.

v: circumvent, event, invent, prevent, vent.

w: underwent, went.

z: misrepresent, present, represent, resent.

ENTH

t: tenth.
   Plus pen'th*, etc.

ĒNTH

gr: greenth.

t: fourteenth, thirteenth, etc.
   Plus lean'th*, etc.

ENTS

m: accouterments.

t: contents.
   Plus cents, etc.
   Plus cent's, etc.
   Cf. ens.

ENZ

Vowel: ens, Valenciennes.

fl: flense.

g: gens.

l: Fresnel lens, lens.

s: Vincennes.
   Plus en+s.
   Plus den's, etc.

ĒENZ

b: baked beans, Boston baked beans,

gr: greens.

r: smithereens.

s: Essenes.

t: teens.
   Plus en+s.

EP

h: hep.

k(c): cèpe.

p: pep.

pr: prep.

r: demirep, rep.

sk(sc): skep.

st: footstep, misstep, overstep, step, steppe.

ĒP

ch: cheap, cheep, chepe*.

d: adeep, deep.

h: aheap, heap.

k(c): keep, upkeep.

kl: clepe*.

kr: creep.

l: leap, outleap, overleap.

n: neap.

p: bopeep, peep, underpeep.

r: reap.

s: seep.

sh: barbary sheep, sheep.

sl: asleep, beauty sleep, outsleep, oversleep, sleep.

st: steep.

sw: chimney sweep, ensweep, sweep, swepe*.

thr: threap.

tr: estrepe.

w: beweep, forweep*, outweep, weep.

EPS

ep+s.

Plus step's, etc.

ĒPS

kr: creeps.

Plus ep+s.

Plus sleep's, etc.

EPT

Vowel: inept.

d: adept.

k(c): kept, unkept.

kl: yclept*.

kr: crept.

l: leapt.

p: pepped.

s: accept, except, intercept, sept.

sl: outslept, overslept, slept.

st: misstepped, overstepped, stepped.

sw: swept, unswept.

w: unwept, wept.

ĒPT

h: upheaped.

n: beneaped, neaped.

st: unsteeped.

Plus ep+d.

Plus sleep'd, etc.

EPTH

d: depth.

Plus stepp'th*, etc.

ER

Vowel: air+, aire, arrière, Ayr+, ayre*+, e'er, ere, eyre, heir, howe'er, mid-air, Pierre, portière, vivandiere, whate'er, whatsoe'er, whene'er, where'er, wheresoe'er.

b: bare, bear, Camembert, forbear, threadbare, underbear, upbear.

bl: blare.

ch: armchair, chair, chare, sedanchair.

d: Adair, bedare, dare+, outdare.

f: affair, affaire, charges d'affaires, fair, fare, laissez faire, misfare, thoroughfare, unfair.

fl: flair, flare.

fr: frère.

g: gare.

gl: beglare, glair, glare.

h: hair+, hare+, maidenhair+, mohair+.

hw: anywhere, elsewhere, everywhere, otherwhere, somewhere, where.

j: etagère.

k(c): care, devil-may-care.

kl: claire, clare*, declare, eclair, Sinclair.

kw(qu): quair*.

l: capillaire, lair.

m: beche de mer, mal de mer, mare+.

n: billionaire, commissionaire, concessionaire, debonair, doctrinaire, jardinière, McNair, McNare, millionaire, ne'er, trillionaire, vin ordinaire.

p: compare, despair, disrepair, impair, pair, pare, pear, prepare, prickly pear, repair.

pr: prayer.

r: rare.

s: Sayre.

sh: cropshare, share.

sk(sc): scare.

skw(squ): square, T square.

sn: ensnare, snare.

sp: spare.

st: backstair, cocklestair*, outstare, stair, stare, stere, upstair.

sw: forswear, outswear, sware*, swear, unswear.

t: parterre, proletaire, solitaire, tare, tear, uptear.

TH: there.

ty: portière.

v: trouvère, vair, vare.

w: aware, beware, Delaware, earthenware, outwear, unaware, unbeware*, underwear, ware, wear.

ERD

Vowel: unheired.

b: Baird.

h: black-haired+, golden-haired+, red-haired+, silver-haired+.

k(c): uncared.

l: laird, laired.

p: ill-prepared, impaired, unimpaired, paired, prepared, unpaired, unprepared.

sh: shared, unshared.

sp: spared, unspared.

Plus ar+ed.

ERN

b: bairn.

k(c): cairn.

t: tairn.

ERS

sk(sc): scarce.

ERT

p: peart+.

ERZ

m: unawares, unbewares, unwares.

spr: prayers.

st: backstairs, stairs.

TH: theirs.

Plus ar+s.

Plus chair's, etc.

ES

Vowel: acquiesce, DES, S, S.O.S.

b: Bess, BS, CBS, EbS, PBS.

bl: bless, God bless, noblesse, unbless.

ch: chess.

d: frondesce, shepherdess, stewardess.

dr: address, ambassadress, diving dress, dress, full dress, gala dress, headdress, readdress, redress, underdress, undress.

f: confess, fess.

g: foreguess, guess.

gr: aggress, digress, egress, ingress, transgress.

h: Hess, VHS.

j: jess, turgesce.

kr: accresce, cress, Kress, mustard cress, watercress.

kw(qu): deliquesce.

l: blemishless, bodiless, bottomless, coalesce, colorless, comfortless, conscienceless, convalesce, cultureless, cumberless, dinnerless, effortless, fanciless, fatherless, fathomless, favorless, featureless, fetterless, flavorless, flowerless, fortuneless, gentilesse*, harborless, less, limitless, masterless, meaningless, measureless, merciless, moneyless, motherless, motionless, motiveless, shadeless, shelterless, silverless, slumberless, spiritless, temptationless, unless, valueless, virtueless, weaponless.

m: EMS, intumesce, mess, PMS.

n: abjectedness, abjectness, abstractedness, abstractness, abusiveness, accidentalness, adaptiveness, addictedness, adhesiveness, advantageousness, affectedness, affrontiveness, agedness, aggressiveness, agileness, agreeableness, airiness, alimentiveness, alliterativeness, allusiveness, almightiness, amazedness, ambitiousness, amiableness, amicableness, ampleness, ancientness, angelicalness, angriness, anonymousness, anticness, anxiousness, apishness, apparentness, appeasableness, appositeness, apprehensiveness, approachableness, arbitrariness, ardentness, arduousness, aridness, artfulness, articulateness, artificialness, artlessness, assiduousness, atrociousness, attentiveness, attractiveness, auspiciousness, avariciousness, awfulness, awkwardness, backhandedness, backwardness, balefulness, banefulness, bareheadedness, baroness, barrenness, bashfulness, beastliness, beeriness, beseechingness, besottedness, bitterness, blamelessness, blessedness, blissfulness, blithesomeness, bloatedness, blockishness, bloodguiltiness, bloodiness, bloodlessness, bloodthirstiness, bloomingness, bloomlessness, bluntishness, boastfulness, boisterousness, bonniness, bookishness, boorishness, bootlessness, boundlessness, bounteousness, boyishness, brackishness, brassiness, brawniness, brazenness, breathlessness, brilliantness, brittleness, brokenness, brotherliness, brushiness, brutishness, bulkiness, bumptiousness, bunchiness, burliness, bushiness, buxomness, candidness, canoness, capaciousness, capriciousness, captiousness, carefulness, carelessness, cautiousness, ceaselessness, chalkiness, changefulness, chariness, charmingness, chattiness, cheerfulness, cheeriness, cheerlessness, childishness, childlessness, chilliness, chubbiness, churlishness, clandestineness, clannishness, cleanliness, clearsightedness, cleverness, cliquishness, cloddishness, cloudiness, cloudlessness, clownishness, clumsiness, coldheartedness, collectedness, collusiveness, comeliness, commonness, composedness, comprehensiveness, compulsiveness, conceitedness, conclusiveness, conduciveness, confusedness, conjunctiveness, conscientiousness, consciousness, consecutiveness, conspicuousness, constructiveness, contentedness, contentiousness, contradictiousness, contradictoriness, contrariness, contumaciousness, copiousness, cordialness, corrosiveness, costliness, courageousness, courtliness, covertness, covetousness, crabbedness, craftiness, craggedness, cragginess, creaminess, credulousness, crookedness, cruelness, crustiness, cumbrousness, curiousness, curliness, customariness, daintiness, dampishness, daringness, dauntlessness, dauphiness, deaconess, deadliness, deathfulness, deathiness, deathlessness, debauchedness, deceitfulness, deceptiveness, decisiveness, decorativeness, defectiveness, defenselessness, defiantless, definiteness, deformedness, degenerateness, dejectedness, deliciousness, delightfulness, delightsomeness, deliriousness, delusiveness, dementedness, demoness, depressiveness, derisiveness, desirousness, despitefulness, destructiveness, desultoriness, detersiveness, detractiveness, devotedness, dewiness, diffusedness, diffusiveness, dilatoriness, dilutedness, dinginess, direfulness, disastrousness, discontentedness, discursiveness, disdainfulness, disinterestedness, dismalness, disposedness, disputatiousness, distastefulness, distinctiveness, dizziness, doggedness, dolefulness, doubtfulness, doughtiness, downiness, dreadfulness, dreaminess, dreariness, droughtiness, drowsiness, drunkenness, dumpishness, duskiness, dustiness, dwarfishness, eagerness, earliness, earnestness, earthiness, earthliness, earthly-mindedness, easefulness, easiness, eeriness, effectiveness, efficaciousness, effusiveness, egregiousness, elatedness, emotiveness, emptiness, endearedness, endlessness, enduringness, engagingness, enormousness, entertainingness, equalness, essentialness, estrangedness, evanesce, evasiveness, everlastingness, exaltedness, exceptiousness, excessiveness, exclusiveness,

excursiveness, expansiveness, expeditiousness, expensiveness, explicitness, expressiveness, exquisiteness, extensiveness, facetiousness, factiousness, faithfulness, faithlessness, fallaciousness, false-heartedness, farsightedness, fastidiousness, fatefulness, fatherliness, faultiness, faultlessness, favoredness, fearfulness, fearlessness, feeble-mindedness, feebleness, feignedness, ferociousness, fervidness, fickleness, fictiousness, fictitiousness, fiendishness, fieriness, filminess, finesse, fishiness, fitfulness, fixedness, flabbiness, flaccidness, flakiness, flashiness, fleshiness, fleshlessness, fleshliness, flexibleness, flightiness, flimsiness, flippantness, floridness, floweriness, fluentness, fogginess, foolhardiness, foolishness, foppishness, forcedness, foreignness, forgetfulness, formlessness, forwardness, fractiousness, fragileness, frankheartedness, franticness, fraudlessness, freakishness, freckledness, free-heartedness, fretfulness, friendlessness, friendliness, frightfulness, frigidness, friskiness, frivolousness, frostiness, frothiness, frowardness, frozenness, frugalness, fruitfulness, fruitlessness, frumpishness, fugaciousness, fulsomeness, fumishness, fundamentalness, furiousness, fussiness, fustiness, gaddishness, gallantness, gamesomeness, garishness, garrulousness, gashliness, gastness, gaudiness, generousness, genialness, gentleness, ghastliness, ghostliness, giddiness, giftedness, girlishness, gladfulness, gladsomeness, glariness, glassiness, gloominess, gloriousness, glossiness, godlessness, godliness, goodliness, gorgeousness,

governess, gracefulness, graceless-
ness, graciousness, graphicness,
grassiness, gratefulness, greasiness, greediness, greenishness,
grievousness, griminess, grittiness,
grogginess, groundlessness,
guardedness, guidelessness,
guilefulness, guilelessness,
guiltiness, guiltlessness,
gustfulness, hairiness, handiness,
handsomeness, haplessness,
happiness, hard-heartedness,
hardiness, harmfulness, harmless-
ness, harmoniousness, hastiness,
hatefulness, haughtiness, haziness,
headiness, healthfulness,
healthiness, healthlessness,
heartedness, heartiness, heartlessness, heathenness, heavenliness,
heavenly-mindedness, heaviness,
heedfulness, heedlessness,
heinousness, hellishness,
helpfulness, helplessness,
heterogeneousness, hiddenness,
hideousness, high-mindedness,
hilliness, hoariness, hoggishness,
holiness, hollowness,
homelessness, homeliness,
hopefulness, hopelessness,
horridness, huffishness, humble-
ness, humidness, humorousness,
hurtfulness, huskiness, iciness,
idleness, ignobleness, illicitness,
illiterateness, ill-naturedness,
illuciveness, illustriousness,
imaginativeness, imitativeness,
immaculateness, impartialness,
impassiveness, imperfectness,
imperiousness, imperviousness,
impetuousness, impiousness,
implicitness, imponderousness,
imposingness, impressiveness,
impulsiveness, inattentiveness,
inauspiciousness, incapaciousness,
incautiousness, incidentalness,
incoherentness, incomprehensive-
ness, inconclusiveness, incongru-
ousness, inconsistentness,
inconspicuousness, indebtedness,
indecisiveness, indecorousness,
inefficaciousness, infectiousness,

ingeniousness, ingenuousness,
injuriousness, inkiness,
innoxiousness, inobtrusiveness,
inoffensiveness, insidiousness,
insipidness, instructiveness,
intensiveness, intrusiveness,
inventiveness, invidiousness,
invincibleness, involuntariness,
inwardness, irefulness, irksome-
ness, jaggedness, jauntiness,
jealousness, jettiness, Jewishness,
jolliness, jovialness, joyfulness,
joylessness, joyousness, judiciousness, juiciness, jumpiness, kind-
heartedness, kindliness,
kingliness, knavishness,
knightliness, knottiness, languid-
ness, large-heartedness, lascivious-
ness, lawfulness, lawlessness,
laziness, leafiness, leaflessness,
leaviness*, lengthiness, licentiousness, lifelessness, light-
heartedness, lightsomeness,
likeableness, likeliness, limber-
ness, limpidness, liquidness,
lissomeness, listlessness, literal-
ness, litigiousness, littleness,
liveliness, lividness, livingness,
loathliness, loathsomeness,
loftiness, loneliness, lonesome-
ness, longsomeness, loquacious-
ness, lordliness, loutishness, love-
in-idleness, loveliness, lovingness,
lowliness, loyalness, lucidness,
luckiness, lugubriousness,
luminousness, lumpishness,
lusciousness, lustfulness, lustiness,
maidenliness, maliciousness,
manfulness, manliness, mannerli-
ness, mannishness, manysided-
ness, marchioness, marshiness,
massiness*, massiveness,
matchlessness, mawkishness,
maziness, meagreness, mealiness,
meanness, meatiness, meditative-
ness, mellowness, meltingness,
meretriciousness, merriness,
mightiness, milkiness, mindful-
ness, miraculousness, miriness,
mirthfulness, mirthlessness,
miscellaneousness,

mischievousness, misshapeneness, mistiness, modernness, modishness, momentousness, monkishness, monotonousness, monstrousness, moodiness, mopishness, morbidness, mortalness, mossiness, motherliness, mouldiness, mournfulness, mulishness, multifariousness, mumpishness, murkiness, muskiness, mustiness, mutinousness, mysteriousness, mysticalness, nakedness, narrowmindedness, narrowness, nastiness, nationalness, nativeness, nattiness, naturalness, naughtiness, near-sightedness, nebulousness, necessariness, necessitousness, nectareousness, needfulness, neediness, needlessness, nefariousness, neglectedness, neglectfulness, neighborliness, nervousness, niggardliness, nimbleness, nobleness, noiselessness, noisiness, noisomeness, notableness, notedness, notelessness, nothingness, notoriousness, noxiousness, numberousness, nutritiousness, objectiveness, obligatoriness, obligingness, obliviousness, obsequiousness, observableness, obstreperousness, obtrusiveness, obviousness, odiousness, odoriferousness, odorousness, offensiveness, officiousness, oiliness, oleaginousness, openhandedness, openheartedness, openness, oppressiveness, opprobriousness, orderliness, ostentatiousness, outlandishness, outrageousness, outwardness, painfulness, painlessness, pallidness, paltriness, parlousness, parsimoniousness, passiveness, pawkiness, peaceableness, peacefulness, pearliness, peerlessness, peevishness, pellucidness, penetrativeness, pennilessness, pensileness,

pensiveness, penuriousness, peremptoriness, perfectness, perfidiousness, perfunctoriness, perilousness, perniciousness, perplexedness, perplexiveness, perspicaciousness, perspicuousness, persuasiveness, pertinaciousness, perverseness, pervicaciousness, perviousness, pestilentialness, pettiness, pettishness, piercingness, pig-headedness, pitchiness, piteousness, pithiness, pitiableness, pitifulness, pitilessness, placableness, placidness, plaintiveness, playfulness, playsomeness, pleasantness, pleasingness, plenteousness, pliantness, poachiness, pointedness, pompousness, ponderousness, poorliness, porousness, portliness, positiveness, powerfulness, powerlessness, practicalness, praiseworthiness, prayerfulness, prayerlessness, precariousness, preciousness, precipitousness, precociousness, prejudicialness, preposterousness, presumptuousness, pretentiousness, prettiness, previousness, prickliness, pridefulness, priestliness, priggishness, primitiveness, princeliness, prodigiousness, productiveness, progressiveness, properness, propitiousness, prosiness, prospectiveness, protectiveness, prudishness, public-mindedness, puffiness, pugnaciousness, pulpiness, pulpousness, pulselessness, punctiliousness, puniness, pursiness, pusilanimousness, putridness, quakiness, qualmishness, queasiness, queenliness, quenchlessness, querulousness, quick-sightedness, quickwittedness, quietness, rabidness, raciness, raggedness, raininess, rakishness, rancidness, rapaciousness, rapidness, ravenousness, readiness, rebelliousness, recentness, receptiveness, recklessness, reddishness, reflectiveness, refractiveness, refractoriness, regardlessness, relativeness, relentlessness, remorsefulness, remorselessness, reproachfulness, repulsiveness, resistlessness, resoluteness, respectfulness, responsiveness, restfulness, restiveness, restlessness, restrictiveness, retentiveness, revengefulness, rightfulness, right-handedness, rightmindedness, rigidness, rigorousness, riotousness, robustiousness, rockiness, roguishness, rompishness, roominess, ropiness, rosiness, rottenness, ruddiness, ruefulness, ruggedness, ruthlessness, sacredness, sacrilegiousness, sagaciousness, saintliness, salaciousness, sallowness, salutariness, sanctimoniousness, sandiness, sanguineness, sappiness, satisfactoriness, sauciness, savageness, savingness, savoriness, scaliness, scorchingness, scornfulness, scragginess, scurviness, seaworthiness, secondariness, secretiveness, secretness, sedentariness, seditiousness, seediness, seemingness, seemliness, seldomness, self-conceitedness, self-consciousness, selfishness, self-righteousness, senselessness, sensitiveness, sensuousness, sententiousness, seriousness, shabbiness, shadiness, shadowiness, shagginess, shakiness, shallowness, shamefulness, shamelessness, shapelessness, shapeliness, sheepishness, shieldlessness, shiftiness, shiftlessness, shiningness, shoaliness, short-sightedness, showeriness, showiness, shrewishness, shrubbiness, sickliness, sightlessness, silentness, sulkiness, silliness, simple-mindedness, simpleness, simultaneousness,

sinfulness, singleness, sinlessness, sketchiness, skilfulness, skittishness, shabbiness, slatiness, slavishness, sleaziness, sleepiness, sleeplessness, sleetiness, slenderness, sliminess, slipperiness, slothfulness, sluggishness, smilingness, smokiness, snappishness, sneakiness, snobbishness, sober-mindedness, soberness, sociableness, soft-heartedness, solidness, solitariness, solubleness, somberness, sombrousness, sonorousness, sordidness, sorriness, sorrowfulness, sottishness, spaciousness, sparklingness, speciousness, speckledness, speculativeness, speechlessness, speediness, spiciness, spitefulness, splendidness, sponginess, spontaneousness, sportiveness, spotlessness, spottedness, spottiness, springiness, spriteliness, spuminess, spuriousness, squeamishness, starchiness, starriness, stateliness, steadfastness, steadiness, stealthfulness, stealthiness, steeliness, steepiness*, stickiness, stinginess, stintedness, stolidness, stoniness, storminess, straightforwardness, strenuousness, stringentness, stringiness, stubbiness, stubbornness, studiousness, stuffiness, stuntedness, stupendousness, stupidness, sturdiness, stylishness, subjectiveness, submissiveness, subordinateness, substantialness, subtleness, successfulness, suddenness, sugariness, suggestiveness, suitableness, sulkiness, sullenness, sultriness, sumptuousness, sunniness, superciliousness, superstitiousness, suppleness, suppliantness, surliness, surprisingness, susceptiveness, suspectedness, suspiciousness, swarthiness, sweatiness, sweetishness, talkativeness, tamelessness, tardiness, tastefulness, tastiness, tawdriness, tawniness, tediousness, tempestuousness, temporariness, temptingness, tenaciousness, tender-heartedness, tepidness, testiness, thankfulness, thievishness, thirstiness, thoroughness, thoughtfulness, thoughtlessness, threadiness, thriftiness, thriftlessness, thrivingness, ticklishness, tidiness, timelessness, timeliness, timidness, timorousness, tipsiness, tiresomeness, toilsomeness, toothsomeness, torpidness, torridness, tortuousness, totalness, touchiness, toyishness, tracklessness, traitorousness, tranquilness, transcendentalness, transientness, transitiveness, transitoriness, transparentness, trashiness, treacherousness, tremendousness, tremulousness, tributariness, trickiness, trickishness, tricksiness, trueheartedness, trustfulness, trustiness, trustlessness, trustworthiness, truthfulness, truthlessness, tunefulness, tunelessness, turfiness, turgidness, ugliness, umbrageousness, unanimousness, unbendingness, unblessedness, unboundedness, uncleanliness, uncloudedness, uncourtliness, undauntedness, uneasiness, unexpectedness, unfeignedness, unfriendliness, ungainliness, ungentleness, ungodliness, ungroundedness, unholiness, universalness, unkindliness, unlikeliness, unloveliness, unmanliness, unpreparedness, unquietness, unreadiness, unrighteousness, unruliness, unseaworthiness, unseemliness, unsightliness, unstableness, untowardness, untrustiness, unwieldiness, unwillingness, unwontedness, unworldliness, unworthiness, uppishness, usefulness, uselessness, uxoriousness, vacuousness, vagrantness, valetudinariness, valiantness, validness, vapidness, vexatiousness, viciousness, victoriousness, vigorousness, vindictiveness, viridness, virileness, virtuousness, viscousness, visionariness, vitreousness, vivaciousness, vividness, vociferousness, voluminousness, voluntariness, voluptuousness, voraciousness, vulgarness, waggishness, wakefulness, wantonness, warefulness*, wariness, warm-heartedness, washiness, waspishness, wastefulness, watchfulness, waveringness, waviness, waxiness, waywardness, wealthiness, weariness, wearisomeness, weightiness, welcomeness, whimsicalness, whitishness, wholesomeness, wickedness, wilderness, wilfulness, wiliness, willingness, winsomeness, wiriness, wishfulness, wistfulness, witheredness, witlessness, wittiness, woefulness, womanliness, wondrousness, wontedness, woodiness, wooliness, wordiness, wordishness, worldliness, worldly-mindedness, worshipfulness, worthiness, worthlessness, wrathfulness, wretchedness, wretchlessness, wrongfulness, wrong-headedness, yeastiness, yellowishness, yellowness, yieldingness, youthfulness, zealousness.

p: CPS.

pr: bench press, compress, depress, express, impress, permanent press, suppress.

r: archeress, caress, conqueress, duress, effloresce, mayoress, sorceress, tailoress, votaress.

s: assess, cess, excess, success.

str: stress.

t: giantess, Tess.

tr: ancestress, comfortress, distress, editress, executress, idolatress, inheritress, ministress, monitress, votress, tress.

v: CVS, effervesce.

y: yes.

z: dispossess, possess, repossess.

ĒS

b: obese.

fl: fleece.

g: geese.

gr: grease, grece, Greece, verdigris+.

kr: crease, creese, decrease, increase, Lucrece, popping crease.

l: coulisse, Felice, lease, pelisse, police, release, valise.

m: comice, semese.

n: Berenice, Bernice, Nice, niece.

p: afterpiece, apiece, battlepiece, chimneypiece, fowling piece, frontispiece, mantelpiece, masterpiece, peace, piece, pocketpiece.

pr: caprice.

r: cerise, Clarice, Maurice, Reese, Therise.

s: cease, decease, predecease, surcease.

tr: cantatrice.

ESH

b: tête-bêche.

d: Bangladesh.

fl: flesh.

fr: afresh, crème frâiche, fresh, refresh.

kr: crèche.

m: enmesh, mesh.

n: nesh.

s: secech.

t: Bayou Teche.

thr: thresh.

ĒSH

f: affiche

k(qu): quiche.

l: leash, McLeish, unleash.

n: McNeish.

sh: sheesh

t: schottische.

ESK

Vowel: Kafkaesque, statuesque.

b: arabesque.

d: desk, reading desk.

l: burlesque, naturalesque.

n: gardenesque, Romanesque.

r: barbaresque, chivalresque, Moresque, picaresque, picturesque, plateresque, sculpturesque.

t: Dantesque, gigantesque, grotesque, soldatesque.

EST

Vowel: beamiest, beguilingest, bleariest, breeziest, briniest, burliest, cheeriest, cheerliest, chilliest, chokiest, cleanliest, coziest, costliest, courtliest, creamiest, creepiest, crustiest, curliest, daintiest, dingiest, dizziest, doughtiest, dowdiest, dreamiest, dreariest, drowsiest, dustiest, earliest, easiest, eeriest, emptiest, enviest*, evenest, filmiest, filthiest, fleeciest, flightiest, flimsiest, flintiest, foamiest, friendliest, funniest, fussiest, giddiest, gloomiest, glossiest, goutiest, grimiest, guiltiest, gustiest, happiest, haughtiest, healthiest, heartiest, heaviest, holiest, homeliest, huffiest, hungriest, huskiest, iciest, inkiest, inliest, jolliest, juiciest, kindliest, kingliest, knightliest, likeliest, liveliest, loftiest, loneliest, loveliest, lowliest, merriest, mightiest, moistest, mossiest, mouldiest, muskiest, mustiest, noisiest, pearliest, portliest, princeliest, prosiest, readiest, rescuest*, rosiest, rowdiest, rustiest, sedgiest, seemliest, shiniest, shoddiest, showiest, sightliest, silliest, sketchiest, skinniest, sleepiest, slimiest, smokiest, snuffiest, soapiest, spiciest, spikiest, spongiest, spooniest, springiest, spriteliest, steadiest, stealthiest, stilliest, stingiest, stormiest, stuffiest, sturdiest, sunniest, surliest, thirstiest, thriftiest, Trieste, trustiest, ugliest, unholiest, unreadiest, veriest, wealthiest, weariest, wheeziest, windiest, wintriest, worriest*, yeastiest.

b: best, second best.

bl: blest, unblest.

br: abreast, breast, Brest, unbreast.

ch: chest.

d: affectedest, effectedest, horridest, morbidest, ruggedest, sacredest, solidest, splendidest, stupidest, timidest.

dr: dressed, overdressed, redressed, underdressed, undressed, unredressed.

f: infest, manifest.

g: Gest, guest, unguessed.

h: alkahest, behest, hest.

j: congest, digest, gest, geste, ingest, jessed, jest, predigest, suggest.

kr: crest, increst, undercrest.

kw(qu): acquest*, bequest, quest, request.

l: blestfulest, blissfulest, blithefulest, cheerfulest, cruellest, forcefulest, genialest, guilefulest, hopefulest, libelest*, loyalest, marvelest*, mournfulest, quarrelest*, restfulest, rightfulest, rivalest*, royalest, skilfulest, tearfulest, wilfulest.

m: blithesomest, lissomest, lithesomest, winsomest.

n: determinest*, emblazonest*, freshenest*, funest, glistenest*, hearkenest*, listenest*, livenest*, nest, pardonest*, predestinest*, questionest*.

p: anapest, Budapest, pest.

pr: depressed, hard-pressed, imprest, pressed, unexpressed, unpressed.

r: answerest*, arrest, blisterest*, blunderest*, Bucharest, cardiac arrest, clusterest*, conquerest*, coverest*, dowerest*, Everest, flowerest*, gatherest*, glimmerest*, glowerest*, hungerest*, incumberest*, interest, laborest*, lingerest*, lowerest*, murmurest*, offerest*, pleasurest*, recoverest*, rememberest*, rest, severest*, severest, shimmerest*, shudderest*, slumberest*, sufferest*, sunderest*, temperest*, thunderest*, unrest, vulgarest, wanderest*, wonderest*, wrest.

s: cest, obsessed, palimpsest, preciousest, recessed, witnessest*.

sh: astonishest*, banishest*, languishest*, nourishest*, punishest*, relinquishest*.

str: stressed, unstressed.

t: attest, attributest*, brilliantest, contest, detest, exhibitest*, forfeitest*, inheritest*, inspiritest*, meritest*, obtest, patentest, pleasantest, protest, quietest, silentest, spiritest*, test.

tr: distressed, golden-tressed, tressed, untressed.

v: attentivest, decisivest, derisivest, devest, divest, invest, pensivest, vest, vindictivest.

w: Key West, mellowest, narrowest, northwest, sorrowest*, west, winnowest*.

y: yessed.

z: self-possessed, unprepossessed, zest.

Plus es+d.

ĒST

Vowel: east, northeast, southeast.

b: beast, hartebeest, wildebeest.

d: modiste.

f: feast, harvest feast, wedding feast.

fl: fleeced.

kw(qu): queest.

l: least, policed, underpoliced.

pr: archpriest, priest, unpriest.

t: artiste, batiste.

tr: triste.

y: yeast.

Plus es+d.

ET

Vowel: duet, Harriet, historiette, Joliet, Juliet, Juliette, minuet, oubliette, pirouette, serviette, silhouette, statuette.

b: abet, alphabet, barbette, bet, Thibet, Tibet.

bl: blet.

br: Brett, soubrette.

ch: Chet.

d: cadet, debt, judgment debt, vedette.

f: estafet, estafette.

fl: flet.

fr: fret, frett, unfret*.

g: baguette, beget, courgette, forget, get, misbeget, unget.

gr: aigrette, regret, vinaigrette.

h: het.

hw: whet.

j: ink jet, jet, resistojet, suffragette.

k(c): banquette, barquette, blanquette, coquette, croquette, diskette, etiquette, parroket, parquet, piquet, piquette, tourniquet.

l: ailette, alette, amulet, anjelet, cassolette, coverlet, epaulet, eyelet, flageolet, Gillette, globulet, landaulet, let, Lett, martlet, medalet, novelette, omelet, rivulet, Russian roulette, roulette, toilette, towelette, violet, zonulet.

m: allumette, Calumet, fumette, met, well-met.

n: Annette, Antoinette, Barnett, baronet, bassinet, bayonet, benet, bobinet, brunette, Burnett, cabinet, canzonet, carcanet, castanet, castnet, chansonette, clarinet, coronet, falconet, genet, Internet, Jeannette, lorgnette, luncheonette, lunette, mari-onette, martinet, mignonette, minionette*, Nanette, net, pianette, sarcenet, tabinet, tournette, Usenet, vignette, villanette, wagonette.

p: parapet, pet, pipette.

r: amourette, anchoret, banneret, cellaret, cigarette, farmerette, floweret, formeret, keaderette, leveret, Margaret, minaret, pillaret, ret, Rhett, tabaret, taboret.

s: anisette, backset, beset, audio cassette, chemisette, crossette, crystal set, dancette, dead-set, facette, fossette, ill-set, inset, interset, Lucette, marmoset, muset, offset, overset, poussette, set, sett, sharp-set, smart set, somerset, sunset, thick-set, underset, upset.

sh: brochette, couchette, fourchette, planchette, ricochet.

st: stet.

sw: sweat.

t: motet, octet, quartet, quintet, septet, sestet, sextet.

th: epiteth.

thr: threat.

tr: tret.

v: brevet, corvette, curvet, Olivet, revet, vet.

w: all wet, bewet, wet.

y: yet.

z: anisette, chemisette, gazette, grisette, marmoset, muset, rosette.

ĒT

Vowel: eat, overeat.

b: beat, beet, deadbeat, sea beat, sugar beet.

bl: bleat.

ch: cheat, cheet, escheat.

f: defeat, effete, feat, feet, Lafitte.

fl: fleet.

fr: afreet.

g: geat.

gl: gleet.

gr: greet.

h: dead heat, heat, overheat, reheat.

hw: wheat.

j: vegete.

k(c): lorikeet, parakeet.

kl: cleat, cleet.

kr: accrete, concrete, Crete, discreet, indiscreet, secrete.

l: athlete, delete, elite, leat, leet, obsolete.

m: dead meat, helpmeet, luncheon meat, meat, meet, mete, unmeet.

n: neat.

p: compete, peat, Pete, repeat.

pl: complete, deplete, incomplete, pleat, replete.

r: marguerite, terete.

s: conceit, country seat, county seat, deceit, facete*, judgement seat, mercy seat, preconceit*, receipt, seat, self-conceit, self-deceit, unseat.

sh: balance sheet, sheet, short sheet, winding sheet.

sk(sc): skeet.

sl: sleet.

str: street.

sw: bittersweet, honey-sweet, meadowsweet, suite, sunnysweet, sweet, unsweet.

t: bon appetit, teat.

tr: Dutch treat, entreat, estreat, ill-treat, maltreat, retreat, treat.

tw: tweet tweet.

w: weet.

z: carte de visite.

ETH

Vowel: busieth*, continueth*, eightieth, envieth*, fiftieth, fortieth, ninetieth, rescueth*, seventieth, sixtieth, sorroweth*, thirtieth, twentieth, wearieth*, winnoweth*, worrieth*.

b: Elizabeth, Macbeth.

br: breath.

d: death, 'sdeath*.

kr: Creath.

l: libelleth*, marvelleth*, quarrelleth*, rivalleth*, shibboleth.

m: meth.

n: determineth*, emblazoneth*, glisteneth*, hearkeneth*, listeneth*, liveneth*, pardoneth*, predestineth*, questioneth*.

p: worshippeth*.

r: answereth*, Astoreth, blistereth*, blundereth*, clustereth*, conquereth*, covereth*, dowereth*, flowereth*, gathereth*, glowereth*, hungereth*, incumbereth*, laboreth*, lingereth*, lowereth*, measureth*, murmureth*, offereth*, overpowereth*, overtowereth*, pleasureth*, recovereth*, remembereth*,

severeth*, shimmereth*,
showereth*, shuddereth*,
slivereth*, slumbereth*,
suffereth*, sundereth*,
tempereth*, thundereth*,
ventureth*, wandereth*,
whispereth*, wondereth*.

s: saith*+, Seth, witnesseth*.

sh: astonisheth*, banisheth*,
blemisheth*, languisheth*,
nourisheth*, punisheth*,
relinquisheth*.

t: attributeth*, enspiriteth*,
exhibiteth*, forfeiteth*,
inheriteth*, inspiriteth*,
meriteth*, quieteth*, spiriteth*.

ĒTH

br: breathe, inbreathe, upbreathe.

h: heath.

k(c): Keith.

kw(qu): bequeath.

l: Leith.

n: beneath, 'neath, underneath.

r: wreath.

r: enwreathe, interwreathe,
inwreathe, unwreathe, wreathe.

s: seethe.

sh: ensheathe, insheathe, sheath,
sheathe, unsheathe.

sn: sneath, sneathe.

t: teeth, teethe.

ĒTHD

b: unbreathed.

kw(qu): bequeathed.
Plus eth+d.

ETHS

m: meths.

ETZ

m: Metz.
Plus et+s.
Plus bet's, etc.

ĒTZ

d: Dietz.

k: Keats.
Plus et+s.
Plus meat's, etc.

ĒV

Vowel: Christmas Eve, eave, eve,
naive, New Year's Eve, yestereve*.

b: beeve.

br: breve.

ch: achieve.

d: deev, Khedive.

gr: aggrieve, engrieve*, greave,
grieve.

h: heave, upheave.

k(c): keeve.

kl: cleave.

l: believe, disbelieve, family leave,
interleave, leave, lieve, make-
believe, relieve.

p: peeve.

pr: reprieve.

r: bereave, reave, reeve, shire
reeve*, unreave, unreeve.

s: conceive, deceive, misconceive,
perceive, preconceive, receive,
seave, undeceive.

sh: sheave.

shr: Shreve, shrieve*.

sl: sleave, sleeve.

st: steeve, Steve.

t: recitative.

th: thieve.

tr: retrieve.

v: qui vive, vive.

w: interweave, inweave, unweave,
weave, we've.

ĒVD

l: unbelieved, unrelieved.

r: bereaved.

s: ill-conceived, self-deceived, unperceived.

  Plus ev+s.

  Plus sleeve'd, etc.

EX

Vowel: Generation X, VX, X.
b: Bx.
fl: retroflex.
m: Tex-Mex.
pl: nuplex.
s: safe sex.
v: vex.

EZ

f: fez.
pr: Prez.
s: says.
t: Cortez.

ĒZ

Vowel: Carlylese, ease, heart'sease, Louise, rabies, unease.
b: bise.
br: breeze, sea breeze.
ch: cheese.
d: antipodes, B. V. D.'s, Caryatides, Eumenides, Hesperides, Maimonides, Pierides, Pleiades, Valdez.
f: feaze.
fl: fleas.
fr: cheval-de-frise, enfreeze*, freeze, frieze, unfreeze.
g: Portuguese.
gr: grease.
h: heeze, he's.
hw: wheeze.
j: Jeez.
k(c): keys.
kw(qu): obsequies.
l: Belize, Bengalese, Herakles, Hercules, isosceles, journalese, lees, legalese, Nepaulese, Singhalese, Tyrolese, valise.
m: Annamese, Assamese, Burmese, chemise, mease, remise, Siamese.
n: aboriginese, Arakanese, Aragonese, bee's knees, Bolognese, Ceylonese, chersonese, Chinese, Diogenes, Havanese, Japanese, Javanese, Johnsonese, Leonese, Milanese, Polonese*, Pyrenees, Verones, Viennese.
p: appease, pease, trapeze.
pl: please.
pr: imprese.
r: cerise, computerese, congeries, Navarrese.
s: analyses, antitheses, hypotheses, indices, parentheses, seize, syntheses, vortices.
sh: she's.
skw(squ): squeeze.
sl: sleaze.
sn: sneeze.
spl: displease.
st: stees.
t: agonistes, D. T.'s, Maltese, tease.
TH: these.
tw: tweeze.
v: Genevese.
z: Crohn's disease, disease, Lyme disease, mad cow disease, periphrases.

  Plus e+s.

  Plus sea's, etc.

EZH

n: manège.
r: barège.
t: cortège.

ĒZH

pr: prestige.
t: tige.

(Choose only one word out of each group.)

I

Words including the following accented vowel sounds:

i: as in it; heard also in pretty, breeches, sieve, women, guild, lymph.

ī: as in fine; also in aisle, aye (meaning *yes*), height, eye, lie, choir, buy, by, rye.

Ī

Vowel: AI, ay, aye, black eye, eye, genii, I, incyc*, my eye, sheep's eye, DUI, weather eye, Y.

b: alibi, bi, buy, by, bye, bye-bye, by-and-by, by-the-by, forby, go-by, goodbye, hereby, hush-a-by, incubi, lullaby, passerby, standby, standerby, thereby, underbuy, whereby.

d: ao dai, bedye, die, dye, red dye.

dr: adry, dry, high-and-dry.

f: acidify, alacrify, alkalify, amplify, angelify, Anglify, beatify, beautify, brutify, candify, certify, clarify, classify, cockneyfy, codify, countrify, crucify, damnify, dandify, defy, deify, dignify, disqualify, dissatisfy, diversify, edify, electrify, emulsify, eternify*, exemplify, falsify, fie, fortify, fossilify, Frenchify, fructify, gasify, glorify, gratify, horrify, humanify, identify, indemnify, intensify, justify, labefy, lenify, lignify, liquefy, magnify, modify, mollify, mortify, mystify, notify, nullify, ossify, pacify, personify, petrify, phi, preachify, purify, putrefy, qualify, quantify, ramify, rarefy, ratify, rectify, revivify, saccharify, sanctify, satisfy, scarify, scorify, signify, simplify, solidify, specify, stellify, stiltify, stultify, stupefy,

tabefy, terrify, testify, torpify, torrefy, transmogrify, typify, unify, verbify, verify, versify, vilify, vitrify, vivify, zombify.

fl: butterfly, dragonfly, firefly, fly, gadfly, horsefly, shoofly, outfly.

fr: fry, small fry.

g: fall guy, guy, wise guy.

gr: gri.

h: heigh, hie, high, sky-high.

hw: why.

k(c): chi.

kr: cry, decry, descry, outcry.

l: alkali, ally, belie, CLI, July, lazuli, lie, lye, rely, Thermopylae, underlie.

m: demi*+, demy, my.

n: deny, nigh, nye, termini, well-nigh.

p: apple pie, DPI, espy, humble pie, magpie, mince pie, occupy, pi, pie, preoccupy, sea pie, umble pie*.

pl: apply, comply, imply, multiply, ply, reply, supply.

pr: pry.

r: awry, MRI, rye, wry.

s: prophesy, psi, scye, sigh.

sh: shy, unshy.

sk(sc): ensky, sky, Skye.

sl: sly.

sn: sny.
sp: bespy, spy, weatherspy.
spr: spry.
st: sty.
t: tie, untie.
th: Thai, thigh.
TH: thy*.
tr: try.
v: outvie, vie.
w: DWI, wye, Y.
y: Chevalier+.

IB

b: bib, Bibb.
d: dib.
dr: drib.
f: fib.
g: gib, Gibb.
gl: glib.
j: jib.
kr: crib.
kw(qu): quib*.
l: ad lib.
n: nib.
r: rib.
s: sib.
skw(squ): squib.
tr: contrib.

ĪB

b: imbibe.
br: bribe.
j: gibe, jibe.
k(c): kibe.
skr(scr): ascribe, circumscribe, describe, inscribe, interscribe, prescribe, proscribe, scribe, subscribe, superscribe, transcribe.
tr: diatribe, tribe.

IBD

r: ribbed, rock ribbed.
    Plus ib+d.

ĪBD

skr(scr): inscribed, uninscribed.
    Plus ib+d.

IBZ

d: dibs.
g: Gibbs.
n: his nibs.
    Plus ib+s.
    Plus Bibb's, etc.

ICH

Vowel: itch.
b: bitch.
ch: chich*.
d: ditch.
f: fitch.
fl: flitch.
gl: glitch.
h: hitch, unhitch.
hw: which.
kw(qu): quitch.
l: lich*.
m: miche.
n: niche.
p: pitch.
r: enrich, rich.
s: sich.
skr(scr): scritch.
sn: snitch.
st: chain stitch, feather stitch, stitch.
sw: switch.
tw: twitch.
v: czarevitch.
w: bewitch, Caesarewitch, czarewitch, Gabrilowitch, witch.

ICHT

h: hitched, unhitched.
w: unbewitched, unwitched.
    Plus ich+d.

ĬD

Vowel: id.

b: bid, forbid, outbid, overbid, rebid, unbid, underbid, unforbid.

ch: chid*.

d: did, fordid*, katydid, outdid, overdid, undid.

dr: Madrid.

f: fid.

g: gid.

gr: grid.

h: hid.

k(c): kid.

kw(qu): quid.

l: eyelid, invalid, lid.

m: amid, mid, pyramid.

r: rid.

s: Cid.

sk(sc): skid.

skw(squ): squid.

sl: slid.

st: dermestid.

str: bestrid*, strid*.

thr: thrid*.

w: Clwyd.

ĪD

Vowel: almond-eyed, Arguseyed, calf-eyed, cockeyed, cross-eyed, dioxide, dove-eyed, dull-eyed, eagle-eyed, evil-eyed, eyed, full-eyed, goggle-eyed, green-eyed, hawk-eyed, I'd, ide, lynx-eyed, meek-eyed, monoxide, open-eyed, owl-eyed, ox-eyed, oxide, pale-eyed, peroxide, pie-eyed, pop-eyed, sloe-eyed, snake-eyed, soft-eyed, squint-eyed, wall-eyed.

b: abide, bide, carbide.

br: bride, child bride.

ch: chide.

d: double-dyed, died, dyed, iodide, tie-dyed.

dr: dried, redried, undried.

f: bona fide, confide, countrified, defied, dignified, dissatisfied, diversified, fortified, justified, purified, qualified, sanctified, satisfied, self-satisfied, sulphide, undignified, ungratified, unpurified, unqualified, unsanctified, unsatisfied, vitrified.

fr: fried.

g: guide, misguide.

gl: glide.

gr: gride.

h: formaldehyde, hide, hied, Hyde.

kl: Clyde.

kr: cried.

l: collide, elide, lied, tide, misallied.

m: bromide.

n: nide.

p: pied, unespied.

pl: unapplied.

pr: pride, Pryde, self-pride.

r: deride, deuteride, outride, override, ride.

s: alongside, aside, Barmecide, bedside, beside, broadside, coincide, countryside, decide, deicide, dockside, excide, fireside, foreside, fratricide, herpicide, hillside, homicide, infanticide, insecticide, inside, lakeside, lapicide, liberticide, matricide, mountain side, outside, parenticide, parricide, patricide, regicide, riverside, seaside, side, sororicide, stillicide, subside, suicide, tyrannicide, underside, uxoricide, vaticide, vermicide, vulpicide, waterside, wayside, weatherside.

sk(sc): skied.

skr(scr): undescried.

sl: backslide, landslide, slide.

sn: snide.

sp: spied, unspied.

str: astride, bestride, outstride, stride.

t: Allhallowtide, Bartholomewtide, betide, Christmastide, Eastertide, ebbtide, Embertide, eventide, flood tide, Hallowtide, high tide, Lammastide, lee tide, morning tide, neap tide, noon tide, Passiontide, Shrovetide, Springtide, tide, unbetide, undertide, weathertide, Whitsuntide, Yuletide.

tr: tried, untried.

v: divide, provide, subdivide.

w: nation-wide, statewide, wide, world-wide.

z: preside, reside.

    Plus i+d.

    Plus I'd, guy'd, etc.

IDST

b: bid'st*, forbid'st*.

ch: chid'st*.

d: did'st*.

h: hid'st*.

k(c): kid'st*.

m: amidst, midst.

r: rid'st*.

sl: slid'st*.

IDTH

w: width.

    Plus id+'th*.

ĪDZ

Vowel: ides.

s: besides.

    Plus id+s.

    Plus bride's, etc.

IF

Vowel: if.

b: biff.

ch: handkerchief+, neckerchief+.

d: diff.

gl: glyph, hieroglyph.

gr: griff, hippogriff.

hw: whiff.

j: jiff.

kl: cliff, undercliff.

kw(qu): quiff.

m: miff.

r: Tenerife, Teneriffe.

sk(sc): skiff.

sn: sniff.

st: stiff.

t: tiff.

w: wiff.

ĪF

f: fife.

l: afterlife, artificial life, life, still life.

n: bowie knife, claspknife, jackknife, knife.

r: rife.

str: strife.

w: fishwife, goodwife, housewife, midwife, wife.

IFT

b: biffed.

dr: adrift, drift, genetic drift, snowdrift, spindrift.

g: gift.

hw: whiffed.

kl: cliffed.

l: forelift*, lift, topping lift, uplift.

m: miffed.

r: rift.

s: sift.

sh: shift.

shr: shrift.

skw(squ): squiffed.

sn: sniffed.

sp: spiffed.

sw: chimney swift, swift.

t: tift.

thr: spendthrift, thrift, unthrift.

Plus if+d.

IFTH

f: fifth.

Plus biff'th*, etc.

IG

b: big.

br: brig.

d: dig, infra dig.

f: fig, honey fig.

fr: frig.

g: gig, whirligig.

gr: grig.

gw: whig.

j: jig, thingamajig.

n: nig, renege.

p: guinea pig, pig.

pr: prig.

r: thimblerig, unrig, rig.

s: cig.

sn: snig.

spr: sprig.

sw: swig.

tr: trig.

tw: twig.

w: periwig, wig.

IGD

r: full-rigged, jury-rigged, square-rigged.

w: bewigged.

Plus ig+d.

IGZ

b: Biggs.

br: Briggs.

d: Digges.

h: Higgs.

j: Jigs.

r: Riggs.

w: Wiggs.

Plus ig+s.

Plus prig's, etc.

IJ

Vowel: acreage, alienage, anchorage, alienage, appanage, armitage, average, baronage, beverage, brigandage, brokerage, chaperonage, concubinage, cooperage, equipage, flowerage, foliage, harborage, heritage, hermitage, hospitage, leverage, lineage, matronage, midage, parentage, parsonage, pastorage, pasturage, patronage, peonage, personage, pilgrimage, pilotage, plunderage, porterage, pupilage, quarterage, seigniorage, surplusage, tutorage, vassalage, verbiage, vicarage, vicinage, vilanage*, villeinage.

br: abridged, bridge.

f: anthropophage, theophage.

fr: saxifrage.

l: cartilage, fortilage*, mucilage, tutelage.

m: midge.

n: espionage+, nidge.

r: enridge*, hemorrhage, ridge, upridge.

Plus polysyllables ending in aj.

ĪJ

bl: oblige.

l: Lije.

IJD

br: abridged, unabridged, unbridged.

Plus ij+d.

IK

br: brick.

ch: apparatchik, chick.

d: Benedick, dick.

fl: flick.

fr: Fricke.

h: hick.

k(c): kick.

kl: double-click, click, single-click.

kr: crick.

kw(qu): double-quick, quick.

l: Catholic, lick.

m: mick.

n: arsenic, kinnikinnick, nick.

p: pick.

pr: prick.

r: bishopric, chivalric, choleric, limerick, maverick, plethoric, rhetoric, rick, tumeric.

s: heartsick, lovesick, sic, sick.

sh: chic.

sl: slick.

sn: snick.

sp: spick.

st: bestick, candlestick, fiddlestick, pogostick, singlestick, stich, stick, walking stick, yardstick.

t: arithmetic, heretic, impolitic, lunatic, politic, tic, tick, triptych.

th: thick.

tr: trick.

v: Vic.

w: bailiwick, candlewick, wick.

ĪK

Vowel: Alibi Ike, Ike.

b: allterrain bike, bike, mountain bike, racing bike.

bl: oblique+.

d: dike, dyke, Vandyck, Vandyke.

f: fyke.

h: hike, hitchhike.

k(c): kike.

l: alike, assassinlike, belike*, brotherlike, dislike, fairylike, ghostlike, like, maidenlike, manlike, mislike, peasantlike, starlike, unlike, womanlike, workmanlike.

m: mike.

p: boardingpike, pike, turnpike.

s: cyc, psych.

shr: shrike.

sp: marlinspike, spike.

str: strike, ten strike.

t: tyke.

w: Van Wyck, Wyke.

IKS

d: Dix.

f: afix, crucifix, fix, prefix, suffix, transfix.

h: Hicks, Hix.

l: prolix.

m: admix, commix, immix, intermix, mix.

n: nix, Pnyx.

p: pyx.

r: Ricks, Rix.

s: six.

st: fiddlesticks, Styx.

t: politics.

tr: Beatrix, cicatrix, executrix, inheritrix, Trix.

Plus ik+s.

Plus Dick's, etc.

ĪKS

d: Dykes.

r: Rikes.

s: Sykes.

y: yikes

Plus ik+s.

Plus bike's, etc.

IKST

f: fixed, refixed, transfixed, unfixed.
k(c): kick'st*.
kl: click'st*.
l: lick'st*.
m: admixed, intermixed, mixed, remixed, unmixed.
p: pick'st*.
pr: prick'st*.
st: stick'st*.
tr: cicatrixed, trick'st*.
tw: atwixt, betwixt, 'twixt.

IKSTH

s: sixth.
Plus iks+'th*.

IKT

br: bricked, rebricked.
d: addict, benedict, contradict, interdict, predict.
fl: afflict, conflict, flicked, inflict.
kl: clicked.
l: delict, derelict, licked, relict, unlicked.
p: depict, Pict, unpicked.
s: sicced.
str: astrict, constrict, restrict, strict.
v: convict, evict.
Plus ik+d.

IL

Vowel: ill.
b: bill, crane's bill, spoonbill.
br: brill.
ch: chill.
d: daffodil, dill, spadille.
dr: drill, espadrille, quadrille.
f: chlorophyl, chrysophyl, fill, fulfil, Phil, refill.

fr: befrill, frill.
g: gill.
gr: grill, grille.
h: anthill, downhill, hill, uphill.
j: gill, jill.
k(c): Bozenkill, Cobleskill, kill, kiln, Normans kill.
kw(qu): quill.
l: Lil.
m: gristmill, mill, powdermill, watermill.
n: eau de Nil, juvenile, nil.
p: pill.
pr: prill.
r: puerile, rill.
s: codicil, domicile, imbecile, sill.
shr: shrill.
sk(sc): skill.
skw(squ): squill.
sp: spill.
st: be still, instil, still, stock-still.
sw: swill.
t: distil, infantile, mercantile, 'til, till, until, versatile, vibratile, volatile.
th: thill.
thr: enthrill, thrill.
tr: trill.
tw: twill, 'twill.
v: Amityville, Evansville, Louisville, Seville, vill.
w: free will, good will, ill will, self-will, unwill, whippoorwill, will.
z: Brazil.

ĪL

Vowel: aisle, I'll, isle.
b: bile, Kabyle.
d: crocodile.
f: Anglophile, bibliophile, cinephile, defile, file, Francophile, Germanophile, paper file, refile, single file,

Sinophile, Slavophile, Turkophile, Zionophile, etc.

g: beguile, guile.

hw: awhile, erewhile*, erstwhile*, meanwhile, otherwhile, somewhile, therewhile, while.

k(c): chile, chyle, Kyle.

l: lisle, Lyle.

m: camomile, mile.

n: campanile, enisle*, juvenile, Nile, senile.

p: compile, pile, Pyle, uppile, voltaic pile.

r: puerile, rile.

s: ensile, reconcile, resile.

sm: smile.

sp: spile.

st: diastyle, high-style, in-style, out-of-style, pentastyle, peristyle, stile, style.

t: infantile, mercantile, tile, versatile, vibratile.

v: revile, vile.

w: wile.

　　Plus pie'll, etc.

ILCH

f: filch.

m: milch.

p: pilch.

z: Zilch.

ILD

b: build, rebuild, unbuild, upbuild.

ch: unchilled.

f: unfulfilled.

g: begild, gild, guild.

sk(sc): unskilled.

t: untilled.

w: self-willed, unwilled.

　　Plus il+d.

ĪLD

Vowel: aisled.

ch: child, childe, fosterchild, love child, unchild.

f: defiled, enfiled, filed.

g: beguiled, unbeguiled.

m: mild, unmild.

s: unreconciled.

st: self-styled.

w: unwild, wild, Wilde.

　　Plus il+d.

ILF

s: sylph.

ILJ

b: bilge.

ILK

Vowel: ilk.

b: bilk.

m: milk.

s: silk, spun silk.

ILKS

w: Wilkes.

　　Plus ilk+s.

　　Plus milk's, etc.

ILM

f: film.

ILN

k(c): kiln.

m: Milne

ILS

gr: grilse.

　　Cf. ilts.

ĪLST

hw: whilst.

    Plus beguil'st*, etc.

ILT

b: built, clinker-built, clipper-built, frigate-built, rebuilt, unbuilt, Vanderbilt.

g: begilt, gilt, guilt, regilt, ungilt.

h: basket hilt, hilt.

j: jilt.

k(c): kilt.

kw(qu): quilt.

l: lilt.

m: milt.

s: silt.

sp: spilt, unspilt.

st: stilt.

t: atilt, tilt, uptilt.

w: wilt.

ILTH

f: filth

sp: spilth.

t: tilth.

    Plus befrill'th*, etc.

ILTS

k: kilts.

    Plus ilt+s.

    Cf. grilse.

ĪLZ

hw: otherwhiles, whiles.

j: Giles.

m: Miles.

n: Niles.

w: wiles.

    Plus il+s.

    Plus aisle's, etc.

IM

b: cherubim.

br: brim.

d: bedim, dim.

dr: Sanhedrim.

f: seraphim.

g: gim*.

gl: glim.

gr: grim.

h: him, hymn.

hw: whim.

j: gym, Jim.

k(c): Kim.

kl: Klim.

l: enlimn, limb, limn, prelim.

n: antonym, Nym, pseudonym, synonym.

p: Pym.

r: interim.

pr: prim.

r: rim.

s: Sim.

sh: shim.

shk(sc): skim.

skr(scr): scrim.

sl: slim.

sw: swim.

t: Tim.

tr: betrim, retrim, trim.

v: vim.

z: Zim, zimb.

ĪM

ch: chime.

d: dime.

gr: begrime, grime.

h: Guggenheim, Rosenheim.

k: chyme.

kr: white-collar crime.

kl: climb, clime, upclimb.

l: belime, birdlime, brooklime, lime, Lyme, quicklime, sublime.

m: mime, pantomine.

pr: prime.

r: berhyme, rhyme, rime.

s: cyme.

sl: beslime, slime.

t: aftertime, bedtime, breathing time, daytime, earning time, eating time, face time, harvest time, haying time, lifetime, maritime, meantime, overtime, pairing time, seedtime, sometime, springtime, summertime, thyme, time, wintertime.

Plus I'm.

ĪMD

tr: untrimmed.

Plus im+d.

ĪMD

r: false-rhymed, rhymed, unrhymed.

t: well-timed.

Plus im+d.

IMP

Vowel: imp.

bl: blimp.

ch: chimp.

g: gimp, guimpe.

j: jimp.

kr: crimp.

l: limp.

p: pimp.

pr: primp.

s: simp.

shr: shrimp.

sk(sc): skimp.

skr(scr): scrimp.

t: tymp.

IMPS

gl: glimpse.

Plus imp+s.

Plus imp's, etc.

IMZ

s: Simms.

Plus im+s.

Plus limb's, etc.

ĪMZ

t: betimes, oftentimes, ofttimes, sometimes.

Plus im+s.

Plus chime's, etc.

IN

Vowel: all in, drive-in, genuine, heroine, herein, in, inn, take in, therein, wherein, whipperin, within.

b: been, bin, carabine, has-been, Jacobin.

ch: chin, Japanese Chin.

d: almandine+, codeine+, din, incarnadine+, paladin.

f: caffeine+, fin, Finn, Mickey Finn.

fl: Flynn.

g: agin, begin, gyn.

gl: Glyn, Glynn.

gr: agrin, chagrin, grin, peregrine.

hw: whin.

j: dijinn, gin, gyn, jinn, origin.

k(c): akin, baldachin, cannikin, finikin, kilderkin, kin, manikin, minikin, tigerkin.

kw(qu): harlequin, Quinn.

l: alkaline, aniline, aquiline, bandoline, Berlin, Boleyn, cabaline, chamberlain, coralline, crinoline, crystalline, Evangeline, francolin, Ghibelline, hyaline, javelin, lin, Lynn, mandolin, masculine, opaline, petaline, porcelain, sibyline, tourmaline+, Ursuline, Vaseline, violin, zeppelin.

m: jessamine, Min, sycamine.

n: feminine, Fescennine, pavonine.

p: astropine, belaying pin, chinkapin, chinquapin, pin, repin, underpin, unpin.

pl: discipline.

r: adulterine+, alizarin, anserine+, asperin, Catherine, culverin, glycerine, Katherine, mandarin, saccharine+, sapphirine+, tambourin, viperine, vulturine+.

s: clavecin, moccasin, sin, unsin.

sh: Capuchin, shin.

sk(sc): bearskin, buckskin, sealskin, skin, tiger skin.

sp: sidespin, spin, tailspin.

t: agatine+, argentine+, bulletin, Byzantine+, carotin, Celestine+, Florentine+, gelatin, infantine+, libertine+, Philistine+, tin, vespertine+.

th: thick-and-thin, thin.

tw: twin.

w: win.

ĪN

Vowel: eyne*.

b: bine, carabine, columbine, combine, concubine, woodbine.

br: brine.

ch: chine.

d: anodyne, celandine, condign, dine, dyne, incarnadine, muscadine.

f: affine, confine, define, fine, refine, superfine, trephine.

gr: peregrine.

hw: whine.

j: jine.

k(c): kine.

kl: Clyne, decline, disincline, incline, Klein, Kline, recline.

l: Adaline, Adeline, align, alkaline, aniline, aquiline, caballine, Capitoline, Caroline, coralline, crystalline, Esquiline, Evaline, Evangeline+, Ghibelline+, hyaline, interline, Jacqueline, lifeline, line, loadline, Madeline, Magdalene+, malign, opaline, Pauline+, petaline, receiving line, saline, sibylline, sideline, snowline, timberline, underline, unline, Ursuline, waterline.

m: countermine, intermine, mine, powdermine, sycamine, undermine.

n: Apennine, asinine, back nine, benign, Fescennine, leonine, nine, pavonine, quinine, saturnine, unbenign.

p: Australian pine, Bristlecone pine, opine, pine, porcupine, Proserpine, repine, resupine, supine, unsupine.

r: adulterine+, anserine+, Rhine, saccharine+, sapphirine+, Turnverein, viperine, vulturine+, zollverein.

s: assign, calcine, consign, countersign, ensign, sign, sine, subsign*, syne, undersign.

sh: ashine, beshine, moonshine, outshine, shine, starshine, sunshine.

shr: enshrine, shrine.

sp: spine.

spl: spline.

st: Beckstein, Epstein, Goldstein, Hoffenstein, Holstein+, Liechtenstein, Rubenstein, stein, Weinstein.

sw: swine.

t: agatine+, argentine+, brigantine, Byzantine+, Celestine+, Clementine, Constantine, eglantine, Florentine+, infantine+, libertine+, matutine, palatine,

Philistine+, serpentine, tine, Turpentine, Tyne, valentine, vespertine+.

TH: thine*.

tr: trine.

tw: entwine, intertwine, overtwine, twine, untwine.

v: divine, Irvine, subdivine, vine.

w: apple wine, Esenwein, fortified wine, red wine, white wine, wine.

z: design, lang syne*, resign, syne*.

INCH

Vowel: inch.

ch: chinch.

f: fallow finch, finch, goldfinch, grassfinch.

fl: flinch.

kl: clinch, unclinch.

l: linch, lynch.

p: bepinch, pinch.

s: cinch.

w: winch.

IND

Vowel: Ind.

l: lind, Lynd, Rosalind.

pl: undisciplined.

r: tamarind.

s: abscind, exscind, rescind.

sk(sc): thick-skinned, thin-skinned.

w: stormwind, wind.

Plus in+d.

Plus skin'd, etc.

ĪND

b: bind, inbind, rebind, unbind, underbind, upbind.

bl: blind, colorblind, half blind, purblind, sand blind, snowblind, unblind.

f: find, unconfined, undefined, unrefined.

gr: grind.

h: behind, hind.

k(c): gavelkind, humankind, kind, mankind, unkind, womankind.

kl: disinclined.

kr: crined.

m: master mind, mind, nevermind, remind.

r: rind, rynd.

s: undersigned.

shr: unshrined.

tw: intertwined, overtwined.

w: interwind, rewind, stormwind*, unwind, upwind, wind*, wind.

z: undesigned, unresigned.

Plus in+d.

Plus vine'd, etc.

ING

Vowel: arguing, bandying, bellowing, blarneying, bullying, burying, busying, candying, carrying, continuing, dallying, dishallowing, embodying, empitying, emptying, envying, fancying, farrowing, flurrying, following, foreshadowing, hallowing, harrowing, harrying, issuing, jollying, lazing, lobbying, marrying, monkeying, narrowing, overshadowing, parrying, quarrying, querying, rallying, rescuing, sallying, shadowing, sorrowing, tallying, tarrying, toadying, undervaluing, unpitying, valuing, volleying, wearying, whinnying, winnowing, worrying.

b: bing, Byng.

br: bring.

ch: Ching, I Ching.

d: ding, forwarding, garlanding, hazarding, heralding, jeoparding, placarding, scaffolding, shepherding.

fl: fling.

j: challenging, damaging, discouraging, disparaging, encouraging, envisaging, managing, pillaging, ravaging, savaging, scavenging, voyaging.

k(c): barracking, fairy king, finicking, king, mafeking, Peking, sea king, trafficking, unking.

kl: cling.

l: apparelling, atheling, barreling, bedeviling, bepummelling, beveling, cancelling, caroling, cavilling, channelling, chiselling, chitterling, cudgelling, daughterling, devilling, drivelling, duelling, easterling, enamelling, entrammelling, gambolling, gravelling, grovelling, labelling, levelling, libelling, ling, marshalling, marvelling, modelling, navelling, outrivalling, panelling, pedalling, pencilling, pommelling, quarrelling, revelling, rivalling, snivelling, spiralling, stencilling, tasselling, tinselling, towelling, travelling, tunnelling, underling, unravelling, unrivalling, wassailling.

m: accustoming, blossoming, embosoming, fathoming, Ming, ransoming.

n: abandoning, actioning, auctioning, awakening, bargaining, betokening, blackening, blazoning, broadening, burdening, canoning, cautioning, chastening, christening, compassioning, darkening, deadening, destining, determining, emblazoning, emboldening, enheartening, evening, examining, fashioning, fortokening, freshening, gammoning, gardening, gladdening, happening, hardening, hastening, hearkening, heartening, imagining, imprisoning, lessening, listening, livening, maddening, mentioning, omening, opening, overburdening, predestining, pardoning, passioning, pensioning, questioning, ravening, reasoning, reckoning, saddening, sanctioning, seasoning, sickening, slackening, smartening, stationing, sweetening, unreasoning, visioning, wakening, wantoning, weakening.

p: galloping, ping, walloping, worshipping.

r: altering, angering, answering, armouring, auguring, badgering, bantering, barbering, bartering, battering, beflattering, beggaring, belaboring, beleaguering, belecturing, bepowdering, bescattering, beslabbering, besmearing, bespattering, bewildering, bickering, blathering, blistering, blubbering, blundering, blustering, bolstering, butchering, cankering, cantering, capering, capturing, chartering, chattering, ciphering, clambering, clamoring, clattering, clustering, cockering, coloring, conjecturing, conquering, considering, covering, cowering, cumbering, deciphering, dickering, disfavoring, dishonoring, displeasuring, dissevering, dowering, enamoring, encumbering, enharboring, enring, entering, faltering, favoring, feathering, festering, filtering, fingering, flattering, flavoring, flickering, flittering, flowering, flustering, fluttering, foregathering, furthering, gathering, gesturing, glimmering, glittering, glowering, hammering, hampering, hankering, harboring, hovering, humoring, hungering, incumbering, indenturing, jabbering, laboring, lacquering, lathering, lecturing, lingering, littering, long-suffering, lowering, lumbering, manufacturing, martyring, meandering, measuring, mirroring, mothering, motoring, murdering, murmuring, mustering, muttering, neighboring, numbering, offering, ordering, outnumbering, overmastering, overpowering, overtowering, paltering, pampering, pandering, pattering, peppering, perjuring, pestering, pilfering, plastering, pleasuring, plundering, pondering, pottering, powdering, prospering, puttering, quartering, quavering, quivering, rapturing, recovering, remembering, rendering, ring, roystering, rubbering, rupturing, sauntering, savoring, scampering, scattering, seal ring, severing, shattering, shimmering, shivering, shouldering, showering, shuddering, signet ring, silvering, simmering, simpering, sistering, slandering, slaughtering, slobbering, slumbering, smattering, smoldering, spattering, spluttering, stammering, stuttering, suffering, sugaring, summering, sundering, tampering, tapering, tempering, thundering, tittering, tottering, towering, unfaltering, unflattering, unmurmuring, unremembering, unslumbering, unwandering, unwavering, upholstering, uttering, vaporing, venturing, wandering, watering, wavering, weathering, westering, whimpering, whispering, wintering, wondering.

s: balancing, besing, buttressing, canvassing, Christmasing, conveyancing, embarrassing, focussing, harassing, menacing, outbalancing, overbalancing, practising, promising, purposing, sing, Synge, unpromising, witnessing.

sh: accomplishing, admonishing, astonishing, banishing, blandishing, blemishing, brandishing, burnishing, diminishing, disestablishing, distinguishing, embellishing, enravishing, establishing, famishing, finishing, flourishing, furnishing, garnishing, languishing, lavishing, nourishing, perishing, polishing, publishing, punishing, ravishing, rubbishing, tarnishing, unperishing, vanishing, vanquishing, varnishing.

sl: sling, unsling.

spr: day spring, driving spring, life spring, mainspring, spring, watch spring, weeping spring.

st: afforesting, ballasting, breakfasting, harvesting, sting.

str: heartstring, string, unstring.

sw: full swing, swing.

t: accrediting, attributing, auditing, blanketing, bonneting, buffeting, carpeting, contributing, coveting, crediting, dieting, discrediting, dispiriting, disquieting, distributing, exhibiting, forfeiting, inhabiting, inheriting, inspiriting, junketing, limiting, marketing, meriting, patenting, prohibiting, quieting, racketing, riveting, spiriting, ting, unmeriting, velveting, visiting.

th: anything, everything, thing.

w: bewing, outwing, sea wing, shufflewing, underwing, wing.

INGD

d: dinged.

w: eagle winged, unwinged, winged.

　　Plus ing+d.

INGK

Vowel: black ink, blue ink, ink, red ink.

bl: blink, snow blink.

br: brink.

ch: chink.

d: Dink, Humperdinck, rinky-dink.

dr: drink.

f: Finck, Fink, fink.

g: gink.

j: jink.

k(c): kink.

kl: clink.

l: bobolink, chain-link, enlink, interlink, link, unlink.

m: mink.

p: Deptford pink, meadow pink, pink, sea pink.

pl: plink.

pr: prink.

r: rink.

s: cinque, countersink, sink.

shr: shrink.

sk(sc): skink.

sl: slink.

sp: spink.

st: stink.

t: tink.

th: bethink, forethink*, think, rethink, unthink.

tr: trink.

tw: twink.

w: hoodwink, tiddlywink, wink.

z: zinc.

INGKS

j: Captain Jinks, high jinks, jinx.

l: lynx.

m: minx.

sf: sphinx.

th: methinks.

w: tiddledywinks.

   Plus ingk+s.

   Plus drink's, etc.

INGKT

s: procinct*, succinct.

st: instinct.

t: distinct, extinct, indistinct, tinct.

   Plus ingk+d.

INGZ

n: awakenings.

st: leading strings.

   Plus ing+s.

   Plus king's, etc.

INJ

Vowel: Inge.

b: binge.

d: dinge.

fr: befringe, fringe, infringe.

h: hinge, unhinge.

kr: cringe.

p: impinge.

r: syringe.

s: singe.

skr(scr): scringe.

spr: springe.

str: constringe, perstringe.

sw: swinge.

t: tinge.

tw: twinge.

INJD

s: singed, unsinged.

   Plus inj+d.

INS

Vowel: Ince.

bl: blintz.

ch: chintz.

kw(qu): quince.

m: mince.

pr: merchant prince, prince, unprince.

r: rinse.

s: since.

v: convince, evince, Vince.

w: wince.

   Cf. int+s.

INSK

m: Minsk.
p: Pinsk.
v: Dvinsk.

INT

Vowel: in't.
b: bint.
d: dint.
fl: flint.
gl: glint.
h: hint.
j: septuagint.
kw(qu): quint.
l: lint.
m: calamint, horsemint, mint, peppermint, sodamint, spearmint.
pr: footprint, imprint, misprint, print, reprint.
skw(squ): asquint, squint.
spl: splint.
spr: sprint.
st: stint.
t: aquatint, mezzotint, tint.
v: vint.

ĪNT

h: ahint, behint.
p: cuckoo pint, pint.

INTH

b: terebinth.
pl: plinth.
r: labyrinth.
s: colocynth, hyacinth.
   Plus win'th*, etc.

ĪNTH

n: ninth.
   Plus pine'th*, etc.

INTS

   See int+s.
   Plus stint's, etc.
   Cf. ins.

ĪNTZ

h: Heintz.
p: pints.
   Plus pint's, etc.

INZ

k(c): ods bodikins.
sh: withershins.
w: winze.
   Plus in+s.
   Plus shin's, etc.

ĪNZ

n: Apennines, baseball nines, nines.
t: Tynes.
   Plus in+s.
   Plus wine's, etc.

IP

b: bip.
ch: bargaining chip, chip.
d: dip.
dr: drip.
fl: flip, sherry flip.
gr: grip, grippe.
h: hip, hyp.
hw: horsewhip, whip.
j: gyp.
k(c): kip.
kl: clip.
kw(qu): equip, quip.
l: harelip, lip, underlip.
n: nip.
p: apple pip, pip.
r: rip, unrip.
s: sip.

sh: acquaintanceship, administratorship, agentship, aldermanship, apprenticeship, archonship, babyship, bachelorship, battleship, cardinalship, censorship, chairmanship, championship, chancellorship, chaplainship, chieftainship, churchmanship, churchmembership, citizenship, collectorship, commandership, companionship, consortship, consulship, controllership, copartnership, courtship, cousinship, craftsmanship, creatorship, deaconship, demonship, draughtsmanship, eldership, electorship, emperorship, ensignship, farmership, fathership, fellowship, fireship, generalship, good-fellowship, governorship, guardianship, horsemanship, huntsmanship, impostership, inspectorship, jockeyship, justiceship, ladyship, leadership, lectureship, legislatorship, librarianship, lightship, lordship, marksmanship, marshalship, mastership, membership, Messiahship, neighborship, noviceship,ownership,paintership, partnership, pastorship, penmanship, praetorship, preachership, prelateship, probationship, professorship, proprietorship, questorship, rajahship,rangership, readership, recordership, rectorship, regentship, relationship, reship, scholarship, seamanship, secretaryship, senatorship, sextonship, sheriffship, ship, sizarship, speakership, sponsorship, statesmanship, stewardship, studentship, sultanship, suretyship, survivorship, swordsmanship, training ship, transship, treasure ship, umpireship, unship, viceroyship, virtuosoship, wardenship, warship, workmanship, wranglership.

sk(sc): skip.

skr(scr): scrip.

sl: landslip, slip, underslip.

sn: snip.

str: outstrip, strip, weatherstrip.

t: tip.

tr: atrip, overtrip*, pleasure trip, trip.

y: yip.

z: zip.

ĪP

gr: gripe.

h: hype.

k(c): kipe.

p: bagpipe, blowpipe, hornpipe, Indian pipe, pipe, pitchpipe, windpipe.

r: dead ripe, overripe, ripe, unripe.

sn: guttersnipe, snipe.

st: stipe.

str: stripe.

sw: swipe.

t: antitype, archetype, autotype, daguerrotype, electrotype, graphotype, heliotype, linotype, logotype, monotype, prototype, stereotype, teletype, tintype, type.

tr: tripe.

w: wipe.

IPS

f: Phipps.

kl: eclipse.

l: apocalypse, ellipse.
   Plus ip+s.
   Plus hip's,etc.

ĪPS

kr: cripes.

y: yipes.
   See ip+s.
   Plus pipe's, etc.

IPST

ch: chip'st*.
d: dip'st*.
gr: grip'st*.
hw: whip'st*.
kl: clip'st*, eclipsed, uneclipsed.
kw(qu): equip'st*.
r: rip'st*.
s: sip'st*.
sh: ship'st*.
sk(sc): skip'st*.
sl: slip'st*.
str: strip'st*.
t: tip'st*.
tr: trip'st*.

IPT

kr: crypt.
l: apocalypt.
n: frost-nipped.
skr(scr): manuscript, script, subscript, superscript.
t: tipt.
    Plus ip+d.

ĪPT

gr: griped, hunger-griped.
str: prison-striped, striped.
    Plus ip+d.

IR

Vowel: ear, madrier, Zaire.
b: beer, bier, dry beer, ice beer, ginger beer, root beer.
bl: blear.
ch: cheer, upcheer.
d: bayadere, belvedere, bombardier, brigadier, commandeer, dear, deer, endear, fallow deer, grenadier, halberdier, indear*, killdeer, petar deer, reindeer.
dr: drear.

f: aerosphere, affeer*, atmosphere, ensphere, fear, hemisphere, insphere, interfere, perisphere, planisphere, sphere, undersphere, unsphere.
fl: fleer.
g: bevel gear, friction gear, gear, regear, ungear.
h: adhere, cohere, inhere.
hy: hear, Heer, here, overhear.
j: jeer.
k(c): fakir, kir.
kl: chanticleer, clear.
kw(qu): queer.
l: bandoleer, canceleer, cavalier, chandelier, chevalier, congé d'élire, fusileer, gaselier, gondolier, lear, leer, pistoleer.
m: amir, chimere*, emeer, emir, meer, mere, mir.
n: anear, auctioneer, buccaneer, cannoneer, carabineer, caravaneer, carbineer, chiffonier, domineer, electioneer, engineer, fineer*, gonfalonier, Indianeer, mountaineer, muffineer, mutineer, near, pioneer, scrutineer, sermoneer, souvenir, specksioneer, timoneer, unnear*, veneer.
p: appear, compeer, disappear, peer, pier, reappear.
r: arrear, career, rear, uprear.
s: cere, cuirassier, ensear*, insincere, overseer, sear, seer, sere, sincere.
sh: cashier, financier, shear, sheer, tabasheer.
sk(sc): skeer.
sm: asmear, besmear, smear.
sn: sneer.
sp: spear.
st: steer, stere, timber stere*.
t: austere, charioteer, chocolatier, circuiteer, crocheteer, frontier, garreteer, gazetteer, muleteer,

musketeer, pamphleteer, privateer, pulpiteer, racketeer, sonneteer, targeteer, tear, teer, tier, Tyr+, volunteer.

v: brevier, persevere, revere, severe, veer.

w: weir.

y: Goodyear, year.

z: grand vizier, vizier.

ĪR

Vowel: ire.

b: byre.

br: briar, brier.

d: dire.

f: afire, beacon fire, death fire, fire, galley fire, hell-fire, St. John's fire, signal fire, spitfire, swamp fire, wildfire.

fl: flyer.

fr: friar.

gw: McGuire, Molly Maguire.

h: hire.

j: gyre.

kw(qu): acquire, choir, enquire, inquire, quire, require.

l: liar, lyre.

m: admire, bemire, Meyer, mire, Myer, Untermyer.

p: pyre.

pl: plier.

pr: prior.

s: grandsire, sire.

sh: shire.

skw(squ): esquire, squire, unsquire.

sp: aspire, conspire, expire, inspire, perspire, respire, spire, suspire, transpire.

sw: swire*.

t: attire, entire, flat tire, McIntyre, overtire, radial tire, retire, snow tire, tire, Tyr, tyre.

v: vire.

w: wire.

z: desire.

Cf. iur.

ĪRD

Vowel: flapeared, lopeared, uneared*.

b: beard.

f: unfeared.

p: unpeered.

w: weird.

Plus er+d.

Plus beer'd, etc.

ĪRD

kw(qu): unacquired.

sp: unexpired, uninspired.

z: undesired.

Plus ir+d.

Plus fire'd, etc.

IRS

b: Bierce.

f: fierce.

p: pierce, transpierce.

t: tierce.

IRZ

j: Algiers.

sh: shears, sheers.

Plus er+s.

Plus year's, etc.

IS

b: abyss, bis.

bl: bliss.

d: cowardice, dis, prejudice.

f: artifice, benefice, edifice, orifice.

fr: dentifrice.

gr: ambergris, verdigris.

h: dehisce, hiss.

k(c): French kiss, kiss.

kw(qu): cuisse.

l: acropolis, chrysalis, fortalice, Liss, metropolis, M'liss, necropolis, populace.

m: amiss, dismiss, grimace, miss, remiss, Salamis.

p: piss, precipice.

pr: priss

r: avarice, liquorice, sui generis.

s: abiogenesis, adipogenesis, anabasis, analysis, antithesis, apheresis, aphesis, biogenesis, diaeresis, dialysis, diathesis, ectogenesis, elephantiasis, emphasis, genesis, hypostasis, hypothesis, metabasis, metamorphosis, metastasis, metathesis, nemesis, paralysis, parenthesis, paresis, periphrasis, sis, siss, synthesis.

st: armistice.

sw: Swiss.

t: clematis.

TH: this.

tr: Beatrice, cicatrice, cockatrice.

v: vis.

w: wis*, ywis*.

ĪS

Vowel: camphorice, ice.

b: bice.

br: Brice, Bryce.

d: dice, liar's dice, paradise.

f: fice, sacrifice, suffice.

gr: grice.

l: beggar's lice, lice.

m: mice.

n: gneiss, nice, overnice.

pr: half-price, misprice, off-price, overprice, price, sale price, sticker price.

r: rice.

s: concise, precise, sice, syce.

sl: slice.

sp: allspice, bespice, spice.

spl: splice.

t: entice, tice.

thr: thrice.

tr: trice.

tw: twice.

v: advice, device, edelweiss, vice.

w: Weiss.

z: Zeiss.

ĪSD

pr: mispriced, overpriced.

ISH

Vowel: babyish, Cockneyish, dowdyish.

b: Bysshe.

d: chafing dish, dish.

f: angelfish, cuttlefish, devilfish, fish, flying fish, goldfish, ladyfish, overfish, pilot fish, rainbow fish.

g: Gish.

l: devilish.

n: cnish, McNish, heathenish, kittenish, mammonish, vixenish, womanish.

p: pish.

r: bitterish, cleverish, feverish, gibberish, impoverish, lickerish, ogreish, quakerish, tigerish, vaporish, viperish, vulturish, waterish.

sh: shish.

skw(squ): squish.

sl: slish.

sw: swish.

t: tish.

w: unwish, willowish, wish, yellowish.

ISK

b: bisque.

br: brisk.

d: compact disc, disc, disk, floppy disk.

f: fisc, Fiske.

fr: frisk.

hw: whisk.

l: basilisk, obelisk, odalisque.

r: asterisk, at-risk, high-risk, low-risk, risk, tamarisk.

t: tisk.

ISP

hw: whisp.

kr: crisp, encrisp*.

l: lisp.

w: wisp.

IST

Vowel: atheist, casuist, egoist, essayist, euphuist, Hebraist, Judaist, lobbyist, soloist, vacuist.

b: Arabist.

br: equilibrist.

d: balladist, chiropodist, melodist, methodist, prejudiced, psalmodist, rhapsodist, synodist, threnodist.

f: beneficed, chirographist, fist, gymnosophist, pacifist, philosophist, photographist, steganographist, stenographist, telegraphist, theosophist, topographist, typographist.

fr: frist*.

gl: glist*.

gr: grist.

h: hissed, hist.

hw: whist

j: aerologist, agist, analogist, anthropologist, apologist, archaeologist, biologist, campanologist, chronologist, conchologist, demonologist, dialogist, ecclesiologist, electrobiologist, elegist, entomologist, etymologist, eulogist, fossilogist, genealogist, geologist, gist, gynecologist, lithologist, martyrologist, meteorologist, mineralogist, mythologist, necrologist, neologist, ontologist, ornithologist, pathologist, penologist, petrologist, pharmacologist, philologist, phrenologist, physiologist, pneumatologist, psychologist, seismologist, sociologist, strategist, suffragist, tautologist, technologist, teleologist, toxicologist, zoologist.

k(c): anarchist, bekissed, catechrist, kissed, unkissed.

kw(qu): colloquist, ventriloquist.

l: agricolist, agriculturalist, analyst, animalculist, annalist, annualist, bibliophilist, bibliopolist, bicyclist, bimetalist, cabalist, capitalist, centralist, choralist, classicalist, congregationalist, constitutionalist, controversialist, criminalist, dactylist, devotionalist, dialist, dualist, duellist, educationalist, enamelist, enlist, eternalist, evangelist, experimentalist, externalist, fabulist, fatalist, federalist, feudalist, financialist, formalist, fossilist, funambulist, futilist, glacialist, herbalist, hyperbolist, idealist, immaterialist, immortalist, imperialist, instrumentalist, intellectualist, internationalist, journalist, legal list, liberalist, list, literalist, loyalist, materialist, medalist, memorialist, metalist, ministerialist, monopolist, moralist, nationalist, naturalist, nihilist, nominalist, novelist, oculist, orientalist, philatelist, pluralist, proverbialist, provincialist, psychoanalyst, pugilist, rationalist, realist, revivalist, ritualist, royalist, ruralist, sciolist, scripturalist, sensationalist, sensualist, sentimentalist, sexualist, sibyllist, socialist, somnambulist, specialist, spiritualist, symbolist, textualist, tradionalist, transcendentalist, universalist, verbalist, violist, vitalist, vocabulist, vocalist, zoophilist.

m: academist, agamist*, alchemist, anatomist, animist, antinomist, atomist, bemist, bigamist, deuterogamist, dismissed, economist, epitomist, legitimist, misogamist, missed, mist, monogamist, optimist, pessimist, phlebotomist, physiognomist, polygamist, synonymist, unmissed, volumist, zootomist.

n: abolitionist, accompanist, agonist, alienist, antagonist, botanist, Bourbonist, Brahmanist, Calvinist, canonist, circumlocutionist, coalitionist, colonist, Communist, Confucionist, constitutionist, constructionist, contortionist, conversationist, corruptionist, cremationist, Darwinist, degenerationist, demonist, destinist, destructionist, devotionist, educationist, elocutionist, eudemonist, evolutionist, excursionist, fictionist, galvanist, harmonist, hedonist, Hellenist, humanist, illusionist, imitationist, immersionist, inspirationist, insurrectionist, Latinist, Malthusianist, mammonist, mechanist, miscellanist, misogynist, modernist, Napoleonist, Neoplatonist, obstructionist, opinionist, opportunist, oppositionist, organist, panhellenist, passionist, perfectionist, phenomenist, Philhellenist, pianist, platonist, precisionist, progressionist, prohibitionist, protagonist, protectionist,

pythonist, rabbinist, religionist, repudiationist, resurrectionist, revolutionist, Romanist, satanist, secessionist, Sorbonnist, telephonist, tobacconist, trades-unionist, traditionist, unionist, vaccinist, Vaticanist, visionist.

p: misanthropist, philanthropist, syncopist, theophilanthropist.

r: agriculturist, allegorist, amorist, aphorist, apiarist, arborculturist, arborist, artillerist, augurist, auteurist, colorist, culturist, Eucharist, floriculturist, horticulturist, humorist, mannerist, mesmerist, monetarist, motorist, plagiarist, pleasurist, posturist, rapturist, rigorist, satirist, scripturist, secularist, terrorist, theorist, votarist, wrist.

s: assist, biblicist, cist, classicist, consist, cyst, empiricist, ethicist, exorcist, insist, persist, pharmacist, physicist, publicist, romanticist, sissed, sist, subsist, synthesist, technicist.

sh: schist.

t: absolutist, anagrammatist, despotist, diplomatist, dogmatist, dramatist, egotist, enigmatist, epigrammatist, hypnotist, magnetist, melodramatist, nepotist, numismatist, pietist, pragmatist, prelatist, quietist, schematist, scientist, syncretist, zealotist.

th: amethyst, allopathist, apathist, sympathist.

tr: trist*, tryst.

tw: atwist, entwist, French twist, intertwist, twist, untwist.

v: Bolshevist, comparativist, Menshevist, positivist, subjectivist.

w: unwist*, wist*.

z: coexist, desist, exist, preexist, resist, xyst.

Plus is+d.

ĪST

d: emparadised.

kr: antichrist, Christ.

l: beliced, liced.

t: enticed.

tr: tryst.

Plus is+d.

IT

Vowel: appropriate+, associate+, baccalaureate, collegiate, immediate, impropriate, inappropriate, it, Jesuit, opiate+, poet laureate.

b: bit, bitt, tidbit, unbit.

br: Brit, invertebrate+, vertebrate+.

ch: chit.

d: candidate+.

f: befit, benefit, comfit, counterfeit, fit, misfit, outfit, refit, unfit.

fl: flit

fr: frit.

g: delegate+, git.

gr: grit

h: hit.

hw: whit.

k(c): advocate+, certificate+, delicate, indelicate, intricate, kit, sophisticate, syndicate.

kr: hypocrite.

kw(qu): acquit, quit.

l: articulate+, desolate+, flagellate+, immaculate+, inarticulate, lit, moonlit, postulate+, starlit.

m: admit, animate+, approximate+, commit, conummate+, demit, emit, estimate+, immit, inanimate+, intermit, intimate+, intromit, legitimate+, manumit, mitt, omit, permit, pretermit, recommit, remit, submit, transmit, ultimate+.

n: affectionate+, alternate+, beknit, carbonate+, close-knit, compassionate+, coordinate+, definite, denominate+, designate+, discriminate+, effeminate+, impassionate, incompassionate, indefinite, infinite, inknit*, inordinate, insubordinate, interknit, knit, McNitt, minute+, nit, passionate, subordinate, unfortunate, unknit.

p: pit, Pitt, rifle pit.

r: accurate, commensurate, confederate+, conglomerate, corporate+, degenerate+, deliberate+, desperate, electorate, favorite, illiterate, inmensurate+, incommensurate, inconsiderate, preterite, temperate, triumvirate, writ.

s: cit, outsit, plebescite, sit.

shm: Schmidt.

sk: skit.

sl: slit.

sm: smit.

sp: spit.

spl: split.

spr: bowsprit, sprit.

t: tit, tomtit.

tw: twit.

w: afterwit, DeWitt, motherwit, outwit, towit, unwit*, wit, Witt.

z: apposite, exquisite, opposite, perquisite, prerequisite, requisite.

ĪT

Vowel: Puseyite, Trotskyite.

b: bight, bite, Jacobite, Moabite, Rechabite.

bl: blight.

br: bright.

d: bedight*, dight*, erudite, expedite, indict, indite, overdight*, recondite, troglodyte, undight*.

dw: Dwight.

f: fight, Fite, neophyte, sea fight, zoophyte.

fl: flight.

fr: affright, fright, stage fright.

h: behight*, Farenheit, height, hight*.

hw: snow-white, white.

k(c): box kite, kite, malachite.

kl: heteroclite.

kw(qu): quite, requite.

l: acolyte, actinolyte, aerolite, alight, Baaliet, Carmelite, chrysolite, cosmopolite, crystallite, daylight, dead light, delight, electrolyte, entomolite, grapholite, harbor light, headlight, ichnolite, impolite, Ishmaelite, Islamite, Israelite, light, moonlight, polite, pre-Raphaelite, proselyte, satellite, sea light, siderolite, signal light, starlight, stoplight, sunlight, theodolite, toxophilite, traffic light, twilight, zoolite.

m: Adamite, Adullamite, bedlamite, Bethlehemite, dolomite, dynamite, Elamite, eremite, Gothamite, midshipmite, might, mite, pre-Adamite, rolamite.

n: Aaronite, aconite, aluminite, Ammonite, anight*, Babylonite, beknight, belemnite, benight, Canaanite, disunite, Ebionite, ebonite, goodnight, ignite, knight, mammonite, Maronite, McKnight, midnight, Mormonite, night, overnight, reunite, tonight, unite, vulcanite, yesternight*.

pl: plight, troth plight.

r: anchorite, aright, copyright, downright, enwrite, forthright, meteorite, Mr. Right, Nazarite, outright, rewrite, right, rite, siderite, Sybarite, underwrite, unright*, unwrite, upright, wheelwright, wright, write.

s: anthracite, cite, excite, foresight, incite, insight, oversight, parasite, plebiscite, recite, second sight, sight, site, unsight.

sk(sc): blatherskite.

sl: sleight, slight.

sm: smite.

sp: despite, spite.

spr: sprite, watersprite.

t: airtight, appetite, bipartite, hematite, tight, tripartite, watertight.

tr: contrite, trite.

v: invite, Muscovite.

w: wight.

ITH

fr: frith.

k(c): kith.

l: acrolith, aerolith, lith, monolith, palaeolith.

m: myth.

p: pith.

s: sith*.

sm: Arrowsmith, Ladysmith, smith.

w: forthwith, herewith, therewith, wherewith, with, withe.

ĪTH

Vowel: saith*+.

bl: blithe.

l: lithe.

m: myth.

r: writhe.

s: scythe.

sm: Smythe.

st: stythe.

t: tithe.

w: withe.

ITS

d: ditz.

fr: Fritz.

gl: glitz
kw(qu): quits.
shl: Schlitz.
Plus it+s.
Plus pit's, etc.

ĪTS

l: footlights.
n: anights.
r: last rites.
t: tights.
Plus it+s.
Plus night's, etc.

IV

fl: fliv.
g: forgive, give, misgive.
l: live, outlive, overlive.
s: sieve.
t: ablative, accusative, acquisitive, admonitive, affirmative, alternative, amative, argumentative, causative, coercitive, combative, comparative, compelative, compensative, competitive, complimentative, compulsative, confirmative, consecutive, conservative, contemplative, contributive, correlative, curative, declarative, definitive, degenerative, demonstrative, derivative, derogative, desiccative, diminutive, dispensative, disputative, distributive, evocative, exclamative, executive, expletive, figurative, formative, fugitive, generative, genitive, illustrative, impeditive, imperative, imputative, incarnative, inchoative, incrassative, indicative, infinitive, informative, inquisitive, insensitive, intensative, interrogative, intuitive, laudative, lenitive, lucrative, negative, nominative, nutritive, premonitive, preparative, prerogative, preservative, primitive, prohibitive, provocative, pulsative, punitive, putative, quantitive, recitative, reformative, reparative, representative, restorative, retributive, sanative, sedative, semblative, sensitive, siccative, substantive, superlative, talkative, tentative, transitive, vibrative, vocative.

ĪV

ch: chive.
d: dive, nosedive, powerdive.
dr: chain drive, drive.
f: five, high-five.
h: hive, unhive.
j: gyve, jive.
kl: Clive.
l: alive, come alive, live.
n: connive.
pr: deprive.
r: arrive, derive, rive.
sh: shrive.
shr: shrive.
sk(sc): skive.
st: stive.
str: strive.
thr: thrive.
tr: contrive.
v: revive, survive.
w: wive.
Plus I've.

IVD

l: long-lived+, megatived, outlived, short-lived+, unlived.

ĪVD

l: long-lived+, short-lived+.
pr: deprived.
shr: unshrived
w: unwived.
Plus iv+d.

ĪVZ

Vowel: St. Ives.

f: fives.

l: lives.

n: knives.

Plus iv+s.

Plus hive's, etc.

IZ

Vowel: is

b: biz.

br: briz.

d: Cadiz.

f: fizz, gin fizz, golden fizz, phiz, rum fizz, silver fizz.

fr: befriz, friz.

h: his.

hw: gee whiz, whizz.

kw(qu): quiz.

l: Liz.

m: Ms.

r: Ariz, riz.

s: sizz.

t: 'tis, Tiz.

v: vis.

w: wiz.

ĪZ

Vowel: atheize, dandyize, euphuize, Hebraize, Judaize.

d: aggrandize, balladize, bastardize, dastardize, Finlandize, fluidize, gormandize, jeopardize, liquidize, merchandize, methodize, oxidize, psalmodize, rhapsodize, subsidize, vagabondize.

f: apostrophize, philosophize, sacrifice, theosophize.

g: disguise, guise, otherguise*.

j: apologize, astrologize, battologize, dialogize, doxologize, energize, etymologize, eulogize, genealogize, geologize, lethargize, mythologize, philosogize, syllogize, tautologize, theologize.

k(c): catechize.

kw(qu): soliloquize, ventriloquize.

l: actualize, alcoholize, alkalize, ambrosialize, analyze, angelize, animalize, annalize, annualize, artificialize, brutalize, capitalize, centralize, civilize, collateralize, constitutionalize, conventionalize, criminalize, crystalize, decimalize, demoralize, denationalize, denaturalize, devilize, devitalize, diabolize, dialyze, electrolize, equalize, eternalize, etherealize, evangelize, experimentalize, fabulize, federalize, fertilize, feudalize, focalize, formalize, formulize, fossilize, generalize, gentilize, gospelize, gutturalize, hyperbolize, idealize, idolize, immortalize, imperialize, individualize, internationalize, journalize, legalize, liberalize, literalize, Lize, localize, martialize, materialize, medicalize, memorialize, mineralize, mobilize, modelize, monopolize, moralize, nasalize, nationalize, naturalize, neutralize, novelize, parallelize, paralyze, penalize, personalize, pluralize, proverbialize, provincialize, rationalize, realize, royalize, ruralize, scandalize, scrupulize, sensualize, sentimentalize, sepulchraglize, sequelize, sexualize, signalize, socialize, specialize, spiritualize, sterilize, structuralize, subtilize, symbolize, tantalize, theatricalize, totalize, tranquillize, universalize, utilize, verbalize, visualize, vitalize, vocalize, volatilize.

m: alchemize, amalgamize, anatomize, astronomize, atomize, compromise, demise, economize, emblemize, epitomize, euphemize, macadamize, manumize, minimize, pessimize, physiognomize, pilgrimize, polygamize, remise, surmise, synonymize, systemize, victimize.

n: adonize, Africanize, agonize, agrarianize, albumenize, Americanize, antagonize, attitudinize, botanize, canonize, Christianize, cognize, colonize, dehumanize, detonize, disillusionize, disorganize, ebonize, Edenize, effeminize, euphonize, Europeanize, excursionize, fraternize, galvanize, gelatinize, gluttonize, gorgonize, harmonize, heathenize, Hellenize, histrionize, humanize, impatronize, Italianize, Latinize, libidinize, lionize, Londonize, Mahomedanize, mammonize, matronize, mechanize, modernize, Mohammedanize, organize, oxygenize, paganize, patronize, pavonize, pedestrianize, personize, platitudinize, Platonize, plebeianize, pollenize, Puritanize, recognize, rejuvenize, republicanize, resurrectionize, revolutionize, Romanize, scrutinize, secrarianize, sermonize, Simonize, Socinianize, solemnize, symphonize, synchronize, Teutonize, Timonize, tyrannize, villainize, vulcanize, wantonize.

p: misanthropize, syncopize.

pr: apprise, comprise, door prize, emprize, enterprise, misprize, prize, reprise, surprise, underprize.

r: allegorize, aphorize, arise, augurize, authorize, barbarize, bowdlerize, cauterize, characterize, chimerize, circularize, decolorize, denuclearize, deodorize, etherize, extemporize, familiarize, martyrize, memorize, mercerize, mesmerize, moonrise, panegyrize, particularize, pauperize, peculiarize, plagiarize, polarize, popularize, pulverize,

rapturize, rhetorize, rise, saccharize, satirize, secularize, seigniorize, seniorize, silverize, singularize, soberize, solarize, summarize, sunrise, tabularize, temporize, terrorize, theorize, uprise, vaporize, vulgarize.

s: Anglicize, apotheosize, assize, atticize, capsize, criticize, ecstacize, emblematicize, emphasize, excize, exercise, exorcise, fanaticize, Hebraicize, Hibernicize, hypothesize, incise, italicize, ostracize, scepticize, Scotticize, sice, size, synthesize.

sp: despise.

t: acclimatize, achromatize, advertize, agatize, alphabetize, anathematize, apostatize, appetize, aromatize, baptize, chastise, climatize, demagnetize, democratize, demonetize, denarcotize, deputize, digitize, dogmatize, dramatize, emblematize, enigmatize, epigrammatize, hypnotize, idiotize, legitimatize, magnetize, mediatize, monetize, narcotize, poetize, prelatize, privatize, proselytize, Protestantize, remonetize, robotize, schismatize, sonnetize, stigmatize, synthetize, systematize.

th: sympathize.

tr: geometrize, idolatrize.

v: advise, devise, improvise, revise, supervise.

w: afterwise, anywise, contrariwise, cornerwise, crescentwise, likewise, otherwise, overwise, penny-wise, unwise, weather-wise, wise.

Plus i+s.

Plus sky's, etc.

ĪZD

g: disguised, undisguised.

l: civilized, criminalized, uncivilized.

m: surmised, unsurmised.

n: canonized, uncanonized.

pr: apprised, surprised, unapprised, unprized, unsurprised.

r: authorized, texturized, unauthorized.

s: undersized.

sp: despised, undespised.

t: baptized, unbaptized.

v: advised, ill-advised, unadvised.

Plus iz+d.

IZM

Vowel: altruism, archaism, asteism, atheism, babyism, bluestockingism, bogeyism, boobyism, Cockneyism, dandyism, egoism, euphuism, fairyism, flunkeyism, fogeyism, Ghandiism, Hebraism, heroism, Hinduism, ism, Irishism, jockeyism, Judaism, ladyism, monkeyism, ogreism, pantheism, paroxysm, puppyism, Puseyism, Shintoism, Toryism, Yankeeism, zanyism.

b: abysm.

ch: Chisholm.

d: braggardism, Lollardism, methodism.

f: pacifism, philosophism, theosophism.

g: dialogism.

j: neologism, savagism, syllogism.

k(c): anarchism, catechism, monarchism.

kl: cataclysm.

kr: chrism.

kw(qu): ventriloquism.

l: accidentalism, alcoholism, animalism, anomalism, Baalism, bibliophilism, bibliopolism, bimetalism, brutalism, cabalism, centralism, chloralism, classicalism, clericalism, colloquialism, colonialism, communalism, congregationalism, constitutionalism, denominationalism, devilism, diabolism, dualism, embolism, emotionalism, etherealism, evangelism, fatalism, federalism, feudalism, formalism, fossilism, frivolism, gentilism, hyperbolism, idealism, immaterialism, imperialism, individualism, industrialism, intellectualism, internationalism, journalism, liberalism, literalism, localism, loyalism, materialism, medievalism, moralism, naturalism, nihilism, monimalism, orientalism, parallelism, personalism, phenomenalism, pluralism, pre-Raphaelism, proverbialism, provincialism, pugilism, radicalism, rationalism, realism, revivalism, ritualism, royalism, ruralism, sacerdotalism, sciolism, scoundrelism, scripturalism, sensationalism, sensualism, sentimentalism, socialism, somnambulism, somnolism, structuralism, subtilism*, supernaturalism, symbolism, traditionalism, transcendentalism, tribalism, universalism, vandalism, verbalism, vitalism, vocalism.

m: academism, anatomism, animism, atomism, euphemism, Islamism, legitimism, optimism, pessimism, totemism.

n: abolitionism, actinism, Africanism, agonism, agrarianism, alienism, Americanism, anachronism, Anglicanism, Anglo-Saxonism, antagonism, antiquarianism, bacchanalianism, Bohemianism, Bourbonism, Brahmanism, Buckmanism, Calvinism, chauvinism, Communism, Confucianism, cosmopolitanism, cretinism, Darwinism, demonianism, demonism, determinism, deviationism, epicureanism, equestrianism, Erastianism, eudemonism, euphonism, Fenianism, foreign-ism, galvanism, Germanism, heathenism, hedonism, Helle-nism, Hibernianism, histrionism, humanism, Ibsenism, Italianism, laconism, Latinism, latitudin-arianism, Leninism, libertinism, Londonism, Mahometanism, mammonism, mechanism, modernism, Mohammedanism, Montanism, Mormonism, necessarianism, necessitarianism, Neoplatonism, organism, pagan-ism, patricianism, peanism, pedestrianism, peonism, phenon-onism, Philhellenism, Philistin-ism, Platonism, plebeianism, precisionism, predestinarianism, Presbyterianism, proletarianism, protectionism, Puritanism, pythonism, rabbinism, religion-ism, Republicanism, Romanism, ruffianism, sabbatarianism, satan-ism, Saxonism, secessionism, sec-tarianism, shamanism, Shavian-ism, Socinianism, Stalinism, synchronism, Syrianism, trades-unionism, unionism, Unitarianism, utilitarianism, Utopianism, valetudinarianism, Vaticanism, vegetarianism, vulpinism, Wesleyanism.

pr: prism.

r: agriculturism, aneurism, aphorism, asterism, auteurism, bachelorism, barbarism, behaviorism, bloomerism, characterism, etherism, Fourierism, Hitlerism, mannerism, mesmerism,

monetarism, pauperism, phalansterism, plagiarism, Quakerism, rigorism, secularism, terrorism, tigerism, vampirism, vulgarism, vulturism.

s: aestheticism, agnosticism, Anglicism, asceticism, Asiaticism, biblicism, Catholicism, classicism, criticism, cynicism, demoniacism, ecclesiasticism, eclecticism, electicism, empiricism, esoteric-ism, exorcism, exoticism, fanaticism, fantasticism, Gallicism, Hibernicism, histrionicism, hypercriticism, hypochondriac-ism, Italicism, laconicism, lyricism, metacism, monasticism, mysti-cism, ostracism, peripateticism, philanthropicism, physicism, romanticism, scepticism, scholasticism, Scotticism, solecism, stoicism, Teutonicism, witticism.

sh: fetishism.

t: absolutism, achromatism, anathematism, anti-Semitism, astigmatism, conservatism, demo-cratism, despotism, diamagnetism, diplomatism, dogmatism, egotism, exquisitism, hypnotism, idiotism, Jesuitism, magnetism, nepotism, occultism, patriotism, pedantism, pietism, pragmatism, prelatism, Protestantism, quietism, quixo-tism, rheuma-tism, Semitism, Sovietism, syncretism.

v: atavism, Bolshevism, Menshevism, nativism, positivism, subjectivism.

O

ō: as in bold; also in tone, oh, foam, toe, boulder, glow, owe, seew, yeoman, beau, hautboy, brooch.

ô: as in nor; also in bought, broad, memoir, hall, balk, warm, haul, taught, claw.

oi: as in boil; also in joy.

oo: as in book; also in put, wolf, should.

ōō: as in tool; juice, dew.

ou: as in shout; also in brow, sauerkraut.

Such words as *dew* include a consonantal *y*, pronounced *dyu*, whereas *do* is pronounced *du*. These pronunciations properly rhyme, although for convenience they are not separated here.

(For the vowel sound in none, blood, see under u.)

Ō

Vowel: adagio, braggadocio, cameo, carabao, CEO, Curacao, eau, embroglio, embryo, exofficio, folio, GIGO, HBO, HMO, imbroglio, impresario, intaglio, MBO, mustachio, nunio, O, Oh, olio, oratorio, owe, Papilio, pistachio, portfolio, punctilio, ratio, Romeo, seraglio, studio, TKO, Tokio, vireo.

b: beau, bo, bow, embow*, gazabo, jabot, long bow, oboe, rainbow, sabot, saddle bow.

bl: blow, death blow, low blow.

d: Bordeaux, do, doe, dough, rondeau, Tae Kwon Do.

f: comme il faut, foe.

fl: Flo, floe, cash flow, flow, ice floe, ice flow, inflow, outflow, overflow.

fr: fro, to-and-fro.

g: ago, archipelago, forego, go, indigo, Largo, little go, long ago, outgo, touch-and-go, undergo, vertigo.

gl: aglow, glow, moonglow.

gr: grow, outgrow, overgrow, upgrow.

h: heigh-ho, ho, hoe, Soho, tallyho, Westward ho.

hw: whoa.

j: adagio, banjo, Jo, Joe.

k: calico, haricot, magnifico, Mexico, portico.

kr: crow, escrow, overcrow.

kw: instatuquo, quidproquo.

l: alow, below, buffalo, bummalo, bungalow, cachalot, furbelow, gigolo, hello, hullo, lo, low, Lowe, merlot, rouleau, tableau, tremolo.

m: bon mot, bravissimo, duodecimo, Eskimo, fortissimo, generalissimo, half a mo, mot, mow, pianissimo, proximo, ultimo.

n: domino, foreknow, know, no, unknow.

p: apropos, chapeau, depot, entrepot, malapropos, Po, Poe.

pr: pro.

r: arrow, bureau, death row, Diderot, rho, row, Rowe.

s: Curacao, curassow, how so, morceau, Rousseau, sew, so, so-and-so, so-so, sow, trousseau.

sh: foreshow, raree show, shew*, show.

sl: sloe, slow.

sn: besnow, snow.

st: bestow, stow, Stowe.

t: bateau, chateau, gateau, incognito, manito, mistletoe, plateau, portmanteau, timbertoe, tiptoe, toe, tow, undertow.

TH: although, though.

thr: death throw, overthrow, throe, throw.

tr: detrop, trow.

v: deux chevaux.

w: whoa, woe.

Ô

Vowel: awe, overawe.

b: Baugh, usquebaugh.

br: braw+.

ch: chaw.

d: dauw, daw, dawe*, jackdaw, landau.

dr: draw, overdraw, redraw, undraw, withdraw.

f: faugh, guffaw+.

fl: flaw.

gr: McGraw.

h: haugh, haw, heehaw.

j: jaw, underjaw.

k(c): caw, macaw.

kl: claw.

kr: craw.

l: brother-in-law, daughter-in-law, in-law, law, mother-in-law, pilau, sister-in-law, son-in-law, unlaw.

m: maw.

n: begnaw, gnaw, naw.

p: Auchimpaugh, papaw, paw, Peckinpaugh.

r: raw.

s: Arkansas, foresaw, oversaw, saw, seesaw.

sh: pshaw, Shaw.

sk(sc): scaw.

skw: squaw.

sl: coleslaw, slaw.

sm: sma'.

sp: spa.

str: straw.

t: tau, taw.

th: thaw.

thr: thraw.

y: yaw.

OI

Vowel: oi, oy.

b: altar boy, boy, breeches buoy, buoy, charity boy, loblolly boy, yellow boy.

f: foy.

g: goy.

h: ahoy, hobble-de-hoy, hoy.

j: enjoy, joy, overjoy.

k(c): coy, decoy.

kl: cloy.

l: alloy, Loy, saveloy.

n: annoy, Illinois.

p: poi, sepoy, teapoy.

pl: deploy, employ.

r: corduroy, Pomeroy, viceroy.

s: paduasoy, soy.

str: destroy.

t: toy.

tr: Troy.

v: convoy, Savoy.

OO

Vowel: AU, CPU, ECU, ICU, jus+, SKU, toodledeoo.

b: baboo, bamboo, boo, bugaboo, caribou, debut, imbue, jigaboo, peekaboo, taboo, zebu.

bl: blew, blue, skyblue, true-blue.

br: barley broo, brew, imbrue.

ch: catechou, chew, eschew.

d: adieu, ado, bedew, billet-doux, can-do, chandoo, derring-do, dew, do, due, endew, endue, fordo*, Hindu, honeydew, hoodoo, indue, misdo, mountain dew, night dew, outdo, overdo, overdue, perdu, priedieu, Purdue, residue, skidoo, subdue, sundew, to-do, underdo, undo, undue, voodoo, well-to-do.

dr: drew, withdrew.

f: feu, feverfew, few, kung fu, phew.

fl: blue flu, flew, flu, flue.

g: goo, goo-goo, haut gout, ragout.

gl: glue, igloo, reglue, unglue.

gr: grew, outgrew.

h: ballyhoo, boo-hoo, Elihu, Fitzhugh, hew, hue, Hugh, rough-hew, wahoo, yahoo, yoo-hoo.

hw: to whit to whoo, whew, who.

j: acajou, Jew, kinkajou.

k(c): barbecue, beaucoup, coo, coup, cuckoo, cue, Daikoku, kew.

kl: clew, clue, unclue.

kr: accrue, crew, cru.

kw(qu): aq, BQ, queue.

l: Alu, curlew, halloo, hullabaloo, lieu, loo, view halloo, Zulu.

m: emu, immew, mew, moo, mu, sea mew, unmew.

n: anew, avenue, canoe, entre nous, fire new, foreknew, gnu, ingenue, knew, new, nu, parvenue, renew, retinue, revenue.

p: Depew, napoo, pew, pooh, Pugh, shampoo.

r: gillaroo, kangaroo, karroo, meadow rue, Peru, rat kangaroo, roux, rue, wallaroo, wanderoo.

s: apercu, Daibutsu, ensue, pursue, Sioux, sou, sue, tiramisu.

sh: cachou, cashew, fichu, shoe, shoo.

shr: beshrew*, shrew.

sk(sc): askew, skew.

skr(scr): corkscrew, screw, unscrew.

sl: slew, sloo, slough, slue.

sm: smew.

sp: spew.

spr: sprue.

st: Brunswick stew, stew.

str: bestrew, construe, misconstrue, overstrew, strew.

t: battue, cockatoo, Gentoo, hereinto, hereto, hereunto, hitherto, impromptu, intransitu, manitou, passe partout, set-to, surtout, tattoo, tew, thereinto, thereto, thereunto, thitherto, Timbucktu, to, too, two, virtu, whereinto, whereto, whereunto.

th: thew.

thr: overthrew, threw, through.

tr: true, untrue.

v: interview, preview, rendevous, review, surview*, view.

w: woo.

y: bayou, ewe, I.O.U., yew, you.

z: Kalamazoo, kazoo, zoo.

OU

Vowel: ou.

b: bough, bow, golden bough.

br: brow, highbrow, overbrow.

ch: chow, chowchow, Foochow, Kwangchow, Soochow, Wenchow.

d: dhow, endow, landau+.

fr: frau.

g: hoosegow.

h: anyhow, how, Howe, somehow.

k(c): cow, Hankow.

l: allow, bacalhau, Belau, disallow.

m: mau-mau.

n: enow*, now, NOW.

pl: plough, plow, snowplough, upplow.

pr: prow.
s: sough, sow.
sk(sc): scow.
t: kowtow, Swatow.
TH: thou*.
v: avow, disavow, vow.
w: bow-wow, pow-wow, wow.

ŌB

d: daube.
f: acrophobe.
gl: conglobe, globe.
j: Job.
l: lobe, Loeb.
pr: probe.
r: disrobe, enrobe, rerobe, robe, unrobe.

ÔB

d: bedaub, daub+.
w: nawab+.

ŌŌB

b: boob.
k(c): cube.
r: Reub, rube.
t: boob tube, lighthouse tube, tube.

ŌCH

br: abroach, broach, brooch+.
k: coach, encoach, slow coach.
kr: croche, encroach.
l: loach.
p: poach.
pr: approach, reproach, self-reproach.
r: cockroach, roach.

ÔCH

b: debauch.
n: nautch.

w: anchor watch+, deathwatch, dogwatch, harbor watch+, larboard watch+, outwatch, starboard watch+, watch+.

ŌŌCH

br: brooch+.
h: hooch.
k(c): cooch, hooch-y-cooch.
m: mooch.
p: pooch, putsch.
sp: "spooch."

OUCH

Vowel: ouch.
gr: grouch.
k(c): couch.
kr: crouch.
m: scaramouch.
p: pouch.
sl: slouch.
v: avouch, vouch.

ŌCHD

br: unbroached.
pr: unapproached.
   Plus och+d.
   Plus roach'd,etc.

ŌD

Vowel: ode, owed, unowed.
b: abode, bode, forebode.
bl: blowed.
g: goad.
k(c): code, Napoleonic code, penal code.
kl: Clode.
l: load, lode, overload, reload, unload.
m: alamode, commode, discommode, incommode, mode.
n: node.
p: antipode, lycopode.

pl: explode.

r: arrode*, bridle road, corrode, erode, off-road, on-road, railroad, road, rode.

s: episode.

sp: spode.

st: unbestowed.

str: bestrode, strode.

t: pigeon-toed, toad.

w: dyer's woad, woad.

> Plus o+d.
> Plus bow'd, etc.

ÔD

Vowel: overawed, unawed.

b: bawd.

br: abroad, broad.

fr: defraud, fraud.

g: begod*+, demigod+, gaud god+, river god+, sea god+, ungod+.

j: lantern-jawed, whopper-jawed.

kl: Claud, Claude.

l: belaud, laud.

m: maud, Maude.

pl: applaud.

r: maraud.

> Plus o+d.
> Plus jaw'd, etc.

OID

b: "boid," unbuoyed.

d: pyramidoid.

dr: dendroid.

fl: Floyd.

fr: Freud.

gr: negroid.

j: overjoyed.

k(c): helecoid.

l: alkaloid, celluloid, coralloid, crystalloid, hyaloid, Lloyd, metalloid, mongoloid, paraboloid, petaloid, tabloid, unalloyed, varioloid.

n: actinoid, albuminoid, ganoid.

p: anthropoid.

pl: disemployed, employed, unemployed.

r: aneroid, steroid.

t: deltoid, pachydermatoid.

v: avoid, devoid, ovoid, void.

z: trapezoid.

> Plus oi+d.
> Plus joy'd, etc.

OOD

g: good.

h: angelhood, babyhood, brother-hood, deaconhood, fatherhood, foolhardihood, gentlemanhood, hardihood, hood, kinglihood, kittenhood, ladyhood, likelihood, livelihood, lustihood*, maiden-hood, manhood, matronhood, monkshood, motherhood, neighborhood, orphanhood, parenthood, Robin Hood, sisterhood, spinsterhood, unlikeli-hood, widowerhood, widowhood, womanhood.

k(c): could.

p: Pud.

sh: should.

st: misunderstood, stood, understood, withstood.

w: dead wood, firewood, plastic wood, purplewood, sandalwood, Underwood, wildwood, wood, would.

OOD

br: abrood, brewed, brood, home-brewed, unbrewed.

d: dude, subdued, unsubdued.

f: fast-food, feud, food.

gl: unglued.

h: rainbow-hued.

j: Jude.

kl: conclude, exclude, include, interclude*, occlude, preclude, reclude*, seclude.

kr: crude.

l: allude, collude, delude, elude, illude, interlude, lewd, prelude.

m: mood.

n: denude, nude, subnude, unrenewed.

p: pood.

pr: prude.

r: rood, rude, unrude*, unrued.

s: transude, unpursued.

shr: shrewd.

sl: slewed.

sn: snood.

st: stewed, stude.

str: abstrude*, unstrude.

t: acerbitude*, acritude*, altitude, amaritude*, amplitude, aptitude, assuetude, attitude, beatitude, certitude, claritude*, consuetude, crassitude, decrepitude, definitude, desuetude, disquietude, exactitude, finitude, fortitude, gratitude, habitude, hebetude, inaptitude, incertitude, ineptitude, infinitude, ingratitude, inquietude, insuetude, lassitude, latitude, lenitude, longitude, magnitude, mansuetude, molitude, multitude, necessitude, parvitude, platitude, plenitude, promptitude, pulchritude, quietude, rectitude, senectitude, serenitude*, servitude, similitude, solicitude, torpitude, turpitude, vastitude, verisimilitude, vicissitude.

th: thewed.

tr: detrude, extrude, intrude, obtrude, protrude, retrude, subtrude.

w: unwooed.

y: exude.

Plus u+d.

Plus you'd, etc.

OUD

b: unbowed.

br: beetle-browed.

d: disendowed.

kl: becloud, cloud, encloud, intercloud, overcloud, recloud, thundercloud, uncloud.

kr: crowd, overcrowd.

l: allowed, alound, loud.

pr: proud.

shr: beshroud, disenshroud, enshroud, reshroud, unshroud.

Plus ou+d.

Plus bow'd, etc.

OIDZ

l: Lloyds.

Plus oid+s.

Plus Freud's, etc.

ŌDZ

r: Rhoades, Rhodes.

Plus od+s.

Plus load's, etc.

ŌF

Vowel: oaf.

g: goaf.

l: loaf, quartern loaf, sugar loaf.

sh: chauf.

ÔF

Vowel: log off, long field off+, mouth off+, off+, pairing off+, sign off+, take off+.

d: doff+.

k(c): coff, cough.

kl: cloff.

s: philosophe.

sk(sc): scoff+.

t: toff+, toph.

tr: trough+.

OIF

k(c): coif.

OOF

(h)w: whoof.
r: sunroof+.
w: whoof.

O͞OF

Vowel: oof.
b: opera bouffe.
d: shadoof.
g: goof.
h: behoof, hoof+.
l: aloof, loof.
pr: bulletproof, disproof, fireproof, foolproof, proof, reproof, virtue-proof, waterproof, weatherproof.
r: gable roof, reroof, roof, sunroof+, unroof.
sp: spoof.
t: Tartuffe.
tr: trufe.

ÔFT

Vowel: oft.
kr(cr): croft, undercroft.
l: aloft, hayloft+, loft+.
s: soft+.
t: toft+.
    Plus of+d.

O͞OFT

h: cloven-hoofed, hoofed.
    Plus uf+d.

ŌG

b: bogue, embogue*.
br: brogue.
h: Hoag, Hogue.

l: apologue, astrologue, collogue, horologue.
r: pirogue, prorogue, rogue.
t: togue.
tr: trogue.
v: vogue.

ÔG

Vowel: Og.
b: bog+, bogue, embog.
br: Dannebrog.
ch: Patchogue.
d: bulldog+, dog+, dog-eat-dog, hot dog+, prairie dog+, sun dog+.
f: befog+, defog+, fog+, pettifog+.
fl: flog+.
fr: frog+.
h: groundhog+, hedgehog+, hog+, quahog+.
k(c): cog+, incog, Pokogue.
kl(cl): clog+, reclog+, unclog+.
kw(qu): Quogue.
l: analogue+, apologue+, catalogue+, decalogue, dialogue+, epilogue, log+, monologue, philologue, theologue, travelog+.
sh: shog.
skr(scr): scrog.
t: tog+.
z: Herzog, Zog.

OOG

m: Moog.

O͞OG

f: fugue.

ÔGD

fr: frogged+.
l: waterlogged.
    Plus og+d.
    Plus dog'd, etc.

ÔGZ

t: togs+.

Plus og+s.

Plus grog's, etc.

ŌJ

b: gamboge.
d: doge.
l: horologe.

OOJ

n: noodge.

ŌŌJ

b: gamboge+.
f: demonifuge, febrifuge, insectifuge, subterfuge, vermifuge.
h: huge.
kl: kluge.
l: luge.
skr(scr): Scrooge, scrouge+.
st: stooge.

OUJ

g: gouge.
skr(scr): scrouge+.

ŌK

Vowel: holm oak, live oak, oak, oke, scrub oak.
bl: bloke.
br: broke, dead broke, outbroke, unbroke, upbroke.
ch: artichoke, choke.
d: doke.
f: folk, gentlefolk.
j: joke.
k(c): coak, coke.
kl: cloak, mourning cloak, uncloak.
kr: croak.
l: loke.
m: moke.
p: poke.
r: barogue, Larocque.
s: asoak, soak.
sl: sloke.
sm: besmoke, smoke.
sp: bespoke, forespoke, forspoke, spoke.
st: stoke.
str: counterstroke, death stroke, master stroke, stroke, thunderstroke, understroke.
t: toke, toque.
v: convoke, equivoke, evoke, invoke, provoke, revoke.
w: awoke, woke.
y: reyoke, unyoke, yoke, yolk.

ÔK

Vowel: auk, awk*.
b: balk.
ch: chalk.
d: dawk.
f: Falk.
g: gawk.
h: chicken hawk, hawk, Mohawk, sparrow hawk, tomahawk.
k(c): calk, recalk, uncalk.
l: Lawk.
m: mawk.
p: pawk.
skw(squ): squawk.
st: stalk.
t: fast-talk, talk.
w: cakewalk, catwalk, outwalk, sidewalk, walk.

OOK

b: audio book, book, minute book, pocketbook.
br: brook.
h: hook, rehook, unhook.

k(c): cook, pastry cook.

l: look, outlook, overlook, uplook.

n: Chinook, inglenook, nook.

r: rook.

s: forsook.

sh: shook.

sn: snook.

t: betook, mistook, overtook, partook, took, undertook.

OOK

b: chibouk, rebuke.

d: archduke, beduke, duke, Marmaduke.

fl: fluke.

j: juke.

l: Luke, Mameluke.

n: Chinook.

p: puke.

r: peruke, seruke.

sp: spook.

st: stook.

t: Heptateuch, Hexateuch, Pentateuch.

y: uke.

z: bashibazook.

OKS

Vowel: Oakes.

h: hoax.

k(c): coax.

n: Nokes.

st: stokes.

v: Vokes, vox+.

Plus ok+s.

Plus coke's, etc.

OOKS

h: tenterhooks.

kr: Crookes.

sn: snooks.

Plus ook+s.

Plus book's, etc.

OKT

s: water-soaked.

st: stoked.

v: unprovoked.

Plus ok+d.

Plus choke'd, etc.

OL

Vowel: aureole, capriole, cariole, foliole, gloriole, ole, oriole, petiole, vacuole, variole.

b: bole, boll, bowl, carambole, embowl, wassail bowl.

d: condole, dhole, dole, girandole.

dr: droll.

f: foal.

g: goal, segol.

h: augur hole, blowhole, bunghole, buttonhole, doghole, glory hole, heart-whole, hole, loophole, peephole, pigeonhole, pinhole, porthole, scupperhole, top hole, unwhole*, whole.

j: cajole, jowl.

k(c): borecole, caracole, coal, cole, kohl.

m: mole.

n: carmagnole, knoll, pinole, Seminole.

p: bibliopole, curtain pole, flagpole, Maypole, pole, poll, rantipole, tadpole.

r: banderole, barcarolle, casserole, enroll, French roll, fumarole, furole, fusarole, jellyroll, logroll, parole, payroll, reroll, rigmarole, role, roll, unroll, uproll, virole.

s: camisole, console, feme sole, girasole, half-sole, resole, sole, soul, unsole, unsoul.

sh: shoal, shole.

sk(sc): skoal.

skr(scr): enscroll, inscroll, scroll.

st: stole.

str: stroll.

t: extoll+, pistole, toll.

th: thole.

tr: biological control, comptrol, control, patrol, self-control, troll.

v: vole.

Plus bow'll, etc.

ÔL

Vowel: all, all-in-all, and all, awl, free-for-all, therewithal, vitriol+, wherewithal, withal.

b: ball, baseball, basketball, bawl, blackball, fireball, football, snowball.

br: brawl.

d: baby doll+, doll+.

dr: drawl.

dw: dwal.

f: befall, evenfall, fall, footfall, landfall, nightfall, overfall, pitfall, rainfall, waterfall, windfall.

g: Bengal, gall, Gaul, spur gall.

h: alcohol+, banquet hall, dance hall, hall, haul, judgment hall, overhaul.

k(c): call, caul, cold call, McCall, miscall, protocol+, recall, trumpet call.

kr: crawl, kraal+.

m: bemawl, mall, maul.

p: appal, pall, Paul, pawl, St. Paul.

s: girasol+, parasol+, Saul

sh: shawl.

sk(sc): scall.

skr(scr): scrawl.

skw(squ): squall.

sm: small.

sp: spall, spawl.

spr: sprawl, urban sprawl.

st: boxstall, forestall, install, stall.

t: tall.

thr: bethrall, disenthrall, entrall, thrall.

tr: trawl.

w: caterwaul, sea wall, wall.

y: yawl.

Plus jaw'll, etc.

OIL

Vowel: boiled oil, canola oil, china wood oil, lamp oil, oil, olive oil, sunflower oil.

b: aboil, boil, Boyle, parboil.

br: broil, disembroil, embroil.

d: Doyle, langue d'oil.

f: cinquefoil, counterfoil, foil, quatrefoil, tinfoil, trefoil.

g: "goil."

h: Hoyle.

k(c): coil, Coyle, recoil, uncoil, upcoil.

m: moil, turmoil.

n: noil.

r: roil.

s: assoil*, soil.

sp: despoil, spoil.

t: entoil, estoile, overtoil, toil.

Plus boy'll, etc.

OOL

b: bull, cock-and-bull, Sitting Bull.

f: full.

p: pull.

w: abb wool, cotton wool, lamb's wool, wool.

Cf. principal.

O͞OL

b: buhl, Istanbul, vestibule.

dr: drool.

f: April fool, befool, fool.

g: ghoul.

h: who'll.

k(c): cool, molecule, reticule, ridicule, vermicule.

m: mewl, mule.

p: Liverpool, pool, pule, whirlpool.

r: misrule, overrule, rule, sliderule.

sk(sc): charity-school, school, Sunday school.

sp: spool.

st: ducking stool, footstool, stool, toadstool.

t: O'Toole, toole, Toole, tulle.

th: Thule, Ultima Thule.

y: you'll, Yule.

　　Plus few'll, etc.

OUL

Vowel: owl, screech owl.

d: dowl.

f: afoul, befoul, foul, fowl, guinea fowl, peafowl, seafowl, technical foul, waterfowl.

gr: growl.

h: behowl, howl.

j: jowl.

k(c): cowl.

pr: prowl.

sk(sc): scowl.

ÔLCH

b: Balch.

w: Walch.

ŌLD

Vowel: old.

b: bold, overbold.

f: blindfold, enfold, fold, fourfold, infold, interfold, manifold, multifold, refold, thousandfold, twofold, unfold.

g: gold, marigold, spun gold.

h: afterhold, ahold, anchor hold, behold, copyhold, foothold, freehold, hold, household, leasehold, stronghold, uphold, withhold.

k(c): acold, clay cold, cold, ice cold, stone cold.

m: bullet mould, leaf mold, mold, mould.

p: Leopold.

s: half-soled, high-souled, sold, unsoled.

t: foretold, retold, told, twice-told, untold.

tr: uncontrolled.

w: wold.

　　Plus ol+d.

　　Plus soul'd, etc.

ÔLD

Vowel: auld+.

b: Archibald, bald, blackballed.

g: ungalled.

k(c): so-called, uncalled, unrecalled.

p: palled+, unappalled.

sk(sc): scald.

thr: unentralled.

　　Plus al+d.

　　Plus call'd, etc.

OILD

b: hard-boiled.

s: soiled, unsoiled.

sp: spoiled, unspoiled.

　　Plus oil+d.

　　Plus boil'd, etc.

O͞OLD

r: unruled.
sk(sc): unschooled.
  Plus ul+d.
  Plus fool'd, etc.

OULD

k(c): uncowled.
  Plus oul+d.
  Plus foul'd, etc.

ÔLF

g: golf+.

OOLF

w: wolf.

O͞LN

sw: swoln.

O͞OLP

p: poulp.

ÔLSH

w: Walsh.
  Cf. olch.

O͞LT

b: bolt, rebolt, shacklebolt, thunderfolt, unbolt.
d: dolt.
h: holt.
j: jolt.
k(c): colt, wood colt.
m: molt.
p: poult.
sm: smolt.
v: demivolt, lavolt, revolt, volt.

ÔLT

b: cobalt.
f: default, fault.
g: Galt, gault.
h: halt.
m: malt.
s: assault, basalt, salt, sea salt, somersault.
sm: smalt.
sp: spalt.
v: envault, vault.
z: exalt.

OILT

sp: spoilt.

ÔLTS

f: false.
v: valse.
w: waltz.
  Plus olt+s.
  Plus fault's, etc.

ÔLV

s: absolve+, solve+.
v: devolve+, evolve+, involve+, revolve+.
z: dissolve+, exolve*, resolve+.

ÔLVD

s: unsolved+.
z: undissolved+, unresolved+.
  Plus olv+d.

OOLVZ

w: wolves.

OILZ

  See oil+s.
  Plus Boyle's, etc.

O͞OLZ

g: gules.

j: Jules.

　Plus ul+s.

　Plus rule's, etc.

ŌM

Vowel: ohm, om.

b: Bohm.

br: brome.

d: dome, endome, Teapot Dome.

dr: aerodrome, aquadrome, hippodrome, palindrome.

f: afoam, befoam, foam, seafoam.

fr: Frome.

gl: gloam*.

h: at home, harvest home, holm, home, nobody home, sea holm.

k(c): catacomb, cockscomb, comb, currycomb, honeycomb.

kl: clomb.*

kr: chrome, heliochrome, metallochrome, monochrome, polychrome.

l: loam, Salome.

n: gastronome, gnome, metronome, nom, Nome.

p: pome.

r: Jerome, roam, Rome.

s: chromosome, microsome.

sl: sloam.

t: hecatomb+, tome.

ÔM

h: haum.

m: imaum, maum.

sh: shawm.

OOM

r: room.

t: hecatomb+.

O͞OM

Vowel: Oom, vacuum+.

b: boom, jib boom.

bl: abloom, bloom, embloom, rebloom.

br: broom, brougham, brume.

d: addoom*, doom, foredoom, predoom, redoom.

f: fume, perfume.

fl: flume.

g: legume.

gl: begloom, engloom, gloom.

gr: bridegroom, groom, grume.

h: exhume, inhume, whom.

k(c): coom, coomb.

l: heirloom, illume, loom, powerloom, reloom, relume.

m: simoom.

pl: beplume, displume, plume, unplume.

r: anteroom, dining room, drawing room, dressing room, elbow room, living room, lumber room, reading room, rheum, room, searoom, sunroom.

s: assume, consume, reassume, subsume.

sp: spoom, spume.

t: costume, disentomb, entomb, Khartoum, tomb, untomb.

w: enwomb, womb.

y: Fiume.

z: presume, resume.

O͞OMD

b: full-bloomed.

f: unfumed.

gl: ungloomed.

l: unillumed.

pl: implumed.

　Plus um+d.

　Plus bloom'd, etc.

ŌŌMF

Vowel: oomph.

ÔMP

sw: swamp+.

ŌMZ

h: Holmes.
k: khoms.
s: Soames.

Plus om+s.

Plus loam's, etc.

ŌŌMZ

z: bazooms.

ŌN

Vowel: disown, own.

b: backbone, bone, debone, knucklebone, marrowbone, trombone, whalebone.

bl: blown, flyblown, fresh-blown, full-blown, outblown, unblown.

d: condone, Doane, Dordogne.

dr: drone, ladrone, padrone.

f: antiphone, audiphone, dictaphone, electrophone, gramaphone, graphophone, megaphone, microphone, phone, radiophone, saxophone, telephone, vitaphone, xylophone.

fl: flown, high-flown.

g: begroan, full-grown, grass-grown, groan, grown, half-grown, moss-grown, overgrown, ungrown.

h: hone.

j: Joan.

k(c): Cohn, cone, ochone.

kl(cl): clone.

kr: crone.

l: alone, Athlone, ballon, Boulogne, Cologne, eau de Cologne, loan, lone, malone.

m: bemoan, moan, mown, remown, unmown.

n: foreknown, known, unbeknown, unforeknown, unknown.

ny: beef bourguignon, cabernet sauvignon.

p: corn pone, depone, dispone, impone*, interpone, pone, postpone, propone.

pr: prone.

r: chaperone, cicerone, Rhone, roan.

s: resewn, resown, sewn, sown, unsewn, unsown.

sh: foreshown, shewn*, shone, shown.

sk(sc): scone.

sl: Sloan.

st: brimstone, clingstone, cornerstone, curbstone, flagstone, foundation stone, grindlestone*, grindstone, hailstone, headstone, hearthstone, holystone, imposing stone, keystone, limestone, loadstone, lodestone, milestone, millstone, moonstone, soapstone, stone, whetstone.

t: atone, baritone, intone, macrotone, monotone, semitone, tone, undertone.

thr: dethrone, enthrone, overthrown, throne, thrown, unthrone.

z: calzone, enterprise zone, enzone, zone.

ÔN

Vowel: awn, right-on+.

b: bawn.

br: brawn.

d: dawn+.

dr: drawn, indrawn, redrawn, undrawn, withdrawn.

f: faun, fawn.

g: Oregon+, paragon+, undergone+, woe-be-gone+.

k(c): cawn.

l: lawn.

p: impawn, pawn.

pr: prawn.

s: sawn.

sh: Denishawn, Shawn.

sp: spawn.

sw: swan+.

y: yawn.

OIN

b: Boyne.

f: foin*.

g: Burgoyne.

gr: groin.

j: adjoin, conjoin, disjoin, enjoin, interjoin, join, rejoin, sejoin, subjoin.

k(c): coigne, coin.

kw(qu): quoin.

l: eloign, loin, purloin, sirloin, tenderloin.

m: almoign, Des Moines, frankalmoigne.

O͞ON

b: baboon, boon.

bl: doubloon.

br: Broun, gambroon.

d: bridoon, cardoon, Doon, dune, rigadoon.

dr: gadroon, quadroon, spadroon.

f: buffoon, typhoon.

g: dragoon, goon, lagoon, Rangoon.

h: Calhoun, hewn, Mahoun, rehewn, rough-hewn, unhewn.

j: jejeune, June.

k(c): barracoon, cocoon, Colquoun, coon, lacune, raccoon, tycoon.

kr: croon.

l: balloon, galloon, loon, lune, pantaloon, saloon, shalloon, Walloon.

m: commune, excommune*, harvest moon, honeymoon, immune, intercommune, moon, simoon.

n: afternoon, forenoon, midnoon, noon.

p: expugn*, harpoon, impugn, lampoon, oppugn.

pr: prune.

r: macaroon, maroon, octoroon, picaroon, rune, seroon.

s: bassoon, eftsoon*, gossoon, monsoon, oversoon, soon.

sh: shoon*.

skr(scr): Schroon.

sp: spoon.

str: bestrewn*, overstrewn, strewn.

sw: aswoon, swoon.

t: attune, batoon*, cartoon, entune, festoon, frigatoon, importune, inopportune, musketoon, opportune, platoon, pontoon, ratoon, retune, spitoon, spontoon, tune, untune.

tr: patroon, poltroon, quintroon.

y: picayne.

z: gazon*.

OUN

b: Bowne.

br: brown, Browne, embrown, nut-brown.

d: adown, down, eiderdown, go down, hand-me-down, meltdown, reach-me-down, swans-down, tumble-down, upside-down.

dr: drown.

fr: frown.

g: gown, nightgown, regown, town and gown, ungown.

k: McKown.

kl: clown.

kr: crown, decrown, discrown, recrown, uncrown.
l: lown*.
n: noun, renown.
t: downtown, town, uptown.

ÔNCH

h: haunch+.
kr: craunch+.
l: launch.
p: paunch.
st: stanch+, staunch+.

ŌND

Vowel: unowned.
b: deboned.
fr: Fronde.
m: beau monde, monde, unmoaned.
r: Gironde+.
t: high-toned, unatoned.
z: unzoned, zoned.
  Plus on+d.
  Plus zone'd, etc.

ÔND

  Plus yawn'd, etc.

OIND

k(c): uncoined.
p: dead poind, poind.
  Plus oin+d.
  Plus coin'd, etc.

ŌŌND

kr: crooned.
t: attuned, disattuned, tuned, untuned.
w: wound.
  Plus un+ed.

OUND

b: abound, bound, hellbound, hidebound, homebound, icebound, inbound, ironbound, outbound, outward-bound, rebound, spellbound, super-a-bound, unbound.
br: browned.
d: downed, redound.
f: confound, dumbfound, found, profound.
gr: aground, background, ground, middle ground, pleasure ground, underdround, unground, vantage ground.
h: bloodhound, boozehound, hoarhound, hound, Mahound, smut hound.
kr: flower-crowned, pine-crowned, triple-crowned, etc.
m: mound.
n: renowned.
p: compound, expound, impound, pound, propound.
r: around, merry-go-round, round, surround.
s: resound, sound, unsound.
t: astound.
z: resound.
  Plus oun+d.
  Plus frown'd, etc.

OUNDZ

z: zounds*.
  Plus ound+s.
  Plus sound's, etc.

ÔNG

b: bong+.
d: ding dong+.
fl: flong.
g: dugong, gong+.
j: mahjongg.

k(c): Hong Kong+, King Kong+.

l: allalong, along, belong, day-long, ere long, headlong, lifelong, livelong, long+, nightlong, overlong.

n: scuppernong.

p: ping pong.

pr: prong.

r: wrong.

s: battle song, drinking song, evensong, singsong, song, undersong.

sh: souchong.

st: Stong.

str: headstrong, strong.

t: tong+.

th: thong.

thr: throng.

w: wong.

ÔNGD

r: unwronged.

    Plus ong+d.

    Plus song'd, etc.

ÔNGK

b: bonk+.

h: honk+.

k(c): conch+, conk+, konk+.

t: honky-tonk.

ÔNGST

l: alongst, belong'st*, long'st*, prolong'st*.

r: wrong'st*.

thr: throng'st*.

ÔNGZ

    See ong+s.

    Plus gong's, etc.

OUNJ

l: lounge.

r: scrounge.

OUNS

Vowel: ounce.

b: bounce.

fl: flounce.

fr: frounce.

n: announce, denounce, enounce, pronounce, renounce.

p: pounce.

r: rounce.

tr: trounce.

    Cf. ount+s.

ŌNT

d: don't.

w: won't.

ÔNT

d: daunt+.

fl: aflaunt, flaunt.

g: gaunt+.

h: haunt+.

j: jaunt.

m: romaunt+.

p: Dupont, Helles-pont, pont.

t: ataunt+, taunt+.

v: avaunt*+, vaunt+.

w: want+.

OINT

j: adjoint, conjoint, disjoint, dowel joint, joint.

n: anoint.

p: appoint, championship point, counterpoint, coverpoint, disappoint, dry point, game point, match point, point, reappoint, repoint, steel point, West Point.

r: aroint*.

OUNT

f: fount.

k(c): account, count, discount, miscount, recount, uncount.

m: amount, catamount, dismount, mount, paramount, remount, surmount, tantamount, unmount.

ÔNTS

See ont+s.
Cf. ons.

OUNTS

See ount+s.
Cf. ouns.

ŌNZ

b: bare-bones, lazybones, rolling the bones.

j: Davy Jones, Jones.

n: nones.

Plus on+s.
Plus bone's, etc.

ÔNZ

g: bygones.

Plus on+s.

ŌŌNZ

r: Cameroons.

s: eftsoons*.

Plus un+s.
Plus tunc's, etc.

ŌP

Vowel: ope.
d: dope.

gr: agrope, grope.

h: Cape of Good Hope, hope.

k(c): cope.

l: antelope, cantaloupe, elope, envelope, interlope, lope.

m: mope.

n: nope.

p: antipope, dispope, pope, unpope.

r: footrope, rope.

s: soap.

sk(sc): astroscope, baroscope, bioscope, electroscope, galvano-scope, gyroscope, helioscope, horoscope, hydroscope, kaleido-scope, microscope, polariscope, scope, seismoscope, spectroscope, stereoscope, stethoscope, telescope, thermoscope.

sl: aslope, slippery slope, slope.

st: stope.

sw: swope.

t: taupe, tope.

thr: misanthrope.

tr: heliotrope, trope.

ÔP

g: gaup.
hw: whaup+.
sk(sc): scaup.
y: yawp+.

ŌŌP

b: Betty Boop.

d: boop-boop-a-doop, dupe.

dr: adroop, droop, drupe.

g: goop.

gr: aggroup, group.

h: cock-a-hoop, hoop, unhoop.

hw: whoop.

j: jupe.

k(c): coop, recoup.

kr: croup, Krupp.

l: cantaloupe, Guadeloupe, loop, loop-the-loop, unloop.

p: liripoop, nincompoop, poop.

r: roup.

s: alphabet soup, black bean soup, chicken noodle soup, pea soup, soup, supe, tomato soup.

sk(sc): apple scoop, scoop.

skr(scr): scroop.

sl: sloop.

st: stoop, stoup.

sw: swoop.

tr: troop, troupe.

OOPS

Vowel: oops.

hw: whoops.

OŌPS

Vowel: oops.

Plus up+s.

Plus group's, etc.

ŌPT

h: hoped, unhoped.

s: soaped, unsoaped.

Plus op+d.

Plus slope'd, etc.

ŌR

f: fore+, four+, heretofore+, pinafore+, semaphore+.

fr: frore*.

kr: crore.

sp: spore+.

ÔR

Vowel: excelsior+, meteor+, oar, o'er, or+, ore, Orr, posterior+, urban ore.

b: boar, Boer, bore, Dukhobor, forebore, hellebore.

ch: chore.

d: adore, ambassador+, backdoor, battledore, commodore, corridor+, death's door, door, dor, dore, Ecuador, Labrador, louis d'or, matador, mirador, picador, Salvador, stevedore, Theodore, toreador, troubadour.

f: afore, before, for+, fore+, four+, heretofore+, lophophore, metaphore+, pinafore+, semaphore+, therefore.

fl: first floor, floor.

g: gore.

h: abhor, hoar, Lahore, whore.

j: mortgagor.

k(c): albacore, core, corps, encore.

l: councillor, folklore, galore, lor, lore.

m: Baltimore, evermore, furthermore, more, nevermore, sagamore, sophomore, sycamore.

n: assignor, ignore, nominor, nor+, Nore.

p: outpour, pore, pour, Singapore.

pl: deplore, explore, implore.

r: conqueror, outroar, roar, uproar.

s: dinosaur, footsore, hearsore, ichthyosaur, lessor, outsoar, pleisosaur, soar, sore, upsore.

sh: ashore, foreshore, inshore, offshore, seashore, shore, weather shore.

sk(sc): four score, scaur, score, underscore.

sn: snore.

sp: spore+.

st: restore, store.

sw: foreswore, swore.

t: apparitor+, contributor, guarantor, inheritor, minotaur, orator+, primogenitor+, progenitor+, tore.

th: Thor.

w: man-of-war, outwore, tug-of-war, war, wore.

y: señor, yore.

OOR

b: boor.

bl: Bloor.

d: dure*, endure, perdure, perendure, troubadour*.

h: hewer.

j: abjure, adjure, conjure*.

k(c): cure, epicure, insecure, liqueur*, manicure, pedicure, procure, secure, sinecure, watercure.

l: allure, colure, liqueur, lure.

m: amour, blackamoor, demure, immure, intermure*, moor, Moore, Ostermoor, paramour, unmoor.

n: Kohinoor, manure.

p: guipure, impure, poor, pure.

r: Ruhr.

s: connoisseur.

sh: assure, brochure, cocksure, cynosure, ensure, insure, reassure, reinsure, sure, unsure.

sk: onscure.

sm: smoor.

sp: spoor.

t: amateur+, calenture+, caricature+, detour, immature, mature, premature, restaurateur+, tour.

y: inure, your, you're+.

zh: carte du jour+, du jour*+.

O͞OR

t: contour.

y: you're+.

zh: carte du jour+, du jour*+

  Plus crew're, etc.

  Cf. u'er, u'ur.

OUR

Vowel: hour, our, sustaining hour.

fl: delower, flour.

s: besour, sour.

sk(sc): bescour, rescour, scour.

v: devour.

  Cf. our.

ÔRB

Vowel: orb.

k(c): corb.

s: absorb, desorb, reabsorb, resorb.

ÔRBD

Vowel: full-orbed.

  Plus orb+d.

ÔRBZ

f: Forbes.

  Plus orb+s.

  Plus orb's, etc.

ÔRCH

b: bortsch.

p: porch

sk(sc): scorch.

t: torch.

ÔRD

Vowel: fiord, oared, Ord, Orde.

b: aboard, beaverboard, board, bord, drawing board, ironing board, ledger board, mould board, seaboard, shuffleboard, surfboard, weather board.

d: adored.

f: afford, ford, Ford.

fy: fyord.

g: gourd+, ungored.

h: abhorred, hoard, horde, unhoard, whored.

k(c): accord, chord, concord*, cord, disaccord, harpsichord, lyrichord, masterchord, McCord, misericord, polychord, record.

l: belord, landlord, lord, overlord, unlord.

n: Nord.

pl: undeplored, unexplored, unimplored.

s: broadsword, sword.

st: unrestored.

sw: sward.

w: award, reward, ward.

Plus or+d

Plus store'd, etc.

Plus war'd, etc.

OORD

g: gourd.

h: heard, herd, overheard.

k(c): uncured.

sh: assured, insured, reassured, self-assured, unassured, uninsured.

t: matured, unmatured.

Plus ur+d.

Plus cure'd, etc.

OURD

s: unsoured.

Plus our+d.

Plus flour'd, etc.

ÔRF

d: Diefendorf.

dw: dwarf.

hw: wharf.

k(c): corf.

m: morph.

ÔRG

m: morgue.

ÔRJ

f: forge.

g: disgorge, engorge, gorge, regorge.

j: George, St. George.

ÔRK

Vowel: ork.

b: bork.

d: dork.

f: fork, pitchfork, weeding fork.

k(c): cork, uncork.

p: moo shu pork, pork.

st: stork.

t: torque.

y: New York, York.

ÔRKD

st: storked.

Plus ork+d.

Plus fork'd, etc.

ÔRL

Vowel: orle.

hw: whorl+.

sh: schorl.

ÔRM

Vowel: Orme.

d: dorm.

f: aeriform, aquiform, chloroform, conform, cruciform, cuneiform, deform, deiform, dendriform, diversiform, floriform, form, inform, misform, misinform, multiform, perform,

reform, stelliform, transform,
uniform, vermiform.

k(c): corm.

n: norm.

st: bestorm, snowstorm, storm,
thunderstorm.

sw: swarm, upswarm.

w: sunny warm, unwarm, warm.

ÔRMD

f: unformed, uninformed,
unperformed, unreformed, well-
informed.

st: unstormed.

Plus orm+d.

Plus storm'd, etc.

ÔRMTH

w: warmth.

Plus storm'th*, etc.

ŌRN

b: borne, bourn, forborne,
overborne.

m: bemourn, mourn.

sh: shorn, unshorn.

sw: forsworn, sworn, unsworn.

t: betorn, torn.

w: footworn, outworn, seaworn,
toilworn, waterworn, waveworn,
wayworn, weatherworn, worn.

Cf. orn.

ÔRN

Vowel: Orne.

b: born, cloud-born, first-born,
heaven-born, high-born, inborn,
night-born, reborn, sea-born, sky-
born, stillborn, suborn, true-born,
unborn, virgin-born.

d: adorn, disadorn, readorn.

h: alpenhorn, Cape Horn, cow
horn, dishorn, drinking horn,

foghorn, French horn, greenhorn, horn, Horne, hunting
horn, Langhorne, Matterhorn,
powderhorn, priming horn.

k(c): barleycorn, Capricorn, corn,
longicorn, peppercorn, popcorn,
tricorn, unicorn.

l: forlorn, lorn, lovelorn.

m: morn, yestermorn*.

n: Norn.

p: porn.

sk(sc): bescorn, scorn, self-scorn.

th: blackthorn, buckthorn,
hawthorn, thorn.

w: forewarn, warn.

OORN

b: bourn.

y: "yourn."

ÔRND

d: unadorned.

m: bemourned, mourned,
unmourned.

w: unforewarned.

Plus orn+d.

Plus morn'd, etc.

ÔRP

d: dorp.

th: Oglethorpe, thorp.

w: warp.

ÔRPS

k(c): corpse.

Plus orp+s.

Plus dorp's, etc.

ÔRS

d: dorse*, endorse.

f: enforce, force, perforce,
reinforce.

g: gorse.

h: Crazy Horse, dead horse, hoarse, hobbyhorse, horse, rocking horse, seahorse, stalkinghorse, unhorse.

k(c): corse, course, discourse, intercourse, recourse, watercourse.

m: Morse, remorse.

n: Norse.

s: resource, source.

t: torse.

tr: dextrorse, retrorse, sinistrorse.

v: divorce.

OORS

b: bourse.

y: yours.

ÔRSK

t: torsk.

ÔRST

d: addorsed, endorsed.

h: horsed, Horst, unhorsed.

ŌRT

f: forte+.

ÔRT

Vowel: ort*.

b: abort, bort.

f: fort, forte+.

h: exhort.

k(c): county court, court, decourt*, excort.

kw(qu): quart.

m: amort, mort.

p: comport, davenport, deport, disport, export, import, misreport, passport, port, Porte, rapport, report, sallyport, seaport, transport.

s: assort, consort, re-sort.

sh: short.

sk: skort

sn: snort.

sp: sport.

sw: swart*.

t: contort, detort*, distort, extort, retort.

thw: athwart, thwart.

v: cavort.

w: wart.

z: resort.
   Cf. ort.

ŌRTH

f: forth+, fourth+, henceforth, setter-forth, thenceforth.
   Plus pour'th*, etc.

ÔRTH

Vowel: Orth.

f: back-and-forth+, forth+, fourth+,

n: north.

sw: swarth.
   Plus abhorr'th*, etc.

ÔRTS

kw(qu): quartz.

sh: shorts.

sw: Schwartz, Swarz.
   Plus ort+s.
   Plus short's, etc.

ÔRVZ

hw: wharves.

ŌRZ

d: indoors, outdoors.

f: all-fours, plus-fours.

z: Azores.

Plus or+s.

Plus floor's, etc.

ÔRZ

kw(qu): Louis Quatorze, quatorze.

Plus or+s.

Plus war's, etc.

OORZ

t: Tours+.

Plus ur+s.

Plus cure's, etc.

O͞ORZ

t: Tours+.

ŌS

Vowel: actuose*, foliose, grandiose, otiose.

b: gibbose, globose, verbose.

d: dose, nodose, overdose, underdose.

gr: engross, gross.

k(c): belicose, cose, floccose, glucose, jocose, metempsychose.

kl: close.

l: annulose, cellulose.

m: animose*.

n: albuminose, diagnose.

p: adipose.

r: aggerose, morose.

t: comatose.

ÔS

Vowel: os.

b: Bos, boss+, emboss+, Setebos.

d: doss.

dr: dross+.

f: fosse+.

fl: floss.

g: Gosse.

gl: gloss+.

j: joss+.

k(c): cos.

kr: across, cross+, double-cross, fiery cross+, lacrosse, recross, rosy cross+, weeping cross+.

l: coloss*, loss+.

m: moss+, sea moss+.

s: applesauce, mornay sauce, sauce.

t: toss+.

tr: albatross+.

OIS

b: Boyce.

ch: choice, pro-choice.

j: Joyce, rejoice.

r: Rolls Royce, Royce.

v: invoice, outvoice, voice.

OOS

p: puss.

O͞OS

Vowel: jus+.

b: abuse, caboose, calaboose, chemical abuse, substance abuse.

br: Bruce.

d: adduce, conduce, deduce, deuce, douce, educe, induce, introduce, produce, reduce, reproduce, seduce, superinduce, traduce.

f: diffuse, profuse.

g: goose.

h: Van Hoose.

j: juice.

k(c): Syracuse.

kl: occluse, recluse.

kr: cruse.

l: flower-de-luce, loose, luce, Toulouse, transluce*, unloose.

m: charmeuse, moose, mousse, vamoose.

n: burnoose, hypotenuse, noose, nous+.

p: pappoose, puce.

r: charlotte russe, Roos.

sk(sc): excuse.

sl: sluice, unsluice.

spr: spruce.

str: abstruse.

t: obtuse, pertuse, retuse.

tr: abstruse, truce.

y: disuse, misuse, use.

z: Zeus.

OUS

bl: blouse.

ch: chouse.

d: douse.

gr: grouse.

h: acid house, backhouse, birdhouse, boathouse, bughouse, cat house, chapter house, charnel house, charterhouse, clubhouse, custom house, doghouse, frat house, hothouse, house, madhouse, outhouse, penthouse, pleasure house, poorhouse, prison house, public house, roundhouse, shorehouse, slaughterhouse, sporting house, storehouse, warehouse, workhouse.

kr: Kraus.

l: louse, wood louse.

m: Fliedermaus, flindermouse, flittermouse, Mickey Mouse, mouse.

n: Gnauss, nous+.

r: Rouse.

s: souse.

ŌSH

f: Foch.

g: gauche.

l: guiloche.

ÔSH

b: bosch+.

g: gosh+.

kw(qu): musquash+, quash+.

skw(squ): squash+.

sw: swash+.

w: wash+.

OOSH

b: bramblebush, bush.

p: push.

sq: squoosh.

ŌŌSH

b: bonne bouche, bouche, debouch.

d: douche.

j: "Joosh."

k: Hindu Kush.

l: louche.

m: gobemouche, mouche, Scaramouch.

r: barouche, ruche.

t: cartouche.

ÔSHT

b: caboshed+.

w: "great unwashed," unwashed+.
    Plus osh+d.

ÔSP

w: wasp+.

ŌST

Vowel: oast.

b: boast.

d: dosed.

g: ghost.

gr: engrossed.

h: host.

k(c): coast, seacost.

m: aftermost, bettermost, bottommost, foremost, furthermost, hindermost, hithermost, innermost, lowermost, most, nethermost, northernmost, outermost, southermost, undermost, uppermost, uttermost, westermost.

p: fingerpost, hitchingpost, post, reposte, signpost, soundpost, whipping post.

r: roast.

t: toast.

v: Van Vost.

y: Yost.

Plus os+d.

ÔST

b: cabossed, embossed+.

d: adossed.

fr: frost+, hoarfrost.

h: exhaust.

k(c): accost+, cost+, holocaust, Lacoste+, Pentecost+.

kr: double-crossed, uncrossed.

l: lost+, unlost+.

m: enmossed.

n: geognost.

t: betossed+, sea-tossed+, tempest-tossed+.

Plus os+d.

OIST

f: foist.

h: hoist.

j: joist, unrejoiced.

m: moist.

v: loud-voiced, shrill-voiced, unvoiced.

Plus ois+d.

ŌŌST

b: boost.

br: browst.

d: adduced, deduced, introduced, produced, reduced, reproduced, unproduced, unreproduced.

j: joost.

l: loosed, unloosed.

m: vamoosed.

r: roost, roust.

spr: spruced.

Plus us+d.

Plus juice'd, etc.

OUST

Vowel: oust.

br: browst.

h: unhoused.

r: roust.

Plus ous+d.

ŌT

Vowel: oat.

b: boat, lifeboat, pilot boat, riverboat, sea boat, steam boat.

bl: bloat.

ch: Choate.

d: anecdote, antidote, bedote*, dote, table d'hote.

f: telephote.

fl: afloat, float.

g: billy goat, goat, nanny goat, redingote.

gl: gloat.

gr: groat.

h: haute.

k(c): coat, cote, overcoate, petticoat.

kw(qu): bequote, misquote, quote, requote, unquote.

l: lote*.

m: commote, demote, emote, folk mote, moat, mote, promote, remote, Witenagemot.

n: connote, denote, footnote, note, one-note.

p: capote.

r: garrote, rewrote, rote, underwrote, wrote.

s: creosote.

sh: shoat, shote.

sk(sc): scote.

sl: slote.

sm: smote, unsmote.

st: stoat.

t: asymptote, tote.

thr: throat, sore throat, strep throat.

tr: troat.

v: devote, outvote, redevote, vote.

ÔT

Vowel: aught, ought.

b: bought, dear-bought, rebought, unbought.

br: brought, upbrought.

f: fought, hard-fought, unfought.

fr: fraught, unfraught.

g: ghat+.

k(c): caught, recaught, uncaught, upcaught.

m: maut.

n: aeronaut+, argonaut+, dreadnought, Juggernaut, naught, nought.

r: bewrought*, inwrought, overwrought, rewrought, unwrought, upwrought, wrought.

s: besought, sought, unbesought, unsought.

sl: onslaught.

str: astraught*, bestraught.

t: retaught, self-taught, taught, taut, untaught.

th: afterthought, bethought, forethought, free thought, merry thought, methought*, rethought, thought, unthought.

tr: distraught.

OIT

d: doit.

dr: adroit, droit, maladroit.

k(c): dacoit.

kw(qu): quoit.

pl: exploit.

tr: Detroit.

v: Voight.

OOT

f: afoot, foot, forefoot, pussyfoot, underfoot.

p: put.

O͞OT

b: attribute, beaut, boot, Butte, marabout, unboot.

br: bruit, brute, imbrute.

f: confute, refute.

fl: flute.

fr: first fruit, forbidden fruit, fruit, gallows fruit.

g: argute.

h: cahoot, hoot.

j: jute.

k(c): acute, baldicoot, coot, cute, electrocute, execute, persecute, prosecute, subacute.

kr: en croute, recruit.

l: absolute, dilute, dissolute, galoot, involute, irresolute, loot, lute, pollute, revolute, salute, solute, volute.

m: commute, deafmute, emeute*, immute*, meute, moot, mute, permute, transmute.

n: comminute, cornute, minute+, newt.

p: compute, depute, dispute, disrepute, impute, Rajput, repute, suppute.

r: arrowroot, cheroot, enroot, en route, root, rute, unroot.

s: birthday suite, hirsute, pursuit, soot, suit, versute*.

sh: bumbershoot, chute, outshoot, overshoot, Shute, upshoot.

sk(sc): scoot, scute.

sn: snoot.

t: astute, constitute, destitute, institute, prostitute, substitute, toot.

y: Piute, Ute.

OUT

Vowel: all-out, churn out, diner-out, foul out, hereout*, holing-out, knockout, lookout, out, out-and-out, pig out, spaced-out, strung out, thereout, throughout, whereout, without.

b: about, bout, drinking bout, gadabout, hereabout, knockabout, rightabout, roundabout, roustabout, stirabout, thereabout, whereabout.

d: doubt, redoubt.

dr: drought.

fl: flout.

g: gout.

gr: grout.

h: mahout.

kl: clout.

kr: kraut, sauerkraut.

l: lout.

n: knout.

p: pout.

r: rout.

sh: beshout, shout.

sk(sc): boyscout, girlscout, scout.

sn: snout.

sp: bespout, spout, waterspout.

spr: sprout.

st: stout, stylish stout.

t: tout.

tr: trout.

v: devout.

ŌTH

Vowel: oath.

b: both.

gr: aftergrowth, growth, overgrowth, regrowth, undergrowth.

kl: clothe, reclothe, unclothe.

kw(qu): quoth*.

l: loath, loathe.

m: behemoth+.

sl: sloth+.

th: Thoth.

tr: betroth+, troth+.

ÔTH

br: barley broth, broth.

fr: froth.

g: Goth, Ostrogoth, Visigoth.

k(c): Coth.

kl: broadcloth, cloth, pilot cloth, saddle cloth.

m: behemoth+, moth.

r: Ashtaroth, wroth.

sl: sloth+.

sw: swath.

th: Thoth+.

tr: troth+.

O͞OTH

b: booth, polling booth, voting booth.

k(c): couth, uncouth.

l: Duluth.

r: ruth.

s: forsooth, insooth*, sooth, soothe.

sl: sleuth.

sm: besmooth, smooth.

t: tooth, untooth.

tr: truth, untruth.

y: youth.

O͞OTHD

s: unsoothed.
　Plus uth+d.
　Plus booth'd, etc.

OUTH

dr: drouth
m: bemouth, mouth, mouthe.
s: south.
　Plus allow'th*, etc.

ŌTS

Vowel: Oates.
k(c): Coates.
　Plus ot+s.
　Plus float's, etc.

ÔTS

p: Potts.
　Plus ot+s.
　Plus cot's, etc.

O͞OTS

h: cohoots.
　Plus ut+s.
　Plus suit's, etc.

OUTS

Vowel: outs.
b: hereabouts, thereabouts, whereabouts.
　Plus out+s.
　Plus snout's, etc.

OUZ

b: bouse.
bl: blouse.
br: browse.
dr: drowse.

h: house, rehouse, unhouse.
p: espouse.
r: arouse, carouse, rouse, uprouse.
s: souse.
sp: spouse.
t: touse.
　Plus ou+s.
　Plus vow's, etc.

ŌV

dr: drove.
gr: grove.
h: hove.
j: Jove.
k(c): cove.
kl: clove.
m: mauve.
r: rove.
shr: shrove.
st: stove.
str: strove.
thr: throve.
tr: treasure trove.
w: interwove, inwove, wove.

O͞OV

gr: groove, ingroove.
h: behoove.
hw: who've.
m: amove, move, remove.
pr: approve, disapprove, disprove, improve, prove, reprove.
y: you've.

O͞OVD

m: moved, removed, unmoved, unremoved.
pr: approved, improved, proved, reproved, unapproved, unimproved, unproved, unreproved.

Plus uv+d.

Plus groove'd, etc.

ŌZ

b: Dubose.

br: brose.

ch: chose.

d: doze.

fr: froze, refroze, unfroze.

gl: gloze.

h: half-hose, hose.

kl: close, clothes, disclose, enclose, foreclose, inclose, interclose, reclose, unclose.

m: Mose.

n: nose.

p: compose, decompose, depose, discompose, dispose, expose, impose, indispose, interpose, oppose, pose, predispose, presuppose, propose, recompose, repose, superpose, suppose, transpose.

pr: prose.

r: arose, bramble rose, couleur derose, damask rose, moss rose, rose, tube rose.

TH: those.

Plus o+s.

Plus blow's, etc.

ÔZ

d: Dawes.

g: gauze.

h: Hawes, hawse.

l: lantern jaws.

k(c): because, cause.

kl: clause, Santa Klaus.

p: menopause, pause.

pl: applause.

t: taws.

y: yaws.

Plus o+s.

Plus jaw's, etc.

OIZ

fr: froise.

n: erminois, noise, Noyes.

p: avoirdupois, counterpoise, equipoise, poise.

Plus oi+s.

Plus boy's, etc.

OŌZ

Vowel: ooze.

b: abuse, booze, disabuse.

bl: blues, the blues.

br: bruise.

ch: choose.

f: circumfuse, confuse, diffuse, effuse, fuse, infuse, interfuse, percussion fuse, perfuse, refuse, suffuse, superinfuse, tranfuse.

g: Betelgeuse, guze.

h: Hewes, Hughes.

hw: who's, whose.

k(c): accuse, incuse.

kr: crews, cruise, cruse, Santa Cruz, Vera Cruz.

l: lose.

m: amuse, bemuse, mews, muse.

n: news, noose.

r: peruse, ruse.

s: sues.

sh: shoes.

sk(sc): excuse.

sn: snooze.

t: contuse.

th: enthuse, thuse.

tr: trews, trues.

w: was+.

y: disuse, misuse, use, "youse."

  Plus u+s.

  Plus blue's, etc.

ŌZD

d: dozed.

p: ill-disposed, indisposed, juxtaposed, predisposed, unopposed, well-disposed.

  Plus oz+d.

  Plus rose'd, etc.

ŌZH

l: eloge, loge.

O͞OZD

b: abused, disabused.

f: fused, transfused.

k(c): accused, self-accused.

y: ill-used, used.

  Plus uz+d.

  Plus bruise'd, etc.

O͞OZH

br: Bruges.

n: baba gannouj.

r: rouge.

U

u: as in cup; also in won, done, does, flood, trouble.

u: as in turn; also in fern, err, heard, sir, word, hournal, myrrh, colonel.

For the vowel sound in full, see *oo*.

For the vowel sound in muse; also in beauty, feud, crew, see $\overline{oo}$.

UB

b: Beelzebub, bub, hubbub, sillabub.

bl: blub.

ch: chub, Chubb.

d: dub, overdub, rub-a-dub.

dr: drub.

f: fub.

fl: flub.

gr: grub.

h: hub.

k(c): cub.

kl: battle club, club, Clubb.

n: nub.

p: pub.

r: rub.

s: sub.

shr: shrub.

skr(scr): scrub.

sl: slub.

sn: snub.

st: stub.

t: hot tub, tub.

UCH

d: double dutch, Dutch.

h: hutch.

k(c): cutch.

kl: clutch.

kr: crutch.

m: forasmuch, inasmuch, insomuch, much, mutch, overmuch.

s: such.

sk(sc): scutch.

sm: smutch.

t: master touch, retouch, touch.

UCHD

kl: clutched.

t: untouched.

Plus uch+d.

Plus Dutch'd, etc.

UD

b: bud, Budd.

bl: blood, lifeblood, 'sblood*.

d: dud.

f: fud.

fl: flood.

h: HUD.

j: Judd.

k(c): cud.

l: lud.

m: mud.

r: rud.

s: sud.

sk(sc): scud.

sp: spud.

st: bestud, stud.

th: thud.

UDZ

b: buds.
d: duds.
s: suds.
Plus ud+s.
Plus mud's, etc.

UF

b: blindman's-buff, buff, counterbuff, rebuff.
bl: bluff, Council Bluff.
ch: chough, chuff.
d: duff, Macduff, plum duff.
fl: Fluff.
g: guff.
h: Hough, huff.
k(c): cuff, off-the-cuff, on the cuff.
kl: clough.
l: luff.
m: muff.
n: enough.
p: bepuff, powder puff, puff.
r: rough, ruff.
s: sough.
sk(sc): scuff.
skr(scr): scruff.
sl: slough.
sn: besnuff, snuff.
st: breadstuff, garden stuff, stuff.
t: tough, tuff.

UFS

k(c): fisticuffs.
p: bepuffs.
Plus uf+s.
Plus snuff's, etc.

UFT

b: bepuffed.
sc: scuft.
t: candytuft, tuft.

Plus uf+d.
Plus ruff'd, etc.

UG

b: bug, doodlebug, litterbug.
ch: chug.
d: dug.
dr: drug.
f: fug.
gl: glug.
h: bunny hug, hug.
j: jug.
l: lug.
m: mug.
p: pug.
pl: plug.
r: rag rug, rug.
shr: shrug.
sl: slug.
sm: smug.
sn: snug.
t: tug.
th: thug.
tr: trug.

UGZ

b: go bugs.
dr: drugs.
Plus ug+s.
Plus bug's, etc.

UJ

b: budge.
dr: drudge.
f: fudge.
gr: begrudge, grudge.
kl: kludge.
j: adjudge, forjudge, judge, misjudge, prejudge, rejudge.
n: nudge.
r: Rudge.
sl: sludge.

sm: smudge.
tr: trudge.

UJD

j: adjudged, ill-judged, unjudged.
Plus uj+d.

UK

b: buck, fast buck, megabuck, roebuck, sawbuck, waterbuck.
ch: chuck, woodchuck.
d: beduck, Donald Duck, duck, lame duck, Peking duck, pressed duck, ring-necked duck.
g: guck.
h: huck.
kl: cluck, dumb cluck.
l: chuck-a-luck, ill-luck, Lady Luck, luck, misluck, potluck.
m: amuck, high muck-a-muck, Kalmuck, muck.
n: Canuck.
p: puck.
pl: pluck.
r: laverock, ruck, rukh.
s: suck.
sh: shuck.
st: stuck.
str: awe-struck, dumbstruck, horror-struck, moonstruck, stagestuck, struck, sunstruck, terror-struck, thunderstruck, wonderstruck.
t: nip and tuck, tuck.
tr: truck.
y: yuck.

UKS

b: big bucks.
d: dux.
fl: flux.
kr: crux.
l: lux.

sh: ah shucks, shucks.
t: tux.
Plus uk+s.
Plus luck's, etc.

UKT

d: abduct, aqueduct, beducked, conduct, deduct, duct, educt, eruct, induct, misconduct, oviduct, product*, reduct*, subduct, viaduct.
fr: usufruct.
l: reluct.
pl: good-plucked, plucked, unplucked.
r: eruct.
str: construct, instruct, misconstruct, obstruct, substruct, superstruct.
Plus uk+d.
Plus luck'd, etc.

UL

d: dull.
g: gull, mogul, seagull.
h: ahull, hull.
k(c): barnacle, canticle, chronicle, coracle, cull, miracle, monocle, obstacle, oracle, pinnacle, spectacle, vehicle, versicle.
l: lull.
m: mull.
n: annul, disannul, null.
sk(sc): numskull, scull, skull.
st: stull.
tr: trull.

ULB

b: bulb.

ULCH

g: gulch.
m: mulch.

ULD

m: mulled.
n: annulled.
sk(sc): thick-skulled.
   Plus ul+d.
   Plus lull'd, etc.

ULF

g: engulf, gulf.

ULJ

b: bulge
d: indulge, overindulge.
f: effulge.
m: promulge.
v: divulge.

ULK

b: bulk.
h: hulk.
s: sulk.
sk(sc): skulk.

ULKT

b: bulked.
h: hulked.
m: mulct.
   Plus ulk+d.
   Plus bulk'd, etc.

ULM

k(c): culm.

ULP

g: gulp.
p: pulp.
sk(sc): sculp.

ULS

b: bulse.
d: dulse.

m: mulse.
p: appulse, expulse, impulse, pulse, repulse.
v: convulse.
   Cf. ult+s.

ULT

d: adult, undult.
k(c): cult, difficult, incult, occult.
p: catapult.
s: consult, insult.
z: exult, result.

UM

b: bum.
ch: chum.
dr: drum, hum-drum, kettledrum.
f: fa fe fi fo fum, fe fi fo fum.
g: gum.
gl: glum.
gr: grum.
h: hum.
k(c): become, come, misbecome, overcome, recumb*, succumb.
kl: "clumb."
kr: crum, crumb.
l: curriculum, Lum, pabulum, pendulum, pour l'homme, speculum.
m: mum.
n: benumb, laudanum, numb, platinum, tympanum.
pl: aplomb+, plum, plumb, sugar plum, unplumb.
r: rhumb, rum.
s: some+, sum.
sk(sc): scum.
skr(scr): scrum.
sl: slum.
st: stum.
str: strum.
sw: swum.
t: ad libitum, adytum, tum, tum-tum.

th: thumb.
thr: thrum.
y: yum.

UMD

b: bummed.
g: begummed.
pl: unplumbed.
th: bethumbed.
  Plus um+d.
  Plus some'd, etc.

UMP

Vowel: ump.
b: bump.
ch: chump.
d: dump.
fr: frump.
g: Andy Gump.
gr: grump.
h: hump.
j: jump.
kl: clump.
kr: crump.
l: lump.
m: mump.
p: pump.
pl: plump.
r: rump.
s: sump.
shl: schlump.
sl: slump.
st: stump.
t: tump.
th: bethump, thump.
tr: trump.
w: mugwump.

UMPS

Vowel: umps.
m: mumps
th: bethumps.

Plus ump+s.
Plus chump's, etc.

UN

b: bun, Bunn.
d: done, dun, Dunn, foredone, outdone, overdone, redone, undone.
f: fun.
g: begun, gun, Gunn, minute gun, percussion gun, unbegun.
h: hon, Hun.
k(c): Helicon, pantechnicon.
l: gonfalon, Sally Lunn.
m: cardamon.
n: none, nun, unnun.
p: pun.
r: forerun, hard-run, outrun, overrun, rerun, run, underrun.
s: foster son, garrison, son, stepson, sun, sunn, unison, venison, Whitsun.
sh: shun.
sp: homespun, spun.
st: stun.
t: ton, tun.
w: A1, hard-won, number one, one, one-on-one, won.
z: amazon, benison.
  Cf. Hyperion, etc., under *on*.

UNCH

b: bunch.
br: brunch.
h: hunch.
kl: clunch.
kr: crunch.
l: box lunch, free lunch, lunch.
m: munch.
p: punch.
skr(scr): scrunch.

UND

b: bund, cummerbund, moribund.

d: dunned.

f: fund, refund.

g: unparagoned.

k(c): rubicund, verecund.

m: immund, Rosamond, Rosamund.

p: punned.

s: sunned, unsunned.

sh: shunned.

st: stunned.

t: obrotund, orotund, retund*, rotund.

    Plus un+ed.
    Plus fun'd, etc.

UNG

Vowel: Ung.

b: bung.

br: "brung."

d: dung.

fl: flung.

h: behung*, hung, overhung, underhung, unhung.

kl: clung.

l: brown lung, lung, one lung.

m: among.

p: pung, unrung.

r: rung, unwrung, wither-wrung, wrung.

s: sung.

sl: slung, unslung.

spr: sprung, upsprung.

st: stung.

str: highstrung, strung, unstrung.

sw: swung, unswung.

t: betongue, mother tongue, tongue.

y: young.

UNGD

b: bunged.

l: leather-lunged, loud-lunged.

t: double-tongued, honey-tongued, pleasant-tongued, shrill-tongued, silver-tongued, soft-tongued, tongued, trumpet-tongued.

    Plus ung+ed.
    Plus dung'd, etc.

UNGK

Vowel: unk.

b: bunk, debunk.

ch: chunk.

d: dunk, slam dunk.

dr: drunk.

f: funk.

fl: flunk.

h: hunk.

j: junk.

m: monk.

n: quid nunc.

p: punk.

pl: kerplunk, plunk.

s: sunk.

shr: shrunk.

sk: skunk.

sl: slunk.

sp: spunk.

t: Tunk.

th: thunk.

tr: trunk.

w: "wunk."

UNGKT

b: bunked.

f: defunct, funked.

j: conjunct, disjunct.

p: compunct*.

tr: trunked.

Plus unk+ed.

Plus spunk'd, etc.

UNGST

m: amongst.

Plus ung'st*.

UNJ

bl: blunge.

gr: grunge.

l: allonge*, lunge, muskellunge.

pl: plunge.

sp: dispunge*, expunge, sponge.

UNS

d: dunce.

w: once.

Plus unt+s.

Plus hunt's, etc.

UNT

Vowel: exeunt.

b: Bundt, bunt

bl: Blount, blunt.

br: brunt.

fr: affront, afront, confront, forefront, front, up-front, waterfront.

gr: grunt.

h: hunt, manhunt, witch hunt.

l: Lunt

p: punt.

r: runt.

sh: shunt.

spr: sprunt.

st: stunt.

w: wont.

Plus done't*, etc.

UNTH

m: month.

Plus run'th*, etc.

UP

Vowel: backup, blowing up, blow up, breakup, buildup, buy-up, catchup, checkup, chin-up, cleanup, close-up, cover-up, dial-up, fed up, hang-up, hard-up, holdup, hookup, keyed-up, letup, lineup, linkup, lockup, lookup, makeup, markup, mock-up, paste-up, pickup, pinup, pullup, punch-up, push-up, roundup, send-up, setup, setter-up, slap up, smashup, speed-up, stickup, up, up-and-up, wake-up, warm-up, windup, write-up.

ch: ketchup.

d: dup*.

g: gup.

k(c): buttercup, cup, Dixie Cup, grace cup, grease cup, hiccup, loving cup, stirrup cup, teacup, wassail cup.

kr: crup*, Krupp.

l: Gallup

n: sunup, turnup.

p: pup.

r: larrup.

s: sup.

sk(sc): scup.

t: tup.

w(h): whup.

UPS

See up+s.

Plus cup's, etc.

UPT

k(c): cupped.

r: abrupt, corrupt, disrupt, erupt, incorrupt, interrupt.

s: supped.

t: tupped.

Plus pup'd, etc.

ŬR

Vowel: blearier, borrower, breezier, brinier, burlier, cheerier, chillier, cleanlier, cosier, costlier, creamier, creepier, curlier, dingier, dizzier, doughtier, dowdier, drearier, drowsier, dustier, earlier, easier, eerier, emptier, err, filmier, filthier, fleecier, flightier, flimsier, foamier, friendlier, funnier, fussier, giddier, gloomier, glossier, goutier, grimier, guiltier, happier, healthier, heavier, herb+, hillier, holier, homelier, huffier, hungrier, huskier, icier, inkier, jollier, juicier, kindlier, kinglier, knightlier, likelier, livelier, loftier, lonelier, lovelier, lowlier, merrier, mightier, moldier, mossier, muskier, mustier, narrower, noisier, pearlier, pitier, portlier, princelier, prosier, rosier, rowdier, seemlier, shinier, shoddier, showier, sightlier, sillier, skinnier, sleepier, slimier, soapier, spicier, spikier, spongier, spoonier, springier, spritelier, steadier, stealthier, stingier, stormier, stuffier, sturdier, sunnier, surlier, terrier, thirstier, thriftier, trustier, valuer, wealthier, wearier, wheezier, widower, windier, wintrier.

b: aberr*, birr, BRR, burr, Excalibur.

bl: blur.

br: "brer."

ch: chirr.

f: autobiographer, befur, bibliographer, biographer, chauffeur+, Jennifer, lithographer, lucifer, philosopher, phonographer, photographer, stenographer, topographer, typographer.

fl: fleur, persifleur.

h: Ben Hur, her, herb+.

hw: whirr.

k(c): coeur, concur, cur, incur, Kerr, liqueur+, occur, recur.

kl: chronicler.

l: lur.

m: demur, myrrh.

n: knur.

p: per, purr.

s: chasseur, connoisseur, croque monsieur, friseur, sir.

sh: shirr.

sl: slur.

sp: spur.

st: astir, bestir.

t: amateur+, amphitheater, archiater, banqueter, carpenter, cricketer, deter*, disinter*, distributer, forfeiter, franc-tireur, hauteur*, inter*, litterateur, pleasanter, presbyter, register, restaurateur, rioter, riveter, scimiter, silenter, sophister.

v: aver.

w: were.

z: frisseur.

Cf. ambassador, and other *or* words.

ŬRB

Vowel: urb.

bl: blurb.

k(c): curb.

p: superb.

s: acerb, Serb.

t: disturb, perturb.

v: reverb, verb.

ŬRBD

k(c): curbed, uncurbed.

t: imperturbed, undisturbed, unperturbed.

Plus urb+ed.

Plus Serb'd, etc.

URBZ

b: burbs, suburbs.

URCH

b: birch, weeping birch.

ch: church, unchurch.

l: lurch.

p: perch.

s: research, search.

sm: besmirch, smirch.

URCHT

b: birched, unbirched.

sm: smirched, unsmirched.

Plus urch+ed.

Plus search'd, etc.

URD

b: bird, frigate bird, gallows bird, hedgebird, hummingbird, ladybird, lovebird, mockingbird, nightbird, pilotbird, seabird, snowbird, songbird, stormbird.

f: Ferd.

g: begird, engird, gird, undergird, ungird.

k(c): curd, Kurd, unsepulchred.

n: nerd.

s: absurd, surd.

sh: sherd, shirred.

sn: Mortimer Snerd.

t: deterred, undeterred.

v: Cape Verde, verd.

w: afterword, foreword, word.

Plus ur+ed.

Plus fur'd, etc.

URF

n: Nerf.

s: serf, surf.

sk(sc): scurf.

t: AstroTurf, turf.

URG

Vowel: erg.

b: berg, burg, burgh, Goldberg, Greenberg, Heidelberg, Helderberg, Helleburg, Rosenberg.

s: exergue.

URJ

Vowel: demiurge, urge.

d: dirge.

g: gurge, regurge.

m: emerge, immerge, merge, submerge.

p: purge.

s: serge, surge.

sk(sc): scourge.

sp: spurge.

spl: splurge.

t: deterge, dramaturge, thaumaturge.

v: converge, diverge, verge.

URJD

Vowel: unurged, urged.

sk: scourged, unscourged.

Plus urj+d.

URK

Vowel: irk.

b: Bourke, Burk, Burke.

d: dirk.

f: firk.

j: jerk, jerque, knee-jerk.
kl(cl): clerk, kirk.
kw: quirk.
l: lurk.
m: murk.
p: perk.
r: O'Rourke.
s: cirque.
sh: shirk.
sm: smirk.
st: stirk.
t: Turk.
w: dirty work, fancywork, frostwork, handiwork, masterwork, overwork, underwork, waterwork, wonderwork, work.
y: yerk.

URKT

Vowel: irked.
w: overworked, underworked.
  Plus urk+ed.
  Plus Turke'd, etc.

URKZ

d: Durkes.
y: Yerkes.
  Plus urk+s.
  Plus murk's, etc.

URL

Vowel: earl.
b: burl.
ch: churl.
f: furl, unfurl.
g: charity girl, girl.
h: hurl.

hw: upwhirl, whirl, whorl+.
k: becurl, curl, uncurl, upcurl.
kw: querl.
m: merle.
n: knurl.
p: bepearl, impearl, mother-of-pearl, pearl, pirl, purl, seed pearl.
sk: skirl.
sw: swirl, upswirl.
t: tirl.
th: thurl.
tw: twirl.

URLZ

s: Searles.
  Plus url+s.
  Plus girl's, etc.

URLD

k(c): becurled, curled, uncurled.
p: impearled, pearled.
w: new-world, old-world, Third World, underworld, world.
  Plus url+ed.
  Plus girl'd, etc.

URM

b: berm.
d: derm, pachyderm.
f: affirm, confirm, disaffirm, firm, infirm, reaffirm.
j: germ.
skw: squirm.
sp: sperm.
t: misterm, term.
th: isotherm.
w: grubworm, hookworm, railroad worm, ringworm, tapeworm, worm.

ŪRMZ

See urm+s.
Plus germ's, etc.

ŪRMD

f: affirmed, confirmed, disaffirmed, reaffirmed.
Plus urm+ed.
Plus worm'd, etc.

ŪRN

Vowel: earn, erne, urn.
b: Berne, burn, Byrne, East Berne, O'Byrne, West Berne.
ch: churn.
d: dern, durn.
f: fern.
h: Hearn, Hearne, hern.
j: adjourn, sojourn.
k: kern.
kw: quern.
l: learn, unlearn.
n: inurn.
p: epergne, pirn.
s: concern, discern, lucern, lucerne, secern, unconcern.
sp: spurn.
st: stern.
t: attorn, eterne*, externe, intern, interne, overturn, return, subaltern, taciturn, tern, turn, upturn.
y: yearn.
z: discern.

ŪRND

Vowel: earned, hard-earned, ill-earned, well-earned.
s: concerned, unconcerned.

t: turned, unturned.
z: discerned.
Plus urn+ed.
Plus fern'd, etc.

URNT

Vowel: earnt.
b: burnt, unburnt.
l: learnt, unlearnt.
w: weren't+.

ŪRNT

l: learned, unlearned.

ŪRNZ

b: Burns.
h: Hearn's.
k: Kearns.
Plus urn+s.
Plus fern's, etc.

ŪRP

b: burp.
bl: blurp.
ch: chirp.
s: discerp.
t: extirp*.
tw: twirl.
z: usurp.

ŪRPS

See urp+s.
Plus chirp's, etc.

ŪRPT

ch: chirped.
s: excerpt.

z: usurped.

    Plus urp+ed.

    Plus twirp'd, etc.

ᴜRS

Vowel: coerce, Erse.

b: birse, burse, disburse, imburse, reimburse.

h: hearse, herse, inhearse, rehearse.

k(c): accurse, bicurse, curse, excurse, precurse.

m: amerce, immerse, submerse.

n: foster nurse, nurse, wet nurse.

p: asperse, cutpurse, disperse, purse.

sp: intersperse.

t: sesterce, terce, terse.

v: adverse, averse, converse, diverse, inverse, perverse, reverse, subverse, transverse, traverse, universe, verse.

w: worse.

ᴜRST

Vowel: erst*.

b: burst, outburst, starburst, sunburst.

d: durst.

f: double first, first.

h: hearsed, Hearst, Hurst.

k(c): accursed, accurst, becurst, curst, uncursed.

th: athirst, thirst.

v: unversed, versed, verst.

w: blutwurst, bratwurst, knackwurst, liverwurst, wienerwurst, worst, wurst.

    Plus urs+d.

    Plus curse'd, etc.

ᴜRT

Vowel: inert.

b: Adelbert, Bert, Englebert, Ethelbert.

bl: blurt.

ch: chert.

d: dirt.

fl: flirt.

g: begirt, engirt, girt, gurt, seagirt, ungirt.

h: hurt, unhurt.

k(c): curt, Kurt.

kw: quirt.

l: alert.

p: alapert, expert+, inexpert, pert.

s: assert, cert, concert, disconcert, exsert, insert, intersert, preconcert, syrt.

sh: shirt.

sk: skirt.

skw: squirt.

sp: spirt, spurt.

t: intervert, introvert, invert, obvert.

v: advert, animadvert, avert, controvert, convert, divert, evert, extrovert, invert, pervert, retrovert, revert, subvert, transvert, vert.

w: liverwort, lousewort, motherwort, throughwort, wert*, Wirt, wort.

z: desert, dessert, exert, indesert.

ᴜRTH

Vowel: earth, fuller's earth, inearth, nightearth, unearth.

b: berth, birth, stillbirth.

d: dearth.

f: firth.

g: girth, Gurth.

m: mirth.

p: Perth.

w: net worth, pennyworth, self-worth, unworth, worth.

    Plus furr'th*, etc.

ŪRTZ

n: "nerts."

w: Wurtz.

    Plus urt+s.

    Plus hurt's, etc.

ŪRV

Vowel: Irv.

d: hors d'oeuvre.

h: Herve.

k(c): bell-shaped curve, curve, French curve, incurve, outcurve.

n: nerve, unnerve.

s: conserve, disserve, serve, self-serve, subserve.

sw: swerve.

v: verve.

z: deserve, observe, preserve, reserve.

ŪRVD

z: ill-deserved, undeserved, well-preserved.

    Plus urv+d.

    Plus curve'd, etc.

ŪRVZ

t: turves.

    Plus urv+s.

    Plus curve's, etc.

ŪRZ

f: furze.

    Plus ur+s.

    Plus fir's, etc.

US

b: bus, buss, omnibus+.

f: fuss.

h: Huss.

j: jus+.

k(c): cuss, discuss, excuss, incuss*, percuss.

m: muss.

p: puss*.

r: rhus, Russ.

st: stuss.

TH: thus.

tr: truss, untruss.

USH

bl: blush, outblush, unblush.

br: brush, clothesbrush, underbrush.

fl: flush, outflush, unflush.

g: gush, Lady Gush.

h: hush.

kr: crush.

l: lush.

m: mush.

pl: plush.

r: outrush, rush, uprush.

sl: slush.

t: tush.

thr: hermit thrush, missal thrush, thrush.

USK

b: busk.
br: brusque.
d: adusk, dusk.
f: fusc, subfusk.
h: dehusk, husk.
l: Lusk.
m: musk.
r: rusk.
t: tusk.

USP

k(c): cusp.

UST

b: bust, combust, robust.
d: adust, bedust, dost*, dust, stardust.
f: fussed, fust.
g: angust*, august, disgust, gust.
j: adjust, coadjust, just, unjust.
k(c): discussed.
kr: crust, encrust.
l: lust.
m: must.
pl: nonplussed.
r: rust
tr: betrust, distrust, entrust, mistrust, self-distrust, trust, untrust.
thr: thrust.
  Plus us+ed.
  Plus fuss'd, etc.

UT

b: abut, but, butt, halibut, rebut, scuttle butt, surrebut, water butt.
g: catgut, gut.

gl: glut.
h: hut.
j: jut.
k(c): clear-cut, cut, uncut, woodcut.
kr: crut.
m: Mutt.
n: beech nut, betelnut, Brazilnut, cashew nut, chestnut+, coconut, hazelnut, hickory nut, McNutt, nut, peanut+, walnut+.
p: Lilliput, occiput, putt.
r: rut.
sh: outshut, shut.
sk(sc): scut.
sl: slut.
sm: besmut, smut.
str: astrut, strut.
t: tut, Tutt.
  Cf. so what.

UTH

d: doth*.

UTS

b: butts; ifs, ands, or buts.
f: futz.
kl: klutz.
p: putz.
sm: smuts.
st: Stutz.
  Plus ut+s.
  Plus cut's, etc.

UV

Vowel: hereof, of, thereof, whereof.
b: above, 'bove.
d: dove, mourning dove, turtle dove.

gl: foxglove, glove, unglove.

l: belove*, ladylove, light-o-love, love, self-love, true-love.

sh: shove.

UVD

l: beloved, loved, unbeloved, unloved.

> Plus uv+d.
> Plus dove'd, etc.

UX

br: brux.

UZ

Vowel: Uz.

b: abuzz, buzz.

d: does, doz.

f: fuzz.

k(c): coz.

l: Luz.

ə

ə: This symbol represents the indistinct, neutral vowel sound as in the sound of a in ago, e in over, i in sanity, o in medallion, u in fanciful.

ə

Vowel: Mafia, medallion.
br: vertebrae.
m: MOMA.
r: diaspora.
t: NAFTA.

əD

h: had+.

əL

Vowel: accentual, aerial, allodial, alluvial, amatorial, annual, antediluvial, arboreal, baronial, boreal, casual, colloquial, connubial, consanguineal, consistorial, continual, conventual, dictatorial, diluvial, effectual, empyreal, ethereal, eventual, expurgatorial, funereal, genial, gradual, habitual, hymeneal, immaterial, immemorial, imperial, incorporeal, individual, industrial, ineffectual, infusorial, initial, inquisitorial, intellectual, jovial, memorial, mercurial, ministerial, mutual, nectareal, patrimonial, pedestrial, perennial, perpetual, phantasmagorial, pictorial, postprandial, primordial, professorial, proverbial, punctual, purpureal, quadrennial, remedial, residual, ritual, sartorial, seigneurial, sidereal, terrestrial, territorial, testimonial, trivial, usual, uxorial, ventriloquial, vicarial, victorial, visual, virtual, vitriol.

b: acceptable, accessible, accountable, admissable, adorable, affable, amenable, amiable, attainable, audible, available, avoidable, believable, capable, changeable, combustible, commendable, compatible, comprehensible, constable, contemptible, corruptible, credible, crucible, culpable, curable, damnable, delectable, deplorable, desirable, detestable, flexible, forcible, horrible, illegible, immovable, immutable, impalpable, impassable, impeccable, imperturbable, implacable, impossible, impregnable, improbable, improvable, inaccessible, inadmissible, inaudible, incapable, incomparable, incompatible, incomprehensible, inconceivable, incontestable, incontrovertible, incorruptible, incredible, incurable, indelible, indescribable, indestructible, indispensable, ineffable, ineffaceable, inexcusable, inexhaustible, inexpressible, infallible, inflammable, inflexible, infrangible, inscrutable, insensible, insoluble, insupportable, insupposable, insuppressible, insurmountable, intangible, intelligible, interchangeable, intractible, invaluable, invicible, irascible, irrespressible,

irreproachable, irresistible,
irresponsible, irretrievable,
justifiable, laudable, legible,
Mehitable, mutable, notable,
ostensible, palpable, passable,
perceptible, permissible, placable,
plausible, portable, possible,
praisable, presentable, probable,
procurable, producible, pro-
nounceable, ratable, redeemable,
reliable, reprehensible, respectable, responsible, sensible,
susceptible, syllable, tangible,
tenable, terrible, tractable,
unimpeachable, unmatchable,
unquenchable, visible, voluble.

b: cannibal, herbal.

br: vertebral.

d: antipodal, iridal, pyramidal,
quadrupedal.

f: apocryphal, beautiful,
bountiful, dutiful, fanciful,
masterful, merciful, pitiful,
plentiful, powerful, sorrowful,
thimbleful, unmerciful, weariful,
wonderful, worshipful.

g: conjugal, madrigal, Portugal,
Senegal.

k(c): academical, aesthetical,
alchemical, alexipharmical,
alexiterical, algebraical,
alkalimetrical, allegorical,
alphabetical, amchemistical,
analogical, analytical, anarchical,
anatomical, angelical,
anthological, antithetical,
apologetical, apostolical,
archaeological, arithmetical,
arsenical, ascetical, asthmatical,
astrological, atmospherical,
Babylonical, bacchical, bacterio-
logical, balsamical, barometrical,
basilical, beatifical, biblical,
bibliographical, bibliomaniacal,
bibliophilical, biographical,
biological, botanical, Brahminical,
bureaucratical, cacophonical,
Calvinistical, canonical, caracal,

cartographical, casuistical,
categorical, catholical, cervical,
characteristical, chemical,
cherubical, chimerical, chronological, classical, clerical,
climactical, climatical, clinical,
comical, conical, conventical,
cortical, cosmetical, cosmical,
coxcombical, critical, cryptical,
cubical, cyclical, cylindrical,
cynical, deistical, democratical,
demoniacal, demonological,
diabolical, diacritical,
diagraphical, dialectical,
dialogical, dialogistical, diametrical, diaphonical, didactical,
dietetical, diplomatical, dipsoma-
niacal, dogmatical, dolorifical,
dominical, dramatical, dropsical,
Druidical, dynamical, eccentrical,
ecclesiastical, economical,
ecstatical, ecumenical, egoistical,
egotistical, electrical, elegiacal,
elliptical, emblematical,
emphatical, empirical,
encomiastical, encyclical,
encyclopedical, endemical,
energetical, enigmatical,
enthusiastical, epical, epidemical,
epigrammatical, episodical,
epithetical, equivocal, erotical,
esoterical, ethical, ethnical,
ethnological, etymological,
Eucharistical, eulogistical,
euphemistical, euphonical,
evangelical, exegetical, exoterical,
exotical, extrinsical, fanatical,
fantastical, farcical, finical,
forensical, galvanical, genealogical,
generical, geographical, geological, geometrical, grammatical,
graphical, harmonical, Hebraical,
heliacal, hemispherical, heretical,
heroical, hierarchical, historical,
hygienical, hyperbolical,
hypercritical, hypochondriacal,
hypocritical, hysterical, identical,
idiotical, illogical, immechanical,
inimical, ironical, jesuitical,
juridical, lackadaisical, laical,

lethargical, Levitical, liturgical, logical, lyrical, magical, magnifical, majestical, maniacal, mathematical, mechanical, medical, metaphorical, metaphysical, methodical, Methodistical, metrical, microscopical, misanthropical, monarchical, musical, mystical, mythical, mythological, nautical, nonsensical, numerical, optical, oratorical, paradisaical, parabolical, parenthetical, pathetical, pathological, patronymical, pedagogical, pedantical, penological, periodical, periphrastical, phantasmagorical, Pharisaical, pharmaceutical, philanthropical, philological, philosophical, photographical, phrenological, phthisical, physical, physiological, pietistical, piratical, platonical, pneumatological, poetical, polemical, political, pontifical, practical, pragmatical, problematical, prophetical, psychiatrical, psychical, psychological, puritanical, pyramidical, pyrotechnical, quizzical, radical, reciprocal, rhapsodical, rhetorical, rheumatical, rhythmical, sabbatical, satanical, satirical, scenical, sceptical, schismatical, scholastical, seraphical, sociological, Socratical, sophistical, spasmodical, spherical, sporadical, stoical, strategical, sybaritical, symbolical, symmetrical, synchronical, synodical, synonymical, synoptical, synthetical, systematical, tactical, technical, technicological, theatrical, theological, theoretical, theosophical, topical, topographical, tragical, tropical, typical, typographical, tyrannical, umbilical, uncanonical, vatical, vertical, vortical, whimsical, zodiacal, zoological.

m: animal, decimal, infinitesimal, lachrymal, mall, quadrigesimal, synonymal.

n: aboriginal, affectional, antiphonal, arsenal, bacchanal, banal, canal, cardinal, circumlocutional, communal, complexional, conclusional, conditional, confessional, congressional, constitutional, contradictional, conventional, conversational, criminal, decanal, denominational, descensional, destinal, devotional, diaconal, diagonal, digressional, discretional, divisional, doctrinal, educational, emotional, evolutional, exceptional, fictional, fractional, functional, geminal, germinal, heptagonal, hexagonal, imaginal, imitational, impersonal, inspirational, institutional, instructional, insurrectional, intentional, intercessional, interjectional, international, longitudinal, marginal, matinal, matronal, medicinal, meridional, national, nominal, notional, occasional, octagonal, optional, original, passional, patronal, pentagonal, personal, phenomenal, precautional, probational, processional, professional, progressional, proportional, provisional, rational, recessional, retinal, sensational, synchronal, terminal, traditional, urinal, viminal, virginal, visional, volitional.

p: Episcopal, municipal, principal, principle.

r: admiral, agricultural, arboricultural, architectural, chaparral, collateral, conjectural, corporal, ephemeral, extemporal, falderal, federal, funeral, general, horticultural, inaugural, liberal, literal, littoral, mineral, natural,

pastoral, peripheral, pictural,
preternatural, quadrilateral,
scriptural, sculptural, several,
sideral, supernatural, temporal,
vesperal.

s: sal.

sh: marechal, seneschal, shall.

t: capital, capitol, digital, hospital,
marital, pedestal, pivotal, vegetal.

v: carnival, festival, interval, Val.

ƏLD

r: emerald.

ƏLT

sh: shalt*+.

ƏM

Vowel: aquarium, auditorium,
axiom, compendium, cranium,
crematorium, delirium, emporium, encomium, epithalamium,
equilibrium, exordium, geranium,
gymnasium, medium, millenium,
moratorium, natatorium, odium,
opium, opprobrium, palladium,
pandemonium, pelargonium,
pericardium, petroleum,
premium, radium, residuum,
sanitorium, sensorium, sympo-
sium, tedium, vacuum+.

d: Bumbledom, Cockneydom,
dumb, flunkeydom,
heatherendom, martyrdom,
prud'homme, rascaldom,
Saxondom, Tweedledum.

fr: from+, therefrom+.

gr: pogrom+.

k(c): modicum, viaticum.

m: cardamom, chrysanthemum,
demi*, maximum, minimum.

r: marjoram.

s: adventuresome, burdensome,
cumbersome, drearisome,
frolicsome, humorsome,

intermeddlesome, meddlesome,
mettlesome, quarrelsome,
quietsome, some+, troublesome,
venturesome, wearisome,
worrisome, wranglesome.

ƏN

Vowel: Acadian, accordion,
Alabamian, alabastrian, Albion,
Alexandrian, Algerian, amatorian,
amazonian, amphibian, an+,
antediluvian, Arcadian, Austrian,
Baconian, Barbadian, barbarian,
Batavian, Bavarian, Bezonian,
Bohemian, Briarean, Bulgarian,
Caducean, Caledonian, Cambrian,
Canadian, Cimmerian, Columbian,
comedian, Corinthian, custodian,
Cyprian, Delphian, diluvian,
enchiridion, Endymion, equestrian, Ethiopian, galleon, ganglion,
gargantuan, halcyon, Hesperian,
historian, Hyperion, Indian,
latitudinarian, librarian, Marianne,
meridian, Mexican, nectarean,
oblivion, octogenarian, Olympian,
pedestrian, Peruvian,
platitudinarian, postmeridian,
praetorian, predestinarian,
Presbyterian, pretorian,
procrustean, proletarian,
Promethean, quaternion,
quotidian, Sabbatarian,
Sacramentarian, Stygian,
subterranean, Thespian, tragedian,
utilitarian, Utopian, valerian,
valetudinarian, Valkyrian,
vegetarian, Vesuvian, veterinarian,
vulgarian, Zoroastrian.

d: harridan, Mohammodan,
myrmidon, oppidan.

f: colophon.

g: arrogant, elegant, extravagant,
Gant, litigant, Michigan,
paragon+, suffragan, suffragant,
termagant.

hw: when+.

k(c): African, American, Anglican, barbican, barracan, basilican, can, Copernican, Dominican, Gallican, Helicon+, irenicon+, khan, lexicon+, pantechnicon, pecan, pelican, pemmican, publican, republican, silicon+, stereopticon+, Vatican.

l: Babylon+, encephalon+, gonfalon+.

m: adamant, alderman, cinnamon, clergyman, Cornishman, countryman, Englishman, fireman, fisherman, foremastman, fugleman, gentleman, husbandman, Isle of Man, journeyman, juryman, lighterman, liveryman, man, medicine man, merchantman, merman, midshipman, minuteman, Mussulman, nobleman, ottoman, overman, quarryman, waterman.

n: Parthenon+, phenomenon+, prolegomenon+, put upon+, sine qua non+, upon+.

r: Oberon+, saccharine+.

s: benison, caparison, comparison, jettison, orison, Saracen, unison, venison, Whitsun.

sw: swan+.

t: automation+, charlatan, Chesterton, cosmopolitan, Galveston, metropolitan, Middleton, Neapolitan, puritan, rattan, sacristan, Samaritan, simpleton, singleton, skeleton.

w: Saskatchewan+,

z: amazon+, artisan, bartizan+, courtesan+.

ƏND

g: legend, urban legend.

ƏNK

bl: Blanc.

ƏNS

Vowel: continuance, luxuriance, radiance, suppliance, variance.

g: arrogance, elegance, extravagance.

k(c): insignificance, significance.

l: ambulance+, flagellance, flatulence, jubilance, petulance+, sibilance+, vigilance+.

n: appurtenance, consonance, countenance, discountenance, dissonance, dominance, finance, inconsonance, ordinance, predominance, resonance.

r: deliverance, exuberance, furtherance, ignorance, intemperance, intolerance, preponderance, protuberance, sufferance, tolerance, utterance.

s: complaisance, conversance, impuissance, puissance, reconnaissance.

z: cognizance, incognizance, recognizance.

ƏNT

Vowel: irradiant, luxuriant, miscreant, procreant, recreant, suppliant, variant.

f: elephant, sycophant.

gr: emigrant, immigrant.

k(c): abdicant, applicant, communcant, excommunicant, fabricant, insignificant, intoxicant, mendicant, sacrificant, significant, supplicant, toxicant.

l: altivolant*, ambulant, congratulant, gallant, gratulant, nonchalant+, petulant, postulant, scintillant, sibilant, stimulant, tintinnabulant, undulant, vigilant.

n: agglutinant, altisonant*, appurtenant, consonant, covenaut, determinant, dissonant, dominant, fulminant, germinant, illuminant, imaginant*,

inconsonant, luminant, predominant, resonant, ruminant.

p: anticipant, occupant.

r: adulterant, cormorant,
corroborant, courant, exuberant,
figurant, figurante, ignorant,
intolerant, itinerant, odorant,
predonderant, protuberant, rant,
refrigerant, reiterant, reverberant,
tolerant, vociferant.

s: complaisant+, conversant,
corposant+, impuissant,
incognisant, puissant, recusant.

t: adjutant, annuitant, combatant,
concomitant, dilettant, disputant,
executant, exorbitant, extant+,
habitant, hesitant, incognitant,
inhabitant, irritant, militant,
precipitant, Protestant,
resuscitant, tant*, visitant.

tr: penetrant, recalcitrant.

v: irrelevant, pursuivant, relevant.

ƏR

Vowel: anterior, excelsior+,
exterior, inferior, interior,
meteor+, or, posterior+, ulterior+.

d: ambassador+, calendar,
calender, corridor+, cylinder,
Frondeur, horrider, islander,
lavender, Lowlander, provender,
ruggeder, solider, stupider,
timider, vivider.

f: autobiographer, bibliographer,
biographer*, chauffeur+, for+,
gopher, Jennifer, lithographer,
lucifer, metaphore+, philosopher,
phonographer, photographer,
stenographer, topographer,
typographer.

g: hanger, vinegar.

j: armiger, astrologer, challenger,
conjure, cottager, disparager,
dowager, encourager, forager,
harbinger, manager, messenger,
passenger, philologer, pillager,

porringer, ravager, scavenger,
villager, vintager, voltigeur,
voyager, voyageur.

k(c): massacre, sepulchre.

l: angular, animalcular, annular,
bachelor, binocular, chancellor,
cheerfuller, circular, councillor,
counsellor, consular, crepuscular,
crueller, derailleur, dissimilar,
driveller, enameller, funicular,
globular, insular, irregular,
jocular, jugular, leveller, libeller,
loyaller, marshmeller, mitrailleur,
modeller, modular, molecular,
mournfuller, ocular, particular,
perpendicular, popular, quadrangular, quarreler, regular, reveller,
scapular, secular, similar, singular,
skilfuller, somnambular, spectacular, stellular, tabernacular, tabular,
tintinnabular, titular, traveller,
triangular, tutelar, uvular, valvular,
vehicular, vermicular, vernacular,
versicular, victualler, vice
chancellor, wassailer.

m: astronomer, customer,
gossamer, lissomer, lithesomer,
lonesomer, ransomer, winsomer.

n: almoner, bargainer, blazoner,
burdener, commissioner,
commoner, confectioner, coroner,
determiner, emblazoner,
enlightener, enlivener, evener,
examiner, executioner, fashioner,
foreigner, gardener, governor,
imprisoner, Londoner, mariner,
milliner, nor+, parishioner,
petitioner, practitioner, prisoner,
probationer, questioner, reasoner,
reversioner, wagoner.

p: caliper, diaper, galloper,
gossiper, juniper, worshipper.

r: adulterer, adventureer,
answerer, armorer, armourer,
banterer, barterer, batterer,
bickerer, blunderer, blusterer,
botherer, broiderer, caterer,
cellarer, chafferer, chatterer,

cofferer, conjurer, coverer, decipherer, deliverer, discoverer, embroiderer, emperor, endeavorer, engenderer, favorer, flatterer, flutterer, franc-ti-reur, furtherer, gatherer, harborer, jabberer, lecturer, lingerer, loiterer, malingerer, manufacturer, measurer, murderer, murmurer, murtherer*, mutterer, offerer, palaverer, panderer, pasturer, patterer, pepperer, perjurer, pesterer, pewterer, pilferer, plasterer, plunderer, posturer, poulterer, profferer, quaverer, roisterer, saunterer, slanderer, slaughterer, slumberer, smatterer, sorcerer, splutterer, squanderer, stutterer, succorer, sufferer, swaggerer, tamperer, thunderer, torturer, totterer, treasurer, upholsterer, usurer, utterer, vaporer, venturer, verderer, verderor, wagerer, wanderer, waverer, whimperer, whisperer, wonderer.

s: affiancer, artificer, officer, purchaser, trespasser.

sh: accoucheur, admonisher, banisher, blandisher, burnisher, cherisher, demolisher, embellisher, establisher, languisher, lavisher, nourisher, polisher, publisher, punisher, ravisher, relinquisher, skirmisher, vanquisher.

st: administer, baluster, bannister, canister, forester, gagster, gangster, harvester, maladminister, minister.

t: abature, abbreviature, amateur+, amphitheater, aperture, arbiter, archiater, armature, banqueter, barometer, barrister, breviature, calenture+, candidature, caricature+, carpenter, character, chorister, colporteur, comfiture, comforter, coverture, cricketer, curvature, diameter, discomfiture, distributer,

divestiture, entablature, expenditure, forfeiter, forfeiture, furniture, garmenture, garniture, hexameter, idolater, interpreter, investiture, judicature, Jupiter, ligature, literature+, litterateur, miniature, overture, pentameter, pleasanter, portraiture, presbyter, primogeniture, quadrature, register, restaurateur, rioter, riveter, scimiter, sepulture, signature, silenter, sinister, sophister, tablature, temperature, tetrameter, theater, theater, thermometer, trumpeter, vestiture, visitor.

t: ancestor, apparitor+, auditor, competitor, compositor, conspirator, creditor, depositor, editor, executor, expositor, inquisitor, interlocutor, janitor, legator, monitor, orator+, primogenitor+, progenitor+, proprietor, senator, servitor, solicitor, visitor.

TH: their.

v: miniver.

y: Euer, ewer, seniors, señor.

ƏRB

b: suburb.

ƏRD

Vowel: milliard.

ƏRNT

w: weren't+.

ƏRT

p: peart+.

ƏS

Vowel: abstemious, alias, alimonious, alluvious, amatorius, ambiguous, amphibious, anfractuous, aqueous, arduous, assiduous, beauteous, bounteous, burglarious, caduceus, calcareous, calumnious, censorious, ceremonious, cinereous, commodious, compendious, congruous, consanguineous, conspicuous, contemporaneous, contemptuous, contiguous, continuous, contrarious, contumelious, copious, courteous, Cretaceous, curious, deciduous, deleterious, delirious, denarius, devious, discourteous, disingenuous, dubious, dulcifluous, duteous, envious, equilibrious, erroneous, ethereous, exiduous, expurgatorious, extemporaneous, extraneous, farinaceous, fastidious, fatuous, felonious, furious, glorious, gregarious, habeas paterfamilias, harmonious, herbaceous, heterogeneous, hideous, hilarious, homogeneous, igneous, ignis fatuus, ignominious, illustrious, impecunious, imperious, impervious, impetuous, impious, incendious, incestuous, incommodious, incongruous, inconspicuous, incurious, indubious, industrious, inebrious, ingenious, ingenuous, inglorious, inharmonious, injurious, innocuous, inquisitorious, insensuous, insidious, instantaneous, invidious, laborious, lascivious, ligneous, litigious, lugubrious, luxurious, mellifluous, melodious, meritorious, miscellaneous, multifarious, multivious, mysterious, nauseous, nectareous, nefarious, notorious, nucleus, oblivious, obsequious, obvious, odious, opprobrious, parsimonious, penurious, perfidious, perspicuous, pervious, piteous, plenteous, precarious, predaceous, presumptuous, previous, promiscuous, punctilious, radius, rebellious, salacious, salubrious, sanctimonious, sanguineous, saponaceous, sensuous, serious, setaceous, simultaneous, sinuous, spontaneous, spurious, stentorious, strenuous, studious, subterraneous, sumptuous, supercilious, superfluous, Syrius, tedious, temerarious, tempestuous, tenuous, tortuous, tumultuous, uproarious, us, usurious, uxorious, vacuous, vagarious, vainglorious, valetudinarious, various, vicarious, victorious, virtuous, vitreous, voluptuous.

b: arquebus, Erebus, harquebus, incubus, omnibus+, succubus, syllabus.

br: tenebrous.

d: hazardous, jeopardous, timidous*.

f: boniface.

g: analagous, androphagous, esophagus, gymnophagous, homologous, sarcophagus, tautologous, theophagous, zoophagous.

k(c): abacus, Americus, Leviticus, repercuss.

kr: ludicrous.

l: abaculus, acephalous, acidulous, agriculous, alkalous, amphibolous, anemophilous, angelus, angulous, anomalous, bibulous, bicephalous, bipetalous, cautelous, convolvulous, convolvulus, crapulous, credulous, crepusculous, cumulus, emulous, fabulous, frivolous, garrulous, globulous, hydrocephalous, incredulous, libellous, marvelous, meticulous, miraculous, nautilus, nebulous, pendulous, periculous, perilous, petalous, populous, quarrelous*, querulous, ranunculous, ridiculous, scandalous, scintillous, scrophulous, scurrilous, scrupulous, sedulous, sibilous, stimulus, stridulous, tantalus, tintinnabulous, tremulous, tuberculous, undulous, unscrupulous, ventriculous, verisimilous, vernaculous.

m: animus, anonymous, bigamous, blasphemous, candlemas, diatomous, eponymous, hippopotamous, Hollowmas, infamous, magnanimous, Michaelmas, minimus, monogamous, polygamous, posthumous, pseudonymous, pusillanimous, sunonymous, unanimous, venomous.

n: albuminous, aluminous, androgenous, androgynous, bituminous, burdenouse*, cavernous, conterminous, criminous, diaphanous, endogenous, ferruginous, fluminous, fortitudinous, fuliginous, gelatinous, glutenous, glutinous, gluttonous, membranous, monotonous, mountainous, mucilaginous, multitudinous, mutinous, oleaginous, ominous, platinous, platitudinous, poisonous, ravenous, resinous, ruinous, scrutinous, synchronous, terminus, treasonous, tyrannous, valetudinous, velutinous, verminous, vertiginous, vicissitudinous, villanous, voluminous, voraginous, vortiginous.

p: octopus, platypus, polypus.

r: adulterous, adventurous, aliferous, aligerous, amorous, anserous, arborous, armigerous, augurous, balsamiferous, barbarous, blusterous, boisterous, bulbiferous, cadaverous, cancerous, cankerous, cantankerous, carboniferous, carnivorous, Cerberus, chivalrous, clamorous, dangerous, dexterous, doloriferous, dolorous, fossiliferous, generous, graminivorous, Hesperus, humorous, humerus, imponderous, imposturous, indecorous, inodorous, languorous, lecherous, metalliferous,

murderous, murmurous, numerous, obstreperous, odoriferous, odorous, omnivorous, onerous, oviparous, perjurous, pesterous, pestiferous, phosphorus, ponderous, preposterous, prosperous, rancorous, rapturous, rhinovirus, rigorous, roisterous, sacchariferous, savorous, slanderous, slumberous, somniferous, sulphurous, Tartarus, thunderous, timorous, torturous, traitorous, treacherous, unchivalrous, ungenerous, valorous, vaporous, venturous, verdurous, vigorous, viperous, viviparous, vociferous, vulturous.

s: Pegasus.

t: acclivitous, calamitous, circuitous, covetous, fatuitous, felicitous, fortuitous, gratuitous, immeritous*, impetus, infelicitous, iniquitous, necessitous, pachydermatous, precipitous, riotous, solicitous, ubiquitous, vegetous*.

th: antipathous.

tr: idolatrous.

v: mischievous.

əST

Vowel: ecclesiast+, elegiast+, encomiast+, enthusiast+, orgiast+, scholiast+, symposiast+.

f: steadfast+.

h: hast*+.

m: foremast+, mainmast+, mizzen mast+.

w: wast+.

əT

Vowel: commissariat, compatriot+, lariat, patriot+, proletariat, secretariat.

b: celibate.

f: phut.

g: delegate+.
hw: what+.
kw(qu): adequate, inadequate.
l: chocolate.
n: chestnut, fortunate, obstinate, peanut, proportionate, walnut.

ƏTH

m: behemoth+.
th: the+.

ƏV

h: have+.

ƏW

f: faugh, guffaw+.

ƏZM

k(c): macrocosm, microcosm.

Double Rhymes

(Words Accented on the Syllable before the Last, the Penult; also Called Feminine Rhymes)

A

The accented vowel sounds included are listed under A in Single Rhymes.

ĀAD

n: naiad.
    Plus display ad, etc.
    Plus may add, etc.

ĀAL

    Plus say, Al, etc.

ĀAN

k(c): Biscayan.
    Plus play an, etc.

ĀÄN

f: Phaon.
kr: crayon.
r: rayon.
    Plus stay on, etc.

ĀANS

    Cf. stray ants, etc.

ĀANT

    Plus stray ant, etc.

ĀÄS

k(c): chaos.
t: Taos.

ÄBĀ

s: no sabe, sabe.

ĀBÄB

n: nabob.
    Plus stray bob, etc.

ĀBAN

    Plus play ban, etc.
    Plus babe, Ann *or* an, etc.

ABÄRD

    Plus jab hard, etc.

ABATH

    Cf. grab bath, etc.
    Cf. abeth*.

ABĒ

Vowel: abbey, Abbie.
b: baby.
bl: blabby.
d: dabby.
dr: drabby.
fl: flabby.
g: gabby.

gr: grabby.
k(c): cabby.
kr: crabby.
sh: shabby.
sk(sc): scabby.
sl: slabby.
t: tabby, tame tabby.
  Plus grab, he, etc.

ĀBĒ

Vowel: Abey, Abie.
b: baby.
m: maybe.
r: Rabe.
  Plus stray bee, etc.
  Cf. abi.

ÄBĒ

b: bobby.
h: hobby, Wahabi.
k(c): cobby.
l: Hobby Lobby, lobby.
m: mobby.
n: knobby, nobby.
r: kohlrabi, Rabe.
sk(sc): scobby.
skw: squabby.
sn: snobby.
t: tabi.
  Plus bah, be *or* bee, etc.
  Plus job, be, etc.
  Plus squab, he, etc.
  Cf. job, be *or* bee, etc.

ABES

Vowel: abbess.
  Cf. grab Bess, etc.

ABEST

bl: blabbest*.
d: dabbest*.
dr: drabbest.
g: gabbest*.
gr: grabbest*.
j: jabbest*.
st: stabbest*.
  Cf. jab best, etc.

ÄBEST

r: robbest*.
s: sobbest*.
thr: throbbest*.
  Cf. job best, etc.

ABETH

bl: blabbeth*.
d: dabbeth*.
g: gabbeth*.
gr: grabbeth*.
j: jabbeth*.
s: Sabbath.
st: stabbeth*.
  Cf. stab Beth, etc.

ÄBETH

r: robbeth*.
s: sobbeth*.
thr: throbbeth*.
  Cf. job, Beth, etc.

ĀBĒZ

j: Jabez.
t: tabes.
  Plus stray bees, etc.

ABĪ

r: rabbi.

ABID

r: rabid.
t: tabid.
  Cf. jab hid, etc.

ABIJ

k(c): cabbage.
   Cf. crab age, etc.

ABIK

l: decasyllabic+, discyllabic+, hendecasyllabic+, imparisyllabic+, monosyllabic+, multisyllabic+, octosyllabic+, parisyllabic+, polysyllabic+, quadrisyllabic+, syllabic+, trisyllabic+.

ÄBIK

l: decasyllabic+, discyllabic+, hendecasyllabic+, imparisyllabic+, monosyllabic+, multisyllabic+, octosyllabic+, parisyllabic+, polysyllabic+, quadrisyllabic+, syllabic+, trisyllabic+.

ĀBIL

l: labile.
   Cf. abl.

ĀBĪ

l: lay-by.

ABIN

k(c): cabin, log cabin.
   Plus grab in, etc.
   Plus drab inn, etc.

ĀBĪN

s: Sabine.

ÄBIN

b: bobbin.
d: dobbin.
r: ragged robin, robbin, robin, round robin, wake robin.
   Plus job in *or* inn, etc.
   Cf. throbbin, etc.

ABING

bl: blabbing.
d: dabbing.
f: confabbing.
g: gabbing.
gr: grabbing.
j: jabbing.
k(c): cabbing, taxicabbing.
kr: crabbing.
n: nabbing.
sk(sc): scabbing.
sl: slabbing.
st: stabbing.
t: tabbing.

ÄBING

b: bobbing.
bl: blobbing.
j: jobbing.
k(c): cobbing.
l: lobbing.
m: mobbing.
n: hobnobbing, knobbing.
r: robbing.
s: sobbing.
sn: snobbing.
sw: swabbing.
thr: throbbing.

ÄBINZ

j: Jobbins.
r: Robbins.
   Plus obin+s.

ÄBISH

b: bobbish.
m: mobbish.
n: nobbish.
skw: squabbish.
sn: snobbish.

ABIT

h: cohabit, habit, inhabit, riding habit.
r: rabbet, rabbit.
    Plus grab it, etc.
    Cf. crab bit, etc.

ABJEKT

Vowel: abject.

ÄBJEKT

Vowel: object.

ABL

b: babble.
br: brabble.
d: bedabble, dabble.
dr: bedrabble, drabble.
g: gabble, gibble-gabble.
gr: grabble.
k(c): cabble.
r: rabble, ribble-rabble.
sk(sc): scabble.
skr(scr): scrabble.
    Plus taxicab'll, etc.

ĀBL

Vowel: Abel, able, disable, enable, unable.
b: Babel.
f: fabel.
fl: flable*.
g: gable.
k(c): cable.
l: label.
m: Mabel.
s: sable.
st: stable, unstable.
t: table.
    Plus Abe'll, etc.
    Plus gay bull, etc.

ÄBL

g: gobble.
h: hobble.
k(c): cobble, coble.
n: nobble.
skw: squabble.
w: wabble.
    Plus stob'll, etc.

ABLĒ

b: babbly.
d: dabbly.
dr: drably.
    Plus crab, Lee *or* lea, etc.

ÄBLĒ

k(c): cobbly.
skw: squabbly.
w: wabbly, Wobbly.
    Plus job, Lee *or* lea, etc.

ABLEST

b: babblest*.
br: brabblest*.
d: bedabblest*, dabblest*.
dr: drabblest*.
g: gabblest*.
skr(scr): scrabblest*.
    Plus crab, lest, etc.

ĀBLEST

Vowel: ablest.
k(c): cablest*.
l: lablest*.
st: stablest*.
t: tablest*.
    Plus play blest, etc.
    Plus Abe, lest, etc.

ABLETH

b: babbleth*.
br: brabbleth*.
d: bedabbleth*, dabbleth*.
dr: drabbleth*.
g: gabbleth*.
gr: grabbleth*.
skr(scr): scrabbleth*.

ĀBLETH

k(c): cableth*.
l: lableth*.
n: enableth*.
st: stableth*.
t: tableth*.

ÄBLIN

g: goblin.
　　Plus rob Lynn, etc.

ABLING

b: babbling.
br: brabbling.
d: bedabbling, dabbling.
dr: drabbling.
g: gabbling.
gr: grabbling.
k(c): cabbling.
skr(scr): scrabbling.

ĀBLING

Vowel: disabling.
f: fabling.
k(c): cabling.
l: labling.
n: enabling.
st: stabling, unstabling.
t: tabling.

ÄBLING

g: gobbling.
h: hobbling.
k(c): cobbling.
n: nobbling.
sn: snobling.
skw: squabbling.
w: wabbling.

ABLISH

st: stablish*.
t: disestablish, establish, reestablish.

ABLOID

t: tabloid.
　　Plus grab Lloyd, etc.

ABLUR

b: babbler.
br: brabbler.
d: bedabbler, dabbler.
dr: bedrabbler, drabbler.
g: gabbler.
gr: grabbler.
k(c): cabbler.
sk(sc): scabbler.
skr(scr): scrabbler.
　　Plus cab blur, etc.

ĀBLUR

Vowel: abler, disabler, enabler.
f: fabler.
st: stabler.
t: tabler.
　　Plus gray blur, etc.

ÄBLUR

g: gobbler, turkey gobbler.
h: hobbler.
k(c): blackberry cobbler, cobbler, peach cobbler, sherry cobbler.

n: knobbler, nobbler.
skw: squabbler.
w: wabbler.

ABLƏT

t: tablet.
   Plus crab let, etc.

ÄBŌŌL

gl: globule.
l: lobule.
   Plus job, you'll *or* Yule, etc.

ABRƏ

d: abracadabra.
   Cf. candelabra.

ĀBRĀK

d: daybreak.
   Plus play break, etc.
   Plus Abe, rake, etc.

ABSENS

Vowel: absence.
   Plus crab sense, etc.

ABSENT

Vowel: absent.
   Plus cab sent *or* scent, etc.

ÄBSTUR

l: lobster.
m: mobster.
   Plus job stir, etc.

ÄBSƏN

d: dobson.
j: Jobson.
r: Robson.
   Plus job, son *or* sun, etc.

ABUR

bl: blabber.
d: dabber.
g: gabber.
gr: grabber.
j: gibber-gabber, jabber.
kl: bonnyclabber, clabber.
kr: crabber.
n: knabber, nabber.
sk(sc): scabber.
sl: beslabber, slabber.
st: stabber.
   Plus jab her, etc.
   Cf. abur, etc.

ĀBUR

g: Gheber.
k(c): Caber.
l: belabor, labor.
n: beggar-my-neighbor, neighbor.
s: saber.
t: taber.
v: von Weber, Weber.
   Plus gay burr, etc.

ÄBUR

bl: blobber.
f: Fabre.
j: jobber.
k(c): cobber.
kl: clobber.
l: lobber.
n: knobber.
r: dog robber, robber.
s: sobber.
sl: beslobber, slobber.
sn: snobber.
sw: swabber.
thr: throbber.
   Cf. Fabre.
   Cf. obur.

Plus mob her *or* err, etc.
Plus swab her, etc.

ABURD

j: jabbered.
sk(sc): scabbard.
sl: beslabbered, slabbered.
t: tabard.
  Cf. grab hard, etc.
  Cf. also aburd.

ĀBURD

l: belabored, labored, unlabored.
n: neighbored.
s: sabered.
  Plus gray burred, etc.
  Plus Abe erred, etc.
  Cf. gray beard.

ÄBWEB

k(c): cobweb.
  Plus rob web, etc.

ĀBƏ

f: Faba.
p: copaiba.
  Plus give Abe a, etc.

ÄBƏ

b: Addis Ababa, Ali Baba.
h: Cahaba.
k: Kaaba.
t: Catawba, mastaba.
  Plus daub a, etc.
  Plus squab a, etc.

ĀBƏN

l: Laban.

ABƏS

r: Barabbas.

ABƏT

Vowel: abbot, Abbott.
k(c): Cabot.
s: sabot.
  Cf. grab at *or* it, etc.

ÄBƏT

k(c): Cobbett.
  Plus mob et, etc.
  Cf. job it, etc.

ACHĒ

k(c): catchy.
p: patchy.
sn: snatchy.
  Plus latch, he, etc.

ÄCHĒ

b: botchy.
bl: blotchy.
n: notchy.
spl: splotchy.
  Plus watch he, etc.

ACHEST

h: hatchest*.
k(c): catchest*.
l: latchest*, unlatchest*.
m: matchest*.
p: dispatchest*, patchest*.
skr(scr): scratchest*.
sn: snatchest*.
t: attachest*, detachest*.
th: thatchest*.

ÄCHEST

b: botchest*.
bl: blotchest*.
n: notchest*.
w: watchest*.

ACHETH

b: batcheth*.
h: hatcheth*.
k(c): catcheth*.
l: latcheth*, unlatcheth*.
m: matcheth*.
p: dispatcheth*, patcheth*.
skr(scr): scratcheth*.
sn: snatcheth*.
t: attacheth*, detacheth*.
th: thatcheth*.

ÄCHETH

b̄: botcheth*.
bl: blotcheth*.
n: notcheth*.
w: watcheth*.

ACHEZ

b: batches.
h: hatches.
k(c): catches.
kl: Kaffee Klatches.
l: laches, latches, unlatches.
m: matches.
n: Natchez.
p: dispatches, patches.
skr(scr): scratches.
sn: snatches.
t: attaches, detaches.
th: thatches.
    Plus latch is, etc.

ACHING

b: batching.
h: hatching.
k(c): catching.
kl: kaffee-klatching.
l: latching, unlatching.
m: matching.
p: dispatching, patching.

skr(scr): scratching.
sn: snatching.
t: attaching, detaching.
th: thatching.

ÄCHING

b: botching.
bl: blotching.
n: notching.
sk(sc): scotching.
spl: splotching.
w: watching.

ACHKĒ

l: latchkey.

ACHLES

m: matchless.
p: patchless.
skr(scr): scratchless.
th: thatchless.
    Plus catch less, or Les, etc.

ÄCHMƏN

sk(sc): Scotchman.
w: watchman.
    Plus notch man, etc.

ACHMƏNT

h: hatchment.
k(c): catchment.
p: dispatchment.
r: ratchment*.
t: attachment, detachment.
    Plus hatch meant, etc.

ACHOO͞

st: statue.
    Plus flat, you or ewe, etc.

ĀCHO͞OR

k(c): plicature.
kl: nomenclature.
l: legislature.
n: good nature, ill nature, nature, unnature.
   Plus fate, you're *or* you're, etc.

ACHO͞OT

st: statute.
   Plus that Ute, etc.

ACHUP

k(c): catchup.
m: matchup.
   Plus snatch up, etc.

ACHUR

h: hatcher.
k(c): catcher, cony-catcher, flycatcher.
l: latcher, unlatcher.
m: matcher.
p: dispatcher, patcher.
skr(scr): back-scratcher, scratcher.
sn: body snatcher, snatcher.
st: stature.
t: attacher, detacher.
th: thatcher, Thatcher.
   Plus at your *or* you're, etc.
   Plus catch her, err *or* er, etc.

ÄCHUR

b: botcher.
bl: blotcher.
n: notcher, top-notcher.
spl: splotcher.
w: watcher.
   Plus scotch her *or* err, etc.

ACHWĀ

h: hatchway.
   Plus catch way *or* weight, etc.

ÄCHWURD

w: watchword.
   Plus notch word, etc.

ACHWURK

k(c): catchwork.
p: patchwork.
   Plus match work, etc.

ACHƏL

h: hatch'el.
s: satch'el.
   Plus scratch L, etc.
   Cf. batch'll, etc.

ĀCHƏL

r: Rachel.
v: Vachel.

ACHƏT

h: hatchet.
kr: Bob Cratchet.
l: latchet.
r: ratchet.
   Plus batch it, etc.
   Cf. scratch it, etc.

ÄCHƏT

kr: crotchet.
r: rotchet.
   Plus Scotch et, etc.
   Cf. scotch it, etc.

ĀDĀ

h: heyday.
l: lay day.

m: May day.
p: payday.
pl: playday.
　Plus play day, etc.
　Plus grade A, etc.

ADÄK

h: haddock.
p: paddock.
r: raddocke*.
sh: shaddock.
　Cf. sad dock, etc.

ADĒ

b: baddie, baddy.
d: daddy, sugar daddy.
f: faddy.
h: haddie.
k(c): caddie, caddy.
l: laddie.
p: paddy.
pl: plaidie.
　Plus had he, etc.

ĀDĒ

br: Brady, braidy.
f: fady.
fr: fraidy.
gl: glady.
gr: Grady, O'Grady.
k(c): cadi, cascady.
l: belady, lady, landlady.
m: Maidie(di).
sh: shady.
　Plus made, he, etc.
　Plus say Dee *or* D, etc.

ÄDĒ

b: body, busy-body, embody, lifting body, nobody, somebody.
h: hoddy.

k(c): cadi.
kl: cloddy.
m: Mahdi.
n: noddy.
r: irade, roddy.
s: soddy.
sh: shoddy.
skw: squaddy.
t: toddy.
w: waddy, wadi.
　Plus clod, he, etc.
　Plus wad he, etc.
　Cf. adi.

ÄDĒD

b: able-bodied, bodied, disembodied, embodied, unbodied, unembodied.
t: toddied, well-toddied.
　Cf. oded.

ADEST

Vowel: addest*.
b: baddest.
g: gaddest*.
gl: gladdest.
m: maddest.
p: paddest*.
s: saddest.

ĀDEST

Vowel: aidest*.
br: abradest*, braidest*, upbraidest*.
f: fadest*.
gr: degradest*.
j: bejadest*.
m: madest*.
st: staidest.
sw: dissuadest*, overpersuadest*, persuadest*.
tr: tradest*.

v: evadest*, invadest*, pervadest*.
w: wadest*.

ÄDEST

Vowel: oddest.
m: immodest, modest.
n: noddest*.
pl: ploddest*.
pr: proddest*.
w: waddest*.

ADETH

Vowel: addeth*.
gl: gladdeth*.
p: paddeth*.
   Plus sad death, etc.

ĀDETH

Vowel: aideth*.
br: braideth*, upbraideth*.
f: fadeth*.
j: bejadeth*.
m: madeth*.
n: serenadeth*.
r: raideth*.
sp: spadeth*.
sw: dissuadeth*, overpersuadeth*, persuadeth*.
tr: tradeth*.
v: evadeth*, invadeth*, pervadeth*.
w: wadeth*.
   Plus play death, etc.

ÄDETH

n: noddeth*.
pl: ploddeth*.
pr: proddeth*.
w: waddeth*.
   Cf. God, death, etc.

ADĒZ

d: daddies, sugar daddies.
h: finnan haddies.
k(c): caddies.
l: laddies.
pl: plaidies.
   Plus had ease, etc.

ĀDĒZ

h: Hades.
l: ladies.
   Plus made ease, *or* E's, etc.
   Cf. adez.

ADFOOL

gl: gladful.
m: madful.
s: sadful.
   Plus dad full, etc.

ADIJ

Vowel: adage.
   Plus sad age, etc.

ADIK

Vowel: dyadic, triadic.
g: haggadic.
k(c): decadic.
m: nomadic.
n: monadic, vanadic.
r: faradic, sporadic.
t: Sotadic.
tr: tetradic.
   Plus mad Dick, etc.

ÄDIK

Vowel: hydriodic, iodic, odis, periodic.
k(c): sarcodic.
l: melodic.
m: spasmodic.

n: anodic, hellanodic, synodic.
p: epodic.
r: parodic.
s: episodic, exodic, kinesodic, rhapsodic.
th: methodic.

ADING

Vowel: adding, superadding.
g: gadding.
gl: gladding.
m: madding.
p: padding.

ĀDING

Vowel: aiding, coaiding.
br: abrading, braiding, unbraiding, upbraiding.
f: fading.
gr: degrading, grading, retrograding.
j: bejading, jading.
k(c): ambuscading, barricading, blockading, brocading, cascading.
l: enfilading, lading, overlading, unlading.
n: gasconading, serenading.
r: masquerading, parading, raiding.
s: crusading.
sh: shading.
sp: spading.
sw: dissuading, overpersuading, persuading.
tr: free-trading, trading.
v: evading, invading, pervading.
w: wading.

ÄDING

k(c): codding.
n: nodding.
p: podding.

pl: plodding.
pr: prodding.
w: wadding.

ADIS

Vowel: Addis.
k(c): caddis.
  Cf. bad is, etc.

ÄDIS

b: bodice.
  Cf. goddess.

ADISH

b: baddish.
f: faddish.
gl: gladdish.
k(c): caddish.
m: maddish.
r: radish.
s: saddish.
  Cf. bad dish, etc.

ĀDISH

m: maidish, mermaidish, old-maidish.
st: staidish.
  Plus gay dish, etc.

ÄDISH

g: goddish.
kl: cloddish.

ADIT

Vowel: adit.
  Plus had it, etc.

ADKAP

m: madcap.
  Plus plaid cap, etc.

ADL

Vowel: addle.
d: daddle, skedaddle.
f: faddle, fiddle-faddle.
p: paddle.
r: raddle.
s: English saddle, saddle, unsaddle.
spr: spraddle.
st: staddle.
str: astraddle, bestraddle, straddle.
 Plus lad 'll, etc.
 Cf. mad dull, etc.

ĀDL

kr: cradle, encradle.
l: ladle.
 Plus maid 'll, etc.
 Plus stay dull, etc.

ÄDL

k(c): coddle, mollycoddle.
m: model, remodel.
n: noddle.
sw: swaddle.
t: toddle.
tw: twaddle.
w: waddle.
 Plus God'll, etc.

ADLÄK

p: padlock.
 Plus bad lock, etc.

ADLĒ

b: badly.
br: Bradley.
gl: gladly.
h: Hadley.

m: madly.
s: sadly.
 Plus had Lee *or* lea, etc.

ĀDLĒ

gr: gradely, retrogradely.
st: staidly.
 Plus grayed lea *or* Lee, etc.

ÄDLĒ

g: godly, ungodly.
tw: twaddly.
w: waddly.
 Plus sod, Lee *or* lea, etc.

ADLING

Vowel: addling.
d: daddling, skedaddling.
f: faddling, fiddle-faddling.
p: paddling.
r: raddling.
s: saddling, unsaddling.
spr: spraddling.
str: bestraddling, straddling.

ĀDLING

kr: cradling, encradling.
l: ladling.

ÄDLING

g: godling.
k(c): coddling, codling.
m: modelling, remodelling.
sw: swaddling.
t: toddling.
tw: twaddling.
w: waddling.

ADLUR

Vowel: addler, Adler.
d: daddler, skedaddler.

f: faddler, fiddle-faddler.
p: paddler.
r: raddler.
s: saddler.
str: straddler.

ÄDLŲR

k(c): coddler, mollycoddler.
m: modeller.
sw: swaddler.
t: toddler.
tw: twaddler.
w: waddler.

ĀDLƏS

Vowel: aidless.
bl: bladeless.
br: braidless.
f: fadeless.
g: brigadeless.
gr: gradeless.
k(c): barricadeless, brocadeless.
m: maidless.
n: serenadeless.
r: paradeless.
sh: shadeless.
sp: spadeless.
tr: tradeless.
    Plus played less, etc.

ADMOUTH

b: bad mouth.

ADMUS

k: Cadmus.
    Plus sad muss, etc.

ADMƏN

k(c): Cadman.
    Plus bad man, etc.

ADNĒ

Vowel: Ariadne.
    Plus bad knee, etc.

ADNƏS

b: badness.
gl: gladness.
m: madness.
pl: plaidness.
s: sadness.

ĀDNƏS

st: staidness, unstaidness.

ÄDNƏS

Vowel: oddness.

ADŌ

sh: foreshadow, overshadow, shadow.
    Plus cad owe, etc.
    Cf. sad dough, doe *or* do, etc.

ĀDŌ

b: gambado.
d: dado+.
g: renegado.
k(c): ambuscado*, barricado, stoccado+.
kr: credo.
l: scalado*.
m: fumado.
n: bastinado, carbonado, grenado*, tornado.
p: strappado.
r: desperado+, Laredo.
s: camisado, crusado*.
v: muscovado.
    Plus weigh dough, etc.
    Plus play do, etc.
    Plus wade O, etc.
    Plus maid owe, etc.

ÄDŌ

d: dado+.
k(c): avocado, imbrocado*, Mikado, stoccado+*.
ly: Amontillado.
p: strappado.
pr: Prado.
r: amorado*, Colorado, desperado+, El Dorado.
s: passado.
t: pintado.
v: bravado, travado.
   Plus shah dough, doe, *or* do, etc.

ADŌD

sh: foreshadowed, overshadowed, shadowed, unshadowed.
   Plus sad ode, etc.

ADÔN

b: Abaddon.
   Plus had on, etc.
   Cf. lad don, etc.

ÄDŌŌL

m: module.
n: nodule.
   Plus sod, you'll *or* Yule, etc.

ĀDŌS

tr: extrados, intrados.

ADPŌL

t: tadpole.
   Plus glad pole *or* Pole, etc.

ÄDRƏN

skw: squadron.
   Plus sod run, etc.

ADSUM

gl: gladsome.
m: madsome.
   Plus had some, bad sum, etc.

ÄDSƏN

d: Dodson.
h: Hodson.
   Plus god, sun *or* son, etc.

ÄDUKT

pr: product.
   Cf. ma ducked *or* duct, etc.
   Cf. sod ducked *or* duct, etc.

ADƱR

Vowel: adder.
bl: bladder.
g: gadder.
gl: gladder.
l: ladder, stepladder.
m: madder.
p: padder.
s: sadder.
   Plus had her, etc.
   Plus lad err, etc.

ĀDƱR

Vowel: aider.
br: braider, unbraider, upbraider.
gr: degrader, grader.
k(c): barricader, blockader.
n: gasconader, promenader, serenader.
r: parader, raider.
s: crusader, harquebusader.
st: staider.
sw: dissuader, overpersuader, persuader.
tr: free trader, trader.

v: evader, invader.
w: wader.
Plus degrade her, etc.
Plus made err, etc.

ÄDƱR

Vowel: odder.
d: dodder.
f: fodder.
k(c): cadre, codder.
n: nodder.
p: podder.
pl: plodder.
pr: prodder.
s: soldier.
Plus squad err, etc.
Plus wad her *or* err, etc.

ÄDƱRD

f: foddered.
g: Goddard.
s: soldered.
st: Stoddard.
Cf. trod hard, etc.

ÄDƱRN

m: modern, unmodern.
Plus sod urn, earn, *or* erne, etc.

ĀDUS

gr: gradus.
Plus made us, etc.

ADVENT

Vowel: advent.
Plus bad vent, etc.

ADVƱRB

Vowel: adverb.
Plus sad verb, etc.

ADƏ

d: dada.
Plus glad a, etc.

ĀDƏ

Vowel: Ada.
k(c): cicada+.
n: Grenada+.
v: Veda.
z: Zaida, Zayda.

ÄDƏ

d: Dada.
g: haggada.
k(c): cicada+.
m: armada.
n: Granada, Grenada+, nada, Nada.
s: pasada.
v: Nevada, Sierra Nevada.
Plus wad a, etc.

ĀDƏD

Vowel: aided, unaided.
bl: bladed.
br: abraded, braided, unbraided, upbraided.
f: faded, unfaded.
gl: gladed.
gr: degraded, graded.
j: bejaded, jaded.
k(c): ambuscaded, barricaded, blockaded, brocaded.
n: cannonaded, serenaded.
r: masqueraded, paraded, raided.
s: crusaded.
sh: shaded, unshaded.
sp: spaded.
sw: dissuaded, persuaded.
tr: traded.
v: evaded, invaded, pervaded.
w: waded.

Plus play dead, etc.
Cf. May did, etc.

ADƏD

Vowel: added, superadded.
p: padded.
pl: plaided.
    Plus lad dead, etc.
    Plus lad did, etc.

ÄDƏD

n: nodded.
p: podded.
pl: plodded.
pr: prodded.
s: sodded.
w: wadded.
    Plus sod dead, etc.
    Cf. odid.
    Cf. sod, Ed, etc.

ADƏM

Vowel: Adam, McAdam.
b: Badham.
k(c): macadam.
m: madam.
    Plus had 'em, etc.
    Cf. sad damn, etc.

ÄDƏM

s: Sodom.
    Plus wad 'em, etc.

ADƏN

f: Macfadden, McFadden.
gl: engladden, gladden.
m: madden.
s: sadden.
    Plus bad den, etc.
    Cf. bad hen, etc.

ĀDƏN

Vowel: Aden, Aidenn.
b: Baden, Baden-Baden.
h: menhaden.
l: heavy-laden, laden, overladen, underladen, unladen.
m: bower-maiden, dairymaiden, handmaiden, maiden, mermaiden, milkmaiden, sea-maiden, serving-maiden.
    Plus play dent, etc.
    Cf. grade hen, etc.

ÄDƏN

h: hodden.
s: sodden, watersodden.
tr: trodden, untrodden.
    Plus pod den, etc.
    Cf. aden.
    Cf. quad hen, etc.

ĀDƏNS

Vowel: aidance.
k(c): cadence, decadence.
    Plus gay dance, etc.
    Plus grayed ants *or* aunts, etc.
    Plus play dents *or* dense, etc.
    Cf. adans.

ĀDƏNT

Vowel: aidant.
k(c): cadent, decadent.
r: abradant.
    Plus gay dent, etc.
    Plus old maid aunt *or* ant, etc.
    Cf. adant.

ÄDƏS

g: goddess.
    Cf. bodice.

ĀĒ

hw: wheyey.

kl: clayey.

spr: sprayey.

Plus say he, etc.

ÄĒ

t: Hatay.

Cf. Hawaii.

ÄĒB

s: sahib.

ĀEST

b: bayest*, disobeyest*, obeyest*.

br: brayest*.

fl: flayest*.

fr: defrayest*, frayest*.

g: gayest.

gr: grayest, greyest.

l: allayest, delayest*, inlayest*, layest*, mislayest*, uplayest*, waylayest*.

m: dismayest*.

p: overpayest*, payest*, repayest*, underpayest*.

pl: displayest*, playest*.

pr: prayest*, preyest*.

r: arrayest*, bewrayest*.

s: assayest*, assayist, essayest*, essayist, gainsayest*, missayest*, sayest*.

sl: slayest*.

sp: spayest*.

spr: sprayest*.

st: overstayest*, stayest*.

sw: swayest*.

tr: betrayest, portrayest*.

v: conveyest*, inveighest*, purveyest*, surveyest*.

w: weighest*.

ĀETH

b: disobeyeth*, obeyeth*.

br: brayeth*.

fr: defrayeth*, frayeth*.

k(c): decayeth*.

l: allayeth*, delayeth*, inlayeth*, layeth*, mislayeth*, uplayeth*, waylayeth*.

m: dismayeth*.

p: overpayeth*, payeth*, repayeth*, underpayeth*.

pl: playeth*.

pr: prayeth*, preyeth*.

r: arrayeth*, bewrayeth*.

s: assayeth*, essayeth*, gainsayeth*, missayeth*, sayeth*.

sl: slayeth*.

sp: spayeth*.

st: overstayeth*, stayeth*.

str: strayeth*.

sw: swayeth*.

tr: betrayeth*, protrayeth*.

v: conveyeth*, inveigheth*, purveyeth*, surveyeth*.

w: weigheth*.

AFĀ

k(c): cafe.

Cf. laugh, Fay, etc.

AFĒ

b: baffy.

ch: chaffy.

d: daffy.

dr: draffy.

t: taffy.

Plus laugh, he, etc.

ĀFĒLD

m: Mayfield.

r: Rayfield.

Plus play field, etc.

ĀFER

m: Mayfair.
pl: Playfair.
　Plus weigh fair, etc.

ĀFEST

ch: chafest*.
s: safest, vouchsafest*.
　Plus May fest, etc.

ĀFETH

ch: chafeth*.
j: Japheth.
s: vouchsafeth*.

AFGAN

Vowel: Afghan.

AFIK

gr: anaglyptographic, autobiographic, autographic, bibliographic, biographic, cacographic, calligraphic, cartographic, cinematographic, chirographic, choreographic, chorographic, clinographic, cosmographic, cryptographic, crystallographic, diagraphic, epigraphic, ethnographic, galvanographic, geographic, glyptographic, graphic, heliographic, heterographic, hierographic, historiographic, holographic, homolographic, horologiographic, hydrographic, hyetographic, ichnographic, ideographic, idiographic, lexicographic, lexigraphic, lichenographic, lithographic, logographic, monographic, orographic, orthographic, paleographic, pantographic, paragraphic, pasigraphic, petrographic, photographic, polygraphic, pornographic, scenographic, sciagraphic, seismographic, selenographic, siderographic, sphenographic, stenographic, stereographic, stratigraphic, stratographic, stylographic, tachygraphic, telegraphic, topographic, uranographic, xylographic, zincographic, zoographic.

m: maffick.
r: seraphic.
s: Sapphic.
t: epitaphic.
tr: traffic.

ÄFIK

s: philosophic, theophilosophic, theosophic.
str: antistrophic, apostrophic, catastrophic.
tr: hypertrophic.

ÄFIN

k(c): coffin, encoffin.
g: McGoffin.
　Plus trough in *or* inn, etc.

AFING

ch: chaffing.
g: gaffing.
gr: graffing, heliographing, lithographing, paragraphing, photographing, stenographing, telegraphing.
l: laughing.

ĀFING

ch: chafing, enchafing.
s: vouchsafing.
str: strafing.

ÄFING

kw(qu): quaffing.

AFĪR

s: sapphire.
Plus chaff fire, etc.

AFISH

r: raffish.
Plus half fish, etc.

ÄFISH

Vowel: offish.
sp: spoffish.
Plus prof fish, etc.

AFL

b: baffle.
g: gaffle.
h: haffle.
r: raffle.
skr(scr): scraffle.
sn: snaffle.
y: yaffle.
Plus laugh'll, etc.

ĀFLĒ

s: safely, unsafely.
Plus chafe, Lee, etc.

AFLING

b: baffling.
h: haffling.
k(c): calfling.
r: raffling.
skr(scr): scraffling.
sn: snaffling.

AFLƱR

b: baffler.
h: haffler.
r: raffler.
skr(scr): scraffler.

AFNĒ

d: Daphne.
Plus half knee, etc.

AFŌLD

s: Saffold.
sk(sc): scaffold.
Plus half fold *or* foaled, etc.
Plus half old, etc.
Cf. af'l+d, as baffled, etc.

ĀFOOL

pl: playful.
tr: trayful.
Plus stay full, etc.
Plus Rafe'll, etc.

AFRĀL

t: taffrail.
Plus half rail, etc.

AFRÄN

s: saffron.
Plus calf run, etc.

AFRIK

Vowel: Afric.
Plus half rick, etc.
Cf. calf Frick, etc.

AFSUM

l: laughsome.
Plus half some *or* sum, etc.

AFTĒ

dr: drafty.
gr: grafty.
kr: crafty.
Plus half tea, etc.

ĀFTĒ

s: safety.
    Plus vouchsafe tea, etc.

AFTEST

d: daftest.
dr: draughtest*.
gr: graftest*.
w: waftest*.
    Plus half test, etc.

AFTETH

dr: draughteth*.
gr: grafteth*.
w: wafteth*.

ĀFTHŌRS

dr: draft horse.
sh: shaft horse.
    Plus daft horse, etc.

AFTIJ

w: waftage.
    Plus daft age, etc.

AFTING

dr: drafting.
gr: engrafting, grafting.
h: hafting.
r: rafting.
sh: shafting.
w: wafting.

AFTLES

dr: draftless.
gr: graftless.
kr: craftless.
r: raftless.
sh: shaftless.
    Plus laughed less, etc.

AFTÔN

Vowel: Afton.
gr: Grafton.
    Plus laughed on, etc.

AFTSMƏN

dr: draftsman.
kr: craftsman, handicraftsman.
r: raftsman.
    Plus draughts, man, etc.

AFTƱR

Vowel: after, hereafter, hereinafter, thereafter.
d: dafter.
dr: drafter.
gr: grafter.
h: hafter.
l: laughter.
r: rafter.
w: wafter, wafture.
    Plus laughed her, laughed your, etc.

AFTƏD

dr: drafted.
gr: engrafted, grafted, ingrafted.
r: rafted.
sh: shafted.
w: unwafted+, wafted+.
    Plus laugh, Ted; laughed, Ed, etc.

ÄFTƏD

w: upwafted+, wafted+.
    Cf. afted.

AFƱR

ch: chaffer.
k: Kaffir.
g: gaffer.
gr: graffer*.

l: laugher.
kw: quaffer.
z: zaffer.
  Plus chaff her, etc.
  Plus half fur *or* fir, etc.
  Cf. afur.

AFŬRD

s: Safford.
st: Stafford.
tr: Trafford.
  Plus calf ford, etc.

ĀFƏR

ch: chafer, cockchafer.
s: safer.
w: wafer.
  Plus strafe her, etc.

ÄFƏL

t: rijsttafel.

ÄFƏT

pr: archprophet, profit, prophet, weatherprophet.
s: soffit.
  Plus doff it, etc.
  Plus prof et, etc.

ĀGÄN

d: Dagon.
  Cf. agan.

AGĒ

Vowel: Aggie.
b: baggy.
br: braggy.
dr: draggy.
f: faggy.
fl: flaggy.
g: gaggy.

kr: craggy.
kw(qu): quaggy.
l: laggy.
m: Maggie.
n: knaggy, naggy.
r: raggy.
s: saggy.
sh: shaggy.
skr(scr): scraggy.
sl: slaggy.
sn: snaggy.
sw: swaggy.
t: taggy.
w: waggy.
  Plus rag he, etc.

AGEND

f: fag end.
l: lag end.
  Plus Mag end, etc.

AGEST

br: braggest*.
dr: draggest*.
f: faggest*.
fl: flaggest*.
g: gaggest*.
l: laggest*.
n: naggest*.
w: waggest*.
  Plus hag guest, etc.

ĀGEST

pl: plaguest*.
v: vaguest.
  Plus stay, guest, etc.

AGETH

br: braggeth*.
dr: draggeth*.
f: faggeth*.

fl: flaggeth*.
g: gaggeth*.
l: laggeth*.
n: naggeth*.
r: raggeth*.
w: waggeth*.

AGIJ

b: baggage.
  Plus hag age, etc.

AGING

b: bagging.
br: bragging.
dr: dragging.
f: fagging.
fl: flagging, unflagging.
g: gagging.
j: jagging.
l: lagging.
m: magging.
n: nagging.
r: ragging.
s: sagging.
sh: shagging.
sl: slagging.
sn: snagging.
t: tagging.
w: wagging.

AGIS

h: haggis.
  Cf. bag is, etc.

AGISH

h: haggish.
l: laggish.
n: naggish.
w: waggish.

AGL

d: bedaggle*, boondaggle, daggle.
dr: bedraggle, draggle.
g: gaggle.
h: haggle.
r: raggle.
str: straggle.
t: raggle-taggle.
w: waggel, waggle.
  Plus flag'll etc.
  Cf. drag hell, etc.

AGLING

d: bedaggling*, boondaggling, daggling.
dr: bedraggling, draggling.
g: gaggling.
h: haggling.
r: raggling.
str: straggling.
w: waggling.

AGLUR

d: boondaggler, daggler.
dr: bedraggler, draggler.
h: haggler.
str: straggler.
w: waggler.

AGMAG

k(c): cagmag.
  Plus tag Mag, etc.

AGMƏN

b: bagman.
dr: dragman.
fl: flagman.
r: ragman.
  Plus drag man, etc.

AGMƏNT

fr: fragment.
　Plus flag meant, etc.

AGMĪR

kw: quagmire+.
　Plus drag mire, etc,

AGMĪT

l: stalagmite.
　Plus flag might *or* mite, etc.

AGNĀT

Vowel: agnate.
m: magnate.
st: stagnate.
　Plus flag, Nate, etc.

AGNEƏS

Vowel: Agnes.

AGNUM

m: magnum.

AGNƏNT

st: stagnant.

AGNƏT

m: magnet.
　Plus Mag met, etc.

ĀGŌ

Vowel: San Diego, Tierra del Fuego.
b: lumbago, plumbago, Tobago.
d: dago.
m: imago.
r: farrago, virago, vorago.
s: sago.
　Plus may go, etc.

ÄGŌ

Vowel: Santiago.
k(c): Chicago.
r: farrago.
　Plus shah go, etc.
　Cf. Fargo.
　Cf. dog owe *or* O, etc.

ĀGONG

l: legong.

ĀGŌŌ

Vowel: ague.
　Plus Hague, you, etc.

AGPĪ

m: magpie.
　Plus stag pie, etc.

AGPĪP

b: bagpipe.
　Plus drag pipe, etc.

AGRIK

d: podagric.
r: chiragric.
　Plus drag rick, etc.

ĀGRƏNS

fl: flagrance.
fr: fragrance.
v: vagrants.
　Plus Hague rants, etc.

ĀGRƏNT

fl: flagrant.
fr: fragrant, infragrant.
v: vagrant.
　Plus Hague rant, etc.

ÄGRƏS

pr: progress+.

AGUR

Vowel: agar-agar.
b: bagger, carpetbagger, four-bagger, one-bagger, three-bagger, two-bagger.
br: bragger.
d: dagger.
f: Fagger.
fl: flagger.
g: gagger.
j: jagger.
l: lagger.
m: magger.
n: nagger.
r: ragger.
s: sagger.
sh: shagger.
st: stagger.
sw: swagger.
t: tagger.
w: wagger, wigwagger.
　　Plus drag her, etc.

ĀGUR

m: maigre.
pl: plaguer.
v: vaguer.
　　Plus plague her, etc.

AGURD

h: haggard.
l: laggard.
st: staggard, staggered.
sw: swaggered.
　　Plus drag hard, etc.
　　Plus Mag guard, etc.

AGURT

br: braggart.
t: Taggart.
　　Plus flag art, etc.

ĀGUS

m: archimagus, magus.
r: choragus.
　　Plus plague us, etc.

AGZMƏN

dr: dragsman.
kr: cragsman.
　　Plus drags man, etc.

AGƏ

Vowel: aga.
kw: quagga.
　　Plus bag a, etc.

ĀGƏ

b: rutabaga.
pl: plaga.
s: saga.
　　Plus vague a, etc.

ÄGƏ

Vowel: aga.
d: dagga.
s: saga.

AGƏD

j: jagged.
kr: cragged.
r: ragged.
skr(scr): scragged.
　　Plus hag, Ed, etc.
　　Cf. bag head, etc.

ĀGƏL

pl: plagal.

v: vagal.

    Plus play gal, etc.

    Plus vague, Al, etc.

AGƏN

dr: dragon, pendragon, snap-dragon.

fl: flagon

w: wagon.

    Plus flag on, etc.

ĀGƏN

h: Hagan, Hagen, O'Hagan.

p: pagan.

r: Regan.

    Plus plague Ann *or* an, etc.

    Cf. Dagon.

AGƏT

Vowel: agate, moss agate.

f: fagot.

m: maggot, magot.

    Plus drag it, flag it, etc.

ÄHŌŌ

w: wahoo.

y: yahoo.

    Plus shah, who, etc.

ĀIJ

dr: drayage.

w: weighage.

    Plus play age, etc.

ĀIK

br: algebraic, Alhambraic, Hebraic.

d: Chaldaic, Eddaic, Judaic, sodaic, spondaic.

k(c): Alcaic, archaic, trochaic.

l: laic.

m: Aramaic, Brahmaic, Ptolemaic, Romaic.

n: Cyrenaic, Sinaic.

t: tesseraic.

s: Passaic, pharisaic, saddusaic.

t: altaic, deltaic, Jagataic, voltaic.

z: anti-Mosaic, mosaic, paradisaic, prosaic, stanzaic.

ĀING

b: baying, disobeying, obeying.

br: braying.

fl: flaying.

fr: defraying, fraying.

gr: graying.

h: haying.

k(c): decaying, undecaying.

kl: claying.

l: allaying, belaying, delaying, inlaying, interlaying, laying, mislaying, outlaying, overlaying, relaying, waylaying.

m: amaying, dismaying, maying.

n: neighing.

p: overpaying, paying, prepaying, repaying, underpaying.

pl: displaying, horseplaying, interplaying, playing, underplaying.

pr: praying, preying.

r: arraying, bewraying, disarraying, hurraying.

s: assaying, essaying, foresaying, gainsaying, missaying, saying, soothsaying, unsaying.

sl: slaying.

sp: spaying.

spr: spraying.

st: outstaying, overstaying, staying.
sw: swaying.
tr: betraying, portraying.
v: conveying, inveighing, purveying, surveying.
w: outweighing, unweighing, weighing.

ĀIS

d: dais.
l: Lais.
　　Cf. May is, etc.

ĀISH

g: gayish.
gr: grayish, greyish, silver-grayish.
k: clayish.

ĀIST

br: algebraist.
k(c): archaist.
m: Ptolemaist.
z: prosaist.

ĀIZM

d: Chaldaism.
l: Laism.
z: Mosaism, prosaism.

AJĒ

h: hadji.
k(c): cadgy.
w: howadji.
　　Plus Madge, he, etc.

ĀJĒ

k(c): cagey.
r: ragy.
s: sagy.
st: stagey, stagy.
　　Plus wage he, etc.

ÄJĒ

g: pedagogy.
p: podgy.
st: stodgy.
　　Plus lodge, he, etc.

ĀJED

Vowel: aged.
　　Plus enrage Ed, etc.
　　Plus say, Jed, etc.

ĀJEST

Vowel: agest*.
g: engagest*, gagest*, gaugest*.
r: enragest*, outragest*, ragest*.
s: presagest*, sagest.
st: stagest*.
sw: assuagest*, swagest*.
w: wagest*.
　　Plus May jest, etc.

ĀJETH

Vowel: ageth*.
g: engageth*, gageth*, gaugeth*.
r: enrageth*, outrageth*, rageth*.
s: presageth*.
sw: assuageth*.
w: wageth.

ĀJEZ

Vowel: ages.
g: disengages, engages, gages, gauges, greengages, pre-engages, weathergauges.
k(c): cages, encages.
m: mages.
p: pages.
r: enrages, outrages, rages.
s: presages, sages.
st: stages.

sw: assuages.
w: wages.
  Plus rage is, etc.

AJIK

f: androphagic, lotophagic, omophagic, sarcophagic, theophagic.
l: archipelagic, ellagic, pelagic.
m: magic.
r: hemorrhagic.
tr: tragic.

ÄJIK

g: anagogic, demagogic, epagogic, isagogic, mystagogic, paragogic, pedagogic.
l: aerologic, anthropologic, archaeologic, astrologic, biologic, chronologic, curiologic, demonologic, dialogic, entomologic, epilogic, ethnologic, ethologic, etymologic, eulogic, geologic, gnomologic, hierologic, histologic, horologic, ichthyologic, idealogic, lithologic, logic, martyrologic, meteorologic, mineralogic, morphologic, mycologic, myologic, mythologic, necrologic, neologic, ontologic, ophiologic, pathologic, philologic, phonologic, photologic, phraseologic, physiologic, psychologic, sarcologic, sociologic, tautologic, theologic, tropologic, zymologic.

ÄJIKS

g: pedagogics.
  Plus ojik+s.

AJIN

m: imagine.
  Plus Madge in, etc.

AJIND

m: imagined, unimagined.

AJING

b: badging.
k(c): cadging.

ĀJING

Vowel: aging.
g: engaging, disengaging, gaging, gauging.
k(c): caging, encaging.
p: paging.
r: enraging, outraging, raging.
s: presaging.
st: staging.

ÄJING

d: dodging.
l: disloding, lodging.

ĀJLĒ

s: sagely.
  Plus enrage Lee *or* lea, etc.

ĀJLES

Vowel: ageless.
g: gageless, gaugelss.
k(c): cageless.
p: pageless.
r: rageless.
s: sageless.
st: stageless.
w: wageless.
  Plus page less, etc.

ĀJLING

k(c): cageling.

ĀJMĀT

Vowel: age-mate.

ĀJMƏNT

g: disengagement, engagement, pre-engagement.
k(c): encagement.
r: enragement.
s: presagement.
sw: assuagement.
Plus page meant, etc.

ĀJNƏS

s: sageness.

ÄJSĀL

g: garage sale.

AJƯR

Vowel: agger.
b: badger.
k(c): cadger.
Plus badge her, err *or* er, etc.

ĀJƯR

g: disengager, engager, gager, gauger.
k(c): cager.
m: major, trumpet major.
p: pager.
r: enrager.
s: presager, sager.
st: old-stager, stager.
sw: assuager.
w: wager.
Plus enrage her, etc.

ÄJƯR

d: corn dodger, dodger.
k(c): codger.

l: dislodger, lodger.
r: roger.
Plus lodge her *or* err, etc.

ĀJUS

b: ambagious.
br: umbrageous.
p: rampageous.
r: courageous, oragious, outrageous.
t: advantageous, contagious, disadvantageous.
Plus enrage us, etc.

ÄJƏ

r: maharajah, rajah.

AJƏL

Vowel: agile.
fr: fragile.
Plus Madge ill, etc.

ÄJƏM

d: dodgem.

AJƏNT

p: pageant.
Plus badge aunt *or* ant, etc.

ĀJƏNT

Vowel: agent, reagent.
Plus play gent, etc.

AJƏT

g: gadget.
p: Padgett, Paget.
Plus cadge, it, etc.
Plus sad jet, etc.
Plus Madge et, etc.

ÄJƏZ

d: dodges.

h: Hodges.

l: dislodges, horologes, lodges.

p: hodge-podges.

Cf. Dodge is, etc.

ĀKÄB

Plus stray cob *or* Cobb, etc.

Cf. make cob, etc.

AKAL

p: pack all.

Plus smack all, etc.

AKÄRD

p: Packard.

pl: placard.

Cf. smack hard, etc.

Cf. stack card, etc.

AKĀT

b: baccate.

s: saccate.

Plus smack eight *or* ate, etc.

ĀKĀT

pl: placate.

AKBRĀND

kr: crackbrained.

sl: slack-brained.

Plus Jack brained, etc.

AKBUT

h: hackbut.

s: sackbut.

Plus Jack, but *or* butt, etc.

AKCHŌŌR

f: bitrifacture, facture, manufacture.

fr: fracture.

Plus lacked your, etc.

AKDÔ

j: jackdaw.

Plus sack daw, etc.

ĀKDOUN

br: breakdown.

sh: shakedown.

Plus make down, etc.

AKĒ

bl: blacky.

k: khaki.

kr: cracky.

l: lackey.

n: knacky.

w: wacky.

Plus track, he, etc.

Plus pack key, etc.

ĀKĒ

Vowel: achey.

br: braky.

f: faky.

fl: flaky.

k(c): caky.

kw: quaky.

sh: shaky.

sn: snaky.

Plus snake, he, etc.

Plus take key, etc.

ÄKĒ

s: Nagasaki, sake, saki.

AKEST

b: backest*.
bl: blackest.
h: hackest*.
hw: whackest*.
kl: clackest*.
kr: crackest*.
kw: quackest*.
l: lackest*.
p: packest*, unpackest*.
r: rackest*.
s: ransackest*, sackest*.
sl: slackest.
sm: smackest*.
t: attackest*, tackest*.
tr: trackest*.

ĀKEST

Vowel: achest*.
b: bakest*.
br: breakest*.
f: fakest*.
kw: quakest*.
m: makest*.
p: opaquest.
r: rakest*.
s: forsakest*.
sh: shakest*.
sp: spakest*.
st: stakest*.
t: betakest*, mistakest*, overtakest*, partakest*, takest*, undertakest*.
w: awakest*, wakest*.

ÄKEST

bl: blockest*.
d: dockest*.
fl: flockest*.
fr: frockest*, unfrockest*.
l: lockest*, unlockest*.

m: bemockest*, mockest*.
n: knockest*.
s: sockest*.
sh: shockest*.
sm: smockest*.
st: stockest*.

AKETH

b: backeth*.
bl: blacketh*.
h: hacketh*.
hw: whacketh*.
kl: clacketh*.
kr: cracketh.
kw: quacketh*.
l: lacketh*.
p: packeth*, unpacketh*.
r: racketh*.
s: ransacketh*, sacketh*.
sl: slacketh*.
sm: smacketh*.
t: attacketh*, tacketh*.
tr: tracketh*.

ĀKETH

Vowel: acheth*.
b: baketh*.
br: breaketh*.
f: faketh*.
k(c): caketh*.
kw: quaketh*.
m: maketh*.
r: raketh*.
s: forsaketh*.
sh: shaketh*.
st: staketh*.
t: betaketh*, mistaketh*, overtaketh*, partaketh*, taketh*, undertaketh*.
w: awaketh*, waketh*.

ĀKFOOL

w: wakeful.

Plus make full, etc.

ÄKGRANT

bl: block grant.

ÄKHOUND

r: rock hound.

AKIJ

p: package.
r: wrackage.
s: sackage.
st: stackage.
tr: trackage.

Plus black age, etc.

ĀKIJ

br: breakage.

Cf. snake age, etc.

AKIK

b: bacchic.
m: stomachic.

Cf. back kick, etc.

ĀKIN

br: break-in.

AKING

Vowel: bivouacing.
b: backing.
bl: blacking.
h: hacking.
hw: whacking.
j: jacking.
kl: clacking.
kr: cracking.
kw: quacking.
l: lacking.
n: knacking.
p: packing, unpacking.
r: racking.
s: ransacking, sacking.
sl: slacking.
sm: smacking.
sn: snacking.
st: stacking.
t: attacking, tacking.
tr: tracking.
thw: thwacking.

Cf. black king, etc.

ĀKING

Vowel: aching.
b: baking.
br: braking, breaking, heartbreaking, upbreaking.
f: faking.
fl: flaking.
k(c): caking.
kw: quaking.
m: making, unmaking.
r: raking.
s: forsaking.
sh: shaking.
sl: slaking.
sp: spaking.
st: staking.
t: betaking, mistaking, overtaking, partaking, taking, undertaking, uptaking.
w: awaking, waking.

Plus play king, etc.

AKISH

bl: blackish.
br: brackish.
kw: quackish.
n: knackish.

ĀKISH

r: rakish.
sn: snakish.

AKKLÔTH

p: packcloth.
s: sackcloth.
　　Plus black cloth, etc.

AKLD

sh: unshackled.
　　Plus akl+ed.
　　Plus stack culled, etc.

AKLĒ

bl: blackly.
k(c): cackly.
kr: crackly.
sh: ramshackly, shackly.
t: tackly.
　　Plus track Lee *or* lea, etc.

AKLING

h: hackling.
k(c): cackling.
kr: crackling.
sh: shackling.
t: tackling.

AKLÔG

b: backlog.
h: hacklog.
　　Plus stack log, etc.

AKLUR

h: hackler.
k(c): cackler.
kr: crackler.
sh: shackler.
t: tackler.

AKLƏS

n: knackless.
s: sackless.
tr: trackless.
　　Plus black less, etc.

ĀKLƏT

l: lakelet.
　　Plus snake let, etc.

AKMĒ

Vowel: acme.
l: Lacme.
　　Plus thwack me, etc.

AKMƏN

bl: blackman.
j: jackman.
p: packman.
　　Plus attack man, etc.

AKNĒ

Vowel: acne.
h: hackney.
　　Plus black knee *or* nee, etc.

ĀKNING

w: awakening, wakening.

AKNƏS

bl: blackness.
sl: slackness.

AKŌ

b: tobacco.
sh: shako.
w: wacko, whacko.
　　Plus black owe *or* O, etc.

ĀKŌ

m: Mako.
w: Waco.
Plus stake owe *or* O, etc.

ÄKŌ

ch: Gran Chaco.
gw: guaco.
n: guanaco.
Cf. lock owe, etc.

ĀKÔF

r: rakeoff.
t: takeoff.
Plus snake off, etc.

ĀKÔN

Plus bake on *or* an, etc.
Cf. aken.

ÄKŌŌ

r: bunraku.

ĀKÔRN

Vowel: acorn.
Plus shake horn, etc.
Plus May corn, etc.
Cf. make corn, etc.

AKPÄT

j: jackpot.
kr: crackpot.
Plus stack pot, etc.

AKRID

Vowel: acrid.
Plus Jack rid, etc.

ĀKRING

s: sacring.
Plus make ring, etc.

ĀKRIST

s: sacrist.
Plus shake wrist, etc.

AKRUM

l: simulacrum.
s: sacrum.
Plus black rum, etc.

ĀKRƏD

s: sacred.
Plus stake red, etc.

AKSĒ

br: braxy.
fl: flaxy.
p: Cotopaxi.
t: biotaxy, heterotaxy, homotaxy, taxi.
w: waxy.
Plus Jack see, etc.

AKSĒN

v: vaccine.
Plus track seen *or* scene, etc.

AKSENT

Vowel: accent.
Plus black cent *or* scent, etc.

AKSĒZ

m: Maxie's.
t: taxis.
Plus Jack sees *or* seize, etc.

AKSHUN

Vowel: action, class action, coaction, counteraction, exaction, inaction, interaction, reaction, retroaction, subaction.

d: redaction.

f: arefaction, assuefaction*, benefaction, calefaction, dissatisfaction, faction, labefaction, liquefaction, lubrifaction, madefaction, malefaction, petrifaction, putrefaction, rarefaction, rubefaction, satisfaction, stupefaction, tabefaction, tepefaction, torrefaction, tumefaction.

fr: diffraction, fraction, infraction, refraction.

p: compaction, paction.

str: abstraction.

t: contaction, taction.

tr: attraction, contraction, counteraction, detraction, distraction, extraction, protraction, retraction, subtraction, traction.

z: transaction.

Plus black shun, etc.

AKSHUS

f: factious.

fr: fractious.

AKSID

fl: flaccid.

Plus back, Sid, etc.

AKSIM

m: maxim.

Plus black Sim, etc.

Plus cracks him, etc.

ÄKSIN

Vowel: dioxin.

t: toxin.

AKSIS

Vowel: axis.

n: synaxis.

pr: praxis.

t: taxis.

Cf. taxes, etc.

AKSL

Vowel: axle.

Plus cracks'll, etc.

AKSMƏN

kr: cracksman.

t: tacksman.

Plus backs man, etc.

AKSTĀ

b: backstay.

j: jackstay.

Plus black stay, etc.

AKSTŌN

bl: Blackstone.

Plus crack stone, etc.

Plus cracks tone, etc.

AKSTƏN

br: Braxton.

k(c): Caxton.

kl: Klaxton.

Plus cracks ton *or* tun, etc.

Plus black stun, etc.

AKSWELL

m: Maxwell.

Plus smacks well, etc.

Plus tack swell, etc.

AKSƏN

fl: flaxen.
j: Jackson.
k(c): caxon*.
kl: Klaxon.
s: Anglo-Saxon, Saxon.
w: waxen.
  Plus tacks on, etc.
  Plus black sun *or* son, etc.
  Cf. wax hen, etc.

AKSƏS

Vowel: access, random access.

AKSƏZ

Vowel: axes, battle-axes, hand axes.
l: relaxes.
t: taxes.
w: waxes.

AKTĀT

l: ablactate, lactate.
tr: tractate.
  Plus bract eight *or* ate, etc.
  Plus tracked eight, etc.

AKTEST

Vowel: actest*, counteractest*, enactest*, reactest*.
str: abstractest*.
tr: attractest*, contractest*, detractest*, extractest*, retractest*, subtractest*.
z: axactest, transactest*.
  Plus track test, etc.

AKTETH

Vowel: acteth*, counteracteth*, enacteth*, reacteth*.
str: abstracteth*.
tr: attracteth*, contracteth*, detracteth*, extracteth*, protracteth*, retracteth*, subtracteth*.
z: exacteth*, transacteth*.

AKTFOOL

t: tactful.
  Plus packed full, etc.

AKTIK

d: didactic.
fr: emphractic.
l: catalactic, galactic, lactic, paralactic, prophylactic, stalactic.
pr: eupractic.
t: protactic, syntactic, tactic.
  Plus black tick, etc.

AKTIKS

l: catalactics.
t: tactics.
  Plus aktik+s.

AKTIL

d: dactyl, didactyl, heterodactyl, leptodactyl, pachydactyl, pterodactyl.
t: tactile.
tr: attractile, contractile, protractile, retractile, tractile.
  Plus crack till, etc.
  Plus lacked ill, etc.

AKTING

Vowel: acting, counteracting, double-acting, enacting, overacting, reacting, retroacting, self-acting, underacting.
fr: diffracting, infracting, refracting.
str: abstracting.

tr: attracting, contracting, detracting, distracting, protracting, retracting, subtracting.

z: exacting, transacting.

AKTIS

pr: practise.

Cf. fact is, etc.

AKTĪT

l: stalactite.

Plus black tight, etc.

AKTIV

Vowel: active, coactive, counteractive, enactive, inactive, radioactive, reactive, retroactive.

f: calefactive, liquefactive, olfactive, petrifactive, putrefactive, rarefactive, satisfactive, stupefactive.

fr: diffractive, refractive.

str: abstractive.

tr: attractive, contractive, counterattractive, detractive, distractive, extractive, protractive, retractive, subtractive, tractive.

AKTLĒ

f: matter-of-factly.

p: compactly.

z: exactly.

Plus tracked Lee *or* lea, etc.

AKTLƏS

Vowel: actless.

br: bractless.

f: factless.

t: tactless.

tr: tractless.

Plus stacked less, etc.

AKTMƏNT

n: enactment, re-enactment.

tr: extractment.

Plus bract meant, etc.

AKTNƏS

p: compactness.

t: intactness.

z: exactness.

AKTŌ

f: defacto, ex post facto.

Plus black toe, etc.

Plus tract owe *or* O, etc.

AKTRƏS

Vowel: actress.

f: benefactress, factress, malefactress.

tr: contractress, detractress.

z: exactress.

Plus black tress, etc.

AKTUR

Vowel: acter, actor, enactor.

f: benefactor, factor, limiting factor, malefactor, olfactor, windchill factor.

fr: diffractor, infractor, refractor.

l: phylacter.

m: climacter*.

p: compacter, compactor.

str: abstractor.

tr: attracter, contracter, contractor, detractor, distracter, extracter, protractor, retractor, subtracter, tractor.

z: exacter, transactor.

Plus backed her, etc.

AKTUS

k: cactus.
   Plus lacked us, etc.

ÄKTƱR

d: doctor, family doctor.
k(c): concocter, decocter.
pr: proctor.
   Plus shocked her *or* err, etc.

ÄKTƱRN

n: nocturne.
   Plus shocked urn, earn, *or* erne, etc.
   Plus flock turn, etc.

AKTƏ

eks: exacta.

AKTƏD

Vowel: acted, counteracted, enacted, overacted, reacted, unacted, underacted.
fr: diffracted, refracted.
p: compacted.
str: abstracted.
t: attracted, contracted, detracted, distracted, extracted, protracted, retracted, subtracted.
z: exacted, transacted.
   Plus crack Ted, etc.
   Plus smacked Ed, etc.
   Cf. cracked head, etc.

AKTƏNT

tr: attractant.

ĀKUP

br: breakup.
m: make-up.
w: wake-up.

Plus shake up, etc.
Plus stray cup, etc.
Cf. take cup, etc.

AKƱR

Vowel: Acker.
b: backer.
bl: blacker.
h: hacker.
hw: bushwhacker, whacker.
j: hijacker.
kl: clacker.
kr: cracker, nutcracker, soda cracker.
kw: quacker.
l: lacker, lacquer.
n: knacker.
p: packer, unpacker.
r: racker.
s: ransacker, sacker.
sl: slacker.
sm: smacker.
sn: snacker.
st: stacker.
t: attacker, tacker.
tr: tracker.
   Plus pack her, *or* err, etc.

ĀKƱR

Vowel: acre, God's acre.
b: baker.
br: breaker, heartbreaker, image breaker, lawbreaker, Sabbathbreaker, truce breaker.
f: faker, fakir.
fl: flaker.
kw: Quaker.
m: ballad maker, bookmaker, dressmaker, maker, matchmaker, mischief-maker, pacemaker, peacemaker, watchmaker.
n: nacre.
r: raker.
s: forsaker.

sh: shaker.

st: grubstaker.

t: mistaker, painstaker, partaker, taker, undertaker.

w: awaker.

  Plus shake her, etc.

  Plus stray cur *or* Kerr, etc.

ÄKU̯R

b: knickerbocker.

bl: beta blocker, blocker.

d: docker.

f: Fokker.

fl: flocker.

h: hocker, hougher

k(c): cocker.

kl: clocker.

l: locker.

m: macher, mocker.

n: knocker.

r: patent rocker, rocker.

s: soccer, socker.

sh: shilling shocker, shocker.

sm: smocker.

st: stocker.

  Plus unlock her *or* err, etc.

ĀKURZ

br: breakers.

  Plus aker+s.

ÄKU̯RZ

b: knickerbockers.

  Plus okur+s.

AKUS

b: Bacchus.

fl: Flaccus.

j: jacchus.

  Plus back us, etc.

  Cf. jackass.

AKWĀ

b: backway.

p: packway.

tr: trackway.

  Plus black way, etc.

  Plus crack weigh, etc.

ĀKWĒN

f: fay queen.

m: May queen.

  Plus play queen, etc.

AKWOODZ

b: backwoods.

  Plus track woods, etc.

  Plus smack Wood's, etc.

AKƏ

l: Malacca, polacca.

p: alpaca.

  Plus pack a, etc.

  Plus plaque a, etc.

ĀKƏ

m: Jamaica.

  Plus flake a, etc.

ĀKƏB

j: Jacob.

ĀKƏD

n: naked.

  Plus waked*, etc.

  Plus stray ked, etc.

AKƏL

gr: grackle.

h: hackle.

j: jackal.

k(c): cackle.

kr: crackle.

kw: quackle.
m: macle.
r: rackle.
sh: ramshackle, shackle
t: tackle.
　Plus black'll, etc.

AKƏN

bl: blacken.
br: bracken.
sl: slacken.
　Cf. black hen, etc.

ĀKƏN

Vowel: Aiken.
b: bacon.
m: Jamaican, Macon.
s: forsaken.
sh: shaken, wind-shaken.
t: mistaken, overtaken, taken, undertaken, uptaken.
w: awaken, waken.
　Cf. wake hen, etc.

ÄKƏN

br: Brocken.
h: Conshohocken.
kr: kraken.
　Cf. mock hen, etc.
　Cf. shock hen, etc.

ĀKƏND

b: baconned.
w: awakened, unawakened, wakened.
　Plus make end, etc.

AKƏT

br: bracket.
fl: flacket.
h: Hackett.

j: barn jacket, battle jacket, denim jacket, jacket, jean jacket, leather jacket, suede jacket.
p: packet.
pl: placket.
r: racket, racquet.
t: tacket.
　Plus attack it, etc.
　Plus Jack et, etc.

ÄKƏT

br: brocket.
d: docket.
k(c): cocket.
kr: crocket, Crockett.
l: locket, Lockett.
p: air pocket, hip pocket, impocket, pickpocket, pocket, vest pocket, watch pocket.
r: rocket, skyrocket.
s: socket.
spr: sprocket.
　Cf. cock it, etc.

ALBUM

Vowel: album.
　Plus pal bum, etc.

ĀLBURD

j: jailbird.
　Plus rail bird, etc.

ALBURT

Vowel: Albert.
　Plus pal, Bert, etc.

ALDIK

r: heraldic.
　Plus shall Dick, etc.

ALDĪN

Vowel: Aldine.
  Plus shall dine.

ALĒ

Vowel: alley, Allie.
b: bally.
d: dally, dilly-dally.
g: galley.
h: Hallie.
k: kali.
l: Lallie.
m: O'Malley.
p: pally.
r: rally.
s: Aunt Sally, sally.
sh: chalis, shilly-shally.
t: Talley, tally.
v: Fountain Valley, valley, Valli Valli.
  Plus shall he, etc.

ĀLĒ

Vowel: Aley, Eili Eili.
b: Bailey, bailie.
br: Braley.
d: daily, Daly.
g: gaily.
h: Haley.
k(c): capercaillie, kali.
l: shillaly, ukelele.
m: Mailly, Maley.
n: rationale.
p: Paley.
sh: shaly.
v: vale.
  Plus male, he, etc.
  Plus may Lee *or* lea, etc.

ÄLĒ

Vowel: Ali, Ollie.
b: Bali.

ch: Cholly.
d: Dollie, Dolly.
f: folly.
g: golly.
h: Holley, holly.
j: jolly.
k(c): Colley, collie, Kali, melancholy.
l: loblolly
m: hot tamale, Mollie, Molly, tamale.
n: baccanale, finale.
p: Polly.
r: pastorale, rolley.
t: Tolley.
tr: trolley.
v: volley.
w: Wally.
  Plus doll, he, etc.
  Plus ma Lee, etc.
  Cf. ale, ali.
  Cf. oli.

ALĒD

d: dallied, dilly-dallied.
p: impallid, pallid.
r: rallied.
s: sallied
sh: shilly-shallied.
t: tallied.
v: vallied.

ÄLĒD

j: jollied.
v: volleyed.
  Plus collie'd, etc.

ÄLĒG

k(c): colleague.
  Plus doll, league, etc.

ĀLEST

Vowel: ailest*.
b: bailest*, balest*.
f: failest*.
fr: frailest.
g: regalest*.
h: hailest*, halest, inhalest*.
j: engoalest*, enjailest*.
kw: quailest*.
m: mailest*.
n: nailest*.
p: impalest*, palest.
r: derailest*, railest*.
s: assailest*, outsailest*, sailest*.
sk(sc): scalest*.
t: curtailest*, detailest*, entailest*, retailest*.
tr: trailest*.
v: availest*, prevailest*, unveilest*.
w: bewailest*, wailest*.
    Cf. jail, lest, etc.

ĀLETH

b: baileth*, baleth*.
g: regaleth.
h: exhaleth*, haileth*, inhaleth*.
j: engaoleth*, enjaileth*, jaileth*.
kw: quaileth*.
n: naileth*.
p: impaleth*, paleth*.
r: deraileth*, raileth*.
s: assaileth*, outsaileth*, saileth*.
sk(sc): scaleth*.
t: curtaileth*, detaileth*, entaileth*, retaileth*.
tr: traileth*.
v: availeth*, prevaileth*, unveileth*, veileth*.
w: bewaileth*, waileth*.

ALĒZ, ĀLĒZ, ÄLĒZ

z: Gonzales.
    Plus gray lees, etc.

ĀLFOOL

b: baleful.
p: pailful.
w: wailful.
    Plus ale full, etc.

ALFRED

Vowel: Alfred.
    Plus pal Fred, etc.

ALFƏ

Vowel: alpha.
f: alfalfa.
    Plus Ralph a, etc.

ALGƏM

m: amalgam.

ÄLID

Vowel: olid.
s: solid.
skw: squalid.
st: stolid.

ĀLIF

b: bailiff.
k(c): Caliph.
    Plus jail, if, etc.

ĀLIJ

b: bailage.
t: curtailage, retailage.
    Plus jail age, etc.

ALIK

d: medallic, Vandalic.

f: acrocephalic, brachistocephalic, cephalic, dolichocephalic, encephalic, eurycephalic, macrencephalic, macrocephalic, mesocephalic, microcephalic, phallic, platycephalic.

g: Gallic.

gr: grallic.

k(c): vocalic

r: Uralic.

s: oxalic, salic.

sh: pashalik.

t: bimetallic, italic, metallic, monometallic.

th: thallic.

Plus shall lick, etc.

ĀLIK

g: Gaelic.

m: malic.

s: Salic.

Plus play lick, etc.

ÄLIK

Vowel: Aeolic, variolic, vitriolic.

b: carbolic, diabolic, embolic, hyperbolic, metabolic, parabolic, symbolic.

fr: frolic.

h: alcoholic.

k(c): bucolic, colic, melancholic.

p: bibliopolic, epipolic.

r: rolick.

t: apostolic, diastolic, epistolic, systolic, vicar-apostolic.

tr: petrolic.

ĀLIKS

k(c): calyx.

s: Salix.

Plus play licks, etc.

ALIN, ÄLIN

st: Stalin.

Plus pal in, etc.

ALING

b: caballing.

p: paling.

ĀLING

Vowel: ailing.

b: bailing, baling.

f: failing.

fl: flailing.

gr: grayling, greyling.

h: exhaling, hailing, haling, inhaling.

hw: whaling.

j: jailing.

kw: quailing.

m: blackmailing, mailing.

n: nailing.

p: empaling, impaling, paling.

r: derailing, railing.

s: assailing, outsailing, sailing, wholesaling.

shm: Schmeling.

sk(sc): scaling.

sn: snailing.

t: curtailing, detailing, entailing, retailing, tailing.

tr: trailing.

v: availing, countervailing, prevailing, unveiling, veiling.

w: bewailing, wailing.

ÄLING

d: baby-dolling.

k(c): caracolling.

l: lolling.

t: extolling.

ÄLINZ

h: Hollins.
k(c): Collins, rum Collins, Tom Collins.
r: Rollins.
   Plus doll inns *or* ins, etc.

ALIS

Vowel: Alice, allice.
ch: chalice, Chalis
m: malice.
   Cf. alas, alus.

ÄLIS

h: Hollis.
k(c): Collis.
w: Cornwallis, Wallace, Wallis.
   Cf. portcollis, etc.

ĀLISH

p: palish.
sh: shalish.
st: stalish.

ÄLISH

b: abolish.
m: demolish.
p: polish.

ÄLISHT

b: abolished.
m: demolished, undemolished.
p: polished, unpolished.

ÄLIV

Vowel: green olive, olive, ripe olive.

ALJĒ

Vowel: Algie, Algy.
l: cephalalgy.

ALJIK

f: cephalgic.
r: neuralgic.
t: antalgic, nostalgic, odontalgic.

ĀLKÄR

m: mail car.
r: rail car.
   Plus trail car, etc.

ALKĀT

f: defalcate, falcate.
   Plus pal Kate, etc.

ALKĒR

v: Valkyr.

ALKIN

m: grimalkin.
   Plus shall kin, etc.

ĀLLĒ

fr: frailly.
h: halely.
p: palely.
st: stalely.
   Plus frail Lee *or* lea, etc.
   Cf. ali.

ALMĀT

p: palmate.
   Plus shall mate, etc.

ALMUD

t: Talmud.
   Plus shall mud, etc.

r: neuralgy.
t: nostalgy, odontalgy.
   Plus pal, Gee, etc.
   Cf. algae.

ALJIK

ALMUK

k: Kalmuck.
  Plus shall muck, etc.

ALMƏ

Vowel: Alma.
th: Thalma.
  Plus shall ma, etc.

ĀLMƏNT

Vowel: ailment.
b: bailment.
g: regalement.
h: inhalement.
p: impalement.
r: derailment.
s: assailment.
t: curtailment, entailment, retailment.
v: availment, prevailment.
w: bewailment.
  Plus sale meant, etc.

ĀLNƏS

fr: frailness.
h: haleness.
m: maleness.
p: paleness.
st: staleness.

ALŌ

Vowel: aloe.
f: fallow, summer fallow.
h: Allhallow, dishallow, hallow, unhallow.
k(c): callow.
m: mallow, marshmallow.
s: sallow.
sh: shallow.
t: tallow.
  Plus shall low, etc.
  Plus shall owe *or* O, etc.

ĀLŌ

h: halo.
  Plus whale owe *or* O, etc.
  Plus play low, etc.

ÄLŌ

f: follow.
h: hollo, hollow.
p: Apollo.
sw: swallow.
w: wallow.
  Plus doll owe *or* O, etc.
  Cf. olo.

ALÔN

s: salon.
  Cf. doll on, etc.

ALOO

v: undervalue, value.
  Plus shall you, etc.

ÄLOOM

k(c): colyum.
v: volume.

ĀLOOR

f: failure.
  Plus whale your *or* you're, etc.

ĀLOUT

b: bailout.

ALŌZ

g: gallows.
  Also alo+s

ALPĪN

Vowel: Alpine, cisalpine.
z: transalpine.
  Plus shall pine, etc.

ALPING

sk(sc): scalping.

ĀLSPIN

t: tailspin.
Plus frail spin, etc.

ĀLTĒ

fr: frailty.
Plus pale tea, etc.

ALTŌ

Vowel: alto, rialto.
tr: contralto.
Plus shall toe, etc.

ALUM

Vowel: alum.
Plus pal 'em, etc.

ÄLUM

k(c): Colum, column.
s: solemn.
Plus baby doll 'em, etc.

ALUR

b: caballer.
p: pallor.
v: valor.
Plus shall err, er, *or* her, etc.

ĀLUR

b: bailer, baler.
f: failer.
fl: flailer.
fr: frailer.
g: regaler.
h: haler, inhaler.
hw: whaler.
j: gaoler, jailer.

kw: quailer.
m: mailer.
n: nailer.
p: impaler, paler.
r: derailer, railer.
s: assailer, sailer, sailor, Sayler.
sk(sc): scaler.
skw: squalor.
st: staler.
t: curtailer, detailer, entailer, retailer, tailor, Taylor.
tr: trailer.
v: prevailer, unveiler.
w: bewailer, wailer.
Plus assail her, etc.

ÄLUR

d: dollar.
k(c): choke collar, cholar, collar
l: loller.
s: sollar
sk(sc): scholar.
skw: squalor+.
t: extoller, Toller.
Plus olur.

ALURD

Vowel: Allard.
b: Ballard.
k(c): Callard.
m: mallard.
Cf. valored.

ÄLURD

b: bollard.
d: dollared.
k(c): collard, collared.
l: Lollard.
p: pollard.
sk(sc): scollard.
Plus collar'd etc.

ÄLURZ

d: petrodollars, dollars.

ALUS

g: gallus.
k(c): callous.
  Plus pal us, etc.
  Cf. also alas, alis.

ÄLUSK

m: mollusk.
  Plus doll, Lusk, etc.

ÄLVEST

s: absolvest*, solvest*.
v: devolvest*, evolvest*, involvest*,
revolvest*.
z: dissolvest*, resolvest*.
  Plus doll vest, etc.

ÄLVETH

s: absolveth*, solveth*.
v: devolveth*, evolveth*,
involveth*, revolveth*.
z: dissolveth*, resolveth*.

ALVIJ

s: salvage.
  Plus valve age, etc.

ALVIN

Vowel: Alvin.
k(c): Calvin.
  Plus valve in, etc.

ÄLVING

s: absolving, solving.
v: devolving, evolving, involving,
revolving.
z: dissolving, resolving.

ÄLVMƏNT

v: devolvement, evolvement,
involvement.
  Plus resolve meant, etc.

ALVŌ

s: salvo.

ALVUR

s: quacksalver, salver, salvor.
  Plus valve or, etc.

ÄLVUR

s: absolver, solver.
v: evolver, involver, revolver.
z: dissolver, resolver.
  Plus resolve her *or* err, etc.

ALVURT

k(c): Calvert.

ALVƏ

Vowel: Alva, Alvah.
h: Halveh.
  Plus valve a, etc.

ÄLVƏNT

s: insolvent, solvent.
v: evolvent.
z: dissolvent, resolvent.
  Plus doll vent, etc.

ALWIN

Vowel: Alwin.
  Plus pal win, etc.

ALYŌ

r: seraglio.
t: intaglio.

ALYŮRD

h: halliard, halyard.

ĀLYŮRD

j: gaolyard, jailyard.
k: kailyard.
Plus sail yard, etc.

ĀLYƏ

d: dahlia.
g: regalia.
m: mammalia.
n: Bacchanalia, marginalia, paraphernalia, saturnalia, terminalia.
t: castalia.
tr: Centralia, penetralia.
z: azalea.
Cf. fail you, etc.

ALYƏ, ÄLYƏ

d: dahlia.
Cf. pal you, doll you, etc.

ALYƏN

d: medallion.
sk(sc): rapscallion, rascallion, scallion.
st: stallion.
t: battalion, Italian.
Plus shall yon, etc.

ĀLYƏN

Vowel: alien.
d: Daedalian, Idalian, sesquipedalian.
g: regalian.
j: Phigalian.
m: mammalian, phantasmalian, Pygmalion.
n: bacchanalian, saturnalian, tenaillon, tobacconalian.

p: episcopalian, marsupialian.
r: paralian*.
s: Messalian, universalian.
tr: Australian.
Plus trail yon, etc.
Cf. alian.

ALYƏNT

v: valiant.

ĀLZMƏN

d: dalesman.
hw: whalesman.
s: salesman.
t: talesman.
Plus fails man, etc.

ALƏ

g: gala.
h: Valhalla.
k(c): cala.
Plus shall a, etc.

ĀLƏ

Vowel: Venezuela.
g: gala.
l: shillalah.
Plus sail a, etc.

ÄLƏ

Vowel: Allah.
g: gala.
h: holla.
m: molla.
r: corolla.
Plus parasol a, etc.

ĀLƏB

k(c): Caleb.
Plus sail ebb, etc.

ALƏD

b: ballad.
s: salad.
  Cf. invalid, valid, etc.

ÄLƏJ

k(c): college, cow college.
n: acknowledge, foreknowledge, knowledge, self-knowledge.
  Plus doll edge, etc.

ÄLƏJD

n: acknowledged, unacknowl-edged.
  Plus doll edged, etc.

ALƏK

Vowel: Aleck, smart aleck.
h: Halleck.
t: Talleck.

ÄLƏM

k(c): column.
s: solemn.
  Plus alcohol 'em, etc.

ALƏN

Vowel: Alan, Allen.
g: gallon.
t: talon.
  Plus pal on, etc.
  Plus pal, Ann *or* an, etc.
  Plus shall an, etc.
  Cf. alon.

ÄLƏN

p: pollen.
st: stollen, stolon.
  Cf. doll an, etc.

ĀLƏNGKS

f: phalanx.

ALƏNJ

ch: challenge.

ALƏNJD

ch: challenged, unchallenged.

ALƏNS

b: balance, counterbalance, outbalance, overbalance.
v: valance
  Cf. gallants, talents, etc.

ĀLƏNS

v: valence.
  Cf. sail hence, etc.

ALƏNST

b: balanced, outbalanced, overbalanced, unbalanced.
v: valanced.
  Cf. pallanced, etc.

ĀLƏNT

h: exhalent, inhalent.
s: assailant.
sk(sc): intranscalent, transcalent.
  Plus May lent *or* leant, etc.

ÄLƏNT

p: equipollent, prepollent.

ALƏP

g: gallop.
j: jalap.
sh: shallop.
sk(sc): scallop.
  Cf. pal up, etc.

ÄLƏP

d: dollop.
k(c): collop.
l: lollop.
sk(sc): escalop, scallop.
tr: trollop.
w: wallop.
  Cf. doll up, etc.

ALƏS

b: balas.
d: Dallas.
p: palace, Pallas.
  Plus pal us, etc.
  Cf. alus.
  Cf. alis.

ĀLƏS

d: dayless.
h: hayless.
kl(cl): clayless.
p: payless.
pl: playless.
pr: preyless.
r: rayless.
spr: sprayless.
w: wayless.
  Plus play less *or* Les, etc.

ÄLƏS

s: solace.

ALƏST

b: ballast.
  Plus pal last, etc.

ÄLƏT

b: ballot.
g: gallet.

m: mallet.
p: palate, palette, pallet.
s: sallet.
v: valet.
  Plus Sal et, etc.
  Cf. pal it, etc.
  Cf. shall it, etc.

ÄLƏT

f: La Follette.
k(c): collet.
w: wallet.
  Plus doll, et, etc.
  Cf. alcohol it, etc.

ÄLƏZ

z: Gonzales.

ĀMÄR

t: Tamar.
  Cf. amer.

ĀMĀT

d: daymate.
h: hamate.
kw: desquamate.
pl: playmate.
  Plus say, mate, etc.
  Plus game ate *or* eight, etc.

ÄMBAT

k(c): combat.
w: wombat.
  Plus from bat, etc.

AMBĒ

p: namby-pamby.
  Plus damn bee *or* be, etc.

ÄMBĒ

d: Dombey.
kr: Abercrombie.
z: zombie.
    Plus from bee *or* be, etc.

AMBIK

Vowel: choliambic, choriambic, elegiambic, galliambic, iambic.
r: dithyrambic.

AMBIST

g: gambist.
k(c): cambist.

AMBIT

Vowel: ambit.
g: gambit.
    Plus lamb bit, etc.
    Plus dithyramb it, etc.

AMBL

Vowel: amble, preamble.
br: bramble.
g: gamble, gambol.
r: ramble.
sh: shamble.
sk(sc): scamble, skimble-skamble.
skr(scr): scramble, scrimble-scramble.
    Plus damn bull, etc.
    Cf. ambl.

AMBLEST

Vowel: amblest*.
g: gamblest*.
r: ramblest*.
sh: shamblest.
skr(scr): scramblest*.
    Plus lamb blest *or* blessed, etc.
    Plus dithyramb, lest, etc.

AMBLETH

Vowel: ambleth*.
g: gambleth*.
r: rambleth*.
sh: shambleth*.
skr(scr): scrambleth*.

AMBLING

Vowel: ambling.
br: brambling.
g: gambling.
r: rambling.
sh: shambling.
sk(sc): scambling.
skr(scr): scrambling.

AMBLUR

Vowel: ambler.
g: gambler.
r: rambler.
sh: shambler.
sk(sc): scambler.
skr(scr): scrambler.

AMBLZ

Vowel: ambles.
g: gambles.
r: rambles.
sh: shambles.
skr(scr): scrambles.
    Plus ram bulls, etc.

AMBŌ

Vowel: ambo.
fl: flambeau.
kr: crambo.
s: Sambo.
z: zambo.
    Plus yam, bo *or* beau, etc.

AMBOOSH

Vowel: ambush.
   Plus jam bush, etc.

ĀMBRIK

k(c): cambric.
   Plus claim brick, etc.

ÄMBRUS

s: sombrous.

AMBƯR

Vowel: amber.
k(c): camber.
kl: clamber.
t: tambour.
   Plus damn boor, etc.
   Plus ram burr, etc.

ĀMBƯR

ch: antechamber, chamber.
   Plus same burr, etc.

ÄMBƯR

Vowel: omber, ombre.
h: hombre.
s: somber.
sk(sc): Scomber.
   Plus from burr, etc.

ÄMBƯRG

sh: Schaumburg.

AMBUS

Vowel: iambus.
r: dithyrambus.
   Plus jam bus *or* buss, etc.

AMBƏ

g: gamba.
   Plus lamb, bah!, etc.

AMBƏNT

l: lambent.
   Plus ram bent, etc.

AMDƏ

l: lambda.
   Plus slammed a, etc.
   Plus slam da, etc.

AMĒ

Vowel: Miami.
d: damme.
g: gammy.
kl: clammy.
m: mammy.
r: rammy.
sh: chamois, shammy.
t: tammy.
   Plus slam me, etc.
   Plus slam, he, etc.

ĀMĒ

Vowel: Amy.
fl: flamy.
g: gamy.
m: Mamie.
   Plus pray me, etc.
   Plus game, he, etc.

ÄMĒ

b: balmy.
k(c): calmy.
kw: qualmy.
m: mommy.
p: palmy.
s: salmi.
sw: swami.

t: Tommie, Tommy.
tr: pastrami.
   Plus blah me, etc.
   Plus calm me, etc.
   Plus calm, he, etc.

AMEST

d: dammest*, damnest*.
kr: crammest*.
r: rammest*.
sh: shammest*.
sl: slammest*.
   Plus Ham messed, etc.

ĀMEST

Vowel: aimest*.
bl: blamest*.
f: defamest*.
fl: flamest*, inflamest*.
fr: framest*.
g: gamest*.
kl: acclaimest*, claimest*, declaimest*, disclaimest*, exclaimest*, proclaimest*, reclaimst*.
l: lamest.
m: maimest*.
n: namest*.
sh: shamest*.
t: tamest*.
   Plus May messed, etc.

ÄMEST

b: embalmest*.
k: calmest.
l: salaamest*.
   Cf. calm messed, etc.

AMETH

d: dammeth*, damneth*.
kr: crammeth*.
r: rammeth*.

sh: shammeth*.
sl: slammeth*.

ĀMETH

Vowel: aimeth*.
bl: blameth*.
f: defameth*.
fl: flameth*, inflameth*.
fr: frameth*.
k(c): overcameth*.
kl: acclaimeth*, claimeth*, declaimeth*, disclaimeth*, exclaimeth*, proclaimeth*, reclaimeth*.
l: lameth*.
m: maimeth*.
n: nameth*.
sh: forshameth*, shameth*.
t: tameth*.

ÄMETH

b: embalmeth*.
k(c): calmeth*.
l: salaameth*.

AMFĪR

s: samphire.
   Plus sham fire, etc.

AMFLƏT

p: pamphlet.

ĀMFOOL

bl: blameful.
fl: flameful.
sh: shameful.
   Plus name full, etc.

AMFƱR

k(c): camphor.
   Plus slam for, etc.

AMIJ

d: damage.

Plus sham age, etc.

ÄMIJ

Vowel: homage.

Cf. bombage, etc.

AMIK

d: Adamic, preadamic.

g: agamic, cryptogamic, gamic, monogamic, phanerogamic, polygamic.

gr: monogrammic, parallelogrammic, telegrammic, trigrammic.

h: Abrahamic.

l: epithalamic, Islamic.

n: adynamic, autodynamic, biodynamic, cinnamic, dynamic, electrodynamic, hydrodynamic, hyperdynamic, isodynamic.

r: ceramic, cosmoramic, cycloramic, dioramic, keramic, panoramic.

s: balsamic.

t: potamic.

Cf. slam Mick, etc.

ÄMIK

dr: hippodromic, orthodromic, palindromic.

k(c): comic, serio-comic, tragicomic.

kr: heliochromic, stereochromic.

m: cinnamomic*.

n: agronomic, astronomic, autonomic, economic, gastronomic, isonomic, metronomic, nomic, physiogonomic, taxonomic.

t: anatomic, atomic, diatomic, dystomic, entomic, microtomic, monatomic, phantomic, stereotomic, triatomic.

v: vomic.

ÄMIKS

n: economics, electrogasdynamics, group dynamics, phoronomics.

Plus omik+s.

AMIL

Vowel: amyl.

h: Hammill.

t: tamil.

Plus am ill, etc.

AMIN

f: famine.

g: gamin.

z: examine.

Plus ram in, etc.

AMING

d: damming, damning.

kr: cramming.

l: lambing, lamming.

r: ramming.

sh: shamming.

sl: slamming.

tr: tramming.

ĀMING

Vowel: aiming.

bl: blaming.

f: defaming.

fl: flaming, inflaming.

fr: framing.

g: gaming.

kl: acclaiming, claiming, declaiming, disclaiming, exclaiming, proclaiming, reclaiming.

l: laming.

m: maiming.

n: misnaming, naming, nicknaming, surnaming.

sh: shaming.
t: taming.

ÄMING

b: embalming.
k(c): becalming, calming.
kw: qualming.
l: salaaming.

AMIS

Vowel: amice.
kl: chlamys.
t: tamis.
  Cf. slam miss, etc.

ÄMIS

pr: promise.
  Cf. ma miss, etc.

AMISH

f: affamish, enfamish, famish.
h: haimish, Hamish.
r: rammish.

ĀMISH

l: lamish.
t: tamish.

ÄMISH

Vowel: Amish.
k(c): calmish.
kw: qualmish.

ÄMIST

b: embalmist.
p: palmist.
s: psalmist.
  Plus shah missed *or* mist, etc.
  Cf. calm mist or missed, etc.

AMĪT

s: samite.
  Cf. slam might *or* mite, etc.

ÄMIT

c: comet.
v: vomit.
  Plus from it, etc.

AMKIN

l: lambkin.
  Plus am kin, etc.

ĀMLĒ

g: gamely.
l: lamely.
n: namely.
t: tamely.
  Plus shame, Lee *or* lea, etc.

ÄMLĒ

k(c): calmly.
  Plus balm Lee *or* lea, etc.

AMLING

l: lambling.

ĀMLƏS

Vowel: aimless.
bl: blameless.
f: fameless.
fl: flameless.
fr: frameless.
g: gameless.
kl: claimless.
n: nameless.
sh: shameless.
t: tameless.
  Plus same less, etc.

ÄMLƏS

b: balmless.
kw: qualmless.
p: palmless.
s: psalmless.
Plus calm less, etc.

AMLƏT

h: hamlet.
k(c): camlet.
s: samlet.
Plus jam let, etc.

ÄMLƏT

Vowel: omelet.
Plus from Lett *or* let, etc.

ÄMMƏNT

b: embalmment.
k(c): becalmment.
Plus psalm meant, etc.

ĀMNƏS

g: gameness.
l: lameness
s: sameness.
t: tameness.

ÄMNƏS

k(c): calmness.

AMŌ

w: whammo.

AMPÄRT

r: rampart.
Plus slam part, etc.
Plus vamp art, etc.

AMPĒ

kr: crampy.
v: vampy.
Plus damp, he, etc.
Plus sham pea, etc.

ÄMPĒ

p: Pompey.
Plus swamp, he, etc.

AMPĒR

Vowel: ampere.
Plus sham peer, etc.
Cf. camp here, etc.

AMPEST

d: dampest.
k(c): campest*, decampest*, encampest*.
kr: crampest*.
r: rampest*.
sk(sc): scampest*.
st: stampest*.
tr: trampest*.
v: vampest*.
Plus sham pest, etc.

AMPETH

d: dampeth*.
k(c): campeth*, decampeth*, encampeth*.
kr: crampeth*.
r: rampeth*.
sk(sc): scampeth*.
st: stampeth*.
tr: trampeth*.
v: vampeth*.

AMPING

ch: champing.
d: damping.
k(c): camping, decamping, encamping.
kl: clamping.
kr: cramping.
l: lamping.
r: ramping.
sk(sc): scamping.
st: stamping.
t: tamping.
tr: tramping.
v: vamping.

AMPĪR

v: vampire.
   Plus sham pyre, etc.
   Plus damp ire, etc.
   Cf. camp hire *or* higher, etc.

AMPISH

d: dampish.
sk(sc): scampish.

ÄMPISH

r: rompish.
sw: swampish.
   Plus bomb, pish!, etc.

AMPL

Vowel: ample.
s: ensample*, sample.
tr: trample.
z: example.
   Plus ram pull, etc.
   Plus scamp'll, etc.

ĀMPLAN

g: game plan.

AMPLD

tr: untrampled.
   Plus ampl+d.
   Plus example'd, etc.

AMPLĒ

d: damply.
   Plus camp lea *or* Lee, etc.
   Plus sham plea, etc.

AMPLING

s: ensampling, sampling.
tr: trampling.

ÄMPLISH

k(c): accomplish.
   Plus pomp, Lish, etc.

AMPLUR

Vowel: ampler.
s: sampler.
tr: trampler.
z: exampler.

AMPMƏNT

k(c): decampment, encampment.
   Plus scamp meant, etc.

AMPNƏS

d: dampness.

AMPRĒ

l: lamprey.

AMPSƏN

l: Lampson.
s: Sampson.
   Plus damp sun *or* son, etc.
   Cf. Samson.
   Cf. sham sun *or* sun, etc.

ÄMPTƏD

pr: prompted, unprompted.
  Plus pomp, Ted, etc.
  Plus prompt, Ed, etc.

AMPTƏN

h: Hampton.
kr: Crampton.
  Plus scamp ton *or* tun, etc.
  Plus camped on, etc.

ÄMPTƏN

br: Brompton.
k(c): Compton, Lecompton.
p: Pompton.
  Plus romp, ton *or* tun, etc.
  Plus prompt 'un, etc.

AMPŲR

ch: champer.
d: damper.
h: hamper.
k(c): camper.
kl: clamper.
kr: cramper.
p: pamper.
sk(sc): scamper.
st: stamper.
t: tamper.
tr: trampler.
v: vamper.
  Plus vamp her, err, *or* er, etc.

AMPŲRD

h: hampered, unhampered.
p: pampered.
t: tampered.
  Plus camp heard, etc.
  Plus Sam purred, etc.

AMPŲRZ

ch: champers.
P: Pampers.

AMPUS

gr: grampus.
k(c): campus.
  Plus lamp us, etc.
  Cf. sham puss, etc.

ÄMPUS

p: pompous.
  Plus swamp us, etc.

AMPƏN

d: dampen.
j: jampan.
s: sampan.
t: tampan.
  Plus damn pen, etc.
  Plus sham pan, etc.
  Cf. damp hen, etc.

AMPƏZ

p: pampas.
  Plus Tampa's, grampa's, etc.

AMRÄD

r: ramrod.
  Plus sham rod, etc.

AMRÄK

sh: shamrock.
  Plus slam rock, etc.

ĀMSTŲR

g: gamester.
  Plus fame stir, etc.

AMTRAK

Vowel: Amtrak.

AMUR

d: dammer, damner.

dr: mellowdrammer.

g: gammer.

gl: glamour.

gr: grammar, grammer.

h: hammer, ninnyhammer, sledgehammer, yellowhammer.

j: jammer, Rammer Jammer, windjammer.

kl: clamor.

kr: crammer.

l: lamber.

n: enamor.

r: rammer.

sh: shammer.

skr(sqr): scrammer.

sl: slammer.

st: stammer.

y: yammer.

　　Plus slam her, err, *or* er, etc.

ĀMUR

Vowel: aimer.

bl: blamer.

f: defamer, disfamer.

fl: inflamer.

fr: framer.

g: gamer.

kl: acclaimer, claimer, declaimer, disclaimer, exclaimer, proclaimer, reclaimer.

kr: Kramer.

l: lamer.

m: maimer.

n: misnamer, namer, nicknamer.

sh: shamer.

t: Tamar, tamer, testamur.

　　Plus shame her, err, *or* er, etc.

　　Plus spray myrrh, etc.

ÄMUR

b: Balmer, bomber, embalmer.

k(c): calmer.

p: palmer.

　　Plus calm her, err, *or* er, etc.

　　Plus from her *or* err, etc.

ÄMURS

k(c): commerce.

　　Plus from Erse, etc.

AMWĀ

tr: tramway.

　　Plus sham weigh *or* way, etc.

ÄMZĒ

m: malmsey.

　　Plus calms, he, etc.

AMZƏL

Vowel: amsel.

d: damsel.

　　Plus clam sell, etc.

　　Cf. clams, hell!, etc.

AMZƏN

d: damson.

AMƏ

b: Alabama.

g: digamma.

　　Plus damn a, etc.

ĀMƏ

　　Plus stray, ma, etc.

ÄMƏ

br: Brahma.
dr: docudrama, drama, melo-
drama.
g: gamma.
h: Bahama, Yokahama.
j: pajama, pyjama.
k(c): comma, Kaama, Kama.
l: Dalai Lama, lama, llama, Teshu
Lama.
m: mamma, momma.
r: cosmorama, cyclorama,
diorama, georama, neorama,
panorama, Rama.
y: Fujiyama, Yama.
　Plus from a, etc.
　Plus salaam a, etc.

AMƏK

h: hammock.
m: mammock.
　Plus slam mock, etc.

AMƏL

h: Hamal.
k(c): camel, Campbell.
m: mammal.
n: enamel.
tr: entrammel, trammel.
　Plus ram'll, etc.

AMƏLD

n: enamelled.
tr: untrammelled.

AMƏN

Vowel: Ammon.
d: daman.
g: backgammon, gammon.
m: mammon.

s: salmon.
sh: shaman.
　Plus ham on, etc.
　Plus slam an, etc.

ĀMƏN

Vowel: amen+.
br: Bremen.
d: dayman.
dr: drayman.
fl: flamen.
h: Haman.
k(c): caiman, cayman.
l: layman, Lehmann.
r: foramen.
st: stamen.
v: gravamen.
w: highwayman, Weyman.
z: examen.
　Plus a man.
　Plus weigh men, etc.
　Cf. shame in, etc.

ÄMƏN

Vowel: amen+.
k(c): common, uncommon.
　Plus bomb on or an, etc.

AMƏND

h: Hammond.

ĀMƏND

r: Raymond.

ÄMƏND

Vowel: almond, bitter almond,
Jordan almond.
　Cf. Hammond

AMƏNT

　Plus scram ant or aunt, etc.

ĀMƏNT

Vowel: ament.
fr: defrayment.
kl: claimant, clament.
l: allayment.
p: payment, repayment.
r: raiment.
tr: betrayment.
    Plus treymeant, etc.
    Plus ament.
    Cf. claim ant *or* aunt, etc.

AMƏS

l: Lammas.
t: Tammas.

ĀMƏS

Vowel: Amos.
d: mandamus.
f: famous.
h: hamous
r: biramous, ignoramous.
s: Samos.
sh: Shaemas.
skw: squamous.
    Plus lame us, etc.
    Plus may muss, etc.
    Plus reclaim us, etc.

ÄMƏS

t: Thomas.
    Cf. from us, etc.

AMƏSK

d: damask.
    Plus ham, ask, etc.

AMƏT

g: gamut.
    Cf. damn mutt, etc.

ÄMƏT

d: domett.
gr: grommet.
k(c): comet.
    Cf. from it, etc.
    Cf. mamma met, etc.

AMƏTH

m: mammoth.
    Plus sham moth, etc.

ÄMƏZ

h: Bahamas.
j: cat's pajamas.
    Plus ama+s.

ÄNÄRK

m: monarch.
    Plus on ark *or* arc, etc.

ANĀT

t: tannate.
    Plus Fan ate *or* eight, etc.

ĀNĀT

l: lanate.
p: impanate.
    Plus reign eight, plain ate, etc.

ÄNĀT

k: khanate.
    Plus wan eight *or* ate, etc.

ĀNBŌ

r: rainbow.
    Plus gain beau, bow, *or* bo, etc.

ANCHĒ

br: branchy.
    Plus ranch, he, etc.

ÄNCHĒ

p: paunchy.
Plus launch, he, etc.

ANCHEST

bl: blanchest*.
skr(scr): scranchest*.

ÄNCHEST

l: launchest*.
st: stanchest.
Plus wan chest, etc.

ANCHETH

bl: blancheth*.
skr(scr): scrancheth*.

ÄNCHETH

l: launcheth*.
st: stancheth*.

ANCHING

bl: blanching.
br: branching.
l: avalanching.
r: ranching.

ÄNCHING

l: launching.
st: stanching.

ANCHĪZ

fr: affranchise, disfranchise, enfranchise, franchise.
Plus ranch eyes, etc.

ANCHLƏS

br: branchless.
l: avalanchless.

r: ranchless.
st: stanchless.
Plus blanch less, etc.

ÄNCHLƏS

l: launchless.
p: paunchless.
Plus launch less, etc.

ANCHUR

br: brancher.
r: rancher.
Plus blanch her *or* err, etc.

ÄNCHUR

l: launcher.
st: stancher.
Plus launch her, etc.

ANCHƏT

m: manchet.
pl: planchet.
Plus can Chet, etc.

ANCHƏZ

bl: blanches.
br: branches.
l: avalanches.
r: ranches.
Cf. ranch is, etc.

ÄNCHƏZ

l: launches.
p: paunches.
st: stanches.
Cf. paunch is, etc.

ANDĀT

m: mandate.
Plus plan date, etc.
Plus planned eight *or* ate, etc.

ANDBAG

h: handbag.
s: sandbag.
　　Plus grandbag, etc.

ANDBÄKS

b: bandbox.
s: sandbox.
　　Plus planned box, etc.

ANDBOI

b: bandboy.
s: sandboy.
　　Plus grand boy, etc.

ANDBÔL

h: handball.
s: sandball.
　　Plus grand ball, etc.

ANDCHĪLD

gr: grandchild.
　　Plus banned child, etc.

ANDĒ

Vowel: Andy.
b: bandy.
br: brandy.
d: dandy, jack-a-dandy, Jim-Dandy, Yankee-Doodle Dandy.
gl: glandy.
gr: Rio Grande.
h: handy, unhandy.
k(c): candy, sugar-candy.
m: Mandy.
p: pandy.
r: jaborandi, randy.
s: sandy.
t: Tandy.
　　Plus and he, etc.
　　Plus Ann D., etc.

ÄNDĒ

g: Ghandi.
gr: Rio Grande.
sp: dispondee, spondee.
　　Plus fond, he, etc.
　　Plus on Dee, etc.
　　Cf. andi.

ANDĒD

br: brandied.
k(c): candid, candied.

ĀNDĒR

r: reindeer.
　　Plus plain dear *or* deer, etc.
　　Plus obtained ear, etc.

ANDEST

b: bandest*, disbandest*.
br: brandest*.
gr: grandest.
h: handest*.
l: landest*.
m: commandest*, demandest*, remandest*, reprimandest*.
p: expandest*.
st: standest*, withstandest*.

ÄNDEST

b: bondest*, vagabondest*.
f: fondest.
sk(sc): abscondest*.
sp: correspondest*, despondest*, respondest*.

ANDETH

b: bandeth*, disbandeth*.
br: brandeth*.
h: handeth*.
l: landeth*.

m: commandeth*, demandeth*, remandeth*, reprimandeth*.
p: expandeth*.
st: standeth*, withstandeth*.
   Plus plan death, etc.

ĀNDETH

br: brain death.

ÄNDETH

b: bondeth*, vagabondeth*.
sk(sc): abscondeth*.
sp: correspondeth*, despondeth*, respondeth*.
   Plus on death, etc.

ANDĒZ

Vowel: Andes.
n: Hernandes.
   Plus planned ease, etc.

ANDFAST

h: handfast.
   Plus stand fast, etc.

ANDFIL

l: land fill.

ANDID

b: bandid.
k(c): candid, uncandid.
   Plus anded.
   Plus Ann did, etc.

ANDIJ

b: bandage.
gl: glandage.
st: standage.
   Cf. grand age, etc.

ÄNDIJ

b: bondage, vagabondage.
fr: frondage.
   Cf. beyond age, etc.

ANDING

b: banding, disbanding.
br: branding.
h: handing, unhanding.
l: landing.
m: commanding, countermanding, demanding, remanding, reprimanding.
p: expanding.
s: ampersanding, sanding.
st: notwithstanding, outstanding, standing, understanding, withstanding.
str: stranding.

ÄNDING

b: bonding, vagabonding.
sk(sc): absconding.
sp: coresponding, corresponding, desponding, responding.

ANDISH

bl: blandish.
br: brandish.
gr: grandish.
l: outlandish.
   Plus plan dish, etc.

ANDIST

b: contrabandist.
g: propagandist.

ANDIT

b: bandit.
   Plus hand it, etc.

ANDL

d: dandle.
h: handle, manhandle, mishandle.
k(c): candle.
r: Randall, Randle.
s: sandal.
sk(sc): scandal.
v: vandal.
   Plus brand'll, etc.
   Cf. man dull, etc.

ÄND'L

f: fondle.
r: rondle.
   Plus beyond'll, etc.
   Cf. Don, dull, etc.

ANDLĒ

bl: blandly.
gr: grandly.
   Plus manned, Lee *or* lea, etc.

ÄNDLĒ

f: fondly.
   Plus beyond Lee *or* lea, etc.

ANDLING

br: brandling.
h: handling, manhandling, mishandling.
k(c): candling.

ANDLÔRD

l: landlord.
   Plus sand lord, etc.

ANDLŲR

ch: chandler, tallow chandler.
d: dandler.
h: handler.
k(c): candler.

ANDLƏS

b: bandless.
br: brandless.
gl: glandless.
h: handless.
l: landless.
m: commandless.
s: sandless.
str: strandless.
   Plus stand less *or* Les, etc.

ANDMĀD

h: handmade, handmaid.
   Plus sand made, etc.

ANDMÄRK

l: landmark.
   Plus sand mark, etc.

ANDMƏNT

b: disbandment.
m: commandment, remandment.
   Plus land meant, etc.

ANDNƏS

bl: blandness.
gr: grandness.

ÄNDNƏS

bl: blondless.
f: fondness.

ANDŌ, ÄNDŌ

gr: grando*.
l: Orlando.
m: commando.
n: Ferdinando, Fernando, Hernando.
t: lentando.
   Plus plan dough *or* doe, etc.

ÄNDOO

f: fondu.

Plus Don do, etc.

Cf. cheese fondue, etc.

ANDOOR

gr: grandeur.

Plus land your *or* you're, etc.

ANDOUT

h: handout.

Plus planned out, etc.

Plus man doubt, etc.

ANDRĀL

l: land rail.

ANDRĒ

Vowel: meandry, polyandry.

ch: chandry*.

m: commandry.

sh: shandry.

ÄNDRĒ

l: laundry.

ANDRIK

Vowel: polyandric, theandric.

Plus grand rick, etc.

ANDRIL

m: mandril.

Plus can drill, etc.

Plus planned rill, etc.

ANDRIN

m: salamandrine.

s: Alexandrine.

ANDRUS

Vowel: meandrous, polyandrous.

ANDRƏ, ĀNDRƏ

s: Alessandra, Alexandra, Cassandra.

ÄNDRƏ

k(c): dichondra.

s: Sondra.

ANDRƏL

sp: spandrel.

Cf. hand rail.

ANDRƏS

p: pandress.

Plus can dress, etc.

ANDSAT

l: landsat.

ANDSĪR

gr: grandsire.

Plus fanned sire, etc.

Cf. band's ire, etc.

ANDSKĀP

l: landscape.

Cf. band's cape, etc.

ANDSTAND

b: bandstand.

gr: grandstand.

Plus land stand, etc.

ANDSƏN

gr: grandson.

Plus planned sun *or* son, etc.

ANDUM

m: mandom.
r: memorandum, random.
t: ad captandum, tandem.
z: avizandum.
    Plus land 'em, etc.
    Plus man dumb, etc.

ĀNDUR

m: remainder.
t: attainder.
    Plus obtained her *or* err, etc.

ÄNDUR

b: bonder.
bl: blonder.
f: fonder.
k(c): hypochonder*.
l: launder, Uitlander.
p: ponder.
sk(sc): absconder.
skw: squander.
sp: coresponder, corresponder, desponder, responder.
w: wander.
y: yonder.
    Plus bond her *or* err, etc.
    Plus pawned her *or* err, etc.
    Cf. condor.

ANDURD

Vowel: meandered.
l: philandered.
p: pandered.
sl: slandered.
st: standard.

ANDURZ

fl: bouvier des Flandres.

ÄNDURZ

s: Sanders, Saunders.
    Cf. on durz.
    Cf. glanders.

ANDZMƏN

b: bandsman.
l: landsman.
    Plus commands man, etc.

ANDƏ

g: propaganda.
m: Amanda.
r: jacaranda, Miranda, memoranda, veranda.
    Plus land a, etc.

ÄNDƏ

f: Fonda.
k(c): anaconda.
r: Deronda, Ruanda.
    Plus blonde a, etc.

ANDƏD

b: banded, contrabanded, disbanded.
br: branded, unbranded.
d: deodanded.
gl: glanded, goat-glanded, monkey-glanded.
h: back-handed, black-handed, cleanhanded, closehanded, empty-handed, evenhanded, first-handed, forehanded, four-handed, freehanded, full-handed, handed, hardhanded, heavyhanded, highhanded, lefthanded, light-handed, lilyhanded, neat-handed, open-handed, overhanded, red-handed, right-handed, short-handed, single-handed, swift-handed, two-handed, underhanded, unhanded.

k(c): candid.

l: landed, unlanded.

m: commanded, countermanded, demanded, remanded, reprimanded.

p: expanded.

s: sanded.

str: stranded.

Plus man dead, etc.

Cf. Klan did, etc.

ÄNDƏD

b: bonded.

sk(sc): absconded.

sp: corresponded, desponded, responded.

Plus Don dead, etc.

Cf. Don did, etc.

ANDƏL

m: coromandel.

r: Randall.

ÄNDƏL

r: rondel.

Plus beyond L or el, etc.

Plus Don Dell, etc.

Cf. on d'l.

ANDƏM

f: fandom.

ANDƏN

b: abandon.

l: Landon.

sh: Shandon.

Plus land on, etc.

Plus man don, etc.

ÄNDƏNS

sp: correspondence, despondence, respondence.

Plus Don, dense or dents, etc.

Cf. fond, hence, etc.

ANDƏNT

k(c): candent.

sk(sc): scandent.

m: commandant, demandant, mandant.

Plus banned ant or aunt, etc.

Plus man dent, etc.

ÄNDƏNT

fr: frondent.

sp: corespondent, correspondent, despondent, respondent.

Plus Don dent, etc.

ANDƏR

Vowel: coriander, Leander, meander, oleander.

b: disbander.

bl: blander.

br: brander.

d: dander.

g: gander, goosey-gander.

gl: glander.

gr: grander.

h: backhander, hander, left-hander, right-hander.

k(c): Africander, candor.

l: Greenlander, Icelander, lander, Newfoundlander, philander, Uitlander.

m: commander, demander, gerrymander, Pomander, remander, reprimander, salamander.

n: Menander.

p: expander, pandar, pander.

s: Alexander, sander.

sl: slander.

st: bystander, stander, understander, withstander.

str: strander.
t: dittander.
> Plus commander her *or* err, etc.

ANĒ

Vowel: Annie.
br: branny.
f: Fannie, Fanny.
gr: granny.
k(c): canny, uncanny.
kr: cranny.
l: Lannie.
m: mannie.
n: Nannie.
> Plus plan, he, etc.

ĀNĒ

br: brainy.
ch: Cheyney.
g: Allegheny.
gr: grainy.
l: Delaney.
r: Rainey, rainy.
v: veiny.
z: zany.
> Plus main, he, etc.
> Plus play knee, etc.

ÄNĒ

b: bonnie, bonny.
j: Johnny.
k: Connie.
l: Lonnie.
p: frangipani.
pr: soprani.
r: Ranee, rani, Ronnie.
st: Hindustani.
v: Galvani.
> Plus Don, he, etc.
> Cf. ma, knee, etc.
> Cf. don, he, etc.

ANĒD

kr: crannied.
> Cf. plan, hid, etc.

ANEST

b: bannest*.
f: fannest*.
m: mannest*, unmannest*.
pl: plannest*.
sk(sc): scannest*.
sp: spannest*.
t: tannest.

ĀNEST

Vowel: inanest.
b: urbanest.
ch: chainest*, enchainest*, unchainest*.
d: deignest*, disdainest*, foreordainest*, ordainest*.
dr: drainest*.
f: feignest*, profanest.
fr: refrainest*.
g: gainest*, regainest*.
gr: grainest*.
k(c): canest*.
kr: cranest*.
m: humanest, remainest*.
p: campaignest*, painest*.
pl: complainest*, explainest*, plainest.
r: arraignest*, rainest*, reignest*, reinest*.
s: sanest.
spr: sprainest*.
st: abstainest*, stainest*.
str: constrainest*, restrainest*, strainest*.
t: appertainest*, ascertainest*, attainest*, containest*, detainest*, entertainest*, maintainest*, obtainest*, retainest*, sustainest*.
tr: trainest*.

v: vainest.
w: wanest*.
Plus play nest, etc.

ÄNEST

Vowel: dishonest, honest.
d: donnest*.
k(c): connest*.
n: nonest.
w: wannest.
Plus ma nest, etc.

ANETH

b: banneth*.
f: fanneth*.
m: manneth*, unmanneth*.
pl: planneth*.
sk(sc): scanneth*.
sp: spanneth*.
t: tanneth*.

ĀNETH

ch: chaineth*, enchaineth*, unchaineth*.
d: deigneth*, disdaineth*, foreordaineth*, ordaineth*, preordaineth*.
dr: draineth*.
f: feigneth*, profaneth*.
fr: refraineth*.
g: gaineth*, regaineth*.
gr: graineth*.
k(c): caneth*.
kr: craneth*.
m: remaineth*.
p: paineth*.
pl: complaineth*, explaineth*.
r: arraigneth*, raineth*, reigneth*, reineth*.
spr: spraineth*.
st: abstaineth*, staineth*.

str: constraineth*, restraineth*, straineth*.
t: appertaineth*, ascertaineth*, attaineth*, containeth*, detaineth*, entertaineth*, maintaineth*, obtaineth*, retaineth*, sustaineth*.
tr: traineth*.
w: waneth*.

ÄNETH

d: donneth*.
k(c): conneth*.

ANFĒLD

k(c): Canfield.
Plus plan field, etc.

ANFER

f: fanfare.
Plus plan fair *or* fare, etc.
Plus Banff air, etc.

ĀNFOOL

b: baneful.
d: disdainful.
p: painful.
pl: complainful.
Plus skein full, etc.

ĀNGANG

ch: chain gang.
tr: train gang.
Plus restrain gang, etc.

ANGGAR

h: hangar.
Plus sprang gar, etc.

ANGĒ

f: fangy.
kl: clangy.
sl: slangy.

ANGGRĒ

Vowel: angry.

ANGGUR

Vowel: anger, angor.
kl: clangor.
l: languor.

ANGGWID

l: languid.

ANGGWIJ

l: body language, language, sign language.

ANGGWIN

Vowel: anguine.
s: ensanguine, sanguine.
    Cf. gang win, etc.

ANGGWISH

Vowel: anguish.
l: languish.
    Cf. gang wish, etc.

ANGING

b: banging.
h: hanging, overhanging, paper hanging.
hw: slang-whanging, whanging.
kl: clanging.
r: haranguing.
sl: slanging.
tw: twanging.

ANGKĒ

h: hanky.
kr: cranky.
l: lanky.
p: hanky-panky.
pl: planky.

pr: pranky.
t: tanky.
y: Yankee.
    Plus rang key, etc.

ANGKEST

b: embankest*.
bl: blankest.
d: dankest.
fl: flankest*, outflankest*.
fr: frankest.
kl: clankest*.
l: lankest.
r: rankest.
s: sankest*.
sp: spankest*.
th: thankest*.

ANGKETH

b: embanketh*.
bl: blanketh*.
fl: flanketh*, outflanketh*.
kl: clanketh*.
r: ranketh*.
s: sanketh*.
sp: spanketh*.
th: thanketh*.

ANGKFOOL

pr: prankful.
th: thankful.
    Plus sank full, etc.

ANGKING

b: banking, embanking.
bl: blanking.
fl: flanking, outflanking.
fr: franking.
kl: clanking.
pl: planking.
r: outranking, ranking.
sp: spanking.

t: tanking.
th: thanking.
y: yanking.
   Plus hang king, etc.

ANGKISH

d: dankish.
fr: frankish.
l: lankish.
pr: prankish.
   Plus hang Kish, etc.

ANGKL

Vowel: ankle.
h: hankle.
kr: crankle.
r: rankle.
   Plus spank'll, etc.
   Cf. gang cull *or* kill, etc.

ANGKLĒ

bl: blankly.
d: dankly.
fr: frankly.
l: lankly.
r: rankly.
   Plus thank Lee *or* lea, etc.

ANGKLIN

fr: Franklin.
   Plus ranklin', etc.
   Plus spank Lynn, etc.

ANGKLING

h: hankling.
r: rankling.
   Plus gang cling, etc.

ANGKLƏS

b: bankless.
bl: blankless.

fl: flankless.
kl: clankless.
kr: crankless.
pl: plankless.
pr: prankless.
r: rankless.
sh: shankless.
sp: spankless.
th: thankless.
   Plus hank less, etc.

ANGKLƏT

Vowel: anklet.
   Plus spank let *or* Lett, etc.

ANGKMƏNT

b: bankment, embankment.
fl: outflankment.
   Plus rank meant, etc.

ANGKNƏS

bl: blankness.
d: dankness.
fr: frankness.
kr: crankness.
l: lankness.
r: rankness.

ANGKŌ

b: banco.
m: calamanco.
   Plus spank owe *or* O, etc.

ANGKSHUN

s: sanction.
   Plus bank shun, etc.

ANGKSHUS

Vowel: anxious.

ANGKTUM

s: sanctum.

Plus ranked 'em, etc.

ANGKUR

Vowel: anchor, sheet anchor, unanchor, up-anchor.
b: banker.
bl: blanker.
ch: chancre.
d: danker.
fl: flanker, outflanker.
fr: franker.
h: hanker.
k(c): canker, encanker.
kl: clanker.
kr: cranker.
l: lanker.
pl: planker.
pr: pranker.
r: rancor, ranker.
sh: shanker.
sp: spanker.
t: tanker.
th: thanker.
y: yanker.

Plus yank her *or* err, etc.

ANGKURD

Vowel: anchored, unanchored.
br: brancard.
k(c): cankered.
t: tankard.

Plus angkur+ed.

ANGKWIL

tr: tranquil.

Plus bank will, etc.

ANGKWISH

v: vanquish.

Plus frank wish, etc.

ANGKWƏT

b: banquet.

Plus hank wet, etc.

ANGKƏT

b: banket.
bl: blanket, receiving blanket.

Cf. spank it, etc.

ANGL

Vowel: angle, triangle.
b: bangle.
br: brangle, embrangle.
d: dangle.
j: interjangle, jangle.
l: phalangal.
m: bemangle, mangle, mingle-mangle.
r: quadrangle, Wrangel, wrangle.
sp: bespangle, spangle.
str: strangle.
t: disentangle, entangle, intertangle, sea tangle, tangle, untangle.
tw: twangle.
w: wangle.

Cf. rang gull, etc.

Cf. Wang'll, etc.

ANGLD

f: new-fangled.
sp: spangled, star-spangled.

Plus angl+d.

ANGLĒ

sp: spangly.
t: tangly.

Plus rang, Lee *or* lea, etc.

ANGLING

Vowel: angling.

Plus ang'l+ing.

ANGLUR

Vowel: angler.

Plus ang'l+er.

ANGLƏS

f: fangless.
p: pangless.

Plus hang less, etc.

ANGMƏN

h: hangman.

Plus sang, man, etc.

ANGŌ

d: fandango.
m: mango.
p: Pago Pago, Pango Pango.
t: contango, tango.

Plus gang go, etc.

ANGRŌV

m: mangrove.

Plus plan grove, etc.

ANGSTUR

g: ganster.

Plus sang, stir, etc.

ANGUR

b: banger.
g: ganger.
h: hangar, hanger, paper hanger, straphanger.
hw: slang-whanger.
kl: clangor.
r: haranguer.

Plus hang her *or* err, etc.

ANGWILL

z: Zangwill.

Plus gang will, etc.

ÄNGƏ

d: donga.
k(c): conga.
m: Rancho Cucamonga.

ÄNGƏN

l: longan.

ANHOOD

m: manhood.

Plus scan hood, etc.

ANIJ

m: manage.
p: pannage.
t: tannage.

Cf. scan age, etc.

ĀNIJ

dr: drainage.
kr: cranage.

Cf. main age, etc.

ANIK

Vowel: cyanic, ferricyanic, hydrocyanic, interoceanic, Messianic, oceanic, Ossianic, valerianic.
d: rhodanic.
f: Aristophanic, diaphanic, lexiphanic, theophanic.
g: organic, paganic.
k(c): mechanic, volcanic, vulcanic.
l: Magellanic.
m: aldermanic, Alemannic, Brahmanic, Germanic, Indo-Germanic, Mussulmanic, Romanic, talismanic.
p: panic, tympanic.
st: stannic.
t: botanic, Britannic, charlatanic, montanic, puritanic, quercitannic,

satanic, sultanic, tannic, tetanic, titanic.

v: galvanic.

Cf. man nick *or* Nick, etc.

ÄNIK

Vowel: amphictyonic, embryonic, ganglionic, histrionic, interganglionic, Ionic, Olympionic, Pharaonic, zoonic.

b: bubonic, cabonic.

d: Adonic, Chalcedonic, hedonic, sardonic.

f: antiphonic, cacophonic, cataphonic*, colophonic, diaphonic, euphonic, homophonic, monophonic, phonic, photophonic, polyponic, symphonic, telephonic.

g: agonic, geogonic, jargonic, theogonic.

k(c): conic, draconic, laconic, Tychonic.

kl: cyclonic.

kr: acronyc, chronic, monochronic.

l: Babylonic, colonic.

m: anharmonic, daemonic, demonic, gnomonic, harmonic, hegemonic, mnemonic, pathognomonic, philharmonic, pneumonic, pulmonic, sermonic, Solomonic.

n: canonic.

p: geoponic, hydroponic.

r: Aaronic, ironic, macaronic, Pyrrhonic, stentoronic.

s: masonic, parsonic.

t: architectonic, atonic, crotonic, diatonic, Housatonic, isotonic, Metonic, Miltonic, monotonic, neoplatonic, paratonic, platonic, Plutonic, semitonic, stratonic, tectonic, Teutonic, tonic.

th: pythonic.

v: Slavonic.

Cf. ma nick, etc.

ANIKS

k(c): body mechanics, mechanics.

m: humanics.

p: panics.

Plus anik+s

Cf. plan nix *or* nicks, etc.

ÄNIKS

Vowel: histrionics, onyx.

d: hedonics.

f: phonics.

l: Megalonyx.

m: mnemonics.

p: geoponics, hydroponics.

t: plate tectonics.

Plus onik+s.

ANIL

Vowel: anil.

Plus man ill, etc.

Cf. plan nil, etc.

ANĪL

Vowel: anile.

Cf. man, Nile, etc.

ĀNIM

p: paynim.

Plus gay Nym, etc.

Plus pain him, etc.

ANIN

t: tannin.

Plus plan in *or* inn, etc.

ANING

Vowel: Anning.
b: banning.
f: fanning.
fl: flanning.
k(c): canning.
m: manning, remanning, unmanning.
p: japanning, panning, trepanning.
pl: planning.
sk(sc): scanning
sp: inspanning, outspanning, spanning.
t: tanning.

ĀNING

br: braining.
ch: chaining, enchaining, unchaining.
d: deigning, disdaining, foreordaining, ordaining, preordaining.
dr: draining.
f: feigning, profaning, unfeigning.
fr: refraining.
g: gaining, regaining.
gr: graining, ingraining.
k(c): caning.
kr: craning.
m: remaining.
p: campaigning, champagning, paining.
pl: airplaning, complaining, explaining, hydroplaning, plaining*, planing, uncomplaining.
r: arraigning, deraigning, raining, reigning, reining.
spr: spraining.
st: abstaining, bestaining, staining.
str: constraining, restraining, straining.

t: appertaining, ascertaining, attaining, containing, detaining, entertaining, maintaining, obtaining, pertaining, retaining, sustaining.
tr: entraining, training, uptraining.
v: veining.
w: waning.

ÄNING

d: donning.
k(c): conning.

ANIS

Vowel: anise.
  Cf. man is, etc.

ANISH

b: banish.
f: fannish.
kl: clannish.
m: mannish, Musselmanish.
pl: planish.
r: Alcoranish.
sp: Spanish.
v: evanish, vanish.

ANISH

b: urbanish.
d: Danish.
s: sanish.
v: vainish.

ÄNISH

m: admonish.
st: astonish.
t: tonnish.
w: wannish.

ANIST

Vowel: pianist.
r: Alcoranist.
t: tanist.

ĀNJĒ

m: mangy.
r: rangy.
  Plus strange, he, etc.
  Plus plain gee *or* G, etc.

ĀNJEST

ch: changest*, exchangest*,
interchangest*.
r: arrangest*, derangest*,
disarrangest*, rangest*.
str: strangest.
tr: estrangest*.
  Plus main jest, etc.

ĀNJEMMTH

ch: changeth*, exchangeth*,
interchangeth*.
r: arrangeth*, derangeth*,
disarrangeth*, rangeth*.
tr: estrangeth*.

ĀNJING

ch: changing, counterchanging,
exchanging, interchanging,
unchanging.
r: arranging, deranging,
disarranging,
ranging.
tr: estranging.

ANJL

v: evangel.
  Plus plan jell, etc.

ĀNJL

Vowel: angel.
  Plus range'll, etc.
  Plus reign jell, etc.

ĀNJLĒ

str: strangely.
  Plus mange, Lee *or* lea, etc.

ĀNJLING

ch: changeling.

ĀNJLƏS

ch: changless.
r: rangeless.
  Plus mange less *or* Les, etc.

ĀNJMƏNT

ch: exchangement,
interchangement.
r: arrangement, derangement,
disarrangement.
tr: estrangement.
  Plus mange meant, etc.

ĀNJNEƏS

str: strangeness.

ĀNJƱR

ch: changer, exchanger,
interchanger, money-
changer.
d: danger, endanger.
gr: granger.
m: manger.
r: arranger, bushranger, deranger,
disarranger, ranger.
str: stranger.
tr: tranger.
  Plus change her *or* err, etc.

ANJƏNT

fr: frangent.
pl: plangent.
t: cotangent, tangent.
    Plus fan gent, etc.

ANJƏZ

fl: flanges.
g: Ganges.
l: phalanges.
    Cf. flange is, etc.

ĀNJƏZ

ch: changes, exchanges, inter-changes.
gr: granges.
r: arranges, deranges, disarranges, enranges, ranges.
tr: estranges.
    Cf. mange is, etc.
    Cf. main jizz, etc.

ANKÄK

h: Hancock.
    Plus ran cock, etc.

ANKIN

h: Hankin.
r: Rankin.
    Plus plan kin, etc.
    Plus thank in *or* inn, etc.

ANKING

n: Nanking.
    Plus plan king, etc.
    Cf. angking.

ANKINZ

h: Hankins.
r: Rankins.

Plus thank inns *or* ins, etc.
Plus plan kin's, etc.

ÄNKLĀV

k: conclave.

ANKƏ

Vowel: Bianca.
s: Sanka.
t: tanka.
    Plus spank a, etc.

ANKƏN

fl: flanken.

ĀNLAND

m: mainland.
    Plus Seine land, etc.

ANLĒ

d: Danley.
m: Manley, manly, unmanly.
sp: spick-and-spanly.
st: Stanley.
    Plus plan Lee *or* lea, etc.

ĀNLĒ

Vowel: inanely.
f: profanely.
g: gainly.
m: humanely, mainly.
pl: plainly.
s: insanely, sanely.
v: vainly.
    Plus gain, Lee *or* lea, etc.

ANLING

m: manling.
t: tanling.

ANLƏS

b: banless.
f: fanless.
kl: clanless.
m: manless.
pl: planless.
sp: spanless.
t: tanless.

    Plus ran less *or* Les, etc.

ĀNLƏS

b: baneless, dogbaneless, etc.
br: brainless.
ch: clainless.
dr: drainless.
g: gainless.
gr: grainless.
k(c): caneless.
kr: craneless.
m: domainless, maneless.
p: painless.
r: rainless.
sk: skeinless.
spr: sprainless.
st: stainless.
str: strainless.
sw: swainless.
th: thaneless.
tr: trainless.
v: vaneless.

    Plus insane, Les *or* less

ĀNMƏNT

d: ordainment.
r: arraignment.
t: ascertainment, attainment, obtainment.

    Plus reign meant, etc.

ĀNNƏS

Vowel: inaneness.
f: profaneness.

m: humaneness.
pl: plainness.
s: insaneness, saneness.

ANŌ

Vowel: piano.
h: Hanno.
pr: soprano.

    Plus plan owe *or* O, etc.
    Cf. plan no *or* know, etc.

ĀNŌ

k(c): volcano.
pl: Plano.

    Plus say no *or* know, etc.
    Plus main owe *or* O, etc.

ÄNŌ

Vowel: guano, piano.
pr: soprano.
s: Montesano.

    Cf. on no *or* know, etc.

ÄNRAD

k(c): Conrad.

ĀNSĀ

g: gainsay.

    Plus plain say, etc.

ĀNSĀL

m: mainsail.

    Cf. plain sail, etc.

ANSĒ

Vowel: Ansey.
ch: chancy, mischancy, unchancy.
d: dancy.
f: fancy, sycophancy.
g: extravagancy, termagancy.
k(c): mendicancy, significancy, supplicancy.

kl: Clancey.

l: Delancey, petulancy, sibilancy.

m: aeromancy, aldermancy, alectoromancy, alectryomancy, aleuromancy, alphitomancy*, anthropomancy, astragalomancy, austromancy, axinomancy, belomancy, bibliomancy, botanomancy, captomancy, catoptromancy, ceromancy, chiromancy, cleromancy, coscinomancy, crithomancy, crystallomancy, dactyliomancy, enoptromancy, gastromancy, geomancy, gyromancy, halomancy, hieromancy, hydromancy, ichthyomancy, lecanomancy, lithomancy, meteoromancy, myomancy, necromancy, oenomancy, onomancy, onychomancy, ophiomancy, ornithomancy, pedomancy, psephomancy, psychomancy, pyrmancy, sciomancy, sideromancy, spodomancy, stichomancy, tephramancy.

n: consonancy, Miss Nancy, Nancy.

p: occupancy.

r: exuberancy.

t: exorbitancy, hesitancy, militancy, precipitancy.

   Plus man see, etc.
   Plus manse, he, etc.

ANSĒD

f: fancied.

ANSEST

ch: chancest*.

d: dancest*.

gl: glancest*.

h: enhancest*.

m: romancest*.

pr: prancest.

tr: entrancest*.

v: advancest*.

ANSETH

ch: chanceth*.

d: danceth*.

gl: glanceth*.

h: enhanceth*.

m: romanceth*.

pr: pranceth*.

tr: entranceth*.

v: advanceth*.

   Plus ran, Seth, etc.

ANSFUR

tr: transfer.

   Plus manse fir *or* fur, etc.

ANSHĒ

b: banshee.

   Plus can she, etc.

ANSHUN

m: mansion.

p: expansion.

sk(sc): scansion.

st: stanchion.

   Plus man shun, etc.

ÄNSHUS

k(c): conscious, self-conscious, subconscious, unconscious.

   Cf. launch us, etc.

ANSHƏL

n: financial.

st: circumstantial, substantial, supersubstantial.

   Plus man shall, etc.
   Plus ranch, Al, etc.

ÄNSHƏNS

k(c): conscience.

ANSHƏNT

tr: transient.

ĀNSHƏNT

Vowel: ancient.

ANSING

Vowel: affiancing, fiancing.
ch: chancing.
d: dancing.
gl: glancing.
h: enhancing.
l: lansing, Lansing.
m: chiromancing, necromancing,
etc., romancing.
pr: prancing.
tr: entrancing.
v: advancing.
  Plus man sing, etc.

ANSIS

fr: Frances, Francis.
  Plus plan, sis, etc.

ANSIST

m: romancist.
  Plus span cyst, etc.

ANSIV

p: expansive.
v: advancive.
  Plus plan sieve, etc.

ÄNSIV

sp: coresponsive, corresponsive,
irresponsive, responsive.
  Plus don sieve, etc.

ANSMƏNT

h: enhancement.
tr: entrancement.
v: advancement.
  Plus glance meant, etc.

ĀNSTĀ

m: mainstay.
  Plus plain stay, etc.

ÄNSTRĀTE

m: demonstrate*+, remonstrate.
  Plus Don, straight *or* strait, etc.

ÄNSTRUS

m: monstrous.
  Cf. Don's truss, etc.

ÄNSTRƏNCE

m: monstrance, remonstrance.
  Cf. Don's trance, etc.

ÄNSTƱR

m: monster.
  Plus Don stir, etc.

ÄNSTƏN

j: Johnston.
  Plus Don stun, etc.

ÄNSTƏNT

k(c): constant, inconstant.

ANSƱR

Vowel: Anser, answer.
ch: chancer.
d: belly-dancer, bubble-dancer,
dancer, fan-dancer, hula-dancer,
etc.

g: merganser.
gl: glancer.
k(c): cancer.
l: lancer.
m: chiromancer, geomancer, necromancer, etc., romancer.
pr: prancer.
tr: entrancer.
v: advancer.
  Plus advance her *or* err, etc.

ÄNSŲR

sp: sponsor.
t: tonsor.

ANSƏL

ch: chancel.
h: handsel.
k(c): cancel.
  Plus man sell, etc.
  Plus pants'll, etc.

ANSƏM

h: handsome, hansom, unhandsome.
r: ransom.
tr: transom.
  Plus plan some *or* sum, etc.

ANSƏN

Vowel: Anson.
h: Hanson.
  Plus plan, son *or* sun, etc.

ÄNSƏN

j: Johnson, Jonson.
  Plus Don, son *or* sun, etc.
  Cf. Wisconsin.

ANSƏT

l: lancet.
  Plus man set, etc.
  Plus Vance et, etc.

ANSƏZ

ch: chances, mischances.
d: dances.
gl: glances.
h: enhances.
l: lances.
m: romances.
n: finances.
p: expanses.
pr: prances.
tr: entrances, trances.
v: advances.
  Plus man says, etc.
  Plus dance, Ez, etc.
  Cf. manse is, etc.

ANTĀ

f: Infante.
  Plus plant a, etc.

ÄNTĀ

d: diamante.

ÄNTĀN

m: cismontane, tramontane, ultramontane.

ANTAZM

f: phantasm.
  Cf. aunt has 'em, etc.

ANTĒ

Vowel: ante.
d: Dante.

k(c): bacchante, canty.
p: panty.
r: Duranty, pococurante.
sh: shanty.
sk(sc): scanty.
t: dilettante.
z: zante.
  Plus ant he, etc.
  Plus plant, he, etc.
  Plus plan tea *or* T, etc.
  Plus span tea *or* T, etc.

ĀNTĒ

d: dainty.
f: fainty, feinty.
  Plus plain tea *or* T, etc.
  Plus ain't he, etc.

ÄNTĒ

Vowel: aunty, chianti.
d: andante, Dante.
  Plus aunt, he, etc.
  Cf. can't he, etc.

ANTEST

ch: chantest*, enchantest*.
gr: grantest*.
k(c): cantest*, decantest*, recantest*.
p: pantest*.
pl: implantest*, plantest*, supplantest*.
r: rantest*.
sk(sc): scantest.
sl: slantest*.
  Plus plan test, etc.

ĀNTEST

f: faintest*, feintest*.
kw: acquaintest*, quaintest.

p: paintest*.
t: taintest*.
  Plus main test, etc.

ANTETH

ch: chanteth*, enchanteth*.
gr: granteth*.
k(c): canteth*, decanteth*, recanteth*.
p: panteth*.
pl: implanteth*, planteth*, supplanteth*.
r: ranteth*.
sk(sc): scanteth*.
sl: slanteth.

ĀNTETH

f: fainteth*, feinteth*.
kw: acquainteth*.
p: painteth*.
t: tainteth*.

ANTĒZ

b: corybantes.
d: Dante's, Dantes.
l: atlantes.
  Plus can tease *or* T's, etc.
  Plus plant ease *or* E's, etc.
  Cf. anti+s

ANTHIK

n: oenanthic.
z: xanthic.
  Plus plan thick, etc.

ANTHIN

Vowel: anthine.
m: Rhadamanthine.
k(c): acanthine, tragacanthin.
r: amaranthine.
z: xanthin.

Plus ran thin, etc.

Plus amaranth in *or* inn, etc.

ĀNTHOOD

s: sainthood.

Plus paint hood.

ANTHUR

Vowel: anther.

p: panther.

Plus amaranth her *or* err, etc.

ANTHUS

Vowel: amianthus, ananthous, dianthus, polyanthous, synanthous.

k(c): acanthous, acanthus, anacanthous, canthus.

l: ailanthus, Galanthus.

m: Haemanthus.

n: Chimonanthus.

p: Agapanthus, epanthous.

r: hysteranthous.

Plus amaranth us, etc.

ANTHƏM

Vowel: anthem.

Plus amaranth 'em, etc.

ANTHƏN

x: xanthan.

ĀNTIF

pl: plaintiff.

Plus main tiff, etc.

Plus paint, if, etc.

ÄNTIF

p: pontiff.

Plus Don, tiff, etc.

ANTIJ

pl: plantage*.

v: advantage, disadvantage, vantage.

Cf. scant age, etc.

ÄNTIJ

p: pontage.

w: wantage.

Cf. font, age, etc.

ANTIK

Vowel: antic.

b: corybantic.

d: pedantic, Vedantic.

f: hierophantic, sycophantic.

fr: frantic.

g: gigantic.

l: Atlantic, mid-Atlantic, trans-atlantic.

m: chiromantic, geomantic, hydromantic, mantic, necroman-tic, onomantic, pyromantic, spodomantic, etc., romantic.

n: consonantic.

Plus plan tick, etc.

ÄNTIK

Vowel: Anacreontic.

d: mastodontic.

k(c): archontic.

kw: quantic.

p: pontic.

Plus Don, tick, etc.

ANTIN, ANTĪN

b: Brabantine.

f: chryselephantine, diophantine, elephantine.

g: gigantine*.

m: adamantine.

v: Levantine.
z: byzantine.
  Plus plan tin, etc.
  Plus plant in *or* inn, etc.
  Plus plan tine, etc.

ÄNTIN

k(c): dracontine.
p: Hellespontine, pontine.
  Plus font in *or* inn, etc.
  Plus con tin, etc.
  Cf. tontine.

ANTING

b: banting.
ch: chanting, disenchanting, enchanting.
gr: granting.
h: "hanting."
k(c): canting, decanting, descanting, recanting.
p: panting.
pl: implanting, planting, supplanting, transplanting.
r: ranting.
sk(sc): scanting.
sl: slanting.

ĀNTING

f: fainting, feinting.
kw: acquainting.
p: painting, word painting.
t: attainting, tainting.

ÄNTING

w: wonting.

ANTIST

k: Kantist.
r: ignorantist.

ÄNTIST

d: Vedantist.

ĀNTIV

pl: plaintive.
str: constraintive.

ANTIZM

k: Kantism.
r: ignorantism, obscurantism, pococurantism, rantism.
t: dilettantism.
  Plus plant ism, etc.

ANTL

k(c): cantle.
m: dismantle, immantle, mantel, mantle.
sk(sc): scantle.
  Plus plant'll, etc.

ANTLD

m: dismantled, ivy-mantled, mantled.
  Plus cantle'd, etc.

ANTLĒ

sk(sc): scantly.
sl: aslantly.
  Plus plant lea *or* Lee, etc.

ĀNTLĒ

kw: quaintly.
s: saintly, unsaintly.
  Plus paint Lee *or* lea, etc.

ĀNTLĪK

s: saintlike.
  Plus paint like, etc.

ANTLING

b: bantling.
m: mantling.
sk(sc): scantling.

ANTLUR

Vowel: antler.
m: dismantler, mantler.
p: pantler*.

ANTLƏT

k(c): cantlet.
m: mantlet.
pl: plantlet.
    Plus ant let *or* Lett, etc.

ANTMƏNT

ch: disenchantment, enchant-
ment.
    Plus plant meant, etc.

ANTNƏS

sk(sc): scantness.

ĀNTNƏS

f: faintness.
kw: quaintness.

ANTŌ

k(c): canto.
m: portmanteau.
r: coranto, quo warranto.
t: protanto.
    Plus plan toe, etc.
    Plus plant owe *or* O, etc.

ANT

b: Bantu.
    Plus can two, to, *or* too, etc.

ÄNTRAKT

k(c): contract, land contract.

ANTRÄN

Vowel: Antron.

ANTRĒ

ch: chantry.
p: pantry.
    Plus scan tree, etc.
    Cf. plant tree, etc.

ÄNTRĪT

k(c): contrite, uncontrite.
    Plus Don, trite, etc.
    Plus font right *or* write, etc.

ANTRUM

t: tantrum.
    Plus scant rum, etc.

ANTRƏS

ch: chantress, enchantress.
    Plus plan tress, etc.

ANTUR

b: banter.
ch: chanter, disenchanter,
enchanter.
gr: granter, grantor.
k(c): canter, cantor, decanter,
descanter, recanter, trochanter.
p: panter.
pl: implanter, planter, supplanter,
transplanter.
r: ranter.
st: instanter.
v: Levanter.
    Plus plan tor, etc.
    Plus plant, or, etc.

Plus plant her *or* err, etc.
Cf. antur.

ĀNTƲR

f: fainter, feinter.
kw: acquainter, quainter.
p: painter, word painter.
t: tainter.
    Plus taint her *or* err, etc.

ANTƲRN

l: lantern
    Plus can turn, etc.
    Plus can't erne, urn, *or* earn, etc.

ANTƏ

Vowel: anta.
d: Vedanta.
f: infanta.
l: Atalanta, Atlanta.
s: Santa.
    Plus plant a, etc.
    Cf. plan "tuh," etc.

ÄNTƏ

d: Vedanta
    Cf. want a, etc.

ANTƏD

ch: chanted, enchanted.
gr: granted.
h: "hanted."
k(c): canted, decanted, recanted.
p: panted.
pl: implanted, planted, supplanted.
r: ranted.
sl: slanted.
    Plus plan, Ted, etc.
    Plus scant, Ed, etc.

ĀNTƏD

f: fainted, feinted.
kw: acquainted, unacquainted.
p: bepainted, depainted*, painted.
s: besainted, sainted, unsainted.
t: attainted, tainted, unattainted, untainted.
    Plus paint, Ed, etc.
    Plus pain, Ted, etc.

ÄNTƏD

w: wonted.
    Plus on, Ted, etc.
    Plus font, Ed, etc.

ANTƏL

dr: quadrantal.
g: gigantal*.
n: consonantal.
    Plus plant, Al, etc.

ÄNTƏL

d: peridontal.
f: fontal.
fr: frontal.
z: horizontal.
    Plus font, Al, etc.

ANTƏM

b: bantam.
f: phantom.
    Plus scant 'em, etc.

ÄNTƏM

kw: quantum.
    Plus font 'em, etc.

ANTƏN

d: Danton.
k(c): Canton.

kl: Clanton.

skr(scr): Scranton.

st: Stanton.

    Plus plant on, etc.

    Plus plan tun *or* ton, etc.

ÄNTƏN

w: wanton.

    Plus Don, ton *or* tun, etc.

    Cf. fronton.

ÄNTƏNS

kw: acquaintance.

    Plus paint aunts *or* ants, etc.

ANƱR

b: banner.

f: fanner.

k(c): canner.

l: lanner.

m: manner, manor.

p: japanner, trepanner.

pl: planner.

sk(sc): scanner.

sp: spanner.

t: tanner.

v: vanner.

    Plus ran her *or* err, etc.

ĀNƱR

Vowel: inaner.

ch: chainer, enchainer, unchainer.

d: disdainer, ordainer.

dr: drainer.

f: feigner, profaner.

fr: refrainer.

g: gainer, Gaynor, regainer.

gr: grainer.

p: campaigner, champagner.

pl: complainer, explainer, plainer.

r: arraigner.

s: insaner, saner.

st: abstainer, bestainer, nonabstainer, stainer.

str: constrainer, restrainer, strainer.

t: appertainer, ascertainer, attainer, container, detainer, entertainer, maintainer, obtainer, retainer, sustainer.

tr: trainer, uptrainer.

v: vainer.

w: cordwainer.

    Plus gain her *or* err, etc.

ÄNƱR

Vowel: dishonor, honor.

b: Bonner.

g: goner.

k(c): conner, Connor, O'Conner, O'Connor.

m: marathoner.

w: Wanner.

    Plus on her *or* err, etc.

ANƱRD

b: bannered, unbannered.

m: ill-mannered, mannered, unmannered, well-mannered.

    Plus tanner'd, etc.

ÄNƱRD

Vowel: dishonored, honored, time-honored, unhonored.

ÄNƱRZ

k(c): Conners, Connors, O'Conners, O'Connors.

    Plus onur+s.

ĀNUS

Vowel: anus.

h: heinous.

j: Janus.
k(c): incanous.
v: Silvanus, veinous.
    Plus ordain us, etc.

ANVƏL

Vowel: anvil.
d: Danville.
gr: Granville.
m: Manville.

ANVƏS

k(c): canvas, canvass.

ĀNWURK

br: brainwork.
ch: chainwork.
pl: plainwork.
    Plus explain work, etc.

ANYUR

p: pannier.
s: droit du seigneur.
    Cf. can your *or* you're, etc.

ANYURD

l: lanyard.
sp: Spaniard.
    Plus man yard, etc.

ÄNYURD

p: poniard.
    Plus con yard, etc.

ANYƏL

d: Daniel.
sp: Brittany spaniel, spaniel, water spaniel.
th: Nathaniel.
    Plus can yell, etc.

ANYƏN

b: banyan.
k(c): canyon.
p: companion.

ANZĒ

p: chimpanzee, pansy.
t: tansy.
    Plus plans, he, etc.

ANZĒN

f: fanzine.

ANZFĒLD

m: Mansfield.
    Plus plans field, etc.

ÄNZŌ

f: Alphonso, Alphonzo.
l: Alonzo.
    Plus dons owe *or* O, etc.

ĀNZVƏL

j: Janesville.
z: Zanesville.

ANZƏ

g: extravaganza, ganza.
gr: granza.
n: bonanza.
p: Panza.
r: Carranza.
st: stanza.
    Plus plans a, etc.

ANƏ

Vowel: Anna, Christiana, Diana, fistiana, Georgiana, Indiana, ipecacuanha, Joanna, Juliana, Louisiana, Pollyana; also

Jeffersoniana, Johnsoniana,
Lincolniana, Shakespeariana, etc.

b: Urbana.

d: bandana.

f: Stephana.

h: Hanna, Hannah, Susquehanna.

k(c): Americana, etc., canna,
Texarkana.

m: manna.

s: Roxana.

t: Montana, sultana.

v: Havana, savanna, Savannah.

z: hosanna, Susanna.

Plus plan a, etc.

ĀNƏ

Vowel: Ana, fistiana, Nicotiana,
poinciana, Santa Ana; also
Jeffersoniana, Johnsoniana,
Shakespeariana, etc.

j: Cartagena.

k(c): Americana, etc., arcana.

p: campana.

m: vox humana.

n: anana.

sh: scena.

t: Curtana.

Plus explain a, etc.

ÄNƏ

Vowel: fistiana, Guiana, iguana,
liana; also Jeffersoniana,
Johnsoniana, Shakespeariana, etc.

d: belladonna, donna, Madonna,
primadonna.

f: aqua tofana.

g: Fata Morgana.

hw: marijuana.

k(c): Americana, etc., gymkhana.

n: anana, banana, zenana.

r: kerana, purana.

s: Messana.

t: Curtana, sultana.

th: thana.

v: nirvana.

w: Tia Juana.

z: hosanna.

Plus on a, etc.

Plus wan a, etc.

ANƏK

b: bannock.

j: jannock.

Plus can knock, etc.

ANƏL

Vowel: annal.

ch: channel.

d: Dan'l.

fl: flannel.

k(c): cannel.

p: empanel, impanel, panel,
rocker panel, unpanel.

skr(scr): scrannel.

st: stannel.

Cf. plan'll, etc.

ĀNƏL

Vowel: anal.

b: banal.

Plus Blaine'll, etc.

Plus brain, Al, etc.

Cf. brain all, etc.

ÄNƏLD

d: Donald, MacDonald,
McDonald.

r: Ronald.

ANƏLZ

Vowel: annals.

Plus anal+s.

ANƏN

f: fanon.
k(c): cannon, canon.
sh: Balleyshannon, Shannon.
    Plus ran on, etc.

ĀNƏNT

pl: complainant.
    Plus plain aunt *or* ant, etc.

ĀNƏS

g: gayness.
gr: grayness, greyness.
    Plus plain S, etc.

ANƏT

g: gannet.
gr: granite, pomegranate.
j: Janet.
kw: quannet.
pl: planet.
    Cf. plan it, etc.

ÄNƏT

b: bluebonnet, bonnet, graybonnet, unbonnet.
s: sonnet.
    Plus Don et, etc.
    Cf. don it, etc.

ĀŌ

d: deo.
k(c): cacao.
tr: tetrao.

ÄÔN

g: Gaon.
    Plus spa on, etc.

ĀÔTH

b: Sabaoth.

ÄPÄ

t: tapa.

APCHOOR

k(c): capture, recapture.
r: enrapture, rapture.
    Plus strapped your *or* you're, etc.

APĒ

ch: chappy.
g: gappy, gapy.
h: happy.
n: knappy, nappy.
p: pappy.
s: sappy.
skr(scr): scrappy.
sn: snappy.
    Plus clap, he, etc.

ĀPĒ

g: gapy.
kr: crapy.
skr(scr): scrapy.
t: red-tapey.
    Plus drape, he, etc.

ÄPĒ

ch: choppy.
dr: droppy.
fl: floppy.
h: hoppy.
k(c): copy.
kr: croppy.
l: loppy.
m: moppy.
p: opium poppy, poppy.

s: soppy.
sh: shoppy.
sl: sloppy.
　　Plus top, he, etc.

APEST

fl: flappest*.
kl: clappest*.
l: lappest*.
m: mappest*.
n: nappest*.
r: enwrappest*, rappest*,
wrappest*.
s: sappest*.
sl: slappest*.
sn: snappest*.
tr: trappest*.

ĀPEST

Vowel: apest*.
dr: drapest*.
g: gapest*.
k(c): escapest*.
r: rapest*.
sh: shapest*.
skr(scr): scrapest*.
　　Plus gay pest, etc.

ÄPEST

ch: choppest*.
dr: droppest*.
h: hoppest*.
l: loppest*.
m: moppest*.
p: poppest*.
pr: proppest*.
sh: shoppest*.
st: stoppest*.
t: overtoppest*, toppest*.
　　Cf. droppest*, etc.

APETH

fl: flappeth*.
kl: clappeth*.
l: lappeth*.
m: mappeth*.
n: nappeth*.
r: enwrappeth*, rappeth*,
wrappeth*.
s: sappeth*.
sl: slappeth*.
sn: snappeth*.
tr: trappeth*.

ĀPETH

Vowel: apeth*.
dr: drapeth*.
g: gapeth*.
k(c): escapeth*.
r: rapeth*.
sh: shapeth*.
skr(scr): scrapeth*.

ÄPETH

ch: choppeth*.
dr: droppeth*.
h: hoppeth*.
l: loppeth*.
m: moppeth*.
p: poppeth*.
pr: proppeth*.
sh: shoppeth*.
st: stoppeth*.
t: overtoppeth*, toppeth*.

ĀPGŌT

sk(sc): scapegoat.
　　Plus drape goat, etc.

ĀPGRĀS

sk(sc): scapegrace.
　　Plus drape Grace, etc.

ÄPHED

h: hophead.
Plus stop head, etc.

ÄPĪ

p: Popeye.
Plus stop, I *or* eye, etc.
Cf. flop pie, etc.

APID

r: rapid.
s: sapid.
v: vapid.
Cf. map hid, etc.

ÄPIJ

pr: proppage.
st: stoppage.
Cf. drop age, etc.

APIK

l: jalapic, Lappic.
Cf. trap pick, etc.

ÄPIK

Vowel: Ethiopic, myopic, presbyopic.
k(c): acopic.
kl: Cyclopic.
n: canopic.
sk: dichroscopic, electroscopic, galvanoscopic, helioscopic, horoscopic, hydroscopic, hygroscopic, kaleidoscopic, laryngoscopic, metoscopic, microscopic, necroscopic, pantascopic, periscopic, spectroscopic, stereoscopic, stethoscopic, telescopic.
t: metatopic, topic.
thr: anthropic, misanthropic, philanthropic, psilanthropic, theanthropic, theophilanthropic.
tr: allotropic, geotropic, heliotropic, isotropic, tropic.
Cf. drop pick, etc.

ÄPIKS

t: topics.
tr: tropics.
Plus opik+s
Cf. stop hicks, etc.

ĀPIN

r: rapine.
Plus play pin, etc.

APING

ch: chapping.
d: dapping.
fl: flapping.
g: gaping, gapping.
k(c): capping, handicapping.
kl: clapping.
l: lapping, overlapping.
m: mapping.
n: napping.
r: enwrapping, rapping, unwrapping, wrapping.
s: sapping.
skr(scr): scrapping.
sl: slapping.
sn: snapping.
str: strapping, understrapping, unstrapping.
t: tapping.
tr: entrapping, trapping.
y: yapping.

ĀPING

Vowel: aping.
dr: draping.
g: gaping.
k(c): escaping.
r: raping.

sh: shaping.
skr(scr): scraping.
t: taping.

ÄPING

ch: chopping.
dr: bedropping, dropping, eavesdropping.
fl: flopping.
h: hopping.
hw: whopping.
k(c): copping.
kl: clip-clopping.
kr: cropping.
l: lopping.
m: mopping.
p: popping.
pl: plopping.
pr: propping.
s: sopping.
sh: shopping.
sl: slopping.
st: stopping.
str: stropping.
sw: swapping.
t: overtopping, topping.
w: Wapping.

APIS

l: lapis.
t: tapis.

ĀPIS

Vowel: apis.
l: lapis.
r: Serapis.
t: tapis.

APISH

n: knappish.
sn: snappish.

ĀPISH

Vowel: apish.
p: papish
    Plus say pish, etc.

ÄPISH

f: foppish.
sh: shoppish.
    Cf. stop, pish!, etc.

ĀPIST

p: papist.
r: rapist.
sk(sc): landscapist.
t: red-tapist.

ĀPIZM

p: papism.
t: red-tapism.

APL

Vowel: apple, Big Apple, love apple, pineapple.
ch: antechapel, chapel, Chappell.
d: dapple.
gr: grapple.
n: knapple*.
r: rappel.
sk(sc): scapple.
skr(scr): scrapple.
thr: thrapple.
    Plus map'll, etc.

ĀPL

k(c): capel.
m: maple.
p: antipapal, papal.
st: staple, wool staple.
    Plus crape'll, etc.
    Cf. play pull, etc.

ÄPL

h: hopple.
p: popple.
st: estoppel, stopple.
t: overtopple, topple.
  Plus mop'll, etc.
  Cf. crop pull, etc.

APLĒ

h: haply.
  Plus map lea, *or* Lee, etc.

ĀPLĒ

sh: shapely.
  Plus drape Lee *or* lea, etc.
  Plus stay plea, etc.

APLIN

ch: chaplain, Chaplin.
  Plus map Lynn, etc.

APLING

d: dappling.
gr: grappling.
l: lapling*.
s: sapling.

ÄPLING

f: fopling.
t: overtoppling, toppling.

ĀPLZ

n: Naples.
st: staples.
  Plus apl+s.
  Cf. dray pulls, etc.

APLƏS

h: hapless.
k(c): capless.

n: napless.
s: sapless.
sl: slapless.
  Plus slap less, etc.

ĀPLƏS

Vowel: apeless.
gr: grapeless.
k(c): capeless, escapeless.
kr: crapeless.
n: napeless.
r: rapeless.
sh: shapeless.
skr(scr): scrapeless.
t: tapeless.
  Plus drape less *or* Les, etc.

APLƏT

ch: chaplet.
  Plus slap Lett *or* let, etc.

APMƏN

ch: Chapman.
k(c): Capman.
n: Knapman.
  Plus trap man, etc.

ÄPNÄT

t: topknot.
  Plus crop not *or* knot, etc.

APNƏL

gr: grapnel.
shr: shrapnel.
  Plus trap Nell *or* knell, etc.

ĀPRƏL

Vowel: April.
  Plus drape rill, etc.

APSANJ

l: Lapsang.

ÄPSĒ

dr: dropsy.
k(c): copsy.
m: Mopsy.
t: Topsy.
  Plus drop see, etc.

APSHUN

k(c): caption, recaption.
l: collapsion*, elapsion*.
tr: contraption.
  Plus slap shun, etc.

ÄPSHUN

Vowel: option.
d: adoption.
  Plus crop shun, etc.

APSHUS

k(c): captious.

APSING

l: collapsing, lapsing, relapsing.
  Plus trap sing, etc.

ÄPSIS

k(c): lycopsis.
l: ampelopsis.
n: synopsis.
t: thanatopsis.
  Plus stop sis, etc.

APSŌN

d: dapsone.

APSTŲR

t: tapstur.
  Plus clap stir, etc.
  Plus elapsed her *or* err, etc.

APSTƏN

k(c): capstan.
  Plus wraps tan, etc.
  Cf. slap stun, etc.

APTEST

Vowel: aptest, inaptest.
d: adaptest*.
r: raptest.
  Plus map test.

ÄPTIK

Vowel: optic.
k(c): Coptic.
n: synoptic.
t: autoptic.
  Plus stop tick, etc.

APTIN

k(c): captain.
  Plus wrap tin, etc.
  Plus wrapped in *or* inn, etc.

APTIV

d: adaptive.
k(c): captive.

APTIZM

b: anabaptism, baptism.

APTLĒ

Vowel: aptly, inaptly.
r: raptly.
  Plus scrapped, Lee *or* lea, etc.

APTNƏS

Vowel: aptness, inaptness, unaptness.

r: raptness.

APTRAP

kl: claptrap.
   Plus slap trap, etc.
   Plus snapped wrap *or* rap, etc.

ÄPTRIK

Vowel: catadioptric.

APTUR

Vowel: apter.
ch: chapter.
d: adapter.
k(c): captor, recaptor.
r: rapter.
   Plus wrapped her *or* err, etc.

APTƏD

d: adapted.
   Plus slap Ted, etc.
   Plus wrapped Ed, etc.

ÄPTƏD

Vowel: co-opted.
d: adopted.
   Plus cop, Ted, etc.
   Plus dropped, Ed, etc.

APUR

d: dapper.
fl: flapper, flyflapper.
g: gaper.
k(c): capper, handicapper.
kl: clapper.
l: lapper, overlapper.
m: mapper.

n: napper.
r: enwrapper, rapper, unwrapper.
s: sapper.
skr(scr): scrapper.
sl: slapper.
sn: red snapper, snapper, snipper-snapper, whipper-snapper.
str: strapper, understrapper, unstrapper.
t: tapper, wire tapper.
tr: entrapper, trapper.
y: yapper.
   Plus slap her *or* err, etc.

ĀPUR

Vowel: aper.
dr: draper, undraper.
g: gaper.
k(c): caper, escaper.
p: construction paper, flypaper, newspaper, paper, sandpaper.
r: raper.
s: sapor.
sh: shaper, unshaper.
sk(sc): landscaper.
skr(scr): scraper, skyscraper.
t: taper, tapir.
v: vapor.
   Plus say purr *or* per, etc.
   Plus scrape her *or* err, etc.

ÄPUR

Vowel: Opper.
ch: chopper, meat chopper.
dr: dropper, eavesdropper, eye dropper.
fl: flopper.
gr: Gropper.
h: clodhopper, finale hopper, grasshopper, hopper.
hw: whopper.

k(c): copper.
kl: clopper.
kr: cropper, sharecropper.
l: lopper.
m: mopper.
p: joy-popper, popper.
pl: plopper.
pr: improper, proper, propper.
s: sopper.
sh: shopper, window shopper.
sl: slopper.
st: stopper.
str: stropper.
sw: swapper.
t: overtopper, tiptopper, topper.
Plus chop her *or* err, etc.

ĀPU̇RZ

p: papers, walking papers.
Plus apur+s.

APUS

p: pappus.
tr: trappous.
Plus slap us, etc.

APWING

l: lapwing.
Plus flap wing, etc.

APƏ

k: kappa.
Plus strap a, etc.

ÄPƏ

gr: groppa.
j: Joppa.
p: poppa.
Plus stop a, etc.

APƏN

h: happen.
Cf. slappin', etc.
Cf. gap in, etc.
Cf. tap pen, etc.

ĀPƏN

k(c): capon.
sh: misshapen, unshapen.
t: tapen.
Plus scrape on, etc.
Cf. say pun, etc.

APƏT

l: lappet.
t: tappet.
Cf. trap, pet, etc.
Cf. trap it, etc.

ÄPƏT

m: moppet.
p: poppet.
Plus pop et, etc.
Cf. stop it, etc.

ÄRĀ

m: moiré.
p: Poiret.
sw: soirée.
Plus star A, etc.
Plus ma ray, etc.

ARAB

Vowel: Arab.
sk(sc): scarab.

ARANT

Vowel: arrant.

ÄRBĒ

d: Darby, Derby.
  Plus scar bee *or* be, etc.
  Plus garb he, etc.

ÄRBEL

b: barbel.
k(c): car bell.
t: Tarbell.
  Plus scar bell *or* Belle, etc.

ÄRBIJ

g: garbage.
  Cf. barb age, etc.

ÄRBL

b: barbel.
g: garbel, garble.
m: emmarble, marble.
  Plus garb'll, etc.
  Cf. arbel.
  Cf. far bull, etc.

ÄRBLING

g: garbling.
m: marbling.

ÄRBLUR

g: garbler.
m: marbler.

ÄRBOIL

p: parboil.
  Plus gar boil, etc.
  Plus barb oil, etc.

ÄRBÔRD

k(c): carboard.
l: larboard.
st: starboard.

  Plus jar board, etc.
  Cf. garb hoard, etc.

ÄRBROIL

ch: charbroil.

ÄRBUR

Vowel: arbor.
b: barber, Barbour.
h: enharbor, harbor, unharbor.
  Plus garb her *or* err, etc.
  Cf. garb, or, etc.

ÄRBƏN

k(c): carbon.
sh: charbon.
  Plus garb on, etc.

ÄRCHĒ

Vowel: Archie, archy.
l: larchy.
st: starchy.
  Plus march, he, etc.

ÄRCHEST

Vowel: archest*, enarchest*.
m: marchest*.
p: parchest*.
st: starchest*.
  Plus scar chest, etc.

ÄRCHETH

Vowel: archeth*, enarcheth*.
m: marcheth*.
p: parcheth*.
st: starcheth*.

ÄRCHING

Vowel: arching, overarching.
m: countermarching, marching,
  outmarching, overmarching.

p: parching.
st: starching.

ÄRCHMƏNT

Vowel: archment.
p: emparchment, parchment.
Plus march meant, etc.

ÄRCHNƏS

Vowel: archness.

ÄRCHU̯R

Vowel: archer.
l: Larcher.
m: marcher.
p: parcher, popcorn parcher.
st: starcher.
Plus starch her *or* err, etc.

ÄRCHWĀ

Vowel: archway.
Plus march way, etc.

ÄRCHƏZ

Vowel: arches, overarches.
l: larches.
m: countermarches, marches, outmarches.
p: parches.
st: starches.
Cf. starch is, etc.

ÄRDÄRM

y: yardarm.
Plus guard arm, etc.

ÄRDĒ

h: foolhardy, hardy.
t: tardy.
Plus scarred, he, etc.
Plus mar Dee *or* D, etc.

ÄRDĒN

n: nardine.
s: sardine.
Plus szar dean, etc.

ÄRDEST

b: bombardest*.
g: disregardest*, guardest*, regardest*.
h: hardest.
k(c): discardest*, false-cardest*.
l: lardest*.
r: retardest*.

ÄRDETH

b: bombardeth*.
g: disregardeth*, guardeth*, regardeth*.
k(c): discardeth*, false-cardeth*.
l: lardeth*.
t: retardeth*.
Plus mar death, etc.

ÄRDFOOL

g: disregardful, guardful, regardful.
Plus nard full, etc.

ÄRDIK

Vowel: bezoardic.
b: bardic, Lombardic.
k(c): anacardic, pericardic.
Plus bar Dick, etc.

ÄRDING

b: bombarding.
g: disregarding, guarding, regarding, unguarding.
h: Harding.
k(c): carding, discarding, false-carding, placarding, wool carding.

l: larding.
t: retarding.

ÄRDL

Vowel: McArdle.
b: Bardle.
Plus card'll, etc.
Cf. scar dull, etc.

ÄRDLĒ

h: hardly.
Plus bard, Lee *or* lea, etc.

ÄRDLƏS

g: guardless, regardless.
k(c): cardless.
Plus hard, Les *or* less, etc.

ÄRDMƏNT

b: bombardment.
t: retardment.
Plus card meant, etc.

ÄRDNING

g: gardening.
h: hardening.
p: pardoning.

ÄRDNƱR

g: gardener.
h: hardener.
p: pardner, pardoner.

ÄRDNƏS

h: hardness.

ÄRDŌ

b: bombardo, Lombardo.
k(c): bocardo.
n: Leonardo.

Plus card owe *or* O, etc.
Plus scar dough *or* doe, etc.

ÄRDSHIP

g: guardship.
h: hardship.
Plus starred ship, etc.

ÄRDƱR

Vowel: ardor.
b: bombarder.
g: disregarder, guarder, regarder.
h: harder.
k(c): carder, discarder, false-carder, wool carder.
l: larder.
t: retarder.
Plus marred her *or* err, etc.

ÄRDWƱRK

y: yardwork.

ÄRDZMƏN

g: guardsman.
Plus retards man, etc.

ÄRDƏD

b: bombarded.
g: disregarded, guarded, regarded, unguarded, unregarded.
k(c): carded, discarded.
l: larded.
sh: sharded.
t: retarded, unretarded.
Plus hard, Ed, etc.
Plus tsar dead, etc.

ÄRDƏL

f: fardel.
Plus hard L *or* el, etc.
Plus scar, Dell, etc.

ÄRDƏN

b: bombardon.

g: beer garden, garden, rock garden, sea garden.

h: caseharden, enharden, harden.

p: pardon.

Plus guard on, etc.

Plus mar den, etc.

Plus scar, Don, etc.

ÄRDƏND

h: casehardened, hardened, weather-hardened.

p: pardoned, unpardoned.

Plus czar donned, etc.

ÄRDƏNT

Vowel: ardent.

g: gardant, regardant.

Plus hard aunt *or* ant, etc.

Plus tsar dent, etc.

Cf. ardent.

ÄRĒ

b: barry.

ch: charry.

k(c): shikaree.

kw: quarry.

n: Carbonari.

s: aracari, sorry.

sk(sc): scarry.

sp: sparry.

st: starry.

t: tarry.

Plus far, he, etc.

Cf. par, he, etc.

Cf. ari.

ARĒD

Vowel: arid.

h: harried.

k(c): carried, miscarried.

m: intermarried, remarried, unmarried.

p: parried.

t: tarried.

ÄREST

b: barrest*, debarrest*, unbarrest*.

j: jarrest*.

m: marrest*.

sk(sc): scarrest*.

sp: sparrest*.

st: starrest*.

t: tarrest*.

Cf. car rest, etc.

Cf. far rest, etc.

ÄRETH

b: barreth*, debarreth*, unbarreth*.

j: jarreth*.

m: marreth*.

sk(sc): scarreth*.

sp: sparreth*.

st: starreth*.

t: tarreth*.

ÄRFISH

g: garfish.

st: starfish.

Plus tar fish, etc.

Cf. far in, etc.

ÄRGIN

b: bargain.

ÄRGL

b: argle-bargle.

g: gargle.

ÄRGŌ

Vowel: Argo, argot.
b: embargo.
d: Dargo.
f: Fargo, Wells Fargo.
k(c): cargo, supercargo.
l: largo, Largo.
m: Margot.
sp: Spargo.
t: botargo.
    Plus scar go, etc.

ÄRGO͞O

Vowel: argue.

ÄRGƏN

Vowel: argon.
d: Dargan.
g: Gargan.
j: jargon.
    Plus scar gone, etc.

ÄRGƏT

t: target.
    Plus spar get, etc.

ÄRIK

h: Amharic.
    Cf. far rick, etc.

ÄRING

b: barring, debarring, disbarring, unbarring.
ch: charring.
j: jarring.
m: marring.
sk(sc): scarring.
sp: sparring.
st: starring.
t: tarring.
    Cf. scar ring, etc.

ÄRINJ

Vowel: Agent Orange+, burnt orange+, orange+.

ÄRJEST

ch: chargest*, dischargest*, overchargest*.
l: enlargest*, largest.
    Plus far jest, etc.

ÄRJETH

ch: chargeth*, dischargeth*, overchargeth*.
l: enlargeth*.

ÄRJIK

th: lethargic.

ÄRJIN

m: margin.
    Plus bar gin, etc.

ÄRJING

b: barging.
ch: charging, discharging, overcharging.
l: enlarging.

ÄRJLĒ

l: largely.
    Plus barge, Lee *or* lea, etc.

ÄRJMƏNT

l: enlargement.

ÄRJUR

b: barger.
ch: charger, discharger, overcharger, surcharger, undercharger.

l: enlarger, larger.
sp: sparger.

    Plus charge her *or* err, etc.

ÄRJƏNT

Vowel: argent.
s: sergeant.

    Plus star gent, etc.

ÄRJƏT

g: garget.
p: parget.

    Plus scar jet, etc.

ÄRJƏZ

b: barges.
ch: charges, discharges, over-charges.
l: enlarges.
m: marges.
t: targes.

ÄRKAL

    Plus far, Cal, etc.
    Plus ark, Al, etc.

ÄRKAZM

s: sarcasm.

    Plus far chasm, etc.
    Cf. park has 'em, etc.

ÄRKĒ

Vowel: matriarchy, patriarchy.
b: barky.
d: darky.
g: oligarchy.
l: larky.
m: marquis.
r: heterarchy, hierarchy.
t: heptarchy.

    Plus spark, he, etc.
    Plus far key, etc.

ÄRKEST

b: barkest*, embarkest*.
d: darkest.
m: markest*, remarkest*.
st: starkest.

ÄRKETH

b: barketh*, embarketh*.
m: marketh*, remarketh*.

ÄRKIK

Vowel: matriarchic, patriarchic.
g: oligarchic.
n: anarchic, antianarchic, monarchic.
r: hierarchic.
t: climatarchic, heptarchic.

    Plus far kick, etc.

ÄRKIN

l: Larkin

    Plus far kin, etc.
    Plus dark inn *or* in, etc.

ÄRKING

b: barking, disembarking, embarking.
h: harking.
k(c): carking.
l: larking, skylarking.
m: marking, remarking.
p: parking.

    Plus far king, etc.

ÄRKISH

d: darkish.
l: larkish.
sp: sparkish.

ÄRKIST

g: oligarchist.
r: hierarchist.
t: heptarchist.

ÄRKĪVZ

Vowel: archives.
  Plus mark Ives, etc.
  Cf. dark hives, etc.

ÄRKL

d: darkle.
sp: sparkle.
  Plus mark'll, etc.
  Cf. far cull, etc.

ÄRKLAND

p: parkland.

ÄRKLĒ

d: darkly.
kl: clarkly, clerkly.
st: starkly.
  Plus spark, Lee or lea, etc.

ÄRKLING

d: darkling.
sp: sparkling.

ÄRKLƏT

p: parklet.
sp: sparklet.
  Plus mark, let or Lett, etc.

ÄRKNUR

d: darkener.
h: hearkener.

ÄRKNƏS

d: darkness.

ÄRKŌ

Vowel: arco.

ÄRKŌL

ch: charcoal.
  Plus far coal or Cole, etc.
  Cf. dark hole, etc.

ÄRKSPUR

l: larkspur.
  Plus spark spur, etc.
  Plus marks purr or per, etc.

ÄRKSƏM

d: darksome.
  Plus spark some or sum, etc.
  Cf. sparks hum, etc.

ÄRKTIK

Vowel: Arctic.
t: Antarctic.
  Plus mark tick, etc.

ÄRKUR

b: barker, embarker.
d: darker.
h: harker.
l: larker.
m: marcor, marker.
p: parker.
sh: sharker.
sp: sparker.
st: starker.
  Plus mark her or err, etc.

ÄRKWIS

  Plus dark wis*, etc.

ÄRKƏL

Vowel: matriarchal, patriarchal.
g: oligarchal.

n: anarchal, monarchal.
r: hierarchal, squirearchal.

ÄRKƏN

d: bedarken, darken, endarken.
h: hearken.
  Plus far ken, etc.

ÄRKƏT

m: market.
  Plus lark et, etc.
  Cf. spark it, etc.

ÄRLÄK

ch: charlock.
h: harlock.
  Plus mar lock, etc.
  Cf. Harlech.

ÄRLĒ

Vowel: Arleigh.
b: barley.
ch: Charley, Charlie.
f: Farley.
h: Harley.
k(c): McCarley.
m: marli.
n: gnarly.
p: parley.
  Plus scar, Lee *or* lea, etc.
  Plus snarl, he, etc.

ÄRLIK

g: garlic, pilgarlick.
s: sarlyk.
  Plus scar lick, etc.

ÄRLĪK

st: starlike.
z: czarlike, etc.

ÄRLIKT

g: garlicked.

ÄRLING

d: darling.
h: Harling.
sn: snarling.
sp: sparling.
st: starling.

ÄRLIT

f: farlit.
st: starlit.
  Plus scar lit, etc.
  Plus snarl it, etc.

ÄRLĪT

st: starlight.
  Plus far light, etc.

ÄRLƱR

n: gnarler.
sn: snarler.
  Plus snarl her *or* err, etc.

ÄRLUS

p: parlous.
  Plus snarl us, etc.

ÄRLƏND

f: Farland, McFarland.
g: engarland, garland.
p: McParland.
  Plus scar land, etc.
  Plus snarl and, etc.

ÄRLƏR

p: massage parlor, parlor.

ÄRLƏS

g: cigarless, garless.
k(c): carless.
sk(sc): scarless.
st: starless.
t: catarrhless.
z: czarless, etc.
  Plus far less, etc.

ÄRLƏT

k(c): carlet.
h: harlot.
sh: Charlotte.
sk(sc): scarlet.
st: starlet.
v: varlet.
  Plus jar let *or* Lett, etc.
  Plus mar lot, etc.
  Cf. arlet.

ÄRMĀD

b: barmaid.
  Plus far maid *or* made, etc.

ÄRMĒ

Vowel: army.
b: barmy.
  Plus scar me, etc.
  Plus harm, he, etc.

ÄRMEST

Vowel: armest*, disarmest*.
ch: charmest*.
f: farmest*.
h: harmest*.
l: alarmest*.
  Plus gar messed, etc.

ÄRMETH

Vowel: armeth*, disarmeth*.
ch: charmeth*.

f: farmeth*.
h: harmeth*.
l: alarmeth*.

ÄRMFOOL

Vowel: armful.
ch: charmful.
h: harmful, unharmful.
  Plus charm full, etc.

ÄRMIK

f: alexipharmic, lexipharmic.
t: ptarmic.
  Plus far Mick, etc.

ÄRMIN

h: harmine.
k(c): carmine, encarmine.
  Plus harm in *or* inn, etc.
  Plus scar, Min, etc.

ÄRMING

Vowel: arming, disarming, forearming, unarming.
ch: charming, uncharming.
f: baby farming, dairy farming, dirt farming, farming.
h: harming, unharming.
l: alarming, unalarming.
  Plus far Ming, etc.

ÄRMLƏS

Vowel: armless.
ch: charmless.
h: harmless.
  Plus alarm less *or* Les, etc.

ÄRMLƏT

Vowel: armlet.
ch: charmlet.
  Plus farm let *or* Lett, etc.

ÄRMU̯R

Vowel: armor, chain armor, plate armor.

ch: charmer, serpent charmer, snake charmer.

f: baby farmer, dairy farmer, dirt farmer, farmer.

h: harmer.

l: alarmer.

　　Plus harm her, etc.

　　Plus far myrrh, etc.

ÄRMƏN

k(c): carmen.

　　Plus bar men, etc.

ÄRMƏNT

b: debarment, disbarment.

g: garment.

s: sarment.

　　Plus scar meant, etc.

ÄRMƏT

Vowel: armet.

k(c): carmot.

m: marmot.

　　Plus car met, etc.

　　Cf. harm it, etc.

ÄRNĀT

k(c): carnate*, incarnate.

　　Plus far, Nate, etc.

　　Plus barn ate *or* eight, etc.

ÄRNĒ

bl: blarney.

k(c): carney.

l: Killarney.

　　Plus far knee, etc.

　　Plus yarn, he, etc.

ÄRNHƏM

f: Farnham.

　　Plus barn ham, etc.

　　Cf. Barnum, Farnum.

ÄRNIJ

k(c): carnage.

　　Cf. barn age, etc.

ÄRNING

d: darning.

y: yarning.

ÄRNISH

g: garnish.

t: tarnish.

v: desert varnish, varnish.

ÄRNISHT

g: garnished, ungarnished.

t: tarnished, untarnished.

v: unvarnished, varnished.

ÄRNLĒ

d: Darnley.

　　Plus barn, Lee *or* lea, etc.

ÄRNU̯R

d: darner.

g: garner.

y: yarner.

　　Plus darn her *or* err, etc.

ÄRNU̯RD

b: Barnard.

　　Plus marnard, etc.

　　Cf. garnered.

ÄRNƏL

ch: charnel, uncharnel.
k(c): carnal, carnel*.
  Plus barn, Al, etc.

ÄRNƏLD

Vowel: Arnold.
  Plus darn old, etc.

ÄRNƏS

f: farness.
h: harness.

ÄRŌ

b: borrow.
m: amorrow, good morrow, Morro, morrow, tomorrow.
kl: claro.
n: Carbonaro.
s: sorrow.
t: taro.
  Plus shah row *or* roe, etc.
  Cf. scar owe *or* O, etc.
  Cf. ma row *or* roe, etc.

ÄRŌD

b: borrowed.
s: sorrowed, unsorrowed.
  Cf. car ode *or* owed, etc.
  Cf. ma rode *or* road, etc.

ÄRPĒ

h: harpy.
k(c): carpy.
  Plus sharp, he, etc.

ÄRPEST

h: harpest*.
k(c): carpest*.
sh: sharpest.
  Plus mar pest, etc.

ÄRPETH

h: harpeth*.
k(c): carpeth*.

ÄRPING

h: harping.
k(c): carping.
sh: sharping.
  Plus czar ping, etc.

ÄRPIST

h: harpist.

ÄRPNES

sh: sharpness.

ÄRPUR

h: harper.
k(c): carper.
sh: sharper.
  Plus sharp her *or* err, etc.
  Plus far purr *or* per, etc.

ÄRPƏT

k(c): carpet.
  Plus scar pet, etc.
  Cf. sharp it, etc.

ÄRSHƏL

m: earl marshal, field marshal, immartial, marshal, Marshall, martial, unmartial.
p: impartial, partial.
  Plus scar shall, etc.

ÄRSLĒ

p: parsley.
  Plus farce, Lee, etc.

ÄRSUR

p: parser.
sp: sparser.
  Plus far, sir, etc.
  Plus farce her *or* err, etc.

ÄRSƏL

t: metatarsal, tarsal.
p: parcel.
s: sarcel*.
v: varsal.
  Plus car, Sal, etc.
  Plus scar sell, etc.

ÄRSƏN

Vowel: arson.
k(c): Carson.
l: Larsen, Larson.
p: parson.
  Plus mar son *or* sun, etc.

ÄRSƏZ

f: farces.
p: parses.
s: sarses.
  Plus Carr says, etc.

ÄRTĒ

h: hearty.
k(c): McCarty.
p: charter party, exparte, party.
t: Astarte.
  Plus mar tea *or* T, etc.
  Plus start, he, etc.

ÄRTEST

d: dartest*.
k(c): cartest*.
p: departest*, impartest*, partest*.

sm: smartest.
st: startest*, upstartest*.
  Plus far test, etc.

ÄRTETH

d: darteth*.
k(c): carteth*.
p: departeth*, imparteth*, parteth*.
sm: smarteth*.
st: starteth*, upstarteth*.

ÄRTFOOL

Vowel: artful.
  Plus heart full, etc.

ÄRTHĒ

k(c): McCarthy.

ÄRTHEST

f: farthest.

ÄRTHING

f: farthing.

ÄRTHUR

Vowel: Arthur.
f: farther.
  Plus hearth err *or* her, etc.

ÄRTHƏ

m: Martha.
  Plus hearth a, etc.

ÄRTIN

m: martin.
  Plus scar tin, etc.
  Plus start inn *or* in, etc.
  Cf. artan, arten, arton.

ÄRTING

d: darting.
h: hearting, sweet hearting.
k(c): carting, uncarting.
p: departing, imparting, parting.
sm: smarting.
st: starting, upstarting.

ÄRTIST

Vowel: artist.
ch: Chartist.

ÄRTĪT

p: bipartite.
Plus scar tight, etc.

ÄRTL

d: dartle.
st: startle.
Plus cart'll, etc.

ÄRTLĒ

p: partly.
sm: smartly.
t: tartly.
Plus start Lee *or* lea, etc.

ÄRTLING

st: startling.

ÄRTLƏS

Vowel: artless.
ch: chartless.
h: heartless.
Plus start less *or* Les, etc.

ÄRTLƏT

h: heartlet.
m: martlet.
t: tartlet.
Plus start let *or* Lett, etc.

ÄRTMƏNT

p: apartment, compartment, department, impartment.
Plus start meant, etc.

ÄRTNƏS

sm: smartness.
t: tartness.

ÄRTRIJ

k(c): cartridge.
p: partridge.
Plus start ridge, etc.

ÄRTƱR

b: barter.
ch: charter.
d: darter.
g: garter.
k(c): carter.
m: bemartyr, martyr, protomartyr, unmartyr.
p: departer, imparter, parter.
sm: smarter.
st: self-starter, starter, upstarter.
t: tartar.
Plus cart her *or* err, etc.

ÄRTWĀ

k(c): cartway.
p: part-way.
Plus smart way *or* weight, etc.

ÄRTƏD

Vowel: arted.
ch: charted, uncharted.
d: darted.
h: broken-hearted, chicken-hearted, cold-hearted, double-hearted, down-hearted, faint-hearted, false-hearted, flint-hearted, frank-hearted,

free-hearted, full-hearted, gentle-hearted, great-hearted, half-hearted, hard-hearted, hare-hearted, hearted, hen-hearted, high-hearted, iron-hearted, kind-hearted, large-hearted, leaden-hearted, light-hearted, lion-hearted, marble-hearted, open-hearted, pale-hearted, pigeon-hearted, proud-hearted, public-hearted, right-hearted, sad-hearted, shallow-hearted, simple-hearted, single-hearted, soft-hearted, stony-hearted, stout-hearted, tender-hearted, traitor-hearted, true-hearted, unhearted, warm-hearted, weak-hearted, wise-hearted.

k(c): carted.

p: departed, imparted, parted, triparted, unimparted.

sm: smarted.

st: started, up-started.

Plus car, Ted, etc.

Plus start, Ed, etc.

ÄRTƏN

b: barton.

g: kindergarten.

h: dishearten, enhearten, hearten.

k(c): carton.

m: marten.

sm: smarten.

sp: Spartan.

t: tartan.

Plus mar ton *or* tun, etc.

Plus start an *or* Ann, etc.

Cf. scar ten, etc.

Cf. arten, arton.

ÄRUR

b: barrer, debarrer, disbarrer.

m: marrer.

sp: sparrer.

t: tarrer.

z: bizarrer.

Plus scar her *or* err, etc.

ÄRVĒ

g: Garvey.

h: Harvey.

Plus starve, he, etc.

Plus far, Vee, etc.

ÄRVEST

h: harvest.

st: starvest*.

Plus mar vest, etc.

ÄRVING

k(c): carving.

st: starving.

ÄRVLING

m: marvelling.

st: starveling.

ÄRVUR

k(c): carver.

m: marver.

st: starver.

Plus starve her *or* err, etc.

ÄRVƏL

k(c): carvel.

l: larval.

m: marvel.

Plus carve, Al, etc.

Plus starve el *or* L, etc.

ÄRVƏLD

m: marvelled.

ÄRVƏN

k(c): carven.

ĀRƏ

l: cordillera.
m: dulcamara, Marah.
  Plus play Ra, etc.

ÄRƏ

Vowel: tiara.
h: Sahara.
k(c): caracara, cascara.
m: Gemara.
r: Ferrara.
t: solfatara.
  Plus far a, etc.
  Cf. are a, etc.
  Cf. ora.

ÄRƏL

k(c): coral.
kw: quarrel.
m: immoral, moral, unmoral.
s: sorrel.

ÄRƏM

l: alarum.
  Plus scar 'em, etc.

ÄRƏN

k: Karen.
l: McLaren.

ÄRƏNJ

Vowel: mock orange, orange.
  Cf. mar, Inge, etc.

ÄRƏNT

w: warrant.
  Plus far ant _or_ aunt, etc.
  Cf. orent.
  Cf. for rent, etc.

ASÄK

h: hassock.
k(c): cassock.

ASĀT

kr: incrassate.
  Plus class ate _or_ eight, etc.

ASCHŌŌR

p: pasture.
  Plus classed your _or_ you're, etc.

ÄSCHU̱R

p: imposture, posture.
  Plus lost your _or_ you're, etc.

ASĒ

br: brassie, brassy.
ch: chassis.
g: gassy, Malagasy.
gl: glassy.
gr: grassy.
h: Tallahassee.
kl: classy.
l: lassie.
m: massy.
r: morassy.
s: sassy.
  Plus pass, he, etc.

ĀSĒ

gr: Gracie.
l: Lacey, lacy.

pr: precis.
r: racy.
　　Plus face, he, etc.
　　Plus may see, etc.

ASEST

kl: classest*.
kr: crassest.
m: amassest*, massest*.
p: passest*, surpassest*.

ĀSEST

b: abasest*, basest, debasest*.
br: bracest*, embracest*.
ch: chasest*.
f: defacest*, effacest*, facest*.
gr: begracest*, disgracest*,
gracest*
l: belacest*, enlacest*,
interlacest*, lacest*, unlacest*.
p: oupacest*, pacest*.
pl: displacest*, placest*,
replacest*.
r: erasest*, racest*.
sp: spacest*.
tr: retracest*, tracest*.

ASETH

kl: classeth*.
m: amasseth*, masseth*.
p: passeth*, surpasseth*.

ĀSETH

b: abaseth*, baseth*, debaseth*.
br: braceth*, embraceth*.
ch: chaseth*.
f: defaceth*, effaceth*, faceth*.
gr: begraceth*, disgraceth*,
graceth*.
l: belaceth*, enlaceth*,
interlaceth*, laceth*, unlaceth*.

p: outpaceth*, paceth*.
pl: displaceth*, placeth*,
replaceth*.
r: eraseth*, raceth*.
sp: spaceth*.
tr: retraceth*, traceth*.
　　Plus Say, Seth, etc.

ĀSFOOL

gr: disgraceful, graceful,
ungraceful.
　　Plus space full, etc.

ASHĀ

k(c): cachet.
s: sachet.
t: attaché.
　　Plus smash a, etc.

ASHBÔRD

d: dashboard.
spl: splashboard.
　　Plus crash board *or* bored, etc.

ASHĒ

Vowel: ashy.
fl: flashy.
h: hashy.
m: mashie, mashy.
pl: plashy.
sl: slashy.
spl: splashy.
tr: trashy.
　　Plus thrash, he, etc.
　　Cf. thrash, she, etc.

ASHEST

d: dashest*.
fl: flashest*.
g: gashest*.

k(c): cashest*.
kl: clashest*.
kr: crashest*.
l: lashest*.
m: mashest*.
n: gnashest*.
sl: slashest*.
sm: smashest*.
spl: splashest*.
thr: thrashest*.

ASHETH

d: dasheth*.
fl: flasheth*.
g: gashesth*.
k(c): casheth*.
kl: clasheth*.
kr: crasheth*.
l: lasheth*.
m: masheth*.
n: gnasheth*.
sl: slasheth*.
sm: smasheth*.
spl: splasheth*.
thr: thrasheth*.

ASHFOOL

b: bashful, unbashful.
g: gashful.
r: rashful.
     Plus sash full, etc.

ASHING

b: abashing, bashing.
d: balderdashing, dashing.
f: fashing.
fl: flashing.
g: gashing.
h: hashing.
k(c): cashing.
kl: clashing.

kr: crashing.
l: lashing, unlashing.
m: mashing.
n: gnashing.
pl: plashing.
sl: slashing.
sm: smashing.
spl: splashing.
thr: thrashing.

ASHLĒ

Vowel: Ashleigh, Ashley.
fl: flashly.
g: gashly.
     Plus thrash Lee *or* lea, etc.

ASHLĪT

d: dash light.
fl: flash light.

ASHMƏN

Vowel: ashman.
fl: "flash man."
     Plus crash man, etc.

ĀSHŌ

r: distribution ratio, Horatio, ratio+.
     Plus play show, etc.

ASHSEKS

k: cache-sex.

ASHUR

Vowel: Asher.
b: basher.
br: brasher.
d: dasher, haberdasher.
fl: flasher.
g: gasher.
k(c): casher, check casher.

kl: clasher.
kr: crasher.
l: lasher, unlasher.
m: masher.
n: gnasher.
p: pasher.
r: rasher
sl: slasher.
sm: baggage-smasher, smasher.
spl: splasher.
thr: thrasher.

Plus smash her *or* err, etc.

ĀSHUS

Vowel: alliaceous, coriaceous, foliaceous, liliaceous, scoriaceous.

b: bibacious, bulbaceous, fabaceous, herbaceous, sabaceous, sebaceous.

d: audacious, edacious, lardaceous, mendacious, mordacious, orchidaceous, perdaceous.

dr: cylindraceous.

f: tophaceous, torfaceous.

g: fugacious, funcaceous, sagacious, saxifragaceous.

gr: disgracious, gracious, misgracious, ungracious.

gw: linguacious*.

k(c): efficacious, inefficacious, micaceous, perspicacious, pervicacious, procacious, salicaceous.

kr: execratious*.

kw: loquacious, sequacious.

l: amylaceous, capillaceous, corallaceous, fallacious, ferulaceous, filaceous, marlaceous, palacious*, perlaceous, ranunculaceous, salacious, schorlaceous, violaceous.

m: contumacious, fumacious, gemmaceous, palmaceous, pomaceous.

n: acanaceous, arenaceous, carbonaceous, erinaceous, farinaceous, gallinaceous, minacious, pectinaceous, pertinacious, pugnacious, resinaceous, saponaceous, tenacious, turbinaceous, vinaceous.

p: capacious, incapacious, lappaceous, rampacious, rapacious.

r: camphoraceous, feracious, furfuraceous, piperaceous, porraceous, pulveraceous, stercoraceous, veracious, voracious.

s: vexatious.

sp: spacious.

t: cactaceous, cetaceous, cretaceous, crustaceous, disputatious, flirtatious, frumentaceous, ostentatious, psitaceous, rutaceous, sarmentaceous, setaceous, testaceous, truttaceous.

th: acanthaceous.

v: olivaceous, vivacious.

z: rosaceous.

ASHVIL

Vowel: Ashville.
n: Nashville.

ĀSHƏL

b: abbatial.
f: craniogacial, facial, unifacial.
gl: glacial.
l: palatial, relatial.
r: racial.
sp: spatial.

Plus May shall, etc.

Cf. basial.

ASHƏN

Vowel: ashen.

f: fashion.

p: compassion, impassion, master passion, passion.

Plus smash Hun.

Plus rash 'un, etc.

Cf. Circassian.

Cf. ashi+an.

Cf. crash shun.

ĀSHƏN

Vowel: abbreviation, actuation, acupunctuation, affiliation, alleviation, amplication, annunciation, appreciation, appropriation, arcuation, Asian, asphyxiation, association, attenuation, aviation, calumniation, columniation, conciliation, consubstantiation, continuation, creation, delineation, denunciation, depreciation, despoliation, deviation, diffareation, differentiation, dimidiation, discontinuation, dissociation, domiciliation, effectuation, effoliation, emaciation, enucleation, enunciation, evacuation, eventuation, excoriation, excruciation, exfoliation, expaition, expatiation, expatriation, expoliation*, expropriation, extenuation, fasciation, filiation, fluctuation, foliation, friation*, glaciation, gloriation*, graduation, habituation, humiliation, ideation, illaqueation, inappreciation, inchoation, indexation, individuation, inebriation, infatuation, ingratiation, initiation, insinuation, intercolumniation, interlineation, intermediation, irradiation, laniation, laureation, licentiation, lineation, lixiviation, luxuriation, maleficiation, malleation, materiation, mediation, mutuation*, negotiation, obviation, otiation*, palliation, permeation, perpetuation, procreation, pronunciation, propitiation, punctuation, radiation, reconciliation, recreation, renunciation, repatriation, repudiation, retaliation, satiation, self-renunciation, sinuation, situation, spoliation, striation, sublineation, substantiation, superannuation, trabeation, transubstantiation, tripudiation, tumultuation, valuation, variation, vindemiation, vitiation.

b: accubation, approbation, cubation*, decubation, disapprobation, exacerbation, incubation, jobation, libation, perturbation, probation, recubation*, reprobation, shock probation, titubation.

bl: ablation, oblation, sublation.

br: adumbration, antilibration, celebration, cerebration, equilibration, libration, lucubration, revibration, tenebration, vibration.

d: accommodation, backwardation, commendation, consolidation, defraudation, degradation, denudation, deoxidation, depredation, dilapidation, elucidation, emendation, exudation, fecundation, foundation, frondation*, gradation, gravidation, incommodation, ingravidation, intimidation, inundation, invalidation, lapidation, laudation, liquidation, nodation, nudation, oxidation, predacean, predation, recommendation, recordation, retardation, retrogradation, secundation, sudation, transudation, trepidation, trucidation, validation.

dr: hydration.

f: philosophation*.

fl: afflation, deflation, efflation, exsufflation, inflation, insufflation, stagflation, sufflation.

g: abnegation, abrogation, aggregation, allegation, alligation, arrogation, castigation, circumnavigation, colligation, compurgation, congregation, conjugation, corrugation, delegation, derogation, divagation, divulgation, expurgation, fumigation, homologation, instigation, interrogation, irrigation, legation, levigation, litigation, mitigation, navigation, negation, noctivigation, nugation*, objurgation, obligation, profligation, prolongation, promulgation, propogation, prorogation, purgation, relegation, renegation, rogation, segregation, subjugation, subligation, subrogation, superrogation, surrogation, variegation.

gr: conflagration, deflagration, disintegration, emigration, immigration, integration, intermigration, migration, reintegration, transmigration.

h: Haitian, Haytian.

k(c): abdication, abjudication, acidification, adjudication, advocation, allocation, altercation, amplification, Anglification, application, authentication, averruncation, avocation, basification, beatification, beautification, behavior modification, bifurcation, brutification, calcification, calorification, caprification, certification, clarification, classification, codification, collocation, communication, complication, confiscation, convocation, cornification, coruscation, damnification, debarkation, decalcification, decortication, dedication, defalcation, defecation, deification, deltafication, demarcation, deprecation, dessication, detruncation, dislocation, disqualification, divarication, diversification, domestication, dulcification, duplication, edification, education, electrification, embrocation, equivocation, eradication, evocation, excommunication, exemplification, explication, exsiccation, extrication, fabrication, falcation, falsification, florification, flossification, fortification, fossilification, frication*, fructification, furcation, gasification, generification, glorification, granitification, gratification, horrification, hypothecation, identification, imbrication, implication, imprecation, inapplication, incarnification, inculcation, indemnification, indication, intensification, intercommunication, interlocation, interstratification, intoxication, intrication, invocation, jollification, justification, lapidification, liquification, location, lubrication, magnification, mastication, medication, mellification*, mendication, modification, mortification, multiplication, mummification, mundification, mystification, nidification, nigrification, nitrification, notification, nudification, nullification, obfuscation, ossification, ozonification, pacation, pacification, palification, panification, personification, petrification, piscation, placation, plebification, plication, predication, prevarication, prognostication, prolification, provocation, publication, purification, quadruplication, quantification, radication*, ramification, ratification, reciprocation, rectification, relocation, replication, resinification, revivification, revocation, rhetorication*, rubification, rustication, sacrification, salification, sanctification, sanguification, saponifacation, scarification, scorification, siccation, signification, silicification, simplification, solidification, sophistication, specification, speechification, spiflication, stratification, stultification, sublimification, suffocation, sulcation, supplication, syllabication, syllabification, testification, thurification, translocation, transmogrification, triplication, truncation, typification, unification, vacation, vellication, verification, versification, vesication, vilification, vindication, vitrification, vivification, vocation.

kr: consecration, deconsecration, desecration, execration, obsecration.

kw: adequation, equation, inadequation, inequation, liquation.

l: accumulation, adulation, ambulation, angulation, annihiliation, annulation, appelation, articulation, assimilation, assimulation, blood relation, bombilation, calculation, cancellation, cantillation, capitulation, carbunculation, castellation, circulation, circumvallation, coagulation, collation, compellation, compilation, confabulation, congelation, congratulation, consolation, constellation, contravellation, copulation, correlation, crenellation, cupellation, decollation, delation, denticulation, dentilation, deoppilation, deosculation, depilation, depopulation, desolation,

dilation, dissimulation, distillation, ejaculation, ejulation*, elation, emasculation, emulation, etiolation, evolation*, exhalation, expostulation, flagellation, floccillation, geniculation, gesticulation, glandulation, granulation, graticulation, gratulation, hariolation, illation, immaculation, immolation, inarticulation, inhalation, inoculation, inosculation, installation, instillation, insulation, intercalation, interpellation, interpolation, interrelation, isolation, jaculation, jubilation, lallation, legislation, machicolation, maculation, manipulation, matriculation, modulation, mutilation, nidulation, noctambulation, obnubilation, orbiculation, oscillation, osculation, pandiculation, peculation, perambulation, percolation, pestillation, population, postillation, postulation, prolation, pullalation, recapitulation, regelation, regulation, relation, reticulation, revelation, scintillation, serrulation, sibilation, simulation, somnambulation, speculation, stellation, stimulation, stipulation, strangulation, stridulation, suggilation, tabulation, tessellation, tintinnabulation, titillation, tralation*, transolation*, translation, tremulation, triangulation, tribulation, tubulation, ululation, undulation, ustulation, vacillation, vacuolation, vapulation, ventilation, vermiculation, vexillation, violation, vitriolation.

m: acclamation, acclimation, affirmation, amalgamation, animation, approximation, chrismation, confirmation, conformation, consummation, cremation, Dalmatian, decimation, declamation, defamation, deformation, desquamation, detamation, estimation, exclamation, exhumation, formation, inanimation, incremation, inflammation, information, inhumation, intimation, lachrymation, legitimation, malformation, proclamation, racemation, reclamation, reformation, sublimation, summation, transanimation, transformation, ultimation, vigesimation.

n: abacination, abalienation, abomination, accrimination, acumination, adornation, agglutination, agnation, agnomination, alienation, alternation, annomination, assassination, assignation, cachination, calcination, carnation, cognation, combination, commination, condemnation, condonation, consternation, contamination, co-ordination, coronation, crimination, culmination, damnation, declination, denomination, deoxygenation, desalination, designation, destination, determination, devirgination, discrimination, disinclination, dissemination, divination, doctrination, domination, donation, effemination, elimination, emanation, examination, explanation, expugnation, extermination, fascination, ferrumination, fibrination, foreordination, fraternation, fulmination, gelatination, gemination, germination, glutination, gunation, hallucination, hibernation, imagination, immanation, impanation, impersonation, impregnation, impugnation, incarnation, inclination, indetermination, indignation, indiscrimination,

indoctrination, ingemination, inordination, insubordination, intonation, lamination, lancination, lunation, machination, miscegenation, nation, nomination, obstination, oppugnation, ordination, origination, oxygenation, ozonation, pagination, patination, pectination, peregrination, perfectionation, personation, phonation, pollination, predestination, predomination, procrastination, profanation, pronation, propination*, propugnation, ratiocination, recrimination, rejuvenation, remanation, resignation, resupination, rose carnation, ruination, rumination, salination, semination, signation, stagnation, subordination, subornation, supination, 'tarnation, termination, turbination, vaccination, vaticination, venation, venenation, vernation*.

p: anticipation, disculpation, dissipation, emancipation, exculpation, extirpation, forcipation, inculpation, occupation, palpation, participation, preoccupation, syncopation, usurpation.

pl: contemplation.

pr: stupration.

r: aberration, abjuration, acceleration, adjuration, admiration, adoration, adulteration, aeration, aggeration, agglomeration, alliteration, alteration, amelioration, annumeration, aration, aspiration, asseveration, auguration, blusteration, botheration, cameration, cineration, circumgryration, coloration, commemoration, commensuration, commiseration, confederation, configuration, conglomeration, conjuration, consideration, co-operation, corporation, corroboration, declaration, decoration, defloration, degeneration, deliberation, deliration, deploration, depuration, desideration, desperation, deterioration, deterration, discoloration, disfiguration, disoperation, disseveration, duration, edulcoration, elaboration, enumeration, evaporation, evisceraton, exaggeration, exasperation, exhilaration, exoneration, expectoration, expiration, exploration, federation, feneration*, figuration, fissipation, flusteration, fulguration, furfuration, generation, glomeration, gyration, immoderation, imploration, inauguration, inauration*, incameration, incarceration, incineration, inconsideration, incorporation, induration, inspiration, instauration, inteneration, intoleration, invigoration, iteration, laceration, liberation, maceration, marmoration, maturation, melioration, mensuration, moderation, murmuration, narration, numeration, obliteration, obscuration, oneration, operation, oration, perforation, peroration, perspiration, preparation, preponderation, procuration, protuberation, ration, recuperation, refrigeration, regeneration, reiteration, remuneration, reparation, respiration, restoration, reverberation, roboration, saburration, saturation, separation, serration, sideration, subarrhation, sulphuration, suppuration, suspiration, susurration, temeration*, titration, titteration, toleration, tractoration, transfiguration, transliteration, transpiration, trituration, ulceration,

vaporation, veneration, verberation, vituperation, vociferation.

s: adversation, Alsatian, annexation, cassation, cessation, coaxation, compensation, conversation, descussation, dispensation, elixation*, fixation, fluxation, inspissation, intensation, laxation, luxation, malveration, presensation, pulsation, quassation, relaxation, sation*, sensation, succassation, suspensation, taxation, tergiversation, vexation.

st: aerostation, afforestation, bustation, chain station, police station, polling station, railroad station, station.

str: administration, demonstration, fenestration, frustration, maladministration, ministration, monstration*, registration, remonstration.

t: ablactation, absentation, acceptation, acclimatation, accreditation, adaptation, adhortation, affectation, agitation, alimentation, amputation, annotation, argentation, argumentation, arrestation, assentation, attestation, attrectation*, augmentation, auscultation, bioinstrumentation, capitation, castrametation, cementation, cetacean, circumnutation, citation, cogitation, cohabitation, commutation, compotation, computation, concertation, confrontation, confutation, connotation, consultation, co-optation, crepitation, crustacean, crustation, debilitation, decantation, decapitation, decrepitation, degustation, dehortation, delectation, delimitation, dementation, denotation, dentation, deportation, deposition, deputation, detestation, devastation, dictation, digitation, dilatation, disputation, dissention, dissertation, documentation, dotation, equitation, eructation, exaltation, excitation, excogitation, exercitation, exhortation, expectation, experimentation, exploitation, exportation, exultation, facilitation, fermentation, flagitation, flirtation, flotation, fomentation, frequentation, frumentation, gestation, gravitation, gustation, habilitation, habitation, hebetation, hesitation, hortation, humectation, imitation, importation, imputation, inaffectation, incantation, infestation, ingurgitation, inhabitation, instrumentation, insultation*, integumentation, interdigitation, intermutation, interpretation, invitation, irritation, jactitation, lactation, lamentation, levitation, limitation, manifestation, meditation, molestation, mutation, natation, necessitation, nictation, nictitation, nobilitation, notation, occultation, orientation, ornamentation, oscitation, ostentation, palpitation, perfectation, permutation, pernoctation, perscrutation, plantation, pollicitation, potation, precipitation, premeditation, presentation, prestidigitation, protestation, quartation, quotation, recantation, recitation, refutation, rehabilitation, representation, reptation, reputation, resuscitation, retractation, rotation, saltation, salutation, sanitation, sciscitation*, scrutation, sedimentation, segmentation, solicitation, sputation*, sternutation, sublimation, supplantation, supplementation, supportation,

sustentation, temptation, testacean, testamentation, testation, tractation, transmutation, transplantation, transportation, vegetation, visitation.

thr: Thracian.

tr: arbitration, concentration, filtration, illustration, infiltration, interpenetration, lustration, oblatration, orchestration, penetration, perlustration, perpetration, prostration, recalcitration, self-concentration, sequestration.

v: acervation, activation, aggravation, captivation, conservation, cultivation, corvation, depravation, deprivation, derivation, elevation, enervation, estivation, excavation, innervation, innovation, lavation, levation*, nervation, Novatian, novation, observation, ovation, preservation, reservation, salivation, salvation, self-preservation, starvation.

z: acclimatization, accusation, actualization, aggrandization, alcoholization, alkalization, allegorization, Americanization, analysation, anathematization, anglicization, animalization, aromatization, atomization, authorization, brutalization, canalization, canonization, capitalization, carbonization, catechization, causation, cauterization, centralization, characterization, Christianization, civilization, colonization, crystallization, decentralization, demonetization, demoralization, denationalization, denization, deodorization, de-Stalinization, detonization*, economization, effinization, electrization, electrolyzation, endenization*, enthronization, equalization, eternization, etherealization, evangelization, extemporization, externalization, extravasation, familiarization, fertilization, feudalization, formulization, fossilization, fraternization, galvanization, gelatinization, generalization, harmonization, Hellenization, hepatization, Hibernization, hominization, humanization, hybridization, idealization, immortalization, improvisation, individualization, Judaization, Latinization, legalization, literalization, localization, macadamization, magnetization, martyrization, materialization, maximization, mediatization, mesmerization, metallization, methodization, mobilization, modernization, monetization, moralization, nasalization, naturalization, neologization, neutralization, normalization, organization, ozonization, paralyzation, patronization, pauperization, pausation, phonetization, pluralization, polarization, porphyrization, pulverization, realization, recognization, recusation, remonetization, secularization, sensualization, solarization, solemnization, specialization, spiritualization, stigmatization, subtilization, syllogization, symbolization, synchronization, systematization, tabularization, tantalization, tartarization, temporization, theorization, tranquilization, trullization, utilization, vaporization, verbalization, vitalization, vitriolization, vocalization, volatilization, volcanization, vulcanization.

Plus may shun, etc.

ASHƏND

f: fashioned, old-fashioned, unfashioned.

p: dispassioned, impassioned, passioned, unimpassioned, unpassioned.

ĀSHƏNS

p: patience.

ĀSHƏNT

p: impatient, patient.

ASHƏZ

Vowel: ashes.
b: abashes, bashes.
d: dashes.
f: fashes.
fl: flashes, hot flashes.
g: gashes.
h: hashes, rehashes.
k(c): caches, cashes.
kl: clashes.
kr: crashes.
l: lashes, unlashes.
m: mashes.
n: gnashes.
pl: plashes.
r: rashes.
s: sashes.
sl: slashes.
sm: smashes.
spl: splashes.
t: moustaches, mustaches.
thr: thrashes.
    Plus hash, Ez, etc.
    Cf. hash is, etc.

ASID

Vowel: acid.
pl: placid.
    Cf. pass hid, etc.

ĀSĪD

b: bayside.
br: braeside.
w: wayside.
    Plus May sighed *or* side, etc.
    Plus face, I'd *or* eyed, etc.

ASIJ

br: brassage.
p: passage.
    Cf. class age, etc.

ASIK

Vowel: Liassic, Triassic.
b: sebacic.
kl: classic.
r: boracic, Jurassic, thoracic.
t: potassic.
    Cf. Class sick, etc.

ĀSIK

b: basic, bibasic, dibasic, quadribasic, tribasic.
f: aphasic.
    Plus stay sick, etc.

ASIL

f: facile.
gr: gracile.
    Plus class ill, etc.

ÄSIL

d: docile+, dossil.
f: fossil.
    Plus cross'll, etc.
    Plus cross ill, etc.

ASIN

s: assassin.
    Plus class in *or* inn, etc.
    Cf. mass sin, etc.

ĀSIN

b: basin.
    Plus face in *or* inn, etc.
    Cf. asn, ason.

ÄSIN

d: spadasin.
    Plus en masse in *or* inn, etc.
    Plus ma sin, etc.

ASING

g: gassing.
kl: classing, underclassing.
m: amassing, massing.
p: overpassing, passing, surpassing.
    Cf. class sing, etc.

ĀSING

b: abasing, basing, bassing, debasing, self-abasing.
br: bracing, embracing, underbracing.
ch: chasing, girl chasing, skirt chasing, etc., steeplechasing.
f: defacing, effacing, facing, outfacing.
gr: begracing, disgracing, gracing.
k(c): casing, uncasing.
l: belacing, enlacing, interlacing, lacing, relacing, tight lacing, unlacing.
p: outpacing, pacing.
pl: displacing, misplacing, placing, replacing.
r: boat racing, erasing, foot racing, horse racing, racing, yacht racing.
sp: interspacing, spacing.
tr: retracing, tracing.
    Plus may sing, etc.

ÄSIP

g: gossip.
    Cf. cross hip, etc.
    Cf. moss sip, etc.

ASIS

    Cf. asez.
    Cf. class is, etc.

ĀSIS

Vowel: oasis.
b: basis.
f: phasis.
gl: glacis.
    Plus say, sis, etc.
    Cf. face is, face's, faces, etc.

ÄSIS

b: proboscis.
    Cf. loss, sis, etc.

ASIT

t: tacit.
    Plus class it, etc.
    Cf. asset.

ASIV

m: massive.
p: impassive, passive.
    Cf. class sieve, etc.

ĀSIV

sw: assuasive, dissuasive, persuasive, suasive.
v: evasive, invasive, pervasive.
    Plus stray sieve, etc.

ÄSKÄ

hw: ayahuasca.

ASKÄR

g: Madagascar.
l: Lascar.
    Plus class car, etc.
    Cf. askur.

ASKEST

Vowel: askest*.
b: baskest*.
m: bemaskest*, maskest*, unmaskest*.
t: taskest*.

ASKETH

Vowel: asketh*.
b: basketh*.
m: bemasketh*, masketh*, unmasketh*.
t: tasketh*.

ASKING

Vowel: asking.
b: basking.
m: bemasking, masking, unmasking.
t: overtasking, tasking.
    Plus class kind, etc.

ASKŌ

Vowel: fiasco.
b: tabasco.
l: Belasco.
t: tasco.
    Plus task owe *or* O, etc.

ASKUR

Vowel: asker.
b: basker.
g: Madagascar.
k(c): casker, casquer.

l: Lascar.
m: masker, unmasker.
  Plus ask her *or* err, etc.
  Plus class cur, etc.

ÄSKUR

Vowel: Oscar.
  Cf. hoss car, etc.
  Cf. cross scar, etc.

ASKUS

m: Damascus.
  Plus ask us, etc.
  Plus class cuss, etc.

ASKWITH

Vowel: Asquith.
  Plus bask with, etc.

ASKƏ

b: Athabaska.
br: Nebraska.
l: Alaska.
  Plus ask a, etc.

ASKƏL

h: Haskell.
p: paschal.
r: rascal.
  Plus task'll, etc.
  Plus class cull, etc.

ASKƏT

b: basket, bread basket, flower basket.
fl: flasket.
g: gasket.
k(c): casket.
l: lasket.
t: tasket.
  Cf. ask it, etc.

ASL

k(c): castle.
r: wrastle.
t: detassel, entassel, tassel.
v: envassal, vassal.
  Plus class'll, etc.

ĀSLĒ

b: basely.
pl: commonplacely.
  Plus trace, Lee *or* lea, etc.

ĀSLƏS

Vowel: aceless.
b: baseless.
f: faceless.
gr: graceless.
k(c): caseless.
l: laceless.
m: maceless.
p: paceless.
pl: placeless.
r: raceless.
sp: spaceless.
tr: traceless.
  Plus lace less, etc.

ASLƏT

h: haslet.
t: taslet.
  Plus class let *or* Lett, etc.

ĀSLƏT

br: bracelet.
  Plus face let *or* Lett, etc.

ĀSMAN

  Plus face man, etc.

ASMIN, AZMIN

j: jasmine.

  Plus class *or* razz, Min, etc.

ASMƏN

g: gasman.

gl: glassman.

kl: classman, underclassman, upperclassman.

  Plus surpass man, etc.

ĀSMƏN

b: baseman, first baseman, second baseman, third baseman.

l: laceman.

p: paceman.

pl: placeman.

r: raceman.

ASMƏNT

m: amassment.

r: harassment.

  Plus class meant, etc.

ĀSMƏNT

b: abasement, basement, debasement, self-abasement, subbasement.

br: embracement.

f: defacement, effacement.

gr: begracement.

k(c): casement, encasement.

l: belacement, enlacement, interlacement.

pl: displacement, misplacement, placement, replacement.

r: erasement.

tr: retracement.

  Plus space meant, etc.

ASN

f: fasten.

  Cf. casson.

  Cf. class in, etc.

ĀSN

ch: chasten, enchasten.

h: hasten.

  Cf. asin, ason.

  Cf. face in, etc.

ĀSNUR

ch: chastener.

h: hastener.

ASNƏS

kr: crassness.

ASŌ, ÄSŌ

b: basso.

g: Sargasso.

l: lasso.

t: Tasso.

  Plus class owe *or* O, etc.

ĀSŌ

s: sayso.

  Plus play so, sow, *or* sew, etc.

  Plus place owe *or* O, etc.

ASPEST

g: gaspest*.

gr: graspest*.

kl: claspest*, enclaspest*, unclaspest*.

r: raspest*.

  Plus mass pest, etc.

ASPETH

g: gaspeth*.
gr: graspeth*.
kl: claspeth*, enclaspeth*, unclaspeth*.
r: raspeth*.

ASPIK

Vowel: aspic.
  Plus class pick, etc.

ASPING

g: gasping.
gr: engrasping, grasping.
kl: clasping, enclasping, unclasping.
r: rasping.
  Plus class ping, etc.

ÄSPIS

h: hospice.

ÄSPISH

w: waspish.
  Plus toss, pish!, etc.

ÄSPƱR

pr: prosper.
  Plus cross per *or* purr, etc.
  Plus wasp her *or* err, etc.

ÄSPƏL

g: gospel.
  Plus wasp'll, etc.

ASPƏN

Vowel: aspen.
  Plus mass pen, etc.
  Cf. claspin', etc.

ASPƏR

Vowel: asper.
g: gasper.
gr: grasper.
j: jasper.
k(c): Caspar, Casper.
kl: clasper, enclasper, unclasper.
r: rasper.
  Plus grasp her *or* err, etc.
  Plus mass purr *or* per, etc.

ĀSTÄR

d: day-star.
  Plus play star, etc.
  Plus face tar, etc.
  Plus waist, are, etc.

ASTĒ

bl: blasty.
m: masty.
n: epinasty, nasty.
pl: genioplasty, plasty.
v: vasty.
  Plus class tea, tee, *or* T, etc.
  Plus outclassed, he, etc.

ĀSTĒ

h: hasty.
p: pasty.
t: tasty.
  Plus face tea, tee, *or* T, etc.
  Plus displaced, he, etc.

ASTEL

p: pastel.
  Plus class tell, etc.

ASTEST

f: fastest.
k(c): castest*.

l: lastest*, outlastest*.
tr: contrastest*.
v: vastest.
   Plus mass test, etc.

ĀSTEST

b: bastest*.
ch: chastest.
h: hastest*.
p: pastest*.
t: foretastest*, tastest*.
w: wastest*.
   Plus face test, etc.

ASTETH

f: fasteth*.
k(c): casteth*.
l: lasteth*, outlasteth*.
tr: contrasteth*.

ĀSTETH

b: basteth*.
h: hasteth*.
p: pasteth*.
t: foretasteth*, tasteth*.
w: wasteth*.

ĀSTFOOL

t: distasteful, tasteful.
w: wasteful
   Plus placed full, etc.

ASTIF

m: mastiff.
   Plus class tiff, etc.
   Plus past, if, etc.

ĀSTIJ

w: wastage.
   Cf. faced age, etc.

ÄSTIJ

h: hostage.
   Cf. lost age, etc.

ASTIK

Vowel: chiliastic, ecclesiastic, encomiastic, enthusiastic, orgiastic, parasceuastic, scholiastic.
b: bombastic.
bl: amphiblastic.
br: Hudibrastic.
dr: drastic.
fr: antiphriastic, metaphrastic, paraphrastic, periphrasitc.
k(c): dichastic, sarcastic.
kl: anaclastic, clastic, iconoclastic, plagioclastic.
l: elastic, gelastic, ineleastic, scholastic.
m: antonomastic, docimastic, mastic, onomastic, paronomastic.
n: dynastic, gymnastic, monastic, pleonastic.
pl: bioplastic, ceroplastic, dentoplastic, emplastic, esemplastic, galvanoplastic, neoplastic, phelloplastic, plastic, proplastic, protoplastic.
r: pederastic, peirastic.
sp: spastic.
t: fantastic.
tr: tetrastich.
   Plus class tick, etc.
   Cf. mass stick, etc.

ÄSTIK

Vowel: eteostic*.
k(c): pentacostic.
kr: acrostic, paracrostic.
n: agnostic, diagnostic, geognostic, gnostic, prognostic.

Plus loss tick, etc.
Cf. lost stick, etc.

ASTIKS

Vowel: ecclesiastics.
l: elastics.
n: gymnastics.
pl: phelloplastics.
t: fantastics.
    Plus astik+s.

ÄSTIL

h: hostile.
    Plus loss till, etc.

ASTĪM

p: pastime.
    Plus fast, I'm, etc.
    Plus class time, etc.

ASTING

bl: blasting.
f: fasting.
g: flabbergasting.
k(c): casting, forecasting, recasting.
l: everlasting, lasting.
tr: contrasting.
    Plus mass sting, etc.

ĀSTING

b: basting.
h: hasting.
p: pasting.
t: foretasting, tasting.
w: unwasting, wasting.
    Plus play sting, etc.

ĀSTINGZ

h: Hastings.
    Plus asting+s.

ASTLĒ

f: steadfastly.
g: ghastly.
l: lastly.
v: vastly.
    Plus massed, Lee *or* lea, etc.

ĀSTLƏS

b: bastless.
h: hasteless.
p: pasteless.
t: tasteless.
w: waistless, wasteless.
    Plus placed less, etc.

ASTMƏNT

bl: blastment.
tr: contrastment.
    Plus fast meant, etc.

ASTNING

f: fastening.

ASTNƏS

f: fastness.
v: vastness.

ÄST   M

k(c): costume.

ĀSTRĒ

p: pastry.
    Plus place tree, etc.

ÄSTRICH

Vowel: ostrich.
    Plus lost rich, etc.

ASTRIK

g: cacogastric, digastric, gastric, hypogastric, perigastric.

   Plus mass trick, etc.

   Plus outclassed rick, etc.

ASTRUS

Vowel: disastrous.

ASTRƏL

Vowel: astral, subastral.

d: cadastral.

ÄSTRƏL

k(c): costrel.

r: lamellirostral, longirostral, rostral.

   Cf. nostril.

ASTRƏN

Vowel: apastron.

pl: plastron.

   Cf. fast run, etc.

ASTƱR

Vowel: aster, Astor, China aster, geaster, Goniaster, oleaster, piaster, Zoroaster.

b: alabaster.

bl: blaster.

d: cadastre.

f: faster.

g: flabbergaster.

k(c): caster, castor, criticaster, forecaster, grammaticaster, medicaster.

l: interpilaster, pilaster.

m: bandmaster, barrack master, burgomaster, bushmaster, grand master, master, overmaster, postmaster, quartermaster, schoolmaster, taskmaster.

n: canaster.

p: pastor.

pl: beplaster, court plaster, plaster, shin plaster, sticking plaster.

s: disaster.

t: Latinitaster, poetaster.

tr: contraster.

v: vaster.

z: disaster.

   Plus cast her *or* err, etc.

ĀSTƱR

b: baster.

ch: chaster.

p: paster.

t: foretaster, taster.

w: waster.

   Plus waste her *or* err, etc.

ÄSTƱR

sh: shaster.

   Plus en massed her, etc.

   Plus shah stir, etc.

ASTƱRD

b: bastard.

d: dastard.

l: pilastered.

m: mastered, overmastered, unmastered.

pl: beplastered, plastered.

ASTUS

r: Erastus, Rastus.

   Plus cast us, etc.

ASTYUN

b: bastion.

   Cf. Erastian.

ASTƏ

sh: Shasta.

   Plus past a, etc.

ASTƏD

bl: blasted, unblasted.
f: fasted.
g: flabbergasted.
l: lasted, outlasted.
m: masted, undermasted.
tr: contrasted.
　　Plus mass, Ted, etc.
　　Plus past, Ed, etc.

ĀSTƏD

b: basted, unbasted.
h: hasted.
p: pasted, unpasted.
t: tasted, untasted.
w: long-waisted, short-waisted, unwasted, waisted, war-wasted, wasted.
　　Plus face, Ted, etc.
　　Plus disgraced, Ed, etc.

ASTƏN

Vowel: Aston.
g: Gaston.
　　Plus mass ton *or* tun, etc.
　　Plus fast 'un, etc.

ASŬR

k(c): antimacassar.
m: amasser, masser.
p: passer, surpasser.
pl: placer.
　　Plus pass her *or* err, etc.

ĀSŬR

b: abaser, baser, debaser.
br: bracer, embracer.
ch: ambulance chaser, chaser, girl chaser, skirt chaser, steeplechaser.
f: defacer, effacer, facer.
gr: begracer, disgracer, gracer.
k(c): encaser.
l: belacer, interlacer, lacer, unlacer.
m: grimacer, macer.
p: outpacer, pacer.
pl: displacer, misplacer, placer, replacer.
r: eraser, foot racer, horse racer, racer.
sp: spacer.
tr: retracer, tracer.
　　Plus chase her *or* err, etc.
　　Plus play, sir, etc.

ÄSŬR

v: kirschwasser.
　　Plus en masse her.

ASƏ

d: Hadassah.
n: Manasseh.
　　Plus class a, etc.
　　Cf. "yas suh."

ĀSƏ

Vowel: Asa.
m: Amassa.
　　Plus face a, etc.

ĀSƏL

b: basal.
　　Plus race, Al, etc.
　　Plus play, Sal, etc.

ÄSƏM

bl: blossom, orange blossom.
gl: odontoglossum.
p: opossum, possum.
　　Plus boss 'em, etc.

ASƏN

k(c): casson.
　　Cf. fasten.
　　Plus class on *or* an, etc.

ĀSƏN

gr: Grayson.

j: Jason.

k(c): caisson.

m: mason.

Plus place on *or* an, etc.

Plus play, sun *or* son, etc.

ĀSƏNS

b: abaisance*, obeisance.

j: adjacence, interjacence.

n: connascence, renascence.

pl: complacence.

Plus say sense, scents, *or* cents, etc.

Cf. chase hence, etc.

ĀSƏNT

b: obeisant.

d: "daycent."

j: adjacent, circumjacent, interjacent, jacent, subjacent, superjacent.

n: connascent, enascent*, naissant, nascent, renaissant, renascent.

pl: complacent, uncomplacent.

r: indurascent, "ray sent."

Plus play sent, scent, *or* cent, etc.

ASƏT

Vowel: asset.

b: basset, Bassett.

br: brasset.

f: fascet.

pl: placet.

Plus class et, etc.

Cf. tacit.

Cf. pass it, etc.

Cf. class set, etc.

ASƏZ

Vowel: asses, jack asses.

br: brasses.

g: gases.

gl: field glasses, glasses, granny glasses, looking glasses, sunglasses, window glasses, etc.

gr: grasses.

kl: classes.

l: lasses, "lasses," molasses.

m: amasses, masses.

p: passes, surpasses.

r: morasses.

s: sasses.

t: demitasses.

v: crevasses.

Plus pass, Ez, etc.

Cf. pass is, etc.

ĀSƏZ

Vowel: aces.

b: bases, basses, counterbasses, debases.

br: braces, embraces.

ch: chases, steeplechases.

f: defaces, effaces, faces, outfaces.

gr: begraces, disgraces, graces.

k(c): cases, ukases, uncases.

l: belaces, enlaces, interlaces, laces, unlaces.

m: grimaces, maces.

p: footpaces, outpaces, paces.

pl: commonplaces, displaces, hiding places, misplaces, places, replaces, resting places, trysting places.

r: chariot races, foot races, horse races, races.

sp: breathing spaces, interspaces, spaces.

tr: retraces, traces.

v: vases.

Plus ace, Ez, etc.
Plus May says, etc.
Cf. ace is, etc.

ÄTASH

p: potash.
Plus got ash, etc.

ATCHEK

h: hatcheck.

ATĒ

b: batty.
ch: chatty.
f: fatty.
h: Hatty.
k(c): catty, Katty.
m: Mattie, matty.
n: Cincinnati, natty.
p: Pattie, patty.
r: ratty.
Plus skat, he, etc.

ĀTĒ

Vowel: ate, eighty.
h: Haiti, Hayti.
k: Katie.
l: Jubilate.
m: maty.
pl: platy.
sl: slaty.
t: exnecessitate.
w: weighty.
Plus state he, etc.
Plus play tea *or* T, etc.

ÄTĒ

d: dotty.
kl: clotty.
l: Lottie.
n: knotty.

sp: spotty.
t: totty.
Plus what he, etc.
Cf. hot tea, etc.

ATEST

b: battest*.
ch: chattest*.
f: fattest.
fl: flattest.
p: pattest*.
Cf. mat test, etc.

ĀTEST

Vowel: alleviatest*, appreciatest*,
associatest*, createst*,
graduatest*, radiatest*,
repudiatest*.
b: abatest*, baitest*, debatest*.
br: celebratest*.
d: accommodatest*.
g: conjugatest*.
gr: gratest*, greatest.
h: hatest*.
k(c): abdicatest*, advocatest*,
communicatest*, deprecatest*,
indicatest*, vacatest*.
kr: consecratest*.
l: accumulatest*, annihilatest*,
articulatest*, assimulatest*,
calculatest*, dilatest*, ejaculatest*,
emulatest*, latest, regulatest*,
relatest*, translatest*, violatest*.
m: animatest*, matest*.
n: contaminatest*, fascinatest*.
p: anticipatest*.
pl: contemplatest*, plaitest*.
pr: pratest*.
r: adulteratest*, beratest*,
commemoratest*, decoratest*,
exaggeratest*, liberatest*,
narratest*, overratest*, ratest*,
toleratest*, underratest*.
sk: skatest*.

sl: slatest*.

st: statest*.

t: agitatest*, cogitatest*, devastatest*, dictatest*, hesitatest*, imitatest*, irritatest*, necessitatest*.

tr: frustratest*.

v: aggravatest*, captivatest*, cultivatest*, elevatest*.

w: awaitest*, waitest*, etc.

    Plus play test, etc.

ÄTEST

bl: blottest*.

d: dottest*.

g: begottest*, gottest*.

h: hottest.

j: jottest*.

kl: clottest*.

l: allotest*.

n: knottest*.

pl: plottest*.

r: garottest*, rottest*.

s: besottest*.

sh: shottest*.

skw: squattest*.

tr: trottest*.

w: wottest*.

y: yachtest*, etc.

    Cf. yacht test, etc.

ATETH

b: batteth*.

ch: chatteth*.

f: fatteth*.

p: patteth*.

ĀTETH

Vowel: alleviateth*, appreciateth*, associateth*, createth*, graduateth*, radiateth*, repudiateth*.

b: abateth*, baiteth*, debateth*.

br: celebrateth*.

d: accommodateth*.

g: conjugateth*.

gr: grateth*.

h: hateth*.

k(c): abdicateth*, advocateth*, communicateth*, deprecateth*, indicateth*, vacateth*.

kr: consecrateth*.

l: accumulateth*, annihilateth*, articulateth*, assimulateth*, calculateth*, dilateth*, ejaculateth*, emulateth*, regulateth*, relateth*, translateth*, violateth*.

m: antimateth*, mateth*.

n: contaminateth*, fascinateth*.

p: anticipateth*.

pl: contemplateth*, plaiteth*.

pr: prateth*.

r: adulterateth*, berateth*, commemorateth*, decorateth*, exaggerateth*, liberateth*, narrateth*, overrateth*, rateth*, tolerateth*, underrateth*.

sk: skateth*.

sl: slateth*.

st: stateth*.

t: agitateth*, cogitateth*, devastateth*, dictateth*, hesitateth*, imitateth*, irritateth*, necessitateth*.

tr: frustrateth*.

v: aggravateth*, captivateth*, cultivateth*, elevateth*.

w: awaiteth*, waiteth*, etc.

ÄTETH

bl: blotteth*.

d: dotteth*.

g: begotteth*, gotteth*.

j: jotteth*.

kl: clotteth*.

l: alloteth*.

n: knotteth*.

pl: plotteth*.
r: garotteth*, rotteth*.
s: besotteth*.
sh: shotteth*.
skw: squatteth*.
tr: trotteth*.
w: wotteth*.
y: yachteth*.

ĀTĒZ

n: panates.
　Plus rate ease *or* E's, etc.
　Plus play tease *or* T's, etc.

ĀTFOOL

f: fateful.
gr: grateful, ungrateful.
h: hateful.
　Plus plate full, etc.

ATFOOT

fl: flatfoot.
　Plus that foot, etc.

ATFÔRM

pl: platform.
　Plus that form, etc.

ATHED

f: fathead.
fl: flathead.
　Plus cat head, etc.

ATHFOOL

r: wrathful.
　Plus lath full, etc.

ĀTHFOOL

f: faithful.
　Plus wraith full, etc.

ATHIK

m: chrestomathic, philomathic, polymathic.
n: orthonathic, prognathic.
p: allopathic, antipathic, electropathic, felspathic, heteropathic, homeopathic, hydropathic, idiopathic, neuropathic, osteopathic, psychopathic, telepathic, theopathic.
sp: spathic.
　Cf. wrath thick, etc.

ÄTHIK

g: Gothic, Moesogothic, Ostrogothic, Visigothic.
　Cf. cloth thick, etc.

ĀTHING

b: bathing.
l: lathing.
pl: plaything.
　Plus stray thing, etc.
　Cf. scathing.

ÄTHING

sw: swathing, unswathing.

ATHLĒT

k: decathlete.
t: pentathlete.

ATHLƏS

b: bathless.
p: pathless.
r: wrathless.
　Plus lath, less, *or* Les, etc.

ĀTHLƏS

f: faithless.
sk(sc): scatheless.
　Plus wraith less *or* Les, etc.

ATHOO

m: Matthew.
  Plus path you *or* ewe, etc.

ĀTHÔS

b: bathos.
p: pathos.

ATHUR

bl: blather.
g: forgather, gather, ungather, upgather.
l: lather.
r: rather+.

ĀTHUR

b: bather.
  Plus scathe her *or* err, etc.

ÄTHUR

b: bother.
f: father, fother.
p: pother.
r: rather+.
sw: swather.
  Cf. othur.

ATHURZ

sl: slathers.
  Plus athur+s.

ÄTHƏ

n: Jagannatha.
  Cf. maranatha.

ĀTHƏM

f: fathom.

ÄTHƏM

g: Gotham+.
  Plus wroth, am, etc.

ATHƏMD

f: fathomed, unfathomed.

ATHƏN

l: lathen.
  Cf. wrath, an, etc.

ĀTHƏN

n: Elnathan, Nathan.
  Plus faith, an, etc.
  Cf. "haythan."

ATHƏNZ

Vowel: Athens.

ĀTĪ

n: antenati, illuminati.
r: literati.
  Plus plate, I *or* eye, etc.
  Plus stray tie, etc.

ATID

Vowel: caryatid.
  Cf. ated.
  Cf. flat hid, etc.

ATĪD

b: bat-eyed.
k(c): cat-eyed.
  Plus flat, I'd *or* eyed, etc.

ÄTID

r: carotid, parotid.
  Cf. oted.

ĀTIF

k(c): caitiff.
  Plus play tiff, etc.
  Plus plate, if, etc.

ÄTIJ

k(c): cottage.
p: pottage.
w: wattage.
    Cf. what age, etc.

ATIK

Vowel: acroatic, Adriatic, Asiatic, attic, caryatic, Eleatic, fluviatic, Hanseatic, muriatic, pancreatic, sciatic, viatic.

b: acrobatic, adiabatic, ecbatic*, hyperbatic, isodiabatic, sabbatic.

f: emphatic, lymphatic, phosphatic, sulphatic.

kr: aristocratic, arithmocratic, autocratic, bureaucratic, democratic, idiocratic, mobocratic, ochlocratic, pancratic, pantisocratic, plutocratic, Socratic, theocratic, timocratic.

kw: aquatic, subaquatic.

l: palatic, prelatic, villatic.

m: achromatic, acousmatic, acromonogrammatic, anagrammatic, aphorismatic, apophthegmatic, aromatic, asthmatic, automatic, axiomatic, categorematic, chromatic, climatic, commatic, dalmatic, diagrammatic, diaphragmatic, dichromatic, dilemmatic, diplomatic, dogmatic, dramatic, emblematic, endermatic, enigmatic, epigrammatic, grammatic, hierogrammatic, idiomatic, isochromatic, kinematic, lipogrammatic, mathematic, melodramatic, miasmatic, monochromatic, monogrammatic, noematic*, numismatic, paradigmatic, paralleogrammatic, pathematic, phantomatic, phlegmatic, pleochromatic, pneumatic, poematic, polychromatic, pragmatic, prismatic, problematic,

proceleusmatic, rhematic, rheumatic, Sarmatic, schematic, schismatic, smegmatic, somatic, stigmatic, stromatic, symptomatic, systematic, thematic, theomatic, traumatic, trigrammatic, truismatic, zeugmatic, zygomatic.

n: agnatic, aplanatic, fanatic, morganatic.

p: hepatic.

pl: platic.

r: erratic, hieratic, operatic, piratic, quadratic.

st: aerostatic, anastatic, astatic, ecstatic, geostatic, hydrostatic, hypostatic, prostatic, static, thermostatic.

t: majestatic*, protatic.

tr: magistratic.

v: lavatic, sylvatic, vatic.

y: hallelujatic.

    Plus that tick, etc.

ÄTIK

Vowel: antipatriotic, chaotic, epizootic, idiotic, macrobiotic, otic, patriotic, semeiotic, zootic.

d: anecdotic.

dr: hidrotic.

gl: epiglotic, glottic.

k(c): narcotic, psychotic, sarcotic.

kr: acrotic.

kw: aquatic.

l: ankylotic, culotic, Nilotic, sansculotic.

m: demotic, endosmotic, osmotic, zymotic.

n: henotic, hypnotic.

p: despotic, nepotic.

pl: anaplotic.

r: carotic, chlorotic, cirrhotic, erotic, escharotic, neurotic, pyrotic, sclerotic.

s: expotic, quixotic.

t: aptotic.

z: exotic.

    Plus ma tick, etc.

ATIKS

m: mathematics, pneumatics.

st: aerostatics, electrostatics, hydrostatics, hygrostatics, statics.

    Plus atik+s.

ĀTIM

Vowel: seriatim.

b: verbatim.

r: literatim.

    Plus hate him, etc.

    Plus play, Tim, etc.

ĀTĪM

d: daytime.

m: Maytime.

pl: playtime.

    Plus hay time, etc.

    Plus hate, I'm, etc.

ATIN

l: Latin.

m: matin.

p: patine.

pl: platen.

s: satin.

st: somatostatin.

    Plus flat in *or* inn, etc.

    Cf. Manhattan.

    Cf. aten.

ATING

b: batting.

ch: chatting.

f: fatting.

m: matting.

p: patting.

pl: platting.

r: ratting.

t: tatting.

v: vatting.

ĀTING

Vowel: abbreviating, accentuating, alleviating, appreciating, appropriating, associating, attenuating, calumniating, conciliating, creating, delineating, depreciating, deviating, differentiating, dissociating, emaciating, evacuating, excruciating, expatiating, expiating, extenuating, fluctuating, graduating, humiliating, inebriating, infatuating, infuriating, ingratiating, initiating, insinuating, irradiating, luxuriating, mediating, negotiating, obviating, palliating, permeating, perpetuating, propitiating, punctuating, radiating, recreating, satiating, undeviating, vitiating.

b: abating, baiting, bating, debating, incubating, rebating, unabating.

br: celebrating.

d: accommodating, dating, dilapidating, elucidating, intimidating, inundating, invalidating, liquidating, radioactive dating, unaccommodating, validating.

f: feting.

fl: inflating.

fr: freighting.

g: abnegating, aggregating, castigating, congregating, conjugating, corrugating, delegating, derogating, fumigating, instigating, interrogating, investigating, irrigating, navigating, promulgating, propagating, relegating, subjugating, variegating.

gr: disintegrating, emigrating, grating, immigrating, migrating.

h: hating.

k(c): abdicating, advocating, authenticating, collocating, communicating, complicating, confiscating, dedicating, deprecating, dislocating, duplicating, educating, equivocating, eradicating, excommunicating, extricating, fabricating, fornicating, implicating, imprecating, indicating, intoxicating, invocating, locating, lubricating, masticating, prevaricating, prognosticating, quadruplicating, reciprocating, rustricating, sophisticating, suffocating, supplicating, vacating, vindicating.

kr: consecrating, desecrating, execrating.

l: accumulating, annihilating, articulating, assimulating, calculating, capitulating, circulating, coagulating, confabulating, congratulating, depopulating, dilating, dissimulating, ejaculating, emulating, expostulating, flagellating, formulating, gesticulating, granulating, gratulating, immolating, inoculating, insulating, interpolating, isolating, legislating, manipulating, matriculating, modulating, mutilating, oscillating, osculating, perambulating, percolating, populating, postulating, recapitulating, regulating, relating, scintillating, simulating, speculating, stimulating, stipulating, tabulating, titillating, translating, undulating, vacillating, ventilating, violating.

m: amalgamating, animating, approximating, consummating, cremating, decimating, estimating, intimating, mating.

n: abominating, alienating, alternating, assassinating, contaminating, criminating,

culminating, denominating, designating, determinating, detonating, discriminating, disseminating, dominating, eliminating, emanating, fascinating, fulminating, germinating, illuminating, impersonating, impregnating, incriminating, indiscriminating, nominating, originating, peregrinating, personating, predominating, recriminating, rejuvenating, ruminating, terminating, undiscriminating, vaccinating.

p: anticipating, dissipating, emancipating, infanticipating, participating, syncopating.

pl: armor plating, contemplating, copperplating, electroplating, nickel-plating, plaiting, plating.

pr: prating.

r: accelerating, adulterating, aerating, ameliorating, annumerating*, augurating, berating, commemorating, confederating, co-operating, corroborating, decorating, degenerating, deliberating, deteriorating, elaborating, enumerating, evaporating, exaggerating, exasperating, exhilarating, exonerating, expectorating, federating, generating, inaugurating, incarcerating, invigorating, iterating, liberating, moderating, narrating, obliterating, operating, overrating, perforating, rating, recuperating, refrigerating, reiterating, remunerating, reverberating, saturating, separating, tolerating, underrating, venerating, verberating, vituperating, vociferating.

s: compensating, sating.

sk: skating.

sl: slating.

st: overstating, reinstating, stating, understating.

str: demonstrating, frustrating, illustrating.

t: agitating, amputating, cogitating, debilitating, decapitating, devastating, dictating, facilitating, felicitating, gravitating, hesitating, imitating, incapacitating, irritating, meditating, militating, mitigating, necessitating, palpitating, precipitating, premeditating, resuscitating, vegetating.

tr: arbitrating, concentrating, penetrating, perpetrating.

v: aggravating, cultivating, derivating, elevating, excavating, innovating, renovating, titivating.

w: awaiting, waiting, weighting.

ÄTING

bl: blotting.
d: dotting.
j: jotting.
kl: clotting, unclotting.
l: alloting.
n: knotting, reknotting, unknotting.
p: potting, unpotting.
pl: plotting, underplotting, unplotting.
r: garotting, rotting.
s: besotting, sotting.
skw: squatting.
sp: spotting, sunspotting.
t: toting.
tr: trotting.
y: yachting.

ATĪR

s: satire.
Plus that ire, etc.
Cf. flat tire, etc.

ATIS

br: brattice.
l: lattice.
Cf. Pattie's, that is, etc.

ĀTIS

gr: gratis.
Cf. Katie's plate is, etc.

ÄTIS

gl: epiglottis, glottis.

ATISH

f: fattish.
fl: flattish.
k(c): cattish.

ÄTISH

s: sottish.
sk(sc): Scottish.

ÄTIST

l: sans-culottist.

ĀTIV

Vowel: alleviative, annunciative, appreciative, appropriative, associative, continuative, creative, denunciative, depreciative, enunciative, initiative, insinuative, palliative, procreative, pronunciative, radiative, recreative, retaliative.

b: approbative, incubative, reprobative.

d: consolidative, dative, elucidative.

g: abrogative, aggregative, investigative, mitigative, propagative.

k(c): communicative, deprecative, duplicative, eradicative, explicative, imbricative, implicative, incommunicative, justificative, modificative, prognosticative, purificative, qualificative, replicative, significative, suffocative, supplicative, velicative, verificative, vindicative, vivificative.

kr: execrative.

l: accumulative, assimilative, coagulative, collative, copulative, cumulative, dilative, emulative, legislative, manipulative, oscillative, speculative, stimulative, translative, undulative, ventilative, violative.

m: animative, approximative, estimative.

n: agglutinative, contaminative, co-ordinative, criminative, denominative, designative, determinative, discriminative, disseminative, dominative, emanative, germinative, glutinative, illuminative, imaginative, incriminative, indiscriminative, native, opinionative, originative, predestinative, recriminative, retinocrinative, subordinative, terminative.

p: anticipative, participative.

r: accelerative, agglomerative, alliterative, alterative, ameliorative, commemorative, commiserative, confederative, co-operative, corroborative, decorative, degenerative, deliberative, desiderative, edulcorative, elaborative, enumerative, evaporative, exaggerative, exonerative, federative, generative, incorporative, inoperative, iterative, lacerative, operative, perforative, recuperative, refrigerative, regenerative, reiterative, remunerative,

reverberative, separative, suppurative, vituperative.

s: sative*.

st: stative.

t: agitative, authoritative, cogitative, gravitative, hesitative, imitative, incogitative, interpretative, irritative, meditative, qualitative, quantitative, resuscitative, vegetative.

tr: administrative, interpenetrative, ministrative, penetrative.

v: innovative.

ĀTKÄR

st: estate car.

ATKINZ

Vowel: Atkins.

b: Batkins.

   (But not Watkins.)

   Plus flat kin's, etc.

ÄTKINZ

Vowel: Otkins.

w: Watkins.

   Plus not kin's, etc.

ÄTKƏ

l: latke.

ATL

Vowel: Seattle.

b: battell, battle, embattle.

ch: chattel.

k(c): cattle.

pr: prattle.

r: death rattle, rattle.

t: tattle, tittle-tattle.

   Plus that'll, etc.

ÄTL

b: bottle.
d: dottle.
gl: epiglottal, glottal.
m: mottle.
p: pottle.
t: tottle.
thr: throttle.
tw: twattle.
w: wattle.
　　Plus hot'll, etc.

ATLĒ

f: fatly.
fl: flatly.
p: patly.
r: rattly.
　　Plus that, Lee *or* lea, etc.

ĀTLĒ

Vowel: appropriately, inappropriately.
d: sedately.
gr: greatly.
k(c): delicately, indelicately.
kw: adequately, inadequately.
l: articulately, desolately, disconsolately, immaculately, inarticulately, lately.
m: approximately, consummately, illegitimately, intimately, legitimately, ultimately.
n: affectionately, alternately, compassionately, effeminately, extortionately, fortunately, unfortunately.
r: accurately, considerately, desperately, elaborately, illiterately, immoderately, inconsiderately, intemperately, irately, literately, moderately, temperately.

st: stately.
str: straightly, straitly.
　　Plus fate, Lee *or* lea, etc.

ÄTLĒ

h: hotly.
m: motley.
　　Plus not, Lee *or* lea, etc.

ATLĪN

d: dateline.

ATLING

b: battling.
f: fatling.
g: gatling.
k(c): catling.
pr: prattling.
r: rattling.
t: tattling.

ÄTLING

b: bottling.
m: mottling.
thr: throttling.
tw: twattling.
w: wattling.

ATLⱯR

b: battler.
pr: prattler.
r: rattler.
st: Statler.
t: tattler.

ATLƏS

Vowel: atlas.
h: hatless.
v: cravatless.
　　Plus at+less.
　　Plus flat, less *or* Les, etc.

ĀTLƏS

b: baitless.
d: dateless.
fr: freightless.
g: gaitless, gateless.
gr: grateless.
h: hateless.
m: mateless.
r: rateless.
st: stateless.
t: estateless.
w: weightless.
　　Plus skate, less *or* Les, etc.

ÄTLƏS

bl: blotless.
d: dotless.
j: jotless.
k(c): cotless.
kl: clotless.
l: lotless.
n: knotless.
p: potless.
r: rotless.
s: sotless.
sp: spotless.
t: totless.
tr: trotless.
　　Plus what less *or* Les, etc.

ÄTMƏN

Vowel: Ottman.
k(c): cotman.
　　Plus got man, etc.

ĀTMƏNT

b: abatement.
fr: afreightment.
st: instatement, overstatement, reinstatement, statement, understatement.
　　Plus hate, meant, etc.

ÄTMƏNT

l: allotment.
s: besotment.
　　Plus what meant, etc.

ATNƏS

f: fatness.
fl: flatness.
p: patness.

ĀTNƏS

Vowel: inappropriateness.
d: sedateness.
gr: greatness.
l: lateness.
n: innateness, ornateness.
r: considerateness.
str: straightness.

ÄTNƏS

h: hotness.
hw: whatness.

ATŌ

pl: plateau.
sh: chateau.
　　Plus flat owe *or* O, etc.

ĀTŌ

k(c): Cato.
m: pomato+, tomato+.
pl: Plato.
r: literato.
t: potato.
　　Plus may toe, etc.
　　Plus hate owe *or* O, etc.

ÄTŌ

Vowel: otto.
bl: blotto.
d: ridotto.

g: legato, obbligato.
gr: grotto.
k(c): pizzicato, staccato.
l: lotto, mulatto.
m: motto, pomato+, tomato+.
n: annato.
r: enamorato.
s: risotto.
sh: chateau.
w: Watteau.
    Plus not owe *or* O, etc.
    Plus shah toe, etc.
    Plus yacht owe *or* O, etc.
    Cf. oto.

ATOUT

fl: flat out.

ÄTPANTS

h: hot pants.

ĀTRĒ

b: bay tree.
m: may tree.
    Plus spray tree, etc

ATRIK

Vowel: hippocratic, iatric, kinesiatric, theatric.
m: matric.
p: Patrick, St. Patrick.
    Plus flat rick, etc.
    Cf. hat trick, etc.

ĀTRIKS

Vowel: aviatrix, impropriatrix, mediatrix.
k(c): cicatrix.
m: matrix.
r: generatrix.
t: imitatrix, spectatrix, testatrix.
tr: administratix.

Plus hate ricks, etc.
Plus play tricks, etc.

ATRIS, ĀTRIS

m: matrice.
    Cf. atres.

ĀTRƏ

p: Cleopatra.

ĀTRƏD

h: hatred.
    Plus great red *or* read, etc.
    Plus may tread, etc.

ÄTRƏL

d: dottrel.
k(c): Cottrell.

ĀTRƏN

m: matron.
n: natron.
p: patron.
    Cf. plate run, etc.

ATRƏS

l: mulattress.
m: mattress.
    Plus flat tress, etc.

ĀTRƏS

t: dictatress, imitatress, spectatress.
tr: traitress.
w: waitress.
    Plus gay tress, etc.

ÄTSĒ

m: Motsie.
t: hotsy-totsy.
    Plus what see, etc.

ATSMƏN

b: batsman.
   Plus flats, man, etc.

ĀTSMƏN

st: statesman.
   Plus plates, man, etc.

ÄTSMƏN

sk(sc): Scotsman.
y: yachtsman.
   Plus blots, man, etc.

ATSƏN

b: Batson.
m: Matson.
   Plus that son *or* sun, etc.

ÄTSƏN

w: Watson.
   Plus what son *or* sun, etc.

ATUM

str: stratum, etc.
   Plus bat 'em, etc.
   Cf. atom.

ĀTUM

d: datum.
l: postulatum.
m: pomatum, ultimatum.
r: desideratrum, erratum.
str: stratum, substratum,
superstratum.
   Plus hate 'em, etc.

ÄTUM

d: datum.
m: pomatum.
   Cf. got 'em, etc.

ATUP

ch: chat up.

ATƱR

Vowel: attar.
b: batter.
bl: blatter.
ch: chatter.
f: fatter.
fl: beflatter, flatter.
h: hatter, Mad Hatter.
kl: clatter, clitter-clatter.
l: latter.
m: matter, subject matter.
p: bepatter, patter.
pl: platter.
r: ratter.
s: satyr.
sh: shatter.
sk(sc): bescatter, scatter.
sm: smatter.
sp: bespatter, spatter.
spl: splatter.
t: tatter.
   Plus bat her *or* err, etc.

ĀTƱR

Vowel: abbreviator, alleviator,
ameliorater, annunciator,
appropriator, aviator, calumniator,
conciliator, creator, delineator,
denunciator, depreciator, deviator,
enunciator, expatiator, expiator,
extenuator, gladiator, humilator,
initiator, insinuator, mediator,
negotiator, officiator, palliator,
permeator, propitiator, radiator,
repudiator, retailiator.

b: abator, baiter, debater,
incubator.

d: consolidater, dater, depredater,
elucidator, emendator, intimida-
tor, laudator, liquidator, sedater.

fl: inflater.

fr: affreighter, frater, freighter.

g: abnegator, abrogator, alligator, castigator, compurgator, conjugator, fumigator, gaiter, instigator, interrogator, investigater, irrigator, litigator, mitigator, navigator, promulgator, propagator, subjugator, superrogator.

gr: disintegrator, grater, greater, migrater, regrater.

h: hater.

k(c): abdicator, adjudicator, authenicator, cater, confiscator, dedicator, duplicater, educator, equivocater, eradicator, extricator, fabricator, fornicator, hypothecator, indicator, invocator, locater, lubricator, masticator, pacificator, piscator, prevaricator, prognosticator, reciprocater, rusticator, sophisticator, supplicator, versificator, vindicator.

kr: consecrator, crater, execrater.

kw: equator.

l: accumulator, adulator, annihilator, assimilator, calculator, demodulator, depopulator, dissimulator, ejaculator, flagellator, formulator, gesticulator, humiliator, inoculator, insulator, interpolator, later, legislator, manipulator, modulator, mutilator, oscillator, osculator, perambulator, percolator, regulator, relater, scintillator, simulator, speculator, stimulator, stipulator, tabulator, titilator, translator, vacillator, ventilator, violator.

m: alma mater, amalgamater, cremator, dura mater, imprimatur, mater, pia mater, Stabat Mater.

n: alienator, comminator, contaminator, criminator, denominator, designator, desseminator, eliminator, emanator, exterminator, fascinator, germinator, illuminator, impersonator, incriminator, nominator, originator, peregrinator, personator, predominator, procrastinator, ruminator, vaccinator, vaticinator.

p: emancipator, pater.

pl: contemplator, plaiter, plater.

pr: prater.

r: accelerator, aspirator, asseverator, berater, collaborator, commemorator, commiserator, cooperator, corroborator, decorator, deliberator, elaborator, enumerator, evaporator, exaggerator, exhilarator, exonerator, expectorator, federator, first-rater, generator, imperator, incarcerator, incorporator, invigorator, liberator, moderator, narrator, obliterator, operator, perforator, procurator, rater, refrigerator, regenerator, reiterator, respirator, second-rater, separator, third-rater, venerator, vituperator, vociferator.

s: satyr, tergiversator.

sk(sc): figure skater, skater, speed skater, water skater.

sl: slater.

st: Free Stater, reinstater, stater.

str: administrator, demonstrator, illustrator, remonstrator, straighter, straiter.

t: agitator, annotator, cogitator, commentator, compotator, computator, decapitator, devastor, dictater, dictator, facilitator, felicitator, hesitator, imitator, irritator, meditator, palpitater, precipitator, prestidigitator, resuscitator, scrutator, spectator, "tater," testater.

tr: arbitrator, arch traitor, concentrator, frustrator, perpetrator, traitor.

v: aggravator, captivator, conservator, cultivator, elevator, excavator, innovator, renovator, titivator.

w: awaiter, dumb-waiter, waiter.

Plus mate her *or* err, etc.

ÄTŲR

Vowel: ottar, otter.

bl: blotter.

d: dotter.

h: hotter.

j: jotter.

k(c): cottar, cotter.

kl: clotter.

n: knotter, unknotter.

m: alma mater, mater, Stabat Mater.

p: pater, potter.

pl: complotter, plotter, underplotter, unplotter.

r: garotter, rotter.

skw: squatter.

sp: spotter.

sw: swatter.

t: totter.

tr: bogtrotter, globetrotter, trotter.

y: yachter.

Plus got her or err, etc.

Plus swat her *or* err, etc.

ARŲRN

p: pattern, willow pattern.

s: Saturn.

sl: slattern.

Plus that urn, erne, *or* earn, etc.

Cf. that turn, etc.

ATUS

r: apparatus.

st: status.

str: stratous, stratus.

Plus bat us, etc.

ĀTUS

Vowel: hiatus, meatus.

fl: afflatus.

n: senatus.

r: apparatus, literatus, saleratus.

Plus hate us, etc.

ĀTWĀ

g: gateway.

st: stateway.

str: straightway.

Plus late weigh *or* way, etc.

ÄTWĀ

Vowel: Otway.

Plus what way, etc.

ÄTWĪR

h: hot wire.

ATƏ

str: strata.

Plus sat a, etc.

ĀTƏ

Vowel: eta.

b: albata, beta+.

br: Invertebrata, Vertebrata.

d: data+.

l: postulata.

m: ultimata.

r: errata, prorata.

str: strata.

t: dentata.

th: theta.

z: zeta.

Plus state a, etc.

ÄTƏ

Vowel: reata.

d: data+.

g: regatta.

k(c): imbrocata, terracota.

l: aballata, Carlotta, Lotta.

m: yerba mata.

n: serenata, sonata.

r: inamorata, Mahratta, prorata.

t: batata cantata.

Plus what a, etc.

ATƏD

Vowel: caryatid.

b: batted.

ch: chatted.

dr: dratted.

f: fatted.

h: hatted, high-hatted, top-hatted.

m: matted.

p: patted.

pl: plaited, platted.

Plus that, Ed, etc.

ĀTƏD

Vowel: abbreviated, accentuated, actuated, affiliated, alleviated, ampliated, annunciated, appreciated, appropriated, asphyxiated, associated, asteriated, attenuated, calumniated, circumstantiated, conciliated, created, delineated, depreciated, deviated, differentiated, dissociated, effectuated, emaciated, enunciated, eventuated, excoriated, expatiated, expatriated, expiated, extenuated, fluctuated, graduated, habituated, humiliated, impropriated, inebriated, infatuated, infuriated, ingratiated, initiated, insinuated, irradiated, luxuriated, negotiated, obviated, officiated, palliated, permeated, perpetuated, propitiated, punctuated, radiated, recreated, repatriated, repudiated, retaliated, satiated, situated, substantiated, superannuated, unappropriated, uncreated, variated, vitated.

b: abated, approbated, baited, bated, debated, incubated, unabated.

br: celebrated.

d: accommodated, antedated, consolidated, dated, dilapidated, elucidated, intimidated, inundated, invalidated, liquidated, validated.

f: fated, feted, ill-fated.

fl: efflated, inflated.

fr: freighted.

g: abnegated, abrogated, aggregated, arrogated, castigated, congregated, conjugated, corrugated, delegated, derogated, fumigated, gaited, gated, heavy-gaited, instigated, interrogated, investigated, irrigated, levigated, mitigated, navigated, obligated, propagated, relegated, segregated, subjugated, unmitigated, variegated.

gr: disintegrated, emigrated, grated, immigrated, migrated.

h: hated.

k(c): abdicated, ablocated, adjudicated, advocated, allocated, authenticated, bifurcated, certificated, collocated, communicated, complicated, confiscated, dedicated, deprecated, dislocated, domesticated, duplicated, educated, equivocated, eradicated, excommunicated, extricated, fabricated, implicated, imprecated, indicated, intoxicated, invocated, located, lubricated, masticated, medicated, placated, plicated, predicated, prevaricated, prognosticated, reciprocated, rusticated, silicated, sophisticated, spifflicated, suffocated, supplicated, syndicated, unauthenticated, unsophisticated, vacated, vindicated.

kr: consecrated, desecrated, execrated.

kw: antiquated.

l: accumulated, acidulated, annihilated, annulated, armillated, articulated, assimilated, assimulated, belated, calculated, capitulated, castellated, circulated, coagulated, collated, confabulated, congratulated, copulated, correlated, crenellated, depopulated, desolated, dilated, dissimulated, ejaculated, elated, emasculated, emulated, evacuated, expostulated, flagellated, formulated, gesticulated, granulated, gratulated, immolated, incastellated, inoculated, insulated, interpolated, isolated, legislated, manipulated, matriculated, mentholated, methylated, modulated, mucleated, mutilated, oscillated, osculated, perambulated, percolated, populated, postulated, recapitulated, regulated, related, scintillated, sibilated, similated, speculated, stimulated, stipulated, tabulated, tessellated, titillated, translated, triangulated, ululated, undulated, unrelated, vacillated, ventilated, violated.

m: amalgamated, approximated, consummated, cremated, decimated, estimated, intimated, mated, sublimated.

n: abominated, alienated, alternated, assassinated, carbonated, comminated, contaminated, co-ordinated, coronated, culminated, denominated, designated, detonated, discriminated, disseminated, dominated, eliminated, emanated, exterminated, fascinated, foreordinated, fulminated, germinated, illuminated, impersonated, incriminated, indoctrinated, marinated, nominated, opinionated,

originated, peregrinated, personated, predestinated, predominated, procrastinated, recriminated, rejuvenated, ruminated, subordinated, terminated, unilluminated, vaccinated.

p: addlepated, anticipated, dissipated, dunderpated, emancipated, idle-pated, participated, rattlepated, shallowpated, syncopated.

pl: armorplated, contemplated, copperplated, electroplated, nickel-plated, plaited, plated, silver-plated.

pr: prated.

r: accelerated, adulterated, aerated, agglomerated, ameliorated, annumerated*, aspirated, asseverated, augurated, aurated, berated, camphorated, commemorated, commiserated, confederated, conglomerated, co-operated, corroborated, decorated, degenerated, deliberated, desiderated, deteriorated, deuterated, elaborated, enumerated, evaporated, exaggerated, exasperated, exhilarated, exonerated, expectorated, federated, generated, inaugurated, incarcerated, incinerated, incorporated, indurated, invigorated, iterated, jasperated, liberated, macerated, moderated, narrated, obliterated, operated, overrated, perforated, rated, recuperated, refrigerated, regenerated, reiterated, remunerated, reverberated, saturated, separated, tolerated, triturated, undecorated, underrated, venerated, vituperated, vociferated.

s: compensated, sated, tergiversated.

sk: skated.

sl: slated.

st: instated, overstated, reinstated, stated, understated, unstated.

str: demonstrated, undemonstrated.

t: agitated, amputated, annotated, capacitated, cogitated, crepitated, debilitated, decapitated, devastated, dictated, exorbitated, facilitated, gravitated, hesitated, imitated, incapacitated, irritated, meditated, militated, necessitated, palpitated, precipitated, premeditated, rehabilitated, resuscitated, unpremeditated, vegetated.

tr: arbitrated, concentrated, frustrated, illustrated, penetrated, perpetrated.

v: aggravated, captivated, cultivated, elevated, excavated, innovated, renovated, salivated, titivated.

w: awaited, heavy-weighted, waited, weighted.

> Plus say, Ted, etc.
> Plus plate, Ed, etc.

ÄTƏD

Vowel: cheviotted.

bl: blotted, unblotted.

d: dotted, undotted.

j: jotted.

kl: clotted, unclotted.

l: alloted, lotted.

n: knotted, unknotted.

p: potted, unpotted.

pl: plotted, underplotted, unplotted.

r: carotid, garotted, rotted, unrotted.

s: besotted, sotted.

sh: shotted.

sk(sc): wainscotted.

skw: squatted.

sl: slotted.

sp: bespotted, blood-bespotted, blood-spotted, spotted, unspotted.

t: totted.

tr: trotted.

> Plus not Ed, etc.

ĀTƏL

f: fatal.

n: natal, postnatal, prenatal.

st: Statal.

> Plus plate, Al, etc.

ATƏM

Vowel: atom.

> Plus bat 'em, etc.

ÄTƏM

b: bottom.

> Plus got 'em, etc.
> Cf. hot tum, etc.

ATƏN

b: baton, batten.

f: fatten.

fl: flatten.

h: Hatton.

p: paten.

r: ratten.

> Cf. atin.
> Plus flat on *or* an, etc.

ĀTƏN

d: Dayton.

kl: Clayton.

l: Leighton.

p: peyton.

s: Satan.

> Plus mate an, etc.
> Plus may tun *or* ton, etc.
> Plus great 'un, etc.
> Cf. atn.

ÄTƏN

g: begotten, first-begotten, forgotten, gotten, hard-gotten, ill-gotten, misbegotten, misgotten, unbegotten, unforgotten, ungotten.

gr: Groton.

k(c): cotton, sea-island cotton.

r: rotten.

t: Fort Totten, Totten.

Cf. hot ten, etc.

Cf. got hen, etc.

Cf. oten.

ĀTƏNT

bl: blatant.

l: latent.

n: natant.

p: patent.

st: statant.

Plus rate aunt *or* ant, etc.

Plus play-tent, etc.

Cf. mate tent, flat tent, etc.

ĀŪR

b: disobeyer, obeyer.

br: brayer.

fl: flayer.

fr: affrayer, defrayer.

g: gayer.

gr: grayer, greyer.

h: hayer.

l: allayer, belayer, deep scattering layer, delayer, inlayer, interlayer, layer, mislayer, outlayer, overlayer, relayer, waylayer.

m: dismayer, mayor.

n: matineer, neigher.

p: payer, prepayer, repayer, underpayer.

pl: displayer, player, underplayer.

pr: prayer, preyer.

r: arrayer, disarrayer, hoorayer.

s: assayer, essayer, gainsayer, missayer, soothsayer.

sl: slayer.

sp: spayer.

spr: sprayer.

st: outstayer, stayer.

str: strayer.

sw: swayer.

tr: betrayer, portrayer.

v: conveyer, inveigher, purveyor, surveyor.

w: outweigher, weigher.

z: viseer.

Plus betray her *or* err, etc.

ĀVĀ

Vowel: ave.

AVÄK

h: havoc.

AVĀL

Vowel: avail.

tr: travail.

Plus have ale *or* ail, etc.

AVĒ

n: navvy.

s: no savvy, savvy.

Plus Slav, he, etc.

Cf. peccavi.

ĀVĒ

d: affidavy, Davie, Davy.

g: agave.

gr: gravy.

k(c): cavy, peccavi.

n: navy.

r: ravy.

sl: slavey.

w: wavy.

Plus shave, he, etc.

ĂVĒ

Plus salve, he, etc.

ĀVEST

br: bravest.

g: forgavest*, gavest*.

gr: engravest*, gravest.

h: behavest*.

kr: cravest*.

l: lavest*.

p: pavest*.

pr: depravest*.

r: ravest*.

s: savest*.

sh: shavest*.

sl: beslavest*, enslavest*, slavest.

w: waivest*, wavest*.

Plus play vest, etc.

ĂVEST

sw: suavest.

ĀVETH

br: braveth*.

g: forgaveth*, gaveth*.

gr: engraveth*, graveth*.

h: behaveth*.

kr: craveth*.

l: laveth*.

p: paveth*.

pr: depraveth*.

r: raveth*.

s: saveth*.

sh: shaveth*.

sl: beslaveth*, enslaveth*, slaveth*.

w: waiveth*, waveth*.

ĀVĒZ

d: Davies.

Plus gravy's, etc.

Plus grave ease, etc.

AVID

Vowel: avid.

gr: gravid.

p: inpavid, pavid.

Cf. Slav hid, etc.

ĀVID

d: David.

Cf. av+d*.

Cf. slave hid, etc.

AVIJ

r: ravage.

s: savage.

sk(sc): scavage.

Cf. Slav age, etc.

AVIK

gr: gravic.

sl: Pan-Slavic, Slavic.

AVIN

s: savin.

sp: spavin.

Cf. have inn *or* in, etc.

AVING

h: having.

s: salving.

ĀVING

br: braving, outbraving.

gr: engraving, graving, steel engraving, wood engraving.

h: behaving, misbehaving.

k(c): caving.
kr: craving.
l: belaving, laving.
p: paving.
pr: depraving.
r: raving.
s: laborsaving, lifesaving, saving, timesaving.
sh: shaving.
sl: beslaving, enslaving, slaving.
st: staving.
w: finger waving, flag waving, marcel waving, waiving, waving.

ÄVING

h: halving.
k(c): calving.
s: salving.

ĀVIS

Vowel: rara avis.
d: Davis.
kl: clavis.
m: mavis.
  Cf. slave is, navy's etc.

AVISH

l: lavish.
r: enravish, ravish.
t: McTavish.

ĀVISH

br: bravish.
n: knavish.
sl: slavish.

AVIT

d: davit.
  Plus salve it, etc.

ĀVIT

d: affidavit.
k: indicavit.
  Plus shave it, etc.

AVL

g: gavel.
gr: gravel.
r: ravel, unravel.
tr: travel.
  Plus Slav'll, etc.
  Cf. cavil.

ĀVL

n: naval, navel.
  Plus slave'll, etc.

ÄVL

gr: grovel.
h: hovel.
n: novel.
  Plus of 'll, etc.

AVLD

gr: gravelled.
r: ravelled, unravelled.
tr: travelled, untravelled.
  Plus gavel'd, etc.

ĀVLĒ

br: bravely.
gr: gravely.
n: knavely.
sw: suavely.
  Plus shave, Lee, etc.

ÄVLĒ

Vowel: souavely.
sw: suavely.
  Plus Slav, Lee or lea, etc.

ĂVLIN

j: javelin.
r: ravelin.
   Plus have, Lynn, etc.

ĀVLING

sh: shaveling.

ĀVLƏS

gr: graveless.
k(c): caveless.
sl: slaveless.
st: staveless.
w: waveless.
   Plus brave less *or* Les, etc.

ĀVMƏNT

gr: engravement.
l: lavement.
p: pavement.
pr: depravement.
sl: enslavement.
   Plus shave meant, etc.

ĀVNƏS

br: braveness.
gr: gravenss.
sw: suaveness.

ĀVŌ, ÄVŌ

br: bravo.
t: octavo.
   Plus shave owe *or* O, etc.

ĂVƏR

d: cadaver.
h: haver.
l: palaver.
sl: beslaver.
   Plus have her *or* err, etc.

ĀVƏR

br: braver.
f: disfavor, favor, marriage favor, misfavor.
fl: flavor.
gr: engraver, graver, steel engraver, wood engraver.
kl: claver.
kr: craver.
kw: demiquaver, quaver, semiquaver.
l: laver.
p: Papaver, paver.
pr: depraver.
r: raver.
s: lifesaver, saver, savor, timesaver.
sh: shaver.
sl: enslaver, slaver.
sw: suaver.
w: finger waver, marcel waver, waiver, waver.
   Plus enslaver her *or* err, etc.

ÄVƏR

l: palaver.
sw: suaver.
   Plus Slav err *or* her, etc.

ÄVƏRB

pr: proverb.
   Cf. Slav herb, etc.

ĀVƏRD

f: favored, ill-favored, well-favored.
fl: flavored.
kw: quavered.
s: savored.
w: wavered.
   Plus shaver'd, etc.

AVŲRN

k(c): cavern.
t: tavern.
   Plus Slav urn, erne, *or* earn, etc.

ÄVUS

t: Gustavus.
   Plus salve us, etc.

ĀVYŲR

h: behavior, havior, misbehavior.
p: Pavier, pavior.
s: savior.
z: Xavier.
   Cf. clavier.

ÄVƏ

br: brava.
gw: guava.
j: Java.
kl: balaclava.
l: lava.
s: cassava.
   Plus salve a, etc.

ĀVƏN

gr: engraven*, graven.
h: haven.
kr: craven.
sh: shaven.
   Cf. save an, etc.

ÄVƏN

d: daven.

ĀWIN

r: rawin.

ĀWĪR

h: haywire.
   Plus play wire, etc.

ĀWÔRN

spr: spray-worn.
w: wayworn.
   Plus day worn, etc.

ĀWŲN

d: Day One.

ĀWŲRD

h: Heyward.
w: wayward.
   Plus play ward, etc.

ÄWŲRD

v: vaward*.

ĀYÄRD

b: Bayard.
   Plus play yard, etc.

ĀYŌ

m: Mayo.
   Cf. kayo, K. O.
   Cf. play owe *or* O, etc.

ĀYOO

   Cf. pay you, etc.

ĀYƏ

Vowel: ayya.
gl: Aglaia.
n: naia.
s: calisaya.
z: Isaiah.
   Cf. play a, etc.

ĀYƏN

l: Himalayan, Malayan.
t: Altaian, Cataian.
   Cf. play an, etc.

AZDAK
n: NASDAQ.

ĀZĒ
bl: blazy.
d: African daisy, daisy, lackadaisy, whoops-a-daisy.
fr: paraphrasy, phrasy.
h: hazy.
j: jasey.
kr: crazy.
l: lazy.
m: mazy.
  Plus maze, he, etc.
  Plus Z *or* Zee, etc.

ÄZĒ
g: ghazi.
w: ghawazi.
  Plus Shiraz, he, etc.

ĀZEST
bl: blazest*.
br: braisest*.
d: dazest*.
fr: paraphrasest*, phrasest*.
g: gazest*.
gl: glazest*.
h: hazest*.
m: amazest*.
pr: bepraisest*, praisest*.
r: raisest*, razest*, upraisest*.
  Plus gay zest, etc.

ĀZETH
bl: blazeth*.
br: braiseth*.
d: dazeth*.
fr: paraphraseth*, phraseth*.

g: gazeth*.
gl: glazeth*.
h: hazeth*.
m: amazeth*.
pr: bepraiseth*, praiseth*.
r: raiseth*, razeth*, upraiseth*.

ÄZHING
fl: camouflaging, persiflaging.
r: garaging.

AZHOUND
j: jazzhound.
  Plus has hound, etc.

AZHƱR
Vowel: azure.

ĀZHƱR
Vowel: azure.
br: brazier, embrasure.
fr: Frasier, Frazier.
gl: glazier.
gr: grazier.
r: erasure, razure.
  Cf. praise your, you're, *or* "yer," etc.

ĀZHƏN
br: abrasion, dermabrasion.
k(c): occasion.
r: erasion.
sw: dissuasion, persuasion, suasion.
v: evasion, invasion.
  Cf. Caucasian
  Cf. azhian.

ĀZHƏR
tr: arbitrager, arbitrageur.

AZIL

b: Basil.
Cf. azl.
Cf. jazz ill, etc.

ĀZIN

r: raisin.
Plus praisin', etc.
Plus stays in *or* inn, etc.

ĀZING

bl: ablazing, blazing, outblazing, trail blazing, upblazing.
br: braising, brazing.
d: dazing.
fr: paraphrasing, phrasing.
g: gazing, outgazing, stargazing.
gl: glazing.
gr: grazing.
h: hazing.
l: lazing.
m: amazing, bemazing*.
pr: bepraising, praising, self-praising.
r: consciousness-raising, flag raising, hellraising, raising, upraising.

AZL

b: Basil
d: bedazzle, dazzle, razzle-dazzle.
fr: frazzle.
Plus jazz'll, etc.

ÄZL

n: nozzle.
s: sozzle.
shn: schnozzle.
Plus Boz'll, etc.

AZLING

d: dazzling.
fr: frazzling.

ĀZLƏS

bl: blazeless.
h: hazeless.
m: maizeless, mazeless.
pr: praiseless.
v: vaseless.
Plus craze less *or* Les, etc.

AZMĒ

k(c): chasmy.
Plus has me, etc.

AZMIK

Vowel: miasmic.
pl: bioplasmic, protoplasmic.
Plus jazz, Mick, etc.

ÄZMIK

d: endosmic.
k(c): cosmic, macrocosmic, microcosmic.
Cf. was Mick, etc.

AZMUS

r: Erasmus.
Plus jazz muss, etc.

AZMƏ

Vowel: asthma, miasma.
f: Phasma.
pl: plasma, protoplasma.
t: phantasma.
Plus jazz, ma, etc.

AZMƏL

Vowel: miasmal.
pl: protoplasmal.
t: phantasmal.

ĀZMƏNT

m: amazement.
pr: appraisement, praisement.
  Plus craze meant, etc.

ĀZUR

Vowel: Eleazer.
bl: blazer.
fr: Fraser, paraphraser, phraser.
g: gazer, geyser, stargazer, upgazer.
gl: glazer.
h: hazer.
l: lazer.
pr: appraiser, dispraiser, praiser, self-praiser.
r: raiser, razer, upraiser.
  Plus daze her *or* err, etc.

AZURD

h: biohazard, haphazard, hazard.
m: mazard*, mazzard.
  Cf. jazz hard, etc.

AZƏ

Vowel: piazza.
pl: plaza.
z: cazazza.
  Plus jazz a, etc.

ĀZƏ

g: Gaza.
  Cf. raise a, etc.

ÄZƏ

g: Gaza.

ĀZƏL

h: hazel, witch hazel.
n: nasal.
pr: appraisal.
  Plus raise, Al, etc.

ĀZƏN

bl: blazon, emblazon.
br: brazen.
gl: glazen.
p: diapason.
sk: skazon.
  Plus blaze on *or* an, etc.

ÄZƏNJ

l: lozenge.

ÄZƏT

kl: closet.
p: deposit, interposit, juxtaposit, posit, reposit.
  Cf. was it, etc.

ĀZƏZ

b: baizes.
bl: blazes, great blue blazes.
br: braises.
d: daisies, dazes.
f: phases.
fr: paraphrases, phrases.
g: gazes, stargazes.
gl: glazes.
gr: grazes.
h: hazes, smoke hazes.
kr: crazes.
m: amazes, bemazes*, mazes.
n: mayonnaises.
pr: praises.
r: raises, razes.
sh: chaises.
v: vases.
  Plus craze is, etc.

ĀƏ

z: Isaiah+.

ĀƏL

b: Baal.
fr: defrayal.
tr: betrayal, portrayal.
v: surveyal.

ĀƏNS

b: abeyance.
v: conveyance, purveyance, surveyance.

ĀƏNT

b: abeyant.

E

The accented vowel sounds included are listed under **E** in Single Rhymes.

ĒÄN

Vowel: aeon.
d: odeon.
f: pheon.
kr: Creon.
l: Leon, Ponce de Leon, Richard Coeur De Lion.
n: neon.
p: paeon, peon.
th: pantheon.
Plus we on *or* an, etc.
Cf. ean.

ĒBAĀS

fr: free base.

ĒBĒ

f: Pheoebe.
h: Hebe.
j: heebee-jeebee.
t: TB, Teebie.
Plus we be, etc.

ĒBIL

t: T-Bill.

EBING

Vowel: ebbing, unebbing.
w: webbing.

EBL

j: djebel.
p: pebble.

r: archrebel, rebel.
tr: treble.
Plus well 'll, etc.

ĒBL

f: enfeeble, feeble.
Plus see bull, etc.
Plus glebe 'll, etc.

ĒBŌ

n: Nebo.
s: placebo.
z: gazebo.
Plus see beau, bow *or* bo, etc.
Plus glebe owe, etc.

ĒBÔRD

fr: freeboard.
k: keyboard.
s: seabosard.
Plus tree bored *or* board, etc.

ĒBÔRN

fr: freeborn.
s: seaborn.
Plus we born, etc.

ĒBOUND

r: rebound.

EBPAĀJ

w: Web page.

ĒBRAÄK

p: pibroch.
   Plus glebe rock, etc.

ĒBROŌ

h: Hebrew.
   Plus we brew, etc.

ĒBRƏ

z: zebra.

EBSĪT

w: Web site.

EBUR

Vowel: ebber.
w: von Weber, webber, Weber.
   Plus web her, etc.

ĒBUR

g: Gheber.
   Plus see burr, etc.
   Plus glebe err *or* her, etc.

EBƏN

Vowel: ebon.
   Plus web on, etc.

ĒBƏN

Vowel: Eben.
   Cf. grebe hen, etc.

ĒBƏ

m: amoeba.
r: Reba, zareba.
s: Seba.
sh: Bath Sheba, Sheba.
   Plus glebea, etc.

ĒBƏS

f: Phoebus.
gl: glebous.
r: rebus.
   Plus glebe us, etc.

ECHĀ

v: ceviche.

ECHED

r: wretched.
   Plus ech+ed.*

ECHEST

Vowel: etchest*.
f: fetchest*.
r: retchest*.
sk: sketchest*.
str: outstretchest*, stretchest*.

ĒCHEST

bl: bleachest*.
p: impeachest*.
pr: preachest*.
r: forereachest*, overreachest*, reachest*.
s: beseechest*, sea chest.
skr(scr): screechest*.
t: tea chest, teachest*.
   Plus see chest, etc.

ECHETH

Vowel: etcheth*.
f: fetcheth*.
r: retcheth*.
sk: sketcheth*.
str: outstretcheth*, stretcheth*.

ĒCHETH

bl: bleacheth*.
p: impeacheth*.

pr: preacheth*.
r: forereacheth*, overreacheth*, reacheth*.
s: beseecheth*.
skr(scr): screecheth*.
t: teacheth*.

ĒCHEĒ

b: beachy, beechy.
bl: bleachy.
br: breachy.
kw: queachy.
p: campeechy, peachy.
pr: preachy, teachy-preachy.
r: reachy, reechy.
skr(scr): screechy.
sp: speechy.
t: teachy.
tr: Beatrice.
    Plus beach, he, etc.

ECHEĒ

f: fetchy.
sk: sketchy.
str: stretchy.
t: tetchy.
v: vetchy.
    Plus vetch, he, etc.

ĒCHING

b: beaching.
bl: bleaching.
br: breaching, breeching.
l: leaching, leeching.
p: impeaching, peaching.
pr: preaching.
r: forereaching, overreaching, reaching.
s: beseeching.
skr(scr): screeching.
t: foreteaching, teaching.

ECHING

Vowel: etching.
f: fetching.
r: retching.
sk: sketching.
str: outstretching, stretching.

ĒCHLƏS

b: beachless, beechless.
br: breachless.
p: peachless.
r: reachless.
sp: speechless.
t: teachless.
    Plus impeach less, etc.

ĒCHMƏNT

p: impeachment.
pr: preachment.
s: beseechment.
    Plus peach meant, etc.

ECHUP

k(c): catch up, ketchup.
    Plus fetch up, etc.

ECHƱR

Vowel: etcher.
f: fetcher.
fl: fletcher.
l: lecher.
r: retcher.
sk: sketcher.
str: stretcher.
tr: treacher*.
    Plus stretch her *or* err, etc.

ĒCHƱR

b: Beecher.
bl: bleacher.

br: breacher, breecher.
f: feature.
kr: creature.
l: leacher, leecher.
p: impeacher, peacher.
pr: preacher.
r: forereacher, overreacher, reacher.
s: beseecher.
skr(scr): screecher.
t: teacher.
    Plus feet, you're *or* your, etc.
    Plus reach her, err *or* er, etc.
    Cf. echur.

ĒCHƱRD

f: featured, hard-featured, ill-featured, well-featured.
    Plus creature'd, etc.
    Cf. echur+ed.

ECHƏZ

Vowel: etches.
f: fetches.
fl: fletches.
k: ketches.
r: retches, wretches.
sk: sketches.
str: outstretches, stretches.
v: vetches.
    Cf. ketch is, etc.

ĒCHƏZ

b: beaches, beeches.
bl: bleaches.
br: breaches, breeches.
l: leeches.
p: impeaches, peaches.
pr: preaches.
r: forereaches, overreaches, reaches, sea-reaches.

s: beseeches.
skr(scr): screeches.
sp: speeches.
t: teaches.
    Cf. peach is, etc.

ĒDBED

r: reedbed.
s: seedbed.
w: weedbed.
    Plus need bed, etc.

EDBĒT

d: deadbeat.
    Plus red beet, etc.

EDBŌLT

d: dead bolt.

EDBREST

r: redbreast.
    Plus dead breast, etc.

EDBRIK

r: redbrick.

EDBUG

b: bedbug.
r: redbug.
    Plus spread bug, etc.

EDDÄG

r: red dog+.

EDDÔG

r: red dog+.

EDDWRF

r: red dwarf.

EDĒ

Vowel: Eddie, eddy.
fr: Freddy.
l: leady.
r: already, ready, reddy, unready.
shr: shreddy.
st: steady, unsteady.
t: teddy.
thr: thready.
  Plus said he, etc.

ĒDĒ

b: beady.
d: deedy, indeedy.
gr: greedy.
h: heedy, unheedy.
kr: creddy.
l: Leedy.
n: needy.
p: encyclopedy.
pr: predy*.
r: reedy.
s: seedy.
sp: speedy.
  Plus bleed, he, etc.
  Plus wee D, etc.

ĒDĒP

n: kneedeep.
s: seadeep.
thr: three deep.
  Plus tree deep, etc.

EDEST

dr: dreadest.
h: beheadest*.
r: reddest.
sh: sheddest*.
spr: outspreadest*, spreadest*.
thr: threadest*.
tr: treadest*.
w: weddest*.

ĒDES

sp: speed chess.

ĒDEST

bl: bleedest*.
br: breedest*.
d: deedest*.
f: feedest*, overfeedest*, underfeedest*.
h: heedest*.
l: leadest*, misleadest*.
n: kneadest*, needest*.
p: impedest*, stampedest*.
pl: pleadest*.
r: readest*.
s: accedest*, cedest*, concedest*, exceedest*, intercedest*, precedest*, proceedest*, recedest*, secedest*, seedest*, succeedest*, supercedest*.
sp: speedest*.
w: weedest*.

EDETH

dr: dreadth*.
h: beheadeth*, headeth*.
sh: sheddeth*.
shr: shreddeth*.
spr: out-spreadeth*, overspreadeth*, spreadeth*.
thr: threadeth*.
tr: treadeth*.
w: weddeth*.
  Cf. led death, etc.

ĒDETH

bl: bleedeth*.
br: breedeth*.
d: deedth*.
f: feedeth*, overfeedeth*, underfeedeth*.
h: heedeth*.
l: leadeth*, misleadeth*.

n: kneadeth*, needeth*.
p: impedeth*, stampedeth*.
pl: pleadeth*.
r: readeth*.
s: accedeth*, cedeth*, concedeth*, exceedeth*, intercedeth*, precedeth*, proceedeth*, recedeth*, secedeth*, seedeth*, succeedeth*, supercedeth*.
sp: speedeth*.
w: weedeth*.
Plus see death, etc.
Cf. Edith.

EDEX

f: Fedex.

EDĒZ

t: teddies.
Plus edi+s.

EDFAST

st: steadfast.
Plus tread fast, etc.

EDFOOL

dr: dreadful.
Plus bed full, etc.

ĒDFOOL

d: deedful
h: heedful, unheedful.
m: meedful.
n: needful, unneedful.
sp: speedful.
Plus reed full, etc.

ĒDGRŌN

r: reedgrown.
s: seedgrown.
w: weedgrown.

Plus we'd groan, etc.
Plus he'd grown, etc.

ĒDGROUS

r: red grouse.

EDHED

d: deadhead.
r: redhead.
Plus spread head, etc.

EDHĒT

d: dead-heat.
r: red-heat.
Plus fed heat, etc.

EDIK

Vowel: Eddic.
y: Samoyedic.
Cf. red, Dick, etc.

ĒDIK

m: comedic.
p: cyclopaedic, encyclopaedic.
v: Vedic.
Plus see, Dick, etc.

ĒDIKT

Vowel: edict.

EDING

b: bedding, embedding.
dr: dreading.
h: beheading, heading.
l: leading.
r: redding.
sh: shedding.
shr: shredding.
sl: sledding.
spr: bespreading, outspreading, overspreading, spreading.
st: steading.

t: tedding.
thr: threading.
tr: treading.
w: wedding.

ĒDING

b: beading.
bl: bleeding, love-lies-bleeding, unbleeding.
br: breeding, inbreeding, interbreeding.
d: deeding.
f: feeding, overfeeding, underfeeding.
h: heeding, unheeding.
l: leading, misleading.
n: kneading, needing.
p: impeding, stampeding.
pl: interpleading, pleading.
r: misreading, reading, reeding.
s: acceding, ceding, conceding, exceeding, interceding, preceding, proceeding, receding, retroceding, seceding, seeding, succeeding, superseding.
sp: Godspeeding, outspeeding, speeding.
w: weeding.

EDISH

Vowel: eddish.
d: deadish.
r: reddish.
    Cf. spread dish, etc.

ĒDISH

sw: Swedish.

EDIT

Vowel: edit, sub-edit.
kr: accredit, credit, discredit, miscredit.
    Plus you said it, etc.

ĒDITH

Vowel: Edith.
    Cf. edeth.

EDKÄRD

r: red card.

EDKLĀ

r: red clay.

EDL

h: heddle.
m: intermeddle, medal, meddle.
p: bipedal, pedal, peddle, tripedal.
r: reddle.
tr: treadle.
    Plus bed 'll, etc.
    Cf. dead dull, etc.

ĒDL

b: beadle.
d: daedal.
hw: wheedle.
n: needle.
p: bipedal, centipedal, millipedal, semipedal.
tw: tweedle.
    Plus feed 'll, etc.
    Cf. see dull, etc.

EDLÄK

d: deadlock.
h: headlock.
w: wedlock.
    Plus dread lock, etc.

EDLÄKS

dr: dreadlocks.

EDLĒ

d: deadly.
m: chance-medley, medley.
r: redly.
  Plus dead lea *or* Lee, etc.

EDLĪN

br: breadline.
d: deadline.
h: headline.
  Plus spread line, etc.

EDLING

m: intermeddling, meddling.
p: peddling.

ĒDLING

hw: wheedling.
n: needling.
r: reedling.
s: seedling.

EDLĪT

d: deadlight.
r: redlight.
  Plus spread light, etc.

ĒDOUT

r: readout.

EDLUR

m: intermeddler, meddler, medlar.
p: pedlar, peddler, pedler.
tr: treadler.

ĒDLUR

hw: wheedler.
n: needler.

EDLƏM

b: Bedlam.
  Plus dead lamb, etc.

EDLƏND

h: headland.
  Plus red land, etc.

EDLƏS

b: bedless.
br: breadless.
dr: dreadless.
h: headless.
l: leadless.
  Plus spread less, etc.

ĒDLƏS

br: breedless.
d: deedless.
h: heedless.
kr: creedless.
n: needless.
s: seedless.
sp: speedless.
st: steedless.
w: weedless.
  Plus impede less, etc.

EDMIL

tr: treadmill.

EDMƏN

Vowel: Edman.
d: deadman.
h: headman.
r: redman.
st: Stedman.
  Plus spread man, etc.

ĒDMAN

fr: Bruce Friedman.

ĒDMƏN

fr: Friedman.
s: seedman.
> Plus need man, etc.

EDNES

r: redness.

EDNƏ

Vowel: Edna.

EDNƏS

d: deadness.
r: redness.

EDŌ

m: meadow.
> Plus bed owe *or* O, etc.

ĒDŌ

b: libido.
kr: credo.
l: Lido, Toledo.
p: stampedo, torpedo.
r: teredo.
> Plus dough *or* doe, etc.
> Plus need owe *or* O, etc.

EDREST

b: bedrest.
h: headrest.
> Plus dead rest, etc.

ĒDRƏ

s: exedra.
th: ex-cathedra.

ĒDRƏL

Vowel: diedral.
h: decahedral, didecahedral, dihedral.
th: cathedral, procathedral.

EDSHU̇RT

r: redshirt.

ĒDSTÄK

f: feedstock.

EDSTŌN

h: headstone
> Plus dead stone, etc.
> Plus bed's tone, etc.

ĒDTĪM

f: feedtime.
s: seedtime.
> Plus need time, etc.

ĒDUKS

r: redux.

ĒDUM

fr: freedom.
s: cedum.
> Plus need 'em, etc.
> Plus we dumb, etc.

EDU̇R

Vowel: edder.
b: bedder, embedder.
ch: Cheddar.
d: deader.
dr: dreader.
h: beheader, double-header, header, triple-header.

l: leader.
r: redder.
sh: shedder.
shr: shredder.
spr: bespreader, spreader.
t: tedder.
thr: threader, unthreader.
tr: treader.
 Plus spread her, etc.

ĒDƏR

bl: bleeder.
br: breeder, inbreeder,
interbreeder.
f: feeder, overfeeder,
underfeeder.
h: heeder, unheeder.
l: leader, misleader, ringleader.
n: kneader, needer.
p: impeder, stampeder.
pl: impleader, interpleader,
pleader.
r: reader, scripture-reader,
Talmud-reader.
s: acceder, anteceder, cedar, ceder,
conceder, exceeder, interceder,
preceder, proceeder, receder,
retroceder, seceder, seeder,
succeeder, superseder.
sp: speeder.
w: weeder.
 Plus lead her *or* err, etc.

EDWĀ

h: headway.
 Plus bread weigh *or* way, etc.

EDWOOD

d: deadwood.
r: redwood.
 Plus spread wood, etc.

EDWƱRD

Vowel: Edward.
b: bedward.
 Plus deadward, etc.

EDZMƏN

h: headsman.
l: leadsman.
 Plus spreads man, etc.

ĒDZMƏN

b: beadsman, bedesman.
s: seedsman.
 Plus needs man, etc.

EDZŌ

m: intermezzo, mezzo.
 Plus beds owe *or* O, etc.

EDƏ

Vowel: Edda.
n: Nedda.
 Plus spread a, etc.

ĒDƏ

dr: ola podrida.
l: Leda.
th: Theda.
v: Veda, Vida.
w: Ouida.
 Plus need a, etc.

EDƏD

b: bedded, embedded, imbedded.
dr: dreaded, undreaded.
h: addle-headed, arrowheaded,
bare-headed, beetle-headed,
beheaded, blunder-headed,
bullheaded, chuckleheaded,
clearheaded, dunder-headed,

fatheaded, feather-headed, fiddle-headed, flatheaded, giddy-headed, gross-headed, headed, heavy-headed, hoary-headed, hotheaded, hydra-headed, idle-headed, Janus-headed, light-headed, long-headed, manyheaded, muddleheaded, pigheaded, puddingheaded, puzzleheaded, rattleheaded, shock-headed, sleekheaded, softheaded, thickheaded, trundleheaded, warmheaded, weakheaded, wrongheaded.

l: leaded.

sl: sledded.

shr: shredded.

t: tedded.

thr: threaded, unthreaded.

w: unwedded, wedded.

Plus lead, Ed, etc.

Cf. head did, etc.

Cf. head dead, etc.

ĒDƏD

b: beaded.

d: deeded.

h: heeded, unheeded.

n: kneaded, needed.

p: impeded, stampeded.

pl: pleaded.

r: reeded.

s: acceded, anteceded, ceded, conceded, exceeded, interceded, preceded, proceeded, receded, retroceded, seceded, seeded, succeeded, superseded.

sp: speeded.

w: unweeded, weeded.

Plus she did, etc.

Cf. need did, etc.

EDƏN

d: deaden.

l: leaden.

r: redden.

thr: threaden.

Cf. redden, etc.

ĒDƏN

Vowel: Eden.

r: reeden.

sw: Sweden.

Plus sea den, etc.

Cf. reed hen, etc.

ĒDƏNS

kr: credence.

s: antecedence, intercedence, precedence.

Cf. antecedents, etc.

EDƏNT

p: pedant.

Plus red ant *or* aunt, etc.

ĒDƏNT

kr: credent.

n: needn't.

s: antecedent, decedent, intercedent, precedent, retrocedent, sedent.

Plus knee dent, etc.

ĒEST

f: feest*.

fl: fleest*.

fr: freest.

gr: agreest*.

r: refereest*.

s: foreseest*, overseest*, seest*.

w: weest*.

ĒETH

f: feeth*.

fl: fleeth*.

fr: freeth*.
gr: agreeth*.
r: refereeth*.
s: foreseeth*, overseeth*, seeth*.

ĒFDƏM

ch: chiefdom.
　Plus grief dumb, etc.

ĒFĒ

b: beefy.
l: leafy.
r: reefy.
sh: sheafy.
　Plus grief, he, etc.

ĒFIJ

l: leafage.
　Cf. grief age, etc.

EFIK

l: malefic.
str: peristrephic.

ĒFKĀK

b: beefcake.

ĒFLET

l: leaflet.

ĒFLƏS

br: briefless.
ch: chiefless.
gr: griefless.
l: leafless.
sh: sheafless.
　Plus leaf less, etc.

EFNƏS

d: deafness.

ĒFŌM

s: seafoam.
　Plus tree foam, etc.

EFO͞OJ

r: refuge.
　Cf. deaf, huge, etc.

ĒFO͞OL

gl: gleeful.
　Plus tree full, etc.

ĒFOUL

p: peafowl.
s: seafowl.
　Plus she foul *or* fowl, etc.

EFRĒ

j: Geoffrey, Jeffrey.

ĒFSTĀK

b: beefsteak.
　Plus reef stake *or* steak, etc.

ĒFTIN

ch: chieftain.
　Plus leafed in, etc.
　Plus leaf tin, etc.

EFTNƏS

d: deftness.

EFᴜL

d: deafer.
f: feoffor.
h: heifer.
z: zephyr.
　Plus cleff err *or* her, etc.

ĒFŪR

b: beefer.
br: briefer.
ch: chiefer.
l: liefer.
r: reefer.
　　Plus enfeoff her *or* err, etc.
　　Cf. me for, etc.

EFƏN

d: deafen.
　　Cf. Strephon.

ĒFƏS

s: Cephas.
　　Cf. Josephus.

EGĒ

Vowel: eggy.
dr: dreggy.
l: leggy.
p: peggy.
　　Plus beg he, etc.

EGING

Vowel: egging.
b: begging.
k: kegging, unkegging.
l: legging.
p: pegging, unpegging.

ĒGING

l: leaguing.
t: fatiguing.
tr: intriguing.

ĒGL

Vowel: bald eagle, eagle, sea eagle.
b: beagle.

gr: gregal.
kl: kleagle.
l: illegal, legal.
r: regal, viceregal.
v: inveigle.
　　Plus McTeague'll, etc.
　　Cf. sea gull.

ĒGLŪR

b: beagler.
v: inveigler.

EGMƏNT

s: segment.
　　Plus leg meant, etc.

EGNER

st: Wallace Stegner.

EGNƏNT

pr: impregnant, pregnant.
r: queenregnant, regant.

ĒGŌ

Vowel: ego.
s: Otsego.
w: Oswego.
　　Plus fee go, etc.

ĒGRĒN

p: pea-green.
s: sea-green.
　　Plus tree green, etc.

ĒGRŌ

n: Negro.
　　Plus league row, etc.

ĒGRƏS

Vowel: egress.
n: Negress.
r: regress.

EGRO̅O̅M

l: legroom.

EGƏR

Vowel: egger.
b: beggar.
l: booklegger, bootlegger, legger.
p: pegger.
s: seggar.
　Plus peg her *or* err, etc.

ĒGƏR

Vowel: eager, eagre, overeager.
l: beleaguer, leaguer.
m: meagre.
t: fatiguer.
tr: intriguer.
　Plus league her *or* err, etc.

ĒGƏRT

s: seagirt.
　Plus tree girt, etc.

ĒGƏ

d: Talladega.
m: omega.
r: Riga.
v: Vega.
　Plus league a, etc.

ĒGƏL

l: paralegal.

EĪK

f: caffeic.
p: mythopoeic.
r: rheic.
t: xanthoproteic.

EĪN

z: zein.
　Plus see in *or* inn, etc.

EĪNG

b: being, inbeing, well-being.
dr: dreeing.
f: feeing.
fl: fleeing.
fr: freeing.
gr: agreeing, disagreeing.
j: geeing.
kr: decreeing.
n: kneeing.
r: refereeing.
s: clear-seeing, foreseeing, overseeing, seeing, unforeseeing, unseeing.
sh: heliskiing, skiing.
sk: skiing.
spr: spreeing.
t: guaranteeing, teeing.
tr: treeing.

EĪST

d: deist.
k(c): manicheist.
th: antitheist, hylotheist, monotheist, polytheist, theist.

EĪT

b: albeit, so be it.
　Plus see it, etc.

EĪZM

d: deism.
k(c): Manicheism.
s: Parseeism, Phariseeism, Sadduceeism.
t: absenteeism, Sutteeism.
th: antitheism, autotheism, cosmotheism, henotheism, hylotheism, monotheism, polytheism, sciotheism, theism.
w: weism.

EJBɄRD

h: hedgebird.
s: sedgebird.
    Plus ledge bird, etc.
    Plus hedge burred, etc.

EJĒ

Vowel: edgy.
h: hedgy.
kl: cledgy.
l: ledgy.
s: sedgy.
v: veggie.
w: wedgy.
    Plus sledge, he, etc.

ĒJĒ

f: Fiji.
    Plus knee, gee *or* G, etc.
    Plus siege, he, etc.

EJEST

dr: dredgest*.
fl: fledgest.
h: hedgest*.
l: allegest*.
pl: impledgest*, pledgest*.
w: wedgest*.

EJETH

dr: dredgeth*.
fl: fledgeth*.
h: hedgeth*.
l: allegeth*.
pl: impledgeth*, pledgeth*.
w: wedgeth*.

EJING

Vowel: edging.
dr: dredging.
fl: fledging.
h: enhedging, hedging.
k: kedging.
l: alleging, ledging.
pl: mispledging, interpledging, pledging.
sl: sledging.
w: wedging.

EJLING

fl: fledgeling.
h: hedgeling.

ĒJMƏN

l: liegeman.
    Plus siege, man, etc.

ĒJMƏNT

s: besiegement.
    Plus liege meant, etc.

EJɄR

Vowel: edger.
dr: dredger.
h: hedger.
l: alleger, ledger, leger*.
pl: pledger.
sl: sledger.
    Plus dredge her *or* err, etc.

ĒJU̇R

s: procedure, supersedure.
Cf. need your, etc.

ĒJU̇RK

n: knee jerk.

EJWOOD

Vowel: Edgewood.
w: Wedgewood.
Plus hedge would *or* wood, etc.

ĒJƏ

w: ouija.
Plus siega, a, etc.
Plus see Jah, etc.

ĒJƏN

l: collegian, legion.
r: region, under-region.
Cf. ejian.

EJƏND

l: legend.
Plus hedge end, etc.

ĒJƏNS

l: allegiance.
Cf. see, gents, etc.

ĒJƏNT

r: regent.
Plus see, gent, etc.

ĒJƏS

gr: egregious.
l: sacrilegious.
Cf. obleege us, etc.

EJƏZ

Vowel: edges.
dr: dredges.
h: hedges.
k: kedges.
l: alleges, ledges.
pl: pledges.
sl: sledges.
w: wedges.

EKĀD

d: decade.
Plus wreck aid, etc.

ĒKÄK

l: Leacock.
m: meacock*.
p: peacock.
Plus see cock, etc.

ĒKAP

n: knee cap.

EKCHOŌR

f: confecture.
j: conjecture, projecture.
l: belecture, lecture.
t: architecture.
Plus protect your, etc.

ĒKĒ

bl: bleaky.
ch: cheeky, cheek-to-cheeky.
fr: freaky.
kl: cliquey.
kr: creaky.
l: cock-a-leekie, leaky.
p: peeky.
r: reeky.
s: hide-and-seeky.

sh: shieky.
shr: shrieky.
skw: squeaky.
sl: sleeky.
sn: sneaky.
str: streaky.
t: teaky.
v: Bolsheviki, Mensheviki.
w: veni, vidi, vici.
  Plus see key, etc.
  Plus seek, he, etc.

EKEST

ch: checkest*.
d: bedeckest*, deckest*.
r: reckest*, wreckest*.

ĒKEST

bl: bleakest, obliquest+.
l: leakest*.
m: meekest.
n: uniquest.
p: peekest*.
r: reekest*.
s: seekest*.
sh: shiekest.
shr: shriekest*.
skw: squeakest*.
sl: sleekest.
sn: sneakest*.
sp: bespeakest*, speakest*.
str: streakest*.
w: weakest.

EKETH

ch: checketh*.
d: bedecketh*, decketh*.
r: recketh*, wrecketh*.

ĒKETH

l: leaketh*.
r: reeketh*, wreaketh*.

s: seeketh*.
shr: shrieketh*.
skw: squeaketh*.
sn: sneaketh*.
sp: bespeaketh*, speaketh*.
str: streaketh*.

EKFƏST

br: breakfast, continental
breakfast.

ĒKĪD

bl: oblique-eyed.
m: meek-eyed.
w: weak-eyed.
  Plus cheek, I'd *or* eyed, etc.

EKING

ch: checking.
d: bedecking, decking.
fl: flecking.
n: necking.
p: henpecking, pecking.
r: bewrecking, recking, wrecking.
tr: trekking.
  Cf. neck, king, etc.

ĒKING

Vowel: eking.
ch: cheeking, cheek-to-cheeking.
kl: cliqueing.
kr: creaking.
l: leaking.
p: peeking.
r: reeking, wreaking.
s: seeking, self-seeking.
sh: sheiking.
shr: shrieking.
skw: squeaking.
sl: sleeking.

sn: sneaking.
sp: bespeaking, forespeaking, speaking.
str: streaking.
tw: tweaking.
   Plus see, king, etc.

EKISH

p: henpeckish, peckish.

ĒKISH

bl: bleakish.
fr: freakish.
gr: Greekish.
kl: cliquish.
m: meekish.
p: peakish.
sn: sneakish.
w: weakish.

ĒKL

tr: treacle.
   Plus ekal.

EKL

d: deckle.
fr: befreckle, freckle.
h: heckle.
j: Jeckyll.
k: keckle.
s: Seckel.
sh: shekel.
sp: bespeckle, speckle.
   Plus wreck 'll, etc.

EKLĒ

fr: freckly.
sp: speakly.
   Plus wreck, Lee *or* lea, etc.

ĒKLĒ

bl: bleakly, obliquely+.
m: meekly.
n: uniquely.
sl: sleekly.
tr: treacly.
w: biweekly, triweekly, weakly, weekly.
   Plus weak Lee *or* lea, etc.

EKLING

fr: freckling.
h: heckling.
k: keckling.
sp: speckling.

ĒKLING

w: weakling.

EKLUR

fr: freckler.
h: heckler.

EKLƏS

f: feckless.
fl: fleckless.
n: necklace.
r: reckless.
sp: speckless.
   Plus check less, etc.

EKMĀT

ch: checkmate.
d: deckmate.
   Plus wreck mate, etc.

EKNIK

t: philotechnic, polytechnic, pyrotechnic, technic, theotechnic.
   Plus deck nick *or* Nick, etc.

EKNING

b: beckning.
r: reckning, unreckning.

ĒKNƏS

bl: bleakness, obliqueness+.
m: meekness.
n: uniqueness.
sl: sleekness.
t: antiqueness.
w: weakness.

EKŌ

Vowel: echo, reecho.
d: dekko.
g: gecko.
s: secco.
Plus wreck owe *or* O, etc.

ĒKŌ

f: beccafico, fico.
kl: Cliquot.
n: Nikko.
Plus clique owe *or* O, etc.

ĒKRAB

p: pea-crab.
s: sea-crab.
tr: tree-crab.
Plus flee crab, etc.
Plus weak Rab, etc.

ĒKRIPT

d: decrypt.

ĒKRƏT

s: secret.

EKSÄN

Vowel: exon, Exxon.

EKSCHŲR

t: intertexture, texture.

EKSĒ

k: kexy.
l: kyriolexy.
pl: apoplexy.
pr: prexy.
r: pyrexy.
Plus wreck see, etc.
Plus wrecks he, etc.

EKSĒM

l: lexeme.

EKSĒN

r: rexine.

EKSEST

fl: flexest*.
n: annexest*.
pl: perplexest*.
s: unsexest*.
v: vexest*.

EKSETH

fl: flexeth*.
n: annexeth*.
pl: perplexeth*.
s: unsexeth*.
v: vexeth*.
Plus wreck Seth, etc.

EKSHUN

f: affection, confection, defection, disaffection, disinfection, effection, imperfection, infection, perfection.
fl: deflection, flection, genuflexion, inflection, irreflection, reflection.

j: abjection, adjection, antirejection, dejection, ejection, injection, insubjection, interjection, objection, projection, rejection, subjection, trajection.

l: bielection, collection, dilection, election, intellection, lection, predilection, prelection, recollection, reelection, selection.

n: connection.

pl: complexion.

r: correction, direction, erection, incorrection, indirection, insurrection, misdirection, rection, resurrection.

s: bisection, dissection, insection, intersection, rhythm section, section, trisection, venesection, vivisection.

sp: circumspection, inspection, introspection, prospection, retrospection.

t: detection, protection.

v: circumvection, convection, evection, provection.

    Plus wreck shun, etc.

EKSHUS

f: infectious.

EKSĪL

Vowel: exile.

fl: flexile.

    Plus decks aisle *or* isle, etc.

    Plus wrecks, I'll, etc.

EKSIK

r: anorexic.

EKSING

fl: flexing, inflexing.

n: annexing.

pl: perplexing.

s: unsexing.

v: vexing.

EKSIS

l: Alexis.

n: Nexis.

    Plus neck, sis, etc.

EKSIT

Vowel: exit.

    Plus wrecks it, etc.

    Plus deck, site, etc.

EKSTĪL

s: bissextile, sextile.

t: textile.

    Plus wreck still, etc.

    Plus wrecks till, etc.

EKSTĪM

fl: flextime.

EKSTRIN

d: dextrin.

t: textrine.

EKSTRUS

d: ambidextrous, dextrous.

s: ambisextrous.

EKSTŲR

d: ambidexter, dexter.

    Plus wreck stir, etc.

EKSTƏN

s: sexton.

    Plus wrecks ton *or* tun, etc.

    Plus wreck stun, etc.

EKSTƏNT

Vowel: extant.
s: sextant.
Plus wrecks ant *or* aunt, etc.

EKSUR

fl: flexor.
n: annexer.
pl: perplexer.
s: unsexer.
v: vexer.
Plus wrecks her *or* err, etc.
Plus wreck, sir, etc.

EKSUS

n: nexus.
pl: plexus.
Plus wrecks us, etc.
Cf. Texas.

EKSWURK

s: sex work.

EKSƏR

fl: deflexure, flexure, inflexure.
pl: plexure.
Plus wrecks your, etc.

EKSƏS

t: Texas.
Plus vex ass, etc.
Plus wreck sass, etc.
Cf. vex us, etc.

EKTEST

f: affectest*, disinfectest*, effectest*, infectest*.
fl: reflectest*.
gl: neglectest*.

j: abjectest, ejectest*, injectest*, interjectest*, objectest*, projectest*, rejectest*, subjectest*.
l: collectest*, electest*, recollectest*, selectest*.
n: connectest*.
p: expectest*, suspectest*.
r: directest, erectest, resurrectest*.
sp: inspectest*, respectest*.
t: detectest*, protectest*.
Plus wreck test, etc.

EKTETH

f: affecteth*, disinfecteth*, effecteth*, infecteth*.
fl: reflecteth*.
gl: neglecteth*.
j: ejecteth*, injecteth*, interjecteth*, objecteth*, projecteth*, rejecteth*, subjecteth*.
l: collecteth*, electeth*, recollecteth*, selecteth*.
n: connecteth*.
p: expecteth*, suspecteth*.
r: directeth*, erecteth*, misdirecteth*, resuurrecteth*.
s: bisecteth*, dissecteth*, trisecteth*, vivisecteth*.
sp: inspecteth*, respecteth*.
t: detecteth*, protecteth*.

EKTFOOL

gl: neglectful.
sp: disrespectful, respectful.
Plus object full, etc.

EKTIK

h: hectic.
k(c): cachectic.
kl: eclectic.

l: acatalectic, analectic, bracycatalectic, catalectic, dialectic, hypercatalectic.

p: pectic.

pl: apoplectic.

Plus wreck tick, etc.

EKTIKS

l: dialectics.

Plus ektik+s.

EKTĪL

j: projectile.

s: insectile, sectile.

Plus wreck till, etc.

Plus recked ill, etc.

EKTIN

l: lectin.

p: pectin.

Plus wrecked in *or* inn, etc.

Plus wreck tin, etc.

EKTING

f: affecting, disinfecting, effecting, infecting.

fl: deflecting, reflecting.

gl: neglecting.

j: ejecting, injecting, interjecting, objecting, projecting, rejecting, subjecting.

l: collecting, electing, recollecting, selecting.

n: connecting, disconnnecting.

p: expecting, suspecting, unsuspecting.

r: directing, erecting, misdirecting, resurrecting.

s: bisecting, dissecting, trisecting, vivisecting.

sp: inspecting, respecting, self-respecting.

t: detecting, protecting.

EKTIV

f: affective, cost-effective, defective, effective, ineffective, infective, perfective, refective.

fl: deflective, inflective, irreflective, reflective.

gl: neglective.

j: injective, objective, rejective, subjective.

l: collective, elective, recollective, selective.

m: humective.

n: connective.

r: corrective, directive., erective.

s: sective.

sp: circumspective, inspective, introspective, irrespecitve, perspective, prospective, respective, retrospective.

t: detective, protective.

v: invective.

EKTIZM

kl: ecclectism.

s: sectism.

EKTMƏNT

j: ejectment, projectment, rejectment.

Plus neglect meant, etc.

EKTNƏS

j: abjectness.

l: selectness.

r: correctness, directness, erectness, incorrectness, indirectness.

EKTRÄN

l: electron.
   Plus select run, etc.

EKTRIK

l: analectric, dielectric, electric, idioelectric.
   Plus wreck trick, etc.
   Plus wrecked rick, etc.

EKTRUM

l: electrum.
pl: plectrum.
sp: spectrum.
   Plus wrecked rum, etc.

EKTRƏL

sp: spectral.

EKTRƏS

l: electress.
r: directress, rectress.
sp: inspectress.
t: protectress.
   Plus wreck tress, etc.

EKTƱR

f: disinfecter, infecter.
fl: deflector, flector, reflector.
gl: neglecter.
h: Hector.
j: ejector, injecter, interjecter, objector, projector, rejecter, subjecter.
l: collector, elector, lector, prelector, recollecter, selector.
n: connector, nectar.
p: expecter, prospector, suspecter.
r: corrector, director, erecter, misdirector, rector, resurrecter.

s: bisecter, dissecter, sector, trisector, vivisector.
sp: disrespector, inspector, respecter, spectre.
t: detector, protector.
v: vector.
   Plus ektur.
   Plus wrecked, or, etc.
   Plus wrecked her *or* err, etc.

EKTƱRD

h: hectored.
n: nectared.
r: rectored.

EKTƏ

tr: trifecta.

EKTƏD

f: affected, confected, defected, disaffected, disinfected, effected, ill-affected, infected, perfected, unaffected.
fl: ideflected, flected*, inflected, reflected.
gl: neglected.
j: dejected, ejected, injected, interjected, objected, projected, rejected, subjected.
l: collected, elected, prelected, recollected, selected.
n: connected, disconnected, unconnected.
p: expected, suspected, unexpected, unsuspected.
pl: complected, dark-complected, light-complected.
r: corrected, directed, erected, misdirected, resurrected.
s: bisected, dissected, intersected, vivisected.
sp: inspected, respected.

t: detected, obtected, protected, unprotected.
v: invected.
    Plus wreck, Ted, etc.
    Plus wrecked, Ed, etc.

EKTƏL

r: colorectal.

EKTƏNT

f: disinfectant.
fl: reflectant.
m: humectant.
n: annectent.
pl: amplextant.
sp: aspectant, expectant, inexpectant, respectant, suspectant, unexpectant.
    Plus wrecked ant *or* aunt, etc.

EKTƏS

p: pectous.
sp: conspectus, prospectus.
    Plus inspect us, etc.

ĒKUM

m: vade-mecum.
s: caecum.
    Plus we come, etc.
    Plus streak 'em, etc.

EKUR

b: Becker.
br: brekker.
ch: checker, chequer, exchequer.
d: bedecker, decker, two-decker, three-decker.
fl: flecker.
p: henpecker, pecker, wood-pecker.

r: wrecker.
tr: trekker.
    Plus wreck her *or* err, etc.

ĒKUR

b: beaker.
bl: bleaker, Bleecker, obliquer+.
ch: cheeker, chicquer.
kl: cliquer.
kr: creaker.
l: leaker.
m: meeker.
p: peeker.
r: reeker.
s: seeker, self-seeker.
shr: shrieker.
skw: squeaker.
sl: sleeker.
sn: sneaker.
sp: bespeaker, speaker, stump-speaker.
tw: tweaker.
w: weaker.
    Plus tweak her *or* err, etc.
    Plus see cur, etc.

EKURZ

ch: checkers.
    Plus ekur+s

ĒKURZ

sn: sneakers.
    Plus ekur+s.

ĒKWƏL

Vowel: co-equal, equal, inequal.
s: sequel.
    Plus peek well, etc.
    Plus we quell, etc.

ĒKWƏNS

fr: frequence, infrequence.
s: sequence.
   Cf. seek whence, etc.

ĒKWƏNT

fr: frequent, infrequent.
s: sequent.
   Plus creek went, etc.

EKƏ

b: Rebecca.
m: Mecca.
   Plus wreck a, etc.

ĒKƏ

ch: Chica.
m: Meeka.
n: Dominica.
p: Topeka.
pr: paprika.
r: Costa Rica, eureka, Frederica, Fredrika, Ulrica.
sp: Spica.
th: bibliotheca, glyptotheca, zootheca.
y: Tanganyika.
   Plus wreak a, etc.

ĒKƏL

f: faecal.
s: caecal.
th: bibliothecal, thecal.
tr: treacle.
   Plus meek'll, etc.
   Plus we cull, etc.
   Cf. see, Cal, etc.

EKƏN

b: beckon.
r: reckon.
   Plus fleck on *or* an, etc.

ĒKƏN

b: beacon.
d: archdeacon, deacon.
m: meeken.
w: weaken.
   Plus speak an *or* on, etc.
   Cf. ekon.

EKƏND

s: second.
   Plus ekon+ed.
   Cf. ekond.

ĒKƏND

f: fecund, infecund.

EKƏNT

p: impeccant, peccant.
   Plus wreck ant *or* aunt, etc.

ĒKƏNT

k(c): piquant, precant, secant.
   Plus he can't, etc.
   Plus flee Kant *or* cant, etc.
   Plus meek ant *or* aunt, etc.

ELĀT

b: debellate, flabellate.
p: appellate, interpellate.
pr: prelate.
s: ocelate.
st: constellate, stellate.
   Plus Nell ate *or* eight, etc.
   Cf. Nell late, etc.

ELBĒ

s: Herbert Selby Jr.

ELBŌ

Vowel: elbow, tennis elbow.

ELBÔRN

h: hell-born.
w: well-born.
　Plus shell born, etc.

ELBOUND

h: hellbound.
sp: spellbound.
　Plus well bound, etc.

ELBᴜR

g: Jack Gelber.

ELBᴜRT

Vowel: Elbert.
　Plus smell, Bert, etc.

ELBӘ

Vowel: Elba.
m: Melba, peach Melba.
　Plus smell, bah!, etc.
　Cf. Elbe.

ELCHEST

b: belchest*.
skw: squelchest*.
w: welchest*.
　Plus swell chest, etc.

ELCHETH

b: belcheth*.
skw: squelcheth*.
w: welcheth*.

ELCHING

b: bleching.
skw: squelching.
w: welching.

ELCHᴜR

b: belcher.
skw: squalcher.
w: welcher.
　Plus squelch her *or* err, etc.

ĒLDĒ

w: unwieldy.
　Plus concealed, he, etc.

ELDEST

Vowel: eldest.
h: heldest*.
w: weldest*.

ĒLDEST

sh: shieldest*.
w: wieldest*.
y: yieldest*.

ELDETH

h: heldeth*.
w: weldeth*.
　Plus tell death, etc.

ĒLDETH

sh: shieldeth*.
w: wieldeth*.
y: yieldeth*.
　Plus feel death, etc.

ĒLDFER

f: fieldfare.
　Plus yield fair *or* fare, etc.

ELDING

g: gelding.
m: melding.
w: welding.
  Plus bell ding, etc.

ĒLDING

f: fielding.
sh: enshielding, shielding, unshielding.
w: wielding.
y: unyielding, yielding.

ELDUM

s: seldom.
sw: swelldom.
  Plus smell dumb, etc.
  Plus meld 'em, etc.

ELDUR

Vowel: elder.
g: Gelder, Van Gelder.
m: melder.
w: welder.
  Plus held her, etc.

ELDƏ

n: Nelda.
s: Griselda.
z: Griselda, Zelda.
  Plus held a, etc.

ĒLDƏD

f: fielded.
sh: shielded, unshielded.
w: wielded.
y: yielded.
  Plus wheel dead, etc.
  Plus concealed, Ed, etc.
  Cf. wheel did, etc.

ĒLDƏNS

y: yieldance.
  Plus heel dance, etc.
  Cf. field ants *or* aunts, etc.

ELĒ

Vowel: Elly.
b: belly, casus belli, potbelly.
ch: Botticelli, vermicelli.
d: Delhi, Odelly.
f: felly.
h: helly*, rake helly.
j: jelly.
k(c): Kelly, O'Kelly.
n: Nellie.
r: Barelly, Corelli.
s: cancelli.
sh: Shelley, shelly.
sk: Skelly.
sm: smelly.
t: Donatelli, Pietro Locatelli.
  Plus tell, he, etc.

ĒLĒ

Vowel: Ealey, Ely.
fr: freely.
h: Healey.
hw: wheely.
k(c): Keeley.
kr(cr): Robert Creeley.
m: mealy.
r: Bareilly, Bareli.
s: seely.
st: steely.
  Plus wheel, he, etc.
  Plus see Lee *or* lea, etc.
  Cf. genteely.

ELĒD

b: bellied.
j: jellied.

ELEST

b: rebellest*.
ch: cellist, violon-cellist.
dw: dwellist*.
f: fellist*.
kw: quellest*.
n: knellest*.
p: compellest*, dispellest*, expellest*, impellest*, propellest*, repellest*.
s: excellest*, sellect*, underscllest*.
sh: shellest*.
sm: smellest*.
sp: spellest*.
sw: swellest*.
t: foretellest*, tellest*.
y: yellest*.
   Cf. yell, lest, etc.

ĒLEST

d: dealest*.
f: feelest*.
h: healest*.
hw: wheelest*.
j: congealest*.
l: lealest.
n: annealest*, kneelest*.
p: appealest*, pealest*, peelest*, repealest*.
r: reelest*.
s: concealest*, sealest*.
skw: squealest*.
sp: spielest*.
st: stealest*, steelest*.
t: genteelest*.
r: revealest*.
   Plus sea, lest, etc.

ELETH

b: rebelleth*.
dw: dwelleth.

f: felleth*.
kw: quelleth*.
sm: smelleth*.
n: knelleth*.
p: compelleth*, dispelleth*, expelleth*, impelleth*, propelleth*, repelleth*.
s: excelleth*, selleth*, underselleth*.
sh: shelleth*.
sp: spelleth*.
sw: swelleth*.
t: foretelleth*, telleth*.
y: yelleth*.

ĒLETH

d: dealth*, double-dealth*.
f: feeleth*.
h: healeth*.
hw: wheeleth*.
j: congealeth*.
n: annealeth*, kneeleth*.
p: appealeth*, pealeth*, peeleth*, repealeth*.
r: reeleth*.
s: concealeth*, sealeth*.
skw: squealeth*.
st: stealeth*, steeleth*.
v: revealth*.

ELFER

w: welfare.
   Plus spell fair *or* fare, etc.
   Plus elf air *or* heir, etc.

ELFIK

d: Delphic.
gw: Guelphic.

ELFIN

Vowel: elfin.
d: delphin*, delphine.
   Plus pelf in *or* inn,e tc.

ELFĪR

h: hellfire.
Plus smell fire, etc.

ELFISH

Vowel: elfish.
p: pelfish.
s: selfish, unselfish.
sh: shellfish.
Plus tell fish, etc.

ELFŌN

s(c): cell phone.

ĒLFOOL

s: seelful.
w: wealful.
z: zealful.
Plus meal full, etc.

ELFRĒ

b: belfry.
p: pelfry.
Cf. sell free, etc.

ĒLĪ

Vowel: Eli.
Plus we lie *or* lye, etc.
Plus wheel eye *or* I, etc.

ELID

j: gelid.
Cf. shell lid, etc.

ELIJ

p: pellage.
Cf. smell age, etc.

ĒLIJ

hw: wheelage.
k: keelage.
Plus feel age, etc.

ELIK

b: bellic.
h: parhelic.
j: angelic, archangelic, evangelic, superangelic.
k(c): nickelic.
m: melic, pimelic.
r: relic.
t: Aristotelic, Pentelic, philatelic, telic.
Cf. smell, lick, etc.

ĒLIK

h: parhelic.
Plus bee lick, etc.

ĒLIKS

f: Felix.
h: helix.
Plus sea licks, etc.

ĒLĪN

b: beeline.
f: feline.
s: sealine.
Plus me line, etc.

ELING

b: belling, rebelling.
dw: dwelling.
f: felling.
j: jelling.
kw: quelling.
l: paralleling.
n: knelling, sentinelling.
p: could-compelling, compeling, dispelling, expelling, impelling,

propelling, repelling.
s: excelling, selling, underselling.
sh: Schelling, shelling.
shm: Schmeling.
sm: smelling.
sp: misspelling, spelling.
sw: swelling.
t: foretelling, fortune-telling, telling.
w: welling.
y: yelling.

ĒLING

Vowel: Ealing.
b: automobiling.
d: dealing, double-dealing, interdealing, misdealing, New-Dealing, underdealing.
f: feeling, fellow-feeling, unfeeling.
h: healing, heeling, self-fealing, unhealing.
hw: wheeling, free-wheeling.
j: congealing, Darjeeling, uncongealing.
k(c): keeling.
n: annealing, kneeling.
p: appealing, pealing, peeling, repealing.
r: reeling.
s: ceiling, concealing, sealing, unseeling.
sh: shealing.
skw: squealing.
st: stealing, steeling.
v: revealing.

ELINT

Vowel: elint.

ELIS

Vowel: Ellis.
tr: trellis.
    Cf. smell is, etc.

ELISH

b: embellish.
h: hellish.
r: disrelish, relish.
sw: swellish.

ELKIN

Vowel: Stanley Elkin.

ELKUM

w: welcome.
    Plus whelk 'em, etc.
    Plus smell come, etc.

ĒLLĪF

r: real-life.

ELMET

h: helmet.
    Plus well met, etc.
    Cf. helm it, etc.

ELMING

h: dishelming, helming, unhelming.
hw: overwhelming, whelming.
    Plus tell Ming, etc.

ELMUR

Vowel: Elmer.
    Plus overwhelm her *or* err, etc.

ELMƏ

Vowel: Elma.
s: Selma.
th: Thelma.
v: Velma.
    Plus well, ma, etc.
    Plus overwhelm a, etc.

ELMƏN

Vowel: Elman.
b: bellman.
w: Wellman.
  Plus smell, man, etc.
  Plus overwhelm Ann
or an, etc.

ĒLMƏNT

j: congealment.
p: repealment.
s: concealment.
v: revealment.
  Plus steal meant, etc.

ELNƏS

f: fellness.
w: wellness.

ELŌ

Vowel: duello, niello.
b: bellow, Saul Bellow.
ch: cello, Monticello, violoncello.
d: Sordello.
f: felloe, fellow, good fellow,
play-fellow.
g: bargello.
h: hello.
j: Jello.
m: mellow.
n: prunello, punchinello.
p: acapello, cobra-dicapello.
r: morello, saltarello.
t: brocatello, Donatello.
v: scrivello.
y: yellow.
  Plus smell owe *or* O, etc.
  Cf. smell low, etc.

ĒLŌ

f: phyllo+.
k: kilo+.
l: Don De Lilo.

ELÖÏ

t: tell-all.

ELŌD

m: unmellowed.
  Plus elo+ed.

ELŌZ

b: bellows.
  Plus elo+s.

ELO͞OD

pr: prelude
  Plus well, you'd, etc.

ELO͞OJ

d: deluge.
  Cf. well, huge, etc.

ELPĒ

k: kelpie.
  Plus whelp, he, etc.

ELPFOOL

h: helpful, self-helpful, unhelpful.
  Plus whelpful, etc.

ELPING

h: helping.
y: yelping.

ELPLƏS

h: helpless.
hw: whelpless.
y: yelpless.
　　Plus help less, etc.

ELPUR

h: helper, self-helper.
y: yelper.
　　Plus help her *or* err, etc.

ĒLRĪT

w: John Brooks Wheelwright.

ĒLSKIN

Vowel: eelskin.
s: sealskin.
　　Plus feel skin, etc.

ELSƏ

Vowel: Elsa.
　　Cf. melts a, etc.

ELSƏN

k: kelson.
n: half-Nelson, Nelson.
　　Plus well, son *or* sun, etc.

ELTDOUN

m: meltdown.

ELTHĒ

h: healthy.
st: stealthy.
w: wealthy.
　　Plus wealth, be, etc.

ELTHFOOD

h: health food.

ELTEST

b: beltest*.
f: feltest*.
m: meltest*.
p: peltest*.
sm: smeltest*.
w: weltest*.
　　Plus swell test, etc.

ELTETH

b: belteth*.
f: felteth*.
m: melteth*.
p: pelteth*.
sm: smelteth*.
w: welteth*.

ELTIK

k(c): Celtic, Keltic.
　　Plus well tick, etc.

ELTING

b: belting, unbelting.
f: felting.
m: melting.
p: pelting.
sm: smelting.
w: welting.

ELTLƏS

b: beltless.
f: feltless.
k(c): Celtless.
p: peltless.
w: weltless.
　　Plus felt less, etc.

ELTRĒ

p: peltry.
w: weltry.
　　Cf. swell tree, etc.

ELTŪR

b: belter.
f: felter.
k(c): kelter.
m: melter.
p: pelter.
sh: inshelter, shelter.
sk: helter-skelter.
sm: smelter.
sp: spelter.
sw: swelter.
w: welter.
  Plus felt err *or* her, etc.

ELTŪRD

sh: unsheltered.
  Plus elter+ed.

ELTƏ

d: delta.
p: pelta.
  Plus pelt a, etc.

ELTƏD

b: belted, unbelted.
f: felted.
m: melted.
p: pelted.
sm: smelted.
w: welted.
  Plus well, Ted, etc.
  Plus felt, Ed, etc.

ELUM

b: antebellum, cerebellum, flabellum.
j: flagellum.
v: vellum.
  Plus tell 'em, etc.
  Plus well, Lum, etc.

ELŪR

b: rebeller.
dw: cave-dweller, dweller.
f: feller.
g: geller.
h: heller, Joseph Heller.
k: keller.
kw: queller.
m: lamellar, "meller."
p: appellor, cloud-compeller, compeller, dispeller, expeller, impeller, propeller, repeller, screw-propellor, twin-propeller.
s: cellar, exceller, Sellar, seller, underseller, wine-cellar.
sh: sheller.
sm: smeller.
sp: speller.
st: interstellar, stellar.
sw: sweller.
t: foreteller, fortune-teller, tale-teller, teller.
w: Weller.
y: yeller.
  Plus tell her *or* err, etc.

ĒLŪR

d: dealer, double-dealer, interdealer, misdealer, New-Dealer.
f: feeler.
h: healer, heeler, wardheeler.
hw: four-wheeler, wheeler.
j: congealer.
k(c): keeler.
n: annealer, kneeler.
p: appealer, pealer, peeler, repealer.
r: reeler.
s: concealer, seeler.
skw: squealer.
sp: spieler.

st: stealer, steeler.
v: revealer.
    Plus steal her *or* err, etc.

ELⱮRZ

s: Sellars, Sellers.
    Plus elur+s.

ELUS

j: jealous.
p: apellous.
s: procellous.
t: entellus, vitellus.
z: overzealous, zealous.
    Plus sell us, etc.

ELVING

d: delving.
h: helving.
sh: shelving.

ELVISH

Vowel: elvish.

ELVⱮR

d: delver.
h: helver.
sh: shelver.
    Plus shelve, her, etc.

ELVƏT

v: velvet.
    Plus swell vet, etc.

ĒLYƏ

b: lobelia.
d: Bedelia, Cordelia, Delia.
f: Ophelia.
l: Lelia.
m: Amelia, camellia, Rumelia.

n: Cornelia.
r: Aurelia.
s: Cecelia, Celia, St. Cecelia.

ĒLYƏN

d: Delian, Mendelian.
m: chameleon.
    Cf. elion.

ELYƏN

b: rebellion.
h: hellion.
    Cf. elian.

ELYƏS

b: rebellious.

ELZƏ

Vowel: Elsa.
    Plus smells a, etc.

ELƏ

Vowel: Aella, Ella, Louella.
b: Bella, Isabella, Rosabella, umbella.
br: umbrella.
ch: Valpolicella.
d: Adela, Della.
f: fellah.
m: lamella.
n: Fifinella, gentianella, Nella, Pimpinella, prunella.
p: acapella, capella.
r: lirella, Littorella.
s: MarMarcella.
st: stella.
t: fenestella, patella, scutella, tarantella.
    Plus tell a, etc.

ĒLƏ

b: Bela.
d: seguidilla.
g: narghila, narghile.
h: gila.
kw: sequela.
l: Leila.
m: philomela.
s: Selah.
sh: Shiela.
st: stele.
  Plus squeal a, etc.
  Plus knee, la!, etc.

ELƏN

Vowel: Ellen.
f: enfellon, felon.
h: Helen.
j: Magellan.
kl: McClellan.
m: Mellen, Mellon, melon, watermelon.
t: Atellan.
w: Llewellyn.
  Plus smell on *or* an, etc.
  Plus tell Ann *or* an, etc.
  Cf. elen.
  Cf. tell an *or* on, etc.

ELƏNT

p: appellant, impellant, interpellant, propellant, repellant.
v: divellant, revellant.
  Plus swell ant *or* aunt, etc.

ELƏP

v: develop, envelop.
  Cf. smell up, etc.

ELƏT

h: helot.
z: zealot.
  Cf. tell Lot, etc.

ĒMĀL

f: female.
sh: shemale.
  Plus see male, etc.

EMBLĒ

s: assembly.
tr: trembly.

EMBL

s: assemble, dissemble, semble.
tr: tremble.
z: resemble.

EMBLD

s: undissemled.
  Plus embl+d.

EMBLIJ

s: assemblage.

EMBLING

s: assembling, dissembling.
tr: trembling.
z: resembling.

EMBLUR

s: assembler, dissembler.
tr: trembler.
z: resembler.

EMBLƏM

Vowel: emblem.

EMBLƏNS

s: assembiance, dissemblance, semblance.
z: resemblance.

EMBLƏNT

s: semblent.
z: resemblent.

EMBRƏL

m: bimembral, trimembral.

EMBRƏNS

m: remembrance.

EMBUR

Vowel: ember.
m: dismember, disremember, member, remember.
s: December.
v: November.
    Plus stem burr, etc.

EMBURD

m: dismembered.
    Plus embur+ed.

EMĒ

d: demi.
j: gemmy, jemmy.
kl: Clemmy.
l: lemme.
s: semi.
    Cf. hem me, etc.

ĒMĒ

b: beamy.
dr: daydreamy, dreamy.
gl: gelamy.
kr: creamy.

m: Mimi.
s: seamy.
skr(scr): screamy.
st: steamy.
str: streamy.
t: teemy.
    Plus see me, etc.
    Plus dream he, etc.

EMEST

d: condemnest*.
h: hemmest*.
j: begemmest*.
st: stemmest*.

ĒMEST

b: beamest*.
d: deemest*, misdeemest*, redeemest*.
dr: dreamest*.
f: blasphemest*.
gl: gleamest*.
kr: creamest*.
pr: aupremest.
s: seemest*.
skr(scr): screamest*.
st: steamest*.
str: streamest*.
t: esteemest*, teemest*.
tr: extremest.

EMETH

d: condemneth*.
h: hemmeth*.
j: begemmeth*.
st: stemmeth*.
t: contemneth*.

ĒMETH

b: beameth*.
d: deemeth*, misdeemeth*,

redeemeth*.
dr: dreameth*.
g: blasphemeth*.
gl: gleameth*.
kr: creameth*.
s: seemeth.
skr(scr): screameth*.
st: steameth*.
t: esteemeth*, teemeth*.

ĒMFOOL

b: beamful.
dr: dreamful.
sk(sc): schemeful.
t: teemful.
   Plus dream full, etc.

EMIK

d: academic, endemic, epidemic, pandemic.
j: stratagemic.
k(c): alchemic, chemic.
l: polemic.
r: theoremic.
t: systemic, totemic.
   Cf. hem Mick, etc.

ĒMIK

n: anemic.
s: racemic.
   Plus see Mick, ctc.

EMING

d: condemning, self-condemning.
fl: Fleming.
h: hemming.
j: begemming, gemming.
l: lemming.
st: stemming.
t: contemning.

ĒMING

b: beaming.
d: deeming, redeeming.
dr: day-dreaming, dreaming.
f: blaspheming.
gl: gleaming.
kr: creaming.
s: beseeming, seeming, summer-seeming, unbeseeming.
sk(sc): scheming.
skr(scr): screaming.
st: steaming.
str: mainstreaming, overstreaming, streaming.
t: esteeming, teeming.

EMISH

bl: blemish, unblemsih.
fl: flemish.

ĒMISH

b: beamish.
   Cf. ice-creamish, etc.

EMISHT

bl: blemished, unblemished.

EMIST

k(c): chemist.
   Cf. hem mist *or* missed, etc.

ĒMIST

sk(sc): schemist.
tr: extremist.
   Plus see mist *or* missed, etc.

EMĪT, ĒMĪT

s: Semite.
   Cf. hem might *or* mite, etc.

ĒMLAND

dr: dreamland.
  Plus deem land, etc.

ĒMLĒ

pr: supremely.
s: seemly, unseemly.
tr: extremely.
  Plus dream, Lee *or* lea, etc.

ĒMLƏS

b: beamless.
dr: dreamless.
kr: creamless.
s: seamless.
sk(sc): schemeless.
str: streamless.
  Plus esteem less, etc.

ĒMLƏT

str: streamlet.
  Plus dream let *or* Lett, etc.

EMNÄN

m: Agamemnon, Memnon.

ĒMŌ

kr: Cremo.
n: Nemo.
pr: a tempo primo, primo, supremo.
  Plus dream owe *or* O, etc.
  Plus see, Mo, etc.

EMŌ

m: memo.
  Plus hem owe *or* O, etc.

ĒMPÄRK

th: theme park.

EMPEST

t: tempest.
  Plus hem pest, etc.

EMPĪR

Vowel: empire.
  Plus condemn pyre, etc.

EMPL

s: Semple.
st: stemple
t: temple.
  Plus hemp'll, etc.

EMPLĀT

t: contemplate, template.
  Plus them plate, etc.
  Plus Kemp, late, etc.

EMPLUR

t: templare.
z: exemplar.

EMPSHUN

Vowel: coemption, emption, preemption.
d: ademption, redemption.
r: diremption.
z: exemption.
  Plus hemp shun, etc.

EMPSTUR

d: dempster.
s: sempster.
  Plus hemp stir, etc.

EMPTĒ

Vowel: empty.
  Plus hemp tea, etc.

EMPTEST

t: attemptest*, temptest*.
z: exemptest*.
  Plus hemp test, etc.

EMPTETH

t: attempteth*, tempteth*.
z: exempteth*.

EMPTING

Vowel: preempting.
t: attempting, tempting.
z: exempting.

EMPTIV

Vowel: preemptive.
d: redemptive.

EMPTRƏS

d: redemptress.
t: temptress.
  Plus help tress, etc.

EMPTƱR

Vowel: preemptor.
k(c): unkempter.
t: attempter, tempter.
z: exempter.
  Plus tempt her *or* err, etc.

EMPTƏD

Vowel: preempted.
t: attempted, tempted, unat-
tempted, untempted.
z: exempted.
  Plus help, Ted, etc.

EMPƱRD

t: ill-tempered, tempered,
untempered.
  Plus Kemp erred, etc.
  Plus Shem purred, etc.

ĒMSONG

dr: dream song.
th: theme song.
  Plus scheme song, etc.

ĒMSTƱR

d: deemster.
s: seamster.
t: teamster.
  Plus scheme stir, etc.

EMSƏN

Vowel: Empson.
kl: Clemson.
  Plus condemn son *or* sun, etc.

ĒMTĒM

dr: dream team.

EMƱR

d: condemner.
h: hemmer.
j: begemmer.
st: stemmer.
t: contemner.
  Plus gem her *or* err, etc.

ĒMƱR

b: beamer.
d: redeemer.
dr: day-dreamer, dreamer.
f: blasphemer, femur.
gl: gleamer.
l: lemur.
r: reamer.
s: seamer, seemer.
sk(sc): schemer.
skr(scr): screamer.
st: steamer.
str: streamer.
t: teemer.

Cf. emir.
Plus dream err *or* her, etc.
Plus see myrrh, etc.

ĒMYŲR

pr: premier.
Cf. dream yer, etc.

EMƎ

Vowel: Emma.
j: gemma.
l: analemma, dilemma, lemma, neurilemma, trilemma.
r: maremma.
st: stemma.
Plus hem a, etc.
Plus hem, ma, etc.

ĒMƎ

Vowel: empyema, seriema.
b: bema.
d: edema, myxedema.
l: Lima.
r: Rima, terzarima.
sk(sc): schema.
t: blastema, Fatima.
th: erythema.
z: eczema.
Plus seem a, etc.

ĒMƎL

h: hemal.
t: blastemal.
Plus dream, Al, etc.
Cf. deem all, etc.

ĒMƎN

b: beeman.
d: agathadaemon, cacodemon, demon, eudaemon.
fr: freeman.
g: G-man.

h: he man.
l: leman.
s: able seaman, merchant seaman, seaman, semen.
t: teaman.
Plus dream an *or* Ann, etc.
Plus fee man, etc.
Plus seem an *or* on, etc.
Cf. Bremen.
Cf. eman.

EMƎNT

kl: clement, inclement.
Cf. hem meant, ctc.

ĒMƎNT

gr: agreement, disagreement.
kr: decreement.
Plus sea meant, etc.

EMƎNZ

kl: Clemens.
Cf. lemons.

ĒMƎS

d: Nicodemus.
r: Remus.
Plus dream us, etc.
Plus see muss, etc.

EMƎT

Vowel: Emmett.
Plus Lem et, etc.
Cf. condemn it, etc.

ENĀ

p: penne.

ENĀT

p: pennate.
Plus then ate *or* eight, etc.
Cf. Then, Nate, etc.

ĒNÄK

Vowel: Enoch.
   Plus we knock, etc.

ENBĀS

b: pen-based.

ENCHÄNT

   Plus bench aunt *or* ant, etc.

ENCHEST

bl: blenchest*.
dr: bedrenchest*, drenchest*.
kl: clenchest*, unclenchest*.
kw: quenchest*.
r: wrenchest*.
tr: intrenchest*, retrenchest*, trenchest*.
   Plus pen chest, etc.

ENCHETH

bl: blencheth*.
dr: bedrencheth*, drencheth*.
kl: clencheth*, unclencheth*.
kw: quencheth*.
r: wrenctheth*.
tr: intrencheth*, retrencheth*, trencheth*.

ENCHING

b: benching.
bl: blenching.
dr: bedrenching, drenching.
kl: clenching, unclenching.
kw: quenching, unquenching.
r: wrenching.
tr: intrenching, retrenching, trenching.

ENCHLƏS

kw: quenchless.
   Plus ench+less.
   Plus French, Les *or* less, etc.

ENCHMƏN

fr: Frenchman.
h: henchman.
   Plus stench, man, etc.

ENCHMƏNT

tr: intrenchment, retrenchment.
   Plus French meant, etc.

ENCHPRES

b: bench press.
fr: French Press.

ENCHƱR

b: bencher, debenture.
bl: blencher.
d: indenture.
dr: bedrencher, drencher.
kl: clencher, unclencher.
kw: quencher.
r: wrencher.
t: tenture.
tr: trencher, retrencher, trencher.
v: adventure, misadventure, peradventure, venture.
   Plus French err, etc.
   Plus sent your, etc.
   Plus scent you're, etc.
   Plus wrench her, etc.

ENCHƏNT

tr: trenchant.

ENDƏ

Vowel: merienda.

ENDÄL

Plus mend, Al, etc.

ENDÄNS

Plus men dance, etc.
Cf. lend aunts *or* ants, etc.

ENDÄNT

Plus send aunt *or* ant, etc.

ENDĒ

b: bendy.
f: Effendi.
tr: trendy.
w: Wendy.
Plus friend, he, etc.
Plus then Dee *or* D, etc.

ENDEST

Vowel: endest*.
b: bendest*, unbendest*.
bl: blendest*, interblendest*.
f: defendest*, fendest*, offendest*.
fr: befriendest*.
h: apprehendest*, comprehendest*, reprehendest*.
l: lendest*.
m: amendest*, commendest*, emendest*, mendest*, recommendest*.
p: appendest*, dependest*, expendest*, suspendest*.
r: rendest*.
s: ascendest*, condescendest*, descendest*, sendest*.
sp: spendest*.
t: attendest*, contendest*, extendest*, intendest*, pretendest*, subtendest*, superintendest*, tendest*.
v: vendest*.
w: wendest*.

ENDETH

Vowel: endeth*.
b: bendeth*, unbendeth*.
bl: blendeth*, interblendeth*.
f: defendeth*, fendeth*, offendeth*.
fr: befriendeth*.
h: apprehendeth*, comprehendeth*, reprehendeth*.
l: lendeth*.
m: amendeth*, commendeth*, emendeth*, mendeth*, recommendeth*.
p: appendeth*, dependeth*, expendeth*, suspendeth*.
r: rendeth*.
s: ascendeth*, condescendeth*, descendeth*, sendeth*.
sp: spendeth*.
t: attendeth*, contendeth*, extendeth*, intendeth*, pretendeth*, subtendeth*, superintendeth*, tendeth*.
v: vendeth*.
w: wendeth*.
Plus then death, etc.

ENDIK

w: Wendic.
Plus then, Dick, etc.

ENDING

Vowel: ending, unending.
b: bending, unbending.
bl: blending, interblending.
f: defending, forfending*, ofeending*, unoffending.
fr: befriending, unfriending.
h: apprehending, comprehending, reprehending.
l: forelending*, lending.
m: amending, commending, emending, mending, recommending.

p: appending, depending, expending, impending, pending, perpending, suspending.

r: heart-rending, rending.

s: ascending, condescending, descending, sending, transcending.

sp: forespending*, misspending, spending.

t: attending, contending, distending, extending, intending, portending, pretending, subtending, superintending, tending, unattending, unpretending.

tr: trending.

v: vending.

w: wending.

ĒNDISH

f: fiendish.

Plus clean dish, etc.

ENDLĒ

fr: friendly, unfriendly.

Plus lend, Lee *or* lea, etc.

ENDLƏS

Vowel: endless.

fr: friendless.

Plus lend less, etc.

ENDMENT

Plus bend meant, etc.

ENDMƏNT

fr: befriendment.

m: amendment.

t: intendment.

ENDŌ

Vowel: dimenuendo, innuendo.

s: crescendo, decrescendo.

Plus then dough *or* doe, etc.

Plus lend, owe *or* O, etc.

ENDRƏN

d: liriodendron, lithodendron, rhododendron, toxicodendron.

Cf. end run, etc.

ENDSHIP

fr: friendship.

Plus lend ship, etc.

ENDƲR

Vowel: ender, tail-ender, week-ender.

b: bender.

bl: blender, interblender.

f: defender, fender, offender.

fr: befriender.

h: apprehender, comprehender, reprehender.

j: engender, gender.

l: lender, moneylender.

m: amender, commender, emender, mender, recommender.

p: depender, expender, perpender, suspender.

r: render, surrender.

s: ascender, descender, sender.

sl: slender.

sp: spender.

spl: splendor.

t: attender, contender, entender*, extender, intender, pretender, tender.

v: vendor.

w: wender.

Plus send her, Ur, err *or* er, etc.

ENDƲRD

r: unsurrendered.

Plus endur+ed.

ENDWĀZ

Vowel: endways.

Plus defend ways *or* weighs, etc.

ENDƏ

Vowel: hacienda.
b: Benda.
br: Brenda.
j: agenda, corrigenda.
l: delenda.
z: Zenda.

Plus lend a, etc.

ENDƏD

Vowel: ended.
b: bended.
bl: blended, interblended, unblended.
f: defended, fended, offended, undefended.
fr: befriended, friended, unbefriended, unfriended.
h: apprehended, comprehended, misapprehended, reprehended.
m: amended, commended, emended, mended, recommended.
p: appended, depended, expended, impended, suspended.
r: rended*.
s: ascended, consescended, descended, reascended, transcended.
t: attended, contended, distended, extended, inextended, intended, portended, pretended, subtended, superintended, tended, unattended, unextended.
tr: trended.
w: wended.

Plus men dead, etc.
Plus send, Ed, etc.
Cf. splendid.
Cf. ten did, etc.

ENDƏL

b: prebendal.
s: sendal.
tr: trendle.

ENDƏM

d: addendum, credendum.
j: agendum, corrigendum.
r: referendum.

Plus lend 'em, etc.
Plus men dumb, etc.

ENDƏNS

p: dependence, impendence, independence, interdependence, pendence*.
s: ascendance, condescendance, descendance, transcendance.
spl: resplendence.
t: attendance, superintendence, tendance.

Cf. defendants.

ENDƏNT

f: defendant.
p: appendant, dependant, dependent, equipendent, impendent, independent, interdependent, pendant, pendant.
s: ascendant, descendant, descendent, transcendent.
spl: resplendent, splendent, transplendent.
t: attendant, contendant, fligh attendant, intendant, superintendent.

ENDƏS

m: tremendous.
p: stupendous.

Plus defend us, etc.

ĒNĀJ

t: teenage.

Plus mean age, etc.

ENEĬ

Vowel: any.
b: Benny.
d: Denny.
f: fenny.
j: jenny, spinning jenny.
k: Kenny, Kilkenny.
m: many.
p: Henny-Penny, Penney, penny, true-penny.
r: Rennie.
t: tenney.
w: wenny.

Plus then he, etc.

ĒNĒ

Vowel: eeni.
ch: Cheney, Cheyney, fantoccini, fetuccini.
n: finis, McFeeney.
gr: greeny.
gw: linguine
j: emalangeni, Eugenie, genie, lilangeni.
kr: Hippocrene.
kw: queenie.
l: Selene, tortellini.
m: meany, meeni.
s: grissini.
sh: sheeny.
spl: spleeny.
sw: Sweeney.
t: teeny.
v: visne.
w: weeny.
z: Tetrazini.

Plus bee knee, etc.

Plus 16 E, etc.

ENELM

k: Kenelm.

Plus glen elm, etc.

ENEST

d: dennest*.
k: kennest*.
p: pennest*, unpennest*.

ĒNEST

gl: gleanest*.
gr: greenest.
k: keenest.
kl: cleanest.
l: leanest.
m: demeanest*, meanest.
r: serenest.
skr(scr): bescreenest*, screenest*.
v: contravenest*, convenest*, intervenest*, supervenest*.
w: weanest*, weenest*.

Plus sea nest, etc.

ENETH

d: denneth*.
k: Kenneth.
p: penneth*, unpenneth*.

ĒNETH

gl: gleaneth*.
k: keeneth*.
kl: cleaneth*.
l: leaneth*.
m: demeaneth*, meaneth*.
skr: bescreeneth*, screeneth*.
v: contraveneth*, conveneth*, interveneth*, superveneth*.
w: weaneth*, weeneth*.

ENĒZ

b: bennies.
j: spinning jennies.
p: pennies.

ENGTHĒ

l: lengthy.

ENHÔLZ

kr: Edward Krenholz.

ĒNHÔRN

gr: greenhorn.
   Plus seen horn, etc.

ĒNĪD

gr: greeneyed.
k: keeneyed.
   Plus clean eyed, etc.

ĒNIJ

gr: greenage.
r: careenage.

ENIK

ch: lichenic.
d: Edenic.
f: alphenic, phenic.
fr: phrenic.
j: anthropogenic, chronogenic, crystallogenic, deuterogenic, Diogenic, diplogenic, embryogenic, eugenic, glyccogenic, hypoallergenic, hysterogenic, metagenic, nitrogenic, organogenic, oxygenic, paragenic, parthenogenic, pathogenic, phosphorogenic, photogenic, protogenic, pyrogenic, pythogenic, thermogenic, zoogenic.
k(c): lichenic.
l: galenic, geoselenic, Hellenic, Panhellenic, Philhellenic, selenic.

m: ecumenic.
r: irenic.
s: Saracenic, scenic.
spl: splenic.
st: tungstenic.
sth: sthenic.
t: Prutenic*.
th: asthenic, callisthenic, Demosthenic, neurasthenic, parthenic.
   Plus pen nick *or* Nick, etc.

ĒNIK

s: scenic.
   Plus me, Nick, etc.

ENIKS

g: cryogenics.

ĒNING

Vowel: eaning.
b: shebeening.
gl: gleaning.
gr: greening.
k(c): keening.
kl: cleaning.
kw: queening.
l: leaning, upleaning.
m: bemeaning, demeaning, doublemeaning, meaning, unmeaning, well-meaning.
pr: preening.
s: scening.
sh: machining.
skr(scr): screening.
v: advening, contravening, convening, intervening, subvening, supervening.
w: overweening, weaning, weening.
y: yeaning.

ENINGZ

j: Jennings.
　　Plus ening+s.

ĒNINGZ

skr(scr): screening.
　　Plus ening+s.

ENIS

d: Dennis.
t: tennis.
　　Cf. menace, tenace.

ENISH

pl: plenish, replenish.
r: Rhenish.
w: wennish.

ĒNISH

gr: greenish.
k: keenish.
kl: cleanish.
kw: queenish.
l: leanish.
m: meanish.
spl: spleenish.

ĒNIST

pl: plenist.
sh: machinist.
t: routinist.
z: magazinist.

ENIZ

　　Plus fen is, etc.

ENJIN

Vowel: engine, Rankine-cycle engine.
　　Plus then gin, djinn *or* jinn, etc.

ENJING

v: avenging, revenging, venging*.

ENJUR

v: avenger.
　　Plus avenge her *or* err, etc.

ENJƏNS

v: vengeance.

ENLĒ

h: Henley.
kl: cleanly+, uncleanly.
s: Senley.
sh: Schenley.
　　Plus then lea *or* Lee, etc.

ĒNLĒ

gr: greenly.
k(c): keenly.
kl: cleanly+.
kw: queenly.
l: leanly.
m: meanly.
r: serenely.
s: obscenely.
　　Plus green lea *or* Lee, etc.

ĒNLIGHT

gr: green light.

ĒNLING

w: weanling.
y: yeanling.

ENMƏN

f: fenman.
p: panman.
　　Plus then man, etc.

ĒNNƏS

gr: greenness.
k: keenness.
kl: cleanness, uncleanness.
l: leanness.
m: meanness.
r: sereneness.
s: obsceneness.

ĒNŌ

Vowel: Eno.
b: bambino, beano.
d: tondino.
k: baldachino, keno, maraschino.
n: pianino.
p: Filipino, pinot.
r: merino, peacherino, peperino, Reno, San Marino, Sereno, vetturino.
s: Casino.
t: andantino, festino, Latino, Valentino.
　　Plus see no *or* know, etc.
　　Plus clean owe *or* O, etc.

ENŌLD

　　Plus then old, etc.

ENÔN

　　Plus den on *or* an, etc.

ENŌŌ

v: venue.

ENSÄL

　　Plus expense, Al, etc.
　　Cf. expense, all, etc.

ENSĀT

d: condensate.
p: compensate.

s: insensate.
t: intensate.
　　Plus men sate, etc.
　　Plus expense ate *or* eight, etc.

ENSEST

d: condensest*, densest.
f: fencest*.
m: commencest*.
p: dispensest*, recompensest*.
s: incensest*.
t: intensest.

ENSETH

d: condenseth*.
f: fenceth*.
m: commenceth*.
p: dispenseth*, recompenseth*.
s: incenseth*.
　　Plus then saith *or* Seth, etc.

ENSĒZ

Vowel: amanuenses.
j: Albigenses.
m: menses.
　　Plus then sees, etc.
　　Plus expense ease, etc.

ENSFÔRTH

h: benceforth.
hw: whenceforth.
TH: thenceforth.
　　Plus fence fourth *or* forth, etc.

ENSIK

r: forensic.

ENSHÄL

　　Plus men shall, etc.
　　Plus bench, Al, etc.
　　Cf. bench all, etc.

ĒNSHIP

d: deanship.

kw: queenship.

Plus clean ship, etc.

ENSHOŌR

s: censure.

ENSHƏL

Vowel: expediential, experiential, influential, obediential, sapiential, sciential.

d: confidential, credential, evidential, jurisprudential, precedential, presidential, providential, prudential, residential, rodential.

j: agential, bigential, indulgential*, intelligential, tengential.

kw: consequential, inconsequential, sequential.

l: pestilential, querulential.

n: exponential.

r: conferential, deferential, differential, inferential, irrevential, preferential, referential, reverential, torrential, transferential.

s: coessential, essential, inessential, nonessential, quintessential, reminiscential, super-essential, unessential.

t: equipotential, existential, penitential, potential, sentential.

z: omnipresential.

ENSHƏN

h: apprehension, comprehension, deprehension*, inapprehension, incomprehension, misapprehension, preapprehension, prehension, reprehension.

j: bottle gentian, gentian.

kl: declension.

m: demension, mention.

p: pension, propension, suspension.

s: accension, ascension, condescension, descension, dissension, recension.

st: abstention.

t: attention, co-extension, contention, detention, distention, extension, inattention, inextension, intension, intention, obtention, ostension, portention, ppretneion, retention, tension, thermotention.

v: circumvention, contravention, convention, intervention, invention, obvention, prevention, subvention, supervention.

z: presention*.

Plus pen shun, etc.

ENSHƏND

m: unmentioned.

p: unpensioned.

t: well-intentioned.

Plus enshun+ed.

ENSHƏS

Vowel: conscientious.

l: pestilentious, silentious.

s: dissentious, licentious.

t: contentious, pretentious, sententious.

Cf. drench us, etc.

ENSING

d: condensing.

f: fencing.

m: commencing.

p: dispensing, recompensing.

s: incensing.

ENSIV

Vowel: influencive.

d: condensive.

f: defensive, indefensive*, inoffensive, offensive, self-defensive.

h: apprehensive, comprehensive, inapprehensive, incomprehensive, reprehensive, unapprehensive.

p: expensive, inexpensive, pensive, recompensive, suspensive.

s: ascensive, condescensive, descensive, incensive*.

t: capital-intensive, distensive, extensive, intensive, labor-intensive, ostensive, protensive, tensive.

Plus men sieve, etc.

ENSLƏS

f: defenseless, fenceless, offenseless.

p: expenseless.

s: senseless.

Plus dense less, etc.

Cf. tents less, etc.

ENSMAN

l: lensman.

ENSMENT

Plus dense meant, etc.

Cf. tents meant, etc.

ENSMƏNT

m: commencement.

s: incensement.

ENSNƏS

d: denseness.

m: immenseness.

p: propenseness.

t: intenseness, tenseness.

ENSÔN

Plus then, son *or* sun, etc.

ENSŌOR

Plus hense your *or* you're etc.

ENSPĒ

t: ten-speed.

ĒNSTEST

m: means test.

ENSUR

d: condenser, denser.

f: fencer.

h: prehenser.

m: commencer.

p: dispenser, recompenser.

s: censer, censor, incensor*.

sp: spencer, Spenser.

t: extensor, intenser, tensor.

Plus men, sir, etc.

Plus condense her, err *or* Ur, etc.

ENSUS

s: census.

Plus fence us, etc.

ENSƏL

h: prehensile.

m: bimensal, commensal, mensal.

p: pencil, pensile.

r: forensal.

st: stencil.

t: extensile, tensile, utensil.

Plus hence, ill, etc.

Plus pen sill, etc.

Plus fence 'll, etc.

ENSƏLD

p: pencilled.
st: stencilled.
t: utensilled.

ENSƏN

b: Benson.
h: Henson.

ENTĀ

Vowel: Agua Caliente,
aguardiente, dolce farniente.
d: presidente.
k(c): contradicente.
l: festinolete.
p: diapente.
s: cognoscente.

ENTĀNS

Cf. bent ants, *or* aunts, etc.

ENTĀNT

Plus lent aunt *or* ant, etc.

ENTĀT

d: bidentate, dentate, edentate,
quadridentate, tridentate.
m: commentate, dementate.
Plus Lent ate *or* eight, etc.
Plus then Tate, etc.

ENTĒ

h: Henty.
m: tormenty.
pl: plenty.
tw: one-and-twenty, two-and-
twenty, etc., twenty.
Plus then tea, etc.
Plus lent, he, etc.
Plus scent, he, etc.
Cf. enti.

ENTEST

b: bentest*.
d: indentest*.
kw: frequentest*.
l: relentest*.
m: augmentest*, cementest*,
commentest*, complementest*,
complimentest*, fermentest*,
fomentest*, lamentest*,
ornamentest*, supplementest*,
tormentest*.
p: repentest*.
r: rentest*.
s: absentest*, accentest*,
assentest*, consentest*,
dissentest*, sentest*, scentest*.
t: contentest*.
v: circumventest*, inventest*,
preventest*, ventest*.
z: misrepresentest*, presentest*,
representest, resentest*.
Plus hen test, etc.
Cf. entist.

ENTETH

b: benteth*.
d: indenteth*.
kw: frequeneth*.
l: relenteth*.
m: augmenteth*, cementeth*,
commenteth*, complementeth*,
complimenteth*, fermenteth*,
fomenteth*, lamenteth*,
ornamentath*, supplementeth*,
tormenteth*.
p: repenteth*.
r: renteth*.
s: absenteth*, accenteth*,
assenteth*, consenteth*,
dissenteth*, scenteth*.
t: contenteth*.
v: circumventeth*, inventeth*,
preventeth*, venteth*.
z: misrepresenteth*, presenteth*,
representeth*, resenteth*.

ENTFOOL

v: eventful, uneventful.
z: resentful.
  Plus tent full, etc.

ENTHOUS

p: penthouse.
  Plus rent house, etc.

ENTIJ

s: percentage.
v: ventage.
  Cf. lent age, etc.

ENTIK

d: identic.
j: argentic.
th: authentic.
  Plus then tick, etc.

ENTĪL

j: Gentile.
  Plus men tile, etc.
  Plus sent aisle *or* isle, etc.
  Plus scent, I'll, etc.

ENTIN

d: Tridentine.
kw: Quentin, San Quentin.
  Plus went in, sent inn, etc.
  Plus then, tin, etc.

ENTING

d: denting, indenting.
kw: frequenting.
l: relenting, unrelenting.
m: augmenting, cementing, commenting, complementing, complimenting, dementing, fermenting, fomenting, lamenting, ornamenting, self-tormenting, supplementing, tormenting.

p: repenting, unrepenting.
r: renting.
s: absenting, accenting, assenting, consenting, dissenting, scenting, unconsenting.
t: contenting, tenting.
v: circumventing, inventing, preventing, venting.
z: misrepresenting, presenting, representing, resenting.

ENTIS

m: noncomposmentis.
p: appentice*, pentice*.
pr: apprentice, prentice, Prentiss.

ENTIST

d: dentist.
pr: apprenticed.
v: preventist.
  Cf. entest.

ENTIV

d: pendentive.
s: assentive, incentive.
t: attentive, inattentive, irrentive, retentive.
v: adventive, circumventive, inventive, preventive.
z: presentive, resentive*.

ENTLĒ

d: evidently.
j: gently.
l: insolently.
n: eminently.
s: innocently.
t: impotently, intently.
  Plus ent+ly.
  Plus scent, Lee *or* lea, etc.

ENTLƏS

d: dentless.
l: relentless.
m: cementless, lamentless.
r: rentless.
s: centless, scentless.
t: tentless.
    Plus accidentless, etc.
    Plus meant less, etc.

ENTMƏNT

l: relentment.
t: contentment, discontentment.
z: presentment, representment, resentment.
    Plus scent meant, etc.

ENTNƏS

t: intentness.

ENTŌ

ch: cinquecento, quattrocento.
l: lento, polento.
m: divertimento, memento, pimento, portamento, pronuncia-mento, rifacimento, Sacramento.
s: cento.
    Plus then toe, etc.
    Plus cent owe *or* O, etc.

ENTRÄNS

    Plus again trance, etc.
    Plus dent Rance, etc.

ENTRĀT

s: concentrate.
    Plus rent rate, etc.

ENTRE

v: danse du ventre.

ENTRĒ

Vowel: entry.
j: gentry.
s: sentry.
    Plus again tree, etc.

ENTRIK

s: acentric, anthropocentric, andocentric, barycentric, centric, concentric, eccentric, geocentric, gynecocentric, heliocentric, paracentric, selenocentric.
    Plus men trick, etc.
    Plus bent rick, etc.

ENTRƏL

s: central.
v: ventral.

ENTRƏNS

Vowel: entrance.

ENTRƏS

m: tormentress.
v: inventress.
    Plus again tress.

ENTUM

m: momentum, sarmentum.
r: Tarentum.
    Plus bent 'em, etc.
    Plus again tum, etc.

ENTƱR

Vowel: enter, reenter.
d: denter, indenter.
kw: frequenter.
l: lentor, relenter.
m: augmenter, cementer, commenter, experimenter,

fermenter, fomenter, lamenter, ornamenter, supplementer, tormenter, mentor.

p: repenter.

r: renter.

s: assenter, centaur, center, concenter, day-care center, dead center, dissenter, precentor, succentor.

st: stentor.

t: contenter, tenter.

v: circumventor, inventer, preventer, venter.

z: misrepresenter, presenter, representer, resenter.

> Plus bent her *or* err, etc.
>
> Plus fen tor, etc.
>
> Plus scent, or, etc.
>
> Cf. entor, entur.

ENTURD

Vowel: entered.

s: self-centered.

> Plus entur+ed.
>
> Plus scent erred, etc.

ENTUS

gw: unguentous.

m: immomentous, ligamentous, momentous, pigmentous, sarmentous.

t: pedententous, portentous.

> Plus sent us, etc.

ENTƏ

j: magenta.

l: polenta.

m: Pimenta.

s: placenta.

> Plus sent a, etc.

ENTƏD

d: dented, indented, precendented, unprecedented.

kw: frequented, unfrequented.

l: relented.

m: augmented, battlemented, cemented, commented, complimented, demented, fermented, fomented, lamented, ornamented, supplemented, tormented, unlamented, unornamented, untormented.

p: repented, unrepented.

r: rented.

s: absented, accented, assented, consented, dissented, scented, sweet-scented.

t: contented, discontented, ill-contented, tented, untented, well-contented.

v: circumvented, invented, prevented, unprevented, vented.

z: misrepresented, presented, represented, resented.

> Plus then, Ted, etc.
>
> Plus rent, Ed, etc.

ENTƏL

Vowel: oriental.

d: accidental, antecedental, bidental, coincidental, dental, dentil, dentile, incidental, labiodental, linguadental, occidental, transcendental, tridental.

j: argental, falcon gentle, gentle, ungentle.

k: kentle*.

l: Lental, lentil.

m: alimental, argumental, atramental, complemental, complimental, departmental, detrimental, developmental, documental, elemental,

excremental, experimental,
firmamental, fragmental,
fundamental, governmental,
impedimental, instrumental,
ligamental, medicamental,
mental, monumental,
nutrimental, ornamental,
parliamental, pedimental,
pigmental, predicamental,
recremental, regimental,
rudimental, sacramental,
segmental, sentimental, supple-
mental, temperamental,
tenemental, testamental.
n: continental, intercontinental.
r: parental, rental.
s: cental, placental.
tr: trental.

  Plus bent, Al, etc.
  Plus gent 'll, etc.
  Cf. ental, men tall, bent all, etc.

ENTƏNS

p: repentance, unrepentance.
s: sentance.

ENTƏNT

p: repentant, unrepentant.
z: representant.

ĒNUM

fr: frenum.
pl: plenum.

  Plus be numb, etc.
  Plus gasoline 'em, etc.

ENU̱R

f: Fenner.
k: Kenner.
p: penner.
t: contra-tenor, counter-tenor, first
tenor, second tenor, tenner, tenor.

  Plus den her, err or Ur, etc.

ĒNU̱R

b: shebeener.
gl: gleaner.
gr: greener.
k: keener.
kl: cleaner.
l: leaner.
m: demeanor, mesner, misde-
meanor.
r: serener.
s: obscener, seiner.
sh: machiner.
skr(scr): screener.
v: contravener, convener,
intervener, supervener.
w: weaner, wiener.
z: magaziner.

  Plus seen her, err, Ur, or er, etc.

ENU̱RD

l: Leonard.
t: teored.

  Plus tenor'd.
  Cf. enur+d.

ĒNUS

j: genus.
l: Silenus.
v: venous, Venus.

  Plus wean us, etc.

ENVĒ

Vowel: envy.

ENVIL

Vowel: Vienville.
gl: Glenville.
gr: Grenville.

ENVŮR

d: Denver.

ĒNYŌ

ch: latticinio.
n: El Niño.
p: jalapeño.

ĒNYÔR

s: monsignor, scignior, senior, signor.
Cf. demean your, etc.

ĒNYUS

j: genius.
Cf. enius.

ĒNYƏL

j: congenial.
Cf. enial.

ĒNYƏN

m: Armenian.
Cf. enian.

ĒNYƏNS

l: lenience.
Cf. eniens.

ĒNYƏNT

v: convenient.
Cf. enient.

ENZDĀ

w: Wednesday.
Plus hens day, etc.

ENZĒ

Vowel: Rienzi.
fr: frenzy.
k: McKenzie.
Plus hens, he, etc.

ENZĒN

b: divinylbenzene.

ENZŌ

r: Lorenzo.
Plus hens owe *or* O, etc.

ENZƏ

Vowel: influenza.
d: cadenza.
Plus when's a, etc.
Plus hens a, etc.

ENZƏN

v: venison.
Plus hens on *or* an, etc.

ENZƏZ

kl: cleanses.
l: lenses.
Cf. hens is, etc.

ENƏ

Vowel: duenna, Sienna, Vienna.
h: Gehenna, henna.
s: senna.
t: dish antenna, antenna.
v: Ravenna.
Plus when a, etc.

ĒNƏ

Vowel: hyena.
b: Sabina+, verbena.
br: Sabrina+

d: Merdina, Modena.

dr: alexandrina.

g: Gina.

j: gena, Georgina, Regina+.

k(c): coquina, Corinna+.

kw: Queena.

l: Catalina+, galena, Helena, Lena, Magdalena, Paulina, Selena, semolina.

m: Wilhelmina, Mina.

p: philopena, subpoena.

r: arena, czarina, farina+, Rina, Serena, signorina, tsarina.

s: Lucina+, Messina, scena, Teresina.

t: Argentina, catena, cavatina, Celestina, Christina, Clementina, concertina, Faustina, fontina, Justina, scarlatina, sestina, Tina+.

tr: Katrina+.

th: Athena.

z: maizena.

Plus wean a, etc.

ENƏL

f: fennel, Fennell.

k: kennel, unkennel.

t: antennal.

Plus men'll, etc.

Plus when, Al, etc.

Cf. when all, etc.

ĒNƏL

p: penal.

pl: plenal*.

r: adrenal, renal.

sh: machinal.

v: venal.

w: weanel.

Plus mean, Al, etc.

ENƏLD

r: Reynold.

ENƏLDZ

r: Reynolds.

ENƏM

d: denim.

v: envenom, venom.

Plus pen 'em, etc.

Plus pen him, etc.

Cf. denim.

ENƏN

l: Lenin.

p: pennon.

t: tenon.

Plus ten in, etc.

ENƏNT

p: pennant.

t: lieutenant, sub-lieutenant, tenant, Tennant.

Plus then ant *or* aunt, etc.

ENƏS

m: menace.

t: tenace.

Cf. tennis.

ĒNƏS

Vowel: Enas, Enos.

z: Zenas.

Cf. seen us, etc.

Cf. enus.

ENƏT

b: Bennett.

j: jennet.

r: rennet.

s: senate.
t: tenet.

   Plus men et, etc.
   Cf. then it, etc.
   Cr. then net, etc.

ĒŌ

Vowel: Eo.
kl: Cleo, Clio+.
l: Leo.
n: neo.
r: Rio+.
th: Theo.
tr: trio+.

   Plus we owe *or* O, etc.

ĒŌL

kr: Creole.

   Plus see Ole, etc.

ĒPDÄG

sh: sheepdog+.

EPĒ

Vowel: Eppie.
k: kepi.
p: peppy.
pr: preppy.
st: one-steppy, two-steppy.
t: tepee.

   Plus step, he, etc.

ĒPĒ

ch: cheepy.
h: heapy.
k: kepi.
kr: creepy.
s: seepy.
sh: sheepy.
sl: sleepy.

st: steepy.
sw: sweepy.
t: tepee.
w: weepy.

   Plus tree pea, etc.
   Plus T.P., etc.

ĒPEST

ch: cheapest, cheepest*.
d: deepest.
h: heapest*.
k: keepest*.
kr: creepest*.
l: leapest*, overleapest*.
p: peepest*.
r: reapest*.
sl: outsleepest*, oversleepest*, sleepest*.
st: steepest.
sw: sweepest*.
w: weepest*.

   Plus tree pest, etc.

ĒPETH

ch: cheepeth*.
h: heapeth*.
k: keepeth*.
kr: creepeth*.
l: leapeth*, overleapeth*.
p: peepeth*.
r: reapeth*.
sl: outsleepeth*, oversleepeth*, sleepeth*.
sw: sweepeth*.
w: weepeth*.

   Cf. tree pith, etc.

ĒPFRĒZ

d: deep freeze.

EPID

l: lepid

t: tepid.

tr: intrepid, trepid.

Cf. step hid, etc.

ĒPIJ

s: seepage.

sw: sweepage.

Cf. deep age, etc.

EPIK

Vowel: epic, orthoepic.

Cf. step pic, etc.

ĒPING

ch: cheeping.

d: Deeping.

h: heaping.

k: housekeeping, keeping, safekeeping.

kr: creeping.

l: leaping, overleaping.

p: peeping.

r: reaping.

s: seeping, seiping.

sl: outsleeping, oversleeping, sleeping, unsleeping.

st: steeping.

sw: sweeping.

w: unweeping, weeping.

Plus we ping, etc.

ĒPISH

d: deepish.

sh: sheepish.

st: steepish.

ĒPL

p: beautiful people, empeople*, people, unpeople.

st: steeple.

Plus reap'll, etc.

Cf. tree pull, etc.

ĒPLƏS

sl: sleepless.

w: weepless.

Plus creepless *or* Les, etc.

ĒPNƏS

ch: cheapness.

d: deepness.

sl: sleepness.

st: steepness.

EPÔN

Plus step on *or* an, etc.

EPSĒ

l: catalepsy, epilepsy, nympholepsy.

p: apepsy, dyspepsy, eupepsy.

Plus step see, etc.

EPSHUN

r: abreption*, arreption*, ereption, obreption, subreption, surreption.

s: apperception, conception, contraception, deception, exception, imperception, inception, interception, introsusception, intussusception, misconception, perception, preconception, preperception, reception, self-deception.

Plus step shun, etc.

EPSIS

l: analepsis, epanalepsis, metalepsis, paralepsis, prolepsis, syllepsis.

s: aspsis.

sk: skepsis.

Plus step, sis, etc.

ĒPŌ

r: repo.

ĒPŌN

k: Kepone.

ĒPSHÄT

ch: cheap shot.

ĒPSKIN

sh: sheepskin.

Plus keep skin, etc.

EPTED

Plus step, Ted, etc.
Plus kept, Ed, etc.

EPTEST

d: adeptest.
s: acceptest*, exceptest*, interceptest*.

Plus pep test, etc.

EPTETH

s: accepteth*, excepteth*, intercepteth*.

EPTIK

kl: kleptic.
l: acataleptci, analeptic, cataleptic, epileptic, metaleptic, neuroleptic, nympholeptic, oganoleptic, proleptic, ylleptic.
p: bradypeptic, dyspeptic, eupeptic, peptic.
s: antiseptic, aspeptic, septic.
sk(sc): sceptic.

Plus step tick, etc.

EPTING

s: accepting, excepting, incepting, intercepting.

EPTIV

s: acceptive, conceptive, contra-ceptive, deceptive, exceptive, imperceptive, inceptive, insusceptive, interceptive, intussusceptive, irrecptive, perceptive, preceptive, receptive, susceptive.

EPTNƏS

Vowel: ineptness.

EPT   N

n: Neptune.

Plus pep tune, etc.

EPTUR

d: adepter.
s: accepter, excepter, inceptor, intercepter, preseptor, scepter, susceptor.

Plus kept her, Ur, err *or* er, etc.

EPTƏD

s: accepted, excepted, inter-cepted.

EPTƏNS

s: acceptance.

Plus kept ant *or* aunts, etc.

EPTƏNT

r: reptant.
s: acceptant, exceptant.

Plus kept aunt *or* ant, etc.

EPUR

h: hepper.
l: leper.
p: pepper.
st: high-stepper, one-stepper, overstepper, two-stepper, stepper.

Plus pep her, err *or* Ur, etc.

ĒPŬR

Vowel: Ypres.

ch: cheaper, cheeper.

d: deeper.

h: heaper.

k: hedge-keeper, housekeeper, keeper, shopkeeper, wicket-keeper.

kr: creeper, wallcreeper.

l: leaper.

p: peeper.

r: reaper.

sl: sleeper.

st: steeper.

sw: sweeper.

w: weeper.

Plus we purr *or* per, etc.

Plus keep her, err *or* Ur, etc.

EPŬRD

j: jeopard.

l: leopard.

p: peppered.

sh: shepherd.

Plus step erred, etc.

Cf. step heard, etc.

ĒPWÔK

sh: sheepwalk.

sl: sleepwalk.

Plus creep, walk, etc.

EPƏN

w: weapon.

ĒPƏN

ch: cheapen.

d: deepen.

st: steepen.

Cf. creep, hen, etc.

ERÄ

b: guayabera.

ĒRÄNS

Cf. erens.

Cf. near ants, *or* aunts, etc.

ĒRÄNT

Plus near aunt *or* ant, etc.

Cf. erent.

ERĀT

s: serrate.

Plus near rate, etc.

Plus her ate *or* eight, etc.

ĒRDLĒ

w: wierdly.

Plus beard, Lee *or* lea, etc.

ĒRDƏD

b: bearded.

Plus deer dead, etc.

Cf. deer did, etc.

Cf. reared, hid, etc.

ERĒ

b: beriberi, berry, blackberry, blueberry, bury, dewberry, huckleberry, Juneberry, logan-berry, mulberry, raspberry, strawberry, whortle-berry.

ch: cherry, chokecherry, Pondicherry.

d: Derry.

f: ferry.

g: Gerry.

hw: wherry.

j: Gerry, Jerry, Tom and Jerry.

k: kerry.

m: merry.

n: millinery, stationary.

p: Peary, perry.

s: lamasery.

sh: sherry.

sk: skerry.

t: cemetery, monastery, presbytery, Terry.

v: very.

Cf. ari.

ĒRĒ

Vowel: aerie, eerie, Erie.

b: beery.

bl: bleary.

ch: cheery, uncheery.

d: dearie, deary.

dr: dreary, Dundreary.

j: jeery.

kw: quaere, query.

l: Cavalieri, leary, leery, O'Leary.

p: peri.

r: Miserere.

sf: sphery.

sm: smeary.

sn: sneery.

t: teary.

v: veery.

w: aweary, forweary*, life-weary, overweary, weary.

Plus dear, he, etc.

ERĒD

b: berried, buried, unburied.

ch: cherried.

f: ferried.

hw: wherried.

s: serried.

ĒRĒD

kw: queried.

w: unwearied, war-wearied, wearied, world-wearied.

Cf. near hid, etc.

ĒREST

ch: cheerest*.

d: dearest, endearest*.

dr: drearest.

f: fearest*, interferest*.

g: gearest*.

h: adherest*, coherest*, hearest*, overhearest*.

j: jeerest*.

kl: clearest.

kw: queerest.

l: leerest*.

m: merest.

n: nearest.

p: appearest*, disappearest*, peerest*, reappearest*.

r: careerest*, rearest*, unrearest*, uprearest*.

s: insincerest, searest*, serest, sincerest.

sh: shearest*, sheerest.

sm: besmearest*, smearest*.

sn: sneerest*.

sp: spearest*.

st: steerest*.

t: austerest.

v: perseverst*, reverest*, severst, veerest*.

Cf. dear, rest, etc.

ĒRETH

ch: cheereth*.

d: endeareth*.

f: feateth*, interfereth*.

g: geareth*.

h: adhereth*, heareth*, overheateth*.

j: jeereth*.

kl: cleareth*.

l: leereth.

p: appeareth, disappeareth*, peereth*, reappeareth*.

r: careereth, reareth, upreareth*.

s: seareth*.
sh: sheareth*.
sm: besmeareth*, smeareth*.
sn: sneereth*.
sp: speareth*.
st: steereth*.
v: persevereth*, revereth*, veereth*.

ERĒZ

b: berries, buries.
ch: cherries.
f: ferries.
hw: wherries.
sh: sherries.

ĒRĒZ

d: dearies.
kw: queries.
s: mini-series, series.
w: overwearies, wearies.
    Plus here is, etc.

ĒRFŌN

Vowel: earphone.
    Plus near phone, etc.

ĒRFOOL

Vowel: earful.
ch: cheerful, uncheerful.
f: fearful, unfearful.
sn: sneerful.
t: tearful.
    Plus beer full, etc.

ERHED

Vowel: airhead.

ĒRĪD

bl: blearyeyd.
kl: cleareyed.

t: teareyed.
    Plus near eyed *or* I'd, etc.
    Cf. near ride, etc.

ERIF

sh: sheriff.
    Cf. eraf.

ĒRIJ

kl: clearage.
p: peerage, pierage.
r: arrearage.
st: steerage.
    Cf. near age, etc.
    Cf. peer rage, etc.

ERIK

Vowel: Eric.
b: suberic.
d: derrick.
f: atmospheric, chromospheric, ferric, helisphric, hemispheric, peripheric, perispheric.
h: Herrick.
kl: cleric.
l: valeric.
m: anisomeric, chimeric, Homeric, isomeric, mesmeric, numeric.
n: generic.
p: siperic.
sf: spheric.
t: alexteric, amphoteric, climacteric, enteric, esoteric, exoteric, hysteric, icteric, masseteric, neoteric, phylacteric.

ERIKS

t: esoterics, hysterics.
    Plus erik+s.

ERĪL

f: Fair Isle.

ĒRIN

Vowel: Erin.

Plus see, Rinn, etc.

ĒRING

Vowel: earing.

bl: blearing.

ch: cheering, upcheering*.

d: Dearing, endearing.

f: fearing, interering.

g: gearing, ungearing.

h: adhering, cohering, hearing, overhearing, reharing.

j: jeering.

kl: clearing.

kw: queering.

l: gondoliering, Edware Learing, leering.

n: aucioneering, cannoneering, domineering, electioneering, engineering, genetic engineering, mountaineering, nearing, pioneering, veneering.

p: appearing, disappearing, peering, reappearing.

r: careering, rearing, uprearing.

s: searing.

sh: cashiering, shearing.

sk: skeering.

sm: besmearing, smearing.

sn: sneering.

sp: spearing.

st: steering.

t: privateering, volunteering.

v: persevering, revering, veering.

Cf. earring.

Cf. hear ring, etc.

ERIS

f: ferris.

t: terrace, teris.

ERISH

ch: cherish.

p: perish.

ERIT

h: disherit, disinherit, inherit.

m: demerit, immerit*, merit.

Cf. hear it, etc.

Cf. eret.

ĒRLĒ

ch: cheerly.

d: dearly.

kl: clearly.

kw: queerly.

l: cavalierly.

m: merely.

n: nearly.

s: sincerely.

t: austerely.

v: severely.

y: yearly.

Plus clear, Lee, *or* lea, etc.

ĒRLING

sh: shearling.

st: steerling.

y: yearling.

ĒRLƏS

Vowel: earless.

ch: cheerless.

f: fearless.

g: gearless.

j: jeerless.

p: peerless.

sp: spearless.

t: tearless.

y: yearless.

Plus smear less, etc.

ĒRMƏNT

d: endearment.
s: cerement.
   Plus cheer meant, etc.

ĒRNƏS

d: dearness.
kl: clearness.
kw: queerness.
n: nearness.
s: sincereness.
t: austerenss.
v: severness.

ĒRŌ

h: hero.
l: lillibullero.
n: Nero, Robert De Niro.
s: Ciro.
z: zero.
   Plus she row *or* roe, etc.

ERL

f: ferrule, ferule.
p: perule.
sf: spherule.

ĒRM

s: searoom.
t: tearoom.
   Plus wee room, etc.

ĒRV

k: kiruv.

ĒRŌS

Vowel: Eros.

ERPLĀ

Vowel: airplay.

ĒRSING

p: ear-piercing, piercing, transpiercing.
   Plus hear sing, etc.

ĒRSNƏS

f: fierceness.

ĒRSUR

f: fiercer.
p: piercer.
   Plus here, sir, etc.
   Plus pierce her, err *or* Ur, etc.

ĒRSƏN

gr: Grierson.
m: Mearson.
p: Pearson, Pierson.
   Plus cheer son *or* sun, etc.

ERUB

ch: cherub.

ĒRUN

r: rerun.

ERUR

Vowel: error.
t: terror.

ĒRUR

ch: cheerer.
d: dearer, endearer.
f: fearer, interferer.
fl: fleerer.

h: adherer, hearer, overhearer.
j: jeerer.
kl: clearer.
kw: queerer.
l: leerer.
n: elctioneerer, nearer.
p: appearer, disappearer, peerer.
r: rearer.
s: searer.
sh: shearer.
sm: besmearer, smearer.
sn: sneerer.
sp: spearer.
st: steerer.
t: austerer, teerer.
v: perseverer, reverer, severer, veerer.
Plus cheer her, Ur *or* err, etc.
Cf. mirror.

ERWUN

sq: square one.

ERƏ

t: ciguatera.

ERƏN

h: heron.

ĒRƏS

s: serous.
skl(scl): sclerous.
Plus cheer us, etc.

ERƏS

f: ferrous.

ĒRZMƏN

st: steersman.
t: privateersman.
Plus nears man, etc.

ĒRƏ

Vowel: Caira, era.
d: madeira.
g: gerah.
h: hera.
k: Kirah.
l: lira, tirra-lira.
m: chimera.
v: Vera.
Cf. here a, etc.

ERƏF

s: seraph
t: teraph.
Cf. sheriff.

ERƏL

b: beryl, chrysoberyl.
m: Merrill, James Merrill.
p: peril
st: sterile.
Cf. eral.

ĒRƏL

f: feral.
sf: spheral.
Plus here, Al, etc.
Cf. eril.
Cf. hear all, etc.

ERƏLD

j: Gerald.
h: herald, Herrold.
   Cf. imperilled, etc.

ERƏNS

b: aberrance.

ĒRƏNS

f: interference.
h: adherence, coherence, incoherence, inherence.
kl: clearance.
p: appearance, disappearance, reappearance.
r: arrearance.
v: perseverance.
   Cf. erans.
   Cf. terence.
   Cf. near hence, etc.

ERƏNT

b: aberrant.

ĒRƏNT

j: vicegerent.
h: adherent, coherent, inadherent, incoherent, inherent.
kw: querent.
v: perseverent.
   Cf. near rent, etc.

ERƏS

t: terrace.
   Cf. eris.

ERƏT

f: ferret.
t: terret.
   Cf. erit.

ĒSĀJ

pr: presage.
   Plus he, sage, etc.
   Plus peace, age, etc.

ĒSBAK

l: lease-back.

ESCHƏN

j: congestion, digestion, indiges-
tion, ingestion, suggestion.
kw: question.

ESCHƏND

j: well-digestioned.
kw: questioned, unquestioned.

ESĒ

b: Bessie.
dr: dressy, undressy.
j: Jesse, Jessie.
kr: Cressy.
m: messy.
t: Tessie.
tr: tressy.
   Plus dress, he, etc.
   Cf. dress, see?, etc.
   Cf. in esse.

ĒSĒ

fl: fleecy.
gr: greasy.
kr: Crecy, creasy.
   Plus tree see, etc.
   Plus peace, he, etc.

ESED

bl: blessed.
   Plus es+ed*.
   Plus Yes, Ed, etc.
   Cf. Tess said, etc.

ĒSEL

b: B cell.
t: T cell.

ĒSENT

Plus sea scent *or* cent, etc.

ĒSEPT

pr: precept.

ĒSES

r: recess.

ESEST

Vowel: acquiescest*.
bl: blessest*.
dr: addressest*, dressest*, redressest*, undressest*.
f: confessest*, professest*.
g: guessest*.
gr: digressest*, progressest*, transgressest*.
pr: compressest*, depressest*, expressest*, impressest*, oppresest*, pressest*, repressest*, suppressest*.
r: caressest*.
s: assessest*.
tr: distressest*.
z: possessest*.

ĒSEST

fl: fleecest*.
gr: greaset*.
kr: creasest*, decreasest*, increaseset*.
l: leasest*, releasest*.
s: ceasest*.

ESETH

Vowel: acquiesceth*.
bl: blesseth*.
dr: addresseth*, dresseth*, redresseth*, undresseth*.
f: confesseth*, profeseth*.
g: guesseth*.
gr: digresseth*, progresseth*, transgresseth*.
pr: compresseth*, depresseth*, expresseth*, impresseth*, oppresseth*, presseth*, represseth*, suppresseth*.
r: caresseth*.
s: assesseth*.
tr: distresseth*.
z: possesseth*.

ĒSETH

fl: fleeceth*.
gr: greaseth*.
kr: creaseth*, decreaseth*, increaseth*.
l: leaseth*, releaseth*.
s: ceaseth*.

ESFOOL

s: successful.
Plus es+full.

ĒSFOOL

p: peaceful, unpeaceful.
pr: capriceful.
Plus niecefull, etc.

ESHĒ

fl: fleshy.
m: meshy.
Plus fresh, he, etc.

ESHEST

fr: freshest, refreshest*.
m: enmeshest*, immeshest*.
thr: threshest*.

ESHETH

fr: refresheth*.
m: enmesheth*, immeseth*,
mesheth*.
thr: thresheth*.

ĒSHĒZ

sp: endangered species, species.
　Plus see she's, etc.

ESHING

fr: refreshing.
m: meshing.
thr: threshing.

ESHINGZ

fl: fleshings.
　Plus eshing+s.

ESHLĒ

fl: fleshly, unfleshly.
fr: freshly.
　Plus mesh, Lee *or* lea, etc.

ESHLƏS

fl: fleshless.
m: meshless.
　Plus fresh less, etc.

ESHMƏN

fr: freshman.
　Plus flesh, man, etc.

ESHMƏNT

fr: refreshment.
　Plus flesh meant, etc.

ESHNƏS

fr: freshness.

ĒSHÔR

s: seashore.
　Plus flee shore, etc.

ĒSHUN

pl: depletion.

ESHƱR

fl: flesher.
fr: fresher, refresher.
m: mesher.
pr: acupressure, pressure.
thr: thresher.
tr: tressure.
　Plus refresh her *or* err, etc.

ESHUS

pr: precious.
　Plus enmesh us, etc.

ĒSHUS

s: facetious.
sp: specious.
　Plus unleash us, etc.

ESHƏL

p: especial.
sp: special.
　Plus fresh, Al, etc.

ESHƏN

f: confession, profession.
fr: freshen.
gr: aggression, digression,
egression, ingression,
introgression, progression,

regression, retrogression, transgression.

h: hessian.

kr: discretion, indiscretion.

pr: compression, decompression, depression, expression, impression, intropression, oppression, reimpression, repression, suppression.

s: accession, cession, concession, insession*, intercession, obsession, precession, procession, recession, retrocession, secession, session, succession, supersession.

z: dispossession, possession, prepossession, repossession, self-possession.

Plus fresh un, etc.

Cf. less shun, etc.

ĒSHƏN

gr: Grecian.

kr: accretion, concretion, secretion.

l: deletion.

n: internecion.

pl: completion, depletion, impletion, incompletion, repletion.

Plus we shun, etc.

Cf. eshian, eshun.

ESHƏNZ

s: quarter-sessions.

Plus eshun+s.

ĒSĪD

l: leeside.

s: seaside.

Plus she sighed, etc.

Plus tree side, etc.

Plus fleece, I'd or eyed, etc.

ESIJ

m: message.

p: pesage.

pr: expressage, presage.

Cf. long dress age, etc.

ESIK

d: geodesic.

n: eugenesic.

Cf. less hick, etc.

ESING

Vowel: acquiescing.

bl: blessing.

dr: addressing, dressing, redressing, undressing, water-dressing.

f: confession, professing.

g: guessing.

gr: digressing, progressing, retrogressing.

j: jessing*, unjessing*.

l: coalescing, convalescing.

m: messing.

pr: compressing, depressing, expressing, impressing, oppressing, pressing, repressing, suppressing.

r: caressing.

s: assessing, excessing.

str: stressing.

tr: distressing.

y: yessing.

z: dispossessing, possessing, prepossessing, repossesssing, unprepossessing.

ĒSING

fl: fleecing.

gr: greasing.

kr: creasing, decreasing, increasing.

l: leasing, policing, releasing.
p: piecing.
s: ceasing, surceasing, unceasing.

ĒSIS

Vowel: diesis, deesis.
j: exegesis.
kr: catachresis.
l: ochlesis.
m: mimesis.
n: amnesis, anamnesis.
p: aposiopesis.
r: apheresis, diaphoresis, iontophoresis, plasmapheresis, perichoresis, synteresis.
sk(sc): schesis.
t: erotesis, paracentesis.
th: anesthesis, anthesis, hyperesthesis, mathesis, thesis.
tm: tmesis.
    Plus spree, sis, etc.
    Cf. esus.
    Cf. fleeces, etc.

ESIV

dr: redressive.
gr: aggressive, congressive, digressive, progressive, regressive, retrogressive, transgressive.
kr: concrescive, crescive.
pr: compressive, depressive, expressive, impressive, inexpressive, oppressive, repressive, suppressive, unexpressive.
s: accessive, concessive, excessive, recessive, successive.
z: possessive.
    Cf. Bess sieve, etc.

ĒSIV

h: adhesive, cohesive.
    Plus he sieve, etc.

ESKĒ

p: pesky.
r: deReszke.
    Plus desk, he, etc.
    Plus dress key, etc.

ESKNƏS

Vowel: statuesqueness.
r: picturesqueness.
t: grotesqueness.

ESKŌ

d: tedesco.
fr: al fresco, fresco.
    Plus desk ow *or* O, etc.

ESK

f: fescue.
r: rescue.
    Plus bless cue *or* queue, etc.
    Plus desk you, etc.

ĒSK   L

b: B-school.

ĒSKWER

t: T square.
    Plus see square, etc.

ESKƏ

j: Modjeska.
l: Valeska.
tr: Tresca.
    Plus desk, a, etc.

ĒSL

    Cf. esil.

ESL

dr: redressal.
j: Jessel.
n: nestle, unnestle.
p: pestle.
r: wrestle.
s: Cecil.
tr: trestle.
v: vessel.
  Plus mess 'll, etc.

ESLING

n: nestling.
p: pestling.
r: restling.

ESLUR

n: nestler.
r: wrestler.

ĒSLƎS

fl: fleeceless.
kr: creaseless.
l: leaseless.
p: peaceless.
pr: capriceless.
s: ceaseless.
  Plus piece less, etc.

ESMĀT

m: messmate.
  Plus bless mate, etc.

ĒSMĒL

p: piecemeal.
  Plus release meal, etc.

ESMƎN

pr: pressman.
y: yesman.
  Plus bless man, etc.

ĒSMƎN

l: policeman.
  Plus fleece, man, etc.

ESMƎNT

dr: redressment.
pr: impressment.
s: assessment
  Plus undress meant, etc.

ĒSNƎS

b: obeseness.

ESPIT

r: respite.
  Plus cress pit, etc.
  Cf. yes, spit, etc.

ESPUR

h: Hesper.
v: vesper.
  Plus yes, purr *or* per, etc.

ESTÄL

  Plus rest, Al, etc.
  Cf. rest all *or* awl, etc.

ESTÄN

  Plus rest an *or* Ann, etc.

ESTÄNT

  Plus rest, aunt *or* ant, etc.

ESTĀT

t: intestate, testate.
  Plus rest ate *or* eight, etc.
  Plus dress, Tate, etc.
  Cf. less, state, etc.

ESTĒ

ch: chesty.
kr: cresty.
r: resty.
t: testy.
y: yesty*.
　Plus bless tea, etc.
　Plus dressed, he, etc.
　Cf. adeste.

ĒSTĒ

b: beastie, bheesty.
y: yeasty.
　Plus peace, tea, etc.
　Plus feast, he, etc.

ESTED

v: vested.

ESTĒJ

pr: prestige.

ESTEST

b: bestest*.
br: breastest*.
f: infestest*, manifestest*.
j: digestest*, jestest*, suggestest*.
kr: crestest*.
kw: questest*, requestest*.
l: molestest*.
n: nestest*.
r: arrestest*, intterestest*, restest*, wrestest*.
t: attentest*, contestest*, detestest*, protestest*, testest*.
v: divestest*, investest*.
　Plus dress test, etc.

ESTETH

b: besteth*.
br: breaseteth*.
f: infeseteth*, manisfesteth*.
j: digesteth*, jesteth*, suggesteth*.
kr: cresteth*.
kw: questeth*, requesteth*.
l: molesteth*.
n: nesteth*.
r: arresteth*, interesteth*, resteth*, wresteth*.
t: attesteth*, contesteth*, detesteth*, protesteth*, testeth*.
v: divesteth*, investeth*.

ESTĒZ

Vowel: Estes.
　Cf. test is, etc.

ESTFOOL

bl: blestful.
j: jestful.
r: resful, unrestful.
　Plus chest full, etc.

ESTIJ

v: vestige.

ESTIK

b: asbestic.
gr: agrestic.
h: alkahestic.
j: gestic, majestic.
kr: ctachrestic.
l: telestic, telestich.
m: domestic.
n: anamestic.
p: anapestic.
　Plus success tick, etc.
　Cf. bless stick, etc.

ĒSTĪL

fr: freestyle.

ESTIN

b: abestine.

d: clandestine, destine, Destinn, predestine.

s: sestine.

t: intestine.

Plus dressed in *or* inn, etc

Plus bless tin, etc.

ESTIND

d: destined, predestined, undestined.

Plus cress tinned, etc.

ĒSTING

Vowel: easting.

f: feasting.

pr: unpriesting.

y: yeasting.

ESTING

b: besting.

br: breasting.

f: infesting, manifesting.

j: congesting, digesting, ingesting, jesting, suggesting.

kr: cresting.

kw: questing, requesting.

l: molesting.

n: nesting.

r: arresting, disinterestin, interesting, resting, uninteresting, unresting, wresting.

t: attesting, contesting, detesting, protesting, testing, **v:** divesting, investing, reinvesting, vesting.

v: divesting, investing, reinvesting, vesting.

w: westing.

ESTIV

f: festive, infestive.

j: congestive, digestive, suggestive.

p: tempestive.

r: restive.

t: attestive.

ĒSTLĒ

b: beastly.

pr: priestly, unpriestly.

Plus east lea *or* Lee, etc.

ESTLING

n: nestling.

r: wrestling.

w: westling.

ESTLƏS

br: breastless.

g: guestless.

j: jestless.

kr: crestless.

kw: questless.

r: restless.

Plus dressed less, etc.

ESTMƏNT

r: arrestment.

v: divestment, investment, vestment.

Plus chest meant, etc.

ESTŌ

f: manifesto.

pr: presto.

Plus dress toe, etc.

Plus best owe *or* O, etc.

ĒSTŌN

fr: freestone.

k: keystone.

Plus see stone, etc.
Plus case tone, etc.

ESTRĀT

kw: sequestrate.
n: fenestrate.
    Plus best rate, etc.
    Plus success trait, etc.

ESTRIK

k(c): orchestric.
l: palaestric.
    Plus dress trick, etc.
    Plus blessed rick, etc.

ESTRIN

p: rupestrine.

ESTRƏL

k(c): kestrel, orchestral.
m: trimestral.
n: fenestral.
p: campestral.
s: ancestral.
    Plus dress trull, etc.

EST   R

j: gesture.
pr: purpresture.
v: divesture, investure, revesture, vesture.
    Plus dressed your *or* you're, etc.

ESTUR

Vowel: ester, Esther.
b: bester, Bestor.
br: breaster, double-breaster, single-breaster.
ch: Chester.

f: fester, infester.
h: Hester.
j: digester, jester, suggester.
kw: quster, requester, sequester.
l: Leicester, Lester, molester.
m: mid-semester, semester, trimester.
n: Dnester, nestor.
p: pester, Lester de Pester.
pr: prester*.
r: arrester, rester, wrester.
t: attester, contester, protester, tester.
v: divester, investor, Sylvester, vester.
w: norwester, souwester.
y: yester*.
    Plus blessed her, etc.
    Plus Bess stir, etc.

ĒSTUR

Vowel: downeaster, Easter, northeaster, southeaster.
f: feaster.
n: Dniester.
    Plus feast her *or* err, etc.
    Plus she stir, etc.

ESTURD

kw: sequestered, unsequesterd.
    Plus estur+ed.

ESTURN

h: hestern*.
w: northwestern, southwestern, western.
y: yestern*.
    Plus mess turn *or* tern, etc.
    Plus blessed urn, earn *or* erne, etc.

ĒSTURN

Vowel: eastern.

Plus pieced urn, earn *or* erne, etc.

Plus cease, tern *or* turn, etc.

Plus see stern, etc.

ESTUS

b: asbestos, asbestus.
s: cestus.

Plus infest us, etc.

ESTWURD

w: westward.

Plus best ward, etc.

ĒSTWURD

Vowel: eastward.

Plus policed ward, etc.

ESTƏ

Vowel: siesta.
d: podesta.
v: Vesta, Zend Avesta.

Plus detest a, etc.

ESTƏD

b: bested.
br: breasted, chicken-breasted, double-breasted, marble-breasted, pigeon-breasted, single-breasted, unbreasted.
ch: chested.
f: infested, manifested, ininfested.
j: congested, digested, indigested, ingested, jested, predigested, rediegested, suggested, undigested.
kr: castle-crested, crested, foam-crested, uncrested.

kw: quested, requested.
l: molested, unmolested.
n: nested.
r: arrested, disinterested, interested, rested, unrested, wrested.
t: attentest, conested, detested, protested, tested.
v: divested, invested, sable-vested, vested.

Plus bless Ted, etc.

Plus rest, Ed, etc.

ESTƏL

f: festal.
v: vestal.

ESTƏN

b: Beston, sebeston.
h: Heston.
v: Avestan.
w: Weston.

Plus best on *or* an, etc.

Plus bless ton *or* tun, etc.

ESTƏNT

j: decongestant, gestant.
t: contestant.

ESUR

Vowel: acquieser.
bl: blesser.
dr: addresser, dresser, redresser, undresser.
f: confessor, professor.
g: guesser.
gr: aggressor, digressor, progressor, transgressor.
l: lesser.
m: messer.
pr: compressor, depressor, impressor, oppressor, presser, represser, suppressor.

r: caresser.

s: antecessor, assessor, cesser, excesser, intercessor, predecessor, successor.

tr: distresser.

z: possessor.

Plus possess her *or* err, etc.

Plus yes, sir, etc.

ĒSƱR

fl: fleecer.

gr: greaser.

kr: creaser, decreaser, increaser.

l: leaser, releaser.

p: piecer.

Plus niece, her *or* err, etc.

Plus see, sir, etc.

ĒSUS

kr: Croesus.

r: Rhesus.

Plus fleece us, etc.

ESƏ

l: Walesa

m: mesa.

t: contessa.

ĒSƏ

l: Elisa, Felica,.

r: Theresa.

ESƏL, ĒSƏL, ISƏL

d: Diesel.

s: Cecil.

Plus see still, peace'll etc.

ESƏN

l: lessen, lesson.

Plus dress on *or* an, etc.

ĒSƏN

gl: Gleason.

l: Leisen.

Plus see, son *or* sun, etc.

ESƏNS

Vowel: acquiescence, essence, quiescence.

b: contabescence, erubescence, exacerbescence*, subescence, rubescence.

d: candescence, frondescence, incandescence, iridescence, plapidescence*, recrudescnece, viridescence.

j: turgescence.

k(c): glaucescence.

kr: accresscence, concrescence, excrescence, supercrescence.

kw: deliquescence.

l: adolescence, calescence, coalescence, convalescence, emolescence, hyalescence, incalescence, incoalescence, obsolescence, opalescence, revalescence, virilescence.

m: detumescence, fremescence, intumescence, spumescence, tumescence.

n: evanescence, juvenescence, rejuvenescence, senescence.

p: torpescence.

r: arborescence, calorescence, efflorescence, florescence, fluorescence, inflorescence, phosphorescence, reflorescence, revirescence.

t: delitescence, fructescence, frutescence, lactescence, latescence, quintessence.

tr: petrescence, putrescence, vitrescence.

v: defervescence, effervescence, ineffervescence.

Cf. less sense, etc.

ĒSƏNS

d: indecence.

ESƏNT

Vowel: acquiesent, quiescent.

b: albescent, erubescent, herbescent, pubescent, rubescent.

d: incandescnt, iridescent, lapidescent, recrudescent, viridescent.

f: rufescent.

gr: nigrescent.

gw: languescent.

j: jessant, turgescent, sugescent.

k(c): glaucessent.

kr: accresscent, crescent, decrescent, excrescent, increscent, supercrescent.

kw: deliquescent, liquescent.

l: aolescent, alkalescent, coalescent, convalescent, incalescent, obsolescent, opalescent, revalescent, spinulescent, violescent.

m: detumescent, fremescent, spumescent, tumescent.

n: evanescent, gangrenescent, ignescent, juvenescent, rejuvenescent, senescent, spinescent.

p: torpescent.

pr: depressant.

r: arobrescent, efflorescent, florescent, fluorescent, maturescent, phosphorescent, virescent.

s: cessant, incessant, marcescent.

t: delitescent, fructescent, frutescent, lactescent, latescent, lutescent, suffrutescent.

tr: petrescent, putrescent, vitrescent.

v: effervescent, fervescent, flavescent, ineffervescent.

Cf. dress sent, etc.

ĒSƏNT

d: decent, indecent.

r: recent.

ESƏZ

Vowel: acquiesces.

bl: blesses.

dr: addresses, dresses, redresses, undresses.

f: confesses, professes.

g: guesses.

gr: digresses, progresses, regresses.

j: jesses.

kr: cresses, water-cresses.

l: coalesces, convalesces.

m: messes.

n: finesses.

pr: compresses, depesses, expresses, impresses, oppresses, presses, represses, suppresses.

r: caresses.

s: assesses, excesses, obsesses, recesses, S-O-S's, successes.

str: stresses.

tr: distresses, tresses.

v: effervesces.

z: dispossesses, possesses, repossesses.

Plus words ending in es+es.

Plus Yes's, tress's, etc.

Cf. yes is, etc.

ĒSƏZ

fl: fleeces.

gr: greases.

kr: creases, decreases, increses, krises.

l: leases, pelisses, releases, valises.

n: nieces.

p: battle-pieces, mantlepieces, peaches, pieces.

pr: caprices.
s: ceases.
   Plus police's, etc.
   Cf. peace is, etc.

ĒTAS

v: gravitas.

ETDOUN

l: let down.

ETĒ

Vowel: Ettie.
b: Bettie, betty.
br: libretti.
ch: concetti.
d: Vendetti.
f: confetti, Irish confetti.
fr: fretty.
g: spaghetti.
gr: Alligretti.
h: Hettie, Hetty.
j: jetty.
l: Lettie, Letty.
n: Nettie, netty.
p: petit, petty, Repetti.
pr: "pretty."
s: spermaceti.
sw: sweaty.
z: Donizetti, Rossetti, Vanizetti.
   Plus sweat, he, etc.

ĒTĒ

m: meaty.
p: peaty.
s: spermaceti.
sl: sleety.
sw: sweetie, sweety.
tr: entreaty, treaty.
   Plus street, he, etc.

ETEST

b: abettest*, bettest*.
fr: frettest*.
g: begettest*, forgettest*, gettest*.
gr: regrettest*.
hw: whettest*.
k: coquesttest*.
l: lettest*.
n: bayonesttest*, benettest*, nettest*.
p: pettest*.
s: back-settest*, besettest*, oversettest*, settest*, upsettest*.
w: wettest.
   Cf. wet test, etc.

ĒTEST

Vowel: eatest*, overeatest*.
b: beatest*.
bl: bleatest*.
ch: cheatest*.
f: defeatest*, effetest.
fl: fleetest.
gr: greetest*.
h: heatest*, overheatest*.
kr: discreetest.
l: deletest*, elitest.
m: meetest*.
n: neatest.
p: competest*, repeatest*.
pl: completest, repletest*, incompletest, pleatest*, repletest.
s: receiptest*, seatest*, unseatest*.
sw: sweetest.
tr: entreatest*, ill-treatest*, maltreatest*, retreatest8, treatest*.
   Cf. etist, e.g., defeatist, etc.

ETETH

b: abetteth*, betteth*.
fr: fretteth*.

g: begetteth*, forgetteth*, getteth*.
gr: regretteth*.
hw: whetteth*.
k(c): coquetteth*.
l: letteth*.
n: bayonetteth*, benetteth*, netteth*.
p: petteth*.
s: setteth*, besetteth*.
w: bewetteth*, wetteth*.

ĒTETH

Vowel: eateth*, overeateth*.
b: beateth.
bl: bleateth*.
ch: cheateth*.
f: defeateth*.
gr: greeteth*.
h: heather*, overheateth*.
l: deleteth*.
m: meeteth*, meteth*.
p: competeth*, repeateth*.
pl: completeth*, depleteth*, pleateth*.
s: receipteth*, seateth*, unseateth*.
tr: entreateth*, maltreateth*, retreateth*, treateth*.

ĒTĒZ

sw: sweeties.
tr: entreaties, treaties, treatise.

ETFOOL

fr: fretful.
g: forgetful.
gr: regretful.
Plus net full, etc.

ĒTFOOL

s: deceitful, seatful.
Plus treat full, etc.

ETHĒ

d: deathy.
Plus breath, he, etc.

ĒTHĒ

h: heathy.
l: Lethe, lethy.
Plus underneath, he, etc.

ETHIKS

Vowel: ethics, situation ethics.

ĒTHING

br: breathing, inbreathing, incense-breathing, terror-breathing.
kw: bequeathing.
r: enwreathing, interwreathing, inwreathing, wreathing.
s: seething.
sh: ensheathing, sheathing, unsheathing.
t: teething.

ETHLĒ

d: deathly.
Plus breath, Lee, etc.

ETHLƏS

br: breathless.
d: deathless.
Plus shibboleth less, etc.

ĒTHLƏS

r: wreathless.
sh: sheathless.
Plus beneath less, etc.

ĒTHMƏNT

kw: bequeathment.
r: wreathment.
sh: ensheathment.
 Plus seethe meant, etc.

ETHNIK

Vowel: ethnic.
l: holethnic.
 Plus death nick *or* Nick, etc.

ETHRƏN

br: brethren.

ETHWISH

w: death wish.

ETHUR

b: blether.
f: feather, pin-feather, tail-feather, unfeather, white feather.
g: altogether, together.
h: heather.
hw: whether.
l: hell-for-lether, lether, patent leather, whitleather.
n: nether.
t: tether, untether.
w: aweather, bellwether, weather, wether.

ETHURD

f: unfeathered.
w: weathered.
 Plus ethur+ed.

ĒTHUR

Vowel: either, ether.
br: breather, lung-breather, mud-breather, water-breather.

kw: bequeather.
n: neither.
r: enwreather, wreather.
s: seether.
sh: sheather.
 Plus beneath her, etc.
 Plus seethe her *or* err, etc.

ETHƏD

m: method.
 Plus death odd, etc.

ETHƏL

Vowel: ethal, ethyl, Ethel.
b: Bethel.
d: diethyl.
m: Methyl.
 Cf. death 'll, etc., ethil.
 Plus breath 'll, death ill, etc.

ĒTHƏL

Vowel: ethal.
kw: bequeathal.
l: lethal.
 Plus underneath, Al, etc.
 Plus seethe, Al, etc.

ĒTHƏN

Vowel: Ethan.
b: Elizabethan.
h: heathen.
r: wreathen.
 Plus beneath, Ann *or* an, etc.
 Cf. seethe hen, etc.
 Cf. seethe an *or* Ann, etc.

ETID, ĒTID

f: fetid, fetid.
 Cf. eted, eted.

ĒTIJ

Vowel: eatage.

ch: cheatage, escheatage.

kl: cleatage.

m: metage.

Cf. sweet age, etc.

ETIK

Vowel: abietic, aloetic, dianoetic, galactopoietic, mythopoetic, noetic, onomatopoetic, poetic.

b: alphabetic, diabetic, quodlibetic, tabetic.

d: geodetic.

f: Japhetic, prophetic.

j: apologetic, energetic, Enna Jettick, exegetic, Gangetic, inergetic, strategetic.

k(c): catechetic.

kr: syncretic.

l: amuletic, athletic, auletic, collectic, homiletic, Lettic, ochletic.

m: arithmetic, Baphometic, cometic, cosmetic, emetic, hermetic, logarithmetic, metic, mimetic.

n: abiogenetic, agamogenetic, biogenetic, biomagnetic, diamagnetic, electromagnetic, epigenetic, eugenetic, frenetic, genetic, histogenetic, homogenetic, kinetic, magnetic, ontogenetic, palinogenetic, pangenetic, parthenogenic, pathogenetic, phonetic, phrenetic, phylogenetic, polygenetic, splenetic, threnetic.

r: alexipyretic, anchoretic, diaphoretic, diuretic, emporetic, Masoretic, paretic, plethoretic, theoretic.

s: ascetic, copacetic, docetic, quesrcetic.

t: dietetic, erotetic, peripatetic, zetetic.

th: aesthetic, allopathetic, anesthetic, antipathetic, antithetic, apathetic, bathetic, epithetic, hypotehtic, idiopathetic, nomothetic, parathetic, parenthetic, pathetic, polysynthetic, sympathetic, synthetic, theopathetic.

v: Helvetic.

Cf. yet tick, etc.

ĒTIK

kr: Cretic.

r: Rhaetic.

s: acetic, cetic.

Plus pea tick, etc.

ETIKS

Vowel: poetics.

j: apologetics, exegetics.

l: athletics, homiletics.

t: dietetics.

th: aesthetics.

Plus etik+s.

ETING

Vowel: minuetting.

b: abetting, betting.

bl: bletting.

fr: fretting.

g: begetting, forgetting, getting.

gr: regretting.

hw: whetting.

j: jetting.

k(c): coquetting, croquetting.

l: letting.

n: benetting, mosquiot netting, netting.

p: petting.

r: retting.

s: back setting, besetting, intersetting, oversetting, setting, somersetting, undersetting, upsetting.

sw: sweating.

v: brevetting, curvetting.

w: wetting.

z: gazetting.

ĒTING

Vowel: beef-eating, clay-eating, crow-eating, dirt-eating, dung-eating, eating, fire-eating, flesh-eating, frog-eating, humble pie-eating, grass-eating, hay-eating, lotus-eating, man-eating, overeating, smoke-eating, toad-eating, undereating.

b: beating, browbeating, drum-beating, jungle-beating, rug-beating, slave-beating, swift-beating, wife-beating.

bl: bleating.

ch: cheating, escheating.

f: defeating.

fl: fleeting.

gr: greeting.

h: heating, overheating, underheating.

k: Keating.

kl: cleating.

kr: concreting, secreting.

m: meeting, meting.

n: ncating.

p: competing, repeating.

pl: completing, pleating.

s: receipting, seating, unseating.

sh: sheeting.

sl: sleeting.

sw: bitter-sweeting, sweeting.

tr: entreating, ill-treating, maltreating, retreating, treating.

ETIS

l: Lettice, lettuce.

ĒTIS

th: Thetis.

Cf. etus.

ETISH

f: fetish.

k(c): coquettish, croquettish.

l: Lettish.

p: pettish.

w: wettish.

Cf. pet, tish!, etc.

ĒTIST

f: defeatist.

kr: accretist.

s: conceitist, county-seatist, mercy-seatist, self-conceitist, self-deceitist.

sw: honey-sweetiest.

tr: Dutch-treatist.

Cf. etest.

ĒTIT

b: beatit.

Pus etit.

ĒTIV

kr: accretive, concretive, decretive, discretive, secretive.

pl: completive, depletive, repletive.

ĒTIZ

Plus Crete is, etc.

Plus see 'tis*, etc.

ĒTLĒ

f: featly*.
fl: fleetly.
kr: concretely, discreetly, indiscreetly.
l: obsoletely.
m: meetly, unmeetly.
n: neatly.
pl: completely, imcomletely.
sw: sweetly.
　　Plus feet, Lea *or* lea, etc.

ETLING

n: nettling.
s: settling, unsettling.

ETLƏS

d: debltess.
thr: threatless.
　　Plus wet less, etc.

ETMƏNT

b: abetment.
d: indebtment.
s: besetment.
v: brevetment, revetment.
　　Plus pet meant, etc.

ĒTMƏNT

tr: entreatment, ill-treatment, maltreatment, mistreatment, treatment.
　　Plus sweet meant, etc.

ĒTOŌN

h: heat moon.

ETNƏS

s: setness.
w: wetness.

ĒTNƏS

f: effeteness, featness.
fl: fleetness.
kr: concreteness, discreetness.
l: obsoleteness.
m: meetness.
n: neatness.
pl: completeness, incompleteness, repleteness.
sw: sweetness.

ETŌ

br: libretto.
ch: concetto.
g: ghetto.
gr: allegretto.
k(c): zucchetto.
l: stilleto.
m: palmetto.
n: sonnetto.
p: rispetto.
r: amaretto, amoretto, lazaretto.
s: falsetto.
z: terzetto.
　　Plus wet toe, etc.

ĒTŌ

l: Leto.
k: mosquito.
n: Benito, bonito, San Benito.
t: Tito.
v: veto.
　　Plus see toe, etc.
　　Plus sweet owe *or* O, etc.

ĒTÄKS

d: detox.

ĒTŌS

s: Cerritos.

ĒTRÄK

sh: sheet rock.
  Plus fleet rock, etc.

ĒTRĒ

p: Petrie.
  Plus bee tree, etc.

ETRIK

m: actinometric, alkalimetric, anemometric, anisometric, audiometric, barometric, bathymetric, calorimetric, clinometric, chlorometric, chronometric, diametric, dimetric, electrometric, endosmometric, eudiometric, gasometric, geometric, goniometric, geometric, goniometric, gravimetric, hexametric, hydrometric, hygrometric, hypsometric, isobarometric, isometric, logometric, magnetometric, metric, micrometric, monometric, ozonometric, pedometric, photometric, stereometric, symmetric, tasimetric, thermometric, trigonometric, trimetric, volumetric.
st: obstetric.
  Plus wet rick, etc.
  Cf. wet trick, etc.

ETRIKS

m: cliometrics.

ETRŌ

r: retro.

ETRᴜM

ch: chetrum.

ETRUS, ĒTRUS

kw: triquetrous.
p: petrous, saltpetrous.

ETRƏL, ĒTRƏL

m: diametral.
p: petrel, stormy petral.

ETSKAN

p: PET scan.

ĒTUM

b: zibetum.
fr: fretum.
n: pinetum.
r: arboretum.
  Plus meet 'em, etc.

ETᴜR

Vowel: Ettor.
b: abbetter, better.
bl: bletter.
d: debtor.
f: enfetter, fetter.
fr: fretter.
g: begetter, forgetter, getter, go-getter.
gr: regreatter.
hw: whetter.
j: jetter.
l: dead letter, letter, red letter.
n: netter.
p: petter.
r: carburetor.
s: besetter, image setter, Irish setter, setter, somersetter, typersetter.
sw: sweater.

v: curvetter.

w: wetter.

Plus get her *or* err, etc.

ĒTUR

Vowel: beef-eater, cake-eater, clay-eater, crow-eater, dirt-eater, dung-eater, eater, fireeater, flesh-eater, frog-eater, grass-eater, hay-eater, humble pie-eater, lotus-eater, man-eater, overeater, smoke-eater, toadeater, undereater.

b: beater, browbeater, drum-beater, goldbeater, jungle-beater, rug-beater, slave-beate, wife-beater.

bl: bleater.

ch: cheater, escheater.

f: defeater.

gr: greeter.

h: heater, overheater, superheater, water heater.

j: Jeeter.

kr: secreter.

l: decaliter, hectoliter, liter.

m: centimeter, Demeter, gas meter, kilometer, meeter, meter, metre, water meter.

n: neater.

p: competer, Peter, repeater, St. Peter, saltpeter.

pl: completer, depleter, repleter.

pr: praetor.

s: one-seater, receipter, seater, three-seater, two-seater, unseater.

sk: skeeter.

sw: sweeter.

t: teeter.

tr: entreater, ill-treater, maltreater, mistreater retreater, treater.

Plus greet her, err *or* Ur, etc.

ETURD

f: fettered, unfettered.

l: lettered, unlettered.

Plus etur+ed.

ĒTURZ

l: woman of letters.

p: Peters, St. Peters.

Plus etur+s.

Plus cheater 's, etc.

ĒTUS

Vowel: quietus.

f: fetus.

s: acetous, Cetus.

Plus greet us, etc.

Plus et is.

ETWĀ

j: Jetway

ETWURK

fr: fretwork.

n: network.

Plus get work, etc.

ETƏ

Vowel: arietta, comedietta, Etta, Henrietta.

ch: concetta.

d: codetta, vendetta.

gr: Greta.

l: burletta.

m: animetta, lametta.

n: minetta, Netta.

r: biretta, operetta, Retta.

s: CETA.

y: Yetta.

z: mosetta, Rosetta.

Plus met a, etc.

ĒTƏ

Vowel: eta.
b: beta(+).
ch: cheetah.
fl: Fleta.
k: Akita, Chiquita, Marquita.
l: Leta.
m: Meta.
n: Anita, Juanita, Nita.
r: Rita.
s: Carmencita.
t: Tita.
th: theta(+).
z: zeta(+), Zita.
    Plus beat a, etc.

ETƏD

Vowel: pirouetted.
b: abetted, betted.
bl: bletted.
d: indebted.
fr: fretted, interfretted, unfretted.
gr: regretted.
kw: whetted.
j: jetted.
k: coquetted.
n: bayonetted, neetted, coronetted, cornetted, netted, unnetted.
p: petted, unpetted.
sw: sweated.
v: brevetted, curvetted.
w: wetted.
z: gazetted.
    Plus met, Ed, etc.
    Cf. fetid.

ĒTƏD

bl: bleated.
ch: cheated, escheated.
f: defeated, undefeated.

gl: gleeted.
gr: greeted.
h: heated, reheated, overheated, wine-heated.
kl: cleated.
kr: accredted, excreted, secreted.
l: deleted.
m: meted, unmeeted, unmeted.
n: neated.
p: competed, repeated.
pl: completed, depleted, uncomleted.
s: conceited, receipted, seated, self-conceited, unseated.
sh: sheeted.
sl: sleeted.
tr: entreated, evil-treated, ill-treated, maltreated, retreated, treated.
    Plus heat, Ed, etc.
    Plus see, Ted, etc.
    Cf. fetid.

ETƏL

b: abettal.
ch: Chettle.
f: fettle.
gr: Gretel.
k: Kettle.
m: Babbitt metal, death metal, heavy metal, metal, mettle, Monel metal, type metal, white metal.
n: nettle, stinging nettle.
p: petal, Popocatapetl.
s: resettle, settle.
    Plus pet'll, etc.

ĒTƏL

b: beetle, betel, elm leaf beetle.
f: fetal.
kr: decretal.
    Plus meet Al, etc.

ETƏLD

m: high-mettled.
n: nettled.
p: petalled.
s: settled, unsettled.
　　Plus etd+d, *or* ed.

ETƏN

br: Breton, Bretton.
fr: fretten*.
thr: threaten.
　　Plus sweat on *or* an, etc.
　　Cf. eten
　　Cf. fret hen, etc.

ĒTƏN

Vowel: eaten, Eaton, Eton, moth-eaten, overeaten, uneaten, worm-eaten.
b: beaten, Beaton, storm-beaten, tempest-beaten, unbeaten, weatherbeaten.
hw: wheaten.
j: Zyzzogeton.
k(c): chiton, Keaton, Keyton.
kr: Cretan, cretin.
s: Seaton, Seyton.
sw: sweeten.
　　Plus see ten, etc.
　　Plus see ton *or* tun, etc.
　　Plus street on, *or* an, etc.
　　Cf. et, etc.
　　Cf. sweet hen, etc.

ĒUM

b: amoebaeum.
d: TeDeum.
l: mausoleum.
n: athenaeum, peritoneum, prytaneum.
s: solosseum, lyceum.
t: bronteum.

z: museum.
　　Plus fee 'em, etc.

ĒUR

f: feer.
fl: fleer.
fr: freer.
gr: agreer.
s: overseer, seer, sight-seer.
　　Plus free her *or* err, etc.

ĒUS

b: plumbeous, scarabaeus.
f: corypheus.
p: onomatopoeous.
r: choreus.
t: gluteus.
　　Plus see us, etc.

EVĒ

b: bevy.
ch: chevy.
h: heart-heavy, heavy, topheavy.
kl: cleavy.
l: levee, levy.
n: nevvy.
sh: Chevvy.

ĒVĒ

Vowel: Evie.
ch: Cheevy.
l: Levy, McLevy.
　　Plus weave, he, etc.
　　Plus see V, etc.

ĒVEST

ch: achievest*.
gr: grievest*.
h: heavest*, upheavest*.
kl: cleavest*.
l: believest*, disbelievest*,

leavest*, relievest*.
pr: repreivest*.
r: bereavest*.
s: conceivest*, deceivest*, perceivest*, receivest*.
th: theivest*.
tr: retrievest*.
w: inweavest*, weavest*.

ĒVETH

ch: achieveth*.
gr: grieveth*.
h: heaveth*, upheaveth*.
kl: cleaveth*.
l: believeth, disbelieveth*, leaveth*, relieveth*.
pr: reprieveth.
r: bereaveth*.
s: conceiveth*, deceiveth*, perceiveth*, receiveth*.
th: theiveth*.
tr: retrieveth*.
w: inweaveth*, weaveth*.

ĒVĪ

l: Levi.
　　Plus grieve eye, etc.
　　Plus grieve, I, etc.

ĒVIJ

kl: cleavage.
l: leavage.
　　Cf. grieve, age, etc.

EVIN

l: levin*.
pl: replevin.
　　Cf. eva, even.

ĒVING

ch: achieving.
gr: aggrieving, grieving.

h: heaving, upheaving.
kl: cleaving.
l: believing, disbelieving, leaving, relieving, unbelieving.
pr: repreiving.
r: bereaving.
s: conceiving, deceiving, misconceiving, perceiving, preconceiving, receiving, undeceiving.
sh: sheaving.
st: steeving.
th: theiving.
tr: retrieving.
w: interweaving, inweaving, unweaving, weaving.

ĒVINGZ

l: leavings.
　　Plus eving+s.

ĒVISH

p: peevish.
th: thievish.

ĒVLAND

kl(cl): Cleveland.

ĒVLƏS

l: leaveless.
sh: sheaveless.
sl: sleeveless.
　　Plus grieve less *or* Les, etc.

ĒVMƏNT

ch: achievement.
r: bereavement.
tr: retrievement.
　　Plus sleeve meant, etc.

ĒVNING

Vowel: evening.

ĒVŌ

r: Antananarivo.

ĒV

pr: preview.
Plus sea view, etc.
Plus deceive you, etc.

EVRĒ

Vowel: every.

EVUR

Vowel: ever, forever, however, howsoever, whatever, whatsoever, whencesoever, whenever, whensoever, whereever, wheresoever, whichever, whichsoever, whithersoever, whoever, whosoever, whosesoever, whosoever.
d: endeavor.
kl: clever.
l: cantilever, lever.
n: never.
s: assever, dissever, sever, unsever.

ĒVUR

Vowel: naiver.
b: beaver.
br: brever*.
ch: achiever.
d: Danny Deever.
f: cabin fever, enfever, ever, hay fever, jungle fever, sea fever, spring fever, yellow fever.
gr: aggriever, griever.
h: ballast heaver, coal heaver, Guadalquiver, heaver, upheaver.
k: keever.

kl: cleaver.
l: believer, cantilever, disbeliever, interleaver, leaver, lever, liever, livre, make-believer, reliever, unbeliever.
pr: repriever.
r: bereaver, reaver, reever, reiver.
s: conceiver, deceiver, misconceiver, perceiver, preconceiver, receiver, undeciver, wide receiver.
sh: sheaver.
tr: retriever.
w: interweaver, weaver, weever.
Plus grieve her, err *or* Ur, etc.

EVURD

s: severed, unsevered.
Plus evur+ed.

ĒVUS

gr: grievous.
j: longevous.
m: primevous.
Plus leave us, etc.

ĒVƏ

Vowel: Eva.
d: diva, Kamadeva, Mahadeva.
k: Kivah.
n: Geneva.
v: viva.
Plus cleave a, etc.

EVL, EVƏL

b: bevel.
d: bedevil, devil.
gr: Greville.
k: kevel.
l: level, sea level, spirit level, water level.

n: Neville.
r: revel.
sh: dishevel.
    Plus Bev'll, etc.
    Plus Chev'll, etc.
    Plus evel.

ĒVƏL

Vowel: coeval, evil, king's evil, medieval.
h: upheaval.
j: longeval.
m: primeval.
shr: shrieval.
tr: retrieval.
w: weevil.
    Plus leave ill, etc.
    Plus sleeve'll, etc.
    Cf. eval.

EVƏLZ

d: blue-devils.
    Plus evil+s.

EVƏN

Vowel: Evan.
d: Devon.
h: heaven.
l: Chapter 11, eleven, leaven.
s: seven.
    Cf. even.

ĒVƏN

Vowel: even, goodeven*, Halloween, uneven, yestereven*.
r: unbereaven*.
st: Stephen, Steven.

EVƏND

l: leavened, unleavened.

ĒVƏNS

ch: achievance.
gr: grievance.
s: perceivance.
tr: retrievance.
    Plus believ aunts *or* ants, etc.
    Cf. Levant's.

EVƏNTH

l: eleventh.
s: seventh.

ĒVƏNZ

st: Stevens, St. Stevens.
    Plus even's, etc.

ĒWĀ

l: leeway.
s: seaway.
    Plus tree way, etc.

ĒWIT

p: peewit.
    Plus see wit, etc.

ĒWƱRD

l: leeward.
s: seaward.
    Plus Marie, ward, etc.

ĒYƏ

p: Cassiopeia, etc.
    See ea.

ĒYƏN

p: Tarpeian, etc.
    See ean.

EZDĀL

Vowel: Esdale.
   Plus says, Dale, etc.

ĒZDĀL

t: Teasdale.
   Plus freeze dale, etc.

ĒZĒ

Vowel: easy, free-and-easy, speakeasy, uneasy.
b: Zambezi.
br: breezy.
ch: cheesy.
fr: freezy.
gr: greasy.
hw: wheezy.
kw: queasy.
sl: sleazy.
sn: sneezy.
   Plus trees he, etc.

EZHƱR

l: leisure.
m: admeasure, measure, outmeasure.
pl: displeasure, pleasure.
tr: entreasure, treasure.
   Plus fez, you're *or* your, etc.

ĒZFRĀM

fr: freeze frame.

ĒZHƱR

l: leisure.
s: seizure.
   Plus squeeze your *or* you're, etc.

EZHƱRD

l: leisured, unleisured.
m: immeasured, measured, unmeasured.
pl: pleasured, unpleasured.
tr: treasured, untreasured.
   Plus treasured'd, etc.

ĒZHƱRD

l: leisured, unleisured.
   Plus seize 'd, etc.

ĒZHƏ

d: Zimabwe Rhodesia
n: magnesia.
   Cf. ezia.

ĒZHƏN

h: adhesion, cohesion, inadhesion, inhesion.
l: lesion, Milesian, Silesian.
p: trapezian.
   Cf. ezian.

ĒZIKS

sk: skeeziks.

ĒZING

Vowel: easing.
br: breezing.
fr: freezing.
gr: greasing.
hw: wheezing.
p: appeasing.
pl: displeasing, pleasing, self-pleasing, unpleasing.
s: foreseizing, seizing.
skw: squeezing.
sn: sneezing.
t: teasing.

ĒZIT

ch: cheese it.
   Plus breeze it, etc.

EZL

b: embezzle.
   Plus fez'll, etc.
   Cf. ezel.

EZLUR

b: embezzler.

ĒZMŌ

r: verismo.

ĒZMƏNT

Vowel: easement.
p: appeasement.
   Plus trees meant, etc.

ĒZŌ

r: chorizo.

EZRƏ

Vowel: Ezra.
   Plus fez, Ra, etc.

ĒZUR

Vowel: easer.
b: beezer.
fr: deep freezer, freezer, friezer.
g: geezer.
gr: greaser.
hw: wheezer.
l: leaser.
n: Ebenezer.
p: appeaser.
pl: pleaser.

s: Caesar.
skw: squeezer.
sn: sneezer.
t: teaser.
tw: tweezer.
   Plus squeeze her *or* err, etc.

EZURT

d: desert.
   Cf. says hurt, etc.

ĒZURZ

tw: tweezers.
   Plus ezur+s.

ĒZUS

j: Jesus.
   Plus tease us, etc.

ĒZƏ

Vowel: Louisa.
l: Liza.
p: Pisa.
   Plus sees a, etc.

EZƏL

b: bezel.
   Cf. ez'l.

ĒZƏL

Vowel: easel.
t: teasel, Teazle.
w: weasel.
   Plus these 'll, etc.

ĒZƏLZ

Vowel: easels.
m: measles.
   Plus ezel+s.

ĒZƏN

kw: Quezon.

r: reason, unreason.

s: season, seizin, unseason.

tr: treason.

Plus trees on *or* an, etc.

Cf. ezin, ezon.

EZƏNS

pl: pleasance.

pr: omnipresence, presence.

Plus fez, aunts *or* ants.

Cf. ezant+s, ezent+s.

ĒZƏNS

Vowel: easance.

f: defeasance, malfeasance, misfeasance.

Plus please aunts *or* ants, etc.

EZƏNT

f: pheasant.

p: peasant.

pl: displeasant, pleasant, unpleasant.

pr: omnipresent, present.

Plus says, aunt *or* ant, etc.

ĒƏ

b: dahabeah, obeah.

ch: Lucia, Kampuchea.

d: idea, Medea.

f: ratafia.

j: Hygeia.

k: Latakia.

m: Crimea.

n: dyspnea.

p: Cassiopea, meloepia.

pr: Cypraea.

r: Ave Maria, cavalleria, diarrhea, gonorrhea, logorrhea, Maria, rhea, ria, spiraea.

s: panacea.

t: yautia.

th: Althaea, Dorothea.

tr: Astrea.

x: dyslexia.

y: onomatopoeia, pathopoeia, pharmacopoeia.

z: Hosea, Zea.

Plus see a, etc.

ĒƏL

b: Belial.

d: beau ideal, ideal, unideal.

j: Arctogaeal, laryngeal, pharyngeal.

n: hymeneal.

r: empyreal, real, unreal.

Plus see, Al, etc.

ĒƏM

br: Librium.

ĒƏN

b: amoebean, Caribbean, Maccabean, Melibean, Niobean, plebeian, Sabaean.

bl: Hyblaean.

ch: Manichaean, Medicean.

d: Andean, antipodean, Archimedean, Assidean, Chaldean, Judean, Pandean, Vendean.

f: nymphean, Orphean, Sisyphean.

j: Aegean, amphigean, apogean, Argean, Augean, laryngean, Paleogaean, perigean, phalangean, pharyngean.

k(c): Achean, ditrochean, trochean.

l: Galilean, Mausolean, Zoilean.

m: Anomoean, Cadmean, Crimean, Nemean.

n: Adonean, Etnean, Hasmonaean, hymenean, Linnaean, Pyrenean.

p: cyclopean, European, Indo-European, paean, pampean, Parthenopean.

pr: Cypraean.

r: Berean, Cytheran, empyrean, epicurean, Pythagorean, terpsichorean.

s: Circean, colossean, Laodicean, lyncean, Medicean, Pharisean, Sadducean, Tennessean, theodicean.

t: adamantean, Atlantean, gigantean, protean.

th: lethean.

tr: astraean.

Plus see an *or* Ann, etc.

Ē∂S

k(c): Zaccheus.

n: Aeneas.

Cf. fee us, etc.

I

The accented vowel sounds included are listed under I in Single Rhymes.

ĪAD

d: dyad.
dr: dryad, hamadryad.
m: Jeremiad.
pl: Pleiad.
tr: triad.
　Plus why add *or* ad, etc.

ĪADZ

h: Hyads.
　Plus iad+s.

ĪAK

gw: guiac.
j: elegiac.
k: kayak.
z: phrenesiac.

ĪAM

Vowel: iamb.
pr: Priam.
s: Siam+.
　Plus I am, etc.
　Cf. I amb.

ĪAT

f: fiat.
m: Myatt.
　Plus try at, etc.
　Cf. iet.

ĪAZM

m: miasm.

ĪBAK

b: buyback.

IBDIS

r: Charybdis.

IBĒ

k: Kibbee.
l: libbey, Libby.
t: Tibbie.
　Plus bib, he, etc.

IBEST

f: fibbest*.
gl: glibbest.
j: jibbest*.
　Plus rib best, etc.

ĪBEST

b: imbibest*.
j: gibest.
skr(scr): ascribest*,
circumscribest*, describest*,
inscribest*, prescribest*,
proscribest*, subscribest*,
superscribest*, transcribest*.
　Plus buy best, etc.

IBETH

f: fibbeth*.
j: jibbeth*.
　Cf. rib, Beth, etc.

ĪBETH

b: imbibeth*.
j: gibeth*.
br: bribeth*.
skr(scr): ascribeth*,
circumscribeth*, describeth*,
inscribeth*, prescribeth*,
proscribeth*, subscribeth*,
superscribeth*, transcribeth*.
  Plus lie, Beth, etc.

IBING

f: fibbing.
j: jibbing.
r: ribbing.
skw: squibbing.

ĪBING

b: imbibing.
br: bribing.
j: gibing.
skr(scr): ascribing, circumscrib-
ing, describing, inscribing,
prescribing, proscribing,
subscribing, superscribing,
transcribing.
  Plus buy, Byng, etc.

IBL

b: ashkabibble.
d: dibble.
dr: dribble.
fr: fribble.
gr: gribble.
k: Kibble.
kr: cribble.
kw: quibble.
n: nibble.
skr(scr): scribble.
thr: thribble.
  Plus bib'll, etc.

ĪBL

b: Bible.
l: libel.
tr: tribal.
  Plus jibe'll, etc.
  Plus sly bull, etc.

IBLD

cr: cribbled.
r: ribald+.
th: Theobald.
  Plus bil+d.

IBLĒ

dr: dribbly.
gl: glibly.
kw: quibbly.
n: nibbly.
skr(scr): scribbly.
thr: thribbly.
tr: tribbly.
  Cf. rib, Lee *or* lea, etc.

IBLEST

d: dibblest*.
dr: dribblest*.
kw: quibblest*.
n: nibblest*.
skr(scr): scribblest*.
  Plus ibl+est*.
  Plus ribblest, etc.

IBLETH

d: dibbleth*.
dr: dribbleth*.
kw: quibbleth*.
n: nibbleth*.
skr(scr): scribbleth*.
  Plus ibl+eth*.

IBLIK

n: niblick.
  Plus rib lick, etc.

IBLING

d: dibbling.
dr: dribbling.
fr: fribbling.
k: kibbling.
kr: cribbling.
kw: quibbling.
n: nibbling.
skr(scr): scribbling.
str: Stribling.
tr: tribbling.

ĪBLŌ

b: by-blow.
fl: flyblow.
  Plus shy blow, etc.
  Plus tribe low *or* lo, etc.

IBLUR

d: dibbler.
dr: dribbler.
fr: fribbler.
k: kibbler.
kr: cribbler.
kw: quibbler.
n: nibbler.
skr(scr): scribbler, transcribbler.

IBLƏT

dr: driblet.
j: giblet.
tr: triblet.
  Plus fib let, etc.

ĪBÔL

Vowel: eyeball.
h: highball.

sk: skyball.
  Plus why bawl *or* ball, etc.
  Plus tribe all *or* awl, etc.

ĪBÔLD

p: piebald.
  Plus ibol+ed.
  Plus why bald, balled, *or* bawled, etc.

IB̄N

tr: tribune+.

IB̄T

tr: attribute, contribute, distribute, redistribute, retribute, tribute.
  Plus rib Ute, etc.

ĪBÔRN

h: highborn.
sk: sky-born.
  Plus why born, etc.

ĪBRĀT

l: equilibrate, librate.
v: vibrate.
  Plus tribe rate, etc.

ĪBROU

Vowel: eyebrow.
h: highbrow.
  Plus try brown, etc.
  Plus tribe row, etc.

ĪBRƏNT

v: vibrant.
  Plus tribe rant, etc.
  Plus why, Brant, etc.

IBSƏN

Vowel: Ibsen, Ibson.
d: Didson.
g: Gibson.
　　Plus rib, son *or* sun, etc.
　　Cf. ibson.

IBUR

b: bibber, wine bibber.
d: dibber.
f: fibber.
gl: glibber.
j: flibbergibber, gibber, jibber.
kr: cribber.
l: adlibber.
n: nibber.
skw: squibber.
　　Plus rib her *or* err, etc.

ĪBUR

b: imbiber.
br: briber.
f: fiber.
j: giber.
l: Leiber, liber.
skr(scr): ascriber, circumscriber, describer, inscriber, prescriber, proscriber, scriber, subscriber, transcriber.
t: Tiber.
　　Plus why burr, etc.
　　Plus tribe err, er, Ur, *or* her, etc.

ĪBƏ

p: copiba.
z: Ziba.
　　Plus describe a, etc.

IBƏLD

r: ribald+.
t: Theobald.

IBƏN

g: gibbon.
r: blue ribbon, red ribbon, ribbon, white ribbon.
　　Plus rib on *or* an, etc.

IBƏNZ

g: Fitzgibbons, Gibbons.
　　Plus ibon+s.

IBƏT

h: adhibit, cohibit, exhibit, inhibit, prohibit.
j: flibbertigibbet, gibbet.
t: Tibbett.
z: zibet.
　　Plus sib et, etc.
　　Cf. ibit.
　　Cf. glib bet, etc.

ICHĒ

Vowel: itchy.
b: bitchy.
f: fitchy.
p: pitchy.
r: Richie.
st: stitchy.
sw: switchy.
w: witchy.
　　Plus which he, etc.

ICHEST

h: hitchest*.
p: pitchest*.
r: enrichest*, richest*.
st: stitchest*.
sw: switchest*.
w: bewitchest*, witchest*.

ICHETH

h: hitcheth*.
p: pitcheth*.

r: enricheth*.
st: stitcheth*.
sw: switcheth*.
w: bewitcheth*, witcheth*.

ICHING

Vowel: itching.
d: ditching.
h: hitching.
m: miching.
p: pitching.
r: enriching.
st: stitching.
sw: switching.
tw: twitching.
w: bewitching, witching.

ICHLƏS

Vowel: itchless.
h: hitchless.
st: stitchless.
sw: switchless.
w: witchless.
    Plus pitch less, etc.

ICHMƏNT

r: enrichment.
w: bewitchment.
    Plus which meant, etc.

ICHNƏS

r: richness.

ICHUR

Vowel: itcher.
d: ditcher.
h: hitcher.
p: pitcher.
r: enricher, richer.
st: sticher.
sw: switcher.

tw: twitcher.
w: bewitcher.
    Plus bewitch her *or* err, etc.

ICHURD

pr: pritchard.
r: Richard.

ĪCHUS

r: righteous.

ICHƏL

k: Kitchell.
m: Mitchell.
sw: switchel.
tw: Twichell.
    Plus switch'll, etc.

ICHƏN

k: kitchen.
l: lichen.
    Cf. rich hen, etc.
    Cf. rich in, etc.

ICHƏT

f: fitchet, Fitchett.
pr: Pritchett.
tw: Twichett.
w: witchet.
    Plus witch et, etc.
    Cf. bewitch it, etc.

ICHƏZ

Vowel: itches.
b: bitches.
br: breeches, britches.
d: ditches.
fl: flitches.
h: hitches.
n: niches.
p: pitches.

r: enriches, riches.
skr(scr): scritches.
st: stitches.
sw: switches.
tw: twitches.
w: bewitches.
w: witches.
  Cf. which is, etc.

ĪDĀ

fr: Friday+.

ĪDBÄR

s: sidebar.

IDĒ

b: biddy, chickabiddy.
d: Diddy.
g: giddy.
k: kiddy.
m: middy.
st: stiddy.
w: Dinwiddie, "widdy."
  Plus did he, etc.

ĪDĒ

d: didy.
f: bonafide+.
fr: Friday+.
l: Leidy.
t: tidy, untidy.
v: vide.
  Plus why'd he *or* side, he, etc.
  Plus try Dee *or* D, etc.

ĪDĒD

t: tidied.
  Plus why did, etc.
  Cf. ided.

IDEST

b: biddest*, forbiddest*,
overbiddest*, underbiddest*.
k: kiddest*.
l: liddest*.
m: pyramiddest*.
r: riddest*.
sk: skiddest*.

ĪDEST

b: abidest*, bidest*.
br: bridest*.
ch: chidest*.
f: confidest*.
fr: friedest.
g: guidest*.
gl: glidest*.
h: hidest*.
l: collidest*, elidest*.
pr: pridest*.
r: deridest*, overridest*, ridest*.
s: coincidest*, decidest*, sidest*,
subsidest*.
sl: backslidest*, slidest*.
str: stridest*.
t: tidest*.
v: dividest*, providest*,
subdividest*.
w: widest.
z: presidest*, residest*.

IDETH

b: biddeth*, forbiddeth*,
overbiddeth*, underbiddeth*.
k: kiddeth.
l: liddeth*.
m: pyramideth*.
r: riddeth*.
sk: skiddeth*.

ĪDETH

b: abideth*, bideth*.
br: brideth*.

ch: chideth*.
f: confideth*.
g: guideth*.
gl: glideth*.
h: hideth*.
l: collideth*, elideth*.
pr: prideth*.
r: derideth*, overrideth*, rideth*.
s: coincideth*, decideth*, sideth*, subsideth*.
sl: slideth*.
str: strideth*.
t: betideth*, tideth*.
v: divideth*, provideth*, subdivideth*.
z: presideth*, resideth*.
　　Plus why death, etc.

ĪDIJ

g: guidage.
h: hidage.
　　Cf. hide age, etc.

IDIK

Vowel: druidic.
m: pyramidic.
r: juridic.
t: fatidic.

IDING

b: bidding, forbidding, outbidding, overbidding, underbidding, unforbidding.
k: kidding, nokidding.
l: lidding.
r: ridding.
sk: skidding.

ĪDING

b: abiding, biding, law-abiding.
br: briding.

ch: chiding.
f: confiding.
g: guiding, misguiding.
gl: gliding.
h: hiding.
l: colliding, eliding.
n: niding.
pr: priding.
r: deriding, outriding, overriding, riding.
s: coinciding, deciding, siding, subsiding.
sl: backsliding, sliding.
str: bestriding, outstriding, striding.
t: betiding.
v: dividing, providing.
z: presiding, residing.

IDINGZ

g: Giddings.
　　Plus iding+s.

ĪDINGZ

t: tidings.
　　Plus iding+s.

IDL

b: Biddle.
d: diddle, flumaddidle.
f: fiddle.
gr: griddle.
kw: quiddle.
l: Liddle.
m: middle.
p: piddle.
r: riddle, unriddle.
t: rumtum tiddle, tiddle.
tw: twiddle.
y: yiddle.
　　Plus kid'll, etc.

ĪDL

Vowel: idle, idol, idyll.
br: bridal, bridle.
s: gratricidal, homicidal, infanticidal, matricidal, parricidal, patricidal, regicidal, sidle, suicidal, uxoricidal, tyrranicidal.
t: tidal.
>   Plus wide, Al, etc.
>   Plus bride 'll, etc.
>   Plus guide ill, I'd ill, etc.
>   Plus try dill, etc.

IDLD

f: fiddled.
>   Plus dil+d.

ĪDLD

br: bridled, unbridled.
>   Plus idl+d.

ĪDLĒ

br: bridely.
w: widely.
>   Plus pride, Lee *or* lea, etc.

IDLEST

f: fiddlest*.
r: riddlest*, unriddlest*.
tw: twiddlest*.
>   Plus hid, lest, etc.

ĪDLEST

Vowel: idlest.
br: bridlest*.
>   Plus hide, lest, etc.

IDLETH

f: fiddleth*.
r: riddleth*. unriddleth*.
tw: twiddleth*.

ĪDLETH

Vowel: idleth*.
br: bridleth*.

IDLĪF

m: midlife.

IDLING

d: diddling.
f: fiddling.
k(c): kidling.
m: middling.
r: riddling.
tw: twiddling.

ĪDLING

Vowel: idling.
br: bridling.
s: sidling.

IDLINGZ

m: middlings.
>   Plus idling+s.

ĪDLĪT

g: guidelight.
s: side light.
>   Plus spied light, etc.

IDLUR

d: diddler.
f: fiddler.
p: piddler.
r: riddler.
t: tiddler, Tom Tiddler.
tw: twiddler.

ĪDLUR

Vowel: idler.
br: bridler.

IDNĒ

k(c): kidney.
s: Sidney, Sydney.
  Plus hid knee, etc.

ĪDNƏS

p: piedness.
w: wideness.

IDŌ

k(c): kiddo.
w: widow.
  Plus did owe *or* O, etc.

ĪDŌ

d: Dido.
f: Fido.
  Plus try dough *or* doe, etc.
  Plus bride owe *or* O, etc.

ĪDR L

s: slide-rule.
  Plus abide rule, etc.
  Plus why drool, etc.

IDUR

b: bidder, forbidder, outbidder, overbidder, underbidder.
k(c): kidder.
r: ridder.
s: consider.
sk: skidder.
  Plus lid her, etc.

ĪDUR

Vowel: eider.
ch: chider.
f: confider.
g: guider, misguider.
gl: glider.
h: hider.
l: collider, elider.
n: nidor.
r: derider, outrider, rider, Rough Rider.
s: cider, coincider, decider, insider, one-sider, outsider, sider, subsider.
shn: Schneider.
sl: backslider, slider.
sn: Snider, Snyder.
sp: spider.
str: bestrider, strider, stridor.
v: divider, provider, subdivider.
w: Fulenwider, wider.
z: presider, resider.
  Plus tied her, tried, or *or* Orr, etc.
  Cf. id ur.

IDURD

s: considered, ill-considered, unconsidered.
  Plus skidder'd, etc.

ĪDƏ

Vowel: Ida.
l: Lida.
n: Oneida.
r: Rida.
v: Vida.
  Plus I'd a, spied a, etc.

IDƏD

b: bidded, overbidded, underbidded.
k: kidded.
l: invalided, lidded.
m: pyramidded.
r: ridded.
sk: skidded.
  Plus did, Ed, etc.

ĪDƏD

b: abided, bided.
br: brided.
ch: chided.
f: confided.
g: guided, misguided, unguided.
gl: glided.
l: collided, elided.
pr: prided.
r: derided.
s: coincided, decided, lopsided, many-sided, one-sided, sided, slab-sided, subsided, two-sided, undecided.
sl: backslided, landslided.
str: strided.
t: betided, tided.
v: divided, provided, subdivided, undivided, unprovided.
z: presided, resided.
  Plus pride, Ed, etc.
  Plus why dead, etc.
  Cf. tidied.
  Cf. why did, etc.

IDƏN

b: bidden, forbidden, God-forbidden, unbidden, unforbidden.
ch: chidden.
h: hidden.
m: kitchen midden, midden.
r: hagridden, overridden, priest-ridden, riddent, unridden, wife-ridden.
sl: slidden.
str: stridden.

ĪDƏN

dr: Dryden.
g: guidon.

l: Leyden.
s: Poseidon, Dison.
w: widen.
  Plus my den, etc.
  Plus spied on *or* an, etc.
  Plus Hi, Don, etc.
  Cf. Idon, Leydoen.
  Cf. wide hen, etc.

IDƏNS

b: forbiddance.
r: riddance.
  Plus rid aunts *or* ants, etc.
  Cf. kid dance, etc.

ĪDƏNS

b: abidance.
g: guidance, misguidance.
s: subsidence.
  Plus deride aunts *or* ants, etc.
  Plus why dance, etc.

ĪDƏNT

b: bident.
g: guidant.
r: rident.
str: strident.
tr: trident.
v: dividant.
  Plus guide aunt *or* ant, etc.
  Plus why dent, etc.

IDƏNZ

s: Siddons.
  Cf. idans.

ĪE

w: Hawaii.
  Cf. Hatay.

ĪEST

Vowel: eyest*.

b: buyest*.

d: beyest*, diest*, dyest*.

dr: driest.

f: amplifiest*, beautifiest*, brutifiest*, certifiest*, clarifiest*, classifiest*, crucifiest*, defiest*, deifiest*, dignifiest*, diversifiest*, edifiest*, electrifiest*, falsifiest*, fortifiest*, glorifiest*, gratifiest*, horrifiest*, identifiest*, justifiest*, liquefiest*, magnifiest*, modifiest*, mollifiest*, mortifiest*, mystifiest*, notifiest*, nullifiest*, ossifiest*, pacifiest*, personifiest*, purifiest*, qualifiest*, ratifiest*, rectifiest*, sanctifiest*, satisfiest*, signifiest*, simplifiest*, specifiest*, stupefiest*, terrifiest*, testifiest*, typifiest*, verifiest*, versifiest*, vilifiest*, vitrifiest*.

fl: fliest*.

fr: friest*.

h: hiest*, highest*.

kr: criest*, decriest*.

l: alliest*, beliest*, liest*, reliest*.

n: deniest*, nighest*.

p: occupiest*.

pl: appliest*, compliest*, impliest*, multipliest*, pliest*, repliest*, suppliest*.

pr: pryest*.

r: awryest*, wryest*.

s: prophesidest*, sighest*.

sh: shyest.

skr(scr): descriest*.

sl: slyest.

sp: bespyest*, espiest*, spyest.

spr: spryest.

t: tiest*, untiest*.

tr: tryest*.

v: outviest*, viest*.

ĪETH

Vowel: eyeth*.

b: buyeth*.

d: bedyeth*, dieth*, dyeth*.

dr: drieth*.

f: amplifieth*, plus all words in the F group under *iest*, with termination change to *eth*.

fl: flieth*.

fr: frieth*.

h: hieth*.

kr: crieth*, decrieth*.

l: allieth*, belieth*, lieth*, relieth*.

n: denieth*.

p: occupieth*.

pl: applieth*, complieth*, implieth*, multiplieth*, plieth*, replieth*, supplieth*.

pr: pryeth*.

s: prophesieth*, sigheth*.

sh: shyeth*.

skr(scr): descrieth*.

sp: bespyeth*, espieth*, spyeth*.

t: tieth*, untieth*.

tr: tryeth*.

v: outvieth*, vieth*.

IFĒ

j: jiffy.

kl: cliffy.

sn: sniffy.

sp: spiffy.

skw: squiffy.

Plus if he, etc.

IFEST

hw: whiffest*.

sn: sniffest*.

st: stiffest.

IFETH

hw: whiffeth.
sn: sniffeth.

IFIK

Vowel: deific.
b: morbific, rubific, tabific.
br: tenebrific.
d: acidific, grandific, lapidific.
gl: anaglyphic, diaglyphic, glyphic, hieroglyphic, lithoglyphic, petroglyphic, photoglyphic, phytoglyphic, triglyphic.
j: algific.
l: mellific, prolific.
n: cornific, damnific, finific, magnific, omnific, somnific, vulnific.
r: aurific, calorific, colorific, dolorific, frigorific, honorific, horrific, humorific, mirific, sacrific, sonorific, soporific, spoprific, sudorific, terrific, torporific, vaporific.
s: classific, lucific, mucific, ossific, pacific, pulsific, sensific, siccific, specific.
t: beatific, incoherentific, lactific, pontific, scientific.
tr: petrific.
v: salvific, vivific.

IFIKS

l: dermatoglyphics.

IFING

hw: whiffing.
sn: sniffing.
t: tiffing.

IFISH

m: miffish.
sn: sniffish.

st: stiffish.
t: tiffish.
skw: squiffish.
    Cf. if fish, etc.

IFL

hw: whiffle.
p: piffle.
r: riffle.
sn: sniffle.
    Plus tiff'll, etc.
    Cf. Riff full, etc.

ĪFL

Vowel: Eiffel.
r: rifle.
st: stifle.
tr: trifle.
    Plus eye full, I full, etc.
    Plus wife'll, etc.
    Cf. life full, etc.

ĪFLĒ

r: rifely.
w: wifely.
    Plus strife, Lee *or* lea, etc.

ĪFLĪK

l: lifelike.
w: wifelike.
    Plus strife like, etc.

IFLING

hw: whiffling.
p: piffling.
r: riffling.
sn: sniffling.

ĪFLING

r: rifling.
st: stifling.
tr: trifling.

IFLƏR

hw: whiffler.
p: piffler.
r: riffler.
sn: sniffler.

ĪFLƏR

r: rifler.
st: stifler.
tr: tribler.

ĪFLƏS

f: fifeless.
l: lifeless.
n: knifeless.
str: strifeless.
w: wifeless.
    Plus fife less, etc.

IFTĒ

dr: drifty.
f: fifty, fifty-fifty.
kl: clifty.
n: nifty.
r: rifty.
sh: shifty.
thr: thrifty.
    Plus drift, he, etc.
    Plus sniff tea, etc.

IFTEST

dr: driftest*.
l: liftest*, upliftest*.
r: riftest*.
sh: shiftest*.

s: siftest*.
sw: swiftest.
    Plus sniff test, etc.

IFTETH

dr: drifteth*.
l: lifteth*, uplifteth*.
r: rifteth*.
sh: shifteth*.
s: sifteth*.

IFTHÔNG

d: diphthong.
tr: triphthong.
    Plus sniff thong, etc.

IFTING

dr: drifting.
l: lifting, shoplifting, uplifting.
r: rifting.
sh: shifting.
s: sifting.

IFTLƏS

dr: driftless.
r: riftless.
sh: shiftless.
thr: thriftless.
    Plus sniffed less, etc.

IFTNƏS

sw: swiftness.

IFTƏR

dr: drifter.
l: lifter, shoplifter, uplifter.
s: sifter.
sh: sceneshifter, shifter.
sw: swifter.
    Plus sniffed her *or* err, etc.

IFŬR

d: differ.
sn: sniffer.
st: stiffer.
　　Plus biff her *or* err, etc.

ĪFŬR

f: fifer.
l: lifer.
n: knifer.
r: rifer.
s: cipher, decipher.
　　Plus strife her *or* err, etc.
　　Plus try fur *or* fir, etc.
　　Cf. try for, etc.

IFTƏD

dr: drifted.
g: gifted, ungifted.
l: lifted, uplifted.
r: rifted.
sh: shifted.
s: sifted.
　　Plus if, Ted.

IFTƏN

kl: Clifton.
　　Plus drift on *or* an, etc.
　　Plus if ton *or* tun, etc.

IFƏN

b: biffin.
gr: griffon.
st: stiffen.
t: tiffin.
　　Plus stuff in *or* inn, etc.
　　Cf. ifen, ifon, ifn.
　　Cf. if an *or* on, etc.
　　Cf. stiff fin, etc.

ĪFƏN

h: hyphen.
s: siphon.
t: Typhon.
　　Plus wife on *or* an, etc.
　　Plus dry fen, etc.

IFƏT

hw: whiffet.
　　Cf. sniff it, etc.

IGBĒ

d: Digby.
　　Plus big bee *or* be, etc.

IGĒ

b: biggy.
p: piggy.
spr: spriggy.
tw: twiggy.
w: piggy-wiggy.
　　Plus big he, etc.

IGEST

b: biggest.
d: diggest*.
j: jiggest*.
n: renegest*.
r: riggest*.
sw: swiggest*.
tr: triggest*.

IGETH

d: diggeth*.
j: jiggeth*.
n: renegeth*.
r: riggeth*.
sw: swiggeth*.

IGING

d: digging.
g: gigging.
j: jigging.
r: rigging, thimblerigging, unrigging.
spr: sprigging.
sw: swigging.
tr: trigging.
tw: twigging.
w: wigging.

IGINZ

dw: Dwiggins.
h: Higgins.
w: Wiggins.

IGISH

hw: whiggish.
p: piggish.
pr: priggish.
    Plus swig, Gish, etc.

IGL

g: giggle.
h: higgle
j: jiggle.
n: niggle.
r: wriggle.
skw: squiggle.
sn: sniggle.
w: wiggle.
    Plus pig'll, etc.

ĪGLAS

Vowel: eyeglass.
sp: spyglass.
    Plus try glass, etc.

IGLD

g: giggled.
h: higgled.
j: jiggled.
n: niggled.
r: wriggled.
skw: squiggled.
sn: sniggled.
w: wiggled.

IGLĒ

g: giggly, higgly, jiggly, squiggly, wiggly, wriggly.
w: Piggly Wiggly.
    Plus gig, Lee *or* lea, etc.

IGLEST

g: gigglest*, higglest*, jigglest*, squigglest*, wigglest*, wrigglest*.
    Cf. Pig, lest, etc.

IGLETH

g: giggleth*, higgleth*, jiggleth*, squiggleth*, wiggleth*, wriggleth*.

ĪGLIF

d: diglyph.
tr: monotriglyph, triglyph.

IGLING

g: giggling, higgling, jiggling, squiggling, wiggling, wriggling.

IGLUR

g: giggler, higgler, jiggler, squiggler, wiggler, wriggler.

IGMĒ

p: pygmy.
    Cf. big me, etc.

IGMƏ

n: enigma.
s: sigma.
st: stigma.
　　Plus pig, ma, etc.

IGMƏNT

f: figment.
p: pigment.
　　Plus sprig meant, etc.

IGNĪT

Vowel: ignite.
l: lignite.
　　Plus big night, etc.

IGNUM

l: lignum.
s: eccesignum.
　　Plus pig numb, etc.

IGNƏL

s: signal.

IGNƏNS

l: malignance.
　　Plus pig, Nance, etc.

IGNƏNT

d: indignant.
l: malignant.
n: benifnant.

IGNƏT

s: cygnet, signet.
　　Plus big net, etc.

IGO

l: caligo, fuligo, Loligo.
t: impetigo.
　　Plus pig owe *or* O, etc.

ĪGŌ

Vowel: Igoe.
sl: Sligo.
　　Plus why go, etc.

ĪGÔN

b: bygone.
tr: tribone.
　　Plus sky gone, etc.

ĪGRES

t: tigress.
　　Cf. Digress+.

IGUR

b: bigger.
ch: chigger.
d: digger, gold digger, grave digger.
f: "figger."
g: gigger.
j: jigger.
l: ligger.
n: nigger.
pr: prigger.
r: market rigger, outrigger, rigger, rigor, thimble-rigger.
sn: sniffer.
spr: sprigger.
sw: swigger.
tr: trigger.
tw: twigger.
v: vigor.
　　Plus pig, or, twig her *or* err, etc.

ĪGUR

l: liger.
n: Niger.
t: tiger.

IGU̇RD

f: "figgered."

j: bejiggered, jiggered.

n: nigard, unniggard.

sn: sniffered.

Plus vigor'd, etc.

IGYU̇R

f: configure, disfigure, figure, prefigure, transfigure.

l: ligure.

Plus rig your *or* you're, etc.

ĪGƏ

s: saiga.

IGƏN

b: bigun.

l: Ligon.

Plus pig on *or* an, etc.

IGƏND

br: brigand.

Plus fig and, etc.

IGƏT

b: bigot.

j: gigot.

sp: spigot.

g: frigate.

Plus pig ate *or* eight, etc.

Cf. dig it, rig it *or* at, etc.

Cf. big gate, etc.

ĪING

Vowel: eyeing, Iing.

b: alibiing, buying, byuing, hushabying, lullabying, underbuying.

d: bedying, dyeing, dying, undying.

dr: adrying, drying.

f: acidifying, amplifying, beautifying, brutifying, candifying, certifying, clarifying, classifying, codifying, countrifying, crucifying, damnifying, dandifying, defying, deifying, dignifying, disqualifying, dissatisfying, diversifying, dulcifying, edifying, electrifying, emulsifying, exemplifying, falsifying, fortifying, Frenchifrying, fructifying, frying, glorifying, gratifying, horrifying, humanifying, identifying, imdemnifying, intensifying, justifying, labifying, liquefying, magnifying, modifying, mollifying, mortifying, mystifying, notifying, nullifying, ossifying, pacifying, personifying, petrifying, preachifying, purifying, putrefying, qualifying, ramifying, rarefying, ratifying, rectifying, revivifying, sanctifying, satisfying, scarifying, scorifying, self-satisfying, signifying, simplifying, solidifying, specifying, stultifying, stupefying, terrifying, testifying, torpifying, torrefying, typifying, unifying, unsatisfying, verifying, versifying, vilifying, vitrifying, vivifying.

fl: butterflying, flying, kiteflying.

fr: frying.

g: guying.

h: hieing.

kr: crying, decrying, outcrying, uncrying.

l: allying, belying, lying, outlying, relying, self-relying, underlying.

n: denying, self-denying.

p: occupying, piing, preoccupying.

pl: applying, complying, implying, multiplying, plying, replying, supplying, uncomplying.

pr: prying.

s: prophesying, sighing, unsighing.
sh: shying.
sk: skying.
skr(scr): descrying.
sp: bespying, espying, spying.
t: tieing, untying.
tr: trying.
v: outvying, viewing.

ĪJAK

h: highjack.
Plus try, Jack *or* jack, etc.

IJID

fr: frigid.
r: rigid.

IJING

br: abridging, bridging.
r: ridging.

ĪJING

bl: disobliging, obliging.

IJIT

Vowel: "ijjit."
br: Bridget, Brigit.
d: digit.
f: fidget.
g: Gidget.
m: midget.
Plus bridge it, etc.

IJUR

br: abridger, bridger.
Plus midge err *or* her, etc.

ĪJƏ

b: Abijah.
l: Elijah.
Plus oblige a, etc.

IJƏL

s: sigil.
str: strigil.
v: vigil.
Plus midge'll, etc.

IJƏN

l: irreligion, religion.
p: pigeon.
w: widgeon.
Plus bridgeon *or* an, etc.

IJƏS

d: prodigious.
l: irreligious, religious.
t: litigious.
Plus bridge us, etc.
Cf. sacrilegious.

ĪJƏST

bl: disobligest*, obligest*.
d: digest.
Plus try jest, etc.

IKĀT

s: siccate.
Plus tick ate *or* eight, etc.
Cf. tick, Kate, etc.

IKCHUR

p: depicture, impicture, picture, word picture.
str: stricture.
Plus mixed your *or* you're, etc.
Plus kicked your *or* you're, etc.

IKĒ

br: bricky.
d: dickey.
f: Ficke.
h: doohickey.

kw: quickie.
n: Nicky.
r: iginrickey, rickey.
s: sickie.
st: sticky.
t: Rikki-Tikki.
tr: tricky.
v: Vicky.
  Plus trick he, etc.

ĪKĒ

sp: spiky.
  Plus like, he, etc.
  Plus my key, etc.
  Cf. Psyche.

IKEST

fl: flickest*.
k(c): kickest*.
kl: clickest*.
kw: quickest.
l: lickest*.
p: pickest*.
pr: prickest*.
sl: slickest*.
st: stickest*.
t: tickest*.
th: thickest.
tr: trickest*.

ĪKEST

bl: obliquest+.
l: dislikest*, likest*.
sp: spikest*.
str: strikest*.

IKETH

fl: flicketh*.
k: kicketh*.
kl: clicketh*.
l: licketh*.

p: picketh*.
pr: pricketh*.
st: sticketh*.
t: ticketh*.
tr: tricketh*.

ĪKETH

l: disliketh*, liketh*.
sp: spiketh*.
str: striketh*.

IKETS

r: rickets.
  Plus iket+s.
  Plus Pickett's, etc.

ĪKIK

s: psychic.
  Plus try kick, etc.

ĪKIKS

s: psychics.
  Plus sly kicks, etc.

IKING

br: bricking.
gl: glicking.
k: high kicking, kicking.
kl: clicking.
kr: cricking.
l: licking.
n: nicking.
p: hand-picking, picking, pocket picking.
pr: pricking.
s: siccing.
sl: slicking.
sn: snicking.
st: besticking, pigsticking, sticking, walking sticking.
t: ticking.

th: thicking.
tr: tricking.
w: wicking.

ĪKING

b: biking.
d: dyking.
h: hiking, hitchhiking.
l: disliking, liking, misliking, well-liking.
p: piking.
sp: spiking.
str: striking.
v: viking.
  Plus my king, etc.

IKISH

br: brickesh.
s: sickish.
sl: slickish.
th: thickish.

IKL

ch: chicle.
f: fickle.
m: mickle.
n: nickel.
p: pickle.
pr: prickle.
s: sickle.
st: stickle.
str: strickle.
t: tickle.
tr: trickle.
  Plus flick'll, etc.

ĪKÄN

Vowel: icon.
  Plus strike on, etc.
  Plus sky con, etc.

ĪKL

m: Michael.
s: cycle, epicycle, psychal, recycle.
  Plus strike 'll.

IKLĒ

kw: quickly.
pr: prickly.
s: sickly.
sl: slickly.
st: stickly.
th: thickly.
tr: trickly.
  Plus quick, Lee *or* lea, etc.

ĪKLĒ

bl: obliquely+.
l: belikely, likely, unlikely.
  Plus strike Lee *or* lea, etc.

IKLEST

f: ficklest.
p: picklest*.
pr: pricklest*.
s: sicklest*.
st: sticklest*.
t: ticklest*.
tr: tricklst*.
  Plus quick, lest, etc.

IKLETH

p: pickleth*.
pr: prickleth*.
s: sickleth*.
st: stickleth*.
t: tickleth*.
tr: trickleth*.

ĪKLIK

s: bicyclic, cyclic, encyclic, epicyclic, geocyclic.

Plus Mike lick, etc.
Plus my click, etc.

ĪKLIN

s: prostacyclin.

IKLING

ch: chickling.
p: pickling.
pr: prickling.
t: tickling.
tr: trickling.

ĪKLING

s: cycling.

IKLISH

pr: pricklish.
t: ticklish.

ĪKLIST

s: cyclist.
    Plus strike list, etc.

ĪKLŌN

s: cyclone.
    Plus Mike, lone *or* loan, etc.

IKLUR

f: fickler.
pr: prickler.
st: stickler.
str: strickler.
t: tickler.

IKNIK

p: picnic.
str: strychnic.
    Plus stick Nick *or* nick, etc.

IKNĪN

str: strychnine.

IKNING

kw: quickening.
s: sickening.
th: thickening.

IKNƏS

kw: quickness.
s: lovesickness, sickness.
sl: slickness.
th: thickness.

ĪKNƏS

bl: obliqueness+.
l: likeness, unlikeness.

ĪKÔR

Vowel: ichor.
    Plus strike, or, etc.

ĪKOUNT

v: viscount.
    Plus my count, etc.

IKSCHUR

f: affixture, fixture.
m: admixture, immixture,
incommixture, intermixture,
mixture.

IKSĒ

d: dixey, Dixie.
n: nixie, water nixie.
p: pixie.
tr: tricksy, Trixie.
    Plus kicks, he, etc.
    Plus trick, see, etc.

IKSEST

f: affixest*, fixest*, prefixest*, transfixest*.
m: intermixest*, mixest.

IKSET

kw: quickset.
th: thickset.
   Plus trick set, etc.

IKSETH

f: affixeth*, fixeth*, prefixeth*, transfixeth*.
m: intermixeth*, mixeth*.

IKSHƏN

d: addiction, benediction, contradiction, diction, indiction, interdiction, jurisdiction, malediction, prediction, valediction.
f: affixion, crucifixion, fiction, prefixion, suffixion, transfixion.
fl: affliction, confliction, infliction.
fr: affriction, friction.
l: dereliction, reliction.
p: depiction.
str: abstriction, constriction, obstriction, restriction.
v: conviction, eviction.
   Plus trick shun, etc.

IKSHUS

d: contradictious.
f: fictious*.

IKSING

f: affixing, fixing, prefixing, transfixing.
m: admixing, intermixing, mixing.

Plus trick sing, etc.
Cf. tricks sing, etc.

IKSTĒ

s: all sixty, sixty.
   Plus mix tea, etc.
   Plus fixed, he, etc.

IKSTƯR

tr: trickster.
   Plus fixed her, etc.
   Plus quick, stir, etc.

IKSƏN

d: Dickson, Dixon.
h: hickson, Hixon.
m: mixen.
v: vixen.
   Plus sticks on, etc.
   Plus trick sun *or* son, etc.
   Plus wicks on *or* an, etc.
   Cf. sticks an, etc.

IKTĀT

d: dictate.
n: nictate.
   Plus quick, Tate, etc.
   Plus tricked, ate *or* eight, etc

IKTEST

d: addictest*, contradictest*, interdictest*, predictest*.
fl: afflictest*, conflictest*, inflictest*.
p: depictest*.
str: constrictest*, restrictest*, strictest*.
v: convictest*, evictest*.
   Plus quick test, etc.

IKTETH

d: addicteth*, contradicteth*, interdicteth*, predicteth*.
fl: afflicteth*, conflicteth*, inflicteth*.
p: depicteth*.
str: constricteth*, restricteth*.
v: convicteth*, evicteth*.

IKTIK

Vowel: deictic, endeictic, epideictic, ictic.
d: apodictic.
    Plus quick tick, etc.

IKTING

d: addicting, contradicting, interdicting, predicting.
fl: afflicting, conflicting, inflicting.
p: depicting.
str: constricting, restricting.
v: convicting, evicting.

IKTIV

d: addictive, benedictive, contradictive, indictive, interdictive, jurisdictive, predictive, vindictive.
f: fictive.
fl: afflictive, conflictive, inflictive.
p: depictive.
str: constrictive, restrictive, unrestrictive.
v: convictive, evictive.

IKTLĒ

l: derelictly.
str: strictly.
    Plus picked Lee *or* lea, etc.

IKTNƏS

str: strictness.

IKTƱR

d: contradicter, predicter.
f: fictor*.
fl: afflicter, conflicter, inflicter.
l: lictor.
p: depicter, Pictor.
str: boa constrictor, constrictor, restricter, stricter.
v: convicter, evictor, victor.
    Plus picked her *or* err, etc.
    Cf. iktur.

IKTUS

Vowel: ictus.
d: Benedictus.
n: acronyctous.
    Plus picked us, etc.

IKTƏD

d: addicted, contradicted, interdicted, predicted.
fl: afflicted, conflicted, inflicted, self-inflicted.
l: relicted.
p: depicted.
str: constricted, restricted, unrestricted.
v: convicted, evicted.
    Plus quick, Ted, etc.
    Plus picked Ed, etc.

IKTƏM

d: dictum, obiterdictum.
v: victim.
    Plus kick tum, etc.
    Plus restrict 'em, etc.
    Plus quick, Tim, etc.
    Plus tricked him, etc.

IKUR

b: bicker.
d: dicker.
fl: flicker.
k: high kicker, kicker.
kl: clicker.
kw: quicker.
l: licker, liquor.
n: cominicker, nicker.
p: berry picker, picker.
pr: pricker.
s: sicker.
sl: slicker.
sn: snicker.
st: sticker.
t: ticker.
th: thicker.
tr: tricker.
v: vicar.
w: wicker.
    Plus pick her *or* err, etc.

ĪKUR

b: biker.
bl: obliquer+.
d: diker.
h: hiker, hitchhiker.
l: liker.
p: piker.
r: Riker.
sp: spiker.
str: striker.
    Plus like her *or* err, etc.
    Plus why cur *or* Kerr, etc.

IKURD

l: liquored.
p: pickard.
r: Rickard.

Plus picker'd, etc.
Cf. pick hard, etc.
Cf. Ikard, ikurd.

IKURZ

n: nickers.
    Plus kiur+s.

IKWID

l: liquid.
    Plus pick wid, etc.

ĪKƏ

l: balalaika.
m: mica, Micah.
p: pica, pika.
r: lorica.
sp: spica.
    Plus strike a, etc.

IKƏD

w: wicked.
    Plus nick, Ed, etc.
    Plus ik+ed*.

ĪKƏL

m: Carmichael, Michael.
    Plus strike'll, etc.
    Cf. ikl.

IKƏN

ch: chicken.
kw: quicken.
s: sicken.
str: horror-stricken, stricken, terror-stricken, wonder-stricken.
th: thicken.
w: wicken.
    Cf. strick hen, etc.

ĪKƏN

l: lichen, liken, unliken.
Plus my ken, etc.
Cf. strike hen, etc.

IKƏNZ

ch: chickens.
d: Dickens, the dickens.
sl: slickens.
Plus iken+s.

ĪKƏS

f: ficus.
p: Picus.
sp: spicous.
Plus like us, etc.
Plus why cuss, etc.

IKƏT

kl: clicket.
kr: cricket.
p: picket, Pickett.
pr: pricket, Prickett.
r: Rickett.
t: ticket, walking ticket.
th: thicket.
w: wicket.
Plus stick et, etc.
Cf. stick it, etc.

ĪLƏ

Vowel: Ila.
h: Hyla.
l: Delilah, Lila, Lilah.
Plus smile, a, etc.

ĪLAK

l: lilac.
Plus why lack, etc.

ĪLÄK

h: hillock.
sh: Shylock.
Plus try lock, etc.
Cf. will lock, etc.

ĪLAKS

l: Lilacs.
sm: smilax.
Plu style ax *or* acts, etc.
Plus why lax, etc.

ĪLÄN

n: nylon.
p: pylon.
tr: trylon.
Plus smile on, etc.
Plus why, Lon, etc.

ĪLÄRK

r: phylarch.
sk: skylark.
Plus buy lark, etc.
Plus style ark *or* arc, etc.

ĪLASH

Vowel: eyelash.
Plus try lash, etc.
Plus style ash, etc.

ILĀT

s: penicillate.
Plus ill eight *or* ate, etc.
Cf. Will, late, etc.

ILBURT

f: filbert.
g: Gilbert.
w: Wilbert.
Plus thrill Bert, etc.

ILDEST

b: buildest*.
g: begildest*, gildest*.

ĪLDEST

m: mildest.
w: wildest.

ILDETH

b: buildeth*.
g: begildeth*, gildeth*.
   Plus still death, etc.

ĪLDHOOD

ch: childhood.
   Plus styled hood, etc.

ILDING

b: building, castle-building, house building, rebuilding, ship-building, unbuilding.
g: begilding, gilding, regilding, ungilding.

ĪLDING

ch: childing.
w: wilding.

ĪLDISH

ch: childish.
m: mildish.
w: wildish.
   Plus style dish, etc.

ĪLDLĒ

ch: childly.
m: mildly.
w: wildly.
   Plus styled, Lee or lea, etc.

ĪLDLĪK

ch: childlike.
   Plus mild like, etc.

ĪLDLƏS

ch: childless.
m: mildless.
   Plus styled less or Les, etc.

ĪLDNƏS

m: mildness, unmildness.
r: riledness.
w: wildness.

ILDRƏD

m: Mildred.
   Plus still dread, etc.

ILDRƏN

ch: children.
   Plus killed wren, etc.

ILDUR

b: builder, castle-builder, home builder, house-builder, rebuilder, ship builder, unbuilder.
ch: childer*.
g: begilder, gilder, builder.
w: bewilder, wilder*.
   Plus filled her or err, etc.

ĪLDUR

m: milder.
w: wilder.
   Plus styled her or err, etc.

ĪLDWOOD

w: wildwood.
   Plus mild wood or would, etc.

ILDƏ

h: Hilda.
t: matilda, Matilda.
Plus killed a, etc.

ILDƏD

b: builded.
g: begilded, gilded, guilded, ungilded.
Plus still dead, etc.
Plus stilled, Ed, etc.
Cf. Phil did, etc.

ILĒ

Vowel: illy.
b: Billee, Billie, billy.
ch: Chile, chili, chilly.
d: daffy-down-dilly, Piccadilly.
f: filly.
fr: frilly.
g: gillie.
gr: grilly.
h: hilly.
l: day lily, lily, meadow lily, piccalilli, pon lily, tiger lily, water lily, wood lily.
m: Millie, Milly.
n: willy-nilly.
s: silly.
shr: shrilly.
sk: skilly.
st: stilly.
t: Tillie, Tilly.
thr: thrilly.
tr: trilly.
w: Willie, Willy.
Plus still he, etc.

ĪLĒ

dr: drily.
h: highly.

r: O'Reilly, Reilly, Riley, wryly.
s: ancile.
sh: shyly.
sl: slily.
w: wily.
Plus while he, etc.

ILĒD

l: lilied.

ILEST

Vowel: ilest.
ch: chillest.
dr: drillest.
f: fillest*, fulfillest*, overfillest*.
fr: befrillest*, frillest*.
gr: grillest*.
k: killest*.
m: millest*.
shr: shrillest.
sp: spillest*.
st: instillest*, stillest.
sw: swillest*.
t: distillest*, tillest*.
thr: enthrillest*, thrillest*.
tr: trillest*.
w: willest*.
Cf. kill, lest, etc.

ĪLEST

f: defilest*, filest*.
g: beguilest*.
hw: whilest*.
p: compilest*, pilest*.
r: rilest*.
s: reconcilest*.
sm: smilest*.
st: stylest*.
v: revilest*, vilest.
w: wilest*.
Plus try, lest, etc.

ILETH

ch: chilleth*.
dr: drilleth*.
f: filleth*, fulfilleth*, overfilleth*.
fr: befrilleth*, frilleth*.
gr: grilleth*.
k(c): killeth*.
m: milleth.
sp: spilleth*.
st: instilleth*.
sw: swilleth*.
t: distilleth*, tilleth*.
thr: enthrilleth*, thrilleth*.
tr: trilleth*.
w: willeth*.

ĪLETH

f: defileth*, fileth*.
g: beguileth*.
hw: whileth*.
p: compileth*, pileth*, uppileth*.
r: rileth*.
s: reconcileth*.
sm: smileth*.
st: styleth*.
t: tileth*.
v: revileth*.
w: wileth*.

ILĒZ

ch: chilies.
f: fillies.
g: gillies.
l: lilies, etc.
s: sillies.
w: the Willies.
    Plus ili+s.

ILFOOL

sk: skillful, unskillful.
w: wilful.
    Plus still full, etc.

ĪLFOOL

g: guileful.
sm: smileful.
w: wileful.
    Plus style full, etc.

ILFUR

p: pilfer.
    Plus sylph err *or* her, etc.
    Plus still fur *or* fir, etc.
    Cf. ill for, etc.

ILGRIM

m: Milgrim.
p: pilgrim.
    Plus still grim, etc.

ILID

    Cf. still hid, etc.

ĪLID

Vowel: eyelid.
    Plus sky lid, etc.

ILIJ

gr: grillage.
p: pillage.
t: tillage.
thr: thrillage.
v: village.
    Cf. will age, etc.

ILIK

d: idyllic, odylic.
m: amylic.
r: Cyrillic.
s: basilic, salicylic.
t: dactylic, macrodactylic, zygodactylic.
th: methylic.
    Cf. still lick, etc.

ILIN

kw: McQuillin.
m: MacMillin.
  Plus still in *or* inn, etc.
  Cf. ilan, ilon, etc.

ĪLĪN

sk: skyline.
st: styline.
  Plus try line, etc.

ILING

b: billing.
ch: chilling.
dr: drilling.
f: filling, fulfilling, overfilling, refilling, upfilling.
fr: befrilling, frilling.
gr: grilling.
k: killing.
m: milling.
sh: shilling.
shr: shrilling.
sp: spilling.
st: instilling, stilling.
sw: swilling.
t: distilling, tilling.
thr: enthrilling, thrilling.
tr: trilling.
w: unwilling, willing.

ĪLING

f: defiling, filing.
g: beguiling, guiling, time beguiling.
hw: whiling.
p: compiling, piling, repiling, unpiling, uppiling.
r: riling.

s: reconciling.
sm: smiling.
st: styling.
t: tiling.
v: reviling.
w: wiling.

ILINGZ

b: Billings.
  Plus iling+s.

ILIP

f: fillip, Philip.
  Cf. still lip, etc.

ILIPS

f: fillips, Phillips, Philipse.
  Cf. still lips, etc.

ILIS

f: Phyllis.
r: Amaryllis.
t: Myrtillis.
w: Willis, Wyllis.

ĪLISH

st: stylish.

ĪLĪT

dr: dry light.
h: high light.
sk: skylight.
st: stylite.
tw: twilight.
z: xylite.
  Plus why light, etc.

ILIZM

h: hylism.
l: Carlylism.

ĪLIZM

h: hylism.
l: Carlylism.

ILJOI

k(c): killjoy.
  Plus still joy, etc.

ILKÄKS

f: Philcox.
s: Silcox.
w: Wilcox.
  Plus still cocks, etc.

ILKĒ

m: milky.
s: silky.
w: Willkie.
  Plus milk, he, etc.
  Plus will key, etc.

ILKING

b: bilking.
m: milking.

ILKƏN

m: milken.
s: silken.
  Cf. Milk an *or* on, etc.

ĪLLƏS

g: guileless.
sm: smileless.
w: wileless.
  Plus style, Les *or* less, etc.

ILMĒ

f: filmy.
  Plus thrill me, etc.

ILMÔR

f: Filmore.
g: Gilmore.
  Plus thrill more, etc.
  Plus film oar *or* o'er, etc.

ILMƏN

b: billman.
g: Gilman.
gr: grillman.
h: hillman.
m: millman, Milman.
st: Stillman.
  Plus kill man, etc.

ILMƏNT

f: fulfillment.
st: instillment.
t: distillment.
  Plus skill meant, etc.

ĪLMƏNT

f: defilement.
g: beguilement.
s: exilement, irreconcilement,
reconcilement.
v: revilement.
  Plus style meant, etc.

ILNUR

m: Milner.

ILNƏS

Vowel: illness.
ch: chillness.
shr: shrillness.
st: stillness.

ĪLNƏS

n: juvenileness.
v: vileness.

ILŌ

b: billow, embillow.
d: armadillo, grenadillo, peccadillo.
gr: negrillo.
k(c): killow*, kilo+.
p: pillow.
v: pulvillo*.
w: weeping willow, willow.
 Plus still owe *or* O, etc.
 Cf. fill low, etc.

ĪLŌ

f: phyllo+.
h: high-low.
m: milo.
s: silo.
 Plus try low *or* Lowe, etc.
 Plus smile owe *or* O, etc.

ILŌD

p: pillowed, unpillowed.
 Plus ilo+ed.

ĪLOID

st: styloid.
z: xyloid.
 Plus why, Lloyd, etc.

ILPIN

g: Gilpin.
 Plus still pin, etc.

ILR̄M

gr: grillroom.
st: stillroom.
 Plus thrill room, etc.

ILSĪD

h: hillside.
r: rill side.
 Plus still side *or* sighed, etc.

ILSƏN

g: Gilson.
st: Stilson.
w: Wilson.
 Plus fill son *or* sun, etc.

ILTĒ

g: guilty.
s: silty.
st: stilty.
 Plus milt, he, etc.

ILTEST

j: jiltest*.
k(c): kiltest*.
kw: quiltest*.
l: liltest*.
t: tiltest*.
w: wiltest*.
 Plus skill test, etc.

ILTETH

j: jilteth*.
k(c): kilteth*.
kw: quilteth*.
l: lilteth*.
t: tilteth*.
w: wilteth*.

ILTHĒ

f: filthy.
 Plus spilth, he, etc.

ILTING

j: jilting.
k(c): kilting.

kw: quilting.
l: lilting.
s: silting.
t: tilting.
w: wilting.

ILTUR

f: filter, infilter, philter.
j: jilter.
k(c): kilter.
kw: quilter.
t: tilter.
w: wilter.
    Plus tilt her *or* err, etc.

ILTƏN

ch: Chilton.
h: Hilton.
m: Milton.
st: Stilton.
t: Tilton.
    Plus fill ton *or* tun, etc.
    Plus wilt on, etc.

ĪLUM

f: phylum.
s: asylum.
w: Wylam.
    Plus file 'em, etc.
    Plus why, Lum, etc.

ILUR

Vowel: iller.
b: biller.
ch: chiller.
d: killer-diller.
dr: driller.
f: filler, fulfiller.
fr: befreiller, friller.
gr: griller.
k(c): killer, giant killer, lady-killer, man-killer.

m: Joe Miller, miller.
p: caterpillar, pillar.
s: maxillar, siller.
sh: Schiller.
shr: shriller.
sp: spiller.
st: instiller, stiller.
sw: swiller.
t: distiller, Rototiller, tiller.
th: thiller.
thr: thriller.
tr: triller.
w: ill-willer, willer.
    Plus thrill her *or* err, etc.

ĪLUR

f: befilar, defiler, filar, filer.
g: beguiler.
h: Huyler.
m: miler, half-miler, quarter-miler, two-miler, etc.
p: compiler, piler, uppiler.
r: riler.
s(sc): reconciler.
sk: Schuyler.
sm: smiler.
st: stylar.
t: tiler, Tyler.
v: reviler, viler.
w: Weyler, wiler.
z: Van Zuyler, zuyler.
    Plus beguile her, *or* err, etc.

ILUS

br: fibrillous.
g: aspergillus.
j: orgillous.
s: bacillus.
v: favillous, villus.
    Plus thrill us, etc.

ILVUR

s: silver.

Plus still ver*, etc.

ILVƏN

s: sylvan.

Plus fill van, etc.

Cf. Kill von, etc.

ILYUN

b: billion, tourbillion.

d: mandillion, modillion.

l: lillian.

m: million, vermillion.

n: nonillion.

p: pllion.

r: carillon, quadrillion.

s: decillion.

st: stillion.

t: cotillion, octillion, postillion, quintillion, sextillion.

tr: trillion.

v: pavillion.

Cf. villian.

ILYUNTH

b: billionth.

m: millionth.

n: nonillionth.

r: quadrillionth.

s: decillionth.

t: actillionth, quintillionth, sextillionth.

tr: trillionth.

ILYUR

b: atrabiliar.

m: familiar.

s: auxiliar, conciliar, domiciliar.

Cf. iliur.

ILYURDZ

b: billiards.

m: milliards.

Plus fill yards, etc.

ILYƏM

g: Gilliam.

w: William.

Plus still yam, etc.

ILYƏNS

br: brillance.

Cf. ilians, iliens.

ILYƏNT

br: brilliant.

Cf. iliant, ilient.

ILƏ

Vowel: Illa.

b: Sybilla.

d: bobadilla, cedilla, codilla, granadilla, sabadilla, sapodilla, squidilla.

l: Lilla, Lillah.

m: armilla, bismillah, Camilla.

n: anilla, granilla, manila, manilla, vanilla.

r: barilla, camarilla, cascarilla, gorilla, guerilla, rachilla, sarsaparilla, sasparilla.

s: Drusilla, Maxilla, Priscilla, Scylla.

t: flotilla, mantilla, Tilla.

v: villa.

Plus kill a, etc.

ĪLƏM

hw: whilom.

Plus beguile 'em, etc.

ILƏN

d: Dillon.
v: arch villain, villain, villein.
  Plus kill an *or* Ann, etc.
  Cf. ilan.
  Cf. ilon.

ĪLƏND

Vowel: island, Long Island, Rhode Island, etc.
h: highland.
r: Ryland.
sk: skyland.
t: Thailand.
  Plus my land, etc.
  Plus smile and, etc.

ĪLƏNS

s: silence.
  Cf. violence.
  Cf. style hence, etc.

ĪLƏNT

s: silent
  Plus sky lent, etc
  Cf. violent

ĪLƏS

s: Silas.
v: Vilas.
  Plus my lass, etc.
  Plus Nile ass, etc.

ILƏT

b: billet.
f: fillet.
m: millet.
r: rillet.
sk: skillet.
w: willet, Willett.
  Plus still et, etc.

ĪLƏT

Vowel: eyelet, islet.
p: pilot, sky pilot.
st: stylet.
  Plus sky let, etc.
  Plus try lot, etc.
  Cf. ilet.

ĪMAKS

kl: anticlimax, climax.
  Plus rhyme ax, etc.
  Plus why, Max, etc.

ĪMĀT

pr: primate.
  Plus prime, ate *or* eight, etc.
  Plus why mate, etc.

IMBL

f: fimble.
g: gimbal, Gimbel.
n: nimble.
s: cymbal, symbol.
t: tymbal.
th: thimble.
w: wimble.
  Plus trim bull, etc.

IMBŌ

b: bimbo.
k(c): akimbo, kimbo.
l: limbo.
  Plus him, beau, bo *or* bow, etc.

IMBRƏL

hw: whimbrel.
t: timbrel.

IMBUR

Vowel: imber.
l: limber, unlimber.
t: timber, timbre.
   Plus slim burr, etc.

IMBURD

t: timbered, untimbered.
   Plus imbur+ed.

IMBUS

l: limbus.
n: nimbus.
   Plus him buss *or* bus, etc.

IMBƏ

b: bimbah.
r: marimba.
s: simbah.

IMĒ

g: gimme.
hw: whimmy.
j: jimmy.
sh: shimmy.
   Plus gi me, etc.
   Plus trim, he, etc.

ĪMĒ

bl: blimy.
gr: grimy.
l: limey, limy.
r: rimy, rhymy.
sl: beslimy, slimy.
st: stymie.
th: thymy.
   Plus try me, etc.
   Plus rhyme, he, etc.

IMEST

br: brimmest*.
d: dimmest.
gr: grimmest.
pr: primmest.
sk: skimmest*.
sl: slimmest.
sw: swimmest*.
tr: trimmest.

ĪMEST

ch: chimest*.
gr: begrimest*.
kl: climbest*.
l: sublimest.
pr: primest.
r: berhymest*, rhymest*.
sl: beslimest*.

IMETH

br: brimmeth*.
d: dimmeth*.
sk: skimmeth*.
sw: swimmeth*.
tr: trimmeth*.

ĪMMETH

ch: chimeth*.
gr: begrimeth*.
kl: climbeth*.
pr: primeth*.
r: berhymeth*, rhymeth*.
sl: beslimeth*.

IMFLAM

fl: flimflam.
   Plus nymph lam *or* lamb, etc.

IMID

t: timid.
  Cf. Jim hid, etc.

IMIJ

Vowel: image.
skr(scr): scrimmage.
  Cf. dim age, etc.

IMIK

b: cherubimic.
k(c): alchimic, cacochymic.
m: mimic, pantomimic.
n: eponymic, homonymic, metonymic, metronymic, patronymic, synonymic.
t: etymic.
th: lipothymic.
z: zymic.
  Plus try Mick, etc.

IMING

br: brimming.
d: bedimming, dimming.
gr: grimming.
sk: skimming.
sl: slimming.
sw: swimming.
tr: betrimming, trimming.

ĪMING

ch: chiming.
gr: begriming, griming.
kl: climbing.
l: beliming, liming.
pr: priming, pump priming.
r: berhyming, rhyming.
sl: besliming, sliming.
t: timing.
  Plus buy Ming, etc.

ĪMIST

r: rhymist.
t: timist.
  Plus pie missed *or* mist, etc.

IMIT

l: limit.
  Plus dim it, etc.

IMJAMZ

j: jimjams.
  Plus hymn jams, etc.

IMKRAK

j: gimcrack.
  Plus him crack, etc.

IML

fr: Friml.
g: gimmal.
gr: Grimmell.
h: Himmel.
k(c): kimmel.
  Plus limb 'll, etc.

IMLĒ

d: dimly.
gr: grimly.
pr: primly.
sl: slimly.
tr: trimly.
  Plus him, Lee *or* lea, etc.

ĪMLĒ

l: sublimely.
pr: primely.
t: timely, untimely.
  Plus rhyme, Lee *or* lea, etc.

IMLƏS

br: brimless.
h: hymnless.
hw: whimless.
l: limbless.
r: rimless.
sw: swimless.
v: vimless.
   Plus skim less *or* Les, etc.

ĪMLƏS

ch: chimeless.
gr: grimeless.
kr: crimeless.
l: limeless.
r: rhymeless, rimeless.
sl: slimeless.
t: thymeless, timeless, overtimeless.
   Plus lime less *or* Les, etc.
   Plus I'm less *or* Les, etc.

IMNĒ

ch: chimney.
   Plus slim knee, etc.

IMNƏL

h: hymnal.
s: simnel.

IMNƏS

d: dimness.
gr: grimness.
pr: primness.
sl: slimness.
tr: trimness.

ĪMNƏS

l: sublimeness.
pr: primeness.

IMPĒ

Vowel: impi, impy.
kr: crimpy.
sk: skimpy.

IMPING

Vowel: imping.
bl: blimping.
kr: crimping.
l: limping.
pr: primping.
shr: shrimping.
sk: skimping.
skr(scr): scrimping.
   Plus him ping, etc.

IMPISH

Vowel: impish.
   Plus him? Pish!, etc.

ĪMPIT

l: limepit.
sl: slimepit.
   Plus rhyme pit *or* Pitt, etc.

IMPL

d: dimple.
kr: crimple.
p: pimple.
r: rimple.
s: simple.
w: bewimple, wimple.
   Plus limb pull, etc.

IMPLĒ

d: dimply.
kr: crimply.
l: limply.
p: pimply.
s: simply.
   Plus limp, Lee, *or* lea, etc.

IMPLEST

d: dimplest*.
kr: crimplest*.
p: pimplest*.
r: rimplest*.
s: simplest.
w: wimplest*.
  Plus limp, lest, etc.

IMPLETH

d: dimpleth*.
kr: crimpleth*.
p: pimplet*.
r: rimpleth*.
s: simpleth*.
w: wimpleth*.

IMPLING

Vowel: impling.
d: dimpling.
kr: crimpling.
p: pimpling.
r: rimpling.
shr: shrimpling.
w: wimpling.

IMPLUR

d: dimpler.
kr: crimpler.
r: rimpler.
s: simpler.
w: wimpler.

IMPUR

hw: whimper.
kr: crimper.
l: limper.
s: simper.
shr: shrimper.

sk: skimper.
skr(c): scrimper.
  Plus skimp her *or* err, etc.

IMPƏT

l: limpet.
  Plus him, pet, etc.

IMRŌZ

pr: primrose.
  Plus limb rose, etc.

IMSHI

Vowel: imshi.
  Plus limb, sh, etc.

ĪMSTUR

r: rhymester.
  Plus time stir, etc.

IMSƏN

j: jimson.
  Plus him, son *or* sun, etc.

IMUR

Vowel: immer.
br: brimmer.
d: dimmer.
g: gimmer.
gl: glimmer.
gr: grimmer.
h: hymner.
l: limner.
pr: primer, primmer.
s: simmer.
sh: shimmer.
sk: skimmer.
sl: slimmer.
sw: swimmer.
tr: trimmer.
z: zimmer.

Plus limn her, etc.
Cf. trim myrrh, etc.

ĪMŬR

ch: chimer.
gr: begrimer.
h: Hergesheimer, Laubenheimer.
kl: lineman's climber, climber,
social climber.
l: sublimer.
pr: primer.
r: rhymer.
t: old-timer, timer.
    Plus time her *or* err, etc.

ĪMUS

pr: primus.
r: rimous.
s: Simous.
t: timeous, untimeous.
    Plus beslime us, etc.

IMZĒ

fl: flimsy.
hw: whimsey.
sl: slimsy.
    Plus limbs, he, etc.
    Cf. him see, etc.

IMZƏN

kr: crimson, encrimson.
    Plus limbs on *or* an, etc.

ĪMƏ

Vowel: Ima.
l: Lima.
m: Jemima.
s: cyma.
    Plus rhyme a, etc.
    Plus I'm a, etc.

ĪMƏL

k(c): isocheimal.
kr: isocrymal.
pr: primal.
    Plus time, Al, etc.

IMƏN

r: Rimmon.
s: persimmon.
w: women.
    Plus limb on *or* an, etc.
    Cf. imon.

ĪMƏN

d: daiman.
h: Hymen.
p: pieman.
s: Simon.
t: Timon.
w: Wyman.
    Plus iman.
    Plus why, man, etc.
    Cf. why, men, etc.

ĪMƏND

d: diamond.
    Plus Wyman'd, etc.

IMƏNZ

s: persimmons, Simmons.
    Plus Rimmon's

ĪMƏT

kl: climate.

ĪNĀT

b: binate.
kw: quinate.
    Plus mine ate *or* eight, etc.

INCHEST

fl: flinchest*.
kl: clinchest*.
l: lynchest*.
p: pinchest*.
   Plus skin chest, etc.

INCHETH

fl: flincheth*.
kl: clincheth*.
l: lyncheth*.
p: pincheth*.

INCHING

fl: flinching, unflinching.
kl: clinching.
l: lynching.
p: pinching.

INCHUR

fl: flincher.
kl: clincher.
l: lyncher.
p: pincher.
   Plus pinch her, etc.

INCHURZ

p: pinchers.
   Plus inchu+s.

INDĒ

l: Lindy.
s: Lucindy.
sh: shindy.
w: windy.
   Plus thinned, he, etc.

ĪNDEST

b: bindest*.
bl: blindest*.

f: findest*.
gr: grindest*.
k: kindest.
m: remindest*.
w: windest*.

ĪNDETH

b: bindeth*.
bl: blindeth*.
f: findeth*.
gr: grindeth*.
m: mindeth*, remindeth*.
w: windeth*.
   Plus wine, death, etc.

ĪNDFOOL

m: mindful, remindful, unmindful.
   Plus dined full, etc.

INDIG

sh: shindig.
   Plus kin dig, etc.

INDIK

Vowel: indic.
s: syndic.
   Plus win, Dick, etc.

ĪNDING

b: binding, inbinding, unbinding, upbinding.
bl: blinding.
f: finding.
gr: grinding.
m: minding, reminding.
w: unwinding, upwinding.

INIS

p: pinnace.

INDL

br: brindle.
dw: dwindle.
k: enkindle, kindle, rekindle.
sp: spindle.
sw: swindle.
  Plus wind'll, etc.
  Plus kin dull, etc.

INDLD

br: brindled.
  Plus indl+d.

INDLĒ

h: Hindley.
sp: spindly.
  Plus thinned, Lee *or* lea, etc

ĪNDLĒ

bl: blindly.
k: kindly, unkindly.
  Plus mind, Lee *or* lea, etc.

INDLEST

br: brindlest*.
dw: dwindlest*.
k: enkindlest*, kindlest*, rekindlest*.
sw: swindlest*.
  Plus wind, lest, etc.

INDLETH

br: brindleth*.
dw: dwindleth*.
k: enkindleth*, kindleth*, rekindleth*.
sw: swindleth*.

INDLING

br: brindling.
dw: dwindling.

k: enkindling, kindling, rekindling.
sw: swindling.

INDLUR

dw: dwindler.
k: kindler.
sw: swindler.

ĪNDNƏS

bl: blindness, color blindness.
k: kindness, loving kindness, unkindness.

INDŌ

w: bay window, launch window, window.
  Plus inn dough *or* doe, etc.

INDRƏNS

h: hindrance.

INDRƏD

k: kindred.
  Plus inn dread, etc.
  Plus thinned red, etc.

INDUR

fl: flinder.
h: hinder.
p: pinder.
s: cinder, rescinder.
t: tinder.
  Plus skinned her *or* err, etc.

ĪNDUR

b: binder, spellbinder.
bl: blinder.
f: faultfinder, finder, pathfinder, waterfinder.
gr: grinder, organ-grinder.
h: hinder.

k: kinder.
m: minder, reminder.
w: sidewinder, stem-winder, winder.

Plus bind her *or* err, etc.

INDƏ

l: Belinda, Ethelinda, Linda.
r: Chlorinda, Dorinda.
s: Lucinda.

Plus skinned a, etc.

INDƏD

br: brinded*.
s: abscinded, exscinded, interscinded, rescinded.
w: long-winded, short-winded, winded.

Plus kin dead, etc.

Cf. kin did, etc.

ĪNDƏD

bl: blinded, self-blinded, snow-blinded.
m: alike-minded, bloody-minded, carnal-minded, double-minded, earthly minded, even-minded, evil-minded, fair-minded, feeble-minded, fleshly minded, free-minded, high-minded, light-minded, like-minded, low-minded, minded, narrow-minded, public-minded, reminded, simple-minded, sober-minded, strong-minded, worldly minded.
r: rinded.
w: winded.

Plus shine, dead, etc.
Plus dined, Ed, etc.
Cf. mine did, etc.

INDƏN

l: linden, Lindon.
m: Minden.

Plus inn den, etc.

INĒ

b: Binney.
ch: chinny.
d: Dinny.
f: finny.
g: guinea, New Guinea.
gr: grinny.
h: hinny.
hw: whinney.
j: jinny, Virginny.
m: ignominy, Minnie.
n: ninny, pickaninny.
p: pinny.
pl: Pliny.
sh: shinney.
sk: skinny.
skw: squinny.
sp: spinney.
t: Tinney, tinny.
v: vinny.

Plus din, he, etc.

ĪNĒ

br: briny.
ch: chinie.
h: Heine.
hw: whiney.
l: liney, outliney.
m: miny.
p: piney.
sh: moonshiny, shiny, sunshiny.
sp: spiny.
t: tiny.
tw: twiney.

v: viny.
w: winy.
Plus mine, he, etc.

INEST

d: dinnest*.
g: beginnest*.
gr: grinnest*.
p: pinnest*.
s: sinnest*.
sk: skinnest*.
sp: spinnest.
th: thinnest.
w: winnest.
Cf. thin nest, etc.

ĪNEST

b: combinest*.
d: condignest*, dinest*.
f: confinest*, definest*, finest, refinest*, superfinest.
hw: whinest*.
kl: declinest*, inclinest*, reclinest*.
l: Malignest, outlinest*, underlinest*.
m: minest*, underminest*.
n: benignest.
p: pinest*, supinest.
s: assignest*, consignest*, countersignest*, reassignest*, signest*, undersignest*.
sh: outshinest*, shinest*.
shr: enshrinest*.
tw: entwinest*, intertwinest*, overtwinest*, twinest*, untwinest*.
v: divinest*.
w: winest*.
z: designest*, resignest*.
Plus high nest, etc.

INETH

d: dinneth*.
g: beginneth*.
gr: grinneth*.
j: ginneth*.
p: pinneth*.
s: sinneth*.
sk: skinneth*.
sp: spinneth*.
w: winneth*.

ĪNETH

b: combineth*.
d: dineth*.
f: confineth*, defineth*, refineth*.
hw: whineth*.
kl: declineth*, inclineth*, reclineth*.
l: maligneth*, outlineth*, underlineth*.
m: mineth*, undermineth*.
p: pineth*, repineth*.
s: assigneth*, consigneth*, countersigneth*, reassigneth*, signeth*, undersigneth*.
sh: outshineth*, shineth*.
shr: enshrineth*.
tw: entwineth*, intertwineth*, overtwineth*, twineth*, untwineth*.
v: divineth*.
w: wineth*.
z: designeth*, resigneth*.

INFOOL

s: sinful.
Plus skin full, etc.

INFƏNT

Vowel: infant.

INGBŌLT

k: kingbolt.
r: ringbolt, wringbolt.
  Plus bring bolt, etc.

INGDÄNG

d: ding-dong+.

INGDUV

r: ringdove.
  Plus bring dove, etc.

INGDƏM

k: kingdom.
  Plus sting dumb, etc.

INGĒ

kl: clingy.
spr: springy.
st: stingy.
str: stringy.
sw: swingy.
w: wingy.
  Plus bring, he, etc.

INGED

w: winged.
  Plus ing+ed*.
  Plus bring, Ed, etc.

INGEST

br: bringest*.
gl: flingest*.
r: ringest*, wringest*.
s: singest*.
sl: slingest*.
spr: springest*.
st: stingest*.
str: stringest*.
sw: swingest*.
w: outwingest*, wingest*.

INGETH

br: bringeth*.
fl: flingeth*.
kl: clingeth*.
r: ringeth*, wringeth*.
s: singeth*.
sl: slingeth*.
spr: springeth*.
st: stingeth*.
str: stringeth*.
sw: swingeth*.
w: outwingeth*, wingeth*.

INGGĒ

d: dinghy.
  Cf. Feringhee.

INGGL

Vowel: ingle.
d: dingle.
j: jingal, jingle.
kr: cringle, Kriss Kringle.
m: commingle, immingle, intermindle, mingle.
s: single, surcingle.
sh: shingle.
spr: springal.
sw: swingle.
t: tingle.
tr: tringle.
  Plus sing, gull, etc.

INGGLD

m: unmingled.
  Plus springald.
  Plus ingl+d.

INGGLĒ

j: jingly.
m: mingly.
s: singly.

sh: shingly.
t: tingly.
    Plus sing glee, etc.

INGGLEST

j: jinglest*.
m: minglest*.
t: tinglest*.

INGLETH

j: jingleth*.
m: mingleth*.
t: tingleth*.

INGGLING

j: jingling.
k: kingling.
m: intermingling, mingling.
s: singling.
t: tingling.
w: wingling.

INGGLISH

Vowel: English.
t: tinglish.

INGGLUR

j: Jingler.
m: intermingler, mingler.
sh: shingler.
t: tingler.

INGGŌ

b: bingo.
d: dingo.
gr: gringo.
j: jingo.
l: lingo.
m: flamingo.

r: Ringo.
st: stingo.
    Plus wing go, etc.

INGGUR

f: finger, forefinger, index finger.
l: linger, malinger.

INGGURD

f: light-fingered, rosy-fingered, web-fingered.
    Plus inggur+ed.

INGGUS

d: dingus.
    Plus sing, Gus, etc.

INGGWISH

t: contradistinguish, distinguish, extinguish.

INGGWƏL

l: bilingual, lingual.

INGGƏ

h: anhinga.

INGING

br: bringing, upbringing.
d: dinging.
fl: flinging.
kl: clinging.
r: enringing, ringing, wringing.
s: plain singing, singing.
sl: slinging, unslinging.
spr: springing.
st: stinging.
str: restringing, stringing, unstringing, upstringing.
sw: swinging.
w: outwinging, winging.

INGKCHUR

s: cincture, encincture.
t: tincture.
  Plus winked you're *or* your, etc.

INGKCHURD

s: cinctured, encinctured, uncinctured.
t: tinctured, untinctured.

INGKĒ

Vowel: inky.
bl: blinky.
d: dinky.
k: kinky.
p: pinky.
z: zincky.
  Plus think, he, etc.

INGKEST

Vowel: inkest*.
bl: blinkest*.
ch: chinkest*.
dr: drinkest*.
kl: clinkest*.
l: linkest*.
p: pinkest.
s: sinkest*.
shr: shrinkest*.
sl: slinkest*.
st: stinkest*.
th: bethinkest*, thinkest*.
w: hoodwinkest*, winkest*.

INGKETH

Vowel: inketh*.
bl: blinketh*.
ch: chinketh*.
dr: drinketh*.
kl: clinketh*.
l: linketh*.

p: pinketh*.
s: sinketh*.
shr: shrinketh*.
sl: slinketh*.
st: stinketh*.
th: bethinketh*, thinketh*.
w: hoodwinketh*, winketh*.

INGKGŌ

g: ginkgo.
  Plus sink go, etc.

INGKĪD

bl: blink-eyed.
p: pink-eyed.
  Plus think, I'd *or* eyed, etc.

INGKING

Vowel: inking.
bl: blinking, unblinking.
ch: chinking.
dr: drinking.
kl: clinking.
l: enlinking, interlinking, linking, relinking, unlinking.
pr: prinking.
r: rinking.
s: sinking.
shr: shrinking, unshrinking.
sl: slinking.
st: stinking.
th: bethinking, freethinking, thinking, unthinking.
w: hoodwinking, unwinking, winking.
  Plus bring kind, etc.

INGKL

Vowel: inkle.
kw: crinkle.
r: wrinkle.
spr: bewprinkle, sprinkle.

t: tinkle.
tw: twinkle.
w: periwinkle, winkle.
  Plus pink'll, etc.

INGKLD

r: unwrinkled.
  Plus ingkl+d.

INGKLĒ

kr: crinkly.
p: pinkly.
r: wrinkly.
t: tinkly.
tw: twinkly.
  Plus think, Lee, or lea, etc.

INGKLEST

kr: crinklest*.
r: wrinklest*.
spr: sprinklest*.
t: tinklest*.
tw: twinklest*.
  Plus think, lest, etc.

INGKLETH

kr: crinkleth*.
r: wrinkleth*.
spr: sprinkleth*.
t: tinkleth*.
tw: twinkleth*.

INGKLING

Vowel: inkling.
kr: crinkling.
r: wrinkling.
spr: besprinkling, sprinkling.
t: tinkling.
tw: twinkling.

INGKLUR

r: wrinkler.
spr: sprinkler.
t: tinkler.
tw: twinkler.

INGKŌ

st: stinko.
  Plus drink owe or O, etc.

INGKSHƏN

t: contradistinction, distinction,
extinction, indistinction,
intinction.
  Plus drink shun, etc.

INGKTIV

t: contradistinctive, distinctive,
instinctive.

INGKTNƏS

s: succinctness.
t: distinctness, indistinctness.

INGKUN

l: Lincoln.
p: pinkun.
  Plus think an or on, etc.

INGKUR

Vowel: inker.
bl: blinker.
dr: drinker.
kl: clinker.
l: enlinker, linker.
p: pinker.
pr: prinker.
r: rinker.
s: sinker.
shr: shrinker.
sl: slinker.

st: stinker.
t: tinker.
th: bethinker, freethinker, thinker.
w: hoodwinker, tiddledywinker, winker.
　　Plus shrink her *or* err, etc.

INGKUS

r: ornithorhynchus, oxyrhynchus.
s: scincus.
z: zincous.
　　Plus shrink us, etc.

INGKƏT

tr: trinket.
　　Cf. think it, etc.

INGLĪK

k: kinglike.
spr: springlike.
w: winglike.
　　Plus thing like, etc.

INGLƏS

k: kingless.
r: ringless.
spr: springless.
st: stingless.
w: wingless.
　　Plus bring less *or* Les, etc.

INGLƏT

k: kinglet.
r: ringlet.
spr: springlet.
w: winglet.
　　Plus bring Lett *or* let, etc.

INGRƏM

Vowel: Ingram.
　　Plus thin gram, etc.

INGSÔNG

s: singsong.
spr: spring song.
　　Plus bring song, etc.

INGTĪM

r: ringtime.
spr: springtime.
　　Plus bring time, etc.

INGUR

br: bringer, firebringer, news bringer.
d: dinger, humdinger.
fl: flinger.
hw: whinger.
kl: clinger.
r: bell ringer, clotheswringer, ringer, wringer.
s: balladsinger, mastersinger, Meistersinger, minnesinger, singer.
sl: mudslinger, slinger, unslinger.
spr: springer.
st: stinger.
str: stringer.
sw: swinger.
w: winger.
　　Plus bring her, Ur *or* err, etc.

INGƏM

b: Bingham.
　　Plus bring 'em, etc.

INIK

b: Jacobinic, rabbinic.
d: Odinic.
f: delphinic, finic.
j: polygynic.
kl: aclinic, clinic, isoclinic, monoclinic.
kw: quinic.

l: Franklinic.
m: Brahminic, fulminic.
p: pinic.
r: mandarinic.
s: cynic.
t: actinic, adiactinic, diactinic, narcotinic, nicotinic, platinic.
v: vinic.
   Plus win, Nick *or* nick, etc.

ĪNIK

k(c): kinic.
p: pinic.
v: vinic.
   Plus try, Nick *or* nick, etc.

INIM

m: minim.
   Plus win him, etc.
   Cf. Louyhnhmn.

INING

Vowel: inning.
ch: chinning.
d: dinning
g: beginning.
gr: grinning.
j: cotton ginning, ginning.
p: pinning, underpinning, unpinning.
s: sinning, unsinning.
sh: shinning.
sk: skinning.
sp: spinning.
t: tinning.
th: thinning.
tw: twinning.
w: winning.

ĪNING

b: combining.
br: brining.

d: dining.
f: confining, defining, fining, refining, trephining.
hw: whining.
j: jining.
kl: declining, inclining, reclining.
l: aligning, interlining, lining, maligning, outlining, relining, underlining.
m: countermining, intermining, mining, undermining.
p: opining, phining, repining.
s: assigning, consigning, countersigning, signing, subsigning.
sh: beshining, moonshining, outshining, shining.
shr: enshrining, shrining.
tw: entwining, intertwining, overtwining, twining, untwining.
v: divining.
w: wining.
z: designer, resigning.

ININGZ

Vowel: innings.
   Plus ining+s.

INISH

f: finish, Finnish
m: diminish.
t: tinnish.
th: thinnish.

INISHT

m: diminished, undiminished.
   Plus inish+ed.

INIST

l: violinist.
   Cf. in+est.

ĪNĪT

f: finite.
kr: crinite.
  Plus try night *or* knight, etc.

INJĒ

d: dingy.
fr: fringy.
kr: cringy.
st: stingy.
sw: swingy.
tw: twingy.
  Plus binge, he, etc.

INJEST

fr: befringest*, fringest*,
imfringest*, infringest*.
h: hingest*, unhingest*.
kr: cringest*.
s: singest*.
sw: swingest*.
t: tingest*.
tw: twingest*.
  Plus thin jest, etc.

INJETH

fr: befringeth*, fringeth*,
imfringeth*, infringeth*.
h: hingeth*, unhingeth*.
kr: cringeth*.
s: singeth*.
sw: swingeth*.
t: tingeth*.
tw: twingeth*.

INJING

fr: fringing, infringing.
h: hinging, unhinging.
kr: cringing.
s: singeing.
sw: swingeing.

t: tingeing.
tw: twingeing.

INJLƏS

fr: fringless.
h: hingeless.
sw: swingless.
t: tingeless.
tw: twingeless.
  Plus cringe, Les *or* less, etc.

INJMƏNT

fr: infringement.
h: unhingement.
p: impingement.
  Plus binge meant, etc.

ĪNJUJ

l: line judge.

INJU̇R

Vowel: injure.
fr: fringer, infringer.
h: hinger.
j: ginger.
kr: cringer.
s: singer.
tw: twinger.
  Plus unhinge her *or* err, etc.

INJƏNS

t: contingence.
  Cf. ingen+s.

INJƏNT

f: fingent.
fr: refringent.
p: impingent.
r: ringent.
str: astringent, constringent,
restringent, stringent.

t: contingent, tingent*.
  Plus thin gent, etc.

INJƏZ

b: binges.
d: dinges.
fr: befringes, fringes, infringes.
h: hinges, unhinges.
kr: cringes.
p: impinges.
s: singes.
skr(scr): scringes.
spr: springes.
str: constringes, perstringes.
sw: swinges.
t: tinges.
tw: twinges.
  Plus thin jizz, etc.
  Cf. hinge is, etc.

ĪNKLAD

p: pine-clad.
v: vine-clad.
  Plus mine clad, etc.

INKUM

Vowel: income.
  Plus skin come, etc.

INKRĒS

Vowel: increase.
  Plus skin crease, etc.

ĪNKROUND

p: pine-crowned.
v: vine-crowned.
  Plus shine, crowned, etc.

INKWISH

l: relinquish.
v: vinquish.
  Cf. think wish, etc.

INKƏ

Vowel: Inca.
  Plus think a, etc.
  Cf. Katinka, Katrinka.

INLĒ

Vowel: inly.
f: Finley.
g: McGinley.
k(c): McKinley.
th: thinly.
  Plus skin, Lee *or* lea, etc.

ĪNLĒ

d: condignly.
f: finely, superfinely.
l: aquilinely, malignly.
n: benignly, caninely, saturninely.
p: supinely.
v: divinely.
  Plus fine, Lee *or* lea, etc.

INLƏND

Vowel: inland.
f: Finland.
  Plus thin land, etc.

ĪNLƏND

r: Rhineland.
v: Vineland.
  Plus wine land, etc.

INLƏS

d: dinless.
f: finless.

l: ginless.
k(c): kinless.
p: pinless.
s: sinless.
sk: skinless.
t: tinless.
w: winless.
　　Plus din less *or* Les, etc.

ĪNMƏNT

f: confinement, refinement.
kl: inclinement.
l: alignment, interlinement.
s: assignment, consignment.
tw: entwinement.
z: designment, resignment.
　　Plus mine meant, etc.

INNƏS

th: thinness.
　　Cf. in es.

ĪNNƏS

d: condignness.
f: fineness, superfineness.
l: salineness.
p: supineness.
v: divineness.

INŌ

m: minnow.
w: winnow.
　　Plus inn owe *or* O, etc.
　　Cf. inn know *or* no, etc.

ĪNŌ

Vowel: Aino.
b: albino.
f: damfino.
r: rhino.
d: juredivino.

　　Plus why no *or* know, etc.
　　Plus mine owe *or* O, etc.

ĪNÔF

s: sign off.
　　Plus mine off, etc.

IN

s: sinew, unsinew.
t: continue, discontinue, retinue.
　　Plus skin ewe *or* you, etc.
　　Plus skin ewe *or* you, etc.
　　Cf. skin new, etc.

IN   D

s: sinewed, unsinewed.
t: continued, discontinued.
　　Plus win, you'd, etc.

INSĒ

kw: Quincy.
r: rinsey.
　　Plus skin, see, etc.
　　Plus prince, he, etc.

INSENS

Vowel: incense.
　　Plus skin sense, etc.
　　Cf. St. Vincent's.

INSEST

Vowel: incest.
m: mincest*.
pr: princessed.
r: rinsest*.
v: convincest*, evincest*.
w: wincest*.

INSETH

m: minceth*.
r: rinseth*.

v: convinceth*, evinceth*.
w: winceth*.
　　Plus kin, Seth, etc.

INSHƏL

v: provincial.
　　Plus kin shall, etc.
　　Plus winch, Al, etc.

INSING

m: mincing.
r: rinsing.
v: convincing, evincing, unconvincing.
w: wincing.
　　Plus skin, sing, etc.

INSIV

v: evincive.
　　Plus skin sieve, etc.

INSL

t: tinsel.
　　Plus skin sell, etc.
　　Plus prince 'll, etc.
　　Cf. Insull.

INSLĒ

pr: princely.
　　Plus quince, Lee *or* lea, etc.

INSMƏNT

v: convincement, evincement.
　　Plus quince meant, etc.

INSTRƏL

m: minstrel.

INSTUR

m: minster, Westminster.
sp: spinster.
　　Plus skin stir, etc.

INSUM

w: winsome.
　　Plus skin some *or* sum, etc.

INSUR

m: mincer.
r: rincer.
v: convincer.
w: wincer.
　　Plus tin, sir, etc.
　　Plus convince her *or* err, etc.

INSURZ

p: pincers.
　　Plus insur+s.

INSƏNT

v: St. Vincent, Vincent.
　　Plus inn sent *or* scent, etc.

INSƏS

pr: princess.

INTĒ

d: Dinty.
fl: flinty.
g: McGinty.
gl: glinty.
l: linty.
skw: squinty.
　　Plus thin tea, etc.

ĪNTĒ

n: ninety.
　　Plus fine tea, etc.
　　Plus pint, he, etc.

INTEST

gl: glintest*.
h: hintest*.
m: mintest*.
pr: imprintest*, misprintest*, printest*.
spr: sprintest*.
st: stintest*.
t: tintest*.
    Plus skin test, etc.

INTETH

gl: glinteth*.
h: hinteth*.
m: minteth*.
pr: imprinteth*, misprinteth*, printeth*.
spr: sprinteth*.
st: stinteth*.
t: tinteth*.

INTHIK

r: labyrinthic.
s: absinthic.
    Plus skin thick, etc.

INTHIN

b: terebinthine.
r: labyrinthine.
s: hyacinthine.
    Plus skin thin, etc.

INTĪD

fl: flint-eyed.
skw: squint-eyed.
    Plus thin tied or tide, etc.
    Plus print, I'd or eyed, etc.

INTIJ

m: mintage.
v: vintage.
    Cf. printage age, etc.

INTING

d: dinting.
gl: glinting.
h: hinting.
m: minting.
pr: imprinting, misprinting, printing.
skw: squinting.
spr: sprinting.
st: stinting.
t: aqua tinting, tinting.

INTL

kw: quintal.
l: lintle.
p: pintle.
    Plus hint'll, etc.
    Plus twin tell, etc.

INTŌ

p: pinto.
sh: Shinto.
t: mezzotinto.
    Plus skin toe, or tow, etc.
    Plus print owe or O, etc.

INTRÄN

Vowel: intron.

INTRĒ

spl: splintry.
v: vintry.
w: wintry.
    Plus thin tree, etc.

INTRƏST

Vowel: interest, self-interest.
spl: splinterest.
w: winterest*.
    Plus hint rest, etc.

INTᴜR

d: dinter.
h: hinter.
m: minter.
pr: imprinter, printer.
skw: squinter.
spl: splinter.
spr: sprinter.
st: stinter.
t: aquatinter, tinter.
w: winter.
  Plus print her *or* err, etc.

INTƏD

d: dinted.
gl: glinted.
h: hinted.
m: minted.
pr: imprinted, misprinted, printed.
skw: squinted.
spr: sprinted.
st: stinted.
t: rainbow-tinted, rosy-tinted, tinted.
v: vinted.
  Plus print, Ed, etc.
  Plus kin, Ted, etc.

INᴜR

Vowel: inner.
b: Bynner.
ch: chinner.
d: dinner, after-dinner.
f: finner.
g: beginner.
gr: grinner.
j: cotton ginner, ginner.
p: pinner, unpinner.
s: sinner.
sh: shinner.
sk: skinner.
sp: spinner.
t: tinner.
th: thinner.
tw: twinner.
w: breadwinner, winner.
  Plus inn her *or* err, etc.

ĪNᴜR

b: combiner.
d: diner.
f: confiner, definer, finer, refiner.
hw: whiner.
kl: decliner, incliner, recliner.
l: liner, maligner, penny-aliner, reliner, underliner.
m: calciminer, miner, minor, underminer.
n: benigner.
p: piner, repiner, supiner.
s: assigner, calciner, consigner, signer.
sh: shiner.
shr: enshriner, shriner.
st: Steiner.
tw: entwiner, intertwiner, twiner.
v: diviner.
w: winer.
z: archdesigner, designer, resigner.
  Plus fine her *or* err, etc.

ĪNᴜS

b: binous.
k(c): echinus.
l: linous, Linus, salinous.
m: minus.
p: lupinus, Pinus.
r: Rhynus.
s: sinus.
sp: spinous.
  Plus fine us, etc.

INWŲRD

Vowel: inward.
    Plus thin ward, etc.

INYUN

b: Binyon.
m: dominion, minion.
p: opinion, pinion.
    Plus skin yon*, etc.
    Cf. inian.

INYUND

m: dominioned, minioned.
p: opinioned, pinioned, self-opinioned.

INZĒ

kw: quinsey.
l: Lindsay, Linsey, linsey.
    Plus pins, he, etc.

INZIK

tr: extrinsic, intrinsic.

INZŲR

w: Windsor.
    Plus pins or, etc.

INƏ

m: Minna.
r: Corinna+, Erinna.
    Plus tin, a, etc.

ĪNƏ

Vowel: Ina.
b: Sabina+.
br: Sabrina+.
ch: China.
d: Dinah.
gr: Melegrina.

h: Heine.
j: Jaina, Regina+.
k(c): Shekina, trichina.
l: Adelina, Angelina, Carolina, Catalina+, Evelina, Messalina, North Carolina, salina, semolina, South Carolina.
m: Mina.
n: Nina.
r: farina+, Platyrhyna.
s: Lucina+.
t: Tina+.
tr: Katrina+.
    Plus fine a, etc.

ĪNƏL

b: binal.
f: final, semifinal.
kl: acclinal, anticlinal, declinal, isoclinal, periclinal, synclinal.
kr: crinal, endocrinal.
kw: equinal*.
n: caninal.
r: rhinal.
s: officinal, piscinal.
sp: cerebrospinal, spinal.
t: matutinal.
tr: trinal.
v: Vinal.
    Plus mine, Al, etc.

INƏN

l: linen.
    Cf. thin hen, etc.
    Cf. win in, etc.

INƏS

Vowel: Inness.
g: Guinness.
t: laurestinus.
    Cf. pinnace.

ĪNƏS

dr: dryness.
h: highness.
n: nighness.
r: wryness.
sh: shyness.
sl: slyness.
spr: spryness.

INƏT

l: linnet.
m: minute.
sp: spinet.
　　Cf. thin net, etc.
　　Cf. in it, etc.

ĪŌ

Vowel: Io.
h: heigh-ho.
kl: Clio+.
r: Rio+.
tr: trio+.
　　Plus why ow *or* O, etc.

ĪÔF

l: lie-off.

ĪUR

pr: prior.
　　Plus sky or, etc.
　　Cf. iur.

IPCHUR

skr(scr): scripture.
　　Plus clipped your *or* you're, etc.

IPĒ

ch: chippy.
d: dippy.
gr: grippy.

l: Lippo Lippi, lippy.
n: nippy.
s: Mississippi.
sh: shippy.
sn: snippy.
z: zippy.
　　Plus ship he, etc.

ĪPĒ

Vowel: I.P.
p: pipy.
sw: swipey.
　　Plus stripe, he, etc.

IPEST

ch: chippest*.
d: dippest*.
dr: drippest*.
fl: flippest.
gr: grippest*.
hw: horsewhippest*, whippest*.
j: gyppest*.
kl: clippest*.
kw: equippest*.
n: nippest*.
r: rippest*.
s: sippest*.
sh: shippest*.
sk: skippest*.
sl: slippest*.
sn: snippest*.
str: outstrippest*, strippest*.
t: tippest*.
tr: trippest*.
　　Cf. ship pest, etc.

ĪPEST

p: Pipest.
r: ripest.
t: typest*, typist.
w: wipest*.
　　Plus why pest, etc.

IPETH

ch: chippeth*.
d: dippeth*.
dr: drippeth*.
fl: flippeth*.
gr: grippeth*.
hw: horse-whippeth*, whippeth*.
j: gyppeth*.
kl: clippeth*.
kw: equippeth*.
n: nippeth*.
r: rippeth*.
s: sippeth*.
sh: shippeth*.
sk: skippeth*.
sl: slippeth*.
sn: snippeth*.
str: outstrippeth*, strippeth*.
t: tippeth*.
tr: trippeth*

ĪPETH

gr: gripeth*.
p: pipeth*.
t: typeth*.
w: wipeth*.

IPID

s: insipid.

IPIJ

k(c): kippage.
skr(scr): scrippage.
str: strippage.
　　Cf. skip age, etc.

IPIK

h: hippic.
l: phillippic.

t: atypic, daguerreotypic, electrotypic, homotypic, idiotypic, monotypic, phonotypic, stereotypic.
　　Cf. ship pick, etc.

IPIN

p: pippin.
　　Plus ship in *or* inn, etc.
　　Cf. skippin', etc.

IPING

ch: chipping.
d: dipping.
dr: dripping.
gr: gripping.
hw: horsewhipping, whipping.
j: gypping.
kl: clipping.
kw: equipping, quipping.
n: nipping.
p: pipping.
r: ripping.
s: sipping.
sh: shipping, transhipping.
sk: skipping.
sl: slipping.
sn: snipping.
str: outstripping, overstripping, stripping.
t: tipping.
tr: atripping, tripping.

ĪPING

gr: griping.
p: Peiping, piping.
str: striping.
sw: swiping.
t: stereotyping, typing.
w: wiping.
　　Plus I ping, etc.

IPISH

gr: grippish.
h: hippish, hyppish.
sn: snippish.
   Cf. strip, pish!

IPL

gr: grippal.
kr: becripple, cripple.
n: nipple.
r: ripple.
s: sipple.
st: stipple.
sw: swiple.
t: tipple.
tr: triple.
   Plus ship'll, etc.
   Cf. ship pull, etc.

ĪPL

s: disciple.
t: ectypal.
   Plus why, pal, etc.
   Plus trip, Al, etc.
   Cf. stripe all, etc.

IPLĒ

kr: cripply.
r: ripply.
st: stipply.
tr: triply.
   Plus ship, Lee *or* lea, etc.

IPLING

k(c): Kipling.
kr: crippling.
r: rippling.
st: stippling.
str: strippling.
t: tippling.

IPLUR

kr: crippler.
t: tippler.

IPLƏT

l: liplet
r: ripplet.
s: siplet.
tr: triplet.
   Plus ship let *or* Lett, etc.

IPMƏNT

kw: equipment.
sh: shipment, transhipment.
   Plus quip meant, etc.

ĪPNƏS

r: dead-ripeness, overripeness, ripeness, underripeness, unripeness.

IPŌ

h: hippo.
j: gippo*.
l: Lippo.
   Plus ship owe *or* O, etc.

ĪPRƏS

s: cypress.
   Plus my press, etc.

IPSĒ

j: gypsy.
k(c): Poughkeepsie.
sk: Skipsey.
t: tipsy.
   Plus ships, he, etc.
   Plus ship, see, etc.

IPSHƏN

j: Egyptian.
n: conniption.
skr(scr): ascription, circumscription, conscription, description, inscription, prescription, proscription, rescription, subscription, superscription, transcription.
    Plus ship shun, etc.

IPSINGK

l: lip-sync.

IPSIS

l: ellipsis.
tr: tripsis.
    Plus skip, sis, etc.

IPSŌ

d: dipso.

IPTIK

d: diptych.
gl: anaglyptic, glyptic.
kl: ecliptic.
kr: cryptic, holocryptic.
l: apocalyptic, iatraliptic.
st: stypic.
tr: triptych.
    Plus ship tick, etc.

IPTIV

skr(scr): adscriptive, ascriptive*, circumscriptive, descriptive, indescriptive, inscriptive, prescriptive, proscriptive, rescriptive, transcriptive.

IPUR

ch: chipper.
d: Big Dipper, dipper.

dr: dripper.
fl: flipper*.
gr: gripper.
hw: horsewhipper, whipper.
j: gyper.
k(c): kipper, Yom Kippur.
kl: clipper.
n: gallinipper, nipper.
p: pipper.
r: Jack the Ripper, ripper.
s: sipper.
sh: shipper, transhipper.
sk: skipper.
sl: lady's slipper, slipper.
sn: snipper.
str: outstripper, overstripper, stripper.
sw: swipper*.
t: tipper.
tr: tripper.
z: zipper.
    Plus whip her *or* err, etc.

ĪPUR

d: diaper.
gr: griper.
l: Leiper.
p: bagpiper, piper.
r: riper.
sn: sniper.
str: striper.
sw: swiper.
t: daguerreotyper, electrotyper, linotyper, monotyper, stereotyper, typer.
v: viper.
w: wiper.
    Plus why purr *or* per, etc.
    Plus stripe her *or* err, etc.

IPURD

k: kippered.
sk: skippered.

sl: slippered.
Plus zipper'd, etc.

IPƏ

l: Philippa.
p: Pippa.
Plus skip a, etc.

ĪPƏN

r: enripen, ripen.
Plus my pen, etc.
Cf. swipe hen, etc.

ĪPƏND

r: ripened.
st: stipend.
Plus why penned, etc.
Plus stripe end, etc.

IPƏNT

fl: flippant.
tr: trippant.
Plus ship pant, etc.
Plus skip ant *or* aunt, etc.

IPƏT

s: sippet.
sk: skippet.
sn: snippet.
t: tippet.
Plus skip it, etc.

ĪRĀT

Vowel: irate+.
j: circumgyrate, dextrogyrate, gyrate.
l: lyrate.
Plus fire ate *or* eight, etc.
Plus why rate, etc.
Cf. fire rate, etc.

ĪRĒ

Vowel: Dies Irae, eyrie.
d: dairi, diary.
kw: acquiry*, enquiry, inquiry.
m: miry.
n: praemunire.
skw: squiry.
sp: spiry.
t: retiree.
w: wiry.
Plus fire, he, etc.
Cf. iri.
Cf. fiery and Iuri.
Cf. Erie, and eri.

ĪRĒM

b: bireme.
tr: trireme.
Plus buy ream, etc.

ĪRĒN

p: Pyrene.
skw: squireen.

ĪREST

d: direst.
f: firest*.
h: hirest*.
kw: acquirest*, enquirest*, inquirest*, requirest*.
m: admirest*, bemirest*, mirest*.
p: pyrest*, umpirest*.
sp: aspirest*, conspirest*, expirest*, inspirest*, perspirest*, respirest*, suspirest*, transpirest*.
t: attirest*, retirest*, tirest*.
w: wirest*.
z: desirest*.
Plus why rest, etc.

ĪRETH

f: fireth*.
h: hireth*.
kw: acquireth*, enquireth*, inquireth*, requireth*.
m: admireth*, bemireth*, mireth*.
p: pyreth*, umpireth*.
sp: aspireth*, conspireth*, expireth*, inspireth*, perspireth*, respireth*, suspireth*, transpireth*.
t: attireth*, retireth*, tireth*.
w: wireth*.
z: desireth*.

ĪRFLĪ

f: firefly.
    Plus desire fly, etc.

ĪRFOOL

Vowel: ireful.
d: direful.
    Plus desire full, etc.

IRID

Vowel: irid.
v: virid.
    Cf. he rid, etc.

IRIK

j: panegyric.
l: lyric.
p: empiric, Pyrrhic.
t: buutyric, satiric, satyric.
    Cf. Viereck.

IRIL

s: Cyril.
v: virile.
    Cf. irel.

ĪRING

f: firing.
h: hiring.
kw: acquiring, enquiring, inquiring, requiring.
l: lyring.
m: admiring, bemiring, miring.
p: pyring.
skw: squiring.
sp: aspiring, conspiring, expiring, inspiring, perspiring, respiring, suspiring, transpiring, unaspiring.
t: attiring, retiring, tiring, untiring.
z: desiring, undesiring.

ĪRIS

Vowel: iris.
s: Isiris.
    Cf. desire is, etc.

ĪRISH

Vowel: Irish.
    Cf. mirish, etc.

IRIST

j: panegyrist.
l: lyrist+.

ĪRIST

Vowel: irised.
l: lyrist+.
    Plus why wrist, etc.

IRIT

sp: dispirit, inspirit, master spirit, party spirit, spirit.
    Cf. fear it, etc.

IRL

b: Birrell.
skw: squirrel.

t: Tirrell.

Plus stir L *or* ell, etc.

Cf. Cyril, Tyrol, virile.

ĪRLING

h: hireling.

skw: squireling.

ĪRMƏN

f: fireman.

Plus desire, man, etc.

ĪRMƏNT

kw: acquirement, requirement.

m: bemirement.

sp: aspirement.

t: retirement.

Plus fire meant, etc.

ĪRNƏS

d: direness.

t: entireness.

ĪRŌ

j: autogiro, gyro.

k(c): Cairo.

t: tyro.

Plus why row *or* roe, etc.

Plus fire owe *or* O, etc.

ĪRŌD

b: byroad.

h: highroad.

Plus sky road, etc.

Plus fire ode *or* owed, etc.

ĪRŌS

j: gyrose.

v: virose.

Plus why rose, etc.

Cf. squire hose, etc.

ĪRSĪD

f: fireside.

Plus desire sighed *or* side, etc.

ĪRSUM

Vowel: iresome.

t: tiresome.

Plus fire some *or* sum, etc.

IRUP

ch: chirrup.

st: stirrup.

s: syrup.

Plus her *or* err up, etc.

IRƱR

m: mirror.

Cf. erur.

ĪRƱR

f: firer.

h: hirer.

kw: acquirer, enquirer, inquirer, requirer.

m: admirer, bemirer, mirer.

p: pyrer.

skw: squirer.

sp: aspirer, conspirer, expirer, inspirer, perspirer, respirer, transpirer, unaspirer.

t: attirer, retirer, tirer.

z: desirer.

Plus desire her *or* err, etc.

ĪRUS

p: apyrous, Epirus, papyrus.

s: Cyrus.

v: rhinovirus, virus.

z: desirous.

Plus hire us, etc.

ĪRWŬRKS

f: fireworks
w: wireworks.
 Plus desire works, etc.

IRƏ

s: sirrah.

ĪRƏ

Vowel: Ira.
f: Sapphira.
j: hegira.
k: Kirah.
l: Lyra.
m: Almira, Elmira, Myra, Palmyra.
th: Thyra.
 Plus hire a, etc.

ĪRƏL

j: gyral.
sp: spiral.
t: retiral.
 Plus inquire, Al, etc.

ĪRƏM

h: Hiram.
 Plus buy ram, etc.
 Plus fire 'em, etc.

ĪRƏN

b: Byron.
ch: Chiron.
j: gyron.
s: lepidosiren, siren.
v: environ, viron.
 Plus why wren, etc.
 Plus fire on *or* an, etc.
 Plus fire hen, etc.

ĪRƏNT

j: gyrant.
kw: inquirent.
sp: aspirant, conspirant, expirant, spirant.
t: archtyrant, tyrant.
v: semipirvirent, virent.
 Plus irant.
 Plus fire aunt *or* ant, etc.
 Plus why rant, etc.

ĪRƏT

p: pirate.
 Cf. fire at, etc.

ĪSĀL

sk: skysail.
tr: trysail.
 Plus why sale *or* sail, etc.
 Plus ice ail *or* ale, etc.

ISCHÄRJ

d: discharge.

ISCHIF

m: mischief.

ISCHƏN

kr: anti-Christian, Christian.
 Plus miss Chan, etc.

ISĒ

m: missi.
s: sissy.
 Plus kiss, he, etc.

ĪSĒ

Vowel: icy.
n: nisi.

sp: spicy.
t: Datisi.
　Plus why see, etc.

ISEST

h: hissest*.
k(c): kissest*.
m: dismissest*, missest*.

ĪSEST

f: sacrificest*, sufficest*.
n: nicest.
pr: pricest*.
s: conciset, precisest.
sl: slicest*.
sp: bespicest*, spicest*.
spl: splicest*.
t: enticest*.

ISETH

h: hisseth*.
k(c): kisseth*.
m: dismisseth*, misseth*.

ĪSETH

f: sacrificeth*, sufficeth*.
pr: priceth*.
sl: sliceth*.
sp: bespiceth*, spiceth*.
spl: spliceth*.
t: enticeth*.
　Plus why, Seth, etc.

ISĒZ

l: Ulysses.
　Cf. isez.
　Cf. miss seas or seize, etc.

ISFOOL

bl: blissful, unblissful.
m: remissful.
　Plus kiss full, etc.

ISHĒ

d: dishy.
f: fishy.
sw: swishy.

ISHEST

d: dishest*.
f: fishest*.
sw: swishest*.
w: wishest*.

ISHETH

d: dishcth*.
f: fisheth*.
sw: swisheth*.
w: wisheth*.

ISHFOOL

d: dishful.
w: wishful.
　Plus knish full, etc.

ISHING

d: dishing.
f: fishing.
sw: swishing.
w: ill-wishing, well-wishing, wishing.

ISHUR

d: disher.
f: Fischer, fisher, fissure, king-fisher.

sw: swisher.

w: ill-wisher, well-wisher, wisher.

 Plus swish her *or* err, etc.

ISHUS

b: ambitious.

d: expeditious, injudicious, judicious, seditious.

f: beneficious, inofficious, officious, veneficous.

j: flagitous.

l: cilicious*, delicious, gentilitious*, malicious, natalitious, satellitious, silicious.

m: pumicious, vermicious.

n: pernicious, puniceous.

p: auspicious, inauspicious, piceous, propitious, suspicious.

pl: multiplicious.

pr: capricious.

r: avaricious, lateritious, sericeous.

s: exitious*.

st: superstitious.

t: addititious, adjectitious, adscititious, adventitious, arreptitious*, ascititious, ascriptitious, deglutitious, factitious, fictitious, obreptitious, profectitious, secretitious, stillatitious, supposititious, surreptitious, tralatitious.

tr: meretricious, nutritious, obstetricious*.

v: vicious.

z: suppositious.

 Plus wish us, etc.

ISHƏ

l: Delicia.

t: Letitia.

 Plus wish a, etc.

ĪSHƏ

l: Elisha.

ISHƏL

d: extrajudicial, judicial, prejudicial.

f: artificial, beneficial, edificial, inartificial, official, sacrificial, superficial.

l: gentilitial, natalitial, policial.

m: comitial.

n: initial, tribunicial.

s: exitial*.

st: interstitial, volstitial.

t: accrementitial, recrementitial, susticial.

 Cf. we shall, etc.

 Plus wish, Al, etc.

ISHƏN

Vowel: circuition*, fruition, intuition, tuition.

b: adhibition, ambition, exhibition, imbibition, inhibition, prohibition.

br: Hebrician, rubrician.

d: addition, audition, condition, deperdition*, edition, erudition, expedition, extradition, perdition, precondition, redition, redition*, rendition, sedition, superaddition, tradition, vendition.

f: fission.

j: logician, magician.

l: abolition, coalition, demolition, ebullition, Galician, nolition, Paulician, resilition, volition.

m: academician, admission, adomician, commission, demission, dismission, emission, immission, insubmission, intermission, intromission, irremission, manumission, mission, obdormition, omission, permission, readmission, remission, submission, transmission, vomition.

n: abannition*, admonition, affinition, ammunition, cognition, definition, epinician, egnition, illinition, inanition, inition, mechanician, monition, munition, neoplatonician, Phoenician, precognition, premonition, punition, pyrotechnician, recognition, reunition, submonition, tribunition.

p: Apician, suspicion.

pl: simplician*.

r: abligurition*, apparition, futurition, parturition, preterition, rhetorician.

s: insition.

st: superstition.

t: accremention, acoustician, aglution, arithmetician, bipartition, competition, deglutition, denitition, departition, dialectician, hydrostatician, magnetician, mathematician, optician, partition, petition, politician, practician, repetition, sortition, statistician, tactician, tralatition, tripartition.

tr: attrition, contrition, detrition, electrician, geometrician, metrician, nutrition, obstetrician, patrician.

z: acquisition, apposition, composition, contraposition, decomposition, disposition, disquisition, exposition, imposition, indisposition, inquisition, interposition, juxtaposition,

musician, opposition, perquisition, physician, position, predisposition, preposition, presupposition, proposition, recomposition, reposition, requisition, superposition, supposition, transposition, transition.

Plus ishun.

ISHƏNS

f: deficience, efficience, insufficience, maleficience, proficience, self-sufficience.

n: omniscience.

sp: perspicience, prospicience.

ISHƏNT

f: beneficient, calorificient, coefficient, deficient, efficient, indeficient, inefficient, insufficient, maleficient, perficient*, proficient, self-sufficient, sufficient.

j: objicient.

l: volitient.

n: omniscient.

ISHƏP

b: bishop.

Cf. fish up, etc.

ISH

Vowel: issue.

t: tissue.

Plus miss you *or* ewe, etc.

ISID

v: viscid.

ISIK

l: salicic.
t: masticic.

ISIN

t: datiscin.
v: viscin.
  Plus bliss in, etc.

ISING

h: dehiscing, hissing.
k(c): kissing.
m: dismissing, missing.

ĪSING

Vowel: icing.
d: dicing.
f: sacrificing, self-sacrificing, self-sufficing, sufficing.
pr: pricing.
sl: slicing.
spl: splicing.
t: enticing.
  Plus why sing, etc.

ĪSIS

Vowel: isis.
kr: crisis.
t: phthisis.
  Cf. is+es.
  Cf. rice is, etc.

ISIT

l: elicit, illicit, licit, solicit.
pl: explicit, implicit.
  Plus kiss it, etc.

ISITH

m: misseth.

ISIV

m: admissive, commissive, demissive*, dismissive, emissive, interissive, irremissive, missive, nonsubmissive, omissive, permissive, promissive, remissive, submissive, transmissive.
  Cf. this sieve, etc.

ĪSIV

l: collisive.
r: derisive.
s: decisive, incisive, indecisive.
tr: cicatrisive.
v: divisive.
  Plus why sieve, etc.

ISKĀT

f: confiscate.
v: inviscate.
  Plus bliss, Kate, etc.
  Plus disc eight *or* ate, etc.

ISKĒ

fr: frisky.
hw: whiskey, Irish whiskey, etc.
r: risky.
  Plus this key, etc.
  Plus whisk, he.

ISKEST

br: briskest.
fr: friskest*.
hw: whiskest*.
r: riskest*.

ISKETH

fr: frisketh*.
hw: whisketh*.
r: risketh*.

ISKFOOL

fr: friskful.
r: riskful.
   Plus risk full, etc.

ISKIN

gr: griskin.
s: siskin.
   Plus this kin, etc.
   Plus whisk in *or* inn, etc

ISKING

br: brisking.
fr: frisking.
hw: whisking.
r: risking.
   Plus this king, etc.

ISKIT

b: biscuit.
   Plus bliss, Kit, etc.
   Plus risk it, etc.

ISKŌ

kr: Crisco.
s: Fransisco, San Francisco.
   Plus risk owe *or* O, etc.
   Cf. this Co., etc.

ISKUR

br: brisker.
fr: frisker.
hw: bewhisker, wisker.
r: risker.
   Plus risk her *or* err, etc.

ISKURZ

hw: whiskers.
   Plus iskur+s.

ISKƏ

r: Mariska.

ISKƏL

d: discal.
f: fiscal.
l: oeliscal.
   Plus kiss, Cal, etc.
   Plus whisk, Al, etc.

ISKƏS

b: hibiscus.
d: discous, discus.
k(c): trochiscus.
n: lemniscus, meniscus.
s: abaciscus.
t: lentiscus.
v: viscous.
   Plus risk us, etc.

ISKƏT

br: brisket.
fr: frisket.
t: tisket.
   Cf. risk it, etc.

ISL

b: abyssal.
br: bristle.
f: fissile.
gr: gristle.
hw: whistle.
m: dismissal, missal, missile.
p: epistle.
s: scissel, scissile.
th: thistle.
   Plus kiss'll, this'll, etc.
   Cf. Isil, isl.

ISLĒ

br: bristly.
gr: gristly.
th: thistly.
   Plus bliss, Lee *or* lea, etc.

ĪSLĒ

n: nicely.
s: Cicely, concisely, precisely.
   Plus price, Lee *or* lea, etc.

ISLING

br: bristling.
hw: whistling.

ĪSLƏS

Vowel: iceless.
d: diceless.
m: miceless.
pr: priceless.
sp: spiceless.
spl: spliceless.
v: adviceless, viceless, etc.
   Plus price less *or* Les, etc.

ĪSMƏNT

f: self-sufficement, sufficement.
t: enticement.
   Plus lice meant, etc.

ISMUS

Vowel: isthmus.
   Plus this muss, etc.
   Cf. Christmas.

ISN

gl: glisten.
kr: christen.
l: listen, relisten.
   Plus this'n, etc.
   Cf. this sun *or* sun, etc.

ISNING

gl: glistening.
kr: Christening.
l: listening.

ĪSNƏS

n: niceness, overniceness.
s: conciseness, preciseness.

ISNƏS

m: remissness.
th: thisness.

ISPĒ

kr: crispy.
l: lispy.

ISPEST

kr: crispest.
l: lispest*.
   Plus this pest, etc.

ISPETH

kr: crispeth*.
l: lispeth*.

ISPIN

kr: Crispin, St. Crispin.
   Plus this pin, etc.

ISPING

kr: crisping.
l: lisping.
   Plus this ping, etc.

ISPUR

hw: stage whisper, whisper.
kr: crisper.
l: lisper.
   Plus this purr *or* per, etc.
   Plus crisp her *or* err, etc.

ISTFĪT

f: fistfight.

ISTL

kr: crystal.
l: listel.
p: pistol, pocket pistol, water pistol.

Plus kissed, Al, etc.

ĪSTDƏM

kr: Christdom.

Plus sliced dumb, etc.

ISTĒN

l: Philistine+.
pr: pristine+.
s: Sistene+.

ISTEST

l: enlistest*, listest*.
s: assistest*, consistest*, insistest*, subsistest*.
tw: twistest*.
z: desistest*, existest*, persistest*, resistest*.

Plus this test, etc.

ISTETH

l: enlisteth*, listeth*.
m: misteth*.
s: assisteth*, consisteth*, insisteth*, subsisteth*.
tw: twisteth*.
z: desisteth*, existeth*, persisteth*, resisteth*.

ISTFOOL

m: mistful.
w: wistful.

Plus fist full, etc.

ISTIK

Vowel: altruistic, atheistic, casuistic, deistic, egoistic, Hebraistic, Judaistic, monotheistic, pantheistic, polytheistic, theistic, tritheistic.

d: Buddhistic, methodistic, sadistic, Talmudistic.

f: fistic, philosophistic, sophistic.

gw: linguistic.

h: Elohistic.

j: aphlogistic, bibleopegistic, dialogistic, epilogistic, eulogistic, logistic, neologistic, palogistic, syllogistic.

k(c): anarchistic, catechistic.

kr: paleocrystic.

l: annalistic, anomalistic, ballistic, bibliopolistic, cabalistic, cameralistic, curialistic, dualistic, electroballistic, evangelistic, familistic, fatalistic, idealitic, individualistic, journalistic, liberalistic, materialistic, naturalistic, nibilistic, nominalistic, parallelistic, pugilistic, rationalistic, realistic, ritualistic, sciolistic, sensualistic, socialistic, somnambulistic, spiritualistic, stylistic, universalistic.

m: alchemistic, animistic, euphemistic, interimistic, mystic, optimistic, pessimistic.

n: agonistic, anachronistic, antagonistic, Calvinistic, canonistic, chauvinistic, communalistic, communistic, eudemonistic, Hellenistic, humanistic, illuministic, Latinistic, monistic, synchronistic, unionistic.

p: papistic, philanthropistic.

pl: simplistic.

r: adiaphoristic, aoristic, aphoristic, characteristic, eristic, Eucharistic, euhemeristic, formularistic, humoristic, juristic, polaristic, puristic, touristic.

s: cystic, solecistic.

sh: fetichistic, schistic.

t: absolutistic, anabaptistic, artistic, baptistic, egotistic, pietistic, quietistic, statistic.

tr: belletristic, patristic.

v: atavistic, Jehovistic.
  Plus this tick, etc.

ISTIKS

j: sphragistics.

l: ballistics.

m: mystics.

n: agonistics.

st: stylistics.

t: statistics.
  Plus istik+s.
  Plus dismiss ticks, etc.
  Cf. dismiss sticks *or* Styz, etc.

ISTIN

j: antiphlogistine, phlogistine.

l: Philistine+.

s: Sistene+.

th: amethystine.
  Plus this tin, etc.
  Plus kissed in *or* inn, etc.

ISTING

l: enlisting, listing.

m: misting.

s: assisting, consisting, insisting, subsisting.

tw: entwisting, intertwisting, twisting, untwisting.

z: desisting, persisting, resisting, unresisting.

ISTIV

z: persistive, resistive.

ISTL

P: pistil
  Plus wrist ill, etc.
  Plus this till, etc.
  Cf. This still, etc.

ISTLƏS

l: listless.

tw: twistless.

z: resistless.
  Plus missed less *or* Les, etc.

ISTMAS

  Plus missed mass, etc.

ISTMƏNT

j: agistment.

l: enlistment.
  Plus wrist meant, etc.

ISTRƏL

m: mistral.

ISTRƏM

tr: tristram.
  Plus this tram, etc.
  Plus missed ram, etc.

ISTRƏS

m: mistress.
  Plus this tress, etc.

ISTƱR

Vowel: Istar.

b: bister.

bl: blister, water blister.

gl: glister.

j: agistor, magister.

l: enlister, lister.

m: mister.

s: assister, foster sister, half sister, insister, sister, stepsister, sobsister, subsister.

tw: intertwister, twister, untwister.

w: Wister.

z: exister, nonresister, passive resister, persister, resister.

Plus missed her *or* err, etc.

ISTURN

s: cistern.

Plus bliss turn, etc.

ISTUS

sh: schistous.

th: acathistus.

Plus missed us, etc.

ISTƏ

l: ballista, Callista.

n: enista.

t: Baptista.

v: Buena Vista, vista.

Plus assist a, etc.

ISTƏD

f: closefisted, fisted, hardfisted, ironfisted, tightfisted, two-fisted.

l: black-listed, enlisted, listed, white-listed.

m: misted.

s: assisted, consisted, cysted, encysted, insisted, subsisted, unassisted.

tw: entwisted, intertwisted, twisted, untwisted.

z: desisted, existed persisted, pre-existed, resisted.

Plus kiss Ted, etc.

Plus missed Ed, etc.

ISTƏM

s: decimal system, system.

Plus kissed 'em, etc.

Cf. miss tum, etc.

ISTƏN

tr: Tristan.

Plus this tan, etc.

ISTƏNS

d: distance, equidistance, long distance.

s: assistance, consistence, inconsistence, insistence, subsistence.

z: coexistence, desistance, existence, inexistence, nonexistence, persistence, pre-existence, resistance.

Cf. istant+s.

Cf. kissed aunts *or* ants, etc.

ISTƏNT

d: distant, equidistant.

s: assistant, consistent, inconsistent, insistent, subsistent.

z: coexistent, existent, inexistent, nonexistent, nonresistant, persistent, pre-existent, resistant.

Plus this tent, etc.

Plus kissed aunt *or* ant, etc.

ISUR

h: dehiscer, hisser.

k: kisser.

m: dismisser, misser, remisser.

Plus hiss her *or* err, etc.

ĪSUR

d: dicer.

f: sacrificer.

g: geyser.
n: nicer.
s: conciser, preciser.
sl: meat slicer, potato slicer, slicer.
sp: spicer.
spl: splicer.
t: enticer.
    Plus why, sir, etc.
    Plus ice her *or* err, etc.

ISUS

Vowel: Issus.
b: byssus.
m: "missus."
s: narcissus.
    Plus kiss us, etc.

ISƏ

l: Elissa, Lissa, Melissa.
r: Clarissa, Nerissa.
    Plus miss a, etc.

ĪSƏL

d: paradisal.
    Plus ice, Al, etc.
    Plus why, Sal, etc.

ISƏM

l: lissome.
    Cf. this sum *or* some, etc.

ĪSƏN

b: bison.
d: Dyson.
gr: grison.
h: hyson.
t: Tyson.
v: vison.
    Plus why, son *or* sun, etc.

ISƏNS

h: dehiscence, indehiscence.
n: reminiscence.
p: concupiscence, resipiscence.
t: fatiscence.
v: reviviscence.
    Cf. bliss sense, scents *or* cents, etc.

ĪSƏNS

l: dog license, fishing license, hunting license, license, marriage license, poetic license.
    Plus buy sense, scents, *or* cents, etc.
    Cf. lice, hence, etc.

ISƏNT

h: dehiscent, indehiscent.
n: reminiscent.
v: reviviscent.
    Cf. bliss sent, scent *or* cent, etc.

ISƏZ

b: abysses.
bl: blisses.
d: prejudices.
f: artifices, benefices, edifices.
h: hisses.
k(c): kisses.
m: dismisses, misses.
p: precipices.
sw: Swisses.
tr: cockatrices.
    Plus this is, etc.

ITĒ

d: banditti, ditty.
fl: flitty.
gr: gritty.
k: kitty.

m: committee, Mittie.
p: pity, self-pity.
pr: pretty.
s: city.
w: witty.
   Plus with, he, etc.

ĪTĒ

bl: blighty.
d: Aphrodite.
fl: flighty.
hw: whity.
m: almighty, mighty, mity.
tr: Amphritrite.
v: arborvitae, ligum vitae.
   Plus might he, etc.
   Plus my tea, etc.
   Cf. iti.

ITĒD

d: dittied.
p: pitied, unpitied.
s: citied.
   Cf. ited.

ĪTEK

h: high-tech.

ITEST

b: bittest*, unbittest*.
f: benefitest*, fittest, refittest*.
fl: flittest*.
h: hittest*.
kw: acquittest*, quittest*.
m: admittest*, committest*, omittest*, permittest*, remittest*, submittest*.
n: knittest*.
p: pittest*.
s: sittest*.
sl: slittest*.
sp: spittest*.
spl: splittest*.
tw: twittest*.
w: outwittest*.

ĪTEST

b: bitest*.
bl: blightest*.
br: brightest.
d: indictest*, inditest*.
f: fightest*.
fr: affrightest*.
hw: whitest.
kw: requitest*.
l: alightest*, delightest*, impolitest, lightest, politest.
m: mightest*.
n: beknightest*, knightest*, reunitest*, unitest*.
pl: plightest*.
r: rightest, uprightest, writest*.
s: citest*, excitest*, incitest*, recitest*, sightest*.
sl: sleightest*, slightest*.
sm: smitest*.
sp: spitest*.
t: tightest.
tr: tritest.
v: invitest*.
   Plus high test, etc.

ITETH

b: bitteth*, unbitteth*.
f: benefiteth*, fitteth*, refitteth*.
fl: flitteth*.
h: hitteth*.
kw: acquitteth*, quitteth*.
m: admitteth*, committeth*, omitteth*, permitteth*, remitteth*, submitteth*.
n: knitteth*.
p: pitteth*.

s: sitteth*.
sl: slitteth*.
sp: spitteth*.
spl: splitteth*.
tw: twitteth*.
w: outwitteth*.

ĪTETH

b: biteth*.
bl: blighteth*.
d: indicteth*, inditeth*.
f: fighteth*.
fr: affrighteth*.
kw: requiteth*.
l: alighteth*, delighteth*,
lighteth*.
m: mighteth*.
n: beknighteth*, knighteth*,
reuniteth*, uniteth*.
pl: plighteth*.
r: righteth*, writeth*.
s: citeth*, exciteth*, inciteth*,
reciteth*, sighteth*.
sl: sleighteth*, slighteth*.
sm: smiteth*.
sp: spiteth*.
v: inviteth*.

ĪTĒZ

r: pyrites, sorites.
Plus fight ease, etc.
Plus why tease *or* teas, etc.

ITFOOL

f: fitful.
w: witful.
Plus knit full, etc.

ĪTFOOL

fr: frightful.
l: delightful.

m: mightful.
r: rightful.
sp: despiteful, spiteful.
spr: sprightful.
Plus bright full, etc.

ITHĒ

p: pithy.
pr: prithee.
sm: smithy.
st: stithy.
w: withy.
Plus myth, he, etc.
Plus with, he, etc.

ĪTHĒ

bl: blithy.
l: lithy.
Plus why the *or* thee*, etc.
Plus scythe, he, etc.

ĪTHEST

bl: blithest.
l: lithest.
r: writhest*.

ĪTHETH

r: writheth*.

ĪTHFOOL

bl: blitheful.
l: litheful.
Plus scythe full, etc.

ITHIK

l: eolithic, lithic, megalithic,
microlithic, monolithic, neolithic,
palaeolithic, trilitic.
m: mythic.
n: ornithic.

ĪTHING

n: nithing*.
r: writhing.
s: scything.
t: tithing.
tr: trithing.

ITHM

r: logarithm, polyrhythm, rhythm.
Plus with 'em, etc.

ITHMIK

r: logarhythmic, polyrhythmic, rhythmic.
Plus with Mick, etc.

ĪTHÄN

p: python.
Plus stithe on *or* an, etc.

ĪTHNƏS

bl: blitheness.
l: litheness.

ĪTHSUM

bl: blithesome.
l: lithesome.
Plus scythe some *or* sum, etc.

ITHUR

bl: blither.
d: dither.
h: behither*, hither.
hw: anywhither, nowhither, somewhither, whither.
sl: slither.
sw: swither.
th: thither.
w: wither.
Plus with her *or* err, etc.

ĪTHUR

Vowel: either+.
bl: blither.
n: neither+.
r: writher.
t: tither.
Plus scythe her *or* err, etc.

ITHURD

w: unwitherered, withered.
Plus ithur+ed.

ITHURZ

w: withers.
Plus ithur+s.

ITIK

Vowel: Jesuitic, Sinaitic.
b: cenobitic, Jacobitic, trilobitic.
d: hermaphroditic, troglodytic.
dr: dendritic.
f: anthropomorphitic, eophitic, epiphytic, mephitic, necrophytic, xerophytic, zoophytic.
j: gingitic.
k(c): conchitic, rachitic.
kl: euclitic, heteroclitic, proclitic.
kr: critic, diacritic, hypercritic, hypocritic, oneirocritic.
l: acrolitic, actinolitic, analytic, anxiolytic, biolytic, catalytic, dialytic, electrolytic, Israelitic, nummulitic, oolitic, paralytic, theodolitic, tonsillitic, toxophilitic, variolitic, zeolitic.
m: Adamitic, dolomitic, eremitic, Hamitic, Islamitic, palmitic, pre-Adamitic, Semitic, Shemitic, Stalagmitic.
n: aconitic, granitic, lignitic, sagenitic, selenitic, syenitic, Titanitic, tympanitic, uranitic.

r: Cabiritic, diphtheritic, margaritic, Nazaritic, phosphoritic, pleuritic, porphyritic, sybaritic.

s: anthracitic, parasitic.

t: hematitic, stalactitic, steatitic, strontitic.

thr: arhritic.

v: Levitic.

ITIKS

l: analytics.

Plus itic+s.

ĪTIN

k(c): chitin.

Cf. iten, iton.

ITING

b: bitting, unbitting.

f: befitting, benefitting, counterfeiting, fitting, misfitting, refitting, steamfitting, unbefitting, unfitting.

fl: flitting.

gr: gritting.

h: hardhitting, hitting, pinchhitting.

kw: acquiting, quitting.

m: admitting, committing, emitting, manumitting, omitting, permitting, pretermitting, recommitting, remitting, submitting, transmitting, unremitting, unsubmitting.

n: knitting.

p: pitting.

s: outsitting, sitting.

sk: skitting.

sl: slitting.

sp: spitting.

spl: hairsplitting, rail splitting, splitting.

tw: twitting.

w: outwitting, unwitting, witting.

ĪTING

b: backbiting, biting.

bl: blighting.

d: expediting, indicting, inditing.

f: cockfighting, fighting, fist fighting.

fr: affrighting, frighting.

hw: whiting.

k(c): kiting.

kw: requiting.

l: acyliting, alighting, delighting, lighting.

m: dynamiting.

n: beknighting, disuniting, igniting, knighting, reuniting, uniting.

pl: plighting.

r: copyrighting, copy writing, handwriting, righting, underwriting, writing.

s: citing, exciting, inciting, reciting, sighting.

sl: slighting.

sm: smiting.

sp: spiting.

v: inviting.

ĪTIS

b: phlebitis.

d: carditis, endocarditis, pericaditis.

fr: nephritis.

j: laryngitis, meningitis, pharyngitis.

k(c): bronchitis, rachitis, trahitis.

l: colitis, hyalitis, tonsillitis.

r: neuritis.

s: appendicitis.

thr: arthritis.

tr: gastritis.

Cf. itus.

ITISH

br: British.
sk: skittish.

ĪTISH

hw: whitish.
l: Ishmaelitish, Israelitish, lightish.
m: eremitish.
n: Canaanitish.
r: anchoritish.
t: tightish.

ĪTIV

d: expeditive.
t: appetitive.

ITL

Vowel: 'ittle.
br: brittle, peanut brittle.
hw: whittle.
kw: acquittal.
l: belittle, little.
m: committal, noncommittal, remittal, transmittal.
n: knittle.
sk: skittle.
sp: lickspittle, spital*, spittle*.
t: tittle.
v: victual.
w: wittle
    Plus bit'll, etc.
    Cf. It'll.

ĪTL

t: entitle, title.
    Plus light 'll, etc.
    Cf. ital.

ITLĒ

f: fitly, unfitly.
    Plus hit Lee *or* lea, etc.

ĪTLĒ

br: brightly.
hw: Whiteley, whitely.
l: impolitely, lightly, politely.
n: Kneightly, knightly, nightly, unknightly.
r: forthrightly, rightly, uprightly.
s: sightly, unsightly.
sl: slightly.
spr: sprightly.
t: tightly.
tr: tritely.
    Plus write, Lee *or* lea, etc.

ITLEST

br: brittlest.
hw: whittlest*.
l: belittlest*, littlest.
v: victualest*.
    Plus hit, lest, etc.

ITLETH

hw: whittleth*.
l: belittleth*.
v: victualeth*.

ITLING

hw: whittling.
k: kitling.
t: titling.
w: witling.

ĪTLING

t: entitling, titling.

ITLIST

h: hit list.

ITLUR

br: brittler.
h: Hitler.

hw: whittler.
l: belittler, littler.
v: victualler.

ITLZ

sk: skittles.
v: victuals.
   Plus itl+s.

ITMƏNT

f: fitment, refitment.
kw: acquitment.
m: commitment, remitment.
   Plus grit meant, etc.

ĪTMƏNT

d: indictment.
fr: affrightment, frightment.
s: excitement, incitement.
v: invitement.
   Plus light meant, etc.

ITNĒ

hw: Mt. Whitney, Whitney.
j: jitney.
   Plus hit knee, etc.

ĪTNING

br: brightening.
fr: frightening.
h: heightening.
hw: whitening.
l: lightening, lightning, sheet lightning.
t: tightening.

ĪTNƱR

br: brightener.
fr: frightener.

h: heightener.
hw: whitener.
l: lightener.
   Cf. whiten her *or* err, etc.

ITNƏS

f: fitness, unfitness.
w: eyewitness, witness.

ĪTNƏS

br: brightness.
hw: whiteness.
l: impoliteness, lightness, politeness.
r: rightness, uprightness.
sl: slightness.
t: tightness.
tr: triteness.

ĪTPEN

l: lightpen.

ĪTRĀT

n: nitrate.
t: titrate.
   Plus bright rate, etc.

ĪTRĒ

m: mitry.
n: nitry*.

ITRIK

s: citric.
v: vitric.
   Plus hit rick, etc.

ĪTRIK

n: nitric.
   Plus bright rick, etc.

ITSĒ

b: itsy bitsy+.
fr: Fritzy+.
r: Ritzy+.
Plus his, he, etc.

ĪTSTIK

n: nightstick.
Plus bright stick, etc.

ITUR

b: bitter, embitter.
f: befitter, benefiter, counterfeiter, fitter, misfitter, refitter, steam fitter, unfitter.
fl: flitter.
fr: fritter.
g: go-gitter.
gl: glitter.
gr: gritter.
h: hitter.
j: jitter.
kr: critter.
kw: acquitter, quitter.
l: litter.
m: admitter, committer, emitter, intermitter, intromitter, manumitter, omitter, permitter, pretermitter, recommitter, remitter, submitter, transmitter.
n: knitter.
p: pitter.
s: outsitter, sitter.
sl: slitter.
sp: spitter.
spl: log splitter, rail splitter, splitter.
t: titter.
tw: atwitter, twitter.
w: outsitter, witter.
Plus hit her *or* err, etc.

ĪTUR

Vowel: iter.
b: arbeiter, backbiter, biter.
bl: blighter.
br: brighter.
d: indicter, inditer.
f: cockfighter, fighter, fist fighter.
fl: first-flighter, flighter, second-flighter, etc.
hw: whiter.
k: check kiter, kiter.
kw: requiter.
l: alighter, cigarette lighter, lighter, impoliter, lamplighter, lighter, moonlighter, politer.
m: bemitre, dynamiter, miter, unmiter.
n: igniter, niter.
pl: plighter.
r: copyrighter, copy writer, righter, typewriter, underwriter, writer.
s: citer, exciter, inciter, reciter, sighter.
sl: slighter.
sm: smiter.
t: tighter.
tr: triter.
v: inviter.
Plus smite her *or* err, etc.

ITURD

b: embittered, unembittered.
Plus itur+ed.

ITURN

b: bittern.
fl: flittern.
g: gittern.
Plus hit urn, erne, *or* earn, etc.

ITŬRZ

b: Angosturabitters, bitters, orange bitters, etc.

Plus itur+s.

ĪTVŬRS

l: light verse.

ĪTWĀT

l: lightweight.

Plus might wait *or* weight, etc.

ĪTWIT

n: nitwit.

Plus hit wit, etc.

ĪTWŬRD

r: rightward.

ITZI

b: itsy-bitsy+.
fr: Fritzy+.
r: Ritzy+.

ITƏD

b: bitted, unbitted.
f: befitted, benefited, counterfeited, fitted, refitted, unbenefited, unfitted.
fl: flitted.
g: gitted.
gr: gritted.
kw: acquitted, quitted.
m: admitted, committed, emitted, intermitted, manumitted, omitted, permitted, recommitted, remitted, submitted, transmitted, unremitted.
n: interknitted, knitted.
p: pitied, pitted.
r: writted.
s: citied.

sl: slitted.
sp: spitted.
spl: splitted.
spr: bowspritted.
t: titted.
tw: twitted.
w: afterwitted, blunt-witted, fat-witted, half-witted, lean-witted, outwitted, quick-witted, ready-witted, sharp-witted, short-witted, subtle-witted, underwitted, witted.

Plus hit, Ed, etc.

ĪTƏD

b: bighted.
bl: blighted.
d: bedighted, dighted*, indicted, indited, undighted*.
fl: eagle-flighted.
fr: affrighted, frighted, unaffrighted, unfrighted.
k: kited.
kw: required, unrequired.
l: alighted, delighted, lighted, unlighted.
m: dynamited.
n: beknighted, benighted, ignited, knighted, nighted, reunited, unbenighted, united.
pl: plighted, trothplighted, unplighted.
r: righted, unrighted.
s: cited, clear-sighted, eagle-sighted, excited, farsighted, foresighted, incited, long-sighted, nearsighted, over-sighted, quick-sighted, recited, second-sighted, sharp-sighted, short-sighted, sighted, sited, unsighted.
sl: slighted.
sp: despited, spited.
tr: attrited, detrited.
v: invited.

Plus bright, Ed, etc.
Plus tie, Ted, etc.

ĪTƏL

kw: requital.
s: cital*, parasital, recital.
t: entitle, title.
tr: detrital.
v: vital.
> Plus fight'll, etc.
> Plus smite, Al, etc.

ĪTƏLZ

v: vitals.
> Plus ital+s.

ĪTƏM

Vowel: item.
> Plus smite 'em, etc.
> Cf. ad infinitum.

ITƏN

b: bitten, flea-bitten, fly-bitten, hunger-bitten, weather-bitten.
br: Britain, Britten, Briton.
f: Fitton.
k: kitten.
l: litten*, red-litten*.
m: mitten.
r: underwritten, unwritten, written.
sm: conscience-smitten, heart-smitten, smitten, sun-smitten, terror-smitten, unsmitten.
> Plus hit an *or* on, etc.
> Plus lit on *or* an, etc.
> Cf. hitten, etc.

ĪTƏN

br: brighten.
fr: frighten.
h: heighten.
kw: whiten.
k(c): chitin, chiton.
l: enlighten, lighten.

t: tighten, Titan.
tr: triton.
> Plus fight on *or* an, etc.
> Plus light on *or* an, etc.
> Plus smite an, etc.
> Plus why ten, etc.
> Cf. iten, itin.
> Cf. why tan *or* ton, etc.

ITƏNS

kw: acquittance, quittance.
m: admittance, omittance, permittance, remittance, transmittance.
p: pittance.
> Cf. hit aunts *or* ants, etc.

ITƏNT

m: emittent, intermittent, intromittent, remittent.
> Cf. hit tent, etc.

ĪTƏS

t: Titus.
tr: detritus.
v: St. Vitus, Vitus.
> Plus smite us, etc.

ĪUMF

tr: triumph.
> Plus sky, umph, etc.

Ī N

tr: triune.

ĪUR

Vowel: eyer.
b: Bayer, Beyer, buyer.
br: briar, brier, sweetbrier.
d: dyer, never-say-dier.
dr: drier, dryer.

f: amplifier, beautifier, certifier, clarifier, classifier, codifier, crucifier, defier, defyer, deifier, degnifier, disqualifier, diversifier, edifier, electrifier, exemplifier, falsifier, fortifier, fructifier, glorifier, gratifier, horrifier, identifier, indemnifier, intensifier, justifier, liquefier, magnifier, modifier, mollifier, mortifier, mystifer, notifier, nullifier, pacifier, personifier, petrifier, purifier, putrefier, qualifier, ramifier, ratifier, rectifier, revivifier, sanctifier, satisfier, scarifier, scorifier, simplifier, signifier, specifier, speechifier, stultifier, stupefier, terrifier, testifier, typifier, verifier, versifier, vilifier, vivifier.

fl: flier, highflier, kiteflier.

fr: black friar, friar, frier, gray friar, white friar.

g: lammergeier.

h: hier, higher.

kr: crier, cryer, decryer, descrier, town crier.

l: liar, lier, relier.

m: Biedermeier, Mayer, Meier, Meyer, Myer, Untermeyer, Untermyer.

n: denier, nigher.

p: occupier.

pl: applier, complier, implier, multiplier, replier, supplier.

pr: prior, pryer.

r: wryer.

s: prophesier, sigher.

sh: shyer.

sk: skyer.

sl: slyer.

sp: spyer.

spr: spryer.

t: tier, tyer, untier.

tr: tier, trioer.

v: vier.

   Plus why her *or* err, etc.

ŬRN

Vowel: grappling iron, iron, lofting iron.

   Plus my urn, erne, *or* earn, etc.

ŬRZ

m: Meyers, Myers.

pl: pliers.

   Plus iur+s.

ŪS

k(c): antibacchius, bacchius.

p: pious, Pius.

pr: nisiprius.

r: Darius.

   Cf. Elias, ias.

ĬVBAK

g: giveback.

ĬVĒ

ch: chivvy.

d: divi-divi, divvy.

l: Livy.

pr: privy.

t: tantivy, tivy.

   Plus forgive, he, etc.

ĪVĒ

Vowel: ivy.

   Plus thrive, he, etc.

ĬVĒD

ch: chivvied.

d: divvied.

l: livid.

pr: privied.

v: vivid.

   Plus Livy'd, etc.

ĪVĒD

Vowel: ivied.

    Plus thrive, he'd etc.

IVEST

g: forgivest*, givest*, misgivest*.
l: livest*, outlivest*, relivest*.

ĪVEST

d: divest*.
dr: drivest*.
l: livest*.
n: connivest*.
pr: deprivest*.
r: arrivest*, derivest*, rivest*.
shr: shrivest*.
str: strivest*.
thr: thrivest*.
tr: contrivest*.
v: revivest*, survivest*.

    Plus my vest, etc.

IVETH

g: forgiveth*, giveth*, misgiveth*.
l: liveth*, outliveth*, reliveth*.

ĪVETH

d: diveth*.
dr: driveth*.
n: conniveth*.
pr: depriveth*.
r: arriveth*, deriveth*, riveth*.
shr: shriveth*.
str: striveth*.
thr: thriveth*.
tr: contriveth*.
v: reviveth*, surviveth*.

IVIK

s: civic.

IVING

g: forgiving, giving, lawgiving, life-giving, misgiving, thanksgiving, unforgiving.
l: everliving, living, outliving.

ĪVING

d: diving.
dr: driving.
h: hiving.
n: conniving.
pr: depriving.
r: arriving, deriving.
shr: shriving.
str: striving.
thr: thriving.
tr: contriving, uncontriving.
v: surviving.
w: wiving.

IVLĒ

t: positively.

ĪVLĒ

l: lively.

    Plus thrive, Lee *or* lea, etc.

IVLING

shr: shrivelling.
sn: snivelling.

ĪVMƏNT

pr: deprivement.
v: revivement.

    Plus C live meant, etc.

IVNƏS

g: forgiveness, unforgiveness.

IVRING

kw: quivering.
l: delivering.
sh: shivering.
sl: slivering.
    Plus give ring, etc.

IVƏR

fl: flivver.
g: forgiver, giver, Indian giver, misgiver.
kw: quiver.
l: cantiliver, deliver, freeliver, liver, outliver.
r: river, Spoon River, etc.
sh: shiver.
sk: skiver.
sl: sliver.
st: stiver.
t: tiver.
    Plus give her *or* err, etc.

ĪVƏR

d: diver, pearl diver.
dr: driver, slave driver.
f: fiver.
h: hiver.
j: gyver.
l: aliver, liver.
n: conniver.
pr: depriver.
r: arriver, deriver, river.
shr: shriver.
sk: skiver.
sl: sliver.
st: stiver.
str: striver.
thr: thriver.
tr: contriver.
v: reviver, surviver.
    Plus shrive her *or* err, etc.

IVƏRD

kw: quivered.
l: delivered, lily-livered, pigeon-livered, white-livered, yellow-livered.
sh: shivered, unshivered.
sl: slivered.
    Plus giver'd, etc.

ĪVUS

kl: acclivous, declivous, proclivous.
l: salivous.
    Plus shrive us, etc.

IVYƏL

tr: trivial.
    Cf. ivial.

ĪVƏ

l: saliva.
s: Saiva, Siva.
sh: shiva.
    Plus I've a, shrive a, etc.

IVƏL

dr: drivel.
r: rivel*.
s: civil, uncivil.
shr: shrivel.
sn: snivel.
sw: swivel.
    Plus forgive 'll, etc.

ĪVƏL

k(c): archival.
l: salival.
r: arrival, nonarrival, outrival, rival.
t: adjectival, conjunctival, estival, imperatival, nominatival.
v: revival, survival.

Plus alive, Al, etc.
Plus why, Va, etc.

ĬVƏN

b: Biven.
dr: driven, overdriven, storm-driven, underdriven, undriven, weather-driven.
g: forgiven, given, unforgiven.
r: riven.
shr: shriven, unshriven.
skr(scr): scriven.
str: striven.
thr: thriven.
　Cf. given hen, etc.

ĪVƏN

Vowel: Ivan.
l: enliven.
　Plus why van *or* von, etc.
　Cf. deprive hen, etc.

ĪVƏNS

n: connivance.
r: arrivance.
tr: contrivance.
v: survivance.
　Plus Why, Vance, etc.
　Cf. thrive, ants *or* aunts, etc.

ĪVƏNT

n: connivent.
tr: trivant.
　Plus arrive, aunt *or* ant, etc.
　Plus why vent, etc.

ĬVƏT

d: divot.
gr: grivet.
p: pivot.
pr: privet.
r: rivet, unrivet.
s: civet.
tr: trivet.
　Plus Bivet, etc.
　Cf. give it, etc.
　Cf. give at, etc.

ĪVƏT

pr: private.
　Plus I've ate, *or* eight, etc.
　Cf. deprive it, etc.

ĪWĀ

b: byway.
h: highway.
sk: skyway.
　Plus try way *or* weigh, etc.

ĪWÄL

dr: dry wall.

ĪZDĀL

gr: Grisdale.
　Plus is dale, etc.

ĬZDƏM

w: wisdom.
　Plus is dumb, etc.

ĬZĒ

b: busy.
d: dizzy.
fr: frizzy.
j: jizzy.
l: Lizzie, Lizzy, tin lizzie.
t: tizzy.
　Plus is he, etc.

ĪZĒ

s: sizy.
　Plus cries, he, etc.

IZĒD

b: busied, unbusied.
d: dizzied.
  Plus Lizzie'd, etc.
  Cf. is hid, etc.

IZEST

f: fizzest*, gin fizzest*.
fr: frizzest*.
hw: whizzest*.
kw: quizzest*.
s: sizzest*.

ĪZEST

d: merchandisest*.
g: disguisest*.
j: apologizest*, eulogizest*.
k(c): catechizest*.
l: civilizest*, mobilizest*,
monopolizest*, realizest*.
m: compromisest*, premisest*,
surmisest*.
n: agonizest*, organizest*,
patronizest*, recognizest*,
solemnizest*, tyrannizest*.
pr: comprisest*, prizest*,
surprisest*.
r: ariest*, rearisest*, risest*,
theorizest*, uprisest*.
s: criticizest*, emphasizest*,
excisest*, exercisest*, exorcisest*,
sizest*.
sp: despiseth*.
t: advertisest*, baptizest*,
chastisest*, dramatizest*.
th: sympathizest*.
v: advisest*, devisest*,
improvisest*, revisest*,
supervisest*.
w: wisest.

IZETH

f: fizzeth*, gin fizzeth*.
fr: frizzeth*.

hw: whizzeth*.
kw: quizzeth*.
s: sizzeth*.

ĪZETH

d: merchandiseth*.
g: disguiseth*.
j: apologizeth*, eulogizeth*.
k(c): catechizeth*.
l: civilizeth*, mobilizeth*,
monopolizeth*, realizeth*.
m: compromiseth*, premiseth*,
surmiseth*.
n: agonizeth*, organizeth*,
patronizeth*, recognizeth*,
solemnizeth*, tyrannizeth*.
pr: compriseth*, prizeth*,
surpriseth*.
r: ariseth*, reariseth*, riseth*,
theorizeth*, upriseth*.
s: criticizeth*, emphasizeth*,
exciseth*, exerciseth*,
exorciseth*, sizeth*.
sp: despiseth*.
t: advertiseth*, baptizeth*,
chastiseth*, dramatizeth*.
th: sympathizeth*.
v: adviseth*, deviseth*,
improviseth*, reviseth*,
superviseth*.

IZHƱR

s: scissure.
  Plus is your or you're, etc.

IZHƏN

l: aillision, collision, elision,
illision.
pr: misprision.
r: derision, irrision.
s: abscission, concision, decision,
excision, imprecision, incision,
indecision, precision, recision,
rescission, scission.

v: cable television, division, envision, prevision, provision, revision, subdivision, supervision, television, vision.

Cf. izian.

IZHƏND

v: provisioned, visioned.

Plus izhun+ed.

IZIJ

v: visage.

Cf. whizz age, etc.

IZIK

d: paradisic.
f: metaphysic, physic.
t: phthisic.

IZIKS

f: metaphysics, physics.
t: phthisics.

IZING

f: fizzing, gin fizzing, phizzing.
fr: befrizzing, frizzing.
hw: whizzing.
kw: quizzing.

ĪZING

Vowel: Hebraizing.

d: aggrandizing, gormandizing, hybridizing, jeopardizing, methodizing, standardizing, subsidizing.
g: disguising.
j: apologizing, eulogizing.
k(c): catechizing.
kw: soliloquizing.
l: analyzing, brutalizing, capitalizing, centralizing, civilizing, crystallizing, demoralizing,

equalizing, eternalizing, evangelizing, fertilizing, generalizing, idealizing, idolizing, immortalizing, journalizing, localizing, materializing, mobilizing, monopolizing, moralizing, neutralizing, paralyzing, rationalizing, realizing, ruralizing, scandalizing, signalizing, specializing, sterilizing, symbolizing, tantalizing, totalizing, tranquilizing, utilizing, visualizing, vitalizing, vocalizing, volatilizing.

m: compromising, demising, economizing, macadamizing, minimizing, premising, surmising, uncompromising.

n: agonizing, antagonizing, canonizing, colonizing, disorganizing, galvanizing, harmonizing, modernizing, organizing, patronizing, recognizing, revolutionizing, revolutionizing, scrutinizing, sermonizing, solemnizing, tyrannizing.

pr: apprising, comprising, enterprising, prizing, surprising, underprizing.

r: arising, authorizing, cauterizing, characterizing, deodorizing, familiarizing, mesmerizing, pauperizing, plagiarizing, pulverizing, rising, secularizing, summarizing, temporizing, terrorizing, theorizing, uprising, vaporizing, vulgarizing.

s: Anglicizing, capsizing, Catholicizing, criticizing, emphasizing, exercising, exorcising, italicizing, sizing.

sp: despising.

t: advertising, apostatizing, appetizing, baptizing, chastizing, dramatizing, hypnotizing, magnetizing, stigmatizing, systematizing.

th: sympathizing.

v: advising, devising, improvising, revising, supervising.

IZIT

Vowel: what is it.
v: visit.
　　Plus is it, etc.

ĪZKRAK

w: wisecrack.
　　Plus skies crack, etc.

IZL

ch: chisel, enchisel.
dr: drizzle.
f: fizzle.
fr: frizzle.
gr: grizzle.
kr: crizzle.
m: mizzle.
s: sizzle.
sw: swizzle.
tw: twizzle.
　　Plus Liz'll, etc.

IZLD

gr: grizzled.
　　Plus izl+d.

IZLĒ

ch: chiselly.
dr: drizzly.
fr: frizzly.
gr: grisly, grizzly.
　　Plus is, Lee *or* lea, etc.

IZLING

ch: chiseling.
dr: drizzling.
f: fizzling.
fr: befrizzling, frizzling.
gr: grizzling.
m: mizzling.

s: sizzling.
sw: swizzling.

IZM

s: bruxism.
w: izzum wizzum.
　　Plus izm.

IZMĒ

pr: prismy.
　　Plus is me, etc.

IZMIK

kl: cataclysmic, clysmic.
l: embolismic.
r: aphorismic.
s: paroxysmic.
　　Plus is, Mick, etc.

IZMƏL

b: abysmal.
d: dismal, Great Dismal.
k(c): catechismal.
kl: cataclysmal.
kr: chrismal.
l: embolismal.
r: aneurismal.
s: paroxysmal.
t: baptismal, rheumatismal.
　　Plus prism, Al, etc.

ĪZMƏN

pr: prizeman.
s: exciseman.
　　Plus wise man, etc.

ĪZMƏNT

d: aggrandizement.
pr: apprizement.
s: assiement.

t: baptizement.
  Plus skies meant, etc.

IZMƏS

b: strabismus.
s: accismus.
t: tarantismus*.
tr: trismus.
  Plus Liz muss, etc.

IZMƏT

k: kismet.
  Plus Liz met, etc.

IZNƏS

b: business.
  Cf. izines.

ĪZNƏS

w: wiseness.

IZƱR

fr: befrizzer, frizzer.
kw: quizzer.
s: scissor.
v: visor.

ĪZƱR

d: aggrandizer, gormandizer, hybridizer.
g: disguiser, geyser, muiser.
j: apologizer, eulogizer.
k(c): catechizer, Kaiser, Keyser, Kyser.
l: analyzer, civilizer, dialyser, elisor, equalizer, fertilizer, generalizer, idolizer, moralizer, realizer, scandalizer, sterilizer, tantalizer, tranquilizer, vitalizer, vocalizer.
m: atomizer, economizer, epitomizer, itemizer, miser, surmiser, victimizer.

n: agonizer, canonizer, colonizer, disorganizer, galvanizer, harmonizer, humanizer, lionizer, organizer, scrutinizer, sermonizer, solemnizer, synchronizer, tyrannizer, vulcanizer.
pr: appriser, priser, surpriser.
r: authorizer, cauterizer, deodorizer, extemporizer, pauperizer, polarizer, pulverizer, riser, temporizer, terrorizer, theorizer, upriser, vaporizer, vulgarizer.
s: assizer, capsizer, exerciser, exorciser, incisor, sizer.
sp: despiser.
t: advertiser, appetizer, baptizer, chastiser, dogmatizer, magnetizer, proselytizer, stigmatizer.
th: sympathizer.
v: adviser, deviser, devisor, divisor, improviser, reviser, superviser.
w: wiser.
  Plus tries, her, etc.

IZƱRD

  Cf. izard.

ĪZƱRD

v: visored.

IZƱRZ

s: scissors.
  Plus izur+s.

ĪZƏ

Vowel: Isa, Iza.
l: Eliza, Liza.
r: coryza.
  Plus why's a, etc.
  Plus realize a, etc.

ĪZƏK

Vowel: Isaac.

ĪZƏL

pr: comprisal, surprisal.
v: revisal.
   Plus skies, Al, etc.

IZƏM

kr: chrisom.
l: ruralism.
   Cf. izm.

IZƏN

d: bedizen, dizen.
m: mizzen.
pr: imprison, prison.
r: arisen, rearisen, risen.
t: ptisan.
w: wizen.
   Cf. hisn.
   Cf. is on *or* an, etc.

ĪZƏN

d: bedizen, dizen.
l: Kyrieeleison.
p: pizen.
r: horizon.
   Plus eyes on *or* an, etc.
   Cf. wise hen, etc.

ĪƏ

b: Tobiah.
d: Jebediah, Obadiah, Zebediah.
f: St. Sophia, Sophia.
k: Hezekiah, Zedekiah.
l: Thalia.
m: Jeremiah.
n: assthenia, Beniah, gorgoneria, Zephaniah.
r: Amariah, Ave Maria, Azariah, Beriah, Black Maria, Maria, Uriah, Zacharish.

s: Josiah, messiah.
str: stria.
tr: latria.
v: via.
z: Isaiah+, Keziah.
   Plus buy a, etc.

ĪƏL

d: dial, moon dial, sundial.
f: phial.
h: basihyal.
kr: decrial, descrial.
n: denial, genial, self-denial.
p: espial.
pl: supplial.
r: rial*.
tr: retrial, trial.
v: bass viol, vial, viol.

ĪƏN

Vowel: ion.
br: Brian, Bryan.
k(c): Chian.
l: dandelion, lion, sea lion, thalian.
n: genian.
r: Orian, Orion, O'Ryan, Ryan.
s: Ixion, scion.
st: styan.
t: altaian.
z: Zion.
   Plus try an, etc.
   Plus ian.
   Plus try on, etc.

ĪƏND

v: viand.
   Plus try and, etc.

ĪƏNDZ

v: viands.

Cf. try hands, etc.

ĪƏNS

f: affiance, defiance.

l: alliance, mesalliance, misalliance, reliance, self-reliance.

pl: appliance, compliance, incompliance, suppliance.

s: computer science, information science, library science, science.

Plus sly ants *or* aunts, etc.

Cf. iant+s.

ĪƏNT

f: affiant, calorifient, defiant.

j: giant.

kl: client.

l: alliant, reliant, self-reliant.

pl: compliant, pliant.

s: inscient, scient.

Plus spy ant *or* aunt, etc.

Cf. iant.

ĪƏS

Vowel: eyas.

b: bias, Tobias, unbias.

l: Elias, Lias.

m: Jeremias.

n: ananias.

s: Josias, Messias.

th: Matthias.

Cf. ius.

Cf. try us, etc.

ĪƏT

Vowel: eyot.

d: diet, liquid diet.

kw: disquiet, inquiet, quiet, unquiet.

p: piet, piot.

r: riot.

s: Sciot.

Plus pie, et, etc.

Cf. try it *or* etc.

Cf. iat.

O

The accented vowel sounds included are listed under O in Single Rhymes.

ŌA

t: toea.

ŌAB

j: Joab.
m: Moab.
Plus so, Ab, etc.

ŌBĀT

gl: globate.
l: lobate.
pr: probate.
Plus globe eight *or* ate, etc.
Plus throw bait, etc.

ŌBĒ

Vowel: obi.
d: adobe, dhobi.
f: hydrophoby.
g: Gobi.
gl: globy.
k: Kobe.
Plus so be *or* bee, etc.
Plus globe, he, etc.

ŌBELT

sn: Snowbelt.

ŌBEST

pr: probest*.
r: disrobest*, enrobest*, robest*, unrobest*.
Plus throw best, etc.

ÔBEST

d: bedaubest*, daubest*.
Plus saw best, etc.

ŌBETH

pr: probeth*.
r: disrobeth*, enrobeth*, robeth*, unrobeth*.
Plus glow, Beth, etc.

ÔBETH

d: bedaubeth*, daubeth*.
Plus saw Beth, etc.

ŌBĪ

g: go by.
Plus so buy, by, *or* bye, etc.
Plus globe, I *or* eye, etc.

ŌBĒL, ŌBIL

m: automobile, immobile, mobile.
Plus owe bill *or* O Bill, etc.
Plus globe ill, etc.
Cf. so, Beale, etc.

ŌBING

gl: globing.
pr: probing.
r: disrobing, enrobing, robing, unrobing.
Plus so, Byng, etc.

ŌBL

n: danseur noble, ennoble, ignoble, noble, unnoble.
s: Sobel.
> Plus throw bull, etc.
> Plus globe 'll, etc.

ŌBŌ

Vowel: oboe.
h: hobo.
k: kobo.
l: lobo.
z: zobo.
> Plus so, bo, beau, *or* bow, etc.
> Plus robe owe *or* O, etc.

ŌBOI

Vowel: O boy!
d: doughboy.
> Plus show boy, etc.
> Plus robe, oil, etc.

ŌBÔL

k(c): COBOL.
n: no ball.
sn: snowball.
> Plus throw ball, etc.

ÔBŌNZ

j: jaw bones.
s: saw bones.
> Plus straw bones, etc.
> Plus daub owns, etc.

ŌBŌS

f: Phobos.

ŌBŌT

sh: showboat.
> Plus so boat, etc.

ŌBRŌ

d: Dobro.

ŌBROU

l: lowbrow.
n: nobrow.
> Plus show brow *or* brau, etc.

ŌBRƏ

d: dobra.
k(c): cobra.

ŌBSƏN

j: Jobson.
r: Robeson, Robson.
> Plus globe, son *or* sun, etc.

ŌBUR

k: Kober.
pr: prober.
r: disrober, enrober, rober.
s: sober.
t: October.
> Plus no burr, etc.
> Plus globe her *or* err, etc.

ÔBUR

d: bedauber, dauber.
k(c): Micawber.
> Plus raw burr, etc.
> Plus daub her, etc.

ÔBURN

Vowel: auburn.
> Plus daub urn, earn, *or* erne, etc.
> Plus saw burn, etc.

ŌBƏ

g: dagoba.
r: arroba, bonaroba*.
t: Manitoba.
  Plus globe, a, etc.

ÔBƏL

b: bauble.
  Plus saw bull, etc.
  Plus daub 'll, etc.

ŌBƏS

Vowel: obus.
gl: globus.
k(c): jacobus.
  Plus woe bus *or* buss, etc.
  Plus enrobe us, etc.

ŌCHEST

br: broachest*.
kr: encroachest*.
p: poachest*.
pr: approachest*, reproachest*.
  Plus slow chest, etc.

ÔCHEST

b: debauchest*.
  Plus saw chest, etc.

ŌCHETH

br: broacheth*.
kr: encroacheth*.
p: poacheth*.
pr: approacheth*, reproacheth*.

ÔCHETH

b: debaucheth*.

ŌCHFOOL

pr: reproachful.

ŌCHING

br: broaching.
k(c): coaching.
kr: encroaching.
p: poaching.
pr: approaching, reproaching.

ÔCHING

b: debauching.

ŌCHMƏNT

kr: encroachment.
pr: approachment.
  Plus coach meant, etc.

ŌCHUR

br: broacher.
kr: encroacher.
p: poacher.
pr: approacher, reproacher, self reproacher.
  Plus coach her *or* err, etc.

ÔCHUR

b: debaucher.

ŌCHƏZ

br: broaches, brooches.
k(c): coaches, stage coaches, train coaches.
kr: encroaches.
l: loaches.
p: poaches.
pr: approaches, reproaches, self reproaches.
r: roaches.
  Cf. roach is, etc.

ŌDĒ

w: woady.
  Plus road, he, etc.

ÔDĒ

b: bawdy.
d: dawdy.
g: gaudy.
m: Maudie.
s: Saudi+.
  Plus outlawed, he, etc.
  Plus saw Dee, etc.

ŌDEST

b: bodest*, forebodest*.
g: goadest*.
l: loadest*, overloadest*,
unloadest*.
pl: explodest*.
r: corrodest*.

ÔDEST

br: broadest.
fr: defraudest*.
l: belaudest*, laudest*.
pl: applaudest*.
r: maraudest*.

ŌDETH

b: bodeth*, forebodeth*.
g: goadeth*.
l: loadeth*, overloadeth*,
unloadeth*.
pl: explodeth*.
r: corrodeth*.
  Plus slow death, etc.

ÔDETH

fr: defraudeth*.
l: belaudeth*, laudeth*.
pl: applaudeth*.
r: maraudeth*.
  Plus law death, etc.

ŌDIK

Vowel: odic.
  Plus so, Dick, etc.

ŌDIN

Vowel: Odin.
b: Bodin.
w: Wodin.
  Plus low din, etc.
  Plus load in *or* inn, etc.
  Cf. oden.

ŌDING

b: boding, foreboding.
g: goading.
l: loading, overloading, unloading.
m: outmoding.
pl: exploding.
r: corroding, eroding.

ÔDING

fr: defrauding.
l: belauding, lauding.
pl: applauding.
r: marauding.

ŌDIST

k(c): codist.
m: modist.
n: palinodist.

ÔDIT

Vowel: audit.
pl: plaudit.
  Plus outlawed it, etc.

ÔDKAST

br: broadcast.
  Plus gaud cast, etc.

ŌDL

m: modal.
n: internodal, nodal, trinodal.
y: yodel.
    Plus code'll, etc.
    Cf. Odal.

ÔDL

d: dawdle.
k(c): bicaudal, caudal, caudle.
    Plus gald'll, etc.

ÔDLIN

m: maudlin.
    Plus laud Lynn, etc.

ŌDMAP

r: road map.

ŌDŌ

d: dodo.
m: Quasimodo.
    Plus slow dough *or* doe, etc.
    Plus code owe *or* O, etc.

ÔDRĒ

b: bawdry.
t: tawdry.

ŌDSHŌ

r: road show.

ŌDSTÄR

l: lodestar.
    Plus showed star, etc.
    Plus goads tar, etc.

ŌDSTŌN

l: loadstone, lodestone.
t: toadstone.

Plus road stone, etc.
Cf. road's tone, etc.

ŌDSTƱR

g: goadster.
r: roadster.
    Plus mode stir, etc.

ŌDƱR

Vowel: malodor, Oder, odor.
b: boder, foreboder.
d: decoder.
g: goader.
l: loader, muzzle-loader, unloader.
pl: exploder.
r: corroder, eroder.
    Plus goad her *or* err, etc.

ÔDƱR

br: broader.
fr: defrauder.
l: belauder, lauder.
pl: applauder.
r: marauder.
s: sawder, soft sawder.
    Plus awed her *or* err, etc.

ŌDUS

m: modus.
n: nodous.
    Plus owed us, etc.

ŌDƏ

g: pagoda.
k(c): coda.
n: trinoda.
r: Baroda, Rhoda.
s: baking soda, brandy and soda, ice cream soda, soda, whisky and soda.
    Plus owed a, etc.

ŌDƏD

b: boded, foreboded.
g: goaded.
k(c): coded, decoded.
l: loaded, loded, overloaded, unloaded.
m: outmoded.
pl: exploded.
r: corroded, eroded.
w: woaded.
  Plus show dead, etc.
  Plus show did, etc.
  Plus code, Ed.
  Cf. toaded.

ÔDƏD

fr: defrauded.
l: belauded, lauded.
pl: applauded.
r: marauded.
  Plus saw dead, etc.
  Plus sawed, Ed, etc.

ŌDƏN

b: foreboden*.
w: Woden.
  Plus low den, etc.
  Cf. Odin, Bodin.

ÔDƏN

br: broaden.
l: loden.
  Plus saw den, etc.

ŌDƏNT

pl: explodent.
r: corrodent, erodent, rodent.
  Plus slow dent, etc.

ŌĒ

b: Bowie.
bl: blowy.
d: doughy.
fl: Floey.
gl: glowy.
j: Joey.
k(c): Cowie.
kl: Chloe.
m: Moe.
sh: showy.
sn: snowy.
t: towy.
v: evoe.
z: Zoe.
  Plus owe *or* O, he, etc.

ÔĒ

fl: flawy.
j: jawy.
str: strawy.
th: thawy.
  Plus saw he, etc.
  Cf. ai.

ŌED

k(c): coed.
  Plus beau, Ed, etc.
  Cf. tow head, etc.

ŌEST

Vowel: owest*.
bl: blowest*.
fl: flowest*, overflowest*.
g: foregoest*, goest*, outgoest*, undergoest*.
gl: glowest*.
gr: growest*, outgrowest*, overgrowest*.
h: hoest*.
kr: crowest*, outcrowest*, overcrowest*.
l: lowest.
m: mowest*.
n: foreknowest*, knowest*.

r: rowest*.
s: sewest*, sowest*.
sh: foreshowest*, showest*.
sl: slowest.
sn: snowest.
st: bestowest*, stowest*.
t: towest*, undertowest*.
thr: overthrowest*, throwest*, upthrowest*.
tr: trowest*.

ÔEST

Vowel: awest*, overawest*.
dr: drawest*, withdrawest*.
l: outlawest*.
r: rawest.

ŌETH

Vowel: oewth*.
bl: bloweth*.
fl: floweth*, overfloweth*.
g: foregoeth*, goeth*, outgoeth*, undergoeth*.
gl: gloweth*.
gr: groweth*, outgroweth*, overgroweth*.
h: hoeth*.
kr: croweth*, outcroweth*, overcroweth*.
l: loweth*.
m: moweth*.
n: foreknoweth*, knoweth*.
r: roweth*.
s: seweth*, soweth*.
sh: foreshoweth*, showeth*.
sn: snoweth*.
st: bestoweth*, stoweth*.
t: toweth*, undertoweth*.
thr: overthroweth*, throweth*, upthroweth*.
tr: troweth*.

ÔETH

Vowel: aweth*, overaweth*.
dr: draweth*, withdraweth*.
l: outlaweth*.

ŌFĒ

s: Sophie.
str: strophe.
tr: trophy.
    Plus loaf, he, etc.
    Plus low fee, etc.

ÔFĒ

k(c): coffee.
sp: spoffy.
t: toffy.
    Plus off, he, etc.

ŌFĪL

pr: profile.
    Plus slow file, etc.
    Plus loaf, I'll, aisle, *or* isle, etc.

ÔFING

Vowel: offing.
d: doffing.
g: golfing.
k(c): coughing.
sk(sc): scoffing.

ÔFIS

Vowel: office, war office.

ÔFISH

Vowel: standoffish.
kr: crawfish.
    Plus law, fish, etc.

ÔFL

Vowel: awful, offal.
l: lawful, unlawful
w: waffle.
　　Plus cough'll, craw full, toff'll, etc.
　　　Cf. oful.

ÔFN

Vowel: often.
s: soften.

ŌF

t: tofu.

ÔFRENCH

l: law French.

ÔFSHÔR

Vowel: offshore.

ÔFSĪD

Vowel: offside.

ÔFTĒ

l: lofty.
s: softy.
　　Plus oft* he, etc.
　　Plus cough tea, etc.

ÔFTEST

l: loftest*.
s: softest.
　　Plus soph test, etc.

ÔFTLĒ

s: softly.
　　Plus scoffed, Lee *or* lea, etc.

ÔFTƏR

kr: crofter.
l: lofter.
s: softer.
　　Plus scoffed her *or* err, etc.

ÔFTƏD

l: lofted.
　　Plus scoff, Ted, etc.
　　Plus scoffed, Ed, etc.

ŌFƱR

Vowel: Ophir.
g: gofer, gopher.
l: loafer.
sh: chauffeur.
　　Plus oaf her *or* err, etc.
　　Plus owe for, fur, *or* fir, etc.

ÔFƱR

Vowel: offer.
d: doffer.
g: goffer, golfer.
k(c): coffer, cougher.
pr: proffer.
sk(sc): scoffer.
　　Plus scoff her *or* err, etc.

ŌFƏ

s: sofa.
　　Plus load a, etc.

ŌFƏL

w: woeful.
　　Plus snow full, etc.

ŌFƏT

t: Tophet.
　　Plus loaf et, etc.
　　Cf. loaf it, etc.

ŌGĒ

b: bogey, bogie.
d: dogie.
f: fogey, old fogey.
st: stogie.
y: yogi.
  Plus rogue, he, etc.

ÔGĒ

b: boggy.
d: doggy.
f: foggy.
fr: froggy.
gr: groggy.
j: joggy.
kl: cloggy.
s: soggy.
  Plus frog, he, etc.

ÔGHWHIP

d: dog whip.
  Plus hog whip, etc.

ÔGIN

n: noggin.
  Plus frog in *or* inn, etc.

ÔGING

b: bogging.
d: dogging.
f: befogging, fogging.
fl: flogging.
j: jogging.
k(c): cogging.
kl: clogging, unclogging.
n: nogging.
sl: slogging.
t: togging.

ŌGISH

r: rogueish.
  Plus rogue, Gish, etc.

ÔGISH

d: doggish.
h: hoggish.
  Cf. tog, Gish, etc.

ÔGJAM

l: logjam.

ŌGL

Vowel: ogle.
b: bogle.
f: fogle.
  Plus rogue'll, etc.
  Cf. slow gull, etc.

ÔGL

b: boggle.
k(c): coggle.
d: boondoggle.
g: goggle, synagogal.
j: joggle.
t: toggle.
  Plus dog'll, etc.
  Plus frog, Al, etc.

ÔGLING

b: boggling.
d: boondoggling.
g: goggling.
j: joggling.

ŌGLUR

Vowel: ogler.

ÔGLUR

b: boggler.
d: boondoggler.
g: goggler.
j: joggler.

ÔGMĪR

kw: quagmire+.
　　Plus frog mire, etc.

ŌGRAM

pr: deprogram, program, programme.
　　Plus slow gram, etc.
　　Plus rogue ram, etc.

ŌGRES

Vowel: ogress.
pr: progress+.

ÔGSTÄR

d: dogstar.
　　Plus hog star, etc.
　　Plus hogs tar, etc.

ÔGTROT

d: dogtrot.
j: jogtrot.
　　Plus frog trot, etc.
　　Plus water-logged, rot, etc.

ŌGUR

Vowel: ogre.
　　Plus rogue her *or* err, etc.

ÔGUR

Vowel: auger, augur.
d: dogger.
f: befogger, pettifogger.

fl: flogger.
h: hogger, whole-hogger.
j: jogger.
k(c): cogger.
kl: clogger.
l: logger.
m: mauger.
n: inauger.
sl: slogger.
t: togger.
　　Plus flog her *or* err, etc.

ÔGWOOD

b: bogwood.
d: dogwood.
l: logwood.
　　Plus clog wood *or* would, etc.

ŌGƏ

r: Ticonderoga.
sn: snoga.
t: Saratoga, toga.
y: yoga.
　　Plus prorogue a, etc.

ÔGƏ

k(c): Sylacauga.
m: Chicamauga.
t: Autauga.

ŌGƏL

d: dogal.
　　Plus rogue, Al, etc.
　　Plus slow gal, etc.

OGƏN

b: tobaggan.
g: McGoggan.
　　Plus dog an, etc.

ŌGƏN

br: brogan.
h: Hogan.
sl: slogan.
  Plus prorogue an, etc.

ŌGƏS

b: bogus.
  Plus prorogue us, etc.
  Plus so, Gus, etc.

ÔGƏST

Vowel: august.
  Plus raw gust, etc.

ŌHED

t: towhead.
  Plus no head, etc.
  Cf. doed.

ŌHEN

k(c): Cohen.
  Plus throw hen, etc.

ŌHŌ

s: SoHo

ŌHUNK

b: Bohunk.
  Plus no hunk, etc.

OIBL

f: foible.
  Plus toy bull, etc.

OICH   R

pl: exploiture.
v: voiture.
  Plus quoit, you're *or* your, etc.

OIDƱR

br: broider, embroider.
m: "moider."
v: avoider, voider.
  Plus cloyed her *or* err, etc.

OIDƏD

v: avoided, voided.
  Plus boy dead, etc.
  Cf. boy did, etc.

OIDƏL

Vowel: oidal.
b: rhomboidal.
dr: dendroidal.
f: typhoidal.
gr: negroidal.
k(c): conchoidal, discoidal, trochoidal.
kl: cycloidal.
l: colloidal, coralloidal, metalloidal, paraboloidal.
m: prismoidal, sigmoidal.
n: conoidal, crinoidal, ethnoidal, ganoidal.
r: asteroidal, hemispheroidal, saccharoidal, spheroidal.
s: ellipsoidal.
t: elephantoidal, planetoidal, prismatoidal.
th: lithoidal.
v: ovoidal.
  Plus employed Al, etc.

OIDƏN

h: hoyden.
  Plus boy den, etc.
  Cf. avoid hen, etc.

OIDƏNS

v: avoidance.
   Plus boy dance, etc.
   Plus destroyed ants *or* aunts,
etc.

OIĒ

pl: employe, employee.
   Plus joy he, etc.

OIEST

b: buoyest*.
j: enjoyest*, joyest*.
k(c): coyest, decoyest*.
kl: cloyest*.
n: annoyest*.
pl: deployest*, employest*.
str: destroyest*.
t: toyest*.
v: convoyest*.

OIETH

b: buoyeth*.
j: enjoyeth*, joyeth*.
k(c): decoyeth*.
kl: cloyeth*.
n: annoyeth*.
pl: deployeth*, employeth*.
str: destroyeth*.
t: toyeth*.
v: convoyeth*.

OIFOOL

j: joyful.
   Plus boy full, etc.

OIIJ

b: buoyage.
l: alloyage.
v: voyage.
   Cf. boy age, etc.

OIING

b: buoying.
j: enjoying, joying.
k(c): decoying.
kl: cloying.
n: annoying.
pl: deploying, employing.
str: destroying.
t: toying.
v: convoying.

OIISH

b: boyish.
k(c): coyish.
t: toyish.

ŌIJ

fl: flowage.
st: stowage.
t: towage.
   Cf. throw age, etc.

ŌIK

kr: dichroic, melanochroic,
pleochroic, xanthochroic.
n: dypnoic.
r: heroic, mock-heroic, unheroic.
st: Stoic.
tr: Troic.
z: azoic, benzoic, Cenozoic
Eozoic, hylozoic, hypnozoic,
Mezozoic, Neozoic, Palaeozoic,
protozoic.

OILĒ

Vowel: oily.
d: doily.
k(c): coyly.
r: roily.
   Plus toil, he, etc.
   Plus boy, Lee *or* lea, etc.

OILEST

b: boilest*.
br: broilest*, embroilest*.
f: foilest*.
k(c): coilest*, recoilest*, uncoilest*.
r: roilest*.
s: soilest*.
sp: despoilest*, spoilest*.
t: toilest.
    Plus boy, lest, etc.
    Cf. toil, lest, etc.

OILETH

b: boileth*.
br: broileth*, embroileth*.
f: foileth*.
k(c): coileth*, recoileth*, uncoileth*.
r: roileth*.
s: soileth*.
sp: despoileth*, spoileth*.
t: toileth*.

OILING

b: boiling.
br: broiling, embroiling, pan broiling.
f: foiling.
k(c): coiling, recoiling, uncoiling.
m: moiling.
r: roiling.
s: assoiling, soiling.
sp: despoiling, spoiling.
t: toiling.

OILMƏNT

br: embroilment.
k(c): recoilment.
sp: despoilment.
    Plus toil meant, etc.

OILUR

Vowel: oiler.
b: boiler.
br: broiler, embroiler.
f: foiller.
k(c): coiler, recoiler, uncoiler.
r: roiler.
s: soiler.
sp: despoiler, spoiler.
t: toiler.
    Plus roil her *or* err, etc.

OILƏT

Vowel: oillet.
t: toilet.
    Plus boy let *or* Lett, etc.
    Plus Hoyle et, etc.
    Cf. spoil it, etc.

OIMƏN

h: hoyman.
k(c): decoyman.
t: toyman.
    Plus joy, man, etc.

OIMƏNT

j: enjoyment.
pl: deployment, employment.
    Plus coy meant, etc.

OINDUR

j: rejoinder.
    Plus coined her *or* err, etc.

ŌING

Vowel: Ohing, owing.
b: beauing, bowing, oboeing.
bl: blowing, bugle-blowing, glass-blowing, horn-blowing, nose-blowing, trumpet blowing.
fl: flowing, inflowing, outflowing, overflowing, unflowing.

g: easygoing, foregoing, going, outgoing, seagoing, thoroughgoing, undergoing.

gl: glowing.

gr: growing, outgrowing, overgrowing, upgrowing.

h: hoeing.

kr: cockcrowing, crowing, overcrowing.

l: helloing, lowing.

m: mowing.

n: foreknowing, knowing, self-knowing, unknowing.

r: rowing.

s: sewing, sowing.

sh: foreshowing, showing.

sl: slowing.

sn: snowing.

st: bestowing, stowing.

str: strowing*.

t: tiptoeing, toeing, towing, undertowing.

thr: overthrowing, throwing.

ÔING

Vowel: awing, overawing.

ch: chawing.

dr: drawing, overdrawing, wiredrawing, withdrawing.

f: guffawing.

h: hee-hawing.

j: jawing.

k(c): cawing.

kl: clawing.

l: lawing, outlawing.

g: begnawing, gnawing.

p: pawing.

s: sawing, seesawing.

sh: pshawing.

str: strawing.

t: tawing.

th: thawing.

y: yawing.

OINIJ

k(c): coinage.

Cf. loin age, etc.

OINING

gr: groining.

j: adjoining, conjoining, disjoining, enjoining, joining, rejoining, subjoining.

k(c): coining.

l: purloining.

OINTGÄRD

p: point guard.

OINTING

j: disjointing, jointing.

n: anointing.

p: appointing, disappointing, pointing.

OINTLƏS

j: jointless.

p: pointless.

Plus anoint Les or less, etc.

OINTMƏNT

Vowel: ointment.

j: disjointment.

n: anointment.

p: appointment, disappointment.

Plus counterpoint meant, etc.

OINTƱR

j: disjointer, jointer.

n: anointer.

p: appointer, disappointer, pointer.

Plus disjoint her or err, etc.

OINTƏD

j: conjointed, disjointed, jointed, unjointed.

n: anointed, unanointed.

p: appointed, disappointed, pointed, unpointed.

    Plus coin, Ted, etc.

OINƱR

j: conjoiner, enjoiner, joiner.

k(c): coiner.

l: purloiner.

    Plus purloin her *or* err, etc.

OINƏS

k(c): coyness.

OIRĪD

j: joyride.

    Plus boy ride, etc.

ŌIS

l: Lois.

p: Powys.

ŌISH

sh: night-showish, showish.

sn: snowish.

    Cf. so wish, etc.

OISING

j: rejoicing, unrejoicing.

v: voicing.

    Plus boy sing, etc.

OISLƏS

ch: choiceless.

v: voiceless.

    Plus rejoice less, etc.

OISTIK

j: joystick.

    Plus boy stick, etc.

    Plus voice tick, etc.

OISTING

f: foisting.

h: hoisting.

j: joisting.

    Plus boy sting, etc.

OISTRƏL

k(c): coystrel.

kl: cloistral.

OISTƱR

Vowel: oyster, pearl oyster.

d: Ralph Roister, Doister.

f: foister.

h: hoister.

kl: cloister, encloister, uncloister.

m: moister.

r: royster.

    Plus joy stir, etc.

    Plus rejoiced her *or* err, etc.

OISƏM

n: noisome.

t: toysome.

    Plus cloy some *or* sum, etc.

OITĒ

k(c): dacoity.

t: hoity-toity.

    Plus enjoy tea, etc.

    Plus quoit, he, etc.

OITRING

l: loitering.

n: reconnoitring.

    Plus quoit ring, etc.

OITUR

dr: adroiter.
g: goiter.
l: loiter.
n: reconnoiter.
pl: exploiter.
Plus quoit her *or* err, etc.

OITƏD

d: doited.
kw: quoited.
pl: exploited, unexploited.
Plus boy Ted, etc.
Plus adroit, Ed, etc.

OIUR

b: Boyar, Boyer.
j: enjoyer.
k(c): coyer, decoyer.
n: annoyer.
pl: deployer, employer.
str: destroyer, self-destroyer.
t: toyer.
Plus enjoy her *or* err, etc.

OIUS

j: joyous.
Plus destroy us, etc.

OIZĒ

n: noisy.
Plus joys, he, etc.

OIZING

n: noising.
p: poising.

OIZƏN

f: foison*.
p: empoison*, poison.
t: toison*.
Plus annoys an *or* on, etc.

OIZƏNZ

f: foisons.
p: poisons.

OIZƏZ

b: boyses.
n: noises.
p: poises.
Cf. noise is, etc.

OIƏ

g: Goya.
Plus employ a, etc.

OIƏL

l: disloyal, loyal.
r: pennyroyal, royal, surroyal.
Plus employ Al, etc.

OIƏNS

b: buoyance.
j: joyance.
n: annoyance.
v: clairvoyance.
Cf. enjoy ants *or* aunts, etc.

OIƏNT

b: buoyant, flamboyant.
n: annoyant.
t: chatoyant.
v: clairvoyant, prevoyant.
Plus enjoy aunt *or* ant, etc.

ŌJĀ

Vowel: o.j.

ŌJĒ

g: anagoge, apagoge, epagoge, paragoge.
Plus doge, he, etc.
Plus O, Gee, etc.

ŌJƱRN

s: sojourn.
　　Plus doge earn, urn, *or* erne, etc.

ŌJƏN

tr: Trojan.
　　Plus show Jan, etc.

ŌJƏNT

k(c): cogent.
　　Plus slow gent, etc.

ŌKĀ

Vowel: O.K., okay.
kr: croquet.
r: roquet.
t: Tokay.
　　Plus slow, Key *or* K, etc.

ŌKÄN

Vowel: ryokan.

ŌKĒ

tr: toche, trochee.
　　Plus slow key, etc.
　　Plus joke, he, etc.
　　Cf. oki.

ŌKEST

ch: chokest*.
j: jokest*.
kl: cloakest*.
kr: croakest*.
s: soakest*.
sm: smokest*.
sp: spokest*.
v: convokest*, evokest*, invokest*,
provokest*, revokest*.
y: unyokest*, yokest*.

ÔKEST

b: balkest*.
st: stalkest*.
t: talkest*.
w: walkest*.

ŌKTAG

Vowel: oaktag.

ŌKUM

Vowel: oakum.
h: hokum.
　　Plus soak 'em, etc.
　　Plus so come, etc.

ŌKUND

j: jocund.

ŌKƱR

Vowel: mediocre, ocher.
br: broker, stockbroker.
ch: choker.
j: joker.
kl: cloaker, uncloaker.
kr: croaker.
p: poker.
s: soaker.
sm: smoker.
st: stoker.
str: stroker.
v: convoker, evoker, invoker,
provoker, revoker.
y: yoker.
　　Plus choke her *or* err, etc.

ÔKƱR

b: balker.

ch: chalker.
g: gawker.
h: hawker, jayhawker, tomahawker.
k(c): calker.
m: mawker.
skw: squawker.
st: deel stalker, stalker.
t: talker.
w: jaywalker, shopwalker, sleepwalker, streetwalker, walker.
   Plus stalk her *or* err, etc.

ŌKUS

f: focus.
h: hocus, Hohokus.
kr: autumn crocus, crocus.
l: locus.
p: hocus-pocus.
   Plus stroke us, etc.
   Plus slow cuss, etc.

ÔKUS

d: Daucus.
gl: glaucous.
k(c): caucus.
r: raucous.
   Plus outtalk us, etc.
   Plus straw cuss, etc.
   Cf. Baucis.

ŌKUST

f: focussed, unfocussed.
l: honey locust, locust, sweet locust.
   Plus okus+ed.

ÔKWŲRD

Vowel: awkward.
   Plus talk, ward, etc.

ŌKƏ

Vowel: tapioca.
b: Boca, saltimbocca.
k(c): coca.
m: mocha.
p: polka.
   Plus joke a, etc.

ŌKƏL

b: bocal.
f: bifocal, focal, phocal.
l: local.
s: socle.
v: vocal.
y: yokel.
   Plus joke'll, etc.

ŌKƏN

Vowel: oaken.
b: Hoboken.
br: broken, heartbroken, unbroken.
sp: bespoken, fair-spoken, fine-spoken, fore-spoken, free-spoken, outspoken, soft-spoken, spoken, unspoken.
t: betoken, foretoken, token.
   Cf. spoke an *or* on, etc.
   Cf. Shamokin.

ŌLAK

p: Polack.
   Plus show lack, etc.

ŌLÄK

m: Moloch.
r: rowlock.
   Plus throw lock, etc.

ŌLBÄR

r: roll bar.

ÔLCHUN

f: falchion.
  Plus Balch 'un, etc.

ŌLDĒ

Vowel: golden oldie, oldie.
f: foldy.
m: moldy.
  Plus bold, he, etc.
  Plus shoal Dee, etc.

ÔLDĒ

b: baldy.

ŌLDEST

Vowel: oldest.
b: boldest.
f: enfoldest*, foldest*, infoldest*,
interfoldest*, refoldest*,
unfoldest*.
h: beholdest*, holdest*,
upholdest*, withholdest*.
k(c): coldest.
m: moldest*.
sk(sc): scoldest*.
t: toldest*.

ÔLDEST

b: baldest.
sk(sc): scaldest*.

ŌLDETH

f: enfoldeth*, foldeth*,
infoldeth*, interfoldeth*,
refoldeth*, unfoldeth*.
h: beholdeth*, holdeth*,
upholdeth*, withholdeth*.
m: moldeth*.
sk(sc): scoldeth*.
  Plus soul death, etc.

ÔLDETH

sk(sc): scaldeth*.
  Plus call death, etc.

ŌLDFAST

h: hold fast.
  Plus sold fast, etc.

ŌLDHƏM

Vowel: Oldham.
  Plus scold 'em, etc.
  Cf. whole, dumb, etc.

ŌLDING

f: enfolding, folding, infolding,
interfolding, refolding, unfolding.
h: beholding, holding, slave
holding, upholding, withholding.
m: molding, moulding, weather
molding.
sk(sc): scolding.

ÔLDING

b: balding.
p: Paulding.
sk(sc): scalding.
sp: Spaulding.

ŌLDISH

Vowel: oldish.
k(c): coldish.
  Plus whole dish, etc.

ŌLDKÄL

k: cold call.

ŌLDLĒ

b: boldly.
f: manifoldly.
k(c): coldly.
  Plus controlled lea *or* Lee, etc.

ŌLDMƏN

Vowel: Oldman.
g: Goldman.
Plus told man, etc.

ŌLDMƏNT

f: enfoldment.
h: withholdment.
Plus cold meant, etc.

ŌLDNƏS

Vowel: oldness.
b: boldness.
k(c): coldness.

ŌLDRUMZ

d: doldrums.
Plus parasol drums, etc.

ÔLDRƏN

k(c): caldron.
p: pauldron.
Cf. called run, etc.

ŌLDSMITH

g: goldsmith.
Plus bold smith, etc.

ŌLDUR

Vowel: older.
b: bolder, boulder.
f: bill folder, enfolder, folder, infolder, interfolder, refolder, unfolder.
h: beholder, bond holder, bottle holder, freeholder, hand holder, holder, householder, landholder, leaseholder, shareholder, slaveholder, stockhholder, upholder, withholder.

k(c): colder.
m: molder, pattern molder.
p: polder.
sh: shoulder.
sk(sc): scolder.
sm: smolder.
Plus told her *or* err, etc.

ÔLDUR

Vowel: alder.
b: balder, Baldur.
sk(sc): scalder.
Plus called her *or* err, etc.

ŌLDURD

b: bouldered.
m: moldered.
sh: broad shouldered, shouldered.
sm: smoldered.
Plus boulder'd, etc.

ÔLDWIN

b: Baldwin.
Plus called, win *or* Wynn, etc.

ÔLDƏ

Vowel: Alda.
Plus called a, etc.

ŌLDƏD

f: blind-folded, enfolded, infolded, manifolded, refolded, unfolded.
m: molded.
sk(sc): scolded.
Plus foal dead, etc.
Plus cold, Ed, etc.
Cf. soul did, etc.

ŌLDƏN

Vowel: olden.
b: embolden.
g: golden.
h: beholden, holden,
misbeholden, withholden.

    Plus coal den, etc.

ÔLDƏN

Vowel: Alden.

    Plus call den, etc.

ŌLĒ

Vowel: Ole.
b: Stromboli.
f: Foley.
h: holey, holy, unholy, wholly.
k(c): coaly.
kr: Croley, Crowley.
l: lowly.
m: Moley, moly.
p: poly, roly-poly.
sh: shoaly, sholy.
sl: slowly.
str: strolly.

    Plus so Lee *or* lea, etc.
    Plus soul, he, etc.
    Cf. olli.

ÔLĒ

hw: whally.
k(c): Macaulay, Macauley.
skw: squally.
spr: sprawly.

    Plus tall, he, etc.
    Plus saw Lee *or* lea, etc.

ŌLER

r: roller.

ŌLEST

b: bowlest*.
d: condolest,* dolest*.
dr: drollest.
j: cajolest*.
p: pollest*.
r: enrollest*, Holy Rollest*,
rollest*, unrollest*, uprollest*.
s: consolest*.
str: strollest*.
t: tollest*.
tr: controllest*, patrollest*,
trollest*.

    Plus grow, lest, etc.

ÔLEST

b: bawlest*.
br: brawlest*.
dr: drawlest*.
f: fallest*.
h: haulest*.
k(c): callest*, overcallest*,
recallest*.
kr: crawlest*.
m: bemaulest*, maulest*.
p: appalest*.
skr(scr): scrawlest*.
skw: squallest*.
sm: smallest.
spr: sprawlest*.
st: forestallest*, stallest*.
t: tallest.
thr: enthrallest*.
tr: trawlest*.

    Cf. call, lest, etc.

ŌLETH

b: bowleth*.
d: condoleth*, doleth*.
j: cajoleth*.

p: polleth*.

r: enrolleth*, Holy Rolleth*, rolleth*, unrolleth*.

s: consoleth*.

str: strolleth*.

t: tolleth*.

tr: controlleth*, patrolleth*, trolleth*.

ÔLETH

b: bawleth*.

br: brawleth*.

dr: drawleth*.

f: falleth*.

h: hauleth*.

k(c): calleth*, overcalleth*, recalleth*.

kr: crawleth*.

m: bemauleth*, mauleth*.

p: appaleth*.

skr(scr): scrawleth*.

skw: squalleth*.

spr: sprawleth*.

st: forestalleth*, stalleth*.

thr: enthralleth*.

tr: trawleth*.

ÔLFIN

d: dolphin.

Plus alcohol fin, etc.

Plus golf in *or* inn, etc.

ÔLFING

g: golfing.

ŌLFOOL

b: bowlful.

d: doleful.

s: soulful.

Plus hole full, etc.

ÔLFUR

g: golfer.

Cf. alcohol fur, fir, *or* for, etc.

ÔLFƏS

d: Adolphus, Dollfuss, Rodolphus, Rudolphus.

Cf. golf us, etc.

ÔLGĀM

b: ball game.

ŌLHOUS

p: pollhouse.

t: tollhouse.

Plus soul house, etc.

ŌLĪ

k: E. coli.

ŌLĪF

l: lowlife.

Plus no life, etc.

ÔLIJ

h: hallage*, haulage.

st: stallage.

Cf. call age, etc.

ÔLIK

Vowel: aulic, interaulic.

dr: hydraulic.

g: Gallic.

Plus saw lick, etc.

ŌLĪN

b: running bowline

ÔLIN

p: tarpaulin.

Plus haul in *or* inn, etc.

Plus saw Lynn, etc.

ŌLING

b: bolling, bowling.
d: condoling, doling.
dr: drolling.
f: foaling.
g: goaling.
h: holing.
j: cajoling.
k(c): caracoling, coaling.
p: poling, polling.
r: enrolling, Holy Rolling, parolling, rolling, unrolling, uprolling.
s: consoling, half soling, soling.
sh: shoaling.
sk: skoaling.
skr(scr): inscrolling, scrolling.
str: strolling.
t: extolling, tolling.
tr: controlling, patrolling, trolling.

ÔLING

b: balling, baseballing, basketballing, bawling, blackballing, footballing, snowballing.
br: brawling.
dr: drawling.
f: befalling, falling.
g: galling.
h: hauling, overhauling.
k(c): calling, miscalling, overcalling, recalling, undercalling.
kr: crawling.
m: bemauling, mauling.

p: appalling, palling, Pawling.
sh: shawling.
skr(scr): scrawling.
skw: squalling.
spr: sprawling.
st: forestalling, stalling, installing.
thr: enthralling, thralling.
tr: trawling.
w: caterwauling, unwalling, walling.

ŌLISH

dr: drollish.
p: Polish.

ÔLISH

g: Gaulish.
skw: squallish.
sm: smallish.
t: tallish.

ÔLIT

k: whatchamacallit.

ŌLJŲR

s: dead soldier, soldier.

ÔLKNŲR

f: falconer.

ŌLKƏ

p: polka.

Plus stole Kaa, etc.

ÔLKƏN

f: falcon, gerfalcon, soar falcon, sore falcon.

Plus talc on *or* an, etc.

ŌLLĒ

dr: drolly.
h: wholly.
s: soley.
  Plus soul, Lee *or* lea, etc.
  Cf. oli, oli.

ÔLMŌST

Vowel: almost.
  Plus call most, etc.

ŌLMƏN

h: Holman.
k(c): coalman, Coleman, Colman.
t: tollman.
  Plus soul, man, etc.

ŌLMƏNT

d: condolement.
j: cajolement.
r: enrollment.
tr: controlment.
  Plus soul meant, etc.

ÔLMƏNT

p: appallment, epaulement.
st: instalment, installment.
thr: disenthrallment, enthrall-
ment.
  Plus call meant, etc.

ŌLNƏS

dr: drollness.
h: wholeness.
s: soleness.

ÔLNƏS

Vowel: allness.
sm: smallness.
t: tallness.

ŌLŌ

b: bolo.
p: polo, water polo.
s: solo.
  Plus grow low, etc.
  Plus goal owe *or* O, etc.

ÔLPÄRK

b: ball park.

ÔLSĒD

p: palsied.
  Plus small, Sid, etc.

ÔLSHOOD

f: falsehood.
  Plus waltz, Hood, etc.

ÔLSNƏS

f: falseness.

ÔLSŌ

Vowel: also.
  Plus small, so, etc.

ŌLSTÄR

p: polestar.
  Plus whole star, etc.

ÔLSTŌN

g: gallstone.
  Plus small stone, etc.

ŌLSTŬR

b: bolster.
h: holster, shoulder holster, upholster.
　　Plus soul stir, etc.

ÔLSTƏN

Vowel: Alston.
b: Balston.
r: Ralston.
　　Plus hall stun, etc.

ŌLSƏM

d: dolesome.
h: wholesome.
　　Plus troll some *or* sum, etc.

ŌLSƏN

Vowel: Olsen, Olson.
j: Jolson.
t: Tolson, Toulson.
　　Plus bowl, son *or* sun, etc.

ÔLTĒ

f: faulty.
m: malty.
s: salty.
v: vaulty.
　　Plus small tee, etc.
　　Plus fault, he, etc.

ŌLTEST

b: boltest*, unboltest*.
j: joltest*.
m: moltest*.
v: revoltest*.
　　Plus soul test, etc.

ÔLTEST

f: defaultest*, faultest*, foot faultest*.
h: haltest*.
m: maltest*.
s: assaultest*, saltest*.
v: vaultest*.
z: exaltest*.
　　Plus small test, etc.

ŌLTETH

b: bolteth*, unbolteth*.
j: jolteth*.
m: molteth*.
v: revolteth*.

ÔLTETH

f: defaulteth*, faulteth*, foot faulteth*.
h: halteth*.
m: malteth*.
s: assaulteth*, salteth*.
v: vaulteth*.
z: exalteth*.

ŌLTIJ

v: voltage.
　　Cf. coltage, etc.

ÔLTIJ

m: maltage.
v: vaultage.
　　Cf. haltage, etc.

ÔLTIK

b: Baltic, cobaltic.
f: asphaltic.
s: basaltic.
st: peristaltic.
　　Plus small tick, etc.

ŌLTING

b: bolting, unbolting.
j: jolting.
m: molting, unmolting.
v: revolting.

ÔLTING

f: defaulting, faulting, foot faulting.
h: halting.
m: malting.
s: assaulting, salting.
v: vaulting.
z: exalting.

ŌLTISH

d: doltish.
k(c): coltish.

ÔLTLƏS

f: faultless.
m: maltless.
s: saltless.
    Plus fault, less or Les, etc.

ŌLTRĒ

p: poultry.
    Plus whole tree, etc.

ÔLTSƯR

f: falser.
w: waltzer.
    Plus fault, sir, etc.

ŌLTƯR

b: bolter, unvolter.
j: jolter.
k(c): colter.
v: revolter.
    Plus bolt her or err, etc.

ÔLTƯR

Vowel: altar, alter, unalter.
br: Gibraltar.
f: defaulter, faulter, foot faulter.
h: halter.
m: malter.
p: palter.
s: assaulter, psalter, salter.
v: vaulter.
w: McWalter, Walter.
z: exalter.
    Plus halt her or err, etc.

ÔLTƯRN

Vowel: subaltern.
s: saltern.
    Plus small tern or turn, etc.
    Plus fault, earn, erne, or urn, etc.

ŌLTƏD

b: bolted, unbolted.
j: jolted, unjolted.
m: molted, unmolted.
v: revolted.
    Plus colt, Ed, etc.
    Plus soul, Ted, etc.

ÔLTƏD

f: defaulted, faulted, foot faulted.
h: halted.
m: malted.
s: assaulted, salted.
v: vaulted.
z: exalted.
    Plus small, Ted, etc.
    Plus malt, Ed, etc.

ŌLTƏN

b: Bolton.
k(c): Colton.
m: molten, Molton, Moulton.
    Plus bolt on *or* an, etc.
    Plus goal ten, etc.
    Plus whole ton *or* tun, etc.

ÔLTƏN

d: Dalton.
w: Walton.
    Plus fault on *or* an, etc.
    Plus small tun *or* ton, etc.

ŌLUR

b: bowler.
d: condoler, doler, dolor.
dr: droller.
f: foaler.
g: goaler, one-goaler, two-goaler, etc.
j: cajoler.
k(c): coaler, kohler.
m: molar.
p: circumpoler, polar, poler, poller, unipolar.
r: enroller, high roller, Holy Roller, roller, unroller, uproller.
s: consoler, solar.
sh: shoaler.
skr(scr): scroller.
str: stroller.
t: toller.
tr: comptroller, controller, patroller, troller.
    Plus mole or, etc.
    Plus O, Lor', etc.
    Plus shoal her *or* err, etc.
    Cf. olur.

ÔLUR

b: bawler, baseballer, basketballer, footballer, high baller.
br: brawler.
dr: drawler.
f: faller.
h: hauler, overhauler.
k(c): caller, hog caller, train caller.
kr: crawler.
m: bemauler, mauler.
skr(scr): scrawler.
skw: squaller+.
sm: smaller.
spr: sprawler.
st: forestaller, staller.
t: taller.
thr: enthraller.
tr: trawler.
w: caterwauler.
y: yawler.
    Plus haul her *or* err. etc.

ŌLUS

b: bolus, holus-bolus.
d: gladiolus.
r: variolus.
s: sciolus, solus.
    Plus bass-viol us, goal us, etc.

ÔLVING

s: resolving.
v: evolving, revolving.

ÔLWĀZ

Vowel: always.
h: hallways.
    Plus stall weighs *or* ways, etc.

ÔLWŬRT

st: stalwart.

    Plus small wart, etc.

ÔLZĒ

b: ballsy.

ŌLƏ

Vowel: Leola, Ola, scagliola, viola
b: carambola.
d: gondola.
g: Angola, gola.
k(c): Appalachicola, COLA, cola, Coca-Cola, kola, Pensacola.
l: Lola.
m: Ramola, Romola.
n: Nola, seminola.
r: pyrola, Savonarola.
sk(sc): schola.
st: stola.
t: ayatollah.
z: Gorgonzola, Mazola, Zola.

    Plus stole a, etc.

ÔLƏ

f: Eufaula.
m: Guatamala.
p: Paula.

    Plus tall a, etc.

ŌLƏN

d: Dolan, eidolon.
k(c): colon, semicolon.
n: Nolan.
s: Solon.
st: stolen, stolon.

sw: swollen.

    Plus stroll on *or* an, etc.
    Plus droll an *or* on, etc.
    Cf. olan, olen, olon.

ÔLƏN

f: chop-fallen, fallen, windfallen.

    Cf. call an *or* on, etc.

ŌLƏND

b: Boland, Bowland.
l: lowland.
n: Noland.
r: Roland, Rowland.

    Plus stole, and, etc.
    Plus glow, land, etc.

ŌLƏNT

ch: cholent.
s: Solent.
v: non volent.

    Plus no Lent, etc.

ÔLƏS

fl: flawless.
j: jawless.
kl: clawless
l: lawless.
m: mawless.
s: sawless.

    Plus gnaw less *or* Les, etc.

ŌMAD

Vowel: ohmad*.
n: nomad.

    Plus so mad, etc.
    Plus Rome ad *or* add, etc.

ŌMĒ

Vowel: Naomi, Ohme.
f: foamy.
h: homey, homy.
l: loamy.
r: roamy.
    Plus show me, etc.

ÔMĒ

m: Maumee.
    Plus saw me, etc.

ŌMIK

br: bromic, hydrobromic.
kr: chromic, polychromic.
n: gnomic.
    Plus slow, Mick, etc.

ŌMĪN

br: bromine, theobromine.
    Plus know mine, etc.

ŌMING

f: befoaming, foaming.
gl: gloaming.
h: homing.
k(c): coaming, combing.
r: roaming.
    Plus show Ming, etc.

ŌMISH

r: Romish.

ŌMLĒ

h: homely.
    Plus roam, Lee *or* lea, etc.

ŌMLƏS

f: foamless.
h: homeless.
k(c): combless.
    Plus Rome less, etc.

ŌMLƏT

h: homelet.
t: tomelet.
    Plus Nome let, etc.

ŌMŌ

d: major-domo.
h: Ecce Homo, homo.
k(c): Como.
kr: chromo.
pr: promo.
    Plus show Mo, etc.
    Plus Rome owe *or* O, etc.

ŌMSPUN

h: homespun.
    Plus Rome spun, etc.

ŌMSTED

h: homestead.
    Plus Nome stead, etc.

ŌMƱR

Vowel: omer
g: gomer.
h: homer, Homer.
k(c): beachcomber, comber,
Comer, wool comber.
n: misnomer.
r: roamer.
v: vomer.
    Plus roam her *or* err, etc.

ŌMWỰRD

h: homeward.
   Plus Rome ward, etc.

ŌMWỰRK

h: homework.

ŌMƏ

Vowel: Oma.
b: aboma.
br: theobroma.
g: zygoma.
k(c): coma, glaucoma, Kaposi's sarcoma, sarcoma, Tacoma.
l: Point Loma.
n: Sonoma.
pl: diploma.
r: aroma, Roma.
s: soma.
st: stoma.
t: Natoma.
   Plus home, a, etc.

ŌMƏL

d: domal.

ŌMƏN

Vowel: omen.
b: bowman.
f: foeman.
n: agnomen, cognomen, praenomen.
r: Roman.
sh: showman.
y: yeoman.
   Plus show men, etc.
   Plus snow, man, etc.

ŌMƏND

Vowel: ill-omened, omened.
   Plus Rome end, etc.
   Plus so mend, etc.

ŌMƏNT

m: defining moment, moment.
st: bestowment.
   Plus glow meant, etc.

ŌNĀT

d: donate.
z: zonate.
   Plus throne ate *or* eight, etc.
   Plus go, Nate, etc.

ÔNDĒ

r: arrondi.
   Plus fawned, he, etc.

ŌNDEF

st: stone-deaf.
t: tone-deaf.
   Plus throne deaf, etc.
   Plus throned F, etc.

ÔNDỰR

l: launder.
m: Maunder.
   Plus pawned her, *or* err, etc.

ÔNDỰRZ

m: maunders.
s: Saunders.
   Plus pawned hers or errs, etc.

ŌNĒ

Vowel: Oney.
b: bony.

d: douppioni.
dr: drony.
f: phony.
h: Mahoney.
k(c): Coney, cony.
kr: crony.
l: aloney, baloney, bologny, Maloney.
m: alimony, antimony, matrimony, parsimony, patrimony, sancti-mony, testimony.
p: pony.
r: cicerone, lazzaroni, macaroni.
st: stony.
t: tony.
tr: ministrone.
    Plus known he, etc.
    Plus slow knee *or* nee, etc.

ÔNĒ

br: brawny.
l: lawny.
p: Pawnee.
s: sawney.
sh: Shawnee.
skr(scr): scrawny.
sw: Swanee.
t: mulligatawny, orange-tawny, Punxatawnee, tawny.
w: Sewanee.
y: yawny.
    Plus lawn, he, etc.
    Plus saw knee, etc.
    Cf. oni.

ŌNEST

Vowel: disownest*, ownest*.
d: condonest*.
dr: dronest*.
gr: groanest*, grownest.

h: honest*.
l: loanest*, lonest.
m: bemoanest*, moanest*.
p: postponest*.
st: stonest*.
t: atonest*, intonest*, tonest*.
thr: dethronest*, enthronest*, thronest*.
    Plus low nest, etc.

ŌNETH

Vowel: disowneth*, owneth*.
d: condoneth*.
dr: droneth*.
gr: groaneth*.
h: honeth*.
l: loaneth*.
m: bemoaneth*, moaneth*.
p: postponeth*.
st: stoneth*.
t: atoneth*, intoneth*, toneth*.
thr: dethroneth*, enthroneth*, throneth*.

ÔNGDĀ

l: long day.

ÔNGEST

l: longest.
str: strongest.

ÔNGĒZ

l: longies.

ÔNGFOOL

r: wrongful.
s: songful.
thr: throngful.
    Plus gong full, etc.

ÔNGGŌ

b: Bongo.
k(c): Congo.
  Plus wrong go, etc.

ÔNGGƯR

k(c): conger.
l: longer.

ÔNGHER

l: long hair.

ÔNGING

l: belonging, longing, prolonging.
r: wronging.
thr: thronging.

ÔNGISH

l: longish.
pr: prongish.
s: songish.
str: strongish.

ÔNGKĒ

d: donkey.
  Plus strong key, etc.

ÔNGKƯR

h: honker.
k(c): conker, conquer.
  Plus honky tonk her.

ÔNGKƯRZ

b: bonkers.
h: honkers.
k(c): conquers.
y: Yonkers.
  Plus honky-tonk errs *or* hers, etc.
  Plus wrong curs, etc.

ÔNGLĒ

l: longly.
r: wrongly.
  Plus song, Lee *or* lea, etc.

ÔNGNƏS

l: longness.
r: wrongness.

ÔNGRUN

l: long-run.

ÔNGSTƯR

s: songster.
  Plus wrong stir, etc.
  Plus wrong'st* her *or* err, etc.

ÔNGƯR

l: prolonger.
r: wronger.
  Plus strong err *or* her, etc.

ÔNGWĀ

l: Lilongwe.

ÔNGWĀV

l: long wave.
  Plus song wave *or* waive, etc.

ŌNHED

b: bonehead.
  Plus own head, etc.

ŌNIK

f: phonic, telephonic.
y: yonic.
z: zonic.
  Plus slow nick, etc.

ŌNING

Vowel: disowning, owning.
b: boning.
dr: droning.
f: phoning, telephoning.
gr: groaning.
h: honing.
kl: cloning.
l: loaning.
m: bemoaning, moaning.
p: poning, postponing.
st: stoning.
t: atoning, intoning, toning.
thr: dethroning, enthroning, throning.
z: zoning.

ÔNING

Vowel: awning.
d: dawning, undawning.
f: fawning.
p: pawning.
sp: spawning.
y: yawning.

ŌNIS

d: Adonis.
r: Coronis.

ŌNISH

dr: dronish.
l: Babylonish.
    Plus no knish, etc.

ŌNĪT

z: Zonite.
    Plus no night, etc.

ÔNJĒ

k(c): congee.
p: pongee.
    Plus on, Gee!, *or* G. etc.

ŌNLĒ

Vowel: only.
l: lonely.
    Plus known, Lee *or* lea, etc.

ŌNLƏS

b: boneless.
t: toneless.
thr: throneless.
z: zoneless.
    Plus own less, etc.

ŌNMƏNT

Vowel: disownment.
d: condonement.
p: postponement.
t: atonement.
thr: dethronement, enthrone-ment.
    Plus cone meant, etc.

ŌNNƏS

l: loneness.
n: unknowness.
pr: proneness.

ŌNŌ

m: avgolemono.

ŌNSHIFT

l: loanshift.

ŌNSUM

l: lonesome.
    Plus own some *or* sum, etc.

ÔNTĒ

fl: flaunty.
j: jaunty.
  Plus haunt, he, etc.
  Plus lawn tea, etc.

ÔNTEST

d: dauntest*.
fl: flauntest*.
h: hauntest*.
t: tauntest*.
v: vauntest*.
w: wantest*.
  Plus lawn test, etc.

ÔNTETH

d: daunteth*.
fl: flaunteth*.
h: haunteth*.
t: taunteth*.
v: vaunteth*.
w: wanteth*.

ÔNTIJ

w: wantage.
  Cf. flaunt age, etc.

ÔNTING

d: daunting.
fl: flaunting.
h: haunting.
j: jaunting.
t: taunting.
v: vaunting.
w: wanting.

ÔNTLƏS

d: dauntless.
t: tauntless.

v: vauntless.
  Plus jaunt, Les *or* less, etc.

ÔNTLƏT

g: gantlet, gauntlet.
  Plus flaunt Lett *or* let, etc.

ÔNTUR

d: daunter.
fl: flaunter.
g: gaunter.
h: haunter.
j: jaunter.
s: saunter.
t: taunter.
v: vaunter.
  Plus flaunt her *or* err, etc.

ÔNTƏD

d: daunted, undaunted.
fl: flaunted.
h: haunted.
t: taunted.
v: vaunted.
w: help wanted, wanted.
  Plus flaunt, Ed, etc.
  Plus lawn, Ted, etc.

ŌNUR

Vowel: owner.
b: boner.
d: condoner, donor.
dr: droner.
f: phoner, telephoner.
gr: groaner.
h: honer.
l: loner.
m: bemoaner, moaner.
p: postponer.
st: stoner.

t: atoner, intoner, toner.
thr: dethroner, enthroner.
Plus loan, *or* etc.
Plus own her *or* err, etc.
Cf. onur.

ÔNU̯R

Vowel: awner, barley awner.
br: brawner.
f: fawner.
p: pawner.
sp: spawner.
y: yawner.
Plus lawn her *or* err, etc.

ŌNYÄRD

b: boneyard.
Plus own yard, etc.

ŌNƏ

Vowel: Iona, Ona.
b: bona, Carbona.
ch: cinchona.
d: Dona.
j: Jonah.
l: Barcelona, Bellona, Bologna.
m: Cremona, Desdemona, Mona, Pomona, Ramona.
n: annona, Anona, Nona.
r: corona.
z: Arizona, Zona.
Plus own a, etc.

ÔNƏ

f: fauna.
l: Launah.
m: Mauna.
Plus fawn a, etc.

ŌNƏL

b: subumbonal.
r: coronal.
t: tonal.
z: zonal.
Plus phone, Al, etc.

ŌNƏNT

p: component, deponent, exponent, interponent, opponent, proponent.
s: intersonant, sonant.
Plus throne aunt *or* ant, etc.
Cf. onant, onent.

ŌNƏS

Vowel: onus.
b: bonus.
j: Jonas.
l: lowness.
sl: slowness.
t: tonous.
Plus telephone us, etc.
Cf. throne us, etc.

O͞OÄN

gl: gluon.

O͞OÄRD

Cf. view hard, etc.

O͞OÄRT

Plus new art, etc.

O͞OBĒ

b: booby.
l: looby.

r: ruby.
   Plus you be *or* bee, etc.
   Plus Rube, he, etc.

OOBĒD

r: rubied.
   Plus you bid, etc.

OOBIK

k(c): cubic.
p: pubic.
r: cherubic.

OOBING

k(c): cubing.
t: tubing.
   Plus you, Byng, etc.

OOBIT

k(c): cubit.
   Plus you bit, etc.
   Plus tube it, etc.

OOB'L

r: ruble.
   Plus tube'll, etc.
   Cf. you bull, etc.

OOBÔL

k(c): cue ball.
skr(scr): screw ball.
   Plus new ball, etc.
   Plus rube all, etc.

OOBRIK

l: lubric.
r: rubric.
   Plus tube rick, etc.
   Plus new brick, etc.

OOBUR

g: goober.
h: Huber.
t: tuber.
   Plus new burr, etc.

OOBURT

h: Hubert.
   Plus knew, Bert, etc.

OOBƏ

j: juba.
k(c): Cuba.
t: tuba.
   Plus cube a, etc.
   Plus new, bah!, etc.

OOBƏL

j: Jubal.
t: Tubal.
   Cf. Ub'l.

OOBƏN

r: Reuben.
st: Steuben.
   Plus you, Ben, etc.
   Cf. Lubin.
   Cf. tube in, etc.

OOCHĒ

d: Il Duce.
g: Noguchi.
k(c): coochy, hoochy-coochy.
n: panouchi, penuchi.
   Plus brooch, he, etc.
   Cf. Uchi.

ŌŌCHŮR

f: future.
p: puture.
s: suture.
　Plus suit your *or* you're, etc.

ŌŌDĀ

t: today

ŌŌDAD

d: doodad.
　Plus new dad, etc.

OODĒ

g: goody, goody-goody.
w: woody.
　Plus should, he, etc.

ŌŌDĒ

br: broody.
m: moody.
sk(sc): scudi.
　Plus rude, he, etc.

ŌŌDEST

br: broodest*.
kl: concludest*, excludest*, includest*, precludest*, recludest*, secludest*.
kr: crudest.
l: alludest*, deludest*, cludest*, illudest*, lewdest*, preludest*.
n: denudest*, nudest.
r: rudest.
shr: shrewdest.
tr: detrudest*, extrudest*, intrudest*, obtrudest*, protrudest*, retrudest*, subtrudest*.
z: exudest*.
　Cf. udist.

ŌŌDETH

br: broodeth*.
j: Judith.
kl: concludeth*, excludeth*, includeth*, precludeth*, recludeth*, secludeth*.
l: alludeth*, deludeth*, eludeth*, illudeth*, preludeth*.
n: denudeth*.
tr: detrudeth*, extrudeth*, intrudeth*, obtrudeth*, protrudeth*, retrudeth*, subtrudeth*.
z: exudeth*.
　Plus new death, etc.

ŌŌDIK

l: ludic.

OODING

g: gooding.
h: hooding.
p: bag pudding, Indian pudding, pudding.

ŌŌDING

br: abrooding, brooding.
kl: concluding, excluding, including, occluding, precluding, recluding, secluding.
l: alluding, deluding, eluding, illuding, preluding.
n: denuding.
s: transuding.
sn: snooding.
tr: detruding, extruding, intruding, obtruding, protruding, retruding, subtruding.
z: exuding.

OODISH

g: goodish.
w: woodish.
　Cf. should dish, etc.

OͲODISH

pr: prudish.
r: rudish.
shr: shrewdish.
  Plus new dish, etc.

OͲODIST

n: nudist.
pr: prudist.
  Cf. rudest.

OͲODITH

j: Judith.
  Cf. udeth.

OͲOD'L

b: boodle, caboodle.
d: flapdoodle, Yankee doodle.
n: canoodle, noodle.
p: poodle.
y: kiyoodle.
  Plus food'll, etc.

OODLĒ

g: goodly.
  Plus wood, lea *or* Lee, etc.

OͲODLĒ

kr: crudely.
l: lewdly.
n: nudely.
r: rudely.
shr: shrewdly.
  Plus brood, Lee, *or* lea, etc.

OODLUM

h: hoodlum.
  Plus brood, Lum, etc.

OͲODMER

br: broodmare.

OODMƏN

g: goodman.
h: hoodman.
w: woodman.
  Plus should man, etc.

OODNƏS

g: honest-to-goodness, goodness.

OͲODNƏS

kr: crudeness.
l: lewdness.
n: nudeness.
r: rudeness.
shr: shrewdness.

OͲODŌZ

k: kudos.

OͲODUͲR

br: brooder.
kl: concluder, excluder, includer, occluder, precluder, recluder, secluder.
kr: cruder.
l: alluder, deluder, eluder, illuder, preluder.
n: denuder.
r: ruder.
s: transuder.
shr: shrewder.
t: Tudor.
tr: detruder, extruder, intruder, obstruder, protruder, retruder, subtruder.
z: exuder.
  Plus exlude her *or* err, etc.

OͲODƏ

b: Barbuda, Buddha.
j: Judah.

k(c): barracuda, Ishkooda.
m: Bermuda.
  Plus stewed a, etc.

OODƏD

h: hooded.
w: unwooded, wooded.
  Plus hood, Ed, etc.
  Cf. good dead, etc.

O̅O̅DƏD

br: brooded.
d: duded.
kl: concluded, excluded, included, occluded, precluded, recluded*, secluded.
l: alluded, colluded, deluded, eluded, illuded, interluded, preluded, undeluded.
n: denuded.
s: transuded.
sn: snooded.
tr: detruded, extruded, intruded, obtruded, protruded, retruded, subtruded.
z: exuded.
  Plus you dead, etc.
  Cf. you did, etc.

O̅O̅DƏL

f: feudal.
l: paludal.
y: udal.
  Plus rude, Al, etc.

OODƏN

w: wooden.
  Plus good N or en, etc.
  Cf. good den, etc.

O̅O̅DƏNS

pr: jurisprudence, prudence.
  Plus new dense or dents, etc.
  Cf. udent+s.

O̅O̅DƏNT

kl: concludent, occludent.
pr: imprudent, jurisprudent, prudent.
st: day student, night student, student.
  Plus new dent, etc.

O̅O̅Ē

Vowel: ooey.
b: Bowie, buoy.
bl: blooie, bluey.
ch: chewy.
d: bedewy, Dewey, dewy.
f: fooey, pfui.
fl: flooey, fluey.
g: gooey.
gl: gluey.
h: hooey.
k(c): cooee, Coue.
l: Louis.
s: chopsuey.
shw: feng shui.
skr(scr): screwy.
th: thewy.
v: viewy.
  Plus knew he, etc.
  Cf. ui.

O̅O̅ES

j: Jewess.
  Plus new S, etc.

O̅O̅EST

b: imbuest*.
bl: bluest.

br: brewest*, imbrewest*.
ch: chewest*, eschewest*.
d: bedewest*, doest*, enduest*, subduest*, undoest*.
dr: drewest*, withdrewest*.
f: fewest*.
fl: flewest*.
gl: gluest*, ungluest*.
gr: grewest*.
h: hewest*, huest*.
k(c): cooest*.
kr: accruest*.
l: halooest*.
m: mewest*.
n: knewest*, newest, renewest*.
p: shampooest*.
r: ruest*.
s: ensuest*, pursuest*, suest*.
sh: shoest*, shooest*.
shr: beshrewest*.
skr(scr): screwest*, unscrewest*.
sl: slewest*.
sp: spewest*.
st: stewest*.
t: tatooest*.
tr: truest, untruest.
thr: threwest*.
v: interviewest*, reviewest*, viewest*.
w: wooest*.

O͞OETH

b: imbueth*.
bl: blueth*.
br: breweth*, imbreweth*.
ch: cheweth*, escheweth*.
d: bedeweth*, doeth*, endueth*, subdueth*, undoeth*.
dr: dreweth*, withdreweth*.
fl: fleweth*.
gl: glueth*, unglueth*.
gr: greweth*.

h: heweth*, hueth*.
k(c): cooeth*.
kr: accrueth*.
l: hallooeth*.
m: meweth*.
n: kneweth*, reneweth*.
p: shampooeth*.
r: rueth*.
s: ensueth*, pursueth*, sueth*.
sh: shoeth*, shooeth*.
shr: beshreweth*.
skr(scr): screweth*, unscreweth*.
sl: sleweth*.
sp: speweth*.
st: steweth*.
t: tatooeth*.
thr: threweth*.
v: intervieweth*, revieweth*, vieweth*.
w: wooeth*.

O͞OFĒ

r: roofy+.
w: woofy.

O͞OFĒ

g: goofy.
r: roofy+.
sp: spoofy.
   Plus who fee, etc.
   Plus roof, he, etc.

O͞OFĒLD

bl: Bluefield
n: Newfield
   Plus strew field, etc.

OOFING

r: roofing+.
w: woofing.

ŌŌFING

pr: water-proofing.
r: roofing+.
sp: spoofing.

OOFŲR

h: hoofer.
r: roofer+.

ŌŌFŲR

l: aloofer.
r: roofer+.
sp: spoofer.
  Plus new fur *or* fir, etc.
  Plus roof her *or* err, etc.
  Cf. who, for, etc.

ŌŌFƏ

ch: chufa.
st: stufa.
t: tufa.
y: ufa.
  Plus roof a, etc.

ŌŌFƏS

g: goofus.
r: rufous, Rufus.
  Plus roof us, etc.

OOGĒ

w: boogie woogie.

ŌŌGĒ

w: boogie-woogie+.
  Plus knew ghee, etc.
  Plus fugue E, etc.

ŌŌG'L

b: bugle.
d: MacDougall.

f: febrifugal, fugal, vermifugal.
fr: frugal, infrugal.
j: jugal.
  Plus fugue'll, etc.
  Cf. new gull, etc.

ŌŌGLŲR

b: bugler.
f: fugler.

ŌŌGŌ

h: Hugo.
  Plus you go, etc.

OOGŲR

b: boogur.
s: beet sugar, loaf sugar, maple sugar, sugar.

ŌŌGŲR

k(c): cougar.
l: Luger.
  Plus knew gar, etc.

OOGƏ

sh: meshuggah+.

ŌŌGƏ

sh: meshuggah+.
  Plus fugue a, etc.

ŌŌID

dr: druid.
fl: fluid.

ŌŌĪD

bl: blue-eyed.
tr: true-eyed.
  Plus knew I'd *or* eyed, etc.

O͞OIJ

br: brewage.
s: sewage.
   Cf. new age, etc.

O͞OIK

ch: catachuic.
l: toluic.

O͞OIN

br: bruin.
r: blue ruin, ruin.
s: sewen.
   Plus crew in *or* inn, etc.

O͞OING

b: imbuing.
bl: blueing.
br: brewing, inbruing.
ch: chewing, eschewing.
d: bedewing, doing, enduing, mildewing, misdoing, outdoing, overdoing, subduing, undoing, well-doing, wrong-doing.
gl: gluing.
h: hewing.
k(c): barbecuing, cooing, cueing.
kl: clewing, clueing.
kr: accruing, full crewing.
l: hallooing, looing.
m: mewing, mooing.
n: canoeing, renewing.
p: pooh-poohing, shampooing.
r: rueing.
s: ensueing, pursuing, suing.
sh: shoeing.
shr: beshrewing.
skr(scr): screwing, unscrewing.
sp: spewing.
st: stewing.
str: bestrewing, construing, misconstruing, strewing.

t: tatooing.
tr: trueing.
v: interviewing, reviewing, viewing.
w: wooing.
y: eweing.
z: zooing.

O͞OINGZ

d: doings, misdoings.
   Plus uing+s.

O͞OIS

l: Lewis, Louis, St. Louis.
   Cf. Jewess.

O͞OISH

bl: blueish.
gl: glueish.
j: Jewish.
n: newish.
shr: shrewish.
tr: truish.

O͞OKAN

t: toucan.
   Plus you can, etc.

O͞OKĀS

y: ukase.
   Plus new case, etc.
   Plus uke ace, etc.

OOKĒ

b: bookie.
h: hookey, hooky.
k(c): cookie, sugar cookie.
r: rookie.
   Plus cook, he, etc.
   Cf. took key, etc.

O͞OKĒ

fl: fluky.
sn: snooky.
sp: spooky.
  Plus duke, he, etc.
  Plus new key, etc.

O͞OKEST

b: rebukest*.
p: pukest*.

O͞OKETH

b: rebuketh*.
p: puketh*.

OOKING

b: booking.
br: brooking.
h: hooking, unhooking.
k(c): cooking, home cooking.
kr: crooking.
l: ill-looking, looking, overlooking, well-looking.
r: rooking.
  Cf. look, king, etc.

O͞OKING

b: rebuking.
p: puking.
  Plus new king, etc.

OOKLƏT

b: booklet.
br: brooklet.
  Plus crook let *or* Lett, etc.

O͞OKŌ

b: Pernambuco.
d: Duco.
  Plus spook owe *or* O, etc.

O͞OKO͞O

k(c): cuckoo.
  Plus you coo, etc.

OOKUP

h: hookup.
  Plus cook up, etc.

OOKƱR

h: hooker.
k(c): cooker, electric cooker, fireless cooker.
l: looker, overlooker.
sn: snooker.
st: stooker.
  Plus crook her *or* err, etc.

O͞OKƱR

b: rebuker.
fl: fluker.
l: lucre.
p: puker.
y: euchre.
  Plus spook her *or* err, etc.

O͞OKƏ

b: bucca, sambouka.
l: felucca, palooka.
r: garookuh.
t: festucca, fistucca.
y: yukka.
  Plus rebuke a, etc.

OOKƏD

kr: crooked.
  Plus ook+ed*.

O͞OKƏL

d: archducal, ducal.
l: noctiluchal.

n: nuchal.
t: Pentateuchal.
  Plus duke'll, etc.
  Plus spook, Al, etc.

ŌŌKƎN

l: antelucan.

ŌŌKƎS

d: caducous.
f: fucus.
kl: Clucas.
l: leucous, Lucas, noctilucous.
m: mucous, mucus.
r: rukus.
  Plus rebuke us, etc.
  Plus new cuss, etc.

ŌŌLÄ

p: pula.

ŌŌLÄG

g: gulag.

OOLBOOL

b: bulbul.
  Plus pull bull, etc.

OOLĒ

b: bully.
f: fully.
p: pulley.
w: wooly.
  Plus full, Lee *or* lea, etc.

ŌŌLĒ

bl: bluely.
ch: patchouli.
d: Dooley, doolie, duly, unduly.
dr: drooly.

g: guly*.
h: Gilhooley.
k(c): Cooley, coolie, coolly.
l: Gillooley, Gilluly.
n: newly.
r: unruly.
sk(sc): high-schooly.
t: tule.
th: Thule, Ultima Thule.
tr: truly.
  Plus few, Lee *or* lea, etc.

OOLĒD

b: bullied.
p: pullied.
  Cf. wool hid, etc.
  Cf. pull lid, etc.

ŌŌLEST

f: befoolest*, foolest.
k(c): coolest.
p: pulest*.
r: rulest*.
  Plus new, lest, etc.

ŌŌLETH

f: befooleth*.
k(c): cooleth*.
p: puleth*.
r: ruleth*.

ŌŌLIJ

k(c): Coolidge.
  Cf. rule age, etc.

ŌŌLIKS

d: spondulix.
  Plus new licks, etc.

OOLING

b: bulling.
p: pulling.

O͞OLING

dr: drooling.
f: befooling, fooling, no fooling.
k(c): cooling.
m: mewling.
p: puling.
r: misruling, overruling, ruling.
sk(sc): schooling.
sp: spooling.
t: tooling.

OOLISH

b: bullish.
f: fullish.

O͞OLISH

f: foolish, pound-foolish, tom-foolish.
k(c): coolish.
m: mulish.

OOLMƏN

p: Pullman.
w: Woolman.
Plus full, man, etc.

OOLNƏS

f: fulness.

O͞OLNƏS

k(c): coolness.

O͞OLO͞O

l: Honolulu, Lulu.
z: Zulu.
Plus new loo *or* Lou, etc.

O͞OLO͞OS

skr(scr): screwloose.
Plus you loose, etc.

OOLSƏM

f: fulsome.

OOLƏR

b: buller.
f: fuller.
p: puller, wire puller.
Plus pull her *or* err, etc.

O͞OLƏR

dr: drooler.
k(c): cooler, ridiculer, water cooler, wine cooler.
m: mewler.
p: puler.
r: ruler.
sp: spooler.
Plus rule her *or* err, etc.

O͞OLYƏR

k(c): peculiar.

O͞OLYUS

j: Julius.
p: Apulius.
Cf. ulius.

O͞OLƏ

b: Ashtabula, Beulah, Boola-Boola.
h: hula-hula.
l: Loula, Lula, Tallula, Wallula.
y: Eula.
z: Missoula.
Plus rule a, etc.

OOLƏN

w: woolen.
Plus pull N *or* en, etc.
Cf. pull hen, etc.

O͞OLƏP

j: julep.
t: tulip.
  Plus new lip, etc.
  Cf. school hip, etc.

O͞OLƏS

d: dewless.
j: Jewless.
k(c): cueless.
m: mewless.
p: pewless.
skr(scr): screwless.
v: viewless.
  Plus knew less *or* Les, etc.

OOLƏT

b: bullet.
p: pullet.
  Plus bull et, etc.
  Cf. pull it, etc.
  Cf. bull let, etc.

OOMÄT

s: consummate.
  Plus dumb eight *or* ate, etc.

O͞OMÄT

h: exhumate, inhumate.
sp: despumate.
  Plus new mate, etc.
  Plus room eight *or* ate, etc.

O͞OMĒ

bl: bloomy.
br: broomy.
f: fumy.
gl: gloomy.
pl: plumy.
r: rheumy, roomie, roomy.
sp: spumy.
y: Fiume.
  Plus who, me, etc.
  Plus tomb, he, etc.

O͞OMEST

b: boomest*.
bl: bloomest*.
d: doomest*.
f: fumest*, perfumest*.
gr: groomest*.
h: exhumest.
l: illumest*, loomest*.
pl: plumest*.
s: assumest*, consumest*.
t: costumest*, entombest*.
z: presumest*, resumest*.
  Plus who messed, etc.

O͞OMETH

b: boometh*.
bl: bloometh*.
d: doometh*.
f: fumeth*, perfumeth*.
gr: groometh*.
h: exhumeth*.
l: illumeth*, loometh*.
pl: plumeth*.
s: assumeth*, consumeth*.
t: costumeth*, entombeth*.
z: presumeth*, resumeth*.

O͞OMFOOL

bl: bloomful.
d: doomful.

OO͞MID

h: humid.
t: tumid.
   Plus who 'mid*, etc.
   Cf. loom hid, etc.

OO͞MIJ

f: fumage.
pl: plumage.
   Cf. tomb age, etc.
   Cf. new mage, etc.

OO͞MIN

b: albumin.
l: illumine, relumine.
   Plus tomb in, etc.
   Plus who, Min, etc.
   Cf. umen.

OO͞MING

b: booming.
bl: blooming, reblooming.
br: brooming, new-brooming.
d: dooming, predooming.
f: fuming, perfuming.
gl: glooming.
gr: grooming.
h: exhuming.
l: illuming, looming.
pl: pluming.
r: rooming.
s: assuming, consuming, unassuming.
sp: spuming.
t: disentombing, entombing, tombing.
v: vooming.
w: unwombing, wombing.
z: presuming, resuming, unpresuming, zooming.
   Plus new Ming, etc.

OO͞MLƏR

t: tummler.

OO͞MLƏS

bl: bloomless.
br: broomless.
d: doomless.
f: fumeless.
gr: groomless.
l: loomless.
pl: plumeless.
r: roomless.
t: tombless.
   Plus whom, Les *or* less, etc.

OO͞MLƏT

b: boomlet.
gr: groomlet.
pl: plumelet.
   Plus tomb let *or* Lett, etc.

OO͞MSTŌN

t: tombstone.
   Plus room stone, etc.

OO͞MŬR

b: baby boomer, boomer.
bl: bloomer.
d: doomer.
f: fumer, perfumer.
h: good-humor, humor, ill-humor.
l: illumer.
pl: ostrich plumer, plumer.
r: roomer, rumor.
s: assumer, consumer.
t: entomber, tumor.
z: presumer, resumer.
   Plus new myrrh, etc.
   Plus tomb her *or* err, etc.

OͦOMU̽RD

h: good-humored, humored, ill-humored.
r: rumored.
t: tumored.
    Cf. tomb herd *or* heard, etc.

OͦOMU̽RZ

bl: bloomers.
    Plus umur+s.

OͦOMUS

br: brumous.
d: dumous.
f: fumous.
gr: grumous.
h: humous, humus.
pl: implumous, plumous.
sp: spumous.
    Plus bloom us, etc.

OͦOMZDĀ

d: doomsday.
    Plus perfumes day, etc.

OͦOMZMƎN

d: doomsman.
gr: groomsman.
    Plus tombs man, etc.

OͦOMƎ

d: duma.
p: puma.
y: Yuma.
z: mazuma, Montezuma.
    Plus who, ma, etc.
    Plus entomb a, etc.

OOMƎN

w: woman.
    Cf. room an, etc.

OͦOMƎN

b: albumen.
g: legumen.
h: human, inhuman, superhu-man.
n: Newman.
k(c): acumen, catechumen.
l: lumen.
r: rumen.
t: bitumen.
tr: Truman.
    Plus who, man, etc.
    Plus you men, etc.
    Cf. umin.

OͦOMƎNT

b: imbuement.
br: imbruement.
ch: eschewment.
d: induement, subduement.
kr: accrument.
    Plus you meant, etc.

OͦONBÔL

m: moonball.

OͦONDĒ

r: Rundi.

OͦONDEST

kr: croondest*, etc.
w: woundest*.

OͦONDETH

kr: croondeth*, etc.
w: woundeth*.
    Plus noon death, etc.

O͞ONDƏD

w: unwounded, wounded.
   Plus loon dead, etc.
   Cf. loon did, etc.

O͞ONĒ

d: Dooney.
l: loony.
m: Mooney, mooney, moonie, Muni.
p: puisne, puny.
r: Rooney.
sp: spoony.
t: tuney.
   Plus croon he, etc.

O͞ONEST

kr: croonest*.
m: communest*, moonest*.
p: harpoonest*, impugnest*, oppugnest*.
pr: prunest*.
s: soonest*.
sp: spoonest*.
sw: swoonest*.
t: attunest*, entunest*, importunest*, tunest*.
   Plus new nest, etc.

O͞ONETH

kr: crooneth*.
m: communeth*, mooneth*.
p: harpooneth*, impugneth*, oppugneth*.
pr: pruneth*.
sp: spooneth*.
sw: swooneth*.
t: attuneth*, entuneth*, importuneth*, tuneth*.

O͞ONFOOL

r: runeful.
sp: spoonful.
t: tuneful.
   Plus dune full, etc.

O͞ONIK

m: Munich.
p: Punic.
r: runic.
t: tunic.
   Plus you, Nick *or* nick, etc.

O͞ONING

kr: crooning.
l: ballooning.
m: communing, mooning.
n: nooning.
p: expugning, harpooning, impugning, oppugning.
pr: pruning.
sp: spooning.
sw: swooning
t: tuning.

O͞ONIS

t: Tunis.
y: Eunice.

O͞ONISH

f: buffoonish.
tr: poltroonish.

O͞ONIST

l: balloonist.
p: harpoonist.
s: bassoonist.
t: opportunist.

O͞ONIT

y: unit.
> Plus few knit *or* nit, etc.
> Plus tune it, etc.

O͞ONIZM

f: buffoonism.
t: opportunism.
tr: poltroonism.

O͞ONLĪT

m: moonlight.
n: noon light.
> Plus June light, etc.

O͞ONLƏS

j: Juneless.
m: moonless.
r: runeless.
t: tuneless.
> Plus spittoon less *or* Les, etc.

O͞ONNƏS

j: jejuneness, Juneness.
t: inopportuneness, opportuneness.

O͞ONŌ

Vowel: Numero Uno, uno.
br: Bruno.
j: Juno.
> Plus you know *or* no, etc.
> Plus croon owe *or* O, etc.

O͞ONRĪZ

m: moonrise.
> Plus June rise, etc.

O͞ONƱR

b: ballooner, interlunar, lunar, novilunar, plenilunar, semilunar, sublunar, translunar.
g: dragooner.
k(c): lacunar.
kr: crooner.
m: communer, mooner.
p: harpooner, impugner, lampooner, oppugner.
pr: pruner.
s: sooner.
sk(sc): schooner.
sp: spooner.
sw: swooner.
t: attuner, importuner, piano tuner, tuner.
> Plus croon her *or* err, etc.

O͞ONYƱR

j: junior.
> Cf. croon your, etc.

O͞ONYƏN

m: communion, excommunion, intercommunion.
y: disunion, European Union, labor union, reunion, trades-union, union.

O͞ONƏ

k(c): Acuna, kuna, lacuna, vicuna.
l: luna.
p: puna.
r: Peruna.
t: fortuna, tuna.
y: una.
> Plus tune a, etc.

O͞ONƏK

y: eunich.

O͞ONƏL

b: tribunal.
k(c): lacunal.
  Plus tune, Al, etc.

O͞ONƏS

bl: blueness.
f: fewness.
n: newness.
tr: trueness.
  Plus moon S, etc.

O͞OPĒ

dr: droopy.
hw: whoopee.
kr: croupy.
l: loopy.
s: soupy.
sw: swoopy.
  Plus group, he, etc.
  Cf. upi.
  Cf. whoopee.

O͞OPEST

d: dupest*.
dr: droopest*.
gr: groupest*.
hw: whoopest*.
k(c): coopest*, recoupest*.
l: loopest*.
sk(sc): scoopest*.
st: stoopest*.
sw: swoopest*.
tr: troopest*.
  Plus new pest, etc.

O͞OPETH

d: dupeth*.
dr: droopeth*.
gr: groupeth*.

hw: whoopeth*.
k(c): coopeth*, recoupeth*.
l: loopeth*.
sk(sc): scoopeth*.
st: stoopeth*.
sw: swoopeth*.
tr: troopeth*.

O͞OPID

k(c): Cupid.
st: stupid.
  Cf. group hid, etc.

O͞OPING

d: duping.
dr: drooping.
gr: grouping.
h: hooping.
hw: whooping.
k(c): cooping, recouping.
l: looping, loop-the-looping.
sk(sc): scooping.
st: stooping.
sw: swooping.
tr: trooping.
  Plus you ping, etc.

O͞OPL

d: subduple.
dr: quadruple.
p: pupil.
skr(scr): scruple.
t: octuple, quintuple, septuple, sextuple.
  Plus new pill, etc.
  Plus group ill, etc.
  Plus group'll, etc.
  Cf. up'l.

O͞OPLEST

skr(scr): scruplest*.

OͦOPLETH

skr(scr): scrupleth*.

OͦOPLƏT

dr: quadruplet.
t: octuplet, quintuplet, septuplet, sextuplet.

Plus group let *or* Lett, etc.

OͦOPMƏNT

gr: aggroupment.
k(c): recoupment.

Plus swoop meant, etc.

OͦOPON

j: jupon.
k(c): coupon.

Plus group on, etc.

OͦOPUB

br: brew pub.

OͦOPUͤR

d: duper.
dr: drooper.
gr: grouper.
h: hooper.
hw: whooper.
k(c): cooper, recouper.
kr: crouper.
l: looper, loop-the-looper.
s: souper, super.
sk(sc): scooper.
sn: snooper.
st: stooper, stupor.
sw: swooper.
tr: trooper.

Plus group her *or* err, etc.
Plus group, or, etc.
Cf. upur.

OͦOPUͤRT

r: Rupert.

Plus new pert, etc.

OͦOPƏ

p: pupa.
s: supa.

Plus group a, etc.

OͦORAT

j: jurat.

Plus you rat, etc.
Plus pure at, etc.

OͦORĀT

k(c): curate.

Plus demure eight *or* ate, etc.
Plus you rate, etc.

OORBUN

b: Bourbon.

OͦORĒ

d: tandoori.
dr: Drury.
f: fury.
h: houri.
j: de jure, Jewry, jury.
k(c): Curie.
y: ewry.
z: Missouri.

Plus pure, he, etc.

OͦOREKS

l: Lurex.

OͦOREST

d: endurest*.
j: abjurest*, adjurest*, conjurest*.
k(c): curest*, procurest*, securest.
l: allurest*, lurest*.

m: demurest, immurest*, moorest*, unmoorest*.

p: impurest, poorest, purest.

sh: assurest*, ensurest*, insurest*, reassurest*, reinsurest*, surest.

sk(sc): obscurest.

t: immaturest, maturest, tourest*.

Plus who rest, etc.

Cf. urist.

Cf. pure rest, etc.

O͞ORETH

d: endureth*.

j: abjureth*, adjureth*, conjureth*.

k(c): cureth*, procureth*, secureth*.

l: allureth*, lureth*.

m: immureth*, mooreth*, unmooreth*.

sh: assureth*, ensureth*, insureth*, reassureth*, reinsureth*.

sk(sc): obscureth*.

t: matureth*.

O͞ORID

l: lurid.

Plus who rid, etc.

Cf. you're hid, etc.

O͞ORIJ

m: moorage, murage.

Cf. your age, etc.

Cf. you rage, etc.

O͞ORIK

f: hydrosulphuric, sulphuric.

p: purpuric.

t: hydrotelluric, telluric.

Plus new rick, etc.

O͞ORIM

p: purim.

y: urim.

Plus new rim, etc.

Plus cure him, etc.

O͞ORIN

b: burin.

n: neurin, neurine.

t: daturin.

y: urine.

Plus pure in, etc.

O͞ORING

d: during, enduring, everduring.

j: abjuring, adjuring, conjuring, juring, nonjuring.

k(c): curing, procuring, securing.

l: alluring, luring.

m: immuring, mooring, unmooring.

n: manuring.

sh: assuring, ensuring, insuring, reassuring, reinsuring.

sk(sc): obscuring.

sp: spooring.

t: maturing, touring.

y: inuring.

Plus new ring, etc.

O͞ORISH

b: boorish.

m: Moorish.

p: poorish.

t: amateurish.

O͞ORIST

j: jurist.

p: purist.

t: caricaturist, tourist.

Plus new wrist, etc.

O͞ORIZM

p: purism.
t: tourism.

O͞ORLĒ

k: securely.
m: demurely.
p: poorly, purely.
sk(sc): obscurely.
t: maturely.
Plus sure, Lee *or* lea, etc.

O͞ORMƏNT

j: abjurement, conjurement.
k(c): procurement.
l: allurement.
m: immurement.
sk(sc): obscurement.
Plus pure meant, etc.

O͞ORNƏS

k(c): insecureness, secureness.
m: demureness.
p: impureness, poorness, pureness.
sh: sureness.
sk(sc): obscureness.
t: immatureness, matureness.

O͞ORŌ

b: bureau.
d: maduro.
sk(sc): chiaroscuro.
tr: Truro.
Plus you row *or* roe, etc.
Plus pure owe *or* O, etc.

O͞ORUR

d: endurer.
f: furor.

j: abjurer, adjurer, conjurer, grand juror, juror, nonjuror, petty juror, trial juror.
k(c): curer, procurer, securer.
l: allurer, lurer.
m: demurer, immurer, moorer, unmoorer.
n: manurer.
p: impuror, poorer, purer.
sh: assurer, ensurer, insurer, reassurer, reinsurer, surer.
sk(sc): obsecurer.
t: maturer, tourer.
y: inurer.
Plus procure her *or* err, etc.
Plus pure, or, etc.
Cf. uror.

O͞ORUS

k(c): dolichurus.
n: anurous.
t: Arcturus.
y: Eurus, urus.
Plus assure us, etc.

O͞ORƏ

d: pietra dura.
k(c): Cuticura.
p: purpura.
pl: pleura.
s: caesura, cesura, fissura, flexura, sura, surra, surrah.
st: Angostura.
t: appoggiatura, coloratura, datura, Keturah, velatura, vettura.
v: bravura.
z: caesura, cesura.
Plus you're a, etc.

O͞ORƏL

j: jural.
k(c): sinecural.

kr: crural.

l: tellural.

m: antemural, extramural, intermural, intramural, mural.

n: interneural, neural.

pl: pleural, plural.

r: rural.

s: caesural, cesural, commissural, sural.

y: Ural.

z: caesural, cesural.

    Plus pure, Al, etc.

ŌŌRƏNS

d: durance, endurance, perdurance.

l: allurance.

sh: assurance, insurance, reassurance, reinsurance.

    Plus pure ants *or* aunts, etc.

    Plus who rants, etc.

OOSĒ

p: pussy.

ŌŌSĒ

b: Debussy.

d: Il Duce.

g: goosy.

j: juicy.

l: Lucy.

sl: sluicy.

    Plus you see, etc.

    Plus reduce, he, etc.

ŌŌSEST

d: adducest*, conducest*, deducest*, inducest*, introducest*, producest*, reducest*, reproducest*, seducest*, traducest*.

f: profusest.

l: loosest, unloosest*.

spr: sprucest.

str: abstrusest.

ŌŌSETH

d: adduceth*, conduceth*, deduceth*, induceth*, introduceth*, produceth*, reduceth*, reproduceth*, seduceth*, traduceth*.

l: looseth*, unlooseth*.

spr: spruceth*.

    Plus new, Seth, etc.

ŌŌSFOOL

j: juiceful.

y: useful.

    Plus reduce full, etc.

ŌŌSHING

d: douching.

r: ruching.

ŌŌSHUN

b: attribution, contribution, distribution, retribution.

g: redargution.

k(c): allocution, circumlocution, collocution, electrocution, elocution, execution, insecution, interlocution, locution, persecution, prosecution, ventrilocution.

l: ablution, absolution, circumvolution, convolution, devolution, dilution, dissolution, evolution, involution, irresolution, obvolution, pollution, resolution, revolution, Ringer's solution, self-pollution, solution, thermal pollution, volution.

n: comminution, diminution, imminution.

p: Lilliputian.

t: constitution, destitution, institution, prostitution, restitution, substitution.

> Plus you shun, etc.

OͦͦSHUS

l: Lucius.

> Plus debouch us, etc.

OͦͦSHƏ

r: Jerusha.

> Plus new shah, etc.
> Plus debouch a, etc.

OͦͦSHƏL

d: fiducial.
kr: crucial.

> Plus you shall, etc.
> Plus barouche, Al, etc.

OͦͦSID

l: lucid, pellucid, translucid.
m: mucid.

> Plus you, Sid, etc.
> Cf. used.
> Cf. goose hid, etc.

OͦͦSIJ

b: abusage*.
y: usage.

> Cf. goose age, etc.
> Cf. new sage, etc.

OͦͦSING

d: adducing, conducing, deducing, educing, inducing, introducing, producing, reducing, reproducing, seducing, traducing.
l: loosing, unloosing.
spr: sprucing.

> Plus you sing, etc.

OͦͦSIV

b: abusive.
d: conducive, deducive, educive.
f: confusive, diffucive, effusive, infusive, perfusive, transfusive.
kl: conclusive, exclusive, inclusive, inconclusive, reclusive, seclusive.
l: allusive, collusive, delusive, elusive, illusive.
t: contusive.
tr: inobtrusive, intrusive, obtrusive.

> Plus new sieve, etc.

OͦͦSKĒ

br: brewski.

OͦͦSLƏS

j: juiceless.
y: useless.

> Plus goose less *or* Les, etc.

OͦͦSMƏNT

d: conducement, deducement, inducement, reducement, seducement, superinducement, traducement.

> Plus goose meant, etc.

OͦͦSNƏS

f: diffuseness, profuseness.
kl: recluseness.
l: looseness.
spr: spruceness.
str: abstruseness.
t: obtuseness.

OͦͦSŌ

hw: whoso.
kr: Crusoe.

r: Caruso.
tr: trousseau.
 Plus you sew, sow, *or* so, etc.
 Plus goose owe *or* O, etc.

O͞OSTƱR

b: booster.
br: brewster.
f: Fewster.
j: jouster.
r: rooster.
w: Worcester.
 Plus few stir, etc.
 Plus loosed her *or* err, etc.

O͞OSTƏS

y: Eustace.
 Plus boost ace, etc.

O͞OSUM

gr: gruesome.
t: twosome.
 Plus through some *or* sum, etc.

O͞OSƱR

d: adducer, conducer, deducer, inducer, introducer, producer, reducer, reproducer, seducer, traducer.
l: looser.
spr: sprucer.
str: abstruser.
 Plus who, sir, etc.
 Plus loose her *or* err, etc.

O͞OSƏ

d: Medusa.
k(c): Coosa.
l: Tuscaloosa.
p: Tallapoosa.

s: Sousa, Susa.
th: Arethusa.
 Plus reduce a, etc.

O͞OSƏD

d: deuced.
 Plus us+d*.
 Cf. usid.

O͞OSƏL

n: hypotenusal.
tr: protrusile.
 Plus goose ill, etc.
 Plus new sill, etc.
 Plus reduce, Al, etc.

O͞OSƏN

l: loosen, unloosen.
 Cf. reduce hen, etc.

O͞OSƏNS

l: translucence.
n: nuisance.
 Plus few scents, cents, *or* sense, etc.

O͞OSƏNT

d: abducent, adducent, conducent, producent, reducent, traducent.
l: interlucent, lucent, relucent, tralucent*, translucent, unlucent.
 Plus new scent *or* cent, etc.
 Cf. Toussaint.

O͞OSƏZ

b: abuses, cabooses.
d: adduces, conduces, deduces, deuces, educes, induces, introduces, produces, reduces, reproduces, seduces, traduces.

dr: Druses.
j: juices.
k(c): excuses.
l: looses, unlooses.
n: burnooses, nooses.
sl: sluices.
spr: spruces.
tr: truces.
y: uses.
  Plus who says, etc.
  Plus truce, Ez, etc.
  Cf. noose is, etc.

O͞OTĀT

m: immutate.
n: circumnutate.
sk(sc): scutate.
  Plus you, Tate, etc.
  Plus brute eight *or* ate, etc.

O͞OTĒ

b: beauty, booty, botee, Djibouti, freebooty, Jibouti.
d: duty.
fl: fluty.
fr: fruity, tutti-frutti.
g: agouti.
k(c): cootie, cutie.
l: looty.
r: rooty.
s: sooty.
sn: snooty.
  Plus brute, he, etc.
  Plus new tea *or* T, etc.
  Plus newt, he, etc.

O͞OTĒD

b: bootied.
p: putid.
  Cf. uted.
  Cf. boot hid, etc.

O͞OTEST

b: bootest*.
f: confutest*, refutest*.
h: hootest*.
k(c): acutest, cutest, executest*, persecutest*.
kr: recruitest*.
l: dilutest*, lootest*, pollutest*, resolutest, salutest*.
m: commutest*, mutest, transmutest*.
n: minutest.
p: deputest*, disputest*, imputest*.
r: rootest*, uprootest*.
sh: shootest*.
t: astutest, constitutest*, institutest*, substitutest*.
  Plus new test, etc.

O͞OTETH

b: booteth*.
f: confuteth*, refuteth*.
h: hooteth*.
k(c): executeth*, persecuteth*.
kr: recruiteth*.
l: diluteth*, looteth*, polluteth*, saluteth*.
m: commuteth*, muteth*, transmuteth*.
p: deputeth*, disputeth*, imputeth*.
r: rooteth*, uprooteth*.
sh: shooteth*.
t: constituteth*, instituteth*, substituteth*.

O͞OTFOOL

fr: fruitful.
  Plus snoot full, etc.

O͞OTHEST

s: soothest.
sm: smoothest.

O͞OTHFOOL

r: ruthful.
t: toothful.
tr: truthful, untruthful.
y: youthful.
    Plus tooth full, etc.

O͞OTHING

s: soothing.
sm: smoothing.
t: toothing.
    Plus new thing, etc.

O͞OTHLƏS

r: ruthless.
t: toothless.
tr: truthless.
    Plus Ruth, less *or* Les, etc.

O͞OTHNƏS

sm: smoothness.
k(c): uncouthness.

O͞OTHSƏM

t: toothsome.
y: youthsome.
    Plus Ruth, some *or* sum, etc.

O͞OTHƱR

k(c): uncouther.
l: Luther.
s: soother.
sm: smoother.
    Plus soothe her *or* err, etc.
    Plus truth, her, etc.

O͞OTIJ

fr: fruitage.
m: mutage.
sk(sc): scutage.
    Cf. flute age, etc.

O͞OTIK

b: scorbutic.
d: propaedeutic.
n: hermeneutic.
p: therapeutic.
t: emphyteutic.
y: maieutic, toreutic.
z: diazeutic.
    Plus you tick, etc.

O͞OTIL

f: futile.
r: rutile.
s: sutile.
y: inutile.
    Plus few till, etc.
    Plus brute ill, etc.

OOTING

f: footing.
p: putting.

O͞OTING

b: booting, unbooting.
f: confuting, refuting.
fl: fluting.
fr: fruiting.
h: hooting.
k(c): executing, persecuting, prosecuting.
kr: recruiting.
l: diluting, high-faluting, looting, polluting, saluting.
m: commuting, mooting, permuting, transmuting.

n: comminuting.
p: computing, deputing, disputing, imputing.
r: rooting, unrooting, uprooting.
s: suiting.
sk(sc): scooting.
sh: off-shooting, out-shooting, overshooting, shooting.
t: constituting, darn-tooting, instituting, prostituting, reconstituting, substituting, tooting.

OͦOTISH

br: brutish.
s: sootish.
Plus you, Tish, etc.

OͦOTIST

fl: flutist.
l: lutist.
n: hermeneutist.
p: therapeutist.
s: pharmaceutist.

OͦOTIV

d: indutive.
j: coadjutive.
k(c): persecutive.
l: resolutive.
t: constitutive.

OͦOTIZM

br: brutism.
m: mutism.
Plus cute ism, etc.

OͦOTL

br: brutal.
f: footle.
t: tootle.
Plus suit, Al, etc.
Cf. util.

OͦOTLĒ

l: absolutely, posilutely.
Plus cute, Lee *or* lea, etc.

OͦOTLING

f: footling.
t: tootling.

OͦOTLƏS

b: bootless.
fr: fruitless.
Plus suit less, etc.

OͦOTMƏNT

br: imbrutement.
f: confutement.
kr: recruitment.
Plus suit meant, etc.

OͦOTNƏS

k(c): acuteness, cuteness.
l: absoluteness.
m: muteness.
n: minuteness.
s: hirsuteness.
st: astuteness.

OͦOTŌ

m: Maputo.
n: sostenuto.
pl: Pluto.
Plus you toe *or* tow, etc.
Plus brute owe *or* O, etc.

OͦOTRID

p: putrid.
Plus brute rid, ect.

OͦOTRIKS

k(c): persecutrix.
t: tutrix.

Plus new tricks, etc.

Plus cute ricks, etc.

O͞OTRƏL

n: neutral.

O͞OTRƏN

n: neutron.

Cf. brute run, etc.

O͞OTSĒ

w: tootsie-wootsie.

Plus brute see, etc.

Plus lutes, he, etc.

OOTƯR

f: footer.

p: putter.

Plus foot her *or* err, etc.

O͞OTƯR

b: booter, free-booter.

f: confuter, fouter, refuter.

fl: fluter.

h: hooter.

j: coadjutor.

k(c): accoutre, acuter, cuter, executor, persecutor, prosecutor.

kr: recruiter.

l: diluter, looter, luter, polluter, saluter.

m: commuter, mooter, muter, permuter, transmuter.

n: minuter, neuter.

p: computer, deputer, disputer, imputer, pewter.

r: rooter, uprooter.

s: suitor.

sh: chuter, parachuter, peashooter, sharpshooter, shooter.

sk(sc): scooter.

t: astuter, constituter, instituter, prostituter, restitutor, ring-tailed tooter, substituter, tooter, tutor.

Plus flute, or, etc.

Plus loot her *or* err, etc.

Cf. utur.

OOTƏD

f: footed, nimbled-footed.

Plus put, Ed, etc.

O͞OTƏD

b: bebooted, booted, unbooted.

br: bruited.

f: confuted, refuted, unconfuted.

fl: fluted.

fr: fruited.

h: hooted.

k(c): allocuted, electrocuted, elocuted, executed, persecuted, prosecuted, unpersecuted, unprosecuted.

kr: recruited.

l: convoluted, diluted, involuted, looted, polluted, saluted, unpolluted, voluted.

m: commuted, immuted, mooted, transmuted.

n: comminuted.

p: computed, deputed, disputed, imputed, reputed, undisputed.

r: rooted, unrooted, uprooted.

s: sooted, suited, unsuited.

sk(sc): scooted.

t: constituted, instituted, prostituted, self-constituted, substituted, tooted.

Plus fruit, Ed, etc.

Plus you, Ted, etc.

Cf. utid.

O͞OTƏN

br: Brewton.

n: Newton.

t: Teuton.

> Plus brute on *or* an, etc.
>
> Plus brew ton *or* tun, etc.

O͞OYƏNS

b: bouyance.

O͞OYƏNT

b: bouyant.

O͞OU̯R

b: imbuer.

bl: bluer.

br: brewer.

ch: chewer, eschewer, gumchewer, tobacco chewer.

d: bedewer, derring-doer, doer, enduer, evil-doer, misdoer, outdoor, overdoer, subduer, undoer, well-doer, wrong-doer.

f: fewer.

gl: gluer.

h: hewer.

k(c): cooer.

l: hallooer.

m: mewer.

n: canoer, newer, renewer.

p: shampooer.

r: ruer.

s: pursuer, sewer, suer.

sh: horseshoer, shoer.

sk: skewer.

skr(scr): screwer, unscrewer.

st: stewer.

str: bestrewer, misconstruer, strewer.

t: tatooer

tr: truer.

v: interviewer, reviewer, viewer.

w: wooer.

y: ewer.

> Plus due her *or* err, etc.

O͞OU̯RD

l: leeward.

s: Seward, sewered.

sk: skewered.

st: steward.

> Cf. new ward, etc.

O͞OVĒ

m: movie.

> Plus prove he, etc.
>
> Plus knew, Vee *or* V, etc.

O͞OVEST

m: movest*, removest*.

pr: approvest*, disapprovest*, disprovest*, provest*, reprovest*.

> Plus new vest, etc.

O͞OVETH

m: moveth*, removeth*.

pr: approveth*, disapproveth*, disproveth*, proveth*, reproveth*.

O͞OVING

gr: grooving.

m: moving, removing, unmoving.

pr: approving, disapproving, disproving, improving, proving, reproving.

O͞OVMƏNT

m: movement.

p: approvement, improvement.

> Plus behoove meant, etc.

O͞OVU̯R

gr: groover.

h: Hoover.

k(c): Vancouver.

l: Louvre.

m: mover, people mover, remover.
n: maneuver.
pr: approver, disapprover, disprover, improver, prover, reprover.
　Plus groove her *or* err, etc.

O͞OVƏL

m: removal.
pr: approval, disapproval, disproval, reproval.
　Plus groove, Al, etc.
　Plus you, Val, etc.

O͞OVƏN

h: hooven.
pr: proven.
　Cf. improve hen, etc.

O͞OWURD

l: leeward.
st: steward.
　Cf. uurd.

O͞OWURT

st: Stewart, Stuart.

O͞OYƏ

l: alleluia.
　Cf. who "yuh," etc.
　Cf. through you, etc.

O͞OZDĒ

t: Tuesday+.
　Plus bruised, he, etc.
　Plus cruise Dee, etc.

O͞OZĒ

Vowel: oozy.
b: boozy.

d: doozy.
fl: fluzie.
k(c): Jacuzzi.
w: woozy.
　Plus cruise, he, etc.
　Plus knew Zee *or* Z, etc.

O͞OZEST

Vowel: oozest*.
b: abusest*, boozest*.
br: bruisest*.
ch: choosest*.
f: confusest*, diffusest*, fusest*, infusest*, refusest*, suffusest*, transfusest*.
k(c): accusest*, excusest*.
kr: cruisest*.
l: losest*.
m: amusest*, musest*.
r: perusest*.
sn: snoozest*.
y: usest*.
　Plus new zest, etc.

O͞OZETH

Vowel: oozeth*.
b: abuseth*, boozeth*.
br: bruiseth*.
ch: chooseth*.
f: confuseth*, diffuseth*, fuseth*, infuseth*, refuseth*, suffuseth*, transfuseth*.
k(c): accuseth*, excuseth*.
kr: cruiseth*.
l: loseth*.
m: amuseth*, museth*.
r: peruseth*.
sn: snoozeth*.
y: useth*.

O͞OZHUN

b: abusion.

f: affusion, circumfusion, confusion, diffusion, effusion, fusion, infusion, interfusion, perfusion, profusion, refusion, suffusion, transfusion.

kl: conclusion, exclusion, inclusion, interclusion*, occlusion, preclusion, reclusion, seclusion.

l: allusion, collusion, delusion, disillusion, elusion, illusion, prolusion, self-delusion.

str: abstrusion.

t: contusion, pertusion*.

tr: detrusion, extrusion, intrusion, obtrusion, protrusion, retrusion, trusion.

th: Malthusian.

Cf. uzian.

O͞OZIK

m: concrete music, music.

O͞OZING

Vowel: oozing.

b: abusing, boozing.

br: bruising.

ch: choosing.

f: confusing, diffusing, fusing, infusing, interfusing, refusing, suffusing, transfusing.

k(c): accusing, excusing, self-accusing.

kr: cruising.

l: losing.

m: amusing, musing.

p: perusing.

sn: snoozing.

t: contusing.

y: disusing, using.

O͞OZIV

m: amusive, unamusive.

O͞OZ'L

b: bamboozle.

f: foozle, gumfoozle, refusal.

r: perusal.

Plus lose, Al, etc.

O͞OZLUR

b: bamboozler.

f: foozler.

OOZM

b: bosom.

Plus lose 'em, etc.

O͞OZMƏN

n: newsman.

tr: trewsman.

Plus whose man, etc.

O͞OZMƏNT

m: amusement.

Plus news meant, etc.

O͞OZRĒL

n: newsreel.

Plus booze reel, etc.

O͞OZUR

Vowel: oozer.

b: abuser, boozer.

br: bruiser.

ch: chooser.

f: confuser, diffuser, fuser, infuser, interfuser, refuser, suffuser, transfuser.

k(c): accuser, excuser.

kr: cruiser.

l: lollapaloozer, loser.

m: amuser, muser.

sn: snoozer.

y: misuser, nonuser, user.

Plus bruise her *or* err, etc.

OͦOͦZƏ

l: lollapalooza.

Plus who's a, etc.

OͦOͦZƏL

f: refusal.

m: musal.

Plus brews, Al, etc.

Cf. fusil.

OͦOͦZƏN

s: Susan.

Plus who's an, etc.

Plus rues an, etc.

OͦOͦZƏZ

Vowel: oozes.

b: abuses, disabuses.

br: bruises.

ch: chooses.

dr: druses.

f: circumfuses, confuses, diffuses, fuses, infuses, interfuses, refuses, suffuses, transfuses.

k(c): accuses, excuses.

kr: cruises, cruzes.

l: loses.

m: amuses, bemuses, muses.

n: nooses.

r: peruses, ruses.

sn: snoozes.

t: contuses.

y: disuses, misuses, uses.

Plus lose, Ez, etc.

OͦOͦƏL

ch: eschewal.

d: dual, duel, subdual.

f: fuel.

gr: gruel.

h: Hewell.

j: bejewel, jewel.

kr: crewel, cruel.

n: newel, renewal.

r: Reuel.

s: pursual, Sewell.

t: tewel.

v: reviewal.

Plus new el *or* L, etc.

Plus two, Al, etc.

Cf. ual, uel, etc.

OͦOͦƏN

ch: Chouan.

d: duan.

g: Perguan.

Plus view an, etc.

OͦOͦƏNS

ch: eschewance.

n: renewance.

s: pursuance.

Plus view ants *or* aunts, etc.

OͦOͦƏNT

s: pursuant.

tr: truant.

Plus new ant or aunt, etc.

OͦOͦƏT

kr: cruet.

s: suet.

Plus who et, etc.

Cf. do it, etc.

ŌPĀ

k: co-pay.

ŌPAZ

t: topaz.
    Cf. Lopez.
    Cf. opi+s.

ŌPĒ

d: dopey.
h: Hopi.
m: mopy.
s: soapy.
sl: slopy.
sn: snow pea.
    Plus hope he, etc.

ŌPEST

gr: gropest*.
h: hopest*.
k(c): copest*.
l: elopest*, interlopest*, lopest*.
m: mopest*.
r: ropest*.
s: soapest*.
    Plus no pest, etc.

ŌPETH

gr: gropeth*.
h: hopeth*.
k(c): copeth*.
l: elopeth*, interlopeth*, lopeth*.
m: mopeth*.
r: ropeth*.
s: soapeth*.

ŌPFOOL

h: hopeful, unhopeful.
    Plus soap full, etc.

ŌPING

d: doping.
gr: groping.
h: hoping.
k(c): coping.
l: eloping, interloping, loping.
m: moping.
r: roping.
s: soaping.
sl: sloping.
st: stoping.
t: toping.
    Plus no ping, etc.

ŌPISH

m: mopish.
p: popish.
    Plus slow, pish!, etc.

ŌP'L

Vowel: opal.
b: Bhopal.
g: Ghopal.
n: Adrianople, Constantinople, nopal.
    Plus pope'll, etc.
    Cf. no pull, etc.

ŌPLƏS

h: hopeless.
p: popeless.
s: soapless.
    Plus dope less, etc.

ŌPMƏNT

l: elopement.
    Plus soap meant, etc.

ÔPÔ

p: pawpaw.
    Plus gnaw paw, etc.

ŌPŌK

sl: slowpoke.
    Plus no poke, etc.

ŌPSTᵾR

d: dopester.
    Plus soap stir, etc.

ŌPᵾR

d: doper.
gr: groper.
k(c): coper.
l: eloper, loper.
m: moper.
r: roper.
s: soaper.
sl: sloper.
t: toper.
    Plus soap her *or* err, etc.

ÔPᵾR

p: pauper.
sk(sc): scauper.
y: yawper.

ŌPƏ

r: Europa.
    Plus grope a, etc.

ŌPƏN

Vowel: open.
    Plus slow pen, etc.

ŌPƏS

Vowel: opus.
g: lagopous, Lagopus.
n: Canopus.
    Plus so, puss, etc.

ŌRĀ

f: foray.
    Plus so, ray *or* Rae, etc.

ÔRAKS

b: borax.
k(c): corax.
st: storax.
th: thorax.
    Plus so wracks *or* racks, etc.
    Plus store ax *or* acts, etc.

ÔRĀT

fl: deflorate.
kl: chlorate, perchlorate.
n: inaurate.
st: instaurate*.
    Plus so rate, etc.
    Plus adore eight *or* ate, etc.
    Plus war eight *or* ate, etc.
    Plus straw rate, etc.

ÔRBĒ

Vowel: orby.
k(c): corbie.
    Plus war, be *or* bee, etc.

ÔRBID

m: morbid.
    Plus war bid, etc.

ÔRBING

Vowel: orbing.
s: absorbing, resorbing.
    Plus war, Byng, etc.

ÔRB'L

k(c): corbel.
w: warble.
    Cf. war, bull, etc.

ÔRBLUR

w: warbler.

ÔRCHUR

sk(sc): scorcher.
t: torcher, torture, water torture.
    Plus scorch her *or* err, etc.
    Plus short, you're *or* your, etc.
    Cf. scorch your *or* you're, etc.

ÔRCHURD

Vowel: orchard.
t: tortured, untortured.

ÔRDEST

b: boardest*, keyboardist.
f: fordest*
h: hoardest*
k(c): accordest*, recordest*.
l: belordest*, lordest*.
w: awardest*, rewardest*, wardest*.

ÔRDETH

b: boardeth*.
f: fordeth*.
h: hoardeth*.
k(c): accordeth*, recordeth*.
l: belordeth*, lordeth*.
w: awardeth*, rewardeth*, wardeth*.
    Plus for death, etc.
    Plus more death, etc.

ÔRDFOOL

k(c): discordful.
w: awardful.
    Plus lord full, etc.

ÔRDGĀM

b: board game.

ÔRDID

s: sordid.
    Cf. orded.

ÔRDIJ

b: boardage, bordage.
k(c): cordage.
    Cf. lord age, etc.
    Cf. stored age, etc.

ÔRDIK

n: Nordic.

ÔRDING

b: boarding, unboarding, weather boarding.
f: affording, fording.
h: hoarding, unhoarding, uphoarding.
k(c): according, cording, recording, unrecording.
l: belording, lording, unlording.
w: awarding, rewarding, unrewarding, warding.

ÔRDLĒ

l: lordly, unlordly.
    Plus award, Lee *or* lea, etc.

ÔRDSHIP

l: lordship.
w: wardship.
    Plus cord, ship, etc.

ÔRDUR

Vowel: disorder, eating disorder, money order, new world order, order, reorder, unorder.
b: boarder, parlor boarder, border, emborder.
f: forder.
h: hoarder.

k(c): accorder, chorder, corder, recorder, tape recorder, wire recorder.

w: awarder, rewarder, warder.

Plus board her *or* err, etc.

Plus lord her *or* err, etc.

ÔRDᵁRD

Vowel: disordered, ordered, reordered, well-ordered.

Plus ordur+ed.

ÔRDZMƏN

s: swordsman.

Plus fords, man, etc.

ÔRDƏD

b: boarded.

f: afforded, forded, unforded.

h: hoarded, unhoarded, uphoarded.

k(c): accorded, chorded, corded, recorded, unrecorded.

l: belorded, lorded, unlorded.

s: sordid, sworded.

sw: swarded.

w: awarded, rewarded, unrewarded, warded.

Plus lord, Ed, etc.

Plus store dead, etc.

Plus soared, Ed, etc.

Plus war dead, etc.

Cf. war did, etc.

ÔRDƏN

g: Gordon.

j: Jordan.

k(c): cordon.

w: warden, waywarden.

Plus Thor den, etc.

Plus warred on *or* an, etc.

Cf. ordon.

ÔRDƏNS

k(c): accordance, concordance, discordance.

Plus war dance, etc.

Plus ward, aunts *or* ants, etc.

ÔRDƏNT

k(c): accordant, concordant, disaccordant, discordant, inaccordant.

m: mordant.

Plus ward aunt *or* ant, etc.

ÔRĒ

Vowel: aforetiori, aposteriori, apriori, oary.

d: dory, hunky dory.

fl: flory.

g: allegory, category, gory.

gl: glory, Old Glory, vainglory.

h: hoary, whory.

j: Maggiore.

l: Annie Laurie, Laurie, lory.

m: Maury.

s: promissory.

sh: shory.

sn: snory.

st: basement story, cover story, feature story, news story, short story, story.

t: abbreviatory, absolutory, acceleratory, acclamatory, accusatory, additory, adhortatory, adjuratory, admonitory, adulatory, amatory, ambagitory, ambulatory, amendatory, annotatory, annunciatory, appellatory, applicatory, appreciatory, approbatory, aratory, aspiratory, asseveratory, assimilatory, auditory, auxiliatory, bibitory, cachinnatory, calculatory, calumniatory, castigatory, circulatory, commandatory, commendatory, commenoratory,

comminatory, communicatory,
compellatory, compensatory,
conciliatory, condemnatory,
confabulatory, confirmatory,
confiscatory, congratulatory,
conservatory, consolatory,
contributory, corroboratory,
crematory, criminatory,
damnatory, declamatory,
declaratory, dedicatory, defama-
tory, delineatory, demonstratory,
denunciatory, depilatory,
depository, deprecatory,
depreciatory, depredatory,
derogatory, designatory,
desultory, dilatory, disapproba-
tory, discriminatory, dispensatory,
distatory, dormitory, edificatory,
ejaculatory, emendatory,
emulatory, exaggeratory,
exclamatory, exculpatory,
execratory, executory, exhorta-
tory, expiatory, expiratory,
explanatory, expostulatory,
expurgatory, extenuatory,
exterminatory, extirpatory,
feudatory, frigeratory,
funambulatory, gesticulatory,
gladiatory, gradatory, grallatory,
gratulatory, gustatory, gyratory,
habilatory, hallucinatory,
hortatory, imperatory, impreca-
tory, improvisatory, incantatory,
incriminatory, incubatory,
inculpatory, indicatory,
inflammatory, initiatory,
inspiratory, interlocutory,
interrogatory, inventory,
investigatory, invitagory,
invocatory, jaculatory, judicatory,
laboratory, laudatory, libatory,
liberatory, mandatory, mastica-
tory, migratory, monitory,
narratory, natatory, negatory,
negotiatory, nugatory, objurga-
tory, obligatory, observatory,
offertory, oratory, oscillatory,
osculatory, pacificatory, palliatory,
peremptory, perfumatory,
perspiratory, piscatory, plauditory,
postulatory, potatory, predatory,

predicatory, prefatory, premoni-
tory, preparatory, probatory,
procrastinatory, procuratory,
profanatory, prohibitory,
promontory, pronunciatory,
propitiatory, punitory, purgatory,
purificatory, recommendatory,
recriminatory, reformatory,
refrigeratory, refutatory,
regeneratory, remuneratory,
repertory, repository, reprobatory,
reptatory, requisitory, respiratory,
restoratory, retaliatory,
retardatory, retributory, rever-
beratory, revocatory, rogatory,
rotatory, sacrificatory, saltatory,
sanitory, sibilitory, signatory,
significatory, simulatory,
speculatory, sternutatory,
stillatory, stridulatory,
sublimatory, sudatory, supplica-
tory, terminatory, territory, tory,
transitory, transpiratory,
undulatory, usurpatory,
vacillatory, vehiculatory, vibratory,
vindicatory, vomitory.

Plus cacciatore, Il Trovatore,
improvvistore, etc.

Plus shore, he, etc.

Plus war, he etc.

ÔRED

f: forehead.
Cf. orid.

ÔRĒD

gl: gloried.
st: storied.

ÔREST

b: borest*.
d: adorest*.
f: afforest, disafforest, enforrest,
forest.
fl: floorest*.
g: gorest*.

h: abhorrest, hoarest, whorest*.
k(c): encorest*.
n: ignorest*.
p: porest*, pourest*.
pl: deplorest*, explorest*,
implorest*.
r: roarest*.
s: outsoarest*, soarest*, sorest.
sk(sc): scorest*.
sn: snorest*.
st: restorest*, storest*.
w: warrest*.

Plus saw rest, etc.
Plus no rest, etc.

ÔRETH

b: boreth*.
d: adoreth*.
fl: flooreth*.
g: goreth*.
h: abhorreth, whoreth*.
k(c): encoreth*.
n: ignoreth*.
p: poreth*, poureth*.
pl: deploreth*, exploreth*,
imploreth*.
r: roareth*.
s: outsoareth*, soareth*.
sk(sc): scoreth*.
sn: snoreth*.
st: restoreth*, storeth*.
w: warreth*.

ÔRFĒUS

Vowel: Orpheus.
m: Morpheus.

ÔRFIK

Vowel: Orphic.
m: allomorphic, anthropomorphic, automorphic, dimorphic, endomorphic, heteromorphic, ichthyomorphic, idiomorphic, isimorphic, metamorphic,

morphic, ophiomorphic,
pantamorphic, polymorphic,
protomorphic, pseudomorphic,
theomorphic, trimorphic,
zoomorphic.

ÔRFIN

d: endorphin.

ÔRFING

dr: dwarfing.
hw: wharfing.

ÔRFIST

hw: wharfist.
m: anthropomorphist,
metamorphist, etc.

Plus war fist, etc.

ÔRFIT

f: forfeit.

Plus wharf it, etc.

ÔRFIZM

m: allomorphism, amorphism,
anamorphism, anthropomorphism, automorphism, dimorphism, isodimorphism,
isomeromorphism, isomorphism,
isotrimorphism, metamorphism,
monomorphism, pleomorphism,
polymorphism, trimorphism,
zoomorphism.

Plus war fizz 'em, etc.

ÔRFUS

m: amorphous,
anthropomorphous, dimorphous,
isodimorphous, isomorphous,
isotrimorphous, ophiomorphous,
paramorphous, polymorphous,
trimorphous.

Plus wharf us, etc.
Plus war fuss, etc.

ÔRFƏN

Vowel: orphan.
  Plus war fan, etc.
  Plus wharf, Ann *or* an, etc.

ÔRGƏN

Vowel: barrel organ, organ.
d: Dorgan.
g: Demogorgon, Gorgon.
m: Morgan, morgen.
  Plus morgue an *or* on, etc.

ÔRHAND

f: aforehand, beforehand, forehand.
  Plus sore hand, etc.

ÔRHOUS

h: whorehouse.
st: storehouse.
  Plus adore house, etc.

ÔRID

fl: florid.
h: horrid.
t: torrid.
  Plus so rid, etc.
  Cf. forehead.
  Cf. sorehead.

ÔRĪD

kl: bichloride, chloride, perchloride.
s: sore-eyed.
  Plus more, I'd *or* eyed, etc.
  Plus show ride, etc.

ÔRIJ

b: borage.
f: forage.
p: porridge.

sh: shorage.
st: storage.
  Cf. ma rage, etc.
  Cf. more age, etc.
  Cf. scarage, etc.

ÔRIK

Vowel: meteoric, theoric.
d: Doric, elydoric.
f: amphoric, camphoric, lithophosphoric, metaphoric, phosphoric, prophoric, semaphoric, zoophoric.
g: allegoric, amphigoric, paregoric, phantasmagoric, Pythagoric.
k(c): choric.
kl: chloric, euchloric, hydrochloric, perchloric.
l: caloric, peloric, pyloric.
m: armoric, sophomoric.
r: Roerich, roric.
sp: zoosporic.
t: historic, pictoric, prehistoric, unhistoric.
th: plethoric.
y: Yorick.
  Plus no rick, etc.
  Cf. far rick, etc.

ÔRIN

f: foreign.
fl: florin.
  Cf. oren.

ÔRING

Vowel: double oaring, oaring, single oaring.
b: boring.
ch: choring.
d: adoring.
fl: flooring.
g: Goering, goring.

h: abhorring, awhoring, whoring.
k(c): encoring.
l: Loring.
m: Moering.
n: ignoring.
p: poring, pouring.
pl: deploring, exploring, imploring.
r: roaring.
s: outsoaring, soaring, upsoaring.
sh: shoring.
sk(sc): scoring.
sn: snoring.
sp: sporing.
st: restoring, storing.
w: warring.
   Plus so ring, etc.
   Plus Thor ring, etc.

ÔRINJ

Vowel: Agent Orange+, burnt orange+, orange+.

ÔRIS

Vowel: oris.
d: doch an dorris, Doris.
h: Horace.
l: loris.
m: morris.

ÔRĪT

kl: sodium hypochlorite.

ÔRJĒ

Vowel: orgy.
p: Georgy Porgy, porgy.
st: storgy.
   Plus gorge, he, etc.

ÔRJĒZ

Vowel: orgies.
g: gorges.
j: Georges.
p: porgies.
st: storges.
   Plus George's, etc.
   Plus George is, etc.
   Plus war jizz, etc.

ÔRJING

f: forging.
g: disgorging, engorging, gorging, regorging.

ÔRJƏR

f: forger.

ÔRJƏ

b: Borgia.
g: Georgia.
   Plus gorge a, etc.

ÔRJƏL

k(c): cordial.
   Plus gorge, Al, etc.

ÔRJƏS

g: gorgeous.
   Plus George us.

ÔRKĒ

f: forky.
k(c): corky.
   Plus stork, he, etc.
   Plus war key, etc.

ÔRKID

Vowel: orchid.
Plus war, kid, etc.

ÔRKING

d: Dorking.
f: forking.
k(c): corking, uncorking.
Plus war king, etc.

ÔRKƏS

Vowel: orchis.
d: Dorcas.
Cf. war kiss, etc.
Cf. stork us, etc.
Cf. orchis.

ÔRLÄK

Vowel: oarlock.
f: forelock.
w: warlock.
Plus more lock, etc.
Plus Thor lock, etc.

ÔRLĒ

m: Morley.
sk(sc): schorly.
w: warly*.
Plus Thor, Lee or lea, etc.

ÔRLING

sh: shoreling.

ÔRLƏS

Vowel: oarless, oreless.
b: boarless, boreless.
d: doorless.
fl: floorless.
g: goreless.
k(c): coreless, encoreless.

sh: shoreless.
sk(sc): scoreless.
sn: snoreless.
sp: sporeless.
st: storeless.
Plus ignore less or Les, etc.

ÔRMĒ

d: dormy.
st: stormy.
w: warmy.
Plus for me, etc.
Plusd swarm, he, etc.

ÔRMEST

f: conformest*, deformest*, formest*, informest*, performest*, reformest*, transformest*.
st: stormest*.
sw: swarmest*.
w: warmest.
Plus war messed, etc.

ÔRMETH

f: conformeth*, deformeth*, formeth*, informeth*, performeth*, reformeth*, transformeth*.
st: stormeth*.
sw: swarmeth*.
w: warmeth*.

ÔRMING

f: conforming, deforming, forming, informing, nonconforming, performing, reforming, transforming.
st: bestorming, storming.
sw: swarming.
w: warming.
Plus war, Ming, etc.

ÔRMIST

f: conformist, nonconformist, reformist.

    Plus war mist *or* missed, etc.

    Cf. ormest.

ÔRMLĒ

f: uniformly.

w: warmly.

    Plus swarm, Lee *or* lea, etc.

ÔRMLƏS

f: formless.

st: stormless.

sw: swarmless.

    Plus warm, less *or* Les, etc.

ÔRMŌN

h: hormone, human growth hormone.

ÔRMŌST

f: foremost, head-foremost.

    Plus floor most, etc.

ÔRMUR

f: conformer, deformer, former, informer, performer, reformer, transformer.

st: barnstormer, stormer.

sw: swarmer.

w: bed warmer, foot warmer, warmer.

    Plus warm her *or* err, etc.

ÔRMUS

f: multiformous.

k(c): cormous, cormus.

n: abnormous, enormous.

    Plus swarm us, etc.

    Plus war muss, etc.

ÔRMƏL

f: formal, informal, uniformal.

k(c): cormal, cormel.

n: abnormal, anormal, normal.

    Plus warm, Al, etc.

ÔRMƏN

d: doorman.

f: foreman.

fl: floorman.

g: Gorman, O'Gorman.

m: Mormon.

n: Norman.

sh: longshoreman, shoreman.

    Plus more, man, etc.

    Plus war, man, etc.

ÔRMƏNS

d: dormance.

f: conformance, performance.

    Plus swarm ants *or* aunts, etc.

ÔRMƏNT

d: adorement, dormant.

f: conformant, informant.

n: ignorement.

pl: deplorement, explorement, implorement.

st: restorement.

t: torment.

    Plus snore meant, etc.

    Plus swarm aunt *or* ant, etc.

    Plus war meant, etc.

ÔRNĀT

Vowel: ornate.

    Plus war, Nate, etc.

    Plus warn eight *or* ate, etc.

ÔRNĒ

h: Hornie, horny.
k(c): corny.
th: thorny.
  Plus for knee, etc.
  Plus warn, he, etc.

ÔRNEST

b: subornest*.
d: adornest*.
s: soreness.
sk(sc): bescornest*, scornest*.
w: forewarnest*, warnest*.
  Plus Thor nest, etc.

ÔRNETH

b: suborneth*.
d: adorneth*.
sk(sc): bescorneth*, scorneth*.
w: forwarneth*, warneth*.

ÔRNFOOL

m: mournful.
sk(sc): scornful.
  Plus sworn full, etc.
  Plus warn full, etc.

ÔRNING

b: suborning.
d: adorning.
h: dehorning, dishorning, horning.
m: good morning, morning, mourning, yester morning*.
sk(sc): bescorning, scorning.
w: forewarning, warning.

ÔRNIS

Vowel: Aepyornis, Heliornis, Ichthyornis.

k(c): cornice.
n: Dinornis.
t: Gastornis.

ÔRNISH

h: hornish.
k(c): Cornish.

ÔRNLƏS

h: hornless.
sk(sc): scornless.
th: thornless.
  Plus warn less *or* Les, etc.

ÔRNMƏNT

d: adornment.
  Plus corn meant, etc.

ÔRN N

f: forenoon.
  Plus score noon, etc.

ÔRNŲR

b: suborner.
d: adorner.
h: horner, Little Jack Horner.
k: chimney corner, corner.
m: mourner.
sk(sc): bescorner, scorner.
w: forewarner, warner.
  Plus borne her *or* err, etc.
  Plus warn her *or* err, etc.

ÔRNƏ

l: Lorna.
m: cromorna.
n: Norna.
  Plus adorn a, etc.

ÔRNƏT

h: hornet.
k(c): cornet.
Plus war net, etc.
Cf. warn it, etc.

ŌRŌ

Vowel: Oro.
d: Rio d'Oro.
m: Moro.
t: toro.
Plus so row *or* roe, etc.
Plus score owe *or* O, etc.

ÔRPID

t: torpid.
Cf. dorp, hid, etc.

ÔRPƱR

t: torpor.
Plus dorp, or, etc.
Plus warp her *or* err, etc.

ÔRSĒ

g: gorsy.
h: horsy.
Plus war, see, etc.

ÔRSEST

d: endorsest*.
f: enforcest*, forcest*, reinforcest*.
h: hoarsest, horsest*, unhorsest*.
k(c): coarsest, coursest*, discoursest*.
v: divorcest*.

ÔRSETH

d: endorseth*.
f: enforceth*, forceth*, reinforceth*.

h: horseth*, unhorseth*.
k(c): courseth*, discourseth*.
v: divorceth*.
Plus more, Seth, etc.
Plus war, Seth, etc.

ÔRSFOOL

f: forceful.
m: remorseful.
s: resourceful.
Plus course full, etc.
Plus gorse full, etc.

ÔRSHƏN

b: abortion.
p: apportion, disproportion, portion, proportion.
s: consortion.
t: contortion, detortion, distortion, extorsion, intorsion, retorsion, torsion.
Plus score shun, etc.
Plus war, shun, etc.

ÔRSHƏND

p: apportioned, disproportioned, portioned, proportioned, unportioned.
Plus score shunned, etc.

ÔRSING

f: enforcing, forcing, reinforcing.
k(c): coursing, discoursing.
v: divorcing.
Plus floor sing, etc.

ÔRSIV

f: enforcive.
k(c): discoursive.
v: divorcive.
Plus more sieve.

ÔRSLƏS

f: forceless.
h: horseless.
m: remorseless.
s: resourceless, source less.
　　Plus coarse less *or* Les, etc.
　　Plus gorse, less *or* Les, etc.

ÔRSMƏN

h: horseman, light-horseman.
n: Norseman.
　　Plus gorse, man, etc.

ÔRSMƏNT

d: endorsement.
f: deforcement, enforcement, forcement, reinforcement.
v: divorcement.
　　Plus course meant, etc.
　　Plus gorse meant, etc.

ÔRSNƏS

h: hoarseness.
k(c): courseness.

ÔRSÔNG

w: war song.
　　Plus Thor song, etc.

ÔRSUR

d: endorser.
f: enforcer, forcer, reinforcer.
h: hoarser, horser, unhorse.
k(c): coarser, courser, discourser.
v: divorcer.
　　Plus divorce her *or* err, etc.
　　Plus gorse err *or* her, etc.

ÔRSWIP

h: horsewhip.
　　Plus Norse whip, etc.

ÔRSƏL

d: dorsal, dorsel.
m: morsel.
t: torsel.
tr: dextrorsal.
　　Plus war, Sal *or* sell, etc.
　　Plus Morse L *or* el, etc.

ÔRSƏM

f: foursome.
　　Plus score some *or* sum, etc.

ÔRSƏN

Vowel: Orson.
h: hoarsen.
k(c): coarsen.
　　Plus war, sun *or* son, etc.

ÔRTĒ

f: forte, forty, pianoforte.
s: sortie.
sn: snorty.
sw: swarty*.
w: warty.
　　Plus for tea, etc.
　　Plus more tea, etc.
　　Cf. orta.

ÔRTEKS

k(c): cortex.
v: vortex.
　　Plus war, Tex, etc.
　　Plus quart, Exe *or* ex, etc.

ÔRTEST

b: abortest*.
k(c): courtest*, escortest*.
p: disportest*, exportest*, importest*, reportest*, supportest*, transportest*.
s: assortest*, consortest*, sortest*.

sh: shortest.
sn: snortest*.
sp: sportest*.
sw: swartest.
t: contortest*, detortest*, distortest*, extortest*, retortest*.
thw: thwartest*.
z: exhortest*, resortest*.
　　Plus floor test, etc.
　　Plus war tést, etc.

ÔRTETH

b: aborteth*.
k(c): courteth, escorteth*.
p: disporteth*, exporteth*, importeth*, reporteth*, supporteth*, transporteth*.
s: assorteth*, consorteth*, sorteth*.
sn: snorteth*.
sp: sporteth*.
t: contorteth*, detorteth*, distorteth*, extorteth*, retorteth*.
thw: thwarteth*.
z: exhorteth*, resorteth*.

ÔRTGĪD

k(c): court guide.
p: port guide.
　　Plus sport guide *or* guyed, etc.

ÔRTHĒ

sw: swarthy.
　　Plus north, he, etc.

ÔRTHWURLD

f: fourth world.

ÔRTIJ

sh: shortage.
　　Cf. quart age, etc.

ÔRTĪM

f: aforetime, beforetime.
　　Plus more time, etc.
　　Plus court, I'm, etc.

ÔRTING

b: aborting.
k(c): courting, escorting.
s: assorting, consorting, sorting.
sn: snorting.
p: desporting, disporting, exporting, importing, reporting, supporting, transporting.
sp: sporting.
t: contorting, detorting, distorting, extorting, retorting.
thw: thwarting.
z: exhorting, resorting.

ÔRTIV

Vowel: ortive.
b: abortive.
p: transportive.
sp: sportive.
t: contortive, distortive, retortive, tortive.

ÔRT'L

ch: chortle.
hw: whortle*.
　　Plus quart'll, etc.
　　Cf. ortal.

ÔRTLĒ

k(c): courtly, uncourtly.
p: portly.
sh: shortly.
　　Plus quart, Lee *or* lea, etc.
　　Plus sport, Lee *or* lea, etc.

ÔRTLƏND

k(c): Courtland.
p: Portland.
  Plus sport land, etc.

ÔRTMƏNT

p: comportment, deportment, disportment, transportment.
s: assortment.
  Plus short meant, etc.
  Plus sport meant, etc.

ÔRTNĪT

f: fortnight.
  Plus sort nit, etc.

ÔRTO͞ON

f: beforetune, enfortune, fortune, misfortune.
p: importune.
  Plus war tune, etc.

ÔRTRƏS

f: fortress.
  Plus Thor tress, etc.

ÔRTRƏT

p: portrait.
  Plus floor trait, etc.
  Plus court rate, etc.

ÔRTSHIP

k(c): courtship.
  Plus sport ship, etc.

ÔRTSMƏN

sp: sportsman.
  Plus court's man, etc.

ÔRTƱR

b: aborter.
k(c): courter, escorter.
kw: last quarter, quarter, weather quarter.
m: mortar.
p: disporter, exporter, importer, porter, reporter, supporter, transporter.
s: assorter, consorter, sorter, wool sorter.
sh: shorter.
sn: snorter.
sp: sporter.
t: contorter, detorter, distorter, extorter, retorter.
thw: thwarter.
z: exhorter, resorter.
  Plus court her *or* err, etc.
  Plus thwart her *or* err, etc.

ÔRTƱRZ

kw: quarters, summer quarters, winter quarters.
  Plus ortur+s.

ÔRTWĀV

sh: shortwave.
  Plus quart wave *or* waive, etc.

ÔRTƏD

b: aborted.
k(c): courted, escorted.
p: disported, exported, imported, reported, supported, transported.
s: assorted, consorted, sorted, unsorted.
sn: snorted.
sp: sported.
t: contorted, detorted, distorted, extorted, retorted.

thw: thwarted.
z: exhorted, resorted.
  Plus fort, Ed, etc.
  Plus more, Ted, etc.
  Plus quart, Ed, etc.
  Plus war, Ted, etc.

ÔRTƏL

Vowel: aortal.
ch: chortle.
m: immortal, mortal.
p: portal, transportal.
  Plus fort, Al, etc.
  Plus quart'll, etc.
  Cf. ort'l.
  Cf. war till, etc.

ÔRTƏM

m: postmortem.
  Plus sort'em, etc.

ÔRTƏN

g: Gorton.
h: Horton.
m: Morton.
n: Norton.
sh: shorten.
  Plus war, ten, etc.
  Plus war ton *or* tun, etc.

ÔRTƏNS

p: importance, supportance, transportance.
  Plus quart, ants *or* aunts, etc.
  Plus support aunts *or* ants, etc.

ÔRTƏNT

p: important, portent.
  Plus quart, aunt *or* ant, etc.
  Plus more tent, etc.

ÔRUM

Vowel: variorum.
f: forum.
j: jorum.
k(c): decorum, indecorum.
kw: quorum.
l: ad valorem.
  Plus shore 'em, etc.
  Plus no rum, etc.

ÔRƱR

b: borer, wood borer.
d: adorer.
fl: floorer.
g: gorer.
k(c): corer, decorer*, encorer.
n: ignorer.
p: outpourer, porer, pourer.
pl: deplorer, explorer, implorer.
r: roarer.
s: outsoarer, soarer, sorer.
sk(sc): scorer.
sn: snorer.
st: restorer, storer.
  Plus restore her *or* err, etc.

ÔRUS

h: Horus.
k(c): chorus, decorous, indecorous.
l: pylorus.
n: canorous, sonorous.
p: imporous, porous.
s: brontosaurus, dolichosaurus, hadrosaurus, ichthyosaurus, megalosaurus, mososaurus, nanosaurus, pleiosaurus, plesiosaurus, protosaurus, regnosaurus, saurus, teleosaurus, thesaurus, tyrannosaurus.
t: Metaurus, Taurus, torous, torus.
  Plus implore us, etc.
  Plus war us, etc.

ÔRWÔRN

w: warworn.

Plus Thor worn, etc.

ÔRWŬRD

f: flash forward, foreward, forward, henceforward, straightforward, thenceforward.

n: norward.

sh: shoreward.

Plus score ward, etc.

Plus shore word, etc.

Plus war ward, etc.

ÔRZMƏN

Vowel: oarsman.

Plus implores man, etc.

ÔRƏ

Vowel: aura, Ora.

d: Andorra, Dora, Dumb-Dora, Eldora, Endora, Eudora, Floradora, Pandora, Theodora.

fl: flora, passiflora.

g: Angora.

h: hora.

k(c): Cora.

l: Laura.

m: Gomorrah, Marmora, Maura.

n: Eleonora, Leonora, Nora, signora.

r: Aurora.

s: Chamaesaura, Masora.

t: Torah.

z: Zorah.

Plus glow, Ra, etc.

Plus adore a, etc.

Plus for a, etc.

Plus saw Ra, etc.

ÔRƏL

Vowel: aural, oral.

fl: floral, trifloral.

h: horal.

k(c): choral, coral, red coral.

kl: chloral.

l: laurel.

n: binaural.

r: auroral, sororal.

th: thoral.

Plus sore, Al, etc.

Plus war, Al, etc.

Cf. oral, oral.

ÔRƏLD

th: Thorold.

Cf. quarrelled.

Cf. car old, etc.

ÔRƏM

Vowel: Orem.

ÔRƏN

sp: sporran.

w: rabbit warren, warren.

Plus for an, etc.

Cf. foreign.

ÔRƏNS

h: abhorrence.

d: Dorrance.

fl: Florence.

l: Lawrence, St. Lawrence.

t: torrents.

w: warrants.

Cf. orens.

Cf. straw rents, etc.

ÔRƏNT

h: horrent.

s: soarant.

t: torrent.
v: vorant.
w: death warrant, warrant.
  Plus core, aunt *or* ant, etc.
  Plus go rant, etc.
  Cf. abhorrent.

ÔSCHUN

z: exhaustion.

ŌSĒ

j: Josie.
l: Losey.
  Plus go see, etc.

ÔSĒ

Vowel: Aussie.
b: bossy.
dr: drossy.
fl: Flossie, flossy.
gl: glossy.
m: mossy.
p: posse.
s: saucy.
t: tossy.
  Plus cross he, etc.
  Plus straw see, etc.
  Plus sauce, he, etc.
  Cf. cross, see, etc.

ŌSEST

d: dosest*, overdosest*.
gr: grossest.
k(c): jocosest.
kl: closest.
n: diagnosest*.
r: morosest.

ÔSEST

b: embossest*.
gl: glossest*.

kr: crossest*.
t: tossest*.

ŌSETH

d: doseth*, overdoseth*.
n: diagnoseth*.
  Plus no, Seth, etc.

ÔSETH

b: embosseth*.
gl: glosseth*.
kr: crosseth*.
t: tosseth*.

ÔSFĀT

f: phosphate.
  Plus cross fate, etc.

ÔSHĒ

b: Boschy, boshy.
skw: squashy.
sl: sloshy.
sw: swashy.
t: toshy.
w: washy, wishy-washy.
  Plus wash, he, etc.
  Cf. ma, she, etc.

ÔSHING

skw: squashing.
sl: sloshing.
sw: swashing.
w: washing.

ŌSHUN

Vowel: Boeotian, ocean.
g: Goshen.
gr: groschen.
k(c): nicotian.
l: Laotion, lotion.

m: commotion, emotion, locomotion, motion, promotion, remotion.

n: notion, prenotion.

p: potion.

v: devotion, indevotion, self-devotion.

Plus so shun, etc.

ÔSHUN

k(c): caution, incaution, precaution.

Plus law shun, etc.

ŌSHUR

g: gaucher.

k(c): kosher.

ÔSHUR

j: josher.

k: cosher.

skw: squasher.

sw: swasher.

w: washer.

Plus slosh her, etc.

ŌSHUS

k(c): precocious.

p: nepotious.

r: ferocious.

tr: atrocious.

Plus gauche us, etc.

ÔSHUS

k(c): cautious, incautious, precautious.

ŌSHƏ

Vowel: OSHA.

ŌSHƏL

s: antisocial, intersocial, social, unsocial.

Plus throw shall, etc.

Plus gauche, Al, etc.

ÔSIJ

s: sausage.

ÔSIK

f: fossick.

gl: glossic.

Cf. loss, sick, etc.

ŌSIL

d: docile+, indocile.

Plus no sill, etc.

Plus dose'll, etc.

ŌSING

d: dosing.

gr: engrossing.

Plus go sing, etc.

ÔSING

b: bossing, embossing.

d: dossing.

gl: glossing.

kr: crossing, grade crossing, railroad crossing.

t: tossing.

ŌSIS

Vowel: apotheosis, enantiosis, heliosis, ichthyosis, meiosis.

f: anamorphosis, morphosis.

g: zygosis.

k(c): metempsychosis, narcosis, psychosis, sarcosis.

kr: necrosis.

l: ankylosis, tuberculosis.

m: endosmosis, exosmosis, osmosis, reverse osmosis, zymosis.

n: carcinosis, diagnosis, enosis, geognosis, hypnosis, prognosis.

p: hypotyposis.

pl: anadiplosis, epanadiplosis.

r: amyotrophic lateral sclerosis, chorosis, cirrhosis, heterosis, leptospirosis, morosis, neurosis, scirrhosis, sorosis, syrosis.

t: halitosis, metasomatosis, metemptosis, metensomatosis, proemtosis, ptosis.

th: epanorthosis.

Plus no, sis, etc.

ŌSIV

pl: explosive, inexplosive.

r: corrosive, erosive.

Plus no sieve, etc.

ÔSKĒ

b: bosky.

Plus cross key, etc.

ÔS'L

d: dosel*, dossil.

f: fossil.

gl: hypoglossal.

j: jostle.

l: colossal.

p: apostle.

t: tossel.

thr: throstle.

w: wassail.

Plus cross'll, etc.

ÔSLĒ

kr: crossly.

Plus loss, Lee *or* lea, etc.

ÔSLƱR

h: hostler.

j: jostler.

r: Rossler.

ŌSNƏS

b: verboseness.

gr: grossness.

k(c): jocoseness.

kl: closeness.

r: moroseness.

ŌSŌ

Vowel: arioso, gracioso, virtuoso.

fr: Phroso.

r: amoroso, doloroso.

s: soso.

Plus go so, sow *or* sew, etc.

Plus gross owe *or* O, etc.

ÔSTĀT

k(c): laticostate, quadricostate.

p: apostate.

pr: prostate.

Plus crossed eight *or* ate, etc.

Plus cross, Tate, etc.

ÔSTĒ

fr: frosty.

Plus cross tea *or* T, etc.

Plus crossed, he, etc.

ŌSTEST

b: boastest*.

k(c): coastest*.

m: mostest.

p: postest*.

r: roastest*.

t: toastest*.

Plus gross test, etc.

ŌSTETH

b: boasteth*.

k(c): coasteth*.

p: posteth*.

r: roasteth*.
t: toasteth*.

ŌSTHOUS

Vowel: oasthouse*.
p: posthouse.
Plus boast house, etc.

ŌSTIJ

p: postage.
Cf. coast age, etc.

ÔSTIK

k(c): catacaustic, caustic, diacaustic, encaustic.
Plus sauce tick, etc.
Plus straw stick, etc.

ŌSTING

b: boasting.
k(c): coasting.
p: posting.
r: roasting.
t: toasting.
Plus no sting, etc.

ÔSTING

fr: frosting.
k(c): accosting, costing.
z: exhausting.
Plus saw sting, etc.
Cf. loss sting, etc.

ÔSTIV

k(c): costive.
z: exhaustive, inexhaustive.

ÔSTL

h: hostel.
k(c): costal, infracostal, intercostal, Pentecostal, supracostal.
Plus cost'll, etc.

ŌSTLĒ

g: ghostly.
m: mostly.
Plus coast, Lee or lea, etac.

ÔSTLĒ

k(c): costly.
Plus crossed, Lee or lea, etc.

ŌSTMÄRK

p: postmark.
Plus ghost, mark!, etc.

ŌSTMƏN

p: postman.
Plus ghost, man, etc.

ŌSTÔRM

sn: snowstorm.
Plus go, storm, etc.

ÔSTRĀT

pr: prostrate.
r: rostrate.
Plus frost rate, etc.
Plus cross straight or strait, etc.

ÔSTRIL

n: nostril.
Plus crossed rill, etc.
Plus loss trill, etc.
Cf. ostral.

ÔSTRƏL

Vowel: austral.
kl: claustral.

ÔSTRƏM

n: nostrum.
r: rostrum.
Plus lost rum, etc.

ŌSTŬR

b: boaster.
k(c): coaster.
p: four-poster, poster.
r: roaster.
t: toaster.
thr: throwster.
    Plus roast her *or* err, etc.
    Plus no stir, etc.

ÔSTŬR

Vowel: auster.
f: foster.
gl: Gloster, Gloucester.
k(c): accoster, coster, pentecoster.
n: Paternoster.
r: roster.
z: exhauster.
    Plus saw stir, etc.
    Plus holocaust her *or* err, etc.
    Plus bossed her *or* err, etc.
    Cf. loss stir, etc.

ÔSTŬRN

p: postern.
    Plus loss turn *or* tern, etc.
    Plus crossed urn, erne, *or* earn, etc.
    Cf. cross stern, etc.

ŌSTƏD

b: boasted.
k(c): coasted.
p: posted, unposted.
r: roasted.
t: toasted.
    Plus gross, Ted, etc.
    Plus grossed, Ed, etc.

ÔSTƏD

fr: frosted.
k(c): accosted.
z: exhausted.
    Plus cross, Ted, etc.
    Plus crossed, Ed, etc.
    Plus sauce, Ted, etc.

ŌSTƏL

k(c): coastal.
p: postal.
    Plus most, Al, etc.

ÔSTƏL

    Plus lost, Al, etc.

ÔSTƏN

Vowel: Austen, Austin.
b: Boston.
    Plus cross ten, etc.
    Plus cross tin, etc.
    Plus lost in, etc.
    Cf. osten.

ŌSTƏS

h: hostess.
    Plus gross, Tess, etc.

ÔSTƏS

f: Faustus.
    Plus sauced us, etc.
    Plus straw stuss, etc.

ŌSŬR

d: doser.
gr: engrosser, grocer, grosser.
k(c): jocoser.
kl: closer.

r: moroser.
> Plus dose her *or* err, etc.
> Plus no, sir, etc.

ÔSƱR

b: baosser, embosser.
ch: Chaucer.
d: dosser.
gl: glosser.
j: josser.
kr: crosser.
s: saucer.
t: tosser.
> Plus naw, sir, etc.
> Plus sauce her *or* err, etc.
> Plus toss her *or* err, etc.
> Cf. toss, sir, etc.

ŌSƏ

m: Formosa, mimosa.
r: amorosa.
> Plus gross a, etc.

ÔSƏN

d: Dawson.
l: Lawson.
r: Rawson.
> Plus craw, son *or* sun, etc.

ÔSƏS

l: colossus, molossus.
> Plus cross us, etc.

ÔSƏT

b: bosset.
f: faucet.
k(c): cosset.
p: posset, sack posset.

> Plus straw set, etc.
> Cf. toss it, etc.
> Cf. sauce it, etc.

ŌTĀT

n: denotate*, notate.
r: rotate.
> Plus go, Tate, etc.
> Plus note eight *or* ate, etc.

ŌTĒ

Vowel: oaty.
bl: bloaty.
d: dhoty, Dotey, Doty, doughty.
fl: floaty.
g: goaty.
k(c): Coty.
l: Loti.
thr: throaty.
y: coyote.
> Plus quote, he, etc.
> Plus no tea, etc.

ÔTĒ

h: haughty.
n: naughty.
> Plus caught, he, etc.
> Plus saw tea, etc.

ŌTEST

d: dottest*.
fl: floatest*.
gl: gloatest*.
kw: misquotest*, quotest*.
m: demotest*, promotest*.
n: denotest*, notest*.
v: devotest*, votest*.
> Plus no test, etc.

ÔTEST

k(c): caughtest*.
n: Argonautest*, Juggernautest*.
th: merry-thoughtest*, etc.
   Plus saw test, etc.

ŌTETH

d: doteth*.
fl: floateth*.
gl: gloateth*.
kw: misquoteth*, quoteth*.
m: demoteth*, promoteth*.
n: denoteth*, noteth*.
v: devoteth*, voteth*.

ÔTETH

k(c): caughteth*.
n: Argonauteth*, Juggernauteth*.
th: merry-thoughteth*, etc.

ÔTFOOL

th: thoughtful.
   Plus brought full, etc.

ÔTHĒ

fr: frothy.
m: mothy.
   Plus cloth, he etc.

ŌTHEST

kl: clothest*.
l: loathest*.

ŌTHETH

kl: clotheth*.
l: loatheth*.

ŌTHFOOL

l: loathful.
sl: slothful.

Plus growth full, etc.
Plus clothe, full, etc.

ÔTHFOOL

r: wrathful+.
   Plus swath full, etc.

ŌTHING

kl: clothing.
l: loathing.

ÔTHMƏNT

tr: betrothment.
   Plus Thoth meant, etc.

ŌTHŌ

Vowel: Otho.
kl: Clotho.
   Plus Thoth owe *or* O, etc.

ŌTHOOK

b: boathook.
k(c): coathook.
   Plus note hook, etc.
   Cf. so took, etc.

ÔTHÔRN

h: hawthorn.
k(c): Cawthorn.
   Plus saw thorn, etc.

ŌTHSƏM

l: loathsome.
   Plus clothe some *or* sum, etc.

ÔTHƯR

Vowel: author.
   Plus wroth, her *or* err, etc.

ŌTHƏ

kw: quotha.

ŌTHƏL

tr: betrothal.
 Plus quoth Al, etc.

ŌTHƏM

g: Gotham+.
j: Jotham.
 Plus sloth, am, etc.

ŌTIJ

d: anecdotage, dotage.
fl: floatage, flotage.
 Cf. quote age, etc.

ŌTIK

Vowel: otic.
 Plus no tick, etc.

ÔTIK

n: aeronautic, Argonautic, nautic.
 Plus straw tick, etc.

ŌTING

b: boating, steamboating.
bl: bloating.
d: anecdoting, doting.
fl: floating, nonfloating, unfloating.
gl: gloating, ungloating.
k(c): coating, uncoating.
kw: misquoting, quoting, unquoting.
m: demoting, promoting.
n: denoting, noting, unnoting.
t: toting.
thr: throating.
v: devoting, voting.

ÔTING

n: Argonauting, Juggernauting.
th: merry-thoughting.

ŌTISH

d: dotish.
g: goatish.

ŌTIST

d: anecdotist.
n: noticed, unnoticed.
sk(sc): Scotist.

ŌTIV

m: emotive, locomotive, motive, promotive.
v: votive.

ÔTLƏS

th: thoughtless.
 Plus brought less, etc.

ŌTMƏN

b: boatman.
g: goatman.
 Plus quote, man, etc.

ŌTMƏNT

m: demotement.
n: denotemenet.
v: devotement.
 Plus quote meant, etc.

ŌTŌ

Vowel: Kyoto.
f: photo.
g: fagotto.
s: De Soto.
t: in toto.
v: divoto, ex voto.
 Plus note owe *or* O, etc.
 Plus so toe, etc.

ÔTUM

Vowel: autumn.
  Plus caught 'em, etc.

ŌTƱR

Vowel: oater.
b: boater.
bl: bloater.
d: doter.
fl: floater.
gl: gloater.
k(c): coater, frock coater.
kw: misquoter, quoter.
m: demoter, hydromotor, locomotor, magnetomotor, motor, promoter, pulmoter, rotomotor, trimotor, vasomotor.
n: denoter, noter.
r: rotor.
sk(sc): scoter.
t: toter.
v: devoter, fagot voter, voter.
  Plus devote her *or* err, etc.

ÔTƱR

d: daughter.
sl: slaughter.
w: backwater, firewater, fizz water, giggle water, milk-and-water, soda water, water.
  Plus caught her *or* err, etc.

ŌTƏ

Vowel: iota.
fl: flota.
k(c): Dakota, North Dakota, South Dakota.
kw: quota.
r: rota.
s: Minnesota.
  Plus quote a, etc.

ŌTƏD

Vowel: oated.
b: boated, steamboated.
bl: bloated.
d: doted, anecdoted.
fl: floated, refloated.
g: goated.
gl: gloated.
k(c): coated, frock coated, particoated, petticoated.
kw: misquoted, quoted.
m: demoted, moated, promoted.
n: denoted, noted, unnoted.
t: toted.
thr: lily-throated, swan-throated, throated.
v: devoted, self-devoted, voted.
  Plus so, Ted, etc.
  Plus quote, Ed, etc.

ÔTƏD

n: Argonauted, Juggernauted.
th: merry-thoughted.
  Plus brought, Ed, etc.
  Plus saw, Ted, etc.

ŌTƏL

d: anecdotal, antidotal, dotal, extradotal, sacerdotal.
n: notal.
r: rotal, sclerotal
t: teetotal, total.
  Plus quote, Al, etc.
  Cf. ot'l.

ŌTƏM

kw: quotum.
skr(scr): scrotum.
t: teetotum.

Plus float on *or* an, etc.
Plus no ton *or* tun, etc.
Plus so ten, etc.
Plus taught an, etc.

ŌTƏN

Vowel: oaten.
kr: Croton.
pr: proton.
　　Plus note 'em, etc.

ÔTƏN

l: Lawton.
r: Rawton.
　　Plus claw ton *or* tun, etc.

ŌTƏNT

fl: flotant.
p: potent, prepotent.
　　Plus no tent, etc.

ŌTƏS

kr: macrotous.
l: lotus.
n: Gymnotus.
　　Plus quote us, etc.

OUCHEST

k(c): couchest*.
kr: crouchest*.
p: pouchest*.
v: avouchest, vouchest*.
　　Plus allow chest, etc.

OUCHETH

k(c): coucheth*.
kr: croucheth*.
p: poucheth*.
v: avoucheth, voucheth*.

OUCHING

gr: grouching.
k(c): couching.
kr: crouching.
p: pouching.
sl: slouching.
v: avouching, vouching.

OUCHUR

g: Goucher.
gr: groucher.
k(c): coucher.
kr: croucher.
p: poucher.
sl: sloucher.
v: avoucher, voucher.
　　Plus avouch her *or* err, etc.

OUDĒ

d: dowdy, pandowdy.
g: Goudy.
h: howdie, howdy.
kl: cloudy, uncloudy.
kr: crowdy.
pr: proudy.
r: rowdy.
s: Saudi+.
shr: shroudy.
　　Plus vowed he, etc.
　　Plus vow Dee *or* D, etc.
　　Cf. summa cum laude.

OUDEST

kl: becloudest*, cloudest*, overcloudest*.
kr: crowdest*, overcrowdest*.
l: loudest.
pr: proudest.
shr: enshroudest*, shroudest*.

OUDETH

kl: becloudeth*, cloudeth*, overcloudeth*.
kr: crowdeth*, overcrowdeth*.
shr: enshroudeth*, shroudeth*.
  Plus vow death, etc.

OUDING

kl: beclouding, clouding, overclouding.
kr: crowding, overcrowding.
shr: beshrouding, enshrouding, shrouding, unshrouding.

OUDISH

l: loudish.
pr: proudish.
  Plus allow dish, etc.

OUDLĒ

l: loudly.
pr: proudly.
  Plus vowed, Lee *or* lea, etc.

OUDNƏS

l: loudness.
pr: proudness.

OUDƱR

ch: chowder, clam chowder.
kr: crowder.
l: louder.
p: baking powder, bepowder, powder, seidlitz powder.
pr: prouder.
  Plus allowed her *or* err, etc.

OUDƏ

h: howdah.
  Plus crowd a, etc.

OUDƏD

kl: beclouded, clouded, overclouded, unbeclouded, unclouded.
kr: crowded, overcrowded, undercrowded.
shr: enshrouded, shrouded, unshrouded.
  Plus vow dead, etc.
  Plus vowed, Ed, etc.
  Cf. scow did, etc.

OUĒ

d: Dowie.
z: zowie.
  Plus now he, etc.
  Plus now we, etc.

OUEST

b: bowest*.
d: endowest*.
k(c): cowest*.
l: allowest*, disallowest*.
pl: ploughest*.
v: avowest*, disavowest*, vowest*.
  Cf. now west, etc.

OUETH

b: boweth*.
d: endoweth*.
k(c): coweth*.
l: alloweth*, disalloweth*.
pl: plougheth*.
v: avoweth*, disavoweth*, voweth*.

OUHAND

k(c): cowhand.
pl: ploughhand.
  Plus vow hand, etc.

OUING

b: bowing.
d: endowing.
k(c): cowing.
l: allowing, disallowing.
pl: ploughing, plowing.
r: rowing.
v: avowing, disavowing, vowing.

OULĒ

k(c): Cowley.
kr: Crowley.
p: Powley.
r: Rowley.
    Plus bow, Lee *or* lea, etc.

OULEST

f: foulest.
gr: growlest*.
h: howlest*.
pr: prowlest*.
sk(sc): scowlest*.
    Plus now, lest, etc.

OULETH

gr: growleth*.
h: howleth*.
pr: prowleth*.
sk(sc): scowleth*.

OULING

f: fouling, fowling.
gr: growling.
h: howling.
pr: prowling.
sk(sc): scowling.

OULISH

Vowel: owlish.
f: foulish.

OULƏR

f: fouler, fowler.
gr: growler.
h: howler.
pr: prowler.
sk(sc): scowler.
y: yowler.
    Plus howl her *or* err, etc.

OULƏT

Vowel: owlet.
h: howlet*.
    Plus now let *or* Lett, etc.
    Cf. prowl it, etc.

OUMƏNT

d: endowment.
v: avowment.
    Plus plough meant, etc.

OUNBAG

br: brown bag.

OUNBELT

br: brown belt.

OUNDEST

b: aboundest*, boundest*,
reboundest*, superaboundest*.
f: confoundest*, foundest*,
profoundest.
gr: groundest*.
h: houndest*.
p: compoundest*, expoundest*,
impoundest*, poundest*,
propoundest*.
r: roundest, surroundest*.
s: soundest.
t: astoundest*.
w: woundest*.
z: resoundest*.

OUNDETH

b: aboundeth*, boundeth*, reboundeth*, superaboundeth*.
f: confoundeth*, foundeth*.
gr: groundeth*.
h: houndeth*.
p: compoundeth*, expoundeth*, impoundeth*, poundeth*, propoundeth*.
r: roundeth*, surroundeth*.
s: soundeth*.
t: astoundeth*.
w: woundeth*.
z: resoundeth*.
   Plus go down, death, etc.

OUNDHĒL

r: round heel.

OUNDIJ

gr: groundage.
p: poundage.
s: soundage.
   Cf. clowned age, etc.

OUNDING

b: abounding, bounding, rebounding, superabounding, unbounding.
d: redounding.
f: confounding, dumfounding, founding.
gr: grounding.
h: hounding.
p: compounding, expounding, impounding, pounding, propounding.
r: rounding, surrounding.
s: big-sounding, high-sounding, sounding.
t: astounding.
w: wounding.
z: resounding.

OUNDLĒ

f: profoundly.
r: roundly.
s: soundly, unsoundly.
   Plus crowned, Lee *or* lea, etc.

OUNDLING

f: foundling.
gr: groundling.

OUNDLƏS

b: boundless.
gr: groundless.
s: soundless.
   Plus crowned less *or* Les, etc.

OUNDNƏS

f: profoundness.
r: roundness.
s: soundness, unsoundness.

OUNDRĒ

f: foundry.

OUNDRƏL

sk(sc): scoundrel.

OUNDTURN

r: round turn.

OUNDUR

b: bounder, rebounder.
f: confounder, dumbfounder, founder, iron founder, profounder, type founder.
fl: flounder.
h: hounder.
p: compounder, expounder, four-pounder, etc., impounder, pounder, propounder.
r: rounder, surrounder.

s: sounder.
t: astounder.
z: resounder.
Plus bound her *or* err, etc.

OUNDƏD

b: abounded, bounded, rebounded, superabounded, unbounded.
d: redounded.
dr: "drownded."
f: confounded, dumbfounded, founded, unfounded, wellfounded.
gr: grounded, ungrounded.
h: hounded.
m: mounded.
p: compounded, expounded, impounded, pounded, propounded.
r: rounded, surrounded.
s: sounded, unsounded.
t: astounded.
w: wounded.
z: resounded.
Plus clown dead, etc.
Plus clowned, Ed, etc.
Cf. clown did, etc.

OUNDƏL

r: roundel.
Plus down dell, etc.
Plus sound L *or* el, etc.

OUNDƏN

b: bounden.
Plus clown den, etc.

OUNĒ

br: browni, brownie.
d: downy.
fr: frowny.

kl: clowny.
t: towny.
Plus down, he, etc.

OUNEST

br: brownest.
dr: drownest*.
fr: frownest*.
kr: crownest*.
Plus now nest, etc.

OUNETH

br: browneth*.
dr: drowneth*.
fr: frowneth*.
kr: crowneth*.

OUNING

br: browning.
d: downing.
dr: drowning.
fr: frowning.
g: gowning, ungowning.
kl: clowning, unclowning.
kr: crowning, discrowning, uncrowning.
t: intowning.

OUNISH

br: brownish.
fr: frownish.
kl: clownish.

OUNJEST

l: loungest*.
Plus clown jest, etc.

OUNJETH

l: loungeth*.

OUNJING

l: lounging.

OUNJUR

l: lounger.

OUNLƏS

fr: frownless.
g: gownless.
kr: crownless.
Plus down, Les *or* less, etc.

OUNPLĀ

d: downplay.

OUNSEST

b: bouncest*.
fl: flouncest*.
n: announcest*, denouncest*, pronouncest*, renouncest*.
p: pouncest*.

OUNSETH

b: bounseth*.
fl: flounceth*.
n: announceth*, denounceth*, pronounceth*, renounceth*.
p: pounceth*.
Plus down, Seth, etc.

OUNSING

b: bouncing.
fl: flouncing.
n: announcing, denouncing, pronouncing, renouncing.
p: pouncing.
tr: trouncing.
Plus clown sing, etc.

OUNSĪZ

d: downsize.

OUNSMƏNT

n: announcement, denouncement, pronouncement, renouncement.
Plus bounce meant, etc.

OUNSUR

b: bouncer.
fl: flouncer.
n: announcer, denouncer, pronouncer, renouncer.
p: pouncer.
tr: trouncer.
Plus down, sir, etc.
Plus counts err *or* her, etc.

OUNSƏZ

Vowel: ounces.
b: bounces.
fl: flounces.
n: announces, denounces, pronounces, renounces.
p: pounces.
tr: trounces.
Plus clown says, etc.
Plus bounce, Ez, etc.

OUNTĒ

b: bounty.
k(c): county, viscounty.
m: mounty.
Plus mount, he, etc.
Plus down tea, etc.

OUNTEST

k(c): accountest*, countest*, discountest*, miscountest*, recountest*.
m: amountest*, dismountest*, mountest*, remountest*, surmountest*.
Plus clown test, etc.

OUNTETH

k(c): accounteth*, counteth*, discounteth*, miscounteth*, recounteth*.

m: amounteth*, dismounteth*, mounteth*, remounteth*, surmounteth*.

OUNTIN

f: drinking fountain, fountain, water fountain.

m: catamountain, mountain.

Plus mount in, etc.

Plus down tin, etc.

OUNTING

k(c): accounting, counting, discounting, miscounting, recounting.

m: amounting, dismounting, mounting, remounting, surmounting.

OUNTƲR

k(c): accounter, counter, discounter, encounter, recounter, reencounter.

m: mounter, remounter, surmounter.

Plus mount her *or* err, etc.

OUNTƏD

k(c): accounted, counted, discounted, miscounted, recounted, uncounted, unrecounted.

m: amounted, dismounted, mounted, remounted, surmounted, unmounted.

Plus down, Ted, etc.

Plus mount, Ed, etc.

OUNTƏS

k(c): countess.

Plus down, Tess, etc.

OUNƲR

br: browner.

d: downer.

dr: drowner.

fr: frowner.

kr: crowner.

Plus down her *or* err, etc.

OUNWƲRD

d: downward.

t: townward.

Plus gown ward, etc.

OUNZMƏN

g: gownsman.

t: townsman.

Plus downs man, etc.

ŌƲR

Vowel: ower.

bl: blower, glass blower, whistle blower.

fl: flower.

g: foregoer, goer, outgoer, undergoer.

gl: glower.

gr: flower grower, grower, wine grower.

h: hoer.

l: lower.

m: mower.

n: foreknower, knower.

s: sewer, sower.

sh: foreshower, shower.

sl: slower.

st: bestower, stower.

t: tower.

thr: overthrower, thrower.
Plus know her *or* err, etc.

ÔUR

Vowel: overawer.
dr: drawer, wire drawer, with-drawer.
f: guffawer.
j: "jawer."
k(c): cawer.
kl: clawer.
n: gnawer.
p: pawer.
r: rawer.
s: sawer.
t: tawer.
Plus draw her *or* err, etc.

ŌURD

l: lowered.
t: toward, untoward.
Plus snow heard *or* herd, etc.
Plus so ward, etc.

OURĒ

d: dowry.
fl: floury, flowery.
h: houri.
k(c): cowrie.
v: avowry.
Plus shower, he, etc.
Cf. ouuri.

OUREST

fl: deflowerest*.
s: sourest.
sk(sc): bescourest*, scourest*.
b: devourest*.
Plus now rest, etc.

OURETH

fl: deflowereth*.
s: soureth*.
sk(sc): bescoureth*, scoureth*.
v: devoureth*.

OURING

fl: deflowering, flouring.
s: souring.
sk(sc): bescouring, off-scouring, scouring.
v: devouring.
Plus now ring *or* wring, etc.
Cf. ouuring.

OURLĒ

Vowel: hourly.
s: sourly.
Plus flower, Lee *or* lea, etc.

OURNƏS

s: sourness.

OURUR

fl: deflower.
s: sourer.
sk(sc): scourer.
v: devourer.
Plus sour her *or* err, etc.

OUSFROU

h: hausfrau.

OUSTING

Vowel: ousting.

OUSƏN

d: Dowson.
Plus how, son *or* sun, etc.

OUTĒ

d: doughty.
dr: droughty.
g: gouty.
gr: grouty.
l: louty.
m: mao-tai, "moughty."
p: pouty.
sn: snouty.
t: touty.
 Plus out, he, etc.
 Plus now tea, etc.

OUTEST

d: doubtest*.
fl: floutest*.
kl: cloutest*.
p: poutest*.
sh: shoutest*.
sk(sc): scoutest*.
sp: spoutest*.
spr: sproutest*.
st: stoutest.
v: devoutest.
 Plus now test, etc.

OUTETH

d: doubteth*.
fl: flouteth*.
kl: clouteth*.
p: pouteth*.
sh: shouteth*.
sk(sc): scouteth*.
sp: spouteth*.
spr: sprouteth*.

OUTING

Vowel: outing.
b: bouting.
d: doubting, undoubting.
fl: flouting.

gr: grouting.
kl: clouting.
kr: sauerkrauting.
l: louting.
n: knouting.
p: pouting.
r: routing.
sh: beshouting, shouting.
sk(sc): scouting.
sp: bespouting, spouting.
spr: besprouting, resprouting, sprouting, unsprouting.
t: touting.
tr: trouting.

OUTKART

t: Tout court.

OUTLĒ

st: stoutly.
v: devoutly.
 Plus shout, Lee *or* lea, etc.

OUTLƏT

Vowel: outlet.
tr: troutlet.
 Plus clout let *or* Lett, etc.

OUTNƏS

st: stoutness.
v: devoutness.

OUTƱR

Vowel: down-and-outer, out-and-outer, outer.
b: bouter.
d: doubter, nondoubter.
fl: flouter.
j: jowter.
kl: clouter.
kr: sauerkrauter.

n: knouter.
p: puter.
r: router.
sh: shouter.
sk(sc): scouter.
sp: spouter.
spr: sprouter.
st: stouter.
t: touter.
v: devouter.
w: Wouter.
> Plus clout her *or* err, etc.

OUTƏD

Vowel: outed.
b: bouted.
d: doubted, misdoubted, redoubted, undoubted.
fl: flouted.
g: gouted.
gr: grouted.
kl: clouted.
kr: sauerkrauted.
n: knouted.
p: pouted.
sh: shouted.
sk(sc): scouted.
sn: snouted.
sp: spouted.
spr: resprouted, sprouted, unsprouted.
t: touted.
tr: trouted.
> Plus lout, Ed, etc.
> Plus now, Ted, etc.

OUƱR

b: bauer, bower, embower, imbower.
br: Brower.
d: dower, endower.

fl: beflower, cauliflower, day flower, deflower, enflower, flower, gilliflower, Mayflower, moon-flower, passion flower, sunflower, wallflower, windflower.
g: Gower.
gl: glower.
k(c): cower.
l: allower, lower.
p: candlepower, empower, horsepower, manpower, over-power, power, waterpower.
pl: plougher, plower.
r: rower.
sh: shower, thundershower.
t: beacon tower, church tower, fire tower, overtower, tower, watch-tower.
v: avower, vower.
> Plus endow her *or* err, etc.
> Cf. our.

OUƱRD

h: Howard.
k: coward.
sh: showered, unshowered.
t: towered, untowered.
> Plus ouur+ed.

OUƱRZ

p: Powers.
> Plus ouur+s.

OUWOU

b: bowwow.
p: powwow.
w: wow wow.
> Plus now wow, etc.

OUZĒ

b: bowsie.
bl: blousy.
dr: drowzy.

fr: frowzy.
l: lousy.
m: mousy.
  Plus allows he, etc.
  Plus now Z *or* Zee, etc.

OUZEST

b: bousest*.
br: browsest*.
dr: drowsest*.
h: unhousest*.
r: arousest*, carousest*, rousest*,
uprousest*.
sp: espousest*.

OUZETH

b: bouseth*.
br: browseth*.
dr: drowseth*.
h: unhouseth*.
r: arouseth*, carouseth*,
rouseth*, uprouseth*.
sp: espouseth*.

OUZIJ

h: housage.
sp: espousage, spousage.
  Cf. blouse age, etc.

OUZING

b: bouzing.
bl: blousing.
br: browsing.
h: housing.
r: arousing, carousing, rousing.

OUZUR

b: bouzer.
br: browser.
h: houser.
m: mauser, mouser.

r: arouser, rouser.
shn: schnauzer.
t: Towser.
tr: trouser.
y: yowzer.
  Plus rouse her *or* err, etc.

OUZURZ

tr: trousers.
  Plus ouzur+s.

OUZƏL

Vowel: ousel.
h: housel.
r: arousal, carousal.
sp: espousal, spousal.
t: tousle.
  Plus drowse'll, etc.

OUZƏND

th: thousand.
  Plus rouse and, etc.

OUZƏS

bl: blouses.
br: browses.
h: houses.
r: arouses, carouses, rouses.
sp: espouses, spouses.
  Cf. browse is, etc.

OUƏL

b: bowel, embowel.
d: dowel.
h: Howell.
p: Powell.
pr: Prowell.
r: rowel.
t: towel.
tr: trowel.
v: vowel.

Plus plough, Al, etc.
Cf. oual.
Cf. plough will, etc.
Cf. plough well, etc.

OUƏN

g: gowan, McGowan.
r: rowan, rowen.
Plus allow an, etc.

OUƏNS

l: allowance, disallowance.
v: avowance, disavowance.
Plus plough ants *or* aunts, etc.

OUƏS

pr: prowess.
Cf. now, West, etc.

OUƏT

h: Howett.
j: Jowett.
Cf. plough wet, etc.
Cf. plough it, etc.

ŌVĒ

ch: anchovy.
gr: grovy.
k(c): covy.
Plus clove, he, etc.

ŌVĪN

Vowel: ovine.
b: bovine.
Plus no vine, etc.

ŌVING

r: roving.
shr: shroving.

ŌVŌ

Vowel: ab ovo.
n: de novo.
Plus clove owe *or* O, etc.

ŌVƱR

Vowel: flopover, half-seas-over, moreover, over, pushover, rollover, walkover.
d: Dover.
dr: drover.
kl: clover, sweet clover.
pl: plover.
r: rover, sea rover.
st: stover.
tr: trover.
Plus drove her *or* err, etc.

ŌVƱRZ

t: estovers.
Plus ovur+s.

ŌVƏ

h: Jehovah.
n: Canova, Cassanova, nova, Villa Nova.
Plus clove a, etc.

ŌVƏL

Vowel: oval.
Plus rove, Al, etc.

ŌVƏN

h: hoven.
k: De Koven.
kl: cloven, uncloven.
w: interwoven, inwoven, woven.
Cf. clove hen, etc.

ŌWHER

n: nowhere.
  Plus go where, etc.

ŌWURD

fr: forward.
  Plus go, ward, etc.
  Cf. toward.

ŌYŌ

y: yo-yo.

ŌYUR

Vowel: oyer.
b: bowyer.

ÔYUR

l: lawyer.
s: sawyer, topsawyer.

ŌYƏZ

Vowel: oyez.
  Plus go, "yez," etc.

ŌZBUD

r: rosebud.
  Plus nose bud, etc.

ŌZDĪV

n: nosedive.
  Plus foes, dive, etc.

ŌZĒ

d: dozy.
k(c): cozy.
n: nosy.
p: posy.
pr: prosy.
r: Rosie, rosy.
  Plus rose, he, etc.

ÔZĒ

g: gauzy.
k(c): causeway, causey.
l: lawsie.
  Plus claws, he, etc.

ŌZĒD

p: posied.
r: rosied.
  Cf. nose hid, etc.

ŌZEST

d: dozest*.
kl: closest*, disclosest*, enclosest*, inclosest*.
p: composest*, decomposest*, deposest*, discomposest*, disposest*, exposest*, interposest*, juxtaposest*, opposest*, posest*, presupposest*, proposest*, recomposest*, reimposest*, reposest*, superimposest*, supposest*, transposest*.
  Plus no zest, etc.

ŌZETH

d: dozeth*.
kl: closeth*, discloseth*, encloseth*, incloseth*.
p: composeth*, decomposeth*, disposeth*, exposeth*, interposeth*, juxtaposeth*, opposeth*, presupposeth*, proposeth*, recomposeth*, reimposeth*, reposeth*, superimposeth*, supposeth*, transposeth*.

ŌZGĀ

n: nosegay.
  Plus rose gay, etc.

ŌZGÄRD

n: nose guard.

ŌZHU̞R

Vowel: osier.
d: Dozier.
h: hosier.
kr: crosier.
kl: closure, disclosure, foreclosure, inclosure.
p: composure, discomposure, disposure, exposure, reposure.
  Plus foes, your *or* you're, etc.

ŌZHƏN

br: ambrosian.
pl: explosion, implosion.
r: corrosion, erosion.
  Cf. ozian, etc.

ŌZING

d: dozing.
h: hosing.
kl: closing, disclosing, enclosing, foreclosing, inclosing, unclosing.
n: nosing.
p: composing, decomposing, deposing, discomposing, disposing, exposing, imposing, interposing, juxtaposing, opposing, posing, predisposing, presupposing, proposing, recomposing, reposing, supposing, transposing, unimposing.

ÔZING

k(c): causing.
p: pausing.

ÔZIV

pl: applausive, plausive, unapplausive.
  Plus claw sieve, etc.

ÔZJÄB

n: nose job.

ŌZŌ

b: bozo.
  Plus rose owe *or* O, etc.

ŌZOIL

r: rose oil.

ŌZŌN

Vowel: ozone.
  Plus rose own, etc.

ŌZU̞R

d: bulldozer, dozer.
gl: glozer.
h: hoser.
kl: closer, discloser, encloser, forecloser, incloser, uncloser.
p: composer, deposer, disposer, exposer, imposer, interposer, juxtaposer, opposer, poser, predisposer, presupposer, proposer, reimposer, reposer, superimposer, supposer, transposer.
r: roser.
  Plus close her *or* err, etc.

ÔZU̞R

h: hawser.
k(c): causer, first causer.
p: pauser.
  Plus claws her *or* err, etc.

ŌZƏ

n: Spinoza.
r: Rosa.
  Plus glows a, etc.

ŌZƏL

p: desposal*, disposal, interposal, opposal, presupposal, reposal, supposal, transposal.

r: rosal.

Plus knows, Al, etc.

ŌZƏN

ch: chosen, forechosen.

fr: frozen.

h: hosen*.

p: Posen.

r: rosen*.

skw: "squozen."

ŌZƏZ

ch: choses.

d: dozes.

gl: glozes.

kl: closes, discloses, encloses, forecloses, incloses, uncloses.

m: Moses.

n: noses.

p: composes, decomposes, deposes, discomposes, disposes, exposes, imposes, indisposes, interposes, juxtaposes, opposes, poses, predisposes, presupposes, proposes, recomposes, reimposes, reposes, superimposes, superposes, supposes, transposes.

r: bramble roses, damask roses, moss roses, roses, tuberoses, wild roses.

Plus Joe says, etc.

Cf. nose is, etc.

ÔZƏZ

g: gauzes.

k(c): causes.

kl: clauses.

p: pauses.

v: vases.

Plus maw says, etc.

Cf. gauze is, etc.

ŌƏ

b: boa, Gilboa, jerboa.

m: moa, Samoa.

n: Genoa, Noah, quinoa.

pr: proa.

st: stoa.

z: entozoa, epizoa, metazoa, protozoa, spermatazoa.

Plus owe *or* O, a etc.

Cf. Aloha.

ŌƏL

j: Joel.

kr: Crowell.

l: Lowell.

n: Noel.

st: bestowal.

Plus slow el, ell *or* L, etc.

Plus go, Al, etc.

ÔƏL

dr: withdrawal.

Plus straw, Al, etc.

ŌƏM

p: poem.

pr: proem.

Plus throw 'em, etc.

ŌƏN

Vowel: Owen.

b: Bowen.

k(c): Cohen.

z: entozoon, epizoon, phytozoon, zoon.

Cf. Rowan.

ŌƏT

p: poet.

Cf. go it, etc.

U

The accented vowel sounds included are listed under **B** in Single Rhymes.

UBCHER

k(c)l: club chair.

UBING

bl: blubbing.
d: dubbing.
dr: drubbing.
gr: grubbing.
kl: clubbing.
n: nubbing.
r: rubbing.
s: subbing.
skr(scr): scrubbing.
sn: snubbing.
st: stubbing.
t: tubbing.

UBISH

gr: grubbish.
k(c): cubbish.
kl: clubbish.
r: rubbish.
t: tubbish.

UBJEKT

s: subject.

UB'L

b: bubble, hubble-bubble.
d: body double, double, redouble.
gr: grubble*.
h: Hubbell.
n: nubble.
r: rubble.
st: stubble.
tr: trouble.
Plus tub'll, etc.

UBLD

b: bubbled.
d: doubled, redoubled.
st: stubbled.
tr: troubled, untroubled.
Plus rubble'd, etc.

UBLĒ

b: bubbly.
d: doubley.
n: knubbly, nubbly.
r: rubbly.
st: stubbly.
Plus tub, Lee *or* lea, etc.

UBLEST

b: bubblest*.
d: doublest*, redoublest*.
tr: troublest*.
Plus tub, lest, etc.

UBLET

d: doublet.
Plus tub let *or* Lett, etc.

UBLETH

b: bubbleth*.
d: doubleth*, redoubleth*.
tr: troubleth*.

UBLIK

p: Khmer Republic, public, republic.

Plus cub lick, etc.

UBLING

b: bubbling.
d: doubling, redoubling.
tr: troubling.

UBLISH

p: publish, republish.

UBLUR

b: bubbler.
d: doubler.
tr: troubler.

UBLUS

tr: troublous.

UBSTĀK

gr: grubstake.
Plus cubs take, etc.
Plus tub stake *or* steak, etc.

UBSTANS

Plus cub stance, etc.

UBSTƏNS

s: substance.

UBTEKST

s: subtext.

UBUR

bl: blubber.
d: dubber.
dr: drubber, tub drubber.
gr: grubber, money-grubber.

kl: clubber.
l: landlubber, lubber.
r: indiarubber, rubber.
skr(scr): scrubber.
sl: slubber.
sn: snubber.
st: stubber.
t: tubber.
Plus rub her *or* err, etc.

UBURD

bl: blubbered.
h: Hubbard, mother hubbard.
k(c): cupboard.
r: rubbered.

UBURN

st: stubborn.
Cf. cub born, etc.

UCHBÄB

d: Dutch bob.

UCHĒ

d: archduchy, duchy.
kl: clutchy.
sm: smutchy.
t: touchy.
Plus crutch, he, etc.

UCHES

d: archduchess, Dutchess.
s: suchess
Cf. such chess, etc.

UCHEST

kl: clutchest*.
sm: smutchest*.
t: retouchest*, touchest*.

UCHETH

kl: clutcheth*.
sm: smutcheth*.
t: retoucheth*, toucheth*.

UCHING

kl: clutching.
sk(sc): scutching.
sm: smutching.
t: retouching, touching.

UCHUR

d: Dutcher.
kl: clutcher.
sk(sc): scutcher.
sm: smutcher.
t: retoucher, toucher.
  Plus touch her *or* err, etc.

UCHƏN

k(c): escutcheon, McCutcheon.
  Plus nuch on *or* an, etc.

UCHƏZ

h: hutches.
kl: clutches.
kr: crutches.
sk(sc): scutches.
sm: smutches.
t: retouches, touches.
  Cf. Dutch is, etc.

UDÄK

p: puddock.
r: ruddock.
  Plus mud, dock, etc.

UDĒ

b: buddy.
bl: bloody.

k(c): cuddy.
m: muddy.
p: puddy.
r: ruddy.
st: studdy, study.
  Plus blood, he, etc.

UDĒD

bl: bloodied.
m: muddied.
r: ruddied.
st: studied, unstudied.
  Cf. uded.
  Cf. blood did, etc.

UDEST

b: buddest*.
fl: floodest*.
sk: scuddest*.
st: studdest*.
th: thuddest*.

UDETH

b: buddeth*.
fl: floodeth*.
sk(sc): scuddeth*.
st: studdeth*.
th: thuddeth*.
  Cf. blood death, etc.

UDING

b: budding.
fl: flooding.
sk(sc): scudding.
sp: spudding.
st: bestudding, studding.

UDĪT

l: Luddite.

UD'L

b: buddle.
f: fuddle.
h: huddle.
k(c): cuddle.
m: bemuddle, muddle.
n: nuddle.
p: puddle.
r: ruddle.
sk(sc): scuddle.
   Plus mud'll, etc.

UDLĒ

d: Dudley.
   Plus brood, Lee *or* lea, etc.

UDLEST

h: huddlest*.
k(c): cuddlest*.
m: bemuddlest*, muddlest*.
p: puddlest*.
   Plus mud, lest, etc.

UDLETH

h: huddleth*.
k(c): cuddleth*.
m: bemuddleth*, muddleth*.
p: puddleth*.

UDLING

f: fuddling.
h: huddling.
k(c): cuddling.
m: bemuddling, muddling.
p: puddling.
sk(sc): scuddling.

UDLUR

f: fuddler.
h: huddler.
k(c): cuddler.

m: muddler.
p: puddler.

UDSIL

m: mudsill.

UDSƏN

h: Hudson.
j: Judson.
   Plus blood, son *or* sun, etc.

UDUR

Vowel: udder.
br: "brudder."
d: dudder.
fl: flooder.
m: mudder.
p: pudder.
r: rudder.
sh: shudder.
sk(sc): scudder.
   Plus flood her *or* err, etc.

UDWURM

b: budworm.

UDZĒ

s: sudsy.
   Plus buds, he, etc.

UDƏD

b: budded.
bl: blooded.
fl: flooded.
sk(sc): scudded.
sp: spudded.
st: bestudded, studded.
th: thudded.
   Cf. udid.
   Cf. stud dead, etc.

UDƏN

s: sudden.

Plus blood den, etc.

UFĒ

b: buffy.
bl: bluffy.
ch: chuffy.
fl: fluffy.
h: huffy.
p: puffy.
pl: pluffy.
sl: sloughy.
sn: snuffy.
st: stuffy.

Plus rough, he, etc.

UFEST

b: rebuffest*.
bl: bluffest.
gr: gruffest.
k(c): cuffest*.
l: luffest*.
m: muffest*.
p: bepuffest*, puffest*.
r: roughest.
sl: sloughest*.
sn: snuffest*.
st: stuffest.
t: toughest.

Cf. snuff fest, etc.

UFETH

b: rebuffeth*.
bl: bluffeth*.
k(c): cuffeth*.
l: luffeth*.
m: muffeth*.
p: bepuffeth*, puffeth*.
r: rougheth*.
sl: slougheth*.

sn: snuffeth*.
st: stuffeth*.

UFHOUS

r: roughhouse.

Plus tough house, etc.

UFIN

m: muffin, ragamuffin.
p: puffin.

Plus enough in *or* inn, etc.
Cf. tough fin *or* Finn, etc.

UFING

bl: bluffing.
fl: fluffing.
h: huffing.
k(c): cuffing.
l: luffing.
p: puffing.
r: roughing.
sl: sloughing.
sn: snuffing.
st: stuffing.

UFISH

Vowel: uffish.
gr: gruffish.
h: huffish.
r: roughish.
t: toughish.

Cf. tough fish, etc.

UF'L

b: buffle.
d: duffle.
m: bemuffle, muffle, unmuffle.
r: ruffle, unruffle.
sh: double shuffle, shuffle.
sk(sc): scuffle.
sn: snuffle.

tr: truffle.

Plus tough'll, etc.

UFL'D

m: bemuffled, muffled, unmuffled.
r: ruffled, unruffled.
sh: shuffled.
sk(sc): scuffled.

Plus truffle'd, etc.

UFLĒ

bl: bluffly.
gr: gruffly.
m: muffly.
r: roughly, ruffly.
sk(sc): scuffly.
sl: sluffly.
sn: snuffly.
t: toughly.
tr: truffly.

Plus enough, Lee *or* lea, etc.

UFLEST

m: bemufflest*, mufflest*, unmufflest*.
r: rufflest*.
sh: shufflest*.
sk(sc): scufflest*.

Plus snuff, lest, etc.

UFLETH

m: bemuffleth*, muffleth*, unmuffleth*.
r: ruffleth*.
sh: shuffleth*.
sk(sc): scuffeth*.

UFLING

m: bemuffling, muffling, unmuffling.
r: ruffling, unruffling.

sh: shuffling.
sk(sc): scuffing.
sn: snuffing.

UFLUR

m: muffler, unmuffler.
r: ruffler.
sh: shuffler.
sk(sc): scuffler.
sn: snuffler.

UFLUV

t: tough love.

UFNƏS

bl: bluffness.
gr: gruffness.
r: roughness.
t: toughness.

UFTĒ

m: mufti.
t: tufty.

Plus enough tea, etc.

UFTƏD

t: tufted.

Plus rough, Ted, etc.
Plus snuffed, Ed, etc.

UFƱR

b: buffer.
bl: bluffer.
d: duffer.
gr: gruffer.
h: huffer.
k(c): cuffer.
l: luffer.
m: muffer.
p: puffer.
r: rougher.

s: suffer.
sk(sc): scuffer.
sn: snuffer.
st: stuffer.
t: tougher.
　　Plus rough her *or* err, etc.
　　Cf. rough fur *or* fir, etc.

UFƏN

r: roughen.
t: toughen.

UFƏT

b: buffet.
m: Muffett.
t: tuffet.
　　Cf. rough it, etc.

UGBĒ

r: Rugby.
　　Plus bug be or bee, etc.

UGĒ

b: buggy.
dr: druggie.
m: muggy.
p: puggi, puggy.
sl: sluggy.
　　Plus drug, he, etc.

UGEST

dr: druggest*.
h: huggest*.
j: juggest*.
l: luggest*.
m: muggest*.
pl: pluggest*.
shr: shruggest*.
sl: sluggest*.
sm: smuggest.

sn: snuggest.
t: tuggest*.
　　Cf. druggist.

UGETH

dr: druggeth*.
h: huggeth*.
j: juggeth*.
l: luggeth*.
m: muggeth*.
pl: pluggeth*.
shr: shruggeth*.
sl: sluggeth*.
t: tuggeth*.

UGHOUS

b: bughouse.
　　Plus rug house, etc.

UGIJ

l: luggage.
　　Cf. drug age, etc.

UGING

dr: drugging.
h: hugging.
j: jugging.
l: lugging.
m: mugging.
pl: plugging.
shr: shrugging.
sl: slugging.
t: tugging.

UGINZ

m: Muggins.
　　Plus drug inns *or* ins, etc.

UGISH

m: muggish.
sl: sluggish.

sm: smuggish.
sn: snuggish.

UGIST

dr: druggist.
    Cf. ugest.

UG'L

g: guggle.
j: juggle.
sm: smuggle.
sn: snuggle.
str: death struggle, struggle.
    Plus bug'll, etc.

UGLĒ

Vowel: plug-ugly, ugly.
g: guggly.
j: juggly.
sm: smugly.
sn: snuggly.
str: struggly.
    Plus drug, Lee *or* lea, etc.

UGLEST

j: jugglest*.
sm: smugglest*.
sn: snugglest*.
str: strugglest*.
    Plus drug, lest, etc.

UGLETH

j: juggleth*.
sm: smuggleth*.
sn: snuggleth*.
str: struggleth*.

UGLING

g: guggling.
j: juggling.
sm: smuggling.

sn: snuggling.
str: struggling.

UGLUR

j: juggler.
sm: smuggler.
sn: snuggler.
str: struggler.

UGNƏS

sm: smugness.
sn: snugness.

UGOUT

d: dugout.
    Plus jug out, etc.

UGUR

b: bugger.
dr: drugger.
h: hugger.
l: lugger.
m: hugger-mugger, mugger.
pl: plugger.
r: rugger.
shr: shrugger.
sm: smugger.
sn: snugger.
t: tugger.
    Plus hug her *or* err, etc.

UGURD

sl: sluggard.
    Cf. ugur+ed.

UGWUMP

m: mugwump.

UGƏD

r: rugged.
    Cf. ug+ed*.

UGƏT

dr: drugget.
n: nugget.
   Cf. rug get, etc.
   Cf. slug it, etc.

UJĒ

p: pudgy.
sl: sludgy.
sm: smudgy.
   Plus judge, he, etc.

UJEST

b: budgest*.
dr: drudgest*.
gr: begrudgest*.
j: adjudgest*, judgest*,
misjudgest*, prejudgest*.
n: nudgest*.
sl: sludgest*.
sm: smudgest*.
tr: trudgest*.

UJETH

b: budgeth*.
dr: drudgeth*.
gr: begrudgeth*.
j: adjudgeth*, judgeth*,
misjudgeth*, prejudgeth*.
n: nudgeth*.
sl: sludgeth*.
sm: smudgeth*.
tr: trudgeth*.

UJING

b: budging.
dr: drudging.
f: fudging.
gr: begrudging, grudging,
ungrudging.

j: adjudging, forejudging, judging,
misjudging, prejudging, rejudg-
ing.
n: nudging.
sl: sludging.
sm: smudging.
tr: trudging.

UJMƏNT

j: judgment.
   Plus grudge meant, etc.

UJUR

b: budger.
dr: drudger.
f: fudger.
gr: begrudger, grudger.
j: adjudger, forejudger, judger,
misjudger, prejudger, rejudger.
n: nudger.
sl: sludger.
sm: smudger.
tr: trudger.

UJƏL

k(c): cudgel.
   Plus drudge'll, etc.

UJƏN

bl: bludgeon.
d: dudgeon.
g: gudgeon.
m: curmudgeon.
   Plus judge on *or* an, etc.

UJƏT

b: budget.
   Cf. grudge it, etc.

UJƏZ

b: budges.
dr: drudges.
f: fudges.
gr: begrudges, grudges.
j: adjudges, forejudges, judges, misjudges, prejudges, rejudges.
n: nudges.
sl: sludges.
sm: smudges.
tr: trudges.
    Cf. judge is, etc.

UKCHŲR

str: deep structure, restructure, structure, substructure, super-structure.
    Plus plucked your *or* you're, etc.

UKĒ

d: ducky.
l: lucky, unlucky.
m: mucky.
pl: plucky.
t: Kentucky.
w: wucky.
y: yucky.
    Plus ruck, he, etc.

UKEST

b: buckest*.
d: duckest*.
pl: pluckest*.
s: suckest*.

UKETH

b: bucketh*.
d: ducketh*.
pl: plucketh*.
s: sucketh*.

UKING

b: bucking.
ch: chucking.
d: ducking.
kl: clucking.
m: mucking.
pl: plucking.
s: sucking.
sh: shucking.
t: tucking.
tr: trucking.

UKISH

b: buckish.
m: muckish.
p: puckish.

UK'L

b: buckle, parbuckle, unbuckle.
br: bruckle.
ch: chuckle.
h: huckle.
m: muckle.
n: knuckle.
s: suckle, honeysuckle.
tr: truckle.
    Plus luck'll, etc.

UK'LD

b: buckled, unbuckled.
ch: chuckled.
k(c): cuckold.
n: knuckled.
s: suckled.
tr: truckled.

UKLES

l: luckless.
    Plus pluck less, etc.

UKLEST

b: bucklest*, unbucklest*.
ch: chucklest*.
s: sucklest*.
  Plus duck, lest, etc.

UKLETH

b: buckleth*, unbuckleth*.
ch: chuckleth*.
s: suckleth*.

UKLING

b: buckling, unbuckling.
ch: chuckling.
d: duckling, ugly duckling.
n: knuckling.
s: suckling.
tr: truckling.

UKLUR

b: buckler, swashbuckler.
ch: chuckler.
n: knuckler.
s: suckler.
tr: truckler.

UKŌLD

k(c): cuckold.
  Plus luck, old, etc.
  Cf. uk'ld.

UKRĀK

m: muckrake.
  Plus pluck rake, etc.

UKSĒ

l: Biloxi.
  Plus bucks, he, etc.

UKSHƏN

d: abduction, adduction, conduction, deduction, diduction*, eduction, induction, introduction, manuduction, nonconduction, obduction, overproduction, production, reduction, reproduction, seduction, subduction, superinduction, traduction.
fl: affluxion, defluxion, effluxion, fluxion, influxion.
r: ruction.
s: suction.
str: construction, deconstruction, destruction, instruction, misconstruction, obstruction, reconstruction, self-destruction, substruction, superstruction.
  Plus luck shun, etc.

UKSIV

fl: influxive.
  Plus pluck sieve, etc.

UKSTUR

h: huckster.
  Plus luck stir, etc.
  Plus pluck'st* her or err, etc.

UKSUM

b: buxom.
l: lucksome.
  Plus pluck some or sum, etc.

UKTEST

d: adductest*, conductest*, deductest*, inductest*.
str: constructest*, instructest*, misconstructest*, obsructest*.
  Plus muck test, etc.

UKTETH

d: abducteth*, conducteth*, deducteth*, inducteth*.

str: constructeth*, instructeth*, misconstructeth*, obstructeth*.

UKTING

d: abducting, conducting, deducting, inducting, misconducting, nonconducting.

str: constructing, instructing, nonobstructing, obstructing.

UKTIV

d: adductive, conductive, deductive, inductive, introductive, nonconductive, overproductive, productive, reconductive, reductive, reproductive, seductive, superinductive, traductive, underproductive.

str: constructive, destructive, instructive, obstructive, reconstructive, self-destructive, superstructive.

UKTRƏS

d: conductress, seductress.

str: instructress, introductress.

Plus pluck tress, etc.

UKTƱR

d: abductor, adductor, conductor, ductor, eductor, inductor, introductor, manuductor, nonconductor.

str: constructor, destructor, instructor, obstructor.

Plus plucked her *or* err, etc.

UKTƏD

d: abducted, conducted, deducted, inducted.

fr: fructed.

str: constructed, instructed, misconstructed, obstructed, superstructed, unobstructed.

Plus pluck Ted, etc.

Plus deduct Ed, etc.

UKTƏL

d: ductile, inductile, productile.

Plus pluck till, etc.

UKTƏNS

l: reluctance.

Plus deduct aunts *or* ants, etc.

UKTƏNT

l: reluctant.

Plus plucked ant *or* aunt, etc.

UKƱR

b: bucker.

ch: chucker, chukker.

d: ducker.

kl: clucker.

m: mucker.

p: pucker.

s: all-day sucker, sapsucker, seersucker, succor, sucker.

t: tucker.

tr: trucker.

Plus tuck her *or* err, etc.

UKƏ

ch: chukka.

Plus pluck a, etc.

UKƏT

b: bucket.

l: Luckett.

p: Puckett.

s: sucket.

t: Nantucket, Pawtucket, tucket.

Cf. pluck it, etc.

ULÄK

h: hullock*.
r: rowlock.
  Cf. dull lock, etc.

ULCHUR

k(c): agriculture, apiculture, arboriculture, aviculture, culture, floriculture, horticulture, inculture, pisciculture, self-culture, sylviculture, terraculture, viticulture.
m: multure.
v: culture vulture, vulture.
  Plus consult your *or* you're, etc.

ULDƏ

h: Hulda.
  Plus sculled a, etc.

ULĒ

d: dully.
g: Gulley, gully.
h: hully.
k(c): cully.
s: sully.
t: Tully.
  Plus dull, he, etc.

ULĒD

g: gullied.
s: sullied, unsullied.
  Cf. trull hid, etc.

ULEST

d: dullest.
k(c): cullest*.
l: lullest*.
n: annullest*.
sk(sc): scullest*.
  Plus trull, lest, etc.

ULETH

d: dulleth*.
g: gulleth*.
l: lulleth*.
n: annulleth*.
sk(sc): sculleth*.

ULFUR

s: sulphur.
  Plus dull fur *or* fir, etc.
  Plus engulf her *or* err, etc.
  Cf. Gulfer.
  Cf. scull for, etc.

ULGĀT

m: promulgate.
v: vulgate.
  Plus dull gate, etc.

ULGUR

b: bulgur.
v: vulgar.
  Plus dull gar, etc.

ULIJ

Vowel: ullage.
g: gullage.
s: sullage.
  Cf. dull age, etc.

ULIN

m: McMullin, mullein.
  Plus dull in *or* inn, etc.
  Cf. ulen.

ULING

d: dulling.
g: gulling.

h: hulling.
k(c): culling.
l: lulling.
m: mulling.
n: annulling.
sk(sc): sculling.

ULINZ

m: McMullins, mulleins, Mullins.
   Plus dull inns *or* ins, etc.

ULISH

d: dullish.
g: gullish.

ULJEST

b: bulgest*.
d: indulgest*.
f: effulgest*.
m: promulgest*.
v: divulgest*.
   Plus dull jest, etc.

ULJETH

b: bulgeth*.
d: indulgeth*.
f: effulgeth*.
m: promulgeth*.
v: divulgeth*.

ULJING

b: bulging.
d: indulging.
f: effulging.
m: promulging.
v: divulging.

ULJMƏNT

d: indulgment.
v: divulgment.
   Plus bulge meant, etc.

ULJUR

b: Bulger.
d: indulger.
m: promulger.
v: divulger.
   Plus divulge her *or* err, etc.

ULJƏNS

d: indulgence, self-indulgence.
f: efflugence, refulgence.
   Cf. dull gents, etc.
   Cf. bulge hence, etc.

ULJƏNT

d: indulgent, self-indulgent.
f: circumfulgent, effulgent,
fulgent, interfulgent, profulgent,
refulgent.
m: emulgent.
   Plus trull, gent, etc.

ULJƏZ

b: bulges.
d: indulges.
f: effulges.
m: promulges.
v: divulges.
   Plus bulge, Ez, etc.

ULKĀT

k(c): inculcate.
s: sulcate, trisulcate.
   Plus dull, Kate, etc.
   Plus hulk eight *or* ate, etc.

ULKĒ

b: bulky.
h: hulky.
s: sulky.

Plus dull key, etc.

Plus bulk, he, etc.

ULKING

b: bulking.

h: hulking.

s: sulking.

sk: skulking.

Plus dull king, etc.

ULKUR

b: bulker.

s: sulker.

sk: skulker.

Plus hulk her *or* err, etc.

ULMƏN

Vowel: Ullman.

Plus dull man, etc.

ULNƏS

d: dullness.

ULŌ

h: hullo.

n: nullo.

Plus trull owe *or* O, etc.

ULPĀT

k(c): disculpate, exculpate, inculpate.

Plus dull pate, etc.

ULPCHUR

sk(sc): sculpture.

Plus pulped your *or* you're, etc.

ULPĒ

g: gulpy.

p: pulpy.

Plus sculp, he, etc.

ULPEST

g: gulpest*.

p: pulpest*.

sk(sc): sculpest*.

Plus dull pest, etc.

ULPETH

g: gulpeth*.

p: pulpeth*.

sk(sc): sculpeth*.

ULPIN, ULPĪN

v: vulpine (*or* pin).

Plus dull pine *or* dull pin, etc.

Plus sculp in *or* inn, etc.

ULPIT

p: bully pulpit, pulpit.

ULPRIT

k(c): culprit.

Plus pulp writ, etc.

ULPTUR

sk(sc): sculptor.

Cf. pulped her *or* err, etc.

ULSEST

m: mulsest.*

p: repulsest*.

v: convulsest*.

ULSETH

m: mulseth*.

p: repulseth*.

v: convulseth*.

ULSHUN

m: demulsion, emulsion.

p: appulsion, compulsion,

expulsion, impulsion, propulsion, pulsion, repulsion.

v: avulsion, convulsion, divulsion, evulsion, revulsion.

Plus trull shun, etc.

ULSING

p: pulsing, repulsing.
v: convulsing.

Plus trull sing, etc.

ULSIV

m: emulsive.

p: appulsive, compulsive, expulsive, impulsive, propulsive, pulsive, repulsive.

v: convulsive, divulsive, revulsive.

Plus dull sieve, etc.

ULSTŮR

Vowel: Ulster.

ULSŮR

Vowel: ulcer.
p: repulser.

Plus trull, sir, etc.

Plus convulse her *or* err, etc.

ULSƏT

d: dulcet.

Plus trull set, etc.

ULTĒ

k(c): difficulty.

ULTEST

k(c): occultest*.
s: consultest*, insultest*.
z: exultest*, resultest*.

Plus dull test, etc.

ULTETH

k(c): occulteth*.
s: consulteth*, insulteth*.
z: exulteth*, resulteth*.

ULTING

k(c): occulting.
s: consulting, insulting.
z: exulting, resulting.

ULTIV

s: consultive.
z: exultive.

ULTNƏS

d: adultness.
k(c): occultness.

ULTRĒ

s: sultry.

ULTŮR

s: consulter, insulter.
z: exulter, resulter.

Plus occult her *or* err, etc.

ULTƏD

k(c): occulted.
s: consulted, insulted.
z: exulted, resulted.

Plus dull, Ted, etc.

Plus result, Ed, etc.

ULTƏN

s: sultan.

Plus dull tan, etc.

Plus occult an *or* Ann, etc.

ULTƏNS

z: exultance, resultance.

Plus consult aunts *or* ants, etc.

ULTƏNT

z: exultant, resultant.
   Plus insult aunt *or* ant, etc.

ULƱR

d: duller, meduller.
g: guller.
h: huller.
k(c): color, culler, discolor, miscolor, multicolor, recolor, rose-color, technicolor, tricolor, watercolor.
kr: cruller.
l: luller.
m: Muller.
n: annuller.
sk(sc): sculler.
   Plus dull her *or* err, etc.

ULƱRD

d: dullard.
k(c): colored, discolored, high-colored, overcolored, particolored, party-colored, peach-colored, rosy-colored, sky-colored, wine-colored.
   Plus cruller'd. etc.

ULYUN

k(c): cullion.
m: mullion.
sk(sc): scullion.

ULƏ

d: medulla.
m: mullah.
n: nullah.
p: ampulla.
   Plus dull a, etc.

ULƏN

k(c): Cullen.
m: McMullin, mullein.
s: sullen.
   Cf. dull in *or* inn, etc.

ULƏT

g: gullet.
k(c): cullet.
m: mullet.
   Cf. scull it, etc.

UMBAT

k(c): combat.
   Plus some bat, etc.
   Cf. wombat.

UMBIK

l: columbic.
pl: plumbic.

UMB'L

Vowel: humble*, umbel.
b: bumble.
f: fumble.
gr: grumble.
h: humble.
j: bejumble, jumble.
kr: crumble.
m: mumble.
r: rumble.
sk(sc): scumble.
st: stumble.
   Cf. some bull, etc.

UMB'LD

h: humbled, unhumbled.
   Plus umb'l+d.

UMBLĒ

h: humbly.
j: jumbly.
kr: crumbly.
st: stumbly.
t: tumbly.

UMBLEST

f: fumblest*.
gr: grumblest*.
h: humblest*.
j: jumblest*.
kr: crumblest*.
m: mumblest*.
r: rumblest*.
st: stumblest*.
t: tumblest*.
    Plus some blest, etc.

UMBLETH

f: fumbleth*.
gr: grumbleth*.
h: humbleth*.
j: jumbleth*.
kr: crumbleth*.
m: mumbleth*.
r: rumbleth*.
st: stumbleth*.
t: tumbleth*.

UMBLING

f: fumbling.
gr: grumbling.
h: humbling.
j: jumbling.
kr: crumbling.
m: mumbling.
r: rumbling.
st: stumbling.
t: tumbling.

UMBLUR

dr: drumbler.
f: fumbler.
gr: grumbler.
h: humbler.
j: jumbler.
kr: crumbler.
m: mumbler.
r: rumbler.
st: stumbler.
t: tumbler.

UMBŌ

g: gumbo.
j: Jumbo, Mumbo-Jumbo.
m: Mumbo.
    Plus some beau, bo, *or* bow, etc.

UMBOOL

tr: Trumbull.
    Plus some bull, etc.

UMBRĀT

Vowel: inumbrate, obumbrate.
d: adumbrate.

UMBRIJ

Vowel: umbrage.

UMBRIL

t: tumbril.
    Plus come, Brill, etc.

UMBRUS

k(c): cumbrous.
n: penumbrous.
sl: slumbrous, unslumbrous.

UMBUG

h: humbug.
    Plus some bug, etc.

UMBᴜR

h: Humber.

k(c): cumber, disencumber, encumber.

l: lumbar, lumber.

n: 800 number, 900 number, number, outnumber, Reynolds number.

sl: slumber.

Plus some burr, etc.

UMBᴜRD

n: numbered, outnumbered, unnumbered.

Plus umbur+ed.

Plus some bird, etc.

UMBƏ

r: rumba.

Plus dumb *or* doom, bah!, etc.

UMBƏL

d: dumbbell.

Plus some bell, etc.

UMBƏNT

c: accumbent, decumbent, incumbent, procumbent, recumbent, superincumbent.

Plus some bent, etc.

UMDRUM

h: humdrum.

Plus come, drum, etc.

UMĒ

d: dummy.

g: gummy.

kr: crumby, crummie.

l: lummy.

m: mummy.

pl: plummy.

r: auction rummy, English rummy, four-hand rummy, Java rummy, Michigan rummy, rummy.

sk(sc): scummy.

skr(scr): scrummy.

t: tummy.

thr: thrummy.

y: yummy.

Cf. hum me, etc.

UMEST

d: dumbest.

dr: drummest*.

g: gummest*.

gl: glummest.

h: hummest*.

k(c): becomest*, comest*, overcomest*, succumbest*.

n: numbest.

r: rummest.

str: strummest.

Cf. bum messed, etc.

UMETH

dr: drummeth*.

g: gummeth*.

h: hummeth*.

k(c): becometh*, cometh*, overcometh*, succumbeth*.

str: strummeth*.

UMFIT

k(c): comfit.

Plus some fit, etc.

UMFÔRT

k(c): comfort.

Plus some fort, etc.

UMFRĒ

h: Humphrey.
   Plus some free, etc.

UMFRĒZ

h: Humphreys.
   Plus some "friz," etc.

UMFƏL

Vowel: triumphal.

UMFƏNT

Vowel: triumphant.

UMIJ

ch: chummage.
r: rummage.
skr(scr): scrummage.
   Cf. some mage, etc.
   Cf. some age, etc.

UMIM

th: Thummim.
z: Zamzummim.
   Plus drum him, etc.

UMIN

k(c): cumin, cummin.
   Plus rum in or inn, etc.

UMING

b: bumming.
ch: chumming.
dr: drumming.
g: gumming.
h: humming.
k(c): becoming, coming,
forthcoming, overcoming,
shortcoming, succumbing,
unbecoming.

kr: crumbing.
m: mumming.
n: benumbing, numbing.
pl: plumbing, plumming.
s: summing.
skr(scr): scrumming.
sl: slumming.
str: strumming.
th: thumbing.
   Cf. some Ming, etc.

UMINGZ

k(c): comings, shortcomings,
Cummings.
   Plus uming+s.

UMLĒ

ch: Chumley.
d: dumbly.
gl: glumly.
n: numbly.
r: rumly.
s: cumbersomely, frolicsomely,
humorsomely, troublesomely, etc.
   Plus come, Lee *or* lea, etc.

UMNUR

s: Sumner.

UMNƏL

l: columnal.
t: autumnal.

UMNƏS

d: dumbness.
gl: glumness.
n: numbness.

UMÔN

k(c): come on.
s: summon.
  Plus dumb on *or* an, etc.

UMPCHĀNJ

ch: chump change.

UMPĒ

b: bumpy.
ch: chumpy.
d: dumpy.
fr: frumpy.
gr: grumpy.
h: humpy.
j: jumpy.
kl: clumpy.
kr: crumpy.
l: lumpy.
m: mumpy.
pl: plumpy.
r: rumpy.
sl: slumpy.
st: stumpy.
th: thumpy.
  Plus thump, he, etc.

UMPEST

b: bumpest*.
d: dumpest*.
h: humpest*.
j: jumpest*.
l: lumpest*.
p: pumpest*.
pl: plumpest*.
st: stumpest*.
th: bethumpest*, thumpest*.
tr: trumpest*.
  Plus some pest, etc.

UMPETH

b: bumpeth*.
d: dumpeth*.
h: humpeth*.
j: jumpeth*.
l: lumpeth*.
p: pumpeth*.
st: stumpeth*.
th: bethumpeth*, thumpeth*.
tr: trumpeth*.

UMPING

b: bumping.
d: granny dumping, dumping.
h: humping.
j: broad-jumping, bunjee jumping, high-jumping, jumping.
kl: clumping.
l: galumping, lumping.
m: mumping.
p: pumping.
pl: plumping.
sl: slumping.
st: stumping.
th: bethumping, thumping.
tr: trumping.
  Plus some ping, etc.

UMPĪR

Vowel: umpire.
  Plus chump ire, etc.
  Plus some pyre, etc.

UMPISH

b: bumpish.
ch: chumpish.
d: dumpish.
fr: frumpish.
gr: grumpish.
h: humpish.

j: jumpish.
l: lumpish.
m: mumpish.
pl: plumpish.
sl: slumpish.
   Plus dumb, pish!, etc.

UMPKIN

b: bumpkin.
p: pumpkin.
   Plus thump kin, etc.
   Cf. Lumkin.

UMP'L

kr: crumple.
r: rumple, unrumple.
   Plus stump'll, etc.
   Cf. some pull, etc.

UMPLEST

kr: crumplest*.
r: rumplest*, unrumplest*.
   Plus trump, lest, etc.

UMPLETH

kr: crumpleth*.
r: rumpleth*, unrumpleth*.

UMPLING

d: dumpling.
kr: crumpling.
r: rumpling, unrumpling.

UMPNƏS

pl: plumpness.

UMPŌ

b: Bumpo.
   Plus some Poe or Po, etc.

UMPSHUN

g: gumption.
s: assumption, consumption, subsumption.
z: presumption, resumption.
   Plus trump shun, etc.

UMPSHUS

b: bumptious.
skr(scr): scrumptious.

UMPTIV

s: assumptive, consumptive, subsumptive.
z: presumptive, resumptive.

UMPᵾR

b: bumper.
d: dumper.
j: broad-jumper, counter-jumper, high-jumper, jumper.
l: lumper.
m: mumper.
p: pumper.
pl: plumper.
sl: slumper.
st: stumper.
th: bethumper, thumper, tub-thumper.
tr: trumper.
   Plus trump her or err, etc.
   Plus some purr or per, etc.

UMPƏS

k(c): compass, encompass.
r: rumpus.
   Cf. some pass or puss, etc.
   Cf. umpas.

UMPƏT

kr: crumpet.
str: strumpet.
tr: trumpet.
　　Plus some pet, etc.
　　Plus chump et, etc.
　　Cf. trump it, etc.

UMTU̇R

s: Fort Sumter, sumter.
　　Cf. trumped her *or* err, etc.

UMU̇R

b: bummer.
d: dumber.
dr: drummer.
g: gummer.
gl: glummer.
gr: grummer.
h: hummer.
k(c): comer, Cummer, incomer, late-comer, newcomer.
m: mummer.
n: number.
pl: plumber.
r: rummer.
s: midsummer, St. Martin's summer, summer.
sk(sc): scummer.
skr(scr): scrummer.
str: strummer.
　　Plus numb her *or* err, etc.
　　Cf. some myrrh, etc.

UMU̇RZ

s: Somers.
　　Plus umur+s.

UMZĒ

kl: clumsy.
m: mumsie.
　　Plus some Z *or* Zee, etc.

UMƏK

h: hummock.
st: stomach.
　　Cf. some mock, etc.
　　Cf. some muck, etc.

UMƏKS

h: hummocks.
l: lummox.
st: stomachs.

UMƏL

h: hummel.
p: bepummel, pommel, pummel.
　　Plus drum'll, etc.

UMƏND

dr: Drummond.
s: summoned.
　　Cf. numb and, etc.

UMƏS

h: hummus.
p: pumice.
　　Cf. come, miss, etc.

UMƏT

gr: grummet.
pl: plummet.
s: summit.
　　Plus dumb it, etc.
　　Plus Lum et, etc.
　　Cf. umet.
　　Cf. some mitt, etc.
　　Cf. numb it, etc.

UNBELT

s: sunbelt.

UNCHĒ

b: bunchy.
h: hunchy.

kr: crunchy.
p: punchy.
    Plus lunch, he, etc.

UNCHEST

b: bunchest*.
h: hunchest*.
kr: crunchest*.
l: lunchest*.
m: munchest*.
p: punchest*.
skr(scr): scrunchest*.
    Plus one chest, etc.

UNCHETH

b: buncheth*.
h: huncheth*.
kr: cruncheth*.
l: luncheth*.
m: muncheth*.
p: puncheth*.
skr(scr): scruncheth*.

UNCHĒZ

m: munchies.

UNCHING

b: bunching.
br: brunching.
h: hunching.
kr: crunching.
l: lunching.
m: munching.
p: punching.
skr(scr): scrunching.

UNCHKIN

m: munchkin.

UNCHƯR

b: buncher.
br: bruncher.

h: huncher.
kr: cruncher, number cruncher.
l: luncher.
m: muncher.
p: cowpuncher, puncher.
skr(scr): scruncher.
    Plus lunch her *or* err, etc.

UNCHƏN

br: bruncheon.
l: luncheon.
n: nuncheon.
p: puncheon.
sk(sc): scuncheon.
tr: truncheon.

UNCHƏZ

b: bunches.
br: brunches.
h: hunches.
kr: crunches.
l: lunches.
m: munches.
p: punches.
skr(scr): scrunches.

UNDĀN

m: antemundane, extramundane, inframundane, intermundane, intramundane, mundane, supermundane, supramundane, ultramundane.
    Plus stun Dane *or* deign, etc.

UNDĀT

k(c): fecundate, secondate.
    Plus one date, etc.
    Plus stunned ate *or* eight, etc.

UNDĒ

b: Bundy.
f: fundi, Fundy.

g: salmagundi.
gr: Grundy, Mrs. Grundy.
l: Lundy.
m: Monday+.
s: Sunday+.
   Plus sunned, he, etc.
   Cf. shun day, etc.

UNDEST

f: fundest*.

UNDETH

f: fundeth*.
   Plus one death, etc.

UNDIN

r: hirundine.
   Plus begun din, etc.
   Plus stunnned in, etc.

UNDING

f: funding, refunding.

UNDIT

p: pundit.
   Plus stunned it, etc.

UND'L

b: bundle, unbundle.
tr: trundle.
   Plus fund'll, etc.
   Cf. one dull, etc.

UNDLEST

b: bundlest*, unbundlest*.
tr: trundlest*.
   Plus fund, lest, etc.

UNDLETH

b: bundleth*, unbundleth*.
tr: trundleth*.

UNDLING

b: bundling, unbundling.
tr: trundling.

UNDRĒ

s: sundry.
th: thundry*.

UNDRUS

w: wondrous.
   Plus fund, Russ, etc.

UNDRUM

r: carborundum.
   Plus fund 'em, etc.
   Plus one dumb, etc.
   Cf. condom.

UNDRƏD

h: hundred.
   Plus one dread, etc.

UNDUN

l: London.
   Plus fun done, etc.
   Plus stunned an, etc.
   Cf. undone.

UNDᵁR

Vowel: down-under, there under, under.
bl: blunder.
d: dunder.
f: refunder.
g: Gunder.
pl: plunder.

s: asunder, dissunder, sunder.
t: rotunder.
th: enthunder, thunder.
w: wonder.
  Plus stunned her *or* err, etc.

UNDƏD

Vowel: undead.
f: funded, refunded.
t: retunded*.
  Plus one dead, etc.
  Plus gunned, Ed, etc.
  Cf. one did, etc.

UNDƏNS

b: abundance, superabundance.
d: redundance.
  Plus sun dance, etc.
  Plus stunned aunts *or* ants, etc.

UNDƏNT

b: abundant, superabundant.
d: redundant.
  Plus stunned aunt *or* ant, etc.

UNEST

f: funnest*.
g: gunnest*.
p: punnest*.
r: outrunnest*, overrunnest*, runnest*.
sh: shunnest*.
st: stunnest*.
w: wonnest*.

UNETH

f: funneth*.
g: gunneth.
p: punneth*.

r: outrunneth*, overrunneth*, runneth*.
sh: shunneth*.
st: stunneth*.
w: wonneth*.

UNGG'L

b: bungle.
j: jungle.
  Cf. one gun, etc.

UNGGLING

b: bungling.
j: jungling.

UNGGUR

h: enhunger, hunger.
m: ballad monger, borough monger, fish monger, gossip monger, ironmonger, monger, Munger, scandalmonger.
y: younger.

UNGKĀT

r: averruncate.
tr: detruncate, truncate.
  Plus monk ate *or* eight, etc.
  Plus rung, Kate, etc.

UNGKCHUR

j: conjuncture, juncture.
p: acupuncture, puncture.
  Plus chunked your *or* you're, etc.

UNGKĒ

ch: chunki.
f: funky.
fl: flunkey.
h: hunky.
j: junkie.
m: monkey, powder monkey, spider monkey.

p: punkie.
sp: spunky.
  Plus drunk, he, etc.
  Plus hung key, etc.

UNGKFISH

m: monkfish.

UNGKFŌOD

j: junk food.

UNGKIN

p: punkin.
  Plus hung kin, etc.
  Plus chunk in *or* inn, etc.
  Cf. ungken.

UNGKISH

f: funkish.
m: monkish.
sk: skunkish.
  Plus hung Kish, etc.

UNGKL

Vowel: uncle.
b: carbuncle.
d: peduncle.
r: caruncle.
tr: truncal.
  Plus monk, Al.
  Plus hung, Cal, etc.

UNGKŌ

b: bunco.
j: junco.
  Plus drunk owe *or* O, etc.

UNGKRÄK

p: punk rock.

UNGKSHUN

Vowel: extremeunction, inunction, unction.
f: defunction, function.
j: adjunction, conjunction, disjunction, injunction, interjunction, Josephson junction, junction, sejunction*, subjunction*.
p: compunction, expunction, interpunction, punction.
  Plus drunk shun, etc.

UNGKSHUS

Vowel: unctious.
b: rambunctious.
p: compunctious.

UNGKTIV

j: abjunctive, adjunctive, conjunctive, disjunctive, subjunctive.
p: compunctive.

UNGKUM

b: Buncombe, bunkum.
  Plus chunk 'em, etc.
  Plus rung come, etc.

UNGKUR

b: bunker.
d: dunker.
dr: drunker.
f: funker.
fl: flunker.
h: hunker.
j: junker.
p: punker.
t: tunker.
  Plus dunk her *or* err, etc.

UNGKURD

b: bunkered.
d: Dunkard.
dr: drunkard.
　　Plus flung curd *or* Kurd, etc.
　　Cf. drunk hard, etc.

UNGKUS

d: aduncous.
h: dohunkus.
j: juncous.
　　Plus shrunk us, etc.
　　Plus hung cuss, etc.

UNGKƏN

dr: drunken.
s: sunken.
shr: shrunken.
　　Plus hung, Ken, etc.
　　Cf. drunk hen, etc.

UNGKƏT

j: junket.
pl: Plunkett.
　　Plus drunk, et, etc.
　　Cf. drunk it, etc.

UNGLING

y: youngling.

UNGRĒ

h: hungry.

UNGSTUR

t: tonguester.
y: youngster.
　　Plus dung stir, etc.

UNGUR

l: lunger, one-lunger.
　　Plus hung her *or* err, etc.

UNĒ

b: bunny.
f: dofunny, funny.
g: gunny.
h: honey, wild honey.
m: acrimony, agrimony, alimony, antimony, matrimony, money, parsimony, patrimony, sanctimony.
r: runny.
s: sonny, sunny, unsunny.
t: Tunney, tunny.
　　Plus fun he, etc.
　　Cf. stun knee, etc.

UNIJ

d: dunnage.
g: gunnage.
t: tonnage.
　　Cf. stun age, etc.

UNIN

r: run-in.
　　Plus sun in *or* inn, etc.

UNING

d: dunning.
f: funning.
g: gunning.
k(c): cunning.
p: punning.
r: gun running, outrunning, overrunning, running.
s: sunning.
sh: shunning.
st: stunning.

UNISH

h: Hunnish.
p: punish.

UNJĒ

gr: grungy.
pl: plungy.
sp: spongy.
  Plus lunge, he, etc.

UNJEST

l: lungest*.
p: expungest*.
pl: plungest*.
sp: spongest*.
  Plus one jest, etc.

UNJETH

l: lungeth*.
p: expungeth*.
pl: plungeth*.
sp: spongeth*.

UNJING

l: lunging.
p: expunging.
pl: plunging.
sp: sponging.

UNJUN

d: dungeon.
pl: plungeon*.
  Cf. none, John, etc.

UNJUR

bl: blunger.
l: lunger.
p: expunger.
pl: plunger.
sp: sponger.
  Plus plunge her *or* err, etc.

UNJƏNT

p: pungent.
  Plus fun gent, etc.

UNJƏZ

l: lunges.
p: expunges.
pl: plunges.
sp: sponges.

UNKƏN

d: Duncan.
  Plus one can, etc.
  Plus drunk an *or* on, etc.
  Cf. ungkin.

UNLƏS

r: runless.
s: sonless, sunless.
  Plus none less *or* Les, etc.

UNMƏN

g: gunman.
  Plus one man, etc.

UNRŌOF

s: sunroof.

UNSĒ

d: duncey.
m: Munsey.
  Plus fun, see, etc.

UNSHIP

g: gunship.

UNSTUR

g: gunster.
p: punster.

Plus fun stir.
Plus dunced her *or* err, etc.
Cf. Munster.

UNSTƏN

d: Dunstan.
f: funston.
Plus dunced an *or* on, etc.
Plus once tan, ton, *or* tun, etc.

UNTĒ

p: punty.
r: runty.
st: stunty.
Plus bunt, he, etc.
Plus one tea, etc.

UNTEST

b: buntest*.
bl: bluntest.
fr: affrontest*, confrontest*.
gr: gruntest*.
h: huntest*.
p: puntest*.
sh: shuntest*.
st: stuntest*.
Plus one test, etc.

UNTETH

b: bunteth*.
bl: blunteth*.
fr: affronteth*, confronteth*.
gr: grunteth*.
h: hunteth*.
p: punteth*.
sh: shunteth*.
st: stunteth*.

UNTING

b: bunting, red bunting, yellow bunting.

fr: affronting, confronting, fronting.
gr: grunting.
h: brush hunting, head-hunting, hunting, lion hunting, scalp hunting, tail hunting.
p: punting.
sh: shunting.
st: stunting.

UNTLƏS

fr: frontless.
w: wontless.
Plus stunt less *or* Les, etc.

UNTNƏS

bl: bluntness.
st: stuntness.

UNTŌ

j: junto.
Plus one toe, etc.
Plus runt owe *or* O, etc.

UNTOO

Vowel: unto.
Plus won, two, to, *or* too, etc.

UNTRĒ

k(c): country.
Plus one tree, etc.

UNTSVIL

bl: Blountsville.
h: Huntsville.

UNTƱR

b: bunter.
bl: blunter.
fr: affronter, confronter.
g: Gunter.

gr: grunter.
h: fortune-hunter, headhunter, hunter, legacy hunter, lion hunter, scalp hunter.
p: punter.
sh: shunter.
st: stunter.
    Plus bunt her *or* err, etc.

UNTƏD

b: bunted.
bl: blunted, unblunted.
fr: affronted, confronted, fronted.
gr: grunted.
h: hunted.
p: punted.
sh: shunted.
st: stunted.
w: unwonted, wonted.
    Plus runt, Ed, etc.
    Plus none, Ted, etc.

UNTƏL

fr: frontal.
gr: disgruntle, gruntle.
p: contrapuntal.
    Plus punt, Al, etc.

UNUR

d: dunner.
g: gunner.
p: punner.
r: gunrunner, outrunner, overrunner, rumrunner, runner.
st: stunner.
    Plus dun her *or* err, etc.

UNYƏN

Vowel: onion, wild onion.
b: bunion, Bunyan.

m: munnion.
r: ronyon*.
tr: trunnion.

UNƏL

f: funnel.
g: gunwale.
r: runnel.
t: tunnel.
tr: trunnel.
    Plus gun'll, etc.

UNƏT

p: punnet.
r: runnet.
    Cf. fun it, etc.
    Cf. dun net, etc.

UPĒ

g: guppy.
k(c): cuppy, hiccoughy, hiccupy.
p: puppy.
y: yuppie.
    Plus up, he, etc.

UPEST

k(c): cuppest*.
s: suppest*.
t: tuppest*.
    Cf. pup pest, etc.

UPET

p: puppet.
    Cf. cup it, etc.
    Cf. cup, pet, etc.

UPETH

k(c): cuppeth*.
s: suppeth*.
t: tuppeth*.

UPFISH

p: pupfish.

UPGRĀD

Vowel: upgrade.

UPING

k(c): cupping.
s: supping.
t: tupping.

UPISH

Vowel: uppish.
p: puppish.

UPL

k(c): couple, uncouple.
s: supple.
> Plus pup'll, etc.

UPLEST

k(c): couplest*, uncouplest*.
s: supplest.

UPLETH

k(c): coupleth*, uncoupleth*.

UPLUR

k(c): coupler, uncoupler.
s: suppler.

UPSHUN

r: abruption, corruption, disruption, eruption, incorruption, interruption, irruption, ruption.
> Plus pup shun, etc.

UPSHƏL

n: antenuptial, nuptial, postnuptial.
> Plus cup shall, etc.

UPSKĀL

sk(c): upscale.

UPTEST

br: abruptest.
r: corruptest, interruptest*.
> Plus pup test, etc.

UPTETH

r: corrupteth*, interrupteth*.

UPTIK

t: uptick.

UPTING

r: corrupting, erupting, interrupting.

UPTIV

r: corruptive, disruptive, eruptive, incorruptive, interruptive, irruptive.

UPTLĒ

br: abruptly.
r: corruptly, incorruptly.
> Plus supped, Lee *or* lea, etc.

UPTNƏS

br: abruptness.
r: corruptness, incorruptness.

UPTUR

br: abrupter.
r: corrupter, disrupter, erupter, incorrupter, interrupter, irrupter.
> Plus supped her *or* err, etc.

UPTƏD

r: abrupted, corrupted, disrupted, interrupted, irrupted.

Plus pup, Ted, etc.
Plus supped, Ed, etc.

UPŬR

Vowel: upper.
k(c): cupper.
kr: crupper.
s: supper.
sk(sc): scupper.
t: Tupper.
    Plus sup her *or* err, etc.

UPWŬRD

Vowel: upward.
    Plus cup ward, etc.

UPƏNS

Vowel: come-uppance.
thr: thruppence.
    Plus sup ants *or* aunts, etc.

URĒ

d: dhurrie+, durrie+.

ŬRBÄR

d: durbar.
    Plus stir bar, etc.

ŬRBĀT

s: acerbate.
t: perturbate.
    Plus curb eight *or* ate, etc.
    Plus cur bait, etc.

ŬRBĒ

d: demolition derby, Derby, Kentucky Derby.
h: herby.
k: Kirby.
t: Iturbi.

Plus stir bee *or* be, etc.
Plus curb, he, etc.

ŬRBEST

bl: blurbest*.
k(c): curbest*.
t: disturbest*, perturbest*.
    Plus stir best, etc.

ŬRBETH

bl: blurbeth*.
k(c): curbeth*.
t: disturbeth*, perturbeth*.
    Plus stir, Beth, etc.

ŬRBID

h: herbid.
t: turbid.
    Plus stir bid, etc.
    Cf. curb hid, etc.

ŬRBĪN

t: turbine.
    Plus cur been, etc.
    Plus curb in *or* inn, etc.
    Cf. urban.

ŬRBING

bl: blurbing.
k(c): curbing.
t: disturbing, perturbing.
    Plus err, Byng, etc.

ŬRBƏR

b: Berber.
bl: blurber.
f: Ferber.
g: Gerber.
k(c): curber.
p: superber.
t: disturber, perturber.

Plus her burr, etc.
Plus curb her *or* err, etc.

URBƏRT

h: Herbert.
Plus stir, Bert *or* Burt, etc.
Cf. curb hurt, etc.

URBƏL

h: herbal.
v: verbal.
Plus curb Al, etc.

URBƏN

Vowel: urban.
b: Bourbon, suburban.
t: turban.
Plus curb an, etc.
Plus her ban, etc.

URBƏNS

t: disturbance.
Plus curbants, etc.
Plus curb ants *or* aunts, etc.

URBƏT

b: burbot.
sh: sherbet.
t: turbot.
Plus curb Ott, etc.
Plus Herb et, etc.
Plus her bet, etc.
Cf. curb hot, etc.

URCHEST

b: birchest*.
l: lurchest*.
p: perchest*, purchased (*or* chast).
s: searchest*.
sm: smirchest*.

Plus her chaste *or* chased, etc.
Plus her chest, etc.
Cf. purchased.

URCHETH

b: bircheth*.
l: lurcheth*.
p: percheth*.
s: searcheth*.
sm: smircheth*.

URCHIF

k: kerchief.

URCHING

b: birching.
ch: churching.
l: lurching.
p: perching.
s: searching.
sm: besmirching, smirching.

URCHLƏS

ch: churchless.
sm: smirchless.
Plus perch less *or* Les, etc.

URCH

v: easy virtue, virtue.
Plus hurt you, etc.

URCHUR

b: bircher.
l: lurcher.
n: nurture.
p: percher.
s: besmircher, searcher, smircher.
Plus hurt, you're *or* your, etc.
Cf. urchur.

URCHƏN

b: birchen.
    Cf. urchin.
    Cf. church hen, etc.

URCHƏNT

m: merchant.
p: perchant*.
    Plus myrrh chant, etc.
    Plus church ant *or* aunt, etc.

URCHƏS

p: purchase (*or* chas).
    Plus church ass, etc.
    Cf. her chase, etc.

URCHƏZ

b: birches.
ch: churches.
l: lurches.
p: perches.
s: researches, searches.
sm: besmirches, smirches.
    Cf. church is, etc.

URDBOOK

h: herdbook.
w: wordbook.
    Plus stirred book, etc.

URDĒ

b: birdy, birdie.
g: hurdy-gurdy.
k(c): curdy.
st: sturdy.
w: wordy.
    Plus heard, he, etc.

URDEST

g: begirdest*, engirdest*, girdest*.
h: heardest*, herdest*.
s: absurdest.

URDETH

g: begirdeth*, engirdeth*, girdeth*.
h: heardeth*, herdeth*.
    Plus stir death, etc.

URDIKT

v: verdict.

URDING

g: begirding, engirding, girding, ungirding.
h: herding.
w: wording.

URDJUR

v: verdure.
    Plus heard your *or* you're, etc.
    Cf. perjure.

URD'L

g: begirdle, engirdle, girdle, hurdle.
k(c): curdle.
    Plus word'll, etc.
    Cf. cur dull, etc.

URDSMITH

w: wordsmith.

URDZMƏN

h: herdsman.
w: wordsman.
    Plus birds, man, etc.

ŬRDƏD

g: begirded, engirded, girded.
h: herded.
k(c): curded.
sh: sherded.
w: worded.
Plus her dead, etc.
Plus bird, Ed, etc.

ŬRDƏN

b: burden, Burdon, disburden, overburden, unburden.
g: guerdon.
Plus heard an *or* on, etc.
Plus Jordan.
Cf. urden.

ŬRDƏR

b: Burder.
g: engirder, girder.
h: goat-herder, herder, sheep-herder.
m: murder, self-murder.
s: absurder.
th: thirder.

ŬRĒ

b: burry.
bl: blurry.
d: dhurrie+, durrie+.
f: firry, furry.
fl: flurry.
h: hurry.
hw: whirry.
k(c): Curie, curry.
l: lurry.
m: Murray.
s: surrey.
sk(sc): hurry-scurry, scurry.

sl: slurry.
w: worry.
Plus myrrh, he, etc.

ŬRĒD

fl: flurried, unflurried.
h: hurried, unhurried.
k(c): curried, uncurried.
sk(sc): scurried.
w: unworried, worried.
Cf. myrrh hid, etc.

ŬREST

Vowel: errest*.
bl: blurrest*.
f: conferrest*, deferrest*, inferrest*, preferrest*, referest*, transferrest*.
k(c): concurrest*, incurrest*.
m: demurrest*.
p: purrest*.
sh: shirrest*.
sl: slurrest*.
st: bestirrest*, stirrest*.
t: interrest*.
Cf. her rest, etc.

ŬRETH

Vowel: erreth*.
bl: blurreth*.
f: conferreth*, deferreth*, inferreth*, preferreth*, referreth*, transferreth*.
k(c): concurreth*, incurreth*.
m: demurreth*.
p: purreth*.
sh: shirreth*.
sl: slurreth*.
st: bestirreth*, stirreth*.
t: interreth*.

ŬRĒZ

fl: flurries.
h: hurries.
k(c): curries.
sk(sc): scurries.
w: worries.
    Plus surrey's, etc.
    Plus myrrh is, etc.

ŬRFĒ

d: Durfey.
m: Murphy.
s: surfy.
sk(sc): scurfy.
t: turfy.
    Plus her fee, etc.
    Plus serf, he, etc.

ŬRFIT

s: surfeit.
    Plus fir fit, etc.
    Plus turf it, etc.

ŬRF ̄M

p: perfume.
    Plus stir fume, etc.

ŬRFRĪ

st: stir-fry.

ŬRFƏKT

p: imperfect, perfect.

ŬRFƏS

s: resurface, surface.

ŬRGĀT

j: objurgate.
p: expurgate.
v: virgate.

Plus her gate, etc.
Plus erg eight *or* ate, etc.

ŬRGLƏR

b: burglar.
g: gurgler.

ŬRGŌ

t: atergo.
v: Virgo.

ŬRGR

b: burgher.
j: jerguer*.
    Plus erg her *or* err, etc.

ŬRGUS

Vowel: demiurgus.
m: Mergus.
t: thaumaturgus.
    Plus myrrh, Gus, etc.
    Plus erg us, etc.

ŬRGƏL

b: burgle.
g: gurgle.
    Plus erg'll, etc.
    Cf. her gull, etc.

ŬRIJ

k(c): courage, discourage, encourage.
m: demurrage.
    Cf. her age, etc.
    Cf. her rage, etc.

URIK

m: myrrhic.
    Cf. her rick, etc.

ŬRING

Vowel: erring, unerring.
bl: blurring.
f: conferring, deferring, inferring, preferring, referring, transferring.
g: Goering.
hw: whirring.
k(c): concurring, incurring, nonconcurring, occurring, recurring.
m: demurring.
p: purring.
sh: shirring.
sl: slurring.
sp: spurring.
st: astirring, bestirring, stirring.
t: disinterring, interring.
    Cf. herring.
    Cf. her ring, etc.

ŬRISH

b: burrish.
fl: flourish.
k(c): currish.
n: nourish, overnourish, undernourish.

ŬRISHT

fl: flourished.
n: nourished, overnourished, undernourished.

ŬRIT

t: turret.
    Cf. fir it, etc.

ŬRJĒ

Vowel: aciurgy, periergy*.
d: dirgie.
kl: clergy.

l: metalurgy.
t: dramaturgy, thaumaturgy.
    Plus urge, he, etc.

ŬRJEST

Vowel: urgest*.
d: dirgest*.
m: emergest*, mergest*, submergest*.
p: purgest*.
s: surgest*.
sk(sc): scourgest*.
spl: splurgest*.
v: convergest*, divergest*, vergest*.
    Plus her jest, etc.

ŬRJETH

Vowel: urgeth*.
d: dirgeth*.
m: emergeth*, mergeth*, submergeth*.
p: purgeth*.
s: surgeth*.
sk(sc): scourgeth.*
spl: splurgeth*.
v: convergeth*, divergeth*, vergeth*.

URJID

t: turgid.
    Cf. verge hid, etc.

ŬRJIK

Vowel: demiurgic, theurgic.
l: metallurgic.
n: energic.
r: chirurgic.
t: dramaturgic, liturgic, thaumaturgic.

ᴜ̆RJING

Vowel: urging.
d: dirging.
m: emerging, immerging, merging, submerging.
p: purging.
s: surging.
sk(sc): scourging.
spl: splurging.
v: converging, diverging, verging.

ᴜ̆RJIST

l: metallurgist.
t: dramaturgist, thaumaturgist.
  Plus her gist, etc.

URJ   S

v: verjuice.
  Plus myrrh juice, etc.

ᴜ̆RJᴜ̆R

Vowel: urger.
d: dirger.
m: emerger, merger, submerger.
p: perjure, purger.
sk(sc): scourger.
spl: splurger.
v: converger, diverger, verger.
  Plus dirge her *or* err, etc.
  Cf. verdure.
  Cf. urge her *or* err, etc.

ᴜ̆RJᴧN

b: burgeon.
s: surgeon.
sp: spurgeon.
st: sturgeon.
v: virgin.
  Plus her gin, etc.
  Plus serge in *or* inn, etc.

ᴜ̆RJᴧNS

m: emergence, submergence.
s: resurgence.
t: deturgence.
v: convergence, divergence.
  Plus her gents, etc.
  Cf. urge hence, etc.

ᴜ̆RJᴧNT

Vowel: urgent.
m: emergent.
s: assurgent, insurgent, resurgent.
spl: splurgent.
st: abstergent.
t: detergent, turgent.
v: convergent, divergent, vergent.
  Plus her gent, etc.

ᴜ̆RJᴧZ

Vowel: urges.
d: dirges.
m: emerges, merges, submerges.
n: Boanerges.
p: asperges, purges.
s: serges, surges.
sp: spurges.
spl: splurges.
v: converges, diverges, verges.
  Cf. serge is, etc.

ᴜ̆RKĒ

d: Durkee.
j: herky-jerky, jerky.
kw: quirky.
l: lurky.
m: mirky, murky.
p: perky.
sh: shirky.
sm: smirky.

t: talk turkey, turkey.
 Plus work, he, etc.
 Plus her key, etc.

URKEST

j: jerkest*.
kl: clerkest*.
l: lurkest*.
sh: shirkest*.
sm: smirkest*.
w: workest*.

URKETH

j: jerketh*.
kl: clerketh*.
l: lurketh*.
sh: shirketh*.
sm: smirketh*.
w: worketh*.

URKFER

w: workfare.

URKIN

f: firkin.
g: gherkin.
j: jerkin.
m: merkin*.
 Plus work in *or* inn, etc.
 Plus her kin, etc.

URKINZ

f: Firkins.
p: Perkins.
 Plus urkin+s.
 Plus her kin's, etc.
 Plus work inns *or* ins, etc.

URKING

j: jerking.
kl: clerking.

l: lurking.
p: perking.
sh: shirking.
sm: smirking.
w: aworking, hard-working, working.
 Plus her king, etc.

URKISH

kw: quirkish.
t: Turkish.

URKIT

s: circuit.
 Plus her kit, etc.
 Plus work it, etc.

URKLĒ

kl: clerkly.
s: circly.
 Plus work, Lee *or* lea, etc.

URKLING

s: circling.
 Plus her cling, etc.

URKLƏT

s: circlet.
 Plus Turk let *or* Lett, etc.

URKMƏN

t: Turkman.
w: workman.
 Plus shirk, man, etc.

URKOIZ

t: turquoise.

URKSHÔP

w: Santa's workshop, sheltered workshop, workshop.

URKSƏM

Vowel: irksome.
m: mirksome.
    Plus work some, etc.
    Cf. works 'em, etc.

URKUR

b: burker.
j: jerker, jerquer.
l: lurker.
sh: shirker.
sm: smirker.
w: wonder worker, worker.
    Plus work her *or* err, etc.
    Plus her cur, etc.

URKUS

f: bifurcous.
kw: Quercus.
s: circus.
    Plus her cuss, etc.
    Plus work us, etc.
    Cf. work house.

URKƏL

m: Merkle.
p: Lupercal.
s: circle, encircle, quality circle, semicircle.
t: turkle.
v: novercal.
    Plus work'll, etc.
    Cf. urk'l.

URLDLĒ

w: unwordly, worldly.
    Plus furled, Lee *or* lea, etc.

URLDLING

w: worldling.

URLĒ

Vowel: early.
b: Burleigh, burly, hurly-burly.
ch: churly.
g: girlie, girly.
h: Hurley.
hw: whirly.
k(c): curly.
n: knurly*.
p: pearly*.
s: surly.
sw: swirly.
sh: Shirley.
tw: twirly.
    Plus her, Lee *or* lea, etc.

URLEST

f: furlest*, unfurlest*.
h: hurlest*.
hw: whirlest*.
k(c): curlest*.
sw: swirlest*.
tw: twirlest*.
    Plus myrrh, lest, etc.

URLETH

f: furleth*, unfurleth*.
h: hurleth*.
hw: whirleth*.
k(c): curleth*.
sw: swirleth*.
tw: twirleth*.

URLHOOD

g: girlhood
    Plus whirl hood, etc.

URLIN

m: merlin.
p: pearlin.

Plus pearl in *or* inn, etc.
Plus her, Lynn, etc.

URLING

f: furling, unfurling.
h: herling, hurling.
hw: upwhirling, whirling.
k(c): curling, uncurling, upcurling.
p: pearling, purling.
sk: skirling.
sp: Sperling.
st: sterling, Stirling.
sw: swirling.
tw: twirling.

URLISH

ch: churlish.
g: girlish.
p: pearlish.

URLOIN

p: purloin.
s: sirloin.
    Plus her loin, etc.

URL

k(c): curlew.
p: purlieu.
    Plus Pearl, who, etc.
    Plus myrrh, Lou *or* loo, etc.

URLUR

b: burler.
f: furler.
h: hurler.
hw: whirler
k(c): curler.
p: pearler, purler.

sk: skirler.
sw: swirler.
tw: twirler.
    Plus whirl her, etc.

URLƏ

l: schefflera.

URMĀD

m: mermaid.
    Plus her maid *or* made, etc.

URMAN

f: firman.
g: cousin german, German.
m: merman.
s: sermon.
    Plus her man, etc.

URMĒ

d: taxidermy.
g: germy.
n: Nurmi.
w: wormy.
    Plus firm, he, etc.
    Plus stir me, etc.

URMEST

f: confirmest*, firmest, infirmest.
skw: squirmest*.
t: termest*.
w: wormest*.
    Plus purr messed, etc.

URMETH

f: confirmeth*.
skw: squirmeth*.
t: termeth*.
w: wormeth*.

ŬRMĒZ

h: Hermes.
k: kermes.
　Plus term ease *or* E's, etc.

ŬRMƏ

Vowel: Irma.
b: Burma.
d: derma.
f: terra firma.
s: syrma.
w: Burma-Wurma.
　Plus term a, etc.

ŬRMƏL

d: dermal, epidermal, hypodermal, pachydermal, taxidermal.
th: diathermal, geothermal, hydrothermal, isogeothermal, isothermal, synthermal, thermal.
　Plus squirm, Al, etc.

ŬRMƏNS

f: affirmance, confirmance, disaffirmance.
　Plus her manse, etc.
　Plus term aunts *or* ants, etc.

ŬRMƏNT

f: affirmant, deferment, ferment, preferment, referment.
t: determent, disinterment, interment.
v: averment.
　Plus myrrh meant, etc.

ŬRMĪK

d: dermic, endermic, epidermic, hydrodermic, hypodermic, pachydermic, sclerodermic, taxidermic.
th: adiathermic, diathermic, geothermic, isogeothermic, thermic.
　Plus her Mick, etc.

ŬRMIN

Vowel: ermine.
d: determine.
v: vermin.
　Plus worm in *or* inn, etc.
　Plus stir Min, etc.
　Cf. urman.

ŬRMIND

Vowel: ermined.
t: determined, undetermined.
　Plus worm inned, etc.

ŬRMING

f: affirming, confirming, firming.
skw: squirming.
t: terming.
w: worming.
　Plus her Ming, etc.

ŬRMIS

d: dermis, epidermis.
　Plus her miss, etc.

ŬRMISH

sk: skirmish.
w: wormish.

ŬRMIT

h: hermit.
p: permit.
　Plus term it, etc.
　Plus her mitt, etc.

ŪRMĪT

t: termite.

Plus myrrh might *or* mite, etc.

ŪRMLĒ

f: firmly.

t: termly.

Plus squirm, Lee *or* lea, etc.

ŪRMOIL

t: turmoil.

Plus her moil, etc.

Plus sperm oil, etc.

ŪRMŪR

f: affirmer, confirmer, firmer, infirmer.

m: bemurmur, murmur.

skw: squirmer.

t: termer, termor.

w: wormer.

Plus squirm her, etc.

Plus her myrrh, etc.

ŪRNÄRD

b: Bernard.

Plus myrrh, nard, etc.

Cf. burn hard, etc.

ŪRNĀT

t: alternate, subalternate, ternate.

th: cothurnate.

Plus tern ate *or* eight, etc.

Plus her, Nate, etc.

ŪRNĒ

b: Berney, Birney, burny-burny.

f: ferny.

g: Gurney.

j: journey.

t: attorney, tourney, Turney.

Plus earn, he, etc.

Plus her knee, etc.

ŪRNED

l: learned, unlearned.

Plus urn+ed*.

ŪRNEST

Vowel: earnest, Ernest, overearnest.

b: burnest*.

ch: churnest*.

j: adjournest*, sojournest*.

l: learnest*.

s: concernest*, discernest*.

sp: spurnest*.

st: sternest.

t: overturnest*, returnest*, turnest*.

y: yearnest*.

Plus her nest, etc.

Cf. erne nest, etc.

ŪRNETH

Vowel: earneth*.

b: burneth*.

ch: churneth*.

j: adjourneth*, sojourneth*.

l: learneth*.

s: concerneth*, discerneth*.

sp: spurneth*.

t: overturneth*, returneth*, turneth*.

y: yearneth*.

z: discerneth*.

ŪRNING

Vowel: earning, urning.

b: burning, heart-burning, overburning, sunburning.

ch: churning.

j: adjourning, sojourning.

l: book learning, learning, unlearning.

s: concerning, discerning, undiscerning.

sp: spurning.

t: overturning, returning, table-turning, turning, upturning.

y: yearning.

z: discerning, undiscerning.

ŪRNISH

b: burnish.

f: furnish.

ŪRNISHT

b: burnished, unburnished.

f: furnished, unfurnished.

ŪRNKĒ

t: turnkey

ŪRNMƏNT

j: adjournment, sojournment.

s: concernment, discernment, secernment.

t: attornment.

z: discernment.

Plus erne meant, etc.

ŪRNŌ

f: inferno.

st: Sterno.

Plus burn owe *or* O, etc.

Plus fir no *or* know, etc.

ŪRNOUT

b: burnout.

ŪRNUM

b: laburnum.

Plus turn 'em, etc.

Plus her numb, etc.

ŪRNŪR

Vowel: earner.

b: back burner, barn burner, burner.

j: adjourner, sojourner.

l: learner.

s: discerner.

sp: spurner.

st: sterner.

t: overturner, returner, turner.

y: yearner.

z: discerner.

Plus burn her *or* err, etc.

ŪRNƏ

m: Myrna.

sm: Smyrna.

v: taverna, Verna.

Plus turn a, etc.

ŪRNƏL

Vowel: diurnal, hodiernal, semidiurnal, urnal.

b: hibernal.

f: infernal, paraphernal.

j: journal.

k(c): colonel, kernel.

p: supernal.

s: lucernal.

st: sternal.

t: coeternal, diuternal, eternal, external, fraternal, hesternal,

internal, maternal, nocturnal,
paternal, sempiternal.

v: cavernal, vernal.

Plus burn, Al, etc.

ᴜRN∂NT

s: secernant.

t: alternant.

v: vernant.

Plus turn aunt *or* ant, etc.

ᴜRN∂S

f: furnace, Furness.

s: sternness.

th: cothurnus.

Plus burn us, etc.

Plus turn S, etc.

Cf. burn ace, etc.

ᴜRŌ

b: borough, burrow.

f: furrow.

th: thorough.

Plus her owe *or* O, etc.

Cf. her roe *or* row, etc.

ᴜRŌD

b: burrowed.

f: furrowed, unfurrowed.

Plus her ode, etc.

Cf. her road *or* rode, etc.

ᴜRŌZ

b: Burroughs, Burrows.

Plus uro+s.

Plus her rows *or* roes, etc.

ᴜRPENT

s: serpent.

Plus her pent, etc.

ᴜRPEST

b: burpest*.

ch: chirpest*.

z: usurpest*.

Plus her pest, etc.

ᴜRPETH

b: burpeth*.

ch: chirpeth*.

t: turpeth.

z: usurpeth*.

ᴜRPĒZ

b: Burpee's.

Plus deter peas, etc.

ᴜRPING

b: burping.

ch: chirping.

z: usurping.

Plus her ping, etc.

ᴜRP'L

p: empurple, purple.

Plus chirp'll, etc.

Cf. her pull, etc.

ᴜRPᴜR

b: burper.

ch: chirper.

z: usurper.

Plus twirp err *or* her, etc.

ᴜRP∂S

p: purpose.

Plus her puss, etc.

Cf. chirp us, etc.

U̶RSĒ

m: gramercy, mercy, Mersey.
p: Percy, pursy.
s: Circe, Searcy.
v: controversy.
　Plus her see, etc.
　Plus purse, he, etc.

U̶RSED

k(c): accursed.
　Plus urs+d*.

U̶RSEST

Vowel: coercest*.
b: disbursest*, reimbursest*.
h: rehearsest*.
k(c): accursest*, becursest*, cursest*.
m: immersest*.
n: nursest*.
p: dispersest*.
sp: interspersest*.
v: conversest*, reversest*, traversest*.

URSET

t: tercet.
　Plus her set, etc.
　Cf. nurse it, etc.

U̶RSETH

Vowel: coerceth*.
b: disburseth*, reimburseth*.
h: rehearseth*.
k(c): accurseth*, becurseth*, curseth*.
m: immerseth*.
n: nurseth*.
p: disperseth*.

sp: intersperseth*.
v: converseth*, reverseth*, traverseth*.
　Plus her, Seth, etc.

U̶RSHIP

w: worship.
　Plus her ship, etc.

U̶RSHUM

t: nasturtium.
　Plus Hirsch 'em, etc.

U̶RSHUN

Vowel: coercion.
k(c): discursion, excursion, incursion, recursion.
m: demersion, emersion, immersion, mersion*, submersion.
p: apertion*, aspersion, dispersion.
s: assertion, concertion*, disconcertion, insertion, intersertion*, self-assertion.
sp: inpersion*, interspersion.
st: abstersion.
t: extersion*, nasturtion, tertian.
v: animadversion, aversion, circumversion*, contraversion, controversion, conversion, diversion, eversion, introversion, obversion, perversion, retroversion, reversion, subversion, version.
z: desertion, exertion.
　Plus fur shun, etc.
　Cf. ursian.

U̶RSHƏL

m: commercial, uncommercial.
t: tertial.
v: controversial.

Plus myrrh shall, etc.
Plus Hirsch, Al, etc.

ᴜʀsɪɴɢ

Vowel: coercing.
b: disbursing, reimbursing.
h: rehearsing.
k(c): accursing, becursing, cursing.
m: immersing.
n: nursing.
p: dispersing.
v: conversing, reversing, transversing, traversing, versing.
  Plus her sing, etc.

ᴜʀsɪᴠ

Vowel: coercive.
k(c): cursive, decursive, discursive, excursive, incursive, precursive.
p: aspersive, dispersive.
st: abstersive.
t: detersive.
v: animadversive, aversive, conversive, eversive, perversive, subversive.
  Plus her sieve, etc.

ᴜʀsᴍəɴᴛ

b: disbursement, imbursement, reimbursement.
m: amercement.
  Plus purse meant, etc.

ᴜʀsɴəs

t: terseness.
v: adverseness, averseness, perverseness.

ᴜʀsᴛē

th: thirsty.

Plus burst, he, etc.
Plus worse tea, etc.

ᴜʀsᴛᴇsᴛ

b: burstest*.
th: thirstest*.
w: worstest*.
  Plus purse test, etc.

ᴜʀsᴛᴇᴛʜ

b: bursteth*.
th: thirsteth*.
w: worsteth*.

ᴜʀsᴛɪɴɢ

b: bursting.
th: thirsting.
w: worsting.

ᴜʀsᴛᴋās

w: worst-case.

ᴜʀsᴛᴜʀ

b: burster.
th: thirster.
w: worster.
  Plus her stir, etc.
  Plus cursed her *or* err, etc.

ᴜʀsᴛəᴅ

b: bursted.
th: thirsted.
w: worsted.
  Plus first, Ed, etc.
  Plus purse, Ted, etc.
  Plus her stead, etc.

ᴜʀsᴜʀ

Vowel: coercer.
b: bursar, disburser, reimburser.
h: hearser, rehearser.

k(c): accurser, antecursor*, curser, cursor, precursor.

m: amercer, commercer, immerser, mercer.

n: nurser.

p: disperser, purser.

v: converser, perverser, reverser, traverser, verser.

w: worser.

Plus curse her, etc.

URSUS

Vowel: ursus.

k(c): excursus.

th: thyrsus.

v: versus.

Plus curse us, etc.

URSƏ

Vowel: ursa.

v: vice-versa.

Plus immerse a, etc.

URSƏL

Vowel: ursal.

h: rehearsal.

t: tercel.

v: controversal, reversal, transversal, universal, versal*.

Plus curse, Al, etc.

Plus her Sal, etc.

URSƏN

f: McPherson.

g: Gerson.

p: anchor person, chair person, lay person, person.

Plus her son, etc.

URSƏNT

k(c): recursant.

v: aversant, versant.

Plus curse aunt *or* ant, etc.

URSƏZ

Vowel: coerces.

b: disburses, reimburses.

h: hearses, rehearses.

k(c): accurses, becurses, curses.

m: amerces, immerses, submerses.

n: nurses.

p: disperses, purses.

sp: intersperses.

t: terces.

v: converses, reverses, traverses, verses.

Plus myrrh says, etc.

Plus hearse, Ez, etc.

URTDRES

sh: shirtdress.

URTĒ

ch: cherty.

d: dirty.

fl: flirty.

g: Gertie.

th: thirty.

Plus hurt, he, etc.

Plus her tea, etc.

URTĒN

th: thirteen.

Plus spurt e'en*, etc.

URTEST

bl: blurtest*.

h: hurtest*.

k(c): curtest.

p: pertest.

s: assertest*, concertest*, disconcertest*, insertest*.

sk: skirtest*.

skw: squirtest*.

sp: spurtest*.

v: advertest*, avertest*, controvertest*, convertest*, divertest*, invertest*, pervertest*, revertest*, subvertest*.

z: desertest*, exertest*.

Plus her test, etc.

URTETH

bl: blurteth*.

h: hurteth*.

s: asserteth*, concerteth*, disconcerteth*, inserteth*.

sk: skirteth*.

skw: squirteth*.

sp: spurteth.

v: adverteth*, averteth*, controverteth*, converteth*, diverteth*, inverteth*, perverteth*, reverteth*, subverteth*.

z: deserteth*, exerteth*.

URTHĒ

Vowel: earthy.

w: noteworthy, seaworthy, trustworthy, unworthy, worthy.

Plus worth, he, etc.

Cf. stir the _or_ thee*, etc.

URTHEST

f: furthest.

URTHFOOL

m: mirthful.

w: worthful.

Plus berth full, etc.

URTHLƏS

b: birthless.

m: mirthless.

w: worthless.

Plus earth less _or_ Les, etc.

URTHUR

f: further.

URTHƏ

b: Bertha.

h: Hertha.

Plus worth a, etc.

URTHƏN

Vowel: earthen.

b: burthen, disburthen, unburthen.

Plus myrrh then, etc.

Cf. mirth, hen, etc.

URTING

bl: blurting.

fl: flirting.

h: hurting.

s: asserting, concerting, disconcerting, inserting, interserting, preconcerting, self-asserting.

sh: shirting, unshirting.

sk: skirting, unskirting.

skw: squirting.

sp: spurting.

v: adverting, averting, controverting, converting, diverting, interverting, inverting, perverting, retroverting, reverting, subverting.

z: deserting, exerting.

URTIS

k(c): Curtis.

Cf. Gertie's, hurt his, etc.

URTIV

f: furtive.

s: assertive, self-assertive.

v: divertive, revertive.

z: exertive.

ÛRT'L

f: fertile.
h: hurtle.
hw: whortle.
k: kirtle.
m: myrtle.
sp: spurtle.
t: turtle.
  Plus squirt'll, etc.
  Cf. her, till, etc.

ÛRTLĒ

Vowel: inertly.
k(c): curtly.
l: alertly.
p: expertly, inexpertly, pertly.
  Plus hurt, Lee *or* lea, etc.

ÛRTLƏS

sh: shirtless.
sk: skirtless.
  Plus hurt, Les *or* less, etc.

ÛRTNƏS

Vowel: inertness.
k(c): curtness.
l: alertness.
p: expertness, inexpertness,
  pertness.

ÛRTR   D

g: Gertrude.
  Plus Bert, rude, etc.

ÛRTSĒ

k(c): curtsey.
  Plus Bert, see, etc.

ÛRTÛR

bl: blurter.
fl: flirter.

h: hurter.
k(c): curter.
p: perter.
s: asserter, disconcerter, inserter,
  preconcerter.
skw: squirter.
sp: spurter.
v: adverter, animadverter, averter,
  catalytic converter, converter,
  diverter, inverter, perverter,
  subverter.
z: exerter.
  Plus hurt her, etc.

ÛRTƏ

b: Alberta, Elberta.
  Plus pert a, etc.

ÛRTƏD

bl: blurted.
fl: flirted.
kw: quirted.
s: asserted, concerted, discon-
  certed, inserted, interserted,
  preconcerted.
sh: shirted, unshirted.
sk: skirted, unskirted.
skw: squirted.
sp: spurted.
v: adverted, averted, converted,
  diverted, inverted, perverted,
  reverted, subverted, undiverted,
  unperverted.
z: deserted, exerted.
  Plus her Ted, etc.
  Plus hurt Ed, etc.

ÛRTƏN

b: Berton.
g: Gurton.
k(c): curtain, encurtain.
l: Lurton.

m: Merton.
s: certain, incertain*, uncertain.
   Plus chert on *or* an, etc.
   Plus her ton *or* tun, etc.
   Plus hurt an *or* on, etc.
   Cf. her tan, etc.

ƱRTƏNS

v: advertence, inadvertence, misadvertence.
   Plus her tents *or* tense, etc.
   Cf. squirt, hence, etc.

ƱRUP

st: stirup.
   Plus her up, etc.
   Cf. irup.

ƱRƱR

bl: blurrer.
f: conferrer, deferrer, inferrer, preferrer, transferrer.
k(c): concurrer, incurrer.
m: demurrer.
p: purrer.
sh: shirrer.
sl: slurrer.
sp: spurrer.
st: bestirrer, stirrer.
t: interrer.
v: averrer.
   Plus spur her *or* err, etc.

ƱRUS

s: susurrous.
w: wurrus.
   Plus blur us, etc.

ƱRVĀT

k(c): curvate, incurvate, recurvate.

n: enervate, trinervate.
s: acervate.
   Plus conserve eight *or* ate, etc.

ƱRVĒ

n: nervy.
sk(sc): scurvy.
t: topsy-turvy.
   Plus swerve, he, etc.

ƱRVĒN

n: nervine+.

ƱRVEST

k(c): curvest*.
n: unnervest*.
s: conservest*, servest*.
sw: swervest*.
z: deservest*, observest*, preservest*, reservest*.
   Plus her vest, etc.

ƱRVETH

k(c): curveth*.
n: unnerveth*.
s: conserveth*, serveth*.
sw: swerveth*.
z: deserveth*, observeth*, preserveth*, reserveth*.

ƱRVID

f: fervid, perfervid.
t: topsy-turvied.
   Cf. curve hid, etc.

ƱRVIL

ch: chervil.
s: servile.
   Plus curve ill, etc.
   Cf. swerve hill, etc.

URVĪL

s: servile.

Plus her vile, etc.

Plus swerve, I'll, isle *or* aisle, etc.

URVIN

n: nervine+.

s: cervine.

Plus swerve in *or* inn, etc.

URVING

Vowel: Irving.

k(c): curving, incurving, outcurving.

n: nerving, unnerving.

s: conserving, serving, time-serving.

sw: swerving, unswerving.

z: deserving, observing, preserving, reserving, undeserving, unobserving.

URVIS

p: Purvis.

s: disservice, interservice, lip service, merchant service, sea service, service, unservice.

URVLƏS

k(c): curveless.

n: nerveless.

sw: swerveless.

Plus deserve less, etc.

URVUR

f: fervor.

n: nerver, unnerver.

s: conserver, server, time-server.

sw: swerver.

z: deserver, game preserver, life preserver, observer, preserver, reserver.

Plus swerve her *or* err, etc.

URVUS

k(c): recurvous.

n: nervous.

Plus swerve us, etc.

URVƏ

n: Minerva, Nerva.

Plus serve a, etc.

URVƏL

k(c): curval*.

s: acerval*.

Plus swerve, Al, etc.

URVƏNS

f: fervence*.

z: inobservance, observance, unobservance.

Plus stir Vance *or* vents, etc.

Plus swerve ants *or* aunts, etc.

Cf. urvant+s.

URVƏNT

f: fervent.

k(c): curvant, recurvant.

s: conservant, servant.

z: inobservant, observant, unobservant.

Plus stir vent, etc.

Plus swerve aunt *or* ant, etc.

URWIN

Vowel: Erwin, Irwin.

m: Merwin.

Plus her win *or* Wynn, etc.

ᵁRZDĀ

th: Thursday.

Plus furze day *or* dey, etc.

ᵁRZĒ

f: furzy.
j: jersey.
k: kersey.
m: Mersey.

Plus furze, he, etc.
Plus stir Zee *or* Z, etc.

ᵁRZHUN

k(c): discursion, excursion, incursion.
m: demersion.
p: aspersion, dispersion, Persian.
v: animadversion, aversion, conversion, diversion, introversion, inversion, perversion, reversion, subversion, version.

ᵁRZHƏ

p: Persia.

ᵁRƏL

b: Burrell.
skw: rock squirrel, squirrel.

Cf. irel.

ᵁRƏNS

k(c): concurrence, incurrence, intercurrence, occurrence, recurrence.
f: transference.
t: deterrence.

Plus her rents, etc.

ᵁRƏNT

k(c): Benguela Current, concurrent, currant, current, decurrent, intercurrent, recurrent, undercurrent.
s: susurrant.
t: deterrent.

Plus fir rent, etc.
Plus stir aunt *or* ant, etc.

ᵁRƏT

t: turret.

Cf. fir it, etc.

USCHUN

b: combustion.
d: adustion*.
f: fustian.

USĒ

f: fussy.
h: hussy.
m: mussy.

Plus cuss, he, etc.

USEST

b: bussest*.
k(c): cussest*, discussest*.
f: fussest*.
m: mussest*.
tr: trussest*.

USETH

b: busseth*.
k(c): cusseth*, discusseth*.
f: fusseth*.
m: musseth*.
tr: trusseth*.

USHĒ

bl: blushy.
br: brushy.
g: gushy.

l: lushy.
m: mushy.
r: rushy.
sl: slushy.
  Plus crush, he, etc.

USHEST

bl: blushest*.
br: brushest*.
fl: flushest*.
g: gushest*.
h: hushest*.
kr: crushest*.
r: rushest*.

USHETH

bl: blusheth*.
br: brusheth*.
fl: flusheth*.
g: gusheth*.
h: husheth*.
kr: crusheth*.
r: rusheth*.

USHING

bl: blushing, unblushing.
br: brushing.
fl: flushing.
g: gushing.
h: hushing.
kr: crushing.
l: lushing.
r: onrushing, rushing, uprushing.

USHUN

k: concussion, discussion, incussion, percussion, recussion, repercussion, succussion.
pr: Prussian.
r: Russian.

USHŲR

Vowel: usher.
bl: blusher.
br: brusher.
fl: flusher, four-flusher.
g: gusher.
h: husher.
kr: crusher.
l: lusher.
m: musher.
pl: plusher.
r: rusher.
  Plus crush her *or* err, etc.

USHUS

l: luscious.
  Plus crush us, etc.

USHƏ

pr: Prussia.
r: Russia.
  Plus crush a, etc.

USHƏN

pr: Prussian.
r: Russian.
  Plus crush an *or* Ann, etc.

USHƏZ

bl: blushes.
br: brushes.
fl: flushes.
g: gushes.
h: hushes.
kr: crushes.
l: lushes.
m: mushes.
pl: plushes.
r: onrushes, rushes, uprushes.

t: tushes.
thr: thrushes.
Plus hush, Ez, etc.

USING

b: busing, bussing.
f: fussing.
k(c): cussing, discussing.
m: mussing.
tr: trussing, untrussing.

USIV

k(c): concussive, discussive,
percussive, repercussive,
successive.
Cf. muss sieve, etc.

USKĀT

f: infuscate, obfuscate.
r: coruscate.
Plus muss Kate, etc.
Plus musk ate *or* eight, etc.

USKĒ

d: dusky.
h: husky.
m: musky.
t: tusky.
Plus musk, he, etc.
Plus thus key, etc.

USKEST

d: duskest*.
h: huskest*.

USKETH

d: dusketh*.
h: husketh*.

USKIN

b: buskin.
r: Ruskin.

Plus thus kin, etc.
Plus husk in *or* inn, etc.

USKING

d: dusking.
h: husking.
t: tusking.
Plus muss king, etc.

USKŌŌL

j: majuscule.
n: minuscule.
p: crepuscule, opuscule.
Plus husk, you'll, etc.
Cf. us cool, etc.

USKUR

h: husker.
t: tusker.
Plus tusk her *or* err, etc.
Plus muss cur, etc.

USKƏN

d: dusken.
kr: Della Cruscan.
l: molluscan.
t: Tuscan.
tr: Etruscan.
Plus buscan, etc.
Plus musk an, etc.

USKƏT

b: busket.
m: musket.

US'L

b: bustle.
h: hustle.
j: justle.
m: muscle, mussel.
p: corpuscle, opuscle.

r: rustle.
t: tussle.
  Plus muss'll, etc.
  Cf. thus sell, etc.

USLEST

b: bustlest*.
h: hustlest*.
r: rustlest*.
t: tusslest*.
  Plus crust, lest, etc.

USLETH

b: bustleth*.
h: hustleth*.
r: rustleth*.
t: tussleth*.

USLING

b: bustling.
h: hustling.
m: muscling.
r: rustling.
t: tussling.
  Cf. us sling, etc.

USLUR

b: bustler.
h: hustler.
r: rustler.
t: tussler.

US'LZ

br: Brussels.
  Plus us'l+s.

USTĀT

kr: incrustate.
  Plus just ate *or* eight.
  Plus muss, Tate, etc.

USTĒ

b: busty.
d: dusty.
f: fustie, fusty.
g: gusty.
kr: crusty.
l: lusty.
m: musty.
r: rusty.
tr: trusty.
  Plus bust, he, etc.

USTEST

b: robustest.
d: dustest*.
g: disgustest*.
j: adjustest*, justest.
kr: encrustest*.
l: lustest*.
r: rustest*.
thr: thrustest*.
tr: distrustest*, entrustest*,
mistrustest*, trustest*.
  Plus fuss test, etc.

USTETH

d: dusteth*.
g: disgusteth*.
j: adjusteth*.
kr: encrusteth*.
l: lusteth*.
r: rusteth*.
thr: thrusteth*.
tr: distrusteth*, entrusteth*,
mistrusteth*, trusteth*.

USTFOOL

l: lustful.
tr: distrustful, mistrustful,
overtrustful, trustful, untrustful.
  Plus just full, etc.

USTIK

f: fustic.
r: rustic.
   Plus us tin, etc.

USTIN

d: Dustin.
j: Justin.
   Plus rust in *or* inn, etc.
   Plus us tin, etc.

USTING

b: busting.
d: bedusting, dusting.
g: disgusting.
j: adjusting, coadjusting, self-adjusting.
kr: crusting, encrusting.
l: lusting.
r: rusting.
thr: thrusting.
tr: betrusting, distrusting, entrusting, mistrusting, overtrusting, trusting, unmistrusting.

USTINGZ

d: dustings.
h: hustings.
l: lustings.
thr: thrustings.

USTIS

j: injustice, justice.
k(c): Custis.
   Cf. dust is, etc.
   Cf. rusty's, etc.

USTIV

b: combustive.
j: adjustive.

USTLĒ

b: robustly.
g: augustly.
j: justly, unjustly.
   Plus must, Lee *or* lea, etc.

USTMƏNT

j: adjustment, maladjustment.
kr: encrustment.
   Plus rust meant, etc.

USTNƏS

b: robustness.
g: augustness.
j: justness.

USTŌ

b: basso robusto, robusto.
g: gusto.
   Plus just owe *or* O, etc.
   Plus muss toe, etc.

USTRĀT

fr: frustate.
l: illustrate.
   Plus must rate, etc.
   Plus fuss trait, etc.
   Cf. cuss straight, etc.

USTRIN

k(c): lacustrine.
l: palustrine.

USTRUM

fl: flustrum.
l: lustrum.
   Plus must rum, etc.
   Cf. us strum, etc.

USTRUS

bl: blustrous.
l: lustrous.

USTRƏL

k(c): lacustral.
l: lustral, palustral.

USTUM

k(c): custom.
r: Rustum.
　　Plus bust 'em, etc.

USTƱR

b: buster, filibuster, robuster, trust buster.
bl: bluster.
d: duster, knuckle duster.
fl: fluster.
j: adjuster, coadjuster, juster.
k(c): Custer.
kl: cluster.
l: lacklustre, luster, lustre.
m: muster.
thr: thruster.
tr: distruster, truster.
　　Plus thrust her *or* err, etc.

USTƱRD

b: bustard.
bl: blustered.
fl: flustered.
k(c): custard.
kl: clustered.
l: lustered.
m: Dijon mustard, mustard, mustered.
　　Plus Custer'd, etc.
　　Cf. just stirred, etc.

USTUS

g: Augustus.
j: Justus.
　　Plus fussed us, etc.

USTƏ

g: Augusta.
j: Justa.
　　Plus must a, etc.

USTƏD

b: busted, combusted.
d: bedusted, dusted.
f: fusted.
g: disgusted.
j: adjusted, coadjusted, self-adjusted.
kr: crusted, encrusted.
l: lusted.
r: rusted.
tr: betrusted, distrusted, entrusted, mistrusted, overtrusted, trusted.
　　Plus must, Ed, etc.
　　Plus fuss, Ted, etc.

USƱR

f: fusser.
k(c): cusser, discusser.
m: musser.
tr: trusser.
　　Plus fuss her *or* err, etc.
　　Cf. fuss, sir, etc.

USƏT

g: gusset.
r: russet.
　　Cf. discuss it, etc.
　　Cf. bus set, etc.

USƏZ

b: buses, busses.
f: fusses.
k(c): cusses, discusses.
m: musses.
tr: trusses, untrusses.
    Plus Gus's, etc.
    Plus buss, Ez, etc.

UTĒ

b: butty.
g: gutty.
j: jutty.
n: nutty.
p: putty, Silly Putty.
r: rutty.
sm: smutty.
t: tutty.
    Plus but he, etc.

UTEST

b: abuttest*, buttest*, rebuttest*.
g: guttest*.
gl: gluttest*.
j: juttest*.
p: puttest*.
r: ruttest*.
str: struttest*.
    Cf. smut test, etc.

UTETH

b: abutteth*, butteth*, rebutteth*.
g: gutteth*.
gl: glutteth*.
j: jutteth*.
p: putteth*.
r: rutteth*.
str: strutteth*.

UTHING

d: dothing*.
n: nothing.

UTHUR

Vowel: other.
br: brother, Charter brother, foster brother, half brother, lodge brother.
m: carth mother, foremother, foster mother, mother, step-mother.
n: another.
sm: smother.
t: tother.

UTHURN

s: Sothern, southern.

UTING

b: abutting, butting, rebutting.
g: gutting.
gl: glutting.
j: jutting.
k(c): cross-cutting, cutting, glass cutting.
n: nutting.
p: putting.
r: rutting.
sh: shutting.
str: strutting.

UTISH

r: ruttish.
sl: sluttish.

UT'L

b: abuttal, rebuttal.
g: guttle.

k(c): cuttle.
r: ruttle.
s: subtle, suttle.
sh: shuttle.
sk(sc): scuttle.
t: Tuttle.
   Plus Tutt'll, etc.

UTLEST

s: suttlest*.
sk(sc): scuttlest*.
   Plus cut, lest, etc.

UTLETH

s: suttleth*.
sk(sc): scuttleth*.

UTLING

g: guttling.
s: sutling.
sk(sc): scuttling.

UTLƱR

b: butler.
k(c): cutler.
s: subtler, sutler.
sk(sc): scuttler.

UTLƏS

k(c): cutlass.
   Plus strut, lass, etc.

UTLƏT

k(c): cutlet.
   Plus butt Lett or let, etc.

UTÔF

k(c): cutoff+.

UTRƏS

b: buttress.
   Plus cut trees, etc.

UTƱR

Vowel: utter.
b: abutter, bread-and-butter, butter, lemon butter, peanut butter, rebutter.
f: futter.
fl: flutter.
g: gutter.
gl: glutter.
k(c): cutter, pilot cutter, woodcutter.
kl: clutter.
m: mutter.
n: nutter.
p: putter.
r: rutter.
s: sutter.
sh: shutter.
sk(sc): scutter.
sp: sputter.
spl: splutter.
st: stutter.
str: strutter.
   Plus but her or err, etc.

UTƱRD

Vowel: uttered, unuttered.
   Plus utur+ed.

UTWƱRK

sk(sc): scut work.

UTƏD

b: abutted, butted, rebutted.
g: gutted.

gl: glutted.
j: jutted.
p: putted.
r: rutted.
str: strutted.
Plus strut, Ed, etc.

UTƏN

b: bachelor button, button.
d: Dutton.
gl: glutton.
h: Hutton.
m: mutton.
n: nut'n
s: Sutton.
Plus strut on *or* an, etc.

UVBUG

l: love bug.

UVĒ

d: dovey, lovey-dovey.
k(c): covey.
l: lovey.
Plus shove he, etc.

UVEST

gl: glovest*, unglovest*.
l: lovest*.
sh: shovest*.

UVETH

gl: gloveth*, ungloveth*.
l: loveth*.
sh: shoveth*.

UVHĀT

l: love-hate.

UVING

gl: gloving, ungloving.
l: loving, self-loving, unloving.
sh: shoving.

UVLĪF

l: love life.

UVLƏS

gl: gloveless.
l: loveless.
Plus shove, Les *or* less, etc.

UVUR

gl: glover.
k(c): cover, discover, recover, rediscover, tablecover, uncover.
l: lover.
pl: plover.
sh: shover.
Plus love her *or* err, etc.

UVURN

g: govern.
Plus love urn, erne, *or* earn, etc.

UVƏD

l: beloved.
Plus uv+d*.
Plus shove, Ed, etc.

UVƏL

sh: shovel.
sk(sc): scovel.
Plus dove'll, etc.
Cf. ovel.

UVƏN

Vowel: oven
k(c): coven.
sl: sloven.
    Cf. shove hen, etc.

UVƏT

l: lovat.

UZBƏND

h: husband.
    Plus fuzz band, etc.

UZĒ

b: buzzy.
f: fuzzy.
h: hussy.
    Plus does he, etc.

UZEST

b: buzzest*.
f: fuzzest*.

UZETH

b: buzzeth*.
f: fuzzeth*.

UZEZ

b: buzzes.
f: fuzzes.

UZIN

d: dozen.
k(c): cousin, cozen.
    Plus buzz in *or* inn, etc.
    Cf. buzzin', etc.

UZING

b: buzzing.
f: fuzzing.

UZINZ

d: dozens.
k(c): cousins, couzens, cozens.
    Plus buzz ins *or* inns, etc.

UZ'L

f: fuzzle*.
g: guzzle.
m: bemuzzle, muzzle, unmuzzle.
n: nuzzle.
p: monkey puzzle, puzzle.
    Plus buzz'll, etc.

UZLEST

g: guzzlest*.
m: bemuzzlest*, muzzlest*, unmuzzlest*.
n: nuzzlest*.
p: puzzlest*.
    Plus buzz lest, etc.

UZLETH

g: guzzleth*.
m: bemuzzleth*, muzzleth*, unmuzzleth*.
n: nuzzleth*.
p: puzzleth*.

UZLIN

m: muslin.
    Plus buzz, Lynn, etc.

UZLING

g: guzzling
m: bemuzzling, muzzling, unmuzzling.
n: nuzzling.
p: puzzling.

UZLUR

g: guzzler.
m: muzzler.
n: nuzzler.
p: puzzler.

UZUM

w: izzum-wuzzum.
   Plus does 'em, etc.

UZUR

b: buzzer.
f: fuzzer.
   Plus buzz her *or* err, etc.

UZURD

b: buzzard, turkey buzzard.
   Cf. fuzz hard, etc.s

UZWURD

b: buzz word.

Triple Rhymes

(Words Accented on the Antepenult, the Second Syllable from the Last)

A

The accented vowel sounds included are listed under **A** in Single Rhymes.

Archaic Verb-Forms among Triple Rhymes—Archaic verb forms ending in **-eth** and **-est,** which form triple rhymes, are not listed. You can easily find them, however, by locating present participles of verbs which form triple rhymes (neighboring, carrying, etc.) and altering the suffixes to the desired archaic forms: neighborest*, neighboreth*, carryest*, carryeth*).

ABĒEST

fl: flabbiest.
sh: shabbiest.

ABĒNES

fl: flabbiness.
sh: shabbiness.
sk(sc): scabbiness.
sl: slabbiness.

ĀBĒƏ

l: labia.
r: Arabia.
sw: Suabia.
  Plus baby a, etc.

ĀBĒƏN

f: Fabian.
r: Arabian, Sorabian.
s: Sabian.
sw: Swabian.
  Plus baby an, etc.

ABĒƏR

fl: flabbier.
g: gabbier.
sh: shabbier.
  Plus tabby, her, etc.

ABIDNES

r: rabidness.
t: tabidness.

ABIKƏL

l: monosyllabical, polysyllabical.
r: Arabical*.
 Plus crabby Cal, etc.

ABILĒ

fl: flabbily.
sh: shabbily.
 Plus slabby lea, etc.

ABITO͞OD

h: habitude.
t: tabitude.
 Plus cab etude, etc.

ABLMENT

b: babblement.
br: brabblement.
d: dabblement.
g: gabblement.
r: rabblement.
 Plus babble meant, etc.

ĀBLNES

s: sableness.
st: stableness, unstableness.

ABLƏTIV

Vowel: ablative.
b: bablative.

ABŌLƏ

r: parabola.
t: metabola.

ABO͞OLĀT

f: confabulate.
t: tabulate.
 Plus grab you, late, etc.

ABO͞OLĒS

f: fabulous.
n: tintinnabulous.
p: pabulous.
s: sabulous.

ABO͞OLIST

f: fabulist.
k(c): vocabulist.
 Plus nab you, list, etc.

ABO͞OLUM

n: tintinnabulum.
p: pabulum.
t: acetabulum.
 Plus grab you, Lum, etc.

ABO͞OLƏR

f: confabular.
n: tintinnabular.
p: pabular.
t: tabular.

ÄBO͞OLƏR

gl: globular.
l: lobular.

ABƏFĪ

l: dissyllabify, labefy, syllabify.
t: tabefy.
 Plus cabby, fie!, etc.

ĀBƏLƏR

g: gabeler.
l: labeller.
 Plus label her, etc.

ABƏNET

k(c): cabinet.
t: tabinet.
 Plus flabby net, etc.

ÄBƏNET

b: bobbinet.
r: robinet.
   Plus Dobbin et, etc.
   Plus hobby net, etc.

ÄBƏRĒ

b: bobbery.
d: daubery+.
j: jobbery, stock-jobbery.
r: robbery.
sl: slobbery.
sn: snobbery.
   Plus slobber, he, etc.
   Plus rob her, he, etc.

ĀBƏRING

l: belaboring, laboring, unlaboring.
n: neighboring.
   Plus say, Bo, ring, etc.
   Plus May beau ring, etc.

ÄBƏRING

kl: clobbering.
sl: slobbering.
   Plus jobber ring, etc.
   Plus fob, her ring, etc.
   Plus rob a ring, etc.

ĀBƏRƏR

l: laborer.
t: taborer.

ABƏSIS

n: anabasis.
t: catabasis, metabasis.
   Plus grab a sis, etc.

ACHƏBƏL

k(c): catchable.
m: immatchable, matchable, unmatchable.
skr(scr): scratchable.
t: attachable, detachable.
   Plus catch a bull, etc.

ACHƏRĀT

m: maturate.
s: saturate, super-saturate.
   Plus Pat, you're eight, etc.
   Plus Matt, you rate, etc.

ACHƏRƏL

n: natural, preternatural, supernatural.

ADĀƏS

m: Amadeus.

ÄDĒECLÄK

b: body clock.

ĀDEDNES

f: fadedness.
gr: degradedness.
j: bejadedness, jadedness.
sh: shadedness.
sw: persuadedness.

ÄDELƏR

m: modeller.
   Plus coddle her, etc.

ĀDĒUM

l: palladium.
n: vanadium.
r: radium.
st: stadium.
   Plus lady, um, etc.

ADĒƏS

m: Amadeus.
th: Thaddeus.
  Plus caddie us, etc.

ĀDĒƏN

b: Barbadian.
k(c): Acadian, Arcadian, Orcadian.
l: Palladian.
m: nomadian.
n: Canadian.
  Plus shady an.

ĀDĒƏNT

gr: gradient.
r: irradiant, radiant.
  Plus lady aunt, etc.

ÄDIFĪ

k(c): codify.
m: modify.
  Plus body, fie!, etc.
  Cf. nod of eye, etc.

ÄDIKƏL

Vowel: periodical.
k(c): codical, episcodical.
m: spasmodical.
n: monodical, nodical, synodical.
s: episodical, prosodical, rhapsodical.
th: methodical.
  Plus body, Cal, etc.
  Plus melodic, Al, etc.

ADITIV

Vowel: additive.
tr: traditive.

ADŌING

sh: foreshadowing, overshadowing, shadowing.

ĀDƏBƏL

gr: biodegradable, photodegradable.
sh: shadable.
sw: persuadable.
tr: tradable.
v: evadible.
w: wadable.
  Plus trade a bull, etc.

ÄDƏMĪZ

s: sodomize.

ÄDƏRIK

Vowel: Theoderic.
r: Roderick.
  Plus fodder rick, etc.
  Plus prod a rick, etc.

ÄDƏRING

d: doddering.
f: foddering.
  Plus odder ring, etc.
  Plus God, her ring, etc.
  Plus trod a ring, etc.

ÄDƏTĒ

Vowel: odditi.
m: commodity, incommodity.
  Plus sod it, he, etc.
  Plus toddy, tea, etc.

ÄFÄRĒS

Vowel: zoophorous.
g: mastigophorous.
l: phyllophorous.

n: actinophorous, adenophorous.
r: pyrophorous.
s: isophorous.
t: galactophorous.
tr: electrophorous.
  Plus offer us, etc.

AFĒƏ

gr: dysgraphia.
m: Mafia.

AFIKƏL

gr: autobiographical, autographical,
bibliographical, biographical,
calligraphical, cartographical,
cosmographical, diagraphical,
ethnographical, geographical,
glossographical, graphical,
lexicographical, lexigraphical,
orthographical, paleontographical,
photographical, physiographical,
phytographical, pterylographical,
topographical, typographical.
r: seraphical.
  Plus traffic, Al, etc.
  Plus daffy Cal, etc.
  Cf. traffic all, etc.

ÄFIKƏL

s: philosophical, theosophical.
tr: trophical.
  Plus coffee, Cal, etc.

ÄFILĒS

Vowel: Theophilus.
d: acidophalus.
l: xylophilous.
m: anemophilous.

ÄFILIST

Vowel: bibliophilist, zoophist.
s: Russophilist.
  Plus coffee list, etc.

ÄFILIZM

Vowel: bibliophilism.
r: necrophilism.
s: Russophilism.

AFTILĒ

dr: draughtily.
kr: craftily.
  Plus crafty lea, etc.

AFTƏRHOURZ

Vowel: after-hours.

AFTƏRWURD

Vowel: afterword.

AFTƏRWURLD

Vowel: afterworld.

ÄFƏGĒ

Vowel: ichthyophagy, theophagy.
n: chthonophagy.
p: anthropophagy, hippophagy.
r: zerophagy.
t: pantophagy, phytophagy.

ÄFƏGĪ

Vowel: theophagi.
d: cardophagi.
dr: androphagi.
k(c): sarcophagi.
p: anthropophagi, hippophagi.
r: heterophagi.
t: Lotophagi, pantophagi.
th: lithophagi.
  Plus off a guy, etc.

ÄFƏGIST

Vowel: geophagist, ichthyophagist.
p: hippophagist.
t: galactophagist, pantophagist.

ÄFƏGƏN

Vowel: theophagan, zoophagan.

k(c): sarcophagan.

r: saprophagan.

Cf. off again, etc.

ÄFƏGƏS

Vowel: geophagous, ophiophagous, theophagous, zoophagous.

dr: androphagous.

k(c): batrachophagous, sarcophagus.

l: hylophagous, xylophagous.

p: anthropophagous, hippophagous.

r: necrophagous, saprophagous.

s: esophagus.

t: galactophagous, pantophagous, phytophagous.

th: lithophagous.

ÄFƏNĒ

Vowel: theophany.

g: laryngophony.

k(c): cacophony.

m: homophony.

n: Satanophany.

r: microphony.

t: photophony, tautophony.

th: orthophony.

Plus off a knee, etc.

AFƏNƏS

Vowel: diaphanous.

ÄFƏNĒS

dr: hydrophanous.

gr: hygrophanous.

k(c): cacophonous.

l: megalophonous.

m: homophonous.

n: monophanous.

r: pyrophanous.

Plus soften us, etc.

Cf. scoff in us, etc.

ÄFƏRING

Vowel: offering, peace offering.

k(c): coffering.

pr: proffering.

Plus offer ring, etc.

Plus doff her ring, etc.

AGEDLĒ

j: jaggedly.

r: raggedly.

Plus cragged lea, etc.

AGEDNES

j: jaggedness.

kr: craggedness.

r: raggedness.

AGĒNES

b: bagginess.

kr: cragginess.

n: knagginess.

sh: shagginess.

skr(scr): scragginess.

AGLĀDĒ

b: bag lady.

ÄGNÄMĒ

Vowel: craniognomy, physiognomy.

th: pathognomy.

Plus hog know me, etc.

AGNETSKO͞OL

m: magnet school.

ÄGRƏFĒ

Vowel: autobiography, balneography, bibliography, biography, dactyliography, geography, hagiography, haliography, heliography, heresiography, historiography, horologiography, ichthyography, ideography, neography, ophiography, oreography, osteography, paleography, physiography, sciography, semeiography, stereography, symbolaeography, tacheography, zoography.

d: pseudography.

dr: dendrography, hydrography.

f: glyphography.

g: logography.

k(c): cacography, calcography, lexicography, pharmacography, phycography, psychography, zincography.

l: chromoxylography, crystallography, epistolography, hyalography, metallography, pterylography, stelography, stylography, xylography.

m: cosmography, demography, microcosmography, nomography, pentamography, phantamography, pneumography, psalmography, seismography, thermography.

n: Christianography, ethnography, galvanography, hymnography, ichnography, iconography, lichenography, mechanography, monography, organography, paneiconography, phonography, pornography, scenography, selenography, sphenography, steganography, stenography, uranography.

p: anthropography, stereotypography, topography, typography.

r: chirography, chorography, heterography, hierography, horography, neurography, rhyparography, siderography, xylopyrography.

s: glossography, gypsography, isography, nosography.

t: autography, chartography, chromatography, chromophotopography, climatography, cryptography, glyptography, heliotography, hematography, histography, hyetography, numismatography, odontography, paleontography, pantography, perspectography, photography, phytography, plastography, stratography, toreumatography.

th: anthography, lithography, orthography.

tr: petrography.

ÄGRƏFIST

Vowel: museorgraphist, palaeographist, zoographist.

l: metallographist.

m: psalmographist.

n: lichenographist, mechanographist, monographist, organographist, phonographist, selenographist, sphenographist, steganographist, uranographist.

p: typographist.

r: chirographist, siderographist.

t: photographist.

th: orthographist.

ÄGRƏFƏR

Vowel: autobiographer, bibliographer, biographer, geographer, haliographer, heresiographer,

historiographer, horologix-
ographer, osteographer,
palaeographer, zoographer.

b: iambographer.

dr: hydrographer.

f: glyphographer.

g: logographer.

k(c): calcographer, lexicographer,
zincographer.

l: crystallographer, zylographer.

m: cosmographer, mimographer,
nomographer, psalmographer.

n: chronographer, ethnographer,
hymnographer, lichenographer,
monographer, phonographer,
selenographer, sphenographer,
stenographer.

p: topographer, typographer.

r: chorographer, hierographer.

s: glossographer.

t: cartographer, chartographer,
cryptography, glyptographer,
photographer.

th: lithographer, mythographer,
orthographer.

tr: petrographer.

ĀGRƏNSĒ

fl: flagrancy.

fr: fragrancy.

v: vagrancy.

ÄGƏMĒ

d: endogamy.

n: coenogamy, monogamy.

r: deuterogamy.

s: misogamy.

z: exogamy.

ÄGƏMĒS

d: endogamous.

n: monogamous, phaenogamous.

r: heterogamous, phanerogamous.

z: exogamous.

ÄGƏMIST

Vowel: neogamist.

n: monogamist.

r: deuterogamist.

s: misogamist.

Plus fog, a mist, etc.

AGƏNIST

Vowel: agonist.

t: antagonist, protagonist.

AGƏNĪZ

Vowel: agonize.

t: antagonize.

Plus dragon eyes, etc.

AGƏNIZM

Vowel: agonism.

t: antagonism.

AGƏRĒ

f: faggery.

j: jaggery.

r: raggery.

w: waggery.

z: zigzaggery.

AGƏRING

st: staggering.

sw: swaggering.

Plus dagger ring, etc.

AGƏRƏR

st: staggerer.

sw: swaggerer.

Plus dagger her, etc.

ÄGƏTIV

r: derogative, interrogative, prerogative.

ĀIKƏL

br: algebraical, Hebraical.
k(c): archaical.
l: laical.
s: paradisaical, pharisaical.

ÄJDƏLƏR

m: modular.
n: nodular.

ĀJĒSNES

br: umbrageousness.
p: rampageousness.
r: courageousness, outrageousness.
t: advantageousness, disadvanta-geousness.

ĀJĒƏN

l: pelagian.
m: magian.
n: Brobdignagian.
    Cf. contagion, etc.

ÄJĒƏN

b: gambogian.
l: archaeologian, astrologian, geologian, mythologian, neologian, philologian, theologian.
    Plus doge, Ian, etc.

AJIKƏL

m: magical.
tr: tragical.

ÄJIKƏL

g: demagogical, synagogical.
l: aerological, amphibiological, amphibological, analogical, anthological, anthropological, archaeological, astrological, bibliological, biological, bryological, chronological, climatological, conchological, cosmological, craniological, demonological, deontological, dialogical, doxological, Egyptological, entomological, etiological, etymological, genealogical, geological, glossological, glottological, homological, hydrological, ichnological, ideological, illogical, lithological, logical, mazological, metalogical, meteorological, mythological, necrological, neological, neurological, nosological, odontological, organological, ornithological, orological, osteological, paleonto-logical, pantological, paralogical, penological, perissological, petrological, philological, phraseological, phrenological, physiological, phytological, pneumatological, pomological, psychological, selenological, semeiological, Sinological, sociological, spectrological, symbological, tautological, technicological, technological, teleological, teratological, terminological, theological, toxicological, tropological, universological, zoological, zoophytological, zymological.
    Plus pedagogic, Al, etc.
    Plus stodgy, Cal, etc.

ĀJƏBƏL

g: gaugeable.
sw: assuageable.
    Plus enrage a bull, etc.

AJƏLNES

Vowel: agileness.
fr: fragileness.

ÄJƏNĒ

Vowel: abiogeny, biogeny,
embryogeny, geogeny, ostoogeny,
zoogeny.
l: philogeny, phylogeny.
m: homogeny.
n: ethnogeny, hymenogeny,
monogeny.
p: anthropogeny.
pr: progeny.
r: heterogeny.
s: misogyny.
t: histogeny, odontogeny,
ontogeny, photogeny, protogyny.
th: pathogeny.
    Plus stodgy knee, etc.
    Cf. dodge a knee, etc.

ÄJƏNIST

Vowel: abiogenist, biogenist.
l: philogynist.
n: monogenist.
r: heterogenist.
s: misogynist.

ĀJƏNSĒ

Vowel: agency.

AJƏNĒS

Vowel: oleaginous.
b: lumbaginous.
l: cartilaginous, mucilaginous.
r: farraginous, voraginous.
    Plus imagine us, etc.

ÄJƏNĒS

d: endogenous.
dr: hydrogenous.
m: thermogenous.
p: hypogynous.
r: pyrogenous.
s: exogenous.
th: lithogenous.
tr: nitrogenous.

ÄJƏNĒ

Vowel: geogony, physiogony,
theogony, zoogony.
m: cosmogony.
t: autogony.
th: pathogony.
    Cf. dodge a knee, etc.

ÄJƏNIST

Vowel: theogonist.
m: cosmogonist.

AJƏNƏL

m: imaginal.
p: paginal.
v: vaginal.

AKCHO͞OƏL

Vowel: actual.
f: factual.
t: tactual.
    Plus smacked you, Al, etc.

ĀKDANSING

br: break dancing.

ĀKĒNES

fl: flakiness.
kw(qu): quakiness.
sh: shakiness.
sn: snakiness.

ÄKĒNES

k(c): cockiness.
r: rockiness.
st: stockiness.

AKETBÔL

r: racketball.

AKETED

br: bracketed.
j: jacketed.
r: racketed.
    Plus packet, Ed, etc.

AKETING

br: bracketing.
j: jacketing.
r: racketing.

AKĒƏN

Vowel: Noachian.
t: eustachian.
tr: batrachian.
    Plus wacky an, etc.

AKISHNES

br: brackishness.
n: knackishness.
sl: slackishness.

ÄKITSHIP

r: rocket ship.

AKLƏMĀT

kl: acclimate.

AKMUNĒ

bl: black money.

AKŌŌLĀT

j: ejaculate, jaculate.
m: bimaculate,
immaculate, maculate.
    Plus track, you late!, etc.

AKŌŌLƏR

Vowel: piacular.
n: supernacular, tabernacular,
vernacular.
r: oracular.
t: spectacular, tentacular.

AKŌŌLƏS

Vowel: piaculous.
b: abaculus.
n: vernaculous.
r: miraculous, oraculous.

ÄKRÄMĒ

Vowel: heliochromy,
stereochromy.
l: metallochromy.
n: monochromy.

AKRITY

Vowel: acrity*.
l: alacrity.

AKRƏNISM

n: anachronism.
t: metachronism.

ÄKRƏNƏS

s: isochronous.
t: tautochronous.

ÄKRƏSĒ

Vowel: hagiocracy, idiocrasy,
neocracy, plousiocracy, theocracy,
theocrasy.

b: mobocracy, snobocracy.
g: logocracy.
k(c): gynaecocracy.
l: ochlocracy.
m: arithmocracy, democracy, nomocracy, timocracy.
n: cottonocracy, monocracy.
p: hypocrisy, shopocracy.
r: hierocracy.
s: pantisocracy.
t: aristocracy, autocracy, despotocracy, gerontocracy, pedantocracy, plantocracy, plutocracy, stratocracy.
v: slavocracy.

ÄKRƏTIZM

m: democratism.
s: Socratism.

AKSHƏNƏL

f: factional.
fr: fractional.
p: pactional.
 Plus exaction, Al, etc.

AKSHƏSNES

f: factiousness.
fr: fractiousness.

ÄKSIKƏL

d: orthodoxical, paradoxical.
t: toxical.
 Plus proxy, Cal, etc.
 Plus toxic, Al, etc.

AKSƏBƏL

l: relaxable.
t: taxable.
 Plus packs a bull, etc.

AKTEDNES

str: abstractedness.
tr: contractedness, distractedness, protractedness.

AKTIKƏL

d: didactical.
pr: practical.

AKTILƏS

d: didactylous, hexadactylous, leptodactylous, pachydactylous, pterodactylous.
 Plus tactile, us, etc.

AKTIVNES

Vowel: activeness.
f: putrefactiveness.
fr: refractiveness.
str: abstractiveness.
tr: attractiveness, contractiveness, detractiveness, distractiveness, protractiveness.

AKTO͞ORING

f: manufacturing.
fr: fracturing.
 Plus manufacture, ring, etc.

ÄKTÔRSHIP

d: doctorship.
pr: proctorship.
 Plus blocked her ship, etc.
 Plus concocter, ship, etc.

AKTƏBƏL

fr: infractible, irrefractible, refractible.
p: compactible.
t: intactible, tactable.

tr: attractible, contractable, detractible, distractible, extractible, intractable, retractable, tractable.

Plus tracked a bull, etc.

AKTƏRĒ

f: dissatisfactory, factory, manufactory, olfactory, satisfactory, unsatisfactory.
fr: refractory.
l: lactary, phylactery.
tr: detractory, tractory.

ÄKŪLƏR

Vowel: ocular.
j: jocular.
l: locular.
n: binocular, monocular.
v: vocular.

ĀKWĒƏS

Vowel: aqueous, subaqueous.
r: terraqueous.

ĀKƏBƏL

Vowel: acheable.
br: breakable, unbreakable.
p: impacable, pacable.
pl: implacable, placable.
sh: shakable, unshakable.
t: mistakable, undertakable, unmistakable.

Plus make a bull, etc.

AKƏRĒ

h: hackery.
j: hijackery.
kw(qu): quackery.
n: knick-knackery.
th: Thackeray.
z: Zackary.

ĀKƏRĒ

b: bakery.
f: fakery, fakiry.
r: rakery.

ÄKƏRĒ

kr: crockery.
m: mockery.
r: rockery.

Plus socker, he, etc.

ĀKƏRIZM

f: fakirism.
kw(qu): Quakerism.
sh: Shakerism.

ÄKƏTIV

l: locative.
v: invocative, provocative, vocative.

ÄLÄGƏS

m: homologous.
r: heterologous.
s: isologous.
t: tautologous.

Plus hollow, Gus, etc.

ÄLÄING

f: following.
h: holloing, hollowing.
sw: swallowing.
w: wallowing.

Plus hollow wing, etc.
Plus doll, O wing, etc.

ÄLÄƏR

f: follower.
h: hollower.

sw: swallower.
w: wallower.
    Plus swallow her, etc.

ALBƏTRÔS

Vowel: albatross.

ALENTĪN

b: Ballantine.
v: Valentine.

ALĒĀT

m: malleate.
p: palliate.
t: retaliate.
    Plus Hally ate, etc.
    Plus Sallie, eight, etc.

ALĒING

d: dallying.
r: rallying.
s: sallying.
t: tallying.

ĀLĒNES

d: dailiness.
sk(sc): scaliness.

ALĒUM

p: pallium.
th: thallium.

ALĒƏ

Vowel: aliya, aliyah.

ĀLĒƏ

d: Adalia, Fidelia, Sedalia.
g: regalia.
l: echolalia, Eulalia.
t: Attalia.

th: Athalia, Thalia.
tr: Australia, Centralia.
z: azalea, Rosalia.
    Plus Bailey, a, etc.
    Cf. alya.

ALĒƏR

d: dallier.
r: rallier.
s: sallier.
t: tallier.
    Plus rally her, etc.

ĀLĒƏS

b: Sibelius.
d: Delius.
    Plus scaly, us, etc.
    Cf. alias.

ALFƏWĀV

Vowel: alpha wave.

ALIBƏR

k(c): caliber, Excalibur.
    Plus valley burr, etc.

ÄLIDLĒ

s: solidly.
skw: squalidly.
st: stolidly.
    Plus solid Lee, etc.

ALIDNES

p: impallidness, pallidness.
v: invalidness, validness.

ÄLIDNES

s: solidness.
skw: squalidness.
st: stolidness.

ÄLIKSUM

fr: frolicsome.
r: rollicksome.
    Plus alcoholic sum *or* some, etc.
    Plus frolics 'em *or* um, etc.

ÄLIKƏL

b: diabolical, hyperbolical, parabolical, symbolical.
f: follicle.
p: bibliopolical.
t: apostolical.
th: catholical.
    Plus colic, Al, etc.
    Plus jolly, Cal, etc.

ÄLISHING

b: abolishing.
m: demolishing.
p: polishing.

ÄLISHƏR

b: abolisher.
m: demolisher.
p: polisher.
    Plus abolish her *or* err, etc.

ALISƏN

Vowel: Alison.
k(c): Callison.
m: Mallison.
    Plus rally, son, etc.

ÄLITĒ

j: jollity.
kw: equality, inequality, quality.
p: interpolity, isopolity, polity.
v: frivolity.
    Plus holly tea *or* T, etc.
    Plus doll it, he, etc.

ÄLIVƏR

Vowel: Oliver.
b: Bolivar.
t: Taliaferro, Tolliver.
    Plus olive her *or* err, etc.

ALJĒƏ

r: neuralgia.
t: nostalgia.

ALŌEST

h: hallowest.
k(c): callowest.
s: sallowest.
sh: shallowest.

ALŌISH

s: sallowish.
sh: shallowish.
t: tallowish.

ÄLO͞OBƏL

s: insoluble, soluble.
v: voluble.
    Plus loll, you bull, etc.

ÄLO͞OTIV

s: solutive*.
v: supervolutive.
    Cf. evolutive, revolutive.

ALŌJIZM

Vowel: dialogism.
n: analogism.
r: paralogism.

ALŌNES

k(c): callowness.
f: fallowness.

s: sallowness.
sh: shallowness.

ALŌƏR

k(c): callower.
h: hallower.
s: sallower.
sh: shallower.
t: tallower.
　　Plus hallow her.

ÄLVƏBƏL

s: absolvable, insolvable, solvable.
z: dissolvable, indissolvable, resolvable.
　　Plus involve a bull, etc.

ÄLVƏNSĒ

s: insolvency, solvency.
v: revolvency.
　　Cf. insolvent, see?, etc.

ĀLYENIZM

Vowel: alienism.
d: sesquipedalianism.
n: bacchanalianism, saturnalianism.
p: episcopalianism.
s: universalianism.

ĀLƏBƏL

b: bailable.
h: exhalable, inhalable.
m: mailable, unmailable.
s: assailable, sailable, saleable, unassailable, unsailable, unsaleable.
t: retailable.
v: available, unavailable.
　　Plus for sale, a bull, etc.

ALƏFĪ

k(c): alkalify, calefy*.
s: salify.
　　Plus Sallie, fie!, etc.

ÄLƏJĒ

Vowel: aesthesiology, agriology, alethiology, amphibiology, archaeology, arteriology, astrotheology, balneology, bibliology, biology, bryology, conchyliology, craniology, dactyliology, dicaeology, ecclesiology, electrobiology, electrophysiology, embryology, endemiology, entozoology, epidemiology, etiology, genesiology, geology, hagiology, historiology, hygiology, ichthyology, ideology, liturgiology, microgeology, myology, neology, noology, ology, oology, ophiology, osteology, palaeology, palaeozoology, palaetiology, pantheology, phraseology, physiology, phytophysiology, semeiology, sociology, soteriology, speciology, stoichiology, teleology, testaceology, theology, thereology, zoology.

b: amphibology, phlebology, symbology.

d: methodology, monadology, orchiology, periodology, pteridology, suicidology, tidology.

dr: dendrology, hydrology.

f: morphology.

fr: nephrology.

g: bugology, fungology, laryngology, pharyngology.

k(c): cacology, conchology, ethnomusicology, filicology, gynecology, lexicology, malacology, muscology, mycology, pharmacology, phycology, psychology, sarcology, toxicology.

kr: macrology, micrology, necrology.

l: angelology, cephalology, hylology, philology, psilology.

m: atomology, cosmology, desmology, entomology, epistemology, etymology, gnomology, homology, miasmology, nomology, ophthalmology, orismology, paromology, pneumology, pomology, potamology, seismology, spasmology, spermology, syndesmology, thermology, zymology.

n: actinology, aphnology, arachnology, asthenology, botanology, campanology, chronology, demonology, eccrinology, emmenology, enteradenology, ethnology, galvanology, gnomonology, hymenology, hymnology, ichnolithnology, ichnology, iconology, kinology, lichenology, membranology, menonology, monology, neurypnology, oceanology, onology, organology, ornithichnology*, palaeoethnology, parthenology, penology, phenomenology, phonology, phrenology, punnology, quinology, runology, selenology, sinology, splanchnology, splenology, synchronology, technology, terminology, termonology, uranology, urbanology, urinology, urononology, vulcanology.

p: anthropology, apology, topology, tropology, typology.

r: aerology, astrometerology, barology, enterology, futurology, heterology, hierology, horology, hysterology, ichorology, martyrology, meteorology, neurology, oneirology, orology, papryology, pharology, ponerology, pyrology, therology.

s: adenochirapsology, dosology, doxology, glossology, gypsology, misology, nosology, osmonosology, paradoxology, parisology, perissology, posology, psychonosology, taxology, threpsology, universology.

t: aesthematology, agmatology, aretology, aristology, battology, bromatology, brontology, Christology, chromatology, climatology, cryptology, deontology, dermatology, dialectology, dittology, Egyptology, emetology, eschatology, gigantology, glottology, histology, hyetology, insectology, leptology, mantology, numismatology, odontology, onomatology, ontology, otology, palaeontology, palaeophytology, pantology, parasitology, patronomatology, photology, phytology, pneumatology, primatology, protophytology, pyritology, scientology, sematology, sitology, skeletology, somatology, Sovietology, spermatology, statistology, stromatology, symptomatology, systematology, tautology, teratology, thanatology, toreumatology, zoophytology.

th: anthology, ethology, lithology, mythology, ornithology, pathology, phytolithology, phytopathology.

tr: astrology, electrology, gastrology, metrology, petrology, spectrology.

v: ovology.

z: mazology.

Plus hollow, Gee!, etc.

ÄLƏJIST

Vowel: agriologist, archaeologist, Assyriologist, biologist, craniologist, crustaceologist, ecclesiologist, electrobiologist, embryologist, geologist, hagiologist, ichthyologist, ideologist, myologist, neologist, noologist, oologist, ophiologist, osteologist, palaeologist, palaetiologist, pantheologist, phraseologist, physiologist, sociologist, teleologist, theologist, thereologist, zoologist.

b: symbologist.

d: orchiologist, pseudologist, pteridologist, suicidologist.

dr: dendrologist, hydrologist.

f: morphologist.

k(c): conchologist, lexicologist, mycologist, pharmacologist, psychologist, sarcologist, toxicologist.

kr: necrologist.

l: philologist.

m: cosmologist, entomolygist, etymologist, pomologist, seismologist, zymologist.

n: campanologist, chronologist, demonologist, ethnologist, galvanologist, hymnologist, hypnologist, monologist, palaeoethnologist, phonologist, phrenologist, quinologist, runologist, sinologist, technologist, urbanologist, vulcanologist.

p: anthropologist, apologist.

r: aerologist, hierologist, horologist, martyrologist, meteorologist, neurologist, oneirologist, orologist, papyrologist, pyrologist, therologist.

s: glossologist, gypsologist, nosologist, universologist.

t: battologist, deontologist, dermatologist, Egyptologist, glottologist, histologist, mantologist, numismatologist, onomatologist, ontologist, palaeontologist, pantologist, photologist, phytologist, pneumatologist, primatologist, saintologist, scientologist, tautologist, teratologist.

th: ethologist, lithologist, mythologist, ornithologist, pathologist, phytolithologist, phytopathologist.

tr: astrologist, petrologist.

z: mazologist, etc.

ÄLƏJĪZ

Vowel: geologize, neologize, sociologize, theologize, zoologize.

l: philologize.

m: entomologize, etymologize.

p: apologize.

s: doxologize.

t: battologize, tautologize.

tr: astrologize, etc.

ÄLƏJƏR

Vowel: geologer, osteologer, physiologer, theologer.

d: sockdolager.

l: philologer.

m: etymologer.

n: acknowledger, botanolager, phonologer, phrenologer.

r: horologer.

th: mythologer.

tr: astrologer.

ALƏNSBĒM

b: balance beam.

ALƏSIS

Vowel: dialysis, radiolysis.

n: analysis.

r: paralysis.

t: catalysis.

Plus rally, sis!, etc.

ALƏTĒ

Vowel: actuality, artificiality, bestiality, circumstantiality, confidentiality, congeniality, connubiality, consubstantiality, conviviality, cordiality, corporeality, curiality, duality, essentiality, ethereality, eventuality, exterritoriality, geniality, graduality, ideality, immateriality, imparitality, imperiality, inconsequentiality, individuality, ineffectuality, intellectuality, joviality, lineality, materiality, mutuality, officiality, parochiality, partiality, potentiality, provinciality, prudentiality, punctuality, reality, sensuality, seriality, sexuality, sociality, speciality, spirituality, substantiality, superficiality, triality, triviality, unusuality, veniality, visuality.

b: verbality.

d: alamodality, feudality, modality, pedality, sesquipedality, sodality.

g: conjugality, egality, frugality, illegality, legality, regality.

gr: integrality.

k(c): Biblicality, classicality, comicality, cosmicality, fantasticality, finicality, inimicality, intrinsicality, laicality, locality, logicality, practicality, radicality, rascality, reciprocality, technicality, theoreticality, verticality, vocality, whimsicality.

m: abnormality, animality, formality, informality.

n: banality, carnality, constitutionality, conventionality, criminality, externality, feminality, finality, impersonality, intentionality, irrationality, meridionality, mesnality, nationality, notionality, originality, penality, personality, proportionality, rationality, sectionality, septentionality, signality, tonality, traditionality, venality.

p: municipality, principality.

r: conjecturality, corporality, ephemerality, generality, gutterality, immorality, laterality, liberality, literality, morality, naturality, plurality, preternaturality, rurality, severality, spirality, supernaturality, temporality.

s: orthodoxality, universality.

t: accidentality, brutality, elementality, fatality, fundamentality, horizontality, hospitality, immortality, instrumentality, mentality, mortality, occidentality, orientality, sentimentality, totality, transcendentality, vitality, vegetality.

tr: centrality, dextrality, magistrality, neutrality, spectrality.

v: rivality.

z: causality, nasality.

Plus bally tea, etc.

ÄLƏJĒ

Vowel: genealogy, genethlialogy.

b: pyrobalogy*.

m: mammalogy.

n: analogy.

r: mineralogy, paralogy, petralogy, tetralogy.

t: crustalogy.

ÄLƏJIST

Vowel: dialogist, genealogist.

k(c): decalogist.

m: mammalogist.

n: analogist, penalogist.

r: mineralogist.

Plus shallow gist, etc.

ÄLƏJĪZ

Vowel: dialogize, genealogize.

n: analogize.

r: paralogize.

ALƏRĒ

g: gallery.
r: raillery*.
s: salary.

ĀLƏRĒ

n: nailery.
r: raillery.

ÄLƏTRĒ

Vowel: bibliolatry, geolatry, gyneolatry, heliolatry, icthyolatry, idiolatry, Mariolatry, ophiolatry, physiolatry, zoolatry.
b: symbolatry.
d: idolatry, lordolatry.
kr: necrolatry.
m: cosmolatry.
n: demonolatry.
p: anthropolatry, topolatry.
r: hierolatry, pyrolatry.
t: thaumatolatry.
th: litholatry.
tr: astrolatry.
  Plus corolla tree, etc.
  Plus doll a tree, etc.

ÄLƏTRƏS

b: symbolatrous.
d: idolatrous.
  Plus extol a truss, etc.
  Plus corolla truss, etc.

ÄLƏTƏR

Vowel: bibliolater, heliolater, Mariolater.
d: idolater.
n: iconolater.
r: pyrolater.
  Plus doll ate her, etc.

AMBŌŌLĀT

Vowel: ambulate, deambulate.
n: funambulate, somnambulate.
r: perambulate.

AMBŌŌLIST

n: funambulist, somnambulist.
t: noctambulist.

AMBŌŌLIZM

n: funambulism, somnambulism.
t: noctambulism.

ÄMĒNƏ

g: antilegomena, prolegomena.
n: phenomena.
p: paralipomena.
  Cf. common a, etc.

ĀMĒƏ

l: lamia.
t: Mesopotamia.
  Plus Mamie, a, etc.

ĀMFƏLNES

bl: blamefulness.
sh: shamefulness.

AMIKƏL

Vowel: amical.
n: dynamical.
s: balsamical.
  Plus mammy, Cal, etc.
  Plus ceramic, Al, etc.

ÄMIKƏL

d: domical.

k(c): comical, coxcombical, tragicomical.

n: agronomical, astronomical, economical, iconomachcal.

t: anatomical, atomical, zootomical.

    Plus from me, Cal, etc.

    Plus tommie, Cal, etc.

AMINĀTE

l: laminate+.

t: contaminate.

    Plus clammy, Nate, etc.

ÄMINĀT

Vowel: ominate*.

b: abominate.

d: dominate, predominate.

k(c): comminate.

n: agnominate, denominate, nominate, prenominate.

    Plus bomb in eight *or* ate, etc.

ÄMINĒ

d: dominie.

h: Chickahomini, hominy.

    Plus from a knee, etc.

    Plus Tommie, knee, etc.

    Cf. Romany.

ÄMINƏL

d: abdominal.

n: cognominal, nominal, prenominal, surnominal.

    Plus bomb in, Al, etc.

ÄMINƏNS

d: dominance, predominance.

pr: prominence.

ÄMINƏNT

d: dominant, predominant, subdominant, superdominant.

pr: prominent.

    Plus bomb in aunt *or* ant, etc.

ÄMINƏS

Vowel: ominous.

d: abdominous, dominus.

g: prolegomenous.

    Plus bomb in us, etc.

ÄMISTRĒ

p: palmistry.

s: psalmistry.

AMITY

Vowel: amity.

l: calamity.

    Plus mammy, tea, etc.

ĀMLESNES

Vowel: aimlessness.

bl: blamelessness.

d: damelessness.

f: famelessness.

n: namelessness.

sh: shamelessness.

t: tamelessness.

AMO͞OLƏS

f: famulus.

h: hamulus.

r: ramulous.

AMŌRƏS

Vowel: amorous.

gl: glamorous.

kl: clamorous.

    Plus hammer us, etc.

ÄMPACTDISC

k(c): compact disc.

AMPĒƏN

ch: champion.
k(c): campion.
t: tampion.

AMPƏRING

h: hampering.
p: pampering.
sk(sc): scampering.
t: tampering.
  Plus damper ring, etc.

AMPƏRƏR

h: hamperer.
p: pamperer.
sk(sc): scamperer.
t: tamperer.
  Plus vamper, her, etc.

AMƏBƏL

gr: programmable.

ĀMƏBƏL

bl: blamable, unblamable.
fr: framable.
kl: claimable, irreclaimable, reclaimable, unreclaimable.
n: namable, unnamable.
t: tamable, untamable.

AMƏNĪT

Vowel: Ammonite.
l: laminate.+
m: Mammonite.
  Cf. backgammon night, etc.

ÄMƏKĒ

Vowel: alectryomachy, sciomachy, theomachy.
g: logomachy.
k(c): psychomachy.
n: iconomachy, monomachy.
t: gigantomachy.
  Plus from a key, etc.
  Plus comma key, etc.

AMƏNIZM

m: Mammonism.
sh: Shamanism.

AMƏNƏ

l: lamina.
st: stamina.
  Plus famine, a, etc.

ÄMƏNƏN

g: prolegomenon.
n: phenomenon.
  Cf. common on, etc.

AMƏRĒ

gr: gramarye*.
m: mammary.
  Plus slam Marie, etc.

AMƏRING

h: hammering.
kl(cl): clamoring.
st: stammering.
y: yammering.
  Plus hammer ring, etc.
  Plus slam her ring, etc.

AMƏRƏN

k(c): Decameron.
t: Heptameron.
  Plus grammar on, etc.
  Plus ram her on, etc.

AMƏRƏR

h: hammerer.
kl: clamorer.
st: stammerer.
y: yammerer.
    Plus hammer her, etc.

ÄMƏRĒS

gl: glomerous*.
s: isomerous.
    Plus bomb her, us, etc.

ÄMƏTHĒ

l: philomathy.
t: chrestomathy.

AMƏTIST

dr: dramatist, melodramatist.
gr: epigrammatist, grammatist,
hierogrammatist, lipogrammatist.

AMƏTIV

Vowel: amative.
kl: exclamative.

AMƏTĪZ

dr: dramatize.
gr: anagrammatize,
diagrammatize, epigrammatize.
    Plus Alabama ties, etc.

ÄMƏTRĒ

Vowel: biometry, craniometry,
eudiometry, geometry, goniom-
etry, rheometry, stereometry,
stoichiometry.
d: odometry.
dr: hydrometry.
gr: hygrometry.
h: Mahometry.
k(c): helicometry, stichometry.

kr: micrometry.
m: pneumometry, seismometry.
n: chronometry, galvanometry,
ozonometry, planometry,
trigonometry.
r: barometry, horometry,
pyrometry, saccharometry.
s: gasometry, hypsometry.
t: photometry.
th: orthometry, pathometry.
    Cf. from a tree, etc.

ÄMƏTƏR

Vowel: absorptometer, audiometer,
craniometer, diameter, eudiometer,
geometer, goniometer, heliometer,
oleometer, pluviameter,
pluviometer, radiometer, rheom-
eter, stereometer, viameter.
b: tribometer.
br: ombrometer.
d: odometer, pedometer,
speedometer, udometer.
dr: dendrometer, hydrometer.
f: graphometer.
g: logometer.
gr: hygrometer.
k(c): echometer, tachometer,
trochometer.
kr: macrometer, micrometer.
l: cephalometer
m: dynamometer, endosmometer,
geothermometer, seismometer,
thermometer, zymometer.
n: actinometer, chronometer,
clinometer, declinometer,
dynameter, galvanometer,
micronometer, monometer,
ozonometer, phonometer,
planometer, salinometer,
sonometer, tannometer,
vinometer, volumenometer.
p: nauropometer.
r: barometer, horometer,
peirameter, parameter, pyrometer,

saccharometer, spherometer, tetrameter.

s: drosometer, hexameter, hypsometer, pulsometer.

t: altometer, chartometer, chromatometer, lactometer, magnetometer, octameter, optometer, pantometer, pentameter, photometer, platometer, pneumatometer, refractometer, stratometer, voltameter.

th: bathometer, stethometer.

tr: astrometer, electrometer, spectrometer.

z: piezometer.

Plus from it, her, err, *or* er, etc.

Plus vomit her, etc.

ÄNÄGRƏF

kr: chronograph.

m: monograph.

Cf. phonograph.

ÄNÄMĒ

f: morphonomy.

k(c): economy.

l: dactylonomy.

r: agronomy, Deuteronomy, heteronomy.

s: isonomy, taxonomy.

t: autonomy.

tr: astronomy, gastronomy.

ÄNÄMIST

k(c): economist.

n: synonymist.

p: eponymist.

r: agronomist.

t: autonomist.

tr: gastronomist.

ÄNÄMĪZ

k(c): economize.

tr: astronomize, gastronomize.

ÄNÄMƏR

tr: astronomer, gastronomer.

ANCHESTER

gr: Granchester.

m: Manchester.

Plus branchy stir.

ANDĒNES

d: dandiness.

h: handiness.

s: sandiness.

ÄNDERĒ

n: nondairy.

ANDIFĪ

d: dandify.

k(c): candify.

Plus brandy? Fie!, etc.

ANDGLĪDING

h: hand gliding.

ÄNDŌŌIT

k(c): conduit+.

ANDRĒƏN

Vowel: meandrian*.

n: Menandrian.

z: Alexandrian.

ANDƏBƏL

m: commandable, countermandable, demandable, reprimandable.

s: sandable.

st: understandable.

Plus stand a bull, etc.

ANDƏRĒS

p: panderous.
sl: slanderous.
   Plus slander us, etc.

ANDƏRING

Vowel: meandering.
l: philandering.
p: pandering.
sl: slandering.
   Plus gander ring, etc.

ÄNDƏRING

l: laundering.
p: pondering.
skw: squandering.
w: unwandering, wandering.
   Plus yonder ring, etc.
   Plus beyond her ring, etc.
   Plus beyond a ring, etc.
   Cf. onduring.

ANDƏRSƏN

Vowel: Anderson.
s: Sanderson.
   Plus gander, son, etc.
   Plus grander sun, etc.

ANDƏRƏR

Vowel: meanderer.
l: philanderer.
p: panderer.
sl: slanderer.
   Plus slander her, etc.

ÄNDƏRƏR

l: launderer.
p: ponderer.
skw: squander.

w: wanderer.
   Plus fonder, her, etc.
   Plus fond o' her, etc.

ĀNĒAK

m: bibliomaniac, dipsomaniac,
eleutheromaniac, kleptomaniac,
maniac, megalomaniac, monomaniac, nymphomaniac, pyromaniac.

ĀNĒAL

kr: cranial.
m: domanial.
r: subterraneal.
   Plus zany, Al, etc.

ÄNĒKLÔZ

d: Delaney clause.

ÄNELĒ

d: Donnely.
k(c): Connoly.
   Plus McConnell, he, etc.

ĀNĒUM

d: succedaneum.
kr: cranium, pericranium.
r: geranium, uranium.
t: titanium.

ĀNĒƏ

Vowel: Lithuania.
b: Albania.
d: succedanea*.
kr: Ukrainia.
l: miscellanea.
m: Anglomania, bibliomania,
decalcomania, demonomania*,
dipsomania, eleutheromania,
erotomania, Gallomania,

kleptomania, logomania, mania, megalomania, metromania, monomania, nymphomania, pyromania, Rumania, Tasmania.

r: Urania.

t: Aquitania, Lusitania, Mauretania, Ruritania, Titania, Tripolitania.

v: Pennsylvania, Sylvania, Transylvania.

ĀNĒƏN

Vowel: cyanean, Lithuanian.

b: Albanian.

k(c): volcanian.

kr: Ukrainian.

m: Alcmanian, Rumanian, Sandemanian, Tasmanian.

r: circumforanean, extemporanean, Iranian, Mediterranean, subterranean, Turanian, Uranian.

t: Aquitanian, Mauretanian, Tripolitanian.

v: Pennsylvanian, Transylvanian.

Plus zany, an, etc.

ĀNĒƏS

br: membraneous.

d: antecedaneous, succedaneous.

l: miscellaneous, porcelaneous.

r: arraneous, circumforaneous, contemporaneous, extemporaneous, exterraneous, mediterraneous*, subterraneous, temporaneous, terraneous.

t: coetaneous, cutaneous, dissentaneous, instantaneous, momentaneous, simultaneous, spontaneous, subcutaneous.

tr: extraneous.

Plus brainy, us, etc.

ĀNFƏLĒ

b: banefully.

d: disdainfully.

p: painfully.

ĀNFƏLNES

d: disdainfulness.

g: gainfulness.

p: painfulness.

ANGBUSTƏRZ

g: gang busters.

ANGKƏBƏL

b: bankable.

ANGKƏRĒS

k(c): cankerous.

t: cantankerous.

Plus anchor us, etc.

ANGKƏRING

Vowel: anchoring.

h: hankering.

k(c): cankering, encankering.

Plus rancor ring, etc.

ANGKƏRMAN

Vowel: anchor man

ANGLSOM

Vowel: anglesome.

r: wranglesome.

t: tanglesome.

Plus mangle some, etc.

ANGŌŌLƏR

Vowel: angular, triangular.

r: quadrangular.

sl: slangular.
t: octangular, pentangular, rectangular.

ANIBƏL

h: Hannibal.
k(c): cannibal.
Cf. anabl.

ANIFĪ

m: humanify.
s: insanify, sanify.
Plus Fannie? Fie!

ÄNIFĪ

p: saponify.
s: personify.
Plus Desdemona, fie!, etc.
Cf. ozonify.

ANIGƏN

br: Brannigan.
fl: Flannigan.
l: Mullanigan.
n: shenannigan.

ANIKIN

m: manikin.
p: panikin.
Plus panic in, etc.
Plus Fannie kin, etc.

ÄNIKƏ

m: harmonica.
r: veronica.
Plus tonic, a, etc.

ANIKƏL

k(c): mechanical.
m: Brahmanical.
p: panicle.

r: tyrannical.
t: botanical, charlatanical.
v: galvanical.
Plus canny Cal, etc.
Plus panic, AL, etc.

ÄNIKƏL

b: Sorbonical.
f: antiphonical, diaphonical, euphonical, tautophonical.
k(c): conical, iconical.
kr: acronycal, antichronical, chronicle, synchronical.
l: Babylonical.
m: harmonical.
n: canonical, uncanonical.
p: geoponical.
r: ironical.
s: thrasonical.
t: architectonical, tonical.
Plus cyclonic, Al, etc.
Plus bonnie, Cal, etc.

ÄNIKƏN

kr: chronicon.
m: harmonicon.

ÄNIMĒ

Vowel: polyonomy.
m: homonomy.
n: synonomy.
r: paronomy.
t: metonomy.
Plus Ranee me, etc.
Cf. onomi.

ANIMƏS

Vowel: animus.
l: pusillanimous.
n: magnanimous, unanimous.

t: multanimous.
  Plus Annie muss, etc.

ÄNIMƏS

Vowel: polyonymous.
d: pseudonymous.
m: homonymous.
n: anonymous, synonymous.
p: eponymous.
r: heteronymous, paronymous.
t: autonomous.

ANISHING

b: banishing.
pl: planishing.
v: vanishing.

ÄNISHING

m: admonishing, monishing*.
st: astonishing.

ANISHMENT

b: banishment.
v: evanishment, vanishment.
  Plus Spanish meant, etc.

ÄNISHMENT

m: admonishment, premonishment.
st: astonishment.
  Plus wannish meant, etc.

ÄNISIZM

Vowel: histrionicism.
k(c): laconicism.
t: Teutonicism.

ANISTƏR

b: banister.
g: ganister.

k(c): canister.
  Plus Fannie stir, etc.

ANITĒ

Vowel: Christianity, inanity.
b: inurbanity, urbanity.
d: mundanity.
f: profanity.
g: inorganity, paganity.
k(c): volcanity.
m: aldermanity, gigmanity, humanity, immanity, inhumanity.
r: subterranity.
s: insanity, sanity.
v: vanity.
  Plus Fannie, tea *or* T., etc.

ANJƏBƏL

fr: frangible, infrangible, refrangible.
t: intangible, tangible.

ANJƏNSĒ

pl: plangency.
t: tangency.

ÄNKŌJĒN

Vowel: oncogene.

ANŌGRƏF

Vowel: pianograph.
v: galvanograph.

ANO͞OLĀT

Vowel: annulate.
gr: granulate.
p: campanulate.
  Plus fan you, late, etc.

ANŌŌLə

gr: granula.
k(c): cannula.

ANŌŌLƏR

Vowel: annular.
k(c): cannular.
n: penannular.

ANŌŌƏL

Vowel: annual.
m: manual.
   Cf. Manuel, Immanuel.

ÄNŌPŌŌL

m: monopole.

ANŌSKŌP

f: diaphanoscope.
v: galvanoscope.

ANSHĒĀT

st: circumstantiate, substantiate, transubstantiate.
   Plus man, she ate, etc.

ANSIVNES

p: expansiveness.
v: advanciveness.

ANSƏMEST

h: handsomest.
r: ransomest*.

ANSƏMUR

h: handsomer.
r: ransomer.
   Plus plan summer, etc.

ANTHRŌPē

Vowel: physianthropy, theanthropy, zoanthropy.
k(c): lycanthropy.
l: aphilanthropy, philanthropy, theophilanthropy.
p: apanthropy.
s: misanthropy.
   Plus can throw pea, etc.

ANTHRŌPIST

l: philanthropist, psylanthropist, theophilanthropist.
s: misanthropist.

ANTHRŌPIZM

Vowel: theanthropism.
l: psilanthropism, theophilanthropism.

ÄNTIFĪ

kw(qu): quantify.

ANTIKNES

fr: franticness.
g: giganticness.
m: romanticness.

ANTISĪD

f: infanticide.
g: giganticide.
   Plus aunty sighed, etc.
   Plus anti side, etc.
   Plus ant, he sighed, etc.

ANTƏBƏL

gr: grantable.
pl: plantable.

ANTƏRING

b: bantering.
k(c): cantering.
    Plus plant her ring, etc.
    Plus grant a ring, etc.

ANTƏRƏR

b: banterer.
k(c): canterer.
    Plus enchanter, her, etc.

ANƏBƏL

k(c): cannibal.
s: insanable*, sanable.
t: tannable.
    Plus can a bull, etc.

ĀNƏBƏL

ch: chainable.
d: ordainable.
dr: drainable, undrainable.
g: gainable.
pl: explainable, unexplainable.
spr: sprainable.
str: constrainable, overstrainable, strainable.
t: ascertainable, attainable, containable, detainable, maintainable, obtainable, sustainable, unattainable, unobtainable.
tr: restrainable, trainable.
    Plus gain a bull, etc.

ANƏLING

ch: channeling.
p: panelling.

ANƏRĒ

gr: granary.
k(c): cannery.

p: panary.
st: stannary.
t: charlatanery, tannery.
    Plus manner, he, etc.

ĀNƏRĒ

k(c): chicanery.
l: lanary*.
pl: planary.

ANƏRET

b: banneret.
l: lanneret.
    Plus manner, et, etc.

ÄPĒDISK

fl: floppy disk.

APĒEST

h: happiest.
s: sappiest.
sn: snappiest.

APĒNES

h: happiness.
s: sappiness.
sn: snappiness.

ÄPĒNES

ch: choppiness.
s: soppiness.
sl: sloppiness.

APĒOUR

h: happy hour.

APĒƏR

h: happier.
s: sappier.
sn: snappier.

APIDLĒ

r: rapidly.
s: sapidly.
v: vapidly.

APIDNES

r: rapidness.
s: sapidness.
v: vapidness.

ÄPIKƏL

sk(sc): metoposcopical, micro-scopical.
t: topical.
tr: allotropical, subtropical, tropical.
thr: misanthropical.
   Plus floppy, Cal, etc.
   Plus kaleidoscopic, Al, etc.

APILĒ

h: happily.
s: sappily.
sn: snappily.
   Plus happy Lee, etc.

ÄPINGPLUG

p: popping plug.

APŌLIS

Vowel: Minneapolis.
n: Annapolis, Indianapolis.

ÄPSIKƏL

dr: dropsical.
m: mopsical.
p: Popsicle.
   Plus Topsy, Cal, etc.

ÄPTIKƏL

Vowel: optical.
t: autoptical.
   Plus Coptic, Al, etc.

ÄPTƏRĒS

d: lepidopterous.
kr: macropterous.
th: orthopterous.

ÄPŪLĀT

k(c): copulate.
p: depopulate, populate.
   Plus stop, you late, etc.

ĀPƏBƏL

dr: drapable.
k(c): capable, escapable, incapable, inescapable.
p: papable.
sh: shapable.
   Plus drape a bull, etc.

ÄPƏLIS

Vowel: Heliopolis.
kr: acropolis, necropolis.
m: cosmopolis, Demopolis.
tr: metropolis.

ÄPƏLIST

Vowel: bibliopolist.
k(c): pharmacopolist.
n: monopolist.

ÄPƏLĪT

m: cosmopolite.
tr: metropolite.
   Cf. shah polite, etc.

ĀPƏRĒ

Vowel: apery.
dr: drapery.
gr: grapery.
n: napery.
p: papery.
v: vapory.
Plus caper, he, etc.

ÄPƏRĒ

f: foppery.
k(c): coppery.
Plus stop her, he, etc.
Plus sharecropper, he, etc.

ĀPƏRING

k(c): capering.
p: papering.
t: tapering.
v: vaporing.
Plus paper ring, etc.

ĀPƏRƏR

k(c): caperer.
p: paperer.
v: vaporer.
Plus taper her, etc.

ÄPƏTHĒ

Vowel: enantiopathy,
homoeopathy, ideopathy,
osteopathy, theopathy.
dr: hydropathy.
k(c): psychopathy.
l: allopathy.
n: somnopathy.
r: heteropathy, neuropathy.
s: isopathy.

ÄPƏTHIST

Vowel: homoeopathist, osteo-
pathist.
dr: hydropathist.
l: allopathist, hylopathist.
n: somnopathist.

ÄRÄING

b: borrowing.
m: morrowing, tomorrowing.
s: sorrowing.

ÄRÄƏR

b: borrower.
s: sorrower.
Plus tomorrow her, etc.
Cf. car, O her, etc.

ÄRBƏNĀT

k(c): carbonate+.

ÄRBƏNIT

k(c): carbonate+.

ÄRBƏRING

b: barbering.
h: harboring.
Plus garb, a ring, etc.

ÄRDĒNESS

h: foolhardiness,
hardiness.
t: tardiness.

ÄRDĒƏN

g: guardian.
k(c): pericardian.
Plus tardy, an, etc.
Plus tardy Ann, etc.

ĀRĒĀT

k(c): vicariate.
v: variate.
  Plus Mary ate, etc.
  Plus nary eight, etc.

ĀRĒEST

ch: chariest.
v: variest*.
w: wariest.

ÄRĒNES

st: starriness.
t: tarriness.

ÄRĒŌ

k(c): comprimario.

ĀRĒUM

Vowel: glaciarium.
b: barium, columnbarium, herbarium.
d: tepidarium.
kw: aquarium.
r: honorarium, sacrarium, terrarium, xeroterrarium.
t: sanitarium, termitarium
v: aquavivarium, vivarium.
  Plus vary 'em, etc.
  Plus vary, um, etc.

ĀRĒƏ

Vowel: area.
g: Bulgaria.
k(c): Caria.
l: caballeria, Calceolaria, Hilaria, malaria.
r: cineraria.
s: adversaria.
t: dataria, digitaria, wistaria.

Plus Mary a, etc.
Plus gay rhea, etc.
Cf. aria.
Cf. pariah.

ĀRĒƏL

Vowel: actuarial, areal.
d: calendarial, diarial*.
k(c): vicarial.
l: malarial.
p: puparial.
s: commissarial, glossarial.
t: nectarial, notarial, secretarial.
v: ovarial.
  Plus stay real, etc.

ĀRĒƏN

Vowel: apiarian, Arian, Aryan, Briarean, diarian, estuarian, sententiarian.
b: barbarian.
br: librarian.
d: abecedarian, Darien, lapidarian, stipendarian.
f: Rastafarian.
g: Bulgarian, Hungarian, Megarian, vulgarian.
gr: agrarian.
k(c): Carian, Icarian.
kw(qu): antiquarian, aquarian, ubiquarian.
l: atrabilarian.
m: grammarian.
n: adessenarian, altitudinarian, Apollinarian, attitudinarian, centenarian, disciplinarian, doctrinarian, latitudinarian, lunarian, millenarian, miscellenarian, nonegenarian, octogenarian, platitudinarian, plenitudinarian, predestinarian, septuagenarian, sexagenarian, valetudinarian, veterinarian.

p: Parian, reparian.

s: necessarian, sublapsarian, supralapsarian.

t: alphabetarian, anecdotarian, antisabbatarian, antitrinitarian, dietarian, equalitarian, experimentarian, futilitarian, humanitarian, libertarian, limitarian, necessitarian, nectarian, parliamentarian, proletarian, sabbatarian, sacramentarian, Tartarean, tractarian, trinitarian, ubiquitarian, unitarian, utilitarian, vegetarian.

v: Bavarian, ovarian, Varian.

z: Caesarian, Janizarian.

  Plus Mary Ann, etc.

  Plus vary an, etc.

ĀRĒƏNT

p: omniparient.

tr: contrariant.

v: variant.

  Plus Mary, aunt, etc.

  Plus wary ant, etc.

ARĒƏR

b: barrier.

f: farrier.

h: harrier.

k(c): carrier.

m: marrier.

t: tarrier.

  Plus carry her, etc.

  Plus Harry err, etc.

  Plus Harry, er, etc.

ĀRĒƏR

ch: charier.

w: warier.

  Plus Mary err, etc.

  Plus Carey, er, etc.

  Plus vary her, etc.

ĀRĒƏS

f: multifarious, nefarious, omnifarious.

g: gregarious, vagarious.

k(c): calcareous, precarious, vicarious.

kw(qu): Aquarius.

l: atrabilarious, hilarious, malarious.

n: arenarious, denarius, quadragenarious, testitudinarious, valetudinarious.

p: viparious.

r: honorarious, temerarious.

t: frumentarious, nectarious, Sagittarius, tartareous.

tr: arbitrarious, contrarious.

v: various.

  Plus vary us, etc.

ARĒƏT

l: lariat.

s: commisariat.

t: proletariat, prothonotariat, secretariat.

  Plus tarry at, etc.

  Cf. ariet.

ÄRIDLĒ

fl: floridly.

h: horridly.

t: torridly.

  Plus forehead, Lee, etc.

ARIET, ARIƏT

h: Harriet.

k(c): Iscariot.

m: Marryatt, Marriott.

  Plus tarry at, etc.

  Cf. ariat.

ARIFĪ

k(c): saccharify.
kl: clarify.
sk(sc): scarify.
　　Plus Carrie, fie!, etc.

ÄRIFĪ

h: horrify.
t: historify, torrefy.
　　Plus sorry, fie!, etc.

ARIGAN

g: Garrigan.
h: Harrigan.
l: Larrigan.

ARIING

h: harrying.
k(c): carrying.
m: marrying.
t: tarrying.

ÄRIKƏL

Vowel: oracle.
f: metaphorical.
g: allegorical, categorical, tautegorical.
k(c): coracle.
t: historical, oratorical, pictorical, rhetorical.
　　Plus sorry, Cal, etc.
　　Plus Doric, Al, etc.

ARINGTƏN

b: Barrington, Great Barrington.
f: Farrington.
h: Harrington.
k(c): Carrington.
　　Cf. bearing ton, etc.

ÄRIŌ

n: scenario.
s: impresario.
　　Plus starry, Oh, etc.
　　Plus starry, owe, etc.
　　Cf. Lothario.

ARISƏN

g: garrison.
h: Harrison.
　　Plus marry, son, etc.
　　Plus tarry, sun, etc.

ÄRITĒ

Vowel: anteriority, deteriority, exteriority, inferiority, interiority, meliority, posteriority, priority, superiority.
j: majority.
n: minority.
r: sorority.
th: authority.
y: juniority, seniority.
　　Plus Dorrit, he, etc.
　　Plus sorry tea, etc.

ARIƏN

k(c): carrion.
kl: clarion.
m: Marian, Marion.
　　Plus carry an, etc.

ARITŌŌD

kl: claritude*.
m: amaritude*.

ÄRKIKƏL

Vowel: archical.
l: hylarchical.

n: monarchical.
r: hierarchical, tetrarchical.
  Plus darky, Cal, etc.

ÄRLƏTƏN

sh: charlatan.
t: tarlatan.

ÄRMINGLĒ

ch: charmingly.
f: farmingly.
h: harmingly.
l: alarmingly.
  Plus harming Lee, etc.
  Plus farming lea, etc.

ÄRNISHING

g: garnishing.
t: tarnishing.
v: varnishing.

ÄRNISHƏR

g: garnisher.
t: tarnisher.
v: varnisher.
  Plus varnish err, *or* er.
  Plus varnish her.

ARŌĒ

Vowel: arrowy.
m: marrowy.
sp: sparrowy.
y: yarrowy.
  Plus farrow, we, etc.

ARŌEST

h: harrowest*.
n: narrowest.

ARŌING

b: wheelbarrowing.
h: harrowing.
n: narrowing.

ARŌƏR

h: harrower.
n: narrower.
  Plus sparrow err, *or* er.
  Plus harrow her, etc.

ÄRSƏNĒ

l: larceny.
p: coparceny.
  Plus arson, he, etc.

ÄRSƏNƏR

l: larcener.
p: coparcener, parcener.
  Plus parson, her, etc.

ÄRSHƏLIZM

m: martialism.
p: partialism.

ÄRTEDNES

h: false-heartedness, fickle-heartedness, frank-heartedness, free-heartedness, hard-heartedness, kind-heartedness, light-heartedness, open-heartedness, soft-heartedness, tender-heartedness, true-heartedness, warm-heartedness.
p: departedness.

ÄRTHRŌSKŌP

Vowel: arthroscope.

ÄRTIK′L

Vowel: article.
p: particle.

ÄRTIZƏN

Vowel: artisan.
b: bartizan.
p: partisan.

ÄRTLESLĒ

Vowel: artlessly.
h: heartlessly.
   Plus smart, Leslie, etc.
   Plus start, Les, Lee, etc.

ÄRTLESNES

Vowel: artlessness.
h: heartlessness.

ÄRTƏRING

b: bartering.
ch: chartering.
m: martyring.
   Plus gartering, etc.

ÄRTƏRƏR

b: barterer.
ch: charterer.
   Plus martyr her, etc.
   Plus garter err, *or* er, etc.

ARƏBƏL

Vowel: arable.
p: parable.

ĀRƏNĪT

Vowel: Aaronite.
m: Maronite.
   Cf. Charon night, etc.

ARƏSING

b: embarrassing.
h: harassing.
   Plus Tara, sing, etc.

ARƏSMENT

b: embarrassment.
h: harassment.
   Plus arras meant, etc.

ARƏTĒ

Vowel: familiarity, peculiarity, rectilinearity.
b: barbarity.
ch: charity, uncharity.
d: solidarity.
g: vulgarity.
kl: clarity.
l: angularity, cirularity, dissimilarity, globularity, hilarity, insularity, irregularity, jocularity, molecularity, muscularity, particularity, perpendicularity, piacularity, polarity, popularity, pupilarity, rectangularity, regularity, secularity, similarity, singularity, titularity, triangularity, vascularity.
p: disparity, fissiparity, gemmiparity, imparity, omniparity, parity, viviparity.
pl: exemplarity.
   Plus carry tea, etc.

ARƏTIV

kl: declarative.
n: narrative.
p: comparative, preparative, reparative.

ASĒNES

br: brassiness.
gl: glassiness.
gr: grassiness.

kl: classiness.
m: massiness.
s: sassiness.

ĀSĒNES

l: laciness.
r: raciness.

ÄSĒNES

dr: drossiness.
fl: flossiness.
gl: glossiness.
m: mossiness.
   Cf. sauciness.

ÄSESING

pr: processing.

ÄSESƏR

pr: processor.

ĀSFƏLNES

gr: disgracefulness, gracefulness, ungracefulness.

ÄSFƏRƏS

b: Bosphorus.
f: phosphorous, phosphorus.
   Plus loss for us, etc.

ĀSHĒAT

gl: glaciate.
gr: ingratiate.
m: emaciate.
p: expatiate.
s: insatiate, satiate.
   Plus the way she ate, etc.

ASHĒNES

Vowel: ashiness.
fl: flashiness.
tr: trashiness.

ASHĒƏN

k(c): Circassian.
n: Parnassian.
   Plus flashy an, etc.
   Cf. ashun.

ASHƏNĀT

p: compassionate, dispassionate, impassionate, incompassionate, passionate.
   Plus fashion, ate, etc.
   Plus Circassian eight, etc.

ASHƏNƏL

n: binational, cross-national, international, multi-national, national.
p: passional.
r: irrational, rational.
   Plus fashion, Al, etc.

ĀSHƏNƏL

Vowel: associational, creational, ideational.
b: probational.
d: gradational.
g: congregational.
gr: emigrational.
k(c): educational.
l: relational.
n: denominational, terminational.
r: gyrational, inspirational, respirational.
s: conversational, sensational.
st: stational.
t: dissertational, imitational, representational, rotational.
v: conservational, derivational, observational.
   Plus nation, Al, etc.

ASHƏNING

f: fashioning.
p: compassioning, passioning.

ĀSHƏNIST

Vowel: repudiationist.
fl: inflationist.
gr: emigrationist, immigrationist.
k(c): convocationist, educationist.
l: annihilationist, isolationist.
m: cremationist.
p: emancipationist.
r: degenerationist, inspirationist, liberationist, restorationist.
s: annexationist, conversationist.
t: annotationist, imitationist, transmutationist.
v: innovationist, preservationist.
z: causationist.

ĀSHƏNLES

d: foundationless.
gr: emigrationless, immigrationless.
r: inspirationless.
s: conversationless.
t: imitationless, temptationless.
Plus one nation less, etc.

ĀSHƏNƏR

b: probationer, reprobationer.
d: foundationer.
l: oblationer.
r: restorationer.
st: stationer.
Plus indignation, her, etc.
Plus nation err *or* er, etc.

ASHƏRĒ

d: haberdashery.
f: fashery.
s: sashery.
Plus rasher, he, etc.

ĀSHƏSNES

d: audaciousness, edaciousness, mendaciousness.

f: ineffaciousness.
g: fugaciousness, sagaciousness.
gr: graciousness, ungraciousness.
k(c): efficaciousness, perspicaciousness.
l: fallaciousness, salaciousness.
m: contumaciousness.
n: pertinaciousness, pugnaciousness, tenaciousness.
p: capaciousness, incapaciousness, rapaciousness.
r: veraciousness, voraciousness.
s: vexatiousness.
sp: spaciousness.
t: disputatiousness, ostentatiousness.
v: vivaciousness.

ASITĒ

b: bibacity.
d: audacity, edacity, mendacity, mordacity.
g: fugacity, sagacity.
k(c): dicacity*, perspicacity, pervicasity, procacity.
kw(qu): loquacity, sequacity.
l: bellacity, salacity.
m: contumacity.
n: minacity, pertinacity, pugnacity, saponacity, tenacity.
p: capacity, incapacity, opacity, rapacity.
r: feracity, veracity, voracity.
v: vivacity.
Plus classy tea, etc.
Plus tacit, he, etc.

ÄSITĒ

Vowel: actuosity, anfractuosity, curiousity, dibuosity, ebriosity, foliosity, furiosity, grandiosity, hideosity, impecuniosity, impetuosity, ingeniosity, eleosity, otiosity, preciocity, pretiosity, religiosity, sensuosity, sinuosity, speciosity, tortuosity, unctuosity, viciosity, virtuosity, vitiosity.

b: gibbosity, glebosity, globosity, verbosity.

br: tenebrosity.

d: docity, nodosity.

g: fungosity, rugosity.

k(c): muscosity, precocity, spicosity, varicosity, viscosity.

kw(qu): aquosity.

l: angulosity, callosity, fabulosity, glandulosity, gulosity, musculosity, nebulosity, pilosity, ridiculosity, sabulosity, scrupulosity, tumulosity, velocity, villosity.

m: animosity, anonymosity, fumosity, gemmosity, gummosity, plumosity, rimosity.

n: caliginosity, carnosity, fuliginosity, glutinosity, libidinosity, luminosity, spinosity, vinosity.

p: pomposity.

pr: reciprocity.

r: ferocity, generosity, ponderosity, porosity, saporosity, scirrhosity, serosity, torosity, tuberosity, vociferosity.

str: monstrosity.

tr: atrocity.

v: nervosity.

  Plus cross it, he, etc.
  Plus Flossie, tea, etc.
  Plus posset, he, etc.
  Cf. faucet, he, etc.

ASIVLĒ

m: massively.

p: impassively, passively.

  Plus lascive Lee, etc.

ASIVNES

m: massiveness.

p: impassiveness, passiveness.

ĀSIVNES

sw: dissuasiveness, persuasiveness, suasiveness.

v: evasiveness, pervasiveness.

ÄSKÄPĒ

Vowel: cranioscopy, geoscopy, stereoscopy.

l: geloscopy.

n: organoscopy, retinoscopy, uranoscopy.

p: metoposcopy.

r: hieroscopy, horoscopy, meteoroscopy, oneiroscopy.

t: omoplatoscopy.

th: ornithoscopy, stethoscopy.

ÄSKÄPIST

Vowel: stereoscopist.

kr: microscopist.

p: netoposcopist.

r: oneiroscopist.

th: ornithoscopist, stethoscopist.

ASKETBÔL

b: basketball.

ASPINGLĒ

g: gaspingly.

r: raspingly.

  Plus clasping Lee, etc.

ASPƏRTĀM

Vowel: aspartame.

ĀSTĒƏ

m: gynecomastia.

ĀSTFUƏLĒ

t: distastefully, tastefully.

w: wastefully.

  Plus chased fully, etc.

ASTICƏL

Vowel: ecclesiastical, encomiastical, enthusiastical.
l: elastical.
n: gymnastical.
t: fantastical.
  Plus nasty, Cal, etc.

ĀSTILĒ

h: hastily.
p: pastily.
t: tastily.
  Plus pasty, Lee, etc.

ASTISIZM

Vowel: ecclesiasticism.
l: scholasticism.
n: monasticism.
t: fantasticism.
  Plus nasty schism, etc.

ASTRĒƏN

Vowel: Zoroastrian.
b: alabastrian.
k(c): Lancastrian.

ASTRŌFĒ

n: epanastrophe.
t: catastrophe.

ASTƏRDĒ

b: bastardy.
d: dastardy.
  Plus bastard, he, etc.

ASTƏRĒ

k: dicastery.
m: mastery, self-mastery.
pl: plastery.

ASTƏRING

m: mastering, overmastering.
pl: beplastering, plastering.
  Plus faster ring, etc.

ASTƏRSHIP

m: mastership.
p: pastorship.
  Plus faster ship, etc.
  Plus passed her ship, etc.

ASURĒ

br: bracery, embracery.
tr: tracery.

ASƏBƏL

n: renascible.
p: impassible, passable, passible, surpassable.
r: irascible.
  Plus classy bull, etc.

ĀSƏBƏL

ch: chasable.
f: effaceable, ineffaceable.
r: erasible.
tr: retraceable, traceable.
v: evasible.
  Plus race a bull, etc.

ÄSƏFĒ

Vowel: theosophy.
l: philosophy, psylosophy.
n: gymnosophy.
  Plus cross off, he, etc.

ÄSƏFIST

Vowel: theosophist.
l: philosophist.
n: deipnosophist, gymnosophist.

r: chirosophist.
Plus loss, Oh fist, etc.

ÄSƏFĪZ

Vowel: theosophize.
l: philosophize.

ÄSƏFƏR

Vowel: theosopher.
l: philosopher, psilosopher.
Cf. cross off her, etc.

ASƏHÔL

g: gasohol.

ASƏNĀT

b: abbacinate.
f: fascinate.
r: deracinate.
s: assassinate, exacinate.
Plus classy, Nate, etc.
Plus class in eight, etc.
Plus mass innate, etc.

ÄSƏNĀT

Vowel: ratiocinate.
tr: patrocinate*.
Plus loss innate, etc.
Plus loss in eight *or* ate, etc.
Plus glossy, Nate, etc.

ĀSƏNSĒ

j: adjacency,
interjacency.
pl: complacency.
Plus renascence, he, etc.

ASƏRĀT

l: lacerate.
m: emacerate, macerate.

Plus pass her eight, etc.
Plus first classer ate, etc.

ÄTÄMIST

Vowel: ichthyotomist, zootomist.
b: phlebotomist.
t: phytotomist, etc.
Plus lot o' mist, etc.
Plus blotto mist *or* missed, etc.

ĀTANDSWICH

b: bait-and-switch.

ATĒNES

ch: chattiness.
f: fattiness.
n: nattiness.

ĀTĒNES

sl: slatiness.
w: weightiness.

ÄTĒNES

d: dottiness.
n: knottiness.
sn: snottiness.
sp: spottiness.

ĀTFƏLĒ

f: fatefully.
gr: gratefully.
h: hatefully.
Plus mate fully, etc.

ĀTFƏLNES

f: fatefulness.
gr: gratefulness.
h: hatefulness.

ATHĒSIS

Vowel: diathesis.
r: parathesis.

ĀTHĒƏN

b: Sabbathian.
p: Carpathian.

ATHƏKƏL

m: chrestomathical.
p: anthropopathical.

ATHƏRING

bl: blathering.
g: foregathering, gathering, upgathering, woolgathering.
l: lathering.
    Plus lather, ring, etc.

ATHƏRƏR

g: forgatherer, gatherer, tax gatherer, toll gatherer, up gatherer.
l: latherer.
    Plus lather her, etc.

ATIFĪ

Vowel: beatify.
gr: gratify.
r: ratify.
str: stratify.
    Plus Mattie, fie!, etc.
    Plus cat, if I, etc.
    Plus flat, if eye, etc.

ATIKƏ

Vowel: Attica, sciatica.
m: dalmatica.
p: hepatica.
    Plus attic, a, etc.

ATIKƏL

b: abbatical, sabbatical.
f: emphatical.
kr: aristocratical, autocratical, bureaucratical, democratical, Socratical.
m: acroamatical, anathematical, anidiomatical, apophlegmatical, apophthegmatical, asthmatical, automatical, axiomatical, climatical, diplomatical, dogmatical, dramatical, emblematical, enigmatical, epigrammatical, grammatical, hebdomatical, idiomatical, mathematical, phantasmatical, pragmatical, primatical, schismatical, spasmatical.
n: fanatical.
r: leviratical, piratical, separatical.
st: aerostatical, statical.
t: apostatical, ecstatical.
v: vatical.
    Plus batty, Cal, etc.
    Plus attic, Al, etc.

ÄTIKƏL

d: anecdotical.
g: bigotical.
l: zealotical.
p: despotical.
r: erotical.
s: exotical.
    Plus dotty, Cal, etc.
    Plus erotic, Al, etc.

ATINĀT

l: gelatinate, Palatinate.
    Plus satin ate *or* eight, etc.
    Plus rat innate, etc.
    Plus batty, Nate, etc.

ATINĪZ

l: gelatinize, Latinize.
pl: platinize.
  Plus satin eyes, etc.

ATINƏS

l: gelatinous.
pl: platinous.
  Plus Latin us, etc.
  Plus fat in us, etc.

ATISĪZ

m: emblematicize, grammaticize.
n: fanaticize.
  Plus Hattie sighs, etc.
  Cf. Hattie's eyes, etc.

ATISIZM

Vowel: Asiaticism.
m: grammaticism.
n: fanaticism.

ATITŌŌD

Vowel: attitude, beatitude.
gr: gratitude, ingratitude.
l: latitude.
pl: platitude.
  Plus pat it, you'd, etc.
  Plus cat etude, etc.

ĀTIVNES

n: nativeness.
r: alliterativeness.
t: imitativeness.
tr: penetrativeness.

AT'LĪT

p: patellite*.
s: satellite.

Plus Mattie, light, etc.
Plus pat, he light, etc.

AT'LMENT

b: battlement, embattlement.
pr: prattlement.
t: tattlement.
  Plus cattle meant, etc.

ATŌŌLĀT

gr: congratulate, gratulate.
sp: spatulate.
  Plus Matt, you late?, etc.

ATRIKƏL

Vowel: theatrical.
l: idolatrical.

ATRISĪD

fr: fratricide.
m: matricide.
p: patricide.

ĀTRƏNIJ

m: matronage.
p: patronage.

ĀTRƏNĪZ

m: matronize.
p: patronize.

ĀTRƏNƏL

m: matronal.
p: patronal.
  Plus natron, Al, etc.

ÄTWĪLƏR

r: Rottweiler.

ĀTƏBĀS

d: database.

ATƏBƏL

Vowel: come-atable.
b: combatable.
p: compatible, imcompatible, impatible*, patible.
   Plus pat a bull, etc.

ĀTƏBƏL

Vowel: creatable.
b: abatable, baitable, debatable.
gr: gratable.
h: hatable.
l: collatable, dilatable, regulatable, translatable, untranslatable.
m: matable.
r: beratable, ratable.
st: statable.
   Plus fete a bull, etc.

ATƏMĒ

Vowel: atomy.
n: anatomy.

ÄTƏMĒ

Vowel: ichthyotomy, stereotomy, tracheotomy, zootomy.
b: bottomy, phlebotomy.
k(c): bronchotomy, dichotomy.
l: encephalotomy.
m: dermotomy.
p: apotome, hippopotamy.
sk(sc): scotomy.
t: phytotomy.
   Plus lot o' me, etc.
   Plus blotto me, etc.
   Plus bottom, he, etc.
   Cf. hippopotami.

ATƏMIST

Vowel: atomist.
n: anatomist.

ATƏMĪZ

Vowel: atomize.
n: anatomize.

ATƏMIZM

Vowel: atomism.
n: anatomism.

ATƏMƏS

Vowel: diatomous.
r: paratomous.

ÄTƏNĒ

b: botanee, botany, geobotany.
k(c): cottony.
n: monotony.
   Plus rotten, he, etc.
   Plus not a knee, etc.

ĀTƏNSĒ

l: latency.
p: patency.
   Plus Satan, see, etc.

ĀTƏRĒ

kr: obsecratory.
l: recapitulatory.
n: ratiocinatory.

ATƏRĒ

b: battery.
fl: flattery.
sh: shattery.
sl: slattery.
t: tattery.
   Plus clatter, he, etc.

ÄTƏRĒ

l: lottery.
p: pottery.
t: tottery.
tr: trottery.
  Plus squatter, he, etc.
  Plus got her, he, etc.

ÄTƏRING

w: watering.

ATƏRƏL

l: bilateral, collateral, equilateral, lateral, quadrilateral, unilateral.
  Plus matter, Al?, etc.

ATƏRƏN

k(c): cateran.
l: Lateran.
  Plus matter, Ann, etc.

ATƏRING

b: battering.
bl: blattering.
ch: chattering.
fl: beflattering, flattering.
kl: clattering.
p: bepattering, pattering.
sh: shattering.
sk(sc): bescattering, scattering.
sm: smattering.
sp: bespattering, spattering.
spl: splattering.
  Plus patter ring, etc.
  Plus pat a ring, etc.

ATƏRƏR

b: batterer.
bl: blatterer.
ch: chatterer.
fl: flatterer.
kl: clatterer.
p: patterer.
sh: shatterer.
sk(sc): scatterer.
sm: smatterer.
spl: splatterer.
  Plus batter her, etc.
  Plus batter err *or* er, etc.

ĀVĒƏ

gr: Belgravia.
n: Scandinavia.
p: Pavia.
r: Moravia.
sl: Jugo-Slavia.
t: Batavia, Octavia.
  Plus navy, a, etc.
  Plus way, via, etc.

ĀVĒƏN

Vowel: avian.
gr: Belgravian.
n: Scandinavian.
r: Moravian.
sh: Shavian.
sl: Jugo-Slavian.
t: Batavian.
  Plus wavy, Ann *or* an, etc.

AVIJING

r: ravaging.
sk(sc): scavaging.

AVIJƏR

r: ravager.
s: savager.
sk(sc): scavager.
  Plus ravage her, etc.
  Plus savage err *or* er, etc.

AVISHING

l: lavishing.
r: enravishing, ravishing.

AVISHMENT

l: lavishment.
r: enravishment, ravishment.

ĀVISHNES

n: knavishness.
sl: slavishness.

AVISHƏR

l: lavisher.
r: ravisher.
    Plus ravish her, etc.
    Plus lavish, err *or* er, etc.

AVITĒ

gr: gravity.
k(c): cavity, concavity.
pr: depravity, pravity.
sw: suavity.
    Plus navvy tea, etc.

AVITƏN

gr: graviton.

AVƏLING

gr: graveling.
r: ravelling, unravelling.
tr: travelling.

ÄVƏLING

gr: groveling.
h: hoveling.
    Cf. shoveling.

AVƏLƏR

r: raveller, unraveller.
tr: traveller.
    Plus gavel her, etc.
    Plus gavel err *or* er, etc.

AVƏNDƏR

ch: chavender.
l: lavender.

AVƏNĒZ

h: Havanese.
j: Javanese.

ĀVƏRĒ

br: bravery.
gr: gravery.
n: knavery.
s: savory, unsavory.
sl: slavery.

ĀVƏRING

f: favoring.
fl: flavoring.
kw(qu): quavering.
s: savoring.
w: unwavering,
wavering.
    Plus braver ring, etc.

ĀVƏRƏR

f: favorer.
fl: flavorer.
kw(qu): quaverer.
w: waverer.
    Plus favor her, etc.
    Plus flavor err *or* er, etc.

AVƏRƏS

d: cadaverous.
p: papaverous.
  Plus beslaver us, etc.

ĀVƏRĒS

fl: flavorous.
s: savorous.
  Plus favor us, etc.

ĀZĒNES

h: haziness.
kr: craziness.
l: laziness.
m: maziness.

ÄZĒƏR

Vowel: osier.
d: Dozier.
h: hosier.
k(c): cozier.
kr: crosier.
n: nosier.
pr: prosier.
r: rosier.
  Plus posy her, etc.

ĀZƏBƏL

pr: praisable.
r: raisable.

sw: persuasible, suasible.
  Plus raise a bull, etc.
  Plus Gaza bull, etc.

ĀZƏRDISC

l: laser disc.

ÄZƏTIV

p: contrapositive, positive.

ĀƏBƏL

fr: defrayable.
p: impayable, payable, repayable, unpayable.
pr: prayable, unprayable.
sw: swayable, unswayable.
tr: portrayable, unportrayable.
v: conveyable, unconveyable.
  Cf. weigh a bull, etc.

ĀƏRĒ

Vowel: aery.
f: faerie*.

ĀƏTĒ

g: gaiety.
l: laity.

ĀƏTRƏL

l: laetrile.

E

The accented vowel sounds included are listed under **E** in Single Rhymes.

ĒBRĒƏS

Vowel: ebrious.
n: funebrious, inebrious, tenebrious.

ECHĒNES

sk: sketchiness.
t: tetchiness.

ĒCHƏBƏL

bl: bleachable.
p: impeachable, unimpeachable.
r: reachable, unreachable.
t: teachable, unteachable.
    Plus teach a bull, etc.

ECHƏRĒ

l: lechery.
tr: treachery.

ECHƏRƏS

l: lecherous.
tr: treacherous.
    Plus stretcher us, etc.

ĒDĒĀT

m: immediate, intermediate, mediate.
    Plus needy ate *or* eight, etc.

EDĒEST

h: headiest.
r: readiest.
st: steadiest, unsteadiest.

ĒDĒEST

b: beadiest.
gr: greediest.
n: neediest.
r: reediest.
s: seediest.
sp: speediest.
w: weediest.

EDĒNES

h: headiness.
r: readiness, unreadiness.
st: steadiness, unsteadiness.
thr: threadiness.

ĒDĒNES

gr: greediness.
n: neediness.
s: seediness.
sp: speediness.
w: weediness.

ĒDĒUM

m: medium.
t: tedium.
    Cf. te deum.

ĒDĒƏL

m: bimedial, intermedial, medial, remedial.
p: pedial.

ĒDĒƏN

j: tragedian.
m: comedian, median.
p: encyclopedian.

ĒDĒƏNS

b: disobedience, obedience.
p: expedience, inexpedience.

ĒDĒƏNT

b: disobedient, obedient.
gr: ingredient.
p: expedient, inexpedient.

EDĒƏR

h: headier.
r: readier.
st: steadier, unsteadier.
  Plus already her, etc.
  Plus already err *or* er, etc.

ĒDĒƏR

b: beadier.
gr: greedier.
n: needier.
r: reedier.
s: seedier.
sp: speedier.
w: weedier.
  Plus speedy her, etc.
  Plus weedy err *or* er, etc.

ĒDĒƏS

m: intermedious.
t: tedious.

  Plus weedy, us, etc.
  Cf. see *deus*, etc.

ĒDFƏLNES

h: heedfulness, unheedfulness.
n: needfulness, unneedfulness.

EDIKĀT

d: dedicate.
m: medicate.
pr: predicate.
  Plus ready, Kate, etc.
  Plus medic ate *or* eight, etc.

EDIKƏL

m: medical.
p: pedicle.
  Plus ready, Cal, etc.
  Plus medic, Al, etc.

EDIKƏNT

m: medicant.
pr: predicant.
  Plus ready cant *or* Kant, etc.
  Plus encyclopedic ant *or* aunt, etc.

ĒDINƏS

b: rubedinous.
s: mucedinous.
tr: putredinous.
  Plus weed in us, etc.

EDITED

Vowel: edited.
kr: accredited, credited, discredited, miscredited, unaccredited.
  Plus ready, Ted, etc.
  Plus credit, Ed, etc.

EDITING

Vowel: editing.
kr: accrediting, crediting, discrediting, miscrediting.

EDITƏR

Vowel: editor.
kr: creditor.
    Plus said it, or, etc.
    Plus credit, or, etc.

ĒDLESLĒ

h: heedlessly.
n: needlessly.
    Plus heed, Leslie, etc.
    Plus heedless Lee, etc.

ĒDLESNES

h: heedlessness.
n: needlessness.

EDYOͦOͦLƏS

kr: credulous, incredulous.
s: sedulous.
    Plus schedule us, etc.

EDƏBƏL

Vowel: edible.
dr: dreadable.
kr: credible, incredible.
    Plus fed a bull, etc.
    Plus ready bull, etc.

ĒDƏBƏL

b: obedible.
p: impedible.
pl: pleadable, unpleadable.
r: readable, unreadable.
s: exceedable.
    Plus feed a bull, etc.
    Plus Theda bull, etc.

EDƏLĒ

h: headily.
r: readily.
st: steadily, unsteadily.
    Plus ready, Lee, etc.
    Plus head alee, etc.

ĒDƏLĒ

gr: greedily.
n: needily.
sp: speedily.
    Plus weedy lea *or* Lee, etc.
    Plus speed alee, etc.

EDƏMƏNT

p: impediment, pediment.
s: sediment.
    Plus ready meant, etc.

EDƏRƏL

f: federal.
h: hederal.

ĒDƏRSHIP

l: leadership.
r: readership.
    Plus cedar ship, etc.
    Plus feed her ship, etc.

EDƏTIV

r: redditive.
s: sedative.

ĒFĒNES

b: beefiness.
l: leafiness.

EFƏRƏNS

d: deference.
pr: preference.
r: cross-reference, reference.

EFƏRƏNT

Vowel: efferent.
d: deferent.
  Plus clef for rent, etc.

EFƏSƏNS

l: maleficence.
n: beneficence.

EFƏSƏNT

l: maleficent.
n: beneficent.

EGĒNES

dr: dregginess.
l: legginess.

EGNƏNSĒ

pr: pregnancy.
r: regnancy.
  Cf. regnant, see, etc.

EGƏBƏL

b: beggable.
l: legable.
  Plus peg a bull, etc.

ĒGƏLIZM

l: legalism.
r: regalism.

ĒGƏLNES

g: regalness.
l: illegalness, legalness.

EGƏRĒ

Vowel: eggery.
b: beggary.
gr: Gregory.

ĒGƏRLĒ

Vowel: eagerly, overeagerly.
m: meagerly.
  Plus intriguer, Lee, etc.

ĒGƏRNES

Vowel: eagerness, overeagerness.
m: meagerness.

ĒJĒƏN

Vowel: Fuegian.
l: collegian.
w: Norwegian.

EJƏBƏL

l: allegeable, illegible, legible.
  Plus hedgy bull, etc.

ĒJƏSNES

gr: egregiousness.
l: sacrilegiousness.

EKCHO͞OƏL

f: effectual, ineffectual.
l: intellectual, lectual.
  Cf. henpecked you all, etc.

EKCHƏRƏL

j: conjectural.
t: architectural.
  Plus lecture, Al, etc.
  Cf. lecture all, etc.

EKCHƏRƏR

j: conjecturer.
l: lecturer.
  Plus lecture her, err, *or* er, etc.

ĒKĒNES

ch: cheekiness.
kr: creakiness.
l: leakiness.
skw(squ): squeakiness.
sn: sneakiness.

ĒKILĒ

ch: cheekily.
kr: creakily.
l: leakily.
skw(squ): squeakily.
sl: sleekily.
sn: sneakily.
    Plus streaky lea *or* Lee, etc.
    Plus streak a lee, etc.

ĒKISHNES

fr: freakishness.
kl: cliquishness.
sn: sneakishness.

EKRƏMƏNT

d: decrement.
r: recrement.

EKSHƏNƏL

f: affectional.
fl: inflectional.
j: interjectional.
pl: complexional.
r: correctional, insurrectional.
s: intersectional, sectional.
t: protectional.
    Plus direction, Al, etc.

EKSHƏNIST

f: perfectionist.
r: insurrectional, resurrectionist.
t: protectionist.

EKSHƏNĪZ

r: resurrectionize.
s: sectionize.
    Plus projection eyes, etc.

EKSIVNES

fl: reflexiveness.
pl: perplexiveness.

EKSƏBƏL

fl: flexible, inflexible, reflexible.
n: nexible.
    Plus apoplexy, bull, etc.

EKSƏTĒ

fl: reflexity.
pl: complexity, intercomplexity, perplexity.
v: convexity.
    Plus prexy, tea, etc.

EKTEDNES

f: affectedness, disaffectedness, infectedness.
j: adjectedness, dejectedness.
p: suspectedness, unsuspectedness

EKTIKƏL

l: dialectical.
pl: apoplectical.

EKTIVLĒ

f: affectively, defectively, effectively, ineffectively, infectively, perfectively, refectively.
fl: deflectively, inflectively, irreflectively, reflectively, unreflectively.
j: injectively, objectively, rejectively, subjectively.
l: collectively, electively,

neglectively, recollectively, selectively.

m: humectively.

n: connectively.

r: correctively, directively, erectively.

s: sectively.

sp: circumspectively, inspectively, introspectively, irrespectively, perspectively, prospectively, respectively, retrospectively.

t: detectively, protectively.

v: invectively.

Plus detective, Lee, etc.

EKTIVNES

f: defectiveness, effectiveness, ineffectiveness.

fl: reflectiveness.

j: objectiveness, subjectiveness.

l: collectiveness.

sp: prospectiveness.

t: protectiveness.

EKTƏBƏL

f: affectible, defectible, effectible, indefectible, perfectible.

fl: reflectible.

j: objectable, rejectable.

l: collectible, delectable, indelectable.

p: expectable, respectable, suspectable.

r: correctible, erectable.

s: dissectible.

sp: respectable.

t: detectible.

Plus wrecked a bull, etc.

EKTƏFĪ

j: objectify.

r: rectify.

EKTƏRĀT

l: electorate.

r: directorate, rectorate.

sp: expectorate.

t: protectorate.

Plus Hector ate *or* eight, etc.

Plus wrecked a rate, etc.

EKTƏRĒ

f: refectory.

n: nectary.

r: correctory, directory, rectory.

s: sectary.

Plus rector, he, etc.

EKTƏRƏL

l: electoral.

p: pectoral.

r: rectoral.

s: sectoral.

t: protectoral.

Plus Hector, Al, etc.

EKTƏTŌŌD

n: senectitude.

r: rectitude.

EKYŌŌLƏR

l: molecular.

s: secular.

sp: specular.

EKYŌŌLĀT

p: peculate.

sp: speculate.

Plus wreck, you late, etc.

EKYŌŌTIV

s: consecutive, executive, subsecutive.

EKƏBƏL

p: impeccable, peccable.
s: seccable*.
    Plus wreck a bull, etc.

ĒKƏBƏL

sp: speakable, unspeakable.
    Plus weak a bull, etc.

EKƏNING

b: beckoning.
r: dead-reckoning, reckoning.

ELEGĀT

d: delegate.
r: relegate.
    Plus Kelly gate, etc.

ĒLĒƏ

Vowel: Elia.
b: lobelia.
d: Bedelia, Cordelia, Delia, Fidelia.
f: Ophelia.
l: Lelia.
m: Amelia, Camelia.
n: Cornelia.
r: Aurelia.
s: Cecelia, Celia.
v: Vilia.
    Plus steely a, etc.
    Cf. elya.

ELĒƏN

j: evangelian.
s: selion.
w: Boswelian, Cromwelian.
    Plus smelly an *or* Ann, etc.
    Plus smell, Ian, etc.
    Cf. elyan, elyun.

ĒLĒƏN

Vowel: Ismaelian.
d: Delian.
f: aphelion, Mephistophelean.
g: Hegelian.
h: perihelion.
m: chameleon.
n: carnelian.
t: Aristotelian.
th: anthelion.
v: Macchiavelian.
    Plus steely an *or* Ann, etc.
    Plus feel, Ian, etc.
    Cf. elyan.

ĒLĒƏS

b: Sibelius.
d: Delius.
n: Cornelius.
r: Aurelius.
    Plus genteely us, etc.
    Cf. helios.
    Cf. elyus.

ELFISHNES

Vowel: elfishness.
s: selfishness, unselfishness.

ELIKƏL

b: bellical.
h: helical.
j: angelical, evangelical.
p: pellicle.
    Plus jelly, Cal, etc.
    Plus bellie, Al, etc.

ELISHING

b: embellishing.
r: relishing.

ELISHMƏNT

b: embellishment.
r: relishment.
  Plus hellish meant, etc.

ELŌEST

b: bellowest.
m: mellowest.
y: yellowest.

ELŌING

b: bellowing.
ch: celloing.
m: mellowing.
y: yellowing.

ELŌƏR

b: bellower.
ch: celloer.
m: mellower.
y: yellower.
  Plus good-fellow her, err, *or* er,
etc.

ELTHĒEST

h: healthiest.
st: stealthiest.
w: wealthiest.

ELTHĒƏR

h: healthier.
st: stealthier.
w: wealthier.
  Plus wealthy her, err *or* er, etc.

ELTHILĒ

h: healthily.
st: stealthily.
w: wealthily.
  Plus wealthy lea *or* Lee, etc.

ELTƏRĒ

sh: sheltery.
sm: smeltery.
  Plus swelter, he.

ELTƏRING

sh: sheltering.
w: weltering.
  Plus felt her ring, etc.
  Plus smelter ring, etc.
  .

ELTƏRƏR

sh: shelterer.
w: welterer.
  Plus shelter her, etc.

ELYŌŌLƏR

s: cellular, intercellular, unicellu-
lar.
st: stellular.

ELƏBƏL

d: delible, indelible.
f: fellable.
j: gelable, ingelable.
p: compellable, expellable.
sp: spellable.
t: tellable.
  Plus umbrella bull, etc.
  Plus tell a bull, etc.

ĒLƏBƏL

h: healable.
j: congealable.
p: peelable, repealable.
s: concealable, inconcealable.
v: revealable.
  Plus steal a bull, etc.

ELƏNĒ

f: felony.
m: melony.
   Plus watermelon, he, etc.

ELƏRĒ

s: celery.
st: stellary.
   Plus seller, he, etc.

ELƏSLĒ

j: jealously.
z: overzealously, zealously.

ELƏTIV

p: compellative.
r: correlative, relative.

ELƏTƏN

sk: skeleton.
   Plus smelly ton *or* tun, etc.
   Cf. gelatin.
   Cf. smell it on, etc.

EMBƏRING

m: dismembering, membering, remembering, unremembering.
s: Decembering.
v: Novembering.
   Plus ember ring, etc.

EMƏNSTRĀTE

m: demonstrate*+.

ĒMĒƏ

f: Euphemia.
h: Bohemia.
k(c): leukemia.

n: anemia.
r: uremia.
   Plus schemy a, etc.

ĒMĒƏL

d: academial, endemial, vindemial.
gr: gremial.
r: uremial.

ĒMĒNES

dr: dreaminess.
kr: creaminess.
st: steaminess.

ĒMĒƏN

Vowel: prooemion.
d: academian.
h: Bohemian.
th: anthemion.
   Plus steamy on, etc.
   Cf. emian.

ĒMĒƏR

b: beamier.
dr: dreamier.
kr: creamier.
pr: premier.
   Plus steamy, err, er, *or* her, etc.

EMIKƏL

d: academical, endemical, epidemical.
k(c): alchemical, chemical, electrochemical.
l: polemical.
   Plus gemmy, Cal, etc.

ĒMILĒ

b: beamily.
dr: dreamily.

kr: creamily.
st: steamily.
  Plus steamy lea *or* Lee, etc.

EMNƏTĒ

d: indemnity.
l: solemnity.

EMŌNĒ

n: anemone.
p: Agapemone.
s: Gethsemane.
  Plus lemon, he, etc.

EMPƏRƏR

Vowel: emperor.
t: temperer.
  Plus sic semper, err, er, *or* her, etc.

EMYO͞OLƏNT

t: temulent.
tr: tremulent.
  Plus Clem, you lent, etc.

EMYO͞OLƏS

Vowel: emulous.
tr: tremulous.

ĒMƏBƏL

d: redeemable.
dr: dreamable.
t: esteemable.
  Plus redeem a bull, etc.

EMƏNĀT

f: effeminate.
j: geminate, ingeminate.
s: disseminate, inseminate, seminate.
  Plus gemmy, Nate, etc.

EMƏNƏL

f: feminal.
j: geminal.
s: seminal.

EMƏRƏL

f: ephemeral, femoral.
n: nemoral.

EMƏRƏLD

Vowel: emerald.
f: aphemeralled.

EMƏRĒ

Vowel: Emery, Emory.
j: gemmery.
m: memory.
  Plus tremor, he, etc.

ĒMƏRĒ

dr: dreamery.
kr: creamery.
  Plus schemer, he, etc.
  Cf. we, Murray, etc.

EMƏRIST

f: ephemerist.
h: euhemerist.
  Plus condemn her wrist, etc.

EMƏTIST

bl: emblematist.
r: theorematist.

ĒMƏTIST

sk(sc): schematist.
th: thematist.

ENCHŌŌƏL

s: accentual.
v: adventual, conventual, eventual.

Plus sent you, Al, etc.

ENCHŌŌĀT

s: accentuate.
v: eventuate.

Plus meant you ate *or* eight, etc.

ENDENSĒ

p: dependency, equipendency*, impendency, independency, interdependency.
s: ascendency, transcendency.
spl: resplendency.
t: attendency, intendency, superintendency, tendency.

Plus dependence, he, etc.

ENDĒƏS

p: compendious.
s: incendious.

ENDLESLĒ

Vowel: endlessly.
fr: friendlessly.

Plus end, Leslie, etc,
Plus endless, he, etc.

ENDLESNES

Vowel: endlessness.
fr: friendlessness.

ENDƏBƏL

f: defendable.
h: comprehendible, uncomprehendible.
l: lendable.
m: amendable, commendable, mendable, recommendable.
p: dependable.
r: rendible.
s: ascendable, descendable, unascendable.
t: extendible.
v: invendible, vendible.

Plus vend a bull, etc.
Plus hacienda bull, etc.

ENDƏREST

j: engenderest*.
r: renderest*, surrenderest*.
sl: slenderest.
t: tenderest.

Plus mend her rest, etc.
Plus defender rest, etc.
Plus friend arrest, etc.
Plus mend a rest, etc.

ENDƏRING

j: engendering, gendering.
r: rendering, surrendering.
t: tendering.

Plus mend her ring, etc.
Plus mend a ring, etc.
Plus tender ring, etc.

ENDƏRLĒ

sl: slenderly.
t: tenderly.

Plus gender, Lee, etc.

ENDƏRNES

sl: slenderness.
t: tenderness.

ENDƏRƏR

j: engenderer.
r: renderer, surrenderer.

sl: slenderer.
t: tenderer.
Plus surrender her, etc.

ENDƏSLĒ

m: tremendously.
p: stupendously.

ENETING

j: jenneting.
r: renneting.

ĒNĒUM

l: selenium.
s: proscenium.
z: xenium.

ĒNĒƏ

d: gardenia.
fr: schizophrenia.
j: Eugenia.
m: Armenia.
th: neurosthenia, Parthenia.
z: Xenia.
Plus Sweeny, a, etc.

ENĒƏL

Vowel: biennial, triennial.
kw: quinquennial.
l: millenial.
r: perennial, quadrennial.
s: decennial, duodecennial, vicennial.
t: centennial, octennial, septennial.
v: novennial.

ĒNĒƏL

j: congenial, genial, primigenial, uncongenial.

m: demesnial, menial.
v: venial.
Plus meany, Al, etc.

ĒNĒƏN

f: Fenian.
l: Hellenian, Madrilenian.
m: Armendian, Estremenian.
r: Cyrenian.
th: Athenian, Ruthenian.
Plus Selene, an *or* Ann, etc.
Plus mean, Ian, etc.

ĒNĒƏNS

l: lenience.
v: convenience, inconvenience.
Cf. enyens.

ĒNĒƏNT

l: lenient.
v: advenient, convenient, inconvenient, intervenient, introvenient, supervenient.
Cf. enyent.

ĒNĒƏS

j: extrageneous, genius, heterogenious, homogenious, ingenious, nitrogenious, primigenious.
l: selenious.
m: pergameneous.
s: arsenious.
Plus genie us, etc.

ENIFÔRM

p: penniform.
t: antenniform.
Plus penny form, etc.

ENIKƏL

m: catechumenical, ecumenical.
r: sirenical.
s: arsenical, scenical.
  Plus Hellenic, Al, etc.

ENISƏN

b: benison
v: venison
  Cf. penny, son *or* sun, etc.

ENITIV

j: genitive, primogenitive.
l: lenitive.
spl: splenitive.

ENITŌŌD

l: lenitude.
pl: plenitude.
r: serenitude.
  Plus men etude, etc.

ENIZƏN

d: denizen, endenizen.

ENSHĒĀT

s: essentiate, licentiate.
t: potentiate.
  Plus then she ate *or* eight, etc.

ENSHĒƏNT

s: assentient, consentient,
dissentient, insentient,
presentient, sentient.

ENSHƏNƏL

s: ascensional, descensional.
t: extensional, intentional.
v: conventional, preventional.
  Plus mention, Al, etc.

ENSHƏNIST

s: ascensionist, recensionist.
t: extensionist.

ENSHƏRĒ

d: residentiary.
t: penitentiary.

ENSHƏSNES

Vowel: conscientiousness.
s: licentiousness.
t: contentiousness, pretentiousness.

ENSIKƏL

r: forensical.
s: nonsensical.

ENSIVNES

f: inoffensiveness, offensiveness.
h: comprehensiveness.
p: expensiveness, pensiveness.
t: extensiveness, intensiveness.

ENSLESLĒ

f: defenselessly.
s: senselessly.
  Plus hence, Leslie, etc.
  Plus senseless, Lee *or* lea, etc.

ENSLESNES

d: defenselessness.
s: senselessness.

ENSƏBƏL

d: condensable, incondensable.
f: defensible, indefensible.
h: comprehensible, depre-
hensible, incomprehensible,
reprehensible.
p: dispensable, indispensable,
suspensible.

s: insensible, sensible, subsensible.

t: distensible, extensible, ostensible, tensible.

ENSƏTĒ

d: condensity, density.

m: immensity.

p: propensity.

t: intensity, tensity.

Plus men see tea, etc.

ENSƏRĒ

f: defensory.

h: prehensory, reprehensory.

p: dispensary, suspensory.

s: incensory, sensory.

t: ostensory.

ENSƏTIV

d: condensative.

f: defensative.

p: compensative, dispensative, pensative.

s: insensitive, sensitive.

t: intensitive.

ENTIKYŌŌL

d: denticule.

l: lenticule.

ENTIKƏL

d: denticle, identical.

th: authentical.

v: conventical, conventicle.

Plus twenty, Cal, etc.

ENTIVNES

m: alimentiveness.

t: attentiveness, inattentiveness, retentativeness.

v: inventiveness.

ENT'LĒ

d: accidentally, incidentally, transcendentally.

m: experimentally, fundamentally, instrumentally, sentimentally.

Plus rental lea *or* Lee, etc.

Plus sent alee, etc.

ENT'LIST

Vowel: Orientalist.

d: Occidentalist, transcendentalist.

m: experimentalist, fundamentalist, instrumentalist, sentimentalist.

Plus sent a list, etc.

Plus rental list, etc.

ENT'LĪZ

Vowel: Orientalize.

m: experimentalize, sentimentalize.

Plus monumental lies, etc.

Plus monumental eyes, etc.

ENT'LIZM

Vowel: Orientalism.

d: accidentalism, transcendentalism.

m: elementalism, sentimentalism.

ENT'LNES

d: accidentalness, incidentalness.

j: gentleness, ungentleness.

m: fundamentalness, instrumentalness, sentimentalness.

ENTƏBƏL

kw(qu): frequentable.

m: fermentable.

r: rentable.

v: inventible, preventable.
z: presentable, representable.
  Plus sent a bull, etc.

ENTƏKƏL

p: pentacle.
t: tentacle.

ENTƏMƏNT

s: sentiment.
z: presentiment.
  Plus Henty meant, etc.

ENTƏNƏL

d: dentinal.
s: sentinal.
  Plus San Quentin, Al, etc.

ENTƏRĒ

d: accidentary, dentary.
m: alimentary, complementary, complimentary, elementary, filamentary, instrumentary, integumentary, parliamentary, pigmentary, rudimentary, sacramentary, sedimentary, tegumentary, tenementary, testamentary, unparliamentary.
s: placentary.
  Plus enter, he, etc.

ENTƏSLĒ

m: momentously.
t: portentously.
  Plus sent us, Lee, etc.

ENTƏSNES

m: momentousness.
t: portentousness.

ENTƏTĒ

Vowel: entity, nonentity.
d: identity.
  Plus meant it, he, etc.
  Plus plenty tea, etc.

ENTƏTIVE

kw: frequentative.
m: alimentative, argumentative, augmentative, commentative, complimentative, experimentative, fermentative.
t: pretentative, tentative.
v: preventative.
z: misrepresentative, presentative, representative.

ENYŌŌƏNT

j: genuant*.
t: attenuant.
  Plus then, you ant *or* aunt, etc.

ENYŌŌĀT

t: attenuate, extenuate, tenuate.
  Plus then you ate *or* eight, etc.

ENYŌŌRĒ

p: penury.
  Plus then you're he, etc.

ENYŌŌƏS

j: disingenuous, ingenuous.
str: strenuous.
t: tenuous.

ĒNYƏNSĒ

l: leniency.
v: conveniency, inconveniency.
  Plus mean yen, see?, etc.

ĒNƏBƏL

m: amenable.
v: convenable.
   Plus screen a bull, etc.
   Plus hyena bull, etc.

ENƏRĀT

j: degenerate, generate, ingenerate, progenerate, regenerate.
t: intenerate.
v: venerate.
   Plus pen her, ate *or* eight, etc.
   Plus tenor ate *or* eight, etc.

ENƏRĒ

d: denary.
h: hennery.
s: decennary, senary*.
t: centenary.
v: venery.
   Plus tenner, he, etc.
   Plus tenor, he, etc.
   Plus ten *or* he, etc.

ĒNƏRĒ

d: deanery.
gr: greenery.
pl: plenary.
s: scenery.
sh: machinery.
   Plus cleaner, he, etc.

ENƏSIS

j: abiogenesis, biogenesis, ectogenesis, eugenesis, genesis, heterogenesis, homogenesis, ontogenesis, organogenesis, palingenesis, pangenesis, paragenesis, parthenogenesis, photogenesis, phylogenesis, polygenesis, psychogenesis, xenogenesis.
r: parenesis.
   Plus any sis, etc.
   Cf. tennis's, etc.
   Cf. menaces, etc.

ENƏTĒ

l: lenity.
m: amenity.
r: serenity, terrenity.
s: obscenity.
   Plus penny tea, etc.
   Plus pen it, he, etc.

ENƏTƏR

j: progenitor.
s: senator.
   Plus rennet, or, etc.
   Plus tenet err *or* er, etc.

ĒPĒNES

kr: creepiness.
sl: sleepiness.
st: steepiness.
w: weepiness.

ĒPILĒ

kr: creepily.
sl: sleepily.
   Plus weepy, Lee *or* lea, etc.
   Plus steep alee, etc.

EPTIKƏL

s: antiseptical, aseptical, receptacle, septical.
sk(sc): sceptical.

EPTIVNES

s: deceptiveness, receptiveness, susceptiveness.

EPTƏBƏL

s: acceptable, deceptible, imperceptible, insusceptible, perceptible, receptible, susceptible.

Plus kept a bull, etc.

EPƏRƏS

l: leperous.
str: obstreperous, perstreperous*, streperous.

Plus pepper us, etc.

ERĒEST

b: buriest*.
f: ferriest*.
m: merriest.

ĒRĒEST

Vowel: eeriest.
b: beeriest.
bl: bleariest.
ch: cheeriest.
dr: dreariest.
t: teariest.
w: weariest.

ERĒING

h: herrying, burying.
f: ferrying.
hw: wherrying.

ERĒMAN

f: ferryman.
hw: wherryman.
m: Merriman.

Plus cemetary man, etc.

ERĒMƏNT

m: merriment.

Plus Kerry meant, etc.
Cf. uriment.

ERĒNES

Vowel: airiness, tumultuariness.
ch: chariness.
gl: glariness.
h: hairiness.
n: sanguinariness.
r: temporariness.
t: salutariness, sedentariness, solitariness, ubiquitariness, voluntariness.
tr: arbitrariness, contrariness.
w: wariness.

ĒRĒNES

Vowel: eeriness.
b: beeriness.
bl: bleariness.
dr: dreariness.
t: teariness.
w: weariness.

ĒRĒUM

t: acroterium, apodyterium.
th: dinotherium, megatherium, paleotherium, titanotherium.

Plus weary 'em, etc.
Plus weary her, err, or er, etc.

ĒRĒƏ

b: Liberia.
j: Algeria, Egeria, Nigeria.
k: Valykyria.
p: hesperia.
t: hysteria, icteria*, wisteria.
th: diphtheria, eleutheria, Etheria.

Plus weary a, etc.

ĒRĒƏL

Vowel: aerial.
d: siderial.
f: ferial.
j: managerial.
n: funereal, manereal.
p: imperial.
s: cereal, rhinocerial, serial.
t: arterial, magisterial, material, ministerial, monasterial, presbyterial.
th: etherial.
z: vizierial.
  Plus weary, Al, etc.

ĒRĒƏN

Vowel: aerian, Pierian.
b: Celtiberian, Iberian, Siberian.
d: Abderian.
f: Luciferian.
j: Algerian.
k: Valkyrian.
l: allerion, Keplerian, valerian.
m: Cimmerian.
p: Hesperian, Hyperion, Shakespearean, Shakespearian.
s: Spencerian, Spenserian.
st: phalansterian.
t: criterion, Presbyterian.
th: Wertherian.

ERĒƏR

b: berrier, burier.
m: merrier.
t: terrier.
  Plus bury her, err, *or* er, etc.

ĒRĒƏR

Vowel: eerier.
b: beerier.

bl: blearier, bleerier.
ch: cheerier.
dr: drearier.
f: inferior.
p: superior.
t: anterior, exterior, interior, posterior, tearier, ulterior.
w: wearier.
  Cf. erior.

ĒRĒƏS

d: siderious.
p: imperious.
s: cereous, cereus, serious.
t: deleterious, mysterious.
th: etherious.
  Plus weary us, etc.

ĒRFƏLĒ

ch: cheerfully.
f: fearfully.
t: tearfully.
  Plus smear fully, etc.
  Plus tearful, he, etc.

ĒRFƏLNES

ch: cheerfulness.
f: fearfulness.
t: tearfulness.

ERFULĒ

k(c): carefully, uncarefully.
pr: prayerfully.
  Plus share fully.

ERFULNES

k(c): carefulness, uncarefulness.
pr: prayerfulness.
sp: sparefulness.
w: warefulness.

ERIDĒZ

Vowel: Pierides.
p: Hesperides.
t: Anterides.
  Plus buried ease *or* he's, etc.

ERIFÔRM

l: scalariform.
p: peariform.
  Plus nary form, etc.
  Plus spare reform, etc.

ERIKƏL

f: atmospherical.
kl: clerical.
m: chimerical, numerical.
s: rhinocerical.
sf: heliospherical, helispherical, spherical, sphericle.
t: alixiterical, climacterical, esoterical, exoterical, hysterical, phylacterical.
  Plus merry, Cal, etc.

ERILĒ

m: merrily.
v: verily.
  Plus cherry, Lee *or* lea, etc.

ĒRILĒ

Vowel: eerily.
ch: cheerily.
dr: drearily.
w: wearily.
  Plus dreary lea *or* Lee, etc.
  Plus drear alee, etc.

ERINGLĒ

bl: blaringly.
d: daringly.

fl: flaringly.
gl: glaringly.
sp: sparingly.
t: tearingly.
  Plus pairing Lee, etc.

ERISHING

ch: cherishing.
p: perishing, unperishing.

ERITĒ

n: debonarity.
r: rarity.
  Plus fairy tea, etc.

ERITED

f: ferreted.
h: disherited, disinherited, inherited.
m: emerited, merited.
  Plus mer'it, Ed, etc.
  Cf. turreted.

ERITING

f: ferreting.
h: inheriting.
m: meriting.

ĒRLESNES

ch: cheerlessness.
f: fearlessness.
p: peerlessness.
t: tearlessness.

ERƏBƏL

Vowel: airable.
b: bearable, unbearable.
d: dareable.
kl: declarable.
p: pairable, repairable.

sw: swearable.
t: tearable.
w: unwearable, wearable.
  Plus tear a bull, etc.

ERƏDĪS

p: imparadise, paradise.
  Plus share a dice, etc.

ERƏGĀT

t: interrogate.
  Cf. urogate.

ĒRƏLIST

p: imperialist.
t: immaterialist, materialist.
  Plus material list, etc.

ĒRƏLIZM

p: imperialism.
t: immaterialism, materialism.

ERƏNSĒ

Vowel: aberrancy, errancy, inerrancy.

ERƏPĒ

th: balneotherapy, hydrotherapy, kinesitherapy, phototherapy, radiotherapy.

ERƏTĒ

j: legerity.
l: celerity.
m: temerity.
p: asperity, prosperity.
s: insincerity, procerity, sincerity.
t: ambidexterity, austerity, dexterity, indexterity, posterity.
v: severity, verity.

Plus merit, he, etc.
Plus merry tea, etc.

ESCHƏRƏL

j: gestural.
v: vestural.

ESHĒNES

fl: fleshiness.
m: meshiness.

ĒSHĒƏN

d: geodesian*.
gr: Grecian.
l: Megalesian, Silesian.
n: gynoecian*, Melanesian, Peloponnesian, Venetian.
p: Capetain.
t: Epictetian.
  Plus fleccy Ann *or* an, etc.
  Cf. eshan, eshun.

ESHĒƏNS

n: nescience.
pr: prescience.

ESHLĒNES

fl: fleshliness, unfleshliness.
fr: freshliness.

ESHƏNIST

gr: progressionist.
pr: impressionist.
s: secessionist, successionist.

ESHƏNƏL

f: confessional, professional.
gr: congressional, digressional, progressional, transgressional.
kr: discretional.
pr: expressional.

s: accessional, intercessional, processional, recessional, retrocessional, sessional, successional.

z: possessional.

Plus confession, Al, etc.

ESHƏNƏR

s: processioner, secessioner.

z: possessioner.

Plus procession her, err, *or* er, etc.

ĒSHƏSNES

s: facetiousness.

sp: speciousness.

ESITĒ

s: necessity.

Plus dress it, he, etc.

ĒSITY

b: obesity.

Plus piece it, he, etc.

ESIVNES

gr: aggressiveness, progressiveness.

pr: depressiveness, expressiveness, impressiveness, inexpressiveness, oppressiveness.

s: excessiveness.

ESTĒNES

r: restiness.

t: testiness.

ĒSTĒNES

r: reastiness.

y: yeastiness.

ESTĒƏL

b: bestial.

gr: agrestial.

l: celestial, supercelestial.

Plus chesty, Al, etc.

ESTIVNES

f: festiveness.

j: suggestiveness.

r: restiveness.

ĒSTLĒNES

b: beastliness.

pr: priestliness.

ESTRĒƏL

d: pedestrial.

m: trimestrial.

r: superterrestrial, terrestrial.

Plus vestry, Al, etc.

ESTRĒƏN

d: pedestrian.

kw(qu): equestrian.

l: palestrian.

p: campestrian.

v: sylvestrian.

Plus vestry, Ann *or* an, etc.

ESTRĒƏS

d: pedestrious.

r: terrestrious.

Plus vestry, us, etc.

ESTYO̅O̅ƏS

p: tempestuous.

s: incestuous.

ESTƏBƏL

j: congestible, digestible, indigestible.

m: comestible.

t: contestable, detestable, incontestable, intestable, testable.

v: divestible.
  Plus dressed a bull, etc.
  Plus siesta, bull, etc.

ESTƏNĀT

d: destinate, predestinate.
f: festinate.
  Plus dressed in eight *or* ate, etc.
  Plus less tin, ate, etc.

ESTƏNƏL

d: destinal.
t: intestinal.

ESTƏRING

f: festering.
p: pestering.
w: westering.
  Plus guessed her ring, etc.
  Plus jester ring, etc.
  Plus at best a ring, etc.

ESƏBƏL

dr: redressible.
gr: transgressible.
kr: concrescible.
pr: compressible, expressible, incompressible, inexpressible, insuppressible, irrepressible, repressible, suppressible.
s: accessible, concessible, inaccessible, incessable, marcessible.
t: fermentescible.
tr: imputrescible, putrescible, vitrescible.
v: effervescible, ineffervescible.
  Plus dressy bull, etc.

ĒSƏBƏL

kr: creasable.
l: releasable.

p: peacable, piecible.
  Plus fleece a bull, etc.

ESƏMƏL

d: decimal.
j: nonagesimal, quadragesimal, septuagesimal, sexagesimal.
t: centesimal, infinitesimal.
  Plus dress him, Al, etc.

ESƏNSĒ

Vowel: acquiescency, quiescency.
b: erubescency, pubescency.
d: incandescency, recrudescency.
j: turgescency.
kr: excrescency.
kw(qu): liquescency.
l: adolescency, alkalescency, convalescency, incalescency.
r: efflorescency.
s: acescency.
t: delitescency.
v: defervescency, effervescency.
  Cf. effervescent, see, etc.

ĒSƏNSĒ

d: decency, indecency.
r: recency.
  Plus Gleason, see, etc.

ĒSƏNTLĒ

d: decently, indecently.
r: recently.
  Plus decent lea *or* Lee, etc.

ESƏRĒ

f: confessary, professory.
p: pessary.
s: intercessory, successary.
  Plus successor, he, etc.

ETĒNES

j: jettiness.
p: pettiness.
sw: sweatiness.

ĒTĒNES

m: meatiness.
p: peatiness.
sl: sleetiness.

ETFƏLĒ

fr: fretfully.
g: forgetfully.
gr: regretfully.
Plus debt fully, etc.

ETFƏULNESS

fr: fretfulness.
g: forgetfulness.
gr: regretfulness.

ETHLESLĒ

br: breathlessly.
d: deathlessly.
Plus breath, Leslie, etc.

ETHLESNES

br: breathlessness.
d: deathlessness.

ETHƏRĒ

f: feathery.
h: heathery.
l: leathery.
w: weathery.
Plus together, he, etc.

ETHƏRING

f: feathering.
l: leathering.

t: tethering.
w: weathering.
Plus together ring, etc.

ETIKYO͞OL

Vowel: poeticule.
r: reticule.
Plus energetic Yule *or* you'll, etc.

ETIKƏL

Vowel: aloetical, noetical, poetical.
b: alphabetical.
j: apologetical, energetical, exegetical.
k(c): catechetical.
l: homiletical.
m: arithmetical, cosmetical, hermetical.
n: planetical.
r: anchoretical, emporetical, heretical, theoretical.
t: dietetical.
th: aesthetical, antipathetical, antithetical, apathetical, epithetical, hypothetical.
Plus jetty, Cal, etc.
Plus emetic, Al, etc.

ETINYO͞O

d: detinue.
r: retinue.
Plus met in you, etc.
Plus Wettin, you, etc.

ETISHLĒ

k(c): coquettishly.
p: pettishly.
Plus Lettish, Lee, etc.

ETISHNES

k(c): coquettishness.
p: pettishness.

ĒTISIZM

l: athleticism.

s: asceticism.

t: peripateticism.

th: aestheticism, estheticism.

ETRIKƏL

m: alkalimetrical, asymmetrical, barometrical, craniometrical, diametrical, geometrical, gnomiometrical, graphometrical, horometrical, isoperimetrical, metrical, perimetrical, planimetrical, pluviometrical, stichometrical, symmetrical, trigonometrical.

st: obstetrical.

Plus photometric, Al, etc.

ETRIMƏNT

d: detriment.

r: retriment*.

ETƏBƏL

g: begetable, forgetable, getable, unforgetable.

gr: regretable.

hw: whetable.

n: bayonestable.

p: petable.

s: setable.

Plus met a bull, etc.

ĒTƏBƏL

Vowel: eatable, uneatable.

b: beatable, unbeatable.

ch: cheatable, escheatable.

f: defeatable.

l: deletable.

p: repeatable.

tr: entreatable.

Plus meet a bull, etc.

ETƏLĒN

s: acetylene.

Plus met a lean, etc.

ETƏLIN

m: metalline.

p: petaline.

Plus metal in *or* inn, etc.

ETƏLIZM

m: bimetallism, monometallism.

p: petalism.

ĒTƏRĒ

Vowel: eatery.

kr: secretory.

pl: completory, depletory, repletory.

ETƏRING

b: bettering.

f: fettering.

l: lettering.

Plus letter ring, etc.

Plus let her ring, etc.

Plus let a ring, etc.

ĒVĒĀT

br: abbreviate.

d: deviate.

l: alleviate.

Plus Levy ate *or* eight, etc.

ĒVĒƏS

d: devious.

pr: previous.

Plus Levy, us, etc.

ĒVISHLĒ

p: peevishly.

th: thievishly.

Plus thievish, Lee *or* lea, etc.

ĒVISHNES

p: peevishness.
th: thievishness.

ĒVƏBƏL

ch: achievable.
gr: grievable.
kl: cleavable.
l: believable, relievable, unbeliev-able.
s: conceivable, deceivable, imperceivable, inconceivable, perceivable, receivable, undeceivable.
tr: irretrievable, retrievable.
    Plus grieve a bull, etc.
    Plus Eva, bull, etc.

EVƏLEST

b: bevelest*.
d: bedevillest*.
l: levellest.
r: revellest*.
sh: dishevellest.
    Plus devil, lest, etc.

EVƏLETH

b: bevelleth*.
d: bedevilleth*.
l: levelleth*.
r: revelleth*.
sh: dishevelleth*.

EVƏLING

b: bevelling.
d: bedevilling.
l: levelling.
r: revelling.
sh: dishevelling.

EVƏLIZM

d: devilism.
l: levelism.

EVƏLƏNS

l: malevolence.
n: benevolence.

EVƏLMƏNT

d: bedevilment, devilment.
r: revelment.
    Plus level meant, etc.

EVƏLOOT

Vowel: evolute.
r: revolute.

EVƏLRĒ

d: devilry.
r: revelry.

EVƏLƏR

b: beveller.
d: bedeviller.
l: leveller.
r: reveller.
sh: disheveller.
    Plus level her, err, *or* er, etc.

EVƏLƏS

l: malevolous.
n: benevolous.
    Plus devil us, etc.

EVƏREST

Vowel: Everest.
d: endeavorest*.

kl: cleverest.
s: severest*.
   Plus clever rest, etc.

EVƏRMƏR

Vowel: evermore.
n: nevermore.
   Plus clever more, etc.

EVƏRƏR

d: endeavorer.
kl: cleverer.
s: severer.
   Plus sever her, err, or er, etc.

EVƏTY

br: brevity.
j: longevity.
l: levity.
   Plus heavy tea, etc.

ĒZĒNES

Vowel: easiness, uneasiness.
br: breeziness.
ch: cheesiness.
gr: greasiness.
hw: wheeziness.
kw(qu): queasiness.
sl: sleaziness.

ĒZĒƏN

f: Ephesian.
kl: ecclesian.
l: Milesian.
n: magnesian, Polynesian.
p: trapesian.
t: artesian, cartesian, etesian.
   Plus easy, Ann or an, etc.

EZIDƏNT

pr: president.
r: resident.

ĒZILĒ

Vowel: easily, uneasily.
br: breezily.
gr: greasily.
hw: wheezily.
   Plus easy lea or Lee, etc.

ĒZINGLĒ

fr: freezingly.
hw: wheezingly.
p: appeasingly.
pl: pleasingly.
t: teasingly.
   Plus pleasing lea or Lee, etc.

ĒZĒƏ, ĒZHĒƏ

b: Zambesia.
d: Rhodesia.
kl: ecclesia.
l: Silesia.
n: amnesia, magnesia.
r: parrhesia.
th: anaesthesia, anesthesia, esthesia.
   Plus easy a, etc.

EZHƏRING

m: measuring.
pl: pleasuring.
tr: treasuring.
   Plus treasure ring, etc.

EZHƏRƏR

m: measurer.
pl: pleasurer.

tr: treasurer.

    Plus treasure her, err, *or* er, etc.

ĒZƏBƏL

f: defeasible, feasible, indefeasible, infeasible.
fr: freezable.
h: cohesible.
p: appeasible, inappeasable, unappeasable.
s: seizable.
skw(squ): squeezable.

    Plus freeze a bull, etc.

ĒZƏNING

r: reasoning, unreasoning.
s: seasoning.

EZƏNTRĒ

f: pheasantry.
p: peasantry.
pl: pleasantry.

    Cf. pleasant tree, etc.

ĒƏBĒL

gr: agreeable, disagreeable.
kr: creable*, decreeable.
m: irremeable.

    Cf. see a bull, etc.

ĒƏLIST

d: idealist.
r: realist.

    Plus see a list, etc.
    Plus real list, etc.

ĒƏLĪZ

d: idealize.
r: realize.

    Plus real eyes, etc.
    Plus real lies, etc.

ĒƏLIZM

d: idealism.
r: realism.

ĒƏLTĒ

f: fealty.
r: realty.

    Plus ideal tea, etc.

ĒƏNIZM

b: Sabaeanism, plebeianism.
p: peanism.
r: epicureanism, Pythagoreanism.
s: Laodiceanism.

ĒƏTĒ

b: plebeity.
d: deity, hermaphrodeity.
l: veleity.
n: contemporaneity, diathermaneity, extraneity, femineity, heterogeneity, homogeneity, instantineity, omneity, personeity, simultaneity, spontaneity.
r: corporeity, incorporeity.
s: aseity, gaseity, seity.
t: multeity.

    Plus see it, he, etc.

I

The accented vowel sounds included are listed under **I** in Single Rhymes.

ĪÄRKĒ

d: diarchy.
tr: triarchy.

IBĒƏ

f: amphibia.
l: Libya.
t: tibia.

IBĒƏL

f: amphibial.
st: stibial.
t: tibial.

IBĒƏN

f: amphibian.
l: Lybian.

IBĒƏS

f: amphibious.
st: stibious.
th: bathybius.

IBITED

h: inhibited, prohibited.
z: exhibited.
  Plus prohibit, Ed, etc.

IBITING

h: inhibiting, prohibiting.
z: exhibiting.

IBITIV

h: inhibitive, prohibitive.
z: exhibitive.

IBYŌŌLƏR

d: infundibular, mandibular.
f: fibular.
v: vestibular.

ĪBƏBƏL

br: bribable.
skr(scr): describable, indescribable, inscribable, scribable, subscribable, undescribable.

ĪBƏSŌM

r: ribosome.

ICHĒNES

b: bitchiness.
i: itchiness.
p: pitchiness.

ICHŌŌĀT

b: habituate.
s: situate.
  Plus bit you ate *or* eight, etc.

ICHŌŌLƏR

p: capitular.
t: titular.

ICHŌŌƏL

b: habitual, obitual.
r: ritual.
  Plus hit you, Al, etc.

ICHƏRĒ

m: michery*.
st: stichery.
w: bewitchery, witchery.

IDĒĀT

m: dimidiate.
s: insidiate.
  Plus kiddy ate *or* eight, etc.
  Plus kid he ate, etc.

IDĒƏL

s: presidial.
t: noctidial.
  Plus chickabiddy, Al, etc.

IDĒƏN

f: nullifidian, ophidian.
g: Gideon.
k(c): rachidian.
l: Lydian.
m: Midian, Numidian.
r: antemeridian, meridian, post meridian, viridian.
s: obsidian.
t: quotidian.
v: Ovidian.

IDĒƏM

Vowel: idiom.
r: iridium, peridium.
  Plus kiddy 'em, etc.

IDĒƏS

d: splendidious.
f: ophidious, perfidious, Phidias.

h: hideous.
s: insidious, parracidious, stillicidious.
t: fastidious.
v: avidious, invidious.
  Plus chickabiddy us, etc.
  Cf. idius.

IDIFĪ

l: solidify.
p: lapidify.
s: acidify.
  Plus kiddy, fie!, etc.

IDIKƏL

Vowel: druidical.
m: pyramidical.
r: juridical, veridical.
  Plus chickabiddy, Cal, etc.

IDINƏS

b: libidinous.
  Plus hid in us, etc.
  Plus hidden us, etc.
  Cf. pinguidinous.

IDITĒ

b: morbidity, rabidity, turbidity.
br: hybridity.
j: frigidity, rigidity, turgidity.
k(c): viscidity.
kr: acridity.
kw(qu): liquidity, quiddity.
l: insolidity, invalidity, gelidity, pallidity, solidity, squalidity, stolidity, validity.
m: humidity, timidity, tumidity.
p: cupidity, insipidity, intrepidity, limpidity, rapidity, sapidity, stupidity, torpidity, trepidity, vapidity.
r: aridity, torridity, viridity.

s: acidity, lucidity, marcidity, pellucidity, rancidity.
sp: hispidity.
t: putidity.
tr: putridity.
v: avidity, gravidity, lividity, pavidity, vividity.
    Plus did it, he, etc.

ID'NNES

b: forbiddenness.
h: hiddenness.

ĪDƏBƏL

f: confidable.
g: guidable.
h: hidable.
l: elidable.
r: deridable, outridable, overridable, ridable.
s: coincidable, decidable, subsidable.
str: bestridable, stridable.
v: dividable, subdividable.
    Plus ride a bull, etc.
    Plus I'd a bull, etc.

IFIKĀT

n: significate.
t: certificate+, pontificate.
    Plus terrific, ate *or* eight, etc.
    Plus sniffy, Kate, etc.

IFIKIT

t: certificate.+

IFIKƏL

n: lanifical*.
r: dolorifical.
s: specifical.
t: beatifical, pontifical.
    Plus jiffy, Cal, etc.
    Plus terrific, Al, etc.

IFIKƏNT

d: mundificant.
kr: sacrificant.
n: insignificant, significant.
    Plus terrific ant, etc.
    Plus sniffy cant *or* Kant, etc.

IFO͞OGƏL

m: vermifugal.
r: febrifugal.
tr: centrifugal.
    Plus skiff, you gal, etc.

IFLO͞OƏS

gw: sanguifluous.
l: fellifluous, mellifluous.
n: ignifluous.
s: culcifluous.
    Plus a Riff flew us, etc.

IFRƏGƏS

r: fedrifragous*.
s: ossifragous, saxifragous.

IFTINES

n: niftiness.
sh: shiftiness.
thr: thriftiness.

IFTLESNES

sh: shiftlessness.
thr: thriftlessness.

IFTƏBƏL

dr: driftable.
l: liftable.
s: siftable.
sh: shiftable.
    Plus shift a bull, etc.

IFƏLĒ

n: niftily.

sh: shiftily.

thr: thriftily.

Plus thrifty Lee *or* lea, etc.

Plus thrift alee, etc.

IFƏNĒ

l: polyphony.

p: epiphany.

s: oxyphony.

t: antiphony.

IFƏRƏL

p: peripheral.

IFƏRƏS

Vowel: oleiferous.

b: bulbiferous, herbiferous, nimbiferous, nubiferous, plumbiferous, sebiferous.

bl: ombliferous.

br: umbriferous.

d: acidiferous, diamondiferous, frondiferous, geodiferous, glandiferous.

g: frugiferous.

gw: sanguiferous.

j: tergiferous.

k(c): conchiferous, siliciferous, succiferous, zinciferous.

kr: luciferous*.

l: aliferous, cheliferous, coralliferous, filiferous, foliferous, fossiliferous, glanduliferous, granuliferous, lamelliferous, maliferous, mammaliferous, melliferous, metalliferous, nickeliferous, pistilliferous, saliferous, stelliferous, tentaculiferous, umbelliferous, umbraculiferous, vasculiferous.

m: armiferous, balsamiferous, flammiferous, fumiferous, gemmiferous, mammiferous, palmiferous, racemiferous, spumiferous.

n: aluminiferous, antenniferous, balaniferous, carboniferous, coniferous, luminiferous, membraniferous, omniferous, ozoniferous, platiniferous, pruniferous, pulmoniferous, resiniferous, saliniferous, somniferous, soniferous, spiniferous, stameniferous, stanniferous, stoloniferous.

p: polypiferous, scopiferous.

r: auriferous, calcariferous, carriferous, doloriferous, ferriferous, floriferous, hederiferous, lauriferous, nectariferous, odoriferous, roriferous, sacchariferous, soporiferous, sudoriferous, thuriferous, tuberiferous, vaporiferous.

s: calciferous, cruciferous, ensiferous*, furciferous, gypsiferous, lanciferous, laticiferous, luciferous, nuciferous, ossiferous, sensiferous, spiciferous, vociferous.

str: monstriferous.

t: ammonitiferous, argentiferous, diamantiferous, fatiferous, fluctiferous, guttiferous, lactiferous, lignitiferous, magnetiferous, margaritiferous, mortiferous, multiferous, noctiferous, oolitiferous, pestiferous, salutiferous, scutiferous, setiferous.

th: lethiferous.

tr: astriferous, nitriferous, ostriferous.

z: quartiziferous.

Plus differ us, etc.

IFƏSƏNS

n: magnificence, munificence.

Plus sniffy sense *or* cents, etc.

IFƏSƏNT

n: magnificent, munificent.
r: mirificent*.
　Plus jiffy sent, cent, *or* scent, etc.
　Plus if he sent, etc.

IFƏSƏR

p: opificer.
t: artificer.
　Plus if he, sir, etc.
　Plus sniffy sir, etc.

IGMƏTIST

n: enigmatist.
st: stigmatist.

IGMƏTĪZ

d: paradigmatize.
n: enigmatize.
st: stigmatize.

IGNĒƏS

Vowel: igneous.
l: ligneous.

IGNƏFĪ

Vowel: ignify.
d: dignify, undignify.
l: lignify, malignify.
s: signify.
　Plus big knee? fie!, etc.

IGNƏNSĒ

d: indignancy.
l: malignancy.
　Plus a pig, Nan, see?, etc.

IGNƏTĒ

d: dignity, indignity.
l: malignity.
n: benignity.

IGO͞OLĀT

f: figulate.
l: ligulate.
　Plus pig, you late, etc.

IGRƏFĒ

k(c): tachygraphy.
l: calligraphy, poligraphy.
p: epigraphy, pseudepigraphy.
s: lexigraphy, pasigraphy.
t: stratigraphy.

IGYO͞OƏS

b: ambiguous.
r: irriguous.
s: exiguous.
t: contiguous.

IGƏMĒ

b: bigamy.
d: digamy.
l: polygamy.
tr: trigamy.

IGƏMIST

b: bigamist.
l: polygamist.
tr: trigamist.
　Plus big a mist, etc.

IGƏMƏS

b: bigamous.
d: digamous.
l: polygamous.
tr: trigamous.

IGƏRĒ

hw: Whiggery.
p: piggery.
w: wiggery.
　Plus bigger, he, etc.

IGƏRƏS

r: rigorous.
v: vigorous.
  Plus trigger us, etc.

IJĒƏN

br: Cantabrigian.
fr: Phrygian.
st: Stygian.
v: vestigian.

IJIDLĒ

fr: frigidly.
r: rigidly.

IJIDNES

fr: frigidness.
r: rigidness.

IJITĒ

d: digity.
f: fidgety.
  Plus midget, he, etc.

IJO͞OĀT

s: assiduate.
v: individuate.
  Plus kid, you ate *or* eight, etc.

IJO͞OLĀT

s: acidulate.
str: stridulate.
  Plus kid, you late, etc.

IJO͞OLƏS

s: acidulous.
str: stridulous.

IJO͞OƏL

v: individual.
z: residual.

Plus hid you, Al, etc.
Cf. amid you all, etc.

IJO͞OƏS

s: assiduous, deciduous,
prociduous, succiduous.
v: viduous.
z: residuous.

IJƏNƏS

b: nubigenous.
d: indigenous.
gw: sanguigenous*.
l: alkaligenous, coralligenous,
fuliginous, melligenous,
polygenous, uliginous.
n: ignigenous, omnigenous,
unigenous.
p: epigenous.
r: marigenous, prurigeous,
terrigenous.
s: oxygenous.
t: gelatigeous, montigenous,
vertigenous, vortigenous.
  Plus bridge in us, etc.

IJƏRĀT

fr: frigerate*, refrigerate.
l: belligerate.
  Plus bridger ate *or* eight, etc.
  Plus ridge, a rate, etc.

IJƏRƏNT

fr: refrigerant.
l: belligerent.
  Plus bridger rent, etc.

IJƏRƏS

d: pedigerous.
k(c): crucigerous.
l: aligerous, belligerous,
coralligerous, piligerous,
proligerous.

m: armigerous, plumigerous.
n: cornigerous, lanigerous,
linigerous, pennigerous,
spinigerous.
p: palpigerous.
r: cirrigerous, immorigerous*.
t: dentigerous, setigerous.
v: navigerous, ovigerous.
   Plus bridge a Russ, etc.

IJƏSNES

d: prodigiousness.
l: religiousness.
t: litigiousness.

IKENING

kw(qu): quickening.
s: sickening.
th: thickening.

IKETĒ

n: pernicketty.
r: rickety.
th: thickety.
   Plus lickety-(split), etc.
   Plus lick it, he, etc.
   Plus picket, he, etc.

IKĒTIK

r: ricky-tick.

IKETING

kr: cricketing.
p: picketing.
t: ticketing.

IKETƏR

kr: cricketer.
p: picketer.
   Plus thicket, her, err, or er, etc.

IKINES

st: stickiness.
tr: trickiness.

IKLINES

pr: prickliness.
s: sickliness.

IKŌLIST

b: plebicolist.
n: ignicolist.
r: agricolist.

IKŌLUS

p: sepicolous.
r: agricolous, terricolous.
   Plus pickle us, etc.

IKŌMUS

r: auricomous.
v: flavicomous.

IKSHƏNƏL

d: contracictional, jurisdictional.
f: fictional.
fr: frictional.
   Plus affliction, Al, etc.

IKSITĒ

f: fixity.
l: prolixity.
s: siccity.
   Plus pixie tea, etc.

IKSƏBƏL

f: fixable.
m: mixable.
   Plus tricks a bull, etc.

IKTIVLĒ

d: vindictively.
str: restrictively.
  Plus vindictive Lee, etc.

IKTIVNES

d: vindictiveness.
str: restrictiveness.

IKTƏRĒ

d: benedictory, contradictory, interdictory, valedictory.
v: victory.
  Plus boa constrictor, he, etc.
  Plus picked her, he, etc.

IKTƏRSKĀL

r: Richter scale.

IKWƏTĒ

b: ubiquity.
l: obliquity.
n: iniquity.
t: antiquity.
  Plus quick wit, he, etc.

IKWƏTƏS

b: ubiquitous.
n: iniquitous.
  Plus slick wit' us, etc.

IKYŌŌLĀT

h: vehiculate.
l: canaliculate.
m: vermiculate.
n: funiculate, geniculate, paniculate.
s: fasciculate, vesiculate.
sp: spiculate.

t: articulate, denticulate, gesticulate, monticulate, particulate, reticulate.
tr: matriculate.
  Plus Nick, you late?, etc.

IKYŌŌLƏ

d: fidicula.
n: Canicula.
t: zeticula.

IKYŌŌLƏM

n: geniculum.
r: curriculum.
  Plus pick you, Lum, etc.

IKYŌŌLƏR

b: cubicular, orbicular.
d: perpendicular, radicular.
h: vehicular.
l: calycular, follicular, pellicular.
m: vermicular.
n: adminicular, canicular, funicular.
r: auricular.
s: acicular, fascicular, versicular, vesicular.
sp: spicular.
t: articular, cuticular, lenticular, particular, quinquarticular, reticular, subcuticular.
tr: ventricular.
v: clavicular, navicular, ovicular.

IKYŌŌLƏS

b: ubiculous.
d: dendiculus, pediculous, pediculus, ridiculous.
l: folliculous.
m: vermiculous.
s: fasciculus, vesiculous.

t: denticulus, meticulous.
tr: ventriculous.

IKƏLĒ

st: stickily.
tr: trickily.
   Plus wick alee, etc.
   Plus trick a Lee, etc.

IKƏLSEL

s: sickle cell.

IKƏMƏNT

d: medicament, predicament.

IKƏTIV

d: abdicative, indicative,
predicative.
fr: fricative.
s: desiccative, exsiccative,
siccative.

ILĒĀT

f: affiliate, filiate.
m: humiliate.
s: concilate, domiciliate.
   Plus Lily ate *or* eight, etc.
   Plus until he ate *or* eight, etc.

ILĒEST

ch: chilliest.
h: hilliest.
s: silliest.
st: stilliest.

ILĒNES

ch: chilliness.
h: hilliness.
s: silliness.

ILĒŌ

t: punctilio.
v: pulvillio.
   Plus Milly owe, etc.
   Plus will he owe, etc.

ILĒƏ

b: memorabilia, notabilia.
d: sedilia.
f: alcoholophilia, androphilia,
Anglophilia, anophilia, copro-
philia, Francophilia, gamophilia,
gynecophilia, haemophilia,
hemophilia, phallophilia,
Russophilia, spasmophilia,
urinophilia, vulvophilia.
   Plus chilly a, etc.

ILĒƏD

Vowel: Iliad.
ch: chiliad.
g: Gilead.
   Cf. Willy had, etc.

ILĒƏN

b: perfectabilian.
d: crocodilian.
j: Vergilian, Virgilian.
l: Lilian, Lillian.
m: Maximilian.
r: Kurilian.
s: Cecilian, Sicilian.
t: Castilian, lacertilian, reptilian.
v: villyan.
z: Brazilian.
   Plus hilly an, etc.
   Cf. il'yun.

ILĒƏR

b: atrabiliar.
s: conciliar, domiciliar.
z: auxiliar.
   Cf. il'yar.

ILFƏLĒ

sk: skilfully, unskilfully.
w: wilfully.
  Plus mill full, Lee, etc.

ĪLFƏLĒ

g: guilefully.
w: wilefully.
  Plus guileful Lee *or* lea, etc.
  Plus pile full, Lee, etc.

ILFƏLNES

sk: skillfulness, unskillfulness.
w: willfulness.

ĪLFƏLNES

g: guilefulness.
w: wilefulness.

ILIFĪ

b: nobilify, stabilify.
s: fossilify.
v: vilify.
  Plus Millie, fie!, etc.
  Plus will he?, fie, etc.

ILIFÔRM

f: filiform.
m: plumiliform.
  Plus Willy form, etc.
  Plus will he form, etc.

ILIGƏN

g: Gilligan.
m: McMilligan, Milligan.
  Plus will again, etc.

ILIJƏR

p: pillager.
v: villager.

ILIKƏ

s: basilica, silica.
z: basilica.
  Plus idyllic a, etc.

ILIKƏL

b: umbilical.
f: filical.
s: basilical, silicle.
z: basilical.
  Plus silly Cal, etc.
  Plus will he, Cal?, etc.

ILINGLĒ

k: killingly.
thr: thrillingly.
tr: trillingly.
w: willingly.
  Plus drilling Lee *or* lea, etc.

ILITED

b: billeted.
f: filleted, unfileted.
  Plus will it, Ed?, etc.
  Plus millet, Ed, etc.
  Plus silly, Ted, etc.

ILITING

b: billeting.
f: filleting.

ILIƏS

b: atrabilious, bilious.
s: supercilious.
t: punctilious.
  Plus willy-nilly us, etc.
  Cf. ilyus.

ILKĒEST

m: milkiest.
s: silkiest.

ĪLŌBĀT

st: stylobate.
tr: trilobate.
Plus silo bait, etc.

ILŌĒ

b: billowy.
p: pillowy.
w: willowy.
Plus armadillo he, etc.

ILŌING

b: billowing.
p: pillowing.
Plus pecadillo wing, etc.

ILYƏNSĒ

br: brillancy.
s: transiliency.
z: resiliency.
Plus million, see, etc.

ILYƏRĒ

b: atrabiliari.
z: auxiliary.

ILƏBĒL

f: fillable, refillable, unrefillable.
k: killable.
s: syllable.
sp: spillable.
t: distillable, tillable, untillable.
thr: thrillable.
Plus kill a bull, etc.
Plus gorilla bull, etc.

ĪLƏBĒL

f: defilable.
g: beguilable.
p: compilable.

s: irreconcilable.
v: revilable.

ILƏJĒ

d: dilogy.
k(c): brachylogy.
l: palilogy.
s: fossilogy.
t: antilogy.
tr: trilogy.
Plus willow gee!, etc.
Plus skill, Oh gee!, etc.

ILƏJĪZ

p: epilogize.
s: syllogize.

ILƏJIZM

p: epilogism.
s: episyllogism, syllogism.

ILƏKWĒ

l: soliloquy.
n: somniloquy.
r: pectoriloquy.
s: pauciloquy.
t: dentiloquy, stultiloquy.
tr: gastriloquy, ventriloquy.
v: suaviloquy.
Plus hillock, we, etc.
Plus hill oak, we, etc.

ILƏKWƏNS

d: blandiloquence, grandiloquence.
n: magniloquence,
somniloquence.
t: stultiloquence.
v: breviloquence.

ILƏKWƏNT

d: blandiloquent, grandiloquent.
l: melliloquent.
n: magniloquent, somniloquent.
r: veriloquent.
s: flexiloquent, pauciloquent.
t: sanctiloquent, stultiloquent.
v: breviloquent, suaviloquent.
  Plus mill oak went, etc.

ILƏKWIST

n: somniloquist.
t: dentiloquist.
tr: gastriloquist, ventriloquist.

ILƏKWĪZ

l: soliloquize.
tr: ventriloquize.

ILƏKWIZM

n: somniloquism.
r: pectoriloquism.
tr: gastriloquism, ventriloquism.

ILƏKWƏS

d: grandiloquous.
n: magniloquous, somniloquous.
r: pectoriloquous.
tr: ventriloquous.

ĪLƏNDƏR

Vowel: islander.
h: highlander.
sk: skylander.
th: Thailander.
  Plus Ryland, her, err, *or* er, etc.
  Plus dry land err, etc.

ILƏRĒ

f: phyllary.
h: Hilary.

p: capillary, pillory.
s: cilery, codicillary, Sillery.
t: artillery, distillery.
  Plus miller, he, etc.
  Cf. iluri.

ILƏTĀT

b: abilitate, debilitate, habilitate, impossibilitate, nobilitate, rehabilitate, stabilitate.
m: militate.
s: faciliate.
  Plus Willy Tate *or* Tait, etc.
  Plus skillet ate *or* eight, etc.
  Plus fill it eight, etc.

ILƏTĒ

b: ability, absorbability, acceptability, accessibilty, accountability, acquirability, adaptability, addibility, admirability, admissibility, adoptability, adorability, advisability, affability, affectibility, agreeability, alienability, alterability, amenability, amiability, amicability, amissibility, appetibility, applicability, ascendibility, associability, attainability, attemptability, attractability, audibility, availability, capability, changeability, cognoscibility, cohesibility, combustibility, communicability, commutability, compatibility, comprehensibility, compressibility, computability, conceivability, condensability, conducibility, conductability, conformability, confusability, contemptibility, contractibility, convertibility, corrigibility, corrodibility, corrosibility, credibility, creditability, culpability, curability, damnability, debility, deceptibility, deducibility, defectibility, demisability, demonstrability, deplorability, descendibility, desirability, despicability, destructibility, determinability, detestability, diffusibility, digestibilty, dilatability, disability, dissolubility, dissolvability, distensibility, divisibility, docibility, durability, edibility, educability, eligibility, equability, exchangeability, excitability, exhaustibility, expansibility, extensibility, fallibility, feasibility, fermentability, flexibility, fluctuability, fluxibility, formidability, frangibility, friability, fusibility, generability, gullibility, habitability, histocompatibility, ignobility, illability, imitability, immeability, immeasurability, immiscibility, immovability, immutability, impalpability, impartibility, impassibility, impeccability, impenetrability, imperceptibility, imperdibility, impermeability, imperturbability, imperviability, implacability, impossibility, impregnability, imprescriptibility, impressibility, impressionability, improbability, imputability, inability, inaccessibility, incognitability, incognoscibility, incombustibility, incommeasurability, incommunicability, incommutability, incompatibility, incomprehensibility, incompressibility, inconceivability, incondensability, incontrovertibility, inconvertibility, incorruptibility, incredibility, incurability, indefatigability, indefeasibility, indefectibility, indelibility, indemonstrability, indestructibility, indigestibility, indiscernibility, indiscerptibility, indispensability, indisputability, indissolubility, indivisibility, indocibility, ineffability, ineffervescibility, ineligibility, inevitability, inexhaustibility, inexorability, inexplicability, infallibility, infeasibility, inflammability, inflexibility, infrangibility, infusibility, inhability, inhabitability,

inheritability, inimitability, innumerability, insanability, insatiability, insensibility, inseparability, insociability, insolubility, instability, insuperability, insurmountability, insusceptibility, intangibility, intelligibility, interchangeability, intractability, invendibility, invincibility, inviolability, invisibility, invulnerability, irascibility, irreconcilability, irreductibility, irremovability, irreparability, irresistibility, irresponsibility, irritability, lability, laminability, laudability, legibility, liability, malleability, manageability, memorability, mensurability, miscibility, mobility, modifiability, modificability, movability, mutability, navigatability, negotiability, nobility, notability, opposability, organizability, ostensibility, palpability, partibility, passibility, peccability, penetrability, perceptibility, perdurability, perfectibility, permissibility, persuasibility, perturbability, placability, plausibility, pliability, ponderability, portability, possibility, practicability, precipitability, preferability, prescriptibility, preventability, probability, producibility, quotability, ratability, readability, receivability, receptibility, redeemability, reductibility, reflectibility, refragability, refrangibility, refutability, reliability, remissibility, removability, remunerability, renewability, reparability, repealability, resistibility, resolvability, respectability, responsibility, reversibility, revocability, risibility, saleability, salvability, sanability, satiability, sensibility, separability, sociability, solubility, solvability, sportability, squeezability, stability, suability, suitability, susceptibility, suspensibility, tamability, tangibility, taxability, temptability, tenability, tensibility, tolerability, torsibility, tractability, transferability, transmissibility, transmutability, transportability, unaccountability, unbelievability, unutterability, vaporability, variability, vegetability, vendibility, venerability, versability, viability, vindicability, visibility, volubility, vulnerability, writability.

d: crocodility.

h: nihility.

j: agility, fragility.

kw: tranquility.

m: humility, versimility.

n: anility, juvenility, senility, vernility.

r: neurility, puerility, scurrility, sterility, virility.

s: docility, facility, fossility, gracility, imbecility, indocility, pensility, tensility.

t: contractility, ductility, fertility, fictility, futility, gentility, hostility, infertility, inutility, motility, subtility, tactility, tortility, tractility, utility, versatility, vibrality, volatility.

v: civility, incivility, servility.

Plus millet, he, etc.

Plus silly tea, etc.

IMBRIKĀT

Vowel: imbricate.

f: fimbricate.

ĪMERĒ

pr: primary.

r: rhymery.

Plus two-timer, he, etc.

IMĒƏN, IMIÔN

d: Endymion.

s: Simeon, simian.

Plus jimmy an *or* Ann, etc.

IMIKƏL

k(c): alchymical.

m: mimical, pantomimical.

n: anonymical, homonymical, inimical, metonymical.

Plus shimmy, Cal, etc.

IMINĀT

kr: accriminate*, criminate, discriminate, incriminate, indiscriminate, recriminate.

l: eliminate.

Plus women ate *or* eight, etc.

Plus vim innate, etc.

Plus limb in eight, etc.

ĪMINES

gr: griminess.

r: rhyminess.

sl: sliminess.

t: thyminess.

IMINĒ

b: Bimini.

j: jiminy.

l: post-liminy.

p: nimini-pimini.

r: Rimini.

Plus women, he, etc.

Plus limb in, he, etc.

Plus shimmy, knee, etc.

IMINUS

kr: criminous.

l: moliminous*.

Plus women *or* persimmon us, etc.

IMINƏL

j: regiminal.

kr: criminal.

l: subliminal.
v: viminal.

> Plus women, Al, etc.
> Plus vim in Al, etc.
> Cf. women all, etc.
> Cf. vim in all, etc.

IMPƏRING

hw: whimpering.
s: simpering.

> Plus simper, ring, etc.

IMPƏRƏR

hw: whimperer.
s: simperer.

> Plus whimper her, etc.

IMYO͞OLĀT

s: assimulate, dissimulate, simulate.
st: stimulate.

> Plus him, you late, etc.

IMYO͞OLƏS

l: limulus.
st: stimulus.

IMƏNUS

d: pedimanous.
j: longimanous.

IMƏRƏS

d: dimerous.
l: polymerous.

> Plus simmer us, etc.

IMƏTĒ

d: dimity.
l: sublimity.

n: anonymity, equanimity, magnanimity, parvanimity, pseudonymity, pusillanimity, sanctanimity, unannimity.
s: proximity.

> Plus limit, he, etc.
> Plus dim it, he, etc.

IMƏTƏR

d: dimeter.
l: alkalimeter, limiter, salimeter.
n: planimeter.
r: calorimeter, perimeter, polarimeter, saccharimeter.
s: dasymeter, focimeter, licimeter, pulsimeter, rhysimeter, scimeter, tasimeter, velocimeter, zymosimeter.
t: altimeter.
tr: trimeter.
v: gravimeter, pelvimeter.

> Plus limit her, err, *or* er, etc.
> Cf. scimitar.

IMƏTRĒ

j: longimetry.
l: alkalimetry.
n: planimetry.
r: calorimetry, isoperimetry, polarimetry, saccarimetry.
s: asymmetry, symmetry.
th: bathymetry.

ĪMƏTYO͞OR

kl: climature.
l: limature*.

> Plus I'm at your, etc.

ĪNANSING

f: financing.

INDIKĀT

Vowel: indicate.
s: syndicate.
v: vindicate.
  Plus windy Kate, etc.

ĪNDKÄRBƏN

bl: blind carbon.

INDƏRĒ

s: cindery.
t: tindery.
  Plus cinder, he, etc.

ĪNDƏRĒ

b: bindery.
gr: grindery.
  Plus blinder, he, etc.

INĒĀT

l: delineate, lineate.
m: miniate.
s: laciniate.
  Plus minnie ate *or* eight, etc.
  Plus thin, he ate, etc.

ĪNEEST

br: briniest.
sh: shiniest.
sp: spiniest.
t: tiniest.

INĒMƏ

k: kinema.
s: cinema.
  Plus skinny ma, etc.

INGĒNES

r: ringiness.
spr: springiness.
str: stringiness.

INĒƏ

d: Sardinia.
j: Virginia.
s: Abyssinia.
v: Lavinia.
z: zinnia.
  Plus whinny a, etc.

INĒƏL

f: finial.
gw: consanguineal, sanguineal.
l: interlineal, lineal.
m: gramineal, stamineal.
p: pineal.
t: pectineal.
  Plus whinny, Al, etc.

INĒƏN

d: Sardinian.
f: Delphinian.
j: anthropophaginian, Carthaginian, viraginian, Virginian.
l: Carolinian.
m: Arminian.
r: czarinian.
s: Abyssinian, Eleusinian, Hercynian, Socinian.
t: Augustinian, Justinian, Palestinean, serpentinean.
w: Darwinian.
  Plus skinny, Ann *or* an, etc.

ĪNĒƏR

br: brinier.
sh: shinier.
sp: spinier.
t: tinier.
  Plus winy, her, err, *or* er, etc.

INĒƏS

d: testudineous.
gw: consanguineous, sanguineous.
j: cartilagineous.
m: flamineous, fulmineous, gramineous, ignominious, stamineous, stramineous, vimineous.
  Plus skinney us, etc.

INGKĒNES

Vowel: inkiness.
k: kinkiness.
p: pinkiness.
sl: slinkiness.

INGKWƏTĒ

j: longinquity*.
p: propinquity.
  Plus pink wit, he, etc.

INGKƏBƏL

dr: drinkable, undrinkable.
s: sinkable, unsinkable.
shr: shrinkable, unshrinkable.
th: thinkable, unthinkable.
  Plus sink a bull, etc.

INIFÔRM

m: aluminiform.
s: laciniform.
t: actiniform.
  Plus finny form, etc.

INIKIN

f: finikin.
m: minikin.
  Plus finny kin, etc.

INIKƏL

b: binnacle, binocle.
f: finical.
kl: clinical, synclinical.
m: adminicle, Brahminical, dominical, flaminical.
p: pinnacle.
s: cynical, Sinical.
  Plus skinny, Cal, etc.

INISHING

f: finishing.
m: diminishing.

INISTRƏL

m: ministral.
s: sinistral.

INISTƏR

m: administer, minister.
s: sinister.
  Plus Minnie stir, etc.
  Plus violinist, her, err, *or* er, etc.

INITĒ

f: affinity, infinity.
gr: peregrinity.
gw: consanguinity, sanguinity.
j: viraginity, virginity.
l: alkalinity, felinity, masculinity, salinity.
n: asininity, femininity.
s: vicinity.
t: Latinity, satinity.
tr: trinity.
v: divinity, patavinity.
  Plus in it, he, etc.
  Plus linnet, he, etc.
  Plus guinea tea, etc.

INITIV

b: combinitive.
f: finitive, infinitive.

INJKĒDINJK

r: rinky-dink.

INJĒNES

d: dinginess.
st: stinginess.

INJĒƏN

r: Thuringian.
v: Carlovingian, Merovingian.
  Plus stingy, Ann *or* an, etc.

INJGƏRING

f: fingering.
l: lingering, malingering.
  Plus finger ring, etc.

INJGƏRƏUR

f: fingerer.
l: lingerer, malingerer.
  Plus finger her, err, *or* er, etc.

INJƏLĒ

d: dingily.
st: stingily.
  Plus fringy, Lee *or* lea, etc.

INJƏNSĒ

fr: refringency.
str: stringency.
t: contingency.
tr: astrinigency.

INLƏNDƏR

Vowel: inlander.
f: Finlander.
  Plus Min land her, etc.

ĪNLƏNDƏR

r: Rhinelander.
v: Vinelander.
  Plus mine, land her, etc.

INŌLIN

kr: crinoline.
kw: quinoline.

INSƏPƏL

pr: Peter Principle, principal, principle.

INTHĒƏN

r: Carinthian, Corinthian, labyrinthian.
s: absinthian, hyacinthian.

INTƏRĒ

pr: printery.
spl: splintery.
w: wintery.
  Plus sprinter, he, etc.

INTƏREST

Vowel: interest.
spl: splinterest*.
w: winterest*.
  Cf. sin to rest, etc.

INTƏRFĀS

Vowel: interface.

INYŌŌĀT

s: insinuate, sinuate.
t: continuate.
  Plus skin you ate *or* eight, etc.
  Plus sinew ate, etc.

INYŌŌƏS

s: sinuous.
t: continuous.
Plus sinew us, etc.

ĪNƏBƏL

b: combinable.
f: definable, finable, indefinable.
kl: declinable, inclinable, indeclinable.
s: assignable, consignable, signable.
z: designable.
Plus assign a bull, etc.
Plus china bull, etc.

INƏMƏNT

l: liniment.
m: miniment*.
Plus whinny meant, etc.
Plus skin he meant, etc.

INƏRBÄX

sk: Skinner Box.

ĪNƏRĒ

b: binary.
f: finary*, finery, refinery.
kw: quinary.
p: alpinery*, pinery.
sw: swinery.
v: vinery.
Plus miner, he, etc.
Cf. inuri.

ĪNƏTIV

b: combinative.
f: finative*.

ĪŌKLĒN

b: bioclean.

ĪŌLƏ

r: variola.
v: viola+.
Plus bass-viol, a, etc.

ĪŌLET

tr: triolet.
v: violet.
Plus sky, O let, etc.
Plus viol let, etc.
Plus Clio let, etc.

ĪŌLIST

s: sciolist.
v: violist.
Plus try, O list, etc.
Plus Clio, list, etc.

ĪŌPĒ

b: presbyopy.
l: Calliope.
m: myope.

ĪŌTƏR

r: rioter.
Cf. ietur.

ĪŌSĒN

m: Miocene.
pl: Pliocene, post-Pliocene.
Plus sky, O scene *or* seen, etc.

IPEDƏL

skw: equipedal.
l: solipedal.

IPLIKĀT

kw: sesquiplicate.
tr: triplicate.
Plus triply, Kate, etc.

IPTIKƏL

kr: cryptical.
l: apocalyptical, elliptical.
  Plus ecliptic, Al, etc.

IPTƏRƏS

d: dipterous.
r: peripterous.
tr: tripterous.

IPYŌŌLĀT

n: manipulate.
st: astipulate, stipulate.
  Plus skip, you late, etc.

IPƏLĒ

l: Gallipoli.
tr: Tripoli.
  Plus ship alee, etc.
  Plus tipple he, etc.
  Plus strip a lea *or* Lee, etc.

IPƏRĒ

fr: frippery.
sl: slippery.
  Plus zipper, he, etc.

IPƏRƏS

Vowel: deiparous, foliiparous.
b: biparous, sebiparous.
d: frondiparous.
l: gemelliparous, polyparous.
m: gemmiparous, tomiparous, vermiparous.
n: criniparous, omniparous, uniparous.
p: opiparous, polypiparous.
r: floriparous, sudoriparous.
s: fissiparous.
t: fructiparous, multiparous.

v: larviparous, oviparous, ovoviparous, viviparous.
  Plus skipper us, etc.

IPƏTHĒ

n: comnipathy.
s: kinesipathy.
t: antipathy.
  Cf. whippeth thee*, etc.

IPƏTHIST

n: somnipathist.
t: antipathist.

IPƏTƏNS

m: armipotence.
n: ignipotence, omnipotence, plenipotence.
  Plus hippo, tense *or* tents, etc.

IPƏTƏNT

l: bellipotent.
m: armipotent.
n: ignipotent, omnipotent, plenipotent.
t: multipotent.
  Plus hippo tent, etc.

IRĒƏN

s: Assyrian, Syrian.
st: Styrian.
t: Tyrian.
  Plus weary an, etc.
  Plus drear, Ian, etc.
  Cf. erian.

IRĒƏS

l: delirious.
s: Sirius.
  Plus weary us, etc.
  Cf. erius.

ĪRFƏLNES

Vowel: irefulness.
d: direfulness.

IRIKƏL

j: panegyrical.
l: lyrical.
m: miracle.
p: empirical.
t: satirical.
   Plus weary, Cal, etc.
   Plus lyric, Al, etc.

IRISIZM

l: lyricism.
p: empiricism.

ĪRƏBƏL

kw: acquirable, requirable.
sp: expirable, perspirable, respirable, transpirable.
t: untirable.
z: desirable.
   Plus hire a bull, etc.
   Plus Elmira bull, etc.

ĪRƏNĒ

Vowel: irony.
j: gyrony.
   Plus Myron, he, etc.
   Plus Cairo knee, etc.

IRƏSĒ

l: deliracy.
sp: conspiracy.
   Plus Kirah, see, etc.
   Plus smear a sea, etc.

ĪRƏSĒ

p: piracy.
t: retiracy.

Plus acquire a sea, etc.
Plus Mira, see, etc.

ĪSBÄR

s: sissy bar.

ĪSĒEST

Vowel: iciest.
sp: spiciest.

ĪSĒNES

Vowel: iciness.
sp: spiciness.

ISHĒĀT

f: maleficiate, officiate.
n: initiate.
p: propitiate.
tr: patriciate.
v: novitiate, vitiate.
   Plus wish he ate, etc.
   Plus swishy, ate *or* eight, etc.

ISHĒƏ

l: Alicia, Delicia, Felicia.
   Plus sissy, a, etc.

ISHƏLĒ

d: judicially, prejudicially.
f: officially, superficially.
   Plus initial, Lee *or* lea, etc.
   Plus initial, he, etc.

ISHƏLIZM

d: judicialism.
f: officialism.

ISHƏNIST

b: exhibitionist, prohibitionist.
d: expeditionist, traditionist.

l: abolitionist, coalitionist.

z: oppositionist, requisitionist.

ISHƏNSĒ

f: beneficiency, deficiency, efficiency, inefficiency, insufficiency, proficiency, self-sufficiency, sufficiency.

l: alliciency.

s: insitiency*.

Plus mission, sea *or* see, etc.

ISHƏNƏL

Vowel: intuitional.

d: additional, conditional, traditional.

l: volitional.

m: commissional.

n: definitional.

t: repetitional.

z: dispositional, disquisitional, inquisitional, positional, prepositional, propositional, suppositional, transitional, transpositional.

Plus mission, Al, etc.

ISHƏNƏR

b: exhibitioner.

d: traditioner.

l: coalitioner.

m: commissioner, missioner.

n: admonitioner.

t: practioner.

Plus patrician her, err, *or* er, etc.

ISHƏSNES

d: expeditiousness, indiciousness, judiciousness, seditiousness.

j: flagitiousness.

l: deliciousness, maliciousness.

n: perniciousness.

p: auspiciousness, inauspiciousness, propitiousness, suspiciousness.

pr: capriciousness.

r: avariciousness.

st: superstitiousness.

t: adventitiousness, fictitiousness.

tr: meretriciousness.

z: suppositiousness.

ĪSIKƏL

Vowel: icicle.

b: bicycle.

tr: tricycle.

Plus spicy, Cal, etc.

ISIMŌ

l: generalissimo.

n: pianissimo.

t: fortissimo, prestissimo.

v: bravissimo.

Plus sissy, Mo, etc.

ISITĒ

Vowel: stoicity.

br: lubricity, rubricity.

d: benedicete, immundicity, impudicity, mendicity, periodicity, pudicity, spheroidicity.

l: catholicity, evangelicity, felicity, infelicity, liceity, publicity, triplicity.

m: endemicity.

n: canonicity, conicity, electrotonicity, tonicity, unicity, volcanicity, vulcanicity.

p: hygroscopicity.

pl: accomplicity, complicity, duplicity, multiplicity, simplicity.

r: caloricity, historicity, splericity.

t: achromaticity, authenticity, causticity, domesticity, elasticity, ellipticity, inelasticity, pepticity, plasticity, rusticity, spasticity, stypticity, verticity.

tr: centricity, electricity.

Plus illicit, he, etc.

Plus kiss it, he, etc.

ISITNES

l: illicitness, licitness.
pl: explicitness, implicitness.

ISITŌŌD

l: solicitude.
s: vicissitude.
sp: spissitude.

Plus this etude, etc.

ĪSIVLĒ

r: derisively.
s: decisively, incisively, indecisively.

ĪSIVNES

r: derisiveness.
s: decisiveness, incisiveness, indecisiveness.

ISKĒEST

fr: friskiest.
r: riskiest.

ISTLISNES

l: listlessness.
z: resistlessness.

ISTƏKĀT

f: sophisticate+.
j: dephlogisticate.

Plus misty, Kate, etc.

Plus mystic ate *or* eight, etc.

ISTƏKIT

f: sophisticate+.

ISTƏKƏL

Vowel: atheistical, casuistical, deistical, egoistical, theistical.
d: methodistical.
f: paragraphistical, sophistical, theosophistical.
gw: linguistical.
j: dialogistical, eulogistical.
k(c): anarchistical, antanarchistical.
l: anomalistical, cabalistical.
m: alchemistical, chemistical, euphemistical, hemistichal, mystical.
n: agonistical, antagonistical, Calvanistical.
r: aoristical, aphoristical, characteristical, eucharistical, puristical.
t: artistical, egotistical, pietistical, statistical.
th: apathistical.

Plus misty, Cal, etc.

ISTƏLĀT

t: distillate+.

ISTƏNSĒ

d: distancy.
s: consistency, inconsistency, subsistency.
z: existency, persistency, preexistency.

Plus distance, he, etc.

ISTƏRĒ

h: history, oral history, psychohistory.
m: mystery.
s: consistory.

Plus blister, he, etc.

Cf. bistonry.

ISƏBƏL

m: admissible, amissable, dismissible, immiscible, incommiscible, irremissable, miscible, omissible, permiscible, permissible, remissible, transmissible.
s: scissible.
  Plus hiss a bull, etc.

ĪSƏLĒ

Vowel: icily.
sp: spicily.
  Plus icy Lee *or* lea, etc.

ISƏNING

gl: glistening.
kr: christening.
l: listening, unlistening.

ISƏNSĒ

n: reminiscency.
v: reviviscency.
  Plus listen, sea *or* see, etc.

ISƏNƏL

d: fidicinal, medicinal.
f: officinal.
t: vaticinal.
v: vicinal.

ISƏNƏR

kr: christener.
l: listener.
  Plus glisten, her *or* er, etc.

ISƏNƏS

n: unisonous.
t: fluctisonous.
  Plus imprison us, etc.

ISƏRĒ

m: admissory, dismissory, emissory, remissory.
s: rescissory.
  Plus dismisser, he, etc.

ĪSƏRĒ

r: derisory.
s: decisory, incisory.
sp: spicery.
  Plus nicer, he, etc.

ITĒNES

fl: flittiness.
gr: grittiness.
pr: prettiness.
w: wittiness.

ĪTĒNES

fl: flightiness.
m: almightiness, mightiness.

ĪTFƏLĒ

fr: frightfully.
l: delightfully.
r: rightfully.
sp: spitefully.
  Plus spiteful, lea *or* Lee, etc.

ĪTHSƏMLĒ

bl: blithesomely.
l: lithesomely.
  Plus blithesome, Lee *or* lea, etc.

ĪTHSƏMNES

bl: blithesomenss.
l: lithesomeness.

ITHƎRWƎRD

h: hitherward.
hw: whitherward.
th: thitherward.
　Plus wither, ward, etc.
　Plus with her ward, etc.

ITHƎSIS

p: epithesis.
t: antithesis.
　Plus pithy, sis, etc.

ITIGĀT

l: litigate.
m: mitigate.
　Plus hit a gate, etc.

ITIGƎNT

l: litigant.
m: mitigant.

ITIKƎL

Vowel: Jesuitical.
kr: acritical, critical, diacritical, hypercritical, hypocritical.
l: analytical, cosmopolitical, electrolytical, political.
m: Abrahamitical, hermitical.
p: pulpitical.
r: anchoritical, soritical.
s: thersitical.
v: Levitical.
　Plus witty, Cal, etc.
　Plus Hamitic, Al, etc.

ĪTLĒNES

n: knightliness.
s: unsightliness.
spr: spriteliness.

IT'LNES

br: brittleness.
l: littleness.

ITZĒEST

gl: glitziest.
r: ritziest.

ITZĒƎR

gl: glitzier.
r: ritzier.

ITƎBƎL

f: fittable.
h: Mehitable.
kw: quittable.
m: admittable, irremitable, transmittable.
　Plus hit a bull, etc.

ĪTƎBƎL

d: indictable, inditable.
kw: requitable.
l: lightable.
n: ignitable, unitable.
r: writable.
s: citable, excitable, incitable.
　Plus fight a bull, etc.

ITƎLĒ

gr: grittily.
pr: prettily.
w: wittily.
　Plus pity, Lee *or* lea, etc.

ITƎRĀT

Vowel: iterate, reiterate.
l: illiterate, literate, obliterate, transliterate.

ITƏREST

b: bitterest, embitterest*.
fr: fritterest*.
gl: glitterest*.
  Plus bitter rest, etc.
  Plus hit arrest, etc.

ITƏRING

b: bittering, embittering.
fr: frittering.
gl: glittering.
t: tittering.
tw: twittering.
  Plus glitter, ring, etc.
  Plus hit her ring, etc.

ITƏRIT

l: literate.

ITƏRMĀT

l: littermate.

ĪTƏTIV

r: writative.
s: excitative, incitative.

IVĀLƏNT

kw: quinquivalent.
n: omnivalent, univalent+.
t: multivalent.
tr: trivalent.

IVĒƏ

l: Bolivia, Livia, Olivia.
tr: trivia.
  Plus Livy, a, etc.

IVĒƏL

l: oblivial.
r: quadrivial.

s: lixivial.
tr: trivial.
v: convivial.
  Plus Livy, Al, etc.

IVĒƏN

l: Bolivian.
v: Vivian, Vivien.
  Plus Livy, Ann *or* an, etc.

IVĒƏS

b: bivious.
l: oblivious.
s: lascivious, lixivious.
t: multivious.
  Plus Livy us, etc.

IVIDNES

l: lividness.
v: vividness.

IVITĒ

pr: privity.
t: captivity.

IVƏBƏL

g: forgivable, givable, unforgivable.
l: livable.
  Plus outlive a bull, etc.

ĪVƏBƏL

dr: drivable.
pr: deprivable.
r: derivable.
tr: contrivable.
v: revivable.
  Plus drive a bull, etc.

IVƏKƏL

kw: equivocal.
n: univocal.

IVƏLĒ

r: Rivoli.
t: Tivoli.
　　Plus give, oh Lee, etc.

IVƏLƏNT

kw: equivalent.
n: univalent+.

IVƏLƏR

dr: driveller.
s: civiller.
sn: sniveller.
　　Plus shrivel her, etc.

ĪVƏNSĒ

n: connivancy.
v: survivancy.

ĪVƏRĒ

Vowel: ivory.
v: vivary.
　　Plus contriver, he, etc.

IVƏRING

l: delivering.
kw: quivering.
sh: shivering.
　　Plus quiver ring, etc.

IVƏRYĒ

l: delivery, gaol delivery, jail delivery, livery.
r: rivery.
sh: shivery.
　　Plus liver, he, etc.

IVƏRƏR

l: deliverer.
kw: quiverer.

sh: shiverer.
　　Plus deliver her, etc.

IVƏRƏS

b: herbivorous.
g: frugivorous.
k(c): piscivorous.
kw: equivorous.
m: vermivorous.
n: carnivorous, graminivorous, granivorous, omnivorous, panivorous, sanguinivorous.
s: fucivorous, ossivorous.
t: insectivorous, phytivorous.
　　Plus deliver us, etc.

IVƏTĒ

kl: acclivity, declivity, proclivity.
s: impassivity, passivity.
t: absorptivity, activity, causativity, cogitativity, collectivity, conducticity, festivity, incogitativity, instinctivity, motivity, nativity, negativity, objectivity, perceptivity, positivity, productivity, receptivity, relativity, sensitivity, subjectivity.
　　Plus civet, he, etc.
　　Plus privy tea, etc.

IVƏTIV

pr: privative.
r: derivative.

IZĒEST

b: busiest.
d: dizziest.

IZĒƏR

b: busier.
d: dizzier.
fr: frizzier.

Plus busy her, err, *or* er, etc.
Cf. vizier.

IZHIƏN

d: Paradisean.
fr: Frisian.
l: Elysian.
r: Parisian.
s: precisian.
  Cf. izhun.

IZHUNƏL

s: transitional+.
v: divisional, provisional, revisional, visional.
  Plus incision, Al, etc.

IZIKƏL

d: paradisiacal.
f: metaphysical, physical, psychophysical.
t: phthisical.

IZITƏR

kw: acquisitor, inquisitor, requisitor.
v: visitor.
  Plus what-is-it, or, etc.

IZƏBƏL

kw: acquisible.
r: risible.
v: divisible, indivisible, invisible, visible.
  Plus quiz a bull, etc.

ĪZƏBƏL

d: oxidizable.
l: analysable, crystallizable, electrolysable, realizable.
m: demisable.
n: organizable, recognizable.

pr: prizable.
r: vaporizable.
s: excisable, exercisable, sizable.
sp: despisable.
t: magnetizable.
v: advisable, devisable.
  Plus prize a bull, etc.

IZƏLĒ

b: busily.
d: dizzily.
  Plus busy lea *or* Lee, etc.

ĪZƏRĒ

r: irrisory.
v: advisory, provisory, revisory, supervisory.
  Plus miser, he, etc.

ĪƏBLĒ

j: justifiably, etc.
l: liably, reliably.
n: deniably, undeniably.
pl: pliably, etc.

ĪƏBƏL

f: acidifiable, classifiable, diversifiable, electrifiable, exemplifiable, falsifiable, fortifiable, justifiable, liquefiable, magnifiable, modifiable, pacifiable, petrifiable, qualifiable, rarefiable, rectifiable, saponifiable, satisfiable, solidifiable, verifiable, vitrifiable.
fr: friable.
l: liable, reliable.
n: deniable, undeniable.
pl: appliable, compliable, impliable, pliable.
tr: triable, viable.
  Plus Hezekiah bull, etc.
  Plus try a bull, etc.

ĪƏDĒZ

dr: hamadryades.
h: Hyades.
pl: Pleiades.

ĪƏKƏL

d: cardiacal, encyclopediacal, prosodiacal, zodical.
dr: hydrochondriacal.
j: elegiacal.
l: heliacal.
n: bibliomaniacal, demoniacal, dipsoniacal, kleptomaniacal, maniacal, megalomaniacal, monomaniacal, nymphomaniacal, pyromaniacal, simoniacal.
s: paradisiacal.
　　Plus Sophia, Cal, etc.

ĪƏNSĒ

kl: cliency.
pl: compliancy, pliancy.
r: riancy.
　　Plus Bryan see, etc.
　　Cf. try and see, etc.
　　Cf. iansi.

ĪƏNTLĒ

f: defiantly.
l: reliantly.
pl: compliantly, pliantly.
　　Plus giant Lee *or* lea, etc.

IƏRĒ

br: briery.
d: diary.
f: fiery.
fr: friary.
pr: priory.
　　Plus higher, he, etc.
　　Cf. iuri.

ĪƏRIST

d: diarist.
p: Piarist.
　　Plus higher wrist, etc.
　　Plus tie a wrist, etc.

ĪƏSIS

dr: hypochondriasis.
t: elephantiasis.
　　Plus try a sis, etc.
　　Cf. try her, sis, etc.

ĪƏSIZM

dr: hypochondriacism.
n: demoniacism.

ĪƏTĒ

b: dubiety, nullibiety, ubiety.
br: ebriety, inebriety, insobriety, sobriety.
d: mediety.
l: filiety.
m: numiety.
n: omniety.
p: impiety, piety.
pr: impropriety, propriety.
r: contrariety, luxuriety*, notoriety, variety.
s: society.
t: satiety.
z: anxiety.
　　Plus riot, he, etc.
　　Plus Nehemiah, tea!, etc.

ĪƏTED

d: dieted.
kw(qu): disquieted, quieted.
r: rioted.
　　Plus fiat, Ed, etc.
　　Plus messiah, Ted, etc.

ĪƏTEST

d: dietest*.
kw(qu): quietest.
r: riotest*.
   Plus messiah test, etc.

ĪƏTING

d: dieting.
kw(qu): disquieting, quieting.
r: rioting.

ĪƏTIST

d: dietist.
kw(qu): quietist.
p: pietist.
pr: proprietist.
r: varietiest.
z: anxietist.

ĪƏTIZM

kw(qu): quietism.
p: pietism.
r: varietism.

ĪƏTƏL

d: dietal.
h: hyetal.
r: parietal, varietal.
   Plus riot, Al, etc.
   Cf. try it, Al, etc.

ĪƏTƏR

d: dieter.
k(c): psychiater.
kw(qu): quieter.
pr: proprietor.
r: rioter.
   Plus quiet her, etc.
   Cf. archiater.

O

The accented vowel sounds included are listed under **O** in Single Rhymes.

ŌBĒƏ

Vowel: obeah.

f: agoraphobia, airphobia, androphobia, Anglophobia, bacteriophobia, claustrophobia, demonophobia, dermatophobia, doraphobia, dysmophophobia, Francophobia, Gallophobia, gamophobia, Germanophobia, gynekophobia, heresyphobia, hydrophobia, lyssophobia, neophobia, pharmacophobia, phobia, phobophobia, photophobia, pyrophobia, Russophobia, sitiphobia, syphilophobia, thanatophobia, toxicophobia, zoophobia.

n: Zenobia.

Plus adobe a, etc.

ÔBERĒ

Cf. strawberry.

ÔBƏRĒ

d: daubery+.

Cf. strawberry.

ÔDĒNES

b: bawdiness.

g: gaudiness.

ŌDĒUM

Vowel: odium.

r: rhodium.

s: sodium.

Plus toady 'em.

ŌDĒƏL

l: allodial.

n: palinodial, threnodial.

s: episodial, prosodial.

t: custodial.

Plus toady, Al.

ŌDĒƏN

r: Herodian, Rhodian.

s: prosodian.

t: custodian.

Plus toady, Ann *or* an.

Plus load, Ian, etc.

ŌDĒƏS

Vowel: odious.

l: melodious.

m: commodious, incommodious.

Plus toady us.

ÔDRĒNES

b: bawdriness.

t: tawdriness.

ÔFƏLĒ

Vowel: awfully.

l: lawfully, unlawfully.

Plus craw full, Lee, etc.

Plus awful, Lee, etc.

ÔFƏLNES

Vowel: awfulness.

l: lawfulness, unlawfulness.

ŌGĒIZM

b: bogeyism.
f: fogeyism.

ŌIKƏL

g: egoical.
r: heroical, unheroical.
st: stoical.
   Plus Mesozoic, Al, etc.
   Plus snowy, Cal, etc.

OINTEDLĒ

j: disjointedly.
p: pointedly.
   Plus disappointed Lee *or* lea, etc.
   Plus join Ted Lee, etc.

OISTƏRING

kl: cloistering.
r: roistering.
   Plus oyster ring, etc.
   Plus foist her ring, etc.
   Plus foist a ring, etc.

OIƏBƏL

j: enjoyable.
pl: employable.
   Plus destroy a bull, etc.
   Cf. Goya bull.

OIƏLĒ

l: loyally.
r: royally.
   Plus pennyroyal, he, etc.
   Plus destroy a lea, etc.

OIƏLIST

l: loyalist.
r: royalist.
   Plus royal list, etc.
   Plus enjoy a list, etc.

OIƏLIZM

l: loyalism.
r: royalism.

OIƏLTĒ

l: loyalty.
r: royalty, viceroyalty.
   Plus pennyroyal tea, etc.

ÔKĒNES

ch: chalkiness.
g: gawkiness.
p: pawkiness.
skw: squawkiness.
t: talkiness.

ŌKƏLĪZ

f: focalize.
l: localize.
v: vocalize.
   Plus yokel eyes, etc.
   Plus tapioca, Lize, etc.

ŌKƏLIZM

l: localism.
v: vocalism.

ŌKƏNLĒ

br: brokenly.
sp: outspokenly.
   Plus token, Lee *or* lea, etc.

ÔKILĒ

ch: chalkily.
g: gawkily.
p: pawkily.
skw: squawkily.
   Plus talky, Lee *or* lea, etc.
   Plus squawk alee, etc.

ÔLABƏL

k(c): recallable.
thr: enthrallable.
Plus call a bull, etc.
Plus Eufala bull, etc.

ŌLĒĀT

f: foliate, infoliate.
sp: spoliate.
Plus holy eight *or* ate, etc.

ŌLĒEST

h: holiest, unholiest.
l: lowliest.

ŌLĒNES

h: holiness, unholiness.
l: lowliness.
sh: shoaliness.

ŌLĒŌ

Vowel: olio.
f: folio, portfolio.
p: Sapolio.
Plus holy owe *or* Oh, etc.
Cf. no, Leo, etc.

ŌLĒUM

f: trifolium.
n: linoleum.
sk(sc): scholium.
tr: petroleum.
Plus holy 'em *or* 'um, etc.
Cf. oleum.
Cf. olium.

ŌLĒƏ

g: Mongolia.
k(c): colia, melancholia.

n: magnolia.
t: Aetolia, Anatolia.
Plus holy a, etc.

ŌLĒƏN

Vowel: Aeolian, Creolian.
b: metabolian.
g: Mongolian.
k(c): melancholian.
m: simoleon.
p: Napoleon.
t: Aetolian, Anatolian, capitolian, Pactolian.
Plus holy an, etc.
Plus holy un, etc.
Plus so, Leon, etc.

ŌLĒƏR

Vowel: olier.
gr: Grolier.
h: holier, unholier.
l: lowlier.
Plus slowly her *or* err, etc.
Plus soul, he err, etc.

ŌLĒƏZ

Plus olia+s.

ÔLIFĒ

d: idolify.
k: disqualify, qualify.
m: mollify.
Plus Polly, fie!, etc.

ÔLIFĪD

d: idolified.
kw: disqualified, qualified, unqualified.
m: mollified.
Plus Polly fie'd, etc.

ÔLTĒEST

f: faultiest.
s: saltiest.

ÔLTĒNES

f: faultiness.
m: maltiness.
s: saltiness.

ÔLTƏRING

Vowel: altering, unaltering.
f: faltering, unfaltering.
p: paltering.
　　Plus Gibralter ring, etc.
　　Plus exalt her ring, etc.
　　Plus exalt a ring, etc.

ÔLTƏRƏR

Vowel: alterer.
f: falterer.
p: palterer.
　　Plus alter her, etc.

ŌLƏBƏL

r: rollable.
s: consolable.
t: extollable, tollable.
tr: controllable, uncontrollable.
　　Plus toll a bull, etc.
　　Plus Angola bull, etc.

ŌLƏRĒ

b: bolary.
j: cajolary.
p: polary.
s: solary.
v: volary.
　　Plus molar, he, etc.
　　Cf. so, Larry, etc.

ŌLƏRĪZ

p: polarize.
s: solarize.
　　Plus goal arise, etc.
　　Plus Lola rise, etc.
　　Plus molar eyes, etc.

ŌMĒŌ

dr: Dramio.
r: Romeo.
　　Plus loamy, O, etc.
　　Plus show me, Oh, etc.

ŌMƏTIZM

kr: achromatism, chromatism.
pl: diplomatism.

ŌNABƏL

l: loanable.
t: tonable, unatonable.
　　Plus stone a bull, etc.
　　Plus Iona bull, etc.

ŌNEAK

m: demoniac, simoniac.
　　Cf. bony yak, etc.

ÔNĒEST

br: brawniest.
t: tawniest.

ŌNĒUM

g: pelargonium.
k(c): zirconium.
m: harmonium, pandemonium, stramonium.
　　Plus Coney 'em, etc.

ŌNĒƏ

Vowel: bryonia, Ionia.
d: Adonia, Donia, Fredonia.

f: aphonia, Euphonia.

fr: Sophronia.

g: begonia, Patagonia.

k(c): Laconia.

l: Cephalonia, valonia.

m: ammonia, pneumonia.

n: bignonia.

s: Ansonia, Sonia.

t: Antonia, Latonia.

v: Slavonia.

   Plus pony, a, etc.

ŌNĒƏL

g: oxygonial*.

l: colonial, intercolonial.

m: ceremonial, demonial, matrimonial, monial, patrimonial, sanctimonial, testimonial.

r: baronial.

   Plus macaroni, Al, etc.

ŌNĒƏN

Vowel: Aonian, halcyonian, Ionian.

b: Serbonian.

d: Aberdonian, Caledonian, Macedonian, Myrmidonian, Sardonian.

f: colophonian.

g: Gorgonean, Patagonian.

k(c): Baconian, Draconian, Heliconian, Laconian.

kth: Chthonian.

l: Babylonian, Chelonian, Thessalonian.

m: Ammonian, demonian, Simonian.

p: Lapponian.

r: Cameronian, Ciceronian, Neronian, Pyrhonian.

s: Ausonian, Grandisonian, Johnsonian, Oxonian.

t: Catonian, Cottonian, Daltonian, Etonian, Miltonian, Newtonian, Plutonian.

v: Devonian, Favonian, Livonian, Slavonian.

z: Amazonian, bezonian.

   Plus bony Ann or an, etc.

ŌNĒƏS

b: Trebonius.

f: euphonious, symphonious.

l: felonious.

m: acrimonious, alimonious, ceremonious, harmonious, inharmonious, matrimonious, parsimonious, querimonious, sanctimonious, solomonious.

r: erroneous.

t: Antonius.

tr: ultroneous.

   Plus macaroni us, etc.

ŌOBĒƏN

n: Danubian, Nubian.

r: rubian.

   Plus booby, Ann or an, etc.

ŌOBĒƏS

d: dubious.

r: rubious.

   Plus booby us, etc.

ŌOBIKƏL

k(c): cubical.

r: cherubical.

   Plus booby, Cal, etc.

   Plus pubic, Al, etc.

ŌOBRĒƏS

g: lugubrious.

l: insalubrious, salubrious.

OOBRIKĀT

l: lubricate.
r: rubricate.
Plus new Brie Kate, etc.

OOBƏLĀT

j: jubilate.
l: volubilate*.
n: enubilate, nubilate, obnubilate.
Plus booby late, etc.
Plus boob elate, etc.

OOBƏRƏS

s: suberous.
t: protuberous, tuberous.
Plus Huber us, etc.

OODĒNES

w: woodiness.
Cf. udines.

OODĒNES

d: dewiness.
gl: gluedyness.
m: moodiness.
Cf. oodines.

OODĒƏS

l: preludious.
st: studious.

OOD'NĪZ

t: attitudinize, platitudinize.
Plus food in eyes, etc.

OOD'NƏL

t: aptitudinal, attitudinal,
consuetudinal, latitudinal,
longitudinal, testitudinal.

Plus brood in, Al, etc.
Plus brood in all, etc.

OOD'NƏS

l: paludinous.
t: fortitudinous, latitudinous,
longitudinous, multitudinous,
platitudinous, solicitudinous,
vicissitudinous.
Plus food in us, etc.

OODƏBƏL

kl: includable, includible.
l: alludable, deludable, ineludible.
tr: protrudable.
Plus brood a bull, etc.
Plus Bermuda bull, etc.
Cf. udabl'l.

OODƏNSĒ

kl: concludency.
kr: recrudency.
p: impudency, pudency.
Plus new den, see, etc.
Cf. students see, etc.

OODƏTĒ

kr: crudity.
n: nudity.
r: rudity.
Plus moody tea, etc.
Plus brood it, he, etc.

OOISHNES

j: Jewishness.
shr: shrewishness.

OOJƏNƏS

n: lanuginous.
r: aeruginous, ferruginous.

s: salsuginous.
    Plus huge in us, etc

O͞OKO͞OLƏNT

l: luculent.
m: muculent.
    Cf. succulent.

OOKƏRĒ

b: bookery.
k(c): cookery.
r: rookery.

O͞OLĒƏN

j: Julian, Julien.
k(c): herculean.
r: cerulean.
    Plus Dooley, Ann *or* an, etc.
    Plus rule, Ian, etc.

O͞OLĒƏS

j: Julius.
p: Apuleius.
    Plus coolie us, etc.
    Cf. ulyus.

O͞OLISHNES

f: foolishness.
m: mulishness.

O͞OLĪT

Vowel: oolite.
z: zoolite.

O͞OLƏTĒ

d: credulity, incredulity, sedulity.
r: garrulity.
    Plus rule it, he, etc.

O͞OMĒNES

gl: gloominess.
r: roominess.
sp: spuminess.

O͞OMĒNƏS

fl: fluminous.
g: leguminous.
l: aluminous, luminous, voluminous.
t: bituminous.
    Plus illumine us, etc.
    Plus doom in us, etc.

O͞OMO͞OLĀT

k(c): accumulate.
t: tumulate.
    Plus whom you late, etc.
    Plus new mule ate, etc.

O͞OMO͞OLƏS

k(c): cumulus.
t: tumulus.

O͞OMƏBƏL

s: assumable, consumable.
z: presumable, resumable.
    Plus entomb a bull, etc.
    Plus Yuma bull, etc.

O͞OMƏNĀT

k(c): acuminate, catechumentate.
l: illuminate, luminate.
r: ferruminate, ruminate.
    Plus two men ate *or* eight, etc.
    Plus gloomy, Nate, etc.
    Plus room in eight, etc.

O͞OMƏNLĒ

w: womanly.
   Cf. umanli.

O͞OMƏNLĒ

h: humanly, inhumanly.
   Plus new man, Lee, etc.
   Cf. womanly.

O͞OMƏNƏNT

l: illuminant, luminant.
r: ruminant.
   Plus acumen, aunt *or* ant, etc.
   Plus new man, aunt, etc.

O͞OMƏRĒ

f: perfumery.
pl: plumery.
r: rumory.
   Plus who, Marie, etc.
   Plus humor, he, etc.
   Cf. roomery.

O͞OMƏRƏL

h: humeral.
n: numeral.
   Plus roomer, Al, etc.
   Plus groom her, Il, etc.

O͞OMƏRƏS

h: humerus, humorous.
n: numcrous.
r: rumorous.
   Plus humor us, etc.
   Plus groom or us, etc.

O͞ONIKĀT

m: communicate, excommunicate.
t: tunicate.

   Plus loony, Kate, etc.
   Plus Punic eight *or* ate, etc.
   Plus new knee, Kate, etc.

O͞ONITIV

p: punitive.
y unitive.

O͞ONƏBƏL

p: expugnable*.
t: tunable.
   Plus festoon a bull, etc.
   Plus vicuna bull, etc.

O͞ONƏFÔRM

k(c): cuneiform.
l: luniform.
y: uniform.
   Plus puny form, etc.
   Plus new knee form, etc.

O͞ONƏRĒ

f: buffoonery.
k(c): cocoonery.
l: pantalooncry, lunary.
tr: poltroonery.
   Plus sooner, he, etc.

O͞ONƏTĒ

m: community, immunity, intercommunity.
p: impunity.
t: importunity, inopportunity, opportunity.
y: triunity, unity.
zh: jejunity.
   Plus loony tea, etc.
   Plus spoon o' tea, etc.

OͦOPƏRĀT

k(c): recuperate.
t: vituperate.
　　Plus super-eight *or* ate, etc.
　　Plus loop her eight, etc.

OͦORĒAT

f: infuriate.
m: muriate.
t: parturiate.
z: luxuriate.
　　Plus jury ate *or* eight, etc.

OͦORĒƏ

ch: Manchuria.
m: Lemuria.
tr: Etruria.
　　Plus fury a, etc.

OͦORĒƏL

g: augurial, figurial.
k(c): mercurial.
m: Muriel.
n: seignurial.
p: purpureal.
　　Plus Missouri, Al, etc.

OͦORĒƏN

d: durian.
l: Silurian.
t: centurian, scripturian.
tr: Etrurian.
y: Urian.
z: Missourian.
　　Plus fury, Ann *or* an, etc.
　　Cf. centurion.

OͦORĒƏNS

pr: prurience.
z: luxuriance.

OͦORĒƏNT

pr: prurient.
r: luxuriant.
s: esurient.
t: parturient, scripturient.
z: luxuriant.

OͦORĒƏS

f: furious, sulphureous.
g: strangurious.
j: injurious, perjurious.
k(c): curious, incurious.
n: penurious.
sp: spurious.
z: luxurious.
zh: usurious.
　　Plus fury, us, etc.

OORITĒE

k(c): insecurity, security.
m: demurity.
p: impurity, purity.
sk(sc): obscurity.
t: immaturity, maturity, prematurity.
　　Plus lure it, he, etc.

OͦORƏBƏL

d: durable, endurable.
k(c): curable, incurable, procurable, securable.
s: assurable, insurable.
　　Plus procure a bull, etc.

OͦORƏFĪ

p: purify.
th: thurify.
　　Plus houri, fie!, etc.

ŌŌRƏLISM

pl: pluralism.
r: ruralism.

OORƏLIST

r: ruralist.
　　Plus neural list, etc.
　　Cf. pluralist.

ŌŌRƏTĒ

k(c): insecurity, security.
m: demurity.
p: impurity, purity.
sk(sc): obscurity.
t: immaturity, maturity,
prematurity.
　　Plus lure it, he, etc.

ŌŌRƏTIV

d: indurative.
k(c): curative.
p: depurative.
t: maturative.

ŌŌSEDLĒ

d: deucedly.
l: lucidly, pellucidly.
m: mucidly.
　　Plus lucid, Lee, etc.

ŌŌSĒƏN

d: Caducean.
f: Confucian.
k(c): Rosicrucian.
l: Tuscaloosian.
　　Plus juicy, Ann *or* an, etc.

ŌŌSHĒƏL

d: fiducial.
kr: crucial.

ŌŌSHƏNƏL

k(c): circumlocutional,
elocutional.
l: evolutional.
t: constitutional, institutional,
substitional.
　　Plus diminution, Al, etc.

ŌŌSHƏNIST

k(c): circumlocutionist,
elocutionist.
l: evolutionist, resolutionist,
revolutionist.
t: constitutionist.

ŌŌSHƏNƏR

k(c): executioner.
l: ablutioner, resolutioner,
revolutioner.
　　Plus institution her, err, *or* er, etc.

ŌŌSIVNES

b: abusiveness.
d: conduciveness.
f: diffusiveness, effusiveness.
kl: conclusiveness, exclusiveness,
inconclusiveness.
l: allusiveness, delusiveness,
elusiveness, illusiveness.
tr: inobtrusiveness, intrusiveness,
obtrusiveness.

ŌŌSƏBƏL

d: adducible, conducible,
deducible, educible, inducible,
irreducible, producible, reduc-
ible, seducible, traducible.
kr: crucible.
　　Plus juicy bull, etc.
　　Plus loose a bull, etc.

OͯOSƏNSĒ

l: lucency, tralucency*, translucency.
Cf. nuisancy.

OͯOSƏRĒ

kl: conclusory, exclusory, reclusory.
l: collusory, delusory, elusory, illusory, lusory, prelusory.
tr: extrusory.
Plus producer, he, etc.
Plus loose her, he, etc.

OͯOTĒƏS

b: beauteous.
d: duteous.
l: luteous.
Plus tutti-frutti us, etc.

OͯOTHFƏLĒ

r: ruthfully.
tr: truthfully.
y: youthfully.
Plus toothful, Lee, etc.

OͯOTHFƏLNES

r: ruthfulness.
tr: truthfulness.
y: youthfulness.

OͯOTHLESLĒ

r: ruthlessly.
tr: truthlessly.
y: youthlessly.
Plus tooth, Leslie, etc.
Plus toothless, Lee, etc.

OͯOTIKƏL

b: scorbutical.
k(c): cuticle.

p: therapeutical.
s: pharmaceutical.
tr: latreutical.
Plus duty, Cal, etc.
Plus hermeneutic, Al, etc.

OͯOT'NĒ

m: mutiny.
skr(scr): scrutiny.
Plus loot in, he, etc.
Plus gluten, he, etc.

OͯOT'NĒR

m: mutineer.
skr(scr): scrutineer.
Plus beauty near, etc.

OͯOT'NƏS

gl: glutinous.
l: velutinous.
m: mutinous.
skr(scr): scrutinous.
Plus boot in us, etc.
Plus gluten us, etc.

OͯOTƏBƏL

f: confutable, refutable.
k(c): executable.
m: commutable, immutable, incommutable, mootable, mutable, permutable, transmutable.
p: computable, disputable, imputable.
s: suitable.
skr(scr): inscrutable, scrutable.
Plus shoot a bull, etc.

OͯOTƏFĪ

b: beautify.
br: brutify.
Plus booty, fie!, etc.

ŌŌTƏFƏL

b: beautiful.
d: dutiful.
 Plus booty full, etc.

ŌŌTƏRĒ

b: bootery, free-bootery.
fr: fruitery.
p: pewtery.
r: rootery.
 Plus looter, he, etc.

ŌŌTƏTIV

f: confutative.
m: commutative.
n: sternutative.
p: disputative, imputative,
putative.
sp: sputative.

ŌŌVĒƏL

fl: effluvial, fluvial.
l: alluvial, antediluvial, dilluvial,
post-diluvial.
pl: pluvial.
z: exuvial.
 Plus movie, Al.

ŌŌVĒƏN

l: antediluvian, diluvian,
postdiluvian.
r: Peruvian.
s: Vesuvian.
 Plus movie, Ann *or* an.
 Plus groove, Ian, etc.

ŌŌVĒƏS

pl: Jupiter Pluvius.
s: Vesuvius.
 Plus movie us.

ŌŌVƏBƏL

m: immovable, irremovable,
movable, removable.
pr: approvable, improvable,
provable, reprovable.
 Plus behoove a bull, etc.

ŌŌZĒƏN

th: Carthusian.
 Cf. uzhun.

ŌŌZƏBƏL

f: confusable, diffusible, fusible,
infusible, transfusible.
k(c): excusable, inexcusable.
l: losable.
m: amusable.
y: usable.
 Plus choose a bull, etc.

ŌŌƏBƏL

d: doable, subduable, undoable.
n: renewable.
s: persuable, suable, unpersuable,
unsuable.
v: reviewable, unreviewable.
 Plus knew a bull, etc.

ŌŌƏLING

d: dueling.
f: fueling, refueling.
gr: grueling.
j: bejewelling, jewelling.

ŌŌƏLƏR

d: dueler.
f: fueler.
j: jeweler.
kr: crueler.
 Plus newel her, err, *or* er, etc.

O͞OƏNƏS

br: bruinous.
pr: pruinous.
r: ruinous.
  Plus knew in us, etc.
  Plus ruin us, etc.

O͞OƏTĒ

d: assiduity.
fl: superfluity.
g: ambiguity, contiguity, exiguity.
k(c): acuity, circuity, conspicuity, innocuity, perspicuity, promiscuity, vacuity.
n: annuity, continuity, discontinuity, ingenuity, strenuity, tenuity.
s: suety.
t: fatuity, gratuity, perpetuity.
  Plus suet tea, etc.
  Plus suet, he, etc.
  Plus sue it, he, etc.

O͞OƏTƏS

k(c): circuitous.
t: fatuitous, fortuitous, gratuitous, pituitous.
  Plus suet us, etc.

ŌPĒNES

d: dopiness.
r: ropiness.
s: soapiness.
sl: slopiness.

ŌPĒƏ

Vowel: Ethiopia, myopia, presbyopia.
k(c): cornucopia.
t: Utopia.
  Plus dopy a, etc.

ŌPĒƏN

Vowel: Ethiopian.
l: Fallopian.
s: Aesopian, Esopian.
t: Utopian.
  Plus ropy an or Ann, etc.

ŌPISHNES

d: dopishness.
m: mopishness.
p: popishness.

ŌPƏRĒ

d: dopery.
p: popery.
r: ropery.
  Plus rope her, he, etc.
  Plus eloper, he, etc.

ÔRCHƏNĀT

f: fortunate, unfortunate.
p: importunate.
  Plus fortune ate or eight, etc.
  Plus escort you, Nate, etc.

ÔRDĒƏL

k(c): cordial.
m: primordial.
s: exordial.

ÔRDĒƏN

g: Gordian.
k(c): accordion.
  Plus Lordy, Ann or an, etc.

ÔRDƏNĀT

Vowel: coordinate+, foreordinate, ordinate.
b: insubordinate+, subordinate+.
  Plus lord innate, etc.
  Cf. Gordon ate or eight, etc.

ÔRDƏNIT

Vowel: coordinate+.
b: insubordinate+, subordinate+.

ÔRDƏRING

Vowel: ordering.
b: bordering.
    Plus order ring, etc.
    Plus award a ring, etc.
    Plus award her ring, etc.

ŌRĒĀT

k(c): excoriate.
s: professoriate.
    Plus lory ate *or* eight, etc.
    Plus more he ate, etc.

ÔRĒĀT

Vowel: aureate.
l: baccalaureate, laureate, poet laureate.
    Plus Maury ate *or* eight, etc.
    Plus war, he ate, etc.

ŌRĒNES

g: goriness.
h: hoariness, whoriness.
t: desultoriness, dilatoriness, peremptoriness.

ŌRĒŌL

Vowel: oriole.
gl: gloriole, glory hole.
    Plus story, Ole, etc.
    Plus lory hole *or* whole, etc.

ÔRĒŌL

Vowel: aureole.
l: laureole*.

ŌRĒUM

b: ciborium.
f: triforium.
k(c): corium.
p: emporium.
s: aspersorium, sensorium.
t: auditorium, crematorium, digitorium, fumatorium, haustorium, inclinatorium, moratorium, praetorium, prospectorium, sanatorium, scriptorium, sudatorium.
th: thorium.
    Plus glory 'em, etc.

ŌRĒƏ

Vowel: Peoria.
f: dysphoria, euphoria.
g: phantasmagoria.
gl: Gloria.
n: Honoria.
p: aporia.
s: infusoria.
sk(sc): scoria.
t: Astoria, Castoria, littoria, Pretoria, Victoria, Waldorf Astoria.
    Plus story a, etc.
    Cf. slow, rhea, etc.

ŌRĒƏL

b: arboreal, boreal.
d: ambassadorial.
g: phantasmagorial.
m: armorial, immemorial, marmoreal, memorial.
n: manorial, seignorial.
p: corporeal, emporial, incorporeal.
s: accessorial, assessorial, censorial, compromissorial, cursorial, fossorial, gressorial, infusorial, insessorial, intercessorial, professorial,

rasorial, risorial, scansorial, sensorial, sponsorial, tonsorial, uxorial.

t: accusatorial, adaptorial, admonitorial, amatorial, ancestorial, auditorial, commentatorial, compurgatorial, consistorial, dedicatorial, dictatorial, directorial, disquitorial, editorial, electorial, equatoreal, escritorial, executorial, expurgatorial, exterritorial, extraterritorial, factorial, gladiatorial, grallatorial, gubernatorial, historial, imperatorial, improvisitorial, inquisitorial, inventorial, legislatorial, mediatorial, mentorial, monitorial, motorial, oratorial, pictorial, piscatorial, preceptorial, prefatorial, proctorial, procuratorial, proprietorial, protectorial, purgatorial, raptorial, rectorial, reportorial, sartorial, sectorial, senatorial, spectatorial, speculatorial, suctorial, territorial, tinctorial, tutorial, victorial, visitatorial.

th: authorial.

Plus gory, Al, etc.

Plus no real, etc.

ŌRĒƏN

b: hyperborean.
d: Dorian.
f: Bosphorian.
g: Gregorian.
m: marmorean.
s: censorian.

t: amatorian, consistorian, dictatorian, gladiatorian, Hectorean, historian, mid-Victorian, Nestorian, oratorian, praetorian, purgatorian, salutatorian, senatorian, stentorian, valedictorian, Victorian.

Plus gory an *or* Ann, etc.

ŌRĒƏS

b: arboreous, laborious.

gl: glorious, inglorious, vainglorious.

n: hippicanorious.

r: uproarious.

s: censorious, lusorious, uxorious.

sk(sc): scorious.

t: amatorious, circulatorious, desultorious, expiatorious, expurgatorious, inquisitorious, meritorious, notorious, oratorious, purgatorious, raptorious, salutatorious, saltatorious, senatorious, stentorious, stertorious, suctorious, ustorious, victorious.

Plus glory us, etc.

ÔRĒƏSLĒ

b: laboriously.

gl: gloriously, ingloriously, vaingloriously.

n: hippicanoriously.

r: uproariously.

s: uxoriously.

t: meritoriously, notoriously, stentoriously, victoriously.

ÔRGƏNĪZ

Vowel: organize.

g: gorgonize.

Plus Morganize, etc.

Plus gorgon eyes, etc.

ŌRIFĪ

gl: glorify.
sk(sc): scorify.

Plus tory, fie!, etc.

ÔRMITĒ

f: conformity, deformity, inconformity, multiformity, nonconformity, uniformity.
n: abnormity, enormity.
　Plus storm it, he, etc.
　Plus war, Mittie, etc.

ÔRMƏTIV

d: dormitive.
f: afformative, formative, informative, reformative, transformative.

ÔRSƏBƏL

f: enforceable, forcible.
v: divorceable.
　Plus force a bull, etc.

ÔRTĒNES

sw: swartiness*.
w: wartiness.

ÔRTIFĪ

f: fortify.
m: mortify.
　Plus warty, fie!, etc.

ÔRTIKƏL

k(c): cortical.
v: vortical.
　Plus forty, Cal, etc.

ÔRTLĒNES

k(c): courtliness, uncourtliness.
p: portliness.

ÔRƏSLĒ

k(c): decorously.
n: sonorously.
p: porously.
　Plus chorus, Lee *or* lea, etc.

ŌRƏBƏL

d: adorable.
h: horrible.
pl: deplorable, explorable.
st: restorable.
　Plus gore a bull, etc.
　Plus Angora bull, etc.s

ŌRƏTIV

pl: explorative.
st: restorative.

ŌSHĒƏN

Vowel: Boeotian.
k(c): Nicotian.
　Cf. oshun.

ŌSHƏNƏL

m: emotional.
n: notional.
v: devotional.
　Plus emotion, Al, etc.

ŌSHƏSNES

k(c): precociousness.
r: ferociousness.
tr: atrociousness.

ŌSIVNES

pl: explosiveness.
r: corrosiveness.

ÔSƏTĒ

p: paucity.
r: raucity.
　Plus cross it, he, etc.
　Plus faucet, he, etc.
　Cf. craw, city, etc.

ŌTEDLĒ

bl: bloatedly.
n: notedly.
v: devotedly.
   Plus quoted Lee, moated lea, etc.
   Plus slow, Ted Lee, etc.

ÔTĒEST

h: haughtiest.
n: naughtiness.

ÔTĒNES

h: haughtiness.
n: naughtiness.

ÔTĒƏR

h: haughtier.
n: naughtier.
   Plus haughty, her, err, *or* er, etc.

ÔTILĒ

h: haughtily.
n: naughtily.
   Plus naughty Lee, etc.
   Plus brought alee, etc.

ŌTƏBƏL

fl: floatable.
kw(qu): quotable.
n: notable.
p: potable.
v: votable.
   Plus tote a bull, etc.
   Plus Minnesota bull, etc.

ŌTƏLIZM

d: sacerdotalism.
t: teetotalism.

ŌTƏRĒ

n: notary.
r: rotary.
v: votary.
   Plus voter, he, etc.
   Plus quote her, he, etc.

ÔTƏRĒ

k(c): cautery.
w: watery.
   Plus brought her, he, etc.
   Plus daughter, he, etc.

ÔTƏRING

sl: slaughtering.
w: watering.
   Plus caught her ring, etc.
   Plus caught a ring, etc.
   Plus daughter ring, etc.

ÔTƏRƏR

sl: slaughterer.
w: waterer.
   Plus daughter, her, etc.
   Plus caught her, her, etc.

ŌTƏTIV

n: connotative, denotative.
r: rotative.

OUDEDNES

kl: cloudedness, uncloudedness.
kr: crowdedness, overcrowdedness.

OUDĒIZM

d: doudyism.
r: rowdyism.

OUDĒNES

d: dowdiness.
kl: cloudiness.
r: rowdiness.

OULƏRĒ

Vowel: owlery.
pr: prowlery.
  Plus foul her, he, etc.
  Plus growler, he, etc.

OUNDEDNES

b: unboundedness.
f: confoundedness,
dumbfoundedness.
gr: ungroundedness.
st: astoundedness.

OUNDLESLĒ

b: boundlessly.
gr: groundlessly.
s: soundlessly.
  Plus boundless lea *or* Lee, etc.

OUNDLESNES

b: boundlessness.
gr: goundlessness.
s: soundlessness.

OUNDƏBƏL

p: compoundable.
s: soundable, unsoundable.
z: resoundable.
  Plus surround a bull, etc.

OUNTƏBƏL

k(c): countable, discountable,
unaccountable.
m: insurmountable, mountable,
surmountable.
  Plus mount a bull, etc.

OUTĒNESS

d: doutiness.
dr: droughtiness.
g: goutiness.

OUZĒNES

dr: drowsiness.
fr: frowsiness.
l: lousiness.

OUƏBƏL

d: endowable.
l: allowable.
v: avowable.
  Plus cow a bull, etc.

OUƏRĒ

b: bowery.
d: dowery.
fl: flowery.
gl: glowery.
l: lowery.
sh: showery.
t: towery.
  Plus flower, he, etc.
  Cf. ouri.

OUƏRING

d: dowering.
fl: deflowering, flowering.
gl: glowering.
k(c): cowering.
l: lowering.
p: empowering, overpowering.
sh: showering.
t: overtowering, towering.

ŌVĒƏL

j: jovial.
n: synovial.
  Plus Hovey, Al, etc.

ŌVĒƏN

j: Jovian.
k(c): Cracovian.
    Plus Hovey, Ann *or* an, etc.

ŌZĒEST

k(c): coziest.
n: nosiest.
pr: prosiest.
r: rosiest.

ŌZĒNES

d: doziness.
k(c): coziness.
n: nosiness.
pr: prosiness.
r: rosiness.

ŌZĒƏ

br: ambrosia.
p: symposia.
    Plus posy, a, etc.

ŌZHĒƏL

br: ambrosial.
r: roseal.
    Plus dozy, Al, etc.

ŌZHĒƏN

br: ambrosian.
    Cf. ozhun.

ŌZILĒ

k(c): cozily.
n: nosily.
pr: prosily.
r: rosily.
    Plus cozy, Lee *or* lea, etc.
    Plus doze alee, etc.

ŌZƏRĒ

Vowel: hosiery.
d: dozery.
p: composery.
r: rosary.

U

The accented vowel sounds included under **U** in Single Rhymes.

UBĒNES

ch: chubbiness.
gr: grubbiness.
shr: shrubbiness.
skr(scr): scrubbiness.
st: stubbiness.

UDĒNES

bl: bloodiness.
m: muddiness.
r: ruddiness.

UD′LĒ

bl: bloodily.
m: muddily.
r: ruddily.
  Plus study, Lee *or* lea, etc.
  Plus mud alee, etc.

UDƏRĒ

d: duddery.
sh: shuddery.
st: studdery.
  Plus udder, he, etc.

UFĒNES

fl: fluffiness.
h: huffiness.
p: puffiness.
st: stuffiness.

UGƏRĒ

p: pugaree.
sn: snuggery.
th: thuggery.
  Plus lugger, he, etc.
  Plus hug her, he, etc.

UK′LĒ

l: luckily.
pl: pluckily.
  Plus lucky lea *or* Lee, etc.

UKSHƏNĀL

d: inductional.
fl: fluxional.
str: constructional, instructional.
  Plus ruction, Al, etc.

UKSHƏNIST

fl: fluxionist.
str: constructionist, destructionist.

UKTIVLĒ

d: inductively, productively.
str: constructively,
deconstructively, instructively.
  Plus instructive, Lee, etc.

UKTIVNES

d: inductiveness, productiveness.
str: constructiveness, destructiveness, instructivenesss.

UKTƏBƏL

d: conductible.
str: destructible, indestructible, instructible.
  Plus deduct a bull, etc.

UKTƏRĒ

d: conductory, introductory, reproductory.
  Plus instructor, he, etc.

UKƏRING

p: puckering.
s: succoring.
  Plus mucker ring, etc.
  Plus pluck a ring, etc.
  Plus pluck her ring, etc.

ULCHƏRIZM

gr: agriculturism, etc.
v: vulturism.
  Cf. ultur plus ism.

ULKĒNES

b: bulkiness.
s: sulkiness.

ULMƏNƏNT

f: fulminant.
k(c): culminant.

ULMƏNĀT

f: fulminate.
k(c): culminate.
  Plus skull me, Nate, etc.

ULSIVLĒ

p: impulsively, repulsively.
v: convulsively.
  Plus emulsive, Lee, etc.

ULSIVNES

p: compulsiveness, impulsiveness, repulsiveness.
v: convulsiveness, revulsiveness.

ULTƏRĒ

d: adultery.
s: consultary.
  Plus consult her, he, etc.
  Plus exulter, he, etc.

ULVƏRIN

k(c): culverin.
p: pulverin.

ULƏRĒ

d: medullary.
g: gullery.
sk(sc): scullery.
  Plus color, he, etc.
  Plus gull err, he, etc.

UMBƏRĒ

Vowel: umbery.
sl: slumbery.
  Plus number, he, etc.

UMBƏRING

k(c): cumbering, encumbering.
l: lumbering.
n: numbering, outnumbering.
sl: slumbering, unslumbering.
  Plus Humber ring, etc.

UMBƏRƏR

k(c): cumberer, encumberer.
l: lumberer.
n: numberer.
sl: slumberer.
  Plus number her, err, *or* er, etc.

UMINGLĒ

h: hummingly.
k(c): becomingly, unbecomingly.
n: benumbingly, numbingly.
str: strummingly.
    Plus strumming, Lee, etc.

UMPCHŌŌƏS

s: sumptuous.
z: presumptuous.

UMPISHNES

d: dumpishness.
fr: frumpishness.
gr: grumpishness.
l: lumpishness.
m: mumpishness.

UMPSHƏSLĒ

b: bumptiously.
skr(scr): scrumptiously.
    Plus bumptious, Lee, etc.

UMƏRĒ

fl: flummery.
m: mummery.
n: nummary.
pl: plumbery.
s: summary, summery.
    Plus dumber, he, etc.
    Plus dumb Marie, etc.

UNDƏRING

bl: blundering.
pl: plundering.
s: sundering.
th: thundering.
w: wondering, unwondering.
    Plus under ring, etc.
    Plus shunned her ring, etc.
    Plus shunned a ring, etc.

UNDƏR SÔNG

Vowel: under song.
th: thunder song.
w: wonder song.
    Plus plunder song, etc.
    Plus shunned her song, etc.

UNDƏRWŲRLD

Vowel: underworld.
w: wonder world.
    Plus plunder world, etc.
    Plus shunned her world, etc.

UNDƏRƏR

bl: blunderer.
pl: plunderer.
s: sunderer.
th: thunderer.
w: wonderer.
    Plus plunder her, err, *or* er, etc.

UNDƏRƏS

bl: blunderous.
th: thunderous.
w: wonderous.
    Plus plunder us, etc.

UNDƏTĒ

b: moribundity.
f: profundity.
k(c): fecundity, jocundity, jucundity, rubicundity.
t: rotundity.
    Plus pundit, he, etc.

UNGƏRING

h: hungering.
m: mongering, scandal-mongering.
    Plus younger ring, etc.

UNILĒ

f: funnily.
s: sunnily.
　　Plus honey, Lee *or* lea, etc.

UNJKSHƏNƏL

f: functional.
j: conjunctional.
　　Plus junction, Al, etc.
　　Plus monk shun, Al, etc.

UNKYO͞OLƏR

Vowel: uncular.
b: carbuncular.
d: peduncular.
r: caruncular.
v: avuncular.

UNTEDLĒ

fr: affrontedly.
st: stuntedly.
w: unwontedly, wontedly.
　　Plus bunted, Lee, etc.

UNƏRē

g: gunnery.
n: nunnery.
　　Plus runner, he, etc.

ᵾRBēƏL

b: suburbial.
v: adverbial, proverbial.
　　Plus Derby, Al, etc.

ᵾRBYO͞OLƏNT

h: herbulent.
t: turbulent.
　　Plus blurb you lent, etc.

ᵾRBƏLIST

h: herbalist.
v: verbalist.
　　Plus disturb a list, etc.

ᵾRBƏLIZM

h: herbalism.
v: verbalism.

ᵾRDƏLĒ

st: sturdily.
w: wordily.
　　Plus third alee, etc.

ᵾRDƏRƏR

m: murderer.
v: verderer.
　　Plus herder, her, etc.
　　Plus heard her, err, etc.

ᵾRēEST

f: furriest.
h: hurriest*.
w: worriest*.

ᵾRēING

fl: flurrying.
h: hurrying.
k(c): currying.
sk(sc): scurring.
w: worrying.

ᵾRēMENT

w: worriment.
　　Cf. eriment.

ᵾRēƏR

f: furrier.
fl: flurrier.
h: hurrier.

k(c): currier.
sk(sc): scurrier.
w: worrier.
  Plus worry her, err, *or* er, etc.

ᴜRFLO̅O̅ᴐS

p: superfluous.
t: subterfluous.

ᴜRISHING

fl: flourishing.
n: nourishing.

ᴜRITED

t: turreted.
  Cf. erited.

ᴜRJIKᴐL

Vowel: demiurgical, theurgical.
kl: clergical.
n: energical.
r: chirurgical.
s: surgical.
t: liturgical, thaumaturgical.
  Plus metallurgy, Cal, etc.
  Plus demiurgic, Al, etc.

ᴜRJᴐNSE̅

Vowel: urgency.
m: emergency.
s: assurgency, insurgency.
t: detergency.
v: convergency, divergency,
vergensy.
  Plus virgin, see, etc.
  Plus divergence, he *or* see, etc.

ᴜRJᴐRE̅

p: perjury, purgery.
r: chirurgery.

s: surgery.
  Plus verger, he, etc.
  Plus scourge her, he, etc.

ᴜRKYO̅O̅LA̅T

b: tuberculate.
s: circulate.
  Plus work, you late, etc.

ᴜRKYO̅O̅LᴐR

b: tubercular.
f: furcular.
s: circular.

ᴜRKYO̅O̅LᴐS

b: tuberculous.
s: surculus, surculous.

ᴜRLE̅EST

Vowel: earliest.
b: burliest.
ch: churliest.
k(c): curliest.
p: pearliest.
s: surliest.

ᴜRLE̅NES

Vowel: earliness.
b: burliness.
k(c): curliness.
p: pearliness.
s: surliness.

ᴜRLISHLE̅

ch: churlishly.
g: girlishly.

ᴜRLISHNES

ch: churlishness.
g: girlishness.

ÛRMƏNĀT

j: germinate.
t: determinate, exterminate, indeterminate, interminate, terminate.
  Plus vermin ate *or* eight, etc.
  Plus worm innate, etc.
  Plus squirm in eight *or* ate, etc.

ÛRMƏNƏL

j: germinal.
t: terminal.
  Plus ermine, Al, etc.
  Plus germ in, Al, etc.
  Cf. vermin, all, etc.

ÛRMƏNƏNT

j: germinant.
t: determinant, terminant.
  Plus ermine aunt *or* ant, etc.
  Plus worm in ant, etc.

ÛRMƏNƏS

t: coterminous, terminus.
v: verminous.
  Plus ermine us, etc.
  Plus term in us, etc.

ÛRNĒƏN

b: Hibernian.
l: Falernian.
t: Saturnian.
z: Avernian.
  Plus attorney, an *or* Ann, etc.
  Plus spurn, Ian, etc.

ÛRNISHING

b: burnishing.
f: furnishing, refurnishing.

ÛRNISHƏR

b: burnisher.
f: furnisher, refurnisher.
  Plus furnish her, etc.

ÛRNƏBƏL

b: burnable.
l: learnable.
t: overturnable, turnable.
z(s): discernible, indiscernible.
  Plus turn a bull, etc.
  Plus Smyrna bull, etc.

ÛRNƏLIST

j: journalist.
t: eternalist.
  Plus infernal list, etc.
  Plus Verna list, etc.

ÛRNƏLĪZ

j: journalize.
t: eternalize, externalize.
  Plus infernal eyes, etc.
  Plus Verna lies, etc.

ÛRNƏLIZM

j: journalism.
t: eternalism, externalism.

ÛRNƏRĒ

f: fernery.
t: turnery.
  Plus burner, he, etc.
  Plus spurn her, he, etc.

ÛRNƏTY

d: modernity.
t: alternity, diuternity, eternity, fraternity, maternity, paternity, sempiternity, taciturnity.

Plus burn it, he, etc.
Plus ferny tea, etc.

URƏGĀT

s: surrogate.
    Cf. erogat.

URPƏNTĪN

s: serpentine.
t: turpentine.

URSHĒƏL

v: controversial.
    Cf. urshal.

URSHƏN

p: Persian.
s: lacertian.
t: Cistercian.
    Cf. asurshan, urzhan.

URSIFÔRM

Vowel: ursiform.
v: diversiform, versiform.
    Plus Circe form, etc.

URSIVNES

Vowel: coerciveness.
k(c): discursiveness, excursiveness.
t: detersiveness.

URSƏBƏL

Vowel: coercible, incoercible.
b: reimbursable.
m: amercable, immersible.
v: conversable, conversible,
irreversible, reversible.
    Plus curse a bull, etc.
    Plus vice versa, bull, etc.

URSƏRĒ

b: bursary.
k(c): cursory, percursory.
n: nursery.
p: aspersory.
v: anniversary, controversary.
    Plus disperser, he, etc.
    Plus curse her, he, etc.

URTHLESNES

m: mirthlessness.
w: worthlessness.

URTIGO

t: vertigo+.

URTƏTOOD

Vowel: inertitude.
s: certitude, incertitude.
    Plus assert it, you'd, etc.

URVƏNSĒ

f: fervency.
s: conservancy.

URVƏTIV

k(c): curvative.
n: enervative.
s: conservative.
z: observative, preservative,
reservative.

URZHƏNIST

k(c): excusionist.
m: immersionist, total-
immersionist.
v: versionist.

URƏBƏL

f: conferrable, inferable, referable, transferable.
m: demurrable.
    Plus stir a bull, etc.

URƏNSĒ

k(c): concurrency, currency, recurrency.
    Plus transference, he, etc.

USKYŌŌLƏR

m: bimuscular, muscular.
p: corpuscular, crepuscular.

USKYŌŌLƏS

m: musculous.
p: corpusculous, crepusculous.

USKƏLĒ

d: duskily.
h: huskily.
m: muskily.
    Plus husky Lee, etc.
    Plus musk alee, etc.

USTĒEST

d: dustiest.
f: fustiest.
g: gustiest.
kr: crustiest.
l: lustiest.
m: mustiest.
r: rustiest.
tr: trustiest.

USTĒNES

d: dustiness.
f: fustiness.
g: gustiness.

kr: crustiness.
l: lustiness.
m: mustiness.
r: rustiness.
tr: trustiness.

USTFƏLĒ

l: lustfully.
tr: distrustfully, mistrustfully, trustfully.
    Plus trustful, he, etc.

USTRĒƏS

d: industrious.
l: illustrious.

USTƏBƏL

b: bustable, combustible, incombustible.
d: dustible.
j: adjustible.
r: rustable.
thr: thrustable.
    Plus Augusta bull, etc.
    Plus thrust a bull, etc.

USTƏLY

d: dustily.
f: fustily.
g: gustily.
kr: crustily.
l: lustily.
m: mustily.
r: rustily.
tr: trustily.
    Plus trusty, Lee *or* lea, etc.
    Plus dust alle, etc.

USTƏRING

bl: blustering.
fl: flustering.

kl: clustering.
m: mustering.
    Plus adjuster ring, etc.
    Plus thrust her *or* a, ring, etc.

UTHƏRĒ

br: brothery.
m: mothery.
sm: smothery.
    Plus other, he, etc.

UTHƏRHOOD

br: brotherhood.
m: motherhood.
    Plus another hood, etc.

UTHƏRING

br: brothering.
m: mothering.
sm: smothering.
w: Wuthering.
    Plus another ring, etc.

UTHƏRLĒ

br: brotherly, unbrotherly.
m: motherly, unmotherly.
s: southerly.
    Plus smoother, Lee *or* Lea, etc.

UTHƏRLĪK

br: brotherlike.
m: motherlike.
    Plus another like, etc.

UTLƏRĒ

b: butlery.
k(c): cutlery.
s: sutlery.
    Plus butler, he, etc.

UT'NĒ

b: buttony.
gl: gluttony.
m: muttony.
    Plus Dutton, he, etc.
    Plus smut on, he, etc.

UTƏRING

Vowel: uttering.
b: buttering.
fl: fluttering.
g: guttering.
m: muttering.
sp: sputtering.
spl: spluttering.
st: stuttering.
    Plus utter ring, etc.
    Plus cut a ring, etc.
    Plus cut her ring, etc.

UTƏRƏR

Vowel: utterer.
b: butterer.
fl: flutterer.
m: mutterer.
sp: sputterer.
spl: splutterer.
st: stutterer.
    Plus utter her *or* err, etc.

UVƏRLĒ

k(c): de Coverley.
l: loverly.
    Plus hover, Lee, etc.
    Plus shove her, Lee, etc.

UZĒNES

b: buzziness.
f: fuzziness.
m: muzziness.
w: wuzziness.

Part II

Guidelines for Effective Rhyme

Where Does Poetry and Song Come from?

Poetry starts inside the mind and heart; it's an expression of the poet's desire, whether conscious or unconscious. Sometimes poets don't know, when they start writing, how the poem will turn out; sometimes they "write to the poem," as William Stafford once put it; sometimes they start with a "triggering" word, phrase, or image, as Richard Hugo put it. Some call this inspiration; others simply call it the unconscious—that pool of images, feelings, thoughts, and experiences each one of us carries with us throughout our lives. Poetry starts in this place, and it leads its readers back to this place—which may be why some people are simply afraid of poetry. Poetry asks more of its readers than prose, and it asks more of poets themselves.

Is the feeling more important than the form? Always. But can the poem exist without its form? Never. There is always a way of putting words together which expresses the poet's feeling and ideas better than other ways of putting words together. It's the job of the intellect in this process to shape the un-formed desire, feelings, or ideas; and, after the poem begins to take shape, it is this intellectual part of the process for which the poet needs to know the best ways of shaping words to make the poem.

Think of it this way: Whenever a poet writes a poem, there are two writers, not one, at work. The first we can call the *creator:* The room is messy with old scraps of newspapers, souvenirs from childhood, photos of picnics and lost loves, wild vines of exotic rainforest flowers. Out of this mess, the feelings, ideas, and words emerge, strong and powerful, insightful and delicate, brief flashes and long-sought gains from experience. The creator lives for the moment of exhilaration when the words emerge and fit together and the poem starts. The creator knows that poetry is life, rooted in dirt and garbage, forcing its way up to the sun. If the creator's room looks like a teenager's bedroom, that's no surprise—it's dangerous for a totally controlled, adult mind to go in there. The creator is the young Marlon Brando yelling "Stella!" or Marilyn Monroe standing above the subway grate, feeling the wind fly up her dress.

But if a poem is just a momentary image, then every teenage diary would be the sonnets of Shakespeare. All poets know that from the creator's room the poem must move—if it is to be a poem at all—into the critic's study. There, books line the walls, the newspaper is folded, the coffee steams with a hint of amaretto, and the exotic flowers of the rainforest have been cut and placed in an elegant vase on top of a desk where pens and pencils are arranged in rows by a pad of paper and a gleaming computer. If the creator's life is a mess, the critic's life is a job: Which word goes where? How does this word sound next to that one? What would happen if this line were moved up to the top of the poem? Every word is weighed and measured, just as if the poem were an experiment in a laboratory, until the poem gains a form.

This book cannot give you life itself; you have your own dirt, garbage, souvenirs, and wonderful exotic flowers. This book depends on your bringing them—"the mess" of your life—to your own poetry. But this book can help provide the elegant vase in which you can place your wonderful exotic flowers, the critic's study where poems are completed and formed.

Sometimes, it's true, you won't need this book—the words will seem to form themselves; your creator will stumble onto some words that bloom the right way and the poem just happens. That's when you need to thank your lucky stars or get down on your knees and offer thanksgiving to whoever is helping your creator. But there will be other times when you have a group of words or a feeling or an idea and it's like discovering an Oscar dress at the local K-Mart—how did it get there? Where can you wear it? You have no idea. This book can give you ideas on how to "wear" or shape your finds into something that looks and feels right.

But let's be clear: Nothing in this book can exist without the creator—that mood, those unformed feelings and ideas that come and develop spontaneously out of your own life. The creator, not the critic, has the last word, always; poetry is life, and life is ultimately something which cannot be measured and controlled by any critic. It's the critic's job to help the creator, not the other way around.

All the poetic forms in this book began, long ago, as un-formed ideas that poets had and played with, trying to make something happen in the words. In school or college, you may have heard about "the poetic tradition," and all those names—Shakespeare, Dante, Dickinson, Wordsworth, Eliot—seem like some big club that you can never be a member of. Forget the academic hype; it was thought up by people who got lost in the critic's study and forgot the creator's room. "The poetic tradition" is people who play with words in the same way musicians play with music or try to find new ways of putting their feelings and ideas together. It's that simple—and that complicated. If you like playing with words, you will want to know more about the poets and poetic forms in this book, in the same way a young jazz musician will want to listen to old Charlie Parker or Miles Davis LP records.

Think of this book, then, as the critic's study—a library of poetic forms, here when you need them, catalogued and explained, ready to help you write your poems, no matter where they come from. You bring the flowers; here is the vase.

Michael S. Allen

Guidelines to Using the Language

Poets and songwriters should write in the language they hear every day. Poetry is best when it is based in the words, word order, and idioms that come from living speech. Poets who try too hard to sound like famous dead poets, using words which "sound poetic," end up making dead poetry—stilted and affected, instead of alive and convincing. Both song and poetry have something to communicate; both are aimed at the emotions of their audience. There never has been a time when the emotions were moved by dead words more than by live words. When poets try too hard to imitate the poetry of the past, they overlook the fact that the great poetry of any age always uses the living speech of that age. Living speech moves people; dead words do not.

If you read a lot of poetry, you will see that, in any age, the words that are different from the living vocabulary stick out like a pimple on a beautiful girl's nose. Sometimes, simply because the girl (or the poem) is beautiful, people think that the pimple (or the dead language) is beautiful too. It's not. The girl (poem) may be beautiful, but the pimple (dead language) can still be a flaw. In some ways, people get the wrong idea about the language of poetry because they have been taught by teachers to accept that whatever Poet X wrote is great. Unfortunately, some teachers have thought that because great poetry sounds different from our everyday speech, the secret of the poetry's greatness lies in the difference, and so when they teach poetry, they stress how different it is from everyday speech. For decades, poetry has been paying a heavy price for this type of mistaken instruction, and people have looked at poetry with distrust because it sounds different from everyday speech. The great poets of today, as of every era, rise about this public distrust precisely because they always use the living speech which they hear all around them.

Always, the result of listening closely to living speech is a poetry which lasts over time. Four centuries ago, a poet wrote these lines:

Macbeth:	Wherefore was that cry?
Seyton:	The queen, my lord, is dead.
Macbeth:	She should have died hereafter;
	There would have been a time for such a word,—
	Tomorrow, and tomorrow, and tomorrow,
	Creeps in this petty pace from day to day,
	To the last syllable of recorded time;
	And all our yesterdays have lighted fools
	The way to dusty death. Out, out brief candle!
	Life's but a walking shadow; a poor player,
	that struts and frets his hour upon the stage,
	And then is heard no more; it is a tale
	told by an idiot, full of sound and fury,
	Signifying nothing.

(from *Macbeth*, William Shakespeare)

William Shakespeare's lines still move us not because he used an Elizabethan vocabulary but because he listened to the living speech of his day. If Shakespeare had tried to imitate too closely the words of Geoffrey Chaucer, a great poet who was long dead when Shakespeare lived, the only people reading Shakespeare now would be scholars who research Chaucer. Luckily, Shakespeare knew one of the secrets of writing poetry: Love the great poets who preceded you, but write only with words you hear every day. Only by using living speech can poets write lines of poetry which will last "tomorrow and tomorrow, and tomorrow."

Use the Language of Life, Not Books

People expect prose to use a living vocabulary; good poets know that the same rule applies to poetry. Perhaps the most American of poets, Walt Whitman once put some straight talk about writing poetry into one of his poems:

Rhymes and rhymers pass away, poems distill'd from poems pass away,

The swarms of reflectors and the polite pass, and leave ashes,

Admirers, importers, obedient persons, make but the soil of literature. . . .

What is this you bring America? . . .

Is it not something that has been better told or done before? . . .

Is it not a mere tale? a rhyme? a prettiness?

Has it not dangled long at the heels of poets?

Can your performance face the open fields and the seaside?

Does it meet modern discoveries, calibres, facts, face to face?

(*Blue Ontario's Shore*, Walt Whitman)

Harsh talk, but true talk. "Can your performance face the open fields and the seaside?" Is it from real life, and not just something like what you read in a book somewhere? The choice is your own. But borrowing words and ideas from another book is doubly removed from the life which all books seek to catch. Let your words, at least, come from your own life, and not from some way you think you should be living.

Use Emotion-Rousing Words

Poetry and song appeal to the emotions. It is important, therefore, to select words which can arouse your reader's or listener's emotions. Short, sharp Anglo-Saxon words are almost always more effective than ponderous polysyllables derived from Latin or Greek. Precise, specific words are as a rule far stronger than general, more abstract words. For example, *peony* is more effective than *flower;* but either is better than *Paeonia officinalis!* Lofty talk about such abstractions as truth, beauty, or justice in song or poetry can simply put people to sleep, especially when compared to the use of more specific words and examples. It's always valuable to use words with strong emotional overtones:

> It's like a jungle sometimes, it makes me wonder
> How I keep from going under
>
> (from *The Message,* Grandmaster Flash and
> the Furious Five)

> A green line, frayed at the end
> where he broke it, two heavier lines,
> and a fine black thread
> still crimped from the strain and snap
> when it broke and he got away.
> Like medals with their ribbons
> frayed and wavering,
> a five-haired beard of wisdom
> trailing from his aching jaw.
>
> (from *The Fish,* Elizabeth Bishop)

Use Figurative and Allusive Words

The highest power of the mind is the power of generalization—that is, finding the likenesses between objects, ideas, etc., no matter how remote the connection. Expressing such likenesses and unlikenesses are what figures of speech do in any language. Sometimes these likenesses are easy to understand—and fun, as in this section of a cute poem where the author imagines chasing a bagel rolling down the street; the only comparison, a simile ("like a bagel"), doesn't appear until the next-to-last line:

Faster and faster it rolled,
with me running after it
bent low, gritting my teeth,
and I found myself doubled over
and rolling down the street
head over heels, one complete somersault
after another like a bagel
and strangely happy with myself.

(from *The Bagel,* David Ignatow)

And sometimes the comparison is more elaborate, as in the following section of a poem where the metaphor, getting grades in school, is used for all the things a wife and mother might do:

My son says I am average,
an average mother, but if
I put my mind to it
I could improve.
My daughter believes
in Pass/Fail and tells me
I pass. Wait 'til they learn
I'm dropping out.

(from *Marks,* Linda Pastan)

Making allusions—referring to something familiar to your reader or listener—also evokes overtones beyond the words themselves. For example, when Coolio says

As I walk through the valley of the shadow of death
I take a look at my life and realise there's nuthin' left

(from *Gangsta's Paradise,* Coolio)

He's making an allusion to *Psalm 23* in the Bible ("Lo, though I walk through the valley of the shadow of death, Thou art with me"). Sometimes allusions are more complicated or deeply embedded in the poem; in the following example, the poet needs the reader to understand that "pullets" is another word for chickens, that Ohio has steel mills and steelworkers, and that much of Ohio is crazy about football:

All the proud fathers are ashamed to go home.
Their women cluck like starved pullets,
Dying for love.

Therefore,
Their sons grow suicidally beautiful
At the beginning of October
And gallop terribly against each other's bodies.

(from *Autumn Begins in Martin's Ferry, Ohio,* James Wright)

There's a problem, though, with allusions. Your audience has to understand them or be able to figure them out. If you read much old poetry, you'll find a host of classical allusions. These can be fun, if you know Greek mythology (not that there's anything wrong with Greek mythology!). And if you read much Shakespeare, you know that he and other Elizabethan poets loved to allude to Greek and Roman mythology and history.

But few people know that Diana means the moon, or Apollo the sun, or Aurora the dawn. Unless you are writing a song or poem for your high school Latin Club, steer clear. Nothing advertises itself as being mediocre poetry as a poem filled with classical allusions; it's bookish and boorish and not alive. It can also be downright silly. Is Saddam Hussein a modern day Mars? Hardly. Do United Airline pilots think of themselves as Icarus? I hope not! (Icarus flew on wings up to the sun, only to have the sun melt his wings and cause him to plummet into the ocean.)

Use Musical, Singable Words

In poetry, where you are trying to appeal to the deeper emotions, it is clear that this appeal cannot be based only on rhyme. The important thing is what the poem has to say, not how it says it. As a rule, rhyme, rhythm, and other features of poetry, like similes and metaphors, should be unobtrusive; when a poem is read aloud or a song is sung, such ornaments should be natural to the poem so that the listener may not even be aware of them except as a faint addition to the pleasure. The appeal of African-American spirituals—some of which have no rhyme at all—is a case in point, but all free verse and even the later poetry of Shakespeare create deep emotional appeal with little or no rhyme at all.

But for most poetry and most poets, the sounds of words—their rhythm, sound patterns, and rhyme—are very important, and for some poets and songwriters, the sounds of words are nearly as important as what they say. For a song lyric, the words should fit with the music and be as singable as possible. In writing either popular lyrics or concert songs, the song writers should familiarize themselves with what other writers of their time are writing, if they wish acceptance and popularity. Here the language should always be from everyday speech. But there is a wide acceptance of a variety of rhymes, from single syllables to triple mosaic rhymes, where three syllables, and often more than one word, are built into a rhyme (as, in *best of it, rest of it; adoring you, imploring you,* etc.). But the more mosaic the rhyme, the more likely the song is comic, as in this example from the Beatles:

Will you still need me, will you still feed me

(from *When I'm Sixty-Four,* The Beatles)

Generally, the most singable sounds are those which use *m, n, l,* or *r* as consonants, coupled with the long *ah,* long *o,* long *i,* long *a,* and short *ah* vowel sounds. Some examples, from those same lads from Liverpool:

long ah: And though the holes were rather small
             They had to count them all
             Now they know how many holes it takes to fill
             the Albert Hall

                        (from *A Day in the Life,* The Beatles)

long o: I don't really want to stop the show,
             But I thought you might like to know

                        (from *St. Pepper's Lonely Hearts Club Band,*
                                            The Beatles)

long i: Will you still be sending me a valentine
             Birthday greetings, bottle of wine

                        (from *When I'm Sixty-Four,* The Beatles)

long a: Waiting to keep the appointment she made
             Meeting a man from the motor trade.

                        (from *She's Leaving Home,* The Beatles)

short ah: Well I just had to laugh
             I saw the photograph

                        (from *A Day in the Life,* The Beatles)

With these kinds of rhymes, the success of the song will depend upon the wideness of its emotional appeal; in the case of the Beatles, that wideness was world-wide.

In proportion as poetry emphasizes rhyme, usually it tends to be lighter in mood. Thus double rhyme should be used sparingly at best in serious poetry,; and triple rhyme hardly ever. But when the progression has arrived at light verse, whose only purpose is to amuse, the process is reversed. In comic and light verse, you *want* repeated, surprising, obtrusive, and even ridiculous rhymes. In American poetry, Ogden Nash, Dorothy Parker, and Phyllis McGinley are prime practitioners of light verse rhymes; in English poetry, there is still no one superior to W. S. Gilbert of Gilbert and Sullivan fame. Here is a stanza of triple mosaic rhymes from *Iolanthe:*

        Go away, madam;
        I should say, madam,
        You display, madam,
            Shocking taste.

> It is rude, madam,
> To intrude, madam,
> with you brood, madam
>   Brazen-faced.

(from *Iolanthe*, W. S. Gilbert)

By any measure, the songwriter who wishes to write light verse must become familiar with the best of W. S. Gilbert.

Some Warnings

Poetry is a living tradition. Poets and songwriters learn from early writers, often modeling themselves on earlier works to get a start in their writing. But there are dangers in following too closely the words and expressions from earlier times. It may lead you to sound poetic but it may also lead you to use old words and dead ideas. Therefore, some warnings are in order:

Watch for Old Words and Expressions

Have you heard anyone lately say *'tis*, or *doth, beshrew* or *wouldst, hath*, or *'gainst*? Probably not. You can find these words in Shakespeare, but that's because he heard them in the late 1500s. They live on in his poetry, but the only kind of poem you could make with them now is a parody of Shakespeare or some other Elizabethan poet. Here are some things to avoid, with some examples of words not to use:

1. Avoid all old pronouns: *thee, thou, thy, thine*, and *ye*. Last century there were still some Quakers who used *thee* and *thou*, but not lately.

2. Avoid all old verb forms: *didst, hast, dost, doth, art, wert, welt, wouldst, shalt*, and the whole tribe of *-est* and *-eth* verb forms (*adorest, adoreth*, etc.), including their contractions (*ador'st, ador'th*, etc.).

3. Avoid all old verbals (verb forms used as adjectives): *bedight, bedimmed, bedewed, beshrew, besprent, bethink*, and *betide*. You might get away with *bedecked, befell*, and maybe even *beribboned*, but I doubt if anyone would believe words like *beclasp, beshadow, befop, betailor, beglue*, or *bemercy* (although I hope one day someone will resurrect *berascal* and *bepretty*). A couple of centuries ago, people stopped "be-doing" things; maybe as the pace of life got faster, the verbs got shorter.

4. Avoid all old words, in general: *wrath, ruth, reft, bethinks, athwart, welkin, rathe, sooth, fardel, bodkin, burthen, murther, burgeon*, etc. These words truly belong to Shakespeare's time; let him have them. They've died since then.

Watch for Rhyme and Rhythm-Induced Forcings

Sometimes when you start a poem with a strong rhythm or rhyme scheme, your first impulse is to keep it going. It's logical—you like what you've got, and you want to keep it going. But then you hit a snag, and you find yourself forcing words into places in the line just to take up space, or you switch words around so the rhythm remains constant. Better to break the constant rhythm, or the rhyme, than to use words poorly or just to take up space. Sometimes the poem you *think* you want to write—the one that you started—is just a springboard to another poem, and the snag you've hit is a message from that other poem, asking you to rethink and revise your original idea. Better to rethink and revise than to force words to do things they have no business doing.

In a good poem or lyric, *every word counts*. If you don't need a word, it shouldn't be there. If you find yourself cutting off part of a word just to fit a rhythm, then the rhythm shouldn't be there. If the order of the words sounds backward or wrong, you should not use that order. If you've omitted a word that is necessary for the reader to understand what you're saying, then you need to put it in.

1. Avoid all rhythm- or rhyme-induced uses of *do*. Of course, if you need, "Do hurry up!" or, "He did turn; I saw him," that's fine. But a lot of poets have used *do* to fill up the rhythm of a line. This is called "padding the line," and it shows in lines such as "When winking merry buds do bloom" or "when stars do shine." Such lines sound forced and unnatural; you can do better.

2. Avoid all rhythm- or rhyme-induced contractions. As with *do*, you should use contractions anywhere you need them, but don't force them. The most unreal contractions are those which omit the first syllable or letter, such as *'tis, 'gainst, 'twas, 'neath, 'fore,* and *'tween*—leave *'twas* to Clement Moore ("'Twas the night before Christmas. . ."). But there has been a host of other forced contractions to save a line's rhythm: *e'er, n'er, e'en, 'gan, 'gins, ta'en,* etc. Whenever you find yourself reaching for one of these words to save a poetic rhythm, change the rhythm or write the poem as free verse. Sometimes fine free verse poems grow out of the busted shells of too-tight rhythm.

3. Avoid all rhythm- or rhyme-induced inversions. An inversion is a grammatical term for upsetting the regular word order: Instead of saying "dawn came," a poet inverts the order to "came the dawn." It's unbelievable whether in prose or poetry. There's an easy rule to remember here: Whenever an inversion is bad in prose, it's also bad in poetry. But some people think that inversions are part of a "poetic license," that such word order is "poetical." In most cases, it's not; here are some examples:

A. To fit a rhyme pattern:

> I turned on swift and frightened feet,
> So that I might the villain greet (instead of "greet the villain")

> Then, straight through the limb,
> Boldly struck he him
> (instead of "he struck him")

B. To fit a line's metric rhythm:

> Where heaves the turf in many a moldering heap.
> (instead of "the turf heaves")

> Now fades the glimmering landscape on the sight.
> (instead of "the glimmering landscape fades")

Both of the rhythm examples are from a famous poem, Thomas Gray's *Elegy Written in a Country Courtyard,* but of course Shakespeare and many other poets did the same thing. The problem is that neither in Shakespeare's day nor in Gray's were grammar rules as fixed as they are now. To make an inversion in a poem now immediately attracts attention *to* the inversion and *away* from the poem. It's the poem and what you are saying that should be important to your readers and listeners; you want them to keep reading, not to stop and try to figure out why you made the inversion.

4. Avoid all rhyme- or rhythm-induced omissions or substitutions. It's very tempting just to leave a word out to keep a line's rhythm, or to get to a word that rhymes. It's a subtle trick, and one practiced by many poets. Sometimes you can get away with it, but sometimes one word omitted will confuse readers and lose them. Worse, you may be tempted to substitute a less exact word so that you will fit a rhythmic or rhyming pattern. Once again, we only have to turn to Mr. Gray to see how to do these things, and why such techniques are too outdated for modern language.

A. Omitting an article:

> For them no more the blazing hearth shall burn,
> Or busy housewife ply her evening care.

It's a small word that's been left out—(the) busy housewife—and maybe you didn't notice it. That's what a poet hopes when a small word is omitted. But it's still best to keep it in, since that poetry is best when it's most like speech.

B. Omitting a pronoun:

> The applause of listening senates to command . . .
> Their lot forbade.

Here, there should be a "them" after forbade. The omitted pronoun helps give the poem a feeling of mystery—which may be what Gray wanted—but it also increases confusion.

C. Using the wrong word:

> Their name, their years, spelt by th' unlettered muse . . .
> And many a holy text around she strews,

Here Gray is reaching for a rhyme for *muse*. He lands on *strews,* but since he's talking about verses carved on tombstones, it's hard to see how *strews* refers to something that takes such effort. You could use *strews* for seeds in a garden or field, or you could even *strew* rose petals before your lover (though it's doubtful many people nowadays would use the word). The problem here is that *strews* once again increases the confusion-level in the poem. Gray forces a rhyme to agree with *muse* and the result is less, not more, understanding. But then, he's not the first nor the last poet to have forced a rhyme. Don't continue this sad tradition. It gives rhyme and poetry a bad name. Prose at its best uses the right word, the perfect word, in each instance; no artificial convention is worth it, if it forces your poetry to use any other word than the perfect word.

Watch Out for Clichés, Hackneyed Phrases, and Plagiarism

English is full of metaphor, and clichés are nothing more than dead metaphors people keep around as a mental shorthand. They're fine for speech, but not for poetry and most songs. Poets and songwriters should create their own metaphors. Readers and listeners have a right to expect no less. Therefore, avoid the old clichés when you write your poems or lyrics:

> red as a rose, white as snow, black as night, the boundless blue, the bounding main, the dewy earth, the purling brook, the golden sun, the sun-kist earth, the whispering breeze, teeth like pearls, eyes like stars or violets or woodland pools, cheeks like roses, throat like a swan, voice like a lark or nightingale,

and so on. If you use those phrases, you're not creating anything new. It is, however, possible to use the preceding phrases, but only in altered states:

> white as Himalayan snow; black as a starless night; the slyly whispering breeze

These are still not all that original, but they're better than letting someone else do your thinking for you. Likewise, watch out for proverbs and maxims. You may want to write a poem *about* a proverb or maxim, and use it in your title or as an epigraph just under the title, or you may want to use a proverb or maxim in an unusual, comic way, but don't put "a miss is as good as a mile" or "the early bird catches the worm" into your poem and expect readers to think it is an original idea. Your readers and listeners are interested in what you have to say—not in something they already know.

Similarly, unless you are going to do another Ezra Pound or T. S. Eliot, and weave other poets' words and stanzas into an epic poem about the downfall of Western civilization, or unless you are going to parody or change substantively the sense of another poet's words, don't steal another poet's words. It's theft and you can get sued, plain and simple. Remember instead that you have your own life, your own words and sounds, ideas and images, and they will be more than enough to lead you into the poems and songs you want to write.

Rhyme

Some History about Rhyme

The sounds in words are of two kinds: vowels and consonants. Of course, this isn't a text on linguistics, but it seems that language development may have been influenced by geography and climate. Generally, in the more northerly countries and languages (Germanic and Slavic languages—and English is a Germanic language), the consonants are heard more clearly, and the words tend to be full of consonants. Conversely, in Romance languages (French, Italian, and Spanish) and languages from sub-tropical and equatorial countries, the vowels dominate and the consonants are subordinate. Of course, there are exceptions—some South African languages have explosive consonants—but generally, the dominance of consonants or vowels seems somehow connected to geography and climate.

The essence of all poetry and song is its use of rhythm and repetition. Repetition is pleasing to the human ear—just think of how babies and young children like to sing songs that repeat words, and how Dr. Seuss's books are based on that idea. As poetry developed within each language, the forms of rhythm and repetition were influenced by the structure of consonants and vowels within the words. Rhyme is not native to English. As a Germanic language full of consonants, repetition of consonant sounds became the basis for alliterative verse, or the repetition of introductory accented consonants in words. This was a requirement of Anglo-Saxon and Old English verse, and although it has faded as a requirement for poetry, English is full of alliterative couplings and phrases, occurring in everyday speech, prose, and poetry: *time and tide, tried and true, bag and baggage, red as a rose, busy as a bee, dead as a doornail, topsy-turvy, shilly-shally, footloose and fancy-free,* etc.

Rhyme seems to have been invented early in the Christian era, probably by priests of the Alexandrian church so that their parishioners could remember certain church teachings or concepts. It spread through Italy and France and was brought over to England after the Norman Conquest (1066). It didn't exert much influence until Middle English replaced Old English; by the time of Chaucer's rhymed couplets in *The Canterbury Tales* (begun 1386), rhyme had become firmly established in English poetry.

The Function of Rhyme

Rhyme is the repetition of an identical accented vowel sound, with the consonants following it, but a difference in the consonants preceding it. Rhyme deals with sound only; spelling makes no difference. Thus *beat* and *great* do not rhyme; but the following words, despite their different spelling, do:

> beat, Crete, greet, elite, suite, conceit, concrete

Unfortunately, English rhyme limits the poet's and songwriter's word usage. For, once a rhyming word has been chosen, the lines that rhyme with it, instead of ending with any of the possible words in the language (something blank verse can do), must end with one of the limited group of words that rhyme with the word first chosen.

But the foundation of rhyme is not wholly negative and limiting. By a sort of paradox, rhyme can become positive and inspiration-awakening. It is always a fault if a rhyme is "dearly bought"—that is, if the second rhyming word is irrelevant, second-rate, or not at all appropriate for the poem. But, once the rhyming word is chosen, the need for selecting from the limited group of rhyming words can spur the creative poetic imagination to weigh and consider all possible uses of those words, and even reconsider and re-organize the poem as a whole. Thus in Clement Woods' poem "The Path," accent verse quatrains rhyming 1, 2, 3, 2, once had been written:

> I guess the little folk must use it,
> Whatever there is that lives in woods,

Wood had to consider the limited number of rhymes to *woods,* and what could be done with each of them; he finally chose the following:

> Bowling the crimson partridge berries,
> Playing leapfrog on toadstool hoods,

which was the kind of playful image Wood needed after the rather nebulous idea in the first two lines. A similar process may take place with the writing of any poem, as long as the poet's mind is not fixed on one particular image or idea and allows the creative process to be fluid and developing.

For another example, look at what W. B. Yeats did with "politics" in writing this short poem just before World War II, in response to German novelist Thomas Mann's statement, "In our time the destiny of man presents its meaning in political terms":

> How can I, that girl standing there,
> My attention fix
> On Roman or on Russian

> Or on Spanish politics?
> Yet here's a travelled man that knows
> What he talks about,
> And there's a politician
> That has read and thought,
> And maybe what they say is true
> Of war and war's alarms,
> But I that I were young again
> And held her in my arms!

(Politics, William Butler Yeats)

Types of Rhyme

Single or Masculine Rhymes

Traditionally, one-syllable rhymes are called single or masculine rhymes. Note that this rhyme may be one of a one-syllable word, or of the final accented syllable of a longer word:

> day, they, bouquet, Bordelais, Kid-n-Play

Double or Feminine Rhymes

Traditionally, two-syllable rhymes are called double or feminine rhymes. Here the identical accented vowels must be both in the second-to-last syllable and in the last syllable:

> ended, bended, pretended, defended, men did.

Triple and Longer Rhymes

Three-syllable or triple rhymes have the accented syllables third from the end of the word, with all following sounds identical:

> breakable, unmistakable, (and some would say:) implacable

These, and longer rhymes, are more suitable to light verse than to serious poetry. But even in light verse, longer rhymes can sometimes cause problems with rhythm. Note how in the following example, the first two lines have four accents, while the last two have only three:

> Rhyme, when I in its I proper I place,
> Lends both I digni- I ty and I grace.
> It is I unmis- I takable
> If it's I not too I breakable.

Now, maybe your poem or song needs a faster rhythm in the third and fourth lines—if so, then the preceding example is fine. But if you are looking for a more regular rhythm, either lengthen the lines—

> It is | always | unmis- | takable
>   If it | doesn't | prove too | breakable.

—or make the whole stanza three-accented verse:

> Rhyme, when | in its | place,
> Lends im- | pressive | grace;
> It is | unmis- | takable
> If it's | not too | breakable.

Minor Accent Rhymes

It is very effective to break the regular flow of rhymes on the major accents by rhyming a major accent with a minor accent, or even by rhyming two minor accents together:

> tree, memory; Spring, shopping; hit, counterfeit; dead, comforted; less, distress

Misplaced Accent Rhymes

Since rhyme was an alien importation, its use at first in English, especially in the popular ballads, was loose and approximate. French may have been the language of the court, but English was still a much more accented language than French, and so misplaced accent rhymes are a linguistic leftover of this conflict between the desire to please those in power and the fundamentals of English. Hence in ballads we find rhyming pairs such as the following:

> plan, woman; sea, Jamie; tree, weary; John, yeoman

For these words to rhyme, the accents in the second words must be misplaced—we don't say wo-MAN, but WO-man. (Perhaps this was the beginning of the famous "poetic license" used by so many great and lesser poets?) Nonetheless, this device can be put to good use in a language which is often hostile to rhyme. For example:

> Death gives no life to the ravished dead;
> But for this your soul has been appointed. . . .

> The choiring angels—and the vast anguish
> That tore her soul when she won her wish. . . .

> You can't ketch God wid no fly-paper—
> But my boy Jesus caught de Lord wid prayer! . . . .

Sugar Plum,
You says yes, I buys a ring;
You 'n' me has a church wedding.

(from *The Glory Road*, Clement Wood)

In reading misplaced accent rhymes aloud, it is clear that these natural trochaic endings (ap-|pointed, anguish, fly-|paper, wedding) should not be read as iambs—that would be too unnatural. Don't take the accent away from its proper place for the sake of the rhyme; that would give us an-guish′, wed-ding′. Instead, keep the natural accent (an′-guish, wed′-ding) but increase the stress on the unaccented syllable, reading the words almost like spondees, with both syllables accented.

Mosaic Rhymes: or Words and Parts of Words

One or both of the rhymes may consist of more than one word:

make it; break it; needed, she did; grab it, rabbit;

This device appears sometimes in serious poetry. It is always at home in popular songs and light verse, and at times it is used with great cleverness, as when George Noel Gordon, Lord Byron, rhymes *intellectual* with *hen-pecked-you-all,* or when Thomas Ingoldsby rhymes *furniture* with *burn it, you're.* Gilbert often uses such couplings:

monotony, got any; cerebellum, too, tell 'em too;
lot 'o news, hypotenuse; din afore, Pinafore;
strategy, sat a gee; way at, Commissariat;

And popular songs are full of examples:

found her, around her; enfold you, hold you;
dream awhile, scheme awhile; direct us, respect us;
jackin' and cappin', packin' and strappin';
flat in, Manhattan; gloomy, to me;
with 'em, rhythm; diss us, business.

In light verse, parts of words may also be used, relying on the visual typography to create both the rhyme and the joke. Classic examples are Lewis Carroll's *soup, two p-* (where the next line begins *-ennyworth*) and George Canning's rhyming *adieu* with *U-* (niversity of Gottingen) and *gru-* (the next line completing the *el* of *gruel*). Gilbert does this cleverly in *Iolanthe:*

Peers shall team in Christendom,
    And a duke's exalted station
Be obtainable by com-
    petitive examination.

(from *Iolanthe*, W. S. Gilbert)

Rhymes of Split Familiar Phrases

An excellent light verse device is to split a familiar phrase at an unexpected point and rhyme it there. Thus, "The early bird catches the worm"
could be rhymed at e*arly, bird,* or *catches:*

> To fling at me, "The early bird
> Catches the worm" is quite absurd.
> I'm sure, if the truth be told,
> That all he catches is a cold.

End Rhyme and Internal Rhyme

Rhymes used at the ends of lines are called end rhymes. Rhymes used
anywhere else within the line are called internal rhymes—including
rhymes used at the beginnings of lines:

> Hold the dam! The flood is rising,
> Crashing, smashing levees down.
> Bold of heart, we're realizing
> It's a task to save the town!

Here *rising* and *realizing, down* and *town* are end rhymes, while *crashing*
and *smashing, hold* and *bold* are internal rhymes. Sometimes internal
rhymes can be fun, even if the message they carry can be a little scary
(okay, so rhyme is contagious!):

> 'Cause when I am in action, there is no time for maxin' or relaxin'
> Just reactin' and subtractin'
> On a sucker MC whose mouth keeps on yappin' and flappin'
> I lose my cool, then I'll be start slappin' and smackin'
> You on a roll, then I'll be start jackin' and cappin'
> No time to lounge, I'm packin' and strappin'

> (from *Strictly Business,* EPMD)

Rhyme is a powerful force in poetry, whether traditional—as end line
rhyme—or internal. Lately, two facts have led to internal rhyme becoming more important for the poet and songwriter: 1) so much recent
poetry has been published in blank and free verse; 2) much rap music
uses internal rhyme. The term "internal rhyme" now is often used to
cover not only full rhymes (*crashing, smashing*) but also the use of
assonance and consonance within the poetic line.

Assonance and Consonance

Assonance, sometimes called *vowel rhyme,* is the repetition of the last
accented vowel sound in a word (and sometimes all following vowel
sounds), with a difference in the consonant sounds afterwards. Found
often in Provençal, early French, Spanish, and Portuguese poetry, it can

be found in early English ballads, in many popular song lyrics, and in much recent English poetry in free verse. Sometimes poets use assonance and mistakenly call it rhyme; the following series are not rhymes but are perfectly fine examples of assonance:

> mate, take shape
>
> sleet, deep, meek
>
> line, time
>
> fishes, ditches
>
> eagle, needle
>
> supper, butter

In rap music, assonance is often used in place of rhyme in rapid-fire lines, as in this example, where full rhymes (*rope, pope, dope*) give way to assonance, sometimes called *half-rhyme* (*Farrakhan, understand, man; game, insane*) when used at the ends of lines:

> All the critics you can hang 'em
> I'll hold the rope
> But they hope to the pope
> And pray it ain't dope
> The follower of Farrakhan
> Don't tell me that you understand
> Until you hear the man
> The book of the new school rap game
> Writers treat me like Coltrane, insane

> (from *Don't Believe the Hype,* Public Enemy)

In blank verse and free verse poetry, assonance can keep the lines linked together. In this example, the assonance of *might* and *life* is picked up in later lines when *try* leads by assonance to *drivers* and *lives*; also, the full internal rhymes of *Sunday* and *say* give way to assonance in *laid* and *insane:*

> You might come here Sunday on a whim.
> Say your life broke down. The last good kiss
> you had was years ago. You walk these streets
> laid out by the insane, past hotels
> that didn't last, bars that did, the tortured try
> of local drivers to accelerate their lives.

> (from *Degrees of Gray in Philipsburg,* Richard Hugo)

Sometimes, the use of assonance is more subtle, used almost as distant sound echoes that keep the lines connected. In the following poem, there are different *a* and *i* sounds (here, they are shorter vowels) in the first three lines (*a* sounds) and in the next two lines (*i* sounds):

This year again the bruise-colored oak
hangs on eating my heart out
with its slow change, the leaves at last
spiraling end over end like your
letters home that fall Fridays
in the box at the foot of the hill
saying the old news, keeping it neutral.

(from *Seeing the Bones,* Maxine Kumin)

Consonance

Consonance is pretty much the reverse of assonance: Instead of repeated vowel sounds, consonance is the repetition of consonants. Sometimes *alliteration* is used to include all consonance, but alliteration is usually restricted to the repetition of the same consonant at the beginning of two words, while consonance is usually reserved for repetition of consonant sounds within words. Also like assonance, consonance has been called half-rhyme or off-rhyme and it has found increased use in English poetry in blank and free verse.

Consonance has a long history in English poetry, however, for some of the same reasons as alliteration: the importance of consonant sounds in Anglo-Saxon, Old English, and early English ballads. But the limited number of accurate rhymes in English has made consonance attractive to many poets from Emily Dickinson, who often used it in place of full rhymes, to free verse poets in our time. And so consonance has also been used in two ways: to refer to *full consonance,* where the consonant sounds are closest to rhyme, and to *internal consonance,* where the same consonant sounds appear within words.

Full Consonance

When compared to rhyme, full consonance multiplies the possible combinations of words by about 10 times; moreover, consonance often possesses a freshness that many rhymes lost long ago. For example, *death* has few rhyming mates (*breath, saith* [archaic], and minor accent rhymes like *twentieth* and *Elizabeth*). But consonance adds to this limited group the following:

> faith, wraith, etc.
>
> bath, path, wrath, etc.
>
> beneath, heath, teeth, etc.
>
> myth, with, pith, etc.
>
> growth, both, oath, etc.
>
> broth, cloth, Goth, etc.
>
> booth, ruth, truth, youth, etc.

The increased naturalness of word usage that consonance permits, plus the novelty and freshness of the coupled sounds, is very effective. Consonance may be used exclusively, intermingled formally with rhyme, or used intermittently with rhyme.

Internal Consonance

Think of internal consonance as alliteration that's hiding inside a word. Take an example:

> *To t*ake the road *to* yes*t*erday's *t*errain.

The alliteration of *To, take, to,* and *terrain* is echoed by the internal consonance of the *t* in *yesterday*. The form of consonance has become more important as more free verse has been written; sometimes the use of consonance in free verse is nearly as important as the use of rhyme in traditional poetry. Examples abound. Notice how in the following lines the poet uses *s* sounds to obtain a hissing effect as he describes government authorities spinning the Three Mile Island nuclear accident in the 1970s:

> . . . the utility company continues making little of the accident,
> the slick federal spokesmen still have their evasions in some
> semblance of order.
> Surely we suspect now we're being lied to, . . .
>
> (from *Tar,* C. K. Williams)

Including all the varieties of the *s* sound (in *accident, slick,* and *spokes-*), there are 11 *s* sounds altogether within three lines—it's not hard to hear the hiss. Of course, consonance can also be found in traditional poetry and song lyrics. In the next example, *s* sounds are not nearly as sinister; in this simple but lovely lyric, they connect the stanza to the refrain:

> Certain as the sun
> rising in the east,
> Tale as old as time,
> Song as old as rhyme,
> Beauty and the Beast.
>
> (from *Beauty and the Beast,* Howard Ashman)

It's a small, nearly unnoticeable, point, but consonance continues the alliteration of *Certain* and *sun* through *rising, east, as,* and *Beast.* Did the writer know he was doing this as he wrote the lines? Maybe; or maybe it was just an intuitive sense, developed over years of listening to the sounds of words, that helped him see that these words go together very well to make an award-winning lyric.

Internal consonance can also be found in similar sounds which are related but not identical: Sounds made with the teeth (called dentals) are similar, as are sounds made with the lips (labials), with the teeth and lips (labiodentals), with the nose (nasals), and other sounds (gutturals, sibilants, and liquids). Here is a list:

> Dentals: t, d, th (as in *thin*), *TH* (as in *THis*).
>
> Labials: b, p (*M* is sometimes added).
>
> Labiodentals: f, v.
>
> Nasals: m, n, ng, nk.
>
> Gutturals: g, k, ng.
>
> Sibilants: s, z, sh, zh, ch, j.
>
> Liquids: l, r.

In the following example, note how the *s* and *sh* sounds reinforce each other:

> 'Tis shame that men should use poor maidens so.
>
> (from *The Complaint of Rosamond,* Samuel Daniel)

In this second example, note how Bob Dylan starts his famous song with several labial sounds (b, p) that help to paint a picture of a place where things aren't all right:

> They're selling postcards of the hanging
> They're painting the passports brown
> The beauty parlor is filled with sailors
> The circus is in town
>
> (from *Desolation Row,* Bob Dylan)

Incorrect Rhymes

Strictly speaking, *identities* do not rhyme. None of the words in the following groups rhyme:

> bay, obey, disobey
>
> bare, bear, forbear
>
> lying, underlying, overlying
>
> astrologic, biologic, geologic, pathologic

This rhyming dictionary helps you limit the unintentional misrhyming of identities since the words are properly grouped for rhyming according to one guiding principle:

> *Use only one word from each group.*

Eye rhymes are words spelled alike, but whose differing sounds prevent rhyme. Some of these have long been acceptable in English verse due to the scarceness of rhyme sounds. Among these are:

>   earth, hearth; are, bare; flow, allow; love, prove

These do not rhyme, and could be classified as consonant rhymes. Other permitted consonance and assonance rhymes (half-rhymes) are:

>   heaven, given; was, grass; bliss, is

A common erroneous miscoupling is *real* or *ideal* with *steal,* since the first two words are two syllable rhymes (E´ al) while *steal* is a single syllable (EL).

Light or humorous verse often uses eye rhymes for comic effect, rhyming words spelled similarly but pronounced differently:

>   enough, plough; through, although

Rhymes depend on your hearing them, and with the variety of dialects and regional accents in English, a full rhyme to you may not be a full rhyme to someone in another part of the country. Some people see *north* and *forth* as a full rhyme; others do not. Go with what you know.

Words with differing terminal consonant sounds are not true rhymes but consonant rhymes:

>   main, game; hate, shape; feed, sleet; blame, games;
>
>   miss, kissed; singer, finger; silver, deliver

Mispronunciation should not excuse false rhymes. However, remember the first rule in writing poetry: It comes from speech. If you pronounce a word a certain way that makes it rhyme with another word, use it, even if someone in another part of the country, or speaking a different dialect, pronounces it another way. For example, in Boston, *fork* and *talk* might rhyme, whereas in Ohio they don't. There are, however, some proper nouns and words from foreign languages which need to be respected. *Hades* does not rhyme with *spades; heinous* doesn't rhyme with *Venus; fete* doesn't rhyme with *meet.*

Rhyme-Induced Rhymes

The chief fault in rhymed poetry is using a rhyming word merely for the purpose of rhyming—because you need the rhyme. Examples:

>   We celebrate this merry Christmas,
>   Although we are not on an isthmus.
>
>   Do not speak only to embarrass
>   As Helen may have done to Paris.

Unless you are trying for a cheap joke, don't do this. Rhymed verse is good in proportion as *every word comes in naturally and inevitably*—just as in good prose.

Undesirable Rhymes

There are certain rhymes which have been used so often that they have become clichés and should be avoided unless you are using them in a strikingly original way. Using any of the following in a poem about love or spring has simply been done too many times:

> kiss, bliss; June, moon; love, dove; spring, wing.

A Mental Rhyming Dictionary

Long ago, I invented a mental rhyming dictionary, to be used when a printed one is unavailable. It depends, of course, on some significant memorizing of all the possible consonant sounds in the language. It can also be used, however, as a way of seeing (if not memorizing) the connections between consonant sounds in English:

Single Sounds	*Double*	*Triple*	*Rare*
Vowel (no beginning consonant)			
B	BL, BR		BW
CH			
D	DR		DW
F	FL, FR		
G	GL, GR		GW
H	HW		
J			
K (C)	KL, KR, KW (QU)		
L			
M			
N			
P	PL, PR		PW
R			
S	SK (SC), SL, SM, SN, SP, ST, SW	SKR (SCR), SHW (SQU), SPL, SPR, STR	SV

(continues)

Single Sounds	Double	Triple	Rare
Vowel (no beginning consonant)			
SH	SHR		
T	TR, TW		
th (thin)	thR, thW		
TH (this)			
V			VL
W			
Y			
Z			ZH, ZL

This gives 23 single sounds, 24 double sounds, five triple sounds, and eight rare sounds—60 altogether. Now, apply to this list the sound that you want to rhyme, and write out the rhymes that you can think of. For example, going down the list, the rhymes for *mate* would include the following:

> *single sounds:* ate, abate, date, fact, gate, hate, Kate, late, pate, rate, sate, tete-a-tete, wait
>
> *double sounds:* freight, great, crate, plate, prate, skate, slate, state, trait
>
> *triple sounds:* straight
>
> *rare:* (none)

You can then add the minor accent rhymes. For example:

> syndicate, conglomerate, abbreviate, indicate, intimate

You can follow the same procedure for two-syllable rhymes (using *backing* as an example word to be rhymed):

> hacking, jacking, lacking, lacking, packing, racking, sacking, tacking, blacking, clacking, cracking, quacking, slacking, smacking, stacking, tracking

The same thing can be done with triple or longer rhymes.

Rhythm

The one thing that distinguishes poetry from prose in English is that poetry has a tendency toward regularity or uniformity in rhythm, caused by the repetition of some pattern of accented and unaccented syllables, whereas while prose has a tendency toward variety instead of uniformity in the sounds the words make. The precise dividing line is fairly subjective, and there are excellent prose poems (e.g. Carolyn Forché's *The Colonel*) as well as very poetic prose (e.g. Virginia Woolf's *The Waves*).

However, people can get confused about rhythm (and even confuse rhythm and rhyme), and the history of poetry in English hasn't been much help in overcoming the confusion. There are three main categories of rhythm in English poetry: *accent verse, scansion* (or *metric verse*), and *free verse* (sometimes referred to by its French name, *vers libre*). You may have learned something about scansion in high school or college—and it just seemed like more of the same weirdness that made all poetry seem weird. Actually, you were right: Metric verse is *not* natural to English; it was imported into English from French, Italian, and other romance languages deriving from Latin. English verse probably originated in free verse, but the oldest form of regular rhythm in English poetry is accent verse. So, although we'll have to go back a few centuries to show how accent verse started, it's also one of the most contemporary forms of verse around.

Early Accent Verse in English

Accent verse is poetry with a definite number of accents to each line, with unaccented syllables ranging from none to as many as the poet desires, placed wherever he or she wishes. It was the basic rhythmic form of Anglo-Saxon poetry and continued to exert its influence in Old English poetry even after English began absorbing the French language of the Norman conquerors after 1066. There were three basic requirements of Old English verse:

1. Four accents to each line.

2. A break, or caesura, midway in each line.

3. At least two uses of alliteration in each line (alliteration is the same consonant sound at the beginning of two or more words).

This last requirement has led to accent verse also being called alliterative verse. The following are typical lines from Old English verse, with the accents marked and the alliterations in bold:

> **W**id´sith made ut´terance | his **w**ord´-hoard unlocked´.
>
> (*Widsith,* c. 600 A.D.)

> What! We of **S**pear´-Danes´ | in **s**pent´ days´.
>
> (*Beowulf,* c. 1000 A.D.)

> In a **s**um´mer **s**eason, | when **s**oft´ was the **s**un´.
>
> (*The Vision of Piers Plowman,* William Langland, c. 1350)

When this four-accent verse was used in old (as opposed to "Old") English ballads, the requirements for a midline break (caesura) and alliteration were dropped, although they can be found in some poems. It's important to see the freedom of the accent verse line. Unlike metric verse, where the number of unaccented syllables is fixed in each metric "foot," in accent verse there is no such fixed measurement; any number of unaccented syllables make up an accent verse foot. That freedom can be seen by counting the syllables as well as the accents in the following lines:

> It was´ upon a Scer´ethursday that our Lord´ arose´.
>
> (*Judas,* 13th century)

> He came´ also still´e, there his moth´er was´.
>
> (*Song of the Incantation,* 14th century)

> For I want´ for to go´ to Wid´dicombe fair´.
>
> (*Widdicombe Fair*)

> He court´ed the king's daugh´ter of fair´ England´.
>
> (*Earl Brand*)

These four lines have the following number of syllables each (in bold), and the following of number of syllables in each accented foot:

> *Judas:* **14:** 2, 5, 5, 2.
>
> *Incantation:* **11:** 2, 4, 3, 2.
>
> *Widdicombe Fair:* **11:** 3, 3, 2, 3.
>
> *Earl Brand:* **11:** 3, 4, 2, 2.

Accent verse is as natural to English poetry as Anglo-Saxon words such as *through, house,* and *shot.* Here are some examples which should be familiar:

> Hark, | hark, | the dogs | do bark
>
> The beggars | are coming | to town . . .
>
> Pease | porridge | hot . . .
>
> Three | blind | mice . . .
>
> Deedle deedle | dumpling | my son | John . . .

That's right: Many *Mother Goose* rhymes are in accent verse. In modern poetry, Walter de la Mare wrote *The Listeners* in three-accent verse:

> Though ev- | ery word | he spake
> Fell ech- | oing through the shad- | owiness of the still house.

> (from *The Listeners,* Walter de la Mare)

In that last line, the three feet contain 2, 5, and 7 syllables—something impossible in metric verse.

While four-accent verse is the oldest and most native form of poetry in English, examples of three-accent verse are almost as numerous, and the line can be of any length. Most recently, this most Anglo-Saxon form of poetry has had a resurgence in what would seem at first to be a most un-Anglo-Saxon venue: rap music. The strong drumbeat background and sound effects of much rap music are only part of the music; the poetry, which often rhymes, also has a strong rhythm based not on formal metric scansion, but on accents, as in this example:

> Read'y or not', ref'ugees taking ov'er
> The buf'falo sold'ier, dread' like rast'a
> On the twelve' hour fly' by' in my bomb'er
> crews' went for cov'er now they und'er pushin' up flow'ers
> Sup'erfly, true' lies do' or dies'
> toss me high' only pro'file with my crew' from Lacaille'
> I ref'ugee from Guatan'amo Bay',
> dance' around the bord'er like I'm Cass'ius Clay'

> (from *Ready or Not,* The Fugees)

Writing Accent Verse

In writing accent verse, try to make the various feet as different from each other as possible; if you try to make the unaccented syllables consistent, then you will wind up with metric verse. For a three-accent line, starting with the pattern TUM, TUM, TUM, like three drumbeats, we might get:

Spring! Spring! Spring!
With the flash | of birds | in the tree-limbs,
With soft | tints | of the rainbow
On the buds | and the awakening | blossoms.
No | more | snow,
No chill, | but a balm | in the air,

and so on. Accent verse is especially fitted to popular song lyrics, as in

No' | more pain',
No' | more strain',
Now' | I'm sane', but
I' | had rather be punch'-drunk.

(from *I Wish I Were in Love Again,* Lorenz Hart)

It is also the usual rhythm for chants:

O de Glo'- | ry Road'! | O de Glo'- | ry Road'!
I'm gonter drap' | my load' | upon de Glo'- | ry Road'!

(from *The Glory Road,* Clement Wood)

Fat | black bucks | in a wine- | barrel room . . .
Beat | an empty bar- | rel with the hand- | dle of a broom.

(from *The Congo,* Vachel Lindsay)

In these two and many other chants, feet of four and more syllables are common.

Remember: *Metric verse may correctly be regarded as accent verse clipped and padded into identical feet.*

While all metric verse can be seen and scanned as accent verse (by ignoring the unaccented syllables), it is best to write accent verse with a far freer and more natural rhythm than metric verse ever attains. For our purposes of classification, we will use the term *metric verse* for that subhead of accent verse in which the unaccented syllables, as well as the accented syllables, fit a pattern. We will limit the term *accent verse* to that verse whose unaccented syllables are not regular enough to qualify it as metric verse.

We've spent a lot of time on this topic because it can be a major stumbling block to poetry writers (the others being vocabulary, free verse, and consonance). Listen to and read popular song lyrics— whether rap, rock, pop, or country—and hear how the words and syllables are accented, and the relationship between the accents and the unaccented syllables. That's probably still the best way to understand the naturalness of accent verse, and to get over the idea, promoted in much school and college poetry instruction, that all poetry has to be metric verse. Even poets who are usually taught only as examples of metric verse also wrote in accent verse: Shakespeare (*Anthony and Cleopatra*), Milton (*Samson Agonistes*), and Frost (*Directive*).

Metric Verse

A meter in poetry is the systematic arrangement of accented and unaccented syllables in a poetic line. The syllables are divided into metric feet which have names derived from classical Greek and Latin prosody (the study of metrical versification). If anything in the study of poetic rhythm is scary, it is metric verse, because of all the names of the different metric patterns. A convenient way to cut through the confusion is to remember that there are only two kinds of metrical feet—two-syllable and three-syllable—and they can be grouped as follows, with the minor patterns placed in parentheses:

> Two-syllable feet: iamb, trochee (spondee and pyrrhic)
>
> Three-syllable feet: anapest, amphibrach, dactyl (amphimacer, bacchius, antibacchius, molossus, etc.)

But before we get too far into metric verse, some words about two ways of looking at it: natural and pattern scansion.

Scansion, Natural and Pattern

Scansion, whether of prose or verse (and some prose writers do scan their rhythms), is the division into rhythmical units, called feet, with markings to divide the feet and markings to show accented and unaccented syllables. The first step, then, in scanning your lines of poetry, is to mark your syllables as either accented or unaccented. If you are uncertain about which syllable is accented, consulting a dictionary may help, but simply saying the word or the whole poetic line out loud may help as much, since dictionaries do vary on how words are pronounced and some words are pronounced differently depending on the part of the country (or the kind of English spoken in your country). Once you have marked your accented and unaccented syllables, there are two ways of looking at scansion: natural and pattern.

Natural scansion is the scansion of words as they are naturally used in conversation. At times, natural scansion is as close to accent verse as it is to pattern scansion, since accent verse is more natural to the basic rhythms of English words and sentences. Therefore, the feet in a natural scansion may have more than three syllables, and there may be minor accents, as well as the major ones, in each foot. Here, for example, is a natural scansion of the opening of *Hamlet*'s famous "To be" soliloquy:

To be | or not to be. | That | is the question.
Whether | 'tis nobler | in the mind | to suffer
The slings | and arrows | of outrageous | fortune . . .

(from *Hamlet,* William Shakespeare)

In *pattern scansion,* as we shall see, the pattern calls for *five* accents, but in a more natural scansion of these lines—basing the scansion on reading the lines more like conversation than like poetry—we get four accents for each line. Similarly, the natural scansion of Joyce Kilmer's *Trees* is as follows:

I think | that I shall never | see
A poem | lovely | as a tree.

(from *Trees,* Joyce Kilmer)

Here the pattern, to look ahead again, calls for four accents per line, but a more natural, conversational reading of the lines gives us three accents per line.

Poetry comes from speech and should always be based in speech. Free verse and prose require only natural scansion. Accent verse is also close to natural scansion, marking only the accents and ignoring the unaccented syllables and minor accents. All three forms of rhythm in English are closer to speech than is formal, pattern scansion, which requires more precision—and sometimes that precision makes the poetry less accessible to an audience of readers or listeners.

Pattern scansion is the division of a poetic line into feet, dictated by the structured patterns of classical metrical verse. A classical pattern may call for a line of iambs, or trochees, or any other foot; or it may call for a pattern which alternates kinds of feet, as in Sapphic lines and stanzas. In pattern scansion, words are often divided ruthlessly, and minor accents can be regarded as the major accent of a foot. Also, a foot may be made up of all unaccented syllables (pyrrhic: two unaccented syllables; tribrach: three). In metric scansion, the goal is to fit each foot to the pattern, if possible, and if not, to make it a variation as near to the original as possible. Thus, the quotation from *Hamlet,* since *Hamlet* is blank verse, or iambic pentameter, has five accents per line in pattern scansion:

To be, | or not | to be. | That is | the question.
Whether | 'tis no - | *bler in* | the mind | to suffer
The slings | and ar- | *rows of* | outra- | geous fortune.

Here each line has a permitted extra unaccented syllable at its end. The third foot in the first line, "to be," has a minor accent which become a major accent in pattern scansion. The two italicized feet in lines two and three are pyrrhics, without any accent: ta-ta.

The pattern scansion of the couplet from *Trees*, in four-foot iambic, is *ta TUM, ta TUM, ta TUM, ta TUM,* as shown here:

> I think | that I | shall nev- | er see
> A po- | em love- | *ly as* | a tree.

The pyrrhic in the second line is italicized. Comparing the natural and pattern scansion in both cases, notice how in natural scansion there are fewer feet, with definite accents, and feet which have a variety of syllables; meanwhile, in pattern scansion, there are more feet, with a strict number of syllables in each foot, making some minor accents into major accents.

Let's have some fun with this. Here's a song that most children have heard (and some parents hear too much!) where the natural and pattern scansion differ, and both occur in the song:

> Supercalifragilisticexpialidocious!
> Even though the sound of it is something quite atrocious
> If you say it loud enough
> You'll always sound precocious
> Supercalifragilisticexpialidocious!

> (from *Supercalifragilisticexpialidocious!,* Richard M. and
> Robert B. Sherman)

In normal conversation, Julie Andrews says the word in natural scansion (here the accented syllables are indicated by uppercase):

> SUPercaliFRAGilsiticEXpialiDOcious

Like most ballads, it's a four-foot line; note how the first three accented syllables are each followed by three unaccented syllables (*ercali, ilistic, piali*). But in pattern scansion (and when Julie Andrews slows down the line so the children can understand the magic word), the first line is highly regular trochaic (TUM ta):

> SUPerCALiFRAGilLISTicEXpiALiDOcious

A line of *seven* trochaic feet! (Repeated, by the way, only when Mary Poppins shows off and says the word backward.) The next two lines of this chorus start out in trochaic feet (e.g., EVen THOUGH the SOUND of IT) and end up iambic (is SOMEthing QUITE aTROcious) but it is sung in natural scansion:

> EVen though the SOUND of it is SOMEthing quite aTROcious

And if you don't believe me, just ask a parent of a young child who has recently seen *Mary Poppins:* Kids like to sing the constant pattern trochaic lines (EVen THOUGH the SOUND of IT is SOMEthing QUITE aTROcious), to the dismay and patience-testing of any parent.

The difference between natural and pattern scansion is not just a matter of splitting hairs. When poets learn about scansion and rhythm, it is all too easy to think only of pattern scansion and be lured by the mechanics of measuring out the poetic line in terms of rigid patterns of syllables and feet. The end result can be poetry which is very regular but terribly boring. As great a poet as he was, much of William Wordsworth's poetry is a real snooze-maker—it is so regular in its "ta-TUM" iambic pattern. Since Wordsworth "wrote" whole poems in his head as he walked the hills of the Lake District, his walking reinforced the "ta-TUM" pattern in his lines. He wrote a lot of lines of very regular blank verse—but his poetry has put a lot of English graduate students asleep. Use classical, pattern scansion as a check on your lines, but no more. Here is a rule for writing good, but lively, metric verse:

> *Generally, poetry is natural and effective the more the natural scansion differs from the metric scansion.*

If, when you read aloud your poetry, you find yourself reading only in metric scansion, then your poetry is too regular and will induce sleep. Keep your readers, and your poetry, alive and awake.

Classical Metric Feet and Lines

Here is a table of all the metric feet (with asterisks by those most commonly used):

Name of foot	Scansion	Accent Pronunciation	Examples	Example Scanned
I. Two-Syllable Feet				
*Iamb	˘ ´	ta-TUM	delight, to go	de-light
*Trochee	´ ˘	TUM-ta	going, bread and	go-ing
Pyrrhic	˘ ˘	ta-ta	in a, and the	in a
Spondee	´ ´	TUM-TUM	big book, huge sun	big book
II. Three-Syllable Feet				
*Amphibrach	˘ ´ ˘	ta-TUM-ta	dividing, at ending	di-vid-ing
*Dactyl	´ ˘ ˘	TUM-ta-ta	battlement, end of the	bat-tle-ment

Name of foot	Scansion	Accent Pronunciation	Examples	Example Scanned
Amphimacer	´ ˘ ´	TUM-ta-TUM	antiwar; end the man	an-ti-war
Tribrach	˘ ˘ ˘	ta-ta-ta	and in the	and in the
Molossus	´ ´ ´	TUM-TUM-TUM	great white whale	great white whale
Bacchius	˘ ´ ´	ta-TUM-TUM	a huge bear, adore food	a huge bear
Antibacchius	´ ´ ˘	TUM-TUM-ta	base-stealing	base-stealing

Metric lines: In metric verse, each line is named by the number of feet it contains; thus iambic monometer is a one-foot iambic line, etc. Here is a table with the major types of lines:

Common Name	Classic (Metric) Name	Number of Feet
One-foot	Monometer	1
Two-foot	Dimeter	2
Three-foot	Trimeter	3
Four-foot	Tetrameter	4
Five-foot	Pentameter	5
Six-foot	Hexameter	6
Seven-foot	Heptameter	7
Eight-foot	Octometer	8

Here are some examples of flawless metric lines, divided into feet:

4-foot iambic:	I think | that I | shall nev- | er see
4-foot trochaic:	Then the | little | Hia- | watha
3-foot spondaic:	Great men | grow strong; | all die.
3-foot anapestic:	At the end | of the loft- | iest trail
3-foot amphribrachic:	In going | to Baby- | lon, children
3-foot dactylic:	Caught in the | spell of the | melody
3-foot amphimacer:	Men of Rome, | fight and die, | never yield!

We have already seen that flawlessness is a fault in metric poetry; naturalness comes in proportion as the natural scansion differs from the pattern scansion. But even if you wish to keep your poetry close to the patterns of classical metrics, there are many variations allowed. Iambs and trochees are interchangeable; so are pyrrhics and spondees. Added unaccented syllables are permitted, like grace-notes in music. Similarly, the three most common three-syllabled feet (anapest, amphibrach, and dactyl) are interchangeable; a spondee may be substituted for any of the three. Feet may be mingled formally or informally within the line and in alternate lines—there is room for variation in classical metrics. By liberal use of these variations, patterned metric verse in practice approaches natural scansion and accent verse. As a rule, though, the dominant foot (iamb, usually) remains dominant, to justify the kind of rhythm in the pattern scansion of the poem.

Other Terms in Classical Metric Scansion

The varieties allowed in classical metrics gave rise to frequently combined feet, as the ditrochee, which is two trochees. Moreover, allowing an extra unaccented syllable or omitting a syllable at the beginning of the line gave rise to further terms. Here are a table and a list of the more arcane features of classical metrics:

Name of foot	Scansion	Accent Pronunciation	Example
Ditrochee	´ ˘ ´ ˘	TUM-ta-TUM-ta	softly smiling
Paeon	´ ˘ ˘ ˘	TUM-ta-ta-ta	shadowiness
Choriamb	´ ˘ ˘ ´	TUM-ta-ta-TUM	Kalamazoo
Epitrite, 1st class	˘ ´ ´ ´	ta-TUM-TUM-TUM	
Epitrite, 2nd class	´ ˘ ´ ´	TUM-ta-TUM-TUM	
Epitrite, 3rd class	´ ´ ˘ ´	TUM-TUM-ta-TUM	
Epitrite, 4th class	´ ´ ´ ˘	TUM-TUM-TUM-ta	

Acatalectic verse: A poetic line with the full number of syllables; not defective in the last foot.

Anacrusis: The addition of one or two unaccented syllables to a foot which begins with an accent.

Caesura: A break, usually midway in a poetic line, caused by the ending of a word within a foot. A masculine caesura follows the accented part of a foot, and a feminine caesura follows an unaccented syllable. In classical prosody, caesuras were named even for the precise foot in which they occurred.

Catalectic verse: A poetic line which lacks a syllable at its beginning or which ends in an incomplete foot.

Deiresis: The break caused by the coinciding of the end of a foot with the end of a word.

Enjambment: A sentence which goes beyond one poetic line. Sometimes this becomes an important aspect in the imagery of a poem, as when John Keats, in *To Autumn,* describes a gleaner carrying a bundle on her head:

> . . . or like a gleaner thou dost keep
> Steady thy laden head across a brook. . .

The enjambment of *keep* and *Steady* makes a tension between the natural pause at the end of the line and the connection between the two words as the sentences goes forward; that tension helps to enact the image of the woman trying to keep the bundle steady as she crosses a brook.

Metric Verse: A Review

Of all the metric feet, the iamb (ta TUM) is the most natural in English. The language has about as many unaccented syllables as accented, and a majority of sentences start with an iamb—usually an unaccented article or preposition followed by a word with some accent on its first syllable. Trochees (TUM ta) have the same number of unaccents and accents as iambs, but the emphatic opening on an accented syllable gives an abrupt, staccato effect, like a command or a cry for help. It is no accident that the major kinds of lines and stanzas in English poetry— heroic blank verse, the heroic couplet, ballad meter, named stanzas like the Spenserian stanza, and the Shakespearean sonnet—are all iambic.

Three-syllable feet, like the anapest, amphibrach, and dactyl, are less natural than the iamb and trochee because it is not natural in English to use two unaccents for every accent. To use anapests (ta ta TUM) effectively, you would need to use a lot of Latinate words, such as the natural anapests in *apprehend, coincide, interfere,* and *supersede.* Of course, you can build anapests by putting together several syllables, such as *to the end, with delight,* and *into Rome.* But it is not easy maintaining the anapest as a constant metric pattern.

Likewise, amphibrachs (ta TUM ta) are not natural in English; some natural amphibrachs are *Alaska, delighted, dramatic, O'Reilly,* and *suspended.* An amphibrach can be regarded as an iamb with an extra unaccented syllable, and built up by several syllables—*to end it, chastise her,* and *loving*—and it can be found in verbals with a second syllable accent and an -ing ending: *displaying, portraying, decaying.* Much of the same can be said for dactyls (TUM ta ta), where the natural dactyls are words like *antonym, merriment, heavenly,* and *rhapsody.* But dactyls can often be found in two-syllable verbals that start with an accent and have an -ing ending: *shimmering, happening, hammering.*

Blending anapests or dactyls with another of the three-syllable feet makes more sense than trying to write straight lines of any of the three-syllable feet. Tennyson's famous poem about British imperialism, *The Charge of the Light Brigade,* does a good job of this, making the rhythm enact the galloping hooves that took a whole troop to blind, obedient—but to Tennyson, heroic—death. Here he combines dactyls with amphimacers :

> Stormed at with | shot and shell,
> Boldly they | rode and well.

And later, he uses straight dactyls:

> Cannon to | right of them,
> Cannon to | left of them.

> (from *Charge of the Light Brigade,*
> Alfred Lord Tennyson)

Is the whole poem dactylic verse? I doubt if it mattered to Tennyson; he used what he needed to write this poem which became wildly popular in imperial Britain.

Here's a part of another poem wildly popular in Britain, but by some lads whose only imperialism was in music; if the stanza is seen without the line breaks, it is almost perfect dactyls (the accented syllables in uppercase):

> PICTure yourSELF in a BOAT on a RIVer,
> With TANgerine TREES and MARmalade SKIES
> SOMEbody CALLS you, you ANswer quite SLOWly,
> A GIRL with kaLEIdoscope EYES.

> (from *Lucy in the Sky with Diamonds,* The Beatles)

Here, the dactyls give the song a waltz-like rhythm, lilting and dreamy, appropriate for this LSD-inspired classic. There are breaks in the succession of perfect dactyls: in line 2, where *and* is the only unaccented syllable between *TREES* and *MAR;* and after *SKIES,* where there are no unaccented syllables. Otherwise, the rhythm is constant, like a waltz: ONE-two-three, ONE-two-three. Pattern scansion of the lines would classify lines two and four as catalectic—that is, they each lack an unaccented syllable or two to complete the rhythmic foot. But whether or not each line is perfect dactylic doesn't matter as much as the constant rhythm of the words, to go with the rhythm of the music.

To summarize: Remembering that accent verse is natural to English, and that meter is an alien import, it is not surprising that most poets vary their meters much more than they write straight meter of any sort. Plays from Shakespeare can be dated by his increasing freedom in the use of variations in the iambic line. The same applies to all the best poets. The end of the process is either accent verse or free verse—which is what we often find in the later plays of Shakespeare.

If you use metric verse, always let your natural scansion differ from your pattern scansion; it will increase the vitality of your rhythms and your poetry.

Pleasing effects can be obtained by alternating rhythms in a single line—alternating the rhythms of each couplet, or changing rhythms from stanza to stanza. Keats did it in his odes, and so can you. What matters most is not the adherence to metric pattern, but the right words for what you have to say.

Free Verse

Free verse is poetry which follows no rhythmic convention. There may be passages where the rhythm of words becomes important, and there may be places where the poetry is shaped—such as line endings, to make an enjambment that accentuates meaning. But free verse is best described by what it does not have: It must not have the measured thudding drumbeat of accent verse; it must not have the more precise alternation of accent and unaccent in metric verse; and it also should not show the tendency toward variety that good prose has.

Having said that, it's also important to say that there's no "Free Verse Club" where poets swear off all forms of rhythm like alcoholics in Alcoholics Anonymous give up all forms of alcohol. Poets have been moving in and out of free verse for centuries in various forms, depending on what they wanted to say. The grandfather of modern American poetry, Walt Whitman, provides an excellent case in point. Most of the time, Whitman wrote in free verse, but there were times he wrote in the following:

1. *Metric verse.* Many of Whitman's lyric passages in *Leaves of Grass* are definitely metric, as in the poem "Joy, Shipmate, Joy!" Unrhymed, but with a regular iambic pattern of four feet to the line, it's *not* free verse:

   Our life is closed—our life begins;
   The long, long anchorage we leave,
   The ship is clear at last—she leaps!
   She swiftly courses from the shore.

   (from *Joy, Shipmate, Joy!,* Walt Whitman)

2. *Accent verse.* Whitman must have found that accent verse fit the marching rhythms that surrounded him during the Civil War. Here a six-accent pattern is divided into feet with one major accent in each foot:

Beat! I beat! I drums!— I blow! I bugles! I blow!
Through I the windows I through doors— I burst I like a ruth- I less force!

(from *Beat! Drums! Beat!,* Walt Whitman)

But even in gentler moments, Whitman's rhythms follow accent verse, as in much of *Out the Cradle, Endlessly Rocking.*

3. *Prose.* Whitman's prose, such as the famous *Preface* to the 1855 edition of *Leaves of Grass,* is every bit as capacious and full of catalogues as his poetry, but there is more variety in word choice and less rhythmic structure.

I imagine that there are still some people who say free verse is nothing more than prose chopped up into lines—that was a criticism of Marianne Moore, and indeed, she herself joked that was how she wrote. But her poetry is poetry indeed: Each line is a syllabic unit, and the form she used often led to startling, ironic enjambments which influenced the meaning of her poems. Prose should be seen as just another tool for the poet to use. There's nothing wrong with starting out a poem as prose—freewriting in a journal, or notes dashed off in the middle of the night or after a dream. Poets use whatever writing process works for them, and few sit down with the form of the poet in front of them and just fill in the rhythmic units with words that magically come to them. Think of it this way: There is always a balance in anything; when you write free verse, what you lose in the musical qualities of rhythmic verse are often balanced by a freshness or presence of a human voice in your poem. Indeed, some poets thought of their poems as extensions of their poetry, as Frank O'Hara and Kenneth Koch of what was called "the New York School" of poetry. To them, the poem was freshest, most alive, when it sounded like someone talking.

Robert Frost once drew attention to the care with which free verse must be written. He said that writing free verse was "like playing tennis without a net"; it's a good simile to remember. Without the formal requirements of rhythm, the free verse poet still chooses each word carefully, often finding a "organic form" as the poem unfolds.

Free verse can be rhymed, as in the poems of Ogden Nash. It may also have—indeed, it often has more of—the other poetic features: alliteration, assonance, consonance, and so on. The matter of rhythm alone determines whether it is free verse or not. It is wise to read a lot of poetry, whatever rhythmic form attracts you. Some poets find it natural to write in rhythm, and to them it requires some effort to write free verse and avoid the devices of accent verse and meter. Other poets find it more natural to express themselves without the constraints of meter and accent. A lot of it depends on what you want to say and how you want to say it.

Line Length in Verse

In accent verse, the line length is usually determined by the pattern— so many accents to the line. The "long line" of Anglo-Saxon poetry consisted of four accent feet, usually broken by a pause or caesura. In metric verse, the line length is also fixed by the pattern, even if the number of feet varies from line to line. The classical Greek and Latin line was normally a six-foot line (hexameter), but it was always broken in the middle by a caesura. For centuries, the French norm was the Alexandrine, a six-foot iambic line. In English, the standard line length has been the five-foot iambic (pentameter)—as in Shakespeare's sonnets and plays, the epics of Milton, the heroic couplets of Pope and Dryden, and the blank verse of Wordsworth, Frost, and many others. Many poets have a "signature" line that becomes identified with them, such as Whitman's long lines, or the short lines of H.D., Elinor Wylie, and other modernists poets.

In free verse, there are several ways to determine line length. Whitman followed a natural breath pause at the end of his long lines (and sometimes it seems he could hold a lot of breath!). Other, more contemporary poets, use units of meaning, or break the line for effect at enjambments. William Carlos Williams considered the idea of "free" verse absurd, since all language always had some kind of rhythm; like Whitman, Williams was an American original, and the tension between free and accent verse in his poetry was one of its greatest strengths:

> Good Christ what is
> a poet—if any
>   exists?
>
> a man
> whose words will
>   bite
>   their way
> home—being actual
> having the form
>   of motion

(*The Wind Increases*, W. C. Williams)

The important thing is to find a line length which fits what you need to say; as you write, if you become comfortable with blank verse or short-lined free verse, or rhymed quatrains, and can say what you need to say in that form, then you will be a happy poet! But all good poets also try new things, experiment with different forms, and stretch their abilities into other areas of poetry and song.

Stanza Forms

A stanza is one or more lines (sometimes called verses) of poetry, making a division of the poem or song. A stanza in verse is like a paragraph in prose. Stanzas may be in free, accent, or metric verse, or any combination of these, with any number of feet to each line, and any combination of feet within each line. They may be rhymed of unrhymed, with or without any of the other features of poetry. The one or more lines may, of course, be the whole poem, in which case they are no longer a stanza.

One-Line Stanzas

A poem may have formal stanzas of only one line. Some rhymed alphabet poems follow this pattern, and one-line stanzas can be found in many types of poems:

> This is the house that Jack built
>
> > (from *Mother Goose*)

> Whoever you are, to you endless announcement!
> > (from *Starting from Paumanok*, Walt Whitman)

> fathandsbangrag
> > (from *Portrait of a Pianist*, e. e. cummings)

Stanzas of Two Lines: The Couplet

A stanza (or a poem) of two lines, unrhymed or rhymed, is called a couplet. Probably the most famous unrhymed couplet in American poetry is one that shows the influence of Oriental poetry and haiku:

> The apparition of these faces in the crowd;
> Petals on a wet, black bough.
> > ("In a Station of the Metro," *Personae*, Ezra Pound)

Where the two lines of a couplet stanza rhyme, this is called *couplet rhyming:*

In a deep song voice with a melancholy tone   1
I heard that Negro sing, that old piano moan—   1

(from *The Weary Blues,* Langston Hughes)

The same numbers indicate the lines which rhyme together. Poems may have couplet rhyming where the stanzas are made up of couplets:

"Lights out!" the siren warnings roll.   1
The cities silk, as clack as coal.   1
But that's no cause to cringe in fright: 2
Earth has its blackout every night,   2
Yet, every morning, sunbeams pour   3
Freer, more glorious, than before!   3

(from *World Situation: 1941,* Clement Wood)

Couplet rhyming may also be used in a poem not divided into stanzas; the poem is then said to be *stichic.*

Iambic pentameter couplets, couplet-rhymed, are called *heroic couplets:*

A little learning is a dangerous thing;
Drink deep, or taste not the Pierian spring.

(from *Essay on Criticism,* Alexander Pope)

Pope's poems are often long, and all couplets. Few poets write long poems entirely in couplets anymore, but James Merrill certainly could; here is a brief excerpt from one of his longer passages:

It starts out in the small hours. An interlude
Out of Rossini. Strings in sullen mood
Manage by veiled threats, to recruit a low
Pressure drum and lightning piccolo.
Not until daybreak does the wind machine
Start working. The whole house quakes, and one green
Blind snaps at its own coils like a hurt dragon.
Outside the elm falls for a beachwagon.
And ill-assorted objects fill the sky:
Shingles, fishnet, garbage, doghouse. "Hi,
What's up?" yawns David, as down Water Street
Wild torrents drive. Attempting to reheat
Last night's coffee, toast some raisin bread,
We find our electricity gone dead.

(from *Mirabell's Book of Number,* James Merrill)

Couplets may have end rhyme without couplet rhyming, as when successive couplets are interlinked by rhyming:

The craze to make new forms in verse	1
Possesses poets everywhere.	2
The theory breathes like a prayer;	2
The practice often is a curse.	1

The interlocking may be far more elaborate, as 1, 2; 3, 4; 3, 1; 4, 5; 5, 2, etc.

By far the most popular form is couplets or run-on lines with couplet rhyming. Here is an example which has a surprise ending:

> When I get home at five o'clock,
> I pause outside my door, and knock.
> A gentle rap should let her know
> That now it's time for her to go
> And hide herself in some dark corner.
> I really do it just to warn her,
> And not because I'm scared. I'm blest
> With one small mouse as my house-guest.

(from Guest, Marcia M. Jones)

But sometimes two lines are all you need for a poem, and a couplet can make it complete:

> Naked came I, naked I leave the scene,
> And naked was my pastime in between.

(Epitaph for Someone or Other, J. V. Cunningham)

Stanzas of Three Lines: The Triplet or Tercet

A stanza or poem of three lines is called a triplet or tercet. Tercets have four possible end rhyme schemes within the stanza; all lines can rhyme, as here:

The witch that came (the withered hag)	1
To wash the steps with pail and rag,	1
Was once the beauty Abishag,	1

(from Provide, Provide, Robert Frost)

But there are other possibilities:

They have all gone away	1
From the house on the hill;	2
There is nothing more to say.	1

(from The House on the Hill,
Edwin Arlington Robinson)

The other possibilities are 1, 1, 2; 1, 2, 2. Tercets and other stanzas may be interlocked by rhyme from stanza to stanza—this is called chain rhyming; for example, 1, 2, 1; 3, 2, 3; 4, 3, 4; or 1, 1, 2; 2, 2, 3; 4, 4, 2; or in any other pattern of rhymes.

Terza rima is an Italian pattern of rhymed tercets, interlocked by rhyme in this way: 1, 2, 1; 2, 3, 2; 3, 4, 3; 4, 5, 4; 5, 6, 5; and so forth, usually with a final couplet taking its rhyme sound from the middle line of the previous tercet. The poem can be of any length. As it originated in Italy, terza rima was not divided into stanzas. Dante's *Divina Commedia* is easily the most famous use of this form. In English, it is usually written in five-foot iambic lines (iambic pentameter). In his *Ode to the West Wind*, Shelley used a terza rima pattern of four triplets followed by the usual couplet (1, 2, 1; 2, 3, 2; 3, 4, 3; 4, 5, 4; 5, 5) or 14 lines in all:

If I were a dead leaf thou mightest bear;	1	
If I were a swift cloud to fly with thee;		2
A wave to pant beneath they power, and share	1	
The impulse of thy strength, only less free		2
Than thou, O uncontrollable! If even	3	
I were as in my boyhood, and could be		2
The comrade of thy wanderings over heaven,	3	
As then, when to outstrip thy skyey speed		4
Scarce seemed a vision—I would ne'er have striven	3	
As thus with thee in prayer in my sore need.		4
O! lift me as a wave, a leaf, a cloud!	5	
I fall upon the thorns of life! I bleed!		4
A heavy weight of hours has chained and bowed	5	
One too like thee—tameless, and swift, and proud.	5	

(from *Ode to the West Wind*, Percy Bysshe Shelley)

Shelley can be at times hard to believe with *skyey speed* and other poeticisms; his "I fall upon the thorns of life! I bleed!" has had its share of parody and ridicule. But then, as here, he turns around and writes a couplet which more than makes up for the excesses of the previous lines. This 14-line form is sometimes used as a separate poem, usually without stanza divisions; it is at times called a *terza rima sonnet.*

Stanzas of Four Lines: The Quatrain

A quatrain, a stanza (or poem) of four lines, is the most popular stanza length in English poetry and song. As in all cases, the stanzas may be unrhymed or rhymed; in free verse, accent, or metric verse; with any number of feet to each line; and with any type of feet in each line. Because this stanza form has been so popular, some varieties within the form have been given names:

Ballad meter, ballad measure, or service stanza:

It is an ancient Mariner,	1
And he stoppeth one of three.	2
"By thy long gray beard and glittering eye	3
Now wherefore stopp'st thou me?"	2

(from *The Rime of the Ancient Mariner,*
Samuel Taylor Coleridge)

One of the oldest stanza forms in English, this form originated in accent verse, four-, three-, four-, and three-feet to the lines, and in turn, it was derived from four-accent couplets (see the chapter "Rhythm"). It was later often used in iambic verse with the same number of feet to the line. In the ballads, poets occasionally use longer stanzas, slightly varied from this pattern, as Coleridge does in his famous poem.

Rubaiyat Stanza, in five foot iambic lines:

The Moving Finger writes; and having writ,	1
Moves on; nor all your Piety and Wit	1
Shall lure it back to cancel half a Line,	2
Nor all your Tears wash out a Word of it.	1

(from *Rubaiyat of Omar Khayyam,* Edward Fitzgerald)

In Memoriam Stanza, in four-foot iambic lines:

Ring out false pride in place and blood,	1
The civic slander and the spite;	2
Ring in the love of truth and right,	2
Ring in the common love of good.	1

(from *In Memoriam,* Alfred Tennyson)

Elegiac Stanza, in five-foot iambic lines:

He was always good at these poems about the dead—	1
James, Yeats, his doctor. Now we are left	2
to say to ourselves for him such words as he said	1
But which of us is sufficiently wise or deft?	2

(From *In Memory of W. H. Auden,* David R. Slavitt)

The same rhyming pattern, but in three-foot iambic lines, has been called Gray's stanza. Of course, any of these quatrain rhyme schemes can be adapted to different metric feet or line lengths; the preceding examples have specific names because of their use or their fame in certain poems (such as Tennyson's *In Memoriam*). You could have a four-foot iambic stanza with elegiac rhyming, a five-foot trochaic stanza with

In Memoriam rhyming, etc. Or you could have a 1, 2, 3, 2 rhyme with three four-foot lines followed by a three-foot line, as in this famous song:

> Picture yourself in a boat on a river,
> With tangerine trees and marmalade skies
> Somebody calls you, you answer quite slowly,
> A girl with kaleidoscope eyes.

> (from *Lucy in the Sky with Diamonds*, The Beatles)

The possible quatrain rhyme schemes are as follows, with the ones already given in italics:

> 2 lines rhyming, 2 unrhymed: *1, 2, 3, 2*; 1, 1, 2, 3; 1, 2, 2, 3; 1, 2, 3, 3; 1, 2, 1, 3; 1, 2, 3, 1.

> 3 lines rhyming together, 1 unrhymed: 1, 1, 1, 2; *1, 1, 2, 1*; 1, 2, 1, 1; 1, 2, 2, 2.

> All four lines rhymed: 1, 1, 1, 1; 1, 1, 2, 2, (couplet rhyming); *1, 2, 1, 2*; 1, 2, 2, 1.

Poets and songwriters can make for themselves a similar analysis of the possible rhyme schemes for stanzas of five and more lines.

Rhymed quatrains are commonly found in many church hymns; any rhyming is permissible, but 1, 2, 3, 2 is common in the three common quatrain patterns that follow:

> *Long meter:* four four-foot iambic lines.

> *Common meter:* four iambic lines of 4, 3, 4, 3 feet (the same number of feet as the ballad measure).

> *Short meter:* four iambic lines of 3, 3, 4, 3 feet. (As a couplet of six and seven iambic feet, this was the popular 16th century Poulter's measure.)

The most famous stanza from classical Greece is the Sapphic, written originally in a quantity meter (with long and short syllables stressed by duration not accent) and therefore adapted more easily to English accent verse. The stanza pattern is based on rhythm, and in English it is usually unrhymed. The lines are made up of trochees, dactyls, and sometimes spondees (see the "Rhythm" chapter), following this pattern:

> ´ ˘ | ´ or ˘ | ´ ˘ ˘ | ´ ˘ | ´ or ´ | ´ ˘ ˘ ˘

> ´ ˘ | ´ or ´ | ´ ˘ ˘ | ´ ˘ | ´ or ´ | ´ ˘ ˘ ˘

> ´ ˘ | ´ ˘ | ´ ˘ ˘ | ´ ˘ | ´ or ´ ´ ˘ | ´ ˘ ˘ | ´ ˘

Although not usually rhymed, this pattern may have rhyme, as well as any other device of poetry. Here is a sample:

She beyond all others in deepest dreams comes
back. You shun sleep, lying in darkness, breath held,
hearing that voice over the rustling dry grass
　　breathing in darkness.

Walk for miles each day, with a dog to watch, pen,
paper, ink, try, focus attention somewhere
else. But Mi, Sol, Re go the notes her voice slips
　　into your blind heart.

(from *A Little Song*, Charles O. Hartman)

Stanzas of Five Lines: The Cinquain

Also called the quintain, a cinquain is a stanza or poem in five lines. It is
popularly used in limericks, but also can be found in the tanka and in
invented, tanka-inspired forms (see the "Fixed Forms" chapter). Besides
these, popular cinquain rhyme schemes include 1, 2, 1, 2, 2; 1, 2, 3, 3, 2;
and 1, 2, 3, 2, 2.

One of the possible variations is used by Shelley in his *To a Skylark:*

All the earth and air	1
With thy voice is loud,	2
As, when night is bare,	1
From one lonely cloud	2
The moon rains out her beams, and heaven is overflowed.	2

(from *To a Skylark*, Percy Bysshe Shelley)

The rhythm here is four three-foot trochaic lines, followed by a six-
foot iambic line. A six-foot iambic line, which is used frequently in
French poetry, is called an Alexandrine, and we will see this line again
in the Spenserian stanza.

Edgar Allan Poe also used the cinquain in his *To Helen*, which
contains three cinquains in a poem which uses more than one stanza
form and a variety of rhyme schemes. Using different stanza forms is not
illegal, unless you are writing a fixed form such as a sonnet or a
villanelle. Many great poets have switched stanza forms when it has
helped the poem, when it was natural to what is being said.

Stanzas of Six Lines: The Sestet

A stanza or poem of six lines is called a sestet. It can be found in
Petrarchan (Italian) sonnets, where often the rhyme scheme is 1, 2, 1, 2,
1, 2. But one of its most famous uses in English was in Shakespeare's
Venus and Adonis. In that poem, the stanzas are in iambic pentameter

lines with an alternately rhymed quatrain followed by a couplet (which is, after all, the way Shakespeare ended his sonnets, instead of following the Italian model):

Torches are made to light, jewels to wear.	1
Dainties to taste, fresh beauty for the use,	2
Herbs for their smell, and sappy plants to bear;	1
Things growing to themselves are growth's abuse;	2
Seeds spring from seeds, and beauty breedeth beauty;	3
Thou wast begot—to get it is thy duty.	3

(from *Venus and Adonis,* William Shakespeare)

A favorite stanza form of Robert Burns is a sestet, used here in his "Epistle to J. Lapraik":

Gie me ae spark o' nature's fire,	1
That's a' the larning I desire;	1
Then tho' I drudge thro' dub an' mire	1
At pleugh or cart,	2
My muse, tho' hamely in attire,	1
May touch the heart.	2

(from *Epistle to J. Lapraik,* Robert Burns)

This stanza form is called *tail-rhymed* because of the presence of two or more lines shorter than the others, serving as "tails" to lines in the stanza. John Greenleaf Whittier's *The Last Leaf* is also a tail-rhymed sestet, rhymed 1, 1, 2, 3, 3, 2. Longer examples of tail rhyme include Michael Drayton's *Agincourt*, and Tennyson's *The Charge of the Light Brigade* and *The Lady of Shalott.*

Stanzas of Seven Lines: The Septet

Rhyme Royal (or *Rime Royal*) is easily the most famous seven-line stanza or septet. It's an ancient form in English poetry, adapted from Scottish poetry and first popularized by Chaucer. It is written in iambic pentameter and has a close relationship to Shakespeare's *Venus and Adonis* stanza—all that is added is an additional line between the quatrain and the couplet. Here's how Shakespeare used it:

Why should the worm intrude the maiden bud?
Or hateful cuckoos hatch in sparrows' nests?
Or toads infect fair founts with venom mud?
Or tyrant folly lurk in gentle breasts?
Or kings be breakers of their own behests?
    But no perfection is so absolute
    That some impurity doth not pollute.

(from *The Rape of Lucrece,* William Shakespeare)

The Canopus stanza, first appearing in 1920, eliminated the two concluding couplets and made the septet form more of a narrative form:

He sank into the stubble by her side,	1
Leaving a blankness in the upper night;	2
His lips leant in their urgency of pride	1
Toward her eyes, that made the blackness bright.	2
His lips spoke only to the reddened cheek,	3
And settled to a long-denied delight	2
Upon the goal they had not dared to seek.	3

(from *Canopus*, Clement Wood)

Stanzas of Eight and More Lines

The *ottava rima* is an Italian octave, or stanza of eight lines, and used famously by many English poets, such as Milton, Keats, and Byron. It has six iambic pentameter lines followed by a couplet which is rhymed:

But never mind;—"God save the king!" and kings!
For if *he* don't, I doubt if *men* will longer—
I think I hear a little bird, who sings
The people by and by will be the stronger;
the veriest jade will wince when harness wrings
So much into the raw as quite to wrong her
Beyond the rules of posting,—and the mob
At last falls sick of imitating Job.

(from *Don Juan, VIII, 1,* George Gordon, Lord Byron)

The *Spenserian stanza* is a nine-line stanza very similar to ottava rima, and has often been used in long narrative poems. It has eight lines of iambic pentameter followed by a six-foot iambic line (an Alexandrine), which adds some variety to the final couplet of the stanza. Here's how Keats used it:

And still she slept an azure-lidded sleep,
In blanched linen, smooth, and lavender'd,
While he from forth the closet brought a heap
Of candied apple, quince, and plum, and gourd;
With jellies soother than the creamy curd,
And lucent syrops, tinct with cinnamon;
Manna and dates, in argosy transferr'd
From Fez; and spiced dainties, every one,
From silken Samarcand to cedar'd Lebanon.

(from *The Eve of St. Agnes,* John Keats)

Notice how the Alexandrine line at the end of the stanza slows the poem down with its six stresses (here shown in uppercase), from SILKen

SAMarCAND to CEDar'd LEBanNON. But as lovely as Keat's poem is, Spenser still holds the record on this stanza: 3,848 stanzas written in this form in *The Faerie Queene*. Thomas Chatterton changed the stanza form a little by adding a rhyme—1, 2, 1, 2, 2, 3, 2, 3, 4, 4—but he kept the basic format: eight iambic pentameter lines followed by an Alexandrine; his variation is called a Chatterton stanza.

The stanzas in Keats's four famous odes bear a special place in English poetry. They are usually in iambic pentameter, with a quatrain alternately rhymed (1, 2, 1, 2) followed by a sestet rhymed 3, 4, 5, with different patterns for the last three lines (3, 4, 5; or 4, 3, 5, etc.). "To a Nightingale" shortens the eighth line in each stanza to three feet:

> Thou wast not born for death, immortal Bird!   1
> No hungry generations tread thee down;   2
>
> Thy voice I heard this passing night was heard   1
> In ancient days by emperor and clown: 2
>
> Perhaps the self-same song that found a path   3
> Through the sad heart of Ruth, when, sick for home,   4
>
> She stood in tears amid the alien corn;   5
> The same that oft-times hath   3
> Charm'd magic casements, opening on the foam   4
>
> Or perilous seas, in faery lands forlorn.   5

(from *To a Nightingale,* John Keats)

The omission of the two expected feet in the eighth line is very effective. Here Keats lengthens the last line of the Spenserian stanza, as an inverse of the Alexandrine stanza, to achieve a greater emphasis and depth. By reducing the number of feet in the eighth line, Keats gives greater weight and importance to the last two lines of the stanza. Although, like others in the Romantic movement, Keats used some archaic poeticisms ("Thou," "wast," "thee," etc.), the rest of the vocabulary is specific and evocative: *hungry, tread, path, sad heart, foam,* etc.

In *On a Grecian Urn,* Keats lengthens the eighth line back to the standard iambic pentameter, but he changes the rhyme scheme of the sestet in several of the stanzas. In *To Psyche,* each of the stanzas has a different length and different rhyme schemes. *On Melancholy* has less variety, with only the last stanza having a different rhyme scheme. In most of the odes, Keats uses iambic pentameter in a stanza based on a quatrain followed by a sestet (in one case, a septet) based on three rhyme sounds, always opening 3, 4, 5, and always closing on the 5 sound, with variations as needed.

Odic stanzas need not be uniform or fixed, as Keats' great odes demonstrate. There could be other odic stanzas of greater complexity invented. But the variety in Keats' odes rests on two simple structures: the iambic pentameter quatrain and a sestet based on a 3, 4, 5 rhyme.

Many poems vary the rhyme, meter, and number-of-feet pattern from stanza to stanza. Poe's *To Helen, To One in Paradise, The Conquering Worm,* and *The Haunted Palace* show this in masterly fashion. Stanzas in light verse tend to be regular, even if based on a complex form. The stanza forms and chorus patterns in popular songs tend to vary from decade to decade. Songwriters need to listen closely to the songs of their day to find out the varieties and stanza forms used.

The Fixed Forms

Rules for Formal Verse

Many of the fixed forms have been imported from French, Italian, and other languages, where the sounds of the language make it easier to rhyme. Although poets in English have always experimented and adapted forms, the forms themselves allow for little deviation:

1. No syllable or group of syllables, once you've used it as a rhyme, should be used again as a rhyme in the same poem, even if spelled differently, nor if the whole word is altered by a prefix.

2. The refrain should not be a meaningless repetition of sounds (unless, of course, you're writing "doo-wap" 1950s rock-n-roll). It should aid in the progression of the thought; should come in naturally, and should be repeated in all of its sounds.

Thus, the rules. However, in American poetry, we've been breaking rules since Anne Bradstreet. And that is especially true in American songs, where songwriters in rap and country often use identities. But even in contemporary poetry, sometimes it looks like identities in rhyme are used. Gwendolyn Brooks achieves powerful effect by repeating the same syllable ("We") at the end of each line in "We Real Cool":

> We real cool. We
> Left school. We
>
> Lurk late. We
> Strike straight. We
>
> Sing sin. We
> Thin gin. We
>
> Jazz June. We
> Die soon.

(We Real Cool, Gwendolyn Brooks)

The rhyme, however, is not at the end of each line, but just before it. The repetition of "We" is part of the message of the poem, as it draws attention to the power of the group in the gang.

Sonnets

The sonnet is a poem or stanza of 14 five-foot iambic lines, following one of several rhyme schemes. The two main varieties are the Shakespearean (or Elizabethan) and the Italian (or Petrarchan).

The Italian or Petrarchan Sonnet

Petrarch, a famous Italian poet of the Renaissance, wrote so many sonnets to his lover, Laura, that the Italian sonnet form which he followed has come to bear his name. The sonnet has two parts. The first is an octave (eight-line stanza) made up of two interlocking quatrains: The first and last lines of both quatrains all rhyme, and the middle lines of each quatrain rhyme. If we use numbers for the rhyme sounds, the pattern, or "rhyme scheme," looks like this: 1, 2, 2, 1; 1, 2, 2, 1. After the octave comes a sestet (six-line stanza), which can have a couple of different patterns, but cannot end in a couplet (Shakespeare is the guy who ended sonnets with a couplet—it's an English thing). Traditional sestet rhyme patterns can be 3, 4, 5; 3, 4, 5 or 3, 4, 3; 4, 3, 4. But they can't be a series of couplets with the rhyme pattern 3, 4; 3, 4; 3, 4. Confusing? In the Renaissance, poets took their forms seriously.

Italian sonnets were about one idea or emotion, discussed through the whole poem, but the octave and the sestet treated the idea differently. Sometimes, the different treatment was so different that it was called a "turn"—that is, the sestet "turned" the idea around so that sometimes the poem ended a lot differently than it started. The octave was divided into two quatrains, and the sestet into two three-line stanzas or tercets. The first quatrain stated the idea; the second quatrain elaborated on it. The first part of the sestet treats the idea differently, and the second tercet still differently, but brings the poem to a conclusion with some deeper idea or feeling.

The fixed form of Petrarchan sonnets is not easy to write in English (which may be why Shakespeare used a different sonnet form). Here are two examples, neither of which follows the form completely, but both of which show some of its power. The first, a 20th century sonnet in English, follows a variant of the Petrarchan sonnet developed by William Wordsworth, where the middle rhymes of the second quatrain are different from those of the first quatrain. There may be some allusion to Wordsworth in Cunningham's title, since Wordsworth rejected the heroic or "high style" of the 18th century in favor of a more "flat" style, accessible to more people.

There are, perhaps, whom passion gives a grace,	1
Who fuse and part as dancers on the stage,	2
But that is not for me, not at my age,	2
Not with my bony shoulders and fat face.	1
Yet in my clumsiness I found a place	1
And use for passion: with it I ignore	2*
My gaucheries and yours, and feel no more	2*
The awkwardness of the absurd embrace.	1
It is a pact men make, and seal in flesh	3
To be so busy with their own desires.	4
Their loves may be as busy with their own,	5
And not in union. Though the two enmesh	3
Like gears in motion, each with each conspires	4
To be at once together and alone.	5

(*The Aged Lover Discourses in the Flat Style,*
J. V. Cunningham)

The second is a translation of Petrarch's "Sonnet I"; although the translation doesn't keep to the strict rhyme scheme, it does a good job of keeping Petrarch's original ideas and tone:

O you who hear in scattered rhymes the sound	1
Of that wailing with which I fed my heart	2
In my first youthful error, when in part	2
I was not the same man who treads this ground,	1
May I find mercy, also forgiveness,	1*
Where, after trial, science of love is deep,	2*
For all the ways in which I talk and weep	2*
Between vain hopes, between throes of distress.	1*
But I have seen enough that in this land	3
To the whole people like a tale I seem,	4
So that I feel ashamed of my own name;	5
Of all my raving the harvest is shame,	5
And to repent, and clearly understand	3
That what pleases on earth is a swift dream.	4

(*Sonnet I,* Petrarch)

In sonnet writing, there usually is no internal rhyme (rhymes within the lines). Moreover, in the strictest form, the rhymes within the octave should be different (Cunningham's are not), and the rhymes within the sestet should be distinctly different from those in the octave. English use of the Petrarchan sonnet has tended to accentuate the difference between the octave and the sestet; in Italian versions of this form, there are additional breaks between the two quatrains of the octave and the two tercets of the sestet.

The Miltonic Sonnet

The most successful adaptation of the Italian sonnet was made by John Milton, who emphasized the "turn" by adding a break in the middle of the eighth line, making the last part of the line more a part of the sestet than the octave. A devout Puritan of the mid-17th century, Milton is probably most famous for his epic poem, *Paradise Lost*. The most famous of Milton's sonnets is this one, written after he had gone blind:

When I consider how my light is spent,	1
Ere half my days in this dark world and wide,	2
And that one talent which is death to hide	2
Lodged with me useless, though my soul more bent	1
To serve therewith my Maker, and present	1
My true account, lest He returning chide,	2
"Doth God exact day-labor, light denied?"	2
I fondly ask.	
But Patience, to prevent	1
That murmur, soon replies, "God doth not need	3
Either man's work or his own gifts. Who best	4
Bear his mild yoke, they serve him best. His state	5
Is kingly: thousands at his bidding speed,	3
And post o'er land and ocean wither rest;	4
They also serve who only stand and wait."	5

(*On His Blindess,* John Milton)

Milton's emphasis of the break between the octave and sestet illustrates the way the "turn" became the central feature of the Petrarchan sonnet for poets writing in English. Because there are far fewer rhyming words in English than there are in Italian, English poets have often found it necessary to change the form somewhat, but the contrast between the octave and sestet has remained in all the variations on the Italian form.

The Spenserian Sonnet

Edmund Spenser lived before Milton and Shakespeare and is most noted for his long epic poem *The Faerie Queen,* which is based on a stanza form he invented and which still bears his name: the Spenserian stanza. Like his stanza form, Spenser's sonnet form is built on interlocking rhymes and includes a final couplet. Taken together, it makes for an intricate pattern: 1, 2, 1, 2; 2, 3, 2, 3; 3, 4, 3, 4; 5, 5. It's tough to write the Spenserian stanza, and it's just as tough to write a Spenserian sonnet; it has not become a popular form in English.

The Wyattian Sonnet

Thomas Wyatt, who lived before Spenser, adapted the Italian sonnet by changing the sestet to a series of couplets: 1, 2, 2, 1; 1, 2, 2, 1; 3, 3, 4, 4, 5, 5. Though it is largely ignored, the fact that Wyatt tinkered with the Italian sonnet form so early in the Renaissance emphasizes how English poets have felt compelled to modify the form.

The Shakespearean Sonnet

This is the most popular sonnet form in English—either because Shakespeare popularized it, or perhaps because he saw the alternately rhymed quatrain and the couplet as the most natural and powerful basis for the sonnet form in English. Although the sonnet form is most often named after Shakespeare, the first "Shakespearean" sonnet appeared in English several years before Shakespeare was born. In *Tottel's Miscellany* (1557), Philip Surrey, who, along with Thomas Wyatt, imported the sonnet from Italy, published the first sonnet following the pattern now called Shakespearean. In that collection, Surrey's sonnet had only two rhyme sounds: 1, 2, 1, 2; 1, 2, 1, 2; 1, 2, 1, 2; 1, 1. Edmund Spenser then began to write sonnets, but with an interweaving of rhyme from quatrain to quatrain (see the section "The Spenserian Sonnet"). However, neither of those forms received anything like the popularity of Shakespeare's sonnets.

Compared to the strictures of the Petrarchan sonnet, the Shakespearean sonnet is roomy: three quatrains of different rhymes followed by a "punch-line" couplet at the end: 1, 2, 1, 2; 3, 4, 3, 4; 5, 6, 5, 6; 7, 7. And of course, Shakespeare made the form positively sing:

> Let me not to the marriage of true minds
> Admit impediment. Love is not love
> Which alters when it alteration finds,
> Or bends with the remover to remove:
> O, no; it is an ever-fixed mark
> That looks on tempests, and is never shaken;
> It is the star to every wandering bark,
> Whose worth's unknown, although his height be taken.
> Love's not Time's fool, though rosy lips and cheeks
> Within his bending sickle's compass come;
> Love alters not with his brief hours and weeks,
> But bears it out even to the edge of doom.
> > If this be error, and upon me prov'd,
> > I never writ, nor no man ever lov'd.

> (*Sonnet cxvi*, William Shakespeare)

Wow! Even after four centuries, the language still carries a living voice. Notice that Shakespeare ignored the idea that there should be no internal rhyme; he repeats sounds within several lines (e.g., "Admits impediment"; "alters when it alteration finds"). Moreover, he also never hesitated to vary from the strict iambic form of Petrarch; like all great poets, he knew that poetry existed not for the form's sake, but for the feeling. The resulting naturalness opened up the sonnet form for poets in English, and we have been "playing with" the form ever since. A prolific sonneteer, Shakespeare wrote sonnets that are at the same time stanzas in a sonnet sequence, and also independent poems, able to stand alone.

Sonnets as Stanzas

One of the most popular poetic forms since the Renaissance, sonnets have also been used as stanzas with in a *sonnet sequence*. Two of the more popular sonnet sequences include the following:

The Crown of Sonnets: This is a sequence of seven sonnets where, for the first six poems, the last line of one sonnet becomes the first line of the next sonnet. In the seventh and last sonnet, the last line of the poem is the same as the first line of the first sonnet, thereby making a circle or "crown."

The Sonnet Redoublé: This sequence consists of 15 sonnets, in which the 14 lines of the first sonnet are used, successively, as either the first or the final lines of the next 14 sonnets.

Miscellaneous Sonnets

Combined sonnets: Sonnets with an octave from one type of sonnet (e.g., Petrarchan) and a sestet from another type (e.g., Shakespearean).

Irregular sonnets: 14-line poems in five-foot iambic lines, with a rhyme scheme which doesn't follow one of the traditional sonnet forms. Shelley's "Ozymandias of Egypt," for example, has a Shakespearean opening, but it doesn't follow any established type after that; its rhyme pattern is 1, 2, 1, 2; 1, 3, 4, 3; 5, 4, 5; 6, 5, 6. It's a sonnet because it generally follows the sonnet form, but it doesn't follow any one style too closely. Occasionally sonnets written as light or comic verse have fewer than five feet to the line, but these poems are enjoyable more for their humor than for their adherence to traditional sonnet form.

Terza rima sonnets: See under *terza rima,* in the discussion of tercets.

Writing Sonnets

The Shakespearean sonnet, with its liberal natural rhyme scheme and its absense of artificial stipulations about the development of theme or idea, above all must be written in the same natural flow of words that good prose has. A sonnet that has inversions, archaisms. stilted and warped word order, poeticized ellipses, and so on, is not following in the Bard's footsteps.

Speaking of feet—but the poetic, rhythmic variety— Shakespeare gives us room to roam. He seldom followed strict iambic pentameter, instead substituting trochees, spondees, pyrrhics, anapests, and other feet. A graceful use of double rhyme is also found in his sonnets along with single rhyme. The main requirement in Shakespearean sonnets is that the sonnet begin and end well—the final couplet requirement reinforces this idea. The two most memorable lines in a Shakespearean sonnet are usually the first and the last lines. These cannot be mediocre or anticlimactic; they must be memorable and worth remembering. To play the Bard's game, you need to make sure that one of these two lines is good enough to be retained in your reader's memory, for its essential truth or beauty.

When writing the Italian, Miltonic, or other sonnet—and even more especially when writing more complex fixed forms like the villanelle, chants royal, ballades, or other fixed forms—you need to be careful about your rhymes. It may be helpful to make a chart for your rhymes to remind you of the pattern, and then write the consonants in separate columns for each of your rhyme sounds. Here is an example for an Italian sonnet:

Rhyme Sounds				*Rhyme Scheme*
(1)	**(2)**	**(3)**	**(4)**	
				1
				2
				2
				1
				1
				2
				2
				1
				3
				4
				3
				4
				3
				4

As you write each line, write down, in the appropriate column, the opening consonantal sound that you use. Here is one of the deftest light verse Italian sonnets Clement Wood ever encountered, *Assignment,* by Stephen Schlitzer, illustrating the preceding rhyme-check method:

Rhyme Sounds				Rhyme Scheme		
(1)	**(2)**	**(3)**	**(4)**			
The best authorities in verse agree				1		GR
We must submerge our souls before we rise					2	R
Burn with emotion! Suffer! Sympathize!					2	th
Become the comrades of mortality;				1		T
Be one with the robber, banker, refugee;				1		J
Live! Live! Though life be but a pack of lies;					2	L
Go down to hell, and up to Paradise					2	D
In order to excel in poetry.				1		TR
But I'll be damned before I go to pieces				3		P
Merely to make a sonnet more complete—					4	PL
Assault my neighbor's wife; destroy my nieces,				3		N
Or starve myself in some forlorn retreat;					4	TR
Or let you break my heart with your caprices,				3		PR
To give the world five more iambic feet!					4	F

If this rhyme-check method is valuable in all sonnet forms except the Shakespearean, it is indispensable in the ballade, the chant royal, and many other fixed, French forms.

Syllable-Count Forms

The *haiku* (or *hokku*) is a Japanese form of only three lines. There's no rhyme nor rhythm required, but the whole poem can be only 17 syllables, broken into lines of five, seven, and five syllables. But, to the Japanese, who have been writing haiku for centuries, the poem's form is not as important as its depth of thought. Haiku poetry is heavily influenced by Zen Buddhism; each haiku provides a moment of insight, based in a natural or seasonal description, leading the reader to think and meditate—the spiritual insight is as important as the formal requirements. Matsuo Basho (1644–1694) is probably the most famous haiku writer (note: His most famous haiku resists translation into three lines of English):

> Breaking the silence
> Of an ancient pond,
> A frog jumped into water—
> A deep resonance.

> (Matsuo Basho, translated by Nobuyuki Yuasa)

Another by Basho haiku translates into English with the form intact:

Under cherry trees	(5)
Soup, the salad, fish and all	(7)
Seasoned with petals.	(5)

Some of the best haiku in English were written by Etheridge Knight while he was in prison:

Eastern guard tower
glints in sunset; convicts rest
like lizards on rocks.

This one meets both the formal requirements and the seasonal, natural setting, but another of Knight's haiku creates insight without the natural scene:

To write a blues song
is to regiment riots
and pluck gems from graves.

(both from *Poems from Prison*, Ethridge Knight)

The haiku emerged in Japan several centuries ago, but even older is the tanka, a longer Japanese form of five lines, each having 5, 7, 5, 7, 7 syllables, or 31 syllables in all.

through the icy glaze
of the kitchen window
quick moving clouds
break the harvest moon
into pieces of a puzzle

(*Tanka-Sijo-Haiku Muse*, Neca Maria Stoller)

Longer Japanese poems may be constructed on the tanka form, with the same alternation of five- and seven-syllable lines, ending with a seven-syllable line.

Haiku-Tanka Variations

When Ezra Pound and other modernists started importing Oriental forms and styles into modern poetry in English, they probably didn't foresee what would happen when Oriental poetic forms met up with "Yankee know-how." What resulted was an explosion of experimentation as poets took the basic format of the haiku and tanka and developed other syllable-based forms: the cinquain, lanterne, pensee, quintet, and others. The forms in the following list (compiled by Etta Josephean Murfey) have at their heart a set pattern of syllables in their stanzas:

Name	Inventor	Syllable Count	Remarks
Cinquain	Adelaide Crapsey	2, 4, 6, 8, 2	Usually unrhymed
Double cinquain	Berta Hart Nance	4, 8, 12, 16, 4	No rhythm requirements
Lanterne	Lloyd Frank Merrell	1, 2, 3, 4, 1	Arranged in form like a Japanese lantern—a shaped whimsey
Pensee	Alice Maude Spokes	2, 4, 7, 8, 6	Strong end words
Quintet	Mary Owen Lewis	3, 5, 7, 9, 3	Strong end words
Vignette	Florzari Rock-wood	2, 4, 4, 6, 7, 3	Strong end words
Septet	Mary Owen Lewis	3, 5, 7, 9, 7, 5, 3	
Cameo	Alice Maude Spokes	2, 5, 8, 3, 8, 7, 2	Strong end words
Sept	Etta Josephean Murfey	1, 2, 3, 4, 3, 2, 1	
Hexaduad	Gee Kaye	2, 2, 6, 6, 8, 8, 4, 4, 6, 6, 4, 4	Couplet rhymes
Inverted hexaduad	Gee Kaye	2, 6, 8, 4, 6, 4, 4, 6, 4, 8, 6, 2	Couplet rhymes; the first two lines are transposed for the last two

These are only the tip of the haiku-variation iceberg, but you get the idea: short poems with fixed syllable counts owing some of their pattern to the Japanese forms of haiku and tanka.

Syllabics: The "Marianne Moore Stanza"

Marianne Moore (1887–1972) created free verse poems with syllable count stanzas, often with lines much longer than the shorter syllable-count lines in the haiku-tanka tradition. The first impression is that her poetry is simply prose chopped up into lines, but the line breaks from that "chopping" often lead to a deep, wry wit. A very modern poet, she tossed in quotes from newspapers and magazines, calling attention to our industrial, instead of natural, environment. In "To a Steam Roller," some of the longer lines look and feel like something run over by a steam roller:

To a Steam Roller

The illustration
is nothing to you with the application.
You lack half wit. You crush all the particles down
into close conformity, and then walk back and forth on them.

Sparkling chips of rock
are crushed down to the level of the parent block.
Were not "impersonal judgment in aesthetic
matters, a metaphysical impossibility," you

might fairly achieve
it. As for butterflies, I can hardly conceive
of one's attending upon you, but to question
the congruence of the complement is vain, if it exists.

(*To a Steamroller,* Marianne Moore)

Sometimes simply limiting the number of syllables in a stanza can lead to a good poem. Here, a strict three-syllable line yields a cute poem:

In the burned-
out highway
ditch the throw-

away beer
bottle lands
standing up

unbroken,
like a cat
thrown off

of a roof
to kill it,
landing hard

and dazzled
in the sun,
sight side up;

sort of a
miracle.

(*Beer Bottle,* Ted Kooser)

Although syllable-counting won't help in much songwriting, it reveals one of the main ideas in poetry: a few words well used.

Miscellaneous Forms

The Limerick

The limerick is a five-line Irish poem of fun based on a rigid pattern. It's worth pointing out that the limerick is the only fixed form indigenous to the English language. There are three major forms of the limerick:

1. Those that appeared when published in Boston in 1719, in *Mother Goose's Melodies,* with the first, second, and fifth lines having three feet each, while the its third and fourth lines only have two feet:

    As I was going to Bonner,
    Upon my word of honor,
    I met a pig
    Without a wig,
    As I was going to Bonner.

2. Those written in quatrains, with three lines of three feet and one line of four feet (predominantly anapestic). This is the form used by Edward Lear, who made a whole career writing limericks:

    There was an Old Man of Cape Horn,
    Who wished he had never been born;
    So he sat in a Chair till he died of dispair,
    That dolorous man of Cape Horn.

3. And those which use a new rhyming word in the fifth line, as in this example from *Mother Goose:*

    There was an old soldier of Blister
    Went walking one day with his sister,
    When a cow at one poke
    Tossed her into an oak
    Before the old gentleman missed her.

The third form is the one most used today. By far, the largest number of limericks use a geographical name at the end of the first line: Nome, Greenwich, Twickenham, Birmingham; it calls for real ingenuity to discover words that can rhyme with words like Calcutta, Australia, or Vladivostok. But limerick writers have this ingenuity, and can sometimes turn their turns of phrases into money at limerick-writing contests. The next largest group make use of a proper name: "a sculptor named Phidias," "a young lady named Bright," "A maiden named Maud," and so on. A third group uses a descriptive phrase, such as "A young man very fond of pajamas." The fourth and trickiest group introduces a rhyme which will lead to trick rhyming: "I'd rather have Fingers than Toes," or "'There's a train at 4:04,' said Miss Jenny."

The limerick is usually written in amphribrachs, sometimes with an extra unaccented syllable at the first of a line:

> There was a / young lady / of Lynn,
> Who was so / excessive- / ly thin,
>   That when she / essayed
>   To drink lem- / onade
> She slipped through / the straw and / fell in.

Like all good poetry, a good limerick should sound like someone talking—but even more importantly, the language should be conversational. However, the limerick is comic verse with a twinkle in its eye; tongue-twisting is all part of the game—as well as trick rhyming, punning, eccentric typography, stammering, intentional misspelling to emphasize rhyme, and so on.

> "There's a train at 4:04," said Miss Jenny.
> "Four tickets I'll take; have you any?"
>   Said the man at the door,
>   "Not four for 4:04!
> For four for 4:04 is too many!"

What makes a good limerick? As literary wag Arnold Bennett once pointed out, the best limericks are "unquotable" in polite society.

The Little Willie

A Little Willie is a quatrain that sounds like a children's verse but with a dark, even sadistic, turn. It is patterned on this once-famous quatrain from Col. D. Streamer's (Harry Graham's) *Tender-Heartedness:*

> Little Willie, in bows and sashes,   1
> Fell in the fire and got burned to ashes.   1
> In the winter, when the weather is chilly,   2
> No one likes to poke up Willie.   2

It consists of simple couplets, four stresses to each line—like much children's poetry. But a Little Willie gleefully perverts "family values":

> Father heard his children scream
> So he threw them in the stream;
> Saying, as he drowned the third,
> "Children should be seen, not heard."

Sometimes the form changes, but not the sadism; here, the rhymes alternate:

Baby in the cauldron fell,—	1
See the grief on Mother's brow;	2
Mother loved her darling well,—	1
Darling's quite hard-boiled by now.	2

A true Little Willie is in quatrain form, with a tricky, effective surprise last line; it is imbued with definite sadism, preferably toward some member of one's immediate family. It is definitely *not* politically correct. Therefore, the following poem, published anonymously in a college magazine in the 1930s, though it satisfies none of the fixed form requirements of the Little Willie, can still be classified as such:

> Tobacco is a filthy weed—
>   I like it.
> It satisfies no normal need—
>   I like it.
> It makes you think, it makes you lean,
> It takes the hair right off your bean,
> It's the worst darned stuff I've ever seen,
>   I like it.

Other Forms

Sicilian octave: Eight five-foot iambic lines, rhymed alternately: 1, 2, 1, 2, 1, 2, 1, 2. It is used for a stanza, as well as for a fixed-form poem:

The wind of poetry blows high and strong,	1
But not of its own choice, in alien meter.	2
Instead of miles of formalized ding-dong	1
Preferred by some super-involved frog-eater,	2
Exotic as Kamchatka or Hong-Kong,	1
Give us the homely strain of *Peter, Peter*	2
Pumpkin-Eater to be our festive song;	1
The taste is homelier by far, and sweeter.	2

(*Home Cooking*, Alan Dubois)

Rispetto: a poem from six to ten lines, though usually eight, rhymed 1, 2, 1, 3; 3; 3, 4, 4, and at times, divided into two stanzas:

Having fallen down the manhole,	1
I discovered myself to be	2
in the wrong world. Having no soul	1
was a problem at first for me,	2
but I, Rick de Travaille, ignore	3
the problem now. I split this door	3
where the women are, and I find	4
in the flesh a little peace of mind.	4

(*Rick de Travaille*, Lewis Turco)

Sonnette: A form derived from the Italian sonnet by Sherman Ripley. It has seven five-foot iambic lines, rhymed 1, 2, 2, 1; 3, 2, 3:

In the old days men at times went insane.	1
Frothing and frantic, they would rape and kill	2
And burn in wild destructiveness, until	2
Death ended the madness, amid the rotting slain.	1
Men go berserk still; the dictators	3
Bloodily seek to bend all men to their will,	2
And die, as ever, in the madness called wars.	3

(*Berserk*, Charles Morgan Flood)

Ottava rima (sometimes called the Ariosto stanza, from the renaissance Italian poet who first extensively used it): An Italian form, with eight lines of five-foot iambic lines, rhyming 1, 2, 1, 2, 1, 2, 3, 3. Here is a more contemporary use of the form:

'Tis pity learned virgins ever wed	1
With persons of no sort of education	2
Or gentlemen, who, though well born and bred,	1
Grow tired of scientific conversation:	2
O don't choose to say much upon this head,	1
I'm a plain man, and in a single station,	2
But—Oh! ye lords of ladies intellectual	3
Inform us truly, have they not henpecked you all?	3

(From *Don Juan*, George Gordon, Lord Byron)

Terza rima: An Italian form composed of interlocking Sicilian tercets (also see the discussion under "Tercets"). The first and third lines of a stanza rhyme (1, 2, 1); the second line rhymes with the first and third lines of the next stanza (2, 3, 2; then 3, 4, 3; and so forth). The poem ends with a couplet that rhymes with the second line of the last tercet. In this example, Donald Revell uses the form, often with half-rhymes, to discuss the long-enduring violence in Northern Ireland:

Go north any way and sadness clings to the ground
like fog. The sound of voices goes wrong and can't
be followed. You hear, you breathe cries with a damp wind.

Go north to the ruined counties where girls chant
over pieces of wood called "Doll-Who's-Dead"
and where the streets that you walk are a dead giant

who won't rise. Here, History is the unfed
beast past scaring who comes down from the hills
in daylight. It kills anything, in broad

daylight, then is itself stalked until
the men corner it in some back street. They wave
the town for the next beast the granite hills

won't hold. And here, Journey's End is the grey
wall, bled white in patches, that divides
bare yard from bare yard, the unsaved from the unsaved.

(from *Belfast,* Donald Revell)

Raccontino: A form invented by Etta Josephean Murfey (the term
comes from the Italian for "a brief story"). The form is couplets, with
the even-numbered lines all having the same rhyme:

There is a little whispering that says,   1
Look up, forget the earth; the sky is glowing!   2
I have not scorned the insidious whisper; I   3
Have probed to where lost galaxies are growing   2
In passionate anguish. Yet I tell you, love   4
Within my soul more tempestuous storms are blowing,   2
And all to drive me in the end to you.   5
This is all the wisdom my soul needs knowing.   2

(*The Song of My Heart,* Ben Sterling)

Paean: A form invented by Evelyn M. Watson with 13 lines: a five-foot
iambic quatrain rhymed 1, 2, 1, 2, followed by a triple-rhymed tercet, 3,
3, 3; next, a five-foot couplet (rhymed 1, 2) repeats the theme, followed
by a single line, rhymed 3; a final triplet in five-foot iambs completes the
form: 4, 4, 4. Six-foot accented lines can be used instead of the standard
five-foot accented lines.

Trine: A nine-line poem invented by Watson, where three rhyme
couplets of any length are followed by three single lines which use the
rhymes of the three previous couplets: 1, 1; 2, 2; 3, 3; 1, 2, 3.

Quaterion: A version of the Trine, also by Watson, with four couplets
and a quatrain based on their rhymes: 1, 1; 2, 2; 3, 3; 4, 4; 1, 2, 3, 4.

Donata: Another version, also by Watson, where the main accented
words of the first line of each stanza are used as the rhyming sounds of
the stanza.

Muted rhyme: Occasional rhyme in a blank verse poem, frequently
rising from internal rhymes within the blank verse form.

Line-Repetition Forms

Kyrielle: A poem in quatrains with eight syllables to each line, with the
last line of the first stanza repeated as a refrain of the other stanzas. In
Dirty Dinky, Theodore Roethke takes some amusing liberties with the
refrain, as shown in this part of the poem:

As I was crossing a hot hot Plain,
I saw a sight that caused me pain,
You asked me before, I'll tell you again:
    —It *looked* like Dirty Dinky.

Last night you lay a-sleeping! No!
The room was thirty-five below;
The sheets and blankets turned to snow.
    —He'd got in: Dirty Dinky.

You'd better watch the things you do.
You've better what the things you do.
You're part of him; he's part of you
    —*You* may be Dirty Dinky.

(from *Dirty Dinky,* Theodore Roethke)

Of course, Roethke wrote this poem in part because the kyrielle is the same pattern many church hymns use ("kyrie" comes from the Greek and starts the phrase "Kyrie eleison"—"Lord have mercy!"). Charles Elliott's *Just as I Am,* a standard Protestant hymn, is an example of a church hymn which follows the kyrielle form.

Quatern: A variation of the kyrielle, in which the first line of the first quatrain, used as a refrain, reappears as the second line of stanza two, the third line of stanza three, and the final line of the final quatrain. The form was invented by Vivan Yeiser Laramore, who used lines of four feet each. An example is:

And we have reached the end, you say:
There is a limit to all things,
And each can go his separate way,
Forgetting joint adventurings.

Life has become dull tiny stings,
And we have reached the end, you say,
Each with sick soul that clings, and clings
As if to hamper till doomsday.

Too much "love, honor and obey,"
A role not fit for queens and kings . . .
And we have reached the end, you say—
(How dreadfully the cold word rings!)

Have you forgot that spring of springs
And our high flights, that gathered gay
Stardust to glitter on our wings?
—And we have reached the end, you say!

(*Against an Ultimatum,* Carveth Wells)

Retourne: Another variation of the kyrielle, in which all the lines of the first quatrain are used as refrains. The second line of the first quatrain opens the second quatrain; the third line of the first quatrain opens the third quatrain; and the fourth line of the first quatrain opens the fourth quatrain. Confused? There's more: The last quatrain uses all the lines of the first quatrain, but in reverse order. The form was invented by Diana Douglas. An example of the form is as follows—the *R* designates the refrains:

Love's the winner, after all.	1R
Hunger has an ancient call;	1R'
Death's a friend that all must seek;	2R
Love's a word only hearts can speak.	2R'
Hunger has an ancient call,	1R'
Holding man and beast in thrall;	1
But the spirit's daily bread	3
Always comes from love instead.	3
Death's a friend that all must seek,	2R
Hand in hand and cheek to cheek;	2
But love's spell glows on and on	4
Long after gray death has gone.	4
Love's a word only hearts can speak.	2R'
Death's a friend that all must seek,	2R
Hunger has an ancient call:	1R'
Love's the winner, after all!	1R

(*Eros,* Lois Lodge)

Pantoum (also called *pantun*): A Malayan form, with any number of quatrains, where lines two and four of the first quatrain are repeated as lines three and four of the following quatrain. The lines rhyme 1, 2, 1, 2; 2, 3, 2, 3. With all the repeated lines, ending such a poem can be a problem; it usually ends in one of two ways: 1) a quatrain where the first *repetons* (repeated lines) are in reversed order; or 2) a couplet made up of the repetons, in reversed order. Here, the poem ends with the *un*repeated lines of the first stanza, in reversed order:

In a chain reaction
the neutrons released
split other nuclei
which release more neutrons

The neutrons released
blow open some others
which release more neutrons
and start this all over

blow open some others
and choirs will crumble

and start this all over
with eyes burned to ashes

And choirs will crumble
and fish catch on fire
with eyes burned to ashes
in a chain reaction

The fish catch on fire
because the sun's force
in a chain reaction
has blazed in our minds

Because the sun's force
with plutonium trigger
has blazed in our minds
we are dying to use it

With plutonium trigger
curled and tightened
we are dying to use it
torching our enemies

Curled and tightened
blind to the end
torching our enemies
we sing to Jesus

Blind to the end
split up like nuclei
we sing to Jesus
in a chain reaction

(*Atomic Pantoum,* Peter Meinke)

Chain Verse

Chain Rhyme and Chain Verse

Terza rima is a good example of chain rhyme, where teach stanza
(tercet) is linked by rhyme: 1, 2, 1; 2, 3, 2; 3, 4, 3; 4, 5, 4; 5, 6, 5; the
poem ends with a couplet rhyming with the middle line of the last tercet
(6, 6). Quatrains or other longer stanzas could be similarly linked: 1, 1,
2, 1; 2, 2, 3, 2; 3, 3, 4, 3; 4, 4, 5, 4; and so on. This process could also lead
to a chain of sonnets, with the final rhyme sound in each sonnet
repeated as the opening rhyme sound of the next.

However, the chain link (pardon the pun) may be more than just the
rhyme; it could also be a word, phrase, or even more, whether based on
rhyme or not. The French chain rhyme requires that one word and one
only grow from each line into the next:

Let us gaily carol Spring,
Spring, that sets the world on fire
With a fire that wakes the wing
Of the forest winged choir.
When this choir is gaudiest,
All the flowers are gaudy too,
Flowers ending the bees' quest
For the quested nectar dew.

(*Spring,* Lois Lodge)

Similarly, phrases may be interlocked:

The rarer seen, the less in mind;
The less in mind, the lesser pain;
The lesser pain, less grief I find;
The lesser grief, the greater gain.

(*Lines,* Barnaby Googe)

Another chain verse type, whose form is similar to that found in a crown of sonnets, is to let each stanza's last line become the first line of the next; here, only the repeated lines are identified:

I have an easy chair,	1
Cozy and sloping and deep,	2
When I am seated there,	1
I lull my cares to sleep.	2R
I lull my cares to sleep,	2R
And dreams of all I'd be	
Wake timidly, and creep	
Softly, to hearten me.	3R
Softly, to hearten me,	3R
Your lovely face appears,	
Bringing its ecstasy	
To brighten all my years.	4R
To brighten all my years,	4R
When other faces fade,	

(*Your Face,* Lacey Beck)

The Lai Group

Lai: A poem composed of couplets of five-syllable lines, all having the same rhyme, separated by single lines of two syllables, each having a different rhyme.

The number of lines per stanza is not fixed, nor the number of stanzas. Each stanza has its own rhymes, unconnected to the previous stanzas. In standard typography, with all lines having the same left margin, the smaller and longer lines form a pattern the French poets called *arbe rouche* (a forked tree), a trunk with bare branches:

> Sing, now, most of all!
> Wake the golden fall
> With glee,
> Till both great and small
> Share the bacchanal,
> Each tree
> Quivers to it tall
> Peak, in carnival
> With me!
>
> Sing, before the bright
> Autumn hues take flight
> And go,
> And eternal night
> Spreads its shroud of white
> Thick snow.

(*Song before Dusk,* J. K. Eden)

Virelai Ancien: A lai interlocked by rhyme, in which the short lines of each stanza rhyme with the long lines of the next stanza; in the last stanza, the short lines rhyme with the long lines of the first stanza. Here's such a pattern for a poem with 12-line stanzas: 1, 1, 2, 1, 1, 2, 1, 1, 2, 1, 1, 2; 2, 2, 3, 2, 2, 3, 2, 2, 3, 2, 2, 3; and so on, until the last stanza rhymes (with *s* designating the short lines) s, s, 1, s, s, 1, s, s, 1, s, s, 1. Each rhyme therefore appears twice: once in the long lines, once in the short. Some poets in English have changed the French model by making the lines longer, and even having all lines be the same length:

As I sat sorrowing,	1	
Love came and bade me sing	1	
A joyous song and meet,		2
For see (said he) each thing	1	
Is merry for the Spring,	1	
And every bird doth greet		2
The break of blossoming,	1	
That all the woodlands ring	1	
Unto the young hours' feet.		
Wherefore put off defeat		2
And rouse thee to repeat		2
The chimes of merles that go, . . .		3

and so on until the last stanza:

So for the sad soul's ease	10
Remembrance treasure these	10
Against time's harvesting,	1
That so, when mild Death frees	10
The soul from Life's disease	10
Of strife and sorrowing,	1
In glass of memories	10
The new hope looks and see	1
Through Death a brighter Spring.	1

(*Spring Sadness,* John Payne)

Virelai Nouveau: A lai based on only two rhymes, with the first couplet supplying refrain lines that alternate as the last lines of stanzas; the poem ends with the two refrain lines used in reverse order. Outside of the refrain pattern, there are no requirements for length of stanza or position of the two rhymes:

Goodbye to the Town—goodbye!	1R
Hurrah! for the sea and the sky!	1R'
In the street the flower-girls cry;	1
In the street the watercarts ply;	1
And a fluter, with features awry,	1
Plays fitfully, "Scots, wha hae"—	2
And the throat of the fluter is dry;	1
Goodbye to the Town!—goodbye!	1R
And over the rooftops nigh	1
Comes a waft like a dream of the May;	2
And a lady-bird lit on my tie;	1
And a cockchafer came with the tray;	2
And a butterfly (no one knows why)	1
Mistook my Aunt's cap for a spray;	2
And "next door" and "over the way"	2
The neighbors take wings and fly;	1
Hurrah! for the sea and sky!	1R'

Here 1R and 1R' are the two refrain lines, The next stanzas use the same rhymes in varying order but maintain the refrain pattern: 1, 1, 2, 1, 2, 1, 2, 1, 1R and 1, 2, 1, 2, 1, 2, 1, 1, 1, 1, 1, 1, 1R'. The conclusion is:

So Phyllis, the fawn-footed, hie	1
For a hanson. Ere close of the day,	2
Between us a "world" must lie,—	1
Hurrah! for the sea and the sky!	1R'
Goodbye! to the Town—GOODBYE!	1R

(from *July,* Austin Dobson)

Text-Embroidering Group

Terna con Variazioni

This form could be called "plagiarism without fear"—the poem grows out of the foundation of another familiar poem. The lines of a familiar stanza are used successively as the first line of each stanza; moreover, the rhyme scheme of each stanza is modeled on that of the familiar poem's pattern. The form was invented by Lewis Carroll, in *Rhyme? and Reason?* It's sort of like the way jazz musicians will take a riff or a melodic line and create an entirely new piece of music. The stanza used as the foundation (the text on which the poem is based) is not ordinarily given first, since its meaning is entirely altered in this hybrid creation, but there is no reason that it couldn't appear first, above the new poem. Since the original text can have any rhyme or rhythm scheme, the possible adaptations of this form are endless.

Out of the night that covers me	1R
I rise whene'er the doorbell rings,	3
to let in Mandy, Jane, Marie,	1
With all their frowsy bags and things.	3
Black as the pit, from Pole to Pole,	2R
From Swede, to Irish, Jap, Negro,	4
I greet the cooks, with quaking soul,	2
Who sometimes come—and always go.	4
I thank whatever gods there be	1R'
When one remains a week or more.	5
Yet, they must toe the mark for me;	1
To pert retorts I show the door	5
For my unconquerable soul,	2R'
Applied with vigor, makes it plain	6
I do not fear my bread to roll,	2'
Nor try "Help Wanted" ads again!	6

(*Lament Culinaire,* Margaret Thurston)

Two important notes about this example:

1. The "3" rhyme in the first stanza is the poet's "new" rhyme; the "2" is reserved for the second rhyme of the original (see the second stanza).

2. The foundation, or text, for this poem was widely familiar at the time of the original edition of this book. It's from William Ernest Henley's *Invictus* (1875); widely familiar in the first half of this century, the poem expressed an heroic "rugged individualism" and its struggles ("My head is bloody, but unbowed") in its famous last lines:

I am the master of my fate;
I am the captain of my soul.

In her poem (from pre-1950), Margaret Thurston plays with the heroics of the original as she recounts her difficulties in hiring a cook!

There are, of course, resemblances between this form and the retourné, discussed earlier in the section "Line-Repetition Forms."

Roundeau Redoublé

This is a French, 25-line theme with variations, with the opening stanza used as a text; its four lines are used successively as refrains at the ends of the next four quatrains. The final quatrain ends *without* a rhyme in its final line, and so the form is not a true rondeau. (Note: "John D." refers to John D. Rockefeller.)

Though I am not a bloated millionaire,	1R
Though I'm no blooming DuPont or John D.	2R
Though I have scarce a jitney-piece to spare,	1R'
Life as a whole goes very well with me.	2R'
Imprimis, I am healthy as can be,	2
With appetite that is distinctly there.	1
My meals? Each day I stow away my three,	2
Though I am not a bloated millionaire.	1R
Secundis, when it comes to what I wear,	1
Blue Tux, slack suits—like any Christmas tree,	2
I cut a glittering figure everywhere,	2
Though I'm no blooming DuPont or John D.	1R
I write with pen unbought (so far) and free	2
Stuff that at times makes Proper People swear,	1
And get it published rather frequently—	2
Though I have scarce a jitney-piece to spare.	1R'
"A daughter of the gods, divinely fair"	1
Said "Yes, sir," to my heart's importunate plea,	2
We make a torrid—and a handsome—pair;	1
Life as a whole goes very well with me.	2R
I seem so needful to Society,	2
So high-removed from Plute and Proletaire,	1
That you might think a Superman you see,—	2
That I'm the Cosmic Kid, the Ages' Heir—	1
Though I am not.	R(!)

(*Mainly about Me,* J. K. Eden)

Villanelle

The villanelle is a French form in tercets, all rhymed 1, 2, 1; it ends with a quatrain rhymed 1, 2, 1, 1. The first and third lines of the first stanza are used alternately as the ending refrains each of the stanzas, and both of these lines compose the refrain of the final quatrain. It is usual for the villanelle to be five tercets and a quatrain, although more stanzas may be used, providing that an *odd* number of tercets be used, so that both refrain lines are used equally. Probably the most famous villanelle, which received new life in our culture through its use in the movie *Dangerous Minds,* is Dylan Thomas' elegiac poem on the death of his father:

> Do not go gentle into that good night,
> Old age should burn and rave at close of day;
> Rage, rage, against the dying of the light,
>
> Though wise men at their end know dark is right,
> Because their words had forked no lightning they
> Do not go gentle into that good night.
>
> Good men, the last wave by, crying how bright
> Their frail deeds might have danced in a green bay,
> Rage, rage against the dying of the light.
>
> Wild men who caught and sang the sun in flight,
> And learn, too late, they grieved it on its way,
> Do not go gentle into that good night.
>
> Grave men, near death, who see with flinging sight
> Blind eyes could blaze like meteors and be gay,
> Rage, rage against the dying of the light.
>
> And you, my father, there on the sad height,
> Curse, bless, me now with your fierce tears, I pray.
> Do not go gentle into that good night.
> Rage, rage against the dying of the light.

> (*Do Not Go Gentle into That Good Night,* Dylan Thomas)

Glose

A glose is a Spanish and Portuguese form, a 44-line theme with variations, in which an opening quatrain, sometimes a quotation, is used as a text. The first four lines successively end the next four stanzas; each of those stanzas is 10 lines. In each of those stanzas, the sixth, ninth, and 10th (refrain) lines rhyme on the same sound; the others have rhyme, but there is no required, fixed rhyme scheme. No final refrain is used after the 10th line of the last stanza. In the following example, only the required, fixed rhymes and refrains are identified:

"If I'd as much money as I could tell,	1R
I never would cry old clothes to sell,	1R'
Old clothes to sell, old clothes to sell,	1R"
I never would cry old clothes to sell."	1R*

The flow of my dreams is at youth's high flood,   2
A Spring flood, freighted with strange and new   3
Wonders of stars, and a touch of mud;   2
for all things are sweet to youth's wild blood.   2

And fire-shod visions come to me too   3
Of a people hungry for stars as well,—   1
Hungry for fare that the managered few   3
Grasp and hoard; there's a world to do—   3
Hunger and darkness I could dispel,   1
If I'd as much money as I could tell.   1R

But whether or not, it matters not;   4
I am caught in the mire as well as they;   5
I am bound to squirm in a bitter spot   4
Where blindness grows, and high dreams rot;   4
I coin my visions, to make them pay;   5
I traffic in things that decay and smell,   1
Stopping my ears to the call of gay   5
Life, and the words the visions say: 5
Ah, if I had the heart to rebel   1
I never would cry old clothes to sell!   1R'

But here I stay, and here I stay,   5
And life is only a bitter jest   6
That a madman dreamed, and idiots play;   5
Tossing each precious thing away,   5
Crowning the lowest, strangling the best: 6
And death will come ringing his peddler's bell,   1
And gather the breath out of the breast,   5
Calling out fairest and loveliest   5
Visions, but rags that shrink and swell,—   1
Old clothes to sell, old clothes to sell.   1R"

Well, I can call as well as he—   7
And these dreams he despises so   8
I say will sooner or later be   7
Not dreams, but fair reality—   7
In dreams and rags and mud will flow   8
The dreamer's passion, the will's hard spell;   1
And very death will change, and glow   8
With life; we will reap the dreams we sow;   8
And then, from earth of heaven or hell,   1
I never would cry old clothes to sell!   1R*

(*Rags and Dreams,* Clement Wood)

Each stanza has only three rhyming sounds, but the only rhyming link, from stanza to stanza, is the refrain. Since the text (first quatrain) may following any rhyme scheme, the stanza rhyme scheme can vary, provided the sixth and ninth lines rhyme with the refrain. The glose has even been used in combination with the sonnet form (see above), where an opening sonnet is followed by 14 quatrains, each quatrain ending with a successive line of the opening sonnet.

The Triolet-Rondeau Family

The Triolet

The triolet, a French form originally called a *simple rondeau,* is a poem of eight lines, the first two of which are not a couplet but which serve as a refrain. The first line reappears as the fourth line; the complete refrain reappears as the seventh and eighth lines. The triolet is about shifting perceptions, as in this example:

Viruses, when the lens is right	1R	
change into a bright bouquet.		2R
Are such soft forms of pure delight	1	
viruses? When the lens is right	1R	
instead of swarms of shapeless blight,	1	
we see them in a Renoir way.		2
Viruses when the lens is right	1R	
change into a bright bouquet.		2R

(*First Photos of Flu Virus,* Harold Witt)

Often, in contemporary poetry, the form is altered slightly, as in this powerful adaptation of the triolet form:

> She was in love with the same danger
> everybody is. Dangerous
> as it is to love a stranger,
> she was in love. With the same danger
> an adulteress risks a husband's anger.
> Stealthily death enters a house:
> she was in love with that danger.
> Everybody is dangerous.

(*Triolet,* Sandra McPherson)

The Rondel

The rondel is a French form, a poem of 14 lines with two rhyme sounds. The first two lines become a refrain that reappears in the seventh and eighth lines as well as becoming the ending couplet.

Kiss me, sweetheart; the Spring is here	1R	
And Love is Lord of you and me.		2R
The bluebells beckon each passing bee;		2
The wild wood laughs to the flowered year.	1	

There is no bird in brake or brere,   1
But to his little make sings he,   2
"Kiss me sweetheart; the Spring is here,   1R
And Love is Lord of you and me!"   2R

The blue sky laughs out sweet and clear,   1
The missel-thrush upon the tree   2
Pipes for sheer gladness loud and free;   2

And I go singing to my dear,   1
"Kiss me, sweetheart; the Spring is here,   1R
And Love is Lord of you and me!"   2R

(*Rondel,* John Payne)

Traditionally, the rondel is a love poem; the French, I've heard, are very forgiving if, in the name of love, the form is not followed exactly (as in the last couplet of the following example):

A beautiful snow falls on a bed,   1R
Amazing the man and woman there.   2R
It falls between and over them where   2
Just before they lay close and naked.   1

They wonder if anything they said   1
Or did called down so cold through the air   2
This beautiful snow onto their bed   1R
To amaze any who would love there;   2R

They wonder if snowmen can be wed,   1
And if white is what they'll always wear,   2
And if lovers should sing or shiver   2
As they watch fall the uninvited   1
And beautiful snow onto their bed.   1R

(*Rondel,* Philip Dacey)

The Thirteen-Line Rondel

This is a rondel omitting one of the final refrain lines, either the 13th or 14th.

Summer has seen decay   1R
Of roses white and red,   2R
And Love with wings outspread   2
Speeds after yesterday.   1

Blue skies have changed to grey,   1
And love has sorrow wed;   2
Summer has seen decay   1R
Of roses white and red.   2R

May's flowers outlast not May;   1
And when the hour has fled,   2

Around the roses dead	2
The mournful echoes say—	1
Summer has seen decay.	1R

(*Rondel*, George Moore)

The Rondelet

The rondelet is a French, seven-line poem, of which the first, third, and seventh lines are a four-syllable refrain. The second, fourth, fifth, and sixth lines are eight syllables each. The fourth line rhymes with the refrain, while the other three lines rhyme with each other.

Say what you please,	1R
But know, I shall not change my mind!	2
Say what you please,	1R
Even, if you wish, on your knees—	1
And, when you hear me next defined	2
As something lighter than the wind,	2
Say what you please!	1R

(*Rondelet*, May Probyn)

The Chaucerian Roundel

The Chaucerian roundel (originated by Geoffrey Chaucer, 1340–1400) is a 10-line form of the rondel, where the first line is a refrain repeated in lines 6 and 10, with lines 4 and 7 rhyming with the refrain, and the other lines rhyming with each other, as illustrated here:

"Laugh while you may; for laughter will have an ending!"	1R
I heard it chuckled grossly from a low	2
Valley, whose foul depth I hoped not to know.	2
I swung instead of the high hill, ascending	1
To great the sun. But still a faint echo,	2
"Laugh while you may; laughter will have an ending."	1R
Then, on the crest, I saw what was past mending,	1
And climbed down, and lived on. And long ago	2
I have warned others who strained upward so:	2
"Laugh while you may; laughter will have an ending."	1R

(*Terminal*, Alan Dubois)

The Rondeau

The rondeau, another French form and, next to the triolet, the most popular of the group, is a 15-line poem, of eight- or 10-syllable lines. It has three stanzas of unequal length, with two rhymes and a refrain taken out of the first line. The rhyme scheme is 1, 1, 2, 2, 1; 1, 1, 2, R; 1, 1, 2, 2, 1, R; it is illustrated in the following poem:

> Is it time to go away?
> June is nearly over; hay
> Fattens the barn, the herds are strong,
> Our old fields prosper; these long
> Green evenings will keep death at bay.
>
> Last winter lingered; it was May
> Before a flowering lilac spray
> Barred cold for ever. It was wrong.
> > Is it time now?
>
> Six decades vanished in a day!
> I bore four sons; one lives; they
> Were all good men; three dying young
> Was hard on us. I have looked long
> for these hills to show me where peace lay . . .
> > Is it time now?

> > (*Death of a Vermont Farm Woman*, Barbara Howes)

The Ten-Line Rondeau

This is a rondeau consisting of only 10 lines, together with two additional refrain lines, each of which is the opening word of the first line. Here is the pattern:

> Death, of thy rigor I complain,
> > Thou hast my lady torn from me,
> > And yet wilt not contented be,
> Till from me too all strength be ta'en
> For languishment of heart and brain.
> > What harm did she in life to thee,
> > > Death?
>
> One heart we had between us twain;
> > Which being dead, I too much dree
> > Death, or, like carven saints, we see
> In choir, sans life to live be fain,
> > > Death!

> > (Villon Rondeau, translated by John Payne)

The Roundel

The roundel (note the different spelling from *rondel!*) is a French poem of 11 lines, two of which are shorter refrain lines. The refrain is either the first word of the first line, or, as in the 10-line rondeau, it is a part of the first line; if the latter, the refrain rhymes with the second rhyme (2). The pattern, therefore, is either 1, 2, 1, R; 2, 1, 2; 1, 2, 1, R; or it is 1, 2, 1, 2R; 2, 1, 2; 1, 2, 1, 2R. Algernon Charles Swinburne, a 19th century English master of the form, wrote *A Century of Roundels*—that is, a hundred of them. Here, he talks about poetry:

Far-fetched and dear bought, as the proverb rehearses,	
Is good, or was held so, for ladies; but nought	2
In a song can be good if the turn of the verse is	1
Far-fetched and dear bought.	2R
As the turn of a wave should it wound, and the tought	2
Ring smooth, and as light as the spray that disperses	1
By the gleam of the words for the garb thereof wrought.	2
Let the soul in it shine through the sound as it pierces	1
Men's hearts with possession of music unsought;	2
For the bounties of song are no jealous god's mercies,	1
Far-fetched and dear bought.	2R

(*A Singing Lesson*, Algernon Charles Swinburne)

The Ballade Family

The Ballade—Eight-Line Stanza

The ballade (or ballad) with eight-line stanza, the most popular of this French family of poetic forms, is a poem of 28 lines with three eight-line stanzas and a four-line final stanza or envoy (also spelled *envoi*). Each stanza and the envoy close with a refrain that is identical in sound, although the meaning and spelling may be altered. The strict French rule, requiring eight syllable lines throughout the main stanzas, is not followed in English. The eight-line stanzas should not be broken up into two quatrains, or any other smaller units, but should be coherent sections of the poem.

The major stanzas should have the same rhyme scheme, while the envoy takes the rhyme scheme of the last half of the preceding stanza. The refrain must naturally close each of the main stanzas. Traditionally, the envoy was addressed to some patron of the poet, or to some symbolic or mythical personification, but this rule hasn't been followed much lately (should poets address the National Endowment of the Arts?). However, the traditional idea that the envoy deepens the poem's meaning has been kept as this form has continued into our times. Here is a very nice contemporary use of the form, although Sherwin departs slightly from the rhyme scheme (and note how she uses all lowercase letters to emphasize her theme of the night making "us all lie down the same"):

In the dark all cats are grey.

Old proverb

when you and i draw close at night and play	1
those individual tricks all love keeps by,	2
do you believe i see you or can say	1
which hand beats mine, or by what bones i lie?	2
thrown down by dark, who separates the high	2
from the low card? what flow of skill can claim	3
to tell by taste the mouth that drinks it dry	2
that night which makes us all lie down the same?	3R
you ride the dark, but can you choose the bay	1
from the dark horse, or by your wits descry	2
which cat howled, at that hour when all are grey,	1
or what bitch held and wrung you, by her cry?	2
lift up our bodies and like hawks we fly,	1
circle and soar and, held each one by name,	3
drip, but all holds are equal when we pry	1
that night which makes us all lie down the same.	3R
a tremor and a flash cry holiday	1
and these husks leap. now tell me can we try	2
by touch which millstones grind our grain away	1
or whether in that press we love or die?	2
when the fine fever twists out straight awry,	2
rakes off our soft particulars, how blame,	3
each one, the other's harsh, unseeing eye,	2
that night which makes us all lie down the same?	3R
after those teeth have gripped me by the thigh	2
and made my flesh and yours shake with one flame	3
shall either know which fire is you, which i,	2
that night which makes us all lie down the same?	3R

(*Ballade of the Grindstones,* Judith Johnson)

Writing the Ballade

As with other fixed forms, it is important to have a guide to the form as you write. The eight-line ballade requires five rhymes on the 3 sound (including the refrain), six rhymes on the 1 sound, and 14 rhymes on the 2 sound. That's a lot of rhyming! It will be necessary, therefore, to use something like the rhyme check method described under the Italian sonnet (see "Stanza Forms"). Some other notes on writing ballades:

1. The refrain is so important that you might want to decide on it first. Since the line appears four times in the poem, it must have power, dignity, and a musical quality. One of the most famous refrains comes from Villon's "ladies of old time" ballade:

Mais où sont les neiges d'antan?

This refrain is only weakly translatable in English as "Where are the snows of yesteryear?" Because of the artificial last word, this was barely acceptable. But it proved effective and has lasted as the standard translation of Villon's line, in part because of the repetition of the line throughout the ballade. Some other effective ballade refrains are W. E. Henley's "Into the night go one and all," from *Ballade of Dead Actors,* and Chesterton's sardonic refrain, "I think I shall not hang myself today." It is for its refrain that any ballade is remembered, so choose your ballade refrain well.

2. No sound in the refrain may be changed in any way. It is forbidden to alter "Where are the snows of yesteryear?" to "Here are the snows of yesteryear." But this prohibition applies to sounds only. The words, the spelling, or the punctuation may be altered, as long as the sounds are unchanged. This permits puns and other plays on words, as can often be found in light verse rondeau refrains; such puns and plays on words also have their place in the more extended ballade.

3. It is one of the interesting facts in the history of English poetry that, in the 1890s, when a revival of French forms took place, accent verse was often chosen over metric verse. It's not that the poets couldn't do metric verse, for they were all accomplished poets. But they chose the medium more natural to the language. It's a good idea, if you want to write a ballade, to read several from various times, and get a feel for the best that have been written. This also, of course, applies to other of the fixed forms, especially the long chant royal and the complex sestina.

The Ballade—Ten-Line Stanza

This ballade form has 35 lines, with three stanzas of 10 lines each and an envoy of five lines. The pattern appears in the opening stanza and envoy of the following example; the more traditional envoy takes its rhyme scheme from the last half of the preceding stanza:

Men, brother men, that after us yet live,	1
Let not your hearts too hard against us be;	2
for if some pity of us poor men ye give,	1
The sooner God shall take of you pity.	2
Here we are five or six strung up, you see,	2
And here the flesh that all too well we fed	3
Bit by bit eaten and rotten, rent and shred,	3
And we the bones grow dust and ash withal;	4
Let no man laugh at us discomforted,	3
But pray to God that he forgive us all.	4R

After two more stanzas of the same pattern, the envoy becomes
a prayer:

Prince Jesus, that of all art lord and head,	3
Keep us, that hell be not our bitter bed;	3
We have nought to do in such a master's hall.	4
Be not ye therefore of our fellowhead,	3
But pray to God that he forgive us all.	4R

(from The Epitaph in Form of a Ballad,
Algernon Charles Swinburne)

The French required 10 syllables in each line of the major stanzas,
but English usage varies, especially in Swinburne's ballades, where the
lines vary from 8 to 20 syllables.

Note that the ballade with eight-line stanzas requires 14 rhymes on
the *2* sound, while the longer ballade (10-line stanzas) requires nine
rhymes on the *2* sound and 12 rhymes on the 3 sound. It is obvious that
checking your rhymes—where you write down the opening consonantal
sounds of your rhymes as they are used—is essential for these two forms,
as well as for the rondeau redouble, villanelle, chant royal, and so on.

The Ballade with a Double Refrain

A double refrain can be used with either the eight-line or the 10-line
ballade forms. In the eight-line ballade, the refrains occur as the fourth
and eighth lines of the major stanzas, and as lines 2 and 4 of the envoy,
which is couplet-rhymed; in the 10-line ballade, the refrains occur as the
fifth and sixth lines of the major stanzas, and the fifth line of the envoy. It
is best to have contrasting refrains. The pattern, which is not used much
in contemporary poetry, appears in the following (note how the envoy of
this early 20th century poem is addressed to "Attentive Reader"):

The car-signs lift their urgent lay	1
For Industry's insistent sake:	2
"Buy Today—a Year to Pay!"	1
"What a Whale of a Difference a Few Cents Make!"	2R
"The Kind Your Mother Couldn't Bake—"	2
"The Latest Thing in Patinums."	3
"Cash Registers Make No Mistake!"	2
"Run Your Finger over Your Gums—"	3R
How can your purse resist them, pray?	1
Their words would bugle the dead awake:	2
"The Best by Test!" "An Orange a Day—"	1
"What a Whale of a Difference a Few Cents Make!"	2R
"Eventually, Why Not Now?" "Just Take	2
A Box Home." "Tasty, to the Crumbs!"	3

"You Get the Girl—We Bake the Cake!"	2
"Run Your Finger over Your Gums—"	3R
"Just a Real Good Car." "The Pleasant Way	1
To Relieve a Cough." "They Stood the Quake!"	2
"Join the Regulars!" "This Paint Will Stay!"	1
"What a Whale of a Difference a Few Cents Make!"	2R
"The Fibre That Can Never Break—"	2
"Just Say It with—Chrysanthemums!"	3
"They Fit the Face—" "That Wheaty Flake—"	2
"Run Your Finger over Your Gums—"	3R
Attentive Reader, "For Sprain and Ache"	2
"What a Whale of a Difference a Few Cents Make!"	2R
And through a hundred milleniums	3
"Run Your Finger over Your Gums."	3R

(*Four Out of Every Five,* Alvin Winston)

The Double Ballade

The double ballade is a ballade of six stanzas, either of the eight-line or 10-line pattern, but from which the envoy can be omitted. Each stanza rhymes along the same lines as the models given: either six stanzas of 1, 2, 1, 2, 2, 3, 2, 3R, or six stanzas of 1, 2, 1, 2, 2, 3, 3, 4, 3, 4R. The former requires 24 separate rhymes of the *2* sound; the latter, 18 rhymes each on the *3* sound and the *4* sound.

W. E. Henley (remember him from *Invictus?*) uses an envoy with his double ballades. Here is the opening stanza and the envoy from his *Double Ballade of Life and Fate:*

Fools may pine, and sots may swill,	1
Cynics jibe and prophets rail,	2
Moralists may scourge and drill,	1
Preachers prose, and faint hearts quail.	2
Let them whine, or threate, or wail!	2
'Tis the touch of Circumstance	3
Down to darkness sinks the scale—	2
Fate's a fiddle, Life's a dance.	3R

After five more stanzas:

Boys and girls, at slug and snail	2
And their compeers look askance.	3
Pay your footing on the nail;	2
Fate's a fiddle, Life's a dance.	3R

(from *Double Ballade of Life and Fate,* W.E. Henley)

This double ballade required 12 rhymes on the 1 sound; 8, including the refrain rhyme, on the 3 sound; and a full 26 on the 2 sound. This calls for deft mastery of versification, of course! At times, Henley adapted the double ballade form to stanzas of 11 lines in each of the six stanzas (rhymed 1, 2, 1, 2, 2, 3, 3, 4, 5, 4, 5R) with an envoy rhymed 3, 3, 5, 4, 4, 5R (which was itself an adaptation of the traditional envoy form). As long as you maintain the general pattern of the form, you can adapt the rigid rules to your poem's needs.

The Chant Royal

The chant royal is a poem very similar to the ballade, with five stanzas of 11 lines each, and an envoy of five lines. Each stanza is rhymed according to the rhymes of the first stanza, and the envoy's pattern follows the last five lines of the preceding stanza. Here is an example, rich with old Appalachian words like "frampold" and "sanghunting":

> Born in a notch of the nigh mountains where
> a spring ran from under the porch, on
> the second of April just one hundred years
> ago this month, my grandpa was a weak one
> to start with, premature, weighted a scant
> two pounds twelve ounces. So fragile the aunt
> who tended him that first night feared to move
> him except for feeding and the changing of
> diapers. He slept near the fire in a shoebox
> with one end cut out. Against the odds he would prove
> adequate for survival, withstanding all knocks.

> Because he was puny his mother would rear
> him sheltered, keep him beside her out of the sun
> and rain alike, feed him molasses and sulfur in fear
> of worms and would let him walk, not run,
> to the gap with the others to stand on the slant
> bars while the cows were milked in elegant
> twilight. Pious and hard, she showed her love
> through strictness and was known to reprove
> him for the least resistance. She tried raw fox
> grape juice and teas of the yarb grannies, strove,
> adequate for survival, withstanding all knocks,

> to find faith healers, quacks, to cure
> her youngest. A cousin wrote of Dr. Wilson
> down near Greenville. They took the wagon one clear
> morning and reached the town just as the moon
> rose full. The man at the door said, "I can't
> see you this late," but examined him and began to rant
> on the virtues of tobacco ("Give him a chew.") then shove
> and shoo them out. That night they drove
> all the way back. No telling what unlocks

the vitality: from that day began to grow and rove
adequate for survival, withstanding all knocks.

Frampold as any mountain branch he hunted bees and deer,
carried to mill on Cold Friday and learned the fun
of shivarees and drinking. Saw his father appear
walking through the pasture toward him and beckon,
then vanish when he spoke like any hant,
and die within the month. He heard a panther
scream and follow as he came back through the cove
from hog killing, and stay up nights by the stove
while his brother crisised with fever and tried to mock
death before it cooled him. Nobody who saw the dove
was adequate for survival, withstanding all knocks.

Out sanghunting he met Mrs. Capps and her
daughter sawing crosscut. The girl could stun
with her beauty, hiding bare feet under leaves. Inner
currents stirred. He quit drinking, came to church, and won
her after three weeks courting. But they lived in want
the first year; a child died. He made his covenant
one cold night in the orchard and a trove
came in acres for sale cheap on the creek above
the Andrews place. There he sank a well through rock,
weathered debt, depression, set groves,
adequate for survival, withstanding all knocks.

Envoi

Guardian ghost, inhere herein. Before Jove
may this music honor his example, improve
my time as he invested his, and no less unorthodox
discover significance in the bonds his fate wove
adequate for survival, withstanding all knocks.

(*Chant Royal,* Robert Morgan)

There is a briefer form of the chant royal, with 10 lines to each stanza and six lines in the envoy. In that form, the rhyme scheme is 1, 2, 1, 2, 2, 3, 3, 4, 3, 4R with an envoy of 3, 3, 4, 3, 3, 4R.

The Sestina

The sestina is an unrhymed French form consisting of six sestets (six-line stanzas) and a final envoy of three lines (also called a "tornado"). Instead of rhyme, the poem turns on the end words of the first stanza; the *same* six words must be used as the end words in *all* the lines of the poem. But wait—there's more! First, the order of the words is fixed, from stanza to stanza. Second, those same six words are used both in the middle of, and at the end of, the final stanza. Here is the pattern of the six words, by stanza (represented by Roman numerals): I. 1, 2, 3, 4, 5, 6; II. 6, 1, 5, 2, 4, 3; III. 3, 6, 4, 1, 2, 5; IV. 5, 3, 2, 6, 1, 4; V. 4, 5, 1, 3, 6, 2; VI. 2, 4, 6, 5, 3, 1. And here is the pattern for word use in the envoy: first line: 2, 5; second line: 4, 3; third line: 6, 1.

There has been no explanation of this original Provençal arrangement, but there is an obvious symmetry in stanzas I and IV, and the ending word of the first line in each successive stanza is the last word in the previous stanza. At a time when rhyme has been less used, the sestina has enjoyed a surge of popularity among contemporary poets, but one of the best sestinas belongs to Elizabeth Bishop, where the only change from the form is the order of the words in the final stanza. (The numbers in the following refer, again, not to rhymes, but to the ending words of the lines.)

September rain falls on the house.	1
In the failing light, the old grandmother	2
sits in the kitchen with the child	3
beside the Little Marvel Stove,	4
reading the jokes from the almanac,	5
laughing and talking to hide the tears.	6
She thinks that her equinoctial tears	6
and the rain that beats on the roof of the house	1
were both foretold by the almanac,	5
but only known to a grandmother.	2
The iron kettle sings on the stove.	4
She cuts some bread and says to the child,	3
It's time for tea now; but the child	3
is watching the teakettle's small hard tears	6
dance like mad on hot black stove,	4
the way the rain must dance on the house.	1
Tidying up, the old grandmother	2
hangs up the clever almanac	5
on its string. Birdlike, the almanac	5
hovers half open above the child,	3
hovers above the old grandmother	2
and her teacup full of dark brown tears.	6
She shivers and says she thinks the house	1
feels chilly, and puts more wood in the stove.	4
It was to be, says the Marvel Stove.	4
I know what I know, says the almanac.	5
With crayons the child draws a rigid house	1
and a winding pathway. Then the child	3
puts in a man with buttons like tears	6
and shows it proudly to the grandmother.	2

But secretly, while the grandmother	2
busies herself about the stove,	4
the little moons fall down like tears	6
from between the pages of the almanac	5
into the flower bed the child	3
has carefully placed in the front of the house.	1
Time to plant tears, says the almanac.	6, 5
The grandmother sings to the marvellous stove	2, 4
and the child draws another inscrutable house.	3, 1

(*Sestina,* Elizabeth Bishop)

The sestina requires substantial advanced planning. The end words of the first stanza should be strong, rich words, whose meaning can be turned slightly as they are used in succeeding stanzas. Write down the words for all the six stanzas, in the order they need to be used; then write the poem.

Of all the major forms, the sestina is the only one which is unrhymed. There have been poets, of course, who have mixed rhyme into the form, resulting in occasional couplets that seem at odds with the poem as a whole. Swinburne opted to change the sestina pattern in favor of rhyme, in his sestina, "I saw my soul at rest upon a day." He used two rhyme sounds and altered the rhyme scheme, creating a poem that is half sestina, half rhymed.

The first stanza has a rhyme scheme of 1, 2, 1, 2, 1, 2:

> I saw my soul at rest upon a day
> As a bird sleeping in the nest of night,
> Among soft leaves that gave the starlight way
> To touch its wings but not its eyes with light;
> So that it knew as one in visions may,
> And knew not as men waking, of delight.

Swinburne used this pattern in stanzas 1, 3, and 5, and alternated it with stanzas rhymed 2, 1, 2, 1, 2, 1 in the even-numbered stanzas. The "tornado" is as follows:

> Song, have they day and take thy fill of light
> Before the night be fallen across the way;
> Sing while he may, man hath no long delight—

where the rhyme scheme is 2, 1, 2 at the end of the lines, and 1, 2, 1 in the middle of the lines. But to achieve this simple rhyme scheme, Swinburne needed to change the traditional order of the sestina words to avoid the occasional disruptive, couplet. Here is his sestina word order (note that he has two stanzas beginning with the *6* word):

I. 1, 2, 3, 4, 5, 6; II. 6, 1, 4, 3, 2, 5; III. 6, 5, 1, 4, 3, 2; IV. 2, 5, 6, 1, 4, 3; V. 3, 2, 1, 6, 5, 4; VI. 4, 3, 2, 6, 5, 1; envoy: 1, 4, 2, 3, 5, 6.

This pattern was imitated by several other poets. But Swinburne wasn't done. In *Rizzio's Love-Song,* he used three rhymes, rhyming his first stanza 1, 2, 1, 3, 2, 3, and repeated this rhyme scheme in the fourth stanza. In stanzas II and V, he used a 3, 1, 2, 3, 1, 2, rhyme scheme; in stanzas III and VI, he used a 2, 3, 2, 1, 3, 1 rhyme scheme; and his final stanza is as follows:

> Clothed as with power of pinions, O my heart,
> Fly like a dove, and seek one sovereign flower,
> Whose thrall thou art, and sing for love of love.

Here the end-rhyme scheme is 2, 3, 1, with the internal rhyme scheme of 3, 1, 2. With this new rhyme scheme, he used a word order which was closer to the traditional sestina form:

I. 1, 2, 3, 4, 5, 6; II. 6, 1, 5, 4, 3, 2; III. 2, 6, 5, 1, 4, 3; IV. 3, 2, 1, 6, 5, 4; V. 4, 3, 2, 1, 6, 5; VI. 5, 4, 1, 3, 6, 1; envoy: 6, 2, 3, 4, 5, 1.

Swinburne even wrote a double sestina, 150 lines altogether, based on 12 end words—whew!

Index

' (apostrophe) in phonetic alphabet, 9
* (asterisk) with archaic words, 6

A

a in phonetic alphabet, 9
acatalectic verse, 854
accent verse, 858
  Anglo-Saxon poetry, 845
  early, 845-849
  line length, 859
  metric verse and, 849
  Mother Goose rhymes and, 847
  Whitman, Walt, 857
  writing, 847-849
accent verse. *See also* alliterative verse
accents, 845
  composite rhymes, 3
  major, 1
  minor, 1
  minor accent rhymes, 835
  misplaced accent rhymes, 835-836
  mosaic rhymes, 3
  pattern scansion, 850
  vowels, 1-2
    classical scansion, 1
Against an Ultimatum
    (Carveth Wells), 887
*Aged Lover Discourses in the Flat Style,
    The* (J.V. Cunningham), 873
alliteration
  consonance and, 839
  free verse and, 858
  internal consonance, 841
alliterative verse, 846
allusion, 825
  classical, 825
  Coolio, 824
  Wright, James, 824
allusive words, 823-825
alphabet, phonetic, 7
amphibrachs, 852, 855
  limericks, 883
amphimacer foot, 853
anacrusis, 854

anapest foot, 855-856
Anglo-Saxon poetry, 845
Anthony and Cleopatra
    (William Shakespeare), 849
antibacchius foot, 853
archaic words, 6
Ariosto stanza, 885
article omission, 829
Assignment (Stephen Schlitzer),
    877-878
assonance, 837-839
  blank verse and, 838
  free verse and, 838, 858
  rap music and, 838
Atomic Pantoum (Peter Meinke), 889
audience, 821
Autumn Begins in Martin's Ferry, Ohio
    (James Wright), 824

B

bacchius, 853
Bagel, The (David Ignatow), 824
ballad measure, 864
ballad meter, 864
ballade, 901-903
  double refrain, 904-905
  ten-line stanza, 903-904
ballade family, 901-907
  chant royal, 906-907
  sestina, 907-910
Ballade of the Grindstones
    (Judith Johnson), 902
Basho, Matsuo, 878
Beat! Drums! Beat! (Walt Whitman),
    858
Beatles, 825-826
  A Day in the Life, 826
  Lucy in the Sky with Diamonds,
    856, 865
  She's Leaving Home, 826
  *St. Pepper's Lonely Hearts Club
    Band*, 826
  When I'm Sixty-Four, 825, 826
  The Fish, 823

Beauty and the Beast (Howard Ashman), 840
Beer Bottle (Ted Kooser), 881
Beck, Lacey, *Your Face*, 890
Belfast (Donald Revell), 886
Beowulf, 846
Berserk (Charles Morgan Flood), 885
Bishop, Elizabeth, *Sestina*, 908-909
blank verse, assonance and, 838
Blue Ontario's Shore (Walt Whitman), 822
breaks
  caesura, 854
  deiresis, 855
  midline breaks, 846
Brooks, Gwendolyn, *We Real Cool*, 871
Burns, Robert, *Epistle to J. Lapraik*, 867
Byron, Lord, *Don Juan VIII, 1*, 868

C

c in phonetic alphabet, 9
caesura, 854, 859
caesura (midline break), 846
cameo, 880
Canning, George, 836
Canopus (Clement Wood), 868
Canterbury Tales, The (Geoffrey Chaucer), 832
Carroll, Lewis, 836
  Rhyme? and Reason?, 893
catalectic verse, 855
Caucer, *Rhyme Royal*, 867
ch in phonetic alphabet, 9
chain rhyme, 863, 889-890
  terza rima, 889-890
chain verse, 889-890
chant royal, 906-907
chants, 848
Charge of the Light Brigade (Alfred Lord Tennyson), 856
Chatterton, Thomas, 869
Chant Royal (Robert Morgan), 907
Chaucer, Geoffrey, 867
  Canterbury Tales, The, 832
  language, 822
Chaucerian roundel, 899
choriamb, 854
cinquain, 866, 880
  double cinquain, 880
classic metric scansion, 854
classical allusions, 825
classical metric feet, 852-854
classical pattern scansion, 850
classical scansion, 1

cliched rhymes, 843
cliches, 830-831
climate and language development, 832
Coleridge, Samuel Taylor, *The Rime of the Ancient Mariner*, 864
combined feet, 854
comedy, mosaic rhyme, 825
common meter, 865
Complaint of Rosamond, The (Samuel Daniel), 841
composite rhymes, 3-4
compound rhymes, 1
Congo, The (Vachel Lindsay), 848
consonance, 1, 5, 837-839
  eye rhymes, 842
  free verse, 840
  free verse and, 858
  full consonance, 839-840
  internal consonance, 840-841
  locating in dictionary, 5-6
  Williams, C.K., 840
  See also near rhyme; off rhyme
consonantal openings
  composite rhymes and, 3
  differentiation, 2-3
  mosaic rhymes and, 3
consonantal sounds, 1
consonants, 2
  musical words, 826
  syllabic, 9
contractions, 828
Coolio, *Gangsta's Paradise*, 824
counting syllables, 878-882
couplet rhyming, 860-861
  iambic pentameter, 861
  stichic poetry, 861
couplets, 860-862
  herioc, 861
Crown of Sonnets, The, 876
cummings, e. e., *Portrait of a Pianist*, 860
Cunningham, J.V., sonnets, 872-873
  Aged Lover Discourses in the Flat Style, The, 873
  Epitaph for Somone or Other, 862

D

Dacey, Philip, *Rondel*, 898
dactyl foot, 852, 855-856
  amphimacers combination, 856
Daniel, Samuel, *The Complaint of Rosamond*, 841
Dante, *Divina Commedia*, 863

Death of a Vermont Farm Woman (Barbara Howes), 900

Degrees of Gray in Philipsburg (Richard Hugo), 838

deiresis, 855

de la Mare, Walter, 847
  The Listeners, 847

dental sounds, 841

Desolation Row (Bob Dylan), 841

Dickinson, Emily, 839

dimeter, 853

Dirty Dinky (Theodore Roethke), 886-887

Directive (Robert Frost), 849

ditrochee, 854

Divina Commedia (Dante), 863

do (rhyme induced), 828

Do Not Go Gentle into That Good Night (Dylan Thomas), 895

Dobson, Austin, *July*, 892

Donata, 886

Don Juan VIII, 1 (Lord Byron), 868

Don't Believe the Hype (Public Enemy), 838

Double Ballade of Life and Fate (W.E. Henley), 905-906

double cinquain, 880

double rhymes, 826, 834

Drayton, Michael, *Agincourt*, 867

Dubois, Alan
  Home Cooking, 884
  Terminal, 899

Dylan, Bob, *Desolation Row*, 841

E

e in phonetic alphabet, 9

Earl Brand, 846

Eden, J. K.
  Mainly about Me, 894
  Song before Dusk, 891

eight-line stanza, ballade, 901-903

Elegiac Stanza, 864

Elegy Written in a Country Courtyard (Thomas Gray), 829-830

elements of rhyme, 2

emotion-rousing words, 823

end rhyme, 837

English rhyme, 833

enjambment, 855

Envoi, 906-907

Epistle to J. Lapraik (Robert Burns), 867

Epitaph for Someone or Other (J.V. Cummingham), 862

Epitaph in Form of a Ballad, The (Algernon Charles Swinburne), 904

epitrite, 854

EPMD, *Strictly Business*, 837

Eros (Lois Lodge), 888

Essay on Criticism (Alexander Pope), 861

Eve of St. Agnes, The (John Keats), 868

everyday speech, 821

expressions, old, 827

eye rhymes, 842

F

Faerie Queen, The (Edmund Spenser), 874

false rhymes, mispronunciation, 842

feet, 849
  anapest, 855-856
  classical pattern scansion, 850
  combined, 854
  iamb, 852
  metric, 852-854
  natural scansion, 849
  pattern scansion, 850
  pyrrhic, 850, 852
  spondee, 852
  three-syllable, 852-853
  tribrach, 850
  trochee, 852
  two-syllable, 852

feminine rhymes, 834

figurative words, 823-825

First Photos of Flu Virus (Harold Witt), 897

Fish, The (Elizabeth Bishop), 823

Fitzgerald, Edward, *Rubaiyat of Omar Khayyam*, 864

five-line stanzas, 866

fixed forms, 871-910
  ballade family, 901-907
  chain verse, 889-890
  Lai, 890-892
  line-repetition forms, 886-889
  sonnets, 872-878
  syllable count forms, 878-882
  text-emroidering group, 893-897
  Triolet-Rondeau family, 897-901

Flood, Charles Morgan, *Berserk*, 885

flow, minor accent rhymes, 835

forced rhyme, 828-830
  inversions, 828
  omissions, 829-830
  substitutions, 829

Forche, Carolyn, 845
form
  ballade family
    chant royal, 906-907
    sestina, 907-910
  chain rhyming, 863
  chain verse, 889-890
  cinquain, 866
    double cinquain, 880
  fixed forms, 871-910
  haiku, 860-861
  limericks, 866, 882-883
  line-repetition, 886-889
  Little Willies, 883-884
  ottava rima, 868
  poetry and, 819-820
  quatrains, 865
    Little Willies, 884
    pantun, 888-889
    Quaterns, 887
    Retourne, 888
    rhymed, 865
  Scottish poetry, 867
  septets, 867-868
  sestets, 866-867
  sonnets, 872-878
    as stanzas, 876
    Crown of Sonnets, The, 876
    Italian, 866-867, 872-873
    Sonnet Redouble, The, 876
  Spenserian stanza, 868
  stanzas, 860-870
    eight-line, ballade, 901-903
    Elegiac, 864
    five-line, 866
    four-line, 863-866
    Gray's stanza, 864
    one-line, 860
    Sapphic, 865-866
    seven-line, 867-868
    six-line, 866-867
    ten-line (ballade), 903-904
    three-line, 862-863
    two-line, 860-862
  syllable count, 878-882
formal verse, 871
forms, fixed, 882-910
  ballade family, 901-907
  Lai, 890-892
  sonnets, 872-878
  syllable count forms, 878-882
  text-emroidering group, 893-897
  Triolet-Rondeau family, 897-901
four-line stanzas, 863-866

Four Out of Every Five (Alvin
    Winston), 904-905
free verse, 857-859
  alliteration and, 858
  assonance and, 838, 858
  consonance, 841
  consonance and, 858
  rhythm and, 845
  Whitman, Walt, 857
Frost, Robert, 858, 859
  Directive, 849
  Provide, Provide, 862
Fugees, The, Ready or Not, 847
full consonance, 839-834
function rhyme, 833-834

G–H

geography and language
    development, 832
Gilbert, W. S., Iolanthe, 826-827, 836
Glory Road, The (Clement Wood),
    836, 848
Glose, 895-897
Googe, Barnaby, Lines, 890
Gordon, George Noel, 836
Grandmaster Flash and the Furious
    Five, 823
  The Message, 823
Gray, Thomas, 829-830, 864
  Elegy Written in a Country Courtyard,
    829-830
Gray's stanza, 864
groups of consonant sounds, 2
Guest (Marcia M. Jones), 862
gutteral sounds, 841

hackneyed phrases, 830-831
haiku, 860-861
  See also tanka
half-rhymes, 842
Hamlet (William Shakespeare)
  and iambic pentameter, 850
  and natural scansion, 849-850
  "To be" sililoquy, 849-850
Hart, Lorenz, I Wish I Were in Love
    Again, 848
Hartman, Charles O., A Little Song,
    866
Henley, Willian Ernest
  Double Ballade of Life and Fate,
    905-906
  Invictus, 893
heptameter, 853
heroic couplets, 861

hexaduad, 880
hexameter, 853
history of rhyme, 832
Home Cooking (Alan Dubois), 884
House on the Hill, The (Edwin Arlington Robinson), 862
How Did It Seem to Sylvia? (Gertrud Schnackenberg), 885
Howes, Barbara, *Death of a Vermont Farm Woman*, 900
Hughes, Langston, *The Weary Blues*, 861
Hugo, Richard, *Degrees of Gray in Philipsburg*, 838
hyphens, syllables, 3

I

i in phonetic alphabet, 9
I Wish I Were in Love Again (Lorenz Hart), 848
iambic, sonnets, 872
iambic feet, 852, 855
iambic pentameter, couplet rhyming, 861
iambs
   classical pattern scansion, 850
   trochees interchangeability, 854
Ignatow, David, 824
In Memoriam (Alfred Tennyson), 864
incomplete words, 3-4
incorrect rhymes, 841-842
Ingoldsby, Thomas, 836
inspiration, 819
internal consonance, 839-841
internal rhyme, 837
inversions, 828
inverted hexaduad, 880
Invictus (William Ernest Henley), 893
Iolanthe (W. S. Gilbert), 826-827, 836
irregular sonnets, 876
Italian sonnets, 866-867, 872-873, 885

J-K

Johnson, Judith, *Ballade of the Grindstones*, 902
Jones, Marcia M., *Guest*, 862
Joy, Shipmate, Joy! (Walt Whitman), 857
Judas, 846
July (Austin Dobson), 892

Keats, John
   Eve of St. Agnes, The, 868
   On a Grecian Urn, 869
   On Melancholy, 869
   Spenserian stanzas, 868-869
   To a Nightingale, 869
   To Psyche, 869
Kilmer, Joyce, *Trees*, 850-851
Knight, Etheridge, *Poems from Prison*, 879
Kooser, Ted, *Beer Bottle*, 881
Kumin, Maxine, *Seeing the Bones*, 839
Kyrielle, 886

L

labial sounds, 841
labiodental sounds, 841
Lai, 890-892
Lament Culinaire (Margaret Thurston), 893-894
language
   allusive words, 823-825
      Coolio, 824
      Wright, James, 824
   Bishop, Elizabeth, 823
   development, 832
      Middle English, 832
      Old English, 832
   emotion-rousing words, 823
   figurative words, 823-825
   flaws in, 821
   Geoffrey Chaucer, 822
   guidelines, 820-827
   Ignatow, David, 824
   musical words, 825-827
   Pastan, Linda, 824
   polysyllabic words, 823
   Shakespeare, 822
   Walt Whitman, 822
lanterne, 880
Laramore, Vivan Yeiser, 887
Leaves of Grass (Walt Whitman), 857
light verse
   eye rhymes, 842
   Gilbert, W.S., 826-827
   mosaic rhymes, incomplete words, 3-4
   splitting phrases, 837
limericks, 866, 882-883
Lindsay, Vachel, *The Congo*, 848
line length in verse, 859
line-repetition forms, 886-889
Lines (Barnaby Googe), 890
lines, metric lines, 852-853
liquid sounds, 841
Listeners, The (Walter de la Mare), 847

Little Song, A (Charles O. Hartman), 866
Little Willies, 883-884
Lodge, Lois
  Eros, 888
  Spring, 890
long meter, 865
lyric writing, 825

M

Macbeth (William Shakespeare), 822
Mainly about Me (J. K. Eden), 894
major accent, 1
Mann, Thomas, 833
Marks (Linda Pastan), 824
masculine rhymes, 834
maxims, 831
McPherson, Sandra, *Triolet*, 897
Meinke, Peter, *Atomic Pantoum*, 889
Merrill, James, *Mirabell's Book of Number*, 861
Message, The (Grandmaster Flash and the Furious Five), 823
metaphors, 824
meter
  common meter, 865
  inversions, 829
  long meter, 865
  rhyme's affect on, 1
  short meter, 865
metric feet, 852-854
metric lines, 852-853
metric scansion, classic, 854
metric verse, 849-857
  accent verse and, 848
  flawlessness and, 854
  natural scansion, 857
  rhythm and, 845
  syllables, 849
  See also scansion
metrical feet, 849
Middle English and language development, 832
midline breaks, 846
Milton, John, 849, 868, 874
  Samson Agonistes, 849
  Miltonic sonnets, 874
  On His Blindness, 874
  Paradise Lost, 874
minor accent rhymes, 1, 835
Mirabell's Book of Number (James Merrill), 861
misplaced accent rhymes, 835-836

mispronunciation and false rhymes, 842
molossus foot, 853
monometer, 853
mood, rhyme emphasis, 826
Moore, George, *Rondel*, 898-899
Moore, Marianne, 858, 880-881
  To a Steamroller, 881
Morgan, Robert, *Chant Royal*, 907
mosaic rhyme, 3-4, 836
  accents, 3
  comedy, 825
  light verse, incomplete words, 3-4
Mother Goose rhymes, 847, 860, 882
Murfey, Etta Josephean, 879-880, 886
musical words, 825-827
  consonants, 826
  vowels, 826
muted rhyme, 886

N

nasals sounds, 841
natural scansion, 849
  feet, 849
  metric verse, 857
  pattern scansion comparison, 851-852
near rhyme, 5
  See also consonance; off rhyme
ng in phonetic alphabet, 10
Norman Conquest (1066) and language development, 832

O

o in phonetic alphabet, 10
octaves
  Sicilian, 884
  sonnets, 872
octometer, 853
Ode to the West Wind (Percy Bysshe Shelley), 863
odic stanzas, 870
off rhyme, 5
  See also consonance; near rhyme
Old English
  language development, 832
  verse, 845-847
omissions, 829-830
On His Blindness (John Milton), 874
one-line stanzas, 860
Oriental poetry, 860-861
ottava rima, 868, 885

P

paean, 854, 886
Paperweight, The (Gertrude Schnackenberg), 864
pantoum (pantun), 888-889
Paradise Lost, 874
Pastan, Linda, *Marks*, 824
"The Path" (Clement Wood), 833
pattern scansion, 850-851
    classical, 850
    feet, 850
    natural scansion comparison, 851-852
patterns, inversions, 829
Payne, John
    Rondel, 897-898
    Spring Sadness, 891-892
pensee, 880
pentameter, 853
Petrarchan sonnets, 866-867, 872-873
phonetic alphabet, 7, 9-11
phrases, splitting, 837
plagiarism, 830-831
Poe, Edgar Allan
    cinquains, 866
    Conquering Women, The, 870
    Haunted Palace, The, 870
    To Helen, 866, 870
    To One in Paradise, 870
Poems from Prison, 879
poetic tradition, 820
poetry
    creators, 819
    double ryhme and, 826
    form and, 819-820
    origins, 819-821
    rigidity in, 852
    triggers, 819
Politics (William Butler Yeats), 834
polysyllabic words, 823
Pope, Alexander, *Essay on Criticism*, 861
Portrait of a Pianist (e. e. cummings), 860
Pound, Ezra, "In a Station of the Metro," *Personae*, 860
Probyn, May, *Roundelet*, 899
pronouns, 827, 830
pronunciation, 7
proverbs, 831
Provide, Provide (Robert Frost), 862
Public Enemy, *Don't Believe the Hype*, 838
pyrrhic, 850, 852
    spondees interchangeability, 854

Q

Quaterion, 886
Quaterns, 887
quatrains, 863-866
    Kyrielle, 886
    Little Willies, 884
    octaves, 872
    pantun, 888-889
    Quaterns, 887
    Retourne, 888
    rhymed, 865
quintent, 880

R

Raccontino, 886
Rags and Dreams (Clement Wood), 895-896
rap music, assonance and, 838
Rape of Lucrece, The (William Shakespeare), 867
Ready or Not (The Fugees), 847
Renaissance, sonnets, 876
repetition, 832
Retourne, 888
Revell, Donald, *Belfast*, 885-886
rhyme, 1-2, 832
    accents, 835-836
    chain rhyming, 863, 889-890
    cliched rhymes, 843
    couplet rhyming, 860-861
    double, 826, 834
    emphasis, mood and, 826
    end rhyme, 837
    English rhyme, 833
    eye rhymes, 842
    feminine, 834
    forced, 828-830
    function, 833-834
    half-rhymes, 842
    identities, 841
    incorrect, 841-842
    internal, 837
    masculine, 834
    mosaic, 836
    muted rhyme, 886
    single, 834
    triple, 834-835
    undesirable, 843
Rhyme Royal (*Rime Royal*), 867
rhyme-induced rhymes, 842-843
rhythm, 832, 845-859
    accents, 845
    chants, 848

free verse, 845, 857-859
metric verse, 849-857
verse, 845
Rick de Travaille (Lewis Turco), 884
rigidity in poetry, 852
Rime of the Ancient Mariner, The
　　(Samuel Taylor Coleridge), 864
Ripley, Sherman, 885
Rispetto, 884
Robinson, Edwin Arlington, *The*
　　House on the Hill, 862
Rondeau, 899-900
Rondel (George Moore), 898-899
Rondel (John Payne), 891-898
Rondel (Philip Dacey), 898
Rondelet (May Probyn), 899
Rothke, Theodore, *Dirty Dinky*,
　　886-887
Roundeau Redouble, 894
Roundel, 900-901
Rubaiyat of Omar Khayyam
　　(Edward Fitzgerald), 864
Rubaiyat Stanza, 864

S

Samson Agonistes (John Milton), 849
Sapphic stanzas, 850, 865-866
scansion
　classical, 1
　metric, classic, 854
　metric verse, 849-852
　natural, 849
　　feet, 849
　　metric verse, 857
　pattern, 850
　See also metric verse
Schlitzer, Stephen, *Assignment*,
　　877-878
Schnackenberg, Gertrude
　How Did It Seem to Sylvia?, 885
　The Paperweight, 864
schwa in phonetic alphabet, 11
Scottish poetry, 867
Seeing the Bones (Maxine Kumin), 839
septet, 867-868, 880
service stanza, 864
sestets, 866-867
　turns, 872
sestina, 907-910
Sestina (Elizabeth Bishop), 908-909
seven-line stanzas, 867-868
Shakespeare, 859, 876
　Anthony and Cleopatra, 849
　language, 822

Macbeth, 822
Rape of Lucrece, The, 867
sestets, 866-867
Sonnet cxvi, 875
"To be" sililoquy, 849-850
Venus and Adonis, 866-867
Shakespearean sonnets, 875-876
Shelley, Percy Bysshe
　cinquains, 866
　Ode to the West Wind, 863
　"Ozymandias of Egypt," 876
　tercets, 863
　To a Skylark, 866
short meter, 865
sibilant sounds, 841
Sicilian octaves, 884
simple rondeau, 897
singable words. *See* musical words
Singing Lesson, A (Algernon Charles
　　Swinburne), 901
single rhymes, 834
six-line stanzas, 866-867
Song before Dusk (J. K. Eden), 891
Song of the Incantation, 846
Song of My Heart, The (Ben Sterling),
　　886
song origins, 819-821
Sonnet I (Pertrach), 873
Sonnet cxvi (William Shakespeare),
　　875
Sonnet Redouble, The, 876
sonnet sequences, 876
sonnets, 872-878
　as stanzas, 876
　Crown of Sonnets, The, 876
　Cunningham, J.V., 873
　irregular, 876
　Italian, 866-867, 872-873
　Miltonic, 874
　octaves, 872
　Petrarchan, 872-873
　Shakespearean, 875-876
　Sonnet Redouble, The, 876
　Spenserian, 874
　terza rima sonnets, 863
　writing, 876-878
　Wyattian, 875
sonnette, 885
speech patterns, 821
Spenser, Edmund, *The Faerie Queen*,
　　874, 875
Spenserian sonnets, 874
Spenserian stanza, 868
split words. *See* incomplete words
splitting phrases, 837

spondee, 852
  pyrrhics interchangeability, 854
Spring (Lois Lodge), 890
Spring Sadness (John Payne), 891-892
stanzas
  Ariosto, 903
  ballad measure, 864
  eight or more lines, 868-870
  eight-line, ballade, 901-903
  Elegiac, 864
  five-line, 866
  forms, 860-870
  four-line, 863-866
  Gray's stanza, 864
  Lai, 891
  odic, 870
  one-line, 860
  Rubaiyat Stanza, 864
  Sapphic, 865-866
  seven-line, 867-868
  six-line, 866-867
  sonnets as, 876
  Spenserian, 868
  tail-rhymed, 867
  ten-line (ballade), 903-904
  three-line, 862-863
  two lines, 860-862
Starting from Paumanok
    (Walt Whitman), 860
Sterling, Ben, *The Song of My Heart*,
    886
stichic poetry, 861
Streamer, Col D. (Harry Graham),
    Tender-Heartedness, 883
Strictly Business, EPMD, 837
Stoller, Neca Maria, *Tanka-Sijo-Haiku
    Muse*, 879
substitutions, 829
Supercalifragilisticexpialidocious!
    (Richard M. and Robert B.
    Sherman), 851
Surrey, Philip, *Tottel's Miscellaney*, 875
Swinburne, Algernon Charles
  A Century of Roundels, 901
  The Epitaph in Form of a Ballad, 904
  A Singing Lesson, 901
syllabic consonants, ', 9
syllable count forms, 878-882
  haiku, 860-861, 878-882
    Basho, Matsuo, 878
    Knight, Etheridge, 879
syllables
  double rhymes, 834
  hyphens, 3
  lyric writing, 825

metric verse, 849
single rhymes, 834
triple rhymes, 834-835
unaccented, 847
  accent verse, 845

T

tail-rhymed stanzas, 867
tanka, 879-882
  See also haiku
Tanka-Sijo-Haiku Muse (Neca Maria
    Stoller), 879
Tar (C.K. Williams), 840
Tender-Heartedness, (Col. D. Streamer
    [Harry Graham]), 883
Ten-Line Rondeau, 900
ten-line stanzas, ballade, 903-904
Tennyson, Alfred Lord, 856, 864
  Charge of the Light Brigade, 856, 867
  In Memoriam, 864
  The Lady of Shalott, 867
tercets, 862-863
  Shelley, Percy Bysshe, 863
  terza rima, 863
Terminal (Alan Dubois), 899
Terna con Variazioni, 893-894
terza rima, 863, 885-886, 889-890
tetrameter, 853
text-embroidering group, 893-897
Thirteen-Line Rondel, 898-899
three-line stanzas, 862-863
  See also tercets; triplets
three-syllable feet, 852-853
Thomas, Dylan, *Do Not Go Gentle into
    That Good Night*, 895
Thurston, Margaret, *Lament
    Culinaire*, 893-894
To a Nightingale (John Keats), 869
To Psyche (John Keats), 869
To a Skylark (Percy Bysshe Shelley),
    866
To a Steamroller (Marianne Moore),
    881
To Helen (Edgar Allan Poe), 866
Tottel's Miscellaney (Philip Surrey),
    875
Trees (Joyce Kilmer), 850-851
tribrach, 850, 853
triggers to poetry, 819
trimeter, 853
Trine, 886
Triolet (Sandra McPherson), 897
Triolet-Rondeau family, 897-901
triple rhymes, 834-835

triplets, 862-863
trochaic word endings, 836
trochee, 852
    classical pattern scansion, 850
    iambs interchangeability, 854
Turco, Lewis, *Rick de Travaille*, 884
turns
    sestets, 872
    sonnets (Milton), 874
two-line stanzas, 860-862
two-syllable feet, 852

U–V

u sounds, 6
undesirable rhymes, 843

Venus and Adonis (William
        Shakespeare), 866-867
verb forms, old, 827
vers libre (free verse), 845
verse, 845
    acatalectic, 854
    accent verse
        early, 845-849
        writing, 847-849
    catalectic, 855
    chain verse, 889-890
    formal, 871
    free verse, 845
    line length, 859
    metric, 855-857
    metric verse, 845, 849-857
    Old English, 845-847
    rhythm and, 845
vignette, 880
Villanelle, 895
Virelai Ancien (Lai), 891-892
Virelai Nouveau (Lai), 892
Vision of Piers Plowman (William
        Langland), 846
vowel rhyme. *See* assonance
vowels
    accents, 1
    musical words, 826

W

Watson, Evelyn M., 886
We Real Cool (Gwendolyn Brooks),
        871
Weary Blues, The (Langston Hughes),
        861

Wells, Carveth, *Against an Ultimatum*,
        887
Whitman, Walt, 822, 857
    Beat! Drums! Beat!, 858
    Blue Ontario's Shore, 822
    free verse, 857-858
    Joy, Shipmate, Joy!, 857
    Leaves of Grass, 857-858
    Starting from Paumanok, 860
    Out of the Cradle, Endlessly Rocking,
        858
Whittier, John Greenleaf, *The Last
        Leaf*, 867
Widdicombe Fair, 846
Widsith, 846
Williams, C.K., 840
    Tar, 840
Williams, William Carlos, *The Wind
        Increases*, 859
Winston, Alvin, *Four Out of Every
        Five*, 904-905
Witt, Harold, *First Photos of Flu Virus*,
        897
Wood, Clement, 833
    Canopus, 868
    The Glory Road, 836, 848
    "The Path," 833
    Rags and Dreams, 895-896
    World Situation: 1941, 861
words
    old, 827
    trochaic endings, 836
Wordsworth, William, 852, 859, 872
World Situation: 1941 (Clement
        Wood), 861
Wright, James, *Autumn Begins in
        Martin's Ferry, Ohio*, 824
writing
    accent verse, 847-849
    ballade, 902-903
    sonnets, 876-878
Wyatt, Thomas, 875
Wyattian sonnets, 875
Wylie, Elinor, 859

X–Y–Z

Yeats, William Butler, 833-834
    Politics, 834
Your Face, Lacey Beck, 890
Yuasa, Nobuyuki, 878

Zen Buddhism, haiku and, 878